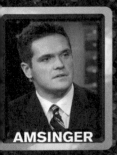
AMSINGER

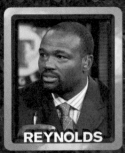
REYNOLDS

VASGERSIAN

GAMMONS

KAAT

COSTAS

ROSE

MILLAR

KENNY

PLESAC

WILLIAMS

LEITER

ALL THE ANALYSIS

They've played the game and covered it for years.
They're the analysts of MLB Network® delivering baseball's best lineup.

All the live games four nights a week.
All the live coverage seven nights a week on MLB TONIGHT™
All the characters of the game on INTENTIONAL TALK™
All the spirited debates about the hottest topics on MLB NOW™.

Together, they bring you OUR NATIONAL PASTIME ALL THE TIME®.

MLB
NETWORK

**OUR NATIONAL PASTIME
ALL THE TIME®**

To find MLB Network in your area, log on to mlbnetwork.com

NATIONAL BASEBALL HALL OF FAME

HALL OF FAME WEEKEND 2013
Experience Cooperstown like never before!
July 26-29, 2013

★ ★ ★ ★ ★

THE HALL OF FAME CLASS OF 2013
HANK O'DAY • JACOB RUPPERT • DEACON WHITE

Featuring a special recognition for Hall of Famers never formally inducted:

LOU GEHRIG
ROGERS HORNSBY

and the entire 1945 Induction Class

★ ★ ★ ★ ★

AWARDS PRESENTATION

Ford C. Frick Award for Excellence in Baseball Broadcasting: Tom Cheek
J.G. Taylor Spink Award for Meritorious Contributions to Baseball Writing: Paul Hagen

PLAN YOUR TRIP TODAY
BASEBALLHALL.ORG *or by calling* 888-HALL-OF-FAME

★ ★

National Baseball Hall of Fame and Museum • Cooperstown, New York
PRESERVING HISTORY. HONORING EXCELLENCE. CONNECTING GENERATIONS.

Baseball america
2013 DIRECTORY

Editor
JOSH LEVENTHAL

Assistant Editors
BEN BADLER, ALEXIS BRUDNICKI J.J. COOPER, AARON FITT, CONOR GLASSEY NATHAN RODE,
JIM SHONERD, BILL WOODWARD

Database and Application Development
BRENT LEWIS

Photo Editor
NATHAN RODE

Design & Production
SARA HIATT MCDANIEL, LINWOOD WEBB

Programming & Technical Development
BRENT LEWIS

Cover Photo
CLIFF WELCH

DISTRIBUTED BY SIMON & SCHUSTER ISBN-13: 978-1-932391-45-9

Baseball america

PRESIDENT/PUBLISHER Lee Folger

EDITORIAL
EDITORS IN CHIEF Will Lingo, John Manuel
EXECUTIVE EDITOR Jim Callis
MANAGING EDITOR J.J. Cooper
NEWS EDITOR Josh Leventhal
NATIONAL WRITER Aaron Fitt
ASSOCIATE EDITOR Matt Eddy
ASSISTANT EDITORS Ben Badler, Conor Glassey,
Nathan Rode, Jim Shonerd

PRODUCTION
DESIGN & PRODUCTION DIRECTOR Sara Hiatt McDaniel
MULTIMEDIA MANAGER Linwood Webb
PRODUCTION MANAGER Inna Cazares

ADVERTISING
DIRECTOR OF ADVERTISING Ryan Johnson
DIRECT MARKETING MANAGER Ximena Caceres
MARKETPLACE MANAGER Kristopher M. Lull
ADVERTISING SALES EXECUTIVE Edward Richards

BUSINESS
CUSTOMER SERVICE Ronnie McCabe, Jocelyn Dantini
MANAGER, FINANCE Susan Callahan
FINANCIAL ADMINISTRATOR Hailey Carpenter
TECHNOLOGY MANAGER Brent Lewis
TECHNOLOGY ASSISTANT Tim Collins

WHERE TO DIRECT QUESTIONS
ADVERTISING: advertising@baseballamerica.com
BUSINESS BEAT: joshleventhal@baseballamerica.com
COLLEGES: aaronfitt@baseballamerica.com
DESIGN/PRODUCTION: production@baseballamerica.com
DRAFT: johnmanuel@baseballamerica.com
HIGH SCHOOLS: nathanrode@baseballamerica.com
INDEPENDENT LEAGUES: jjcooper@baseballamerica.com
MAJOR LEAGUES: jimcallis@baseballamerica.com
MINOR LEAGUES: willlingo@baseballamerica.com
PHOTOS: photos@baseballamerica.com
PROSPECTS: benbadler@baseballamerica.com
REPRINTS: production@baseballamerica.com
SUBSCRIPTIONS/CUSTOMER SERVICE:
customerservice@baseballamerica.com
WEBSITE: customerservice@baseballamerica.com

GrindMedia

GRINDMEDIA MANAGEMENT
SVP, GROUP PUBLISHER Norb Garrett
norb.garrett@grindmedia.com
VP, DIGITAL Greg Morrow
greg.morrow@grindmedia.com
PRODUCTION DIRECTOR Kasey Kelley
kasey.kelley@grindmedia.com
EDITORIAL DIRECTOR–DIGITAL Chris Mauro
chris.mauro@grindmedia.com
FINANCE DIRECTOR Adam Miner
adam.miner@grindmedia.com

ADVERTISING SALES
SALES STRATEGY MGR/PRINT & EVENTS
Chris Engelsman chris.engelsman@grindmedia.com
SALES STRATEGY MGR/DIGITAL Elisabeth Murray
elisabeth.murray@grindmedia.com

DIGITAL
DIRECTOR OF ENGINEERING Jeff Kimmel
jeff.kimmel@grindmedia.com
SENIOR PRODUCT MANAGER Rishi Kumar
rishi.kumar@grindmedia.com
SENIOR PRODUCT MANAGER Marc Bartell
marc.bartell@grindmedia.com
CREATIVE DIRECTOR Peter Tracy
peter.tracy@grindmedia.com

MARKETING AND EVENTS
MARKETING DIRECTOR Jamey Stone
jameystone@grindmedia.com
DIRECTOR OF EVENT OPERATIONS Sean Nielsen
sean.nielsen@grindmedia.com

FACILITIES
MANAGER Randy Ward randy.ward@grindmedia.com
OFFICE COORDINATOR Ruth Hosea
ruth.hosea@grindmedia.com
ARCHIVIST Thomas Voehringer
thomas.voehringer@sorc.com

SOURCE INTERLINK MEDIA

TABLE OF CONTENTS

Fifth Third Field, Toledo, Ohio

MARK CUNNINGHAM

WHAT'S NEW IN 2013

MAJOR LEAGUES

Realignment: Houston Astros move from National League Central to American League West.

TRIPLE-A

Affiliations: Buffalo (International) from Mets to Blue Jays. Las Vegas (Pacific Coast) from Blue Jays to Mets.

Name: Scranton/Wilkes-Barre Yankees (International) become Scranton/Wilkes-Barre RailRiders.

Ballpark: Scranton/Wilkes-Barre RailRiders—PNC Field.

DOUBLE-A

Name: Reading Phillies (Eastern) become Reading Fightin Phils.

Ballpark: Birmingham Barons—Regions Field.

LOW CLASS A

Affiliations: Beloit (Midwest) from Twins to Athletics. Burlington (Midwest) from Athletics to Angels. Cedar Rapids (Midwest) from Angels to Twins. Kane County (Midwest) from Royals to Cubs. Peoria (Midwest) from Cubs to Cardinals. Quad Cities (Midwest) from Cardinals to Astros. Lexington (South Atlantic) from Astros to Royals.

SHORT-SEASON

Affiliations: Batavia (New York-Penn) from Cardinals to Marlins. Jamestown (New York-Penn) from Marlins to Pirates. State College (New York-Penn) from Pirates to Cardinals.

Franchise Move: Hillsboro (Ore.) Hops replace Yakima Bears in Northwest League.

Ballpark: Hillsboro Hops—Hillsboro Ballpark.

ROOKIE

Expansion: New York Yankees add second affiliate in Gulf Coast League. New York Mets join Gulf Coast League.

Map illustrations by Paul Trap

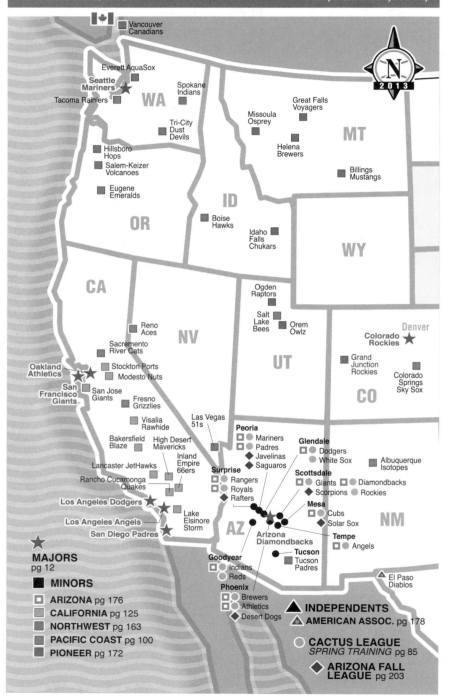

N 2013

Vancouver Canadians

Everett AquaSox

Seattle Mariners

Tacoma Rainiers

WA

Spokane Indians

Great Falls Voyagers

Missoula Osprey

Tri-City Dust Devils

MT

Hillsboro Hops

Helena Brewers

Salem-Keizer Volcanoes

Billings Mustangs

Eugene Emeralds

ID

Boise Hawks

OR

Idaho Falls Chukars

WY

CA

Ogden Raptors

Salt Lake Bees

Orem Owlz

Denver

Colorado Rockies

Reno Aces

NV

Sacramento River Cats

UT

Grand Junction Rockies

Colorado Springs Sky Sox

Oakland Athletics

Stockton Ports

Modesto Nuts

CO

San Francisco Giants

San Jose Giants

Fresno Grizzlies

Visalia Rawhide

Las Vegas 51s

Peoria
☐ ● Mariners
☐ ● Padres
◆ Javelinas
◆ Saguaros

Glendale
☐ ● Dodgers
● White Sox

Albuquerque Isotopes

Bakersfield Blaze

High Desert Mavericks

Inland Empire 66ers

Surprise
☐ ● Rangers
☐ ● Royals
◆ Rafters

Scottsdale
☐ ● Giants ☐ ● Diamondbacks
◆ Scorpions ● Rockies

Lancaster JetHawks

Rancho Cucamonga Quakes

Los Angeles Dodgers

Lake Elsinore Storm

AZ

Mesa
☐ ● Cubs
◆ Solar Sox

Los Angeles Angels

San Diego Padres

Arizona Diamondbacks

Tempe
☐ ● Angels

NM

Goodyear
☐ ● Indians
● Reds

Tucson
Tucson Padres

★

MAJORS
pg 12

■ **MINORS**

☐ **ARIZONA** pg 176

■ **CALIFORNIA** pg 125

■ **NORTHWEST** pg 163

■ **PACIFIC COAST** pg 100

■ **PIONEER** pg 172

Phoenix
☐ ● Brewers
☐ ● Athletics
◆ Desert Dogs

El Paso Diablos

▲ **INDEPENDENTS**

△ **AMERICAN ASSOC.** pg 178

○ **CACTUS LEAGUE**
SPRING TRAINING pg 85

◆ **ARIZONA FALL LEAGUE** pg 203

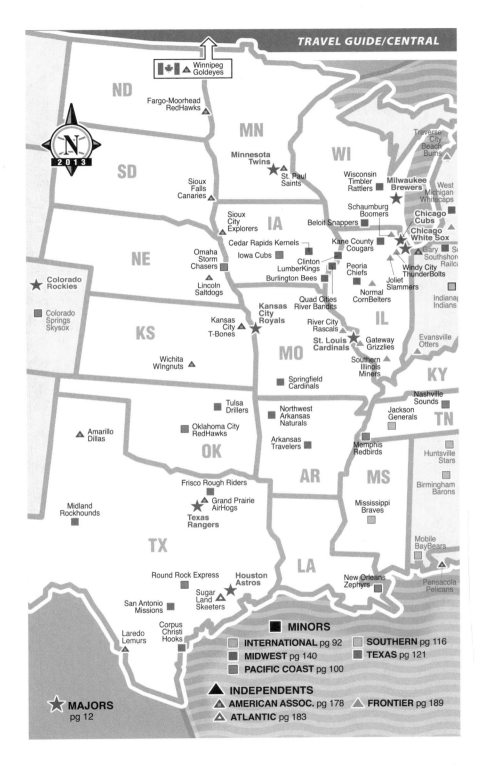

Winnipeg Goldeyes

ND

Fargo-Moorhead RedHawks

MN

Minnesota Twins

St. Paul Saints

WI

Traverse City Beach Bums

N 2013

SD

Sioux Falls Canaries

Wisconsin Timber Rattlers

Milwaukee Brewers

West Michigan Whitecaps

Schaumburg Boomers

Chicago Cubs

Sioux City Explorers

IA

Beloit Snappers

Kane County Cougars

Chicago White Sox

Cedar Rapids Kernels

Gary SouthShore Railca

NE

Omaha Storm Chasers

Iowa Cubs

Clinton LumberKings

Peoria Chiefs

Windy City ThunderBolts

Colorado Rockies

Lincoln Saltdogs

Burlington Bees

Joliet Slammers

Colorado Springs Skysox

KS

Kansas City T-Bones

Kansas City Royals

Quad Cities River Bandits

Normal CornBelters

IL

Indiana Indians

Wichita Wingnuts

River City Rascals

St. Louis Cardinals

Gateway Grizzlies

Evansville Otters

MO

Southern Illinois Miners

KY

Springfield Cardinals

Nashville Sounds

Tulsa Drillers

Northwest Arkansas Naturals

Jackson Generals

TN

Oklahoma City RedHawks

Arkansas Travelers

Memphis Redbirds

Huntsville Stars

Amarillo Dillas

OK

AR

MS

Birmingham Barons

Frisco Rough Riders

Mississippi Braves

Midland Rockhounds

Grand Prairie AirHogs

Texas Rangers

Mobile BayBears

TX

LA

Round Rock Express

Houston Astros

New Orleans Zephyrs

Pensacola Pelicans

San Antonio Missions

Sugar Land Skeeters

Laredo Lemurs

Corpus Christi Hooks

◼ **MINORS**

☐ **INTERNATIONAL** pg 92   ☐ **SOUTHERN** pg 116

◼ **MIDWEST** pg 140   ◼ **TEXAS** pg 121

◼ **PACIFIC COAST** pg 100

▲ **INDEPENDENTS**

△ **AMERICAN ASSOC.** pg 178   △ **FRONTIER** pg 189

△ **ATLANTIC** pg 183

★ **MAJORS**
pg 12

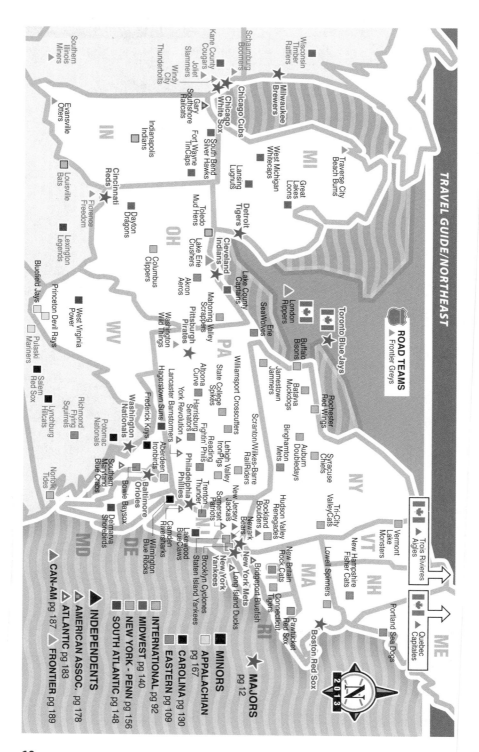

ROAD TEAMS
▶ Frontier Greys

▶ Trois Rivieres Aigles

▶ Quebec Capitales

MINORS

★ **MAJORS** pg 12

★ INTERNATIONAL pg 92
■ EASTERN pg 109
■ CAROLINA pg 130
△ APPALACHIAN pg 167
□ MIDWEST pg 140
□ NEW YORK - PENN pg 156
□ SOUTH ATLANTIC pg 148

INDEPENDENTS

▶ AMERICAN ASSOC. pg 178
▷ ATLANTIC pg 183
▷ CAN-AM pg 187
△ FRONTIER pg 189

Southern Illinois Miners
Kane County Cougars
Schaumburg Boomers
Wisconsin Timber Rattlers
Evansville Otters
Joliet Slammers
Windy City Thunderbolts
Gary SouthShore Railcats
Chicago White Sox
Chicago Cubs
Milwaukee Brewers
Traverse City Beach Bums
Indianapolis Indians
Fort Wayne TinCaps
South Bend Silver Hawks
West Michigan Whitecaps
Lansing Lugnuts
Great Lakes Loons
Louisville Bats
Florence Freedom
Cincinnati Reds
Dayton Dragons
Toledo Mud Hens
Detroit Tigers
Lexington Legends
Columbus Clippers
Lake Erie Crushers
Akron Aeros
Cleveland Indians
Lake County Captains
London Rippers
Erie SeaWolves
Bluefield Jays
Princeton Devil Rays
West Virginia Power
Mahoning Valley Scrappers
Pittsburgh Pirates
Washington Wild Things
Williamsport Crosscutters
Buffalo Bisons
Toronto Blue Jays
Batavia Muckdogs
Jamestown Jammers
Rochester Red Wings
Pulaski Mariners
Salem Red Sox
Lynchburg Hillcats
Richmond Flying Squirrels
Potomac Nationals
Washington Nationals
Frederick Keys
Hagerstown Suns
Lancaster Barnstormers
York Revolution
Harrisburg Senators
Altoona Curve
State College Spikes
Reading Fightin Phils
Lehigh Valley IronPigs
Scranton/Wilkes-Barre RailRiders
Binghamton Mets
Auburn Doubledays
Syracuse Chiefs
Tri-City ValleyCats
Hudson Valley Renegades
Rockland Boulders
New Jersey Jackals
Somerset Patriots
Trenton Thunder
Philadelphia Phillies
Aberdeen Ironbirds
Baltimore Orioles
Bowie Baysox
Southern Maryland Blue Crabs
Delmarva Shorebirds
Wilmington Blue Rocks
Camden Riversharks
Lakewood BlueClaws
Staten Island Yankees
Brooklyn Cyclones
New York Yankees
New York Mets
Long Island Ducks
Newark Bears
Bridgeport Bluefish
Connecticut Tigers
New Britain Rock Cats
New Hampshire Fisher Cats
Vermont Lake Monsters
Lowell Spinners
Pawtucket Red Sox
Portland Sea Dogs
Boston Red Sox
Norfolk Tides

IN

OH

WV

PA

NY

VT

NH

ME

MA

RI

CT

NJ

MD

DE

2013
N

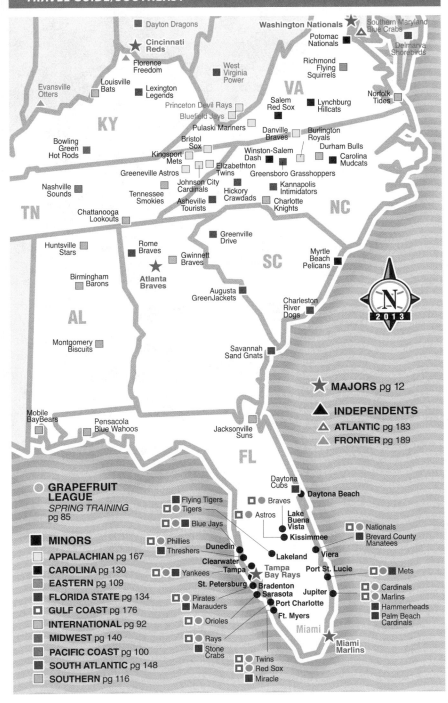

Dayton Dragons
Washington Nationals
Southern Maryland Blue Crabs
Cincinnati Reds
Potomac Nationals
Delmarva Shorebirds
Florence Freedom
West Virginia Power
Richmond Flying Squirrels
Louisville Bats
Lexington Legends
VA
Salem Red Sox
Lynchburg Hillcats
Norfolk Tides
Evansville Otters
Princeton Devil Rays
Bluefield Jays
Pulaski Mariners
Danville Braves
Burlington Royals
KY
Bristol Sox
Durham Bulls
Bowling Green Hot Rods
Kingsport Mets
Winston-Salem Dash
Carolina Mudcats
Greeneville Astros
Elizabethton Twins
Greensboro Grasshoppers
Nashville Sounds
Johnson City Cardinals
Hickory Crawdads
Kannapolis Intimidators
Tennessee Smokies
Asheville Tourists
Charlotte Knights
NC
Chattanooga Lookouts
TN
Greenville Drive
Huntsville Stars
Rome Braves
Gwinnett Braves
Myrtle Beach Pelicans
Birmingham Barons
Atlanta Braves
SC
Augusta GreenJackets
Charleston River Dogs
Savannah Sand Gnats
Montgomery Biscuits
AL

★ MAJORS pg 12

▲ INDEPENDENTS
△ ATLANTIC pg 183
△ FRONTIER pg 189

Mobile BayBears
Pensacola Blue Wahoos
Jacksonville Suns
FL

○ GRAPEFRUIT LEAGUE
SPRING TRAINING pg 85

Daytona Cubs
Daytona Beach
Flying Tigers
Tigers
Braves
Astros
Lake Buena Vista
Kissimmee
Nationals
Brevard County Manatees
Blue Jays
Viera

■ MINORS
▢ APPALACHIAN pg 167
■ CAROLINA pg 130
▢ EASTERN pg 109
■ FLORIDA STATE pg 134
▢ GULF COAST pg 176
▢ INTERNATIONAL pg 92
■ MIDWEST pg 140
■ PACIFIC COAST pg 100
■ SOUTH ATLANTIC pg 148
▢ SOUTHERN pg 116

Phillies
Threshers
Dunedin
Clearwater
Lakeland
Yankees
Tampa
Tampa Bay Rays
Port St. Lucie
Mets
St. Petersburg
Bradenton
Jupiter
Cardinals
Pirates
Sarasota
Port Charlotte
Marlins
Marauders
Ft. Myers
Hammerheads
Orioles
Palm Beach Cardinals
Miami
Rays
Stone Crabs
Miami Marlins
Twins
Red Sox
Miracle

MAJOR LEAGUES

MAJOR LEAGUE BASEBALL

Mailing Address: 245 Park Ave. New York, NY 10167.
Telephone: (212) 931-7800. **Website:** www.mlb.com.
Commissioner: Allan H. "Bud" Selig.
Executive Vice President, Business: Tim Brosnan. **Executive VP, Economics/League Affairs:** Robert Manfred. **Executive VP, Finance/Chief Financial Officer:** Jonathan Mariner. **Executive VP, Administration/Chief Information Officer:** John McHale. **Executive VP, Baseball Development:** Frank Robinson. **Executive VP, Baseball Operations:** Joe Torre.

Baseball Operations

Special Assistant to the Commissioner: Tony La Russa.
Senior VP, Baseball Operations: Joe Garagiola Jr, Kim Ng, Peter Woodfork.
Senior Director, Major League Operations: Roy Krasik. **Consultant:** Lou Melendez. **Director, International Baseball Operations:** Chris Haydock. **Director, Baseball Operations:** Jeff Pfeifer. **Senior Manager, Minor League Operations:** Fred Seymour. **Manager, Amateur Player Administration:** Chuck Fox. **Specialist, Umpire Administration:** Cathy Davis. **Managers, International Talent Development:** Joel Araujo, Juan DeJesus.
Coordinator, Major League Operations: Gina Liento. **Coordinator, On Field Operations:** Stephen Mara. **Administrator, International Baseball Operations:** Shane Barclay. **Coordinator, International Baseball Operations:** Rebecca Seesel. **Senior Administrative Assistant:** Llubia Bussey, Ana Rivas.
Director, Major League Umpiring: Randy Marsh. **Director, Umpiring Development:** Rich Rieker. **Director, Umpire Administration:** Matt McKendry. **Director, Umpire Medical Services:** Mark Letendre. **Umpiring Supervisors:** Cris Jones, Tom Leppard, Chuck Meriwether, Ed Montague, Steve Palermo, Charlie Reliford, Larry Young. **Umpire Evaluator:** Ed Rapuano. **Special Assistant, Umpiring:** Bruce Froemming. **Sure Administrator:** Raquel Wagner.
Video Coordinator: Freddie Hernandez. **Baseball Systems:** Nancy Crofts. **Director, Dominican Operations:** Rafael Perez. **Assistant Manager:** Osiris Ramirez. **Director, Arizona Fall League:** Steve Cobb. **Senior Director, Major League Scouting Bureau:** Frank Marcos. **Assistant Director, Scouting Bureau:** Rick Oliver.

Bud Selig

Baseball Development

VP, Youth/Facilities Development: Darrell Miller. **Director, Baseball Initiatives:** Sylvia Lind. **Manager, Baseball Development:** Ben Baroody.

Security

VP, Security/Facility Management: Bill Bordley.
Director, Security Operations: John Skinner. **Supervisor, Executive Protection:** Charles Hargrove. **Director, Facility Operations:** Paul Hanlon. **Manager, Security Operations:** Harold Brantley. **Manager, Latin America Security Operations:** Tom P. Reilly. **Supervisor, Executive Offices Security Operations:** William Diaz. **Senior Manager, Facility Operations:** Robert Campbell. **Supervisor, Security/Facility Management:** Yenifer Fauche. **Security Analyst:** Christopher Ellis. **Assistant to VP, Security/Facility Management:** Danielle Beckom.

Investigations

Senior VP, Investigations: Dan Mullin.
VP, Investigations: George Hanna. **VP, Educational Programming/Investigative Services:** Earnell Lucas. **Senior Administrative Assistant:** Stephanie Navarrete. **Manager, Investigations:** Nancy Zamudio. **Manager, Investigations/ DR-DOI Office:** Nelson Tejada. **Senior Investigators:** Ed Dominguez, Ricardo Burnham, Awilda Santana, Tom J. Reilly, Ed Maldonado. **Senior Analyst:** Kevin Cepelak. **Research Analyst:** Ariadne Bonano. **Research Coordinators:** Kendall Barreiro, Natalie Romine, Kristin van der Kloot.

Public Relations

Telephone: (212) 931-7878. **Fax:** (212) 949-5654.
Senior VP, Public Relations: Patrick Courtney.
VP, Business Public Relations: Matt Bourne. **Senior Director, Public Relations:** Michael Teevan. **Director, Media Relations:** John Blundell. **Director, Business Public Relations:** Jeff Heckelman. **Manager, Media Relations:** Donald Muller. **Managers, Business Public Relations:** Daniel Queen, Lauren Verrusio. **Specialist, Business Public Relations:** Steven Arocho. **Specialist, Media Relations:** Lydia Panayotidis. **Coordinators, Business Public Relations:** Sarah Leer, Ariel Williams. **Coordinator, Public Relations:** Jennifer Zudonyi. **Senior Administrative Assistant:** Ginger Dillon.

Club Relations

Senior VP, Scheduling/Club Relations: Katy Feeney.
Administrative Assistant, Scheduling/Club Relations: Ana Cruz. **Coordinator, Club Relations:** Bennett Shields. **Senior VP, Club Relations:** Phyllis Merhige. **Senior Administrative Assistant, Club Relations:** Angelica Cintron. **Administrator, Club Relations:** Ian Johns.

Licensing

Senior VP, Licensing: Howard Smith.
VP, Domestic Licensing: Steve Armus. **VP, Hard Goods:** Mike Napolitano. **Senior Director, Consumer Products/ Retail Marketing:** Adam Blinderman. **Director, Licensing/Minor Leagues:** Eliot Runyon. **Senior Director, Non-Authentics:** Greg Sim. **Director, Authentic Collection:** Ryan Samuelson. **Senior Manager, Presence Marketing:** Robin Jaffe.

MAJOR LEAGUES

Publishing/Photographs
VP, Publishing/Photographs: Don Hintze.
Editorial Director: Mike McCormick. **Art Director, Publications:** Faith Rittenberg. **MLB Photographs:** Jessica Foster.

Special Events
Senior VP, Special Events: Marla Miller.
Senior Directors, Special Events: Brian O'Gara, Eileen Buser. **Directors, Special Events:** Jacqueline Secaira-Cotto, Rob Capilli. **Senior Manager, Special Events:** Jeremiah Yolkut. **Managers, Special Events:** Bernie Goon, Keri Harris.

Broadcasting
Senior VP, Broadcasting: Chris Tully.
VP, Broadcast Administration/Operations: Bernadette McDonald. **Senior Director, Broadcasting Business Affairs:** Susanne Hilgefort. **Director, Broadcast Administration/Operations:** Chuck Torres. **Manager, Broadcasting:** Dewey Gong.

Corporate Sales/Marketing
Senior VP, Corporate Sales/Marketing: Lou Koskovolis.
VP, Partnership Marketing: Jeremy Cohen. **VP, National Sales:** Chris Marciani.

Advertising
Senior VP/Chief Marketing Officer: Jacqueline Parkes.
VP, Research/Strategic Planning: Dan Derian. **VP, Design Services:** Anne Occi. **Senior Director, Brand Marketing/Advertising:** Dan Kelleher. **Director, Brand Marketing/Advertising:** Kate Gibson. **Director, Research:** Marc Beck. **Senior Manager, Brand Marketing/Advertising:** Lance Gitlin. **Manager, Brand Marketing/Advertising:** Felicia Principe.

Community Affairs
VP, Community Affairs: Tom Brasuell.
Director, Community Affairs: Celia Bobrowsky. **Director, Reviving Baseball in Inner Cities:** David James.

General Administration
Senior VP, Accounting/Treasurer: Bob Clark.
Senior VP/General Counsel, Labor Relations: Dan Halem. **Senior VP/General Counsel, Business:** Ethan Orlinsky. **Senior VP/General Counsel, BOC:** Tom Ostertag. **Senior VP, Finance:** Kathleen Torres. **Senior VP, Chief Technology Officer:** Mike Morris. **VP, Deputy General Counsel:** Domna Candido.
Senior VP, Diversity/Strategic Alliances: Wendy Lewis. **VP, Human Resources:** Ray Scott. **VP/Deputy General Counsel:** Jennifer Simms. **Director, Baseball Assistance Team:** Joe Grippo. **VP, Office Operations:** Donna Hoder. **Senior Director, Quality Control:** Peggy O'Neill-Janosik. **VP, Recruitment:** John Quinones. **Director, Risk Management/Financial Reporting:** Anthony Avitabile. **Senior Manager, Records:** Mildred Delgado. **Director, Retirement Services:** Rich Hunt. **Director, Benefits/HRIS:** Diane Cuddy.

International
Mailing Address: 245 Park Ave., 31st Floor, New York, NY 10167. **Telephone:** (212) 931-7500. **Fax:** (212) 949-5795.
Senior VP, International Business Operations: Paul Archey.
VP, International Licensing: Denis Nolan. **VP/Executive Producer, International Broadcasting:** Russell Gabay. **VP, Sponsorship/Market Development:** Dominick Balsamo. **VP, World Baseball Classic:** James Pearce. **VP, International Broadcast Sales:** Frank Uddo. **VP, Asia/Managing Director, MLB Japan:** Jim Small. **Managing Director, MLB China:** Leon Xie. **Senior Manager, MLB Europe, Middle East/Africa:** Jason Holowaty. **Director, MLB Australia/Oceania:** Thomas Nicholson. **CEO, Australian Baseball League:** Peter Wermuth.

MLB Western Operations
Office Address: 2415 East Camelback Rd., Suite 850, Phoenix, AZ 85016. **Telephone:** (602) 281-7300. **Fax:** (602) 281-7313.
VP, Western Operations/Special Projects: Laurel Prieb. **Office Coordinator:** Valerie Dietrich.

Major League Baseball Productions
Office Address: One MLB Network Plaza, Secaucus, NJ 07094-2403. **Telephone:** (201) 751-8500. **Fax:** (201) 751-8568.
VP, Executive In Charge of Production: David Gavant. **Executive Producer:** David Check. **Senior Director, Operations:** Shannon Valine. **Senior Manager, Media Management/Tech Ops:** Chris Monico. **Senior Manager, Programming:** Jon O'Sheal. **Senior Manager, Library Licensing:** Nick Trotta. **Senior Writer:** Jeff Scott. **Coordinating Producer, Field Production:** Robert Haddad. **Coordinating Producer:** Adam Schlackman. **Managing Producer:** Kristen Wendland.

Umpires
Lance Barksdale, Ted Barrett, Wally Bell, Dan Bellino, C.B. Bucknor, Vic Carapazza, Mark Carlson, Gary Cederstrom, Eric Cooper, Fieldin Culbreth, Phil Cuzzi, Kerwin Danley, Gary Darling, Bob Davidson, Gerry Davis, Dana DeMuth, Laz Diaz, Mike DiMuro, Rob Drake, Bruce Dreckman, Doug Eddings, Paul Emmel, Mike Everitt, Chad Fairchild, Andy Fletcher, Marty Foster, Greg Gibson, Manny Gonzalez, Brian Gorman, Chris Guccione, Tom Hallion, Angel Hernandez, Ed Hickox, John Hirschbeck, Sam Holbrook, James Hoye, Marvin Hudson, Dan Iassogna, Adrian Johnson, Jim Joyce, Jeff Kellogg, Brian Knight, Ron Kulpa, Jerry Layne, Alfonso Marquez, Tim McClelland, Jerry Meals, Bill Miller, Paul Nauert, Jeff Nelson, Brian O'Nora, Alan Porter, Tony Randazzo, Jim Reynolds, Brian Runge, Paul Schrieber, Dale Scott, Todd Tichenor, Tim Timmons, Larry Vanover, Mark Wegner, Bill Welke, Tim Welke, Hunter Wendelstedt, Joe West, Mike Winters, Jim Wolf.

Events
2013 All-Star Game: July 16 at Citi Field, New York. **2013 World Series:** Unavailable.

AMERICAN LEAGUE

Year League Founded: 1901.
2013 Opening Date: March 31. **Closing Date:** Sept. 29.
Regular Season: 162 games.
Division Structure: East—Baltimore, Boston, New York, Tampa Bay, Toronto. **Central**—Chicago, Cleveland, Detroit, Kansas City, Minnesota. **West**—Houston, Los Angeles, Oakland, Seattle, Texas.
Playoff Format: Two non-division winners with best records meet in one-game wildcard playoff. Wildcard winner and three division champions meet in two best-of-five Division Series. Winners meet in best-of-seven Championship Series.
All-Star Game: July 16, Citi Field, New York (National League vs. American League).
Roster Limit: 25, through Aug 31, when rosters expand to 40.
Brand of Baseball: Rawlings.
Statistician: MLB Advanced Media, 75 Ninth Ave., 5th Floor, New York, NY 10011.

STADIUM INFORMATION

Team	Stadium	Dimensions			Capacity	2012 Att.
		LF	CF	RF		
Baltimore	Oriole Park at Camden Yards	333	410	318	45,971	2,102,240
Boston	Fenway Park	310	390	302	37,493	3,043,003
Chicago	U.S. Cellular Field	330	400	335	40,615	1,965,955
Cleveland	Progressive Field	325	405	325	43,545	1,603,596
Detroit	Comerica Park	345	420	330	41,782	3,028,033
Houston	Minute Maid Park	315	435	326	40,976	1,607,733
Kansas City	Kauffman Stadium	330	410	330	37,903	1,739,859
Los Angeles	Angel Stadium	333	404	333	45,050	3,061,770
Minnesota	Target Field	339	404	328	39,504	2,776,354
New York	Yankee Stadium	318	408	314	52,325	3,542,406
Oakland	O.co Coliseum	330	400	367	34,077	1,679,013
Seattle	Safeco Field	331	401	326	47,447	1,721,920
Tampa Bay	Tropicana Field	315	404	322	41,315	1,559,681
Texas	Rangers Ballpark in Arlington	332	400	325	48,194	3,460,280
Toronto	Rogers Centre	328	400	328	49,539	2,099,663

NATIONAL LEAGUE

Year League Founded: 1876.
2013 Opening Date: April 1. **Closing Date:** Sept. 29.
Regular Season: 162 games.
Division Structure: East—Atlanta, Miami, New York, Philadelphia, Washington. **Central**—Chicago, Cincinnati, Milwaukee, Pittsburgh, St. Louis. **West**—Arizona, Colorado, Los Angeles, San Diego, San Francisco.
Playoff Format: Two non-division winners with best records meet in one-game wildcard playoff. Wildcard winner and three division champions meet in two best-of-five Division Series. Winners meet in best-of-seven Championship Series.
All-Star Game: July 16, Citi Field, New York (National League vs. American League).
Roster Limit: 25, through Aug. 31 when rosters expand to 40.
Brand of Baseball: Rawlings.
Statistician: MLB Advanced Media, 75 Ninth Ave., 5th Floor, New York, NY 10011.

STADIUM INFORMATION

Team	Stadium	Dimensions			Capacity	2012 Att.
		LF	CF	RF		
Arizona	Chase Field	330	407	334	49,033	2,177,617
Atlanta	Turner Field	335	400	330	49,743	2,420,171
Chicago	Wrigley Field	355	400	353	41,160	2,882,756
Cincinnati	Great American Ball Park	328	404	325	42,319	2,347,251
Colorado	Coors Field	347	415	350	50,499	2,630,458
Los Angeles	Dodger Stadium	330	395	330	56,000	3,324,246
Miami	Marlins Park	344	422	335	37,000	2,219,444
Milwaukee	Miller Park	344	400	345	41,900	2,831,385
New York	Citi Field	335	408	330	42,000	2,242,803
Philadelphia	Citizens Bank Park	329	401	330	43,647	3,565,718
Pittsburgh	PNC Park	325	399	320	38,362	2,091,918
St. Louis	Busch Stadium	336	400	335	43,975	3,262,109
San Diego	Petco Park	336	396	322	42,685	2,123,721
San Francisco	AT&T Park	339	399	309	41,503	3,377,371
Washington	Nationals Park	336	402	335	41,546	2,370,794

Arizona Diamondbacks

Office Address: Chase Field, 401 E. Jefferson St, Phoenix, AZ 85004.
Mailing Address: P.O. Box 2095, Phoenix, AZ 85001.
Telephone: (602) 462-6500. **Fax:** (602) 462-6599. **Website:** www.dbacks.com

Ownership
Managing General Partner: Ken Kendrick. **General Partners:** Mike Chipman, Jeff Royer.

BUSINESS OPERATIONS
President/CEO: Derrick Hall. **Executive Vice President, Business Operations:** Cullen Maxey. **Special Assistants to President/CEO:** Luis Gonzalez, Roland Hemond. **Military Affairs Specialist:** Captain Jack Ensch. **Executive Assistant to President/CEO:** Brooke Mitchell. **Executive Assistant to Executive VP, Business Operations:** Katy Bernham.

Broadcasting
VP, Broadcasting: Scott Geyer. **Senior Director, Game Operations/Multi-Media Productions:** Rob Weinheimer. **Senior Manager, Multi-Media Productions:** Jon Willey.

Corporate Partnerships/Marketing
VP, Corporate Partnerships: Steve Mullins. **Director, Corporate Partnership Services:** Kerri White. **VP, Marketing:** Karina Bohn. **Senior Manager, Marketing/Promotions:** Dustin Payne. **Senior Marketing Media Specialist:** Rayme Lofgren.

Ken Kendrick

Finance/Legal
Executive VP/CFO: Tom Harris. **VP, Finance:** Craig Bradley. **Director, Financial Management/Purchasing:** Jeff Jacobs. **Director, Accounting:** Chris James. **Executive Assistant to Managing General Partner/CFO:** Sandy Cox.
Senior VP/General Counsel: Nona Lee. **Senior Director, Legal Affairs/Associate General Counsel:** Caleb Jay.

Community Affairs
VP, Corporate/Community Impact: Debbie Castaldo. **Manager, Community Programs:** Tara Trzinski. **Manager, Community Events:** Robert Itzkowitz. **Manager, Multicultural/Partner Programs:** Julie Romero.

Communications/Media Relations
Senior VP, Communications: Josh Rawitch. **Director, Publications:** Josh Greene. **Director, Player/Media Relations:** Casey Wilcox. **Manager, Player/Media Relations:** Patrick O'Connell. **Manager, Corporate Communications:** Katie Krause. **Coordinator, Communications:** Jim Myers.

Special Projects/Fan Experience
VP, Special Projects: Graham Rossini. **Director, Baseball Outreach/Development:** Jeff Rodin. **Manager, Spring Training Operations/GM, Salt River Fields:** David Dunne.

2013 SCHEDULE
Standard Game Times: 6:40 p.m.; Sun. 1:10.

APRIL
1-3 . . . . St. Louis
5-7 . . . . . . at Milwaukee
8-10 . . . . Pittsburgh
12-14 . . . Los Angeles (NL)
16-18 . . . at New York (AL)
19-21 . . . . . . at Colorado
22-24 . . . at San Francisco
25-28 . . . . Colorado
29-30 . . . San Francisco

MAY
1 . . . . San Francisco
3-5 . . . . . . at San Diego
6-8 . . at Los Angeles (NL)
9-12 . . . . . . Philadelphia

13-15 . . . . Atlanta
17-19 . . . . at Miami
20-22 . . . . . at Colorado
24-26 . . . . . . San Diego
27 . . . . Texas (DH)
29-30 . . . . at Texas
31 . . . . . at Chicago (NL)

JUNE
1-2 . . . . at Chicago (NL)
3-6 . . . . at St. Louis
7-9 . . . . . San Francisco
10-12 . at Los Angeles (NL)
14-16 . . . . at San Diego
17-19 . . . . Miami
21-23 . . . . . . Cincinnati
25-27 . . . at Washington

28-30 . . . . . . at Atlanta

JULY
1-4 . . . . at New York (NL)
5-7 . . . . Colorado
8-10 . . . Los Angeles (NL)
11-14 . . . . . . Milwaukee
19-21 . . . at San Francisco
22-25 . . . . Chicago (NL)
26-28 . . . . . . San Diego
30-31 . . . at Tampa Bay

AUGUST
2-4 . . . . at Boston
6-7 . . . . Tampa Bay
9-11 . . . . . New York (NL)
12-14 . . . . . . Baltimore

16-18 . . . . at Pittsburgh
19-22 . . . . at Cincinnati
23-25 . . . at Philadelphia
26-28 . . . . . . San Diego
30-31 . . . . San Francisco

SEPTEMBER
1 . . . . San Francisco
2-4 . . . . Toronto
5-8 . . . . at San Francisco
9-11 . . at Los Angeles (NL)
13-15 . . . . Colorado
16-19 . . Los Angeles (NL)
20-22 . . . . . at Colorado
23-26 . . . . at San Diego
27-29 . . . . . Washington

GENERAL INFORMATION
Stadium (year opened): Chase Field (1998).
Team Colors: Sedona Red, Sonoran Sand and Black.
Player Representative: Ian Kennedy.
Home Dugout: Third Base.
Playing Surface: Grass.

Human Resources/Information Technology
Senior VP, Chief Human Resources/Diversity Officer: Marian Rhodes. VP, Chief Information Officer: Bob Zweig.

Stadium Operations
VP, Facility Operations/Event Services: Russ Amaral. Senior Director, Security: Sean Maguire. Senior Manager, Security: Greg Green. Director, Facility Services: Jim Hawkins. Director, Engineering: Jim White. Director, Event Services: Bryan White. Event Coordinator: Jeff Gomez. Head Groundskeeper: Grant Trenbeath.

Ticket Sales
Telephone: (602) 514-8400. Fax: (602) 462-4141.
Senior VP, Ticket Sales/Marketing: John Fisher. Director, Season Ticket Services: Cory Parsons. Senior Director, Business Strategy/Operations: Kenny Farrell. Director, Ticket Operations: Josh Simon. Director, Ticket Sales: Ryan Holmstedt.

Travel/Clubhouse
Senior Director, Team Travel/Home Clubhouse Manager: Roger Riley. Manager, Equipment/Visiting Clubhouse: Bob Doty.

BASEBALL OPERATIONS
Executive VP/General Manager: Kevin Towers. Assistant GM: Billy Ryan. VP/Special Assistant to GM: Bob Gebhard. Special Assistant to GM/Major League Scout: Bill Bryk. Special Assistant to GM: Barry Axelrod, Craig Shipley, Jerry Krause. Special Assistant to GM/Advance Scout: Mark Weidemaier. VP, Latin America Operations: Junior Noboa. Director, Baseball Operations: Ryan Isaac. Baseball Operations Assistant: Sam Eaton, Joe Hultzen. Major League Video Coordinator: Allen Campbell. Administrative Assistant: Kristyn Pierce.

Kevin Towers

Major League Staff
Manager: Kirk Gibson.
Coaches: Bench—Alan Trammell; Pitching—Charles Nagy; Batting—Don Baylor; First Base—Steve Sax; Third Base—Matt Williams; Bullpen—Glenn Sherlock; Assistant Batting—Turner Ward.

Medical/Training
Club Physicians: Dr. Michael Lee, Dr. Roger McCoy. Head Trainer: Ken Crenshaw. Assistant Trainer: Ryan DiPanfilo. Strength/Conditioning Coordinator: Nate Shaw. Manual/Performance Therapist: Neil Rampe.

Minor Leagues
Telephone: (602) 462-6500. Fax: (602) 462-6425.
Director, Player Development: Mike Bell. Assistant to Player Development: TJ Lasita. Director, Minor League Administration: Susan Webner. Coordinators: Jeff Pico (field), Mel Stottlemyre, Jr (pitching), Alan Cockrell (hitting), Tony Perezchica (infield), Joel Youngblood (outfield/baserunning), Carlos Hernandez (catching), Hatuey Mendoza (Latin Liaison), Wilfredo Tejada (Dominican field), Andrew Hauser (medical), David Rivera (assistant medical), Vaughn Robinson (strength), Kyle Torgerson (manual performance), Jim Currigan (video), Bob Bensinger (complex).

Farm System

Class	Club (League)	Manager	Hitting Coach	Pitching Coach
Triple-A	Reno (PCL)	Brett Butler	Greg Gross	Mike Parrott
Double-A	Mobile (SL)	Andy Green	Jacob Cruz	Dan Carlson
High A	Visalia (CAL	Bill Plummer	Bobby Smith	Gil Heredia
Low A	South Bend (MWL)	Mark Haley	Jason Camilli	Wellington Cepeda
Short-season	Hillsboro (NWL)	Audo Vicente	JR House	Doug Drabek
Rookie	Missoula (PIO)	Robby Hammock	Wilson Valera	Doug Bochtler
Rookie	Diamondbacks (AZL)	Luis Urueta	Mark Grace	Jeff Bajenaru

Scouting
Telephone: (602) 462-6500. Fax: (602) 462-6425.
Director, Scouting: Ray Montgomery. Director, Pacific Rim Operations: Mack Hayashi. Special Assistant, Pacific Rim Operations: Jim Marshall. Assistant Director, Scouting: Brendan Domaracki. Major League Scouts/Special Assistants to GM: Bill Bryk (Schererville, IN), Todd Greene (Alpharetta, GA), Mike Berger (Oakmont, PA). Pro Scouts: Brian Boehringer (Fenton, MO), Mike Brown (Naples, FL), Bob Cummings (Oak Lawn, IL), Clay Daniel (Jacksonville, FL), Brad Kelley (Scottsdale, AZ), Bill Gayton (San Diego, CA), Pat Murtaugh (West Lafayette, IN), Mike Piatnik (Winter Haven, FL), Tom Romenesko (Santee, CA). Special Assignment Scouts, Independent Leagues: Ron Biga (Chicago, IL), Billy Bryk Jr (Laredo, TX), Chris Carminucci (Southbury, CT). Regional Supervisors: Todd Donovan (East Lyme, CT), Spencer Graham (Gresham, OR), Greg Lonigro (Connellsville, PA), Steve McAllister (Chillicothe, IL), Howard McCullough (Greenville, NC). Area Scouts: John Bartsch (Rocklin, CA), Nathan Birtwell (Nashville, TN), Hal Kurtzman (Lake Balboa, CA), TR Lewis (Marietta, GA), Joe Mason (Millbrook, AL), Rick Matsko (Davidsville, PA), Jeff Mousser (Huntington Beach, CA), James Mouton (Missouri City, TX), Rusty Pendergrass (Missouri City, MO), Donnie Reynolds (Portland, OR), Joe Robinson (St Louis, MO), Tony Piazza (Springfield, MO), JR Salinas (Dallas, TX), Rick Short (Peoria, IL), Doyle Wilson (Phoenix, AZ), George Swain (Wilmington, NC), Frankie Thon Jr (Miami, FL), Luke Wrenn (Lakeland, FL). Part-Time Scouts: Doug Mathieson (Aldergrove, BC), Homer Newlin (Tallahassee, FL), Steve Oleschuk (Verdun, QC), Mike Serbalik (Clifton Park, NY). International Scouting Supervisor: Luis Baez (Santo Domingo, DR). International Scouts: Dominican Republic—Gabriel Berroa, José Ortiz, Rafael Mateo; Panama—José Díaz Perez; Nicaragua—Julio Sanchez; Colombia—Luis Gonzalez; Venezuela—Marlon Urdaneta.

Atlanta Braves

Office Address: 755 Hank Aaron Dr., Atlanta, GA 30315.
Mailing Address: PO Box 4064, Atlanta, GA 30302.
Telephone: (404) 522-7630. **Website:** www.braves.com.

Ownership

Operated/Owned By: Liberty Media.
Chairman/CEO: Terry McGuirk. **Chairman Emeritus:** Bill Bartholomay. **President:** John Schuerholz. **Senior Vice President:** Henry Aaron.

BUSINESS OPERATIONS

Executive VP, Business Operations: Mike Plant. **Senior VP/General Counsel:** Greg Heller.

Finance

Chief Financial Officer: Chip Moore.

Marketing/Sales

Executive VP, Sales/Marketing: Derek Schiller. **VP, Marketing:** Gus Eurton. **VP, Ticket Sales:** Paul Adams. **VP, Corporate Sales:** Jim Allen.

Media Relations/Public Relations

Telephone: (404) 614-1556. **Fax:** (404) 614-1391.
Director, Media Relations: Brad Hainje. **Director, Public Relations:** Beth Marshall.
Publications Manager: Andy Pressley. **Public Relations Coordinator:** Mackenzie Anderson.
Media Relations Manager: Adrienne Midgley. **Media Relations Coordinator:** Jim Misudek.

Terry McGuirk

Stadium Operations

Senior Director, Stadium Operations/Security: Larry Bowman. **Field Director:** Ed Mangan. **Director, Game Entertainment:** Scott Cunningham. **PA Announcer:** Casey Motter. **Official Scorers:** Mike Stamus, Jack Wilkinson.

Ticketing

Telephone: (404) 577-9100. **Fax:** (404) 614-2480.
Director, Ticket Operations: Anthony Esposito.

Travel/Clubhouse

Director, Team Travel/Equipment Manager: Bill Acree. **Visiting Clubhouse Manager:** John Holland.

2013 SCHEDULE

Standard Game Times: 7:10 p.m.; Fri. 7:35; Sun. 1:35.

APRIL
1 . . . . .Philadelphia
3-4. . . . . . .Philadelphia
5-7. . . . . . Chicago (NL)
8-10. . . . . . . at Miami
12-14 . . . at Washington
16-17 . . . . . Kansas City
18-21 . . . at Pittsburgh
22-24 . . . . . at Colorado
26-28 . . . . . . .at Detroit
29-30 . . . . . Washington

MAY
1-2. . . . . . . Washington
3-5 . . . . . .New York (NL)
6-8 . . . . . . .at Cincinnati
9-12 . . . at San Francisco

13-15 . . . . . . at Arizona
17-19 . . . Los Angeles (NL)
20-22 . . . . . . Minnesota
24-26 . . at New York (NL)
27-28 . . . . . . at Toronto
29-30 . . . . .Toronto
31 . . . . Washington

JUNE
1-2. . . . . . . Washington
3-5. . . . . Pittsburgh
6-9. . . at Los Angeles (NL)
10-12 . . . . at San Diego
14-16 . . . .San Francisco
17-20 . . . .New York (NL)
21-23 . . . at Milwaukee
25-26 . . . .at Kansas City

28-30 . . . . .Arizona

JULY
2-4. . . . . .Miami
5-7. . . . . at Philadelphia
8-10 . . . . at Miami
11-14 . . . . Cincinnati
19-21 . . . .at Chicago (AL)
22-25 . . . at New York (NL)
26-28 . . . . St. Louis
29-31 . . . . . . .Colorado

AUGUST
1 . . . . .Colorado
2-4. . . . . . . at Philadelphia
5-7. . . . . at Washington
9-11 . . . . .Miami
12-14 . . . . . .Philadelphia

16-18 . . . . . Washington
20-21 . . . at New York (NL)
22-25 . . . . . .at St. Louis
27-29 . . . . . . Cleveland
30-31 . . . . .Miami

SEPTEMBER
1 . . . . .Miami
2-4. . . . . .New York (NL)
5-8. . . . . at Philadelphia
9-12 . . . . at Miami
13-15 . . . . . San Diego
16-18 . . . . at Washington
20-22 . . . .at Chicago (NL)
23-25 . . . . . .Milwaukee
26-29 . . . . .Philadelphia

GENERAL INFORMATION

Stadium (year opened):
Turner Field (1997).
Team Colors: Red, white and blue.

Player Representative: David Ross.
Home Dugout: First Base.
Playing Surface: Grass.

BASEBALL OPERATIONS

Telephone: (404) 522-7630. **Fax:** (404) 614-3308.
Executive VP/General Manager: Frank Wren.
VP/Assistant GM, Player Development: Bruce Manno. **Executive Assistants:** Annie Lee, Chris Rice.

Frank Wren

Major League Staff

Manager: Fredi Gonzalez.
Coaches: Bench—Carlos Tosca; **Pitching**—Roger McDowell; **Hitting**—Greg Walker; **First Base**—Terry Pendleton; **Third Base**—Brian Snitker; **Bullpen**—Eddie Perez.

Medical/Training

Head Team Physician: Dr. Xavier Duralde.
Trainer: Jeff Porter. **Assistant Trainer:** Jim Lovell.
Director, Strength/Conditioning: Rick Slate. **Major League Strength/Conditioning Coach:** Phil Falco.

Player Development

Telephone: (404) 522-7630. **Fax:** (404) 614-1350.
Director, Minor League Operations: Ronnie Richardson. **Special Assistants to the GM, Player Development:** Jose Martinez, Lee Elia. **Baseball Operations Assistants:** Matt Grabowski, Ron Knight.
Minor League Field Coordinator: Dave Bialas. **Pitching Coordinator:** Dave Wallace. **Hitting Coordinator:** Don Long.
Roving Instructors: Joe Breeden (catching), Doug Dascenzo (outfield/baserunning), Luis Lopez (infield), James Gonzalez (assistant strength/conditioning).

Farm System

Class	Club (League)	Manager	Coach	Pitching Coach
Triple-A	Gwinnett (IL)	Randy Ready	Jamie Dismuke	Marty Reed
Double-A	Mississippi (SL)	Aaron Holbert	Garey Ingram	Dennis Lewallyn
High A	Lynchburg (CL)	Luis Salazar	John Moses	Derek Botelho
Low A	Rome (SAL)	Randy Ingle	Bobby Moore	Derrick Lewis
Rookie	Danville (APP)	Jonathan Schuerholz	Rick Albert	Gabriel Luckert
Rookie	Braves (GCL)	Rocket Wheeler	Carlos Mendez	William Martinez
Rookie	Braves (DSL)	Francisco Santiesteban	Tommy Herrera	Mike Alvarez

Scouting

Telephone: (404) 522-7630. **Fax:** (404) 614-1350.
Assistant GM: John Coppolella.
Special Assistants to GM/Major League Scouts: Dick Balderson (Englewood, CO), Dom Chiti (Auburndale, FL), Matt Carroll (Erdenheim, PA), Jim Fregosi (Tarpon Springs, FL), Dave Holliday (Bixby, OK), Brad Sloan (Brimfield, IL), Jeff Wren (Senoia, GA). **Professional Scouts:** Rod Gilbreath (Lilburn, GA), Lloyd Merritt (Myrtle Beach, SC), John Stewart (Granville, NY).
Director, Scouting: Tony DeMacio. **Office Coordinator, Scouting:** Dixie Keller.
National Crosscheckers: John Flannery (Austin, TX), Deron Rombach (Mansfield, TX). **Regional Crosscheckers: West**—Tom Davis (Ripon, CA), **Southwest**—James "Bump" Merriweather (Glendale, AZ), **East**—Steve Fleming (Louisa, VA), **Midwest**—Terry R. Tripp (Harrisburg, IL), Southeast—Brian Bridges (Rome, GA).
Area Scouts: John Barron (Cameron, TX), Kevin Barry (Kinmundy, IL), Billy Best (Holly Spings, NC), Bill Bliss (Phoenix, AZ), Hugh Buchanan (Snellville, GA), Brett Evert (Salem, OR), Ralph Garr (Richmond, TX), Buddy Hernandez (Orlando, FL), Gene Kerns (Hagerstown, MD), Chris Knabenshue (Fort Collins, CO), Steve Leavitt (Huntington Beach, CA), Rick Sellers (Remus, MI), Dennis Sheehan (Glasco, NY), Don Thomas (Geismar, LA), Terry C. Tripp (Norris, IL), Gerald Turner (Bedford, TX). **Part-Time Scouts:** Dick Adams (Lincoln, CA), Stu Cann (Bradley, IL), Dewayne Kitts (Moncks Corner, SC), Abraham Martinez (Santa Isabel, PR), Lou Sanchez (Miami, FL).
Director, International Scouting/Operations: Johnny Almaraz.
Assistant Director, International Scouting/Operations: Jose Martinez. **International Coordinators: Central American Supervisor**—Luis Ortiz (San Antonio, TX); **Eastern Rim**—Phil Dale (Victoria, Australia).
International Area Supervisors: Matias Laureano (Dominican Republic), Hiroyuki Oya (Japan), Rolando Petit (Venezuela), Manuel Samaniego (Mexico). **Part-Time Scouts:** Neil Burke (Australia), Nehomar Caldera (Venezuela), Junior Carrion (Dominican Republic), Jeremy Chou (Taiwan), Carlos Garcia Roque (Colombia), Raul Gonzalez (Panama), Remmy Hernandez (Dominican Republic), Dargello Lodowica (Curacao), Alfredo Molina (Ecuador), Rafael Motooka (Brazil), Nestor Perez (Spain), Carlos Rodriguez (Venezuela), Jefferson Romero D'Lima (Venezuela), Eduardo Rosario (Venezuela), Miguel Theran (Colombia), Marvin Throneberry (Nicaragua), Carlos Torres (Venezuela).

Baltimore Orioles

Office Address: 333 W Camden St., Baltimore, MD 21201.
Telephone: (888) 848-BIRD. **Fax:** (410) 547-6272.
E-mail Address: birdmail@orioles.com. **Website:** www.orioles.com.

Ownership
Operated By: The Baltimore Orioles Limited Partnership Inc.
Chairman/CEO: Peter Angelos.

BUSINESS OPERATIONS
Executive Vice President: John Angelos. **Executive VP, Business Operations:** Doug Duennes. **VP/Special Liaison to Chairman:** Lou Kousouris. **General Legal Counsel:** Russell Smouse. **Director, Human Resources:** Lisa Tolson. **Director, Information Systems:** James Kline.

Finance
VP/CFO: Robert Ames. **VP, Finance:** Michael D. Hoppes, CPA.

Public Relations/Communications
Telephone: (410) 547-6150. **Fax:** (410) 547-6272.
VP, Communications/Marketing: Greg Bader. **Director, Public Relations:** Monica Barlow. **Manager, Media Relations:** Jeff Lantz. **Coordinator, Baseball Information:** Jay Moskowitz. **Coordinator, Public Relations/New Media:** Amanda Sarver. **Director, Promotions/ Community Relations:** Kristen Schultz.

Peter Angelos

Ballpark Operations
Director, Ballpark Operations: Kevin Cummings. **Head Groundskeeper:** Nicole McFayden.
PA Announcer: Ryan Wagner. **Official Scorers:** Jim Henneman, Marc Jacobson, Ryan Eigenbrode.

Ticketing
Telephone: (888) 848-BIRD. **Fax:** (410) 547-6270.
VP, Ticketing/Fan Services: Neil Aloise. **Assistant Director, Sales:** Mark Hromalik. **Ticket Manager:** Audrey Brown.

Travel/Clubhouse
Coordinator, Team Travel: Kevin Buck.

2013 SCHEDULE
Standard Game Times: 7:05 p.m; Sun. 1:35

APRIL
2-4 . . . . . . at Tampa Bay
5-7 . . . . Minnesota
8 . . . . .at Boston
10-11 . . . . . . .at Boston
12-14 . . at New York (AL)
16-18 . . . . . . .Tampa Bay
19-21 . . . Los Angeles (NL)
22-24 . . . . .Toronto
25-28 . . . . . .at Oakland
29-30 . . . . . .at Seattle

MAY
1 . . . . .at Seattle
2-4 . . . at Los Angeles (AL)
7-9 . . . . Kansas City
10-12 . . . . at Minnesota

14-15 . . . . San Diego
17-19 . . . . . . .Tampa Bay
20-22 . . . .New York (AL)
23-26 . . . . . . at Toronto
27-28 . . . . at Washington
29-30 . . . . . . Washington
31 . . . . Detroit

JUNE
1-2 . . . . Detroit
4-6 . . . . .at Houston
7-9 . . . . . . at Tampa Bay
10-12 . . . Los Angeles (AL)
13-16 . . . . Boston
17-19 . . . . . . .at Detroit
21-23 . . . . . . at Toronto
24-27 . . . . . . Cleveland

28-30 . . . . .New York (AL)

JULY
2-4 . . . . . .at Chicago (AL)
5-7 . . . . at New York (AL)
8-11 . . . . Texas
12-14 . . . . .Toronto
19-21 . . . . .at Texas
22-25 . . . . .at Kansas City
26-28 . . . . Boston
30-31 . . . . Houston

AUGUST
1 . . . . Houston
2-4 . . . . Seattle
6-7 . . . . . . at San Diego
9-11 . . . . at San Francisco
12-14 . . . . . . at Arizona

16-18 . . . . .Colorado
19-21 . . . . . . .Tampa Bay
23-25 . . . . Oakland
27-29 . . . . . . .at Boston
30-31 . . . at New York (AL)

SEPTEMBER
1 . . . . . . .New York (AL)
2-4 . . . . . . .at Cleveland
5-8 . . . . . . Chicago (AL)
9-12 . . . . .New York (AL)
13-15 . . . . . . at Toronto
17-19 . . . . . . .at Boston
20-23 . . . . at Tampa Bay
24-26 . . . . .Toronto
27-29 . . . . Boston

GENERAL INFORMATION
Stadium (year opened): Oriole Park at Camden Yards (1992).
Team Colors: Orange, black and white.

Player Representative: Jim Johnson.
Home Dugout: First Base.
Playing Surface: Grass.

BASEBALL OPERATIONS

Telephone: (410) 547-6107. **Fax:** (410) 547-6271.
Executive Vice President, Baseball Operations: Dan Duquette.
Special Assistants to the Executive VP, Baseball Operations: Brady Anderson, Lee Thomas.
Director, Player Personnel: John Stockstill. **Director, Baseball Administration:** Tripp Norton.
Executive Director, International Scouting: Fred Ferreira. **Assistant Director, Major League Operations:** Ned Rice. **Coordinator, Baseball Operations:** Bill Wilkes. **Coordinator, Baseball Analytics:** Sarah Gelles. **Player Information Analyst:** Tom Duncan. **Video Coordinator:** Michael Silverman. **Advance Scouting Coordinator:** Ben Werthan. **Coordinator, Pro Scouting:** Matt Koizim.

Dan Duquette

Major League Staff
Manager: Buck Showalter.
Coaches: Bench—John Russell; **Pitching**—Rick Adair; **Batting**—Jim Presley; **First Base**—Wayne Kirby; **Third Base**—Bobby Dickerson; **Bullpen**—Bill Castro.

Medical/Training
Club Physician: Dr. William Goldiner. **Club Physician, Orthopedics:** Dr. John Wilckens. **Head Athletic Trainer:** Richie Bancells. **Assistant Athletic Trainer:** Brian Ebel. **Strength/Conditioning Coach:** Joe Hogarty.

Player Development
Telephone: (410) 547-6120. **Fax:** (410) 547-6298.
Director, Minor League Operations: Kent Qualls. **Director, Player Development:** Brian Graham. **Assistant Director, Player Development/Scouting:** Mike Snyder. **Coordinator, Minor League Administration:** J. Maria Arellano. **Coordinator, Player Development:** Cale Cox. **Director, Pitching Development:** Rick Peterson. **Coordinator, Minor League Hitting:** Mike Boulanger. **Coordinator, Organizational Hitting Instructor/Evaluator:** Terry Crowley. **Instructor, Minor League Catching:** Don Werner. **Instructor, Minor League Field:** Matt Martin. **Medical Coordinator:** Dave Walker. **Latin American Medical Coordinator:** Manny Lopez. **Strength/Conditioning Coordinator:** Ryan Driscoll. **Minor League Rehab Pitching Coach:** Scott McGregor. **Minor League Equipment Manager:** Jake Parker. **Pitching Administrator, Florida/DSL:** Dave Schmidt. **Administrator, Sarasota Operations:** Len Johnston.

Farm System

Class	Club (League)	Manager	Hitting Coach	Pitching Coach
Triple-A	Norfolk (IL)	Ron Johnson	Denny Walling	Mike Griffin
Double-A	Bowie (EL)	Gary Kendall	Einar Diaz	Blaine Beatty
High A	Frederick (CL)	Ryan Minor	Torre Tyson	Kennie Steenstra
Low A	Delmarva (SAL)	Luis Pujols	Butch Davis	Justin Lord
Short-season	Aberdeen (NYP)	Matt Merullo	Jon Mathews	Alan Mills
Rookie	Orioles (GCL)	Orlando Gomez	Milt May	Wilson Alvarez
Rookie	Orioles (DSL)	Elvis Morel	D. Pascual/R. Perez	R. Caraballo/M. Jabalera

Scouting
Telephone: (410) 547-6212. **Fax:** 410-547-6928.
Director, Amateur Scouting: Gary Rajsich. **Scouting Administrator:** Brad Ciolek. **National Supervisor:** Danny Haas (Fort Myers, FL). **National Crosschecker:** Matt Haas (Cincinnati, OH). **National Pitching Crosschecker:** James Keller (Sacramento, CA). **West Coast Supervisor:** David Blume (Elk Grove, CA). **Midwest Supervisor:** Jim Richardson (Marlow, OK). **Area Scouts:** Dean Albany (Baltimore, MD), Kelvin Colon (Miami, FL), Adrian Dorsey (Nashville, TN), Thom Dreier (Houston, TX), Kirk Fredriksson (Torrington, CT), Chris Gale (Raleigh, NC), John Gillette (Gilbert, AZ), Ernie Jacobs (Wichita, KS), David Jennings (Spanish Fort, AL), Arthur McConnehead (Atlanta, GA), Rich Morales (Pacifica, CA), Mark Ralston (Carlsbad, CA), David Stockstill (Crane, MO), Bob Szymkowski (Chicago, IL), Jim Thrift (Sarasota, FL), Brandon Verley (White Salmon, WA), Scott Walter (Manhattan Beach, CA). **Special Assignment Scouts:** Wayne Britton (Waynesboro, VA), Darryl Milne (Denver, CO).
Major League Scouts: Dave Engle (San Diego, CA), Jim Howard (Clifton Park, NY), Bruce Kison (Bradenton, FL). **Professional Scouts:** Tom Bourque (Cambridge, MA), Todd Frohwirth (Waukesha, WI), Fred Uhlman Sr (Baltimore, MD). **Consultant, Independent Baseball:** Mal Fichman (Boise, ID). **Part-Time Scouts:** Darin Blair (Lawrenceville, IL), Ellis Dungan (Charlotte, NC), Ken Guthrie (Lantana, TX), Larry Headrick (Glendale, AZ), James Jones (Poway, CA), Frank Kolarek (Baltimore, MD), Tyler Moe (Ontario, Canada), Tim Norris (Baltimore, MD), Harvey Shapiro (Bloomfield, CT), Anibal Zayas (San Lorenzo, Puerto Rico).
Executive Director, International Recruiting: Fred Ferreira. **Executive Advisor, International Baseball:** Ray Poitevint. **Academy Director, Dominican Republic:** Felipe Rojas Alou. **International Scouts:** Calvin Maduro, Brett Ward. **Part-Time International Scouts:** Gustavo Bencid (Venzuela), Joel Bradley (Plantation, FL), Enrique Constante (Dominican Republic), Eric Espinosa (Panama), Jorge Franco (Colombia), Ton Hofstede (Curacao, Europe), Ronald Hurtarte (Guatemala), Juan Linares (Dominican Republic), Ernst Meyer (Curacao), William Morales (Colombia), Carlos Moreno (Venezuela), Justin Prinstein (Europe).

Boston Red Sox

Office Address: Fenway Park, 4 Yawkey Way, Boston, MA 02215.
Telephone: (617) 226-6000. **Fax:** (617) 226-6416.
Website: www.redsox.com

Ownership
Principal Owner: John Henry.
Chairman: Thomas C. Werner. **President/CEO:** Larry Lucchino. **Vice Chairmen:** David Ginsberg, Phillip Morse.

Business Operations/Legal
Executive Vice President/Chief Operating Officer: Sam Kennedy. **Executive VP, Business Affairs:** Jonathan Gilula. **Executive VP/Senior Advisor to the President/CEO:** Charles Steinberg. **Senior VP, Fenway Affairs:** Larry Cancro. **Senior Advisor, Baseball Projects:** Jeremy Kapstein. **General Counsel, Fenway Sports Group LLC:** Ed Weiss. **Senior VP/Assistant General Counsel:** Jennifer Flynn. **Senior VP/Special Counsel:** David Friedman. **VP/Club Counsel:** Elaine Weddington Steward.

Larry Lucchino

Finance
Senior VP/CFO: Steve Fitch. **VP/Controller:** Mark Solitro. **Financial Advisor to the CEO:** Jeff White. **Senior Advisor, Finance/Accounting:** Bob Furbush. **Director, Finance:** Ryan Oremus.

Human Resources/Information Technology
VP, Human Resources: Amy Waryas. **Director, Human Resources:** Mike Danubio. **Director, IT:** Steve Conley. **Director, Business Applications:** Heidi Labritz.

Sales/Corporate Partnerships/Marketing
Senior VP, Corporate Partnerships: Troup Parkinson. **Senior VP, Marketing/Brand Development:** Adam Grossman. **Director, Client Services:** Marcell Bhangoo. **Director, Marketing:** Brian Sullivan. **Director, Broadcasting:** Colin Burch.

Public Affairs/Media
Senior Director, Public Affairs: Pam Kenn. **Director, Media Relations:** Kevin Gregg. **Director, Corporate Communications:** Zineb Curran. **VP/Team Historian:** Dick Bresciani. **Director, Publications:** Debbie Matson.

Ballpark Operations
VP, Fan Services/Entertainment: Sarah McKenna. **Senior Director, Ballpark Operations:** Pete Nesbit. **Director, Facilities:** Jonathan Lister. **Director, Concessions/Merchandise Operations:** Jeff Goldenberg. **Director, Grounds:** Dave Mellor. **Director, Security/Emergency Services:** Charlie Cellucci. **Director, Special Projects:** Fred Olsen. **Director, Business Development:** Tim Zue. **Director, Grounds Emeritus:** Joe Mooney. **Director, Florida Business Operations:** Katie Haas. **Director, Red Sox Productions:** John Carter. **Special Advisor to Florida Operations:** Todd Stephenson.

2013 SCHEDULE
Standard Game Times: 7:10 p.m.; Sun. 1:35

APRIL
1-2 . . . . . at New York (AL)
3-4 . . . . . at New York (AL)
5-7 . . . . at Toronto
8 . . . . Baltimore
10-11 . . . . Baltimore
12-15 . . . . . . Tampa Bay
16-18 . . . . . at Cleveland
19-21 . . . . . Kansas City
22-24 . . . . Oakland
25-28 . . . . Houston
30 . . . . at Toronto

MAY
1-2 . . . . at Toronto
3-5 . . . . at Texas
6-9 . . . . Minnesota

10-12 . . . . Toronto
14-16 . . . . at Tampa Bay
17-19 . . . . at Minnesota
20-22 . . . at Chicago (AL)
23-26 . . . . . . Cleveland
27-28 . . . . . Philadelphia
29-30 . . . at Philadelphia
31 . . . at New York (AL)

JUNE
1-2 . . . . at New York (AL)
4-6 . . . . Texas
7-9 . . . . Los Angeles (AL)
10-12 . . . . at Tampa Bay
13-16 . . . . . at Baltimore
18-19 . . . . . . Tampa Bay
20-23 . . . . . . at Detroit

25-26 . . . . Colorado
27-30 . . . . Toronto

JULY
2-4 . . . . San Diego
5-7 . . . at Los Angeles (AL)
8-11 . . . . at Seattle
12-14 . . . . . at Oakland
19-21 . . . . New York (AL)
22-25 . . . . . Tampa Bay
26-28 . . . . . at Baltimore
30-31 . . . . Seattle

AUGUST
1 . . . . Seattle
2-4 . . . . Arizona
5-7 . . . . at Houston
8-11 . . . . at Kansas City

13-15 . . . . . at Toronto
16-18 . . . . New York (AL)
19-21 . . at San Francisco
23-25 . at Los Angeles (NL)
27-29 . . . . . . Baltimore
30-31 . . . . Chicago (AL)

SEPTEMBER
1 . . . . Chicago (AL)
2-4 . . . . Detroit
5-8 . . . at New York (AL)
10-12 . . . . at Tampa Bay
13-15 . . . . New York (AL)
17-19 . . . . . . Baltimore
20-22 . . . . Toronto
24-25 . . . . . at Colorado
27-29 . . . . . at Baltimore

GENERAL INFORMATION
Stadium (year opened):
Fenway Park (1912).
Team Colors: Navy blue, red and white.

Player Representative: Unavailable.
Home Dugout: First Base.
Playing Surface: Grass.

Ticketing Services/Operations
Telephone: 888-REDSOX6.
Senior VP, Ticketing/Fenway Enterprises: Ron Bumgarner. **VP, Ticketing:** Richard Beaton. **Director, Ticketing:** Naomi Calder. **Director, Premium Sales:** Will Droste. **Director, Fenway Enterprises:** Carrie Campbell.

BASEBALL OPERATIONS

Executive VP/General Manager: Ben Cherington.
VP/Assistant GM: Mike Hazen. **VP/Assistant GM:** Brian O'Halloran. **VP, Player Personnel:** Allard Baird. **Director, Player Personnel:** Dave Finley. **Director, Major League Operations:** Zack Scott. **Director, Baseball Information Services:** Tom Tippett. **Coordinator, Baseball Operations:** Mike Murov. **Software Developer:** Shawn O'Rourke. **Traveling Secretary:** Jack McCormick. **Executive Assistant:** Erin Cox. **Senior Advisor:** Bill James. **Special Assistant to GM:** Jason Varitek.

Ben Cherington

Major League Staff
Manager: John Farrell.
Coaches: Bench—Torey Lovullo; **Pitching**—Juan Nieves; **Hitting**—Greg Colbrunn; **First Base**—Arnie Beyeler; **Third Base**—Brian Butterfield; **Bullpen**—Dana LeVangie; **Assistant Hitting Coach**—Victor Rodriguez; **Bullpen Catcher**—Mani Martinez; **Bullpen Catcher/BP Thrower**—Brian Abraham; **BP Thrower**—Matt Noone; **Staff Assistant**—Ino Guerrero.

Medical/Training
Medical Director: Larry Ronan. **Head Team Orthopedist:** Dr. Peter Asnis. **Sports Medicine Coordinator:** Dan Dyrek. **Head Athletic Trainer:** Rick Jameyson. **Medical Operations Coordinator:** Jim Rowe. **Assistant Trainers:** Brad Pearson, Masai Takahashi. **Strength/Conditioning Coach:** Pat Sandora.

Player Development
Senior Director, Minor League Operations: Raquel Ferreira. **Director, Player Development:** Ben Crockett. **Assistant Director, Player Development:** Duncan Webb. **Assistant Director, Florida Baseball Operations:** Ethan Faggett. **Assistant, Baseball Operations:** Mike Regan. **Field Coordinator:** David Howard. **Latin American Pitching Coordinator:** Goose Gregson. **Minor League Athletic Training Coordinator:** Paul Buchheit. **Minor League Strength/Conditioning Coordinator:** Mike Roose. **Minor League Physical Therapist:** Chip Simpson. **Mental Skills Coach:** Bob Tewksbury. **Coordinator, Player Development Programs:** Laz Gutierrez. **Roving Instructors:** Andy Fox (infield), Chad Epperson (catching), Tim Hyers (hitting), Ralph Treuel (pitching), George Lombard (outfield/baserunning).

Farm System

Class	Club (League)	Manager	Coach(es)	Pitching Coach
Triple-A	Pawtucket (IL)	Gary DiSarcina	Dave Joppie	Rich Sauveur
Double-A	Portland (EL)	Kevin Boles	Rich Gedman	Bob Kipper
High A	Salem (CL)	Billy McMillon	Nelson Paulino	Kevin Walker
Low A	Greenville (SAL)	Carlos Febles	U.L. Washington	Paul Abbott
Short-season	Lowell (NYP)	Bruce Crabbe	Noah Hall	Walter Miranda
Rookie	Red Sox (GCL)	Darren Fenster	Raul Gonzalez/Dave Tomlin	Tom Kotchman/Dick Such
Rookie	Red Sox (DSL)	Jose Zapata	Junior Zamora/Wilton Veras	Amaury Telemaco/Oscar Lira

Scouting
Director, Amateur Scouting: Amiel Sawdaye. **Director, Professional Scouting:** Jared Porter.
Special Assistant, Player Personnel: Eddie Bane. **Assistant Director, Amateur Scouting:** Gus Quattlebaum. **Assistant Director, Player Personnel:** Jared Banner. **Advance Scouting Coordinator:** Steve Langone. **Assistant, International/Amateur Scouting:** Steve Sanders. **Special Assignment Scouts:** Galen Carr (Burlington, VT), Steve Peck (Scottsdale, AZ) Mark Wasinger (El Paso, TX). **Major League Advance Scout:** Dana LeVangie (East Bridgewater, MA). **Major League Scouts:** Bob Hamelin (Charlotte, NC), Dave Klipstein (Roanoke, TX).
Professional Scouts: Jaymie Bane (Parrish, FL), Nate Field (Denver, CO), David Keller (Houston, TX), John Lombardo (Grand Prairie, TX), Matt Mahoney (Scottsdale, AZ), Anthony Turco (Tampa, FL). **Professional Scouting Consultants:** David Cortes (El Centro, CA), Gary Hughes (Aptos, CA), Joe McDonald (Lakeland, FL), Adam Wogan (Brooklyn, NY). **National Scouting Coordinator:** Mike Rikard (Durham, NC). **National Crosschecker:** John Booher (Buda, TX).
Regional Crosscheckers: Southeast—Fred Petersen (Lincoln, NE), **Southwest**—Jim Robinson (Arlington, TX), **Northeast**—Quincy Boyd (Harrisburg, NC), **West**—Dan Madsen (Murrieta, CA). **Area Scouts:** Jon Adkins (Wayne, WV), Tom Battista (Thousand Oaks, CA), Steve Bowden (Kingwood, TX), Chris Calciano (Ocean View, DE), Raymond Fagnant (East Granby, CT), Blair Henry (Naperville, IL), Tom Kotchman (Seminole, FL), Chris Mears (Oklahoma City, OK), Brian Moehler (Marietta, GA), Edgar Perez (Vega Baja, PR), Pat Portugal (Wake Forest, NC), Chris Pritchett (Vancouver, BC), John Pyle (Frankfort IL), Willie Romay (Miami Springs, FL), Demond Smith (Sacramento, CA), Danny Watkins (Tuscaloosa, AL), Vaughn Williams (Phoenix, AZ), Jim Woodward (Claremont, CA). **Part Time Scouts:** Buzz Bowers (Orleans, MA), Rob English (Duluth, GA), Stephen Hargett (St. Augustine, FL), Jay Oliver (Texarkana, TX), Keith Prager (La Verne, CA), Adam Stern (London, Ontario), Terry Sullivan (La Grange, IL).
Director, International Scouting: Eddie Romero. **Coordinator, Latin American:** Todd Claus. **International Crosschecker:** Rolando Pino. **Director, Dominican Academy:** Jesus Alou. **Assistant to the Director, Dominican Academy:** Javier Hernandez. **Dominican Republic Scouting Supervisor:** Manny Nanita. **Dominican Republic Crosschecker:** Victor Rodriguez, Jr. **Coordinator, Pacific Rim Scouting:** Jon Deeble. **International Scouts:** Jonathan Cruz (Dominican Republic), Angel Escobar (Venezuela), Brian Farley (Europe), Cris Garibaldo (Panama), Ernesto Gomez (Venezuela), John Kim (Korea), Louie Lin (Taiwan), Rafael Mendoza (Nicaragua), Dennis Neuman (Aruba/Curacao), Santiago Prada (Colombia), David Tapia (Mexico), Victor Torres (Dominican Republic).

Chicago Cubs

Office Address: Wrigley Field, 1060 W. Addison St., Chicago, IL 60613.
Telephone: (773) 404-2827. **Fax:** (773) 404-4129. **Website:** www.cubs.com.

Ownership
Chairman: Tom Ricketts. **Board of Directors:** Laura Ricketts, Pete Ricketts, Todd Ricketts, Tribune Company. **President, Business Operations:** Crane Kenney.

BUSINESS OPERATIONS
Executive Vice President, Business Operations: Mark McGuire. **Executive VP, Community Affairs/General Counsel:** Michael Lufrano. **Senior VP, Strategy/Development:** Alex Sugarman. **VP, Ticket Sales/Partnerships:** Colin Faulkner. **VP, Communications/Community Affairs:** Julian Green. **VP/CFO:** Jon Greifenkamp. **VP, Ballpark Operations:** Carl Rice. **VP, Human Resources:** Bryan Robinson. **Executive Assistant:** Lorraine Swiatly. **Executive Coordinator, Business Operations:** Sarah Poontong.

Tom Ricketts

Accounting/Finance
Assistant Controller: Mike Van Poucke. **Director, Procurement/Sourcing:** Patrick Meenan.

Ballpark Operations
Senior Director, Wrigley Field Event Operations: Matt Kenny. **Director, Fan Experiences:** Jahaan Blake. **Head Groundskeeper:** Roger Baird. **Public Address Announcer:** Andrew Belleson.

Communications
Manager, Communications: Kevin Saghy. **Social Media/Public Relations Assistant:** Mary Reisert.

Corporate Partnerships/Marketing
Director, Corporate Partnerships: Michael Kirschner. **Senior Director, Marketing:** Alison Miller. **Manager, Broadcast Relations:** Joe Rios. **Manager, Game/Event Production:** Jim Oboikowitch. **Manager, Brand Activation:** John Morrison.

Human Resources/Information Technology
HR Manager, Organization/Staffing: Marisol Widmayer. **HR Manager, Ballpark Operations:** Danielle Alexa. **HR Manager, Program Development:** Rachel Rush. **Director, Information Technology:** Andrew McIntyre. **Manager, IT Infrastructure/Operations:** Sundeep Bhatia. **Manager, Application Development:** Steve Inman.

Legal/Community Affairs
Assistant General Counsel: Lydia Wahlke. **Counsel:** Mike Feldman. **Manager, Community Outreach/Grants/Donations:** Jennifer Dedes-Nowak. **Manager, Community Affairs/Fundraising/Development/Events:** Connie Falcone.

Ticket Sales/Service
Director, Ticket Sales: Brian Garza. **Director, Ticket Operations:** Cale Vennum. **Manager, Fan Service:** Brad Nagel.

2013 SCHEDULE
Standard Game Times: 7:05 p.m., Sun. 1:20.

APRIL		JULY	
1 . . . . at Pittsburgh	13-15 . . . . .Colorado	28-30 . . . . . . .at Seattle	16-18 . . . . St. Louis
3-4 . . . . at Pittsburgh	17-19 . . . . .New York (NL)		19-22 . . . . . Washington
5-7 . . . . at Atlanta	21-23 . . . . at Pittsburgh	2-4 . . . . .at Oakland	23-25 . . . . . at San Diego
8-10 . . . . . . .Milwaukee	24-26 . . . . .at Cincinnati	5-7 . . . . Pittsburgh	26-28 . at Los Angeles (NL)
11-14 . . . . .San Francisco	27-28 . . . .at Chicago (AL)	9-10 . . . Los Angeles (AL)	30-31 . . . . .Philadelphia
16-18 . . . . Texas	29-30 . . . . . Chicago (AL)	11-14 . . . . St. Louis	
19-21 . . . . at Milwaukee	31 . . . . .Arizona	19-21 . . . . . at Colorado	SEPTEMBER
22-24 . . . . .at Cincinnati		22-25 . . . . . . at Arizona	1 . . . . .Philadelphia
25-28 . . . . at Miami	JUNE	26-28 . . at San Francisco	2-4 . . . . .Miami
29-30 . . . . San Diego	1-2 . . . . .Arizona	29-31 . . . . . .Milwaukee	6-8 . . . . .Milwaukee
	4-5 . . at Los Angeles (AL)		9-11 . . . . . .at Cincinnati
MAY	7-9 . . . . Pittsburgh	AUGUST	12-15 . . . . . at Pittsburgh
1-2 . . . . San Diego	10-13 . . . . Cincinnati	1-4 . . . . .Los Angeles (NL)	16-19 . . . . . at Milwaukee
3-5 . . . . Cincinnati	14-16 . . . at New York (NL)	6-8 . . . . . . at Philadelphia	20-22 . . . . Atlanta
7-8 . . . . St. Louis	17-20 . . . . . . .at St. Louis	9-11 . . . . .at St. Louis	23-25 . . . . Pittsburgh
10-12 . . . . at Washington	21-23 . . . . Houston	12-14 . . . . . . Cincinnati	27-29 . . . . . .at St. Louis
	25-27 . . . . . . .Milwaukee		

GENERAL INFORMATION

Stadium (year opened):
Wrigley Field (1914).
Team Colors: Royal blue, red and white.

Player Representative: Unavailable.
Home Dugout: Third Base.
Playing Surface: Grass.

Manager, Ticket Operations: Karry Kerness. Manager, Ticket Operations: Kevin Enerson. Manager, Ticket Sales/Service: Miguel DeJesus.

BASEBALL OPERATIONS

Theo Epstein

Telephone: (773) 404-2827. Fax: (773) 404-4147.
President, Baseball Operations: Theo Epstein. Executive Vice President/General Manager: Jed Hoyer. Assistant GMs: Randy Bush, Shiraz Rehman. Special Assistants: Louie Eljaua, Anthony Iapoce, Tim Wilken.
Special Assistant to GM/Director, Video/Advance Scouting: Kyle Evans. Director, Baseball Operations: Scott Harris. Traveling Secretary: Vijay Tekchandani. Executive Assistant to President/GM: Hayley DeWitte. Coordinator, Advance Scouting: Bobby Basham. Assistant, Baseball Operations: Jeff Greenberg. Baseball Systems: Jeremy Greenhouse. Major League Video Coordinator: Naoto Masamoto. Video Assistant, Advance Scouting: Nate Halm. Video Assistant, Minor League Video: Mitch Duggins.

Major League Staff

Manager: Dale Sveum.
Coaches: Pitching—Chris Bosio; Hitting—James Rowson; Assistant Hitting Coach: Rob Deer; Bench—Jamie Quirk; Third Base—David Bell; First Base—Dave McKay; Bullpen—Lester Strode. Staff Assistants: Mike Borzello, Franklin Font. Bullpen Catcher: Andy Lane.

Medical/Training

Team Physician: Dr. Stephen Adams. Team Orthopedist: Dr. Stephen Gryzlo.
Director, Medical Administration: Mark O'Neal. Head Athletic Trainer: P.J. Mainville. Assistant Athletic Trainers: Ed Halbur, Matt Johnson. Head Physical Therapist: Ryan Mertz. Head Strength/Conditioning Coach: Tim Buss. Sports Psychologist: Dr. Marc Strickland.

Media Relations

Director, Media Relations: Peter Chase. Assistant Director, Media Relations: Jason Carr. Coordinator, Media Relations: Dusty Harrington. Assistant, Media Relations: Safdar Khan.

Player Development

Telephone: (773) 404-4035. Fax: (773) 404-4147.
Senior VP, Scouting/Player Development: Jason McLeod. Director, Player Development: Brandon Hyde. Assistant Director, Player Development/International Scouting: Alex Suarez. Manager, Player Development Administration: Patti James. Player Development/International Scouting Assistant: David Macias. Field Coordinator: Tim Cossins. Coordinators: Derek Johnson (pitching), Anthony Iapoce (hitting), Jose Flores (infield), Lee Tinsley (outfield/baserunning), Carmelo Martinez (lower-level/DSL hitting coordinator), Rick Tronerud (rehab pitching). Training Coordinator: Justin Sharpe. Assistant Training Coordinator: Chuck Baughman. Strength/Conditioning Coordinator: Doug Jarrow. Clubhouse Manager: Dana Noeltner. Manager, Mesa Baseball Administration: Gil Passarella

Farm System

Class	Club (League)	Manager	Hitting Coach	Pitching Coach
Triple-A	Iowa (PCL)	Marty Pevey	Brian Harper	Mike Mason
Double-A	Tennessee (SL)	Buddy Bailey	Desi Wilson	Jeff Fassero
High A	Daytona (FSL)	Dave Keller	Mariano Duncan	Storm Davis
Low A	Kane County (MWL)	Mark Johnson	Tom Beyers	Ron Villone
Short-season	Boise (NWL)	Gary Van Tol	Bill Buckner	David Rosario
Rookie	Cubs (AZL)	Bobby Mitchell	Ricardo Medina/Jimmy Gonzalez	Anderson Tavarez
Rookie	Cubs (DSL)	Yudith Ozorio	Oscar Bernard	Leo Hernandez
Rookie	Cubs (VSL)	Osmin Melendez	Franklin Blanco	Angel Guzman

Scouting

Director, Amateur Scouting: Jaron Madison (Vallejo, CA). Assistant Director, Amateur Scouting: Lukas McKnight (Gurnee, IL). Director, Professional Scouting: Joe Bohringer (Western Springs, IL). Coordinator, Pro Scouting: Andrew Bassett (Chicago, IL). Major League Scout/Special Assistant to the GM: Dave Littlefield (Sewickley, PA). Major League Scouts: Jason Karegeannes (Long Beach, CA), Brad Kullman (Powell, OH). Pro Scouts: Billy Blitzer (Brooklyn, NY), Steve Boros (Kingwood, TX), Jake Ciarrachi (Chicago, IL), Denny Henderson (Orange, CA), Steve Hinton (Mather, CA), Terry Kennedy (Chandler, AZ), Mark Kiefer (Hunt, TX), Ken Kravec (Sarasota, FL), Bob Lofrano (Woodland Hills, CA), Mark Servais (LaCrosse, WI), Keith Stohr (Viera, FL). Amateur Scouting Assistant: Shane Farrell.
National Crosscheckers: Sam Hughes (Atlanta, GA), Matt Dorey (Houston, TX), Ron Tostenson (El Dorado Hills, CA). Crosscheckers: Southeast—Mark Adair (Atlanta, GA), Central—Steve Riha (Houston, TX), West—Matt Dorey (Houston, TX), Midwest/Northeast—Lukas McKnight (Gurnee, IL). Area Scouts: Tim Adkins (Huntington, WV), John Ceprini (Massapequa, NY), Tom Clark (Lake City, FL), Chris Clemons (Robinson, TX), Ramser Correa (Caguas, PR), Jim Crawford (Madison, MS), Jonathan Davis (Nashville, TN), Scott Fairbanks (Walnut Creek, CA), Trey Forkerway (Houston, TX), Al Geddes (Canby, OR), John Koronka (Clairmont, FL), Keith Lockhart (Dacula, GA), Alex Lontayo (Chula Vista, CA), Steve McFarland (Scottsdale, AZ), Tom Myers (Santa Barbara, CA), Ty Nichols (Broken Arrow, OK), Luis Raffan (Miami, FL), Keith Ryman (Jefferson City, TN), Eric Servais (St. Louis Park, MN), Matt Sherman (Norwell, MA), Billy Swoope (Norfolk, VA), Stan Zielinski (Winfield, IL). International Crosschecker/Pacific Rim Supervisor: Paul Weaver (Phoenix, AZ). Coordinator, Pacific Rim/Mexico: Steve Wilson. International Scouts: Hector Ortega (Venezuela), Jose Serra (Dominican Republic), Steve Wilson (Pacific Rim), Brent Phelan (Australia), Manny Esquivia (Colombia), Cirilo Cumberbatch (Panama), Gian Guzman (Dominican Republic), Julio Figueroa (Venezuela) and Min Kyu Sung (Korea).

Chicago White Sox

Office Address: U.S. Cellular, Field, 333 W. 35th St., Chicago, IL 60616.
Telephone: (312) 674-1000. **Fax:** (312) 674-5116. **Website:** www.whitesox.com.

Ownership
Chairman: Jerry Reinsdorf. **Vice Chairman:** Eddie Einhorn.
Board of Directors: Robert Judelson, Judd Malkin, Robert Mazer, Allan Muchin, Jay Pinsky, Lee Stern, Burton Ury, Charles Walsh.
Special Assistant to Chairman: Dennis Gilbert. **Assistant to Chairman:** Barb Reincke.
Coordinator, Administration/Investor Relations: Katie Hermle.

BUSINESS OPERATIONS
Senior Executive Vice President: Howard Pizer.
Senior Director, Information Services: Don Brown. **Senior Director, Human Resources:** Moira Foy. **Senior Coordinator, Human Resources:** Leslie Gaggiano.

Finance
Senior VP, Administration/Finance: Tim Buzard. **Senior Director, Finance:** Bill Waters. **Accounting Manager:** Chris Taylor.

Jerry Reinsdorf

Marketing/Sales
Senior VP, Sales/Marketing: Brooks Boyer. **Senior Director, Business Development/Broadcasting:** Bob Grim. **Senior Director, Game Operations:** Nichole Manning. **Senior Manager, Scoreboard Operations/Production:** Jeff Szynal. **Manager, Game Operations:** Amy Sheridan. **Manager, In-Game Entertainment:** Dan Mielke. **Senior Coordinator, Graphic Apparel/Design:** Lauren Markiewicz.
Director, Corporate Partnerships Sales Development: George McDoniel. **Director, Corporate Partnerships Activation:** Gail Tucker. **Manager, Corporate Partnerships Development:** Jeff Floerke. **Manager, Research/Activation:** Beth Grabowski. **Coordinators, Corporate Partnership Activation:** Lucy Rath, Sarah Gomez.
Director, Ticket Sales: Tom Sheridan. **Manager, Premium Seating Sales:** Rob Boaz.

Media Relations/Public Relations
Telephone: (312) 674-5300. **Fax:** (312) 674-5116.
Senior VP, Communications: Scott Reifert.
Director, Media Relations: Bob Beghtol. **Director, Public Relations:** Lou Hernandez. **Manager, Media Relations:** Ray Garcia. **Manager, Public Relations:** Marty Maloney. **Coordinators, Media Relations/Services:** Joe Roti, Leni Depoister.
Senior Director, Community Relations/Executive Director, CWS Charities: Christine O'Reilly. **Managers, Community Relations:** Laina Myers, Laura Visin. **Manager, Youth Baseball Initiatives:** Kevin Coe.
Director, Mass Communications: Nicole Saunches. **Director, Advertising/Design Services:** Gareth Breunlin. **Manager, Online Communications:** Dakin Dugaw.

2013 SCHEDULE
Standard Game Times: 7:10 p.m.; Sun. 1:10.

APRIL		
1 . . . . Kansas City	13-15 . . . . . at Minnesota	28-30 . . . . Cleveland	12-14 . . . . Detroit

APRIL
1 . . . . Kansas City
3-4 . . . . Kansas City
5-7 . . . . Seattle
9-11 . . . . at Washington
12-14 . . . .at Cleveland
15-18 . . . . . . at Toronto
19-21 . . . . . .Minnesota
22-24 . . . . . . Cleveland
25-28 . . . . . .Tampa Bay
30 . . . . .at Texas

MAY
1-2 . . . . .at Texas
3-5 . . . . .at Kansas City
7-8 . . . . at New York (NL)
10-12 . . . Los Angeles (AL)

13-15 . . . . . at Minnesota
16-19 . . at Los Angeles (AL)
20-22 . . . . Boston
24-26 . . . . .Miami
27-28 . . . . Chicago (NL)
29-30 . . .at Chicago (NL)
31 . . . . .at Oakland

JUNE
1-2 . . . . .at Oakland
3-5 . . . . .at Seattle
6-9 . . . . Oakland
10-12 . . . . . . .Toronto
14-17 . . . . .at Houston
18-20 . . . . at Minnesota
21-23 . . .at Kansas City
25-26 . . . .New York (NL)

28-30 . . . . Cleveland

JULY
2-4 . . . . Baltimore
5-7 . . . . . at Tampa Bay
9-11 . . . . .at Detroit
12-14 . . . . at Philadelphia
19-21 . . . . Atlanta
22-25 . . . . Detroit
26-28 . . . . Kansas City
29-31 . . . . .at Cleveland

AUGUST
1 . . . . .at Cleveland
2-4 . . . . .at Detroit
5-7 . . . . . .New York (AL)
9-11 . . . . .Minnesota

12-14 . . . . Detroit
15-18 . . . . at Minnesota
20-22 . . . .at Kansas City
23-25 . . . . Texas
26-28 . . . . Houston
30-31 . . . . . . .at Boston

SEPTEMBER
1 . . . . .at Boston
2-4 . . . . at New York (AL)
5-8 . . . . . . .at Baltimore
9-11 . . . . Detroit
12-15 . . . . . . Cleveland
16-18 . . . . . .Minnesota
20-22 . . . . . . .at Detroit
24-25 . . . .at Cleveland
26-29 . . . . . Kansas City

GENERAL INFORMATION
Stadium (year opened):
U.S. Cellular Field (1991).
Team Colors: Black, white and silver.
Player Representative: Unavailable.
Home Dugout: Third Base.
Playing Surface: Grass.

Stadium Operations
    Senior VP, Stadium Operations: Terry Savarise. **Senior Director, Event Operations:** Troy Brown. **Senior Director, Park Operations:** Greg Hopwood. **Senior Director, Guest Services/Diamond Suite Operations:** Julie Taylor. **Head Groundskeeper:** Roger Bossard. **PA Announcer:** Gene Honda. **Official Scorers:** Bob Rosenberg, Don Friske.

Ticketing
    Telephone: (312) 674-1000. **Fax:** (312) 674-5102.
    Director, Ticket Operations: Mike Mazza. **Manager, Ticket Accounting Administration:** Ken Wisz.

Travel/Clubhouse
    Director, Team Travel: Ed Cassin.
    Manager, White Sox Clubhouse: Vince Fresso. **Manager, Visiting Clubhouse:** Gabe Morell. **Manager, Umpires Clubhouse:** Joe McNamara Jr.

BASEBALL OPERATIONS
    Exececutive Vice President: Ken Williams.
    Senior VP/General Manager: Rick Hahn.
    VP/Assistant GM: Buddy Bell. **Special Assistants:** Bill Scherrer, Dave Yoakum, Marco Paddy. **Executive Assistant to GM:** Nancy Nesnidal. **Senior Director, Baseball Operations:** Dan Fabian. **Assistant Director, Baseball Operations:** Daniel Zien.

Major League Staff
    Manager: Robin Ventura
    Coaches: Bench—Mark Parent; **Pitching**—Don Cooper; **Batting**—Jeff Manto; **First Base**—Daryl Boston; **Third Base**—Joe McEwing; **Bullpen**—Bobby Thigpen. **Assistant Hitting Coach:** Harold Baines.

Rick Hahn

Medical/Training
    Senior Team Physician: Dr. Charles Bush-Joseph.
    Head Athletic Trainer: Herm Schneider. **Assistant Athletic Trainer:** Brian Ball.
    Director, Conditioning: Allen Thomas.

Player Development
    Senior Director, Minor League Operations: Grace Guerrero Zwit. **Director, Player Development:** Nick Capra. **Assistant Director, Player Development/Scouting:** Del Matthews. **Senior Coordinator, Minor League Administration:** Kathy Potoski. **Manager, Clubhouse/Equipment:** Dan Flood.
    Minor League Field Coordinator: Kirk Champion. **Roving Instructors:** Curt Hasler (pitching), Everado Magallanes (infield), Timothy Laker (hitting), John Orton (catching), Vance Law (special assistant), Doug Sisson (outfield/baserunning), Dale Torborg (conditioning coordinator). **Latin Cultural Coordinator:** Lino Diaz. **Dominican Player Development Academy Coordinator:** Rafael Santana. **Coordinator, Minor League Trainers/Rehabilitation:** Scott Takao. **Coaching Assistant:** Robbie Cummings. **Dominican Field Coordinator:** Julio Valdez.

Farm System

Class	Club (League)	Manager	Coach	Pitching Coach
Triple-A	Charlotte (IL)	Joel Skinner	Brandon Moore	Richard Dotson
Double-A	Birmingham (SL)	Julio Vinas	Gary Ward	Britt Burns
High A	Winston-Salem (CL)	Ryan Newman	Robert Sasser	J.R. Perdew
Low A	Kannapolis (SAL)	Tommy Thompson	Andy Tomberlin	Jose Bautista
Rookie	Bristol (APP)	Bobby Magallanes	Greg Briley	Larry Owens
Rookie	Great Falls (PIO)	Pete Rose, Jr.	Charlie Poe	Brian Drahman
Rookie	White Sox (DSL)	Guillermo Reyes	Angel Gonzalez	Efrain Valdez

Scouting
    Telephone: (312) 674-1000. **Fax:** (312) 674-5105.
    Pro Scouts: Kevin Bootay (Sacramento, CA), Joe Butler (Long Beach, CA), Gary Pellant (Chandler, AZ), Paul Provas (Arlington, TX), Daraka Shaheed (Vallejo, CA), Bill Young (Scottsdale, AZ), John Tumminia (Newburgh, NY), Alan Regier (Gilbert, AZ).
    Director, Amateur Scouting: Doug Laumann (Florence, KY).
    Assistant Director, Scouting/Player Development: Nick Hostetler. **National Crosscheckers:** Nathan Durst (Sycamore, IL), Ed Pebley (Brigham City, UT). **Regional Crosscheckers: East**—Mike Shirley (Anderson, IN), **West**—Derek Valenzuela (Temecula, CA). **Advisor to Baseball Department:** Larry Monroe (Schaumburg, IL).
    Area Scouts: Mike Baker (Santa Ana, CA), Kevin Burrell (Sharpsburg, GA), Alex Cosmidis (Raleigh, NC), Ryan Dorsey (Carmel, IN), Dan Durst (Rockford, IL), Phil Gulley (Morehead, KY), Warren Hughes (Mobile, AL), JJ Lally (San Diego, CA), George Kachigian (Coronado, CA), John Kazanas (Phoenix, AZ), Steve Nichols (Mount Dora, FL), Jose Ortega (Fort Lauderdale, FL), Clay Overcash (Oologan, OK), Andrew Pinter (Raleigh, NC), Joe Siers (Wesley Chapel, FL), Keith Staab (College Station, TX), Adam Virchis (Modesto, CA), Gary Woods (Solvang, CA).
    Part-Time Scouts: Tommy Butler (East Rancho Dominguez, CA), Karl Carswell (Kansas City, MO), Javier Centeno (Guaynabo, PR), John Doldoorian (Whitinsville, MA), Trent Eckstaine (Lemars, IA), Cade Griffis (Addison, TX), Jack Jolly (Murfreeboro, TN), Bryan Maloney (Las Vegas, NV), Dave Mumper (Highlands Ranch, CO), Glenn Murdock (Livonia, MI), Howard Nakagama (Salt Lake City, UT), Al Otto (Schaumburg, IL), Mike Paris (Boone, IA).
    International Scouts: Marino DeLeon (Dominican Republic), Miguel Peguero (Dominican Republic), Guillermo Guillermo Peralta (Dominican Republic), Fermin Ubri (Dominican Republic), Amador Arias (Venezuela), Omar Sanchez (Venezuela).

Cincinnati Reds

Office Address: 100 Joe Nuxhall Way, Cincinnati, OH 45202.
Telephone: (513) 765-7000. **Fax:** (513) 765-7342.
Website: www.reds.com.

Ownership
Operated by: The Cincinnati Reds LLC.
President/CEO: Robert Castellini. **Chairman:** Joseph Williams Jr. **Vice Chairman/Treasurer:** Thomas Williams. **COO:** Phillip Castellini. **Executive Assistant to COO:** Diana Busam. **Secretary:** Christopher Fister.

BUSINESS OPERATIONS
Senior Vice President, Business Operations: Karen Forgus. **VP, Event Services/Merchandising:** Lauren Werner. **Business Operations Assistant/Speakers Bureau:** Emily Mahle. **Senior Director, Diversity/Strategic Initiatives:** Joe Morgan.

Bob Castellini

Finance/Administration
VP, Finance/CFO: Doug Healy. **VP/General Counsel:** James Marx. **Controller:** Bentley Viator. **Assistant to General Counsel/CFO:** Teena Schweier. **Director, Human Resources:** Teddi Mangas-Coon.

Sales
VP, Ticket Sales: John Davis. **Director, Ticket Initiatives:** David Ziegler. **Director, Client Services:** Craig Warman. **Director, Group/Inside Sales:** Sarah Contardo. **Director, Season/Premium Sales:** Mark Schueler. **Director, Client Services:** Craig Warman.

Ticket Operations
Senior Director, Ticket Operations: John O'Brien. **Assistant Director, Ticket Operations:** Ken Ayer. **Season Ticket Manager:** Bev Bonavita. **Group Ticket Manager:** Brad Callahan.

Media Relations
Director, Media Relations: Rob Butcher. **Assistant Director, Media Relations:** Larry Herms. **Assistant Director, Media Relations/Digital Content:** Jamie Ramsey.

Communications/Marketing:
VP, Communications/Marketing: Ralph Mitchell. **Public Relations Manager:** Michael Anderson. **Communications Manager:** Jarrod Rollins. **Advertising Manager:** Audra Sordyl. **Manager, Design/Production:** Jansen Dell. **Director, Promotional Events:** Zach Bonkowski. **Director, Entertainment/Productions:** Adam Lane.

Community Relations
Executive Director: Charley Frank. **Director, Community Relations:** Lindsey Lander. **Manager, Finance/Operations:** Matthew Wagner. **Executive Director, Reds Hall of Fame:** Rick Walls. **Operations Manager/Chief Curator, Reds Hall**

2013 SCHEDULE
Standard Game Times: 7:10 p.m.; Sun. 1:10

APRIL
1 . . . . . . Los Angeles (AL)
3-4 . . . . . Los Angeles (AL)
5-7 . . . . Washington
8-10 . . . . . . .at St. Louis
12-14 . . . . . at Pittsburgh
15-17 . . . . . .Philadelphia
18-21 . . . . Miami
22-24 . . . . . Chicago (NL)
25-28 . . . at Washington
29-30 . . . . . .at St. Louis

MAY
1 . . . . .at St. Louis
3-5 . . . . .at Chicago (NL)
6-8 . . . . Atlanta
10-12 . . . . . .Milwaukee

14-16 . . . . at Miami
17-19 . . . .at Philadelphia
20-22 . . .at New York (NL)
24-26 . . . . Chicago (NL)
27-28 . . . . Cleveland
29-30 . . . . . .at Cleveland
31 . . . . . . .at Pittsburgh

JUNE
1-2 . . . . . . at Pittsburgh
3-5 . . . . .Colorado
7-9 . . . . St. Louis
10-13 . . .at Chicago (NL)
14-16 . . . . . .Milwaukee
17-20 . . . . . . .Pittsburgh
21-23 . . . . . . at Arizona
25-26 . . . . . .at Oakland

28-30 . . . . .at Texas

JULY
1-4 . . . . . . San Francisco
5-7 . . . . Seattle
8-10 . . . . . at Milwaukee
11-14 . . . . . . at Atlanta
19-21 . . . . . . Pittsburgh
22-24 . . . at San Francisco
25-28 . .at Los Angeles (NL)
29-31 . . . . at San Diego

AUGUST
2-4 . . . . St. Louis
6-7 . . . . Oakland
9-11 . . . . San Diego
12-14 . . .at Chicago (NL)

15-18 . . . . at Milwaukee
19-22 . . . . .Arizona
23-25 . . . . . .Milwaukee
26-28 . . . . . .at St. Louis
30-31 . . . . at Colorado

SEPTEMBER
1 . . . . at Colorado
2-5 . . . . St. Louis
6-8 . . . .Los Angeles (NL)
9-11 . . . . . Chicago (NL)
13-15 . . . . at Milwaukee
16-18 . . . . . .at Houston
20-22 . . . . . at Pittsburgh
23-25 . . . .New York (NL)
27-29 . . . . . . .Pittsburgh

GENERAL INFORMATION
Stadium (year opened): Great American Ball Park (2003). **Home Dugout:** First Base.

Player Representative: Mike Leake. **Playing Surface:** Grass. **Team Colors:** Red, white and black.

of Fame: Chris Eckes.

Corporate Sales
VP, Corporate Sales: Bill Reinberger. Corporate Sales Managers: Dave Collins, Dan Lewis, Mark Scherer.

Ballpark Operations
VP, Ballpark Operations: Declan Mullin. Director, Ballpark Operations: Sean Brown. Ballpark Operations Manager: Colleen Rodenberg. Ballpark Operations Superintendent: Bob Harrison. Guest Relations Manager: Jan Koshover. Manager, Technology Business Center: Chris Campbell. Director, Safety/Security: Kerry Rowland. Chief Engineer: Roger Smith. Assistant Chief Engineer: Gary Goddard. Head Groundskeeper: Doug Gallant. Assistant Head Groundskeeper: Derrik Grubbs. Grounds Supervisor: Robbie Dworkin. Senior Clubhouse/Equipment Manager: Bernie Stowe. Home Clubhouse/Equipment Manager: Rick Stowe. Visiting Clubhouse Manager: Mark Stowe.

BASEBALL OPERATIONS

President, Baseball Operations/General Manager: Walt Jocketty. Executive Assistant to GM: Melissa Hill.

VP, Assistant GM: Bob Miller. VP, Scouting/Player Development/International Operations: Bill Bavasi. VP/Special Assistant: Jerry Walker. VP, Baseball Operations: Dick Williams. Senior Advisor: Joe Morgan. Special Assistants: Eric Davis, Mario Soto. Director, Baseball Operations: Nick Krall. Manager, Baseball Systems Development: Brett Elkins. Manager, Baseball Research/Analysis: Sam Grossman. Manager, Video Scouting: Rob Coughlin. Baseball Operations Assistant: Stephanie Ben.

Walt Jocketty

Medical/Training
Medical Director: Dr. Timothy Kremchek. Head Athletic Trainer: Paul Lessard. Assistant Athletic Trainer: Steve Baumann. Stength/Conditioning Coordinator: Matthew Krause. Assistant Athletic Trainer: Tomas Vera.

Major League Staff
Manager: Dusty Baker.
Coaches: Bench—Chris Speier; Batting—Brook Jacoby; Pitching—Bryan Price; First Base—Billy Hatcher; Third Base—Mark Berry; Bullpen—Juan Lopez; Assistant Hitting—Ronnie Ortegon; Assistant Pitching—Mack Jenkins.

Player Development
Director, Player Development: Jeff Graupe. Director, Minor League Administration: Lois Hudson. Arizona Operations Manager: Mike Saverino. Assistant to Arizona Operations Manager: Charlie Rodriguez. Minor League Video Coordinator: Mike Persichilli. Minor League Equipment Manager: Jonathan Snyder. Field Coordinator: Freddie Benavides. Assistant Field Coordinator/Infield Instructor: Bill Doran. Assistant Field Coordinator, Latin America Focus: Joel Noboa. Coordinators: Ryan Jackson (hitting), Mark Riggins (pitching), Darren Bragg (outfield/baserunning), Rick Sweet (catching), Richard Stark (medical), Sean Marohn (strength/conditioning), Patrick Serbus (athletic training). Director, Dominican Republic Academy: Juan Peralta. Physical Therapist/Rehab Coordinator: Brad Epstein.

Farm System

Class	Club (League)	Manager	Coach	Pitching Coach
Triple-A	Louisville (IL)	Jim Riggleman	Tony Jaramillo	Ted Power
Double-A	Pensacola (SL)	Delino DeShields	Dick Schofield	Tom Brown
High A	Bakersfield (CAL)	Ken Griffey	Ray Martinez	Rigo Beltran
Low A	Dayton (MWL)	Jose Miguel Nieves	Alex Pelaez	Tony Fossas
Rookie	Billings (PIO)	Pat Kelly	Kevin Mahar	Tom Browning
Rookie	Reds (AZL)	Eli Marrero	Luis Bolivar	D. Ebert/E. Dessens
Rookie	Reds 1 (DSL)	Luis Saturria	Nilson Antiqua	Luis Montano
Rookie	Reds 2 (DSL)	Unavailable	Cristobal Rodriguez	Luis Andujar

Scouting
Senior Director, Pro/Global Scouting: Terry Reynolds. Senior Director, Amateur Scouting: Chris Buckley. Assistant Director, Amateur Scouting: Paul Person. Special Assistants: Cam Bonifay, J Harrison, Marty Maier, John Morris, Mike Squires, Jeff Taylor. Major League Advance Scout: Shawn Pender. Professional Scouts: Will Harford, Jeff Morris, Steve Roadcap, Dominic Viola.
Crosscheckers: Jeff Barton (Gilbert, AZ), Bill Byckowski (Ontario, Canada), Jerry Flowers (Cypress, TX), Mark McKnight (Tega Cay, SC), Mark Snipp (Humble, TX). Scouting Supervisors: Tony Arias (Miami Lakes, FL), Rich Bordi (Rohnert Park, CA), Jeff Brookens (Chambersburg, PA), Clark Crist (Tucson, AZ), Rex De La Nuez (Burbank, CA), Byron Ewing (Haslet, TX), Rick Ingalls (Long Beach, CA), Ben Jones (Alexandria, LA), Joe Katuska (Cincinnati, OH), Mike Keenan (Manhattan, KS), Brad Meador (Cincinnati, OH), Mike Misuraca (Murrieta, CA), John Poloni (Tarpon Springs, FL), Lee Seras (Flanders, NJ), Perry Smith (Charlotte, NC), Andy Stack (Hartford, WI), Greg Zunino (Cape Coral, FL). Scouts: Nick Carrier (Hemlock, NY), Jim Grief (Paducah, KY), Bill Killian (Stanwood, MI), David Lander (Los Angeles, CA), Denny Nagel (Cincinnati, OH), Marlon Styles (Cincinnati, OH), Mike Wallace (Escondido, CA), John Walsh (Windsor, CT), Roger Weberg (Bemidji, MN).
Director, Latin America Scouting: Tony Arias. Assistant Director, Latin America Scouting: Miguel Machado. Director, Global Scouting: Jim Stoeckel. Scouting Coordinator, Dominican Republic: Richard Jimenez.
International Scouts: Carlos Batista (Dominican Republic), Edward Bens (Dominican Republic), Geronimo Blanco (Colombia), Cesar Castro (Dominican Republic), Frank Coronel (Curacao), Nick Dempsey (South Africa), Leslie Durbridge (Australia), James Henty (Australia), Jason Hewitt (Australia), Evert-Jan't Hoen (Holland), Victor Oramas (Venezuela), Jose Manuel Pujols (Dominican Republic), Tony Rombley (Aruba), Sammy Torreira (Germany), Gareth Jones (Australia), Luke Prokopec (Australia), Anibal Reluz (Panama), Sal Varriale (Italy), Anibal Vega (Nicaragua).

Cleveland Indians

Office Address: Progressive Field, 2401 Ontario St., Cleveland, OH 44115.
Telephone: (216) 420-4200. **Fax:** (216) 420-4396.
Website: www.indians.com.

Ownership
Owner/CEO: Lawrence Dolan. **Chairman/Chief Executive Officer:** Paul Dolan.

BUSINESS OPERATIONS
President: Mark Shapiro.
Senior Vice President, Strategy/Business Analytics: Andrew Miller. **Executive Administrative Assistant:** Marlene Lehky. **Executive VP, Business:** Dennis Lehman. **Executive Administrative Assistant, Business:** Dru Kosik.

Larry Dolan

Corporate Partnerships/Finance
Director, Corporate Partnerships: Ted Baugh. **Manager, Corporate Partnership Services:** Sam Zelasko. **Senior Account Executives, Corporate Partnerships:** Bryan Hoffart, Dominic Polito. **Account Executive, Corporate Partnerships:** Penny Forster. **Senior VP, Finance/CFO:** Ken Stefanov. **VP/General Counsel:** Joe Znidarsic. **Controller:** Sarah Taylor. **Senior Director, Planning/Analysis/Reporting:** Rich Dorffer. **Manager, Accounting:** Karen Menzing. **Manager, Payroll Accounting:** Mary Forkapa. **Concessions Controller:** Marj Ruhl. **Concessions Accounting Manager:** Diane Turner. **Senior Staff Accountant:** Kim Haist.

Human Resources
VP, Human Resources/Chief Diversity Officer: Sara Lehrke. **Manager, Training:** Mailynh Vu. **Manager, Training/Development:** Jennifer Gibson. **Coordinator, Benefits:** Crystal Basile. **Human Resource Generalist:** David Mraz.

Marketing
VP, Marketing/Brand Management: Alex King. **Senior Director, Marketing:** Sanaa Julien. **Manager, Promotions:** Jason Kidik. **Manager, In-Game Entertainment:** Annie Merovich. **Manager, Productions:** Nick Gambone. **Coordinator, Creative Services:** Ashley Churchill. **VP, Concessions:** Kurt Schloss. **Merchandise Manager:** Karen Fox.

Communications/Baseball Information
Telephone: (216) 420-4380. **Fax:** (216) 420-4430.
Senior VP, Public Affairs: Bob DiBiasio. **Senior Director, Communications:** Curtis Danburg. **Director, Baseball Information:** Bart Swain. **Assistant Director, Communications:** Anne Keegan. **Coordinator, Baseball Information:** Court Berry-Tripp. **Coordinator, Communications:** Joel Hammond. **Manager, Digital Asset Creation/Team Photographer:** Dan Mendlik.

Ballpark Operations
VP, Ballpark Operations: Jim Folk. **Director, Facility Maintenance:** Chris Donahoe. **Head Groundskeeper:**

2013 SCHEDULE
Standard Game Times: 7:05 p.m.; Sun. 1:05.

APRIL
2-4	at Toronto
5-7	at Tampa Bay
8-11	New York (AL)
12-14	Chicago (AL)
16-18	Boston
19-21	at Houston
22-24	at Chicago (AL)
26-29	at Kansas City
30	Philadelphia

MAY
1	Philadelphia
3-5	Minnesota
6-9	Oakland
10-12	at Detroit

14-15	at Philadelphia
17-20	Seattle
21-22	Detroit
23-26	at Boston
27-28	at Cincinnati
29-30	Cincinnati
31	Tampa Bay

JUNE
1-2	Tampa Bay
3-5	at New York (AL)
7-9	at Detroit
10-12	at Texas
14-16	Washington
17-19	Kansas City
21-23	Minnesota
24-27	at Baltimore

28-30	at Chicago (AL)

JULY
2-4	at Kansas City
5-8	Detroit
9-11	Toronto
12-14	Kansas City
19-21	at Minnesota
22-24	at Seattle
26-28	Texas
29-31	Chicago (AL)

AUGUST
1	Chicago (AL)
2-4	at Miami
5-8	Detroit
9-11	at Los Angeles (AL)

12-14	at Minnesota
16-18	at Oakland
19-21	at Los Angeles (AL)
23-25	Minnesota
27-29	at Atlanta
30-31	at Detroit

SEPTEMBER
1	at Detroit
2-4	Baltimore
6-8	New York (NL)
9-11	Kansas City
12-15	at Chicago (AL)
16-18	at Kansas City
19-22	Houston
24-25	Chicago (AL)
26-29	at Minnesota

GENERAL INFORMATION
Stadium (year opened):
Progressive Field (1994).
Team Colors: Navy blue, red and silver.

Player Representative: Justin Masterson.
Home Dugout: Third Base.
Playing Surface: Grass.

Brandon Koehnke. **Senior Director, Ballpark Operations:** Jerry Crabb. **Assistant Director, Ballpark Operations:** Brad Mohr. **Assistant Director, Facility Maintenance:** Seth Cooper. **Coordinator, Game Day Staff:** Renee VanLaningham. **Coordinator, Ballpark Services:** Steve Walters.

Information Systems

Director, Software Development/Support: Matt Tagliaferri. **Manager, End-User Support:** Matthew Smith. **Director, Information Technology:** Whitney Kuszmaul. **Programmer Analyst:** Plamen Kouzov.

Ticketing

Telephone: (216) 420-4487. **Fax:** (216) 420-4481.
Director, Ticket Services: Gene Connelly. **Manager, Ticket Services:** Andrew Zaggar. **Manager, Ticket Office:** Katie Smith. **Manager, Ticket Operations:** Eric Fronczek. **Director, Fan Services:** Dave Murray.

Spring Training/Arizona Operations

Manager, Arizona Operations: Ryan Lantz. **Manager, Home Clubhouse:** Fletcher Wilkes.
Director, Team Travel: Mike Seghi. **Home Clubhouse/Equipment Manager:** Tony Amato. **Manager, Video Operations:** Bob Chester. **Visiting Clubhouse Manager:** Willie Jenks.

BASEBALL OPERATIONS

Chris Antonetti

Telephone: (216) 420-4200. **Fax:** (216) 420-4321.
Executive VP/General Manager: Chris Antonetti.
VP, Baseball Operations/Assistant GM: Mike Chernoff.
Director, Baseball Administration: Wendy Hoppel. **Director, Baseball Operations:** Derek Falvey. **Director, Baseball Analytics:** Keith Woolner. **Executive Administrative Assistant:** Marlene Lehky. **Sports Psychologist:** Dr. Charles Maher.

Major League Staff

Manager: Terry Francona.
Coaches: Bench—Sandy Alomar, Jr., **Pitching**—Mickey Callaway, **Hitting**—Ty Van Burkleo, **First Base**—Mike Sarbaugh, **Third Base/Infield**—Brad Mills, **Bullpen**—Kevin Cash.
Assistants, Major League Staff: Armando Camacaro, Francisco Morales.

Medical/Training

Head Team Physician: Dr. Mark Schickendantz. **Director, Medical Services/Head Trainer:** Lonnie Soloff. **Assistant Athletic Trainers:** Jeff Desjardins, Michael Salazar. **Strength/Conditioning Coach:** Joe Kessler.

Player Development

Telephone: (216) 420-4308. **Fax:** (216) 420-4321.
VP, Player Development: Ross Atkins.
Assistant Director, Player Development: Carter Hawkins. **Administrative Assistant:** Nilda Taffanelli. **Advisors, Player Development:** Johnny Goryl, Tim Tolman. **Director, Latin America Operations:** Ramon Pena. **Field Coordinator:** Tom Wiedenbauer. **Coordinators:** Ruben Niebla (pitching), Alan Zinter (hitting), Todd Kubacki (strength/conditioning), Thomas Albert (rehabilitation), Julio Rangel (mental skills), Luis Ortiz (cultural development). **Advisor, Latin America:** Minnie Mendoza. **Latin America Strength/Conditioning Coordinator:** Nelson Perez.

Farm System

Class	Club	Manager	Coach	Pitching Coach
Triple-A	Columbus (IL)	Chris Tremie	Phil Clark	Tony Arnold
Double-A	Akron (EL)	Edwin Rodriguez	Jim Rickon	Greg Hibbard
High A	Carolina (CL)	David Wallace	Rouglas Odor	Jeff Harris
Low A	Lake County (MWL)	Scooter Tucker	Tony Mansolino	Steve Karsay
Short-season	Mahoning Valley (NYP)	Ted Kubiak	Shaun Larkin	Juan Alvarez
Rookie	Indians (AZL)	Anthony Medrano	J. Betances/D. Malave	S. Erickson/D. Swanson
Rookie	Indians (DSL)	Jose Mejia	D. Bautista/C. Fermin	Jesus Sanchez

Scouting

Telephone: (216) 420-4200. **Fax:** (216) 420-4321.
Senior Director, Scouting Operations: John Mirabelli.
Director, Amateur Scouting: Brad Grant. **Assistant Director, Scouting:** Paul Gillispie. **Director, Pro Scouting:** Steve Lubratich. **Assistant Director, Pro Scouting:** Victor Wang. **Advance Scouting Coordinator:** Alex Eckelman. **Assistant Director, International Scouting:** Jason Lynn. **Senior Major League Scouts:** Dave Malpass (Huntington Beach, CA), Don Poplin (Norwood, NC). **Pro Scouts:** Mike Calitri (Tampa, FL), Doug Carpenter (North Palm Beach, FL), Jim Cuthbert (Summit, NJ), Trey Hendricks (Cleveland, OH), Dave Miller (Wilmington, NC), Chris Smith (Montgomery, TX).
Scouting Advisor/Crosschecker: Paul Cogan (Rocklin, CA). **National Crosscheckers:** Scott Barnsby (Huntsville, AL), Bo Hughes (Sherman Oaks, CA). **Regional Crosscheckers:** Kevin Cullen (Frisco, TX), Scott Meaney (Apex, NC), Jason Smith (Long Beach, CA). **Area Scouts:** Steve Abney (Lawrence, KS), Mark Allen (Lake Kiowa, TX), Chuck Bartlett (Starkville, MS), Jon Heuerman (Chandler, AZ), Don Lyle (Sacramento, CA), Bob Mayer (Somerset, PA), Junie Melendez (North Ridgeville, OH), Carlos Muniz (San Pedro, CA), Les Pajari (Angora, MN), Mike Soper (Tampa, FL), Ryan Thompson (Huntington Beach, CA), Brad Tyler (Bishop, GA), Jack Uhey (Ridgefiled, WA), Brent Urcheck (Philadelphia, PA), Kyle Van Hook (Brenham, TX). **Part-Time Scouts:** Bob Malkmus (Union, NJ), Roc Murray (Rocklin, CA), Bill Schudlich (Dearborn, MI), Adam Stahl (Ballwin, MO), Ken Tirpack (Campbell, OH), Jose Trujillo (Bayamon, PR).

Colorado Rockies

Office Address: 2001 Blake St., Denver, CO 80205.
Telephone: (303) 292-0200. **Fax:** (303) 312-2116.
Website: www.coloradorockies.com.

Ownership
Operated by: Colorado Rockies Baseball Club Ltd.
Owner/General Partner: Charles K. Monfort. **Owner/Chairman/Chief Executive Officer:**
Richard L. Monfort. **Executive Assistant to the Owner/General Partner:** Patricia Penfold.
Executive Assistant to the Owner/Chairman/Chief Executive Officer: Terry Douglass.

BUSINESS OPERATIONS
Executive Vice President/Chief Operating Officer: Greg Feasel. **Assistant to Executive
VP/Chief Operating Officer:** Kim Olson. **VP, Human Resources:** Elizabeth Stecklein.

Richard Monfort

Finance
Executive VP/CFO/General Counsel: Hal Roth. **VP, Finance:** Michael Kent. **Senior Director,
Purchasing:** Gary Lawrence. **Coordinator, Purchasing:** Gloria Giraldi. **Senior Director,
Accounting:** Phil Emerson. **Accountants:** Joel Binfet, Laine Campbell. **Payroll Administrator:**
Juli Daedelow.

Marketing/Sales
VP, Corporate Sales: Marcy Glasser. **Assistant to VP, Corporate Sales:** Nicole Ortiz. **Senior Account Executive,
Corporate Sales:** Kari Anderson. **Account Executives:** Dan Lentz, Nate VanderWal. **VP, Community/Retail Operations:**
James P. Kellogg. **Director, Retail Operations:** Aaron Heinrich. **Senior Director, Information Systems:** Bill
Stephani. **Director, Promotions/Special Events:** Jason Fleming. **Director, In-Game Entertainment/Broadcasting:**
Kent Krosbakken. **Senior Director, Advertising/Marketing/Publications:** Jill Campbell. **Supervisor, Advertising/
Marketing:** Sarah Topf. **Coordinator, Multicultural Marketing/Advertising:** Marisol Villagomez.

Communications
Telephone: (303) 312-2325. **Fax:** (303) 312-2319.
VP, Communications: Jay Alves. **Assistant Director, Communications:** Nick Piburn. **Manager, Communications:**
Matt Whewell. **Assistant, Communications/Baseball Operations:** Irma Castaneda.

Ballpark Operations
VP, Ballpark Operations: Kevin Kahn. **Senior Director, Food Service Operations/Development:** Albert Valdes.
Manager, Ballpark Services: Mary Beth Benner. **Senior Director, Guest Services:** Steven Burke. **Head Groundskeeper:**
Mark Razum. **Assistant Head Groundskeeper:** James Sowl. **Groundskeeping Assistant:** James Garner. **Senior Director,
Engineering/Facilities:** James Wiener. **Director, Engineering:** Randy Carlill. **Director, Facilities:** Oly Olsen. **Official
Scorers:** Dave Einspahr, Dave Plati. **Public Address Announcer:** Reed Saunders.

2013 SCHEDULE
Standard Game Times: 6:40 p.m.; Sat. 6:10; Sun. 1:10.

APRIL		
1-3 . . . . at Milwaukee	13-15 . . . .at Chicago (NL)	28-30 . . . . . San Francisco
5-7 . . . . San Diego	16-19 . . . . . San Francisco	
8-10 . . at San Francisco	20-22 . . . . Arizona	**JULY**
12-14 . . . . . at San Diego	24-26 . . at San Francisco	2-4 . . . . Los Angeles (NL)
15-18 . . . .New York (NL)	27-28 . . . . . .at Houston	5-7 . . . . at Arizona
19-21 . . . . Arizona	29-30 . . . . Houston	8-10 . . . . . at San Diego
22-24 . . . . Atlanta	31 . . . . . Los Angeles (NL)	11-14 . at Los Angeles (NL)
25-28 . . . . . . at Arizona		19-21 . . . . . Chicago (NL)
29-30 . at Los Angeles (NL)	**JUNE**	22-25 . . . . .Miami
	1-2 . . . . Los Angeles (NL)	26-28 . . . . . . .Milwaukee
MAY	3-5 . . . . . . .at Cincinnati	29-31 . . . . . . at Atlanta
1 . . . . at Los Angeles (NL)	6-9 . . . . San Diego	
3-5 . . . . .Tampa Bay	11-13 . . . . . Washington	**AUGUST**
7-9 . . . . . .New York (AL)	14-16 . . . . .Philadelphia	1 . . . . at Atlanta
10-12 . . . . . . .at St. Louis	17-19 . . . . . at Toronto	2-4 . . . . . . at Pittsburgh
	20-23 . . at Washington	6-8 . . . .at New York (NL)
	25-26 . . . . . . .at Boston	9-11 . . . . Pittsburgh

12-14 . . . . . . San Diego	
16-18 . . . . . .at Baltimore	
19-22 . . at Philadelphia	
23-25 . . . . at Miami	
26-28 . . . . San Francisco	
30-31 . . . . . . Cincinnati	
SEPTEMBER	
1 . . . . Cincinnati	
2-4 . . . . Los Angeles (NL)	
6-8 . . . . . . at San Diego	
9-11 . . at San Francisco	
13-15 . . . . at Arizona	
16-19 . . . . St. Louis	
20-22 . . . . Arizona	
24-25 . . . . Boston	
27-29 . at Los Angeles (NL)	

GENERAL INFORMATION
Stadium (year opened):
Coors Field (1995).
Team Colors: Purple, black and silver.

Player Representative: Troy Tulowitzki.
Home Dugout: First Base.
Playing Surface: Grass.

Ticketing
Telephone: (303) 762-5437, (800) 388-7625. **Fax:** (303) 312-2115.
VP, Ticket Operations/Sales/Services: Sue Ann McClaren.
Senior Director, Ticket Services, Finance/Technology: Kent Hakes. **Director, Ticket Operations:** Scott Donaldson. **Senior Director, Season Tickets/Renewals/Business Strategy:** Jeff Benner. **Director, Groups/Outbound Sales/Suites:** Matt Haddad. **Manager, Suites/Party Facilities:** Traci Abeyta. **Senior Account Executive:** Todd Thomas.

Travel/Clubhouse
Director, Major League Operations: Paul Egins. **Director, Clubhouse Operations:** Keith Schulz. **Visiting Clubhouse Manager:** Alan Bossart.

BASEBALL OPERATIONS
Telephone: (303) 292-0200. **Fax:** (303) 312-2320.
Executive VP/Chief Baseball Officer/General Manager: Dan O'Dowd. **Assistant to Executive VP/Chief Baseball Officer/GM:** Adele Armagost. **Senior VP, Major League Operations/Assistant GM:** Bill Geivett. **Manager, Baseball Operations/Assistant General Counsel:** Zack Rosenthal. **Assistants, Baseball Operations:** Kent McKendry, Matt Obernauer. **Special Assistant to Baseball Operations:** Pat Daugherty.

Dan O'Dowd

Major League Staff
Manager: Walt Weiss.
Coaches: Bench—Tom Runnells; **Pitching**—Jim Wright; **Assistant Pitching**—Bo McLaughlin; **Hitting**—Dante Bichette; **First Base**—Rene Lachemann; **Third Base**—Stu Cole; **Catching Instructor/Defensive Positioning**—Jerry Weinstein; **Bullpen Catcher**—Pat Burgess; **Strength/Conditioning**—Brian Jordan; **Video**—Brian Jones.

Medical/Training
Senior Director, Medical Operations/Special Projects: Tom Probst. **Medical Director:** Dr. Thomas Noonan. **Club Physicians:** Dr. Allen Schreiber, Dr. Douglas Wyland. **Head Trainer:** Keith Dugger. **Assistant Athletic Trainer:** Scott Gehret.

Player Development
Telephone: (303) 292-0200. **Fax:** (303) 312-2320.
Senior Director, Player Development: Jeff Bridich. **Director, Pitching Operations:** Mark Wiley. **Assistant Director, Player Development:** Zach Wilson. **Coordinator, Minor League Operations:** Walker Monfort. **Head Pitching Coordinator:** Doug Linton. **Assistant Pitching Coordinator:** Bob Apodaca. **Catching Coordinator:** Mark Strittmatter. **Strength/Conditioning Coordinator:** Gabe Bauer. **Assistant Video Coordinator:** Scott Alves. **Peak Performance Coordinator:** Andy McKay.
Rehabilitation Coordinator: Scott Murayama. **Assistant Rehabilitation Coordinator:** Andy Stover. **Equipment Manager:** Jerry Bass.
Supervisors, Development: Duane Espy (Tulsa), Fred Nelson (Modesto), Marv Foley (Asheville), Ron Gideon (Tri-City), Tony Diaz (Grand Junction).

Farm System

Class	Club (League)	Manager	Coach	Pitching Coach
Triple-A	Colorado Springs (PCL)	Glenallen Hill	Dave Hajek	Dave Schuler
Double-A	Tulsa (TL)	Kevin Riggs	Darin Everson	Darryl Scott
High A	Modesto (CAL)	Lenn Sakata	Jon Stone	Dave Burba
Low A	Asheville (SAL)	Fred Ocasio	Mike Devereaux	Joey Eischen
Short-season	Tri-City (NWL)	Drew Saylor	Warren Schaeffer	Frank Gonzales
Rookie	Grand Junction (PIO)	Anthony Sanders	Lee Stevens	Ryan Kibler
Rookie	Rockies (DSL)	Mauricio Gonzalez	F. Nunez/E. Jose	Edison Lora

Scouting
Telephone: (303) 292-0200. **Fax:** (303) 312-2320.
VP, Scouting: Bill Schmidt. **Assistant Director, Scouting:** Danny Montgomery. **Senior Director, Scouting Operations:** Marc Gustafson. **Director, Pro Scouting:** Jon Weil.
Advance Scout: Chris Warren. **Pro Scouts:** Ty Coslow (Louisville, KY), Will George (Woolwich Township, NJ), Jack Gillis (Sarasota, FL), Mike Hamilton (Dallas, TX), Joey Housey (Hollywood, FL), Rick Mathews (Centerville, IA), Mike Paul (Tucson, AZ). **Part-Time Pro Scout:** Fred Wright (Harrisburg, NC). **Special Assignment Scout:** Terry Wetzel (Overland Park, KS).
National Crosschecker: Mike Ericson (Phoenix, AZ), Damon Iannelli (Brandon, MS), Jay Matthews (Concord, NC).
Area Scouts: Julio Campos (Guaynabo, PR) John Cedarburg (Fort Myers, FL), Scott Corman (Lexington, KY), Jordan Czarniecki (Nashville, TN), Jeff Edwards (Missouri City, TX), Chris Forbes (Phoenix, AZ), Mike Garlatti (Edison, NJ), Mark Germann (Atkins, IA), Matt Hattabaugh (Westminster, CA), Darin Holcomb (Seattle, WA), Jon Lukens (Dana Point, CA), Alan Matthews (Atlanta, GA), Jesse Retzlaff (Dallas, TX), Rafeal Reyes (Miami, FL), Ed Santa (Powell, OH), Gary Wilson (Sacramento, CA). **Part-Time Scouts:** Norm DeBriyn (Fayetteville, AR), Marc Johnson (Centennial, CO), Dave McQueen (Bossier City, LA), Greg Pullia (Plymouth, MA).
Senior Director, International Operations: Rolando Fernandez. **Manager, Dominican Operations:** Jhonathan Leyba. **Supervisor, Venezuelan Scouting:** Orlando Medina. **International Scouts:** Phil Allen (Australia), Martin Cabrera (Dominican Republic), Carlos Gomez (Venezuela), Frank Roa (Dominican Republic), Josher Suarez (Venezuela).

Detroit Tigers

Office Address: 2100 Woodward Ave, Detroit, MI 48201.
Telephone: (313) 471-2000. **Fax:** (313) 471-2138. **Website:** www.tigers.com

Ownership
Operated By: Detroit Tigers Inc. **Owner:** Michael Ilitch.
President/CEO/General Manager: David Dombrowski.
Special Assistants to President: Al Kaline, Willie Horton. **Executive Assistant to President/CEO/GM:** Marty Lyon. **Senior VP:** Jim Devellano.

BUSINESS OPERATIONS
Executive Vice President, Business Operations: Duane McLean. **Executive Assistant to Executive VP, Business Operations:** Peggy Thompson.

Mike Ilitch

Finance/Administration
VP/CFO: Stephen Quinn. **Senior Director, Finance:** Kelli Kollman. **Director, Purchasing/Supplier Diversity:** DeAndre Berry. **Accounting Manager:** Sheila Robine.
Financial Analyst: Kristin Jorgensen. **Accounts Payable Coordinator:** Debbi Sword. **Accounts Receivable Coordinator:** Sharon Szkarlat. **Administrative Assistant:** Tracy Rice. **Senior Director, Human Resources:** Karen Gruca. **Director, Payroll Administration:** Maureen Kraatz. **Associate Counsel:** Amy Peterson. **Internal Audit Manager:** Candice Lentz.

Public/Community Affairs
VP, Community/Public Affairs: Elaine Lewis. **Director, Tigers Foundation:** Jordan Field. **Manager, Player Relations:** Sam Abrams. **Manager, Community Affairs:** Alexandrea Thrubis. **Community Affairs Coordinator:** Garnet Conerway. **Administrative Assistants:** Audrey Zielinski/Donna Bernardo.

Sales/Marketing
VP, Corporate Partnerships: Steve Harms. **Director, Corporate Sales:** Steve Cleary.
Senior Director, Corporate Sales: Kurt Buhler. **Corporate Sales Managers:** Soula Burns, John Wolski. **Sponsorship Services Coordinator:** Keri Gallagher.
VP, Marketing: Ellen Hill Zeringue. **Director, Marketing:** Ron Wade. **Marketing Coordinator:** Kate Ready. **Coordinator, Marketing/Promotions Coordinator:** Angela Perez. **Director, Promotions/In-Game Entertainment:** Eli Bayless. **Promotions Manager:** Jared Karner. **VP, Ticket/Suite Sales:** Scot Pett.

Media Relations/Communications
Telephone: (313) 471-2114. **Fax:** (313) 471-2138.
VP, Communications: Ron Colangelo. **Director, Baseball Media Relations:** Brian Britten. **Manager, Baseball Media Relations:** Rick Thompson. **Coordinator, Baseball Media Relations:** Aileen Villarreal. **Director, Broadcasting:** Molly Betensley.

2013 SCHEDULE
Standard Game Times: 7:05 p.m.; Sun. 1:05.

APRIL
1	at Minnesota
3-4	at Minnesota
5-7	New York (AL)
9-11	Toronto
12-14	at Oakland
16-18	at Seattle
19-21	at Los Angeles (AL)
23-25	Kansas City
26-28	Atlanta
29-30	Minnesota

MAY
1	Minnesota
2-5	at Houston
7-8	at Washington
10-12	Cleveland
13-15	Houston
16-19	at Texas
21-22	at Cleveland
23-26	Minnesota
27-28	Pittsburgh
29-30	at Pittsburgh
31	at Baltimore

JUNE
1-2	at Baltimore
4-6	Tampa Bay
7-9	Cleveland
10-12	at Kansas City
14-16	at Minnesota
17-19	Baltimore
20-23	Boston
25-27	Los Angeles (AL)
28-30	at Tampa Bay

JULY
1-4	at Toronto
5-8	at Cleveland
9-11	Chicago (AL)
12-14	Texas
19-21	at Kansas City
22-25	at Chicago (AL)
26-28	Philadelphia
30-31	Washington

AUGUST
2-4	Chicago (AL)
5-8	at Cleveland
9-11	at New York (AL)
12-14	at Chicago (AL)
15-18	Kansas City
20-22	Minnesota
23-25	at New York (NL)
26-29	Oakland
30-31	Cleveland

SEPTEMBER
1	Cleveland
2-4	at Boston
6-8	at Kansas City
9-11	at Chicago (AL)
13-15	Kansas City
16-19	Seattle
20-22	Chicago (AL)
23-25	at Minnesota
27-29	at Miami

GENERAL INFORMATION

Stadium (year opened): Comerica Park (2000).
Team Colors: Navy blue, orange and white.
Player Representative: Alex Avila.
Home Dugout: Third Base.
Playing Surface: Grass.

BASEBALL OPERATIONS

Telephone: (313) 471-2000. **Fax:** (313) 471-2099.
General Manager: David Dombrowski.
VP/Assistant GM: Al Avila. **VP/Legal Counsel:** John Westhoff. **VP, Player Personnel:** Scott Reid. **Special Assistant:** Dick Egan. **Director, Baseball Operations:** Mike Smith. **Executive Assistant to President/GM:** Marty Lyon. **Executive Assistant:** Eileen Surma.

Dave Dombrowski

Major League Staff

Manager: Jim Leyland.
Coaches: Pitching—Jeff Jones; **Batting**—Lloyd McClendon; **First Base**—Rafael Belliard; **Third Base**—Tom Brookens; **Bullpen**—Mike Rojas. **Bench:** Gene Lamont. **Assistant Hitting:** Toby Harrah

Medical/Training

Director, Medical Services/Head Athletic Trainer: Kevin Rand. **Assistant Athletic Trainers:** Steve Carter, Doug Teter. **Strength/Conditioning Coordinator:** Javair Gillett. **Team Physicians:** Dr. Michael Workings, Dr. Stephen Lemos, Dr. Louis Saco (Florida). **Coordinator, Medical Services:** Gwen Keating.

Player Development

Director, Minor League Operations: Dan Lunetta. **Director, Player Development:** Dave Owen. **Director, Minor League/Scouting Administration:** Cheryl Evans. **Director, Latin American Player Development:** Manny Crespo. **Coordinator, Minor League Operations:** Avi Becher. **Administrative Assistant, Minor League Operations:** Marilyn Acevedo. **Minor League Field Coordinator:** Bill Dancy. **Minor League Medical Coordinator:** Corey Tremble. **Minor League Strength/Conditioning Coordinator:** Chris Walter. **Assistant Minor League Strength/Conditioning Coordinator:** Steve Chase. **Minor League Video Operations Assistant:** August Sandri.
Roving Instructors: Bruce Fields (hitting), Kevin Bradshaw (infield), Al Nipper (pitching), Joe DePastino (catching), Gene Roof (outfield/baserunning), Brian Peterson (performance enhancement), Robert "Ghost" Frutchey (minor league clubhouse manager).

Farm System

Class	Club	Manager	Coach	Pitching Coach
Triple-A	Toledo (IL)	Phil Nevin	Leon Durham	A.J. Sager
Double-A	Erie (EL)	Chris Cron	Gerald Perry	Jaime Garcia
High A	Lakeland (FSL)	Dave Huppert	Larry Herndon	Mike Maroth
Low A	West Michigan (MWL)	Larry Parrish	Scott Dwyer	Mike Henneman
Short-season	Connecticut (NYP)	Andrew Graham	Mike Rabelo	Mark Johnson
Rookie	Tigers (GCL)	Basilio Cabrera	Nelson Santovenia	Jorge Cordova

Scouting

Telephone: (863) 413-4112. **Fax:** (863) 413-1954.
VP, Amateur Scouting/Special Assistant to GM: David Chadd. **Director, Amateur Scouting:** Scott Pleis. **Assistant, Amateur Scouting:** Julian Shabazz.
Director, Pro Scouting: Scott Bream. **Major League Scouts:** Jim Olander (Vail, AZ), Mike Russell (Gulf Breeze, FL), Bruce Tanner (New Castle, PA), Jeff Wetherby (Wesley Chapel, FL).
National Crosscheckers: Ray Crone (Cedar Hill, TX), Tim Hallgren (Cape Girardeau, MO). **Regional Crosscheckers: Southeast**—James Orr (Orlando, FL); **Central/Northeast**—Tom Osowski (Franklin, WI); **Midwest**—Mike Hankins (Lee's Summit, MO); **West**—Tim McWilliam (San Diego, CA).
Area Scouts: Bryson Barber (Pensacola, FL), Grant Brittain (Hickory, NC), Bill Buck (Manassas, VA), Rolando Casanova (Miami, FL), Scott Cerny (Rocklin, CA), Murray Cook (Orlando, FL), Tim Grieve (New Braunfels, TX), Garrett Guest (Lockport, IL), Ryan Johnson (Oregon City, OR), Matt Lea (Burbank, CA), Marty Miller (Chicago, IL), Steve Pack (San Marcos, CA), Brian Reid (Gilbert, AZ), Jim Rough (Sharpsburg, GA), Chris Wimmer (Yukon, OK), Harold Zonder (Louisville, KY).
Director, International Operations: Tom Moore. **Director, Latin American Development:** Manny Crespo. **Director, Latin American Scouting:** Miguel Garcia. **Coordinator, Pacific Rim Scouting:** Kevin Hooker. **Director, Dominican Operations:** Ramon Perez. **Coordinator, Dominican Academy:** Oliver Arias. **Venezuelan Scouting Supervisor:** Pedro Chavez. **Coordinator, Venezuelan Academy:** Oscar Garcia. **Scouting Assistant, International Operations:** Giovanni Hernandez.

Houston Astros

Office Address: Minute Maid Park, Union Station, 501 Crawford, Suite 400, Houston, TX 77002.
Mailing Address: PO Box 288, Houston, TX 77001. **Telephone:** (713) 259-8000. **Fax:** (713) 259-8981.
Email Address: fanfeedback@astros.mlb.com. **Website:** www.astros.com.

Ownership
Owner/Chairman: Jim Crane.

BUSINESS OPERATIONS

Jim Crane

President/CEO: George Postolos. **Executive Assistant:** Eileen Colgin.
Senior Vice President, Premium Sponsorships: Jamie Hildrith. **Senior VP, Community Relations/Executive Director, Astros In Action Foundation:** Meg Vallaincourt. **VP/General Manager, Building Operations:** Marcel Braithwaite. **VP, Corporate Partnerships:** Matt Brand. **VP, Building Operations:** Bobby Forrest. **VP, Foundation Development:** Marian Harper. **VP, Ticket Sales/Services:** Jason Howard. **VP, Finance:** Doug Seckel. **VP, Special Events:** Kala Sorenson. **VP, Human Resources:** Larry Stokes.

Media Relations/Community Relations
Telephone: 713-259-8900. **Fax:** 713-259-8025.
Senior Director, Media Relations: Gene Dias. **Managers, Media Relations:** Steve Grande, Dena Propis. **Coordinator, Media Relations:** Chris Peixoto. **Manager, Community Relations:** Dairanetta Spain. **Coordinator, Community Relations:** Maureen Wade. **Assistant Director, Foundation Development:** Allison White. **Manager, Urban Youth Academy:** Daryl Wade. **Coordinator, Urban Youth Academy:** Brandon Denton.

Marketing
Director, Marketing Strategy: Scott Wakeman. **Director, Marketing Analytics:** Mike Dillon. **Director, Social Media:** Kelly George. **Managers, Marketing:** Andrea Andrus, Christie Miller. **Manager, Grass Roots Marketing:** Stephen Richards.

Corporate Partnerships
Director, Strategic Partnerships: Jacqueline Uram. **Account Executives, Corporate Sponsorships:** Keshia Dupas, Jessica Schmidt. **Manager, Corporate Partnership Development:** Melissa Garibay. **Manager, Corporate Partnership Account:** Jarret Nobles.

Events/Human Resources
Director, Special Events Operations: Jonathan Sterchy. **Manager, Special Events Operations:** Cara Lewanda. **Coordinator, Special Events Operations:** Jean Stewart.
Senior Director, Payroll/Employee Benefits: Ruth Kelly. **Payroll Manager:** Jessica Horton. **HR Manager, Recruitment/Internships Program:** Chanda Lawdermilk. **HR Manager, Recruitment/Administration:** Jennifer Springs.

2013 SCHEDULE

Standard Game Times: 7:05 p.m.; Sat. 6:05; Sun. 1:05.

MARCH	
31 . . . . Texas	

APRIL	
2-3 . . . . Texas	
5-7 . . . . Oakland	
8-10 . . . . .at Seattle	
12-14 . at Los Angeles (AL)	
15-17 . . . . . .at Oakland	
19-21 . . . . . . Cleveland	
22-24 . . . . Seattle	
25-28 . . . . . . .at Boston	
29-30 . . at New York (AL)	

MAY	
1 . . . . . at New York (AL)	
2-5 . . . . Detroit	
7-9 . . . . . Los Angeles (AL)	

10-12 . . . . Texas
13-15 . . . . . . .at Detroit
17-19 . . . . at Pittsburgh
20-22 . . . . . Kansas City
24-26 . . . . Oakland
27-28 . . . . . . .Colorado
29-30 . . . . . at Colorado
31 . . at Los Angeles (AL)

JUNE	
1-3 . . at Los Angeles (AL)	
4-6 . . . . Baltimore	
7-9 . . . . . .at Kansas City	
10-12 . . . . . . .at Seattle	
14-17 . . . . . Chicago (AL)	
18-20 . . . . . .Milwaukee	
21-23 . . .at Chicago (NL)	

25-26 . . . . St. Louis
28-30 . . . Los Angeles (AL)

JULY	
1-4 . . . . .Tampa Bay	
5-7 . . . . .at Texas	
9-10 . . . . . . .at St. Louis	
12-14 . . . . . at Tampa Bay	
19-21 . . . . Seattle	
22-24 . . . . Oakland	
25-28 . . . . . . at Toronto	
30-31 . . . . . .at Baltimore	

AUGUST	
1 . . . . .at Baltimore	
2-4 . . . . . . at Minnesota	
5-7 . . . . Boston	
9-12 . . . . Texas	

13-15 . . . . . .at Oakland
16-18 . at Los Angeles (AL)
19-21 . . . . .at Texas
23-25 . . . . .Toronto
26-28 . . . .at Chicago (AL)
29-31 . . . . Seattle

SEPTEMBER	
1 . . . . Seattle	
2-4 . . . . .Minnesota	
5-8 . . . . .at Oakland	
9-11 . . . . .at Seattle	
13-15 . . . Los Angeles (AL)	
16-18 . . . . . . Cincinnati	
19-22 . . . . .at Cleveland	
23-25 . . . . . . .at Texas	
27-29 . . . . .New York (AL)	

GENERAL INFORMATION

Stadium (year opened):
Minute Maid Park (2000).
Team Colors: Navy and orange.

Player Representative: Unavailable.
Home Dugout: First Base.
Playing Surface: Grass.

Stadium Operations
  Director, Stadium Operations: Phillip Pizzo. **Director, Security/Safety:** Chad Ludkey. **Senior Director, Major League Field Operations:** Dan Bergstrom. **Director, Guest Services:** Michael Kenny. **Assistant Director, Guest Services:** Cedrick Edwards. **Authentication Manager:** Mike Acosta.

Ticketing
  Senior Director, Ticket Operations/Strategy: Brooke Ellenberger. **Director, Box Office Operations:** Bill Cannon. **Director, Group Sales:** PJ Keene. **Director, Premium Sales/Service:** Clay Kowalski. **Director, Season Ticket Services:** Alan Latkovic. **Director, Season Ticket Sales:** Creighton Kahoali.

BASEBALL OPERATIONS
  General Manager: Jeff Luhnow.
  Assistant GM: David Stearns. **Special Assistants to the GM:** Craig Biggio, Enos Cabell, Roger Clemens. **Coordinator, Baseball Operations:** Stephanie Wilka.
  Director, Decision Sciences: Sig Mejdal. **Analyst:** Mike Fast. **Senior Technical Architect:** Ryan Hallahan. **Analytics Developer:** Darren DeFreeuw.

Jeff Luhnow

Major League Staff
  Manager: Bo Porter.
  Coaches: Bench—Eduardo Perez; **Pitching**—Doug Brocail; **Hitting**—John Mallee; **First Base**—Dave Clark; **Third Base**—Dave Trembley; **Bullpen**—Dennis Martinez. **Assistant Hitting Coach/Advance Scout:** Dan Radison. **Bullpen Catcher/Catching Coordinator:** Jeff Murphy. **Bullpen Catcher:** Javier Bracamonte.

Team Operations/Clubhouse
  Manager, Team Operations: Dan O'Neill. **Baseball Operations Assistant:** Pete Putila. **Clubhouse Manager:** Carl Schneider. **Visiting Clubhouse Manager:** Steve Perry. **Umpire Attendant/Clubhouse Assistant:** Chuck New. **Clubhouse Attendants:** David Burd, Stacey Gallagher. **Video Coordinator:** Jim Summers.

Medical/Training
  Medical Director: Dr. David Lintner. **Team Physicians:** Dr. Tom Mehlhoff, Dr. Jim Muntz, Dr. Pat McCulloch. **Head Trainer:** Nathan Lucero. **Assistant Trainer:** Rex Jones. **Strength/Conditioning Coach:** Jacob Beiting.

Player Development
  Telephone: (713) 259-8920. **Fax:** (713) 259-8600.
  Director, Player Development: Quinton McCracken. **Assitant Director, Player Development:** Allen Rowin. **Director, Florida Operations:** Jay Edmiston. **Field Coordinator:** Paul Runge. **Advisor, Latin American Development:** Julio Linares. **Minor League Coordinators:** Jamey Snodgrass (medical), Brendan Verner (strength/conditioning), Daniel Roberts (rehab), Ralph Dickenson (hitting), Dyar Miller (pitching), Jeff Albert (hitting rover), Craig Bjornson (pitching rover). **Development Specialists:** Tom Lawless (Triple-A), Mark Bailey (Double-A), Morgan Ensberg (High A), Vince Coleman (Low A). **DSL Coach:** Melvi Ortega. **Dominica Republic Academy Administrator:** Caridad Cabrera.

Farm System

Class	Club	Manager	Hitting Coach	Pitching Coach
Triple-A	Oklahoma City (PCL)	Tony DeFrancesco	Leon Roberts	Steve Webber
Double-A	Corpus Christi (TL)	Keith Bodie	Tim Garland	Gary Ruby
High A	Lancaster (CAL)	Rodney Linares	Darryl Robinson	Don Alexander
Low A	Quad Cities (SAL)	Omar Lopez	Joel Chimelis	Dave Borkowski
Short-season	Tri-City (NYP)	Ed Romero	Russ Steinhorn	Doug White
Rookie	Greeneville (APP)	Josh Bonifay	Cesar Cedeno	Josh Miller
Rookie	Astros (GCL)	Edgar Alfonzo	Marty Malloy	Hector Mercado
Rookie	Astros (DSL)	Johan Maya	Luis Mateo	Rick Aponte

Scouting
  Director, Amateur Scouting: Mike Elias. **Coordinator, Pro Scouting:** Kevin Goldstein. **Coordinator, Amateur Scouting:** Paul Cusick.
  Professional Scouts: Charles Aliano (Land O' Lakes, FL), Hank Allen (Upper Marlboro, MD), Ruben Amaro Sr (Weston, FL), Kenny Baugh (Houston, TX), Ken Califano (Stafford, VA), Alex Jacobs (Lakeland, FL), Justin Lehr (Chandler, AZ), Spike Lundberg (Murrieta, CA), Tim Moore (Sacramento, CA), Paul Ricciarini (Pittsfield, MA), Tom Shafer (Lockport, IL), Will Sharp (Athens, GA).
  National Crosschecker: David Post (Canton, GA). **Regional Supervisors: Midwest**—Ralph Bratton (Dripping Springs, TX), **East**—JD Alleva (Charlotte, NC), **West**—Kris Gross (Newport Beach, CA), **East**—Evan Brannon (St. Petersburg, FL). **Area Scouts:** Tim Bittner (Mechanicsville, VA), Bryan Byrne (Walnut Creek, CA), Brad Budzinski (Huntington Beach, CA), Tim Costic (Stevenson Ranch, CA), Justin Cryer (Hammond, LA), Gavin Dickey (Atlanta, GA), Paul Gale (Keizer, OR), Noel Gonzales (Houston, TX), Troy Hoerner (Middleton, WI), John Martin (Tampa, FL), Mark Ross (Tucson, AZ), Bobby St. Pierre (Port Washington, NY), Jim Stevenson (Tulsa, OK), Nick Venuto (Newton Falls, OH). **Senior Advising Scouts:** Bob King (La Mesa, CA), Bob Poole (Redwood City, CA). **Part-Time Scouts:** Robert Gutierrez (Miami Gardens, FL), Joey Sola (Caguas, PR). **Director, International Scouting:** Oz Ocampo (New York, NY). **International Crosschecker:** Marc Russo (Clearwater Beach, FL). **International Scouts: Venezuela**—Daniel Acuna, Oscar Alvarado, Miguel Chacoa, Jose Palacios; **Dominican Republic**—Rafael Belen, Jose Lima, Francis Mojica, Jose Ortiz; **Colombia**—Carlos Martinez; **Nicaragua**—Leocadio Guevara; **Australia**—Greg Morriss.

Kansas City Royals

Office Address: One Royal Way, Kansas City, MO 64129.
Mailing Address: P.O. Box 419969, Kansas City, MO 64141.
Telephone: (816) 921-8000. **Fax:** (816) 924-0347. **Website:** www.royals.com

Ownership

Operated By: Kansas City Royals Baseball Club, Inc.
Chairman/CEO: David Glass. **President:** Dan Glass. **Board of Directors:** Ruth Glass, Don Glass, Dayna Martz, Julia Kauffman. **Executive Administrative Assistant (Executive Staff):** Ginger Salem.

BUSINESS OPERATIONS

Senior Vice President, Business Operations: Kevin Uhlich. **Executive Administrative Assistant:** Cindy Hamilton. **Director, Royals Hall of Fame:** Curt Nelson.

Finance/Administration

VP, Finance/Administration: David Laverentz. **Director, Finance:** Adam Tyhurst. **Director, Human Resources:** Johnna Meyer. **Director, Risk Management:** Patrick Fleischmann. **Senior Director, Payroll:** Tom Pfannenstiel. **Senior Director, Information Systems:** Brian Himstedt. **Director, Information Systems Operations:** Scott Novak. **Senior Director, Ticket Operations:** Larry Chu. **Director, Ticket Operations:** Chris Darr.

David Glass

Communications/Broadcasting

VP, Communications/Broadcasting: Mike Swanson. **Director, Broadcast Services/Royals Alumni:** Fred White. **Director, Media Relations:** David Holtzman. **Coordinator, Media Services:** Dina Blevins. **Coordinator, Communications/Broadcasting:** Colby Curry.

Publicity/Community Relations

VP, Community Affairs/Publicity: Toby Cook. **Senior Director, Community Relations:** Ben Aken. **Senior Director, Publicity:** Lora Grosshans. **Senior Director, Royals Charities:** Joy Sedlacek. **Director, Community Outreach:** Betty Kaegel.

Ballpark Operations

VP, Ballpark Operations/Development: Bob Rice. **Director, Groundskeeping/Landscaping:** Trevor Vance. **Director, Ballpark Services:** Johnny Williams. **Director, Stadium Engineering/Maintenance:** Todd Burrow.

Marketing/Business Development

VP, Marketing/Business Development: Michael Bucek. **Senior Director, Event Presentation/Production:** Don Constante. **Director, Event Presentation/Production:** Chris DeRuyscher. **Director, Marketing:** Brad Zollars. **Director, Online/Target Marketing:** Erin Sleddens. **Senior Director, Corporate Sponsorships/Broadcast Sales:** Wes Engram. **Senior Director, Client Services:** Michele Kammerer. **Senior**

2013 SCHEDULE

Standard Game Times: 7:10 p.m.; Sat. 6:10; Sun. 1:10.

APRIL
1 . . . . . . .at Chicago (AL)
3-4 . . . . . .at Chicago (AL)
5-7 . . . . . at Philadelphia
8-10 . . . . Minnesota
12-14 . . . . Toronto
16-17 . . . . . . at Atlanta
19-21 . . . . . . .at Boston
23-25 . . . . . . .at Detroit
26-29 . . . . . . Cleveland
30 . . . . .Tampa Bay

MAY
1-2 . . . . .Tampa Bay
3-5 . . . . . . Chicago (AL)
7-9 . . . . . .at Baltimore
10-12 . . . . .New York (AL)

13-15 . at Los Angeles (AL)
17-19 . . . . . .at Oakland
20-22 . . . . . .at Houston
23-26 . . . Los Angeles (AL)
27-28 . . . . St. Louis
29-30 . . . . .at St. Louis
31 . . . . .at Texas

JUNE
1-2 . . . . .at Texas
4-6 . . . . .Minnesota
7-9 . . . . Houston
10-12 . . . . Detroit
13-16 . . . . at Tampa Bay
17-19 . . . .at Cleveland
21-23 . . . . Chicago (AL)
25-26 . . . . .Atlanta

27-30 . . . . . at Minnesota

JULY
2-4 . . . . Cleveland
5-7 . . . . Oakland
8-11 . . . at New York (AL)
12-14 . . . . .at Cleveland
19-21 . . . . Detroit
22-25 . . . . . Baltimore
26-28 . . . .at Chicago (AL)
30-31 . . . . at Minnesota

AUGUST
1 . . . . at Minnesota
2-4 . . . at New York (NL)
5-7 . . . . .Minnesota
8-11 . . . . Boston

12-14 . . . . .Miami
15-18 . . . . . . .at Detroit
20-22 . . . . Chicago (AL)
23-25 . . . . . Washington
27-29 . . . . at Minnesota
30-31 . . . . . . at Toronto

SEPTEMBER
1 . . . . at Toronto
2-5 . . . . Seattle
6-8 . . . . Detroit
9-11 . . . . . .at Cleveland
13-15 . . . . . . .at Detroit
16-18 . . . . . . Cleveland
20-22 . . . . Texas
23-25 . . . . . .at Seattle
26-29 . . . .at Chicago (AL)

GENERAL INFORMATION

Stadium (year opened):
Ewing M. Kauffman Stadium (1973).
Team Colors: Royal blue and white.

Player Representative: Aaron Crow.
Home Dugout: First Base.
Playing Surface: Grass.

Director, Sales/Service: Steve Shiffman. Director, Sales: Theodore Hodges. Director, Ticket Services: Scott Wadsworth.

BASEBALL OPERATIONS

Dayton Moore

Telephone: (816) 921-8000. **Fax:** (816) 924-0347.
Senior VP, Baseball Operations/General Manager: Dayton Moore.
VP, Baseball Operations/Assistant GM: Dean Taylor. **Assistant GM, Scouting/Player Development:** J.J. Picollo. **Assistant GM/International Operations:** Rene Francisco. **Senior Advisor to GM/Scouting/Player Development:** Mike Arbuckle. **Director, Baseball Administration:** Jin Wong. **Director, Pro Scouting:** Gene Watson. **Director, Baseball Analytics:** Mike Groopman. **Assistant Director, Baseball Analytics:** John Williams. **Administrative Assistant to Baseball Operations:** Emily Penning.
Manager, Arizona Operations: Nick Leto. **Senior Advisors:** Art Stewart, Donnie Williams, John Boles. **Special Assistant, Player Personnel:** Louie Medina. **VP, Baseball Operations:** George Brett. **Special Assistants to GM:** Pat Jones, Mike Toomey, Mike Pazik, Jim Fregosi, Jr., Tim Conroy. **Team Travel:** Jeff Davenport. **Video Coordinator:** Mark Topping.

Major League Staff
Manager: Ned Yost.
Coaches: Bench—Chino Cadahia; **Pitching**—Dave Eiland; **Hitting**—Jack Maloof; **Assistant Hitting**—Andre David; **First Base**—Rusty Kuntz; **Third Base**—Eddie Rodriguez; **Bullpen**—Doug Henry.

Medical/Training
Team Physician: Dr. Vincent Key. **Athletic Trainer:** Nick Kenney. **Assistant Athletic Trainer:** Kyle Turner. **Strength/Conditioning:** Ryan Stoneberg.

Player Development
Telephone: (816) 921-8000. **Fax:** (816) 924-0347.
Director, Player Development: Scott Sharp.
Assistant Director, Player Development: Kyle Vena.
Special Assistant: Steve Foster (pitching). **Special Assistant, Player Development/Scouting:** John Wathan.
Coordinators: Tony Tijerina (field), Terry Bradshaw (hitting), Jose Castro (assistant hitting), Glenn Hubbard (infield), Milt Thompson (bunting/baserunning), Chris DeLucia (medical), Tony Medina (Latin America medical), Garrett Sherrill (strength/conditioning), Luis Perez (Latin America strength/conditioning), Sean McQueeney (rehab).

Farm System

Class	Club (League)	Manager	Hitting Coach	Pitching Coach
Triple-A	Omaha (PCL)	Mike Jirschele	Tommy Gregg	Larry Carter
Double-A	Northwest Arkansas (TL)	Brian Poldberg	Nelson Liriano	Jim Brower
High A	Wilmington (CL)	Vance Wilson	Julio Bruno	Steve Luebber
Low A	Lexington (SAL)	Brian Buchanan	Justin Gemoll	Jerry Nyman
Rookie	Idaho Falls (PIO)	Omar Ramirez	Damon Hollins	Steve Merriman
Rookie	Burlington (APP)	Tommy Shields	Abraham Nunez	Carlos Martinez
Rookie	Royals (AZL)	Darryl Kennedy	Pedro Grifol	M. Davis/C. Reyes
Rookie	Royals (DSL)	Ramon Martinez	Unavailable	Rafael Roque

Scouting
Telephone: (816) 921-8000. **Fax:** (816) 924-0347.
Director, Scouting: Lonnie Goldberg.
Manager, Scouting Operations: Linda Smith. **Assistant to Amateur Scouting:** Jack Monahan.
Major League Scouts: Charles Bolton (Indianapolis, IN), Dennis Cardoza (Pilot Point, TX), Mike Pazik (Bethesda, MD), Jon Williams (Imperial, MO), Ron Toenjes (Georgetown, TX), Alec Zumwalt (Winston-Salem, NC).
National Supervisors: Paul Gibson (Center Moriches, NY), Junior Vizcaino (Raleigh, NC). **Regional Supervisors: Canada/Junior Colleges**—Keith Connolly (Fair Haven, NJ), **Midwest**—Mitch Webster (Kansas City, MO), **Southeast**—Gregg Kilby (Tampa, FL), **West**—Dan Ontiveros (Laguna Niguel, CA), **Northeast**—Sean Rooney (Apex, NC).
Area Scouts: Rich Amaral (Huntington Beach, CA), Jason Bryans (Windsor, Canada), Jim Buckley (FL), Keith Connolly (Fair Haven, NJ), Travis Ezi (Baton Rouge, LA), Casey Fahy (Apex, NC), Jim Farr (Williamsburg, VA), Sean Gibbs (Canton, GA), Colin Gonzales (Aliso Viejo, CA), Scott Melvin (Quincy, IL), Alex Mesa (Miami, FL), Ken Munoz (Scottsdale, AZ), Matt Price (Overland Park, KS), Scott Ramsay (Valley, WA), Mitch Thompson (Waco, TX), Max Valencia (Dixon, CA).
Part-Time Scouts: Rick Clendenin (Clendenin, WV), Louis Collier (Chicago, IL), Dan Drake (Riverside, CA), Brian Hiler (Cincinnati, OH), Jerry Lafferty (Kansas City, MO), Chad Lee (Oklahoma City, OK), Brittan Motley (Grandview, MO), Chad Raley (Baton Rouge, LA), Johnny Ramos (Carolina, PR), Jordan Wyckoff (Coatesville, PA).
Latin America Supervisor: Orlando Estevez. **International Scouts:** Richard Castro (Venezuela), Alvin Cuevas (Dominican Republic), Taizo Date (Japan), Alberto Garcia (Venezuela) Juan Indriago (Venezuela), Jose Gualdron (Venezuela); Joelvis Gonzalez (Venezuela), Edson Kelly (Aruba), Juan Lopez (Nicaragua), Nathan Miller (Taiwan), Rafael Miranda (Colombia), Fausto Morel (Dominican Republic), Ricardo Ortiz (Panama), Edis Perez (Dominican Republic), Rafael Vasquez (Dominican Republic), Franco Wawoe (Curacao).

Los Angeles Angels

Office Address: 2000 Gene Autry Way, Anaheim, CA 92806.
Mailing Address: P.O. Box 2000, Anaheim, CA 92803.
Telephone: (714) 940-2000. **Fax:** (714) 940-2205.
Website: www.angels.com.

Ownership
Owner: Arte Moreno. **Chairman:** Dennis Kuhl. **President:** John Carpino.

Business Operations
Chief Financial Officer: Bill Beverage. **Vice President, Finance/Administration:** Molly Taylor Jolly. **Controller:** Cris Lacoste. **Accountants:** Lorelei Largey, Kylie McManus, Jennifer Whynott. **Financial Analyst:** Jennifer Jeanblanc. **Assistant, Accounting:** Linda Chubak. **Assistant, Payroll:** Alison Kelso. **Benefits Manager:** Cecilia Schneider.
Director, Human Resources: Deborah Johnston. **Manager, Recruitment/Training:** Brittany Johnson. **Human Resources Representative:** Mayra Trinidad. **Staffing Analyst:** Kristin Talamantes. **Director, Information Services:** Al Castro. **Senior Network Engineer:** Neil Farris. **Senior Desktop Support Analyst:** David Yun. **Assistant Network Administrator:** Paramjit 'Tiny' Singh. **Helpdesk Assistant:** Kim Davis.

Arte Moreno

Marketing/Corporate Sales
Senior Director, Corporate Sales: Neil Viserto. **Senior Director, Business Development:** Michael Fach. **Corporate Sales Account Executives:** Nicole Provansal, Rick Turner, Matt Wiech. **Sponsorship Services Manager:** Maria Dinh. **Sponsorship Services Coordinators:** Katherine Kaczmarek, Bobby Kowan, Drew Zinser.
VP, Marketing/Ticket Sales: Robert Alvarado. **Marketing Managers:** John Rozak, Kevin Shaw, Ryan Vance. **Marketing Coordinator/Graphic Designer:** Jeff Lee.
Manager, Ticket Sales: Tom DeTemple. **Inside Sales Supervisor:** Josh Hunhoff. **Client Services Representatives:** Ashley Green, Shawn Meyer, Alisa Mitry, Adriana Ryan. **Group Sales Account Executive:** Angel Rodriguez. **Premium Sales Account Executives:** Glenn Griffith, Kyle Haygood. **Ticket Sales Account Executives:** Clint Blevins, Jeff Leuenberger, Jasmin Matthews, Scott Tarlo. **Event Sales/Service Manager:** Courtney Wallace. **Administrative Assistant, Marketing:** Monica Campanis.

Public/Media Relations/Communications
Telephone: (714) 940-2014. **Fax:** (714) 940-2205.
VP, Communications: Tim Mead. **Manager, Communications:** Eric Kay. **Media Relations Representative:** Adam Chodzko. **Administrative Assistant:** Matthew Birch. **Senior Director, Community Relations:** Jenny Price. **Community Relations Coordinator:** Chrissy Vaughn. **Club Photographers:** Debora Robinson, John Cordes, Bob Binder.

Ballpark Operations/Facilities
Senior Director, Ballpark Operations: Brian Sanders. **Director, Ballpark Operations:** Sam Maida. **Event Manager:**

2013 SCHEDULE
Standard Game Times: 7:05 p.m.; Sun. 12:35.

APRIL
1 . . . . .at Cincinnati
3-4 . . . . . . .at Cincinnati
5-7 . . . . .at Texas
9-11 . . . . Oakland
12-14 . . . . Houston
15-17 . . . at Minnesota
19-21 . . . . Detroit
22-24 . . . . Texas
25-28 . . . . . . .at Seattle
29-30 . . . . . .at Oakland

MAY
1 . . . . .at Oakland
2-5 . . . . Baltimore
7-9 . . . . .at Houston
10-12 . . . at Chicago (AL)

13-15 . . . . . Kansas City
16-19 . . . . Chicago (AL)
21-22 . . . . Seattle
23-26 . . . .at Kansas City
27-28 . at Los Angeles (NL)
29-30 . . . Los Angeles (NL)
31 . . . . Houston

JUNE
1-3 . . . . Houston
4-5 . . . . Chicago (NL)
7-9 . . . . .at Boston
10-12 . . . . . at Baltimore
14-16 . . . .New York (AL)
17-20 . . . . Seattle
21-23 . . . . . . Pittsburgh
25-27 . . . . . . .at Detroit

28-30 . . . . . .at Houston

JULY
2-4 . . . . St. Louis
5-7 . . . . Boston
9-10 . . . .at Chicago (NL)
12-14 . . . . .at Seattle
19-21 . . . . Oakland
22-24 . . . . . . .Minnesota
25-28 . . . . . .at Oakland
29-31 . . . . .at Texas

AUGUST
1-4 . . . . .Toronto
5-7 . . . . Texas
9-11 . . . . . .at Cleveland
12-15 . . . at New York (AL)

16-18 . . . . Houston
19-21 . . . . Cleveland
23-25 . . . . .at Seattle
27-29 . . . at Tampa Bay
30-31 . . . . . at Milwaukee

SEPTEMBER
1 . . . . at Milwaukee
2-5 . . . . .Tampa Bay
6-8 . . . . Texas
10-12 . . . . . . at Toronto
13-15 . . . . . . .at Houston
16-18 . . . . . .at Oakland
20-22 . . . . Seattle
23-25 . . . . Oakland
26-29 . . . . .at Texas

GENERAL INFORMATION
Stadium (year opened):
Angel Stadium of Anaheim (1966).
Team Colors: Red, dark red, blue and silver.

Player Representative: Unavailable.
Home Dugout: Third Base.
Playing Surface: Grass.

Calvin Ching. **Security Manager:** Mark Macias. **Field/Ground Maintenance Manager:** Barney Lopas. **Assistant Groundskeeper:** Greg Laesch. **Receptionists:** Sandy Sanford, Margie Walsh.
    Director, Facility Services: Mike McKay. **Assistant Manager, Facility Services:** Linda Fitzgerald. **Purchasing Manager:** Suzanne Peters. **Asset Coordinator:** Daniel Angulo. **Manager, Facility Maintenance:** Steve Preston. **Housekeeping Manager:** Robert Donovan. **Custodial Supervisors:** Nathan Bautista, Pedro Del Castillo, Ray Nells. **Office Assistant:** Jose Padilla.
    Manager, Entertainment/Production: Peter Bull. **Producer, Video Operations:** David Tsuruda. **Associate Producer:** Danny Pitts. **Entertainment Coordinator:** Trina Berberet.

Ticketing
    Manager, Ticket Operations: Sheila Brazelton. **Manager, Ticket Office:** Susan Weiss. **Ticketing Representatives:** Ellen Crooks, Julie Henrick, Clancy Holligan, Cyndi Nguyen, Armando Reyna. **Box Office Representative:** Lisa Martinez

Travel/Clubhouse
    Clubhouse Manager: Keith Tarter. **Assistant Clubhouse Manager:** Shane Demmitt. **Visiting Clubhouse Manager:** Brian Harkins. **Senior Video Coordinator:** Diego Lopez. **Video Coordinator:** Ruben Montano.

BASEBALL OPERATIONS
    General Manager: Jerry Dipoto.
    Assistant GM, Baseball Operations: Matt Klentak. **Assistant GM, Player Development/Scouting:** Scott Servais. **Special Advisor:** Bill Stoneman. **Special Assistants to GM:** Marcel Lachemann, Tim Huff. **Director, Baseball Operations:** Justin Hollander. **Director, Pro Scouting:** Hal Morris. **Coordinator, Baseball Operations:** Jonathan Strangio. **Coordinator, Scouting:** Nate Horowitz. **Baseball Administration Coordinator:** Kathy Mair.

Jerry Dipoto

Major League Staff
    Manager: Mike Scioscia. **Coaches: Bench**—Rob Picciolo; **Pitching**—Mike Butcher; **Batting**—Jim Eppard; **First Base**—Alfredo Griffin; **Third Base**—Dino Ebel; **Bullpen**—Steve Soliz; **Bullpen Catcher**—Tom Gregorio.

Medical/Training
    Medical Director: Dr. Lewis Yocum. **Team Physician:** Dr. Craig Milhouse. **Head Athletic Trainer:** Adam Nevala. **Assistant Athletic Trainer:** Rick Smith. **Minor League Head Athletic Trainer:** Geoff Hostetter. **Strength/Conditioning Coach:** T.J. Harrington. **Minor League Strength/Conditioning Coordinator:** Seth Walsh.

Player Development
    Director, Player Development: Bobby Scales. **Manager, Minor League Operations:** Mike LaCassa. **Minor League Equipment Manager, Arizona:** Brett Crane. **Field Coordinator:** Mike Micucci. **Roving Instructors:** Paul Sorrento (hitting), Orlando Mercado (catching), Bill Lachemann (catching/special assignment), Tyrone Boykin (outfield/baserunning/bunting), Jim Gott (pitching), Kernan Ronan (rehab pitching), Pete Harnisch (special assignment pitching), Geoff Hostetter (training coordinator), Seth Walsh (strength/conditioning), Eric Munson (rehab).

Farm System

Class	Club	Manager	Hitting Coach	Pitching Coach
Triple-A	Salt Lake (PCL)	Keith Johnson	Francisco Matos	Erik Bennett
Double-A	Arkansas (TL)	Tim Bogar	Ernie Young	Mike Hampton
High A	Inland Empire (CAL)	Bill Haselman	Brenton Del Chiaro	Brandon Emanuel
Low A	Burlington (MWL)	Jamie Burke	Nathan Haynes	Trevor Wilson
Rookie	Orem (PIO)	Unavailable	Carson Vitale	Chris Gissell
Rookie	Angels (AZL)	Denny Hocking	Ryan Barba/Brian Betancourth	Matt Wise
Rookie	Angels (DSL)	Charlie Romero	Edgal Rodriguez	Hector Astacio

Scouting
    Director, Amateur Scouting: Ric Wilson.
    Major League/Special Assignment Scouts: Larry Corrigan (Mendota, IL), Timothy Schmidt (San Bernardino, CA), Jeff Schugel (Denver, CO).
    Major League Scouts: Jeff Cirillo (Medina, WA), Mike Koplove (Philadelphia, PA), Tim McIntosh (Stockton, CA), Ken Stauffer (Katy, TX), Gary Varsho (Chili, WI).
    National Crosscheckers: Jeff Malinoff (Lopez, WA), Greg Morhardt (S. Windsor, CT). **Regional Supervisors: Northeast**—Jason Baker (Lynchburg, VA); **Southeast**—Chris McAlpin (Moultrie, GA); **Southern Midwest**—Kevin Ham (Cypress, TX); **Northwest**—Scott Richardson (Sacramento, CA).
    Area Scouts: Dan Archer (Canada), John Burden (Fairfield, OH), Drew Chadd (Wichita, KS), Tim Corcoran (LaVerne, CA), Bobby DeJardin (San Clemente, CA), Jason Ellison (Issaquah, WA), Nick Gorneault (Springfield, MA), John Gracio (Mesa, AZ), Chad Hermansen (Henderson, NV), Todd Hogan (Dublin, GA), Brandon McArthur (Kennesaw, GA), Joel Murrie (Evergreen, CO), Dan Radcliff (Palmyra, VA), Ralph Reyes (Miami, FL), Omar Rodriguez (Puerto Rico), Rudy Vasquez (San Antonio, TX), Rob Wilfong (San Dimas, CA), J.T. Zink (Hoover, AL).
    Director, International Scouting: Carlos Gomez. **International Scouts:** Jason Dunn (Asia), Domingo Garcia (Dominican Republic), Lebi Ochoa (Venezuela Scouting Supervisor), Roman Ocumarez (Dominican Republic Scouting Supervisor), Carlos Ramirez (Venezuela), Rene Rojas (Dominican Republic), Mauro Zerpa (Venezuela).

Los Angeles Dodgers

Office Address: 1000 Elysian Park Ave., Los Angeles, CA 90090.
Telephone: (323) 224-1500. **Fax:** (323) 224-1269. **Website:** www.dodgers.com

Ownership

Chairman: Mark Walter.
President/CEO: Stan Kasten. **Partner:** Earvin 'Magic' Johnson, Peter Guber, Todd Boehly, Robert 'Bobby' Patton, Jr.
Special Advisors to Chairman: Tommy Lasorda, Sandy Koufax, Dr. Frank Jobe, Don Newcombe.

BUSINESS OPERATIONS

Mark Walter

Executive Vice President: Bob Wolfe. **Executive VP/Chief Marketing Officer:** Lon Rosen.
Senior VP/General Counsel: Sam Fernandez. **Senior VP, Planning/Development:** Janet Marie Smith. **Senior VP, External Affairs:** Renata Simril. **Senior VP, Corporate Partnerships:** Michael Young. **Controller:** Eric Hernandez. **Director, Finance:** Paige Bobbitt.

Sales/Partnership

Senior Director, Ticket Sales: David Siegel. **Director, Partnership Administration:** Jenny Oh. **Director, Corporate Partnerships:** Lorenzo Sciarrino. **Director, Business Development:** Schuyler Hoversten. **Director, Premium Sales/Services:** Antonio Morici.

Marketing/Broadcasting

Senior Director, Marketing/Broadcasting: Erik Braverman. **Director, Advertising/Promotions:** Shelley Wagner. **Director, Production:** Greg Taylor. **Director, Graphic Design:** Ross Yoshida.

Human Resources/Legal

Director, Human Resources: Leonor Romero. **Senior Counsel:** Chad Gunderson.

Communications/Community Relations

Assistant Directors, Public Relations: Joe Jareck, Yvonne Carrasco. **Director, Publications:** Jorge Martin. **Director, Community Relations:** Rafael Gonzalez.

Information Technology/Stadium Operations/Security

Senior Director, Information Technology: Ralph Esquibel. **VP, Stadium Operations:** Francine Hughes. **Senior VP, Security:** William Woodward. **Director, Safety/Security:** Michael Betzler. **Director, Fan Services:** Eric George. **Assistant Director, Turf/Grounds:** Eric Hansen.

Ticketing

Telephone: (323) 224-1471. **Fax:** (323) 224-2609.
VP, Ticket Operations: Billy Hunter. **Senior Director, Ticket Operations:** Seth Bluman.

2013 SCHEDULE

Standard Game Times: 7:10 p.m.; Sun. 1:10

APRIL
1-3 . . . . . . San Francisco
5-7 . . . . Pittsburgh
9-11 . . . . . at San Diego
12-14 . . . . . . at Arizona
15-17 . . . . . . San Diego
19-21 . . . . at Baltimore
23-25 . . . at New York (NL)
26-28 . . . . . . Milwaukee
29-30 . . . . Colorado

MAY
1 . . . . Colorado
3-5 . . . . at San Francisco
6-8 . . . . Arizona
10-12 . . . . Miami

13-15 . . . . . . Washington
17-19 . . . . at Atlanta
20-22 . . . . at Milwaukee
24-26 . . . . St. Louis
27-28 . . . Los Angeles (AL)
29-30 . at Los Angeles (AL)
31 . . . . at Colorado

JUNE
1-2 . . . . at Colorado
3-5 . . . . San Diego
6-9 . . . . Atlanta
10-12 . . . . Arizona
14-16 . . . . at Pittsburgh
18-19 . . . at New York (AL)
20-23 . . . at San Diego
24-26 . . . . San Francisco

27-30 . . . . . .Philadelphia

JULY
2-4 . . . . at Colorado
5-7 . . . . at San Francisco
8-10 . . . . . . at Arizona
11-14 . . . . .Colorado
19-21 . . . at Washington
22-24 . . . . . at Toronto
25-28 . . . . . . Cincinnati
30-31 . . . .New York (AL)

AUGUST
1-4 . . . . .at Chicago (NL)
5-8 . . . . . .at St. Louis
9-11 . . . . . . .Tampa Bay
12-14 . . . .New York (NL)

16-18 . . . . at Philadelphia
19-22 . . . . at Miami
23-25 . . . . Boston
26-28 . . . . . Chicago (NL)
30-31 . . . . . . San Diego

SEPTEMBER
1 . . . . San Diego
2-4 . . . . at Colorado
6-8 . . . . .at Cincinnati
9-11 . . . . .Arizona
12-15 . . . . .San Francisco
16-19 . . . . at Arizona
20-22 . . . . at San Diego
24-26 . . at San Francisco
27-29 . . . . .Colorado

GENERAL INFORMATION

Stadium (year opened): Dodger Stadium (1962).
Team Colors: Dodger blue and white.

Player Representative: Clayton Kershaw.
Home Dugout: Third Base.
Playing Surface: Grass.

BASEBALL OPERATIONS

Telephone: (323) 224-1500. **Fax:** (323) 224-1463.
General Manager: Ned Colletti.
VP, Player Personnel: Vance Lovelace. **Special Advisor to the GM:** Gerry Hunsicker. **Special Assistant to the GM:** Pat Corrales. **Director, Baseball Administration:** Ellen Harrigan. **Director, Baseball Contracts/Research/Operations:** Alex Tamin. **Director, Team Travel:** Scott Akasaki. **Director, International/Minor League Relations:** Joseph Reaves. **Manager, Scouting/Travel Administration:** Jane Capobianco. **Advisor, Team Travel:** Billy DeLury. **Major League Video Coordinator:** John Pratt. **Manager, Baseball Research/Operations:** Matt Marks. **Coordinator, Baseball Operations:** Jordan Peikin. **Assistant, Baseball Operations:** Kyle Esecson. **Special Assistants, Player Personnel:** Josh Bard, Juan Castro, Aaron Sele, Jose Vizcaino.
Manager, Dodger Clubhouse: Mitch Poole. **Assistant Manager, Dodger Clubhouse:** Alex Torres. **Clubhouse Attendant:** Jose Castillo. **Manager, Visiting Clubhouse:** Jerry Turner.

Ned Colletti

Major League Staff

Manager: Don Mattingly.
Coaches: Bench—Trey Hillman; **Pitching**—Rick Honeycutt; **Hitting**—Mark McGwire; **First Base**—Davey Lopes; **Third Base**—Tim Wallach; **Bullpen**—Chuck Crim. **Assistant Pitching Coach:** Ken Howell. **Assistant Hitting Coach:** John Valentin. **Instructors:** Manny Mota, Steve Yeager. **Bullpen Catchers:** Rob Flippo, Fumimasa Ishibashi.

Medical/Training

VP, Medical Services: Stan Conte. **Head Athletic Trainer:** Sue Falsone. **Assistant Athletic Trainers:** Nancy Patterson, Greg Harrel. **Strength/Conditioning Coaches:** Stephen Downey, Brandon McDaniel. **Massage Therapist:** Ichiro Tani. **Team Physicians:** Dr. Neal ElAttrache, Dr. John Plosay, Dr. Brian Shafer, Dr. Mary Gendy.

Player Development

Telephone: (323) 224-1500. **Fax:** (323) 224-1359.
VP, Player Development: De Jon Watson.
Field Coordinator: Bruce Hines. **Senior Advisors to Player Development:** Gene Clines, Charlie Hough. **Latin America Special Advisor:** Ramon Martinez. **Senior Manager, Player Development:** Chris Madden. **Coordinator, Minor League Administration:** Adriana Urzua. **Instructor:** Maury Wills. **Coordinators:** Eric Owens (hitting), Rafael Chaves (pitching), Damon Mashore (outfield/baserunning), Pat Listach (infield), Travis Barbary (catching), John Shoemaker (Arizona instruction), Todd Takayoshi (assistant hitting), Richard Knapp (assistant pitching). **Campo Las Palmas Coordinator:** Henry Cruz. **Field Coordinator, Campo Las Palmas:** Antonio Bautista.

Farm System

Class	Club (League)	Manager	Coach	Pitching Coach
Triple-A	Albuquerque (PCL)	Lorenzo Bundy	Franklin Stubbs	Glenn Dishman
Double-A	Chattanooga (SL)	Jody Reed	Orv Franchuk	Hector Berrios
High A	Rancho Cucamonga (CAL)	Carlos Subero	Jay Washington	Matt Herges
Low A	Great Lakes (MWL)	Razor Shines	Mike Eylward	Bill Simas
Rookie	Ogden (PIO)	Damon Berryhill	Esteban Lopez	Scott Radinsky
Rookie	Dodgers (AZL)	P.J. Forbes	Leo Garcia	Kremlin Martinez
Rookie	Dodgers (DSL)	Pedro Mega	Keyter Collado	Alejandro Pena

Scouting

VP, Amateur Scouting: Logan White.
Special Advisor, Amateur Scouting/National Crosschecker: Gib Bodet (San Clemente, CA). **Special Assistant, Amateur Scouting:** Larry Barton (Leona Valley, CA). **National Crosscheckers:** Paul Fryer (Calabasas, CA), John Green (Tucson, AZ). **East Regional Supervisor:** Manny Estrada (Longwood, FL). **Midwest Regional Supervisor:** Gary Nickels (Naperville, IL). **West Regional Supervisor:** Brian Stephenson (Yorba Linda, CA). **Coordinator, Scouting:** Trey Magnuson. **Assistant, Scouting:** Artie Harris.
Area Scouts: Clint Bowers (The Woodlands, TX), Bobby Darwin (Corona, CA), Rich Delucia (Reading, PA), Scott Hennessey (Ponte Verde, FL), Orsino Hill (Sacramento, CA), Calvin Jones (Highland Village, TX), Henry Jones (Vancouver, WA), Lon Joyce (Spartanburg, SC), Jeffrey Lachman (Los Angeles, CA), Marty Lamb (Nicholasville, KY), Scott Little (Cape Girardeau, MO), Dennis Moeller (Stevenson Ranch, CA), Matthew Paul (Slidell, LA), Clair Rierson (Wake Forest, NC), Chet Sergo (Stoughton, WI), Rob Sidwell (Windermere, FL), Dustin Yount (Paradise Valley, AZ). **Part-Time Scouts:** Artie Harris, Luis Faccio, Greg Goodwin, Jimmy Johnston, Rodney Davis. **Scouting Consultant:** George Genovese.
VP, Professional Scouting: Rick Ragazzo. **Special Assistants to the GM:** Ken Bracey, Toney Howell.
Advance Scout: Wade Taylor. **Professional Scouts:** Willie Fraser, Scott Groot, Bill Latham, Carl Loewenstine, Tydus Meadows, Bill Mueller, Steve Pope, John Sanders.
VP, International Scouting: Bob Engle. **Manager, International Scouting:** Roman Barinas. **Executive Director, Asian Operations/Scouting:** Acey Kohrogi. **Senior Scouting Advisor, Dominican Republic:** Ralph Avila. **Coordinator, Pacific Rim:** Pat Kelly. **Coordinator, Latin America:** Patrick Guerrero. **Supervisor, Dominican Republic:** Elvio Jimenez. **Coordinator, Venezuela Operations:** Pedro Avila. **Coordinator, European Operations:** Gene Grimaldi. **Coordinator, Latin America:** Mike Tosar. **Senior Manager, Asian Operations:** Yayoi Sato. **Assignment Scout, Pacific Rim:** Jamey Storvick. **International Scouts:** Gustavo Zapata (Central America), Rolando Chirino (Curacao), Maximo Gross (Dominican), Wilton Guerrero (Dominican), Rafael Rijo (Dominican), Ezequiel Sepulveda (Dominican), Bienvenido Tavarez (Dominican), Marco Mazzieri (Europe), Keiichi Kojima (Japan), Byung-Hwan An (Korea), Mike Brito (Mexico), Jose Briceno (Venezuela), Francisco Cartaya (Venezuela), Camilo Pascual (Venezuela), Oswaldo Villalobos (Venezuela).

Miami Marlins

Office Address: Marlins Park, 501 Marlins Way, Miami, FL 33125
Telephone: (305) 480-1300. **Fax:** (305) 480-3012.
Website: www.marlins.com.

Ownership
Owner/CEO: Jeffrey Loria. **Vice Chairman:** Joel Mael.
President: David Samson. **Special Assistants to Owner:** Bill Beck, Jack McKeon. **Special Assistants to President:** Jeff Conine, Andre Dawson, Tony Perez. **Executive Assistant:** Beth McConville.

Jeffrey Loria

BUSINESS OPERATIONS
Executive Vice President/CFO: Michel Bussiere. **Executive VP, Operations/Events:** Claude Delorme. **VP, Ballpark Operations:** Steve Ethier. **VP, Facilities:** Jeff King. **Director, Ballpark Operations:** Michael Hurt. **Director, Parking:** Michael McKeon. **Director, Security:** Greg Terp. **Director, Grounds:** Chad Mulholland.
Manager, Game Services: Antonio Torres-Roman. **Senior Director, Human Resources:** Ana Hernandez. **Manager, Human Resources:** Brian Estes. **Coordinator, Human Resources:** Michelle Casanova. **Director, Risk Management:** Fred Espinoza.

Finance
Senior VP, Finance: Susan Jaison. **Controller:** Alina Trigo. **Financial Analyst:** Marina Capobianco. **Administrator, Payroll:** Carolina Calderon. **Coordinator, Payroll:** Edgar Perez. **Staff Accountant:** Alina Goni. **Coordinators, Accounts Payable:** Marva Alexander, Tirsa Vasquez. **Coordinator, Finance:** Diana Jorge. **Ballpark Accountant:** Mike Mullane.

Marketing
Senior VP, Marketing/Event Booking: Sean Flynn. **Director, Multicultural Marketing:** Juan Martinez. **Director, Marketing/Promotions:** Matt Britten. **Manager, Multicultural Marketing:** Darling Jarquin. **Manager, Digital/Social Media:** Alex Buznego. **Supervisor, Marketing:** Boris Menier. **Supervisor, Promotions:** Rafael Capdevila. **Specialist, Mobile Marketing:** Mark Warren, Jr. **Director, Creative Services:** Alfred Hernandez. **Manager, Photography/ Publications:** Robert Vigon.

Legal
VP/General Counsel: Derek Jackson. **Associate Counsel:** Ashwin Krishnan. **Associate Counsel/Director, Special Events:** Chelsea Hirschhorn.

Sales/Ticketing
Senior VP, Corporate Partnerships: Brendan Cunningham. **VP, Business Development:** Dale Hendricks. **Director, Corporate Partnerships:** Tony Tome. **Director, Corporate Partnerships:** Heath Price-Khan. **Senior VP, Sales/Service:** Andy Silverman. **Director, Season/Premium Sales:** Sean Flood. **Director, Season Ticket Services:** Spencer Linden.

2013 SCHEDULE
Standard Game Times: 7:10 p.m.; Sun. 1:10

APRIL		
1 . . . . at Washington	14-16 . . . . . . Cincinnati	28-30 . . . . . . San Diego	12-14 . . . . .at Kansas City
3-4. . . . . at Washington	17-19 . . . . . . .Arizona	**JULY**	16-18 . . . . . San Francisco
5-7. . . . at New York (NL)	20-22 . . . .Philadelphia	1 . . . . San Diego	19-22 . . . Los Angeles (NL)
8-10 . . . . Atlanta	24-26 . . . .at Chicago (AL)	2-4. . . . . at Atlanta	23-25 . . . . .Colorado
12-14 . . . . .Philadelphia	27-28 . . . . at Tampa Bay	5-7. . . . . .at St. Louis	27-29 . . . . at Washington
15-17 . . . . . .Washington	29-30 . . . . . .Tampa Bay	8-10 . . . . Atlanta	30-31 . . . . . . at Atlanta
18-21 . . . . .at Cincinnati	31 . . . . . . .New York (NL)	12-14 . . . . . .Washington	
22-23 . . . . at Minnesota	**JUNE**	19-21 . . . . . at Milwaukee	**SEPTEMBER**
25-28 . . . . . Chicago (NL)	1-2. . . . . . .New York (NL)	22-25 . . . . . . at Colorado	1 . . . . at Atlanta
29-30 . . . . .New York (NL)	3-5. . . . . . at Philadelphia	26-28 . . . . Pittsburgh	2-4. . . . . .at Chicago (NL)
	7-9. . . . . at New York (NL)	29-31 . . . .New York (NL)	6-8. . . . . .Washington
MAY	10-12 . . . . . . .Milwaukee		9-12 . . . . Atlanta
1 . . . . . . .New York (NL)	14-16 . . . . St. Louis	**AUGUST**	13-15 . . . at New York (NL)
2-5. . . . . . at Philadelphia	17-19 . . . . . . at Arizona	1 . . . . . . .New York (NL)	16-18 . . . . at Philadelphia
6-8. . . . . . . at San Diego	20-23 . . . at San Francisco	2-4. . . . . . . Cleveland	19-22 . . . . at Washington
10-12 . at Los Angeles (NL)	25-26 . . . . . . Minnesota	6-8. . . . . . . at Pittsburgh	23-25 . . . . .Philadelphia
		9-11 . . . . at Atlanta	27-29 . . . . Detroit

GENERAL INFORMATION
Stadium (year opened): Marlins Park (2012).   **Player Representative:** Steve Cishek.
Team Colors: Red-Orange, Yellow,   **Home Dugout:** Third Base.
Blue, Black, White.   **Playing Surface:** Grass.

Director, Premium Services: Amy Chwick. **Director, Ticket Operations:** Mardi Dilger. **Assistant Director, Ticket Operations:** Michael Nugent. **Director, Retail Operations:** Roger Kitch.

Media Relations/Communications
Senior VP, Communications/Broadcasting: P.J. Loyello. **Director, Media Relations:** Matt Roebuck. **Director, Business Communications:** Carolina Perrina de Diego. **Manager, Media Relations:** Marty Sewell. **Supervisor, Media Relations:** Joe Vieira. **Coordinator, Media Relations:** Jon Erik Alvarez. **Director, Broadcasting:** Emmanuel Muñoz. **Manager, Broadcast:** Nelson Sealy. **Administrative Assistant:** Maria Armella. **Director, Community Outreach:** Angela Smith. **Executive Director, Marlins Foundation:** Alfredo Mesa. **Director, Foundation Partnerships:** Joanne Messing.

Game Presentation/Events
Director, Game Presentation/Events: Larry Blocker. **Manager, Game Presentation/Events:** Luis Dones.

Travel/Clubhouse
Director, Team Travel: Manny Colon. **Equipment Manager:** John Silverman. **Visiting Clubhouse Manager:** Rock Hughes. **Assistant, Clubhouse Attendant:** Domenic Camarda. **Assistant, Clubhouse Attendant:** Lou Assalone.

BASEBALL OPERATIONS

Telephone: (305) 480-1300. **Fax:** (305) 480-3032.
President, Baseball Operations: Larry Beinfest. **VP/General Manager:** Michael Hill. **Executive Assistant to the President, Baseball Operations/VP/GM:** Rita Filbert. **Special Assistant to President, Baseball Operations:** Jim Fleming. **VP, Player Personnel/Assistant GM:** Dan Jennings. **Senior Advisor to Player Personnel:** Orrin Freeman. **Director, Baseball Operations:** Mike Wickham. **Director, Team Travel:** Manny Colon. **Video Coaching Coordinator:** Cullen McRae.

Major League Staff
Manager: Mike Redmond.
Coaches: Bench—Rob Leary; **Pitching**—Chuck Hernandez; **Hitting**—Tino Martinez; **First Base/Infield**—Perry Hill; **Third Base**—Joe Espada; **Bullpen**—Reid Cornelius; **Bullpen Coordinator**—Jeff Urgelles.

Larry Beinfest

Medical/Training
Head Trainer: Sean Cunningham. **Assistant Trainers:** Mike Kozak, Dustin Luepker. **Strength/Conditioning Coach:** Ty Hill. **Team Psychologist:** Robert Seifer.

Player Development
VP, Player Development: Marty Scott. **Director, Player Development:** Brian Chattin. **Assistant Director, Player Development/International Operations:** Marc Lippman. **Supervisor, Player Development/Scouting:** Michael Youngberg. **Baseball Operations Assistant:** Brett West. **Manager, Player Development:** Matt Cabrera.
Field Coordinator: John Pierson. **Pitching Coordinator:** Wayne Rosenthal. **Hitting Coordinator:** Greg Norton. **Infield Coordinator:** Dave Berg. **Outfield/Baserunning Coordinator:** Tarrik Brock. **Catching Coordinator:** Clint Sammons. **Latin Coordinator:** Bobby Ramos. **Training/Rehab Coordinator:** Gene Basham. **Strength/Conditioning Coordinator:** Mark Brennan. **Rehab Coach:** Jeff Schwarz. **Minor League Equipment/Clubhouse Manager:** Mark Brown.

Farm System

Class	Club (League)	Manager	Hitting Coach	Pitching Coach
Triple-A	New Orleans (PCL)	Ron Hassey	Damon Minor	Charlie Corbell
Double-A	Jacksonville (SL)	Andy Barkett	Kevin Randel	John Duffy
High A	Jupiter (FSL)	Andy Haines	Corey Hart	Joe Coleman
Low A	Greensboro (SAL)	Jorge Hernandez	Frank Moore	Blake McGinley
Short-season	Batavia (NYP)	Angel Espada	Rich Arena	Brendan Sagara
Rookie	Marlins (GCL)	Julio Garcia	Bobby Bell	Jeremy Powell

Scouting
Telephone: (561) 630-1816/Pro (561) 630-1809.
VP, Scouting: Stan Meek. **Assistant Director, Scouting:** Gregg Leonard. **Assistant Director, Pro Scouting:** Dan Noffsinger. **Advance Scout:** Joel Moeller (San Clemente, CA).
Professional Scouts: Pierre Arsenault (Pierrefonds, QC), Brendan Hause (Huntington Beach, CA), Matt Kinzer (Fort Wayne, IN), Benny Latino (Hammond, LA), Dave Roberts (Fort Worth, TX), Phil Rossi (Jessup, PA), Tommy Thompson (Greenville, NC).
National Crosschecker: David Crowson (College Station, TX). **Regional Supervisors: Southeast**—Mike Cadahia (Miami, FL); **Northeast**—Carmen Carcone (Canton, GA); **Central**—Steve Taylor (Shawnee, OK); **West**—Scott Goldby (Yuba City, CA); **Canada**—Steve Payne (Barrington, RI).
Area Scouts: Eric Brock (Indianapolis, IN), Christian Castorri (Dacula, GA), Robby Corsaro (Victorville, CA), Matt Gaski (Greensboro, NC), John Hughes (Walnut Creek, CA), Brian Kraft (Bixby, OK), Laz Llanes (Miami, FL), Joel Matthews (Concord, NC), Tim McDonnell (Westminster, CA), Bob Oldis (Iowa City, Iowa), Gabe Sandy (Damascus, OR), Scott Stanley (Peoria, AZ), Ryan Wardinsky (The Woodlands, TX), Mark Willoughby (Hammond, LA), Nick Zumsande (Fairfax, IA).
Director, International Operations: Albert Gonzalez. **International Supervisors:** Sandy Nin (Santo Domingo, Dominican Republic), Wilmer Castillo (Maracay, VZ). **International Scouts:** Hugo Aquero (Dominican Republic), Carlos Avila (Dominican Republic), Luis Cordoba (Panama), Edgarluis J Fuentes (Dominican Republic), Alix Martinez (Dominican Republic), Domingo Ortega (Dominican Republic), Robin Ordonez (Venezuela).

Milwaukee Brewers

Office Address: Miller Park, One Brewers Way, Milwaukee, WI 53214.
Telephone: (414) 902-4400. **Fax:** (414) 902-4053.
Website: www.brewers.com.

Ownership
Operated By: Milwaukee Brewers Baseball Club.
Chairman/Principal Owner: Mark Attanasio.

Mark Attanasio

BUSINESS OPERATIONS
Chief Operating Officer: Rick Schlesinger. **Executive Vice President, Finance/ Administration:** Bob Quinn. **VP, General Counsel:** Marti Wronski. **Senior Director, Business Operations:** Teddy Werner. **Executive Assistant:** Adela Reeve. **Executive Assistant, Ownership Group:** Samantha Ernest. **Executive Assistant/Paralegal:** Kate Rock.

Finance/Accounting
VP/Controller: Joe Zidanic. **Accounting Director:** Vicki Wise. **Payroll Manager:** Vickie Gowan. **VP, Human Resources/Office Management:** Sally Andrist.
VP, Technology/Information Systems: Nick Watson. **Director, Network Services:** Corey Kmichik. **System Support Specialist:** Adam Bauer. **Application Developer:** Josh Krowiorz.

Marketing/Corporate Sponsorships
VP, Corporate Marketing: Tom Hecht. **Senior Director, Corporate Marketing:** Andrew Pauls. **Directors, Corporate Marketing:** Sarah Holbrook, Andrew Lukanich. **VP, Consumer Marketing:** Jim Bathey. **Senior Director, Merchandise Branding:** Jill Aronoff. **Senior Director, Marketing:** Kathy Schwab. **Director, Suite Services:** Kristin Loeser. **Senior Manager, Advertising/Marketing:** Caitlin Moyer. **Coordinator, Marketing/Promotions:** Brittany Luznicky.
VP, Broadcasting/Entertainment: Aleta Mercer. **Director, Audio/Video Productions:** Deron Anderson. **Manager, Entertainment/Broadcasting:** Andrew Olson. **Coordinators, Audio/Video Production:** Scott Powell, Cory Wilson, Matt Morell.

Media Relations/Communications
VP, Communications: Tyler Barnes. **Senior Director, Media Relations:** Mike Vassallo. **Manager, Media Relations:** John Steinmiller. **Coordinator, Media Relations:** Ken Spindler. **Publications Assistant:** Robbin Barnes. **Senior Director, Community Relations:** Katina Shaw. **Director, Alumni Relations:** Dave Nelson. **Coordinator, Community Relations:** Erica Bowring. **Executive Director, Brewers Community Foundation:** Cecelia Gore.

Stadium Operations
Senior Director, Stadium Operations: Bob Hallas. **Director, Grounds:** Justin Scott. **Supervisor, Warehouse:** Patrick Rogo. **VP, Brewers Enterprises:** Jason Hartlund. **Manager, Event Services:** Matt Lehmann. **Manager, Guest Services:** Jennacy Cruz. **Receptionists:** Jody McBee, Susan Ramsdell.

2013 SCHEDULE
Standard Game Times: 7:10 p.m.; Sun. 1:10.

APRIL		JULY	
1-3 . . . . Colorado	13-16 . . . . . at Pittsburgh	28-30 . . . . . at Pittsburgh	15-18 . . . . Cincinnati
5-7 . . . . Arizona	17-19 . . . . . . at St. Louis	**JULY**	19-21 . . . . St. Louis
8-10 . . . at Chicago (NL)	20-22 . . . Los Angeles (NL)	1-4 . . . . . . at Washington	23-25 . . . . . at Cincinnati
12-14 . . . . . . at St. Louis	24-26 . . . . . . Pittsburgh	5-7 . . . . . . New York (NL)	27-29 . . . . at Pittsburgh
16-18 . . . . San Francisco	27-28 . . . . . . Minnesota	8-10 . . . . Cincinnati	30-31 . . . Los Angeles (AL)
19-21 . . . . Chicago (NL)	29-30 . . . . at Minnesota	11-14 . . . . . . at Arizona	
22-24 . . . . at San Diego	31 . . . . . at Philadelphia	19-21 . . . . Miami	**SEPTEMBER**
26-28 . at Los Angeles (NL)		22-25 . . . . . . San Diego	1 . . . . . . Los Angeles (AL)
29-30 . . . . . . Pittsburgh	**JUNE**	26-28 . . . . . at Colorado	2-4 . . . . Pittsburgh
	1-2 . . . . . at Philadelphia	29-31 . . . at Chicago (NL)	6-8 . . . . . at Chicago (NL)
MAY	3-5 . . . . Oakland		10-12 . . . . . . at St. Louis
1 . . . . Pittsburgh	6-9 . . . . . . Philadelphia	**AUGUST**	13-15 . . . . Cincinnati
2-5 . . . . St. Louis	10-12 . . . . at Miami	2-4 . . . . Washington	16-19 . . . . Chicago (NL)
7-8 . . . . Texas	14-16 . . . . at Cincinnati	5-8 . . . at San Francisco	20-22 . . . . St. Louis
10-12 . . . . at Cincinnati	18-20 . . . . . at Houston	9-11 . . . . at Seattle	23-25 . . . . . . at Atlanta
	21-23 . . . . . . Atlanta	13-14 . . . . at Texas	26-29 . . at New York (NL)
	25-27 . . . . Chicago (NL)		

GENERAL INFORMATION
Stadium (year opened): Miller Park (2001).
Team Colors: Navy blue, gold and white.

Player Representative: Unavailable.
Home Dugout: First Base.
Playing Surface: Grass.

Ticketing
Telephone: (414) 902-4000. **Fax:** (414) 902-4056.
Senior Director, Ticket Operations: Regis Bane. **Senior Director, Season Ticket Sales:** Billy Friess. **Director, Group Ticket Sales:** Chris Barlow. **Administrative Assistant:** Irene Bolton.

BASEBALL OPERATIONS

Telephone: (414) 902-4400. **Fax:** (414) 902-4515.
President, Baseball Operations/General Manager: Doug Melvin.
VP/Assistant GM: Gord Ash. **Special Assistant to GM/Pro Scouting/Player Personnel:** Dick Groch. **Special Assistant to GM:** Craig Counsell.
Senior Director, Baseball Operations: Tom Flanagan. **Director, Video Scouting/Baseball Research for Pro Scouting:** Karl Mueller. **Coordinator, Advance Scouting/Baseball Research:** Scott Campbell. **Manager/Coaching Assistant/Digital Media Coordinator:** Joe Crawford. **Senior Administrator, Baseball Operations:** Barb Stark. **Senior Director, Team Travel:** Dan Larrea.

Doug Melvin

Major League Staff
Manager: Ron Roenicke.
Coaches: Bench—Jerry Narron; **Pitching**—Rick Kranitz; **Hitting**—Johnny Narron; **First Base**—Garth Iorg; **Third Base**—Ed Sedar; **Bullpen**—Lee Tunnell; **Outfield Coach**—John Shelby.

Medical/Training
Head Team Physician: Dr. William Raasch. **Head Athletic Trainer:** Dan Wright. **Assistant Athletic Trainer:** Dave Yeager. **Strength/Conditioning Specialist:** Josh Seligman. **Director, Medical Operations:** Roger Caplinger.

Player Development
Special Assistant to GM/Director, Player Development/Training Center: Reid Nichols (Phoenix, AZ). **Special Assistant to GM/Baseball Operations:** Dan O'Brien.
Business Manager, Player Development/Minor League Operations: Scott Martens. **Manager, Administration/Player Development:** Mark Mueller. **Assistant to Director for Staff/Player Development:** Tony Diggs. **Coordinator, Arizona Complex/Video Operations:** Matt Kerls. **Field/Catching Coordinator:** Charlie Greene. **Coordinators:** Frank Neville (athletic training), Rick Tomlin (pitching), Sandy Guerrero (hitting), Bob Miscik (infield), Reggie Williams (roving outfield). **Special Instructor, Player Development:** Don Money.

Farm System

Class	Club (League)	Manager	Coach	Pitching Coach
Triple-A	Nashville (PCL)	Mike Guerrero	Bob Skube	Fred Dabney
Double-A	Huntsville (SL)	Darnell Coles	Kenny Dominguez	Chris Hook
High A	Brevard County (FSL)	Joe Ayrault	Ned Yost IV	Mark Dewey
Low A	Wisconsin (MWL)	Matt Erickson	Dusty Rhodes	David Chavarria
Rookie	Helena (PIO)	Tony Diggs	Unavailable	Elvin Nina
Rookie	Brewers (AZL)	Nestor Corredor	Unavailable	Steve Cline
Rookie	Brewers (DSL)	Jose Pena	Luis De Los Santos	Jose Nunez

Scouting
Telephone: (414) 902-4400. **Fax:** (414) 902-4059.
Director, Professional Scouting: Zack Minasian. **Director, Amateur Scouting:** Bruce Seid. **Assistant Director, Amateur Scouting/Baseball Research:** Tod Johnson. **Manager, Administration/Amateur Scouting:** Amanda Kropp. **Assistant, Pro Scouting:** Ben McDonough.
National Crosschecker: Joe Ferrone (Grosse Pointe, MI). **National Pitching Crosschecker:** Jim Rooney (Chicago, IL). **Regional Supervisors: West**—Corey Rodriguez (Redondo Beach, CA); **East**—Doug Reynolds (Tallahassee, FL).
Pro Scouts: Lary Aaron (Atlanta, GA), Brad Del Barba (Fort Mitchell, KY), Bryan Gale (Wayne, PA), Joe Kowal (Yardley, PA), Cory Melvin (Tampa, FL), Ben McLure (Hummelstown, PA), Tom Mooney (Pittsfield, MA), Andy Pratt (Peoria, AZ), Marv Thompson (West Jordan, UT), Ryan Thompson (Scottsdale, AZ), Derek Watson (Chicago, IL), Tom Wheeler (Martinez, CA), Leon Wurth (Paducah, KY).
Area Scouts: Drew Anderson (Cold Spring, MN), Josh Belovsky (Orange, CA), Tim Collinsworth (McKinney, TX), Mike Farrell (Indianapolis, IN), Manolo Hernandez (Puerto Rico), Dan Huston (Westlake Village, CA), Harvey Kuenn, Jr (New Berlin, WI), Marty Lehn (White Rock, British Columbia, Canada), Justin McCray (Davis, CA), Tim McIlvaine (Tampa, FL), Dan Nellum (Crofton, MD), Scott Nichols (Richland, MS), Brian Sankey (The Hills, TX), Jeff Scholzen (Santa Clara, UT), Jeff Simpson (Scottsdale, AZ), Steve Smith (Kennesaw, GA), Charles Sullivan (Weston, FL), Shawn Whalen (Vancouver, WA), Steffan Wilson (Wayne, PA).
Supervisor, Canada: Jay Lapp (London, Ontario, Canada).
Part-Time Scouts: John Bushart (West Hills, CA), Richard Colpaert (Shelby Township, MI), Don Fontana (Pittsburgh, PA), Joe Hodges (Rockwood, TN), Roger Janeway (Englewood, OH), Johnny Logan (Milwaukee, WI), Ernie Rogers (Chesapeake, VA), JP Roy (Saint Nicolas, Quebec, Canada), Lee Seid (Huntington Beach, CA), Brad Stoll (Lawrence, KS), Nathan Trosky (Carmel, CA).
Director, Latin America Operations/Scouting: Eduardo Brizuela (Dominican Republic/Doral, FL). **Director, Latin America Scouting:** Manny Batista (Vega Alta, PR). **Latin America Scout Supervisors:** Eduardo Sanchez (Dominican Republic), Fernando Veracierto (Venezuela). **Latin America Scouts:** Julio De La Cruz (Dominican Republic), Reinaldo Hidalgo (Venezuela), Alcides Melendez (Venezuela), Jose Morales (Dominican Republic), Clifford Nuitter (Central America), Jose Ramos (Dominican Republic), Edgar Suarez (Venezuela).

Minnesota Twins

Office Address: Target Field, 1 Twins Way, Minneapolis, MN 55403.
Telephone: (612) 659-3400. **Fax:** 612-659-4025. **Website:** www.twinsbaseball.com.

Ownership
Operated By: The Minnesota Twins.
Chief Executive Officer: Jim Pohlad.
Chairman, Executive Board: Jerry Bell. **Executive Board:** Jim Pohlad, Bob Pohlad, Bill Pohlad, Dave St. Peter.

Business Operations
President, Minnesota Twins: Dave St. Peter. **Executive Vice President, Business Development:** Laura Day. **Executive VP, Business Administration/CFO:** Kip Elliott.
Special Assistant to the President/GM: Bill Smith. **Director, Ballpark Development/ Planning:** Dan Starkey. **Executive Assistants:** Danielle Berg, Joan Boeser, Lynette Gittins.

Human Resources/Finance/Technology
VP, Human Resources/Diversity: Raenell Dorn. **Director, Payroll:** Lori Beasley. **Director, Benefits:** Leticia Silva. **Human Resources Generalist:** Holly Corbin. **Senior Director, Finance:** Andy Weinstein. **Senior Manager, Ticket Accounting:** Jerry McLaughlin. **Senior Manager, Accounting:** Lori Windschitl. **Senior Manager, Financial Planning/Analysis:** Mike Kramer. **Senior Director, Procurement:** Bud Hanley. **Manager, Procurement:** Mike Sather.
VP, Technology: John Avenson. **Senior Director, Technology:** Wade Navratil.

Jim Pohlad

Marketing
Senior Director, Brand Marketing: Nancy O'Brien. **Senior Manager, Marketing/Promotions Manager:** Julie Okland. **Director, Emerging Markets:** Miguel Ramos. **Director, Productions/Creative Services:** Joe Pohlad. **Manager, Twins Productions:** Sam Henschen. **Manager, Creative Services:** Matt Semke.

Corporate Partnerships
Senior Director, Corporate Partnership: Jeff Jurgella. **Senior Account Executives:** Doug Beck, Karen Cleary, Jordan Woodcroft. **Coordinators, Corporate Client Services:** Kayleen Alexson, Paulette Cheatham, Joe Morin

Communications
Telephone: (612) 659-3471. **Fax:** (612) 659-3472.
Director, Baseball Communications/Player Relations: Dustin Morse. **Manager, Baseball Communications:** Mitch Hestad. **Coordinator, Publications/Baseball Communications:** Mike Kennedy. **Coordinator, Player Relations/Media Service:** Andrew Heydt. **Senior Director, Corporate Communications/Broadcasting:** Kevin Smith.

Community Relations
Senior Director, Community Relations: Bryan Donaldson. **Manager, Community Relations:** Stephanie Johnson.

2013 SCHEDULE
Standard Game Times: 7:10 p.m.; Sun 1:10.

APRIL			
1 . . . . Detroit	13-15 . . . . . Chicago (AL)	27-30 . . . . . Kansas City	12-14 . . . . Cleveland
3-4 . . . . Detroit	17-19 . . . . Boston	**JULY**	15-18 . . . . . Chicago (AL)
5-7 . . . . . . at Baltimore	20-22 . . . . at Atlanta	1-4 . . . . . . New York (AL)	20-22 . . . . . . .at Detroit
8-10 . . . . . at Kansas City	23-26 . . . . .at Detroit	5-7 . . . . at Toronto	23-25 . . . . . at Cleveland
12-14 . . . . New York (NL)	27-28 . . . . . at Milwaukee	8-11 . . . . . at Tampa Bay	27-29 . . . . . . Kansas City
15-17 . . . Los Angeles (AL)	29-30 . . . . . . .Milwaukee	12-14 . . . at New York (AL)	30-31 . . . . .at Texas
19-21 . . . .at Chicago (AL)	31 . . . . Seattle	19-21 . . . . Cleveland	
22-23 . . . . Miami		22-24 . at Los Angeles (AL)	**SEPTEMBER**
25-28 . . . . Texas	**JUNE**	25-28 . . . . . . .at Seattle	1 . . . . .at Texas
29-30 . . . . . . .at Detroit	1-2 . . . . Seattle	30-31 . . . . . Kansas City	2-4 . . . . .at Houston
	4-6 . . . . . .at Kansas City		6-8 . . . . .Toronto
MAY	7-9 . . . . . at Washington	**AUGUST**	10-12 . . . . Oakland
1 . . . . at Detroit	11-13 . . . . . Philadelphia	1 . . . . Kansas City	13-15 . . . . . .Tampa Bay
3-5 . . . . .at Cleveland	14-16 . . . . Detroit	2-4 . . . . Houston	16-18 . . . at Chicago (AL)
6-9 . . . . .at Boston	18-20 . . . . Chicago (AL)	5-7 . . . . . .at Kansas City	19-22 . . . . . . .at Oakland
10-12 . . . . . . Baltimore	21-23 . . . .at Cleveland	9-11 . . . . .at Chicago (AL)	23-25 . . . . Detroit
	25-26 . . . . at Miami		26-29 . . . . . . Cleveland

GENERAL INFORMATION
Stadium (year opened): Target Field (2010).
Team Colors: Red, navy blue and white.
Player Representative: Glen Perkins.
Home Dugout: First Base.
Playing Surface: Four-way blend of Kentucky Bluegrass.

Manager, Community Programs: Josh Ortiz. **Coordinator, Community Relations:** Gloria Westerdahl.

Ticket Sales/Service
Telephone: 1-800-33-TWINS. **Fax:** (612) 659-4030.
Senior Director, Ticket Sales/Service: Mike Clough. **Director, Suite/Premium Seat Sales/Service:** Scott O'Connell. **Director, Season Sales/Service:** Eric Hudson.

Ticket Operations/Target Field Events
Senior Director, Ticket Operations: Paul Froehle. **Director, Box Office:** Mike Stiles. **Director, Target Field Events/ Tours:** David Christie.

Ballpark Operations
Senior VP, Operations: Matt Hoy. **Senior Director, Ballpark Operations:** Dave Horsman. **Senior Director, Ballpark Systems:** Gary Glawe. **Director, Guest Services:** Patrick Forsland. **Head Groundskeeper:** Larry DiVito. **Manager, Grounds:** Al Kuehner. **Manager, Field Maintenance:** Jared Alley. **Manager, Ballpark Maintenance:** Dana Minion. **Senior Manager, Ballpark Operations:** John McEvoy. **Senior Manager, Guest Services:** Dan Smoliak. **Senior Manager, Premium Services:** Jeffrey Kroll. **Manager, Building Security:** Jeff Reardon. **Manager, Event Security:** Dick Dugan. **PA Announcer:** Adam Abrams. **Equipment Manager:** Rod McCormick. **Visitors Clubhouse:** Jason Lizakowski. **Manager, Major League Video:** Sean Harlin.

BASEBALL OPERATIONS
Telephone: (612) 659-3485. **Fax:** (612) 659-4026.
Executive VP/General Manager: Terry Ryan.
VP, Player Personnel: Mike Radcliff. **Assistant GM:** Rob Antony. **Special Assistants:** Wayne Krivsky, Tom Kelly. **Manager, Major League Administration/Baseball Research:** Jack Goin. **Administrative Assistant to the GM:** Katie Van Der Linden. **Director, Team Travel:** Mike Herman.

Major League Staff
Manager: Ron Gardenhire.
Coaches: Bench—Terry Steinbach; **Pitching**—Rick Anderson; **Batting**—Tom Brunansky; **First Base**—Scott Ullger; **Third Base**—Joe Vavra; **Bullpen**—Bobby Cuellar.

Medical/Training
Club Physicians: Dr. John Steubs, Dr. Vijay Eyunni, Dr. Tom Jetzer, Dr. Jon Hallberg, Dr. Diane Dahm, Dr. Amy Stromwall, Dr. Pearce McCarty, Dr. Rick Aberman. **Head Trainer:** Dave Pruemer. **Assistant Trainers:** Tony Leo, Lanning Tucker. **Strength/Conditioning Coach:** Perry Castellano.

Player Development
Telephone: (612) 659-3480. **Fax:** (612) 659-4026.
Director, Minor League Operations: Brad Steil. **Senior Manager, Minor League Administration:** Kate Townley. **Minor League Coordinators:** Joel Lepel (field), Eric Rasmussen (pitching), Bill Springman (hitting), Paul Molitor (infield/baserunning).

Terry Ryan

Farm System

Class	Club (League)	Manager	Coach	Pitching Coach
Triple-A	Rochester (IL)	Gene Glynn	Tim Doherty	Marty Mason
Double-A	New Britain (EL)	Jeff Smith	Chad Allen	Stu Cliburn
High A	Fort Myers (FSL)	Doug Mientkiewicz	Jim Dwyer	Ivan Arteaga
Low A	Cedar Rapids (MWL)	Jake Mauer	Tommy Watkins	Gary Lucas
Rookie	Elizabethton (APP)	Ray Smith	Jeff Reed	Henry Bonilla
Rookie	Twins (GCL)	Ramon Borrego	Riccardo Ingram/Rudy Hernandez	Ehren Wassermann
Rookie	Twins (DSL)	Jimmy Alvarez	Ramon Nivar	Manuel Santana
Rookie	Twins (VSL)	Asdrubal Estrada	Pablo Torres	Luis Ramirez

Scouting
Telephone: (612) 659-3491. **Fax:** (612) 659-4026.
Director, Scouting: Deron Johnson.
Coordinator, Professional Scouting: Vern Followell. **Senior Manager, Scouting/International Administration:** Amanda Daley. **Administrative Assistant to Scouting:** Rafael Yanez.
Major League Scouts: Ken Compton, Earl Frishman, Bob Hegman, Bill Milos. **Pro Scouts:** Bill Harford, Shaun McGinn, Earl Winn.
Scouting Supervisors: East—Mark Quimuyog, **West**—Sean Johnson, **Southeast**—Billy Corrigan, **Midwest**—Mike Ruth. **Area Scouts:** Trevor Brown (WA), Taylor Cameron (CA), JR DiMercurio (KS), Marty Esposito (TX), John Leavitt (CA), Jeff Pohl (IN), Jack Powell (GA), Greg Runser (TX), Alan Sandberg (TN), Brent Shelton (FL), Elliott Strankman (CA), Ricky Taylor (NC), Freddie Thon (FL), Jay Weitzel (PA), Ted Williams (AZ), John Wilson (NJ), Mark Wilson (MN).
Coordinator, International Scouting: Howard Norsetter.
International Scouts-Full-Time: Cary Broder (Taiwan), Glenn Godwin (Europe, Africa), Fred Guerrero (Coordinator—Dominican Republic), David Kim (Pacific Rim), Luis Lajara (Dominican Republic), Jose Leon (Coordinator—Venezuela, Panama), Eduardo Soriano (Dominican Republic).
International Scouts-Part-Time: John Cortese (Italy), Andy Johnson (Europe), Manuel Luciano (Dominican Republic), Juan Padilla (Venezuela), Franklin Parra (Venezuela), Yan-Yu "Kenny" Su (Taiwan), Koji Takahashi (Japan), Pablo Torres (Venezuela), Lester Victoria (Curacao), Troy Williams (Germany).

New York Mets

Office Address: Citi Field, 126th Street, Flushing, NY 11368.
Telephone: (718) 507-6387. **Fax:** (718) 507-6395.
Website: www.mets.com, www.losmets.com. **Twitter:** @mets, @losmets.

Ownership
Operated By: Sterling Mets LP.
Chairman/Chief Executive Officer: Fred Wilpon. **President:** Saul Katz. **Chief Operating Officer:** Jeff Wilpon. **Board of Directors:** Fred Wilpon, Saul Katz, Jeff Wilpon, Richard Wilpon, Michael Katz, David Katz, Tom Osterman, Steve Greenberg, Stuart Sucherman.

BUSINESS OPERATIONS
Executive Vice President, Business Operations: Dave Howard. **Executive VP/General Counsel:** David Cohen. **VP/Deputy General Counsel:** Neal Kaplan.

Finance
CFO: Mark Peskin. **VP/Controller:** Len Labita. **Assistant Controller/Director:** John Ventimiglia.

Marketing/Sales
Senior VP, Marketing/Communications: David Newman. **Executive Director, Marketing Productions:** Tim Gunkel. **Senior Director, Marketing:** Mark Fine. **Senior Director, Broadcasting:** Lorraine Hamilton. **Director, Marketing Communications:** Jill Grabill. **Director, Community Outreach:** Jill Knee.
Senior VP, Corporate Sales/Services: Paul Asencio. **Senior Director, Corporate Partnerships:** Catherine Marquette. **Director, Corporate Sales:** Matthew Soloff. **Director, Corporate Sales/Partnerships:** Marc Arnberg.

Media Relations
Telephone: (718) 565-4330. **Fax:** (718) 639-3619.
VP, Media Relations: Jay Horwitz. **Senior Director, Media Relations:** Shannon Forde. **Director, Communications:** Danielle Parillo. **Assistant Director, Media Relations:** Ethan Wilson. **Manager, Media Relations:** Robert Hines. **Coordinator, Media Relations:** Jon Kerber.

Ticketing
Telephone: (718) 507-8499. **Fax:** (718) 507-6369.
VP, Ticket Sales/Services: Leigh Castergine. **Senior Director, Group Sales:** Kirk King. **Senior Director, Season Ticket Account Services:** Jamie Ozure. **Senior Director, Ticket Sales:** Katie Mahon. **Senior Director, Premium Sales:** Roberto Beltramini. **Senior Director, Sales Strategy/Operations:** John Morris. **Director, Ticket Fulfillment/Services:** Jarett Parver. **Director, Ticket Operations:** Michael Berman.

Venue Services/Operations
Senior VP, Venue Services/Operations: Mike Landeen. **Executive Director, Venue Services:** Paul Schwartz.

Fred Wilpon

2013 SCHEDULE
Standard Game Times: 7:10 p.m.; Sun. 1:10.

APRIL
1	San Diego
3-4	San Diego
5-7	Miami
8-10	at Philadelphia
12-14	at Minnesota
15-18	at Colorado
19-21	Washington
23-25	Los Angeles (AL)
26-28	Philadelphia
29-30	at Miami

MAY
1	at Miami
3-5	at Atlanta
7-8	Chicago (AL)
9-12	Pittsburgh
13-16	at St. Louis
17-19	at Chicago (NL)
20-22	Cincinnati
24-26	Atlanta
27-28	New York (AL)
29-30	at New York (AL)
31	at Miami

JUNE
1-2	at Miami
4-6	at Washington
7-9	Miami
11-13	St. Louis
14-16	Chicago (NL)
17-20	at Atlanta
21-23	at Philadelphia
25-26	at Chicago (AL)
28-30	Washington

JULY
1-4	Arizona
5-7	at Milwaukee
8-10	at San Francisco
12-14	at Pittsburgh
19-21	Philadelphia
22-25	Atlanta
26-28	at Washington
29-31	at Miami

AUGUST
1	at Miami
2-4	Kansas City
6-8	Colorado
9-11	at Arizona
12-14	at Los Angeles (NL)
15-18	at San Diego
20-21	Atlanta
23-25	Detroit
26-29	Philadelphia
30-31	at Washington

SEPTEMBER
1	at Washington
2-4	at Atlanta
6-8	at Cleveland
9-12	Washington
13-15	Miami
17-19	San Francisco
20-22	at Philadelphia
23-25	at Cincinnati
26-29	Milwaukee

GENERAL INFORMATION
Stadium (year opened): Citi Field (2009).
Team Colors: Blue and orange.
Player Representative: Unavailable.
Home Dugout: First Base.
Playing Surface: Grass.

Manager, Venue Services: Taryn Donovan. Executive Director, Metropolitan Hospitality: Heather Collamore. Director, Metropolitan Hospitality: Gina Pizzutello. Executive Director, Ballpark Operations: Sue Lucchi. Senior Director, Peter Cassano. Director, Ballpark Operations: Mike Dohnert. Director, Landscaping/Field Operations: Bill Deacon. VP, Technology: Tom Festa.

VP, Guest Experience: Craig Marino. Senior Director, Guest Experience: Chris Brown. Manager, Guest Experience: Kieran Nulty. Director, Partner Services: Andy Horner.

Travel/Clubhouse
Clubhouse Manager: Kevin Kierst. Assistant Equipment Manager: Dave Berni. Visiting Clubhouse Manager: Tony Carullo. Manager, Team Travel: Brian Small. Video Editors: Joe Scarola, Sean Haggans.

BASEBALL OPERATIONS
Telephone: (718) 803-4013, (718) 565-4339. Fax: (718) 507-6391.
General Manager: Sandy Alderson.
VP/Assistant GM: John Ricco. Special Assistant to GM: J.P. Ricciardi.
Executive Assistant to GM: June Napoli. Director, Baseball Operations: Adam Fisher.
Manager, Baseball Analytics: Ian Levin. Coordinator, Baseball Systems Development: Joe Lefkowitz. Assistant, Baseball Operations: Jeffrey Lebow.

Sandy Alderson

Major League Staff
Manager: Terry Collins.
Coaches: Bench—Bob Geren; Pitching—Dan Warthen; Batting—Dave Hudgens; First Base—Tom Goodwin; Third Base—Tim Teufel; Bullpen—Ricky Bones.

Medical/Training
Medical Director: Dr. David Altchek. Physician: Dr. Struan Coleman. Trainer: Ray Ramirez.

Player Development
Telephone: (718) 565-4302. Fax: (718) 205-7920.
VP, Scouting/Player Development: Paul DePodesta.
Director, Minor League Operations: Jon Miller. Manager, Minor League Operations: T.J. Barra. Coordinator, International Operations: Ronny Reyes. Director, Player Development: Dick Scott. Coordinator, Instruction/Infield: Kevin Morgan. Hitting Coordinator: Lamar Johnson. Short-Season Hitting Coordinator: Luis Rivera. Pitching Coordinator: Ron Romanick. Short-Season Pitching Coordinator: Miguel Valdes. Catching Coordinator: Bob Natal. Outfield/Baserunning Coordinator: Jack Voigt. Medical Coordinator: Mike Herbst.
Rehab/Physical Therapist: Dave Pearson. Strength/Conditioning: Jason Craig. Senior Advisor: Guy Conti. Pitching Consultant: Al Jackson. Special Instructor: Bobby Floyd. International Field Coordinator: Rafael Landestoy. International Catching Instructor: Ozzie Virgil.

Farm System

Class	Club	Manager	Coach(es)	Pitching Coach
Triple-A	Las Vegas (PCL)	Wally Backman	George Greer	Randy St. Claire
Double-A	Binghamton (EL)	Pedro Lopez	Luis Natera	Glenn Abbott
High A	St. Lucie (FSL)	Ryan Ellis	Benny Distefano	Phil Regan
Low A	Savannah (SAL)	Luis Rojas	Joel Fuentes	Frank Viola
Short-season	Brooklyn (NYP)	Rich Donnelly	Bobby Malek	Marc Valdes
Rookie	Kingsport (APP)	Jon Debus	Yunir Garcia	Jonathan Hurst
Rookie	Mets (GCL)	Jose Carreno	Ender Chavez	Unavailable
Rookie	Mets 1 (DSL)	Jose Leger	M. Martinez/E. Chavez	Francis Martinez
Rookie	Mets 2 (DSL)	Alberto Castillo	L. Hernandez/D. Davalillo	Benjamin Marte

Scouting
Telephone: (718) 565-4311. Fax: (718) 205-7920.
Director, Amateur Scouting: Tom Tanous. Assistant, Amateur Scouting: Bryan Hayes. Director, Pro Scouting: Jim D'Aloia. Professional Scouts: Bryn Alderson (New York, NY), Mack Babitt (Richmond, CA), Conor Brooks (Plymouth, MA), Thomas Clark (Shrewsbury, MA), Tim Fortugno (Elk Grove, CA), Roland Johnson (Newington, CT), Ashley Lawson (Athens, TN), Shaun McNamara (Worcester, MA), Roy Smith (Chicago, IL), Rudy Terrasas (Santa Fe, TX).
Assistant Scouting Director: Marc Tramuta (Fredonia, NY). Regional Supervisors: Southeast—Steve Barningham (Land O'Lakes, FL), West—Doug Thurman (San Jose, CA), Northeast—Scott Hunter (Mount Laurel, NJ), Midwest—Mac Seibert (Cantonment, FL).
Area Supervisors: Cesar Aranguren (Clermont, FL), Jim Blueberg (Carson City, NV), Jim Bryant (Macon, GA), Ray Corbett (College Station, TX), Jarrett England (Murfreesboro, TN), Steve Gossett (Fremont, NE), Tyler Holmes (Forest Park, IL), Tommy Jackson (Birmingham, AL), Fred Mazuca (Tustin, CA), Marlin McPhail (Irmo, SC), Claude Pelletier (St. Lazare, Quebec), Art Pontarelli (Lincoln, RI), Jim Reeves (Camas, WA), Kevin Roberson (Scottsdale, AZ), Max Semler (Allen, TX).
International Supervisor: Mike Silvestri (Davie, FL), Jim Thompson (Philadelphia, PA), Andrew Toussaint (Los Angeles, CA). Director, International Operations: Chris Becerra. Area Supervisor, Dominican Republic: Gerardo Cabrera. Area Supervisor, Venezuela: Hector Rincones. Dominican Crosschecker: Hilario Soriano.
International Scouts: Modesto Abreu (Dominican Republic), Marciano Alvarez (Dominican Republic), Lionel Chatelle (Europe), Alexis De La Cruz (Dominican Republic), Robert Espejo (Venezuela), Harold Herrera (Colombia Supervisor), Gabriel Low (Mexico), Nestor Moreno (Venezuela), Daurys Nin (Dominican Republic), Ismael Perez (Venezuela), Alex Zapata (Panama).

New York Yankees

Office Address: Yankee Stadium, One East 161st Street, Bronx, NY 10451.
Telephone: (718) 293-4300. **Fax:** (718) 293-8431. **Website:** www.yankees.com, www.yankeesbeisbol.com.

Ownership

Managing General Partner/Co-Chairperson: Harold Z. (Hal) Steinbrenner.
General Partner/Co-Chairperson: Henry G (Hank) Steinbrenner. **General Partner/Vice Chairperson:** Jennifer Steinbrenner Swindal. **General Partner/Vice Chairperson:** Jessica Steinbrenner. **Vice Chairperson:** Joan Steinbrenner. **Executive Vice President/Chief International Officer:** Felix Lopez.

Harold Steinbrenner

BUSINESS OPERATIONS

President: Randy Levine, Esq.
COO: Lonn A Trost, Esq.
Senior VP, Strategic Ventures: Marty Greenspun. **Senior VP, Chief Security Officer:** Sonny Hight. **Senior VP/Chief Financial Officer, Yankee Global Enterprises:** Anthony Bruno. **Senior VP, Corporate/Community Relations:** Brian Smith. **Senior VP, Corporate Sales/Sponsorship:** Michael Tusiani. **Senior VP, Marketing:** Deborah Tymon. **VP/CFO, Accounting:** Robert Brown.
CFO/VP, Financial Operations: Scott Krug. **Deputy General Counsel/VP, Legal Affairs:** Alan Chang. **Controller:** Derrick Baio. **VP, Stadium Operations:** Doug Behar.

Communications/Media Relations

Telephone: (718) 579-4460. **Fax:** (718) 293-8414.
Director, Communications/Media Relations: Jason Zillo. **Assistant Director, Media/Player Relations:** Jason Latimer. **Assistant Director, Baseball Information/Public Communications:** Michael Margolis. **Senior Coordinator, Baseball Information:** Lauren Moran. **Coordinator, Media Relations/Publicity:** Kenny Leandry. **Assistant, Media Relations/Publicity:** Alexandra Trochanowski. **Administrative Assistant, Media Relations:** Dolores Hernandez.

Ticket Operations

Telephone: (718) 293-6000. **Fax:** (718) 293-4841.
Senior Director, Ticket Operations: Irfan Kirimca. **Executive Director, Ticket Operations:** Kevin Dart.

2013 SCHEDULE

Standard Game Times: 7:05 p.m.; Sat.-Sun. 1:05.

APRIL		
1 . . . . Boston	14-16 . . . . Seattle	28-30 . . . . . .at Baltimore
3-4 . . . . Boston	17-19 . . . . .Toronto	**JULY**
5-7 . . . . .at Detroit	20-22 . . . . .at Baltimore	1-4 . . . . . . at Minnesota
8-11 . . . . . .at Cleveland	24-26 . . . at Tampa Bay	5-7 . . . . Baltimore
12-14 . . . . . Baltimore	27-28 . . . at New York (NL)	8-11 . . . . Kansas City
16-18 . . . . Arizona	29-30 . . . . .New York (NL)	12-14 . . . . . . Minnesota
19-21 . . . . . . at Toronto	31 . . . . Boston	19-21 . . . . . . .at Boston
22-24 . . . . at Tampa Bay		22-25 . . . . .at Texas
25-28 . . . . Toronto	**JUNE**	26-28 . . . . . .Tampa Bay
29-30 . . . . Houston	1-2 . . . . Boston	30-31 . .at Los Angeles (NL)
	3-5 . . . . Cleveland	
MAY	6-9 . . . . .at Seattle	**AUGUST**
1 . . . . Houston	11-13 . . . . . at Athletics	2-4 . . . . . . at San Diego
3-5 . . . . Oakland	14-16 . at Los Angeles (AL)	5-7 . . . . .at Chicago (AL)
7-9 . . . . . at Colorado	18-19 . . Los Angeles (NL)	9-11 . . . . Detroit
10-12 . . . . .at Kansas City	20-23 . . . . . . .Tampa Bay	12-15 . . . Los Angeles (AL)
	25-27 . . . . Texas	

16-18 . . . . .at Boston	
20-22 . . . . .Toronto	
23-25 . . . . at Tampa Bay	
26-28 . . . . . . at Toronto	
30-31 . . . . Baltimore	
SEPTEMBER	
1 . . . . Baltimore	
2-4 . . . . . . Chicago (AL)	
5-8 . . . . Boston	
9-12 . . . . . .at Baltimore	
13-15 . . . . .at Boston	
17-19 . . . . . . at Toronto	
20-22 . . . . San Francisco	
24-26 . . . . .Tampa Bay	
27-29 . . . . . .at Houston	

GENERAL INFORMATION

Stadium (year opened): Yankee Stadium (2009).
Team Colors: Navy blue and white.

Player Representative: Unavailable.
Home Dugout: First Base.
Playing Surface: Grass.

BASEBALL OPERATIONS

Telephone: (718) 293-4300. **Fax:** (718) 293-0015.
Senior VP/General Manager: Brian Cashman.
Senior VP/Assistant GM: Jean Afterman, Esq. **Assistant GM, Pro Player Personnel:** Billy Eppler. **Senior VP/Special Advisor:** Gene Michael. **Special Advisors:** Reggie Jackson, Yogi Berra. **Special Assistant:** Stump Merrill.
Director, Quantitative Analysis: Michael Fishman. **Assistant, Baseball Operations:** Steve Martone. **Systems Architect:** Brian Nicosia. **Research Assistants:** David Grabiner, Jim Logue, Alex Rubin. **Administrative Assistant:** Mary Pellino.
Director, Mental Conditioning: Chad Bohling. **Coordinator, Mental Conditioning:** Chris Passarella.

Brian Cashman

Major League Staff

Manager: Joe Girardi.
Coaches: Bench—Tony Pena; **Pitching**—Larry Rothschild; **Batting**—Kevin Long; **First Base**—Mick Kelleher; **Third Base**—Rob Thomson; **Bullpen**—Mike Harkey.

Medical/Training

Team Physician, New York: Dr. Christopher Ahmad.
Head Athletic Trainer: Steve Donohue. **Assistant Athletic Trainer:** Mark Littlefield. **Strength/Conditioning Coordinator:** Dana Cavalea.

Player Development

Telephone: (813) 875-7569. **Fax:** (813) 873-2302.
Senior VP, Baseball Operations: Mark Newman. **Director, Player Personnel:** John Kremer. **Director, Player Development:** Pat Roessler. **Assistant Director, Baseball Operations:** Billy Hart. **Administrative Assistant:** Jackie Williams. **Senior Pitching Instructors:** Nardi Contreras, Greg Pavlik. **Pitching Coordinator:** Gil Patterson. **Hitting Instructor:** Tom Slater. **Infield Coordinator:** Carlos Mendoza. **Catching Coordinator:** Julio Mosquera. **Head Athletic Trainer:** Tim Lentych. **Strength/Conditioning Coordinator:** Mike Kicia.

Farm System

Class	Club (League)	Manager	Hitting Coach	Pitching Coach
Triple-A	Scranton/WB (IL)	Dave Miley	Butch Wynegar	Scott Aldred
Double-A	Trenton (EL)	Tony Franklin	Justin Turner	Tommy Phelps
High A	Tampa (FSL)	Luis Sojo	Marcus Thames	Jeff Ware
Low A	Charleston (SAL)	Al Pedrique	P.J. Pilittere	Danny Borrell
Short-season	Staten Island (NYP)	Justin Pope	Ty Hawkins	Carlos Chantres
Rookie	Tampa 1 (GCL)	Tom Nieto	Edwar Gonzalez	Jose Rosado
Rookie	Tampa 2 (GCL)	Mario Garza	Drew Henson	Tim Norton
Rookie	Yankees I (DSL)	Raul Dominguez	Roy Gomez	Jose Duran
Rookie	Yankees II (DSL)	Carlos Mota	Caonabo Cosme	Rudy Guillen

Scouting

Telephone: (813) 875-7569. **Fax:** (813) 873-2302.
VP, Amateur Scouting: Damon Oppenheimer.
Assistant Director, Amateur Scouting: Eric Schmitt. **Manager, Professional Scouting:** Will Kuntz.
Professional Scouts: Gordon Blakely, Ron Brand, Joe Caro, Jay Darnell, Dave DeFreitas, Gary Denbo, Bill Emslie, Abe Flores, Jalal Leach, Pete MacKanin, Bill Mele, Tim Naehring, Greg Orr, Josh Paul, Kevin Reese, Rick Williams, Tom Wilson, Bob Miske. **Special Assignment Scouts:** Jim Hendry, Don Wakamatsu.
Amateur Scouting, National Crosscheckers: Brian Barber, Kendall Carter, Tim Kelly, DJ Svihlik.
Area Scouts: Troy Afenir (Escondido, CA), Andy Cannizaro (Mandeville, LA), Adam Czajkowski (Tampa, FL) Jeff Deardorf (Clermont, FL), Mike Gibbons (Liberty Township, OH), Matt Hyde (Canton, MA), David Keith (Anaheim, CA), Steve Kmetko (Phoenix, AZ), Steve Lemke (Geneva, IL), Mike Leuzinger (Canton, TX), Scott Lovekamp (Lynchburg, VA), Darryl Monroe (Decatur, GA), Jeff Patterson (Yorba Linda, CA), Cesar Presbott (Bronx, NY), Matt Ranson (Topeka, KS), Stewart Smothers (Los Angeles, CA), Mike Thurman (West Linn, OR), Dennis Twombley (Redondo Beach, CA).
Part-time Scouts: Denis Boucher, Carlos Marti, Bill Pintard, Steve Breen, Oscar Martinez, David List, Steve Thornhill.
Director, International Scouting: Donny Rowland. **Assistant Director, International Operations:** Alex Cotto. **International Crosschecker:** Dennis Woody. **Coordinator, International Player Development:** Pat McMahon. **Latin American Crosscheckers:** Victor Mata (Dominican Republic), Ricardo Finol (Venezuela).
Scouting Development Coaches: Argenis Paulino, Jonnathan Saturria.
Dominican Republic Scouts: Esteban Castillo, Raymi Dicent, Arturo Pena, Juan Rosario, Jose Sabino. **Venezuela Scouts:** Alan Atacho, Roney Calderon, Darwin Bracho, Jose Gavidia, Borman Landaeta, Cesar Suarez. **International Scouts:** Carlos Levy (Panama), Edgar Rodriguez (Nicaragua), Luis Sierra (Colombia), Lee Sigman, Leobardo Figueroa, Humberto Soto (Mexico), Doug Skiles (Europe/Netherland Antilles), Ken Su (Taiwan), John Wadsworth (Australia), Ji-Eun Lee (Korea).

Oakland Athletics

Office Address: 7000 Coliseum Way, Oakland, CA 94621.
Telephone: (510) 638-4900. **Fax:** (510) 562-1633. **Website:** www.oaklandathletics.com.

Ownership
Owner/Managing Partner: Lew Wolff.

Lew Wolff

BUSINESS OPERATIONS
President: Michael Crowley. **Executive Assistant to President:** Carolyn Jones. **General Counsel:** Neil Kraetsch. **Senior Counsel:** Ryan Horning.

Finance/Administration
Vice President, Finance: Paul Wong. **Senior Director, Finance:** Kasey Jarcik. **Senior Manager, Payroll:** Kathy Leviege. **Accounting Manager:** Ling Ding. **Senior Accountant, Accounts Payable:** Isabelle Mahaffey.
Director, Human Resources: Kim Kubo. **Human Resources Assistant:** Erica Sahli. **Director, Information Technology:** Nathan Hayes. **Systems Administrator:** David Frieberg. **Office Services Coordinator:** Julie Vasconcellos. **Executive Offices Receptionist:** Maggie Baptist.

Sales/Marketing
VP, Sales/Marketing: Jim Leahey. **Assistant, Sales/Marketing:** Sarina Madnick. **Senior Director, Marketing:** Troy Smith. **Senior Manager, Digital Marketing:** Travis LoDolce. **Manager, Advertising/Marketing:** Amy MacEwen. **Creative Services Manager:** Mike Ono. **Advertising Assistant:** Stella Koh. **Senior Director, Corporate Partnerships:** Darrin Gross. **Director, Partnership Services:** Franklin Lowe. **Senior Account Manager, Corporate Partnerships:** Jill Golden. **Corporate Account Managers:** Jessica Scott, Tim Sommer. **Corporate Service Assistant:** Mitch Tom. **Senior Manager, Promotion/Events:** Heather Rajeski. **Special Events Coordinator:** Caroline Griggs.

Public Relations/Communications
VP, Communications/Broadcasting: Ken Pries. **Director, Public Relations:** Bob Rose. **Senior Manager, Player/Media Relations:** Kristy Mendes. **Baseball Information Manager:** Mike Selleck. **Media Services Manager:** Debbie Gallas. **Coordinator, Media Relations/Broadcast:** Adam Loberstein. **Team Photographer:** Michael Zagaris.
Director, Community Relations: Detra Paige. **Manager, Community Relations/Memorabilia:** Erik Farrell. **Community Relations Assistant:** Melissa Guzman. **Senior Director, Multimedia Services:** David Don. **Stadium Entertainment Production Manager:** Matt Shelton. **Multimedia Services Manager:** Jon Martin. **Public Address Announcer:** Dick Callahan.

Stadium Operations
VP, Stadium Operations: David Rinetti. **Director, Stadium Operations:** Paul La Veau. **Senior Manager, Stadium Operations:** Kristy Ledbetter. **Stadium Services Manager:** Randy Duran. **Guest Services Manager:** Whitney Smith.

2013 SCHEDULE
Standard Game Times: 7:05 p.m.; Sat./Sun. 1:05.

APRIL
1-4 . . . . Seattle
5-7 . . . . .at Houston
9-11 . . at Los Angeles (AL)
12-14 . . . . Detroit
15-17 . . . . Houston
19-21 . . . . . at Tampa Bay
22-24 . . . . . . .at Boston
25-28 . . . . . . Baltimore
29-30 . . . Los Angeles (AL)

MAY
1 . . . . . . Los Angeles (AL)
3-5 . . . at New York (AL)
6-9 . . . . . . .at Cleveland
10-12 . . . . .at Seattle

13-15 . . . . Texas
17-19 . . . . . Kansas City
20-22 . . . . . . .at Texas
24-26 . . . . . .at Houston
27-28 . . . . . San Francisco
29-30 . . . at San Francisco
31 . . . . Chicago (AL)

JUNE
1-2 . . . . Chicago (AL)
3-5 . . . . . . at Milwaukee
6-9 . . . . . .at Chicago (AL)
11-13 . . . . .New York (AL)
14-16 . . . . Seattle
17-20 . . . . .at Texas
21-23 . . . . . . .at Seattle
25-26 . . . . . . Cincinnati

28-30 . . . . St. Louis

JULY
2-4 . . . . . . Chicago (NL)
5-7 . . . . . .at Kansas City
8-10 . . . . . at Pittsburgh
12-14 . . . . Boston
19-21 . at Los Angeles (AL)
22-24 . . . . . .at Houston
25-28 . . . Los Angeles (AL)
29-31 . . . . .Toronto

AUGUST
2-4 . . . . Texas
6-7 . . . . . .at Cincinnati
9-12 . . . . . . at Toronto
13-15 . . . . Houston

16-18 . . . . . . Cleveland
19-21 . . . . Seattle
23-25 . . . . . .at Baltimore
26-29 . . . . . . .at Detroit
30-31 . . . . . .Tampa Bay

SEPTEMBER
1 . . . . .Tampa Bay
2-4 . . . . Texas
5-8 . . . . Houston
10-12 . . . at Minnesota
13-15 . . . . .at Texas
16-18 . . . Los Angeles (AL)
19-22 . . . . . . Minnesota
23-25 . at Los Angeles (AL)
27-29 . . . . . . .at Seattle

GENERAL INFORMATION

Stadium (year opened):
The Coliseum (1968).
Team Colors: Kelly green and gold.

Player Representative: Unavailable.
Home Dugout: Third Base.
Playing Surface: Grass.

Ticket Sales/Operations/Services
Executive Director, Ticket Sales/Operations: Steve Fanelli. **Senior Director, Ticket Services:** Josh Ziegenbusch. **Senior Manager, Ticket Operations:** David Adame. **Ticket Services Manager:** Catherine Glazier. **Suite Services Manager:** Moti Bycel. **Premium Services Manager:** David King. **Ticket Operations Manager:** Anuj Patel. **Director, Ticket Sales:** Brian DiTucci. **Coordinator, Sales/Ticket Operations:** Judy Quinata.

Travel/Clubhouse
Director, Team Travel: Mickey Morabito. **Equipment Manager:** Steve Vucinich. **Visiting Clubhouse Manager:** Mike Thalblum. **Assistant Equipment Manager:** Brian Davis. **Umpire/Clubhouse Attendant:** Matt Weiss. **Clubhouse Assistant:** William Angel. **Arizona Clubhouse Manager:** James Gibson.

BASEBALL OPERATIONS
VP/General Manager: Billy Beane.
Assistant GM: David Forst. **Director, Baseball Operations:** Farhan Zaidi. **Director, Player Personnel:** Billy Owens. **Special Assistants to GM:** Grady Fuson, Chris Pittaro. **Executive Assistant:** Betty Shinoda. **Director, Baseball Administration:** Pamela Pitts. **Video Coordinator:** Adam Rhoden. **Special Assistant to Baseball Operations:** Scott Hatteberg. **Architect/Baseball Systems:** Rob Naberhaus. **Baseball Operations Analyst:** Michael Schatz.

Major League Staff
Manager: Bob Melvin.
Coaches: Bench—Chip Hale; **Pitching**—Curt Young; **Batting**—Chili Davis; **First Base**—Tye Waller; **Third Base**—Mike Gallego; **Bullpen**—Darren Bush.

Billy Beane

Medical, Training
Head Athletic Trainer: Nick Paparesta. **Assistant Athletic Trainers:** Walt Horn, Brian Schulman. **Strength/Conditioning Coach:** Michael Henriques. **Major League Massage Therapist:** Ozzie Lyles. **Coordinator, Medical Services:** Larry Davis. **Team Physicians:** Dr. Allan Pont, Dr. Elliott Schwartz. **Team Orthopedist:** Dr. Jon Dickinson. **Associate Team Orthopedist:** Dr. Will Workman. **Consulting Orthopedist:** Dr. Lewis Yocum. **Arizona Team Physicians:** Dr. Fred Dicke, Dr. Doug Freedberg.

Player Development
Telephone: (510) 638-4900. **Fax:** (510) 563-2376.
Director, Player Development: Keith Lieppman. **Director, Minor League Operations:** Ted Polakowski. **Administrative Assistant, Player Development:** Valerie Vander Heyden. **Minor League Roving Instructors:** Juan Navarrete (infield), Scott Emerson (pitching), Todd Steverson (hitting), Marcus Jensen (catching). **Minor League Instructor:** Ruben Escalera. **Minor League Video Coordinator:** Mark Smith. **Minor League Medical Coordinator:** Jeff Collins. **Minor League Strength/Conditioning Coordinator:** Josh Cuffe. **Special Instructor, Pitching/Rehabilitation:** Garvin Alston. **Minor League Rehabilitation Coordinator:** Nate Brooks. **Manager, Arizona Clubhouse:** James Gibson. **Arizona Assistant Clubhouse Managers:** Chad Yaconetti, Thomas Miller.

Farm System

Class	Club (League)	Manager	Coach	Pitching Coach
Triple-A	Sacramento (PCL)	Steve Scarsone	Greg Sparks	Rick Rodriguez
Double-A	Midland (TL)	Aaron Nieckula	Brian McArn	Don Schulze
High A	Stockton (CAL)	Webster Garrison	Haas Pratt	Jimmy Escalante
Low A	Beloit (MWL)	Ryan Christenson	Casey Myers	John Wasdin
Short-season	Vermont (NYP)	Rick Magnante	Lloyd Turner	Craig Lefferts
Rookie	Athletics (AZL)	Marcus Jensen	Juan Dilone	Carlos Chavez
Rookie	Athletics (DSL)	Ruben Escalera	Rahdames Perez	Gabriel Ozuna

Scouting
Telephone: (510) 638-4900. **Fax:** (510) 563-2376.
Director, Scouting: Eric Kubota (Rocklin, CA). **Assistant Director, Scouting:** Michael Holmes (Winston Salem, NC). **Director, Pro Scouting/Baseball Development:** Dan Feinstein (Lafayette, CA). **Scouting Assistant:** Kate Greenthal (San Francisco, CA). **West Coast Supervisor:** Scott Kidd (Folsom, CA). **Midwest Supervisor:** Ron Marigny (Cypress, TX). **East Coast Supervisor:** Marc Sauer (Tampa, FL). **Special Assignment Scout:** Craig Weissmann (San Diego, CA). **Pro Scouts:** Jeff Bittiger (Saylorsburg, PA), Dan Freed (Lexington, IL), John McLaren (Peoria, AZ), Will Schock (Oakland, CA), Steve Sharpe (Kansas City, MO), Tom Thomas (Phoenix, AZ), Mike Ziegler (Orlando, FL).
Area Scouts: Neil Avent (Greensboro, NC), Yancy Ayres (Topeka, KS), Armann Brown (Houston, TX), Jermaine Clark (Discovery Bay, CA), Jim Coffman (Portland, OR), Ruben Escalera (Carolina, PR), Matt Higginson (Burlington, ON), Rick Magnante (Sherman Oaks, CA), Eric Martins (Diamond Bar, CA), Kevin Mello (Chicago, IL), Kelcey Mucker (Baton Rouge, LA), Trevor Ryan (Tempe, AZ), Trevor Schaffer (Belleair, FL), Rich Sparks (Sterling Heights, MI), Jemel Spearman (Lithonia, GA), JT Stotts (Moorpark, CA), Ron Vaughn (Windsor, CT).
Director, Latin American Operations: Raymond Abreu (Santo Domingo, DR). **Coordinator, International Scouting:** Sam Geaney (Oakland, CA). **Coordinator, Latin American Scouting:** Julio Franco (Carrizal, VZ).
International Scouts: Ruben Barradas (Venezuela), Juan Carlos De La Cruz (Dominican Republic), Angel Eusebio (Dominican Republic), Andri Garcia (Venezuela), Adam Hislop (Taiwan), Lewis Kim (South Korea), Pablo Marmol (Dominican Republic), Juan Mosquera (Panama), Tito Quintero (Colombia), Amaury Reyes (Dominican Republic), Oswaldo Troconis (Venezuela), Juan Villanueva (Venezuela).

Philadelphia Phillies

Office Address: Citizens Bank Park, One Citizens Bank Way, Philadelphia, PA 19148.
Telephone: (215) 463-6000. **Website:** www.phillies.com.

Ownership
Operated By: The Phillies.
President/CEO: David Montgomery. **Chairman:** Bill Giles.

BUSINESS OPERATIONS

David Montgomery

Vice President/General Counsel: Rick Strouse. **VP, Phillies Enterprises:** Richard Deats. **VP, Employee/Customer Services:** Kathy Killian. **Director, Ballpark Enterprises/Business Development:** Joe Giles. **Director, Information Systems:** Brian Lamoreaux. **Director, Employee Benefits/Services:** JoAnn Marano.

Ballpark Operations
Senior VP, Administration/Operations: Michael Stiles. **Director, Operations/Facility:** Mike DiMuzio. **Director, Operations/Events:** Eric Tobin. **Director, Operations/Security:** Sal DeAngelis. **Manager, Concessions Development:** Bruce Leith. **Head Groundskeeper:** Mike Boekholder. **PA Announcer:** Dan Baker. **Official Scorers:** Jay Dunn, Mike Maconi, Joseph Bellina.

Communications
Telephone: (215) 463-6000. **Fax:** (215) 389-3050.
VP, Communications: Bonnie Clark. **Director, Baseball Communications:** Greg Casterioto. **Coordinator, Baseball Communications:** Craig Hughner. **Communications Assistant:** Deanna Sabec. **Baseball Communications Assistant:** Chris Ware.

Finance
VP/CFO: John Nickolas. **Director, Payroll Services:** Karen Wright.

Marketing/Promotions
Senior VP, Marketing/Sales: David Buck. **Manager, Client Services/Alumni Relations:** Debbie Nocito. **Director, Corporate Partnerships:** Rob MacPherson. **Director, Advertising Sales:** Brian Mahoney. **Director, Corporate Sales:** Scott Nickle. **Manager, Advertising Sales:** Tom Sullivan.
Director, Marketing Programs/Events: Kurt Funk. **Director, Entertainment:** Chris Long. **Manager, Broadcasting:** Rob Brooks. **Manager, Advertising/Internet Services:** Jo-Anne Levy-Lamoreaux.

Sales/Tickets
Telephone: (215) 463-1000. **Fax:** (215) 463-9878.
VP, Sales/Ticket Operations: John Weber. **Director, Ticket Department:** Dan Goroff. **Director, Ticket Technology/Development:** Chris Pohl. **Director, Season Ticket Sales:** Derek Schuster. **Manager, Suite Sales/Services:** Tom Mashek.

2013 SCHEDULE
Standard Game Times: 7:05 p.m.; Sun. 1:35

APRIL
1 . . . . at Atlanta
3-4 . . . . at Atlanta
5-7 . . . . Kansas City
8-10 . . . . . New York (NL)
12-14 . . . . . at Miami
15-17 . . . . .at Cincinnati
18-21 . . . . St. Louis
22-25 . . . . . . Pittsburgh
26-28 . . at New York (NL)
30 . . . . . . .at Cleveland

MAY
1 . . . . .at Cleveland
2-5 . . . . Miami
6-8 . . . . at San Francisco
9-12 . . . . at Arizona

14-15 . . . . . . Cleveland
17-19 . . . . . . Cincinnati
20-22 . . . . . at Miami
24-26 . . . . at Washington
27-28 . . . . . . .at Boston
29-30 . . . . Boston
31 . . . . .Milwaukee

JUNE
1-2 . . . . .Milwaukee
3-5 . . . . Miami
6-9 . . . . . . at Milwaukee
11-13 . . . . at Minnesota
14-16 . . . . . at Colorado
17-19 . . . . .Washington
21-23 . . . .New York (NL)
24-26 . . . . at San Diego

27-30 . at Los Angeles (NL)

JULY
2-4 . . . . . . at Pittsburgh
5-7 . . . . Atlanta
8-11 . . . . . .Washington
12-14 . . . . . Chicago (AL)
19-21 . . . at New York (NL)
23-25 . . . . . .at St. Louis
26-28 . . . . . . .at Detroit
30-31 . . . . San Francisco

AUGUST
1 . . . . San Francisco
2-4 . . . . Atlanta
6-8 . . . . . . Chicago (NL)
9-11 . . . . . at Washington

12-14 . . . . at Atlanta
16-18 . . . Los Angeles (NL)
19-22 . . . . .Colorado
23-25 . . . . Arizona
26-29 . . . at New York (NL)
30-31 . . . .at Chicago (NL)

SEPTEMBER
1 . . . . . . .at Chicago (NL)
2-4 . . . . .Washington
6-8 . . . . Atlanta
10-12 . . . . . . San Diego
13-15 . . . at Washington
16-18 . . . . .Miami
20-22 . . . .New York (NL)
23-25 . . . . at Miami
26-29 . . . . at Atlanta

GENERAL INFORMATION

Stadium (year opened): Citizens Bank Park (2004).
Team Colors: Red, white and blue.
Player Representative: Unavailable.
Home Dugout: First Base.
Playing Surface: Natural Grass.

Director, Ticket Services/Intern Program: Phil Feather. **Manager, Season Ticket Services:** Mike Holdren.

Travel/Clubhouse
    Director, Team Travel/Clubhouse Services: Frank Coppenbarger.
    Manager, Visiting Clubhouse: Kevin Steinhour. **Manager, Home Clubhouse:** Phil Sheridan. **Manager, Equipment/Umpire Services:** Dan O'Rourke.

BASEBALL OPERATIONS
    Senior VP/General Manager: Ruben Amaro Jr.
    Senior Advisor to the President/GM: Pat Gillick. **Assistant GM:** Scott Proefrock. **Assistant GM, Player Personnel:** Benny Looper. **Senior Advisor to GM:** Dallas Green. **Special Assistants to GM:** Bart Braun, Charley Kerfeld. **Special Consultant, Baseball Operations:** Ed Wade. **Director, Baseball Administration:** Susan Ingersoll Papaneri. **Director, Professional Scouting:** Mike Ondo. **Baseball Information Analyst:** Jay McLaughlin. **Administrative Assistant, Baseball Operations:** Adele MacDonald. **Baseball Operations Representative:** Chris Cashman.

Major League Staff
    Manager: Charlie Manuel.
    Coaches: Catching—Mick Billmeyer; **Pitching**—Rich Dubee; **Hitting**—Steve Henderson; **Assistant Hitting**—Wally Joyner; **Bullpen**—Rod Nichols; **First Base**—Juan Samuel; **Third Base**—Ryne Sandberg; **Bullpen Catcher**—Jesus Tiamo.

Ruben Amaro Jr.

Medical/Training
    Director, Medical Services: Dr. Michael Ciccotti. **Head Athletic Trainer:** Scott Sheridan. **Assistant Athletic Trainer:** Shawn Fcasni. **Strength/Conditioning Coordinator:** Dong Lien. **Manual Therapy Specialist:** Ichiro Kitano. **Employee Assistance Professional:** Dickie Noles.

Player Development
    Telephone: (215) 463-6000. **Fax:** (215) 755-9324.
    Assistant GM, Player Personnel: Benny Looper. **Director, Player Development:** Joe Jordan.
    Director, Minor League Operations: Lee McDaniel. **Assistant Director, Player Development:** Steve Noworyta. **Special Assistant, Player Development:** Jorge Velandia. **Director, Florida Operations/GM. Clearwater Threshers:** John Timberlake. **Assistant Director, Minor League Operations/Florida Operations:** Joe Cynar. **Coordinator, Internal Operations:** Ray Robles.
    Field Coordinator: Mike Compton. **Coordinators:** James Ready (trainer), Ernie Whitt (catching), Gorman Heimueller (pitching), Paul Fornier (conditioning), Andy Tracy (hitting), Andy Abad (outfield/baserunning), Doug Mansolino (infield).

Farm System

Class	Club (League)	Manager	Coach	Pitching Coach
Triple-A	Lehigh Valley (IL)	Dave Brundage	Sal Rende	Ray Burris
Double-A	Reading (EL)	Dusty Wathan	Frank Cacciatore	Dave Lundquist
High A	Clearwater (FSL)	Chris Truby	John Mizerock	Bob Milacki
Low A	Lakewood (SAL)	Mickey Morandini	Greg Legg	Aaron Fultz
Short-season	Williamsport (NYP)	Nelson Prada	Lino Connell	Les Lancaster
Rookie	Clearwater (GCL)	Roly DeArmas	R. DeLima/R. Henderson	Steve Schrenk
Rookie	Phillies (DSL)	Manny Amador	L. Garcia/C. Henriquez	Alex Conception
Rookie	Phillies (VSL)	Trino Aguilar	S. Navas/H. Ovalles	Les Straker

Scouting
    Assistant GM, Amateur Scouting: Marti Wolever (Scottsdale, AZ).
    Director, Amateur Scouting Administration: Rob Holiday (Philadelphia, PA). **Coordinators, Scouting:** Mike Ledna (Arlington Heights, IL), Bill Moore (Alta Loma, CA).
    Regional Supervisors: Gene Schall (Northeast/Harleysville, PA), Eric Valent (Southeast/Wernersville, PA), Scott Trcka (Central/Hobart, IN), Darrell Conner (West/Riverside, CA).
    Area Scouts: Alex Agostino (Quebec, Canada), Shane Bowers (La Verne, CA), Steve Cohen (Spring, TX), Joey Davis (Ranco Murrieta, CA), Nate Dion (West Chester, OH), Mike Garcia (Moreno Valley, CA), Brad Holland (Gilbert, AZ), Eric Jacques (Bellevue, WA), Aaron Jersild (Alpharetta, GA), Brian Kohlscheen (Norman, OK), Alan Marr (Sarasota, FL), Paul Murphy (Wilmington, DE), Demerius Pittman (Corona, CA), Paul Scott (Rockwall, TX), David Seifert (Paw Paw, IL), Mike Stauffer (Brandon, MS).
    Director International Scouting: Sal Agostinelli (Kings Park, NY). **International Scouts:** Norman Anciani (Panama), Rogel Andrade (Venezuela), Nathan Davison (Australia), Franklin Felida (Dominican Republic), Tomas Herrera (Mexico), Andres Hiraldo (Dominican Republic), Ferenc Jongejan (Netherlands), Allan Lewis (Panama), Gregory Manuel (Aruba), Jesus Mendez (Venezuela), Romulo Oliveros (Colombia), Bernardo Perez (Dominican Republic), Koby Perez (Dominican Republic), Carlos Salas (Venezuela), Claudio Scerrato (Italy), Darryn Smith (South Africa), Everth Valazuez (Venezuela).
    Director, Major League Scouting: Gordon Lakey (Barker, TX). **Special Assignment Scouts:** Howie Frieling (Apex, NC), Dave Hollins (Orchard Park, NY). **Major League Advance Scout:** Craig Colbert. **Professional Scouts:** Sonny Bowers (Hewitt, TX), Dean Jongewaard (Fountain Valley, CA), Jesse Levis (Fort Washington, PA), Jon Mercurio (Coraopolis, PA), Roy Tanner (North Charleston, SC), Del Unser (Scottsdale, AZ), Dan Wright (Cave Springs, AR).

Pittsburgh Pirates

Office Address: PNC Park at North Shore, 115 Federal St., Pittsburgh, PA, 15212.
Mailing Address: P.O. Box 7000, Pittsburgh, PA 15212.
Telephone: (412) 323-5000. **Fax:** (412) 325-4412. **Website:** www.pirates.com. **Twitter:** @Pirates.

Ownership
Chairman of the Board: Robert Nutting.
Board of Directors: Donald Beaver, G. Ogden Nutting, Robert Nutting, William Nutting, Duane Wittman.

BUSINESS OPERATIONS

Frank Coonelly

President: Frank Coonelly. **Executive Vice President/CFO:** Jim Plake. **Executive VP/General Manager, PNC Park:** Dennis DaPra. **Executive VP/Chief Marketing Officer:** Lou DePaoli. **Senior VP, Community/Public Affairs:** Patty Paytas. **VP/General Counsel:** Bryan Stroh.

Finance/Administration/Information Technology
Director, Human Resources: Jamie Holewski. **Senior Director, IT:** Terry Zeigler. **Director, Employee Services:** Patti Mistick. **Senior Director, Business Analytics:** Jim Alexander.

Communications
Fax: (412) 325-4413.
Senior Director, Communications: Brian Warecki. **Director, Baseball Communications:** Jim Trdinich. **Director, Broadcasting:** Marc Garda. **Director, Media Relations:** Dan Hart.

Community Relations
Director, Community Relations: Michelle Mejia. **Manager, Diversity Initiatives:** Chaz Kellem.

Marketing
Senior Director, Marketing/Special Events: Brian Chiera. **Director, Alumni Affairs/Promotions/Licensing:** Joe Billetdeaux. **Director, Advertising/Creative Services:** Kiley Cauvel. **Director, Special Events:** Christine Serkoch.

Corporate Sponsorships
Senior Director, Corporate Sponsorship Sales/Service: Aaron Cohn. **Client Services Managers:** Mike Demars, Brittany Ryce.

Stadium Operations
Senior Director, Ballpark Operations: Chris Hunter. **Senior Director, Security/Contract Services:** Jeff Podobnik. **Director, Field Operations:** Manny Lopez. **Ballpark Operations Manager:** J.J. McGraw.

Florida Operations
Senior Director, Florida Operations: Trevor Gooby. **Manager, Florida Operations:** A.J. Grant.

2013 SCHEDULE
Standard Game Times: 7:05 p.m.; Sun. 1:35.

APRIL		
1 . . . . Chicago (NL)	13-16 . . . . . . .Milwaukee	28-30 . . . . . . .Milwaukee
3-4. . . . . Chicago (NL)	17-19 . . . . Houston	
5-7. . . at Los Angeles (NL)	21-23 . . . Chicago (NL)	**JULY**
8-10 . . . . at Arizona	24-26 . . . . at Milwaukee	2-4. . . . . . . .Philadelphia
12-14 . . . . . . Cincinnati	27-28 . . . . . . .at Detroit	5-7. . . . .at Chicago (NL)
15-17 . . . . St. Louis	29-30 . . . . Detroit	8-10 . . . . Oakland
18-21 . . . . Atlanta	31 . . . . Cincinnati	12-14 . . . .New York (NL)
22-25 . . . . at Philadelphia		19-21 . . . . .at Cincinnati
26-28 . . . . . .at St. Louis	**JUNE**	22-25 . . . . at Washington
29-30 . . . . . at Milwaukee	1-2. . . . . Cincinnati	26-28 . . . . at Miami
	3-5. . . . . at Atlanta	29-31 . . . . St. Louis
MAY	7-9. . . . . .at Chicago (NL)	
1 . . . . at Milwaukee	11-13 . . . . . San Francisco	**AUGUST**
3-5. . . . . . . .Washington	14-16 . . . Los Angeles (NL)	1 . . . . St. Louis
7-8. . . . . Seattle	17-20 . . . .at Cincinnati	2-4. . . . . .Colorado
9-12 . . . at New York (NL)	21-23 . at Los Angeles (AL)	6-8. . . . . Miami
	25-26 . . . . .at Seattle	9-11 . . . . . . at Colorado

13-15 . . . . . .at St. Louis		
16-18 . . . . Arizona		
19-21 . . . . at San Diego		
22-25 . . at San Francisco		
27-29 . . . . .Milwaukee		
30-31 . . . . St. Louis		
SEPTEMBER		
1 . . . . St. Louis		
2-4. . . . . . at Milwaukee		
6-8. . . . . . . .at St. Louis		
9-11 . . . . .at Texas		
12-15 . . . . . Chicago (NL)		
16-19 . . . . . San Diego		
20-22 . . . . . . Cincinnati		
23-25 . . .at Chicago (NL)		
27-29 . . . . .at Cincinnati		

GENERAL INFORMATION
Stadium (year opened): PNC Park (2001).
Team Colors: Black and gold.
Player Representative: Neil Walker.
Home Dugout: Third Base.
Playing Surface: Grass.

Ticketing
Telephone: (800) 289-2827. **Fax:** (412) 325-4404.
Senior Director, Ticket Sales/Service: Christopher Zaber. **Director, Suite Sales/Service:** Terri Smith. **Director, New Business Development:** Travis Apple. **Director, Season Ticket Service/Retention:** Jim Popovich. **Director, Group Sales/Service:** Raven Jemison. **Director, Ticket Operations:** Andrew Bragman.

BASEBALL OPERATIONS

Senior VP/General Manager: Neal Huntington.
Assistant GM, Scouting: Greg Smith. **Assistant GM, Development:** Kyle Stark. **Director, Player Personnel:** Tyrone Brooks. **Director, Baseball Operations:** Kevan Graves. **Director, Baseball Systems Development:** Dan Fox. **Senior Advisor to the GM:** Bill Livesey. **Special Assistants to GM:** Jim Benedict, Marc DelPiano, Jax Robertson, Doug Strange. **Major League Scouts:** Mike Basso, Bob Minor, Steve Williams. **Pro Scouts:** Ricky Bennett, Carlos Berroa, Jamie Brewington, Jim Dedrick, Ron Hopkins, John Kosciak, Alvin Rittman, Gary Robinson, Lewis Shaw. **Coordinator, Baseball Operations:** Alex Langsam. **Baseball Operations Assistant:** Will Lawton. **Quantitative Analyst:** Mike Fitzgerald. **Data Architect:** Josh Smith. **Video Coordinator:** Kevin Roach. **Advance Scouting Coordinator:** Simon Ferrer.

Neal Huntington

Major League Staff
Manager: Clint Hurdle.
Coaches: Bench—Jeff Banister; **Pitching**—Ray Searage; **Hitting**—Jay Bell; **First Base**—Rick Sofield; **Third Base**—Nick Leyva; **Bullpen**—Euclides Rojas; **Coach**—Jeff Branson; **Coach**—David Jauss.

Medical/Training
Medical Director: Dr. Patrick DeMeo. **Team Physician:** Dr. Edward Snell. **Head Major League Athletic Trainer:** Todd Tomczyk. **Assistant Major League Athletic Trainer:** Ben Potenziano. **Head Major League Strength/Conditioning Coach:** Brendon Huttmann. **Assistant Major League Strength/Conditioning Coach/Latin American Strength/Conditioning Coordinator:** Kiyoshi Momose. **Physical Therapist/Rehab Coordinator:** Jeremiah Randall.

Minor Leagues
Director, Minor League Operations: Larry Broadway.
Coordinator, Minor League Operations: Diane DePasquale. **Coordinator, Florida Baseball Operations:** Juan Rodriguez. **Field Coordinator:** Brad Fischer. **Coordinator, Instruction:** Tom Prince. **Outfield/Baserunning Coordinator:** Kimera Bartee. **Pitching Coordinator:** Scott Mitchell. **Infield Coordinator:** Gary Green. **Hitting Coordinator:** Jeff Livesey. **Senior Advisor, Minor League Operations:** Woody Huyke. **Dominican Field Coordinator:** Larry Sutton. **Senior Advisor, Latin American Operations:** Luis Silverio. **Dominican Academy Administrator:** Juan Carlos Mendoza.
Athletic Training Coordinator: Carl Randolph. **Minor League Rehab Coordinator:** Wes Eberlin. **Strength/Conditioning Coordinator:** Mike Winkler. **Athletic Development Coordinator:** Joe Hughes. **Director, Mental Conditioning:** Bernie Holliday. **Mental Conditioning Coordinator:** Tyson Holt.

Farm System

Class	Club (League)	Manager	Coach(es)	Pitching Coach
Triple-A	Indianapolis (IL)	Dean Treanor	Mike Pagliarulo	Tom Filer
Double-A	Altoona (EL)	Carlos Garcia	Ryan Long	Stan Kyles
High A	Bradenton (FSL)	Frank Kremblas	Edgar Varela	Justin Meccage
Low A	West Virginia (SAL)	Michael Ryan	Orlando Merced	Jeff Johnson
Short-season	Jamestown (NYP)	Dave Turgeon	Kory DeHaan	Mike Steele
Rookie	Bradenton (GCL)	Milver Reyes	Mike Lum/Woody Huyke	Miguel Bonilla
Rookie	Pirates (DSL1)	Gera Alvarez	Jonathan Prieto/Cecilio Beltre	Dan Urbina
Rookie	Pirates (DSL2)	Keoni De Renne	Johe Acosta/Osiel Flores	Jairo Cuevas

Scouting
Fax: (412) 325-4414.
Director, Scouting: Joe Delli Carri.
Coordinator: Jim Asher. **National Supervisors:** Jack Bowen (Bethel Park, PA), Jimmy Lester (Columbus, GA), Matt Ruebel (Oklahoma City, OK). **Regional Supervisors:** Jesse Flores (Sacramento, CA), Rodney Henderson (Lexington, KY), Everett Russell (Thibodaux, LA), Greg Schilz (Alexandria, VA). **Area Supervisors:** Rick Allen (Agoura Hills, CA), Matt Bimeal (Baldwin City, KS), Jerome Cochran (Slidell, LA), Jason Cooper (Cave Creek, AZ), Trevor Haley (Conroe, TX), Sean Heffernan (Florence, SC), Greg Hopkins (Beaverton, OR), Phil Huttmann (Plano, TX), Jerry Jordan (Kingsport, TN), Chris Kline (Holyoke, MA), Darren Mazeroski (Panama City Beach, FL), Nick Presto (Palm Beach Gardens, FL), Mike Sansoe (Walnut Creek, CA), Brian Selman (Washington, DC), Brian Tracy (Orange, CA), Anthony Wycklendt (Grafton, WI). **Part-Time Scouts:** Elmer Gray (Pittsburgh, PA), Enrique Hernandez (Puerto Rico).
Director, Latin American Scouting: Rene Gayo. **Full-Time Scouts:** Orlando Covo (Colombia), Nelson Llenas (Dominican Republic), Juan Mercado (Dominican Repuplic), Rodolfo Petit (Venezuela), Victor Santana (Dominican Republic), Cristino Valdez (Dominican Republic), Jesus Chino Valdez (Mexico). **Part-Time Scouts:** Esteban Alvarez (Dominican Republic), Pablo Csorgi (Venezuela), David De La Cruz (Dominican Republic), Denny Diaz (Dominican Republic), Daniel Espitia Garcia (Colombia), Rainford Harris (Jamaica), Jhoan Hidalgo (Venezuela), Jose Lavagnino (Mexico), Javier Magdaleno (Venezuela), Juan Morales (Venezuela), Robinson Ortega (Colombia), Rogelio Osuna (Mexico), Jose Pineda (Panama), Juan Pinto (Mexico), Cesar Saba (Dominican Republic), Cristobal Santoya (Colombia), Gary Sewell (Jamaica), Leon Taylor (Jamaica), Ruben Tinoco (Mexico), Marc Van Zanten (Netherlands Antilles), Darryl Yrausquin (Aruba). **International Scouts:** Fu-Chun Chiang (Korea, Taiwan), Tom Gillespie (Europe), Tony Harris (Australia).

St. Louis Cardinals

Office Address: 700 Clark Street, St. Louis MO 63102.
Telephone: (314) 345-9600. **Fax:** (314) 345-9523. **Website:** www.cardinals.com.

Ownership

Operated By: St. Louis Cardinals, LLC.
Chairman/Chief Executive Officer: William DeWitt, Jr.
President: Bill DeWitt III.
Senior Administrative Assistant to Chairman: Grace Kell. **Senior Administrative Assistant to President:** Julie Laningham.

BUSINESS OPERATIONS

Bill DeWitt III

Finance

Fax: (314) 345-9520.
Senior VP/Chief Financial Officer: Brad Wood. **Director, Finance:** Rex Carter. **Director, Human Resources:** Melissa Hughes
Vice President, Event Services/Merchandising: Vicki Bryant. **Director, Special Events:** Julia Row.

Marketing/Sales/Community Relations

Fax: (314) 345-9529.
Senior VP, Sales/Marketing: Dan Farrell. **Administrative Assistant, VP Sales/Marketing:** Gail Ruhling. **VP, Corporate Marketing/Stadium Entertainment:** Thane van Breusegen. **Director, Scoreboard Operations/Senior Account Executive:** Tony Simokaitis. **Director, Publications:** Steve Zesch.
VP, Community Relations/Executive Director, Cardinals Care: Michael Hall. **Administrative Assistant:** Bonnie Parres.

Media Relations

Fax: (314) 345-9530.
Director, Media Relations: Brian Bartow. **Manager, Media Relations:** Melody Yount.
Media Relations Specialist: Chris Tunno. **Director, Public Relations/Government Affairs:** Ron Watermon. **Public Relations Specialist:** Lindsey Weber. **PA Announcer:** John Ulett. **Official Scorers:** Gary Muller, Jeff Durbin, Mike Smith.

Stadium Operations

Fax: (314) 345-9535.
VP, Stadium Operations: Joe Abernathy.
Administrative Assistant: Hope Baker. **Director, Security/Special Services:** Joe Walsh. **Director, Quality Assurance/Guest Services:** Mike Ball. **Head Groundskeeper:** Bill Findley.

2013 SCHEDULE

Standard Game Times: 7:15 p.m.; Sun. 1:15.

APRIL
1-3 . . . . at Arizona
5-7 . . . . at San Francisco
8-10 . . . . Cincinnati
12-14 . . . . Milwaukee
15-17 . . . . at Pittsburgh
18-21 . . . at Philadelphia
22-24 . . . at Washington
26-28 . . . . . . Pittsburgh
29-30 . . . . Cincinnati

MAY
1 . . . . Cincinnati
2-5 . . . . . at Milwaukee
7-8 . . . .at Chicago (NL)
10-12 . . . ., . . . Colorado

13-16 . . . . .New York (NL)
17-19 . . . . . .Milwaukee
20-22 . . . . at San Diego
24-26 . at Los Angeles (NL)
27-28 . . . . .at Kansas City
29-30 . . . . . Kansas City
31 . . . . San Francisco

JUNE
1-2 . . . . . San Francisco
3-6 . . . . Arizona
7-9 . . . . . . .at Cincinnati
11-13 . . . at New York (NL)
14-16 . . . . at Miami
17-20 . . . . Chicago (NL)
21-23 . . . . Texas
25-26 . . . . . .at Houston

28-30 . . . . . .at Oakland

JULY
2-4 . . . at Los Angeles (AL)
5-7 . . . . Miami
9-10 . . . . Houston
11-14 . . . .at Chicago (NL)
19-21 . . . . . . San Diego
23-25 . . . . .Philadelphia
26-28 . . . . . . at Atlanta
29-31 . . . at Pittsburgh

AUGUST
1 . . . . at Pittsburgh
2-4 . . . . .at Cincinnati
5-8 . . . . Los Angeles (NL)
9-11 . . . . . Chicago (NL)

13-15 . . . . . . Pittsburgh
16-18 . . . .at Chicago (NL)
19-21 . . . . . at Milwaukee
22-25 . . . . Atlanta
26-28 . . . . Cincinnati
30-31 . . . . . at Pittsburgh

SEPTEMBER
1 . . . . at Pittsburgh
2-5 . . . . .at Cincinnati
6-8 . . . . Pittsburgh
10-12 . . . . Milwaukee
13-15 . . . . Seattle
16-19 . . . . at Colorado
20-22 . . . . at Milwaukee
23-25 . . . . . Washington
27-29 . . . . Chicago (NL)

GENERAL INFORMATION

Stadium (year opened): Busch Stadium (2006).
Team Colors: Red and white.

Player Representative: Jon Jay.
Home Dugout: First Base.
Playing Surface: Grass.

Ticketing
Fax: (314) 345-9522.
VP, Ticket Sales/Service: Joe Strohm.
Director, Ticket Sales/Marketing: Martin Coco. **Director, Ticket Sales/Services:** Rob Fasoldt. **Director, Client Relations:** Delores Scanlon.

Travel/Clubhouse
Fax: (314) 345-9523.
Traveling Secretary: C.J. Cherre. **Equipment Manager:** Rip Rowan. **Assistant Equipment Manager:** Ernie Moore. **Visiting Clubhouse Manger:** Jerry Risch. **Video Coordinator:** Chad Blair.

BASEBALL OPERATIONS
Fax: (314) 345-9599.
Senior VP/General Manager: John Mozeliak.
Assistant GM: Mike Girsch. **Executive Assistant:** Linda Brauer. **Senior Special Assistant to GM:** Mike Jorgensen. **Special Assistant to GM:** Cal Eldred. **Director, Player Personnel:** Matt Slater. **Director, Major League Administration:** Judy Carpenter-Barada. **Director, Minor League Operations:** John Vuch.
Director, Scouting: Dan Kantrovitz. **Manager, Baseball Information:** Jeremy Cohen. **Manager, Baseball Development:** Chris Correa. **Quantitative Analysts:** Matt Bayer, Dane Sorensen. **Mechanics Analyst:** Tim Leveque. **Baseball Operations Assistant, Player Development:** Tony Ferreira. **Baseball Operations Assistant, Scouting:** Jared Odom.

John Mozeliak

Player Development
Fax: (314) 345-9519.
Senior Advisor, Minor League Operations: Gary LaRocque.
Minor League Field Coordinator: Mark DeJohn. **Coordinators:** Brent Strom (pitching), Derrick May (hitting), Luis Aguayo (international infield/infield instructor), Barry Weinberg (senior medical advisor), Geoff Gabler (minor league medical), Rene Pena (minor league strength/conditioning). **Minor League Equipment Manager:** Buddy Bates.

Major League Staff
Telephone: (314) 345-9600.
Manager: Mike Matheny.
Coaches: Bench—Mike Aldrete; **Pitching**—Derek Lilliquist; **Hitting**—John Mabry; **Assistant Hitting Instructor**—Benjie Molina; **First Base**—Chris Maloney; **Third Base**—Jose Oquendo; **Bullpen**—Blaise Ilsley; **Bullpen Coach**—Jamie Pogue.

Medical/Training
Medical Advisor: Dr. George Paletta. **Head Trainer:** Greg Hauck. **Assistant Trainer:** Chris Conroy. **Assistant Trainer/Rehabilitation Coordinator:** Adam Olsen. **Strength/Conditioning Coach:** Pete Prinzi.

Farm System

Class	Club (League)	Manager	Hitting Coach	Pitching Coach
Triple-A	Memphis (PCL)	Ron Warner	Mark Budaska	Bryan Eversgerd
Double-A	Springfield (TL)	Mike Shildt	Phillip Wellman	Randy Niemann
High A	Palm Beach (FSL)	Johnny Rodriguez	Roger LaFrancois	Ace Adams
Low A	Peoria (MWL)	Dann Bilardello	Erik Pappas	Jason Simontacchi
Short-season	State College (NYP)	Oliver Marmol	Ramon Ortiz	Dernier Orozco
Rookie	Johnson City (APP)	Joe Kruzel	Roberto Espinoza	Paul Davis
Rookie	Cardinals (GCL)	Steve Turco	Jobel Jimenez	Darwin Marrero
Rookie	Cardinals (DSL)	Fray Peniche	Kleininger Teran	Bill Villanueva

Scouting
Fax: (314) 345-9519.
Professional Scouts: Bruce Benedict (Atlanta, GA), Alan Benes (Town & Country, MO), Chuck Fick (Newbury Park, CA), Ryan Franklin (Shawnee, OK), Jeff Ishii (Chino, CA), Mike Jorgensen (Fenton, MO), Mike Juhl (Indian Trail, NC), Marty Keough (Scottsdale, AZ), Deric McKamey (Bluffton, OH), Joe Rigoli (Parsippany, NJ), Kerry Robinson (Ballwin, MO).
Crosscheckers: Joe Almaraz (San Antonio, TX), Fernando Arango (Davie, FL), Brian Hopkins (Brunswick, OH), Mike Roberts (Hot Springs, AR), Jeremy Schied (Aliso Viejo, CA), Roger Smith (Eastman, GA), Jamal Strong (Vacaville, CA).
Area Scouts: Matt Blood (Durham, NC), Nicholas Brannon (Baton Rouge, LA), Jay Catalano (Nashville, TN), Mike Dibiase (Irvine, CA), Rob Fidler (Atlanta, GA), Mike Garciaparra (Orange, CA), Ralph Garr Jr. (Houston, TX), Charlie Gonzalez (Weston, FL), Aaron Krawiec (Gilbert, AZ), Aaron Looper (Shawnee, OK), Sean Moran (Levittown, PA), Charles Peterson (St Cloud, MN), Juan Ramos (Carolina, PR), Matt Swanson (Ripon, CA).
Part-Time Scouts: Scott Cooper (St. Louis, MO), Manny Guerra (Las Vegas, NV), Dirk Kinney (Kansas City, MO), Jimmy Matthews (Athens, GA), Andre Miller (Santa Barbara, CA), Jared Odom (St Louis, MO), Todd Stein (St. Louis, MO), Dave Silvestri (Chesterfield, MO).
Director, International Operations: Moises Rodriguez. **Assistant, International Baseball Operations:** Luis Morales. **International Crosschecker:** Cesar Geronimo, Jr. **Scouting Supervisor, Dominican Republic:** Angel Ovalles. **Administrator, Dominican Republic Operations:** Aaron Rodriguez.
International Scouts: Jean Carlos Alvarez (Dominican Republic), Rodny Jimenez (Dominican Republic), Omar Rogers (Dominican Republic), Jose Gregorio Gonzalez (Venezuela), Estuar Ruiz (Venezuela), Henry Sandoval (VZ/Dutch Caribbean), Carlos Balcazar (Colombia), Crysthiam Blanco (Nicaragua), Arquimedes Nieto (Panama).

San Diego Padres

Office Address: Petco Park, 100 Park Blvd, San Diego, CA 92101.
Mailing Address: PO Box 122000, San Diego, CA 92112.
Telephone: (619) 795-5000. **E-mail address:** comments@padres.com. **Website:** www.padres.com.
Twitter: @padres. **Facebook:** www.facebook.com/padres

Ownership
Operated By: Padres LP. **Executive Chairman:** Ron Fowler. **President/CEO:** Tom Garfinkel.

BUSINESS OPERATIONS
Senior Vice President, Business Development: Tyler Epp. **Executive VP/Senior Advisor:** Dave Winfield. **Special Assistants to President/CEO:** Tony Gwynn, Trevor Hoffman.

Finance/Administration/Information Technology
Senior VP/CFO: Ronda Sedillo. **Senior VP, Business Administration/General Counsel:** Erik Greupner. **VP, Information Technology:** Steve Reese. **Director, Accounting:** Todd Bollman.

Public Affairs/Communications/Community Relations/Military Affairs
Telephone: (619) 795-5265. **Fax:** (619) 795-5266.
Senior VP, Public Affairs: Sarah Farnsworth. **VP, Community Relations:** Sue Botos. **Director, Military Affairs:** Michael Berenston. **Manager, Player/Media Relations:** Josh Ishoo. **Manager, Communications/Broadcasting:** Shana Wilson. **Manager, Publications/Media Relations:** Fernando Alcala. **Manager, Community Affairs/Padres Foundation:** Nhu Tran. **Manager, Latino Affairs:** Alex Montoya. **Manager, Community Relations:** Veronica Nogueira. **Coordinator, Community Affairs/Padres Foundation:** Christina Papasedero.

Entertainment/Partnerships/Marketing/Creative Services
VP, Corporate Partnerships: Jarrod Dillon. **Director, Entertainment/Production:** Erik Meyer. **Director, Brand Development:** Nicole Smith. **Director, Partnership Development:** Joe Mulford.
Manager, Promotions/Merchandising: Michael Babida. **Manager, In-Park Entertainment:** Mike Grace. **Manager, Entertainment/Production Engineer:** Hendrik Jaehn. **Manager, Game Presentation/Production:** Jennifer Cota. **Manager, Marketing Services:** Harrison Boyd. **Manager, Creative Services:** Oliver Yambao.

Ballpark Operations
VP, Ballpark Operations/GM, Petco Park: Mark Guglielmo. **VP, Petco Park Events:** Jeremy Horowitz.
Director, Security: John Leas. **Director, Event Operations:** Ken Kawachi. **Director, Field Operations:** Luke Yoder. **Director, Guest Services:** Kameron Durham. **Official Scorers:** Jack Murray, Bill Zavestoski.

Ticketing
Telephone: (619) 795-5500. **Fax:** (619) 795-5034.
VP, Ticket Sales/Service/Operations: Jeremy Walls.

Ron Fowler

2013 SCHEDULE
Standard Game Times: 7:05 p.m.; Wed. 3:35; Sat. 5:35; Sun. 1:05

APRIL
1	at New York (NL)
3-4	at New York (NL)
5-7	at Colorado
9-11	Los Angeles (NL)
12-14	Colorado
15-17	at Los Angeles (NL)
19-21	at San Francisco
22-24	Milwaukee
26-28	San Francisco
29-30	at Chicago (NL)

MAY
1-2	at Chicago (NL)
3-5	Arizona
6-8	Miami
10-12	at Tampa Bay
14-15	at Baltimore
16-19	Washington
20-22	St. Louis
24-26	at Arizona
27-28	at Seattle
29-30	Seattle
31	Toronto

JUNE
1-2	Toronto
3-5	at Los Angeles (NL)
6-9	at Colorado
10-12	Atlanta
14-16	Arizona
17-19	at San Francisco
20-23	Los Angeles (NL)
24-26	Philadelphia
28-30	at Miami

JULY
1-4	at Boston
5-7	at Washington
8-10	Colorado
11-14	San Francisco
19-21	at St. Louis
22-25	at Milwaukee
26-28	at Arizona
29-31	Cincinnati

AUGUST
2-4	New York (AL)
6-7	Baltimore
9-11	at Cincinnati
12-14	at Colorado
15-18	New York (NL)
19-21	Pittsburgh
23-25	Chicago (NL)
26-28	at Arizona
30-31	at Los Angeles (NL)

SEPTEMBER
1	at Los Angeles (NL)
2-4	San Francisco
6-8	Colorado
10-12	at Philadelphia
13-15	at Atlanta
16-19	at Pittsburgh
20-22	Los Angeles (NL)
23-26	Arizona
27-29	at San Francisco

GENERAL INFORMATION
Stadium (year opened): Petco Park (2004).
Team Colors: Blue, white, tan and gray

Player Representative: Unavailable.
Home Dugout: First Base.
Playing Surface: Grass.

Director, Ticket Operations: Jim Kiersnowski. **Director, Season Ticket Sales/Services:** Jonathan Tillman. **Director, Group Tickets/Hospitality:** Eric McKenzie. **Director, Business Development:** Robert Davis.

Travel/Clubhouse

Director, Team Travel/Equipment Manager: Brian Prilaman. **Assistant Equipment Manager/Umpire Room Attendant:** Tony Petricca. **Assistant to Equipment Manager:** Spencer Dallin. **Visiting Clubhouse Manager:** David Bacharach.

BASEBALL OPERATIONS

Josh Byrnes

Telephone: (619) 795-5076. **Fax:** (619) 795-5361.
Executive VP/General Manager: Josh Byrnes.
Senior VP, Baseball Operations: Omar Minaya. **VP/Assistant GM:** Fred Uhlman Jr. **VP/Assistant GM:** AJ Hinch. **VP/Assistant GM, Player Personnel:** Chad MacDonald.
Special Assistants, Baseball Operations: Brad Ausmus, Mark Loretta. **Director, Baseball Operations:** Josh Stein. **Director, Team Travel/Equipment Manager:** Brian Prilaman. **Assistant, Baseball Operations/Professional Scouting:** Alex Slater. **Architect, Baseball Systems:** Wells Oliver. **Developer, Baseball Systems:** Brian McBurney. **Advance Scouts, Baseball Operations:** Nick Ennis, Ben Sestanovich. **Video Coordinator, Clubhouse:** Mike Tompkins. **Executive Assistant:** Julie Myers.

Medical/Training

Club Physician: Scripps Clinic Medical Staff. **Head Athletic Trainer:** Todd Hutcheson. **Assistant Athletic Trainer:** Paul Navarro. **Physical Therapist:** Rick Stauffer. **Therapist/Sports Massage:** Philip Kerr. **Strength/Conditioning Coach:** Brett McCabe.

Player Development

Telephone: (619) 795-5343. **Fax:** (619) 795-5036.
VP, Player Development/International Scouting: Randy Smith.
Manager, Player Development/International Operations: Juan Lara. **Manager, Minor Leagues Operations:** Warren Miller. **Equipment Manager, Minor Leagues:** Zach Nelson. **Administrator, Dominican Republic Operations:** Cesar Rizik. **Assistant Administrator, Dominican Republic Operations:** Jesus Negrette. **Roving Instructors:** Randy Johnson (field coordinator), Mike Cather (pitching coordinator), Sean Berry (hitting coordinator), Gary Jones (infield coordinator), Glen Barker (outfield/baserunning coordinator), Evaristo Lantigua (coordinator, Latin American instruction), Joseph Tarantino (medical coordinator), Jordan Wolf (strength/conditioning coordinator), Ryan Bitzel (rehab coordinator).

Farm System

Class	Farm Club (League)	Manager	Coach	Pitching Coach
Triple-A	Tucson (PCL)	Pat Murphy	Tom Tornincasa	Bronswell Patrick
Double-A	San Antonio (TL)	Rich Dauer	Jacque Jones	Jimmy Jones
High A	Lake Elsinore (CAL)	Shawn Wooten	David Newhan	Brian Lawrence
Low A	Ft Wayne (MWL)	Jose Valentin	Morgan Burkhart	Burt Hooton
Short-season	Eugene (NWL)	Jim Gabella	Ivan Cruz	Dave Rajsich
Rookie	Padres (AZL)	Michael Collins	Carlos Sosa	Nelson Cruz
Rookie	Padres (DSL)	Mel Rojas	J. Quezada/J. Guillen	J. Ramirez/J. Pozo

Major League Staff

Manager: Bud Black.
Coaches: Bench—Rick Renteria; **Pitching**—Darren Balsley; **Hitting**—Phil Plantier; **Assistant Hitting**—Alonzo Powell; **First Base**—Dave Roberts; **Third Base**—Glenn Hoffman; **Bullpen**—Willie Blair.

Scouting

Director, Scouting: Billy Gasparino (Venice, CA).
Assistant to Director, Scouting: Eddie Ciafardini (San Diego, CA). **Amateur Scouting Intern:** Matt Thomas (San Diego, CA). **National Crosscheckers:** Bob Filotei (Daphne, AL), Kurt Kemp (Peachtree City, GA).
Supervisors: Sean Campbell (Nashville, TN), Pete DeYoung (Carlsbad, CA), Tim Holt (Allen, TX), Chip Lawrence (Palmetto, FL). **Amateur Scouts:** Justin Baughman (Seattle, WA), Willie Bosque (Winter Garden, FL), Adam Bourassa (Burlington, NC), Jim Bretz (South Windsor, CT), Mark Conner (Hendersonville, TN), Jeff Curtis (Arlington, TX), Lane Decker (Piedmont, OK), Kevin Ellis (Katy, TX), Josh Emmerick (Oceanside, CA), Chris Kelly (Sarasota, FL), Dave Lottsfeldt (Denver, CO), Brent Mayne (Costa Mesa, CA), Russ McNickle (Duluth, GA), Sam Ray (Clayton, CA), Andrew Salvo (Pelham, AL), Jeff Stewart (Normal, IL), Murray, Zuk (Souris, Manitoba). **Part-Time Scouts:** Ed Daub (Binghamton, NY), Hank Krause (Akron, IA), Gary Murphy (Henderson, NV), Jimmy Nelson (West Monroe, LA), Willie Rhonda (Las Lomas Rio Piedras, PR), Cam Walker (Centerville, IA).
Special Assignment Scouts: Chris Bourjos (Scottsdale, AZ), Kevin Jarvis (Franklin, TN), Steve Lyons (San Antonio, TX), Jeff Pickler (Chandler, AZ). **Professional Scouts:** Joe Bochy (Plant City, FL), Jim Elliot (Winston-Salem, NC), Al Hargesheimer (Arlington Heights, IL), Mark Merila (Maple Grove, MN), Matt Smith (Surprise, AZ), John Vander Wal (Grand Rapids, MI), Mike Venafro (Fort Myers, FL), Chris Young (Austin, TX).
Coordinator, Latin American Scouting: Felix Feliz. **Supervisor, Venezuela:** Yfrain Linares. **Supervisor, Central America/Mexico:** Robert Rowley. **International Crosschecker/Coordinator, Pacific Rim:** Trevor Schumm.
International Scouts: Antonio Alejos (Venezuela), Milton Croes (Aruba), Marcial Del Valle (Colombia), Emenegildo Diaz (Dominican Republic), Mayron Isenia (Curacao), Elvin Jarquin (Nicaragua), Martin Jose (Dominican Republic), Victor Magdaleno (Venezuela), Ricardo Montenegro (Panama), Luis Prieto (Venezuela), Ysrael Rojas (Dominican Republic), Jose Salado (Dominican Republic).

San Francisco Giants

Office Address: AT&T Park, 24 Willie Mays Plaza, San Francisco, CA 94107.
Telephone: (415) 972-2000. **Fax:** (415) 947-2800. **Website:** sfgiants.com, sfgigantes.com.

Ownership
Operated by: San Francisco Baseball Associates L.P.

BUSINESS OPERATIONS
President/Chief Executive Officer: Laurence M. Baer. **Special Assistant:** Willie Mays. **Senior Advisor:** Willie McCovey.

Finance
Senior Vice President/Chief Financial Officer: John F. Yee. **VP, Finance:** Lisa Pantages. **Senior VP/Chief Information Officer:** Bill Schlough. **Senior Director, Information Technology:** Ken Logan.

Human Resources/Legal
Chief People Officer: Leilani Gayles. **VP, Human Resources:** Joyce Thomas. **Senior VP/General Counsel:** Jack F. Bair. **VP/Deputy General Counsel:** Elizabeth R. Murphy.

Communications
Telephone: (415) 972-2445. **Fax:** (415) 947-2800.
Senior VP, Communications/Senior Advisor to the CEO: Staci Slaughter. **Senior Director, Broadcast Services:** Maria Jacinto. **Senior Director, Media Relations:** Jim Moorehead. **Media Relations Manager:** Matt Chisholm. **Manager, Hispanic Marketing/Media Relations:** Erwin Higueros. **VP, Public Affairs/Community Relations:** Shana Daum. **VP, Creative Services:** Nancy Donati. **Director, Photography/Archives:** Missy Mikulecky.

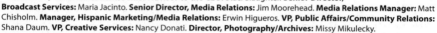

Laurence M. Baer

Business Operations
Senior VP, Business Operations: Mario Alioto. **Managing VP, Sponsorship/New Business Development:** Jason Pearl. **VP, Strategic Revenue Services:** Jerry Drobny. **VP, Sponsor/Special Events Services:** Danny Dann. **Director, Special Events:** Valerie McGuire. **Director, Sponsorship Sales:** Bill Lawrence. **VP, Retail Operations:** Dave Martinez.

Ticketing
Telephone: (415) 972-2000. **Fax:** (415) 972-2500.
Managing VP, Ticket Sales/Services: Russ Stanley. **VP, Sales:** Jeff Tucker. **Director, Season Ticket Sales:** Craig Solomon. **Senior Director, Ticket Services:** Devin Lutes. **Senior Ticket Operations Manager:** Anita Sprinkles. **Senior Box Office Manager:** Todd Pierce. **VP, Client Relations:** Annemarie Hastings.

Marketing
Senior VP, Consumer Marketing: Tom McDonald. **Senior Director, Marketing/Entertainment:** Chris Gargano. **Director, Executive Producer:** Paul Hodges.

2013 SCHEDULE
Standard Game Times: 7:15 p.m.; Sun. 1:05

APRIL
1-3. . . at Los Angeles (NL)
5-7. . . . . St. Louis
8-10 . . . . .Colorado
11-14 . . .at Chicago (NL)
16-18 . . . . . at Milwaukee
19-21 . . . . San Diego
22-24 . . . . .Arizona
26-28 . . . . at San Diego
29-30 . . . . . . at Arizona

MAY
1 . . . . at Arizona
3-5 . . . . Los Angeles (NL)
6-8. . . . . . . .Philadelphia
9-12 . . . . Atlanta

14-15 . . . . . . at Toronto
16-19 . . . . . . at Colorado
20-22 . . . . . Washington
24-26 . . . . . .Colorado
27-28 . . . . . .at Oakland
29-30 . . . . Oakland
31 . . . . .at St. Louis

JUNE
1-2. . . . . at St. Louis
4-5. . . . . .Toronto
7-9. . . . . at Arizona
11-13 . . . . at Pittsburgh
14-16 . . . . . . at Atlanta
17-19 . . . . . . San Diego
20-23 . . . . .Miami
24-26 . at Los Angeles (NL)

28-30 . . . . . at Colorado

JULY
1-4. . . . . . . .at Cincinnati
5-7. . . . Los Angeles (NL)
8-10 . . . . . .New York (NL)
11-14 . . . . . at San Diego
19-21 . . . . .Arizona
22-24 . . . . . . Cincinnati
26-28 . . . . Chicago (NL)
30-31 . . . at Philadelphia

AUGUST
1 . . . . . . at Philadelphia
2-4. . . . . . at Tampa Bay
5-8. . . . . .Milwaukee
9-11 . . . . Baltimore

13-15 . . . . at Washington
16-18 . . . . at Miami
19-21 . . . . Boston
22-25 . . . . Pittsburgh
26-28 . . . . . at Colorado
30-31 . . . . . . at Arizona

SEPTEMBER
1 . . . . at Arizona
2-4. . . . . . at San Diego
5-8. . . . . .Arizona
9-11 . . . . .Colorado
12-15 . at Los Angeles (NL)
17-19 . . at New York (NL)
20-22 . . . at New York (AL)
24-26 . . . Los Angeles (NL)
27-29 . . . . . . San Diego

GENERAL INFORMATION
Stadium (year opened): AT&T Park (2000).
Team Colors: Black, orange and cream.

Player Representative: Matt Cain.
Home Dugout: Third Base.
Playing Surface: Grass.

Administration/Ballpark Operations

Senior VP, Administration: Alfonso G. Felder. **Senior VP, Ballpark Operations:** Jorge Costa. **VP, Ballpark Operations:** Gene Telucci. **Senior Director, Security:** Tinie Roberson. **VP, Guest Services:** Rick Mears. **Head Groundskeeper:** Greg Elliott. **PA Announcer:** Renel Brooks-Moon.

Clubhouse/Travel

Giants Equipment Manager: Miguel Murphy. **Home Clubhouse Assistants:** Brandon Evans, Ron Garcia, David Lowenstein. **Visitors Clubhouse Manager:** Harvey Hodgerney.

BASEBALL OPERATIONS

Telephone: (415) 972-1922. **Fax:** (415) 947-2929.
Senior VP/General Manager: Brian R. Sabean.
VP/Assistant GM, Player Personnel: Dick Tidrow. **VP/Assistant GM:** Bobby Evans. **Special Assistant to GM:** Felipe Alou. **Senior Advisor, Baseball Operations:** Tony Siegle. **Director, Minor League Operations/Quantitative Analysis:** Yeshayah Goldfarb. **Executive Assistant to GM:** Karen Sweeney. **Coordinator, Video Coaching System:** Danny Martin.

Major League Staff

Manager: Bruce Bochy.
Coaches: Bench—Ron Wotus; **Pitching**—Dave Righetti; **Hitting**—Hensley Meulens/Joe Lefebvre; **First Base**—Roberto Kelly; **Third Base**—Tim Flannery; **Bullpen**—Mark Gardner/Bill Hayes.

Brian Sabean

Medical/Training

Team Physicians: Dr. Robert Murray, Dr. Ken Akizuki, Dr. Anthony Saglimbeni. **Head Trainer:** Dave Groeschner. **Assistant Trainers:** Mark Gruesbeck, Anthony Reyes. **Strength/Conditioning Coach:** Carl Kochan. **Coordinator, Medical Administration:** Chrissy Yuen.

Player Development

Director, Player Development: Fred Stanley.
Senior Consultant, Player Personnel: Jack Hiatt. **Special Assistants:** Joe Amalfitano, Jim Davenport. **Director, Arizona Baseball Operations:** Alan Lee. **Special Assistant, Player Development:** Shane Turner. **Coordinator, Minor League Pitching:** Bert Bradley. **Coordinator, Minor League Hitting:** Steve Decker. **Minor League Roving Instructors:** Lee Smith (pitching), Jose Alguacil (infield), Henry Cotto (baserunning/outfield), Kirt Manwaring (catching). **Manager, Player Personnel Administration:** Clara Ho. **Coordinator, Minor League Operations:** Eric Flemming. **Arizona Minor League Operations Assistant:** Gabriel Alvarez. **Baseball Operations Assistant:** Jose Bonilla.

Farm System

Class	Farm Club (League)	Manager	Coach(es)	Pitching Coach
Triple-A	Fresno (PCL)	Bob Mariano	Russ Morman	Pat Rice
Double-A	Richmond (EL)	Dave Machemer	Ken Joyce	Ross Grimsley
High A	San Jose (CAL)	Andy Skeels	Lipso Nava	Michael Couchee
Low A	Augusta (SAL)	Mike Goff	Hector Borg	Steve Kline
Short-season	Salem-Keizer (NWL)	Gary Davenport	Ricky Ward	Jerry Cram
Rookie	Giants (AZL)	Nestor Rojas	Billy Horton	L. McCall/Z. Zimmerman
Rookie	Giants (DSL)	Jesus Tavarez	C. Valderrama/ J. Perra	Marcos Aguasvivas

Scouting

Telephone: (415) 972-2360. **Fax:** (415) 947-2929.
VP/Assistant GM, Scouting/International Operations: John Barr (Haddonfield, NJ).
VP, Pro Scouting/Player Evaluation: Jeremy Shelley. **Senior Advisors, Scouting:** Ed Creech (Moultrie, GA), Doug Mapson (Chandler, AZ), Matt Nerland (Clayton, CA), Paul Turco Sr (Sarasota, FL). **Coordinator, Scouting Administration:** Adam Nieting. **Special Assignment Scouts:** Pat Burrell (Scottsdale, AZ), Lee Elder (Scottsdale, AZ), Tom Korenek (Houston, TX), Darren Wittcke (Gresham, OR). **Advance Scouts:** Steve Balboni (Murray Hill, NJ), Keith Champion (Ballwin, MO). **Major League Scouts:** Brian Johnson (Detroit, MI), Michael Kendall (Rancho Palos Verde, CA), Stan Saleski (Dayton, OH), Paul Turco Jr (Tampa, FL), Tom Zimmer (Seminole, FL). **Senior Consultants, Scouting:** Dick Cole (Costa Mesa, CA).
Supervisors: East—John Castleberry (High Point, NC); **Midwest**—Arnold Brathwaite (Grand Prairie, TX); **West**—Joe Strain (Englewood, CO).
Territorial Scouts: East Region—Ray Callari (Cote Saint Luc, Quebec), Kevin Christman (Noblesville, IN), John DiCarlo (Glenwood, NJ), Donnie Suttles (Marion, NC), Andrew Jefferson (Atlanta, GA), Mike Metcalf (Sarasota, FL), Glenn Tufts (Bridgewater, MA); **Midwest Region**—Lou Colletti (Elk Grove Village, IL), Daniel Murray (Prairie Village, KS), Todd Thomas (Dallas, TX), Hugh Walker (Jonesboro, AR); **West Region**—Brad Cameron (Los Alamitos, CA), Chuck Hensley (Mesa, AZ), Gil Kubski (Valencia, CA), Keith Snider (Stockton, CA), Matt Woodward (Vancouver, WA).
West Coast Video/Area Scout: Colin Sabean (Belmont, CA). **Part-Time Scouts:** Bob Barth (Williamstown, NJ), Jim Chapman (Langley, BC), Felix Negron (Bayamon, PR), Tim Rock (Orlando, FL).
Director, Dominican Operations: Pablo Peguero. **International Crosschecker:** Joe Salermo (Hallandale Beach, FL). **Latin America Crosschecker:** Junior Roman (San Sebastian, PR). **Venezuela Supervisor:** Ciro Villalobos. **Assistant Director, Dominican Operations:** Felix Peguero. **Coordinator, Pacific Rim Scouting:** John Cox. **International Scouts:** Jonathan Arraiz (Venezuela), Jonathan Bautista (Dominican Republic), Phillip Elhage (Curacao/Bonaire/Aruba), Gabriel Elias (Dominican Republic), Edgar Fernandez (Venezuela), Ricardo Heron (Panama), Jeff Kusumoto (Japan), Juan Marquez (Venezuela), Daniel Mavarez (Colombia), Oscar Montero (Venezuela), Sandy Moreno (Nicaragua), Ruddy Moretta (Dominican Republic), Jim Patterson (Australia), Luis Pena (Mexico), Jesus Stephens (Dominican Republic).

Seattle Mariners

Office Address: 1250 First Avenue South, Seattle, WA 98134.
Mailing Address: PO Box 4100, Seattle, WA 98194.
Telephone: (206) 346-4000. **Fax:** (206) 346-4400. **Website:** www.mariners.com.

Ownership
Board of Directors: Minoru Arakawa, John Ellis, Chris Larson, Howard Lincoln, Wayne Perry, Frank Shrontz, Rob Glaser.
Chair/CEO: Howard Lincoln.
President/Chief Operating Officer: Chuck Armstrong.

BUSINESS OPERATIONS

Chuck Armstrong

Finance
Executive Vice President, Finance/Ballpark Operations: Kevin Mather. **VP, Finance:** Tim Kornegay. **Controller:** Greg Massey. **Senior VP, Human Resources:** Marianne Short.

Corporate Business/Marketing
Executive VP, Business/Operations: Bob Aylward. **VP, Corporate Business/Community Relations:** Joe Chard. **Senior Director, Corporate Business:** Ingrid Russell-Narcisse. **Senior Director, Community Relations:** Gina Hasson. **Manager, Community Programs:** Sean Grindley. **VP, Marketing:** Kevin Martinez. **Director, Marketing:** Gregg Greene.

Sales
VP, Sales: Frances Traisman. **Director, Group Business Development:** Bob Hellinger. **Director, Ticket Sales:** Cory Carbary.

Baseball Information/Communications
Telephone: (206) 346-4000. **Fax:** (206) 346-4400.
Senior VP, Communications: Randy Adamack.
Senior Director, Baseball Information: Tim Hevly. **Assistant Director, Baseball Information:** Jeff Evans. **Manager, Baseball Information:** Kelly Munro.
Director, Public Information: Rebecca Hale. **Director, Graphic Design:** Carl Morton.

Ticketing
Telephone: (206) 346-4001. **Fax:** (206) 346-4100.
Senior Director, Ticketing/Parking Operations: Malcolm Rogel. **Director, Ticket Services:** Jennifer Sweigert.

Stadium Operations
VP, Ballpark Operations: Scott Jenkins. **Senior Director, Safeco Field Operations:** Tony Pereira. **Senior Director, Engineering/Maintenance:** Joe Myhra. **Security:** Sly Servance. **Director, Events:** Jill Hashimoto.
VP, Information Services: Dave Curry. **Director, PBX/Retail Systems:** Oliver Roy. **Director, Database/Applications:** Justin Stolmeier. **Director, Procurement:** Sandy Fielder. **Head Groundskeeper:** Bob Christofferson. **Assistant Head

2013 SCHEDULE
Standard Game Times: 7:10 p.m.; Sun. 1:10.

APRIL		JULY	SEPTEMBER
1-4 . . . . .at Oakland	14-16 . . . at New York (AL)	28-30 . . . . . Chicago (NL)	13-15 . . . . . at Tampa Bay
5-7 . . . . . at Chicago (AL)	17-20 . . . . .at Cleveland		16-18 . . . . .at Texas
8-10 . . . . Houston	21-22 . at Los Angeles (AL)	**JULY**	19-21 . . . . . .at Oakland
11-14 . . . . Texas	24-26 . . . . Texas	2-4 . . . . .at Texas	23-25 . . Los Angeles (AL)
16-18 . . . . Detroit	27-28 . . . . . San Diego	5-7 . . . . . . .at Cincinnati	26-28 . . . . Texas
19-21 . . . . .at Texas	29-30 . . . . . at San Diego	8-11 . . . . Boston	29-31 . . . . . .at Houston
22-24 . . . . . .at Houston	31 . . . . at Minnesota	12-14 . . . Los Angeles (AL)	
25-28 . . Los Angeles (AL)		19-21 . . . . . .at Houston	**SEPTEMBER**
29-30 . . . . . . Baltimore	**JUNE**	22-24 . . . . . . Cleveland	1 . . . . .at Houston
	1-2 . . . . . . at Minnesota	25-28 . . . . . . Minnesota	2-5 . . . . .at Kansas City
MAY	3-5 . . . . . . Chicago (AL)	30-31 . . . . . . .at Boston	6-8 . . . . . .Tampa Bay
1 . . . . Baltimore	6-9 . . . . . .New York (AL)		9-11 . . . . Houston
3-5 . . . . at Toronto	10-12 . . . . Houston	**AUGUST**	13-15 . . . . . .at St. Louis
7-8 . . . . . . at Pittsburgh	14-16 . . . . . . .at Oakland	1 . . . . .at Boston	16-19 . . . . . . .at Detroit
10-12 . . . . Oakland	17-20 . at Los Angeles (AL)	2-4 . . . . .at Baltimore	20-22 . at Los Angeles (AL)
	21-23 . . . . Oakland	5-7 . . . . .Toronto	23-25 . . . . . Kansas City
	25-26 . . . . . . Pittsburgh	9-11 . . . . . . .Milwaukee	27-29 . . . . Oakland

GENERAL INFORMATION
Stadium (year opened): Safeco Field (1999). **Player Representative:** Charlie Furbush
Team Colors: Northwest green, **Home Dugout:** First Base.
silver and navy blue. **Playing Surface:** Grass.

Groundskeepers: Tim Wilson, Leo Liebert. **PA Announcer:** Tom Hutyler. **Official Scorer:** Eric Radovich.

Merchandising
    Senior Director, Merchandise: Jim LaShell. **Director, Retail Merchandising:** Julie McGillivray. **Director, Retail Stores:** Doug Orwiler.

Travel/Clubhouse
    Director, Team Travel: Ron Spellecy.
    Clubhouse Manager: Ryan Stiles. **Visiting Clubhouse Manager:** Ted Walsh. **Video Coordinator:** Jimmy Hartley. **Assistant Video Coordinator:** Craig Manning.

BASEBALL OPERATIONS
    Executive VP/General Manager: Jack Zduriencik.
    Assistant GM: Jeff Kingston. **Special Assistants:** Tony Blengino, Roger Hansen, Lee MacPhail, Ken Madeja, Joe McIlvaine, Ted Simmons, Pete Vuckovich.
    Administrator, Baseball Operations: Debbie Larsen.

Major League Staff
    Manager: Eric Wedge.
    Coaches: Bench—Robby Thompson, Pitching—Carl Willis, Batting—Dave Hansen, First Base—Mike Brumley, Third Base—Jeff Datz, Bullpen-Jaime Navarro.

Jack Zduriencik

Medical/Training
    Medical Director: Dr. Edward Khalfayan. **Club Physician:** Dr. Mitchel Storey. **Head Trainer:** Rick Griffin. **Assistant Trainers:** Rob Nodine, Matt Toth. **Stength/Conditioning:** James Clifford.

Player Development
    Telephone: (206) 346-4316. **Fax:** (206) 346-4300.
    Director, Player Development: Chris Gwynn. **Director, Minor League/International Administration:** Hide Sueyoshi. **Administrator, Minor League Operations:** Jan Plein. **Assistant, Minor League Operations:** Casey Brett. **Coordinator, Minor League Instruction:** Jack Howell. **Coordinator, Athletic Training:** Jimmy Southard. **Latin Athletic Trainer Coordinator:** Javier Alvidrez. **Assistant Athletic Trainer:** Ben Fraser. **Roving Instructors:** Chad Uihlein (strength/conditioning), Chris Woodward (infield), Brant Brown (outfield/baserunning), John Stearns (catching), Lee May Jr (hitting), Rick Waits (pitching), Gary Wheelock (rehab pitching), Jose Moreno (Latin America field coordinator), Nasusel Cabrera (Latin America pitching coordinator).

Farm System

Class	Club (League)	Manager	Coach	Pitching Coach
Triple-A	Tacoma (PCL)	Daren Brown	Howard Johnson	Dwight Bernard
Double-A	Jackson (SL)	Jim Pankovits	Cory Snyder	Terry Clark
High A	High Desert (CAL)	James Horner	Roy Howell	Lance Painter
Low A	Clinton (MWL)	Eddie Menchaca	Mike Kinkade	Andrew Lorraine
Short-season	Everett (NWL)	Rob Mummau	Rafael Santo Domingo	Rich Dorman
Rookie	Pulaski (APP)	Chris Prieto	Scott Steinmann	Nasusel Cabrera
Rookie	Peoria (AZL)	Darrin Garner	Andy Bottin	Cibney Bello
Rookie	Mariners (DSL)	Claudio Almonte	M. Pimentel/F. Gerez	Danielin Acevedo
Rookie	Mariners (VSL)	Russell Vasquez	Alex Delgado	Carlos Hernandez

Scouting
    Telephone: (206) 346-4314. **Fax:** (206) 346-4300.
    Director, Professional Scouting: Tom Allison. **Director, Amateur Scouting:** Tom McNamara. **Scouting Administrator:** Hallie Larson.
    Major League Scouts: Tony Blengino (Waukesha, WI), Roger Hansen (Stanwood, WA), Bob Harrison (Long Beach, CA), Greg Hunter (Seattle, WA), Steve Jongewaard (Napa, CA), Bill Kearns (Milton, MA), Lee MacPhail (Shaker Heights, OH), Joe McIlvaine (Newtown Square, PA), John McMichen (Treasure Island, FL), Ken Madeja (Novi, MI), Bill Masse (Manchester, CT), Joe Nigro (Staten Island, NY), Duane Shaffer (Anaheim, CA), Ted Simmons (Chesterfield, MO), Pete Vuckovich (Johnstown, PA), Woody Woodward (Palm Coast, FL).
    National Crosschecker: Mark Lummus (Cleburne, TX). **Territorial Supervisors: West**—Butch Baccala (Weimar, CA), **Northeast**—Alex Smith (Abingdon, MD), **Southeast**—Garrett Ball (Atlanta, GA), **Midwest**—Jeremy Booth (Houston, TX). **Area Supervisors:** Dave Alexander (Lafayette, IN), Ben Collman (Austin, TX), Dustin Evans (Jacksonville, FL), Jesse Kapellusch (Emporia, KS), Steve Markovich (Highlands, NJ), Devitt Moore (Durham, NC), Mike Moriarty (Marlton, NJ), Rob Mummau (Palm Harbor, FL), Brian Nichols (Taunton, MA), Chris Pelekoudas (Goodyear, AZ), Stacey Pettis (Antioch, CA), John Ramey (Wildomar, CA), Joe Ross (Kirkland, WA), Tony Russo (Montgomery, IL), Noel Sevilla (Weston, FL), Bob Steinkamp (Beatrice, NE), Greg Whitworth (Los Angeles, CA), Brian Williams (Cincinnati, OH).
    Director, International Operations: Tim Kissner. **Coordinator, Special Projects International:** Ted Heid (Glendale, AZ). **Coordinator, Canada/Europe:** Wayne Norton (Port Moody, British Columbia). **Administrative Director, Dominican Operations:** Martin Valerio. **Coordinator, Venezuelan Operations:** Emilio Carrasquel (Barquisimeto, Venezuela). **International Scouts:** Luis Molina (Panama), Franklin Taveras, Jr (Dominican Republic), Yasushi Yamamoto (Japan).

Tampa Bay Rays

Office Address: Tropicana Field, One Tropicana Drive, St. Petersburg, FL 33705.
Telephone: (727) 825-3137. **Fax:** (727) 825-3111. **Website:** www.raysbaseball.com.

Ownership
Principal Owner: Stuart Sternberg. **President:** Matt Silverman.

BUSINESS OPERATIONS
Senior Vice President, Administration/General Counsel: John Higgins. **Senior VP, Business Operations:** Brian Auld. **Senior VP:** Mark Fernandez. **Senior VP, Development/Business Affairs:** Michael Kalt. **VP, Development:** Melanie Lenz. **Senior Director, Development:** William Walsh. **Senior Director, Procurement/Business Services:** Bill Wiener, Jr. **Senior Director, Information Technology:** Juan Ramirez. **Director, Human Resources:** Jennifer Tran. **Director, Partner/VIP Relations:** Cass Halpin.

Stuart Sternberg

Finance
VP, Finance: Rob Gagliardi. **Controller:** Patrick Smith.

Marketing/Community Relations
VP, Marketing: Tom Hoof. **Director, Marketing:** Carey Cox. **Senior Director, Community Relations:** Suzanne Luecke.

Communications/Broadcasting
Phone: (727) 825-3242.
VP, Communications: Rick Vaughn. **Director, Communications:** Dave Haller. **Senior Director, Broadcasting:** Larry McCabe.

Corporate Partnerships
Senior Director, Corporate Partnerships: Josh Bullock. **Director, Corporate Partnerships:** Richard Reeves. **Director, Corporate Partnership Services:** Devin O'Connell.

Ticket Sales
Phone: (888) FAN-RAYS.
VP, Sales/Service: Brian Richeson. **Senior Director, Season Ticket Sales/Service:** Jeff Tanzer. **Director, Ticket Operations:** Robert Bennett. **Assistant Director, Ticket Operations:** Ken Mallory.

Stadium Operations
VP, Operations/Facilities: Rick Nafe. **Senior Directors, Stadium Operations:** Scott Kelyman, Tom Karac. **Director, Stadium Operations:** Chris Raineri. **Director, Audio/Visual Services:** Ron Golick. **Head Groundskeeper:** Dan Moeller. **VP, Branding/Fan Experience:** Darcy Raymond. **Director, Customer Service/Stadium Experience:** Eric Weisberg.

2013 SCHEDULE
Standard Game Times: 7:10 p.m.; Sun. 1:40.

APRIL
2-4	Baltimore
5-7	Cleveland
8-10	at Texas
12-15	at Boston
16-18	at Baltimore
19-21	Oakland
22-24	New York (AL)
25-28	at Chicago (AL)
30	at Kansas City

MAY
1-2	at Kansas City
3-5	at Colorado
6-9	Toronto
10-12	San Diego
14-16	Boston
17-19	at Baltimore
20-22	at Toronto
24-26	New York (AL)
27-28	Miami
29-30	at Miami
31	at Cleveland

JUNE
1-2	at Cleveland
4-6	at Detroit
7-9	Baltimore
10-12	Boston
13-16	Kansas City
18-19	at Boston
20-23	at New York (AL)
24-26	Toronto
28-30	Detroit

JULY
1-4	at Houston
5-7	Chicago (AL)
8-11	Minnesota
12-14	Houston
19-21	at Toronto
22-25	at Boston
26-28	at New York (AL)
30-31	Arizona

AUGUST
2-4	San Francisco
6-7	at Arizona
9-11	at Los Angeles (NL)
13-15	Seattle
16-18	Toronto
19-21	at Baltimore
23-25	New York (AL)
27-29	Los Angeles (AL)
30-31	at Oakland

SEPTEMBER
1	at Oakland
2-5	at Los Angeles (AL)
6-8	at Seattle
10-12	Boston
13-15	at Minnesota
16-19	Texas
20-23	Baltimore
24-26	at New York (AL)
27-29	at Toronto

GENERAL INFORMATION
Stadium (year opened): Tropicana Field (1998). **Home Dugout:** First Base.
Team Colors: Dark blue, light blue, yellow. **Playing Surface:** AstroTurf
Player Representative: Matt Moore. Game Day Grass 3D-60 H.

Travel/Clubhouse
    Director, Team Travel: Jeff Ziegler. **Equipment Manager, Home Clubhouse:** Chris Westmoreland. **Visitors Clubhouse Manager:** Guy Gallagher. **Video Coordinator:** Chris Fernandez.

BASEBALL OPERATIONS

Andrew Friedman

    Executive VP, Baseball Operations: Andrew Friedman.
    Director, Baseball Operations: Chaim Bloom, Erik Neander. **Director, Major League Administration:** Sandy Dengler. **Senior Baseball Advisor:** Don Zimmer. **Special Assistant, Baseball Operations:** Rocco Baldelli.
    Architect, Baseball Systems: Brian Plexico. **Director, Baseball Research/Development:** James Click. **Assistant, Baseball Operations Systems:** Matt Hahn. **Developer, Baseball Systems:** Dan Turkenkopf. **Analysts, Baseball Research/Development:** Joshua Kalk, Leland Chen. **Assistant, Baseball Research/Development:** Peter Bendix, Shawn Hoffman. **Assistant, Baseball Operations:** Graham Tyler.

Major League Staff
    Manager: Joe Maddon.
    Coaches: Bench—Dave Martinez; **Pitching**—Jim Hickey; **Hitting**—Derek Shelton; **First Base**—George Hendrick; **Third Base**—Tom Foley; **Bullpen**—Stan Boroski; **Hitting/Catching**—Jamie Nelson.

Medical/Training
    Medical Director: Dr. James Andrews. **Medical Team Physician:** Dr. Michael Reilly. **Orthopedic Team Physician:** Dr. Koco Eaton. **Head Athletic Trainer:** Ron Porterfield. **Assistant Athletic Trainers:** Paul Harker, Mark Vinson. **Strength/Conditioning Coach:** Kevin Barr.

Player Development
    Telephone: (727) 825-3267. **Fax:** (727) 825-3493.
    Director, Minor League Operations: Mitch Lukevics.
    Assistant, Minor League Operations: Jeff McLerran. **Administrator, International/Minor League Operations:** Giovanna Rodriguez.
    Field Coordinators: Jim Hoff, Bill Evers. **Minor League Coordinators:** Skeeter Barnes (outfield/baserunning), Dick Bosman (pitching), Steve Livesey (hitting), Paul Hoover (catching), Matt Quatraro (hitting), Dewey Robinson (pitching), Joe Benge (medical), Joel Smith (rehabilitation/athletic training), Trung Cao (strength/conditioning).
    Equipment Manager: Tim McKechney. **Assistant Equipment Manager:** Shane Rossetti. **Video Coordinator, Baseball Operations:** Ryan Bristow.

Farm System

Class	Club (League)	Manager	Coach	Pitching Coach
Triple-A	Durham (IL)	Charlie Montoyo	Dave Myers	Neil Allen
Double-A	Montgomery (SL)	Billy Gardner Jr.	Ozzie Timmons	R.C. Lichtenstein
High A	Charlotte (FSL)	Brady Williams	Joe Szekely	Bill Moloney
Low A	Bowling Green (MWL)	Jared Sandberg	Manny Castillo	Kyle Snyder
Short-season	Hudson Valley (NYP)	Michael Johns	Dan DeMent	Steve Watson
Rookie	Princeton (APP)	Danny Sheaffer	Reinaldo Ruiz	Darwin Peguero
Rookie	Rays (GCL)	Jim Morrison	W. Rincones/H. Torres	Marty DeMerritt
Rookie	Rays (DSL)	Julio Zorrilla	A. DeFreites/R. Guerrero	Jose Gonzalez/Roberto Yil
Rookie	Rays (VSL)	German Melendez	A. Freire/G. Omaña	J. Moncada/E. Gonzalez

Scouting
    Telephone: (727) 825-3241. **Fax:** (727) 825-3493.
    Director, Scouting: R.J. Harrison (Phoenix, AZ).
    Assistant Director, Amateur Scouting: Rob Metzler. **Administrator, Scouting:** Nancy Berry.
    Director, Pro Scouting: Matt Arnold. **Special Assignment Scouts:** Mike Cubbage (Keswick, VA), Larry Doughty (Leawood, KS), Bobby Heck (Kingwood, TX), Jeff McAvoy (Rotonda West, FL), Fred Repke (Carson City, NV). **Major League Scouts:** Bob Cluck (San Diego, CA). **Professional Scouts:** Michael Brown (Chandler, AZ), Jason Grey (Mesa, AZ), Kevin Ibach (Geneva, IL), Brian Keegan (Matthews, NC), Jim Pransky (Davenport, IA).
    National Crosschecker: Chuck Ricci (Greencastle, PA).
    Eastern Regional Supervisor: Kevin Elfering (Wesley Chapel, FL). **Midwest Regional Supervisor:** Jeff Cornell (Lee's Summitt, MO). **Western Regional Supervisor:** Jake Wilson (Ramona, CA).
    Scout Supervisors: Tim Alexander (Jamesville, NY), Josh Arhart (Garden Grove, CA), James Bonnici (Auburn Hills, MI), Jack Cressend (Mandeville, LA), Rickey Drexler (New Iberia, LA), Jayson Durocher (Phoenix, AZ), J.D. Elliby (Mansfield, TX), Brett Foley (Naperville, IL), Brian Hickman (Fort Mill, SC), Milt Hill (Cumming, GA), Paul Kirsch (Sherwood, OR), Ronnie Merrill (Tampa, FL), Robbie Moen (El Segundo, CA), Brian Morrison (Fairfield, CA), Pat Murphy (Marble Falls, TX), Lou Wieben (Little Ferry, NJ).
    Part-Time Area Scouts: Tom Couston (Sarasota, FL), Jose Hernandez (Miami, FL), Jim Lief (Wellington, FL), Gil Martinez (San Juan, PR), Graig Merritt (Pitts Meadow, Canada), Casey Onaga (Aiea, HI), Jack Sharp (Dallas, TX), Donald Turley (Spring, TX), Peter Woodworth (St. Petersburg, FL).
    Director, Latin American Scouting: Carlos Rodriguez (Tampa, FL). **Special Assistant, International Operations:** Carlos Alfonso (Naples, FL). **Director, Venezuelan Operations:** Ronnie Blanco. **Pacific Rim Coordinator:** Tim Ireland. **Assistant, International Operations:** Patrick Walters. **Consultant, International Operations:** John Gilmore. **International Scouts:** Eddie Diaz (Mexico), Aaron Acosta (Mexico), Javier Robles (Mexico), Chairon Isenia (Curacao), Keith Hsu (Taiwan), Tateki Uchibori (Japan). **Coordinator, Colombia:** Angel Contreras. **Coordinator, Brazil:** Adriano De Souza.

Texas Rangers

Office Address: 1000 Ballpark Way, Arlington, TX 76011.
Mailing Address: P.O. Box 90111, Arlington, TX 76011.
Telephone: (817) 273-5222. **Fax:** (817) 273-5110. **Website:** www.texasrangers.com.

Ownership
Co-Chairman: Ray C. Davis, Bob R. Simpson.
Chairman, Ownership Committee: Neil Leibman. **CEO/President:** Nolan Ryan.

BUSINESS OPERATIONS
Chief Operating Officer: Rick George. **Senior Executive Vice President:** Jim Sundberg.
Executive VP/Chief Financial Officer: Kellie Fischer.
Executive VP, Communications: John Blake. **Executive VP, Business Partnerships/
Development:** Joe Januszewski. **Executive VP, Ballpark/Event Operations:** Rob Matwick.
Executive VP, Rangers Enterprises/Customer Service/Sales: Jay Miller. **Executive VP,
Entertainment/Productions:** Chuck Morgan. **Executive Assistant to CEO/President:**
Courtney Krug. **Executive Assistant to COO/Finance:** Gabrielle Stokes. **Executive Assistant:**
Leslie Dempsey. **Manager, Ownership Concierge Services:** Amy Beam.

Nolan Ryan

Finance/Accounting
VP/Controller: Starr Gulledge. **Assistant Controller:** Brian Thompson. **Payroll Manager:**
Donna Ebersole. **A/P-A/R Manager:** Paula Murphy.

Human Resources/Legal/Information Technology
Senior VP, Human Resources/Risk Management: Terry Turner. **Associate Counsel:** Kate Cassidy. **Managers, Human
Resources:** Shannon Abbott, Shelby Carpenter, Mercedes Riley. **VP, Information Technology:** Mike Bullock. **Manager,
Application Systems:** Bill Edevane.

Ballpark/Event Operations
VP, Security/Parking: Blake Miller. **Assistant VP, Customer Service:** Donnie Pordash. **Director, Parking/Security:**
Mike Smith.

Communications/Community Relations
Assistant VP, Player Relations: Taunee Paur Taylor. **Senior Director, Broadcasting/Communications:** Angie Swint.
Senior Director, Media Relations: Rich Rice. **Assistant Director, Player Relations:** Ashleigh Greathouse. **Manager,
Photography:** Kelly Gavin. **Manager, Media Services:** Brian SanFilippo. **Manager, Publications/Media Relations:** Rob
Morse. **Assistant, Communications:** Amber Sims. **Assistant, Player Relations:** Becky Reed. **VP, Community Outreach/
Executive Director, Foundation:** Karin Morris. **Assistant VP, Community Outreach:** Breon Davis.

Facilities
VP, Ballpark Facilities Operations: Gib Searight. **Director, Grounds:** Dennis Klein. **Director, Ballpark Construction/**

2013 SCHEDULE
Standard Game Times: 7:05 p.m.; Sun. 2:05.

MARCH		
31 . . . . .at Houston	10-12 . . . . . .at Houston	25-27 . . . at New York (AL)	16-18 . . . . Seattle

MARCH
31 . . . . .at Houston

APRIL
2-3 . . . . .at Houston
5-7 . . . . . Los Angeles (AL)
8-10 . . . . . . .Tampa Bay
11-14 . . . . at Seattle
16-18 . . . .at Chicago (NL)
19-21 . . . . Seattle
22-24 . at Los Angeles (AL)
25-28 . . . . . at Minnesota
30 . . . . Chicago (AL)

MAY
1-2 . . . . Chicago (AL)
3-5 . . . . Boston
7-8 . . . . at Milwaukee

10-12 . . . . . .at Houston
13-15 . . . . . .at Oakland
16-19 . . . . Detroit
20-22 . . . . Oakland
24-26 . . . . . . .at Seattle
27 . . . . .at Arizona (DH)
29-30 . . . . Arizona
31 . . . . Kansas City

JUNE
1-2 . . . . Kansas City
4-6 . . . . .at Boston
7-9 . . . . at Toronto
10-12 . . . . . . .Cleveland
13-16 . . . . .Toronto
17-20 . . . . Oakland
21-23 . . . . . .at St. Louis

25-27 . . . at New York (AL)
28-30 . . . . . . Cincinnati

JULY
2-4 . . . . Seattle
5-7 . . . . Houston
8-11 . . . . . .at Baltimore
12-14 . . . . . .at Detroit
19-21 . . . . . . Baltimore
22-25 . . . .New York (AL)
26-28 . . . . .at Cleveland
29-31 . . . Los Angeles (AL)

AUGUST
2-4 . . . . .at Oakland
5-7 . . . at Los Angeles (AL)
9-12 . . . . .at Houston
13-14 . . . . . . .Milwaukee

16-18 . . . . Seattle
19-21 . . . . Houston
23-25 . . . .at Chicago (AL)
26-28 . . . . . . .at Seattle
30-31 . . . . . . Minnesota

SEPTEMBER
1 . . . . Minnesota
2-4 . . . . .at Oakland
6-8 . . . at Los Angeles (AL)
9-11 . . . . Pittsburgh
13-15 . . . . Oakland
16-19 . . . . . at Tampa Bay
20-22 . . . .at Kansas City
23-25 . . . . Houston
26-29 . . . Los Angeles (AL)

GENERAL INFORMATION
Stadium (year opened): Rangers
Ballpark in Arlington (1994).
Team Colors: Royal blue and red.

Player Representative: Derek Holland.
Home Dugout: First Base.
Playing Surface: Grass.

Development: Andrew St. Julian.

Marketing/Game Presentation
VP, Marketing: Becky Kimbro. **Assistant VP, Marketing:** Kelly Calvert. **Senior Director, Promotions/Special Events:** Sherry Flow. **Director, In-Game Entertainment:** Michael Cruz. **Director, Social Media:** Kaylan Eastepp.

Sponsorship/Ticket Sales/Ticket Operations
VP, Partnerships/Client Service: Jim Cochrane. **Senior Director, Media Sales:** Wade Howell. **Director, Partnerships:** Guy Tomcheck. **Manager, Client Services:** Rose Swenson. **VP, Ticket Sales/Service:** Paige Farragut. **Director, Ticket Services:** Mike Lentz. **Manager, Ticket Operations:** Ben Rogers.

BASEBALL OPERATIONS
Telephone: (817) 273-5222. **Fax:** (817) 273-5285.
General Manager: Jon Daniels.
Assistant GM: Thad Levine. **Senior Advisor to the GM:** John Hart. **Senior Special Assistant to the GM, Scouting:** Don Welke. **Senior Advisor to GM:** Tom Giordano. **Director, Baseball Operations:** Matt Vinnola. **Assistant, Baseball Operations:** Matt Klotsche. **Executive Assistant to GM:** Barbara Pappenfus. **Special Assistants to the GM:** Tony Fernandez, Greg Maddux. **Major League Special Assistant:** Scott Littlefield.

Major League Staff
Manager: Ron Washington.
Coaches: Bench—Jackie Moore; **Pitching**—Mike Maddux; **Hitting**—Dave Magadan; **First Base**—Dave Anderson; **Third Base**—Gary Pettis; **Bullpen**—Andy Hawkins.

Medical/Training
Team Physician: Dr. Keith Meister. **Team Internist:** Dr. David Hunter. **Spine Consultant:** Dr. Andrew Dossett. **Head Trainer/Medical Director:** Jamie Reed. **Director, Strength/Conditioning:** Jose Vazquez.

Jon Daniels

Player Development
Telephone: (817) 436-5999. **Fax:** (817) 273-5285.
Senior Director, Player Development: Tim Purpura.
Director, Minor League Operations: Jake Krug. **Special Assistants, Player Development:** Harry Spilman, Mark Connor. **Manager, Cultural Enhancement:** Bill McLaughlin. **Special Assistant:** Dave Oliver. **Assistant, Player Development:** Paul Kruger. **Field Coordinator:** Jayce Tingler. **Coordinators:** Danny Clark (pitching), Randy Ready (hitting), Hector Ortiz (catching), Keith Comstock (rehab pitching), Casey Candaele (infield/baserunning), Brian Dayette (special assignment coach), Napoleon Pichardo (strength/conditioning), Dale Gilbert (medical), TJ Nakagawa (rehab), Joe Mikulik (outfield). **Manager, Minor League Complex Operations:** Chris Guth.

Farm System

Class	Club (League)	Manager	Coach	Pitching Coach
Triple-A	Round Rock (PCL)	Bobby Jones	S. Coolbaugh/S. Owen	Brad Holman
Double-A	Frisco (TL)	Steve Buechele	Jason Hart	Jeff Andrews
High A	Myrtle Beach (CL)	Jason Wood	J. Perez/K. Holmberg	Steve Mintz
Low A	Hickory (SAL)	Unavailable	J. Mashore/H. Miranda	Ryan O'Malley
Short-season	Spokane (NWL)	Tim Hulett	Vinny Lopez	Oscar Marin
Rookie	Rangers (AZL)	Corey Ragsdale	D. McDonald/B. Shouse	Jose Jaimes
Rookie	Rangers (DSL)	Ryley Westman	A. Infante/G. Mercedes	Pablo Blanco

Scouting
Senior Director, Player Personnel: A.J. Preller.
Director, Amateur Scouting: Kip Fagg. **Director, Pro Scouting:** Josh Boyd.
Director, International Scouting: Mike Daly. **ML Special Assistant:** Scott Littlefield. **Special Assistant/Major League Scout:** Greg Smith. **Manager, Amateur Scouting:** Bobby Crook.
Major League Scouts: Russ Ardolina (Rockville, MD), Keith Boeck (Chandler, AZ). **Pro Scouts:** Mike Anderson (Austin, TX), Chris Briones (Reno, NV), Scot Engler (Montgomery, IL), Ross Fenstermaker (Granite Bay, CA), Todd Walther (Hurst, TX), Mickey White (Sarasota, FL).
National Crosscheckers: Mike Grouse (Olathe, KS), Clarence Johns (Atlanta, GA). **Crosschecker:** Phil Geisler (El Granada, CA). **Western Crosschecker:** Casey Harvie (Lake Stevens, WA). **Midwest Crosschecker:** Randy Taylor (Katy, TX). **Eastern Crosschecker:** Ryan Coe (Acworth, GA). **Area Scouts:** Doug Banks (Scottsdale, AZ), Roger Coryell (Ypsilanti, MI), Jay Eddings (Plano, TX), Steve Flores (Temecula, CA), Jonathan George (North Huntingdon, PA), Todd Guggiana (Long Beach, CA), Jay Heafner (Katy, TX), Chris Kemp (Charlotte, NC), Derek Lee (Frankfurt, IL), Gary McGraw (Gaston, OR), Butch Metzger (Sacramento, CA), Takeshi Sakurayama (Manchester, CT), Dustin Smith (Olathe, KS), Cliff Terracuso (Palm Beach Gardens, FL), Derrick Tucker (Woodstock, GA), Frankie Thon (Guaynabo, Puerto Rico), Steve Watson (Austin, TX), Jeff Wood (Birmingham, AL). **Part-Time Scouts:** Buzzie Keller (Seguin, TX), Bob Laurie (Plano, TX), James Vilade (Frisco, TX). **Amateur Video Scout:** Nick English (Pasadena, CA).
Senior Advisor, Pacific Rim Operations: Jim Colborn. **Coordinator, Pacific Rim Operations:** Joe Furukawa (Japan). **Assistant Director, International Scouting:** Gil Kim (Dominican Republic). **Dominican Program Coordinator:** Danilo Troncoso. **Manager, Pacific Rim Operations:** Curtis Jung. **Assistant, International Operations:** Stosh Hoover. **Latin America Crosscheckers:** Roberto Aquino (Dominican Republic), Rafic Saab (Venezuela). **International Scouts:** Willy Espinal (Dominican Republic), Jose Felomonia (Curacao), Jose Fernandez (Florida), Carlos Gonzalez (Venezuela), Chu Halabi (Aruba), Jung-Hua Liu (Taiwan), Bill McLaughlin (Mexico), Rodolfo Rosario (Dominican Republic), Joel Ronda (Puerto Rico), Hamilton Sarabia (Colombia), Eduardo Thomas (Panama), Manuel Velez (Mexico), Hajime Watabe (Japan).

Toronto Blue Jays

Office/Mailing Address: 1 Blue Jays Way, Suite 3200, Toronto, Ontario M5V 1J1.
Telephone: (416) 341-1000. **Fax:** (416) 341-1250. **Website:** www.bluejays.com.

Ownership
Operated by: Toronto Blue Jays Baseball Club. **Principal Owner:** Rogers Communications Inc.

BUSINESS OPERATIONS

Vice Chairman, Rogers Communications: Phil Lind. **President, Rogers Media:** Keith Pelley. **President/CEO, Toronto Blue Jays/Rogers Centre:** Paul Beeston.

VP, Special Projects: Howard Starkman. **Special Assistant to the Organization:** Roberto Alomar. **Executive Assistant to the President/CEO:** Sue Cannell.

Finance/Administration
Senior VP, Business Operations: Stephen R. Brooks. **Executive Assistant:** Donna Kuzoff. **Senior Director/Controller:** Lynda Kolody. **Director, Payroll/Benefits:** Brenda Dimmer. **Director, Risk Management:** Suzanne Joncas. **Senior Manager/Assistant Controller:** Ciaran Keegan. **Financial Business Managers:** Leslie Galant-Gardiner, Tanya Proctor. **Manager, Revenue Reporting/Analysis:** Craig Whitmore. **Manager, Stadium Payroll:** Sharon Dykstra. **Manager, Ticket Receipts/Vault Services:** Joseph Roach.

Paul Beeston

Director, Human Resources: Paulette Soper. **Senior Manager, Human Resources:** Fiona Nugent. **Advisor, Human Resources:** Reena Patel. **Director, Information Technology:** Mike Maybee. **Manager, Revenue Reporting/Analysis:** Craig Whitmore. **Manager, Information Technology:** Anthony Miranda. **VP, Business Affairs/Legal Counsel:** Matthew Shuber. **Executive Assistants:** Liza Daniel, Suey Lau.

Marketing/Community Relations
VP, Marketing/Merchandising: Anthony Partipilo. **VP, Corporate Partnerships:** Mark Ditmars. **Executive Assistant:** Maria Cresswell. **Director, Game Entertainment/Promotions:** Marnie Starkman. **Executive Director, Jays Care Foundation:** Danielle Bedasse. **Directors, Corporate Partnership/Business Development:** John Griffin, Rob Swann. **Directors, Marketing Services:** Natalie Agro, Krista Semotiuk. **Senior Manager, Corporate Partnerships/Business Development:** Mark Palmer. **Senior Manager, Marketing Services:** Honsing Leung. **Executive Assistant:** Darla McKeen.

Communications
Telephone: (416) 341-1301/1302/1303. **Fax:** (416) 341-1250.
VP, Communications: Jay Stenhouse. **Manager, Baseball Information:** Mal Romanin. **Coordinator, Baseball Information:** Erik Grosman. **Coordinator, Communications:** Sue Mallabon.

Stadium Operations
VP, Stadium Operations/Security: Mario Coutinho. **Executive Assistant:** June Sym. **Director, Guest Experience:** Carmen Day. **Manager, Event Services:** Julie Minott. **Manager, Game Operations:** Karyn Gottschalk.

2013 SCHEDULE
Standard Game Times: 7:07 p.m.; Sat/Sun: 1:07

APRIL			
2-4 . . . . Cleveland	14-15 . . . . . San Francisco	27-30 . . . . .at Boston	16-18 . . . . . at Tampa Bay
5-7 . . . . Boston	17-19 . . . at New York (AL)	**JULY**	20-22 . . at New York (AL)
9-11 . . . . . . .at Detroit	20-22 . . . . . . .Tampa Bay	1-4 . . . . Detroit	23-25 . . . . . . .at Houston
12-14 . . . . .at Kansas City	23-26 . . . . Baltimore	5-7 . . . . Minnesota	26-28 . . . . .New York (AL)
15-18 . . . . . Chicago (AL)	27-28 . . . . Atlanta	9-11 . . . . . .at Cleveland	30-31 . . . . . . Kansas City
19-21 . . . . .New York (AL)	29-30 . . . . . at Atlanta	12-14 . . . . .at Baltimore	
22-24 . . . . .at Baltimore	31 . . . . at San Diego	19-21 . . . . . .Tampa Bay	**SEPTEMBER**
25-28 . . at New York (AL)	**JUNE**	22-24 . . Los Angeles (NL)	1 . . . . Kansas City
30 . . . . Boston	1-2 . . . . . at San Diego	25-28 . . . . Houston	2-4 . . . . at Arizona
	4-5 . . . . at San Francisco	29-31 . . . . .at Oakland	6-8 . . . . . . at Minnesota
MAY	7-9 . . . . Texas		10-12 . . Los Angeles (AL)
1-2 . . . . Boston	10-12 . . . .at Chicago (AL)	**AUGUST**	13-15 . . . . . . Baltimore
3-5 . . . . Seattle	13-16 . . . . .at Texas	1-4 . . . at Los Angeles (AL)	17-19 . . . . .New York (AL)
6-9 . . . . . . at Tampa Bay	17-19 . . . . . . .Colorado	5-7 . . . . .at Seattle	20-22 . . . . . . .at Boston
10-12 . . . . . .at Boston	21-23 . . . . Baltimore	9-12 . . . . Oakland	24-26 . . . . . .at Baltimore
	24-26 . . . . . at Tampa Bay	13-15 . . . . Boston	27-29 . . . . . .Tampa Bay

GENERAL INFORMATION
Stadium (year opened): Rogers Centre (1989). **Team Colors:** Blue and white.

Player Representative: Unavailable. **Home Dugout:** Third Base. **Playing Surface:** AstroTurf Gameday 3D Synthetic Turf.

Ticket Operations

Director, Ticket Operations: Justin Hay. **Director, Ticket Services:** Sheila Stella. **Manager, Box Office:** Christina Dodge. **Manager, Ticket Operations:** Scott Hext.

Ticket Sales/Service

VP, Ticket Sales/Service: Jason Diplock. **Executive Assistant:** Stacey Jackson. **Director, Luxury Suite Sales/Service:** Mike Hook. **Director, Ticket Sales:** Franc Rota. **Manager, Group Sales:** Ryan Gustavel. **Manager, Season Ticket Services:** Erik Bobson. **Manager, Ticket Sales:** John Santana.

Travel/Clubhouse

Director, Team Travel/Clubhouse Operations: Mike Shaw. **Equipment Manager:** Jeff Ross. **Clubhouse Manager:** Kevin Malloy. **Visiting Clubhouse Manager:** Len Frejlich. **Video Operations:** Robert Baumander. **Coordinator, Advance Scouting/Video:** Ryan Mittleman. **Director, Team Employee Assistance Program:** Ray Karesky.

BASEBALL OPERATIONS

Senior VP, Baseball Operations/General Manager: Alex Anthopoulos. **VP, Baseball Operations/Assistant GM:** Tony LaCava. **Assistant GMs:** Jay Sartori, Andrew Tinnish. **Special Assistant to the GM:** Dana Brown. **Consultants:** George Bell, Cito Gaston. **Administrator, Baseball Operations:** Heather Connolly. **Baseball Information Analyst:** Joe Sheehan. **Executive Assistant to the GM:** Anna Coppola.

Alex Anthopoulos

Major League Staff

Manager: John Gibbons.

Coaches: Bench—DeMarlo Hale; **Pitching**—Pete Walker; **Hitting**—Chad Mottola; **First Base**—Dwayne Murphy; **Third Base**—Luis Rivera; **Bullpen**—Pat Hentgen.

Medical/Training

Medical Advisor: Dr. Bernie Gosevitz. **Consulting Physician:** Dr. Ron Taylor. **Consulting Team Physicians:** Dr. Irv Feferman, Dr. Noah Forman. **Head Trainer:** George Poulis. **Assistant Trainer:** Mike Frostad. **Strength/Conditioning Coordinator:** Bryan King.

Player Development

Telephone: (727) 734-8007. **Fax:** (727) 734-8162.

Director, Minor League Operations: Charlie Wilson. **Senior Advisor, Player Development:** Tim Leiper. **Minor League Field Coordinator:** Doug Davis. **Senior Roving Instructor:** Rich Miller. **Roving Instructors:** Dane Johnson (pitching), Mike Barnett (hitting), Mike Mordecai (infield), Tim Raines (outfield/baserunning), Sal Fasano (catching). **Rehab Pitching Coach:** Rick Langford. **Latin Affairs Coordinator:** Omar Malave. **Minor League Coordinators:** Jeff Stevenson (rehab), Donovan Santas (strength/conditioning), Chris Joyner (assistant strength/conditioning), Billy Wardlow (equipment). **Consultant:** Sandy Alomar Sr. **Baseball Assistant:** Megan Evans. **Assistant, Latin American Administration:** Blake Bentley. **Assistant, Player Development:** Mike Nielsen. Administrative Assistant: Kim Marsh.

Farm System

Class	Club (League)	Manager	Hitting Coach	Pitching Coach
Triple-A	Buffalo (IL)	Marty Brown	Jon Nunnally	Bob Stanley
Double-A	New Hampshire (EL)	Gary Allenson	Richie Hebner	Tom Signore
High A	Dunedin (FSL)	Bob Meacham	Stubby Clapp	Darold Knowles
Low A	Lansing (MWL)	John Tamargo Jr.	Kenny Graham	Vince Horsman
Short-season	Vancouver (NWL)	Clayton McCullough	Dave Pano	Jim Czajkowski
Rookie	Bluefield (APP)	Dennis Holmberg	Ken Huckaby	Antonio Caceres
Rookie	Blue Jays (GCL)	John Schneider	Paul Elliott	Dave Williams
Rookie	Blue Jays (DSL)	Cesar Martin	Luis Hurtado	Rafael Lazo/Oswald Peraza

Scouting

Director, Professional Scouting: Perry Minasian. **Director, Amateur Scouting:** Brian Parker. **Special Assistant, Amateur Scouting:** Chuck LaMar. **Coordinator, Professional Scouting:** Pete Holmes. **Coordinators, Amateur Scouting:** Harry Einbinder, Matt Bishoff. **Special Assignment Scout:** Russ Bove. **Major League Scouts:** Jim Beattie, Sal Butera, Ed Lynch, Jim Skaalen. **Senior Advisor/Professional Scout:** Mel Didier. **Professional Crosscheckers:** Kevin Briand, Jon Lalonde. **Professional Scouts:** Mike Alberts, Matt Anderson, Jon Bunnell, Steve Connelly, Kimball Crossley, C.J. Ebarb, Bob Fontaine, Kevin Fox, Bryan Lambe, Ted Lekas, Nick Manno, Brad Matthews, David May Jr, Steve Springer, Doug Witt.

Amateur Crosscheckers: Blake Davis, Dean Decillis, Mike Mangan, Tom Burns, Steve Miller, Tim Rooney, Rob St Julien. **Area Scouts:** Joey Aversa (Fountain Valley, CA), Coulson Barbiche (Columbus, OH), Darold Brown (Elk Grove, CA), Mike Burns (Houston, TX), Dan Cox (Santa Ana, CA), Blake Crosby (Gilbert, AZ), Ryan Fox (Yakima, WA), Bobby Gandolfo (Lansdale, PA), Joel Grampietro (Tampa, FL), John Hendricks (Mocksville, NC), Jeff Johnson (Denver, CO), Brian Johnston (Baton Rouge, LA), Randy Kramer (Aptos, CA), Jim Lentine (San Clemente, CA), Mike Medici (Naperville, IL), Nate Murrie (Bowling Green, KY), Matt O'Brien (Clermont, FL), Cliff Pastornicky (Birmingham, AL), Wes Penick (Clive, IA), Michael Pesce (New Hyde Park, NY), Jorge Rivera (Puerto Nuevo, PR), Mike Tidick (Statesboro, GA), Darin Vaughan (Tulsa, OK), Michael Wagner (Addison, TX). **Special Assistant, Latin American Operations:** Ismael Cruz. **Director, Dominican Republic:** Jose Rosario. **Director, Venezuela:** Luis Marquez. **Canada Scouts:** Jamie Lehman (Brampton, ON), Don Cowan (Delta, BC). **International Scouts:** Jairo Castillo (East, DR), Jose Contreras (Oriente, VZ), Ruban Contreras (Santo Domingo, DR), Martin Crespo (Panama City, PN), Luciano del Rosario (San Pedro, DR), Juan Garcia (Oriente, VZ), Rafael Moncada (San Diego Valencia, VZ), Lorenzo Perez (Manoguayabo, DR), Daniel Sotelo (Managua, Nicaragua), Marino Tejada (Santo Domingo, DR), Carlos Villalobos (Costa Atlantica, CO).

Washington Nationals

Office Address: 1500 South Capitol Street SE, Washington, DC 20003.
Telephone: (202) 640-7000. **Fax:** (202) 547-0025.
Website: www.nationals.com.

Ownership
Managing Principal Owner: Theodore Lerner.
Principal Owners: Annette Lerner, Mark Lerner, Marla Lerner Tanenbaum, Debra Lerner Cohen, Robert Tanenbaum, Edward Cohen, Judy Lenkin Lerner.

BUSINESS OPERATIONS
Chief Operating Officer, Lerner Sports: Alan Gottlieb. **COO:** Andrew Feffer. **Senior Vice President, Administration:** Elise Holman. **VP, Government/Municipal Affairs:** Gregory McCarthy. **Senior Director, Client Services/Special Projects:** Britton Stackhouse Miller.

Business Affairs/Legal
VP, Ballpark Enterprises/Guest Services: Catherine Silver. **Director, Ballpark Enterprises:** Maggie Gessner. **Director, Guest Services/Hospitality Operations:** Jonathan Stahl. **Senior Manager, Guest Services** Maurice Ruffin. **VP/Managing Director, Corporate Partnerships/ Business Development:** John Knebel. **Director, Corporate Partnerships:** Allen Hermeling. **Director, Sponsorship Activation:** Kevin Hill. **Senior Manager, Corporate Partnerships:** Samuel Cole.
VP/General Counsel: Damon Jones. **Deputy General Counsel:** Amy Inlander Minniti. **Executive Assistant:** Helena Wise.

Ted Lerner

Finance/Human Resources
Chief Financial Officer: Lori Creasy. **VP, Finance:** Ted Towne. **Director, Accounting:** Kelly Pitchford. **Senior Accountants:** Ross Hollander, Michael Page, Rachel Proctor. **VP, Human Resources:** Alexa Herndon. **Director, Benefits:** Stephanie Giroux. **Manager, Human Resources:** Alan Gromest. **Assistant, Human Resources:** Lynleigh Johnson.

Media Relations/Communications
Senior Director, Baseball Information: John Dever. **Director, Baseball Media Relations:** Mike Gazda. **Coordinator, Baseball Media Relations:** Kyle Brostowitz. **VP/Managing Director, Communications/Brand Development:** Lara Potter. **Director, Creative Services/New Media:** Chad Kurz. **Director, Communications:** Joanna Comfort. **Manager, Communications:** Alexandra Schauffler.

Community Relations
Senior Director, Community Relations: Shawn Bertani. **Manager, Community Relations:** Nicole Murray. **Coordinator, Community Relations:** Kyle Mann.

Marketing/Broadcasting
VP, Marketing/Broadcasting: John Guagliano. **Executive Director, Production/Entertainment/Promotions:**

2013 SCHEDULE
Standard Game Times: 7:05 p.m.; Sun. 1:35

APRIL		
1 . . . . .Miami	10-12 . . . . . Chicago (NL)	25-27 . . . . .Arizona
3-4. . . . . .Miami	13-15 . at Los Angeles (NL)	28-30 . . . at New York (NL)
5-7. . . . . . .at Cincinnati	16-19 . . . . . at San Diego	**JULY**
9-11 . . . . Chicago (AL)	20-22 . . . at San Francisco	1-4. . . . . .Milwaukee
12-14 . . . . Atlanta	24-26 . . . . . .Philadelphia	5-7. . . . . San Diego
15-17 . . . . at Miami	27-28 . . . . Baltimore	8-11 . . . . at Philadelphia
19-21 . . at New York (NL)	29-30 . . . . . .at Baltimore	12-14 . . . . .at Miami
22-24 . . . . St. Louis	31 . . . . at Atlanta	19-21 . . .Los Angeles (NL)
25-28 . . . . . Cincinnati	**JUNE**	22-25 . . . . Pittsburgh
29-30 . . . . at Atlanta	1-2. . . . . at Atlanta	26-28 . . . .New York (NL)
MAY	4-6. . . . . .New York (NL)	30-31 . . . . . . .at Detroit
1-2. . . . . at Atlanta	7-9. . . . . . . .Minnesota	**AUGUST**
3-5. . . . . . at Pittsburgh	11-13 . . . . . at Colorado	2-4. . . . . . at Milwaukee
7-8. . . . . Detroit	14-16 . . . . .at Cleveland	5-7. . . . . Atlanta
	17-19 . . . . at Philadelphia	9-11 . . . . . .Philadelphia
	20-23 . . . . . . .Colorado	

13-15 . . . . .San Francisco	
16-18 . . . . . . at Atlanta	
19-22 . . .at Chicago (NL)	
23-25 . . . .at Kansas City	
27-29 . . . . .Miami	
30-31 . . . .New York (NL)	
SEPTEMBER	
1 . . . . . . .New York (NL)	
2-4. . . . . . .at Philadelphia	
6-8. . . . . at Miami	
9-12 . . . at New York (NL)	
13-15 . . . . . .Philadelphia	
16-18 . . . . Atlanta	
19-22 . . . . .Miami	
23-25 . . . . . .at St. Louis	
27-29 . . . . . . at Arizona	

GENERAL INFORMATION
Stadium (year opened): Nationals Park (2008).
Team Colors: Red, white and blue.

Player Representative: Unavailable.
Home Dugout: First Base.
Playing Surface: Grass.

Jacqueline Coleman. **Director, Consumer Marketing:** Scott Lewis. **Manager, Promotions/Events:** Amanda Hauge. **Manager, Production/Operations:** Dave Lundin. **Producer:** Benjamin Smith. **Editor:** Mark Jackson. **Senior Designer:** Lisa Grondines. **Copy Editor/New Media Manager:** Noah Frank. **Copywriter:** Mike Feigen

Ticketing/Sales

VP/Managing Director, Sales/Client Services: Chris Gargani. **Director, Ticket Sales:** David McElwee. **Senior Director, Ticket Operations:** Tom Jackson. **Director, Ticket Operations:** Derek Younger. **Manager, Box Office:** Tyler Hubbard. **Senior Account Executive, Group Sales:** Brian Beck. **Senior Account Executive, Ticket Sales:** Katherine Mitchell, Kevin Nawrocki. **Manager, Sales Development:** Rob Erwin. **Manager, Premium Sales:** Michael Shane. **Senior Manager, Ticket Services:** Andy Burns. **Manager, Client Services:** Richard Medina.

Ballpark Operations

VP, Facilities: Frank Gambino. **Senior Manager, Ballpark Operations:** Adam Lasky. **Head Groundskeeper:** John Turnour. **Assistant Head Groundskeeper:** Mike Hrivnak. **Assistant Groundskeeper:** Matt Coates. **Director, Security:** Dennis Maroney. **Assistant Manager, Security:** Kathleen Costello. **Director, Engineering Operations:** James Pantazis.

BASEBALL OPERATIONS

Executive VP/General Manager: Mike Rizzo.

Mike Rizzo

Assistant GM: Bryan Minniti. **Special Assistant to GM, Major League Administration:** Harolyn Cardozo. **Senior Advisor to GM:** Phillip Rizzo. **VP, Clubhouse Operations/Team Travel:** Rob McDonald. **Director, Baseball Operations:** Adam Cromie. **Analyst, Baseball Operations:** Sam Mondry-Cohen. **Assistant, Baseball Operations:** Aron Weston. **Assistant, Scouting:** Eddie Longosz. **Coordinator, Advance Scouting:** Erick Dalton. **Assistant, Advance Scouting:** Christopher Rosenbaum.

Major League Staff

Manager: Davey Johnson.
Coaches: Bench—Randy Knorr; **Pitching**—Steve McCatty; **Hitting**—Rick Eckstein; **First Base**—Tony Tarasco; **Third Base**—Trent Jewett; **Bullpen**—Jim Lett.

Medical/Training

Team Medical Director: Dr. Wiemi Douoguih. **Head Trainer:** Lee Kuntz. **Assistant Trainer:** Steve Gober. **Strength/Conditioning Coach:** John Philbin. **Assistant, Strength/Conditioning:** Matt Eiden. **Assistant, Medical Staff:** John Hsu.

Player Development

Assistant GM/VP, Player Development: Bob Boone.
Director, Player Development: Doug Harris. **Director, Minor League Operations:** Mark Scialabba. **Assistant Director, Minor League Operations:** Ryan Thomas. **Director, Florida Operations:** Thomas Bell. **Manager, Florida Operations:** Jonathan Tosches. **Administrative Assistant, Florida Operations:** Dianne Wiebe. **Dominican Republic Academy Administrator:** Fausto Severino.
Coordinators: Bobby Henley (field), Spin Williams (pitching), Rick Schu (hitting), Jeff Garber (infield), Gary Thurman (outfield/baserunning), Gary Cathcart (instruction), Mark Grater (rehab pitching), Mike McGowan (medical/rehab), Landon Brandes (strength/conditioning). **Manager, Minor League Equipment/Clubhouse:** Calvin Minasian.

Farm System

Class	Club	Manager	Coach(es)	Pitching Coach
Triple-A	Syracuse (IL)	Tony Beasley	Troy Gingrich	Greg Booker
Double-A	Harrisburg (EL)	Matt LeCroy	Eric Fox	Paul Menhart
High A	Potomac (CL)	Brian Daubach	Mark Harris	Chris Michalak
Low A	Hagerstown (SAL)	Tripp Keister	Brian Rupp	Franklin Bravo
Short-season	Auburn (NYP)	Gary Cathcart	Luis Ordaz	Sam Narron
Rookie	Nationals (GCL)	Patrick Anderson	Amaury Garcia	Michael Tejera

Scouting

Assistant GM/VP, Player Personnel: Roy Clark.
Director, Scouting: Kris Kline. **Director, Pro Scouting:** Bill Singer. **Director, Player Procurement:** Kasey McKeon. **Special Assistants to GM:** Chuck Cottier, Bob Johnson, Deric Ladnier, Ron Rizzi, Jay Robertson, Bob Schaefer. **Professional Scout:** Mike Daughtry. **Crosscheckers:** Mark Baca, Jimmy Gonzales, Jeff Zona. **Area Supervisors:** Steve Arnieri (Barrington, IL), Fred Costello (Livermore, CA), Reed Dunn (Nashville, TN), Paul Faulk (Myrtle Beach, SC), Ben Gallo (Encinitas, CA) Ed Gustafson (Denton, TX), John Malzone (Needham, MA), Alex Morales (Wellington, FL), Tim Reynolds (Irvine, CA), Eric Robinson (Acworth, GA), Mitch Sokol (Phoenix, AZ), Paul Tinnell (Bradenton, FL), Tyler Wilt (Willis, TX). **Part-Time Area Scouts:** Ray Blano (Miami, FL), Bobby Myrick (Colonial Heights, VA). **Director, Latin American Operations:** Johnny DiPuglia. **Dominican Republic Scouting Supervisor:** Moises De La Mota. **Venezuela Scouting Supervisor:** German Robles.
International Scouts: Modesto Ulloa (Dominican Republic). **Part-Time Scouts:** Pablo Arias (Dominican Republic), Carlos Ulloa (Dominican Republic), Juan Munoz (Venezuela), Salvador Donadelli (Venezuela), Eduardo Rosario (Venezuela), Caryl Van Zanten (Curacao), Miguel Ruiz (Panama).

MEDIA
INFORMATION

LOCAL MEDIA INFORMATION

AMERICAN LEAGUE

BALTIMORE ORIOLES
Radio Announcers: Joe Angel, Fred Manfra. **Flagship Station:** WBAL Radio 1090 AM.
TV Announcers: Mike Bordick, Jim Hunter, Jim Palmer, Gary Thorne. **Flagship Station:** Mid-Atlantic Sports Network (MASN).

BOSTON RED SOX
Radio Announcers: Joe Castiglione, Dave O'Brien. **Flagship Station:** WEEI (850 AM).
TV Announcers: Don Orsillo, Jerry Remy. **Flagship Station:** New England Sports Network (regional cable). **Spanish Radio Announcers:** Oscar Baez, Uri Berenguer. **Flagship Station:** WWZN (1510 AM).

CHICAGO WHITE SOX
Radio Announcers: Ed Farmer, Darrin Jackson, Chris Rongey. **Flagship Station:** WSCR The Score 670-AM.
TV Announcers: Ken Harrelson, Steve Stone. **Flagship Stations:** WGN TV-9, WCIU-TV, Comcast SportsNet Chicago (regional cable).

CLEVELAND INDIANS
Radio Announcers: Tom Hamilton, Jim Rosenhaus. **Flagship Station:** WTAM 1100-AM.
TV Announcers: Rick Manning, Matt Underwood. **Flagship Station:** SportsTime Ohio.

DETROIT TIGERS
Radio Announcers: Dan Dickerson, Jim Price. **Flagship Station:** WXYT 97.1 FM and AM 1270.
TV Announcers: Rod Allen, Mario Impemba. **Flagship Station:** FOX Sports Detroit (regional cable).

HOUSTON ASTROS
Radio Announcers: Brett Dolan, Dave Raymond. **Spanish:** Alex Trevino, Francisco Romero. **Flagship Stations:** KTRH 740-AM, KLAT 1010-AM (Spanish).
TV Announcers: Bill Brown, Jim Deshaies. **Flagship Station:** Fox Sports Net.

KANSAS CITY ROYALS
Radio Announcers: Denny Matthews, Steve Physioc, Steve Stewart. **Kansas City affiliate:** KCSP 610-AM.
TV Announcers: Ryan Lefebvre, Rex Hudler, Joel Goldberg. **Flagship Station:** FOX Sports Kansas City.

LOS ANGELES ANGELS
Radio Announcers: Terry Smith, Mark Langston. **Spanish:** Jose Mota, Amaury Pi-Gonzalez. **Flagship Station:** AM 830, 1330 KWKW (Spanish).
TV Announcers: Victor Rojas, Mark Gubicza. **Flagship Stations:** Fox Sports West (regional cable).

MINNESOTA TWINS
Radio Announcers: Cory Provus, Dan Gladden. **Radio Network Studio Host:** Kris Atteberry. **Radio Engineer:** Kyle Hammer. **Spanish Radio Play-by-Play:** Alfonso Fernandez. **Flagship Station:** 1500 ESPN.
TV Announcers: Bert Blyleven, Dick Bremer. **Flagship Station:** Fox Sports North.

NEW YORK YANKEES
Radio Announcers: John Sterling, Suzyn Waldman. **Flagship Station:** WCBS 880-AM. **Spanish Radio Announcers:** Beto Villa, Francisco Rivera.
TV Announcers: David Cone, Jack Curry, John Flaherty, Michael Kay, Al Leiter, Bob Lorenz, Meredith Marakovits, Paul O'Neill, Ken Singleton. **Flagship Station:** YES Network (Yankees Entertainment & Sports).

OAKLAND ATHLETICS
Radio Announcers: Vince Cotroneo, Ken Korach. **Flagship Station:** KGMZ 95.7 The Game, FM.
TV Announcers: Ray Fosse, Glen Kuiper. **Flagship Stations:** Comcast Sports Net California.

SEATTLE MARINERS
Radio Announcers: Rick Rizzs. **Flagship Station:** KOMO 1000-AM.
TV Announcers: Mike Blowers, Dave Simms. **Flagship Station:** FOX Sports Net Northwest.

TAMPA BAY RAYS
Radio Announcers: Andy Freed, Dave Wills. **Flagship Station:** Sports Animal WDAE 620 AM.
TV Announcers: Brian Anderson, Dewayne Staats, Todd Kalas. **Flagship Station:** Sun Sports.

TEXAS RANGERS
Radio Announcers: Eric Nadel, Matt Hicks; **Spanish**—Eleno Ornelas, Benji Gil. **Flagship Station:** KESN 103.3 FM, KZMP 1540 AM (Spanish).
TV Announcers: Steve Busby, Tom Grieve; Spanish—Victor Villalba, Jose Guzman. **Flagship Stations:** Fox Sports Southwest (regional cable), TXA 21 (Fridays), Time Warner (Spanish).

TORONTO BLUE JAYS
Radio Announcers: Jerry Howarth, Mike Wilner. **Flagship Station:** SportsNet Radio Fan 590-AM.
TV Announcers: Buck Martinez, Pat Tabler. **Flagship Station:** Rogers Sportsnet.

NATIONAL LEAGUE

ARIZONA DIAMONDBACKS
Radio Announcers: Greg Schulte, Tom Candiotti, Jeff Munn, Mike Fetters, Miguel Quintana (Spanish), Oscar Soria (Spanish), Richard Saenz (Spanish). **Flagship Stations:** KTAR 620-AM & ESPN DEPORTES 710-AM (Spanish).
TV Announcers: Steve Berthiaume, Bob Brenly, Luis Gonzalez, Joe Garagiola Sr. **Flagship Stations:** FOX Sports Arizona (regional cable).

ATLANTA BRAVES
Radio Announcers: Jim Powell, Don Sutton. **Flagship Stations:** WCNN-AM 680, The Fan (93.7 FM), WNNX-FM (100.5).
TV Announcers: Chip Caray, Joe Simpson. **Flagship Stations:** FS South and SportSouth (regional cable).

CHICAGO CUBS
Radio Announcers: Pat Hughes, Keith Moreland. **Flagship Station:** WGN 720-AM.
TV Announcers: Len Kasper, Jim Deshaies. **Flagship Stations:** WGN Channel 9 (national cable), Comcast Sports Net Chicago (regional cable), WCIU-TV Channel 26.

CINCINNATI REDS
Radio Announcers: Marty Brennaman, Thom Brennaman, Jeff Brantley, Jim Kelch. **Flagship Station:** WLW 700-AM.
TV Announcers: Chris Welsh, Thom Brennaman, Jeff Brantley. **Flagship Station:** Fox Sports Ohio (regional cable).

COLORADO ROCKIES
Radio Announcers: Jack Corrigan, Jerry Schemmel. **Flagship Station:** KOA 850-AM.
TV Announcers: Drew Goodman, George Frazier, Jeff Huson.

LOS ANGELES DODGERS
Radio Announcers: Vin Scully, Rick Monday, Charley Steiner. **Spanish:** Jaime Jarrín, Fernando Valenzuela, Pepe Yñiguez. **Flagship Stations:** AM570 Fox Sports LA, KTNQ 1020-AM (Spanish).
TV Announcers: Vin Scully, Steve Lyons, Eric Collins. **Flagship Stations:** KCAL 9, PRIME TICKET (regional cable).

MIAMI MARLINS
Radio Announcers: Dave Van Horne, Glenn Geffner. **Flagship Stations:** WAXY 790-AM, WAQI 710-AM (Spanish).
Spanish Radio Announcers: Felo Ramirez, Yiky Quintana.
TV Announcers: Tommy Hutton, Rich Waltz, Jeff Conine, Frank Forte, Craig Minervini, Allison Williams, Preston Wilson, Cliff Floyd. **Spanish TV Announcers:** Cookie Rojas, Raul Striker Jr. **Flagship Stations:** FSN Florida (regional cable).

MILWAUKEE BREWERS
Radio Announcers: Bob Uecker, Joe Black. **Flagship Station:** WTMJ 620-AM.
TV Announcers: Bill Schroeder, Brian Anderson. **Flagship Station:** Fox Sports Net North.

NEW YORK METS
Radio Announcers: Howie Rose, Josh Lewin, Ed Coleman. **Flagship Station:** WFAN 660-AM.
TV Announcers: Gary Cohen, Keith Hernandez, Ron Darling, Ralph Kiner, Kevin Burkhardt. **Flagship Stations:** PIX11-TV, Sports Net New York (regional cable).

PHILADELPHIA PHILLIES
Radio Announcers: Larry Andersen, Scott Franzke, Jim Jackson. **Flagship Stations:** WPHT 1210-AM.
TV Announcers: Tom McCarthy, Gary Matthews, Chris Wheeler. **Flagship Stations:** WPHL PHL17, Comcast SportsNet (regional cable).

PITTSBURGH PIRATES
Radio Announcers: Steve Blass, Greg Brown, Tim Neverett, Bob Walk, John Wehner. **Flagship Station:** Sports Radio 93.7 FM The Fan.
TV Announcers: Steve Blass, Greg Brown, Tim Neverett, Bob Walk, John Wehner. **Flagship Station:** ROOT SPORTS (regional cable).

ST. LOUIS CARDINALS
Radio Announcers: Mike Shannon, John Rooney. **Flagship Station:** KMOX 1120 AM.
TV Announcers: Rick Horton, Al Hrabosky, Dan McLaughlin. **Flagship Stations:** Fox Sports Midwest.

SAN DIEGO PADRES
Radio Announcers: Jerry Coleman, Ted Leitner, Andy Masur, Bob Scanlan. **Flagship Station:** XX Sports Radio 1090-AM/ESPN 1700-AM.
TV Announcers: Dick Enberg, Mark Grant, Tony Gwynn. **Flagship Station:** Fox Sports San Diego.

SAN FRANCISCO GIANTS
Radio Announcers: Mike Krukow, Duane Kuiper, Jon Miller, Dave Flemming. **Spanish:** Tito Fuentes, Erwin Higueros. **Flagship Station:** KNBR 680-AM (English); ESPN Deportes-860AM (Spanish).
TV Announcers: CSN Bay Area—Mike Krukow, Duane Kuiper; **KNTV-NBC 11**—Jon Miller, Mike Krukow. **Flagship Stations:** KNTV-NBC 11, CSN Bay Area (regional cable).

WASHINGTON NATIONALS
Radio Announcers: Charlie Slowes, Dave Jageler. **Flagship Station:** WJFK 106.7 FM.
TV Announcers: Bob Carpenter, FP Santangelo. **Flagship Station:** Mid-Atlantic Sports Network (MASN).

NATIONAL MEDIA INFORMATION

BASEBALL STATISTICS

ELIAS SPORTS BUREAU INC. NATIONAL MEDIA BASEBALL STATISTICS Official Major League Statistician

Mailing Address: 500 Fifth Ave., Suite 2140, New York, NY 10110. **Telephone:** (212) 869-1530. **Fax:** (212) 354-0980. **Website:** www.esb.com.

President: Seymour Siwoff.

Executive Vice President: Steve Hirdt. **Vice President:** Peter Hirdt. **Data Processing Manager:** Chris Thorn.

MAJOR LEAGUE BASEBALL ADVANCED MEDIA Official Minor League Statistician

Mailing Address: 75 Ninth Ave., New York, NY 10011. **Telephone:** (212) 485-3444. **Fax:** (212) 485-3456. **Website:** MiLB.com.

Assistant Director, Stats Operation: Chris Lentine. **Managers of Stats:** Shawn Geraghty, Ian Schwartz. **Stats Supervisors:** Nicole Burdett, Jason Rigatti.

MiLB.COM Official Website of Minor League Baseball

Mailing Address: 75 Ninth Ave, New York, NY 10011. **Telephone:** (212) 485-3444. **Fax:** (212) 485-3456. **Website:** MiLB.com.

Senior Editorial Manager, MiLB.com: Brendon Desrochers. **Director, Minor League Club Initiatives:** Nathan Blackmon. **Club Producers:** Dan Marinis, Danny Wild. **Columnist:** Ben Hill.

STATS

Mailing Address: 2775 Shermer Road, Northbrook, IL 60062. **Telephone:** (847) 583-2100. **Fax:** (847) 470-9140. **Website:** www.stats.com. **Email:** sales@stats.com. **Twitter:** twitter.com/STATSBiznews, twitter.com/STATS_MLB. **CEO:** Gary Walrath. **Executive Vice Presidents:** Steve Byrd, Robert Schur. **Senior Vice President, Sales:** Greg Kirkorsky. **Vice President, Strategic Planning:** Brian Kopp. **Assistant Vice President, Sports Operations:** Allan Spear. **Manager, Baseball Operations:** Jeff Chernow. **Director, Marketing and Communications:** Nick Stamm.

TELEVISION NETWORKS

ESPN/ESPN2

Mailing Address, ESPN Connecticut: ESPN Plaza, Bristol, CT 06010. **Telephone:** (860) 766-2000. **Fax:** (860) 766-2213.

Mailing Address, ESPN New York Executive Offices: 77 W 66th St, New York, NY, 10023. **Telephone:** (212) 456-7777. **Fax:** (212) 456-2930.

Executive Chairman, ESPN, Inc.: George Bodenheimer.

President: John Skipper. **Executive VP, Administration:** Ed Durso. **Executive VP, Content:** Vinnie Malhorta. **Executive VP, Production:** Norby Williamson. **Executive VP, News/Talent/Content Operations:** Steve Anderson. **Senior VP, Programming/Acquisitions:** Carol Stiff. **Senior VP, Production:** Mark Gross. **Senior VP/Executive Producer, Production:** Jed Drake. **Coordinating Producer, Event Production:** Matt Sandulli. **Senior Coordinating Producer, Baseball Tonight:** Jay Levy. **Senior VP, Operations:** Jodi Markley.

Email: Kristen.M.Hudak@espn.com Kristen Hudak, Senior Publicist, Communications

ESPN CLASSIC, ESPNEWS

VP, Strategic Program Planning: John Papa.

ESPN INTERNATIONAL, ESPN DEPORTES

Executive VP/Managing Director, ESPN International: Russell Wolff.

Senior VP, ESPN Deportes: Traug Keller. **General Manager, ESPN Deportes:** Lino Garcia. **VP, ESPN Deportes, Programming:** Freddy Rolon.

FOX SPORTS

Mailing Address, Los Angeles: Fox Network Center, Building 101, Fifth floor, 10201 West Pico Blvd., Los Angeles, CA 90035. **Telephone:** (310) 369-6000. **Fax:** (310) 969-6700.

Mailing Address, New York: 1211 Avenue of the Americas, 20th Floor, New York, NY 10036. **Telephone:** (212) 556-2500. **Fax:** (212) 354-6902. **Website:** www.foxsports.com.

Chairman/CEO, Fox Sports Media Group: David Hill. **Vice Chairman, Fox Sports Media Group:** Ed Goren. **Co-Presidents/Co-COOs:** Randy Freer, Eric Shanks. **Executive VP, Production/Coordinating Studio Producer:** Scott Ackerson. **Executive VP, Production/Field Operations:** Bill Brown. **Executive VP, Programming/Production:** George Greenberg. **Executive VP/Creative Director:** Gary Hartley. **Senior VP, Production:** John Entz. **Senior VP, Prodution:** Jack Simmons. **Senior VP, Field/Technical Opearations, MLB on Fox:** Jerry Steinberg. **Coordinating Producer, MLB on Fox:** Pete Macheska. **Director, Game Production, MLB on Fox:** Bill Webb. **Senior VP, Media Relations:** Lou D'Ermilio. **VP, Communications:** Dan Bell. **Director, Communications:** Ileana Pena. **Publicist:** Eddie Motl.

MLB NETWORK

Mailing Address: 40 Hartz Way, Suite 10, Secaucus, NJ 07094. **Telephone:** (201) 520-6400.

President/CEO: Tony Petitti. **Executive VP, Advertising/Sales:** Bill Morningstar. **Senior VP, Marketing/Promotion:** Mary Beck. **Senior VP, Distribution/Affiliate Sales/Marketing:** Art Marquez. **Senior VP, Programming/Business Affairs:** Rob McGlarry. **Senior VP, Finance/Administration:** Tony Santomauro. **VP, Programming:** Andy Butters. **VP, Engineering/I.T.:** Mark Haden. **VP, Operations/Engineering:** Susan Stone. **Director, Remote Operations:** Tom Guidice. **Director, Studio Operations:** Karen Whritner. **VP, Business Public Relations, Major League Baseball:** Matt Bourne. **Manager, Business Public Relations/Entertainment/Major League Baseball:** Lauren Verrusio.

MAJOR LEAGUES

TURNER SPORTS
Mailing Address: 1015 Techwood Drive, Atlanta, GA 30318. **Telephone:** (404) 827-1700. **Fax:** (404) 827-1339. **Website:** www.tbs.com/sports/mlb.
President: David Levy. **Senior VP, Executive Producer:** Jeff Behnke. **Executive VP, Chief Operating Officer:** Lenny Daniels. **Senior VP, Turner Sports Strategy/Marketing/Programming:** Christina Miller. **Senior VP, Creative/Content:** Craig Barry. **VP, Sports Program Planning:** John Vandegrift. **Executive VP, Turner Sports Ad Sales/Marketing:** Jon Diament. **VP, Production:** Howard Zalkowitz. **Coordinating Producer, MLB:** Glenn Diamond. **Senior VP, Public Relations:** Sal Petruzzi. **Publicist:** Eric Welch.

FOX SPORTS NET
Mailing Address: 10201 W Pico Blvd., Building 103, Los Angeles, CA 90035. **Telephone:** (310) 369-1000. **Fax:** (310) 969-6049.
Chairman/CEO, Fox Sports Media Group: David Hill. **President, Fox National Cable Networks:** Bob Thompson. **President, Fox Regional Cable Sports Networks:** Randy Freer. **Senior VP, Media Relations:** Lou D'Ermilio. **Senior VP, Fox Sports Net/Editor-in-Chief, Fox Sports Interactive Media:** Rick Jaffe.

OTHER TELEVISION NETWORKS

CBS SPORTS
Mailing Address: 51 W 52nd St., New York, NY 10019. **Telephone:** (212) 975-5230. **Fax:** (212) 975-4063.
Chairman: Sean McManus. **Executive VP:** David Berson. **Executive VPs, Programming:** Mike Aresco, Rob Correa. **Executive Producer/VP, Production:** Harold Bryant. **Senior VP, Communications:** LeslieAnne Wade.

CNN SPORTS
Mailing Address: One CNN Center, Atlanta, GA 30303. **Telephone:** (404) 878-1600. **Fax:** (404) 878-0011.
Vice President, Production: Jeffrey Green.

HBO SPORTS
Mailing Address: 1100 Avenue of the Americas, New York, NY 10036. **Telephone:** (212) 512-1000. **Fax:** (212) 512-1751. **President, HBO Sports:** Ken Hershman.

NBC SPORTS
Mailing Address: 30 Rockefeller Plaza, Suite 1558, New York, NY 10112. **Telephone:** (212) 664-2014. **Fax:** (212) 664-6365.
Chairman: Mark Lazarus. **President:** Jon Litner. **President, Programing:** Jonathan Miller. **Executive Producer:** Sam Flood. **Senior VP, Communications:** Greg Hughes.

ROGERS SPORTSNET (Canada)
Mailing Address: 9 Channel Nine Court, Toronto, ON M1S 4B5. **Telephone:** (416) 332-5600. **Fax:** (416) 332-5629. **Website:** www.sportsnet.ca.
President, Rogers Media: Keith Pelley. **President, Rogers Sportsnet:** Scott Moore. **Director, Communications/Promotions:** Dave Rashford.

THE SPORTS NETWORK (Canada)
Mailing Address: 9 Channel Nine Court, Toronto, ON M1S 4B5. **Telephone:** (416) 384-5000. **Fax:** (416) 332-4337. **Website:** www.tsn.ca.

RADIO NETWORKS

ESPN RADIO
Address: ESPN Plaza, 935 Middle St., Bristol, CT 06010. **Telephone:** (860) 766-2000, (800) 999-9985. **Fax:** (860) 589-5523. **Website:** espnradio.espn.go.com/espnradio/index.
GM, ESPN Radio Network: Mo Davenport. **Senior Director, Content:** Scott Masteller. **Senior Director, Operations/Events:** Keith Goralski. **Senior Director, Radio Content/Operations:** Peter Gianesini. **Senior Director, ESPN Deportes Radio:** Freddy Rolon. **Executive Producer:** John Martin. **Senior Director, Engineering:** Kevin Plumb. **Executive Director, Affiliate Relations:** Jim Roberts.

SIRIUS XM SATELLITE RADIO
Mailing Address: 1500 Eckington Place NE, Washington, DC 20002. **Telephone:** (202) 380-4000. **Fax:** 202-380-4500. **Hotline:** (866) 652-6696. **E-Mail Address:** mlb@siriusxm.com. **Website:** www.siriusxm.com.
President/Chief Content Officer: Scott Greenstein. **Senior VP, Sports:** Steve Cohen. **VP, Sports:** Brian Hamilton. **Director, MLB programming:** Chris Eno. **Senior Director, Communications/Sports Programming:** Andrew Fitzpatrick

SPORTS BYLINE USA
Mailing Address: 300 Broadway, Suite 8, San Francisco, CA 94133. **Telephone:** (415) 434-8300. **Guest Line:** (800) 358-4457. **Studio Line:** (800) 878-7529. **Fax:** (415) 391-2569. **E-Mail Address:** editor@sportsbyline.com. **Website:** www.sportsbyline.com. **President:** Darren Peck. **Executive Producer:** Ira Hankin.

YAHOO SPORTS RADIO
Mailing Address: 5353 West Alabama Street, Suite 415, Houston, TX 77056. **Telephone:** (800) 224-2004. **Fax:** (713) 479-5333 . **E-Mail Address formula:** first initial, last name@yahoosportsradio.com. **Website:** www.yahoosportsradio.com.
CEO: David Gow. **CMO:** Graham McKernan. **Senior Programming Director:** Craig Larson.

GENERAL INFORMATION

MAJOR LEAGUE BASEBALL PLAYERS ASSOCIATION

Mailing Address: 12 E. 49th St., 24th Floor, New York, NY 10017. **Telephone:** (212) 826-0808. **Fax:** (212) 752-4378. **E-Mail Address:** feedback@mlbpa.org. **Website:** www.mlbplayers.com.

Year Founded: 1966. **Twitter:** @MLB_Players.

Executive Director: Michael Weiner.

General Counsel: David Prouty. **Senior Advisor:** Rick Shapiro. **Assistant General Counsels:** Heather Chase, Robert Guerra, Bob Lenaghan, Matt Nussbaum. **Senior Labor Counsel:** Ian Penny. **Special Counsel:** Steve Fehr.

Director, Player Relations: Tony Clark. **Chief Administrative Officer:** Martha Child. **Chief Financial Officer:** Marietta DiCamillo. **Special Assistants to the Executive Director:** Bobby Bonilla, Phil Bradley, Rick Helling, Stan Javier, Mike Myers, Steve Rogers. **Player Relations:** Leonor Barua, Virginia Carballo, Allyne Price. **Contract Administrator:** Cindy Abercrombie. **Director, Communications:** Greg Bouris. **Director, Players Trust:** Melissa Persaud. **Accounting Assistants:** Jennifer Cooney, Terri Hinkley, Yolanda Largo. **Program Coordinator:** Hillary Caffarone. **Administrative Assistants:** Aisha Hope, Melba Markowitz, Sharon O'Donnell, Lisa Pepin. **Accounting Assistant:** Deirdre Sweeney. **Receptionist:** Rebecca Rivera.

Director, Business Affairs/Licensing/Senior Counsel, Business: Timothy Slavin. **General Manager, Business Affairs/Media/International:** Richard White. **Director, Licensing/Business Development:** Evan Kaplan. **Senior Category Director, Retail Development/Apparel/Events Director:** Nancy Willis. **Category Director, Interactive Media:** Michael Amin. **New Media Content Director:** Chris Dahl. **Licensing Manager, Hard Goods/Collectibles:** Tom Cerabino. **Licensing Manager, Apparel/Retail Development:** Paul McNeill. **Business Services Manager:** Heather Gould. **Licensing Manager, Apparel/Retail Development:** Paul McNeill. **Executive Assistant, Business Affairs:** Gretchen Mueller. **Licensing Manager:** Paul Zickler. **Licensing Assistant:** Eric Rivera. **Office Services Clerk:** Victor Lugo.

Executive Board: Player representatives of the 30 major league clubs.

MLBPA Association Representatives: Curtis Granderson, Jeremy Guthrie. **Alternate Association Representatives:** Justin Masterson, Carlos Villanueva. **MLBPA Pension Representatives:** Chris Capuano, Craig Breslow. **Alternate Pension Representatives:** Ross Ohlendorf, Kevin Slowey.

SCOUTING

MAJOR LEAGUE BASEBALL SCOUTING BUREAU

Mailing Address: 3500 Porsche Way, Suite 100, Ontario, CA 91764. **Telephone:** (909) 980-1881. **Fax:** (909) 980-7794. **Year Founded:** 1974.

Director: Frank Marcos. **Assistant Director:** Rick Oliver. **Office Coordinator:** Debbie Keedy. **Supervisor-Scouting Operations:** Adam Cali.

Scouts: Rick Arnold (Spring Mills, PA), Ty Boyles (Minneapolis, MN) Andy Campbell (Gilbert, AZ), Mike Childers (Lexington, KY), Craig Conklin (Malibu, CA), Dan Dixon (Temecula, CA), Brad Fidler (Douglassville, PA), Rusty Gerhardt (New London, TX), Dennis Haren (San Diego, CA), Chris Heidt (Rockford, IL), Don Kohler (Asbury, NJ), Mike Larson (Waseca, MN), Johnny Martinez (St Louis, MO), Paul Mirocke (Land O Lakes, FL), Carl Moesche (Gresham, OR), Tim Osborne (Woodstock, GA), Gary Randall (Rock Hill, SC), Kevin Saucier (Pensacola, FL), Harry Shelton (Ocoee, FL), Pat Shortt (South Hempstead, NY), Craig Smajstrla (Pearland, TX), Everett Stull (Northern CA), George Vranau (Simi Valley, CA), Jim Walton (Shattuck, OK).

Supervisor, Canada: Walt Burrows (Brentwood Bay, BC). **Canadian Scouts:** Jason Chee-Aloy (Toronto), Ken Lenihan (Bedford, Nova Scotia), Jasmin Roy (Longueuil, Quebec), Bob Smyth (Ladysmith, BC), Tony Wylie (Anchorage, AK).

Supervisor, Puerto Rico: Pepito Centeno (Cidra, PR). **Latin American Scouts:** Fabio Herrera (Dominican Republic), Alfredo Ulloa (Dominican Republic), Luis Perez (Venezuela), Frank Campos (Venezuela).

Video Technicians: Jabari Barnett (Phoenix, AZ), Matt Barnicle (Long Beach, CA), Rafael Castellanos (Dominican Republic), Wayne Mathis (Cuero, TX), Christie Wood (Raleigh, NC).

PROFESSIONAL BASEBALL SCOUTS FOUNDATION

Mailing Address: 5010 North Parkway Calabasas, Suite 201, Calabasas, CA 91302.

Telephone: (818) 224-3906. **Fax:** (818) 267-5516.

Website: www.probaseballscouts.com.

Mailing Address: 5010 North Parkway Calabasas, Suite 201, Calabasas, CA 91302.

Telephone: (818) 224-3906. **Fax:** (818) 267-5516

Email: cindy.pbsf@yahoo.com. **Website:** www.pbsfonline.com

Chairman: Dennis J. **Gilbert. Executive Director:** Cindy Picerni.

Board of Directors: Bill "Chief" Gayton, Pat Gillick, Derrick Hall, Roland Hemond, Gary Hughes, Jeff Idelson, Dan Jennings, J.J. Lally, Tommy Lasorda, Frank Marcos, Roberta Mazur, Harry Minor, Bob Nightengale, Tracy Ringolsby, John Scotti, Tom Sherak, Dale Sutherland, Kevin Towers, Dave Yoakum, John Young.

SCOUT OF THE YEAR FOUNDATION

Mailing Address: P.O. Box 211585, West Palm Beach, FL 33421. **Telephone:** (561) 798-5897, (561) 818-4329. **E-mail Address:** bertmazur@aol.com.

President: Roberta Mazur. **Vice President:** Tracy Ringolsby. **Treasurer:** Ron Mazur II.

Board of Advisers: Pat Gillick, Roland Hemond, Gary Hughes, Tommy Lasorda.

Scout of the Year Program Advisory Board: Tony DeMacio, Joe Klein, Roland Hemond, Gary Hughes, Dan Jennings, Linda Pereira.

UMPIRES

JIM EVANS ACADEMY OF PROFESSIONAL UMPIRING
Mailing Address: 200 South Wilcox St., #508, Castle Rock, CO 80104. **Telephone:** (303) 290-7411. **E-mail Address:** jeapu@umpireacademy.com. **Website:** www.umpireacademy.com.
Operator: Jim Evans.

PROFESSIONAL BASEBALL UMPIRE CORP
Street Address: 9550 16th Street North, St. Petersburg, FL 33716.
Mailing Address: P.O. Box A, St. Petersburg, FL 33731-1950.
Telephone: (727) 822-6937. **Fax:** (727) 821-5819.
President: Pat O'Conner. **Secretary/VP, Legal Affairs/General Counsel:** D. Scott Poley. **Executive Director, PBUC:** Justin Klemm. **Chief of Instruction/PBUC Evaluator:** Mike Felt. **Field Evaluators/Instructors:** Jorge Bauza, Dusty Dellinger, Matt Hollowell, Larry Reveal, Darren Spagnardi. **Medical Coordinator:** Mark Stubblefield. **Special Assistant, PBUC:** Lillian Patterson.

THE UMPIRE SCHOOL
Mailing Address: P.O. Box A, St. Petersburg, FL, 33731-1950.
Telephone: (877) 799-UMPS. **Fax:** (727) 821-5819.
Email: info@therightcall.net. **Website:** www.therightcall.net.
Executive Director: Justin Klemm. **Chief of Instruction:** Mike Felt. **Curriculum Coordinator:** Larry Reveal. **Lead Rules Instructor:** Jorge Bauza. **Field Leaders:** Dusty Dellinger, Tyler Funneman, Darren Spagnardi. **Medical Coordinator:** Mark Stubblefield. **Administrator:** Andy Shultz.

WENDELSTEDT UMPIRE SCHOOL
Mailing Address: 100 Minges Creek Place, Suite A205, Battle Creek, MI, 49015.
Telephone: 800-818-1690. **Fax:** 888-881-9801. **E-mail Address:** admin@umpireschool.com. **Website:** www.umpire-school.com.

WORLD UMPIRES ASSOCIATION
Mailing Address: P.O. Box 394, Neenah, WI 54957. **Telephone:** (920) 969-1580. **Fax:** (920) 969-1892. **E-mail Address:** worldumpiresassn@aol.com.
Year Founded: 2000.
President: Joe West. **Vice President:** Fielden Culbreth. **Secretary/Treasurer:** Jerry Layne. **Labor Counsel:** Brian Lam. **Administrator:** Phil Janssen.

TRAINERS

PROFESSIONAL BASEBALL ATHLETIC TRAINERS SOCIETY
Mailing Address: 1201 Peachtree St., 400 Colony Square, Suite 1750, Atlanta, GA 30361. **Telephone:** (404) 875-4000, ext. **1. Fax:** (404) 892-8560. **E-mail Address:** rmallernee@mallernee-branch.com. **Website:** www.pbats.com.
Year Founded: 1983.
President: Richie Bancells (Baltimore Orioles). **Secretary:** Mark O'Neal (Chicago Cubs). **Treasurer:** Jeff Porter (Atlanta Braves). **American League Head Athletic Trainer Representative:** Ron Porterfield (Tampa Bay Rays). **American League Assistant Athletic Trainer Representative:** Rob Nodine (Seattle Mariners). **National League Head Athletic Trainer Representative:** Keith Dugger (Colorado Rockies). **National League Assistant Athletic Trainer Representative:** Mike Kozak (Florida Marlins). **Immediate Past President:** Jamie Reed (Texas Rangers).
General Counsel: Rollin Mallernee II.

MUSEUMS

BABE RUTH BIRTHPLACE
Office Address: 216 Emory St., Baltimore, MD 21230. **Telephone:** (410) 727-1539. **Fax:** (410) 727-1652. **E-mail Address:** info@baberuthmuseum.com. **Website:** www.baberuthmuseum.com.
Year Founded: 1973.
Executive Director: Mike Gibbons. **Deputy Director:** John Ziemann. **Chief Curator:** Shawn Herne. **Communications:** Tim Richardson.
Hours: Museum open Tuesday-Sunday: 10 a.m. to 5 p.m. Gift shop open daily, 10 a.m. to 5 p.m. **Closed:** New Year's Day, Thanksgiving and Christmas.

CANADIAN BASEBALL HALL OF FAME AND MUSEUM
Museum Address: 386 Church St., St. Marys, Ontario N4X 1C2. **Mailing Address:** P.O. Box 1838, St. Marys, Ontario N4X 1C2. **Telephone:** (519) 284-1838. **Fax:** (519) 284-1234. **E-mail Address:** baseball@baseballhalloffame.ca.
Website: www.baseballhalloffame.ca.
Year Founded: 1983.
Director, Operations: Scott Crawford.
Museum Hours: May—weekends only; June 1-Oct. 8—Monday-Saturday, 10:30-4 p.m.; Sunday, noon—4 p.m.

FIELD OF DREAMS MOVIE SITE
Address: 28995 Lansing Rd., Dyersville, IA 52040. **Telephone:** (563) 875-8404; (888) 875-8404. **Fax:** (563) 875-7253. **E-mail Address:** info@fodmoviesite.com. **Website:** www.fodmoviesite.com. **Year Founded:** 1989. **Office/Business Manager:** Betty Boeckenstedt. **Hours:** April-November, 9 a.m.-6 p.m.

WORLD OF LITTLE LEAGUE: PETER J. McGOVERN MUSEUM AND OFFICIAL STORE
(FORMERLY LITTLE LEAGUE BASEBALL MUSEUM)
Office Address: 525 Route 15 South, Williamsport, PA 17701. **Mailing Address:** P.O. Box 3485, Williamsport, PA 17701. **Telephone:** (570) 326-3607. **Fax:** (570) 326-2267. **E-mail Address:** museum@littleleague.org.
Website: www.littleleague.org/museum.
Year Founded: 1982.
Vice President/Executive Director: Lance Van Auken
Director of Public Programming and Outreach: Janice Ogurcak Curator: Adam Thompson.
Museum Hours: (Closed for renovations and reopening June 15, 2013) 9 a.m. to 5 p.m. daily. **Closed:** Easter, Thanksgiving, Christmas and New Year's Day

LOUISVILLE SLUGGER MUSEUM AND FACTORY
Office Address: 800 W. Main St., Louisville, KY 40202. **Telephone:** (502) 588-7228, (877) 775-8443. **Fax:** (502) 585-1179.
Website: www.sluggermuseum.org.
Year Founded: 1996.
Executive Director: Anne Jewell.
Museum Hours: Jan. 1-June 30 and Aug. 12-Dec. 31—Mon-Sat 9 a.m.-5 p.m. Sun. 11 a.m.-5 p.m., July 1-Aug. 11— Sun-Thurs 9 a.m.-6 p.m. Fri-Sat 9 a.m.-8 p.m. **Closed:** Thanksgiving and Christmas Day.

NATIONAL BASEBALL HALL OF FAME AND MUSEUM
Address: 25 Main St., Cooperstown, NY 13326. **Telephone:** (888) 425-5633, (607) 547-7200. **FAX:** (607) 547-2044. **E-mail Address:** info@baseballhalloffame.org. **Website:** www.baseballhall.org.
Year Founded: 1939.
Chairman: Jane Forbes Clark. **Vice Chairman:** Joe Morgan. **President:** Jeff Idelson.
Museum Hours: Open daily, year-round, closed only Thanksgiving, Christmas and New Year's Day. 9 a.m.-5 p.m. Summer hours, 9 a.m.-9 p.m. (Memorial Day weekend through the day before Labor Day.)
2013 Hall of Fame Induction Weekend: July 26-29, Cooperstown, NY.

NEGRO LEAGUES BASEBALL MUSEUM
Mailing Address: 1616 E. 18th St., Kansas City, MO 64108. **Telephone:** (816) 221-1920. **Fax:** (816) 221-8424. **E-mail Address:** nlmuseum@hotmail.com. **Website:** www.nlbm.com.
Year Founded: 1990.
President: Bob Kendrick. **Executive Director Emeritus:** Don Motley.
Museum Hours: Tues.-Sat. 9 a.m.-6 p.m.; Sun. noon-6 p.m.

NOLAN RYAN FOUNDATION AND EXHIBIT CENTER
Mailing Address: 2925 South Bypass 35, Alvin, TX 77511. **Telephone:** (281) 388-1134. **FAX:** (281) 388-1135. **Website:** www.nolanryanfoundation.org.
Hours: Mon.-Fri. 9 a.m.-4 p.m. The Exhibit is closed on Sundays.

RESEARCH

SOCIETY FOR AMERICAN BASEBALL RESEARCH
Mailing Address: 4455 East Camelback Rd., Suite D-140, Phoenix, AZ 85018. **Telephone:** (800) 969-7227. **Fax:** (602) 595-5690. **Website:** www.sabr.org.
Year Founded: 1971.
President: Vince Gennaro. **Vice President:** Bill Nowlin. **Secretary:** Todd Lebowitz. **Treasurer:** F.X. Flinn. **Directors:** Ty Waterman, Tom Hufford, Paul Hirsch, Leslie Heaphy. **Executive Director:** Marc Appleman. **Web Content Editor/Producer:** Jacob Pomrenke.

ALUMNI ASSOCIATION

MAJOR LEAGUE BASEBALL PLAYERS ALUMNI ASSOCIATION
Mailing Address: 1631 Mesa Ave., Copper Building, Suite D, Colorado Springs, CO 80906. **Telephone:** (719) 477-1870. **Fax:** (719) 477-1875.
E-mail Address: postoffice@mlbpaa.com. **Website:** www.baseballalumni.com.
Facebook: facebook.com/majorleaguebaseballplayersalumniassociation. **Twitter:** @MLBPAA.
Chief Executive Officer: Dan Foster (dan@mlbpaa.com). **Chief Operating Officer:** Geoffrey Hixson (geoff@mlbpaa.com). **Vice President, Legends Entertainment Group:** Chris Torgusen (chris@mlbpaa.com). **Director, Special Events:** Mike Groll (mikeg@mlbpaa.com). **Director, Administration:** Mary Russell Baucom (maryrussell@mlbpaa.com). **Special Events Coordinators:** Tyler Kourajian (tyler@mlbpaa.com), Rene Viscarra (Rene@mlbpaa.com). **Public Relations Coordinator:** Nikki Warner (nikki@mlbpaa.com). **Director, Memorabilia:** Matthew Hazzard (matt@mlbpaa.com). **Memorabilia Coordinators:** Billy Horn (bhorn@mlbpaa.com), Matt Tissi (mtissi@mlbpaa.com), Greg Thomas (greg@mlbpaa.com). **Membership Development Coordinator:** Kate Hutchinson (Kate@mlbpaa.com).
President: Brooks Robinson.
Chairman: Jim Hannan. **Vice President, Secretary:** Fred Valentine. **Board of Directors:** Sandy Alderson, John Doherty, Denny Doyle, Brian Fisher, Joseph Garagiola Jr., Doug Glanville, Jim "Mudcat" Grant, Rich Hand, Steve Rogers, Will Royster, Jim Sadowski, Jose Valdivielso. **Legal Counsel:** Sam Moore.

MINOR LEAGUE BASEBALL ALUMNI ASSOCIATION
Mailing Address: P.O. Box A, St. Petersburg, FL 33731. **Telephone:** (727) 822-6937. **Fax:** (727) 821-5819. **E-Mail Address:** alumni@minorleaguebaseball.com. **Website:** www.milb.com.

ASSOCIATION OF PROFESSIONAL BALL PLAYERS OF AMERICA

Mailing Address: 101 S. Kraemer Ave., Suite 112, Placentia, CA 92870. **Telephone:** (714) 528-2012. **Fax:** (714) 528-2037.
E-mail Address: ballplayersassn@aol.com. **Website:** www.apbpa.org.
Year Founded: 1924.
President: Roland Hemond. **First Vice President:** Tal Smith. **Second VP:** Stephen Cobb. **Third VP:** Tony Siegle.
Secretary/Treasurer: Dick Beverage. **Membership Services Administrator:** Jennifer Joost-Van Sant. **Membership Services Manager:** Patty Joost.
Directors: Tony Gwynn, Whitey Herzog, Tony La Russa, Tom Lasorda, Brooks Robinson, Nolan Ryan, Tom Seaver, James Leyland, Mike Scioscia.

BASEBALL ASSISTANCE TEAM (BAT)

Mailing Address: 245 Park Ave., 31st Floor, New York, NY 10167.
Telephone: (212) 931-7822, Fax: (212) 949-5433.
Website: www.baseballassistanceteam.com.
Year Founded: 1986.
To Make a Donation: (866) 605-4594.
President: Randy Winn.
Vice President: Bob Watson.
Board of Directors: Steve Garvey, Luis Gonzalez, Adam Jones, Jim Martin, Sam McDowell, Joe Morgan (HOF), Alan Nahmias, Jim Pongracz, Ted Sizemore, Bob Watson, Greg Wilcox, Randy Winn.
Executive Director: Joseph Grippo. **Secretary:** Thomas Ostertag. **Treasurer:** Scott Stamp. **Consultant:** Sam McDowell. **Consultant:** Dr. **Genoveva Javier. Operations:** Dominique Correa, Erik Nilsen.

MINISTRY

BASEBALL CHAPEL

Mailing Address: P.O. Box 302, Springfield, PA 19064. **Telephone:** (610) 999-3600.
E-mail Address: office@baseballchapel.org. **Website:** www.baseballchapel.org.
Year Founded: 1973.
President: Vince Nauss.
Hispanic Ministry: Cali Magallanes, Gio Llerena. **Director, Ministry Operations:** Rob Crose.
Board of Directors: Don Christensen, Greg Groh, Dave Howard, Vince Nauss, Bill Sampen, Walt Wiley.

TRADE/EMPLOYMENT

BASEBALL WINTER MEETINGS

Mailing Address: P.O. Box A, St. Petersburg, FL 33731. **Telephone:** (727) 822-6937. **Fax:** (727) 821-5819. **E-Mail Address:** BaseballWinterMeetings@milb.com. **Website:** www.baseballwintermeetings.com.
2012 Convention: Dec. 9-12, Walt Disney World Swan and Dolphin Resort, Lake Buena Vista, Fla.

BASEBALL TRADE SHOW

Mailing Address: P.O. Box A, St. Petersburg, FL 33731-1950. **Telephone:** (866) 926-6452. **Fax:** (727) 683-9865. **E-Mail Address:** tradeshow@milb.com. **Website:** www.baseballtradeshow.com.
Contact: Noreen Brantner, Sr. Asst. Director, Exhibition Services & Sponsorships.
2013 Show: Dec. 9-11, Walt Disney World Swan and Dolphin Resort, Orlando, FL.

PROFESSIONAL BASEBALL EMPLOYMENT OPPORTUNITIES

Mailing Address: P.O. Box A, St. Petersburg, FL 33731-1950. **Telephone:** 866-WE-R-PBEO. **Fax:** 727-821-5819. **Website:** www.PBEO.com. **Email:** info@pbeo.com. **Contact:** Mark Labban, Manager, Business Development.

BASEBALL CARD MANUFACTURERS

PANINI AMERICA INC.

Mailing Address: Panini America, 5325 FAA Blvd., Suite 100, Irving TX 75061. **Telephone:** (817) 662-5300, (800) 852-8833.
Website: www.paniniamerica.net. **Email:** RM_Marketing@paniniamerica.net
Marketing Manager: Scott Prusha.

GRANDSTAND CARDS

Mailing Address: 22647 Ventura Blvd., #192, Woodland Hills, CA 91364. **Telephone:** (818) 992-5642. **Fax:** (818) 348-9122. **E-mail Address:** gscards1@pacbell.net. **Website:** www.grandstandcards.com.

BRANDT SPORTS MARKETING (FORMERLY MULTIAD SPORTS)

Mailing Address: 8914 N. Prairie Pointe Ct., Peoria, IL 61615. **Telephone:** (800) 348-6485, ext. **5111. Fax:** (309) 692-8378. **VP Brandt Sports Marketing:** Jim Garner. **Website:** http://www.brandtco.com/sports.
Contact: Jim Dougas, jim.douglas@brandtco.com. **Phone:** 309-215-9243. **Fax:** 563-386-4817.
Contact: Dave Mateer, dave.mateer@brandtco.com. **Phone:** 309-215-9248. **Fax:** 563-386-4817.

TOPPS

Mailing Address: One Whitehall St., New York, NY 10004. **Telephone:** (212) 376-0300. **Fax:** (212) 376-0573.
Website: www.topps.com.

UPPER DECK

Mailing Address: 2251 Rutherford Rd., **Carlsbad, CA 92008. Telephone:** (800) 873-7332. **Fax:** (760) 929-6548.
E-mail Address: customer_service@upperdeck.com. **Website:** www.upperdeck.com.

SPRING TRAINING

CACTUS LEAGUE

For spring training schedules, see page 239

ARIZONA DIAMONDBACKS

Major League
Complex Address: Salt River Fields at Talking Stick, 7555 N. Pima Road, Scottsdale, AZ 85256.
Telephone: (480) 270-5000.
Seating Capacity: 11,000 (7,000 fixed seats, 4,000 lawn seats).
Location: From Loop-101, use exit 44 (Indian Bend Road) and proceed west for approximately one-half mile; turn right at Pima Road to travel north and proceed one-quarter mile; three entrances to Salt River Fields will be available on the right-hand side.

Minor League
Complex Address: Same as major league club.

CHICAGO CUBS

Major League
Complex Address: HoHoKam Stadium, 1235 N. Center St, Mesa, AZ 85201. **Telephone:** (480) 668-0500. **Seating Capacity:** 13,100. **Location:** Main Street (US Highway 60) to Center Street, north 1½ miles on Center Street.
Hotel Address: Best Western Dobson Ranch Inn, 1666 S Dobson Rd., Mesa, AZ 85202. **Telephone:** (480) 831-7000.

Minor League
Complex/Hotel Address: Fitch Park, 160 E. Sixth Place, Mesa, AZ 85201. **Telephone:** (480) 668-0500.

CHICAGO WHITE SOX

Major League
Complex Address: Camelback Ranch—Glendale, 10710 West Camelback Road, Glendale, AZ 85037. **Telephone:** (623) 302-5200. **Seating Capacity:** 13,000.
Hotel Address: Comfort Suites Glendale, 9824 W. Camelback Rd, Glendale, AZ 85305. **Telephone:** (623) 271-9005. **Hotel Address:** Renaissance Glendale Hotel & Spa, 9495 W. Coyotes Blvd., Glendale, AZ 85305. **Telephone:** 629-937-3700.

Minor League
Complex/Hotel Address: Same as major league club.

CINCINNATI REDS

Major League
Complex Address: Surprise Stadium, 15754 N. Bullard Ave., Surprise, AZ 85374. **Telephone:** (623) 266-8100. **Seating Capacity:** 10,714. **Location:** I-10 West to Route 101 North, 101 North to Bell Road, left at Bell for seven miles, stadium on left.

Minor League
Complex Address: Same as major league club.
Hotel Address: Holiday Inn Express, 16540 N. Bullard Ave., Surprise, AZ 85374. **Telephone:** (623) 975-5540.

CLEVELAND INDIANS

Major League
Complex Address: Cincinnati Reds Player Development Complex, 3125 S. Wood Blvd, Goodyear, AZ 85338. **Telephone:** (623) 932-6590. **Ballpark Address:** Goodyear Ballpark, 1933 S. Ballpark Way, Goodyear, AZ 85338. **Telephone:** (623) 882-3120.
Hotel Address: Marriott Residence Inn, 7350 N. Zanjero Blvd., Glendale, AZ 85305. **Telephone:** (623) 772-8900. **Fax:** (623) 772-8905.

Minor League
Complex/Hotel Address: Same as major league club.

COLORADO ROCKIES

Major League
Complex Address: Salt River Fields at Talking Stick, 7555 N. Pima Rd., Scottsdale, AZ 85258. **Telephone:** (480) 270-5800. **Seating Capacity:** 11,000. **Location:** From Loop 101 northbound, Take exit 44 (Indian Bend Rd) and turn left, proceeding west for approximately a half mile, turn right at Pima and the ballpark will be located on the right; From Loop 101 southbound, take exit 43 (Via De Ventura) and turn right, proceeding west for a half mile, turn left at the Via De Ventura entrance into the ballpark parking lot. **Visiting Team Hotel:** The Scottsdale Plaza Resort, 7200 North Scottsdale Road, Scottsdale, AZ 85253. **Telephone:** (480) 948-5000. **Fax:** (480) 951-5100.

Minor League
Complex/Hotel Address: Same as major league club.

KANSAS CITY ROYALS

Major League
Complex Address: Surprise Stadium, 15946 N. Bullard Ave., Surprise, AZ 85374. **Telephone:** (623) 222-2222. **Seating Capacity:** 10,700. **Location:** I-10 West to Route 101 North, 101 North to Bell Road, left on Bell for five miles, stadium on left.
Hotel Address: Wigwam Resort, 300 East Wigwam Blvd., Litchfield Park, Arizona 85340. **Telephone:** (623)-935-3811

Minor League
Complex: Same as major league club. **Hotel Address:** Comfort Hotel and Suites, 13337 W. Grand Ave., Surprise, AZ 85374. **Telephone:** (623) 583-3500.

LOS ANGELES ANGELS

Major League
Complex Address: Tempe Diablo Stadium, 2200 W. Alameda, Tempe, AZ 85282. **Telephone:** (480) 858-7500. **Fax:** (480) 438-7583. **Seating Capacity:** 9,558. **Location:** I-10 to exit 153B (48th Street), south one mile on 48th Street to Alameda Drive, left on Alameda.

Minor League
Complex Address: Tempe Diablo Minor League Complex, 2225 W. Westcourt Way, Tempe, AZ 85282. **Telephone:** (480) 858-7558.
Hotel Address: Sheraton Phoenix Airport, 1600 South 52nd Street, Tempe, AZ 85281. **Telephone:** (480) 967-6600.

LOS ANGELES DODGERS

Major League
Complex Address: Camelback Ranch, 10710 West Camelback Rd., Phoenix, AZ 85037. **Seating Capacity:** 13,000, plus standing room.
Location: I-10 or I-17 to Loop 101 West or North, Take Exit 5, Camelback Road West to ballpark. **Telephone:** (623) 302-5000. **Hotel:** Unavailable.

Minor League
Complex/Hotel Address: Same as major league club.

MILWAUKEE BREWERS

Major League
Complex Address: Maryvale Baseball Park, 3600 N. 51st Ave., Phoenix, AZ 85031. **Telephone:** (623) 245-5555. **Seating Capacity:** 9,000. **Location:** I-10 to 51st Ave., north on 51st Ave.
Hotel Address: Staybridge Suites, 9340 West Cabella Drive, Glendale, AZ 85305. **Telephone:** (623) 842-0000

Minor League
Complex Address: Maryvale Baseball Complex, 3805 N. 53rd Ave., Phoenix, AZ 85031. **Telephone:** (623) 245-5600. **Hotel Address:** Same as major league club.

OAKLAND A'S

Major League
Complex Address: Phoenix Municipal Stadium, 5999 E. Van Buren, Phoenix, AZ 85008. **Telephone:** (602) 225-9400. **Seating Capacity:** 8,500. **Location:** I-10 to exit 153 (48th Street), HoHoKam Expressway to Van Buren Street (US Highway 60), right on Van Buren. **Hotel Address:** Doubletree Suites Hotel, 320 N 44th St, Phoenix, AZ 85008. **Telephone:** (602) 225-0500.

Minor League
Complex Address: Papago Park Baseball Complex, 1802 N. 64th St, Phoenix, AZ 85008. **Telephone:** (480) 949-5951. **Hotel Address:** Crowne Plaza, 4300 E. Washington, Phoenix, AZ 85034. **Telephone:** (602) 273-7778.

SAN DIEGO PADRES

Major League
Complex Address: Peoria Sports Complex, 8131 W. Paradise Lane, Peoria, AZ 85382. **Telephone:** (623) 486-7000. **Fax:** (623) 486-7154. **Seating Capacity:** 11,333. **Location:** I-17 to Bell Road exit, west on Bell to 83rd Ave.
Hotel Address: Country Inn and Suites (623) 879-9000, 20221 N 29th Avenue, Phoenix, AZ 85027.

Minor League
Complex/Hotel: Same as major league club.

SAN FRANCISCO GIANTS

Major League
Complex Address: Scottsdale Stadium, 7408 E. Osborn Rd., Scottsdale, AZ 85251. **Telephone:** (480) 990-7972. **Fax:** (480) 990-2643. **Seating Capacity:** 11,500. **Location:** Scottsdale Road to Osborne Road, east on Osborne ½ mile.
Hotel Address: Hilton Garden Inn Scottsdale Old Town, 7324 East Indian School Rd, Scottsdale, AZ 85251.

Telephone: (480) 481-0400.

Minor League
Complex Address: Giants Minor League Complex 8045 E. Camelback Road, Scottsdale, AZ 85251. **Telephone:** (480) 990-0052. **Fax:** (480) 990-2349.

SEATTLE MARINERS

Major League
Complex Address: Peoria Sports Complex, 15707 N. 83rd Ave., Peoria, AZ 85382. **Telephone:** (623) 776-4800. **Fax:** (623) 776-4829. **Seating Capacity:** 11,000. **Location:** I-17 to Bell Road exit, west on Bell to 83rd Ave.
Hotel Address: LaQuinta Inn & Suites, 16321 N. 83rd Ave., Peoria, AZ 85382. **Telephone:** (623) 487-1900.

Minor League
Complex Address: Peoria Sports Complex (1993), 15707 N. 83rd Ave., Peoria, AZ 85382. **Telephone:** (623) 776-4800. **Fax:** (623) 776-4828. **Hotel Address:** Hampton Inn, 8408 W Paradise Lane, Peoria, AZ 85382. **Telephone:** (623) 486-9918.

TEXAS RANGERS

Major League
Complex Address: Surprise Stadium, 15754 N. Bullard Ave., Surprise, AZ 85374. **Telephone:** (623) 266-8100. **Seating Capacity:** 10,714. **Location:** I-10 West to Route 101 North, 101 North to Bell Road, left at Bell for seven miles, stadium on left. **Hotel Address:** Windmill Suites at Sun City West, 12545 W. Bell Rd., Surprise, AZ 85374. **Telephone:** (623) 583-0133.

Minor League
Complex Address: Same as major league club.
Hotel Address: Hampton Inn, 2000 N. Litchfield Rd., Goodyear, AZ 85338. **Telephone:** (623) 536-1313; Holiday Inn Express, 1313 N. Litchfield Rd., Goodyear, AZ 85338.

GRAPEFRUIT LEAGUE

For spring training schedules, see page 241

ATLANTA BRAVES

Major League
Stadium Address: Champion Stadium at ESPN Wide World of Sports Complex, 700 S Victory Way, Kissimmee, FL 34747. **Telephone:** (407) 939-1500.
Seating Capacity: 9,500. **Location:** I-4 to exit 25B (Highway 192 West), follow signs to Magic Kingdom/Wide World of Sports Complex, right on Victory Way.
Hotel Address: World Center Marriott, World Center Drive, Orlando, FL 32821. **Telephone:** (407) 239-4200.

Minor League
Complex Address: Same as major league club. **Telephone:** (407) 939-2232. **Fax:** (407) 939-2225.
Hotel Address: Marriot Village at Lake Buena Vista, 8623 Vineland Ave., Orlando, FL 32821. **Telephone:** (407) 938-9001.

BALTIMORE ORIOLES

Major League
Complex Address: Ed Smith Stadium, 2700 12th Street, Sarasota, FL 34237. **Telephone:** (941) 893-6300. **Fax:** (941) 893-6377. **Seating Capacity:** 7,500. **Location:** I-75 to exit 210, West on Fruitville Road, right on Tuttle Avenue. **Hotel Address:** Homewood Suites by Hilton, 3470 Fruitville Road, Sarasota, FL 34237. **Telephone:** (941) 365-7300.

Minor League
Complex Address: Buck O'Neil Baseball Complex at Twin Lakes Park, 6700 Clark Rd., Sarasota, FL 34241. **Telephone:** (941) 923-1996. **Hotel Address:** Days Inn, 5774 Clark Rd., Sarasota, FL 34233. **Telephone:** (941) 921-7812. **Hotel Address:** AmericInn, 5931 Fruitville Rd., Sarasota, FL 34232. **Telephone:** (941) 342-8778.

BOSTON RED SOX

Major League
Complex Address: JetBlue Park at Fenway South, Fort Myers, FL 33913.
Telephone: (239) 334-4799. **Directions: From the North:** Take I-75 South to Exit 131 (Daniels Parkway); Make a left off the exit and go east for approximately two miles; JetBlue Park will be on your left. **From the South:** Take I-75 North to Exit 131 (Daniels Parkway); Make a right off exit and go east for approximately two miles; JetBlue Park will be on your left.

Minor League
Complex/Hotel Address: Fenway South, Fort Myers, FL 33913.

DETROIT TIGERS

Major League
Complex Address: Joker Marchant Stadium, 2301 Lakeland Hills Blvd., Lakeland, FL 33805. **Telephone:** (863) 686-8075. **Seating Capacity:** 9,000. **Location:** I-4 to exit 33 (Lakeland Hills Boulevard).

Minor League
Complex: Tigertown, 2125 N. Lake Ave., Lakeland, FL 33805. **Telephone:** (863) 686-8075.

HOUSTON ASTROS

Major League
Complex Address: Osceola County Stadium, 631 Heritage Park Way, Kissimmee, FL 34744. **Telephone:** (321) 697-3200. **Fax:** (321) 697-3197.
Seating Capacity: 5,300. **Location:** From Florida Turnpike South, take exit 244, west on US 192, right on Bill Beck Blvd.
Hotel Address: Hilton Grand Vacations Club, 8122 Arrezzo Way, Orlando, FL 32811. **Telephone:** (407) 465-2600. **Fax:** (407) 465-2612.

Minor League
Complex/Hotel Address: Same as major league club.

MIAMI MARLINS

Major League
Complex Address: Roger Dean Stadium, 4751 Main St., Jupiter, FL 33458. **Telephone:** (561) 775-1818. **Telephone:** (561) 799-1346. **Seating Capacity:** 7,000.
Location: I-95 to exit 83, east on Donald Ross Road for one mile to Central Blvd., left at light, follow Central Boulevard to circle and take Main Street to Roger Dean Stadium.
Hotel Address: Palm Beach Gardens Marriott, 4000 RCA Boulevard, Palm Beach Gardens, FL 33410. **Telephone:** (561) 622-8888. **Fax:** (561) 622-0052.

Minor League
Complex/Hotel Address: Same as major league club.

MINNESOTA TWINS

Major League
Complex Address: Lee County Sports Complex/ Hammond Stadium, 14100 Six Mile Cypress Pkwy., Fort Myers, FL 33912. **Telephone:** (239) 533-7610. **Seating Capacity:** 8,100. **Location:** Exit 21 off I-75, west on Daniels Parkway, left on Six Mile Cypress Parkway.
Hotel Address: Hilton Garden Inn, 12600 University Drive, Fort Myers, FL 33907. **Telephone:** (239) 790-3500.

Minor League
Complex/Hotel Address: Same as major league club.

NEW YORK METS

Major League
Complex Address: Mets Stadium, 525 NW Peacock Blvd., Port St. Lucie, FL 34986. **Telephone:** (772) 871-2100.
Seating Capacity: 7,000. **Location:** Exit 121C (St Lucie West Blvd.) off I-95, east ¼ mile, left onto NW Peacock.
Hotel Address: Hilton Hotel, 8542 Commerce Centre Drive, Port St. Lucie, FL 34986. **Telephone:** (772) 871-6850.

Minor League
Complex Address: Same as major league club. **Hotel Address:** Main Stay Suites, 8501 Champions Way, Port St. Lucie, FL 34986. **Telephone:** (772) 460-8882.

NEW YORK YANKEES

Major League
Complex Address: George M. Steinbrenner Field, One Steinbrenner Dr., Tampa, FL 33614. **Telephone:** (813) 879-2244. **Seating Capacity:** 11,076. **Hotel:** Unavailable.

Minor League
Complex Address: Yankees Player Development/Scouting Complex, 3102 N. Himes Ave., Tampa, FL 33607. Telephone: (813) 875-7569. Hotel: Unavailable.

PHILADELPHIA PHILLIES

Major League
Complex Address: Bright House Networks Field, 601 N. Old Coachman Rd., Clearwater, FL 33765. Telephone: (727) 467-4457. Fax: (727) 712-4498. Seating Capacity: 8,500. Location: Route 60 West, right on Old Coachman Road, ballpark on right after Drew Street.
Hotel Address: Holiday Inn Express, 2580 Gulf to Bay Blvd., Clearwater, FL 33765. Telephone: (727) 797-6300. Hotel Address: La Quinta Inn, 21338 US 19 North, Clearwater, FL 33765. Telephone: (727) 799-1565.

Minor League
Complex Address: Carpenter Complex, 651 N. Old Coachman Rd., Clearwater, FL 33765. Telephone: (727) 799-0503. Fax: (727) 726-1793. Hotel Addresses: Hampton Inn, 21030 US Highway 19 North, Clearwater, FL 34625. Telephone: (727) 797-8173. Hotel Address: Econolodge, 21252 US Hwy. 19, Clearwater, FL 34625. Telephone: (727) 799-1569.

PITTSBURGH PIRATES

Major League
Stadium Address (Feb. 22-March 28): McKechnie Field, 17th Ave. West and Ninth Street West, Bradenton, FL 34205. Seating Capacity: 8,500.
Location: US 41 to 17th Ave., west to 9th Street. Workouts from Feb 12-27 held at: Pirate City, 1701 27th St. E., Bradenton, FL 34208.
Telephone: (941) 747-3031. Fax: (941) 747-9549.

Minor League
Complex/Hotel Address: Pirate City, 1701 27th St. E., Bradenton, FL 34208.

ST. LOUIS CARDINALS

Major League
Complex Address: Roger Dean Stadium, 4795 University Dr., Jupiter, FL 33458. Telephone: (561) 775-1818. Fax: (561) 799-1380. Seating Capacity: 6,864. Location: I-95 to exit 58, east on Donald Ross Road for ¼ mile.
Hotel Address: Embassy Suites, 4350 PGA Blvd., Palm Beach Gardens, FL 33410. Telephone: (561) 622-1000.

Minor League
Complex: Same as major league club. Hotel: Double Tree Palm Beach Gardens. Telephone: (561) 622-2260.

TAMPA BAY RAYS

Major League
Stadium Address: Charlotte Sports Park, 2300 El Jobean Road, Port Charlotte, FL 33948. Telephone: (941) 235-5025. Seating Capacity: 6,823 (5,028 fixed seats). Location: I-75 to US-17 to US-41, turn left onto El Jobean Rd.
Hotel Address: Unavailable.

Minor League
Complex Address: Same as major league club.

TORONTO BLUE JAYS

Major League
Stadium Address: Florida Auto Exchange Stadium, 373 Douglas Ave., Dunedin, FL 34698. Telephone: (727) 733-0429. Seating Capacity: 5,509. Location: US 19 North to Sunset Point; west on Sunset Point to Douglas Avenue; north on Douglas to Stadium; ballpark is on the southeast corner of Douglas and Beltrees.

Minor League
Complex Address: Bobby Mattick Training Center at Englebert Complex, 1700 Solon Ave., Dunedin, FL 34698. Telephone: (727) 743-8007. Hotel Address: Baymont Inn & Suites 26508 US 19 North, Clearwater, FL 33761. Telephone: (727) 796-1234.

WASHINGTON NATIONALS

Major League
Complex Address: Space Coast Stadium, 5800 Stadium Pkwy., Viera, FL 32940. Telephone: (321) 633-9200. Seating Capacity: 8,100. Location: I-95 southbound to Fiske Blvd (exit 74), south on Fiske/Stadium Parkway to stadium; I-95 northbound to State Road #509/Wickham Road (exit 73), left off exit, right on Lake Andrew Drive; turn right on Stadium Parkway, stadium is ½ mile on left. Hotel Address: Hampton Inn, 130 Sheriff Drive, Viera, FL. Telephone: (321) 255-6868.

Minor League
Complex Address: Carl Barger Complex, 5600 Stadium Pkwy., Viera, FL 32940. Telephone: (321) 633-8119. Hotel Address: Same as major league club.

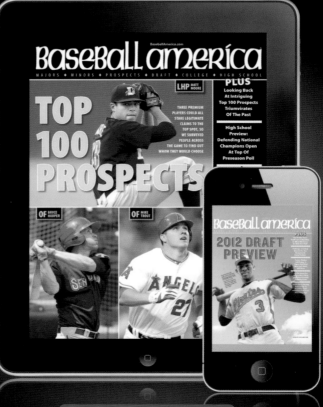

MINOR
LEAGUES

MINOR LEAGUE BASEBALL

NATIONAL ASSOCIATION OF PROFESSIONAL BASEBALL LEAGUES

MINOR LEAGUE BASEBALL

Street Address: 9550 16th Street North, St Petersburg, FL 33716.
Mailing Address: PO Box A, St Petersburg, FL 33731-1950.
Telephone: (727) 822-6937. **Fax:** (727) 821-5819. **Fax (marketing):** (727) 894-4227. **Fax (licensing):** (727) 825-3785.
President/CEO: Pat O'Conner.
Vice President: Stan Brand. **Senior VP, Legal Affairs/General Counsel:** D Scott Poley. **VP, Baseball/Business Operations:** Tim Brunswick. **VP, Business Development:** Tina Gust. **Special Counsel:** George Yund. **Executive Director, Communications:** Steve Densa. **Director, Finance/Accounting:** Sean Brown. **Director, Security/Facility Operations:** Earnell Lucas. **Assistant Director, Legal Affairs:** Louis Brown. **Manager, Baseball Operations/Executive Assistant to the President:** Mary Wooters.

AFFILIATED MEMBERS/COUNCIL OF LEAGUE PRESIDENTS

Pat O'Conner

Triple-A

League	President	Telephone	Fax Number
International	Randy Mobley	(614) 791-9300	(614) 791-9009
Mexican	Plinio Escalante	011-52-555-557-1007	011-52-555-395-2454
Pacific Coast	Branch Rickey	(512) 310-2900	(512) 310-8300

Double-A

League	President	Telephone	Fax Number
Eastern	Joe McEacharn	(207) 761-2700	(207) 761-7064
Southern	Lori Webb	(770) 321-0400	(770) 321-0037
Texas	Tom Kayser	(210) 545-5297	(210) 545-5298

High Class A

League	President	Telephone	Fax Number
California	Charlie Blaney	(805) 985-8585	(805) 985-8580
Carolina	John Hopkins	(336) 691-9030	(336) 464-2737
Florida State	Chuck Murphy	(386) 252-7479	(386) 252-7495

Low Class A

League	President	Telephone	Fax Number
Midwest	George Spelius	(608) 364-1188	(608) 364-1913
South Atlantic	Eric Krupa	(727) 538-4270	(727) 499-6853

Short-Season

League	President	Telephone	Fax Number
New York-Penn	Ben Hayes	(727) 289-7112	(727) 683-9691
Northwest	Mike Ellis	(406) 541 9301	(406) 543-9463

Rookie Advanced

League	President	Telephone	Fax Number
Appalachian	Lee Landers	(704) 252-2656	Unavailable
Pioneer	Jim McCurdy	(509) 456-7615	(509) 456-0136

Rookie

League	President	Telephone	Fax Number
Arizona	Bob Richmond	(208) 429-1511	(208) 429-1525
Dominican Summer	Orlando Diaz	(809) 532-3619	(809) 532-3619
Gulf Coast	Operated by MILB	(727) 456-1734	(727) 821-5819
Venezuela Summer	Unavailable	011-58-241-823-8101	011-58-241-823-8101

NATIONAL ASSOCIATION BOARD OF TRUSTEES

TRIPLE-A
At-large: Ken Young (Norfolk). **International League:** Ken Schnacke (Columbus). **Pacific Coast League:** Sam Bernabe, Chairman (Iowa). **Mexican League:** Cuauhtemoc Rodriguez (Quintana Roo).

DOUBLE-A
Eastern League: Joe Finley, (Trenton). **Southern League:** Stan Logan (Birmingham). **Texas League:** Reid Ryan (Corpus Christi).

CLASS A
California League: Tom Volpe (Stockton). **Carolina League:** Chuck Greenberg (Myrtle Beach). **Florida State League:** Ken Carson, Secretary (Dunedin). **Midwest League:** Tom Dickson (Lansing). **South Atlantic League:** Chip Moore (Rome).

SHORT-SEASON
New York-Penn League: Marv Goldklang (Hudson Valley). **Northwest League:** Bobby Brett (Spokane).

ROOKIE
Appalachian League: Mitch Lukevics (Princeton). **Pioneer League:** Dave Baggott, vice chairman (Ogden). **Gulf Coast League:** Bill Smith (Twins).

PROFESSIONAL BASEBALL PROMOTION CORP
Street Address: 9550 16th Street North, St Petersburg, FL 33716.
Mailing Address: PO Box A, St Petersburg, FL 33731-1950.
Telephone: (727) 822-6937. **Fax:** (727) 821-5819. **Fax/Marketing:** (727) 894-4227. **Fax/Licensing:** (727) 825-3785.
President/CEO: Pat O'Conner.
Senior VP, Legal Affairs/General Counsel: D Scott Poley. **VP, Baseball/Business Operations:** Tim Brunswick. **VP, BIRCO/Business Services:** Brian Earle. **VP, Business Development:** Tina Gust. **VP, Sales/Marketing:** Rod Meadows. **Executive Director, Communications:** Steve Densa. **Director, Finance/Accounting:** Sean Brown. **Director, Information Technology:** Rob Colamarino. **Director, Licensing:** Sandie Hebert. **Director, Business Development:** Scott Kravchuk. **Director, Security/Facility Operations:** Earnell Lucas. **Senior Assistant Director, Exhibition Services/Sponsorships:** Noreen Brantner. **Senior Assistant Director, Event Services:** Kelly Butler. **Assistant Director, Licensing:** Carrie Adams. **Assistant Director, Legal Affairs:** Louis Brown. **Assistant Director, Business Development:** Jill Dedene. **Assistant Director, Accounting:** James Dispanet. **Senior Manager, Corporate Communications:** Mary Marandi. **Senior Account Manager:** Heather Raburn.
Manager, Office Operations: Jeff Carrier. **Manager, Business Development:** Mark Labban. **Contract Manager:** Jeannette Machicote. **Trademark Manager:** Bryan Sayre. **Manager, Baseball Operations/Executive Assistant to President:** Mary Wooters. **Graphic Designer:** Ashley Allphin. **Staff Accountant:** Michelle Heystek. **Administrative Coordinator:** Sheryl Hamilton. **Sales/Account Coordinator:** Gabe Rendón. **Coordinator, Business Services:** Jessica Watts. **Special Assistant to the President/Legal Affairs:** Robert Fountain. **Assistant, Baseball Operations:** Andy Shultz.

PROFESSIONAL BASEBALL UMPIRE CORP
Street Address: 9550 16th Street North, St Petersburg, FL 33716.
Mailing Address: PO Box A, St Petersburg, FL 33731-1950.
Telephone: (727) 822-6937. **Fax:** (727) 821-5819.
President: Pat O'Conner. **Secretary/VP, Legal Affairs/General Counsel:** D Scott Poley. **Executive Director, PBUC:** Justin Klemm. **Chief, Instruction/PBUC Evaluator:** Mike Felt. **Field Evaluators/Instructors:** Jorge Bauza, Dusty Dellinger, Tyler Funneman, Larry Reveal, Darren Spagnardi. **Medical Coordinator:** Mark Stubblefield.

GENERAL INFORMATION

| | Teams | Games | Regular Season | | All-Star Games | |
			Opening Day	Closing Day	Date	Host
International	14	144	April 4	Sept. 2	*July 17	Reno
Pacific Coast	16	144	April 4	Sept. 2	*July 17	Reno
Eastern	12	142	April 4	Sept. 2	July 10	New Britain
Southern	10	140	April 4	Sept. 2	July 17	Jacksonville
Texas	8	140	April 4	Sept. 2	June 25	Nwest Arkansas
California	10	140	April 4	Sept. 2	#June 18	San Jose
Carolina	8	140	April 4	Sept. 2	#June 18	San Jose
Florida State	12	140	April 4	Sept. 2	June 18	Dunedin
Midwest	16	140	April 4	Sept. 2	June 18	Dayton
South Atlantic	14	140	April 4	Sept. 2	June 18	Lakewood
New York-Penn	14	76	June 17	Sept. 4	Aug. 13	Connecticut
Northwest	8	76	June 15	Sept. 1	Aug. 6	Everett
Appalachian	10	68	June 20	Aug. 30	None	
Pioneer	8	76	June 20	Sept. 8	None	
Arizona	13	56	June 20	Aug. 29	None	
Gulf Coast	16	60	June 21	Aug. 28	None	

*Triple-A All-Star Game. #California League vs. Carolina League

INTERNATIONAL LEAGUE

Office Address: 55 South High St, Suite 202, Dublin, Ohio 43017.
Telephone: (614) 791-9300. **Fax:** (614) 791-9009.
E-Mail Address: office@ilbaseball.com. **Website:** www.ilbaseball.com.
Years League Active: 1884-
President/Treasurer: Randy Mobley.
Vice Presidents: Dave Rosenfield, Tex Simone. **Assistant to the President:** Chris Sprague.
Corporate Secretary: Max Schumacher.
Directors: Don Beaver (Charlotte), Rob Crain (Scranton/Wilkes-Barre), Joe Finley (Lehigh Valley), George Habel (Durham), North Johnson (Gwinnett), Joe Napoli (Toledo), Bob Rich Jr (Buffalo), Dave Rosenfield (Norfolk), Ken Schnacke (Columbus), Max Schumacher (Indianapolis), Naomi Silver (Rochester), John Simone (Syracuse), Mike Tamburro (Pawtucket), Gary Ulmer (Louisville).
Office Manager: Gretchen Addison.
Division Structure: North—Buffalo, Lehigh Valley, Pawtucket, Rochester, Scranton/Wilkes-Barre, Syracuse. West—Columbus, Indianapolis, Louisville, Toledo. South—Charlotte, Durham, Gwinnett, Norfolk.
Regular Season: 144 games. **2013 Opening Date:** April 4. **Closing Date:** Sept 2. **All-Star Game:** July 17 at Reno (IL vs Pacific Coast League).

Randy Mobley

Playoff Format: South winner meets West winner in best of five series; wild card (non-division winner with best winning percentage) meets North winner in best of five series. Winners meet in best-of-five series for Governors' Cup championship.
Triple-A Championship Game: Sept 17 at Lehigh Valley (IL vs Pacific Coast League).
Roster Limit: 25. **Player Eligibility:** No restrictions.
Official Baseball: Rawlings ROM-INT.
Umpires: Sean Barber (Lakeland, FL), Toby Basner (Snellville, GA), Ryan Blakney (Wenatchee, WA), Seth Buckminster (Fort Worth, TX), Kelvin Bultron (Canovanas, Puerto Rico), Jon Byrne (Charlotte, NC), Travis Carlson (Lakeland, FL), Chris Conroy (North Adams, MA), Andy Dudones (Uniontown, OH), Mike Estabrook (Boynton Beach, FL), Ian Fazzio (Springfield, MO), Jeff Gosney (Lakeland, FL), Max Guyll (Fort Wayne, IN), Adam Hamari (Marquette, MI), Anthony Johnson (McComb, MS), Will Little (Fall Branch, TN), Ben May (Racine, WI), Brad Myers (Holland, OH), David Rackley (Matthews, NC), Jonathan Saphire (Centerville, OH), David Soucy (Bluffton, SC), Carlos Torres (Acarigua, Venezuela), John Tumpane (Chicago, IL), Chris Vines (Canton, GA), Chad Whitson (Dublin, OH).

STADIUM INFORMATION

| Club | Stadium | Opened | Dimensions | | | Capacity | 2012 Att. |
			LF	CF	RF		
Buffalo	Coca-Cola Field	1988	325	404	325	18,025	515,898
Charlotte	Knights Stadium	1990	335	400	335	10,002	278,676
Columbus	Huntington Park	2009	325	400	318	10,100	611,223
Durham	Durham Bulls Athletic Park	1995	305	400	327	10,000	483,593
Gwinnett	Coolray Field	2009	335	400	335	10,427	327,584
Indianapolis	Victory Field	1996	320	402	320	14,500	595,043
Lehigh Valley	Coca-Cola Park	2008	336	400	325	10,000	622,421
Louisville	Louisville Slugger Field	2000	325	400	340	13,131	561,818
Norfolk	Harbor Park	1993	333	410	318	12,067	384,013
Pawtucket	McCoy Stadium	1946	325	400	325	10,031	510,748
Rochester	Frontier Field	1997	335	402	325	10,840	405,111
*Scranton/WB	PNC Field	2013	330	408	330	10,000	272,168
Syracuse	Alliance Bank Stadium	1997	330	400	330	11,671	349,027
Toledo	Fifth Third Field	2002	320	408	315	10,300	540,400

* Played 2012 home schedule on the road

BUFFALO BISONS

Office Address: Coca-Cola Field, One James D Griffin Plaza, Buffalo, NY 14203.
Telephone: (716) 846-2000. **Fax:** (716) 852-6530.
E-Mail Address: info@bisons.com. **Website:** www.bisons.com.
Affiliation (first year): Toronto Blue Jays (2013).
Years in League: 1886-90, 1912-70, 1998-

OWNERSHIP/MANAGEMENT
Operated By: Rich Products Corp.
Principal Owner/President: Robert Rich Jr. **President, Rich Entertainment Group:** Melinda Rich. **President, Rich Baseball Operations:** Jon Dandes. **Vice President/Treasurer:** David Rich. **VP/Secretary:** William Gisel.
VP/General Manager: Mike Buczkowski. **VP, Finance:** Joseph Segarra. **Corporate Counsel:** Jill Bond, William

Grieshober. **Director, Sales:** Anthony Sprague. **Director, Stadium Operations:** Tom Sciarrino. **Controller:** Kevin Parkinson. **Senior Accountants:** Rita Clark. **Accountant:** Amy Delaney. **Director, Ticket Operations:** Mike Poreda. **Director, Public Relations:** Brad Bisbing. **Director, Game Day Entertainment/Promotions Coordinator:** Matt La Sota. **Sales Coordinators:** Rachel Osucha, Mike Simoncelli. **Account Executives:** Lindsay Carucci, Jeffrey Erbes, Mark Gordon, Jim Harrington, Robert Kates, Geoff Lundquist, Burt Mirti, Frank Mooney. **Ticket Sales Representatives:** Scott Harsch, Victoria Rebman.

Manager, Merchandise: Sara Bukas. **Manager, Office Services:** Margaret Russo. **Executive Assistant:** Tina Lesher. **Community Relations:** Gail Hodges. **Director, Food Services:** Robert Free. **Assistant Concessions Manager:** Roger Buczek. **Head Groundskeeper:** Chad Laurie. **Chief Engineer:** Pat Chella. **Home Clubhouse/Baseball Operations Coordinator:** Scott Lesher. **Visiting Clubhouse Manager:** Dan Brick.

FIELD STAFF
Manager: Marty Brown. **Coach:** Jon Nunnally. **Pitching Coach:** Bob Stanley.

GAME INFORMATION
Radio Announcers: Ben Wagner, Duke McGuire. **No of Games Broadcast:** Home-72, Road-72. **Flagship Station:** WWKB-1520.
PA Announcer: Jerry Reo. **Official Scorers:** Kevin Lester, Jon Dare.
Stadium Name: Coca-Cola Field. **Location:** From north, take I-190 to Elm Street exit, left onto Swan Street; From east, take I-190 West to exit 51 (Route 33) to end, exit at Oak Street, right onto Swan Street; From west, take I-190 East, exit 53 to I-90 North, exit at Elm Street, left onto Swan Street. **Standard Game Times:** 7:05 pm, Sun 1:05. **Ticket Price Range:** $5-18.
Visiting Club Hotel: Adams Mark Hotel, 120 Church St, Buffalo, NY 14202. **Telephone:** (716) 845-5100. **Visiting Club Hotel:** Hyatt Hotel, 2 Fountain Plaza, Buffalo, NY 14202. **Telephone:** (716) 856-1234.

CHARLOTTE KNIGHTS

Office Address: 2280 Deerfield Dr, Fort Mill, SC 29715.
Telephone: (704) 357-8071. **Fax:** (704) 329-2155. **E-Mail Address:** knights@charlotteknights.com. **Website:** www.charlotteknights.com.
Affiliation (first year): Chicago White Sox (1999). **Years in League:** 1993-

OWNERSHIP/MANAGEMENT
Operated by: Knights Baseball, LLC.
Principal Owners: Don Beaver, Bill Allen.
Executive Vice President/Chief Operating Officer: Dan Rajkowski. **General Manager, Baseball Operations:** Scott Brown. **VP, Marketing:** Mark Smith. **VP, Sales:** Chris Semmens.
Director, Special Programs/Events: Julie Clark. **Director, Media Relations:** Tommy Viola. **Director, Broadcasting/Team Travel:** Matt Swierad. **Director, Stadium Operations:** Mark McKinnon. **Facility Manager:** Tom Gorter. **Director, Merchandising:** Becka Leveille. **Business Manager:** Michael Sanger. **Senior Account Executives:** Brett Butler, Tony Furr. **Director, Ticket Sales/Hospitality:** Sean Owens. **Director, Ticket Operations:** Matt Millward. **Director, Community/Team Relations:** Lindsey Roycraft. **Creative Director:** Bill Walker. **Special Event Sales Executive:** Margie Burleson. **Manager, Sponsorship Sales:** Audrey Stanek. **Account Executive:** Mark Krizanik. **Head Groundskeeper:** Eddie Busque. **Assistant Groundskeeper:** Justin Fulbright. **Front Desk Receptionist:** Cindi Craddock.

FIELD STAFF
Manager: Joel Skinner. **Hitting Coach:** Brandon Moore. **Pitching Coach:** Richard Dotson.

GAME INFORMATION
Radio Announcer: Matt Swierad. **No. of Games Broadcast:** Home-72 Road-72. **Flagship Station:** WRHI 1340-AM/94.3-FM. **PA Announcer:** Ken Conrad, Tim Donelli. **Official Scorers:** Jerry Bowers, Dave Friedman, Karl Lyles.
Stadium Name: Knights Stadium. **Location:** Exit 88 off I-77, east on Gold Hill Road. **Ticket Price Range:** $9-15.
Visiting Club Hotel: Comfort Suites, 10415 Centrum Parkway, Pineville, NC 28134. **Telephone:** 704-540-0559.

COLUMBUS CLIPPERS

Office Address: 330 Huntington Park Lane, Columbus, OH 43215.
Telephone: (614) 462-5250. **Fax:** (614) 462-3271. **Tickets:** (614) 462-2757.
E-Mail Address: info@clippersbaseball.com. **Website:** www.clippersbaseball.com.
Affiliation (first year): Cleveland Indians (2009). **Years in League:** 1955-70, 1977-

OWNERSHIP/MANAGEMENT
Operated By: Columbus Baseball Team Inc.
Principal Owner: CBT Inc. **Board of Directors:** Steven Francis, Tom Fries, Wayne Harer, Thomas Katzenmeyer, David Leland, Cathy Lyttle, Richard Smith, McCullough Williams.
President/General Manager: Ken Schnacke. **Assistant GM:** Mark Warren. **Director, Ballpark Operations:** Steve Dalin. **Assistant Director, Ballpark Operations:** Phil Colilla. **Director, Ticket Operations:** Scott Ziegler. **Assistant Director, Ticket Operations:** Eddie Langhenry. **Director, Marketing/Sales:** Mark Galuska. **Assistant Director, Marketing:** Patrick Thompson. **Assistant Director, Sales:** Brittany McKittrick. **Assistant Directors, Promotions:** Seth Rhodes. **Director, Communications/Media/Team Historian:** Joe Santry. **Assistant Director, Media Relations:** Anthony

Slosser. **Assistant Director, Communications:** Ben Leland. **Directors, Broadcasting:** Ryan Mitchell, Scott Leo. **Director, Merchandising:** Krista Oberlander. **Assistant Director, Merchandising:** Robin Vlah. **Director, Group Sales:** Ben Keller. **Assistant Directors, Group Sales:** Brett Patton, Steve Kuilder. **Director, Multimedia:** Josh Glenn. **Assistant Director, Multimedia:** Yoshi Ando.

Director, Finance: Bonnie Badgley. **Executive Assistant to the President/GM:** Ashley Held. **Office Manager:** Melissa Schrader. **Administrative Assistants:** Kevin Smith, Josh Samuel, Emily Poynter. **Director, Sponsor Relationships:** Joyce Martin. **Director, Event Planning:** Micki Shier. **Assistant Director, Event Planning:** Shannon O'Boyle. **Director, Clubhouse Operations:** George Robinson. **Clubhouse Manager:** Matt Pruzinsky. **Ballpark Superintendent:** Gary Delozier. **Head Groundskeeper:** Wes Ganobcik. **Assistant Groundskeeper:** Nick Roe.

FIELD STAFF
Manager: Chris Tremie. **Coach:** Phil Clark. **Pitching Coach:** Tony Arnold. **Trainer:** James Quinlan. **Strength/ Conditioning Coach:** Ed Subel.

GAME INFORMATION
Radio Announcers: Ryan Mitchell, Scott Leo. **No of Games Broadcast:** Home-72, Road-72. **Flagship Station:** WMNI 920AM. **PA Announcer:** Matt Leininger. **Official Scorer:** Jim Habermehl, Ray Thomas.

Stadium Name: Huntington Park. **Location:** From north: South on I-71 to I-670 west, exit at Neil Avenue, turn left at intersection onto Neil Avenue; From south: North on I-71, exit at Front Street (#100A), turn left at intersection onto Front Street, turn left onto Nationwide Blvd; From east: West on I-70, exit at Fourth Street, continue on Fulton Street to Front Street, turn right onto Front Street, turn left onto Nationwide Blvd; From west: East on I-70, exit at Fourth Street, continue on Fulton Street to Front Street, turn right onto Front Street, turn left onto Nationwide Blvd.

Ticket Price Range: $6-20. **Visiting Club Hotel:** Crowne Plaza, 33 Eeast Nationwide Blvd, Columbus, OH 43215. **Telephone:** (877) 348-2424. **Visiting Club Hotel:** Drury Hotels Columbus Convention Center, 88 East Nationwide Blvd, Columbus, OH 43215. **Telephone:** (614) 221-7008. **Visiting Club Hotel:** Hyatt Regency Downtown, 350 North High Street, Columbus, OH 43215. **Telephone:** (614) 463-1234.

DURHAM BULLS

Office Address: 409 Blackwell St, Durham, NC 27701. **Mailing Address:** PO Box 507, Durham, NC 27702.

Telephone: (919) 687-6500. **Fax:** (919) 687-6560.

Website: www.durhambulls.com. **Twitter:** @DurhamBulls

Affiliation (first year): Tampa Bay Rays (1998). **Years in League:** 1998-2013.

OWNERSHIP/MANAGEMENT
Operated By: Capitol Broadcasting Company, Inc.

President/CEO: Jim Goodmon. **Vice President:** George Habel.

General Manager: Mike Birling. **Director, Corporate Partnerships:** Chip Allen. **Director, Marketing:** Scott Carter. **Director, Promotions:** Krista Boyd. **Account Executives, Sponsorship:** Elizabeth Pritchett, Patrick Kinas. **Coordinator, Mascot/Community Relations:** Nicholas Tennant. **Director, Ticket Operations:** Tim Seaton. **Manager, Premium Ticket Sales:** Eli Starkey. **Ticket Sales Associates:** Tim Campbell, JJ Greenstein, Steve Morgan. **Manager, Group Ticket Sales:** Brian Simorka. **Group Sales Associates:** Wes Rowe, Maggie Sullivan, Josh Trezvant. **Account Executives, Tickets:** Tyler Churchill, Dennis Fryer, Lauren Powell.

Director, Special Events: Mary Beth Warfford. **Director, Merchandise/Team Travel:** Bryan Wilson. **Box Office Sales:** Jerry Mach. **Director, Stadium Operations:** Josh Nance. **GM, Concessions:** Tammy Scott. **Assistant GM, Concessions:** Ralph Orona. **Head Groundskeeper, DBAP:** Scott Strickland. **Head Groundskeeper, DAP:** Alpha Jones. **Manager, Business:** Rhonda Carlile. **Supervisor, Accounting:** Theresa Stocking. **Accountant/Receptionist:** NaTasha Jessup. **Manager, Home Clubhouse:** Colin Saunders. **Manager, Visiting/Umpires Clubhouses:** Aaron Kuehner. **Team Ambassador:** Bill Law.

FIELD STAFF
Manager: Charlie Montoyo. **Hitting Coach:** Dave Myers. **Pitching Coach:** Neil Allen. **Trainer:** Mike Sandoval.

GAME INFORMATION
Broadcasters: Patrick Kinas, Ken Tanner. **No. of Games Broadcast:** Home-72, Road-72. **Flagship Stations:** 620-AM The Buzz, 99.9 FM the Fan.

PA Announcer: Tony Riggsbee. **Official Scorer:** Brent Belvin.

Stadium Name: Durham Bulls Athletic Park. **Location:** From Raleigh, I-40 West to Highway 147 North, exit 12B to Willard, two blocks on Willard to stadium; From I-85, Gregson Street exit to downtown, left on Chapel Hill Street, right on Mangum Street. **Standard Game Times:** 7:05 pm, Sunday 5:05. **Ticket Price Range:** $6-14.

Visiting Club Hotel: Durham Marriot at the Civic Center, 201 Foster St, Durham, NC 27701. **Telephone:** (919) 768-6000.

GWINNETT BRAVES

Office Address: 2500 Buford Drive, Lawrenceville, GA 30043.
Mailing Address: PO Box 490310, Lawrenceville, GA 30049.
Telephone: (678) 277-0300. **Fax:** (678) 277-0338.
E-Mail Address: gwinnettinfo@braves.com. **Website:** www.gwinnettbraves.com.
Affiliation (first year): Atlanta Braves (1966). **Years in League:** 1884, 1915-17, 1954-64, 1966-

OWNERSHIP/MANAGEMENT

General Manager: North Johnson. **Assistant GM:** Shari Massengill. **Office Manager:** Tyra Williams. **Ticket Sales Manager:** Ryan Moore. **Ticket Operations Manager:** Josh Holley. **Account Executives:** Steve Kree, Josh Murray, Jerry Pennington, Haile Urquhart, Alex Williams. **Corporate Sales Manager:** Samantha Dunn. **Manager, Marketing/Promotions:** Maggie Neil. **Creative Services Manager:** Andrea Roa. **Community Relations Manager:** Unavailable. **Media Relations Manager:** Dave Lezotte. **Sports Turf Manager:** Chris Ball. **Stadium Operations Manager:** Ryan Stoltenberg. **Stadium Operations Coordinator:** Jonathan Blair. **Facilities Maintenance Manager:** Gary Hoopaugh. **Clubhouse Manager:** Nick Dixon. **ARAMARK General Manager:** Mindy Pevzner.

FIELD STAFF

Manager: Randy Ready. **Coach:** Jamie Dismuke. **Pitching Coach:** Marty Reed. **Trainer:** Mike Graus.

GAME INFORMATION

Radio Announcer: Tony Schiavone. **No. of Games Broadcast:** Home-72 Road-72. **Flagship Station:** WDUN 550-AM and 102.9-FM. **PA Announcer:** Unavailable. **Official Scorers:** Guy Curtright, Jon Schwartz, Frank Barnett, Tim Gaines. **Stadium Name:** Coolray Field. **Location:** I-85 (at Exit 115, State Road 20 West) and I-985 (at Exit 4), follow signs to park. **Ticket Price Range:** $5-30.
Visiting Club Hotel: Courtyard by Marriott Buford/Mall of Georgia, 1405 Mall of Georgia Boulevard, Buford, GA 30519. **Telephone:** (678) 215-8007

INDIANAPOLIS INDIANS

Office Address: 501 W Maryland Street, Indianapolis, IN 46225.
Telephone: (317) 269-3542. **Fax:** (317) 269-3541.
E-Mail Address: indians@IndyIndians.com. **Website:** www.IndyIndians.com.
Affiliation (first year): Pittsburgh Pirates (2005). **Years in League:** 1963, 1998-

OWNERSHIP/MANAGEMENT

Operated By: Indians Inc.
President/Chairman of the Board: Max Schumacher.
Vice President/General Manager: Cal Burleson. **Assistant GM:** Randy Lewandowski. **VP, Corporate Affairs:** Bruce Schumacher. **Director, Tickets/Operations:** Matt Guay. **Director, Corporate Sales/Marketing:** Joel Zawacki. **Director, Business Operations:** Brad Morris. **Director, Merchandising:** Mark Schumacher. **Director, Facilities:** Tim Hughes. **Director, Broadcasting:** Howard Kellman. **Senior Manager, Marketing/Communications:** Amanda Murray. **Senior Manager, Ticket/Premium Services:** Kerry Vick.
Sponsorship Services Manager: Keri Oberting. **Ticket Sales Manager:** Chad Bohm. **Marketing Manager:** Anna Fraser. **Communications Manager:** Brian Bosma. **Operations Manager:** Steve Bray. **Manager, Community Relations/Promotions:** Brian McLaughlin. **Facilities Manager:** Matt Rapp. **Manager, Telecast/Productions:** Scott Templin. **Stadium Maintenance Manager:** Allan Danehy. **Merchandise Manager:** Missy Weaver.
Coordinator, Community Relations/Promotions: Hunter Brown. **IT Consultant:** Sean Couse. **Sponsorship Services Coordinator:** Drew Donovan. **Manager, Ticket Services:** Bryan Spisak. **Communications Coordinator:** Chris Robinson. **Operations Support:** Ricky Floyd. **Sponsorship Sales Account Executive:** Chris Inderstrodt, Christina Toler. **Ticket Sales Executives:** Ryan Barrett, Nathan Butler, Lauren Davis, Ty Eaton, Jonathan Howard. **Operations Support:** Sandra Johnson. **Administrative Assistant:** Sarah McKinney. **Graphic Designer:** Adam Pintar. **Office Manager:** Julie Rumschlag. **Head Groundskeeper:** Joey Stevenson. **Assistant Groundskeeper:** George Peters.
Ticket Sales Assistant: Anaclaudia Cervantes, Kirsten Dickinson, Jason Schroeder, Ben Wiley, Alex Withorn. **Business Operations Assistant:** Ben Cooper. **Marketing Assistant:** Melanie Depoian. **Merchandise Assistant:** Christine Janesky. **Community Relations Assistant:** Alexandra King. **Web Design Assistant:** Chris Miller. **Stadium Operations Assistant:** Corey Pierson. **Video Production Assistant:** Joseph Tichy.

FIELD STAFF

Manager: Dean Treanor. **Hitting Coach:** Mike Pagliarulo. **Pitching Coach:** Tom Filer. **Trainer:** Bryan Housand.

GAME INFORMATION

Radio Announcers: Howard Kellman, Will Flemming.
No. of Games Broadcast: Home-72, Road-72. **Flagship Station:** WNDE 1260-AM.
PA Announcer: David Pygman. **Official Scorers:** Bill McAfee, Gary Johnson, Bill Potter, Kim Rogers.
Stadium Name: Victory Field. **Location:** I-70 to West Street exit, north on West Street to ballpark; I-65 to Martin Luther King and West Street exit, south on West Street to ballpark.

Standard Game Times: 7:05 pm; 1:35 (Wed/Sun), 7:15 (Fri). **Ticket Price Range:** $10-15.
Visiting Club Hotel: Courtyard by Marriott, 601 West Washington, Indianapolis, IN 46204. **Telephone:** (317) 822-9054.

LEHIGH VALLEY IRONPIGS

Office Address: 1050 IronPigs Way, Allentown, PA 18109.
Telephone: (610) 841-7447. **Fax:** (610) 841-1509.
E-Mail Address: info@ironpigsbaseball.com. **Website:** www.ironpigsbaseball.com.
Affiliation (first year): Philadelphia Phillies (2008). **Years in League:** 2008-

OWNERSHIP/MANAGEMENT
Ownership: LV Baseball LP.
President: Chuck Domino. **General Manager:** Kurt Landes.
Assistant GM: Howard Scharf. **Director, Media Relations:** Matt Provence. **Director, New Media:** Jon Schaeffer. **Director, Community Relations:** Sarah Marten. **Director, Merchandise:** Adam Fondl. **Director, Ticket Sales:** Scott Evans. **Director, Ticket Operations:** Amy Schoch. **Director, Group Sales:** Don Wilson. **Director, Marketing:** Ron Rushe. **Marketing Services Managers:** Courtney Novotnak, Erin Stancick. **Director, Creative Services:** Matt Zidik. **Manager, Creative Services:** Justin Vrona. **Director, Promotions:** Lindsey Knupp. **Director, Special Events/Catering:** Mary Nixon. **Manager, Special Events/Catering:** Nick Wootsick. **Director, Concessions:** Alex Rivera. **Manager, Concessions:** Brock Hartranft. **Executive Chef:** Jerry Rogers. **Controller:** Deb Landes. **Manager, Finance:** Michelle Perl.
Director, Stadium Operations: Garrett Fahrmann. **Stadium Operations Managers:** Jason Kiesel, Steve Pump. **Managers, Sponsorship:** Casey Gamard, Ben Muell, Kristin Scheitrum. **Managers, Ticket Operations:** Katie Leonick. **Tickets/Group Representatives:** Ryan Hines, Brad Ludwig, Bri Silovsky. **Director, Field Operations:** Ryan Hills. **Receptionist:** Pat Golden.

FIELD STAFF
Manager: Dave Brundage. **Hitting Coach:** Sal Rende. **Pitching Coach:** Ray Burris. **Trainers:** Chris Mudd. **Strength/Conditioning:** Jason Meredith.

GAME INFORMATION
Radio Announcers: Matt Provence, Jon Schaeffer. **No. Games Broadcast:** 144 (72 Home; 72 Away). **Flagship Radio Station:** ESPN 1240/1320 AM. **Television Station:** TV2. **Television Announcers:** Mike Zambelli, Steve Degler, Matt Provence, Doug Heater. **No. Games Televised:** 72 Home. **PA Announcer:** Tim Chorones. **Official Scorers:** Mike Falk, Jack Logic, David Sheriff, Dick Shute. **Stadium Name:** Coca-Cola Park. **Location:** Take US 22 to exit for Airport Road South, head south, make right on American Parkway, left into stadium. **Standard Game Times:** 7:05 pm, Sat 6:35, Sun 1:35 (April-June), 5:35 (July-Aug).

LOUISVILLE BATS

Office Address: 401 E Main St, Louisville, KY 40202.
Telephone: (502) 212-2287. **Fax:** (502) 515-2255.
E-Mail Address: info@batsbaseball.com. **Website:** www.batsbaseball.com.
Affiliation (first year): Cincinnati Reds (2000). **Years in League:** 1998-

OWNERSHIP/MANAGEMENT
Chariman: Dan Ulmer Jr.
Board of Directors: Edward Glasscock, Gary Ulmer, Kenny Huber, Steve Trager, J Michael Brown.
President/CEO: Gary Ulmer. **Vice President, Business Operations:** James Breeding. **Senior VP, Marketing:** Greg Galiette. **Senior VP, Corporate Sales:** Dale Owens. **VP, Operations/Technology:** Scott Shoemaker. **Director, Baseball Operations:** Josh Hargreaves. **Controller:** Michele Anderson. **Director, Ticket Operations:** Kyle Reh. **Director, Media/Public Relations:** Chadwick Fischer. **Media Relations Assistant:** Nick Curran. **Director, Group Sales:** Bryan McBride. **Director, Broadcasting:** Matt Andrews. **Director, Corporate Suites:** Malcolm Jollie. **Assistant Director, Stadium Operations:** Randy Williams. **Graphic Designer:** Tony Brown. **Assistant Director, Marketing:** Sarah Nordman. **Senior Account Executives:** Hal Norwood, Evan Patrick. **Account Executives:** Brad Wagner, Michael Harmon, Dustin Mercurio, Kevin Gamm. **Assistant Director, Ticket Operations:** Brian Knight. **Groundskeeper:** Tom Nielsen. **Assistant Groundskeeper:** Jason Boston.

FIELD STAFF
Manager: Jim Riggleman. **Hitting Coach:** Tony Jaramillo. **Pitching Coach:** Ted Power. **Trainer:** Jimmy Mattocks.

GAME INFORMATION
Radio Announcers: Matt Andrews. **No. of Games Broadcast:** Home-72, Road-72. **Flagship Station:** WKRD 790-AM. **PA Announcer:** Shayne Duvall. **Official Scorer:** Nick Evans. **Organist:** Bob Ramsey.
Stadium Name: Louisville Slugger Field. **Location:** I-64 and I-71 to I-65 South/North to Brook Street exit, right on Market Street, left on Jackson Street; stadium on Main Street between Jackson and Preston. **Ticket Price Range:** $7-11.
Visiting Club Hotel: Galt House Hotel, 140 North Fourth Street, Louisville, KY 40202. **Telephone:** (502) 589-5200.

NORFOLK TIDES

Office Address: 150 Park Ave, Norfolk, VA 23510.
Telephone: (757) 622-2222. **Fax:** (757) 624-9090.
E-Mail Address: receptionist@norfolktides.com. **Website:** www.norfolktides.com.
Affiliation (first year): Baltimore Orioles (2007). **Years in League:** 1969-

OWNERSHIP/MANAGEMENT
Operated By: Tides Baseball Club Inc.
President: Ken Young.
General Manager: Joe Gregory.
Executive Vice President/Senior Advisor to the President: Dave Rosenfield. **Assistant GM:** Ben Giancola. **Director, Media Relations:** Ian Locke. **Director, Community Relations:** Heather McKeating. **Director, Ticket Operations:** Gretchen Todd. **Director, Group Sales:** Stephanie Hierstein. **Director, Stadium Operations:** Mike Zeman. **Business Manager:** Andrew Garrelts. **Manager, Merchandising:** Ann Marie Piddisi. **Corporate Sponsorships/Promotions:** Jonathan Mensink. **Group/Corporate Sales:** Christina Dewey. **Director, Military Affairs:** John Muszkewycz. **Assistant Director, Stadium Operations:** Mike Cardwell. **Assistant to the Director, Tickets:** Sze Fong. **Event Staff Manager:** Matt Moyer. **Corporate Sponsorships/Promotions:** Mike Watkins. **Media Relations Assistant:** Nate Rowan. **Administrative Assistant:** Lisa Cox.
Head Groundskeeper: Kenny Magner. **Assistant Groundskeeper:** Keith Collins. **Home Clubhouse Manager:** Kevin Casey. **Visiting Clubhouse Manager:** Mark Bunge.

FIELD STAFF
Manager: Ron Johnson. **Hitting Coach:** Denny Walling. **Pitching Coach:** Mike Griffin. **Coach:** Jose Hernandez.

GAME INFORMATION
Radio Announcers: Pete Michaud. **No. of Games Broadcast:** Home-72, Road-72. **Flagship Station:** ESPN 94.1 FM.
PA Announcer: Jack Ankerson. **Official Scorers:** Mike Holtzclaw, Dave Lewis.
Stadium Name: Harbor Park. **Location:** Exit 9, 11A or 11B off I-264, adjacent to the Elizabeth River in downtown Norfolk. **Standard Game Times:** 7:15 pm, Sun 1:15. **Ticket Price Range:** $11-14.
Visiting Club Hotel: Sheraton Waterside, 777 Waterside Dr, Norfolk, VA 23510. **Telephone:** (757) 622-6664.

PAWTUCKET RED SOX

Office Address: One Ben Mondor Way, Pawtucket, RI 02860.
Mailing Address: PO Box 2365, Pawtucket, RI 02861.
Telephone: (401) 724-7300. **Fax:** (401) 724-2140.
E-Mail Address: info@pawsox.com. **Website:** www.pawsox.com.
Affiliation (first year): Boston Red Sox (1973). **Years in League:** 1973-

OWNERSHIP/MANAGEMENT
Operated by: Pawtucket Red Sox Baseball Club, Inc.
President: Mike Tamburro.
Vice President/General Manager: Lou Schwechheimer. **VP, Chief Financial Officer:** Matt White. **VP, Sales/Marketing:** Michael Gwynn. **VP, Stadium Operations:** Mick Tedesco. **VP, Public Relations:** Bill Wanless. **Director, Community Relations:** Jeff Bradley. **Manager, Sales:** Augusto Rojas. **Director, Merchandising:** Eric Petterson. **Director, Media Creation:** Kevin Galligan. **Director, Ticket Sales:** John Wilson. **Director, Warehouse Operations:** Dave Johnson. **Administrative Assistant:** Lauren Dincecco. **Account Executives:** Tom Linehan, Sam Sousa, Mike Lyons, Geoff Sinnott. **Field Superintendant:** Matt McKinnon. **Assistant Groundskeeper:** Kyle Carney. **Director, Security:** Rick Medeiros. **Director, Clubhouse Operations:** Carl Goodreau. **Executive Chef:** Ken Bowdish.

FIELD STAFF
Manager: Gary DiSarcina. **Hitting Coach:** Dave Joppie. **Pitching Coach:** Rich Sauveur. **Trainer:** Jon Jochim.

GAME INFORMATION
Radio Announcers: Unavailable. **No. of Games Broadcast:** Home-72, Away-72. **Flagship Station:** WHJJ 920-AM. **PA Announcer:** Scott Fraser. **Official Scorer:** Bruce Guindon. **Stadium Name:** McCoy Stadium. **Location:** From north, 95 South to exit 2A in Massachusetts (Newport Ave), follow Newport Ave for 2 miles, right on Columbus Ave, follow one mile, stadium on right. From south, 95 North to exit 28 (School Street), right at bottom of exit ramp, through two sets of lights, left onto Pond Street, right on Columbus Ave, stadium entrance on left. From west (Worcester), 295 North to 95 South and follow directions from north. From east (Fall River), 195 West to 95 North and follow directions from south.
Standard Game Times: 7 pm, Sat 6, Sun 1. **Ticket Price Range:** $5-11. **Visiting Club Hotel:** Marriott Courtyard Providence Downtown, 32 Exchange Terrace at Memorial Blvd, Providence, RI 02903. **Telephone:** (401) 272-1191.

ROCHESTER RED WINGS

Office Address: One Morrie Silver Way, Rochester, NY 14608.
Telephone: (585) 454-1001. **Fax:** (585) 454-1056.
E-Mail Address: info@redwingsbaseball.com. **Website:** www.redwingsbaseball.
com.
Affiliation (first year): Minnesota Twins (2003). **Years in League:** 1885-89, 1891-92, 1895-

OWNERSHIP/MANAGEMENT

Operated by: Rochester Community Baseball.
President/CEO/COO: Naomi Silver. **Chairman:** Gary Larder.
General Manager: Dan Mason. **Assistant GM:** Will Rumbold. **Director, Communications:** Mark Rogoff. **Director, Corporate Development:** Nick Sciarratta. **Director, Group Sales/Promotions:** Bob Craig. **Director, Marketing:** Matt Cipro. **Director, Ticket Operations:** Rob Dermody. **Director, Video:** John Blotzer. **Director, Merchandising:** Barbara Moore. **Director, Community Relations:** Danielle Barone. **Manager, Picnic Sales:** Josh Britt. **Controller:** Darlene Giardina. **Director, Human Resources:** Paula LoVerde. **Head Groundskeeper:** Gene Buonomo. **Account Executives:** Eric Friedman, Derek Swanson. **Executive Secretary:** Ginny Colbert. **General Manager, Food Services:** Jeff Dodge. **Director/Catering:** Courtney Trawitz. **Manager, Concessions:** Jeff DeSantis. **Executive Chef:** Mark Feiock. **Warehouse Manager:** Rob Burgett. **Business Manager, Concessions:** Dave Bills.

FIELD STAFF

Manager: Gene Glynn. **Coach:** Tim Doherty. **Pitching Coach:** Marty Mason. **Trainer:** Larry Bennese.

GAME INFORMATION

Radio Announcer: Josh Whetzel. **No. of Games Broadcast:** Home-72, Away-72. **Flagship Stations:** WHTK 1280-AM, WYSL 1040-AM.
PA Announcers: Kevin Spears, Rocky Perrotta. **Official Scorers:** Warren Kozireski, Brendan Harrington.
Stadium Name: Frontier Field. **Location:** I-490 East to exit 12 (Brown/Broad Street) and follow signs; I-490 West to exit 14 (Plymouth Ave) and follow signs. **Standard Game Times:** 7:05 pm, Sun 1:05. **Ticket Price Range:** $7-11.
Visiting Club Hotel: Rochester Plaza, 70 State St, Rochester, NY 14608. **Telephone:** (585) 546-3450.

SCRANTON/WILKES-BARRE
RAILRIDERS

Office Address: 235 Montage Mountain Road, Moosic, PA 18507.
Telephone: (570) 969-2255. **Fax:** (570) 963-6564. **E-Mail Address:** info@swbrailriders.
com. **Website:** www.swbrailriders.com.
Affiliation (first year): New York Yankees (2007). **Years in League:** 1989-

OWNERSHIP/MANAGEMENT

Owned by: SWB Yankees, LLC.
Operated by: SWB Yankees, LLC.
President/General Manager: Rob Crain. **Executive VP, Operations:** Jeremy Ruby. **Executive VP, Business Operations:** Paul Chilek. **VP, Ticket Sales:** Doug Augis. **VP, Marketing/Corporate Services:** Katie Beekman. **VP, Stadium Operations:** Curt Camoni. **VP, Corporate Partnerships:** Mike Trudnak.
Director, Media Relations/Broadcasting: John Sadak. **Media Relations/Broadcasting Assistant:** Andrew Kappes. **Director, Fan Experience:** Cameron Wengrzyn. **Staff Accountant:** William Steiner. **Corporate Partnerships:** Curtis Phair. **Director, Corporate Services/Special Events:** Kristina Knight. **Community Relations Manager:** Ryan Beardsley. **Corporate Services Manager:** Karen Luciano. **Corporate Services Manager:** Lindsey Graham. **Ticket Operations Manager:** Seth Atkinson. **Inside Sales/Customer Account Managers:** Kelly Cusick, Allison Juchem. **Corporate Ticket Sales Executives:** Robert McLane, Mario Scarfalloto. **Group Sales Coordinators:** Katie Kuhn, Amanda Zuzik, Holly Norton, Nick Wenderlich. **Ticket Operations Assistant:** Bryant Guilmette. **Operations Manager:** Rob Galdieri. **Director, Field Operations:** Steve Horne. **Director, Facility Operations:** Joe Villano.

FIELD STAFF

Manager: Dave Miley. **Hitting Coach:** Butch Wynegar. **Pitching Coach:** Scott Aldred. **Coach:** Frank Menechino. **Trainer:** Darren London. **Strength/Conditioning Coach:** Lee Tressel.

GAME INFORMATION

Radio Announcers: John Sadak, Andrew Kappes. **No. of games broadcast:** Home- 72 Road- 72. **Flagship Stations:** 100.7 FM, 1340 WYCK-AM, 1400 WICK-AM, 1440 WCDL-AM, 106.7 FM. **PA Announcer:** Unavailable. **Official Scorer:** Unavailable. **Stadium Name:** PNC Field. **Location:** Moosic, Pa. **Standard Game Times:** 6:35 pm (April/May) 7:05 (June-August), Sun 1:05. **Ticket Price Range:** $7-$16.
Visiting Club Hotel: Radisson Lackawanna Station. **Telephone:** (570) 342-8300.

SYRACUSE CHIEFS

Office Address: One Tex Simone Dr, Syracuse, NY 13208.
Telephone: (315) 474-7833. **Fax:** (315) 474-2658.
E-Mail Address: baseball@syracusechiefs.com. **Website:** www.syracusechiefs.com.
Affiliation (first year): Washington Nationals (2009).
Years in League: 1885-89, 1891-92, 1894-1901, 1918, 1920-27, 1934-55, 1961-

OWNERSHIP/MANAGEMENT
Operated by: Community Owned Baseball Club of Central New York, Inc.
Chairman: Charles Rich. **President:** William Dutch. **Executive Vice President/COO:** Anthony "Tex" Simone.
General Manager: John Simone. **Assistant GM/Director, Marketing/Promotions:** Mike Voutsinas. **Assistant GM, Business:** Don Lehtonen. **Director, Sales:** Paul Fairbanks. **Director, Group Sales:** Victor Gallucci. **Director, Broadcasting/Public Relations:** Jason Benetti. **Assistant Director, Broadcasting/Public Relations:** Kevin Brown. **Director, Merchandising:** Wendy Shoen. **Director, Ticket Office:** Josh Jones. **Administrative Assistant:** Priscilla Venditti. **Turf Manager:** Jon Stewart. **Team Historian:** Ron Gersbacher.

FIELD STAFF
Manager: Tony Beasley. **Hitting Coach:** Troy Gingrich. **Pitching Coach:** Greg Booker. **Trainer:** Unavailable. **Strength Coordinator:** Ryan Pye.

GAME INFORMATION
Radio Announcers: Jason Benetti/Kevin Brown. **No. of Games Broadcast:** Home-72, Away-72. **Flagship Station:** The Score 1260 AM. **PA Announcer:** Dan Rayome. **Official Scorer:** Sam Leo.
Stadium Name: Alliance Bank Stadium. **Location:** New York State Thruway to exit 36 (I-81 South), to 7th North Street exit, left on 7th North, right on Hiawatha Boulevard. **Standard Game Times:** 7 pm, Sun 2, 6. **Ticket Price Range:** $6-10.
Visiting Club Hotel: Ramada Inn, 1305 Buckley Rd, Syracuse, NY 13212. **Telephone:** (315) 457-8670.

TOLEDO MUD HENS

Office Address: 406 Washington St, Toledo, OH 43604.
Telephone: (419) 725-4367. **Fax:** (419) 725-4368.
E-Mail Address: mudhens@mudhens.com. **Website:** www.mudhens.com.
Affiliation (first year): Detroit Tigers (1987). **Years in League:** 1889, 1965-

OWNERSHIP/MANAGEMENT
Operated By: Toledo Mud Hens Baseball Club, Inc.
Chairman of the Board: Michael Miller.
Vice President: David Huey. **Secretary/Treasurer:** Charles Bracken.
President/General Manager: Joseph Napoli.
Chief Marketing Officer: Kim McBroom. **Assistant GM/Director, Corporate Partnerships:** Neil Neukam. **Assistant GM, Ticket Sales/Operations:** Erik Ibsen. **Assistant GM, Food/Beverage:** Craig Nelson. **CFO:** Pam Alspach. **Manager, Promotions:** Michael Keedy. **Communications Director:** Andi Roman. **Director, Ticket Sales/Services:** Thomas Townley. **Accounting:** Sheri Kelly, Brian Leverenz. **Manager, Gameday Operations:** Greg Setola. **Manager, Community Relations:** Cheri Pastula. **Corporate Sales Associate:** Ed Sintic. **Season Ticket/Group Sales Associates:** Frank Kristie, Kyle Moll, John Mulka. **Manager, Online Marketing:** Nathan Steinmetz. **Game Plan Advisor:** Colleen Rerucha. **Special Events Coordinator:** Emily Croll. **Director, Broadcast Services:** Greg Tye.
Graphic Designer: Dan Royer. **Manager, Souvenir Sales:** Craig Katz. **Manager, Swamp Shop:** Stephanie Miller. **Manager, Ballpark Operations:** Ken Westenkirchner. **Office Manager:** Carol Hamilton. **Executive Assistant:** Tracy Evans. **Turf Manager:** Jake Tyler. **Clubhouse Manager:** Joe Sarkisian. **Team Historian:** John Husman.

FIELD STAFF
Manager: Phil Nevin. **Coach:** Leon Durham. **Pitching Coach:** AJ Sager. **Trainer:** Matt Rankin.

GAME INFORMATION
TV Announcers: Jim Weber, Matt Melzak. **No of Games Broadcast:** Home-72. **TV Flagship Station:** BCSN (Buckeye Cable Sports Network).
Radio Announcers: Jim Weber. **No of Games Broadcast:** Home-72 Road-72. **Flagship Station:** WCWA 1230 AM.
PA Announcer: Unavailable. **Official Scorers:** Jeff Businger, Ron Kleinfelter, Guy Lammers.
Stadium Name: Fifth Third Field. **Location:** From Ohio Turnpike 80/90, exit 54 (4A) to I-75 North, follow I-75 North to exit 201-B, left onto Erie Street, right onto Washington Street; From Detroit, I-75 South to exit 202-A, right onto Washington Street; From Dayton, I-75 North to exit 201-B, left onto Erie Street, right on Washington Street; From Ann Arbor, Route 23 South to I-475 East, I-475 east to I-75 South, I-75 South to exit 202-A, right onto Washington Street.
Ticket Price Range: $9.
Visiting Club Hotel: Park Inn, 101 North Summit, Toledo, OH 43604. **Telephone:** (419) 241-3000.

PACIFIC COAST LEAGUE

PACIFIC COAST LEAGUE

Address: One Chisholm Trail, Suite 4200, Round Rock, Texas 78681.
Telephone: (512) 310-2900. **Fax:** (512) 310-8300.
E-Mail Address: office@pclbaseball.com. **Website:** www.pclbaseball.com.
President: Branch B. Rickey.

Vice President: Don Logan (Las Vegas).

Directors: Don Beaver (New Orleans), Sam Bernabe (Iowa), John Pontius (Memphis), Chris Cummings (Fresno), Dave Elmore (Colorado Springs), Aaron Artman (Tacoma), Don Logan (Las Vegas), George King (Round Rock), Marc Amicone (Salt Lake), Gary Green (Omaha), Art Matin (Oklahoma), Josh Hunt (Tucson), Jeff Savage (Sacramento), John Traub (Albuquerque), Frank Ward (Nashville), Stuart Katzoff (Reno).

Director, Business: Melanie Fiore. **Director, Baseball Operations:** Dwight Hall. **Media/Operations Assistant:** Matt Lundgren.

Division Structure: American Conference—Northern: Iowa, Memphis, Nashville, Omaha. Southern: Albuquerque, New Orleans, Oklahoma, Round Rock. Pacific Conference—Northern: Colorado Springs, Reno, Salt Lake, Tacoma. Southern: Fresno, Las Vegas, Sacramento, Tucson.

Regular Season: 144 games. **2013 Opening Date:** April 4. **Closing Date:** Sept 2.

All-Star Game: July 15 at Reno Aces, Reno, Nevada (PCL vs International League).

Branch Rickey

Playoff Format: Pacific Conference/Northern winner meets Southern winner, and American Conference/Northern winner meets Southern winner in best-of-five semifinal series. Winners meet in best-of-five series for league championship.

Triple-A Championship Game: Sept 17 (PCL vs International League).

Roster Limit: 24. **Player Eligibility Rule:** No restrictions.

Brand of Baseball: Rawlings ROM.

Umpires: Gerard, Ascani (San Antonio, TX), Nick Bailey (Big Spring, TX), Jordan Baker (Shawnee, OK), Steve Barga (Mesa, AZ), Lance Barrett (Fort Worth, TX), Cory Blaser (Westminster, CO), Angel Campos (Tucson, AZ), Clint Fagan (Tomball, TX), Jordan Ferrell (Clarksville, TN), Spencer Flynn (Plymouth, MN), Hal Gibson (Marysville, WA), Brian Hertzog (Lake Stevens, WA), Joel Hospodka (Omaha, NE), Kolin Kline (Arvada, CO), Shaun Lampe (Phoenix, AZ), Kellen Levy (Mesa, AZ), Patrick Mahoney (Pittsburg, CA), Brandon Misun (Edmond, OK), Michael Muchlinski (Ephrata, WA), Marcus Pattillo (Jonesboro, AR), Daniel Reyburn (Franklin, TN), Mark Ripperger (Carlsbad, CA), Stuart Scheurwater (Regina, Saskatchewan, Canada), Adam Schwarz (Riverside, CA), Chris Segal (Burke, VA), Gregory Stanzak (Phoenix, AZ), John Tumpane (Oak Lawn, IL), Quinn Wolcott (Puyallup, WA), Thomas Woodring (Boulder, NV).

STADIUM INFORMATION

Club	Stadium	Opened	Dimensions LF	CF	RF	Capacity	2012 Att.
Albuquerque	Isotopes Park	2003	340	400	340	13,279	568,417
Colorado Springs	Security Service Field	1988	350	410	350	8,400	334,245
Fresno	Chukchansi Park	2002	324	402	335	12,500	471,686
Iowa	Principal Park	1992	335	400	335	11,000	509,798
Las Vegas	Cashman Field	1983	328	433	328	9,334	311,516
Memphis	AutoZone Park	2000	319	400	322	14,300	493,706
Nashville	Herschel Greer Stadium	1978	327	400	327	10,700	321,042
New Orleans	Zephyr Field	1997	333	405	332	10,000	329,942
Oklahoma City	RedHawks Field	1998	325	400	325	11,455	399,965
Omaha	Werner Park	2011	310	402	315	9,023	415,650
Reno	Aces Ballpark	2009	339	410	340	9,100	389,860
Round Rock	The Dell Diamond	2000	330	400	325	10,000	595,584
Sacramento	Raley Field	2000	330	405	325	14,014	586,090
Salt Lake	Spring Mobile Ballpark	1994	345	420	315	15,500	515,633
Tacoma	Cheney Stadium	1960	325	425	325	8000	352,032
Tucson	Kino Stadium	1998	340	405	340	11,500	200,991

ALBUQUERQUE ISOTOPES

Office Address: 1601 Avenida Cesar Chavez SE, Albuquerque, NM 87106.
Telephone: (505) 924-2255. **Fax:** (505) 242-8899.
E-Mail Address: info@abqisotopes.com. **Website:** www.abqisotopes.com.
Affiliation (first year): Los Angeles Dodgers (2009). **Years in League:** 1972-2000, 2003-

OWNERSHIP/MANAGEMENT

President: Ken Young. **Vice President/Secretary/Treasurer:** Emmett Hammond. **General Manager:** John Traub. **Assistant GM, Sales/Marketing:** Nick LoBue. **Director, Box Office/Retail Operations:** Chrissy Baines. **Director, Sales/Promotions:** Adam Beggs. **Director, Media Relations:** Laura Verillo. **Director, Stadium Operations:** Bobby Atencio. **Manager, Community Relations/Promotions:** Kim Stoebick. **Manager, Suite Relations:** Paul Hartenberger. **Manager,**

Creative Services: Kris Shepard. **Season Ticket/Group Sales Representatives:** Quentin Andes, Jason Buchta, David Wenigmann, Jordan Vicain. **Director, Accounting/Human Resources:** Cynthia DiFrancesco. **Assistant Director, Retail Operations:** Patrick Westrick. **Assistant Director, Box Office Operations:** Kyle Hamman.

    Stadium Operations Assistant: Nathan McNair. **Director, Field Operations:** Casey Griffin. **Manager, Field Operations:** Gil South. **Home Clubhouse Manager:** Bubba Hearn. **Visiting Clubhouse Manager:** Rick Pollack. **Front Office Assistant:** Mark Otero. **GM, Ovations Foodservices:** Patrick Queeney. **Catering Manager, Ovations Foodservices:** Amanda Baca. **Concession Manager, Ovations Foodservices:** Matt Butler. **Head Chef:** Scott Eastburn.

FIELD STAFF

    Manager: Lorenzo Bundy. **Hitting Coach:** Franklin Stubbs. **Pitching Coach:** Glenn Dishman. **Trainer:** Yosuke Nakajima.

GAME INFORMATION

    Radio Announcer: Robert Portnoy. **No. of Games Broadcast:** Home-72 Road-72. **Flagship Station:** KNML 610-AM. **PA Announcer:** Stu Walker. **Official Scorers:** Gary Herron, James Hilchen.

    Stadium Name: Isotopes Park. **Location:** From 1-25, exit east on Avenida Cesar Chavez SE to University Boulevard; From I-40, exit south on University Boulevard SE to Avenida Cesar Chavez. **Standard Game Times:** 7:05 pm, Sun 6:05. **Ticket Price Range:** $7-$25.

    Visiting Club Hotel: Sheraton Albuquerque Airport Hotel, 2910 Yale Blvd SE, Albuquerque, NM 87106. **Telephone:** (505) 843-7000.

COLORADO SPRINGS SKY SOX

Office Address: 4385 Tutt Blvd, Colorado Springs, CO 80922.
Telephone: (719) 597-1449. **Fax:** (719) 597-2491.
E-Mail address: info@skysox.com. **Website:** www.skysox.com.
Affiliation (first year): Colorado Rockies (1993). **Years in League:** 1988-

OWNERSHIP/MANAGEMENT

    Operated By: Colorado Springs Sky Sox Inc.
    Principal Owner: David Elmore.
    President/General Manager: Tony Ensor. **Assistant GM/Director, Public Relations:** Mike Hobson. **Director, Corporate Sales:** Chris Phillips. **Director, Broadcasting:** Dan Karcher. **Director, Accounting:** Kelly Hanlon. **Director, Ticket Operations:** Whitney Shellem. **Director, Group Sales:** Keith Hodges. **Director, Marketing/Promotions:** Jon Eddy. **Vice President, Field Operations:** Steve DeLeon. **Manager, Graphics/Merchandise:** Erin Moroney. **Manager, Stadium Operations:** Eric Martin. **Manager, Corporate Sales:** Alec Shepherd. **Assistant Director, Group Sales:** Jim Rice. **Event Manager:** Brien Smith. **GM, Diamond Creations:** Don Giuliano. **Executive Chef:** Chris Evans.

    Public Relations Assistant: Dan Kopf. **Stadium Operations Assistant:** Ryan Gaynor. **Assistant, Corporate Sales/Promotions:** Cole Chisholm. **Assistant, Marketing/Promotions:** Wes Kaminski. **Managers, Group Sales:** Mike Marso, Drew Trujillo. **Coordinator, Community Relations/Ticketing:** Alyce Bofferding. **Ticketing Assistant:** Emily Droessler. **Group Sales Assistant:** Charles Mushin. **Receptionist:** Marianne Paine. **Home Clubhouse Manager:** Ricky Grima. **Visiting Clubhouse Manager:** Steve Martin.

FIELD STAFF

    Manager: Glenallen Hill. **Coach:** Dave Hajek. **Pitching Coach:** Dave Schuler.

GAME INFORMATION

    Radio Announcer: Dan Karcher. **No. of Games Broadcast:** Home-72 Road-72. **Flagship Station:** AM 1300 "The Sports Animal." **PA Announcer:** Josh Howe. **Official Scorer:** Marty Grantz, Rich Wastler, Ken Jones.

    Stadium Name: Security Service Field. **Location:** I-25 South to Woodmen Road exit, east on Woodmen to Powers Boulevard, right on Powers to Barnes Road. **Standard Game Times:** 7:05 pm, Sat 6:05, Sun 1:05. **Ticket Price Range:** $5-13.

    Visiting Club Hotel: Hilton Garden Inn, 1810 Briargate Parkway, Colorado Springs, CO 80920. **Telephone:** (719) 598-6866.

FRESNO GRIZZLIES

Office Address: 1800 Tulare St, Fresno, CA 93721.
Telephone: (559) 320-4487. **Fax:** (559) 264-0795.
E-Mail Address: info@fresnogrizzlies.com. **Website:** www.FresnoGrizzlies.com.
Affiliation (first year): San Francisco Giants (1998). **Years in League:** 1998-

OWNERSHIP/MANAGEMENT

    Operated By: Fresno Baseball Club, LLC.
    President: Chris Cummings. **Executive Vice President:** Brian Glover. **Chief Financial Officer:** SuSin Correa. **VP, Sales:** Derek Franks. **VP, Marketing/Stadium Events:** Drew Vertiz.

    Director, Client Services: Andrew Melrose. **Director, Corporate Partnerships:** Jerry James. **Director, Stadium Operations:** Harvey Kawasaki. **Director, Event Operations:** Matt Studwell. **Director, Human Resources:** Ashley Tennell. **Grizzlies Community Fund Manager:** Whitney Campbell. **Community Relations Assistant:** Chris Wilson. **Coordinator,**

Marketing/Promotions: Sarah Loving. **Coordinator, Media Relations:** Chris Kutz. **Coordinator, Stadium/Baseball Operations:** Joe Castillo. **Coordinators, Entertainment/Mascot:** Troy Simeon, Nick Haas. **Graphic Designers:** Sam Hansen, Jennifer Rose. **Inside Sales Manager:** Andrew Milios. **Boxt Office Manager:** Cody Holden. **Senior Group Sales Account Executive:** Adam Gleich.

Corporate Sponsorship Account Executive: Ray Ortiz. **Partnership Executive:** Phillip Kasparian. **Ticket Account Executives:** Marissa Barretta, Ryan Malone, Jon Stockton. **Assistant Ticket Sales Manager:** Brian Boden. **Ticket Sales Assistant:** Andrea Renfro. **Client Services Executive:** Karen Kelly. **Manager, Operations:** Ira Calvin. **Head Groundskeeper:** David Jacinto. **Finance Managers:** Monica Delacerda, Brian Mehlman. **Manager, Team Store:** Lalonnie Calderon. **Manager, Guest Services:** Steve Sodini. **Receptionist:** DeeAnn Hernandez. **GM, Ovations Concessions:** Tim Dickert.

FIELD STAFF

Manager: Bob Mariano. **Hitting Coach:** Russ Morman. **Pitching Coach:** Pat Rice. **Athletic Trainer:** Eric Ortega. **Strength/Conditioning Coach:** Jim Bose.

GAME INFORMATION

Radio Announcer: Doug Greenwald. **No. of Games Broadcast:** Home-72 Road-72. **Flagship Station:** 105.5 FM The Truth (Wilks Broadcasting). **Official Scorer:** Matt Pena. **Stadium Name:** Chukchansi Park. **Location:** 1800 Tulare St, Fresno, CA 93721. **Directions:** From 99 North, take Fresno Street exit, left on Fresno Street, left on Inyo or Tulare to stadium; From 99 South, take Fresno Street exit, left on Fresno Street, right on Broadway to H Street; From 41 North, take Van Ness exit toward Fresno, left on Van Ness, left on Inyo or Tulare, stadium is straight ahead; From 41 South, take Tulare exit, stadium is located at Tulare and H Streets, or take Van Ness exit, right on Van Ness, left on Inyo or Tulare, stadium is straight ahead. **Ticket Price Range:** $9-19. **Visiting Club Hotel:** Holiday Inn Downtown Fresno, 1055 Van Ness, Fresno, CA 93721. **Telephone:** (888) 465-4329.

IOWA CUBS

Office Address: One Line Drive, Des Moines IA 50309. **Telephone:** (515) 243-6111. **Fax:** (515) 243-5152. **Website:** www.iowacubs.com **Affiliation (first year):** Chicago Cubs (1981). **Years in League:** 1969-

OWNERSHIP/MANAGEMENT

Operated By: Raccoon Baseball Inc.
Chairman/Principal Owner: Michael Gartner. **Executive Vice President:** Michael Giudicessi.
President/General Manager: Sam Bernabe. **Shareholder:** Mike Gartner. **VP/Assistant GM:** Nate Teut, Jim Nahas. **VP/CFO:** Sue Tollefson. **VP/Director, Broadcast Operations:** Deene Ehlis.
Director, Media Relations: Randy Wehofer. **Director, Communications:** Scott Sailor. **Director, Marketing/Video Presentation:** Blake Havard. **Director, Ticket Operations:** Kenny Houser. **Director, Luxury Suites:** Brent Conkel. **Assistant Ticket Manager:** Eric Hammes. **Director, Group Sales:** Aaron Roland. **Director, Stadium Operations:** Jeff Tilley. **Manager, Stadium Operations:** Jake Samo. **Assistant, Stadium Operations:** Jerod Davey. **Corporate Relations:** Red Hollis. **Head Groundskeeper:** Chris Schlosser.
Director, Merchandise: Rick Giudicessi. **Accountant:** Lori Auten. **Manager, Cub Club:** Derek Hickey. **Director, Information Technology:** Ryan Clutter. **Landscape Coordinator:** Shari Kramer.

FIELD STAFF

Manager: Marty Pevey. **Hitting Coach:** Brian Harper. **Pitching Coach:** Mike Mason. **Athletic trainer:** Nick Frangella. **Strength/Conditioning:** Ed Kohl.

GAME INFORMATION

Radio Announcers: Deene Ehlis, Randy Wehofer. **No. of Games Broadcast:** Home-72 Road-72. **Flagship Station:** AM 940 KPSZ. **PA Announcers:** Aaron Johnson, Mark Pierce, Corey Coon. **Official Scorers:** Jayme Adam, Michael Pecina. **Stadium Name:** Principal Park. **Location:** I-80 or I-35 to I-235, to Third Street exit, south on Third Street, left on Line Drive. **Standard Game Times:** 7:05 pm; Sun 1:05. **Ticket Price Range:** $4-14. **Visiting Club Hotel:** Embassy Suites, 101 East Locust St, Des Moines IA 50309. **Telephone:** (515) 244-1700.

LAS VEGAS 51S

Office Address: 850 Las Vegas Blvd North, Las Vegas, NV 89101. **Telephone:** (702) 943-7200. **Fax:** (702) 943-7214.
E-Mail Address: info@lv51.com. **Website:** www.lv51.com
Affiliation (first year): New York Mets (2013). **Years in League:** 1983-.

OWNERSHIP/MANAGEMENT

Operated By: SBG, LLC.
Executive Vice President: Don Logan. **General Manager/VP, Marketing:** Chuck Johnson.
VP, Sponsorships: Mike Hollister. **VP, Ticket Operations:** Mike Rodriguez. **VP, Operations/Security:** Nick Fitzenreider. **Controller:** Araxi Demirjian. **Director, Broadcasting:** Russ Langer. **Director, Ticket Sales:** Erik Eisenberg. **Director,**

Community Relations/Customer Service: Melissa Harkavy. Baseball Administration/Travel Director: Denise Korach. Business Development: Larry Brown. Media Relations Director: Jim Gemma. Ticket Operations Assistant: Michelle Taggart. Administrative Assistants: Jan Dillard, Pat Dressel. Account Executives, Ticket Sales: Justin Dunbar, Bryan Frey, Josh Rusnak. Retail Operations Manager: Jason Weber. Sponsorship Services Manager: William Graham. Operations Manager: Chip Vespe.

FIELD STAFF
Manager: Wally Backman. Hitting Coach: George Greer. Pitching Coach: Randy St. Claire. Athletic Trainer: Joe Golia. Strength/Conditioning Coach: Ronald Kenyatta.

GAME INFORMATION
Radio Announcer: Russ Langer. No. of Games Broadcast: Home-72 Road-72. Flagship Station: Fox Sports Radio 920-AM. PA Announcer: Dan Bickmore. Official Scorers: Gary Arlitz, Mark Wasik.
Stadium Name: Cashman Field. Location: I-15 to US 95 exit (downtown), east to Las Vegas Boulevard North exit, one-half mile north to stadium. Standard Game Time: 7:05 pm. Ticket Price Range: $10-14.
Visiting Club Hotel: Golden Nugget Hotel & Casino, 129 Fremont Street, Las Vegas, NV 89101. Telephone: (702) 385-7111.

MEMPHIS REDBIRDS

Office Address: 175 Toyota Plaza, Suite 300, Memphis, TN 38103.
Stadium Address: 200 Union Ave. Memphis, TN 38103.
Telephone: (901) 721-6000. Fax: (901) 842-1222.
Website: www.memphisredbirds.com.
Affiliation (first year): St. Louis Cardinals (1998). Years in League: 1998-

OWNERSHIP/MANAGEMENT
Ownership: Memphis Redbirds Baseball Foundation, Inc. Managed by: Global Spectrum.
General Manager: Ben Weiss. Assistant GM/Director, Sales: Derek Goldfarb.
Director, Operations: Mark Anderson. Coordinator, Operations: Kevin Rooney. Director, Finance: Art Davis. Director, Marketing: Adam Goldberg. Ticket Operations Manager: Travis Trumitch. Ticket Sales Manager: Jason Mott. Marketing Manager: Erin O'Donnell. Media Relations Manager: Michael Whitty. Graphic Designer/Photographer: Allison Rhoades. Special Event Coordinator: Kellie Grabert. Corporate Sales Executive: Corey Bush. Corporate Sales Coordinator: Leigh Eisenberg. Sales Coordinator: Shannon Comerford. Ticket Sales Executives: Corey Gilden, Alex Sides. Staff Accountant: Cindy Neal. Office Coordinator: Linda Smith. Head Groundskeeper: Ed Collins. Chief Engineer: Danny Abbott. Maintenance: Spencer Shields. Groundskeeper: Andrew Strong.

FIELD STAFF
Manager: Ron Warner. Coach: Mark Budaska. Pitching Coach: Bryan Eversgerd. Trainer: Jeremy Clipperton. Strength/Conditioning Coach: Sean Johnson

GAME INFORMATION
Radio Announcer: Steve Selby.
No. of Games Broadcast: Home-72 Road-72. Flagship Station: WHBQ 560-AM. PA Announcer: Unavailable. Official Scorer: JJ Guinozzo.
Stadium Name: AutoZone Park. Location: North on I-240, exit at Union Avenue West, one and half mile to park. Standard Game Times: 7:05 pm, Sat 6:05, Sun 1:35. Ticket Price Range: $6-23. Visiting Club Hotel: Sleep Inn at Court Square, 40 N Front, Memphis, TN 38103. Telephone: (901) 522-9700.

NASHVILLE SOUNDS

Office Address: 534 Chestnut Street, Nashville, TN 37203.
Telephone: (615) 690-HITS. Fax: (615) 256-5684.
E-Mail address: info@nashvillesounds.com. Website: www.nashvillesounds.com
Affiliation (first year): Milwaukee Brewers (2005). Years in League: 1998-

OWNERSHIP/MANAGEMENT
Operated By: MFP Baseball.
Owners: Frank Ward, Masahiro Honzawa.
Vice President/General Manager: Brad Tammen. Assistant GM: Doug Scopel. Assistant GM, Sales/Marketing: Jason Franke. Director, Accounting: Barb Walker. Director, Community Relations: Michael Bigley. Director, Group Sales/Hospitality: Drew Himsworth. Manager, Stadium Operations: Mike Simonson. Manager, Community Relations: Buddy Yelton. Manager, Ticketing: Eric Laue. Manager, Media Relations: Alex Wassel. Manager, Advertising/Marketing: Cliff McArdle. Manager, Corporate Partnerships/Promotions: Brandon Yerger. Senior Account Executive: Kevin Samborski. Account Executives: Josh Barnes, Justin Webster. Office Manager: Sharon Ridley. Head Groundskeeper: Thomas Trotter. Assistant Groundskeeper: Alex Norman. Clubhouse Managers: JR Rinaldi, Cole Filosa.

FIELD STAFF
Manager: Mike Guerrero. Coach: Bob Skube. Pitching Coach: Fred Dabney. Trainer: Aaron Hoback. Strength/

Conditioning Coach: Andrew Emmick.

GAME INFORMATION

Radio Announcer: Jeff Hem. **No of Games Broadcast:** Home-72 Road-72. **Flagship Station:** 102.5 FM (WPRT). **PA Announcers:** Eric Berner, Jim Kiser. **Official Scorers:** Eric Jones, Trevor Garrett, Robert Hernberger, Kyle Parkinson. **Stadium Name:** Herschel Greer Stadium. **Location:** I-65 to Wedgewood exit, west to Eighth Avenue, right on Eighth to Chestnut Street, right on Chestnut. **Standard Game Times:** 7:05 pm, Sat 6:35, Sun 2:05 (April-June), 6:35 (July-Sept). **Ticket Price Range:** $8-14.
Visiting Club Hotel: Holiday Inn Vanderbilt, 2613 West End Avenue, Nashville, TN 37203. **Telephone:** (615) 327-4707.

NEW ORLEANS ZEPHYRS

Office Address: 6000 Airline Dr, Metairie, LA 70003.
Telephone: (504) 734-5155. **Fax:** (504) 734-5118.
E-Mail Address: zephyrs@zephyrsbaseball.com. **Website:** www.zephyrsbaseball.com.
Affiliation (first year): Miami Marlins (2009). **Years in League:** 1998-

OWNERSHIP/MANAGEMENT

Managing Partner/President: Don Beaver.
Executive Director/COO: Ron Maestri. **Minority Owner/Vice President/General Counsel:** Walter Leger. **General Manager:** Mike Schline. **VP, Sales/Marketing/Community Relations:** Jeff Booker. **Director, Broadcasting/Team Travel:** Tim Grubbs. **Color Analyst/Speakers Bureau:** Ron Swoboda. **Director, Media Relations:** Dave Sachs. **Director, Promotions/Merchandise:** Brandon Puls. **Director, Ticket Operations:** Kathy Kaleta. **Director, Community Relations:** Jeremy Thomas. **Director, Finance/Accounting:** Donna Light. **Director, Stadium Operations:** Jose Avila. **Assistant, Stadium Operations:** Brian Adler. **Director, Clubhouse:** Brett Herbert. **Group Outings Coordinators:** Katie Bonaccorso, Greg Herbert, Michael Morse, Tori Stein. **Coordinator, Marketing:** Sarah Wasser.
Head Groundskeeper: Thomas Marks. **Maintenance Coordinator:** Craig Shaffer. **Receptionist:** Susan Radkovich. **Director, Operations, Messina's Inc:** George Messina. **Administrative Assistant, Messina's Inc:** Priscilla Arbello. **Catering Manager, Messina's Inc:** Andrew Messina.

FIELD STAFF

Manager: Ron Hassey. **Hitting Coach:** Damon Minor. **Pitching Coach:** Charlie Corbell. **Trainer:** Chris Olson.

GAME INFORMATION

Radio Announcers: Tim Grubbs, Ron Swoboda. **No. of Games Broadcast:** Home-72 Road-72. **Flagship Station:** WMTI 106.1 FM. **PA Announcer:** Doug Moreau. **Official Scorer:** JL Vangilder. **Stadium Name:** Zephyr Field. **Location:** I-10 West toward Baton Rouge, exit at Clearview Pkwy (exit 226) and continues south, right on Airline Drive (US 61 North) for 1 mile, stadium on left; From airport, take Airline Drive (US 61) east for 4 miles, stadium on right. **Standard Game Times:** 7 pm, Sat 6, Sun 2 (April-May), 6 (June-Sept). **Ticket Price Range:** $6-10.
Visiting Club Hotel: Sheraton Four Points, 6401 Veterans Memorial Blvd, Metairie, LA 70003. **Telephone:** (504) 885-5700.

OKLAHOMA CITY REDHAWKS

Office Address: 2 S Mickey Mantle Dr, Oklahoma City, OK 73104.
Telephone: (405) 218-1000. **Fax:** (405) 218-1001.
E-Mail Address: info@okcredhawks.com. **Website:** www.okcredhawks.com.
Affiliation (first year): Houston Astros (2011). **Years in League:** 1963-1968, 1998-

OWNERSHIP/MANAGEMENT

Operated By: OKC Athletic Club LLC.
Principal Owner: Mandalay Baseball Properties. **President/General Manager:** Michael Byrnes. **VP, Ticketing:** Jenna Byrnes. **Director, Ticket Sales:** Matt Hernandez. **Director, Finance/Accounting:** Jon Shaw. **Director, Facility Operations:** Harlan Budde. **Director, Operations:** Mike Prange. **Director, Sponsor Services:** Chris Hart. **Director, Entertainment:** Leah Watkins. **Director, Food /Beverage:** Travis Johnson. **Manager, Media Relations/Broadcasting:** Alex Freedman. **Manager, Merchandise:** Nancy Simmons. **Manager, Baseball Operations:** Mitch Stubenhofer. **Ticket Office Manager:** Armando Reyes. **Office Manager:** Travis Hunter. **Head Groundskeeper:** Monte McCoy.

FIELD STAFF

Manager: Tony DeFrancesco. **Hitting Coach:** Leon Roberts. **Pitching Coach:** Steve Webber. **Infield Coach:** Tom Lawless. **Athletic Trainer:** Mike Freer. **Strength/Conditioning Coach:** Alex Pounds.

GAME INFORMATION

Radio Announcer: Alex Freedman **No. of Games Broadcast:** Home-72 Road-72.
Station: KGHM-AM 1340 **Website:** www.1340thegame.com. **PA Announcer:** Tom Travis. **Official Scorers:** Jim Byers, Ryan McGhee, Rich Tortorelli.
Location: Bricktown area in downtown Oklahoma City, near interchange of I-235 and I-40, off I-235 take Sheridan exit to Bricktown; off I-40 take Shields exit, north to Bricktown.
Standard Game Times: 7:05 pm, Sun 2:05 (April-May), 6:05 (June-Aug). **Ticket Price Range:** $5-17.

Visiting Club Hotel: Courtyard Oklahoma City Downtown, 2 West Reno Avenue, Oklahoma City, OK 73102. **Telephone:** (405) 232-2290.

OMAHA STORM CHASERS

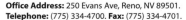

Office Address: Werner Park, 12356 Ballpark Way, Papillion, NE 68046.
Administrative Office Phone: (402) 734-2550. **Ticket Office Phone:** (402) 738-5100. **Fax:** (402) 734-7166.
E-mail Address: info@omahastormchasers.com. **Website:** www.omahastormchasers.com.
Affiliation (first year): Kansas City Royals (1969). **Years in League:** 1998-

OWNERSHIP/MANAGEMENT
Operated by: Alliance Baseball.
Managing Partners: Gary Green, Larry Botel, Eric Foss, Brian Callaghan.
Chief Executive Officer: Gary Green.
President/General Manager: Martie Cordaro.
Assistant GM: Laurie Schlender. **Director, Broadcasting:** Mark Nasser. **Director, Corporate Sales:** Matthew Rau. **Director, Business Development:** Dave Endress. **Director, Community Relations:** Andrea Stava. **Director, Group Sales:** Kyle Schoonover. **Director, Baseball Operations:** Brett Pollock. **Director, Creative Services:** Ben Tupman. **Director, Marketing/Promotions:** Ben Hemmen. **Director, Special Events:** Ben Kratz. **Corporate Sales Executive:** Jason Kinney. **Ballpark Operations Manager:** Brett Myers. **Ticket Operations Manager:** Kaci Long. **Group Operations Manager:** Ryan Worthen. **Media Relations Manager:** Brett Pollock.
Ticket Sales Executives: Andrew Madden, Jenna Grable. **Group Sales Executive:** Cameron Wilson. **Manager, Promotions/Client Services:** Aaron Cox. **Finance Assistant:** Meredith Daniels. **Head Groundskeeper:** Noah Diercks. **Assistant Groundskeeper:** Adam Basinger. **Administrative Assistant:** Dana Becker.

FIELD STAFF
Manager: Mike Jirschele. **Hitting Coach:** Tommy Gregg. **Pitching Coach:** Larry Carter. **Athletic Trainer:** Dave Iannicca. **Strength Coach:** Joey Greany.

GAME INFORMATION
Radio Announcers: Mark Nasser, Brett Pollock. **No. of Games Broadcast:** Home-72, Away-72. **Flagship Station:** KOIL-AM 1180. **PA Announcers:** Craig Evans, Jake Ryan, Matt Siegel. **Official Scorers:** Frank Adkisson, Steve Pivovar, Ryan White.
Stadium Name: Werner Park. **Location:** Highway 370, just east of I-80 (exit 439). **Standard Game Times:** 6:35 pm (April-May), 7:05 (June-Sept), Fri/Sat 7:05, Sun 2:05.
Visiting Club Hotel: Courtyard Omaha La Vista, 12560 Westport Parkway, La Vista, NE 68128. **Telephone:** (402) 339-4900. **Fax:** (402) 339-4901.

RENO ACES

Office Address: 250 Evans Ave, Reno, NV 89501.
Telephone: (775) 334-4700. **Fax:** (775) 334-4701.
Website: www.renoaces.com
Affiliation (first year): Arizona Diamondbacks (2009). **Years in League:** 2009-

OWNERSHIP/MANAGEMENT
President/Managing Partner: Stuart Katzoff.
Partners: Jerry Katzoff, Herb Simon, Steve Simon.
Chief Financial Officer: Todd Steele. **General Counsel:** Brett Beecham. **General Manager:** Rick Parr.
Director, Broadcasting: Ryan Radtke. **Coordinator, Communications:** Shannon Siders. **Director, Marketing Partnerships:** Brady Raggio. **Account Executive, Marketing Partnerships:** JonPaul Ryan. **Director, Ticketing:** Brian Moss. **Account Executives, Group Tickets:** Ashley Belka, Kris Morrow. **Account Executives, Business Development:** Jeff Anderson, Jennifer Crum, Travis Post. **Manager, Client Services:** Adam Kincaid. **Director, Ticket Operations:** Charles Lucas. **Manager, Ticket Operations:** Sarah Bliss. **Director, Marketing:** Brett McGinness.
Coordinator, Promotions: Audrey Hill. **Coordinator, Mascot:** Thomas Norden. **VP, Operations:** David Avila. **Director, Ballpark Operations:** Tara O'Connor. **Coordinator, Ballpark Operations:** Daniel Mulligan. **Manager, Grounds:** Eric Blanton. **Assistant, Grounds:** Lane Pickle. **Manager, Facilities:** Mark Link. **Assistant, Facilities:** Adam Mercado. **Assistant Director, Merchandise:** Linda Hanson. **Controller:** Jerry Meyer. **Senior Staff Accountant:** Melinda Jessee. **Staff Accountant:** Michelle Howson.

FIELD STAFF
Manager: Brett Butler. **Hitting Coach:** Greg Gross. **Pitching Coach:** Mike Parrott. **Trainer:** Joe Metz. **Strength/Conditioning Coordinator:** Mike Schofield.

GAME INFORMATION
Radio Announcer: Ryan Radtke. **No. of Games Broadcast:** Home-72, Away-72. **Flagship Station:** Fox Sports 630 AM. **PA Announcer:** Unavailable. **Official Scorers:** Chad Hartley, Jack Kuestermeyer. **Stadium Name:** Aces Ballpark.
Location: From Carson City (south of Reno): 395 North to I-80 West, Exit 14 (Wells Ave), left on Wells, right at Kuenzli

Street, ballpark on right; From East, I-80 West to exit 14 (Wells Avenue), left on Wells, right on Kuenzli, right at East 2nd Street; From West, I-80 East to Exit 13 (Virginia St), right on Virginia, left on Second, ballpark on left; From North, 395 South to I-80 West, Exit 14 (Wells Ave), left on Wells, right on Kuenzli. **Standard Game Times:** 7:05 pm, 6:35, 1:05. **Ticket Price Range:** $7-30.
Visiting Club Hotel: Silver Legacy Resort Casino. **Telephone:** 775-325-7401.

ROUND ROCK EXPRESS

Office Address: 3400 East Palm Valley Blvd, Round Rock, TX 78665.
Telephone: (512) 255-2255. **Fax:** (512) 255-1558.
E-Mail Address: info@rrexpress.com. **Website:** www.roundrockexpress.com.
Affiliation (first year): Texas Rangers (2011). **Year in League:** 2005-

OWNERSHIP/MANAGEMENT
Operated By: Ryan Sanders Baseball, LP.
Principal Owners: Nolan Ryan, Don Sanders.
Owners: Reid Ryan (CEO), Reese Ryan (CFO), Brad Sanders, Bret Sanders, Jay Miller, Eddie Maloney.
Executive VP, Ryan Sanders Baseball: JJ Gottsch.
Executive Assistants, Ryan Sanders Baseball: Debbie Bowman, Rebecca Gustafson.
President: Dave Fendrick. **Executive VP/General Manager:** George King. **Senior VP/Assistant GM:** Chris Almendarez.
Senior VP, Marketing: Laura Fragoso. **VP, Corporate Sales:** Henry Green. **VP, Ticket Sales:** Gary Franke. **VP, Business Development:** Gregg Miller. **VP, Administration/Accounting:** Debbie Coughlin.
Senior Director, Stadium Operations: David Powers. **Senior Director, United Heritage Center:** Scott Allen. **Senior Director, Ticket Operations:** Ross Scott. **Director, Broadcasting:** Mike Capps. **Director, Communications:** Jill Cacic. **Director, Community Relations:** Tim Jackson. **Director, Entertainment/Promotions:** Derrick Grubbs. **Director, Stadium Maintenance:** Aurelio Martinez. **Manager, Entertainment/Promotions:** Rob Runnels. **Manager, Corporate Partnerships:** Brian Spieles. **Retail Manager:** Debbie Goodman. **Marketing Coordinator:** Whitney Rhoden. **Client Services:** Cade Richardson. **IT Manager, Sam Isham. Stadium Maintenance Manager:** Corey Woods.
Senior Account Executive: Stuart Scally. **Account Executives:** Julia Benavides, Luke Crum, Lindsey Gordon. **Head Groundskeeper:** Garrett Reddehase. **Assistant Groundskeeper:** Phillip Grefrath. **Clubhouse Manager:** Kenny Bufton. **Maintenance Staff:** Raymond Alemon, Ofelia Gonzalez. **Event Staff Coordinator:** Randy Patterson. **Office Manager:** Wendy Abrahamsen.

FIELD STAFF
Manager: Bobby Jones. **Hitting Coach:** Scott Coolbaugh. **Pitching Coach:** Brad Holman. **Coach:** Spike Owen. **Trainer:** Jason Roberts. **Strength Coach:** Ric Mabie.

GAME INFORMATION
Radio Announcers: Mike Capps. **No. of Games Broadcast:** Home-72, Road-72. **Flagship Station:** The Horn 104.9 FM ESPN Radio Austin. **PA Announcer:** Derrick Grubbs. **Official Scorer:** Tommy Tate. **Stadium Name:** Dell Diamond. **Location:** US Highway 79, 3.5 miles east of Interstate 35 (exit 253) or 1.5 miles west of Texas Tollway 130. **Standard Game Times:** 7:05 pm, 6:05, 1:05. **Ticket Price Range:** $7-$14.
Visiting Club Hotel: Hilton Garden Inn, 2310 North IH-35, Round Rock, TX 78681. **Telephone:** (512) 341-8200.

SACRAMENTO RIVER CATS

Office Address: 400 Ballpark Dr, West Sacramento, CA 95691.
Telephone: (916) 376-4700. **Fax:** (916) 376-4710.
E-Mail address: reception@rivercats.com. **Website:** www.rivercats.com.
Affiliation (first year): Oakland Athletics (2000). **Years in League:** 1903, 1909-11, 1918-60, 1974-76, 2000-

OWNERSHIP/MANAGEMENT
Operated By: Sacramento River Cats Baseball Club, LLC.
Owner/CEO: Susan Savage.
General Manager: Jeff Savage. **Executive VP/CFO:** Dan Vistica. **Senior VP, Business Operations:** Chip Maxson. **Director, Corporate Partnerships:** Greg Coletti. **Manager, Corporate Partnerships:** Jim Manker. **Coordinator, Partnership Activation:** Andrew Shipp. **Director, Finance/IT:** Jess Olivares. **Human Resources Manager:** Grace Bailey. **Director, Event Operations:** Ryan Van Sossan. **Community Relations:** Tony Asaro. **Manager, Advertising:** Genene Charles. **Manager, Marketing:** Leslie Lindsey. **Manager, Entertainment/Promotions:** Dane Lund. **Coordinator, Multimedia/Graphic Design:** Mike Villareal. **Graphic Designer:** Sara Molina. **Senior Coordinator, Events/Entertainment:** Samantha Klasing. **Coordinator, Events/Entertainment:** Brittney Broberg. **Mascot Coordinator:** Rhett Holland.
Manager, Public Relations/Baseball Operations: Zak Basch. **New Media/Baseball Information Editor:** Mark Ling. **Manager, Merchandise:** Rose Holland. **Coordinator, Website/Research:** Brent Savage. **Coordinator, Online Sales:** Megan Osgood. **Manager, Operations:** Madeline Strika. **Coordinator, Operations:** Tony Amaral. **Head Groundskeeper:** Chris Shastid. **Coordinator, Grounds:** Marcello Clamar. **Building Superintendent:** Danny Reilly. **Manager, Ticket Operations:** John Krivacic. **Manager, Ticket Sales:** Katie Krivacic. **High School Sports Product Manager:** Samantha

Bottari. **Corporate Account Executives:** Mychal Baker, Erin Gereghty, Zachary Haber, John Watts. **Group Events Account Executives:** Collin Brown, Stephen Caselli, Eric Esposito, Meagan Schreiner. **Inside Sales Representative:** Jessica Wilson. **Executive Assistant:** Angela Kroeker. **Receptionist:** Leah Larot.

FIELD STAFF

Manager: Steve Scarsone. **Hitting Coach:** Greg Sparks. **Pitching Coach:** Rick Rodriguez. **Trainer:** Brad LaRosa. **Strength Coach:** Jared Elliott.

GAME INFORMATION

Radio Announcer: Johnny Doskow. **No. of Games Broadcast:** Home-72 Road-72. **Flagship Station:** Talk 650 KSTE. **PA Announcer:** Greg Lawson. **Official Scorers:** Brian Berger, Ryan Bjork, Mark Honbo. **Stadium Name:** Raley Field. **Location:** I-5 to Business-80 West, exit at Jefferson Boulevard. **Standard Game Time:** 7:05 pm. **Ticket Price Range:** $8-60. **Visiting Club Hotel:** Holiday Inn.

SALT LAKE BEES

Office Address: 77 W 1300 South, Salt Lake City, UT 84115. **Telephone:** (801) 325-2337. **Fax:** (801) 485-6818. **E-Mail Address:** info@slbees.com. **Website:** www.slbees.com. **Affiliation (first year):** Los Angeles Angels (2001). **Years in League:** 1915-25, 1958-65, 1970-84, 1994-.

OWNERSHIP/MANAGEMENT

Operated by: Larry H Miller Baseball Inc. **Principal Owner:** Gail Miller. **CEO, Larry H Miller Group of Companies:** Greg Miller. **Chief Operating Office, Miller Sports Properties:** Steve Miller. **Senior Vice President:** Jim Olson. **VP/General Manager:** Marc Amicone. **Senior VP, Broadcasting:** Chris Baum. **General Counsel:** Robert Tingey. **Director, Corporate Travel:** Judy Adams. **Executive VP, Communications:** Linda Luchetti. **Director, Broadcasting:** Steve Klauke. **Communications Manager:** Hannah Lee. **Senior VP, Strategic Partnerships:** Mike Snarr. **VP, Corporate Partnerships:** Greg Tanner. **VP, Marketing:** Craig Sanders. **VP, Ticket Sales:** Clay Jensen. **Director, Game Operations:** Chance Fessler. **Director, Ticket Sales/Services:** Casey Patterson. **Director, Corporate Partnerships:** Brian Prutch. **Box Office Manager:** Laura Russell. **Ticket/Group Sales Manager:** Brad Jacoway. **VP, Public Safety:** Jim Bell. **VP, Food Services:** Mark Stedman. **Director, Food Services:** Dave Dalton. **Youth Programs Coordinator:** Nate Martinez. **Clubhouse Manager:** Eli Rice.

FIELD STAFF

Manager: Keith Johnson. **Hitting Coach:** Francisco Matos. **Pitching Coach:** Erik Bennett. **Trainer:** Brian Reinker.

GAME INFORMATION

Radio Announcer: Steve Klauke. **No. of Games Broadcast:** Home-72, Away-72. **Flagship Station:** 1280 the Zone (1280 AM). **PA Announcer:** Jeff Reeves. **Official Scorers:** Howard Nakagama, Terry Harward. **Stadium Name:** Spring Mobile Ballpark. **Location:** I-15 North/South exit, east to ballpark at West Temple. **Standard Game Times:** 6:35 (April-May), 7:05 (June-Sept), Sun 1:05. **Ticket Price Range:** $8-24. **Visiting Club Hotel:** Sheraton City Centre, 150 W 500 South, Salt Lake City, UT 84101. **Telephone:** (801) 401-2000.

TACOMA RAINIERS

Stadium/Office Address: 2502 South Tyler St, Tacoma, WA 98405. **Telephone:** (253) 752-7707. **Fax:** (253) 752-7135. **Website:** www.tacomarainiers.com. **Affiliation:** Seattle Mariners (1995). **Years in League:** 1904-1905, 1960-

OWNERSHIP/MANAGEMENT

Owners: The Baseball Club of Tacoma. **President:** Aaron Artman. **Director, Administration/Assistant to the President:** Patti Stacy. **Vice President, Business Development:** Jim Flavin. **Creative Director:** Tony Canepa. **Director, Corporate Partner Services:** Audrey Berglund. **Director, Communications:** Ben Spradling. **Senior Director, Ballpark Operations:** Ryan Schutt. **Director, Ticket Sales:** Shane Santman. **Director, Corporate Sales:** Adam Baker. **Director, Military Relations:** Ryan Latham. **Director, Event/Tickets Services:** Nicole Strunks. **Director, Baseball Operations/Merchandise:** Ashley Roth. **Director, Ticket Operations:** Cameron Badgett. **Head Groundskeeper:** David Schutt. **Events Consultant:** Alyson Jones. **Coordinator, Corporate Partner Services:** Samantha Haas. **Controller:** Brian Coombe. **Accounting:** Elise Schorr. **Senior Corporate Sales Manager:** Thomas Knowlton. **Corporate Sales Managers:** Joe Corona, Emily Green, Ross Richards. **Group Event Coordinator:** Jessica Blengino, Lauren Coombs, Ainsley O'Keefe, Alexandra Snyder. **Home Clubhouse Manager:** Tony Gutierrez.

FIELD STAFF

Manager: Daren Brown. **Coach:** Howard Johnson. **Pitching Coach:** Dwight Bernard. **Trainer:** Tom Newberg. **Trainer:**

B.J. Downie. **Performance Coach:** Rob Fumagelli

GAME INFORMATION

Radio Broadcaster: Mike Curto. **No. of Games Broadcast:** Home-72, Away-72. **Flagship Station:** KHHO 850-AM. **PA Announcer:** Derek Stansbury. **Official Scorers:** Kevin Kalal, Gary Brooks, Michael Jessee. **Stadium Name:** Cheney Stadium. **Location:** From I-5, take exit 132 (Highway 16 West) for 1.2 miles to 19th Street East exit, right on Tyler St for 1/3 mile. **Standard Game Times:** 7 pm, Sun, 1:30. **Ticket Price Range:** $7-$25. **Visiting Club Hotel:** Hotel Murano, 1320 Broadway Plaza, Tacoma, WA 98402. **Telephone:** (253) 238-8000.

TUCSON PADRES

Office Address: 2500 E Ajo Way, Tucson, AZ 85713.
Telephone: (520) 434-1367. **Fax:** (520) 434-1361.
Email address: info@tucsonpadres.com. **Website:** www.tucsonpadres.com.
Affiliation (first year): San Diego Padres (2011). **Years in League:** 1969-2008, 2011-

OWNERSHIP/MANAGEMENT

Operated By: MountainStar Sports.
Vice President/General Manager: Mike Feder. **Senior Advisor:** Jack Donovan. **Business Manager/Director, Merchandising:** Pattie Feder. **Assistant GM:** Eric May. **Director, Game Day Operations:** Debbie Clark. **Director, Sales:** James Jensen. **Director, Ticket Operations:** Tyler Bouchard. **Executive, Sales/Marketing:** Karlee Cordova. **Director, Inside Sales:** Sandy Davis. **Director, Community Relations:** Rudy Bustillos. **Director, Broadcasting/Media Relations:** Tim Hagerty. **Director, Hispanic Marketing:** Francisco Gamez. **Stadium Operations Manager:** Chris Tonner. **Head Groundskeeper:** Andy Beggs. **Home Clubhouse Manager:** TJ Laidlaw.

FIELD STAFF

Manager: Pat Murphy. **Hitting Coach:** Tom Tornincasa. **Pitching Coach:** Bronswell Patrick. **Trainer:** Nathan Stewart. **Assistant Trainer:** Isak Yoon.

GAME INFORMATION

Radio Announcer: Tim Hagerty. **No. of Games Broadcast:** Home-72 Road-72. **Flagship Station:** 1290 AM The Source. **PA Announcer:** Jonas Hunter. **Official Scorer:** Michael Guymon. **Stadium Name:** Kino Stadium. **Location:** 2500 E Ajo Way Tucson, AZ 85713. **Standard Game Times:** 7:05 pm, Sun 1:05. **Ticket Price Range:** $5-10.50. **Visiting Club Hotel:** DoubleTree at Reid Park, 445 South Alvernon Way, Tucson, AZ 85711-4198. **Telephone:** (520) 881-4200.

EASTERN LEAGUE

Office Address: 30 Danforth St, Suite 208, Portland, ME 04101.
Telephone: (207) 761-2700. **Fax:** (207) 761-7064.
E-Mail Address: elpb@easternleague.com. **Website:** www.easternleague.com.
Years League Active: 1923-.
President/Treasurer: Joe McEacharn.
Vice President/Secretary: Charles Eshbach. **VP:** Chuck Domino. **Assistant to President:**
Bill Rosario.
Directors: Ken Babby (Akron), Rick Brenner (New Hampshire), Lou DiBella (Richmond), Josh
Solomon (New Britain), Charles Eshbach (Portland), Joe Finley (Trenton), Bob Lozinak (Altoona),
Art Matin (Erie), Michael Reinsdorf (Harrisburg), Brian Shallcross (Bowie), Craig Stein (Reading),
Mike Urda (Binghamton).
Division Structure: Eastern—Binghamton, New Britain, New Hampshire, Portland, Reading,
Trenton. Western—Akron, Altoona, Bowie, Erie, Harrisburg, Richmond.
Regular Season: 142 games. **2013 Opening Date:** April 4. **Closing Date:** Sept 2.
All-Star Game: July 10 at New Britain. **Playoff Format:** Top two teams in each division meet
in best-of-five series. Winners meet in best-of-five series for league championship.
Roster Limit: 25. **Player Eligibility Rule:** No restrictions. **Brand of Baseball:** Rawlings.
Umpires: Joey Amaral (Columbia, MD), John Bacon (Sherrodsville, OH), Joseph Born
(Lafayette, IN), William Cunha (New York, NY), Ramon De Jesus (Santo Domingo, DR), Brian De
Brauwere (Hummelstown, PA), Eric Gillam (Roscoe, IL), Christopher Gonzalez (Campbell, CA),
Luke Hamilton (Goshen, IN), Thomas Honec (Harrisonburg, VA), Nicolas Lentz (Holland, MI), Nicholas Mahrley (Bartlett,
IL), Jeffrey Morrow (Fenton, MO), Roberto Ortiz (Hopkinsville, KY), Brian Reilly (Grand Rapids, MI), Timothy Rosso (Saddle
Brook, NJ), Matthew Springer (Beaverton, OR), Jansen Visconti (Latrobe, PA).

Joe McEacharn

STADIUM INFORMATION

Club	Stadium	Opened	Dimensions LF	CF	RF	Capacity	2012 Att.
Akron	Canal Park	1997	331	400	337	9,097	256,473
Altoona	Peoples Natural Gas Field	1999	325	405	325	7,210	270,613
Binghamton	NYSEG Stadium	1992	330	400	330	6,012	196,929
Bowie	Prince George's Stadium	1994	309	405	309	10,000	248,210
Erie	Jerry Uht Park	1995	312	400	328	6,000	208,725
Harrisburg	Metro Bank Park	1987	325	400	325	6,300	280,964
New Britain	New Britain Stadium	1996	330	400	330	6,146	339,100
New Hampshire	Northeast Delta Dental Stadium	2005	326	400	306	6,500	377,317
Portland	Hadlock Field	1994	315	400	330	7,368	374,930
Reading	FirstEnergy Stadium	1951	330	400	330	9,000	426,623
Richmond	The Diamond	1985	330	402	330	9,560	438,002
Trenton	ARM & HAMMER Park	1994	330	407	330	6,150	373,355

AKRON AEROS

Office Address: 300 S Main St, Akron, OH 44308.
Telephone: (330) 253-5151. **Fax:** (330) 253-3300.
E-Mail address: info@akronaeros.com. **Website:** www.akronaeros.com.
Affiliation (first year): Cleveland Indians (1989). **Years in League:** 1989-

OWNERSHIP/MANAGEMENT
Operated By: Akron Baseball, LLC.
Principal Owner: Ken Babby.
General Manager/COO: Jim Pfander. **Director, Finance:** Paul Pawlowski. **Director, Promotions:** Christina Shisler.
Director, Public/Media Relations: Adam Liberman. **Director, Broadcasting/Baseball Information:** Dave Wilson.
Director, Merchandise: Courtney Campbell. **Director, Creative Services:** Chris Thomas. **Director, Stadium Operations:**
Adam Horner. **Head Groundskeeper:** Chris Walsh. **Executive Chef:** Jason Kerton. **Assistant Director, Food/Beverage:**
Sam Dankoff. **Coordinator, Suites/Picnics/Community Relations:** Sierra Sawtelle. **Executive Assistant to Owner/
Office Manager:** Emily Ray. **Box Office Manager:** Dan Chesser. **Group Sales Representatives:** Mitch Cromes, Jeremy
Heit. **Ticket Sales Account Executive:** Dee Shilling. **Sponsorship Sales Coordinator:** Juli Donlen.

FIELD STAFF
Manager: Edwin Rodriguez. **Coach:** Jim Rickon. **Pitching Coach:** Greg Hibbard. **Trainer:** Chad Wolfe.

GAME INFORMATION
Radio Announcers: Jim Clark, Dave Wilson. **No of Games Broadcast:** Home-71 Road-71. **Flagship Station:** Fox
Sports Radio 1350-AM. **PA Announcer:** Leonard Grabowski. **Official Scorer:** Unavailable.
Stadium Name: Canal Park. **Location:** From I-76 East or I-77 South, exit onto Route 59 East, exit at Exchange/Cedar,

right onto Cedar, left at Main Street; From I-76 West or I-77 North, exit at Main Street/Downtown, follow exit onto Broadway Street, left onto Exchange Street, right at Main Street. **Standard Game Time:** 7:05 pm, Sun 1:05.

    Ticket Price Range: $5-9. **Visiting Club Hotel:** Unavailable.

ALTOONA CURVE

Office Address: Peoples Natural Gas Field, 1000 Park Avenue, Altoona, PA 16602.
Telephone: (814) 943-5400. **Fax:** (814) 942-9132.
E-Mail Address: frontoffice@altoonacurve.com. **Website:** www.altoonacurve.com.
Affiliation (first year): Pittsburgh Pirates (1999). **Years in League:** 1999-

OWNERSHIP/MANAGEMENT

Operated By: Lozinak Professional Baseball.
Managing Members: Bob & Joan Lozinak. **COO:** David Lozinak. **CFO:** Mike Lozinak. **Chief Administrative Officer:** Steve Lozinak. **General Manager:** Rob Egan. **Senior Advisor:** Sal Baglieri.
Assistant GM, Marketing/Promotions: Matt Hoover. **Director, Finance:** Mary Lamb. **Director, Ticket Operations:** Chris Keefer. **Director, Group Sales:** Corey Homan. **Director, Creative Services:** John Foreman. **Director, Mascot/Brand Development:** Bill Bettwy. **Director, Communications:** Mike Passanisi. **Director, Community Relations:** Elsie Gibney. **Director, Merchandising:** Claire Hoover. **Director, Ballpark Operations:** Kirk Stiffler. **Assistant Operations Manager:** Doug Mattern. **Head Groundskeeper:** Ben Young. **Manager, Concessions:** Glenn McComas. **Assistant Manager, Concessions:** Michelle Anna.
Sponsorship Sales Account Executive: Chuck Griswold. **Ticket Sales Associates:** Steffan Langguth, Luke Johnson. **Associate, Ticket/Communications:** Nathan Bowen. **Associate, Ticket Sales/Operations:** Tim Lozinak. **Administrative Assistant:** Carol Schmittle.

FIELD STAFF

Manager: Carlos Garcia. **Hitting Coach:** Ryan Long. **Pitching Coach:** Stan Kyles. **Trainer:** Mike Zalno.

GAME INFORMATION

Radio Announcers: Mike Passanisi, Nathan Bowen. **No. of Games Broadcast:** Home-71 Road-71. **Flagship Station:** ESPN Radio 1430 (WVAM-AM).
PA Announcer: Rich DeLeo. **Official Scorers:** Ted Beam, Dick Wagner.
Stadium Name: Peoples Natural Gas Field. **Location:** Located just off the Frankstown Road Exit of I-99.
Standard Game Times: 7pm, 6:30 (April-May); Sat 6, Sun 6. **Ticket Price Range:** $5-12.
Visiting Club Hotel: Ramada Altoona, Route 220 and Plank Road, Altoona, PA 16602. **Telephone:** (814) 946-1631.

BINGHAMTON METS

Office Address: 211 Henry St, Binghamton, NY 13901.
Mailing Address: PO Box 598, Binghamton, NY 13902.
Telephone: (607) 723-6387. **Fax:** (607) 723-7779.
E-Mail address: bmets@bmets.com. **Website:** www.bmets.com.
Affiliation (first year): New York Mets (1992). **Years in League:** 1923-37, 1940-63, 1966-68, 1992-

OWNERSHIP/MANAGEMENT

Principal Owners: Bill Maines, David Maines, George Scherer, Michael Urda.
General Manager: Jim Weed. **Assistant GM:** Heith Tracy.
Director, Stadium Operations: Richard Tylicki. **Box Office Manager:** Joe Pascarella. **Director, Video Production:** Unavailable. **Corporate Sales Executive:** Josh Patton. **Director, Community Relations:** Connor Gates. **Special Event Coordinator:** Erica Folli. **Director, Food/Beverage:** Bob Urda. **Scholastic Programs Coordinator:** Lou Ferraro. **Office Manager:** Amy Fancher. **Merchandising Manager:** Lisa Shattuck. **Director, Broadcast/Media Relations:** Tim Heiman. **Sports Turf Manager:** EJ Folli. **Home Clubhouse Manager:** Unavailable.

FIELD STAFF

Manager: Pedro Lopez. **Coach:** Luis Natera. **Pitching Coach:** Glenn Abbott.

GAME INFORMATION

Radio Announcer: Tim Heiman. **No. of Games Broadcast:** Home-71 Road-71. **Flagship Station:** WNBF 1290-AM.
PA Announcer: Chris Schmidt. **Official Scorer:** Steve Kraly. **Stadium Name:** NYSEG Stadium. **Location:** I-81 to exit 4S (Binghamton), Route 11 exit to Henry Street. **Standard Game Times:** 6:35, 7:05 (Fri-Sat), 1:05 (Day Games). **Ticket Price Range:** $7-22.
Visiting Club Hotel: Best Western, 569 Harry L Drive, Johnson City, NY 13790. **Telephone:** (607) 729-9194.

BOWIE BAYSOX

Office Address: Prince George's Stadium, 4101 NE Crain Hwy, Bowie, MD 20716.
Telephone: (301) 805-6000. **Fax:** (301) 464-4911.
E-Mail Address: info@baysox.com. **Website:** www.baysox.com.
Affiliation (first year): Baltimore Orioles (1993). **Years in League:** 1993-

OWNERSHIP/MANAGEMENT
Owned By: Bowie Baysox Baseball Club LLC.
President: Ken Young.
General Manager: Brian Shallcross. **Assistant GM:** Phil Wrye.
Director, Marketing: Brandan Kaiser. **Director, Field/Facility Operations:** Matt Parrott. **Director, Ticket Operations:** Charlene Fewer. **Director, Sponsorships:** Matt McLaughlin. **Promotions Manager:** Chris Rogers. **Communications Manager:** Matt Wilson. **Sponsorship Account Manager:** Josh VerStandig. **Group Events Managers:** Matt McCann, Josh Seils, Danielle White, Sean Foy. **Box Office Manager:** Ryan Barber. **Mascot Coordinator:** Joe Miller. **Stadium Operations Manager:** Andrew Jackson. **Assistant Groundskeeper:** Mike Soper. **Director, Gameday Personnel:** Darlene Mingioli. **Clubhouse Manager:** Andy Maalouf. **Bookkeeper:** Carol Terwilliger.

FIELD STAFF
Manager: Gary Kendall. **Coach:** Einar Diaz. **Pitching Coach:** Blaine Beatty.

GAME INFORMATION
Radio Announcer: Ben Gordon-Goldstein. **No. of Games Broadcast:** 72. **Flagship Station:** www.baysox.com.
PA Announcer: Adrienne Roberson. **Official Scorers:** Bill Hay, Carl Smith, Ted Black, Herb Martinson.
Stadium Name: Prince George's Stadium. **Location:** 1/4 mile south of US 50/Route 301 Interchange in Bowie.
Standard Game Times: 7:05 pm, Sat 6:35, Sun 2:05 (April-June), 6:05 (July-Aug). **Ticket Price Range:** $7-17.
Visiting Club Hotel: Best Western Annapolis, 2520 Riva Rd, Annapolis, MD 21401. **Telephone:** (410) 224-2800.

ERIE SEAWOLVES

Office Address: 110 E 10th St, Erie, PA 16501.
Telephone: (814) 456-1300. **Fax:** (814) 456-7520.
E-Mail Address: seawolves@seawolves.com. **Website:** www.seawolves.com.
Affiliation (first year): Detroit Tigers (2001). **Years in League:** 1999-

OWNERSHIP/MANAGEMENT
Principal Owners: Mandalay Baseball Properties, LLC.
President: Greg Coleman. **Assistant GM, Communications:** Greg Gania. **Assistant GM, Sales:** Mark Pirrello. **Director, Accounting/Finance:** Amy McArdle. **Director, Ticket Sales:** Cody Herrick. **Director, Group Sales:** Dan Torf. **Group Sales Coordinator:** Kevin Forte. **Ticket Operations Assistant:** Seth Pihanich. **Director, Food/Beverage (Pro Sports Catering):** Austin Punzel.

FIELD STAFF
Manager: Chris Cron. **Coach:** Gerald Perry. **Pitching Coach:** Jaime Garcia. **Trainer:** Chris McDonald.

GAME INFORMATION
Radio Announcer: Greg Gania. **No. of Games Broadcast:** Home-71 Road-71. **Flagship Station:** Fox Sports Radio WFNN 1330-AM. **PA Announcer:** Bob Shreve. **Official Scorer:** Les Caldwell.
Stadium Name: Jerry Uht Park. **Location:** US 79 North to East 12th Street exit, left on State Street, right on 10th Street.
Standard Game Times: 7:05 pm, 6:35 (April-May), Sun 1:35.
Ticket Prices: $8-12. **Visiting Club Hotel:** Bel Aire Clarion Hotel, 2800 West 8th St Erie, PA 16505.

HARRISBURG SENATORS

Office Address: Metro Bank Park, City Island, Harrisburg, PA 17101.
Mailing Address: PO Box 15757, Harrisburg, PA 17105.
Telephone: (717) 231-4444. **Fax:** (717) 231-4445.
E-Mail address: information@senatorsbaseball.com. **Website:** www.senatorsbaseball.com.
Affiliation (first year): Washington Nationals (2005). **Years in League:** 1924-35, 1987-

OWNERSHIP/MANAGEMENT
Operated By: Senators Partners, LLC.
Chairman: Michael Reinsdorf. **CEO:** Bill Davidson. **President:** Kevin Kulp.
General Manager: Randy Whitaker. **Assistant GM:** Aaron Margolis.
Accounting Manager: Donna Demczak. **Accounting, Intern:** Gina Wirfel. **Senior Corporate Sales Executive:** Todd Matthews. **Director, Ticket Sales:** Nate DeFazio. **Senior Account Executives:** Jonathan Boles, Jessica Kauffman. **Director, Merchandise:** Ann Marie Naumes. **Director, Stadium Operations:** Tim Foreman. **Head Groundskeeper:**

Brandon Forsburg. **Stadium Operations Coordinator:** Ben Moyer. **Director, Broadcasting/Media Relations:** Terry Byrom. **Broadcaster/Media Relations Intern:** Marshall Kelner. **Director, Community Relations/Box Office Manager:** Emily Winslow. **Community Relations Coordinator:** Mary Kate Holder. **Director, Digital/New Media:** Ashley Grotte. **Game Entertainment Coordinator:** Sean Purcell. **Ticket Sales Interns:** Brett Grove, Sam Musselman, Ryan Reeves, Seth Stover. **Box Office Intern:** Matt McGrady.

FIELD STAFF
Manager: Matt LeCroy. **Coach:** Eric Fox. **Pitching Coach:** Paul Menhart. **Trainer:** John Kotredes. **Strength Coach:** Tony Rogowski.

GAME INFORMATION
Radio Announcers: Terry Byrom, Marshall Kelner. **No. of Games Broadcast:** Home-71 Road-71. **Flagship Station:** 1460-AM.
PA Announcer: Chris Andre. **Official Scorers:** Terry Walters, Bruce Bashore. **Stadium Name:** Metro Bank Park. **Location:** I-83, exit 23 (Second Street) to Market Street, bridge to City Island. **Ticket Price Range:** $5-13.50.
Visiting Club Hotel: Park Inn by Radisson, 5401 Carlisle Pike, Mechanicsburg, PA 17050. **Telephone:** (800) 772-7829.
Visiting Team Workout Facility: Gold's Gym, 3401 Hartzdale Dr, Camp Hill, PA 17011. **Telephone:** (717) 303-2070.

NEW BRITAIN ROCK CATS

Office Address: 230 John Karbonic Way, New Britain, CT 06051.
Mailing Address: PO Box 1718, New Britain, CT 06050.
Telephone: (860) 224-8383. **Fax:** (860) 225-6267.
E-Mail Address: rockcats@rockcats.com. **Website:** www.rockcats.com.
Affiliation (first year): Minnesota Twins (1995). **Years in League:** 1983-

OWNERSHIP/MANAGEMENT
Operated By: Greater Hartford Sports Management, LLC.
Directors: William F Dowling, Coleman B Levy Esq.
President/CEO: William F Dowling. **Vice President:** Evan Levy. **Assistant GM:** Ricky Ferrell.
Director, Broadcasting: Jeff Dooley. **Director, Ticket Operations:** Brendan O'Donnell. **Director, Group Sales:** Jonathan Lissitchuck. **Director, Promotions:** Kim Pizighelli. **Director, Media Relations:** Robert Dowling. **Corporate Sales/Hospitality:** Andres Levy. **Group Sales Manager:** Evan Paradis. **Marketing Coordinator:** Lori Soltis. **Corporate Sponsorship Manager:** Kate Baumann. **Director, Community Relations:** Amy Helbling. **Manager, Corporate Developement:** Steve Kunsey. **Controller:** Jim Bonfiglio. **Director, Stadium Operations:** Eric Fritz. **Client Service Coordinator:** Amanda Goldsmith. **Box Office Manager:** Josh Montinieri. **On-Site Manager, Concessionaire Centerplate:** Sheila Fagan.

FIELD STAFF
Manager: Jeff Smith. **Coach:** Rudy Hernandez. **Pitching Coach:** Stu Cliburn. **Trainer:** Larry Bennese.

GAME INFORMATION
Radio Announcer: Jeff Dooley, Joe D'Ambrosio. **No. of Games Broadcast:** Home-71 Road-71. **Flagship Station:** WTIC 1080-AM/96.5-FM, WMRD 1150-AM.
PA Announcer: Don Steele. **Official Scorer:** Ed Smith.
Stadium Name: New Britain Stadium. **Location:** From I-84, take Route 72 East (exit 35 of Route 9 South (exit 39A), left at Ellis Street (exit 25), left at South Main Street, stadium one mile on right; From Route 91 or Route 5, take Route 9 North to Route 71 (exit 24), first exit. **Ticket Price Range:** $5-18.
Visiting Club Hotel: Holiday Inn Express, 120 Laning St, Southington, CT 06489. **Telephone:** (860) 276-0736.

NEW HAMPSHIRE
FISHER CATS

Office Address: 1 Line Dr, Manchester, NH 03101.
Telephone: (603) 641-2005. **Fax:** (603) 641-2055.
E-Mail Address: info@nhfishercats.com. **Website:** www.nhfishercats.com.
Affiliation (first year): Toronto Blue Jays (2004). **Years in League:** 2004-

OWNERSHIP/MANAGEMENT
Operated By: DSF Sports.
Owner: Art Solomon. **President:** Rick Brenner.
President: Rick Brenner. **Vice President, Sales:** Mike Ramshaw. **VP, Business Operations:** Steve Pratt.
Corporate Controller: Karl Stone. **Director, Box Office Operations:** Tim Hough. **Director, Facilities/Turf:** Shawn Meredith. **Director, Marketing/Public Affairs:** Jenna Raizes. **Director, Broadcast/Media Relations:** Tom Gauthier. **Stadium Operations Manager:** DJ White. **Merchandise Manager:** Justin Stecz. **Community Relations Manager:** Megan Shea. **Sports Turf Manager:** Dan Boyle. **Production/Graphic Design Manager:** Sean Hladick. **Corporate Sales Manager:** Jason Corbeil. **Ticket Sales Account Executives:** Chris Aubertin, Stephanie Fournier, Chris Wall, Matt

Labossiere, Kirby Wade. **Ticket Sales Account Executive/On-Field Promotions:** Jeff Martin. **Executive Assistant/Office Manager:** Kayla Hines. **President, Advantage Food/Beverage:** Tim Restall. **Director, Food/Beverage Operations:** Chris Carlisle. **Executive Chef:** Alan Foley.

FIELD STAFF

Manager: Gary Allenson. **Hitting Coach:** Richie Hebner. **Pitching Coach:** Tom Signore. **Trainer:** Bob Tarpey. **Strength/Conditioning:** Brian Pike

GAME INFORMATION

Radio Announcers: Tom Gauthier, Bob Lipman, Dick Lutsk, Charlie Sherman. **No. of Games Broadcast:** Home-71 Road-71. **Flagship Station:** WGIR 610-AM. **PA Announcer:** Alex James. **Official Scorers:** Chick Smith, Lenny Parker, Greg Royce, Pete Dupuis.

Stadium Name: Northeast Delta Dental Stadium. **Location:** From I-93 North, take I-293 North to exit 5 (Granite Street), right on Granite Street, right on South Commercial Street, right on Line Drive. **Ticket Price Range:** $6-12.

Visiting Club Hotel: Comfort Inn, 298 Queen City Ave, Manchester, NH 03102.

Telephone: (603) 668-2600.

PORTLAND SEA DOGS

Office Address: 271 Park Ave, Portland, ME 04102.
Mailing Address: PO Box 636, Portland, ME 04104.
Telephone: (207) 874-9300. **Fax:** (207) 780-0317.
E-Mail address: seadogs@seadogs.com. **Website:** www.seadogs.com.
Affiliation (first year): Boston Red Sox (2003). **Years in League:** 1994-

OWNERSHIP/MANAGEMENT

Operated By: Portland, Maine Baseball, Inc.
Chairman: Bill Burke.
Treasurer: Sally McNamara. **President:** Charles Eshbach. **Executive Vice President/General Manager:** Geoff Iacuessa. **Senior VP:** John Kameisha. **VP, Financial Affairs/Operations:** Jim Heffley. **Assistant GM, Media Relations:** Chris Cameron. **Assistant GM, Marketing/Promotions:** Liz Riley. **Director, Ticketing:** Dave Strong. **Director, Group Sales:** Brayton Chase. **Director, Video Operations/Corporate Sales Executive:** Brian Murphy. **Ticket Sales Executive/Season Ticket Holder Manager:** Courtney Rague. **Director, Broadcasting:** Mike Antonellis. **Director, Food Services:** Mike Scorza. **Assistant Director, Food Services:** Greg Moyes. **Clubhouse Managers:** Craig Candage Sr, Nick Fox. **Head Groundskeeper:** Rick Anderson.

FIELD STAFF

Manager: Kevin Boles. **Coach:** Rich Gedman. **Pitching Coach:** Bob Kipper. **Trainer:** Brandon Henry.

GAME INFORMATION

Radio Announcer: Mike Antonellis. **No. of Games Broadcast:** Home-71 Road-71. **Flagship Station:** WPEI 95.9 FM. **PA Announcer:** Paul Coughlin. **Official Scorer:** Thom Hinton.

Stadium Name: Hadlock Field. **Location:** From South, I-295 to exit 5, merge onto Congress Street, left at St John Street, merge right onto Park Ave; From North, I-295 to exit 6A, right onto Park Ave. **Ticket Price Range:** $5-10.

Visiting Club Hotel: DoubleTree by Hilton Portland Maine, 363 Maine Mall Rd, South Portland, ME 04106. **Telephone:** (207) 775-6161.

READING FIGHTIN PHILS

Office Address: Route 61 South/1900 Centre Ave, Reading, PA 19605.
Mailing Address: PO Box 15050, Reading, PA 19612.
Telephone: (610) 375-BALL (2255). **Fax:** (610) 373-5868.
E-Mail Address: info@fightins.com. **Website:** www.fightins.com.
Affiliation (first year): Philadelphia Phillies (1967). **Years in League:** 1933-35, 1952-61, 1963-65, 1967-

OWNERSHIP/MANAGEMENT

Operated By: E&J Baseball Club, Inc.
Principal Owner: Reading Baseball LP. **Managing Partner:** Craig Stein.
General Manager: Scott Hunsicker. **Assistant GM:** Ashley Peterson.
Director, Stadium Operations/Concessions: Andy Bortz. **Director, Sales:** Joe Bialek. **Director, Baseball Operations/Merchandise:** Kevin Sklenarik. **Director, PR/Media Relations:** Eric Scarcella. **Director, Ticket Operations:** Mike Becker. **Director, Group Outings:** Matt Hoffmaster. **Director, Communications:** Chris McConney. **Controller:** Kristyne Haver. **Director, Graphic Arts/Game Entertainment:** Matt Jackson. **Assistant Director, Sales:** Anthony Pignetti. **Assistant Director, Group Outings:** Tim McGee, Jon Muldowney. **Assistant Director, Tickets/Administrative Assistant:** Holly Frymyer. **Director, Community Relations/Internship Coordinator:** Mike Robinson.

Video Director: Andy Kauffman. **Director, Adult Beverages/Sales Representative:** Curtis Burns. **Head Groundskeeper:** Dan Douglas. **Office Manager:** Deneen Giesen. **Director, Educational Programs/Music:** Todd Hunsicker. **Merchandising Manager:** Jason Yonkovitch. **Fundraising Manager/Sales Representative:** Andrew Nelson.

FIELD STAFF

Manager: Dusty Wathan. **Coach:** Frank Cacciatore. **Pitching Coach:** Dave Lundquist.

GAME INFORMATION

Radio Announcer: Anthony Oppermann. **No. of Games Broadcast:** Home-71, Away-71. **Flagship Station:** WRAW 1340-AM. **PA Announcer:** Unavailable. **Official Scorers:** Paul Jones, Brian Kopetsky, Josh Leiboff, Dick Shute.

Stadium Name: FirstEnergy Stadium. **Location:** From east, take Pennsylvania Turnpike West to Morgantown exit, to 176 North, to 422 West, to Route 12 East, to Route 61 South exit; From west, take 422 East to Route 12 East, to Route 61 South exit; From north, take 222 South to Route 12 exit, to Route 61 South exit; From south, take 222 North to 422 West, to Route 12 East exit at Route 61 South.

Standard Game Times: 7:05 pm, 6:35 (April-May), Sun 1:05. **Ticket Price Range:** $6-11. **Visiting Club Hotel:** Crowne Plaza Reading Hotel 1741 Papermill Road, Wyomissing, PA 19610. **Telephone:** (610) 376-3811.

RICHMOND FLYING SQUIRRELS

Office Address: 3001 N Boulevard, Richmond, VA 23230.
Telephone: (804) 359-3866. **Fax:** (804) 359-1373.
E-Mail Address: info@squirrelsbaseball.com. **Website:** www.squirrelsbaseball.com.
Affiliation (first year): San Francisco Giants (2009). **Years in League:** 2009-

OWNERSHIP/MANAGEMENT

Operated By: Navigators Baseball LP.
President/Managing Partner: Lou DiBella.
CEM: Chuck Domino. **Vice President/COO:** Todd "Parney" Parnell.
General Manager: Bill Papierniak. **Assistant GM:** Tom Denlinger. **Controller:** Faith Casey. **Assistant Controller:** Jessica Miller. **Director, Corporate Sales:** Ben Terry. **Corporate Sales Executives:** Mike Murphy, Jerrine Lee. **Director, Tickets:** Brendon Porter. **Box Office Manager:** Patrick Flower. **Director, Broadcasting:** Jon Laaser. **Manager, Media Relations:** Jay Burnham. **Creative Services Manager:** Jason Grohoske. **Director, Community Relations:** Stefanie Sacks. **Director, Promotions/In-Game Entertainment:** Kellye Semonich. **Director, Group Sales:** Brandon Greene.
Group Sales Executives: Chris Joyner, Megan Angstadt, Ida Henley, Camp Peery. **Suites/Group Sales Executive:** Elyse Holben. **Executive Director, Food/Beverage/Merchandise:** Ben Rothrock. **Assistant Directors, Food/Beverage:** Eric Freeman, Mike Caddell. **Chef/Catering/Banquet Services:** Gavin Edmunds. **Director, Field Operations:** Steve Ruckman. **Assistant Director, Field Operations:** Cody Harvey. **Director, Stadium Operations:** Tom White.

FIELD STAFF

Manager: Dave Machemer. **Coach:** Ken Joyce. **Pitching Coach:** Ross Grimsley. **Athletic Trainer:** LJ Petra. **Strength/Conditioning Coach:** Brad Lawson.

GAME INFORMATION

Radio Announcers: Jon Laaser, Jay Burnham. **No. of Games Broadcast:** Home-71 Road-71. **Flagship Station:** Sports Radio 910 WRNL-AM. **PA Announcer:** Jimmy Barrett. **Official Scorer:** Scott Day.

Stadium Name: The Diamond. **Capacity:** 9,560. **Location:** Right off I-64 at the Boulevard exit. **Standard Game Times:** 7:05 pm, Sat 6:35, Sun 5:05. **Ticket Price Range:** $7-11. **Visiting Club Hotel:** Comfort Suites at Virginia Center Commons, 10601 Telegraph Road, Glen Allen, VA. **Telephone:** (804) 262-2000.

TRENTON THUNDER

Office Address: One Thunder Road, Trenton, NJ 08611.
Telephone: (609) 394-3300. **Fax:** (609) 394-9666.
E-Mail address: fun@trentonthunder.com. **Website:** www.trentonthunder.com.
Affiliation (first year): New York Yankees (2003). **Years in League:** 1994-

OWNERSHIP/MANAGEMENT

Operated By: Garden State Baseball, LLP.
General Manager/COO: Will Smith.
Senior VP, Corporate Sales/Partnerships: Eric Lipsman. **VP, Stadium Operations:** Ryan Crammer. **Director, Public Relations:** Bill Cook. **Director, Merchandising:** Joe Pappalardo. **Director, Finance/Baseball Operations:** Jeff Hurley. **Director, Community Relations:** Patience Purdy. **Director, Ticket Operations:** Matt Pentima. **Director, Creative/ Audiovisual Services:** Greg Lavin. **Director, Ticket Sales/Corporate Sponsorships:** Patrick McMaster. **Director, Group Sales:** TJ Jahn. **Director, Broadcasting:** Josh Maurer. **Director, Food/Beverage:** Kevin O'Byrne. **Assistant Director, Food/Beverage:** Chris Champion. **Stadium Operations Manager:** Steve Brokowsky.
Office Manager: Susanna Hall. **Group Sales Manager:** Nate Schneider. **Ticket Sales Manager:** Caitlin Reardon. **Group Sales Account Representative:** Lindsey Ravior. **Group Sales Account Representative:** Tom Henninger. **Ticket Sales Account Representatives:** Janelle Alfano, John Belfiore. **Business Development Executive:** Brad McNamara. **Head Groundskeeper:** Ryan Woodley. **Seasonal Group Sales Representative:** Molly Hartman. **Coordinator, Promotions/ Events:** Kelly Wasilewski. **Group Sales Coordinator:** Matt Mango. **Merchandise Assistant:** Lisa Szymendera. **Assistant, Broadcast/Media Relations:** Adam Giardino. **Building Superintendent:** Scott Ribsam.

FIELD STAFF

Manager: Tony Franklin. **Hitting Coach:** Justin Turner. **Pitching Coach:** Tommy Phelps. **Coach:** Luis Dorante. **Trainer:** Scott DiFrancesco. **Strength/Conditioning Coach:** Orlando Crance.

GAME INFORMATION

Radio Announcers: Josh Maurer, Adam Giardino. **No. of Games Broadcast:** Home-71 Road 71. **Flagship Station:** WTSR 91.3 FM. **Official Scorers:** Jay Dunn, Greg Zak. **Stadium Name:** ARM & HAMMER Park.
Location: From I-95, take Route 1 North to Route 29 South, stadium entrance just before tunnel; From NJ Turnpike, take Exit 7A and follow I-195 West, Road will become Rte 29, Follow through tunnel and ballpark is on left.
Standard Game Times: 7:05 pm, Sun 1:05.
Ticket Price Range: $10-13. **Visiting Club Hotel:** Trenton Marriott Downtown. **Telephone:** (609) 421-4000.

SOUTHERN LEAGUE

Mailing Address: 2551 Roswell Rd, Suite 330, Marietta, GA 30062.
Telephone: (770) 321-0400. **Fax:** (770) 321-0037.
Email Address: loriwebb@southernleague.com. **Website:** www.southernleague.com.
Years League Active: 1964-
President: Lori Webb. **Vice President:** Steve DeSalvo.
Directors: Jonathan Nelson (Birmingham), Rich Mozingo (Chattanooga), Miles Prentice
(Huntsville), Reese Smith (Jackson), Peter Bragan Jr (Jacksonville), Steve DeSalvo (Mississippi),
Bill Shanahan (Mobile), Tom Dickson (Montgomery), Quinton Studer (Pensacola), Doug
Kirchhofer (Tennessee).
Media Relations Director: Peter Webb.
Division Structure: North: Birmingham, Chattanooga, Huntsville, Jackson, Tennessee.
South: Jacksonville, Mississippi, Mobile, Montgomery, Pensacola.
Regular Season: 140 games (split schedule). **2013 Opening Date:** April 4. **Closing Date:**
Sept 2.
All-Star Game: July 17, at Jacksonville Suns. **Playoff Format:** First-half division winners meet
second-half division winners in best-of-five series for league championship. **Roster Limit:** 25.
Player Eligibility Rule: No restrictions.

Lori Webb

Brand of Baseball: Rawlings.
Umpires: Jonathan Bailey, John Bostwick, Jose Esteras, Blake Felter, Ryan Goodman, Brandon Henson, Matthew
Jones, Benjamin Leake, Shane Livensparger, Matthew McCoy, Derek Mollica, Robert Moreno, Thomas Newsom III, Garrett
Patterson, Jeremy Riggs.

STADIUM INFORMATION

Club	Stadium	Opened	Dimensions LF	CF	RF	Capacity	2012 Att.
* Birmingham	Regions Field	2013	320	400	325	8,500	204,269
Chattanooga	AT&T Field	2000	325	400	330	6,362	243,051
Huntsville	Joe W. Davis Municipal Stadium	1985	345	405	330	10,488	130,231
Jackson	Ballpark at Jackson	1998	310	395	320	6,000	133,352
Jacksonville	Baseball Grounds of Jacksonville	2003	321	420	317	11,000	293,013
Mississippi	Trustmark Park	2005	335	402	332	7,416	191,639
Mobile	Hank Aaron Stadium	1997	325	400	310	6,000	133,062
Montgomery	Riverwalk Stadium	2004	314	380	332	7,000	244,976
Pensacola	Bayfront Stadium	2012	325	400	335	6,000	328,147
Tennessee	Smokies Park	2000	330	400	330	6,000	251,112

*Team relocates from Regions Park, Hoover, Ala.

BIRMINGHAM BARONS

Office Address: 1400 1st Ave South, Birmingham, AL, 35233.
Mailing Address: PO Box 877, Birmingham, AL, 35201.
Telephone: (205) 988-3200. **Fax:** (205) 988-9698.
E-Mail Address: barons@barons.com. **Website:** www.barons.com.
Affiliation (first year): Chicago White Sox (1986). **Years in League:** 1964-65, 1967-75, 1981-

OWNERSHIP/MANAGEMENT
Principal Owners: Don Logan, Jeff Logan, Stan Logan.
General Manager: Jonathan Nelson.
Director, Broadcasting: Curt Bloom. **Director, Media Relations:** Nick Dobreff. **Director, Sales:** John Cook. **Director,
Tickets:** David Madison. **Director, Production:** Mike Ferko. **Corporate Sales Manager:** Don Leo. **Corporate Event
Planner:** Charlie Santiago. **Director, Retail Sales:** Joseph Cooper. **General Manager, Parkview Catering:** Eric Crook.
Director, Concessions: Taylor Youngson. **Office Manager:** Jennifer Dillard. **Accountants:** Jo Ann Bragan, Randy Prince.
Head Groundskeeper: Daniel Ruggiero.

FIELD STAFF
Manager: Julio Vinas. **Hitting Coach:** Gary Ward. **Pitching Coach:** Britt Burns. **Trainer:** Scott Johnson. **Strength/
Conditioning:** Shawn Powell.

GAME INFORMATION
Radio Announcer: Curt Bloom. **No of Games Broadcast:** Home-70 Road-70. **Flagship Station:** News Radio 105.5
WERC-FM. **PA Announcers:** Derek Scudder. **Official Scorers:** AA Moore, Grant Martin.
Stadium Name: Regions Field. **Location:** I-65 (exit 259B) in Birmingham. **Standard Game Times:** 7:05 pm, Sat 6:30,
Sun 2:05. **Ticket Price Range:** $7-14.
Visiting Club Hotel: Sheraton Birmingham Hotel, 2101 Richard Arrington Junior Boulevard North, Birmingham, AL
35203. **Telephone:** (205) 324-5000.

CHATTANOOGA LOOKOUTS

Office Address: 201 Power Alley, Chattanooga, TN 37402.
Mailing Address: PO Box 11002, Chattanooga, TN 37401.
Telephone: (423) 267-2208. **Fax:** (423) 267-4258.
E-Mail Address: lookouts@lookouts.com. **Website:** www.lookouts.com.
Affiliation (first year): Los Angeles Dodgers (2009). **Years in League:** 1964-65, 1976-

OWNERSHIP/MANAGEMENT

Operated By: Scenic City Baseball LLC.
Principal Owners: Frank Burke, Charles Eshbach.
President/General Manager: Rich Mozingo. **Vice President/Assistant GM:** John Maedel.
Director, Group Sales: Gavin Cox. **Director, Merchandising/Ticketing:** Chrysta Jorgensen. **Director, Media Relations:** Peter Intza. **Director, Concessions:** Steve Sullivan. **Director, Broadcasting:** Larry Ward. **Director, Stadium Operations/Assistant Director, Broadcasting:** Will Poindexter. **Director, Business Administration/Accounting:** Amy Leffew. **Head Groundskeeper:** Joe Fitzgerald. **Group Sales Manager:** Andrew Zito. **Stadium Operations Associate:** Jimmy Phillips. **Concessions Associate:** Suzanne Riggs. **Group Sales Associate:** Melissa Blunk. **Retail Associate:** Ben South. **Ticketing Associate:** Todd Bateman.

FIELD STAFF

Manager: Jody Reed. **Hitting Coach:** Orv Franchuk. **Pitching Coach:** Hector Berrios.

GAME INFORMATION

Radio Announcers: Larry Ward, Will Poindexter. **No. of Games Broadcast:** Home-70 Road-70. **Flagship Station:** 105.1 FM ESPN Chattanooga (WALV-FM). **PA Announcer:** John Maedel. **Official Scorers:** Wirt Gammon, Andy Paul.
Stadium Name: AT&T Field. **Location:** From I-24, take US 27 North to exit 1C (4th Street), first left onto Chestnut Street, left onto Third Street. **Ticket Price Range:** $5-9.
Visiting Club Hotel: Holiday Inn, 2232 Center Street, Chattanooga, TN 37421. **Telephone:** (423) 485-1185.

HUNTSVILLE STARS

Office Address: 3125 Leeman Ferry Rd, Huntsville, AL 35801.
Telephone: (256) 882-2562. **Fax:** (256) 880-0801.
E-Mail Address: starsinfo@huntsvillestars.com. **Website:** www.huntsvillestars.com.
Affiliation (first year): Milwaukee Brewers (1999). **Years in League:** 1985-

OWNERSHIP/MANAGEMENT

Operated By: Huntsville Stars LLC.
President: Miles Prentice.
General Manager: Buck Rogers. **Assistant GM:** Babs Rogers. **Manager, Media:** Nicole Collins. **Director, Broadcasting:** Alex Cohen. **Director, Corporate Sales:** Renee Ducote. **Director, Merchandising/Sales:** Jessica McQueen. **Director, Stadium Operations:** Mike Stowe. **Office Manager:** Earl Grilliot. **Head Groundskeeper:** Kelly Rensel.

FIELD STAFF

Manager: Darnell Coles. **Coach:** Kenny Dominguez. **Pitching Coach:** Chris Hook. **Athletic Trainer:** Steve Patera. **Strength/Conditioning Coach:** Tim Gifford.

GAME INFORMATION

PA Announcer: Matt Mitchell. **Official Scorer:** Don Rizzardi.
Stadium Name: Joe W Davis Municipal Stadium. **Location:** I-65 to I-565 East, south on Memorial Parkway to Drake Avenue exit, right on Don Mincher Drive. **Ticket Price Range:** $5-$20.
Visiting Club Hotel: Holiday Inn, 401 Williams Avenue, Huntsville, AL, 35801. **Telephone:** 256-533-1400.

JACKSON GENERALS

Office Address: 4 Fun Place, Jackson, TN 38305.
Telephone: (731) 988-5299. **Fax:** (731) 988-5246.
E-Mail Address: fun@diamondjaxx.com. **Website:** www.diamondjaxx.com.
Affiliation (first year): Seattle Mariners (2007). **Years in League:** 1998-

OWNERSHIP/MANAGEMENT

Operated by: Jackson Baseball Club LP.
Chairman: David Freeman. **President:** Reese Smith.
General Manager: Jason Compton. **Vice President, Sales/Marketing:** Mike Peasley.
Director, Stadium Operations: Robert Jones. **Manager, Media Relations/Broadcasting:** Chris Harris. **Manager, Ticketing/Merchandise:** Hunter Ellington. **Manager, Catering/Concessions:** Kurt Brown. **Manager, Home Clubhouse Operations:** CJ Fedewa. **Manager, Visiting Clubhouse:** Dustin Smith. **Account Executives:** Nick Hall, Katie Mangrum,

Chris Turpin. **Sales Executives:** Xan Stewart, Clay Fowler. **Sales Executive/Promotions:** Justin Bernhard. **Administrative Assistant:** Laura Bernhard. **Manager, Design/Publications:** Bradley Field. **Accounting Manager:** Charles Ferrell. **Turf Manager:** Marty Wallace.

FIELD STAFF

Manager: Jim Pankovits. **Coach:** Cory Snyder. **Pitching Coach:** Terry Clark. **Trainer:** Matt Toth.

GAME INFORMATION

Radio Announcer: Chris Harris. **No. of Games Broadcast:** Home-70, Away-70. **Flagship Station:** WNWS 101.5 FM. **PA Announcer:** Dan Reeves. **Official Scorer:** Mike Henson. **Stadium Name:** The Ballpark at Jackson. **Location:** From I-40, take exit 85 South on FE Wright Drive, left onto Ridgecrest Road. **Standard Game Times:** 7:05 pm, Sat 6:05, Sun 2:05 or 6:05. **Ticket Price Range:** $6-10. **Visiting Club Hotel:** Doubletree Hotel, 1770 Hwy 45 Bypass, Jackson, TN 38305. **Telephone:** (731) 664-6900.

JACKSONVILLE SUNS

Office Address: 301 A Philip Randolph Blvd, Jacksonville, FL 32202.
Mailing Address: PO Box 4756, Jacksonville, FL 32201.
Telephone: (904) 358-2846. **Fax:** (904) 358-2845.
E-Mail Address: info@jaxsuns.com. **Website:** www.jaxsuns.com.
Affiliation (first year): Miami Marlins (2009). **Years In League:** 1970-

OWNERSHIP/MANAGEMENT

Operated by: Baseball Jax Inc.
Senior Madame Chairman: Mary Frances Bragan.
President: Peter Bragan Jr. **General Manager:** Chris Peters. **Director, Field Operations:** Ed Attalla. **Director, Merchandise:** Brett Andrews. **Assistant GM:** Casey Nichols. **Senior Director, Business Administration:** Barbara O'Berry. **Director, Video Services:** Brian Delettre. **Director, Group Sales:** January Putt Squyres. **Manager, Group Sales:** Trevor Johnson. **Director, Ticket Operations:** Amy Delettre. **Director, Stadium Operations:** JD Metrie. **Director, Community Relations:** Sarah Foster. **Director, Broadcasting:** Roger Hoover. **Manager, Box Office:** Theresa Viets. **General Manager, Ballpark Foods:** Jamie Davis. **Assistant GM, Ballpark Foods/Finance:** Mitch Buska. **Manager, Stadium Operations:** Jarrod Simmons. **Account Executives:** Yogi Brewington, Richard O'Neill.

FIELD STAFF

Manager: Andy Barkett. **Hitting Coach:** Kevin Randel. **Pitching Coach:** John Duffy. **Trainer:** Masanao Fujimoto.

GAME INFORMATION

Radio Announcer: Roger Hoover. **No. of Games Broadcast:** Home-70, Away-70. **Flagship Station:** 94.1 FM-WSOS. **PA Announcer:** Wesley Mitchell. **Official Scorer:** Jason Eliopulos.
Stadium Name: Bragan Field at The Baseball Grounds of Jacksonville. **Location:** I-95 South to Martin Luther King Parkway exit, follow Gator Bowl Blvd around Everbank Field; I-95 North to Exit 347 (Emerson Street), go right to Hart Bridge Expressway, take Sports Complex exit, left at light to stop sign, take left and follow around Everbank Field; From Mathews Bridge, take A Philip Randolph exit, right on A Philip Randolph, straight to stadium.
Standard Game Times: 7:05 pm, Sun 3:05/6:05. **Ticket Price Range:** $7.50-$22.50.
Visiting Club Hotel: Hyatt Regency Jacksonville Riverfront, 225 Coastline Dr, Jacksonville, FL 32202. **Telephone:** (904) 633-9095.

MISSISSIPPI BRAVES

Office Address: Trustmark Park, 1 Braves Way, Pearl, MS 39208.
Mailing Address: PO Box 97389, Pearl, MS 39288.
Telephone: (601) 932-8788. **Fax:** (601) 936-3567.
E-Mail Address: mississippibraves@braves.com. **Website:** www.mississippibraves.com.
Affiliation (first year): Atlanta Braves (2005). **Years in League:** 2005-

OWNERSHIP/MANAGEMENT

Operated By: Atlanta National League Baseball Club Inc.
General Manager: Steve DeSalvo. **Assistant GM:** Jim Bishop. **Ticket Manager:** Nick Anderson. **Merchandise Manager:** Sarah Banta. **Manager, Public Relations/Advertising/Design:** Brian Byrd. **Sales Associates:** Miranda Black, Jacob Newton, Jeff Van, Seth Hunter, Ryan Ladner, Sean Guillotte. **Head Chef:** Tina Funches. **Suites/Catering Manager:** Debbie Herrington. **Stadium Operations Manager:** Matt McCoy. **Promotions/Entertainment Manager:** Brian Prochilo. **Concessions Manager:** Felicia Thompson. **Office Administrator:** Christy Shaw. **Restaurant Manager:** Gene Slaughter. **Director, Field/Facility Operations:** Matt Taylor. **Receptionist:** Christy Guillory.

FIELD STAFF

Manager: Aaron Holbert. **Coach:** Garey Ingram. **Pitching Coach:** Dennis Lewallyn. **Trainer:** Ricky Alcantara.

GAME INFORMATION

Radio Announcer: Kyle Tate. **No. of Games Broadcast:** Home-70 Road-70. **Flagship Station:** WYAB 103.9 FM. **PA Announcer:** Derrel Palmer. **Official Scorer:** Mark Beason. **Stadium Name:** Trustmark Park. **Location:** I-20 to exit

48/Pearl (Pearson Road). **Ticket Price Range:** $6-$20.
   Visiting Club Hotel: Holiday Inn Trustmark Park, 110 Bass Pro Drive, Pearl, MS 39208. **Telephone:** (601) 939-5238.

MOBILE BAYBEARS

Office Address: Hank Aaron Stadium, 755 Bolling Bros Blvd, Mobile, AL 36606.
Telephone: (251) 479-2327. **Fax:** (251) 476-1147.
E-Mail Address: info@mobilebaybears.com. **Website:** www.mobilebaybears.com.
Affiliation (first year): Arizona Diamondbacks (2007). **Years in League:** 1966, 1970, 1997-

OWNERSHIP/MANAGEMENT
   Operated by: HWS Baseball Group.
   Principal Owner: Mike Savit.
   President/COO: Bill Shanahan. **Vice President:** Mike Gorassi. **General Manager:** Heath Bennett.
   Assistant GM, Finance: Betty Adams. **Assistant GM, Corporate Sales:** Mike Callahan. **Director, Community Relations/Creative Services/Press Box:** Ari Rosenbaum. **Director, Ticket Sales:** Bradley Reynolds. **Sales Manager:** John Golz. **Concessions Manager:** Tara Crawford. **Director, Stadium Operations:** Wayne Loeblein. **Director, Broadcast Operations:** Craig Durham. **Account Executive:** Kyne Sheehy. **Coordinator, Sales/Marketing:** Sam Yarin. **Community Relations Assistant:** Christine LaPlante. **Sales Associates:** Travis Hawks, Shannon O'Connor. **Head Groundskeeper:** Caleb Adams. **Stadium Operations Assistant:** Wade Vadakin. **Team Chaplain:** Lorin Barr.

FIELD STAFF
   Manager: Andy Green. **Hitting Coach:** Jacob Cruz. **Pitching Coach:** Dan Carlson.

GAME INFORMATION
   Radio Announcer: Craig Durham. **No. of Games Broadcast:** Home-70, Away-70.
   Website Broadcast: www.baybearsradio.com. **PA Announcer:** Unavailable. **Official Scorers:** Unavailable.
   Stadium Name: Hank Aaron Stadium. **Location:** I-65 to exit 1 (Government Blvd East), right at Satchel Paige Drive, right at Bolling Bros Blvd. **Standard Game Times:** 7:05 pm, Sun 2:05. **Ticket Price Range:** $5-15.
   Visiting Club Hotel: Riverview Plaza, 64 S Water St, Mobile, AL 36602. **Telephone:** (251) 438-4000.

MONTGOMERY BISCUITS

Office Address: 200 Coosa St, Montgomery, AL 36104.
   Telephone: (334) 323-2255. **Fax:** (334) 323-2225. **E-Mail address:** info@biscuits-baseball.com. **Website:** www.biscuitsbaseball.com.
   Affiliation (first year): Tampa Bay Rays (2004). **Years in League:** 1965-1980, 2004-

OWNERSHIP/MANAGEMENT
   Operated By: Montgomery Professional Baseball LLC.
   Principal Owners: Tom Dickson, Sherrie Myers.
   President: Greg Rauch. **General Manager:** Marla Terranova Vickers.
   Sales Director: Scott Trible. **Corporate Account Executive:** Ross Winkler. **Director, Marketing:** Unavailable. **Media Relations:** Aaron Vargas. **Marketing Assistant:** Molly Johnson. **Box Office Manager:** Kyle Kreutzer. **Sponsorship Service Representatives:** Jonathan Vega, Megan Barnes. **Director, Retail Operations:** Steve Keller. **Director, Stadium Operations:** Steve Blackwell.
   Head Groundskeeper: Alex English. **Catering Managers:** Marissa Gordon. **Director, Food/Beverage:** Geoff Siddons. **Director, Business Operations:** Linda Fast. **Assistant Business Manager:** Dewanna Croy. **Administrative Assistant:** Bill Sisk. **Season Ticket Concierge:** Bob Rabon. **Executive Chef:** David Parker, Erin Clendenin. **Corporate Account Executive:** Greg Liebbe. **Group Sales Representatives:** Chris Asa.

FIELD STAFF
   Manager: Billy Gardner Jr. **Coach:** Ozzie Timmons. **Pitching Coach:** RC Lichtenstein.

GAME INFORMATION
   Radio Announcer: Aaron Vargas. **No of Games Broadcast:** Home-70 Road-70. **Flagship Station:** WLWI 1440-AM. **PA Announcer:** Rick Hendrick. **Official Scorer:** Kyle Kreutzer. **Stadium Name:** Montgomery Riverwalk Stadium.
   Location: I-65 to exit 172, east on Herron Street, left on Coosa Street. **Ticket Price Range:** $8-12. **Visiting Club Hotel:** Candlewood Suites.

PENSACOLA BLUE WAHOOS

Office Address: 351 West Cedar Street, Pensacola, FL 32502.
Mailing Address: PO 12587, Pensacola, FL 32591.
Telephone: (850) 934-8444. **Fax:** (850) 791-6256.
E-Mail Address: info@bluewahoos.com. **Website:** www.bluewahoos.com.
Affiliation (first year): Cincinnati Reds (2012). **Years in League:** 2012-

OWNERSHIP/MANAGEMENT
Operated by: Northwest Florida Professional Baseball LLC.
Principal Owner: Quint, Rishy Studer.
President: Bruce Baldwin. **Executive Vice President:** Jonathan Griffith.
Receptionist: Linda Aguado. **Stadium Operations Manager:** Chase Elliott. **Creative Services Manager:** Andrew Demsky. **Director, Sports Turf Management:** Ray Sayre. **Special Events Manager:** Shelley Yates. **Sales Manager:** Travis Painter. **Media Relations Coordinator/Broadcaster:** Tommy Thrall. **Director, Food/Beverage:** Mark Micallef. **Finance Director:** Amber McClure. **Groups Sales Executives:** Leroy Williams, Charlie Ortiz.

FIELD STAFF
Manager: Delino DeShields. **Coach:** Tony Jaramillo. **Pitching Coach:** Tom Brown. **Trainer:** Charles Leddon. **Strength Coach:** Frank Renner.

GAME INFORMATION
Radio Announcers: Tommy Thrall. **No. of Games Broadcast:** Home-70, Away-70. **Flagship Stations:** WBSR ESPN Radio Pensacola 1450 AM & 101.1 FM. **PA Announcer:** Josh Gay. **Official Scorer:** Unavailable.
Stadium Name: Blue Wahoos Ballpark. **Standard Game Times:** 7 pm, Sat 6:30, Sun 4 pm. **Ticket Price Range:** $16-$6.
Visiting Club Hotel: Hilton Garden Inn, Hampton Inn, Homewood Suites.

TENNESSEE SMOKIES

Office Address: 3540 Line Drive, Kodak, TN 37764.
Telephone: (865) 286-2300. **Fax:** (865) 523-9913.
E-Mail Address: info@smokiesbaseball.com. **Website:** www.smokiesbaseball.com.
Affiliation (first year): Chicago Cubs (2007). **Years in League:** 1964-67, 1972-

OWNERSHIP/MANAGEMENT
Operated By: SPBC, LLC.
President: Doug Kirchhofer.
General Manager: Brian Cox. **Assistant GM:** Jeff Shoaf.
Director, Stadium Operations: Bryan Webster. **Director, Community Relations:** Lauren Chesney. **Director, Food/Beverage:** Tony DaSilveira. **Director, Media Relations:** Adam Kline. **Director, Entertainment/Client Services:** Ryan Cox. **Director, Video Production/Graphic Design:** Tim Avery. **Director, Ticket/Retail Operations:** Robby Scheuermann. **Director, Field Operations:** Stuart Morris. **Director, Corporate Ticket Development:** Matt Strutner. **Senior Corporate Sales Executives:** Ken Franz, Dan Blue. **Group Sales Manager:** Rey Regenstreif-Harms. **Group Sales Representatives:** Baylor Love, Michael McMullen, Jason Moody, Will Thompson. **Business Manager:** Suzanne French. **Administrative Assistant:** Tolena Trout.

FIELD STAFF
Manager: Buddy Bailey. **Hitting Coach:** Desi Wilson. **Pitching Coach:** Jeff Fassero. **Trainer:** Scott Barringer. **Strength Coach:** Ryan Clausen.

GAME INFORMATION
Radio Announcer: Mick Gillispie. **No. of Games Broadcast:** Home-70 Road-70. **Flagship Station:** WNML 99.1-FM/990-AM. **PA Announcer:** Unavailable. **Official Scorers:** Jack Tate, Jared Smith, Bernie Reimer.
Stadium Name: Smokies Park. **Location:** I-40 to exit 407, Highway 66 North.
Standard Game Times: 7:15 pm, Sat 6:15 pm, Sun 2/5. **Ticket Price Range:** $6-11.
Visiting Club Hotel: Hampton Inn & Suites Sevierville, 105 Stadium Drive, Kodak, TN 37764. **Telephone:** (865) 465-0590.

TEXAS LEAGUE

Mailing Address: 2442 Facet Oak, San Antonio, TX 78232.
Telephone: (210) 545-5297. **Fax:** (210) 545-5298.
E-Mail Address: texasleague@sbcglobal.net. **Website:** www.texas-league.com.
Years League Active: 1888-1890, 1892, 1895-1899, 1902-1942, 1946-
President/Treasurer: Tom Kayser. **Vice Presidents:** Burl Yarbrough, Bill Valentine.
Corporate Secretary: Eric Edelstein. **Assistant to the President:** Doug Gale.
Directors: Jon Dandes (Northwest Arkansas), Ken Schrom (Corpus Christi), William DeWitt III (Springfield), Dale Hubbard (Tulsa), Scott Sonju (Frisco), Miles Prentice (Midland), Russ Meeks (Arkansas), Burl Yarbrough (San Antonio).
Division Structure: North—Arkansas, Northwest Arkansas, Springfield, Tulsa. South—Corpus Christi, Frisco, Midland, San Antonio.
Regular Season: 140 games (split schedule).
2013 Opening Date: April 4. **Closing Date:** Sept 2. **All-Star Game:** June 25 at Northwest Arkansas. **Playoff Format:** First-half division winners play second-half division winners in best-of-five series. Winners meet in best-of-five series for league championship.
Roster Limit: 25. **Player Eligibility Rule:** No restrictions. **Brand of Baseball:** Rawlings.
Umpires: Matt Benham (Spokane, WA), Ryan Blakney (Wenatchee, WA), Michael Cascioppo (Escondido, CA), Bryan Fields (Lincoln, NE), Ramon Hernandez (Columbia, MD), Pat Hoberg (Urbandale, IA), Gabe Morales (Livermore, CA), Alex Ortiz (Los Angeles, CA), Justin Sassman (Lewisville, TX), Brett Terry (Beaverton OR), Will Thornewell (Austin, TX, Nate White (CarsonCity, NV).

Tom Kayser

STADIUM INFORMATION

Club	Stadium	Opened	Dimensions LF	CF	RF	Capacity	2012 Att.
Arkansas	Dickey-Stephens Park	2007	332	413	330	5,842	308,109
Corpus Christi	Whataburger Field	2005	325	400	315	5,362	388,927
Frisco	Dr Pepper Ballpark	2003	335	409	335	10,216	488,224
Midland	Citibank Ballpark	2002	330	410	322	4,669	301,110
NW Arkansas	Arvest Ballpark	2008	325	400	325	6,500	321,254
San Antonio	Nelson Wolff Municipal Stadium	1994	310	402	340	6,200	301,942
Springfield	John Q. Hammons Field	2003	315	400	330	6,750	352,674
Tulsa	ONEOK Field	2010	330	400	307	7,833	372,624

ARKANSAS TRAVELERS

Office Address: Dickey-Stephens Park, 400 West Broadway, North Little Rock, AR 72114.
Mailing Address: PO Box 55066, Little Rock, AR 72215.
Telephone: (501) 664-1555. **Fax:** (501) 664-1834.
E-Mail address: travs@travs.com. **Website:** www.travs.com.
Affiliation (first year): Los Angeles Angels (2001). **Years in League:** 1966-

OWNERSHIP/MANAGEMENT

Ownership: Arkansas Travelers Baseball Club, Inc.
President: Russ Meeks.
General Manager: Paul Allen.
Director, Broadcasting/Media Relations: Phil Elson. **Director, Finance:** Ann McClure. **Director, In-Game Entertainment:** Tommy Adam. **Director, Merchandise/Licensing:** Rusty Meeks. **Park Superintendent:** Greg Johnston. **Assistant Park Superintendent:** Reggie Temple. **Director, Luxury Suites/Account Executive:** Jared Schein. **Director, Tickets:** Drew Williams. **Director, Community Relations:** Leslie Baker. **Director, Stadium Operations/Account Executive:** Jeff Daley. **Account Executives:** Ben Harrington, Eric Schrader.

FIELD STAFF

Manager: Tim Bogar. **Coach:** Ernie Young. **Pitching Coach:** Mike Hampton. **Trainer:** Mike Metcalfe. **Strength/Conditioning Coach:** Al Sandoval

GAME INFORMATION

Radio Announcers: Phil Elson, Matt Dudas. **No. of Games Broadcast:** Home-70 Road-70. **Flagship Station:** KARN 920 AM. **PA Announcer:** Russ McKinney. **Official Scorers:** Tim Cooper, Todd Traub.
Stadium Name: Dickey-Stephens Park. **Location:** I-30 to Broadway exit, proceed west to ballpark, located at Broadway Avenue and the Broadway Bridge. **Standard Game Time:** 7:10 pm. **Ticket Price Range:** $3-12.
Visiting Club Hotel: Clarion Little Rock, 925 S University Avenue, Little Rock, AR 72204. **Telephone:** (501) 664-5020. **Fax:** (501) 614-3803.

CORPUS CHRISTI HOOKS

Office Address: 734 East Port Ave, Corpus Christi, TX 78401.
Telephone: (361) 561-4665. **Fax:** (361) 561-4666.
E-Mail Address: info@cchooks.com. **Website:** www.cchooks.com.
Affiliation (first year): Houston Astros (2005). **Years in League:** 1958-59, 2005-

OWNERSHIP/MANAGEMENT
Operated By: Ryan-Sanders Baseball.
Principal Owners: Eddie Maloney, Reese Ryan, Reid Ryan, Nolan Ryan, Brad Sanders, Bret Sanders, Don Sanders.
CEO: Reid Ryan. **CFO:** Reese Ryan. **Executive Vice President:** JJ Gottsch.
President: Ken Schrom. **VP/General Manager:** Michael Wood. **VP, Sales:** Adam Nuse. **Director, Sponsor Services:** Elisa Macias. **Director, Retail:** Brooke Milam. **Controller:** Christy Lockard. **Director, Communications:** Matt Rogers. **Director, Broadcasting:** Michael Coffin. **Director, Stadium Operations:** Tina Athans, Jeremy Sturgeon. **Director, Group Sales:** Andy Steavens. **Director, Ballpark Entertainment:** JD Davis. **Director, Season Ticket Services:** Bryan Mayhood. **Account Executives:** Jeff Mackor, Charlie Kovar, Cody Cozart. **Field Superintendent:** Josh Brewer.

Field Staff
Manager: Keith Bodie. **Hitting Coach:** Tim Garland. **Pitching Coach:** Gary Ruby. **Development Specialist:** Mark Bailey. **Athletic Trainer:** Bryan Baca. **Strength Coach:** Trey Weidman.

GAME INFORMATION
Radio Announcers: Michael Coffin, Chris Blake, Gene Kasprzyk. **No. of Games Broadcast:** Home-70 Road-70. **Flagship Station:** KKTX-AM 1360. **PA Announcer:** Lon Gonzalez. **Stadium Name:** Whataburger Field. **Location:** I-37 to end of interstate, left at Chaparral, left at Hirsh Ave. **Ticket Price Range:** $5-14.
Visiting Club Hotel: Omni Hotel, N Shoreline Dr, Corpus Christi, TX 78401. **Telephone:** (361) 886-3553.

FRISCO ROUGHRIDERS

Office Address: 7300 RoughRiders Trail, Frisco, TX 75034.
Telephone: (972) 731-9200. **Fax:** (972) 731-5355.
E-Mail Address: info@ridersbaseball.com. **Website:** www.ridersbaseball.com.
Affiliation (first year): Texas Rangers (2003). **Years in League:** 2003-

OWNERSHIP/MANAGEMENT
Operated by: Mandalay Baseball Properties.
President: Scott Sonju. **Senior Vice President:** Billy Widner.
VP, Partnerships/Communications: Scott Burchett. **VP, Operations:** Mike Poole. **VP, Accounting/Finance:** Dustin Alban. **Director, Operations:** Scott Arnold. **Director, Corporate Partnerships:** Steven Nelson. **Director, Partner Services:** Matt Ratliff. **Director, Partner/Event Services:** Kristin Russell. **Director, Ticket Operations:** Jason Brayman. **Director, Game Entertainment:** Gabriel Wilhelm. **Director, Community Development:** LaShawn Moore.
Head Groundskeeper: David Bicknell. **Director, Maintenance:** Alfonso Bailon. **Assistant Director, Maintenance:** Gustavo Bailon. **Manager, Broadcasting/Media Development:** Alex Vispoli. **Ticket Operations Manager:** Rob Miles. **Partner Services Coordinator:** David Kosydar. **Manager, Marketing/Special Events:** Gabrielle Ganz. **Senior Manager, Group Sales:** Andy Benedict. **Senior Corporate Marketing Manager:** Andrew Sidney.

FIELD STAFF
Manager: Steve Buechele. **Coach:** Jason Hart. **Pitching Coach:** Jeff Andrews. **Trainer:** Carlos Olivas. **Strength/Conditioning:** Eric McMahon.

GAME INFORMATION
Broadcaster: Alex Vispoli. **No. of Games Broadcast:** Home-70, Away-70. **Flagship Station:** Unavailable.
PA Announcer: John Clemens. **Official Scorer:** Larry Bump. **Stadium Name:** Dr Pepper Ballpark. **Location:** Dallas North Tollway to State Highway 121. **Standard Game Times:** 7 pm, Sun 4 (April-June), 6 (July-Sept).
Visiting Club Hotel: Comfort Suites at Frisco Square, 9700 Dallas Parkway, Frisco, TX 75033. **Phone:** (972) 668-9700. **Fax:** (972) 668-9701.

MIDLAND ROCKHOUNDS

Office Address: 5514 Champions Dr, Midland, TX 79706.
Telephone: (432) 520-2255. **Fax:** (432) 520-8326.
Website: www.midlandrockhounds.org.
Affiliation (first year): Oakland Athletics (1999). **Years in League:** 1972-

OWNERSHIP/MANAGEMENT
Operated By: Midland Sports, Inc.
Principal Owners: Miles Prentice, Bob Richmond.

President: Miles Prentice. **Executive Vice President:** Bob Richmond. **General Manager:** Monty Hoppel. **Assistant GM:** Jeff VonHolle. **Assistant GM, Marketing/Tickets:** Jamie Richardson. **Assistant GM, Merchandise/Facilities:** Ray Fieldhouse. **Assistant GM, Media Relations:** Greg Bergman. **Assistant GM/Executive Director, Group Events:** Jeremy Lukas. **Director, Broadcasting/Publications:** Bob Hards. **Director, Business Operations:** Eloisa Galvan. **Director, Ticket Operations:** Michael Richardson. **Head Groundskeeper:** Eric Campbell. **Office Manager:** Frances Warner. **Director, Stadium Operations/Promotions/Special Events:** Manabu Beppu. **Director, Public Relations:** Brian Smith. **Director, Video Board Operations/Sales Associate:** Sean Clement. **Assistant Director, Operations/Sales Associate:** Chris Freeman. **Home Clubhouse Manager:** Derek Smith. **Visiting Clubhouse Manager:** TJ Leonard. **Complex Operations Manager:** CJ Bahr. **Assistant Groundskeeper:** Patrick Barnaby.

FIELD STAFF
Manager: Aaron Nieckula. **Hitting Coach:** Brian McArn. **Pitching Coach:** Don Schulze. **Trainer:** Justin Whitehouse. **Strength/Conditioning:** Terrence Brannic.

GAME INFORMATION
Radio Announcer: Bob Hards. **No. of Games Broadcast:** Home-70, Away-70. **Flagship Station:** KCRS 550 AM. **PA Announcer:** Wes Coles. **Official Scorer:** Steve Marcum. **Stadium Name:** Citibank Ballpark. **Location:** From I-20, exit Loop 250 North to Highway 191 intersection. **Standard Game Times:** 7 pm. **Ticket Price Range:** $7-16. **Visiting Club Hotel:** Sleep Inn and Suites, 5612 Deauville Blvd, Midland, TX 79706. **Telephone:** (432) 694-4200.

NORTHWEST ARKANSAS
NATURALS

Office Address: 3000 S 56th Street, Springdale, AR 72762. **Telephone:** (479) 927-4900. **Fax:** (479) 756-8088. **E-Mail Address:** info@nwanaturals.com. **Website:** www.nwanaturals.com. **Affiliation (first year):** Kansas City Royals (1995). **Years in League:** 1987-

OWNERSHIP/MANAGEMENT
Principal Owner: Rich Products Corp. **Chairman:** Robert Rich Jr. **President, Rich Entertainment:** Melinda Rich. **President, Rich Baseball:** Jon Dandes. **General Manager:** Eric Edelstein. **Assistant GM:** Justin Cole. **Business Manager:** Morgan Helmer. **Marketing/PR Manager:** Regina Van Henkelum. **Stadium Operations Director:** Jeff Windle. **Head Groundskeeper:** Monty Sowell. **Ticket Office Coordinator:** Sam Ahern. **Group Sales Manager:** Mark Zaiger. **Broadcaster/Baseball Operations Coordinator:** Steven Davis. **Sponsorship/Community Relations Coordinator:** Julie Maletto. **Production Coordinator:** Rob Sternberg. **Senior Account Executive:** Dustin Dethlefs. **Assistant Groundskeeper:** Brock White. **Operations Coordinator:** Marshall Schellhardt. **Gameday Staff Coordinator:** Rebekah Carpenter. **Merchandise Coordinator:** Shelby Huff. **Equipment Manager:** Danny Helmer.

FIELD STAFF
Manager: Brian Poldberg. **Coach:** Nelson Liriano. **Pitching Coach:** Jim Brower. **Trainer:** Masa Koyanagi.

GAME INFORMATION
Radio Announcers: Steven Davis. **No. of Games Broadcast:** Home-70, Away-70. **Flagship:** CBS Sports 92.1FM The Ticket (KQSM-FM). **PA Announcer:** Bill Rogers. **Official Scorer:** Chris Ledeker. **Stadium Name:** Arvest Ballpark. **Location:** I-540 to US 412 West (Sunset Ave); Left on 56th St. **Ticket Price Range:** $6-13. **Standard Game Times:** 7 pm, Sun 2 (April/May), 6 (May 27-Sept 2). **Visiting Club Hotel:** Holiday Inn Springdale, 1500 S 48th St, Springdale, AR 72762. **Telephone:** (479) 751-8300.

SAN ANTONIO MISSIONS

Office/Mailing Address: 5757 Highway 90 West, San Antonio, TX 78227. **Telephone:** (210) 675-7275. **Fax:** (210) 670-0001. **E-Mail Address:** sainfo@samissions.com. **Website:** www.samissions.com. **Affiliation (first year):** San Diego Padres (2007). **Years in League:** 1888, 1892, 1895-99, 1907-42, 1946-64, 1968-

OWNERSHIP/MANAGEMENT
Operated by: Elmore Sports Group. **Principal Owner:** David Elmore. **President:** Burl Yarbrough. **General Manager:** Dave Gasaway. **Assistant GMs:** Mickey Holt, Jeff Long, Bill Gerlt. **GM, Diamond Concessions:** Mike Lindal. **Controller:** Ivan Molina. **Director, Broadcasting:** Mike Saeger. **Office Manager:** Delia Rodriguez. **Box Office Manager:** Rob Gusick. **Director, Operations:** John Hernandez. **Director, Group Sales:** George Levandoski. **Director, Public Relations:** Jim White. **Field Superintendent:** Karsten Blackwelder. **Assistant Field Superintendent:** Jaxon Bailey.

FIELD STAFF
Manager: Rich Dauer. **Coach:** Jacque Jones. **Pitching Coach:** Jimmy Jones. **Trainer:** Daniel Turner.

GAME INFORMATION

Radio Announcer: Mike Saeger. **No. of Games Broadcast:** Home-70, Away-70. **Flagship Station:** KKYX 680-AM. **PA Announcer:** Roland Ruiz. **Official Scorer:** David Humphrey. **Stadium Name:** Nelson W Wolff Stadium. **Location:** From I-10, I-35 or I-37, take US Hwy 90 West to Callaghan Road exit. **Standard Game Times:** 7:05 pm, Sun 4:05/6:05. **Visiting Club Hotel:** Holiday Inn Northwest/Sea World. **Telephone:** (210) 520-2508.

SPRINGFIELD CARDINALS

Office Address: 955 East Trafficway, Springfield, MO 65802.
Telephone: (417) 863-0395. **Fax:** (417) 863-0388.
E-Mail address: springfield@cardinals.com. **Website:** www.springfieldcardinals.com.
Affiliation (first year): St. Louis Cardinals (2005). **Years in League:** 2005-

OWNERSHIP/MANAGEMENT

Operated By: St. Louis Cardinals.
Vice President/General Manager: Matt Gifford. **VP, Baseball/Business Operations:** Scott Smulczenski. **VP, Facility Operations:** Bill Fischer. **Director, Ticket Operations:** Angela Deke. **Director, Sales/Marketing:** Dan Reiter. **Manager, Promotions/Productions:** Kent Shelton. **Manager, Market Development:** Scott Bailes. **Manager, Stadium/Game Day Operations:** Aaron Lowrey. **Manager, Public Relations/Broadcaster:** Jeff Levering. **Coordinator, Sales Services:** Lindsay Bone. **Box Office Supervisor/Office Assistant:** Ayrica Batson. **Head Groundskeeper:** Brock Phipps. **AssistantGroundskeeper:** Derek Edwards.

FIELD STAFF

Manager: Mike Shildt. **Coach:** Phillip Wellman. **Pitching Coach:** Randy Niemann. **Trainer:** Scott Ensell. **Strength Coach:** Josh Cue.

GAME INFORMATION

Radio Announcer: Jeff Levering. **No. of Games Broadcast:** Home-70 Road-70. **Flagship Station:** JOCK 98.7 FM. **PA Announcer:** Unavailable. **Official Scorers:** Mark Stillwell, Tim Tourville. **Stadium Name:** Hammons Field. **Location:** Highway 65 to Chestnut Expressway exit, west to National, south on National, west on Trafficway. **Standard Game Time:** 7:10 pm. **Ticket Price Range:** $6-25.
Visiting Club Hotel: University Plaza Hotel, 333 John Q Hammons Parkway, Springfield, MO 65806. **Telephone:** (417) 864-7333.

TULSA DRILLERS

Office Address: 201 N Elgin, Tulsa, OK 74120.
Telephone: (918) 744-5998. **Fax:** (918) 747-3267.
E-Mail Address: mail@tulsadrillers.com. **Website:** www.tulsadrillers.com.
Affiliation (first year): Colorado Rockies (2003). **Years in League:** 1933-42, 1946-65, 1977-

OWNERSHIP/MANAGEMENT

Operated By: Tulsa Baseball Inc.
Co-Chairmen: Dale Hubbard, Jeff Hubbard.
General Manager: Mike Melega. **Assistant GM:** Jason George.
Bookkeeper: Cheryll Couey. **Executive Assistant:** Kara Biden. **Director, Stadium Operations:** Mark Hilliard. **Director, Media/Public Relations:** Brian Carroll. **Director, Ticket Operations:** Brandon Shiers. **Director, Marketing/Business Development:** Rob Gardenhire. **Director, Merchandise:** Tom Jones. **Director, Group Ticket Sales:** Geoff Beaty. **Manager, Promotions:** Michael Taranto. **Head Groundskeeper:** Gary Shepherd. **Manager, Group Sales:** Matt Larson. **Manager, Business Development:** Kevin Butcher. **Manager, Game Entertainment:** Justin Gorski. **Assistant Bookkeeper:** Jenna Higgins. **Account Executive:** Joanna Hubbard. **Mascot Coordinator:** Vincent Pace. **Marketing Assistant:** Jordan Nommay. **Ticket Office Assistant:** Ryan Minahan. **Group Sales Assistant:** Adam Fremd. **Operations Assistant:** Zach Miller. **Merchandise Assistant:** Travis Day. **Media Assistant:** Heath Hicks. **Video Production Assistant:** Kyle Guertin. **Video Production Assistant:** Owen Sloan. **Director, Food Services:** Carter Witt. **Team Photographer:** Rich Crimi. **Director, Concessions:** Wayne Campbell. **Catering Manager/Executive Chef:** Cody Malone.

FIELD STAFF

Manager: Kevin Riggs. **Hitting Coach:** Darin Everson. **Pitching Coach:** Darryl Scott. **Trainer:** Chris Dovey. **Strength Coach:** Brian Buck. **Supervisor, Double-A Development:** Duane Espy.

GAME INFORMATION

Radio Announcer: Dennis Higgins. **No. of Games Broadcast:** Home-70 Road-70. **Flagship Station:** KTBZ 1430-AM. **PA Announcer:** Kirk McAnany. **Official Scorers:** Bruce Howard, Duane DaPron, Larry Lewis, Barry Lewis. **Stadium Name:** ONEOK Field. **Location:** Take I-244 to the Cincinnati/Detroit Exit (#6A); Go north on Detroit Ave, take a right onto John Hope Franklin Blvd, take a right on Elgin Ave. **Standard Game Times:** 7:05 pm, Sun 2:05 (April-June), 7:05 (July-Aug). **Visiting Club Hotel:** Hyatt Regency, 100 E 2nd St, Tulsa, OK 74103. **Telephone:** (918) 582-9000.

CALIFORNIA LEAGUE

Office Address: 3600 South Harbor Blvd, Suite 122, Oxnard, CA 93035.
Telephone: (805) 985-8585. **Fax:** (805) 985-8580.
Website: www.californialeague.com. **E-Mail:** info@californialeague.com.
Years League Active: 1941-1942, 1946-
President: Charlie Blaney. **Vice President:** Tom Volpe.
Directors: Bobby Brett (Rancho Cucamonga), Brad Seymour (Lancaster), Dave Elmore (Inland Empire), Gene Voiland (Bakersfield), Dave Heller (High Desert), Gary Jacobs (Lake Elsinore), Mike Savit (Modesto), Tom Seidler (Visalia), Tom Volpe (Stockton), Dan Orum (San Jose).
Director, Operations/Marketing: Matt Blaney. **Historian:** Chris Lampe. **Legal Counsel:** Jonathan Light. **CPA:** Jeff Hass.
Regular Season: 140 games (split schedule).
2013 Opening Date: April 4. **Closing Date:** Sept 2.
Playoff Format: Six teams. First-half winners in each division earn first-round bye; second-half winners meet wild cards with next best overall records in best-of-three quarterfinals. Winners meet first-half champions in best-of-five semifinals. Winners meet in best-of-five series for league championship.
All-Star Game: vs Carolina League, June 18 at San Jose.
Roster Limit: 25 active (35 under control).
Player Eligibility: No more than two players and one player/coach on active list may have more than six years experience. **Brand of Baseball:** Rawlings.
Umpires: Johnathan Bostwick, Jonathan Burzynski, Paul Clemons, Matt Czajak, Derek Eaton, Blake Felix, Ben Guttenberger, Lee Meyers, Ronnie Teague.

Charlie Blaney

| Club | Stadium | Opened | Dimensions | | | Capacity | 2012 Att. |
			LF	CF	RF		
Bakersfield	Sam Lynn Ballpark	1941	328	354	328	2,700	40,056
High Desert	Mavericks Stadium	1991	340	401	340	3,808	119,028
Inland Empire	San Manuel Stadium	1996	330	410	330	5,000	185,411
Lake Elsinore	The Diamond	1994	330	400	310	7,866	225,769
Lancaster	Clear Channel Stadium	1996	350	410	350	4,500	147,129
Modesto	John Thurman Field	1952	312	400	319	4,000	180,785
R Cucamonga	The Epicenter	1993	335	400	335	6,615	155,903
San Jose	Municipal Stadium	1942	320	390	320	5,208	222,547
Stockton	Banner Island Ballpark	2005	300	399	326	5,200	198,705
Visalia	Rawhide Ballpark	1946	320	405	320	2,468	118,065

BAKERSFIELD BLAZE

Office Address: 4009 Chester Ave, Bakersfield, CA 93301.
Mailing Address: PO Box 10031, Bakersfield, CA 93389.
Telephone: (661) 716-4487. **Fax:** (661) 322-6199.
E-Mail Address: blaze@bakersfieldblaze.com. **Website:** www.bakersfieldblaze.com.
Affiliation: Cincinnati Reds (2011). **Years In League:** 1941-42, 1946-75, 1978-79, 1982-

OWNERSHIP/MANAGEMENT
Principal Owner: Bakersfield Sports Group (Eugene Voiland, Chad Hathaway).
General Manager: Elizabeth Martin. **Assistant GM, Operations:** Philip Guiry. **Assistant GM, Sales:** Mike Candela.
Director, Broadcasting/Media Relations: Dan Besbris. **Director, Groups/Events:** Megan Murphy. **Director, Community Relations:** Carolyne Wood. **Director, Ticketing:** Brianne Gidcumb.

FIELD STAFF
Manager: Ken Griffey. **Hitting Coach:** Ray Martinez. **Pitching Coach:** Rigo Beltran. **Trainer:** Adam Weyer.

GAME INFORMATION
Radio: Dan Besbris. **Flagship Station:** 1230-AM.
PA Announcer: Mike Cushine. **Official Scorer:** Tim Wheeler.
Stadium Name: Sam Lynn Ballpark. **Location:** Highway 99 to California Avenue, east three miles to Chester Avenue, north two miles to stadium. **Standard Game Time:** 7:30 pm. **Ticket Price Range:** $7-10.
Visiting Club Hotel: Double Tree, 3100 Camino Del Rio Court Bakersfield, CA 93308. **Telephone:** (661) 323-7111.

HIGH DESERT MAVERICKS

Stadium/Office Address: 12000 Stadium Way, Adelanto, CA 92301.
Telephone: (760) 246-6287. **Fax:** (760) 246-3197.
E-Mail Address: mbutz@hdmavs.com. **Website:** www.hdmavs.com.
Affiliation: Seattle Mariners (2007). **Years in League:** 1991-

OWNERSHIP/MANAGEMENT

Operated By: Main Street California.
Vice President: Stefanie Brown. **Assistant General Manager:** Mitch Butz.
Director, Corporate Partnerships: Casey Rasmussen. **Director, Marketing/Communications:** Jim Kneer. **Account Executive:** Michelle Alipio. **Director, Food/Beverage:** Daniel Gonzalez. **Head Groundskeeper:** Joe Jimenez.

FIELD STAFF

Manager: Jim Horner. **Hitting Coach:** Roy Howell. **Pitching Coach:** Lance Painter.

GAME INFORMATION

Radio Announcer: None.
PA Announcer: Unavailable. **Official Scorer:** Unavailable.
Stadium Name: Stater Bros Stadium. **Location:** I-15 North to Highway 395 to Adelanto Road. **Standard Game Times:** 7:05 pm; Sun 2:05. **Ticket Price Range:** $5-$8
Visiting Club Hotel: Motel 6, 9757 Cataba Rd, Hesperia, CA 92395. **Telephone:** (760) 947-0094.

INLAND EMPIRE 66ERS

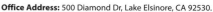

Office Address: 280 South E St, San Bernardino, CA 92401.
Telephone: (909) 888-9922. **Fax:** (909) 888-5251.
Website: www.66ers.com.
Affiliation (first year): Los Angeles Angels of Anaheim (2011). **Years in League:** 1941, 1987-

OWNERSHIP/MANAGEMENT

Operated by: Inland Empire 66ers Baseball Club of San Bernardino.
Principal Owners: David Elmore, Donna Tuttle.
Owner/President: Dave Elmore. **Owner/Chairman:** Donna Tuttle.
General Manager: Joe Hudson. **Assistant GM:** Ryan English. **Assistant GM:** Ryan English.
Director, Ticket Operations/Media Relations: Joey Seymour. **Director, Group Sales:** Steve Pelle. **Director, Marketing/Promotions:** Matt Kowallis. **Corporate Group Executives:** Adam Franey, Sarah Henry. **Community Groups Sales Manager:** Kelsey English. **Groups Sales Manager:** Andrew Pittman. **Stadium Operations Manager:** Jordan Smith. **Creative Director:** Robert Peters. **Administrative Assistant:** Angie Geibel. **Head Groundskeeper:** Rob Gladwell. **Groundskeeper:** Dominick Guerrero. **CFO:** John Fonseca.

FIELD STAFF

Manager: Bill Haselman. **Hitting Coach:** Brent Del Chiaro. **Pitching Coach:** Brandon Emanuel. **Trainer:** Greg Spence. **Strength/Conditioning Coach:** Ben Gaal.

GAME INFORMATION

Radio Announcer: Sam Farber. **Flagship Station:** KCAA 1050-AM. **PA Announcer:** JJ Gould. **Official Scorer:** Bill Maury-Holmes. **Stadium Name:** 66ers Stadium. **Location:** From south, I-215 to 2nd Street exit, east on 2nd, right on G Street; from north, I-215 to 3rd Street exit, left on Rialto, right on G Street. **Standard Game Times:** 7:05 pm; Sun 2:05 (April-June), 5:05 (July-Aug). **Ticket Price Range:** $8-12. **Ticket Price Range:** $5-10. **Visiting Club Hotel:** Hilton San Bernardino, 285 East Hospitality Lane, San Bernardino, CA 92408. **Telephone:** (909) 889-0133.

LAKE ELSINORE STORM

Office Address: 500 Diamond Dr, Lake Elsinore, CA 92530.
Mailing Address: PO Box 535, Lake Elsinore, CA 92531.
Telephone: (951) 245-4487. **Fax:** (951) 245-0305.
E-Mail Address: info@stormbaseball.com. **Website:** www.stormbaseball.com.
Affiliation (first year): San Diego Padres (2001). **Years in League:** 1994-

OWNERSHIP/MANAGEMENT

Owners: Gary Jacobs, Len Simon.
President: Dave Oster.
Vice President/General Manager: Chris Jones. **VP/GM, Events:** Bruce Kessman. **Assistant GMs:** Tracy Kessman, JT Onyett, Raj Narayanan. **Director, Stadium Operations:** Matt Schaffner. **Director, Broadcasting:** Sean McCall. **Assistant Director, Media Relations:** Ryan Mersey. **Group Sales Representatives:** Jason Emerick, Kasey Rawitzer, Eric Theiss.

Senior Graphics/Animation Designer: Mark Beskid. **Assistant Director, Ticketing:** Eric Colunga . **Sponsorship Coordinator:** Dave Barnick. **Director, Mascot Operations:** Patrick Gardenier. **Director, Administration:** Rick Riegler. **Director, Finance:** Marcy Sattelmaier. **Director, Merchandise:** Donna Grunow. **Director, Social Media:** Rachael Recker. **GM, Catering:** Arjun Suresh. **Executive Chef:** Steve Bearse. **Assistant Director, Food/Beverage:** Andrew Nelson. **Director, Grounds/Maintenance:** Peter Hayes. **Maintenance Supervisor:** Jassiel Reza. **Office Manager:** Peggy Mitchell. **Clubhouse Manager:** Terrance Tucker.

FIELD STAFF

Manager: Shawn Wooten. **Hitting Coach:** David Newhan. **Pitching Coach:** Brian Lawerence. **Trainer:** Will Sinon.

GAME INFORMATION

Radio Announcer: Sean McCall. **No. of Games Broadcast:** Home-70 Road-70. **Flagship Station:** Unavailable. **PA Announcer:** Joe Martinez. **Official Scorer:** Lloyd Nixon. **Stadium Name:** The Diamond. **Location:** From I-15, exit at Diamond Drive, west one mile to stadium. **Standard Game Times:** 7:05 pm, Sat 6:05, Sun 2:05 (first half), 6:05 (second half). **Ticket Price Range:** $10-14. **Visiting Club Hotel:** Lake Elsinore Hotel and Casino, 20930 Malaga St, Lake Elsinore, CA 92530. **Telephone:** (951) 674-3101.

LANCASTER JETHAWKS

Office Address: 45116 Valley Central Way, Lancaster, CA 93536. **Telephone:** (661) 726-5400. **Fax:** (661) 726-5406. **E-Mail Address:** info@jethawks.com. **Website:** www.jethawks.com. **Affiliation (first year):** Houston Astros (2009). **Years in League:** 1996-

OWNERSHIP/MANAGEMENT

Operated By: Hawks Nest LLC. **President:** Pete Carfagna. **Vice President:** Brad Seymour. **General Manager:** Derek Sharp. **Assistant GM:** Will Thornhill. **Assistant GM, Tickets/Merchandise:** Will Murphy. **Director, Facility/Baseball Operations:** John Laferney. **Director, Food/Beverage:** Adam Fillenworth. **Community Relations Manager/Account Executive:** Jennifer Adamczyk. **Ticket Account Executives:** Brandon Capelo, Joe Yates.

FIELD STAFF

Manager: Rodney Linares. **Coach:** Darryl Robinson. **Pitching Coach:** Don Alexander. **Infield Coach:** Morgan Ensberg. **Trainer:** Grant Hufford.

GAME INFORMATION

Radio Announcer: Jason Schwartz. **No. of Games Broadcast:** Home-70, Away-70. **Flagship Station:** www.jethawks.com . **PA Announcer:** John Tyler. **Official Scorer:** David Guenther. **Stadium Name:** The Hangar. **Location:** Highway 14 in Lancaster to Avenue I exit, west one block to stadium. **Standard Game Times:** 7 pm, Sun 2 (April-June), 5 (July-Sept). **Ticket Price Range:** $6-12. **Visiting Club Hotel:** Palmdale Hotel, 300 West Palmdale Blvd, Palmdale, CA 93551. **Telephone:** (661) 947-9593.

MODESTO NUTS

Office Address: 601 Neece Dr, Modesto, CA 95351. **Mailing Address:** PO Box 883, Modesto, CA 95353. **Telephone:** (209) 572-4487. **Fax:** (209) 572-4490. **E-Mail Address:** fun@modestonuts.com. **Website:** www.modestonuts.com. **Affiliation (first year):** Colorado Rockies (2005). **Years in League:** 1946-64, 1966-

OWNERSHIP/MANAGEMENT

Operated by: HWS Group IV. **Principal Owner:** Mike Savit. **President:** Bill Shanahan. **Vice President/GM:** Michael Gorrasi. **Assistant GM, Operations:** Ed Mack. **Assistant GM, Sales/Marketing:** Tyler Richardson. **Director, Stadium Operations:** Ryan Thomas. **Director, Broadcasting:** Alex Margulies. **Director, Public Relations:** Justin McKissick. **Account Executive:** Peter Billups.

FIELD STAFF

Manager: Lenn Sakata. **Coach:** Jon Stone. **Pitching Coach:** Dave Burba.

GAME INFORMATION

Radio Announcer: Alex Margulies. **PA Announcer:** Unavailable. **Official Scorer:** Unavailable. **Stadium Name:** John Thurman Field. **Location:** Highway 99 in southwest Modesto to Tuolomne Boulevard exit, west on Tuolomne for one block to Neece Drive, left for 1/4 mile to stadium. **Standard Game Times:** 7:05 pm, Sun 1:05. **Ticket Price Range:** $6-12. **Visiting Club Hotel:** Clarion Inn, 1612 Sisk Rd, Modesto, CA 95350. **Telephone:** (209) 521-1612.

RANCHO CUCAMONGA
QUAKES

Office Address: 8408 Rochester Ave, Rancho Cucamonga, CA 91730.
Mailing Address: PO Box 4139, Rancho Cucamonga, CA 91729.
Telephone: (909) 481-5000. **Fax:** (909) 481-5005.
E-Mail Address: info@rcquakes.com. **Website:** www.rcquakes.com.
Affiliation (first year): Los Angeles Dodgers (2011). **Years in League:** 1993-

OWNERSHIP/MANAGEMENT
Operated By: Brett Sports & Entertainment.
Principal Owner: Bobby Brett.
President: Brent Miles. **Vice President/General Manager:** Grant Riddle. **VP, Tickets:** Monica Ortega. **Assistant GM:** Linda Rathfon. **Director, Group Sales:** Kyle Burleson. **Group Sales Manager:** Matt Sirios. **Director, Season Tickets/Operations:** Dirk Manley. **Director, Promotions:** Matt Franco. **Director, Sponsorships:** Chris Pope. **Director, Accounting:** Amara McClellan. **Account Executives:** Melinda Balandra, Arturo Torres. **Promotions Coordinator:** Kristen Vella. **Public Relations Manager/Voice of the Quakes:** Mike Lindskog. **Office Manager:** Shelley Scebbi. **Director, Food/Beverage:** Peter Neubert.

FIELD STAFF
Manager: Carlos Subero. **Coach:** Jay Washington. **Pitching Coach:** Matt Herges.

GAME INFORMATION
Radio Announcer: Mike Lindskog. **No of Games:** Home-70, Road-70. **Flagship Station:** KSPA AM 1510.
PA Announcer: Chris Albaugh. **Official Scorer:** Ryan Wilson.
Stadium Name: The Epicenter. **Location:** I-10 to I-15 North, exit at Foothill Boulevard, left on Foothill, left on Rochester to Stadium Way. **Standard Game Times:** 7:05 pm. **Ticket Price Range:** $8-12.
Visiting Club Hotel: Best Western Heritage Inn, 8179 Spruce Ave, Rancho Cucamonga, CA 91730. **Telephone:** (909) 466-1111.

SAN JOSE GIANTS

Office Address: 588 E Alma Ave, San Jose, CA 95112.
Mailing Address: PO Box 21727, San Jose, CA 95151.
Telephone: (408) 297-1435. **Fax:** (408) 297-1453.
E-Mail Address: info@sjgiants.com. **Website:** www.sjgiants.com.
Affiliation (first year): San Francisco Giants (1988). **Years in League:** 1942, 1947-58, 1962-76, 1979-

OWNERSHIP/MANAGEMENT
Operated by: Progress Sports Management.
Principal Owners: San Francisco Giants, Heidi Stamas, Richard Beahrs.
President/CEO: Daniel Orum.
Chief Operating Officer/General Manager: Mark Wilson. **Chief Marketing Officer:** Juliana Paoli. **VP, Operations/Assistant GM:** Zach Walter. **VP, Sales:** Ainslie Walter. **VP, Baseball Operations:** Lance Motch. **Director, Player Personnel:** Linda Pereira. **Director, Broadcasting:** Joe Ritzo. **Director, Finance/Human Resources:** Tyler Adair. **Director, Food/Beverage:** Josh Cocke. **Director, Ticketing:** Kellen Minteer. **Account Executive/Camp Coordinator:** Taylor Wilding. **Marketing Coordinator:** Sarah Carpenter. **Coordinator, Finance/Human Resources:** Mike Butera. **Media Relations Coordinator:** Ben Taylor. **Account Executive:** Adam Reid.

FIELD STAFF
Manager: Andy Skeels. **Hitting Coach:** Lipso Nava. **Pitching Coach:** Michael Couchee. **Trainer:** David Getsoff. **Strength/Conditioning Coach:** Dustin Brooks.

GAME INFORMATION
Radio Announcers: Joe Ritzo, Rocky Koplik. **No. of Games Broadcast:** Home-70, Away-70. **Flagship:** www.sjgiants.com. **Television Announcers:** Joe Ritzo, Joe Castellano, Rocky Koplik. **No. of Games Broadcast:** Home-20 on Comcast Hometown Network, 70 on MiLB.TV.
PA Announcer: Russ Call. **Official Scorers:** Brian Burkett, Mike Hohler.
Stadium Name: Municipal Stadium. **Location:** South on I-280, Take 10th/11th Street Exit, Turn right on 10th Street, Turn left on Alma Ave; North on I-280: Take the 10th/11th Street Exit, Turn left on 10th Street, Turn Left on Alma Ave. **Standard Game Times:** 7 pm, Sat 5, Sun 1 (5 after June 30). **Ticket Price Range:** $7-16.
Visiting Club Hotel: DoubleTree by Hilton Hotel San Jose, 2050 Gateway Place, San Jose, CA 95110. **Telephone:** (408) 453-4000.

STOCKTON PORTS

Office Address: 404 W Fremont St, Stockton, CA 95203.
Telephone: (209) 644-1900. **Fax:** (209) 644-1931.
E-Mail Address: info@stocktonports.com. **Website:** www.stocktonports.com.
Affiliation (first year): Oakland Athletics (2005). **Years in League:** 1941, 1946-72, 1978-

OWNERSHIP/MANAGEMENT
Operated By: 7th Inning Stretch LLC.
President: Pat Filippone. **General Manager:** Luke Reiff. **Senior Director, Marketing:** Jeremy Neisser. **Community Relations Manager:** Bailey West. **Manager, Corporate Partnerships/Inside Sales:** Aaron Morales. **Director, Operations:** Bryan Meadows. **Senior Director, Ticket Sales:** Jeff Kaminski. **Director, Ticket Operations:** Tim Pollack. **Account Executive:** Lisa Peterson. **Sponsorship/Ticket Sales Executive:** Greg Bell. **Bookkeeper:** Vang Hang. **Front Office Manager:** Deborah Pelletier. **Ovations General Manager:** Mike Bristow.

FIELD STAFF
Manager: Webster Garrison. **Hitting Coach:** Haas Pratt. **Pitching Coach:** Jimmy Escalante. **Trainer:** Nathan Brooks.

GAME INFORMATION
Radio Announcer: Zack Bayrouty. **No of Games Broadcast:** Home-70, Away-70. **Flagship Station:** KWSX 1280 AM. **TV:** Comcast Hometown Network, Channel 104, Regional Telecast.
PA Announcer: Mike Conway. **Official Scorer:** Paul Muyskens.
Stadium Name: Banner Island Ballpark. **Location:** From I-5/99, take Crosstown Freeway (Highway 4) exit El Dorado Street, north on El Dorado to Fremont Street, left on Fremont.
Standard Game Times: 7:05 pm. **Ticket Price Range:** $6-$12.
Visiting Club Hotel: Hampton Inn Stockton, 5045 South State Route 99 East, Stockton, CA 95215. **Telephone:** (209) 946-1234.

VISALIA RAWHIDE

Office Address: 300 N Giddings St, Visalia, CA 93291.
Telephone: (559) 732-4433. **Fax:** (559) 739-7732.
E-Mail Address: info@rawhidebaseball.com. **Website:** www.rawhide-baseball.com.
Affiliation (first year): Arizona Diamondbacks (2007). **Years in League:** 1946-62, 1968-75, 1977-

OWNERSHIP/MANAGEMENT
President: Tom Seidler.
General Manager: Jennifer Pendergraft. **Executive Assistant:** Erin O'Brien.
Director, Ticketing/Group Events: Charlie Saponara. **Manager, Ticketing:** Dan Makela. **Event Coordinator:** Jessica Massart. **Coordinator, Client Servicing:** Charlie Bennett. **Director, Broadcasting:** Donny Baarns. **Manager, Media Relations:** Josh Jackson. **Manager, Hispanic Marketing/Community Relations:** Jesus Romero. **Director, Ballpark Operations:** Cody Gray. **Head Groundskeeper:** Jason Smith. **Operations Assistant, Food/Beverage:** Chris Lukasiewicz. **Ballpark Operations Assistant:** Les Kissick.

FIELD STAFF
Manager: Bill Plummer. **Hitting Coach:** Bobby Smith. **Pitching Coach:** Gil Heredia. **Trainer:** Takashi Onuki.

GAME INFORMATION
Radio Announcers: Donny Baarns, Josh Jackson. **No. of Games Broadcast:** Home-70, Away-70. **Flagship Station:** KJUG 1270-AM. **PA Announcer:** Brian Anthony. **Official Scorer:** Harry Kargenian.
Stadium Name: Rawhide Ballpark. **Location:** From Highway 99, take 198 East to Mooney Boulevard exit, left at second signal on Giddings; four blocks to ballpark.
Standard Game Times: 7 pm, Sun 2 (first half), 6 (second half). **Ticket Price Range:** $5-20.
Visiting Club Hotel: Lamp Liter Inn, 3300 W Mineral King Ave, Visalia, CA 93291. **Telephone:** (559) 732-4511.

CAROLINA LEAGUE

Office Address: 1806 Pembroke Rd, Suite 2-B, Greensboro, NC 27408.
Mailing Address: same as street address.
Telephone: (336) 691-9030. **Fax:** (336) 464-2737.
E-Mail Address: office@carolinaleague.com. **Website:** www.carolinaleague.com.
Years League Active: 1945-.

President/Treasurer: John Hopkins.

Vice President: Art Silber (Potomac). **Corporate Secretary:** Ken Young (Frederick).

Directors: Tim Zue (Salem), Rex Angel (Lynchburg), Chuck Greenberg (Myrtle Beach), Dave Ziedelis (Frederick), Steve Bryant (Carolina), Jack Minker (Wilmington), Billy Prim (Winston-Salem), Art Silber (Potomac).

Administrative Assistant: Marnee Larkins.

Division Structure: North—Frederick, Lynchburg, Potomac, Wilmington. South—Carolina, Myrtle Beach, Salem, Winston-Salem.

Regular Season: 140 games (split schedule). **2013 Opening Date:** April 4. **Closing Date:** Sept 2.

All-Star Game: June 18 at San Jose (Carolina League vs California League).

Playoff Format: First-half division winners play second-half division winners in best-of-three series; if a team wins both halves, it plays a wild card (team in that division with next-best second-half record). Division series winners meet in best-of-five series for Mills Cup.

John Hopkins

Roster Limit: 25 active. **Player Eligibility Rule:** No age limit. No more than two players and one player/coach on active list may have six or more years of prior minor league service.

Brand of Baseball: Rawlings.

Umpires: Richard Gonzalez (Maryland Heights, MO), Jimmie Hollingsworth (Irmo, SC), JJ January (Columbus, OH), Drew Maher (Huntersville, NC), Dan Merzel (Hopkinton, MA), Mike Patterson II (New Windsor, MD), Junior Valentine (Maryville, TN).

STADIUM INFORMATION

Club	Stadium	Opened	Dimensions LF	CF	RF	Capacity	2012 Att.
Carolina	Five County Stadium	1991	330	400	309	6,500	225,577
Frederick	Harry Grove Stadium	1990	325	400	325	5,400	311,805
Lynchburg	City Stadium	1939	325	390	325	4,281	155,261
Myrtle Beach	TicketReturn.com Field	1999	308	405	328	5,200	220,273
Potomac	Pfitzner Stadium	1984	315	400	315	6,000	191,928
Salem	Salem Memorial Stadium	1995	325	401	325	5,502	178,730
Wilmington	Frawley Stadium	1993	325	400	325	6,532	287,992
Winston-Salem	BB&T Ballpark	2010	315	399	323	5,500	305,515

CAROLINA MUDCATS

Office Address: 1501 NC Hwy 39, Zebulon, NC 27597.
Mailing Address: PO Drawer 1218, Zebulon, NC 27597.
Telephone: (919) 269-2287. **Fax:** (919) 269-4910.
E-Mail Address: muddy@carolinamudcats.com. **Website:** www.carolinamudcats.com.
Affiliation (first year): Cleveland Indians (2012). **Years in League:** 2012-

OWNERSHIP/MANAGEMENT

Operated by: Mudcats Baseball, LLC. **Majority Owner/President:** Steve Bryant.

General Manager: Joe Kremer. **Assistant GM:** Eric Gardner. **Office Manager:** Jackie DiPrimo. **Director, Stadium Operations:** Daniel Spence. **Stadium Operations:** Joel Chavez. **Director, Food/Beverage:** Dwayne Lucas. **Director, Merchandise:** Britni Holman. **Director, Video Operations/Multimedia Productions/Website:** Aaron Bayles. **Director, Tickets:** Stephen Boham. **Director, External Affairs/Corporate Development:** Ricky Ray. **Director, Community Relations:** Lindsey Lynch. **Director, Group Sales/Marketing:** Sean Nickelsen. **Associates, Group Sales:** Jordan Buck, Juan D Toro. **Associate, Group Sales/Luxury Suites:** Everette Blackman. **Director, Field Operations:** John Packer. **Director, Broadcasting/Media Relations:** Darren Headrick. **Promotions:** Gordon Buchanan.

FIELD STAFF

Manager: David Wallace. **Hitting Coach:** Rouglas Odor. **Pitching Coach:** Jeff Harris. **Trainer:** Jeremy Heller.

GAME INFORMATION

Radio Announcer: Darren Headrick. **No. of Games Broadcast:** Home-70, Away-70.

Flagship Station: WGWD 98.5 FM. **PA Announcer:** Ricky Ray. **Official Scorer:** John Hobgood.

Stadium Name: Five County Stadium. **Location:** From Raleigh, US 64 East to 264 East, exit at Highway 39 in Zebulon. **Standard Game Times:** 7:15 pm, Sat 6:15, Sun 2. **Ticket Price Range:** $6-11. **Visiting Club Hotel:** Hampton Inn Wake Forest NC, 12318 Wake Union Church Road, Wake Forest, NC 27587. **Telephone:** (919) 554-0222. **Fax:** (919) 554-1499.

FREDERICK KEYS

Office Address: 21 Stadium Drive, Frederick, MD 21703.
Telephone: (301) 662-0013. **Fax:** (301) 662-0018.
E-Mail Address: info@frederickkeys.com. **Website:** www.frederickkeys.com.
Affiliation (first year): Baltimore Orioles (1989). **Years in League:** 1989-

OWNERSHIP/MANAGEMENT

Ownership: Maryland Baseball Holding LLC.
President: Ken Young. **General Manager:** Dave Ziedelis. **Assistant GMs:** Branden McGee, Adam Pohl. **Director, Ticket Operations:** Felicia Adamus. **Promotions Manager:** Brandon Apter. **Marketing/Sponsorship Manager:** Bridget McCabe. **Public Relations Assistant:** Mike Mueller. **Group Sales Manager:** Matt Miller. **Account Managers:** Donny Lawson, Joe Welch, Catherine Larkin. **Account Manager/Broadcaster:** Tim Murray. **Box Office Assistant:** Jack Greene. **Box Office Assistant:** Ben Sealy. **Stadium Operations Manager:** Kari Collins. **Head Groundskeeper:** Brian Eiche. **Office Manager:** Barb Freund. **Finance Manager:** Tami Hetrick. **General Manager, Ovations:** Anita Clarke.

FIELD STAFF

Manager: Ryan Minor. **Hitting Coach:** Torre Tyson. **Pitching Coach:** Kennie Steenstra. **Athletic Trainer:** Pat Wesley.

GAME INFORMATION

Radio Announcers: Adam Pohl, Tim Murray.
PA Announcer: Andy Redmond. **Official Scorers:** Bob Roberson, Dennis Hetrick, Dave Musil.
Stadium Name: Harry Grove Stadium. **Location:** From I-70, take exit 54 (Market Street), left at light; From I-270, take exit 32 (I-70 Baltimore/Hagerstown) toward Baltimore (I-70), to exit 54 at Market Street. **Ticket Price Range:** $9-12.
Visiting Club Hotel: Best Western, 420 Prospect Blvd, Frederick, MD 21701. **Telephone:** (301) 695-6200.

LYNCHBURG HILLCATS

Office Address: Lynchburg City Stadium, 3180 Fort Ave, Lynchburg, VA 24501.
Mailing Address: PO Box 10213, Lynchburg, VA 24506.
Telephone: (434) 528-1144. **Fax:** (434) 846-0768.
E-Mail address: info@lynchburg-hillcats.com. **Website:** www.Lynchburg-hillcats.com.
Affiliation (first year): Atlanta Braves (2011). **Years in League:** 1966-

OWNERSHIP/MANAGEMENT

Operated By: Lynchburg Baseball Corp.
President: C Rex Angel. **General Manager:** Paul Sunwall. **Assistant GM:** Ronnie Roberts. **Head Groundskeeper/Sales:** Darren Johnson. **Director, Broadcasting:** Erik Wilson. **Director, Food/Beverage:** Zach Willis. **Director, Promotions:** Ashley Stephenson. **Director, Group Sales:** Brad Goodale. **Ticket Manager:** John Hutt. **Office Manager:** Diane Tucker.

FIELD STAFF

Manager: Luis Salazar. **Hitting Coach:** John Moses. **Pitching Coach:** Derek Botelho. **Trainer:** Joe Toenjes.

GAME INFORMATION

Radio Announcer: Erik Wilson. **No. of Games Broadcast:** Home-70 Flagship Station: WZZU-97.9FM.
PA Announcer: Chuck Young. **Official Scorers:** Malcolm Haley, Chuck Young.
Stadium Name: Calvin Falwell Field at Lynchburg City Stadium. **Location:** US 29 Business South to Lynchburg City Stadium (exit 6); US 29 Business North to Lynchburg City Stadium (exit 4). **Ticket Price Range:** $5-9.
Visiting Club Hotel: Best Western, 2815 Candlers Mountain Rd, Lynchburg, VA 24502. **Telephone:** (434) 237-2986.

MYRTLE BEACH PELICANS

Office Address: 1251 21st Ave N, Myrtle Beach, SC 29577.
Telephone: (843) 918-6002. **Fax:** (843) 918-6001.
E-Mail Address: info@myrtlebeachpelicans.com. **Website:** www.myrtlebeachpelicans.com.
Affiliation (first year): Texas Rangers (2011). **Years in League:** 1999-

OWNERSHIP/MANAGEMENT

Operated By: Myrtle Beach Pelicans LP.
Managing Partner: Chuck Greenberg.
General Manager: Andy Milovich. **Senior Director, Business Development:** Guy Schuman. **Senior Group Sales Manager:** Glen Goodwin, Justin Bennent. **Corporate Sales Manager:** Katelyn Guild, Justin Shively. **Director, Broadcasting/Media Relations:** Travis Luian. **Director, Marketing/Promotions:** Jen Borowski. **Community Relations Manager:** Tyler Alewine. **Executive Producer, In-Game Entertainment:** Russ Pinkerton. **Facility Operations Manager:** Mike Snow. **Director, Merchandising:** Dan Bailey. **Director, Food/Beverage:** Brad Leininger. **Clubhouse Manager:** Stan Hunter. **Visiting Clubhouse Manager:** Bob Leber. **Administrative Assistant:** Beth Freitas. **Accounting Assistant:** Karen

Ulyicsni.

FIELD STAFF
Manager: Jason Wood. **Hitting Coach:** Jose Perez. **Pitching Coach:** Steve Mintz. **Athletic Trainer:** Jeff Bodenhamer. **Strength/Conditioning:** Anthony Miller.

GAME INFORMATION
Radio Announcer: Travis Luian. **Flagship Station:** Unavailable. **PA Announcer:** Matt Parris. **Official Scorer:** Steve Walsh.
Stadium Name: Ticketreturn.com Field at Pelicans Ballpark. **Location:** US Highway 17 Bypass to 21st Avenue North, 1/2 mile to stadium. **Standard Game Times:** 7:05 pm; Sun 3:05/6:05. **Ticket Price Range:** $7-13.
Visiting Club Hotel: Hampton Inn-Broadway at the Beach, 1140 Celebrity Circle, Myrtle Beach, SC 29577. **Telephone:** (843) 916-0600.

POTOMAC NATIONALS

Office Address: 7 County Complex Ct, Woodbridge, VA 22192.
Mailing Address: PO Box 2148, Woodbridge, VA 22195.
Telephone: (703) 590-2311. **Fax:** (703) 590-5716.
E-Mail Address: info@potomacnationals.com. **Website:** www.potomacnationals.com.
Affiliation (first year): Washington Nationals (2005). **Years in League:** 1978-

OWNERSHIP/MANAGEMENT
Operated By: Potomac Baseball LLC.
Principal Owner: Art Silber. **President:** Lani Silber Weiss.
Vice President/General Manager: Josh Olerud. **Assistant GM, Ticket Operations:** Zach Prehn. **Director, Media Relations:** Bryan Holland. **Senior Executive, Corporate Partnerships:** Seth Distler. **Director, Food Services:** Jim Johnson. **Director, Stadium Operations:** Aaron Johnson. **Group Sales Account Executives:** Andrew Stinson, Julie Goldberg. **Manager, Community Relations:** Alexis Deegan. **Head Groundskeeper:** Brian Stokes. **Manager, Business Operations:** Shawna Hooke.

FIELD STAFF
Manager: Brian Daubach. **Hitting Coach:** Mark Harris. **Pitching Coach:** Chris Michalak.

GAME INFORMATION
Radio Announcer: Bryan Holland. **No. of Games Broadcast:** Home-70 Road-70. **Flagship:** www.potomacnationals.com. **Official Scorer:** David Vincent, Ben Trittipoe.
Stadium Name: G Richard Pfitzner Stadium. **Location:** From I-95, take exit 158B and continue on Prince William Parkway for five miles, right into County Complex Court. **Standard Game Times:** 7:05 pm, Sat 6:35, Sun 1:05. **Ticket Price Range:** $8-15. **Visiting Club Hotel:** Country Inn and Suites, Prince William Parkway, Woodbridge, VA 22192. **Telephone:** (703) 492-6868.

SALEM RED SOX

Office Address: 1004 Texas St, Salem, VA 24153.
Mailing Address: PO Box 842, Salem, VA 24153.
Telephone: (540) 389-3333. **Fax:** (540) 389-9710.
E-Mail Address: info@salemsox.com. **Website:** www.salemsox.com.
Affiliation (first year): Boston Red Sox (2009). **Years in League:** 1968-

OWNERSHIP/MANAGEMENT
Operated By: Carolina Baseball LLC/Fenway Sports Group.
President: Sam Kennedy. **Vice President/General Manager:** Todd Stephenson.
Senior Assistant GM: Allen Lawrence. **Director, Ticketing:** Steven Elovich. **Director, Creative Services:** Dave Cawley. **Director, Food/Beverage:** Tim Anderson. **Assistant GM/Director, Stadium Operations:** Tracy Schneweis. **Operations:** Matt Bird. **Sales Coordinators:** Shea Maple, Casey Eliff. **Merchandise Manager:** Patrick Pelletier. **Clubhouse Manager:** Tom Wagner.

FIELD STAFF
Manager: Billy McMillon. **Hitting Coach:** Nelson Paulino. **Pitching Coach:** Kevin Walker. **Trainer:** David Herrera.

GAME INFORMATION
Radio Announcer: Evan Lepler. **No. of Games Broadcast:** Home-70 Road-70. **Flagship Station:** WFIR 960-AM.
PA Announcer: Travis Jenkins. **Official Scorer:** Billy Wells. **Stadium Name:** Lewis-Gale Field at Salem Memorial Ballpark. **Location:** I-81 to exit 141 (Route 419), follow signs to Salem Civic Center Complex. **Standard Game Times:** 7:05 pm, Sat 6:05, Sun 4:05. **Ticket Price Range:** $8-11. **Visiting Club Hotel:** Comfort Inn Airport, 5070 Valley View Blvd, Roanoke, VA 24012. **Telephone:** (540) 527-2020.

WILMINGTON BLUE ROCKS

Office Address: 801 Shipyard Dr, Wilmington, DE 19801.
Telephone: (302) 888-2015. Fax: (302) 888-2032.
E-Mail Address: info@bluerocks.com. Website: www.bluerocks.com.
Affiliation (first year): Kansas City Royals (2007). Years in League: 1993-

OWNERSHIP/MANAGEMENT

Operated by: Wilmington Blue Rocks LP.
Honorary President: Matt Minker. President: Tom Palmer. Vice President: Jack Minker. Secretary/Treasurer: Bob Stewart. General Manager: Chris Kemple. Assistant GM: Andrew Layman. Director, Broadcasting/Media Relations: Matt Janus. Assistant Director, Broadcasting/Media Relations: Jeff Arnold. Director, Merchandise: Jim Beck. Merchandise Assistant: Maria Donahue. Director, Marketing: Joe Valenti. Assistant Director, Marketing: Jake Schrum. Marketing Assistant: Kristen Valania. Director, Community Affairs: Kevin Linton. Community Affairs Assistant: Vince Marcucci.
Director, Ticket Sales: Joe Fargnoli. Box Office Assistants: Brandon White, Mark Cunningham. Director, Group Sales: Stefani Rash. Group Sales Executives: Ed Wagner, Megan Holloway. Director, Field Operations: Steve Gold. Office Manager: Elizabeth Kolodziej. Director, Advertising Sales: Brian Radle. Manager, Game Entertainment: Mike Diodati.

FIELD STAFF

Manager: Vance Wilson. Coach: Julio Bruno. Pitching Coach: Steve Luebber. Athletic Trainer: James Stone. Strength/Conditioning Coach: Adam Vish.

GAME INFORMATION

Radio Announcers: John Sadak, Jeff O'Connor. No. of Games Broadcast: Home-70, Away-70. Flagship Station: 89.7 WGLS-FM. PA Announcer: Kevin Linton. Official Scorers: Dick Shute, Adam Kamras.
Stadium Name: Judy Johnson Field at Daniel S Frawley Stadium. Location: I-95 North to Maryland Ave (exit 6), right on Maryland Ave, and through traffic light onto Martin Luther King Blvd, right at traffic light on Justison St, follow to Shipyard Dr; I-95 South to Maryland Ave (exit 6), left at fourth light on Martin Luther King Blvd, right at fourth light on Justison St, follow to Shipyard Dr.
Standard Game Times: 7:05 pm, 6:35 (April-May), Sat 6:05, Sun 1:35. Ticket Price Range: $4-10.
Visiting Club Hotel: Clarion Belle, 1612 N DuPont Hwy, New Castle, DE 19720. Telephone: (302) 299-1408.

WINSTON-SALEM DASH

Office Address: 926 Brookstown Ave, Winston-Salem, NC 27101.
Stadium Address: 951 Ballpark Way, Winston-Salem, NC 27101.
Telephone: (336) 714-2287. Fax: (336) 714-2288.
Website: www.wsdash.com. E-Mail Address: info@wsdash.com.
Affiliation (first year): Chicago White Sox (1997). Years in League: 1945-

OWNERSHIP/MANAGEMENT

Operated by: Sports Menagerie LLC.
Principal Owner: Billy Prim. President: Geoff Lassiter.
Vice President/Chief Financial Officer: Kurt Gehsmann. VP, Baseball Operations: Ryan Manuel. VP, Ticket Sales: CJ Johnson. VP, Corporate Partnerships: Chris Wood. VP, Sponsor Services: Gerri Brommer. Staff Accountant: Yimeng Huo. Director, Marketing/Communications: Brandon Cathey. Associate Director, Creative Services: Caleb Pardick. Associate Director, Events/Marketing: Nikki Caldwell. Director, Entertainment: Gabriel Wilhelm. Director, Media Relations/Broadcasting: Brian Boesch. Media Relations/Broadcasting Assistant: Robert Low. Group Sales Manager: Russell Parmele. Group Sales Representatives: Sarah Baumann, Cameron Harris, Matt Satterfield. Business Development Manager: Darren Hill. Business Development Representatives: Jay Andrews, Brandon Stump.
Sales Coordinator: Kayla Sherrill. Box Office Manager: Chris Loignon. Box Office Supervisor: Kenny Lathan. Head Groundskeeper: Doug Tanis. Director, Stadium Operations: Corey Bugno. Director, Facility Management: Frank DeBerry.

FIELD STAFF

Manager: Ryan Newman. Hitting Coach: Rob Sasser. Pitching Coach: JR Perdew. Athletic Trainer: Josh Fallin. Strength Coach: Tim Rodmaker.

GAME INFORMATION

Radio Announcer: Brian Boesch. No. of Games Broadcast: Home-70, Away-70. Flagship Station: www.wsdash.com. PA Announcer: Cabell Philpott. Official Scorers: Bill Grainger, Todd Bess.
Stadium Name: BB&T Ballpark. Stadium Location: I-40 Business to Peters Creek Parkway exit (exit 5A). Standard Game Times: 7 pm; Sun 2. Visiting Club Hotel: Sundance Plaza Hotel. Telephone: (336) 723-2911.

FLORIDA STATE LEAGUE

Office Address: 115 E Orange Ave Daytona Beach, FL 32114.
Mailing Address: PO Box 349, Daytona Beach, FL 32115.
Telephone: (386) 252-7479. **Fax:** (386) 252-7495.
E-Mail Address: fslbaseball@cfl.rr.com. **Website:** www.floridastateleague.com.
Years League Active: 1919-1927, 1936-1941, 1946-.

President/Treasurer: Chuck Murphy.
Executive Vice President: Ken Carson. **Vice Presidents:** North Division—Ken Carson. South Division—Paul Taglieri. **Corporate Secretary:** C. David Hood. **Special Advisor:** Ben J Hayes.
Directors: Mike Bauer (Jupiter/Palm Beach), Ken Carson (Dunedin), Aaron Moszer (Port Charlotte), Marvin Goldklang (Fort Myers), Trevor Gooby (Bradenton), Ron Myers (Lakeland), Brady Ballard (Daytona), Kyle Smith (Brevard County), Vance Smith (Tampa), Paul Taglieri (St. Lucie), John Timberlake (Clearwater).
Office Manager: Laura LeCras.
Division Structure: North—Brevard County, Clearwater, Daytona, Dunedin, Lakeland, Tampa. South—Fort Myers, Jupiter, Palm Beach, Port Charlotte, St. Lucie, Bradenton.
Regular Season: 140 games (split schedule). **2013 Opening Date:** April 4. **Closing Date:** Sept 2.
All-Star Game: June 15 at Dunedin.
Playoff Format: First-half division winners meet second-half winners in best-of-three series. Winners meet in best-of-five series for league championship.
Roster Limit: 25. **Player Eligibility Rule:** No age limit. No more than two players and one player-coach on active list may have six or more years of prior minor league service.
Brand of Baseball: Rawlings.
Umpires: Ryan Additon (Davie, FL), Joshua Clark (McDonough, GA), Travis Eggert (Gilbert,AZ), John Libka (Mayville, MI), Brian Miller (Cleveland, OH), Alex Ransom (Winfield, MO), Fernando Rodriguez (San Juan, PR), Sean Ryan (Waunakee, WI), Charles Tierney (Louisville, KY), Christopher Tipton (Flint, MI), Alexander Tosi (Lake Villa , IL), Alex Ziegler (Metairie, LA).

Chuck Murphy

STADIUM INFORMATION

Club	Stadium	Opened	Dimensions LF	CF	RF	Capacity	2012 Att.
Bradenton	McKechnie Field	1923	335	400	335	8,654	101,528
Brevard County	Space Coast Stadium	1994	340	404	340	7,500	89,512
Charlotte	Charlotte Sports Park	2009	343	413	343	5,028	117,417
Clearwater	Bright House Field	2004	330	400	330	8,500	177,297
Daytona	Jackie Robinson Ballpark	1930	317	400	325	4,200	143,131
Dunedin	Florida Auto Exchange Stadium	1977	335	400	327	5,509	53,091
Fort Myers	Hammond Stadium	1991	330	405	330	7,900	121,452
Jupiter	Roger Dean Stadium	1998	330	400	325	6,871	73,337
Lakeland	Joker Marchant Stadium	1966	340	420	340	7,828	59,589
Palm Beach	Roger Dean Stadium	1998	330	400	325	6,871	73,954
St. Lucie	Mets Stadium	1988	338	410	338	7,000	92,044
Tampa	Steinbrenner Field	1996	318	408	314	11,026	112,668

BRADENTON MARAUDERS

Mailing Address: 1701 27th Street East, Bradenton, FL 34208.
Telephone: (941) 747-3031. **Fax:** (941) 747-9442.
E-Mail Address: MaraudersInfo@pirates.com. **Website:** www.BradentonMarauders.com.
Affiliation (first year): Pittsburgh Pirates (2010). **Years in League:** 1919-20, 1923-24, 1926, 2010-.

OWNERSHIP/MANAGEMENT
Operated By: Pittsburgh Associates.
Director, Florida Operations: Trevor Gooby. **Manager, McKechnie Operations:** Kris Koch. **Manager, Florida Operations:** AJ Grant. **Concessions Manager:** Terry Pajka. **Manager, Sales/Marketing:** Rachelle Madrigal. **Coordinator, Sales/Marketing:** Stacy Morgan. **Coordinator, Ticket Operations:** Justin Kristich. **Coordinator, Communication/Broadcasting:** Nate March. **Head Groundskeeper:** Victor Madrigal.

FIELD STAFF
Manager: Frank Kremblas. **Coach:** Edgar Varela. **Pitching Coach:** Justin Meccage. **Athletic Trainer:** Dru Scott. **Strength/Conditioning Coach:** Unavailable.

GAME INFORMATION
Radio: Online only. **PA Announcer:** Art Ross. **Official Scorer:** Dave Taylor.

Stadium Name: McKechnie Field. **Location:** I-75 to exit 220 (220B from I-75N) to SR 64 West/Manatee Ave, Left onto 9th St West, McKechnie Field on the left.
Standard Game Times: 6:30 pm, Sun 1 (1st half), 5 (second half). **Ticket Price Range:** $5-10.
Visiting Club Hotel: Courtyard by Marriott Bradenton Sarasota Waterfront, 100 Riverfront Drive West, Bradenton, FL 34205. **Telephone:** (941) 747-3727.

BREVARD COUNTY MANATEES

Office Address: 5800 Stadium Pkwy, Suite 101, Viera, FL 32940.
Telephone: (321) 633-9200. **Fax:** (321) 633-4418.
E-Mail Address: info@spacecoaststadium.com. **Website:** www.manateesbaseball.com.
Affiliation (first year): Milwaukee Brewers (2005). **Years in League:** 1994-

OWNERSHIP/MANAGEMENT

Operated By: Central Florida Baseball Group LLC.
Chairman: Dr Tom Winters. **Vice Chairman:** Dwight Titus. **President:** Charlie Baumann.
General Manager: Kyle Smith.
Assistant GM: Chad Lovitt. **Director, Business Operations/Merchandise:** Kelley Wheeler. **Director, Ticketing/Media:** Frank Longobardo. **Director, Promotions/Community Relations:** Kevin Soto. **Clubhouse Manager:** Ryan McDonald. **Head Groundskeeper:** Doug Lopas. **Team Chaplains:** Donnie Legg, Abraham Medina.

FIELD STAFF

Manager: Joe Ayrault. **Coach:** Ned Yost IV. **Pitching Coach:** Mark Dewey. **Trainer:** Tommy Craig. **Strength/Conditioning Coordinator:** Jonah Mergen.

GAME INFORMATION

PA Announcer: JC Meyerholz. **Radio:** Webcast: www.manateesbaseball.com.
Official Scorer: Brad Dunn. **Stadium Name:** Space Coast Stadium. **Location:** I-95 North to Wickham Rd (exit 191), left onto Wickham, right at traffic circle onto Lake Andrew Drive for 1 1/2 miles through the Brevard County government office complex to the four-way stop, right on Stadium Parkway, Space Coast Stadium 1/2 mile on the left; I-95 South to Rockledge exit (exit 195), left onto Stadium Parkway, Space Coast Stadium is 3 miles on right.
Standard Game Times: 6:35 pm, Sun 5:05. **Tickets:** $7 in advance, $8 day of game.
Visiting Club Hotel: Holiday Inn Hotel & Conference Center, 8928 N Wickham Rd, Viera, FL 32940. **Telephone:** (321) 255-0077.

CHARLOTTE STONE CRABS

Office Address: 2300 El Jobean Rd, Port Charlotte, FL 33948.
Mailing Address: 2300 El Jobean Rd, Building A, Port Charlotte, FL 33948.
Telephone: (941) 206-4487. **Fax:** (941) 206-3599.
E-Mail Address: info@stonecrabsbaseball.com. **Website:** www.stonecrabsbaseball.com.
Affiliation (first year): Tampa Bay Rays (2009). **Years in League:** 2009-

OWNERSHIP/MANAGEMENT

Operated By: Ripken Baseball.
General Manager: Corey Brandt.
Director, Ticket Sales: Michael Warren. **Director, Operations:** Chris Sprunger. **Marketing Manager:** Mary Hegley. **Full Charge Bookkeeper:** Tamera Figueroa. **Accounting Clerk:** Sue Denny. **Manager, Food/Beverage:** Marshall Clapper. **Director, Broadcasting/Media Relations:** Grant McAuley. **Manager, Corporate Sponsorship Sales:** Bill Holohan. **Account Representatives:** Jaime Ferreyros, Katie Hoyt, Hallie Rubins, Patrick Wondrak.

FIELD STAFF

Manager: Brady Williams. **Coach:** Joe Szekely. **Pitching Coach:** Bill Moloney.

GAME INFORMATION

PA Announcer: Josh Grant. **Official Scorer:** Unavailable.
Stadium Name: Charlotte Sports Park. **Location:** I-75 to Exit 179, turn left onto Toldeo Blade Blvd then right on El Jobean Rd. **Ticket Price Range:** $7-11.
Visiting Club Hotel: Days Inn, 1941 Tamiami Trail, Port Charlotte, FL 33948. **Telephone:** 941-627-8900.

CLEARWATER THRESHERS

Office Address: 601 N Old Coachman Rd, Clearwater, FL 33765.
Telephone: (727) 712-4300. **Fax:** (727) 712-4498.
Website: www.threshersbaseball.com.
Affiliation (first year): Philadelphia Phillies (1985). **Years in League:** 1985-

OWNERSHIP/MANAGEMENT
Operated by: Philadelphia Phillies.
Chairman: Bill Giles. **President:** David Montgomery.
Director, Florida Operations/General Manager: John Timberlake. **Assistant Director, Minor League Operations:** Lee McDaniel. **Business Manager:** Dianne Gonzalez. **Assistant GM/Director, Sales:** Dan McDonough. **Assistant GM, Ticketing:** Jason Adams. **Office Administration:** DeDe Angelillis. **Manager, Group Sales:** Dan Madden. **Assistant Manager, Group Sales:** Bobby Mitchell. **Manager, Ballpark Operations:** Jerry Warren.
Operations Assistant: Sean McCarthy. **Coordinator, Facility Maintenance:** Cory Sipe. **Manager, Special Events:** Doug Kemp. **Manager, Community Relations/Promotions:** Amanda Koch. **Clubhouse Manager:** Mark Meschede. **Manager, Food/Beverage:** Brad Dudash. **Assistant, Food/Beverage:** Jon Kerstetter. **Suites Manager:** Wendy Armstrong. **Ticket Office Managers:** Pat Privelege, Kyle Webb. **Group Sales Assistant:** Alyssa Novick. **Audio/Video:** Nic Repper.

FIELD STAFF
Manager: Chris Truby. **Coach:** John Mizerock. **Pitching Coach:** Bob Milacki.

GAME INFORMATION
Radio: None. **PA Announcer:** Don Guckian. **Official Scorer:** Larry Wiederecht.
Stadium Name: Bright House Field. **Location:** US 19 North and Drew Street in Clearwater.
Standard Game Times: 7 pm, Fri/Sat 6:30. **Ticket Price Range:** $5-9.50.
Visiting Club Hotel: La Quinta Inn, 3301 Ulmerton Road, Clearwater, FL, 33762. **Telephone:** (800) 753-3757.

DAYTONA CUBS

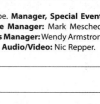

Office Address: 110 E Orange Ave, Daytona Beach, FL 32114.
Telephone: (386) 257-3172. **Fax:** (386) 257-3382.
E-Mail Address: info@daytonacubs.com. **Website:** www.daytonacubs.com.
Affiliation (first year): Chicago Cubs (1993). **Years in League:** 1920-24,1928, 1936-41, 1946-73, 1977-87, 1993-

OWNERSHIP/MANAGEMENT
Operated By: Big Game Florida LLC.
Principal Owner/President: Andrew Rayburn.
General Manager: Brady Ballard.
Assistant GM: Josh Lawther. **Director, Broadcasting/Media Relations:** Robbie Aaron. **Director, Stadium Operations:** JR Laub. **Director, Tickets:** Amanda Earnest. **Director, Sales:** Clint Cure. **Director, Special Events/Community Relations:** Janelle Yonkovitch. **Director, Groups/Merchandise:** Jim Jaworski. **Manager, F&B:** Kevin Dwyer. **Manager, Group Sales:** Erin Killian. **Office Manager:** Tammy Devine. **Head Groundskeeper:** Mike Geiger.

FIELD STAFF
Manager: Dave Keller. **Hitting Coach:** Mariano Duncan. **Pitching Coach:** Storm Davis. **Trainer:** Peter Fagan.

GAME INFORMATION
Radio Announcer: Robbie Aaron. **No. of Games Broadcast:** Home-70, Road-70. **Flagship Station:** AM-1230 WSBB.
PA Announcer: Tim Lecras. **Official Scorer:** Don Roberts.
Stadium Name: Jackie Robinson Ballpark. **Location:** I-95 to International Speedway Blvd Exit (Route 92), east to Beach Street, south to Magnolia Ave east to ballpark; A1A North/South to Orange Ave west to ballpark. **Standard Game Time:** 7:05 p.m. **Ticket Price Range:** $6-12.
Visiting Club Hotel: Holiday Inn Resort Daytona Beach Oceanfront, 1615 S Atlantic Ave Daytona Beach, FL 32218. **Telephone:** (386) 255-0921.

DUNEDIN BLUE JAYS

Office Address: 373 Douglas Ave Dunedin, FL 34698.
Telephone: (727) 733-9302. **Fax:** (727) 734-7661.
E-Mail Address: dunedin@bluejays.com. **Website:** www.dunedinbluejays.com.
Affiliation (first year): Toronto Blue Jays (1987). **Years in League:** 1978-79, 1987-

OWNERSHIP/MANAGEMENT
Director/General Manager, Florida Operations: Shelby Nelson. **Assistant GM:** Janette Donoghue.
Accounting Manager: Gayle Gentry. **Manager, Group Sales/Retail/Community Relations:** Kathi Beckman.

Manager, Sales: Mike Liberatore. **Community Relations Coordinator:** Kyra Hallett. **Ticket Operations Coordinator:** Dan Hilbert. **Administrative Assistant/Receptionist:** Michelle Smith. **Stadium Operations Supervisor:** Leon Harrell. **Stadium Operations Supervisor:** Zac Phelps. **Senior Advisor:** Ken Carson. **Home Clubhouse Attendant:** Nate Barker. **Head Superintendent:** Patrick Skunda. **Assistant Superintedent:** Matt Johnson.

FIELD STAFF
Manager: Bob Meacham. **Hitting Coach:** Stubby Clapp. **Pitching Coach:** Darold Knowles. **Trainer:** Shawn McDermott.

GAME INFORMATION
Radio: None. **PA Announcer:** Unavailable. **Official Scorer:** Unavailable.
Stadium Name: Florida Auto Exchange Stadium. **Location:** From I-275, north on Highway 19, left on Sunset Point Rd for 4 1/2 miles, right on Douglas Ave stadium is 1/2 mile on right.
Standard Game Times: 6:30 pm, Sun 5. **Ticket Price Range:** $7.
Visiting Club Hotel: La Quita, 21338 US Highway 19 North, Clearwater, Fl. **Telephone:** (727) 799-1565.

FORT MYERS MIRACLE

Office Address: 14400 Six Mile Cypress Pkwy, Fort Myers, FL 33912.
Telephone: (239) 768-4210. **Fax:** (239) 768-4211.
E-Mail Address: miracle@miraclebaseball.com. **Website:** www.miraclebaseball.com.
Affiliation (first year): Minnesota Twins (1993). **Years in League:** 1926, 1978-87, 1991-

OWNERSHIP/MANAGEMENT
Operated By: Greater Miami Baseball Club LP.
Principal Owner/Chairman: Marvin Goldklang. **Executive Advisor To The Chairman:** Mike Veeck.
President: Steve Gliner. **VP/General Manager:** Andrew Seymour.
Senior Director, Corporate Sales/Marketing: Terry Simon. **Senior Director, Business Operations:** Suzanne Reaves. **Senior Director, Business Development:** John Kuhn. **Director, Food/Beverage:** Phillip Busch. **Manager, Broadcasting/Multimedia:** Brice Zimmerman. **Broadcasting/Multimedia Assistant:** Adam MacDonald. **Food/Beverage Assistant:** BJ Potter. **Community Relations Manager:** Savannah Martin. **Administrative Assistant/Operations:** Kyle Schmit. **Head Groundskeeper:** Keith Blasingim. **Clubhouse Manager:** Brock Rasmussen.

FIELD STAFF
Manager: Doug Mientkiewicz. **Coach:** Jim Dwyer. **Pitching Coach:** Ivan Arteaga. **Trainer:** Alan Rail.

GAME INFORMATION
Radio Announcer: Brice Zimmerman, Adam MacDonald. **No. of Games Broadcast:** Home-70, Road-70. **Internet Broadcasts:** www.miraclebaseball.com.
PA Announcer: Jay Wyse. **Official Scorer:** Scott Pedersen.
Stadium Name: William H Hammond Stadium. **Location:** Exit 131 off I-75, west on Daniels Parkway, left on Six Mile Cypress Parkway. **Standard Game Times:** 7:05 pm, Sat 6:05; Sun 4:05. **Ticket Price Range:** $5-10.50.
Visiting Club Hotel: Fairfield Inn by Marriot, 7090 Cypress Terrace, Fort Myers, FL 33907. **Telephone:** (239) 437-5600.

JUPITER HAMMERHEADS

Office Address: 4751 Main Street, Jupiter, FL 33458.
Telephone: (561) 775-1818. **Fax:** (561) 691-6886.
E-Mail Address: f.desk@rogerdeanstadium.com. **Website:** www.jupiterhammerheads.com.
Affiliation (first year): Miami Marlins (2002). **Years in League:** 1998-

OWNERSHIP/MANAGEMENT
Owned By: Florida Marlins.
Operated By: Jupiter Stadium, LTD.
General Manager, Jupiter Stadium, LTD: Mike Bauer.
Executive Assistant: Carol McAteer. **Assistant GM, Jupiter Stadium LTD/GM Jupiter Hammerheads:** Melissa Kuper. **Assistant GM, Jupiter Stadium:** Lisa Fegley. **Director, Accounting:** John McCahan. **Corporate Partnerships Manager:** Chris Snyder. **Group Sales Coordinator:** Gary Lohmann. **Marketing/Media Relations Manager:** Kristen Cummins. **Manager, Event Services:** Alex Inman. **Director, Grounds:** Jordan Treadway. **Assistant Directors, Grounds:** Matt Eggerman, Matt Dierdorff. **Stadium Building Manager:** Walter Herrera. **Merchandise Manager:** Lauren Gurley. **Ticket Manager:** Jason Cantone. **Press Box:** Nick Kappel. **Office Manager:** David Vago.

FIELD STAFF
Manager: Andy Haines. **Coach:** Corey Hart. **Pitching Coach:** Joe Coleman.

LAKELAND FLYING TIGERS

Office Address: 2125 N Lake Ave, Lakeland, FL 33805.
Mailing Address: 2125 N Lake Ave, Lakeland, FL 33805.
Telephone: (863) 686-8075. **Fax:** (863) 688-9589.
Website: www.lakelandflyingtigers.com.
Affiliation (first year): Detroit Tigers (1967). **Years in League:** 1919-26, 1953-55, 1960, 1962-64, 1967-.

OWNERSHIP/MANAGEMENT
Owned By: Detroit Tigers, Inc.
Principal Owner: Mike Ilitch. **President:** David Dombrowski. **Director, Florida Operations:** Ron Myers.
General Manager: Zach Burek. **Manager, Administration/Operations:** Shannon Follett. **Ticket Manager:** Ryan Eason. **Group Sales Manager:** Dan Lauer. **Receptionist:** Maria Walls.

FIELD STAFF
Manager: Dave Huppert. **Coach:** Larry Herndon. **Pitching Coach:** Mike Maroth.

GAME INFORMATION
Radio: None. **PA Announcers:** Jacob Roen. **Official Scorer:** Ed Luteran.
Stadium Name: Joker Marchant Stadium. **Location:** Exit 33 on I-4 to 33 South, 1.5 miles on left. **Standard Game Times:** 6:30, Fri 7:11, Sat 6, Sun 1. **Ticket Price Range:** $4-7.
Visiting Club Hotel: Unavailable.

PALM BEACH CARDINALS

Office Address: 4751 Main Street, Jupiter, FL 33458.
Telephone: (561) 775-1818. **Fax:** (561) 691-6886.
E-Mail Address: f.desk@rogerdeanstadium.com. **Website:** www.palmbeachcardinals.com.
Affiliation (first year): St. Louis Cardinals (2003). **Years in League:** 2003-

OWNERSHIP/MANAGEMENT
Owned By: St. Louis Cardinals.
Operated By: Jupiter Stadium LTD.
General Manager, Jupiter Stadium, LTD: Mike Bauer.
Executive Assistant: Carol McAteer. **Assistant GM, Jupiter Stadium LTD/GM Palm Beach Cardinals,** Lisa Fegley. **Assistant GM, Jupiter Stadium:** Melissa Kuper. **Director, Accounting:** John McCahan. **Corporate Partnerships Manager:** Chris Snyder. **Group Sales Coordinator:** Gary Lohmann. **Manager, Marketing/Media Relations:** Kristen Cummins. **Manager, Event Services:** Alex Inman. **Director, Grounds:** Jordan Treadway. **Assistant Directors, Grounds:** Matt Eggerman, Matt Dierdorff. **Stadium Building Manager:** Walter Herrera. **Merchandise Manager:** Lauren Gurley. **Ticket Manager:** Jason Cantone. **Press Box:** Nick Kappel. **Office Manager:** David Vago.

FIELD STAFF
Manager: Johnny Rodriguez. **Hitting Coach:** Roger LaFrancois. **Pitching Coach:** Arthur "Ace" Adams. **Athletic Trainer:** Keith Joynt.

GAME INFORMATION
Radio: None. **PA Announcers:** John Frost, Dick Sanford, Lou Palmer. **Official Scorer:** Lou Villano.
Stadium Name: Roger Dean Stadium. **Location:** I-95 to exit 83, east on Donald Ross Road for 1/4 mile.
Standard Game Times: 6:30 pm; Sun 5. **Ticket Price Range:** $6.50-8.50.
Visiting Club Hotel: Fairfield Inn by Marriott, 6748 Indiantown Road, Jupiter, FL 33458.

ST. LUCIE METS

Office Address: 525 NW Peacock Blvd, Port St Lucie, FL 34986.
Telephone: (772) 871-2100. **Fax:** (772) 878-9802.
Website: www.DigitalDomainPark.com
Affiliation (first year): New York Mets (1988). **Years in League:** 1988-

OWNERSHIP/MANAGEMENT
Operated by: Sterling Mets LP.
Chairman/CEO: Fred Wilpon. **President:** Saul Katz. **Senior Executive Vice President/COO:** Jeff Wilpon.
Director, Florida Operations/General Manager: Paul Taglieri.
Assistant Director, Florida Operations/Assistant GM: Traer Van Allen. **Manager, Sales/Ballpark Operations:** Ryan Strickland. **Manager, Food/Beverage Operations:** Brian Paupeck. **Manager, Group Sales/Community Relations:** Katie Hatch. **Manager, Ticketing/Merchandise:** Clinton Van Allen. **Manager, Media Relations:** Matt Gagnon. **Executive Assistant:** Cynthia Malaspino. **Accountant:** Paula Andreozzi.

FIELD STAFF
Manager: Ryan Ellis. **Hitting Coach:** Benny Distefano. **Pitching Coach:** Phil Regan. **Coach:** Jose Carreno.

GAME INFORMATION
Radio: None.
PA Announcer: Matt Gagnon. **Official Scorer:** Bob Adams.
Stadium Name: Digital Domain Park. **Location:** Exit 121 (St Lucie West Blvd) off I-95, east 1/2 mile, left on NW Peacock Blvd. **Standard Game Times:** 6:30 pm, Sun 1. **Ticket Price Range:** $4-8.
Visiting Club Hotel: SpringHill Suites, 2000 NW Courtyard Circle, Port St Lucie, FL 34986. **Telephone:** (772) 871-2929.

TAMPA YANKEES

Office Address: One Steinbrenner Drive, Tampa, FL 33614.
Telephone: (813) 875-7753. **Fax:** (813) 673-3174.
E-Mail Address: vsmith@yankees.com. **Website:** tybaseball.com.
Affiliation (first year): New York Yankees (1994). **Years in League:** 1919-27, 1957-1988, 1994-

OWNERSHIP/MANAGEMENT
Operated by: New York Yankees LP.
Principal Owner: Harold Z Steinbrenner.
General Manager: Vance Smith.
Assistant GM, Sales/Marketing: Matt Gess. **Community Relations Coordinator:** AmySue Manzione. **Ticket Operations:** Jennifer Magliocchetti. **Head Groundskeeper:** Ritchie Anderson.

FIELD STAFF
Manager: Luis Sojo. **Hitting Coach:** Marcus Thames. **Pitching Coach:** Jeff Ware. **Coach:** Brian Baisley. **Trainer:** Lee Myer. **Strength/Conditioning:** David DeKay.

GAME INFORMATION
Radio: Internet, www.tybaseball.com. **PA Announcer:** Unavailable. **Official Scorer:** Unavailable.
Stadium Name: George M Steinbrenner Field. **Location:** I-275 to Dale Mabry Hwy, North on Dale Mabry Hwy (Facility is at corner of West Dr Martin Luther King Blvd/Dale Mabry Hwy).
Standard Game Times: 7 pm, Sat 6, Sun 1. **Ticket Price Range:** $4-6.

MIDWEST LEAGUE

Office Address: 1118 Cranston Rd, Beloit, WI 53511.
Mailing Address: PO Box 936, Beloit, WI 53512.
Telephone: (608) 364-1188. **Fax:** (608) 364-1913.
E-Mail Address: mwl@midwestleague.com. **Website:** www.midwestleague.com.

Years League Active: 1947-.
President/Treasurer: George H. Spelius.
Vice President/Legal Counsel/Secretary: Richard A. Nussbaum II.
Directors: Andrew Berlin (South Bend), Rick Brenner (Bowling Green), Chuck Brockett (Burlington), Lew Chamberlin (West Michigan), Dennis Conerton (Beloit), Paul Davis (Clinton), Tom Dickson (Lansing), Jason Freier (Fort Wayne), David Heller (Quad Cities), Gary Keoppel (Cedar Rapids), Gary Mayse (Dayton), Brad Seymour (Lake County), William Stavropoulos (Great Lakes), Rocky Vonachen (Peoria), Mike Woleben (Kane County), Rob Zerjav (Wisconsin).
League Administrator: Holly Voss.
Division Structure: East—Bowling Green, Dayton, Fort Wayne, Lake County, Lansing, South Bend, Great Lakes, West Michigan. West—Beloit, Burlington, Cedar Rapids, Clinton, Kane County, Peoria, Quad Cities, Wisconsin.
Regular Season: 140 games (split schedule). **2013 Opening Date:** April 4. **Closing Date:** Sept 2.
All-Star Game: June 18 at Dayton.
Playoff Format: Eight teams qualify. First-half and second-half division winners and wild-card teams meet in best-of-three quarterfinal series. Winners meet in best-of-three series for division championships. Division champions meet in best-of-five final for league championship.
Roster Limit: 25 active. **Player Eligibility Rule:** No age limit. No more than two players and one player-coach on active list may have more than five years experience.
Brand of Baseball: Rawlings ROM-MID. **Umpires:** Unavailable.

George Spelius

STADIUM INFORMATION

Club	Stadium	Opened	Dimensions LF	CF	RF	Capacity	2012 Att.
Beloit	Pohlman Field	1982	325	380	325	3,500	68,867
Bowling Green	Bowling Green Ballpark	2009	312	401	325	4,559	233,208
Burlington	Community Field	1947	338	403	318	3,200	58,195
Cedar Rapids	Veterans Memorial Stadium	2000	315	400	325	5,300	160,064
Clinton	Ashford University Field	1937	335	390	325	4,000	111,760
Dayton	Fifth Third Field	2000	338	402	338	7,230	588,689
Fort Wayne	Parkview Field	2009	336	400	318	8,100	396,531
Great Lakes	Dow Diamond	2007	332	400	325	5,200	259,160
Kane County	Fifth Third Bank Ballpark	1991	335	400	335	7,400	391,102
Lake County	Classic Park	2003	320	400	320	7,273	248,114
Lansing	Cooley Law School Stadium	1996	305	412	305	11,000	345,763
Peoria	Peoria Chiefs Stadium	2002	310	400	310	7,500	190,244
Quad Cities	Modern Woodmen Park	1931	343	400	318	4,024	240,008
South Bend	Coveleski Regional Stadium	1987	336	405	336	5,000	189,575
West Michigan	Fifth Third Ballpark	1994	317	402	327	10,051	362,554
Wisconsin	Fox Cities Stadium	1995	325	400	325	5,500	240,509

BELOIT SNAPPERS

Office Address: 2301 Skyline Dr, Beloit, WI 53511.
Mailing Address: PO Box 855, Beloit, WI 53512.
Telephone: (608) 362-2272. **Fax:** (608) 362-0418.
E-Mail Address: snappy@snappersbaseball.com. **Website:** www.snappersbaseball.com.
Affiliation (first year): Oakland Athletics (2013). **Years in League:** 1982-

OWNERSHIP/MANAGEMENT
Operated by: Beloit Professional Baseball Association Inc.
Chairman: Dennis Conerton. **President:** Perry Folts.
General Manager: Matthew Bosen. **Corporate Sales/Promotions:** Bill Czaja. **Director, Media Relations/Marketing:** Mark Inserra. **Director, Tickets/Merchandise:** Katie Pietrowiak, Head Groundskeeper: Zach Ricketts.

FIELD STAFF
Manager: Ryan Christenson. **Hitting Coach:** Casey Myers. **Pitching Coach:** John Wasdin. **Trainer:** Alan Rail.

GAME INFORMATION

Radio Announcer: Andrew Liebetrau. **No. of Games Broadcast:** 25. **Flagship Station:** 1380-AM ESPN.
PA Announcer: Mark Inserra. **Official Scorer:** Unavailable.
Stadium Name: Pohlman Field. **Location:** I-90 to exit 185-A, right at Cranston Road for 1 1/2 miles; I-43 to Wisconsin 81 to Cranston Road, right at Cranston for 1 1/2 miles.
Standard Game Times: 7 pm, 6:30 (April-May), Sun 2. **Ticket Price Range:** $7-9.
Visiting Club Hotel: Rodeway Inn, 2956 Milwaukee Rd, Beloit, WI 53511. **Telephone:** (608) 364-4000.

BOWLING GREEN HOT RODS

Office Address: Bowling Green Ballpark, 300 8th Avenue, Bowling Green, KY 42101.
Telephone: (270) 901-2121. **Fax:** (270) 901-2165.
E-Mail Address: fun@bghotrods.com. **Website:** www.bghotrods.com.
Affiliation (first year): Tampa Bay Rays (2009). **Years in League:** 2010-

OWNERSHIP/MANAGEMENT

Operated By: DSF Sports.
Owner: Art Solomon. **DSF Sports President:** Rick Brenner.
President: Brad Taylor. **General Manager:** Ryan Gates.
Assistant GM, Operations: Ken Clary. **Controller:** Sally Lancaster. **Director, Ticket Sales:** Mike Mariano. **Creative Services Manager:** Atlee McHeffey. **Broadcast/Media Relations Manager:** Hank Fuerst. **Promotions Manager:** Jennifer Johnson. **Sports Turf Manager:** John Gides. **Box Office Manager:** Greg Heroy. **Account Executives:** Kelci Harris, Adam Smedberg. **Merchandise/Community Affairs Manager:** Michelle Gravert.

FIELD STAFF

Manager: Jared Sandberg. **Coach:** Manny Castillo. **Pitching Coach:** Kyle Snyder. **Trainer:** Chris Tomashoff.

GAME INFORMATION

Radio Announcers: Hank Fuerst, Chris Kleinhans-Schulz. **No. of Games Broadcast:** Home-70, Away-70. **Flagship Station:** WBGN 1340-AM.
PA Announcer: Chris Kelly. **Official Scorers:** Rick Grieve, Chris George.
Stadium Name: Bowling Green Ballpark. **Location:** From I-65, take Exit 26 (KY-234/Cemetery Road) into Bowling Green for 3 miles, left onto College Street for .2 miles, right onto 8th Avenue.
Standard Game Times: 7:05 pm, Sun 2:05 (April-May, Aug-Sept), 5:05 (June-July). **Ticket Price Range:** $7-12. **Visiting Club Hotel:** Home-Towne Suites, 1929 Mel Browning Street, Bowling Green, KY 42104. **Telephone:** (270) 846-3311.

BURLINGTON BEES

Office Address: 2712 Mt Pleasant St, Burlington, IA 52601.
Mailing Address: PO Box 824, Burlington, IA 52601.
Telephone: (319) 754-5705. **Fax:** (319) 754-5882.
E-Mail Address: staff@gobees.com. **Website:** www.gobees.com.
Affiliation (first year): Los Angeles Angels (2013). **Years in League:** 1962-

OWNERSHIP/MANAGEMENT

Operated By: Burlington Baseball Association Inc.
President: Dave Walker.
General Manager: Chuck Brockett.
Assistant GM: Jared Schjei. **Director, Group Outings:** Kim Brockett. **Director, Media Relations:** Brandon Marcus. **Groundskeeper:** TJ Brewer.

FIELD STAFF

Manager: Jamie Burke. **Hitting Coach:** Nathan Haynes. **Pitching Coach:** Trevor Wilson. **Trainer:** Chris Wells. **Strength Coach:** Joe Griffin.

GAME INFORMATION

Radio Announcer: Brandon Marcus. **No. of Games Broadcast:** Home-70, Away-70. **Flagship Station:** KBUR 1490-AM.
PA Announcer: Nathan McCoy. **Official Scorer:** Ted Gutman.
Stadium Name: Community Field. **Location:** From US 34, take US 61 North to Mt Pleasant Street, east 1/8 mile.
Standard Game Times: 6:30 pm, Sun 2. **Ticket Price Range:** $4-8.
Visiting Club Hotel: Pzazz Best Western FunCity, 3001 Winegard Dr, Burlington, IA 52601. **Telephone:** (319) 753-2223.

CEDAR RAPIDS KERNELS

Office Address: 950 Rockford Rd SW, Cedar Rapids, IA 52404.
Mailing Address: PO Box 2001, Cedar Rapids, IA 52406.
Telephone: (319) 363-3887. **Fax:** (319) 363-5631.
E-Mail Address: kernels@kernels.com. **Website:** www.kernels.com.
Affiliation (first year): Minnesota Twins (2013). **Years in League:** 1962-

OWNERSHIP/MANAGEMENT

Operated by: Cedar Rapids Ball Club Inc.
President: Gary Keoppel. **General Manager:** Doug Nelson.
Assistant GM: Scott Wilson. **Sales:** Morgan Hawk. **IT/Communications Manager:** Andrew Pantini. **Sports Turf Manager:** Jesse Roeder. **Director, Ticket/Group Sales:** Andrea Murphy. **Director, Finance:** Charlie Patrick. **Manager, Entertainment/Community Relations:** Brandon Clemens. **Director, Corporate Sales/Marketing:** Jessica Fergesen. **Director, Food/Beverage:** Debra Maier. **Coordinator, History:** Marcia Moran. **Receptionist:** Amber Martin.

FIELD STAFF

Manager: Jake Mauer. **Hitting Coach:** Tommy Watkins. **Pitching Coach:** Gary Lucas. **Trainer:** Ryan Hedwall.

GAME INFORMATION

Radio Announcer: Morgan Hawk. **No. of Games Broadcast:** Home-70, Away-70. **Flagship Station:** KMRY 1450-AM/93.1-FM. **PA Announcers:** Bob Hoyt, Josh Paulson. **Official Scorers:** Steve Meyer, Josh Schroeder.
Stadium Name: Veterans Memorial Stadium. **Location:** From I-380 North, take the Wilson Ave exit, turn left on Wilson Ave, after the railroad tracks, turn right on Rockford Road, proceed .8 miles, stadium is on left; From I-380 South, exit at First Avenue, proceed to Eighth Avenue (first stop sign) and turn left, stadium entrance is on right (before tennis courts).
Standard Game Times: 6:35 pm, Sun 2:05. **Ticket Price Range:** $7-11.
Visiting Club Hotel: Best Western Cooper's Mill, 100 F Ave NW, Cedar Rapids, IA 52405. **Telephone:** (319) 366-5323.

CLINTON LUMBERKINGS

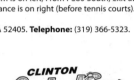

Office Address: Ashford University Field, 537 Ball Park Drive, Clinton, IA 52732. **Mailing Address:** PO Box 1295, Clinton, IA 52733.
Telephone: (563) 242-0727. **Fax:** (563) 242-1433.
E-Mail Address: lumberkings@lumberkings.com. **Website:** www.lumberkings.com.
Affiliation (first year): Seattle Mariners (2009). **Years in League:** 1956-

OWNERSHIP/MANAGEMENT

Operated By: Clinton Baseball Club Inc.
President: Paul Davis.
General Manager: Ted Tornow. **Director, Broadcasting/Media Relations:** Chad Seely. **Director, Operations:** Jason Wright. **Director, Concessions:** Brittany Jones. **Manager, Stadium/Sportsturf:** Chris Mason. **Accountant:** Ryan Marcum. **Assistant Director, Operations:** Morty Kriner. **Director, Facility Compliance:** Tom Whaley. **Office Procurement Manager:** Les Moore. **Clubhouse Manager:** Lynn Cripps.

FIELD STAFF

Manager: Eddie Menchaca. **Coach:** Mike Kinkade. **Pitching Coach:** Andrew Lorraine. **Trainer:** Jeff Kahn. **Strength/Conditioning:** Ryan White.

GAME INFORMATION

Radio Announcer: Chad Seely. **No. of Games Broadcast:** Home-70, Away-70. **Flagship Station:** KCLN 1390-AM.
PA Announcer: Brad Seward. **Official Scorers:** Chris Shaw, Jared Lueders.
Stadium Name: Ashford University Field. **Location:** Highway 67 North to Sixth Avenue North, right on Sixth, cross railroad tracks, stadium on right. **Standard Game Times:** 6:30 pm, 7 (May 31-Aug 16), Sat 6, Sun 2. **Ticket Price Range:** $5-8.
Visiting Club Hotel: Super 8, 1711 Lincoln Way, Clinton IA 52732. **Telephone:** 563-242-8870.

DAYTON DRAGONS

Office Address: Fifth Third Field, 220 N Patterson Blvd, Dayton, OH 45402.
Mailing Address: PO 2107, Dayton, OH 45401.
Telephone: (937) 228-2287. **Fax:** (937) 228-2284.
E-Mail Address: dragons@daytondragons.com. **Website:** www.daytondragons.com.
Affiliation (first year): Cincinnati Reds (2000). **Years in League:** 2000-

OWNERSHIP/MANAGEMENT

Operated By: Dayton Professional Baseball Club LLC/Mandalay Baseball Properties, LLC.
Owners: Mandalay Baseball Properties LLC, Earvin "Magic" Johnson, Archie Griffin.

President: Robert Murphy.
Executive Vice President: Eric Deutsch. **Executive VP/General Manager:** Gary Mayse.
VP, Accounting/Finance: Mark Schlein. **VP, Corporate Partnerships:** Jeff Webb. **VP, Sponsor Services:** Brad Eaton.
Director, Media Relations: Tom Nichols. **Director, Operations:** Andrew Ottmar. **Director, Entertainment:** Kaitlin
Rohrer. **Director, Sponsor Services:** Brandy Guinaugh. **Senior Marketing Manager:** Clint Taylor. **Marketing Managers:**
Erin Beadle, Amanda Fawcett, Lindsey Huerter, Samantha Weaver. **Director, Ticket Sales:** Andrew Aldenderfer. **Director,
Group Sales:** Mike Vujea.
Box Office Manager: Stefanie Mitchell. **Corporate Marketing Managers:** Chad Adams, Sean Allen, Jose de la Vega,
Evan Elkins, Trafton Eutsler, Maurice Hillman, Viterio Jones, Nick Kuchey. **Senior Operations Director:** Joe Eaglowski.
Facilities Operations Manager: Joe Elking. **Baseball Operations Manager:** John Wallace. **Entertainment Assistant:**
Chelsie Cooper. **Director, Merchandising:** Shari Sharkins. **Office Manager/Executive Assistant to the President:**
Leslie Stuck. **Staff Accountant:** Dorothy Day. **Administrative Secretary:** Barbara Van Schaik. **Head Groundskeeper:**
Dan Jennings.

FIELD STAFF
Manager: Jose Miguel Nieves. **Coach:** Alex Pelaez. **Pitching Coach:** Tony Fossas. **Trainer:** Tyler Steele.

GAME INFORMATION
Radio Announcers: Tom Nichols, Bill Spaulding. **No. of Games Broadcast:** Home-70, Away-70. **Flagship Station:**
WONE 980 AM. **Television Announcer:** Tom Nichols. **No. of Games Broadcast:** Home-25. **Flagship Station:** WHIO 7.2.
PA Announcers: Ben Oburn, Kim Parker. **Official Scorers:** Matt Lindsay, Tom Harner, Mike Lucas.
Stadium Name: Fifth Third Field. **Location:** I-75 South to downtown Dayton, left at First Street; I-75 North, right at First
Street exit. **Ticket Price Range:** $7-$15.
Visiting Club Hotel: Comfort Inn, 7125 Miller Lane, Dayton, OH 45414.
Phone: (937) 890-9995. **Fax:** (937) 890-9995.

FORT WAYNE TINCAPS

Office Address: 1301 Ewing St Fort Wayne, IN 46802.
Telephone: (260) 482-6400. **Fax:** (260) 471-4678.
E-Mail Address: info@tincaps.com. **Website:** www.tincaps.com.
Affiliation (first year): San Diego Padres (1999). **Years in League:** 1993-

OWNERSHIP/MANAGEMENT
Operated By: Hardball Capital.
Owner: Jason Freier.
President/General Manager: Mike Nutter. **Vice President Sales/Finance:** Brian Schackow. **VP Corporate
Partnerships:** David Lorenz. **VP Marketing/Promotions:** Michael Limmer. **Director, Group Sales:** Brad Shank. **Assistant
Director, Group Sales:** Jared Parcell. **Director, Ticketing:** Pat Ventura. **Assistant Director, Ticketing/Reading Program
Director:** Paige Salway. **Director, Food/Beverage:** Bill Lehn. **Culinary Director:** Scott Kammerer. **Catering Director:**
Brandon Tinkle. **Manager, Food/Beverage Operations:** Dan Krleski. **Coordinators, Special Events:** Holly Raney, Jen
Walters. **Director, Facilities:** Tim Burkhart. **Assistant Director, Maintenance:** Donald Miller. **Head Groundskeeper:**
Keith Winter. **Assistant Groundskeeper:** Andrew Burnette.
Creative Director: Tony DesPlaines. **Video Production Manager:** Melissa Darby. **Managers, Ticket Sales:** Tyler
Baker, Brent Harring, Austin Allen, Justin Shurley, Erik Lose. **Manager, Corporate Partnerships:** Tom Baxter. **Director,
Broadcasting/Media Relations:** Mike Couzens. **Office Manager:** Cathy Tinney. **Manager, Merchandise:** Karen Schieber.
Assistant Director, Marketing/Community Relations: Abby Naas.

FIELD STAFF
Manager: Jose Valentin. **Hitting Coach:** Morgan Burkhart. **Pitching Coach:** Burt Hooton. **Trainer:** Ricky Huerta.

GAME INFORMATION
Radio Announcers: Mike Couzens, Mike Maahs, John Nolan. **No. of Games Broadcast:** Home-70, Away-70. **Flagship
Station:** WKJG 1380-AM. **PA Announcers:** Jared Parcell, Jim Shovlin. **Official Scorers:** Rich Tavierne, Bill Salyer, Bill Scott,
Chris Bauman.
Stadium Name: Parkview Field. **Location:** Downtown Fort Wayne off of Jefferson Blvd. **Ticket Price Range:** $5-12.50.
Visiting Club Hotel: Downtown Courtyard by Marriott, 1150 S Harrison Street, Fort Wayne, IN 46802. **Telephone:**
(260) 490-3629.

GREAT LAKES LOONS

Office Address: 825 East Main St, Midland, MI 48640.
Telephone: (989) 837-2255. **Fax:** (989) 837-8780.
E-Mail Address: info@loons.com. **Website:** www.loons.com.
Affiliation (first year): Los Angeles Dodgers (2007). **Years in League:** 2007-

OWNERSHIP/MANAGEMENT
Operated By: Michigan Baseball Operations. **Stadium Ownership:** Michigan Baseball Foundation.
Founder/Foundation President: William Stavropoulos.

MINOR LEAGUES

President/General Manager: Paul Barbeau.

Vice President, Facilities/Operations: Matt McQuaid. **VP, Finance:** Jana Chotivkova. **VP, Marketing/Entertainment:** Chris Mundhenk. **VP. Sales/Event Operations:** Scott Litle. **General Manager. Dow Diamond Events:** Dave Gomola. **Assistant GM, Corporate Partnerships/Director, Development (MBF):** Emily Schafer. **Assistant GM, Event Operation:** Ann Craig. **Assistant GM, Production/Entertainment:** Chris Lones. **Assistant GM, Ticket Sales:** Tiffany Seward. **Director, Accounting:** Jamie Start. **Director, Food/Beverage:** Jenny Coleman. **Director, Group Sales:** Tara Bergeron. **Director, Programming:** Jared Sandler. **Director, Programs/Fund Development (MBF):** Patti Tuma. **Director, Ticket Services:** Kevin Schunk. **Assistant to MBF President:** Marge Parker.

Accounting Manager: Kathleen Cifuentes. **Communications Manager:** Steve Livingston. **Concessions Manager:** James Reed. **Corporate Partnerships Manager:** Eric Ramseyer. **Group Sales Manager:** Matt Hoffman. **Retail Manager:** Jenean Clarkson. **Promotions Manager:** Matt C. Hoffman. **Stadium Operations Manager:** Dan Straley. **Catering Coordinator:** Amanda Colmus. **Kitchen Supervisor:** Alec Norris. **Retail Supervisor:** Scott Trybe. **Account Executive:** Rachel Burton. **Corporate Account Executive:** Kevin Rathbun. **Executive Chef:** Andrea Noonan. **Head of Grounds:** Matt Ellis. **Group Sales Coordinator:** Katie Wahl. **Administrative Assistant:** Liz Rousseau.

FIELD STAFF

Manager: Razor Shines. **Hitting Coach:** Mike Eylward. **Pitching Coach:** Bill Simas

GAME INFORMATION

Play-by-Play Broadcaster: Brad Golder. **No. of Games Broadcast:** Home-70, Away-70. **Flagship Station:** ESPN 100.9-FM WLUN.

PA Announcer: Jerry O'Donnell. **Official Scorers:** Terry Wilczek, Larry Loiselle. **Stadium Name:** Dow Diamond. **Location:** I-75 to US-10 W, Take the M-20/US-10 Business exit on the left toward downtown Midland, Merge onto US-10 W/MI-20 W (also known as Indian Street), Turn left onto State Street, The entrance to the stadium is at the intersection of Ellsworth and State Streets. **Standard Game Times:** 6:05 pm (April), 7:05 (May-Sept), Sun 2:05. **Ticket Price Range:** $6-9.

Visiting Club Hotel: Holiday Inn, 810 Cinema Dr, Midland, MI 48642. **Telephone:** (989) 794-8500.

KANE COUNTY COUGARS

Office Address: One Cougar Trail, Geneva, IL 60134.
Telephone: (630) 232-8811. **Fax:** (630) 232-8815.
E-Mail Address: info@kanecountycougars.com. **Website:** www.kccougars.com.
Affiliation (first year): Chicago Cubs (2013). **Years in League:** 1991-

OWNERSHIP/MANAGEMENT

Operated By: Cougars Baseball Partnership/American Sports Enterprises, Inc.
Managing Partners: Mike Woleben, Mike Murtaugh.
General Manager: Curtis Haug.
Senior Director, Finance/Administration: Douglas Czurylo. **Manager, Finance/Accounting:** Lance Buhmann. **Senior Director, Ticketing:** R Michael Patterson. **Senior Ticket Sales Representative:** Alex Miller. **Sales Representatives:** Joe Golota, Derek Weber, Sean Freed. **Director, Ticket Services/Community Relations:** Amy Mason. **Senior Ticket Operations Representative:** Paul Quillia. **Ticket Operations Representative:** Lisa Carrillo. **Director, Security:** Dan Klinkhamer. **Promotions Manager:** Jenni Brechtel. **Promotions Assistant:** Derek Harrigan. **Director, Public Relations:** Shawn Touney. **Design/Graphics:** Emmet Broderick. **Media Placement Coordinator:** Bill Baker. **Webmaster/PA Announcer:** Kevin Sullivan. **Director, Food/Beverage:** Mike Koski. **Business Manager:** Robin Hull.

Kitchen Manager: Jon Williams. **Concessions Manager:** Kyle Larson. **Senior Director, Stadium Operations:** Mike Klafehn. **Head Groundskeeper:** Tyler Carter. **Stadium Maintenance Supervisor:** Jeff Snyder.

FIELD STAFF

Manager: Mark Johnson. **Hitting Coach:** Tom Beyers. **Pitching Coach:** Ron Villone. **Trainer:** Shane Nelson.

GAME INFORMATION

Radio Announcer: Wayne Randazzo. **No. of Games Broadcast:** Home-70, Away-70. **Flagship Station:** WBIG 1280-AM. **PA Announcer:** Kevin Sullivan. **Official Scorer:** Unavailable.

Stadium Name: Fifth Third Bank Ballpark. **Location:** From east or west, I-88 (Ronald Reagan Memorial Tollway) to Farnsworth Avenue North exit, north five miles to Cherry Lane, left into stadium; from northwest, I-90 (Jane Addams Memorial Tollway) to Randall Road South exit, south to Fabyan Parkway, east to Kirk Road, north to Cherry Lane, left into stadium complex. **Standard Game Times:** 6:30 pm, Sun 1. **Ticket Price Range:** $8-14. **Visiting Club Hotel:** Unavailable.

LAKE COUNTY CAPTAINS

Office Address: Classic Park, 35300 Vine Street, Eastlake, OH 44095-3142.
Telephone: (440) 975-8085. **Fax:** (440) 975-8958.
E-Mail Address: bseymour@captainsbaseball.com.
Website: www.captainsbaseball.com.
Affiliation (first year): Cleveland Indians (2003). **Years in League:** 2010-

OWNERSHIP/MANAGEMENT

Operated By: Cascia, LLC.
Owners: Peter and Rita Carfagna, Ray and Katie Murphy.
Chairman/Secretary/Treasurer: Peter Carfagna. **Vice Chairman:** Rita Carfagna. **Vice President:** Ray Murphy. **Senior VP:** Pete E. Carfagna. **VP, General Manager:** Brad Seymour. **Assistant GM, Sales:** Neil Stein. **Senior Director, Media/ Community Relations:** Craig Deas. **Director, Promotions:** Jake Schrum. **Director, Captains Concessions:** John Klein. **Manager, Stadium Operations:** Josh Porter. **Director, Turf Management/Stadium Operations:** Dan Stricko. **Director, Finance:** Rob Demko. **Manager, Ticket Operations/Merchandise:** Jen Yorko. **Manager, Group Sales:** Amy Gladieux. **Director, Special Projects:** Bill Levy. **Senior Ticket Sales Account Excutive:** Andrew Grover. **Ticket Sales Account Executives:** David Kodish, Dan Torf. **Office Assistant:** Jim Carfagna.

FIELD STAFF

Manager: Scooter Tucker. **Coach:** Tony Mansolino. **Pitching Coach:** Steve Karsay.

GAME INFORMATION

Radio Announcer: Craig Deas. **No. of Games Broadcast:** Home-70, Away-70. **Flagship Station:** WELW 1330-AM. **PA Announcer:** Ray Milavec. **Official Scorer:** Glen Blabolil.
Stadium Name: Classic Park. **Location:** From Ohio State Route 2 East, exit at Ohio 91, go left and the stadium is 1/4 mile north on your right; From Ohio State Route 90 East, exit at Ohio 91, go right and the stadium in approximately five miles north on your right.
Standard Game Times: 6:30 pm (April-May), 7 (May-Sept), Sat 1 (April-May), 7 (May-Sept), Sun 1.
Visiting Club Hotel: Comfort Inn & Suites, 7701 Reynolds Road, Mentor, OH 44060. **Telephone:** (440) 951-7333.

LANSING LUGNUTS

Office Address: 505 E Michigan Ave, Lansing, MI 48912.
Telephone: (517) 485-4500. **Fax:** (517) 485-4518.
E-Mail Address: info@lansinglugnuts.com. **Website:** www.lansinglugnuts.com.
Affiliation (first year): Toronto Blue Jays (2005). **Years in League:** 1996-

OWNERSHIP/MANAGEMENT

Operated By: Take Me Out to the Ballgame LLC.
Principal Owners: Tom Dickson, Sherrie Myers.
General Manager: Nick Grueser. **Assistant GM:** Nick Brzezinski. **Director, Business Operations:** Heather Viele. **Corporate Account Executives:** Adam Barber, Kohl Tyrrell. **Group Sales Representatives:** Faith Brooks, Bill Adler. **Manager, Box Office/Team Relations:** Josh Calver. **Season Ticket Concierge:** David Link. **Retail Manager:** Matt Hicks. **Stadium Operations Manager:** Dennis Busse. **Director, Food/Beverage:** Brett Telder. **Concessions Manager:** Andrew Creswell. **Director, Marketing:** Jeremy Smoker. **Marketing Assistant:** Ben Owen. **Sponsorship Service Representatives:** Michaela Vryhof, Ashley Moore. **Administrative Assistant:** Angela Sees. **Business Coordinator:** Stephanie Hart. **Head Groundskeeper:** Mike Kacsor.

FIELD STAFF

Manager: John Tamargo Jr. **Hitting Coach:** Kenny Graham. **Pitching Coach:** Vince Horsman. **Trainer:** Drew Macdonald.

GAME INFORMATION

Radio Announcer: Jesse Goldberg-Strassler. **No of Games Broadcast:** Home-70, Away-70. **Flagship Station:** WQTX 92.1-FM. **PA Announcer:** Unavailable. **Official Scorer:** Unavailable.
Stadium Name: Cooley Law School Stadium. **Location:** I-96 East/West to US 496, exit at Larch Street, north of Larch, stadium on left. **Ticket Price Range:** $8-11. **Visiting Club Hotel:** Unavailable.

PEORIA CHIEFS

Office Address: 730 SW Jefferson, Peoria, IL 61605.
Telephone: (309) 680-4000. **Fax:** (309) 680-4080.
E-Mail Address: feedback@chiefsnet.com. **Website:** www.peoriachiefs.com.
Affiliation (first year): St. Louis Cardinals (2013). **Years in League:** 1983-

OWNERSHIP/MANAGEMENT

Operated By: Peoria Chiefs Community Baseball Club LLC.
President: Rocky Vonachen. **Vice President/General Manager:** Ralph Converse. **Manager, Broadcast/Media:** Nathan Baliva. **Manager, Box Office:** Ryan Sivori. **Director, Corporate Sales/Partnerships:** Brendan Kelly. **Manager, Entertainment/Events:** Courtney Kessler. **Ticket Sales Manager:** Mike Schulte. **Merchandise Manager:** Paige Peugh. **Account Executives:** Sam Annable, Brett Adams, Tim Fritz, Joe Christian, Kevin McClelland. **Head Groundskeeper:** Mike Reno. **Director, Food/Beverage:** Keith Thompson.

FIELD STAFF

Manager: Dann Bilardello. **Hitting Coach:** Erik Pappas. **Pitching Coach:** Jason Simontacchi. **Trainer:** Michael Petrarca.

GAME INFORMATION

Radio Announcer: Nathan Baliva. **No. of Games Broadcast:** Home-70, Away-70. **Flagship Station:** www.peoriachiefs.com, Peoria Chiefs App in iTunes (Free).

PA Announcer: Brendan Burke. **Official Scorers:** Bryan Moore, Nick Siefken. **Stadium Name:** Peoria Chiefs Stadium. **Location:** From South/East, I-74 to exit 93 (Jefferson Street), continue one mile, stadium is one block on left; From North/West, I-74 to Glen Oak Exit, turn right on Glendale which turns into Kumpf Blvd, turn right on Jefferson, stadium on left. **Standard Game Times:** 7 pm, 6:30 (April-May, after Aug 24), Sat 6:30, Sun 5. **Ticket Price Range:** $7-11.

Visiting Club Hotel: Unavailable.

QUAD CITIES RIVER BANDITS

Office Address: 209 S Gaines St, Davenport, IA 52802.
Telephone: (563) 322-6348. **Fax:** (563) 324-3109.
E-Mail Address: bandit@riverbandits.com. **Website:** www.riverbandits.com.
Affiliation (first year): Houston Astros (2013). **Years in League:** 1960-

OWNERSHIP/MANAGEMENT

Operated by: Main Street Iowa LLC, David Heller, Bob Herrfeldt.
General Manager: Harold Craw. **Executive Director:** Stefanie Brown. **Assistant GM:** Andrew Chesser. **VP, Sales:** Shawn Brown. **Director, Client Relations/Events:** Andrea Nolan. **Director, Community Relations, Merchandise:** Brittany Carter. **Director, Marketing/Promotions:** Shane Huff. **Director, Media Relations:** Marco LaNave. **Director, Stadium Operations:** Elliott Sweitzer. **Manager, Box Office:** Andrea Williams. **Manager, Production:** Stacy Issen. **Manager, Special Events:** Shauna Learn. **Account Executives:** Amanda Henzen, Ryan Wright. **Director, Food/Beverage:** Patrick Glackin. **Executive Chef:** Chad Ramenda.

FIELD STAFF

Manager: Omar Lopez. **Hitting Coach:** Joel Chimelis. **Pitching Coach:** Dave Borkowski. **Trainer:** Steve Miller. **Development Specialist:** Vince Coleman.

GAME INFORMATION

Radio Announcer: Unavailable. **No. of Games Broadcast:** Home-70. **Flagship Station:** www.riverbandits.com. **PA Announcer:** Scott Werling. **Official Scorer:** Unavailable.

Stadium Name: Modern Woodmen Park. **Location:** From I-74, take Grant Street exit left, west onto River Drive, left on South Gaines Street; from I-80, take Brady Street exit south, right on River Drive, left on South Gaines Street. **Standard Game Times:** 7 pm; Sun 2 (April-May), 5 (June-Sept). **Ticket Price Range:** $5-13.

Visiting Club Hotel: Clarion Hotel, 5202 Brady St, Davenport, IA 52806. **Telephone:** (563) 391-1230.

SOUTH BEND
SILVER HAWKS

Office Address: 501 W South St, South Bend, IN 46601.
Mailing Address: PO Box 4218, South Bend, IN 46634.
Telephone: (574) 235-9988. **Fax:** (574) 235-9950.
E-Mail Address: hawks@silverhawks.com. **Website:** www.silverhawks.com.
Affiliation (first year): Arizona Diamondbacks (1997). **Years in League:** 1988-.

OWNERSHIP/MANAGEMENT

Owner: Andrew Berlin.
President: Joe Hart.
Assistant GM, Tickets: Andy Beuster. **Director, Corporate Sales/Business Development:** Nick Brown. **Assistant GM, Operations:** Peter Argueta. **Director, Finance/Human Resources:** Cheryl Carlson. **Box Office Manager:** Devon Hastings. **Community Relations/Account Executive:** Erin Kostos. **Account Executives:** Mike Frissore, John Littleton. **Director, Production:** Terry Breen. **Director, Food/Beverage:** Ben Hayes. **Head Groundskeeper:** Joel Reinebold.

FIELD STAFF

Manager: Mark Haley. **Hitting Coach:** Jason Camilli. **Pitching Coach:** Wellington Cepeda. **Trainer:** Masa Abe. **Strength Coach:** Skyler Zarndt.

GAME INFORMATION

Radio Announcer: Unavailable. **Flagship Station:** www.silverhawks.com.
Stadium Name: Stanley Coveleski Regional Stadium. **Location:** I-80/90 toll road to exit 77, take US 31/33 south to South Bend to downtown (Main Street), to Western Avenue, right on Western, left on Taylor.
Standard Game Times: 7:05 pm; Fri 7:35, Sun 2:05. **Ticket Price Range:** $8-10.
Visiting Club Hotel: Unavailable.

WEST MICHIGAN WHITECAPS

Office Address: 4500 West River Dr, Comstock Park, MI 49321.
Mailing Address: PO Box 428, Comstock Park, MI 49321.
Telephone: (616) 784-4131. Fax: (616) 784-4911.
E-Mail Address: playball@whitecaps-baseball.com. Website: www.whitecaps-baseball.com.
Affiliation (first year): Detroit Tigers (1997). Years in League: 1994-

OWNERSHIP/MANAGEMENT

Operated By: Whitecaps Professional Baseball Corp.
Principal Owners: Denny Baxter, Lew Chamberlin.
President: Scott Lane. Vice President, Whitecaps Professional Baseball: Jim Jarecki. VP, Sales: Steve McCarthy. Facility Events Manager: Craig Yust. Operations Manager: Tyler Edema. Director, Food/Beverage: Matt Timon. Community Relations Coordinator: Courtney Galat. Director, Marketing/Media: Mickey Graham. Promotions Manager: Keith Roelfsema. Multimedia Manager: Brian Oropallo. Box Office Manager: Shaun Pynnonen. Groundskeeper: Michael Huie. Facility Maintenance Manager: John Passarelli. Director, Ticket Sales: Chad Sayen.

FIELD STAFF

Manager: Larry Parrish. Coach: Scott Dwyer. Pitching Coach: Mike Henneman. Trainer: TJ Saunders.

GAME INFORMATION

Radio Announcers: Ben Chiswick, Dan Elve. No. of Games Broadcast: Home-70, Away-70. Flagship Station: WBBL 107.3-FM. PA Announcers: Mike Newell, Bob Wells. Official Scorers: Mike Dean, Don Thomas.
Stadium Name: Fifth Third Ballpark. Location: US 131 North from Grand Rapids to exit 91 (West River Drive). Ticket Price Range: $6-14.
Visiting Club Hotel: Holiday Inn Express-GR North, 358 River Ridge Dr NW, Walker, MI 49544. Telephone: (616) 647-4100.

WISCONSIN TIMBER RATTLERS

Office Address: 2400 N Casaloma Dr, Appleton, WI 54913.
Mailing Address: PO Box 7464, Appleton, WI 54912.
Telephone: (920) 733-4152. Fax: (920) 733-8032.
E-Mail Address: info@timberrattlers.com. Website: www.timberrattlers.com.
Affiliation (first year): Milwaukee Brewers (2009). Years in League: 1962-

OWNERSHIP/MANAGEMENT

Operated By: Appleton Baseball Club, Inc.
Chairman: Marc Snyder.
President/General Manager: Rob Zerjav.
Assistant GM/Director, Ticket Sales: Aaron Hahn. Controller: Cathy Spanbauer. Director, Food/Beverage: Ryan Grossman. Director, Stadium Operations/Security: Ron Kaiser. Director, Community Relations: Dayna Baitinger. Director, Media Relations: Chris Mehring. Corporate Partnerships: Ryan Cunniff, Jerrad Radocay. Director, Merchandise: Jay Gruszynski. Box Office Manager: Ryan Moede. Banquet Facility Manager: Jenny Smith. Executive Chef: Tim Hansen. Assistant, Food/Beverage Assistant: Chumley Hodgson. Group Sales: Seth Merrill, Rebecca Sievers, Liz Wockenfus. Creative Director: Ann Mollica. Marketing Coordinator: Hilary Bauer. Entertainment Coordinator: Kevin Ross. Clubhouse Manager: Travis Voss. Office Manager: Mary Robinson. Groundskeeper: Eddie Warczak.

FIELD STAFF

Manager: Matt Erickson. Coach: Dusty Rhodes. Pitching Coach: Dave Chavarria. Trainer: Jeff Paxson.

GAME INFORMATION

Radio Announcer: Chris Mehring. No. of Games Broadcast: Home-70, Away-70. Flagship Station: WNAM 1280-AM. Television Announcers: Bob Brainerd, John Maino, Ted Stefaniak, Brad Woodall. Television Affiliates: Time Warner Cable SportsChannel, WACY-TV. No. of Games Broadcast: 32. PA Announcer: Matt Breska. Official Scorer: Jay Gruszynski.
Stadium Name: Time Warner Cable Field at Fox Cities Stadium. Location: Highway 41 to Highway 15 (00) exit, west to Casaloma Drive, left to stadium.
Standard Game Times: 7:05 pm, 6:35 (April-May), Sat 6:35, Sun 1:05. Ticket Price Range: $5-25.
Visiting Club Hotel: Microtel Inn & Suites, 321 Metro Dr, Appleton, WI 54913. Telephone: (920) 997-3121.

SOUTH ATLANTIC LEAGUE

Office Address: 13575 58th Street North, Suite 141, Clearwater, FL 33760-3721. **Telephone:** (727) 538-4270. **Fax:** (727) 499-6853.

E-Mail Address: office@saloffice.com. **Website:** www.southatlanticleague.com.
Years League Active: 1904-1964, 1979-.
President/Secretary/Treasurer: Eric Krupa.
First Vice President: Chip Moore (Rome). **Second Vice President:** Craig Brown (Greenville).
Directors: Don Beaver (Hickory), Cooper Brantley (Greensboro), Craig Brown (Greenville), Brian DeWine (Asheville), Joseph Finley (Lakewood), Jason Freier (Savannah), Marvin Goldklang (Charleston), Chip Moore (Rome), Bruce Quinn (Hagerstown), Brad Smith (Kannapolis), Bill Shea (Lexington), Glenn Tilley (Augusta), Tom Volpe (Delmarva), Tim Wilcox (West Virginia).
Division Structure: North—Delmarva, Greensboro, Hagerstown, Hickory, Kannapolis, Lakewood, West Virginia. South—Asheville, Augusta, Charleston, Greenville, Lexington, Rome, Savannah.
Regular Season: 140 games (split schedule). **2013 Opening Date:** April 4. **Closing Date:** Sept 2. **All-Star Game:** June 18 at Lakewood.
Playoff Format: First-half and second-half division winners meet in best-of-three semifinal series. Winners meet in best-of-five series for league championship.
Roster Limit: 25 active. **Player Eligibility Rule:** No age limit. No more than two players and one player-coach on active list may have more than five years of experience.
Brand of Baseball: Rawlings.
Umpires: Jordan Albarado (Scott, LA), Ryan Benson (Selden, NY), Jeffrey Carnahan (Crystal River, FL), Scott Costello (Barry, Ontario), Morgan Day (Eros, LA), Douglas Del Bello Jr, (Hamburg, NY), Travis Godec (Pueblo West, CO), Clayton Hamm (Austin, TX), Brian Peterson (Manchester, NJ), Jorge Teran (Barquisimeto, Lara, Venezuela), Richard Tucker (Pearland, TX), Jacob Wilburn (Fort Worth, TX), Lewis Williams (Riverbank, CA), Ryan Wills (Herndon, VA).

Eric Krupa

STADIUM INFORMATION

Club	Stadium	Opened	LF	CF	RF	Capacity	2012 Att.
Asheville	McCormick Field	1992	326	373	297	4,000	155,760
Augusta	Lake Olmstead Stadium	1995	330	400	330	4,322	182,124
Charleston	Joseph P. Riley Jr. Ballpark	1997	306	386	336	5,800	254,002
Delmarva	Arthur W. Perdue Stadium	1996	309	402	309	5,200	231,194
Greensboro	NewBridge Bank Park	2005	322	400	320	7,599	367,077
Greenville	Fluor Field	2006	310	400	302	5,000	347,042
Hagerstown	Municipal Stadium	1931	335	400	330	4,600	87,429
Hickory	L.P. Frans Stadium	1993	330	401	330	5,062	132,696
Kannapolis	CMC-NorthEast Stadium	1995	330	400	310	4,700	132,493
Lakewood	FirstEnergy Park	2001	325	400	325	6,588	410,113
Lexington	Whitaker Bank Ballpark	2001	320	401	318	6,033	295,937
Rome	State Mutual Stadium	2003	335	400	330	5,100	184,983
Savannah	Historic Grayson Stadium	1941	290	410	310	8,000	117,372
West Virginia	Appalachian Power Park	2005	330	400	320	4,300	157,875

Table header note: Dimensions (LF, CF, RF)

ASHEVILLE TOURISTS

Office Address: McCormick Field, 30 Buchanan Place, Asheville, NC 28801.
Telephone: (828) 258-0428. **Fax:** (828) 258-0320.
E-Mail Address: info@theashevilletourists.com. **Website:** www.theashevilletourists.com.
Affiliation (first year): Colorado Rockies (1994). **Years in League:** 1976-

OWNERSHIP/MANAGEMENT
Operated By: DeWine Seeds Silver Dollar Baseball, LLC.
President: Brian DeWine.
General Manager: Larry Hawkins.
Assistant GM: Chris Smith. **Box Office Manager:** Neil Teitelbaum. **Office Manager:** Ryan Straney. **Merchandise/Promotions Manager:** Jon Clemmons. **Community Relations Manager:** Ashley Trobaugh. **Broadcasting/Media Relations Manager:** Doug Maurer. **Group Sales Representatives:** Chris Zolli, Josh Weeks. **Outside Sales Representative:** Bob Jones. **Stadium Operations Director:** Patrick Spence. **Director, Food/Beverage:** Craig Phillips (Pro Sports Catering). **Publications/Website:** Bill Ballew.

FIELD STAFF
Manager: Fred Ocasio. **Hitting Coach:** Mike Devereaux. **Pitching Coach:** Joey Eischen. **Development Supervisor:** Marv Foley. **Trainer:** Billy Whitehead.

GAME INFORMATION
   Radio Announcer: Doug Maurer. **No. of Games Broadcast:** Home-70, Away-70. **Flagship Station:** WRES 100.7-FM.
   PA Announcer: Rick Rice. **Official Scorer:** Jim Baker
   Stadium Name: McCormick Field. **Location:** I-240 to Charlotte Street South exit, south one mile on Charlotte, left on McCormick Place. **Ticket Price Range:** $6-11.
   Visiting Club Hotel: Quality Inn, 1 Skyline Drive, Arden, NC 28704. **Telephone:** (828) 684-6688.

AUGUSTA GREENJACKETS

Office Address: 78 Milledge Rd, Augusta, GA 30904.
Mailing Address: PO Box 3746 Hill Station, Augusta, GA 30914.
Telephone: (706) 736-7889. **Fax:** (706) 736-1122.
E-Mail Address: info@greenjacketsbaseball.com. **Website:** www.greenjacketsbase-ball.com.
Affiliation (first year): San Francisco Giants (2005). **Years in League:** 1988-.

OWNERSHIP/MANAGEMENT
   Ownership Group: AGON Sports & Entertainment.
   Owner: Chris Schoen.
   President: Jeff Eiseman. **General Manager:** Bob Flannery.
   Director, Operations: Brian Marshall. **Director, Ticket Sales:** Ben Burnett. **Accounting:** Debbie Brown. **Group Sales Manager:** Bill Levy. **Corporate Sales Executive:** Dan Szatkowski. **Stadium Operations Manager:** Kyle Titus. **Marketing Manager:** Lindsey McGuire. **Account Executives:** Keaton Kovacs, Anthony Laurendi, Whitney Taylor, Dylan Tobin, Matt Toohey. **Box Office:** Zach Daw. **Media Relations:** Katie Agostin.

FIELD STAFF
   Manager: Mike Goff. **Hitting Coach:** Hector Borg. **Pitching Coach:** Steve Kline. **Trainer:** Garret Havig.

GAME INFORMATION
   Radio: None. **PA Announcer:** Scott Skadan. **Official Scorer:** Ted Miller.
   Stadium Name: Lake Olmstead Stadium. **Location:** I-20 to Washington Road exit, east to Broad Street exit, left on Milledge Road. **Standard Game Times:** 7:05 pm; Sun 2:05. **Ticket Price Range:** $8-15.
   Visiting Club Hotel: Microtel 2909 Riverwest Drive, Augusta, GA. **Telephone:** (706) 481-8010.

CHARLESTON RIVERDOGS

Office Address: 360 Fishburne St, Charleston, SC 29403.
Mailing Address: PO Box 20849, Charleston, SC 29413.
Telephone: (843) 723-7241. **Fax:** (843) 723-2641.
E-Mail Address: admin@riverdogs.com. **Website:** www.riverdogs.com.
Affiliation (first year): New York Yankees (2005). **Years in League:** 1973-78, 1980-

OWNERSHIP/MANAGEMENT
   Operated by: The Goldklang Group/South Carolina Baseball Club LP.
   Chairman: Marv Goldklang. **President:** Mike Veeck. **Director of Fun:** Bill Murray. **Co-Owners:** Dr. Gene Budig, Al Phillips, Peter Freund.
   Executive Vice President/General Manager: Dave Echols.
   Assistant GMs: Andy Lange, Harold Craw. **Director, Stadium Operations:** John Schumacher. **Director, Promotions:** Noel Blaha. **Director, Special Events:** Melissa Azevedo. **Director, Merchandise:** Mike DeAntonio. **Director, Community Relations:** Lauren Allio. **Director, Broadcasting/Media Relations:** Sean Houston. **Box Office Manager:** Ryan Stewart. **Special Events Manager:** Kristen Wolfe. **Manager, Food/Beverage:** Peter Parker. **Assistant Operations:** Harris Seletsky. **Sales Manager:** Jake Terrell. **Sales Representative:** David Cullins. **Business Manager:** Dale Stickney. **Office Manager:** Kristal Lessington. **Head Groundskeeper:** Mike Williams. **Clubhouse Manager:** Kenneth Bassett.

FIELD STAFF
   Manager: Al Pedrique. **Hitting Coach:** PJ Pilittere. **Pitching Coach:** Danny Borrell. **First-Base Coach:** Justin Tordi. **Trainer:** Mike Becker. **Strength/Conditioning Coach:** Joe Giangrasso.

GAME INFORMATION
   Radio Announcer: Sean Houston. **No. of Games Broadcast:** Home-70, Away-70. **Flagship Station:** WTMZ 910-AM.
   PA Announcer: Ken Carrington. **Official Scorer:** Jeremy Helms.
   Stadium Name: Joseph P Riley, Jr. **Ballpark. Location:** From US 17, take Lockwood Drive North, right on Fishburne Street. **Standard Game Times:** 7:05 pm, Sun 5:05. **Ticket Price Range:** $5-18.
   Visiting Club Hotel: Crowne Plaza Charleston, 4381 Tanger Outlet Blvd, N Charleston, SC 29418. **Telephone:** (843) 744-4422.

DELMARVA SHOREBIRDS

Office Address: 6400 Hobbs Rd, Salisbury, MD 21804.
Mailing Address: PO Box 1557, Salisbury, MD 21802.
Telephone: (410) 219-3112. **Fax:** (410) 219-9164.
E-Mail Address: info@theshorebirds.com. **Website:** www.theshorebirds.com.
Affiliation (first year): Baltimore Orioles (1997). **Years in League:** 1996-

OWNERSHIP/MANAGEMENT

Operated By: 7th Inning Stretch, LLP. **Directors:** Tom Volpe, Pat Filippone.
General Manager: Chris Bitters.
Assistant GM: Jimmy Sweet. **Director, Community Relations/Marketing:** Shawn Schoolcraft. **Business Development Executive:** Alyssa Dooyema. **Director, Tickets:** Brandon Harris. **Group Sales Manager:** Fred Schnarrs. **Ticket Sales Manager:** Mike Steinhice. **Ticket Sales Account Executive:** Zac Penman. **Director, Stadium Operations:** Aaron Becker. **Head Groundskeeper:** Dave Super. **Director, Broadcasting/Graphic Design:** Bret Lasky. **Box Office Manager:** Joe Long. **Accounting Manager:** Gail Potts. **Office Manager:** Audrey Vane.

FIELD STAFF

Manager: Luis Pujols. **Coach:** Butch Davis. **Pitching Coach:** Justin Lord. **Trainer:** Greg Svarczkopf.

GAME INFORMATION

Radio Announcer: Bret Lasky. **No of Games Broadcast:** Home-70, Away-70. **Flagship Station:** 960 WTGM.
PA Announcer: Dustin Mills. **Official Scorer:** Gary Hicks.
Stadium Name: Arthur W Perdue Stadium. **Location:** From US 50 East, right on Hobbs Road; From US 50 West, left on Hobbs Road. **Standard Game Times:** 7:05 pm. **Ticket Price Range:** $4-12.
Visiting Club Hotel: Unavailable.

GREENSBORO GRASSHOPPERS

Office Address: 408 Bellemeade St, Greensboro, NC 27401.
Telephone: (336) 268-2255. **Fax:** (336) 273-7350.
E-Mail Address: info@gsohoppers.com. **Website:** www.gsohoppers.com.
Affiliation (first year): Miami Marlins (2003). **Years in League:** 1979-

OWNERSHIP/MANAGEMENT

Operated By: Greensboro Baseball LLC.
Principal Owners: Cooper Brantley, Wes Elingburg, Len White.
President/General Manager: Donald Moore.
Vice President, Baseball Operations: Katie Dannemiller. **CFO:** Benjamin Martin. **Assistant GM/Head Groundskeeper:** Jake Holloway. **Assistant GM, Sales/Marketing:** Tim Vangel. **Director, Ticket Sales:** Erich Dietz. **Coordinator, Ticket Services:** Kyle Smith. **Director, Promotions/Community Relations:** Joey Burridge.
Director, Production/Entertainment: Shawn Russell. **Director, Creative Services:** Amanda Williams. **Director, Merchandise:** Yunhui Bradshaw. **Executive Director, Business Development:** John Redhead. **Group Sales Associates:** Todd Olson, Murray White. **Sales Associate:** Rosalee Brewer. **Director, Stadium Operations:** Chad Green. **Assistant Groundskeeper:** Kaid Musgrave.

FIELD STAFF

Manager: Jorge Hernandez. **Coach:** Frank Moore. **Pitching Coach:** Blake McGinley. **Trainer:** Ben Cates.

GAME INFORMATION

Radio Announcer: Andy Durham. **No. of Games Broadcast:** Home-70, Away-0. **Flagship Station:** WPET 950-AM.
PA Announcer: Jim Scott. **Official Scorer:** Wayne Butler/Wilt Browning.
Stadium Name: NewBridge Bank Park. **Location:** From I-85, take Highway 220 South (exit 36) to Coliseum Blvd, continue on Edgeworth Street, ballpark at corner of Edgeworth and Bellemeade Streets. **Standard Game Times:** 7 pm, Sun 4. **Ticket Price Range:** $6-10.
Visiting Club Hotel: Days Inn 6102 Landmark Center Boulevard, Greensboro, NC 27407. **Telephone:** (336) 553-2763.

GREENVILLE DRIVE

Office Address: 945 South Main St, Greenville, SC 29601.
Telephone: (864) 240-4500. **Fax:** (864) 240-4501.
E-Mail Address: info@greenvilledrive.com. **Website:** www.greenvilledrive.com.
Affiliation (first year): Boston Red Sox (2005). **Years in League:** 2005-

OWNERSHIP/MANAGEMENT

Operated By: Greenville Drive, LLC.
Co-Owner/President: Craig Brown. **Co-Owners:** Roy Bostock, Paul Raether.
General Manager: Mike deMaine. **Senior Vice President:** Nate Lipscomb. **VP, Finance:** Eric Blagg. **VP, Ticket Sales:** Kyle Krebs. **VP, Ballpark Experience:** Eric Jarinko. **Director, Food/Beverage:** Larry Mattson. **Director, Game Entertainment:** Sam LoBosco. **Sponsor Services Manager:** Jennifer Brown. **Production Manager:** Josh Cozzini. **Manager, Special Events/Community Relations:** Samantha Bauer. **Media Relations Manager:** Cameron White. **Coordinator, Corporate Sales/Marketing:** Alex Fiedler. **Senior Account Executive:** Jeff Chiappini. **Account Executive:** Rachel Prindle. **Operations Manager:** Amanda LaVecchia. **Retail Manager:** Wade Mann. **Merchandise Manager:** Steven Seman. **Facilities Manager:** Eric Anastasi. **Head Groundskeeper:** Greg Burgess. **Assistant Groundskeeper:** Ross Groenevelt. **General Accountant:** Connie Pynne. **Office Manager:** Jamie Schafer.

FIELD STAFF

Manager: Carlos Febles. **Hitting Coach:** UL Washington. **Pitching Coach:** Paul Abbott. **Trainer:** Mackenzie Zabbo.

GAME INFORMATION

Radio Announcer: Ed Jenson. **No. of Games Broadcast:** Home-70, Away-0. **Flagship Station:** greenvilledrive.com.
PA Announcer: John Oliver. **Official Scorer:** Sanford Rogers
Stadium Name: Fluor Field. **Location:** From south, I-85S to exit 42 toward downtown Greenville, turn left onto Augusta Road, stadium is two miles on the left; From north, I-85S to I-385 toward Greenville, turn left onto Church Street, turn right onto University Ridge. **Standard Game Times:** 7 pm, Sun 4. **Ticket Price Range:** $6-9.
Visiting Club Hotel: Hampton Inn Greenville-Haywood, 246 Congaree Road, Greenville, SC 29607. **Telephone:** (864) 288-1200.

HAGERSTOWN SUNS

HAGERSTOWN SUNS

Office Address: 274 E Memorial Blvd, Hagerstown, MD 21740.
Telephone: (301) 791-6266. **Fax:** (301) 791-6066.
E-Mail Address: info@hagerstownsuns.com. **Website:** www.hagerstownsuns.com.
Affiliation (first year): Washington Nationals (2007). **Years in League:** 1993-

OWNERSHIP/MANAGEMENT

Principal Owner/Operated by: Hagerstown Baseball LLC.
President: Bruce Quinn. **General Manager:** Bill Farley.
Director, Marketing/Community Relations: Kyle MacBain. **Director, Media Relations:** Eli Pearlstein. **Director, Group Sales:** Josh Mastin. **Stadium Operations/Account Executive:** Andrew Houston. **Director, Human Resources/ Promotions/Entertainment:** Lori Kendall. **Director, Sales/Community Affairs:** Bob Bruchey. **Director, Ticket Operations:** Paul Krenzer. **Assistant, Promotions:** Rachel Hawkins. **Assistant, Marketing:** Hannah Wolfe.

FIELD STAFF

Manager: Tripp Keister. **Hitting Coach:** Brian Rupp. **Pitching Coach:** Franklin Bravo. **Trainer:** TD Swinford.

GAME INFORMATION

Radio Announcer: Eli Pearlstein. **No. of Games Broadcast:** Home-70, Away-70. **Flagship Station:** WJEJ 1240-AM.
PA Announcer: Unavailable. **Official Scorer:** Will Kauffman.
Stadium Name: Municipal Stadium. **Location:** Exit 32B (US 40 West) on I-70 West, left at Eastern Boulevard; Exit 6A (US 40 East) on I-81, right at Eastern Boulevard. **Standard Game Times:** 7:05 pm, Sun 1:05. **Ticket Price Range:** $9-12.
Visiting Club Hotel: Clarion Hotel, 901 Dual Highway, Hagerstown, MD, 21740. **Telephone:** (301) 733-5100.

HICKORY CRAWDADS

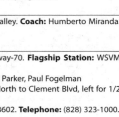

Office Address: 2500 Clement Blvd NW, Hickory, NC 28601.
Mailing Address: PO Box 1268, Hickory, NC 28603.
Telephone: (828) 322-3000. **Fax:** (828) 322-6137.
E-Mail Address: crawdad@hickorycrawdads.com. **Website:** www.hickorycrawdads.com.
Affiliation (first year): Texas Rangers (2009). **Years in League:** 1952, 1960, 1993-

OWNERSHIP/MANAGEMENT

Operated by: Hickory Baseball Inc.
Principal Owners: Don Beaver, Luther Beaver, Charles Young.
President: Don Beaver.
General Manager: Mark Seaman. **Assistant GM:** Charlie Downs.
Director, Promotions: Jared Weymier. **Director, Broadcasting/Media Relations:** Andrew Buchbinder. **Business Manager:** Donna White. **Director, Special Events:** Matt Moes. **Community Relations Coordinator:** Megan Meade. **Clubhouse Manager:** Billy Watkins. **Director, Group Sales:** Kathryn Bobel. **Director, Ticket Operations/Merchandising:** Douglas Locascio. **Head Groundskeeper:** Andrew Tallent. **Director, Food/Beverage:** Teddy Ingraham.

FIELD STAFF

Manager: Unavailable. **Hitting Coach:** Justin Mashore. **Pitching Coach:** Ryan O'Malley. **Coach:** Humberto Miranda. **Trainer:** Jacob Newburn. **Strength/Conditioning:** Wade Lamont.

GAME INFORMATION

Radio Announcer: Andrew Buchbinder. **No. of Games Broadcast:** Home-70, Away-70. **Flagship Station:** WSVM 1490-AM.
PA Announcers: Ralph Mangum, Jason Savage, Steve Jones. **Official Scorers:** Mark Parker, Paul Fogelman
Stadium Name: LP Frans Stadium. **Location:** I-40 to exit 123 (Lenoir North), 321 North to Clement Blvd, left for 1/2 mile. **Standard Game Times:** 7 pm, Sun 5.
Visiting Club Hotel: Crowne Plaza, 1385 Lenior-Rhyne Boulevard SE, Hickory, NC 28602. **Telephone:** (828) 323-1000.

KANNAPOLIS INTIMIDATORS

Office Address: 2888 Moose Rd, Kannapolis, NC 28083.
Mailing Address: PO Box 64, Kannapolis, NC 28082.
Telephone: (704) 932-3267. **Fax:** (704) 938-7040.
E-Mail Address: info@intimidatorsbaseball.com. **Website:** www.intimidatorsbaseball.com.
Affiliation (first year): Chicago White Sox (2001). **Years in League:** 1995-

OWNERSHIP/MANAGEMENT

Operated by: Smith Family Baseball Inc.
President: Brad Smith.
General Manager: Randy Long. **Head Groundskeeper/Director, Stadium Operations:** Billy Ball. **Assistant GM:** Jason Bright. **Director, Broadcasting/Media Relations:** Josh Feldman. **Ticket Sales Managers:** Terry Clark, Adam Hunte. **Seasonal Staff:** Harrison Christian. **Assistant Groundskeeper:** Mitchell Houten.

FIELD STAFF

Manager: Tommy Thompson. **Hitting Coach:** Andy Tomberlin. **Pitching Coach:** Jose Bautista. **Trainer:** Cory Barton. **Strength/Conditioning Coach:** Chad Efron.

GAME INFORMATION

Radio Announcer: Josh Feldman. **No. of Games Broadcast:** Home-70, Away-select games.
Flagship Station: www.intimidatorsbaseball.com.
PA Announcer: Sean Fox. **Official Scorer:** Unavailable.
Stadium Name: CMC-NorthEast Stadium. **Location:** Exit 63 on I-85, west on Lane Street to Stadium Drive.
Standard Game Times: 7:05 pm, Sun 5:05. **Ticket Price Range:** $6-$12.
Visiting Club Hotel: Fairfield Inn by Marriott, 3033 Cloverleaf Pkwy, Kannapolis, NC 28083. **Telephone:** (704) 795-4888.

LAKEWOOD BLUECLAWS

Office Address: 2 Stadium Way, Lakewood, NJ 08701.
Telephone: (732) 901-7000. **Fax:** (732) 901-3967.
E-mail Address: info@blueclaws.com. **Website:** www.blueclaws.com
Affiliation (first year): Philadelphia Phillies (2001). **Years in League:** 2001-

OWNERSHIP/MANAGEMENT

Operated By: American Baseball Company, LLC.
President: Joseph Finley.
General Manager: Brandon Marano. **Assistant GM, Tickets:** Joe Harrington. **Controller:** Bob Halsey. **Director, Marketing:** Mike Ryan. **Director, Promotions:** Hal Hansen. **Director, Community Relations:** Jim DeAngelis. **Director, Sponsorship:** Zack Rosenberg. **Director, Business Development:** Dan DeYoung. **Director, Group Sales:** Jim McNamara. **Director, New Client Development:** Mike Van Hise. **Director, Special Events:** Steve Farago. **Director, Inside Sales:** Lisa Carone. **Director, Corporate Sponsorship:** Chris Tafrow. **Director, Regional Sales:** John Fierko. **Director, Retail Operations:** Lisa Carone.
Senior Manager, Media/Public Relations: Greg Giombarrese. **Senior Manager, Ticket Sales:** Rob Vota. **Senior Manager, Ticket Sales:** Kevin Fenstermacher. **Senior Manager, Ticket Sales:** Andrew Granozio. **Ticket Sales Managers:** Justin Campbell, Annmarie Clifford, Sean MacLeary, Rob McGillick. **Manager, BlueClaws Baseball Academy:** Joe Agnello. **Regional Sales Manager:** Sara Lamont. **Corporate Sales Manager:** Dave Ricci. **Sponsorship Manager:** Amy DeMichele. **Ticket Sales Coordinator:** Libby Rowe. **Premium Services Manager:** Maria Cervino. **Ticket Operations Coordinator:** Paige Selle. **Concourse Operations Manager:** Robert Van Praag. **Manager, Food/Beverage:** Mike Barry. **Executive Administrator:** Lindsay Lubeck. **Clubhouse Manager:** Russ Schaffer. **Head Groundskeeper:** Ryan Radcliffe.

FIELD STAFF

Manager: Mickey Morandini. **Hitting Coach:** Greg Legg. **Pitching Coach:** Aaron Fultz.

GAME INFORMATION

Radio Announcers: Greg Giombarrese, Dan Acheson. **No. of Games Broadcast:** Home-70, Away-70. **Flagship Station:** WOBM 1160-AM.
PA Announcers: Kevin Clark, Mike Stoughton. **Official Scorers:** Joe Bellina, Jared Weiss. **Stadium Name:** FirstEnergy Park. **Location:** Route 70 to New Hampshire Avenue, North on New Hampshire for 2.5 miles to ballpark. **Standard Game Times:** 7:05 pm, 6:35 pm (April-May); Sun 1:05, 5:05 (July-Aug). **Ticket Price Range:** $7-12.
Visiting Team Hotel: Clarion Hotel Toms River, 815 Route 37 West, Toms River, NJ 08755. **Telephone:** (732) 341-3400.

LEXINGTON LEGENDS

Office Address: 207 Legends Lane, Lexington, KY 40505.
Telephone: (859) 252-4487. **Fax:** (859) 252-0747.
E-Mail Address: webmaster@lexingtonlegends.com.
Website: www.lexingtonlegends.com.
Affiliation (first year): Kansas City Royals (2013). **Years in League:** 2001-

OWNERSHIP/MANAGEMENT

Operated By: Ivy Walls Management Co.
Principal Owner: Bill Shea. **President/COO:** Andy Shea.
General Manager: Seth Poteat. **Assistant GM:** Adam English. **Vice President, Facilities:** Gary Durbin.
Director, Stadium Operations/Manager, Human Resource: Shannon Kidd. **Business Manager:** Tina Wright. **Corporate Sales Manager:** Jake Thayer. **Box Office Manager:** David Barry. **Director, Creative Services/Graphic Designer:** Ty Cobb. **Director, Broadcasting/Media Relations:** Keith Elkins. **Senior Account Executive:** Ron Borkowski. **Director, Community Relations/Special Events:** Sarah Bosso. **Promotions Coordinator:** Lauren Shrader. **Production Manager:** Nick Juhasz. **Head Groundskeeper:** Britt Barry. **Facility Specialist:** Steve Moore.

FIELD STAFF

Manager: Brian Buchanan. **Hitting Coach:** Justin Gemoll. **Pitching Coach:** Jerry Nyman. **Athletic Trainer:** Mark Keiser. **Strength/Conditioning Coach:** Nate Dine.

GAME INFORMATION

Radio Announcer: Keith Elkins. **No. of Games Broadcast:** Home-70, Away-70. **Flagship Station:** WLXG 1300-AM.
PA Announcer: Ty Cobb. **Official Scorer:** Unavailable.
Stadium Name: Whitaker Bank Ballpark. **Location:** From I-64/75, take exit 113, right onto North Broadway toward downtown Lexington for 1.2 miles, past New Circle Road (Highway 4), right into stadium, located adjacent to Northland Shopping Center. **Standard Game Times:** 7:05 pm, Wed 12:05, Sun 1:35. **Ticket Price Range:** $4-$24.
Visiting Club Hotel: Ramada Inn and Conference Center, 2143 N Broadway, Lexington, KY 40505. **Telephone:** (859) 299-1261.

ROME BRAVES

Office Address: State Mutual Stadium, 755 Braves Blvd, Rome, GA 30161.
Mailing Address: PO Box 1915, Rome, GA 30162-1915.
Telephone: (706) 368-9388. **Fax:** (706) 368-6525.
E-Mail Address: rome.braves@braves.com. **Website:** www.romebraves.com.
Affiliation (first year): Atlanta Braves (2003). **Years in League:** 2003-

OWNERSHIP MANAGEMENT

Operated By: Atlanta National League Baseball Club Inc.
General Manager: Michael Dunn. **Assistant GM:** Jim Jones.
Director, Stadium Operations: Eric Allman. **Director, Ticket Manager:** Jeff Fletcher. **Director, Culinary Services:** Dave Atwood. **Director, Food/Beverage:** Brad Smith. **Special Projects Manager:** Erin White. **Administrative Manager:** Christina Shaw. **Account Representatives:** John Layng, Kyle Allen. **Head Groundskeeper:** Bryant Powers. **Retail Manager:** Starla Roden. **Warehouse Operations Manager:** Terry Morgan. **Neighborhood Outreach Coordinator:** Laura Harrison.

FIELD STAFF

Manager: Randy Ingle. **Coach:** Bobby Moore. **Pitching Coach:** Derrick Lewis. **Trainer:** Kyle Damschroder.

GAME INFORMATION

Radio Announcer: Unavailable. **No. of Games Broadcast:** Home-70, Away-70. **Flagship Station:** WATG 95.7 FM. **Television:** online streaming romebraves.com (home games).
PA Announcer: Tony McIntosh. **Official Scorers:** Jim O'Hara, Lyndon Huckaby.
Stadium Name: State Mutual Stadium. **Location:** I-75 North to exit 190 (Rome/Canton), left off exit and follow Highway 411/Highway 20 to Rome, right at intersection on Highway 411 and Highway 1 (Veterans MemorialHighway), stadium is at intersection of Veterans Memorial Highway and Riverside Parkway. **Ticket Price Range:** $4-10.
Visiting Club Hotel: Days Inn, 840 Turner McCall Blvd, Rome, GA 30161. **Telephone:** (706) 295-0400.

SAVANNAH SAND GNATS

Office Address: 1401 E Victory Dr, Savannah, GA 31404.
Mailing Address: PO Box 3783, Savannah, GA 31414.
Telephone: (912) 351-9150. **Fax:** (912) 352-9722.
E-Mail Address: info@sandgnats.com. **Website:** www.sandgnats.com.
Affiliation (first year): New York Mets (2007). **Years in League:** 1904-1915, 1936-1960, 1962, 1984-

OWNERSHIP/MANAGEMENT

Operated By: Savannah Professional Baseball, LLC.
President: John Katz.
VP, Business Development: Jeremy Auker. **VP, Food/Beverage:** Scott Burton. **Director, Stadium Operations:** Evan Christian. **Director, Group Sales/Community Affairs:** Ariel Wagner. **Director, Sales:** Jonathan Mercier. **Ticketing Manager:** Joe Shepard. **Graphics Manager:** Vincent Caffiero. **Head Groundskeeper:** Andy Rock. **Account Executives:** Evan DeCamp, Taryn Duncan, Henry Garcia, Sarah Sutton.

FIELD STAFF

Manager: Luis Rojas. **Coach:** Joel Fuentes. **Pitching Coach:** Frank Viola. **Trainer:** Tom Truedson. **Strength/Conditioning Coach:** Jason Griffin.

GAME INFORMATION

Radio Announcer: Toby Hyde. **No. of Games Broadcast:** Home-70, Away-70. **Flagship Station:** WBMQ 960-AM.
PA Announcer: Unavailable. **Official Scorer:** Unavailable.
Stadium Name: Historic Grayson Stadium. **Location:** From I-16 E to 37th Street exit, left on 37th, right on Abercorn Street, left on Victory Drive; From I-95 to exit 16, east on 204, right on Victory Drive, Stadium is on right in Daffin Park.
Standard Game Times: 7:05 pm, Sat 6:05, Sun 2:05. **Ticket Price Range:** $7-10.
Visiting Club Hotel: Fairfield Inn & Suites, 2 Lee Blvd, Savannah, GA 31405. **Telephone:** (912) 351-9150.

WEST VIRGINIA POWER

Office Address: 601 Morris St, Suite 201, Charleston, WV 25301.
Telephone: (304) 344-2287. **Fax:** (304) 344-0083.
E-Mail Address: info@wvpower.com. **Website:** www.wvpower.com.
Affiliation (first year): Pittsburgh Pirates (2009). **Years in League:** 1987-

OWNERSHIP/MANAGEMENT

Operated By: West Virginia Baseball, LLC.
Managing Partner: Tim Wilcox.
General Manager: Tim Mueller. **Assistant GM, Marketing:** Kristin Call. **Assistant GM, Operations:** Jeremy Taylor. **Accountant:** Darren Holstein. **Box Office Manager:** Nikki Mirth. **Director, Food/Beverage:** Nate Michel. **Director, Media Relations:** Adam Marco. **Director, Tickets:** Kevin Buffalino. **Event Planner:** Will Bell. **Groundskeeper:** Brent Szarka. **Production Manager:** Jay Silverman.

FIELD STAFF

Manager: Michael Ryan. **Coach:** Orlando Merced. **Pitching Coach:** Jeff Johnson. **Trainer:** Phillip Mastro.

GAME INFORMATION

Radio Announcer: Adam Marco. **No. of Games Broadcast:** Home-70, Away-70. **Flagship Stations:** ESPN 104.5 FM, WSWW 1490-AM.
PA Announcer: Unavailable. **Official Scorer:** Unavailable.
Stadium Name: Appalachian Power Park. **Location:** I-77 South to Capitol Street exit, left on Lee Street, left on Brooks Street. **Standard Game Times:** 7:05 pm, Sun 2:05. **Ticket Price Range:** $6-9.
Visiting Club Hotel: Holiday Inn and Suites- Charleston West, 400 Second Avenue SW, South Charleston, WV 25303. **Telephone:** (304) 744-4641.

NEW YORK-PENN LEAGUE

Mailing Address: 6161 MLK Street North, Suite 205, St Petersburg, FL 33703.
Telephone: (727) 289-7112. **Fax:** (727) 683-9691.
Website: www.newyork-pennleague.com.
Years League Active: 1939-

President: Ben J Hayes.
President Emeritus: Robert F Julian. **Treasurer:** Jon Dandes (Jamestown). **Secretary:** Doug Estes.
Directors: Tim Bawmann (Lowell), Steve Cohen (Brooklyn), Jon Dandes (Jamestown), Aaron Moszer (Aberdeen), David Daum (Auburn), Bill Gladstone (Tri-City), Marvin Goldklang (Hudson Valley), Chuck Greenberg (State College), Kyle Bostick (Vermont), Michael Savit (Mahoning Valley), Miles Prentice (Connecticut), Naomi Silver (Batavia), Glenn Reicin (Staten Island), Paul Velte (Williamsport).
Office Manager: Laurie Hayes. **Media Intern:** Ben Prueitt. **League Historian:** Charles Wride.
Division Structure: McNamara-Aberdeen, Brooklyn, Hudson Valley, Staten Island. Pinckney-Auburn, Batavia, Jamestown, Mahoning Valley, State College, Williamsport. Stedler-Lowell, Connecticut, Tri-City, Vermont.
Regular Season: 76 games. **2013 Opening Date:** June 17. **Closing Date:** Sept 4.
All-Star Game: Aug 13 at Connecticut. **Playoff Format:** Division winners and wild-card team meet in best-of-three semifinals. Semifinal winners meet in best-of-three series for league championship. **Roster Limit:** 30 active, but only 25 may be in uniform and eligible to play in any given game. **Player Eligibility Rule:** No more than four players 23 or older; no more than three players on active list may have four or more years of prior service. **Brand of Baseball:** Rawlings. **Umpires:** Unavailable.

Ben Hayes

STADIUM INFORMATION

Club	Stadium	Opened	Dimensions LF	CF	RF	Capacity	2012 Att.
Aberdeen	Ripken Stadium	2002	310	400	310	6,000	244,974
Auburn	Falcon Park	1995	330	400	330	2,800	55,810
Batavia	Dwyer Stadium	1996	325	400	325	2,600	33,443
Brooklyn	KeySpan Park	2001	315	412	325	7,500	249,009
Connecticut	Dodd Stadium	1995	309	401	309	6,270	58,086
Hudson Valley	Dutchess Stadium	1994	325	400	325	4,494	161,811
Jamestown	Russell E. Diethrick Jr. Park	1941	335	410	353	3,324	36,078
Lowell	Edward LeLacheur Park	1998	337	400	301	4,842	168,239
Mahoning Valley	Eastwood Field	1999	335	405	335	6,000	109,956
State College	Medlar Field at Lubrano Park	2006	325	399	320	5,412	129,588
Staten Island	Richmond County Bank Ballpark	2001	325	400	325	6,500	141,163
Tri-City	Joseph L. Bruno Stadium	2002	325	400	325	5,000	159,966
Vermont	Centennial Field	1922	323	405	330	4,000	89,977
Williamsport	Bowman Field	1923	345	405	350	4,200	62,901

ABERDEEN IRONBIRDS

Office Address: 873 Long Drive, Aberdeen, MD 21001.
Telephone: (410) 297-9292. **Fax:** (410) 297-6653.
E-Mail Address: info@ironbirdsbaseball.com. **Website:** www.ironbirdsbaseball.com.
Affiliation (first year): Baltimore Orioles (2002). **Years in League:** 2002-

OWNERSHIP/MANAGEMENT
Operated By: Ripken Professional Baseball LLC.
Principal Owner: Cal Ripken Jr. **Co-Owner/Executive Vice President:** Bill Ripken.
General Manager: Aaron Moszer. **Assistant GM:** Kari Rumfield. **Director, Ticket Operations:** Brad Cox. **Director, Retail Merchandising:** Don Eney. **Video Production Manager:** Jason Vaughn. **Manager, Facilities:** Steve Fairbaugh. **Head Groundskeeper:** Patrick Coakley.

FIELD STAFF
Manager: Matt Merullo. **Coaches:** Jon Mathews. **Pitching Coach:** Alan Mills.

GAME INFORMATION
Radio Announcer: Unavailable. **No. of Games Broadcast:** Home-38, Away-38. **Flagship Station:** MiLB.com.

PA Announcer: Unavailable. **Official Scorer:** Unavailable.
Stadium Name: Ripken Stadium. **Location:** I-95 to exit 85 (Route 22), west on 22 West, right onto Long Drive.
Ticket Price Range: $7-16.

AUBURN DOUBLEDAYS

Office Address: 130 N Division St, Auburn, NY 13021.
Telephone: (315) 255-2489. **Fax:** (315) 255-2675.
E-Mail Address: info@auburndoubledays.com.
Website: www.auburndoubledays.com.
Affiliation (first year): Washington Nationals (2011). **Years in League:** 1958-80, 1982-

OWNERSHIP/MANAGEMENT
Operated by: Auburn Community Non-Profit Baseball Association Inc.
President: David Daum. **General Manager:** Adam Winslow.

FIELD STAFF
Manager: Gary Cathcart. **Coach:** Luis Ordaz. **Pitching Coach:** Sam Narron.

GAME INFORMATION
Radio Announcer: Graham Doty. **No of Games Broadcast:** Away-38. **Flagship Station:** Unavailable.
Stadium Name: Falcon Park. **Location:** I-90 to exit 40, right on Route 34 for 8 miles to York Street, right on York, left on North Division Stareet. **Standard Game Times:** 7 pm. **Ticket Price Range:** $5-8. **Visiting Club Hotel:** Unavailable.

BATAVIA MUCKDOGS

Office Address: Dwyer Stadium, 299 Bank St, Batavia, NY 14020.
Telephone: (585) 343-5454. **Fax:** (585) 343-5620.
E-Mail Address: tsick@muckdogs.com. **Website:** www.muckdogs.com.
Affiliation (first year): Miami Marlins (2013). **Years in League:** 1939-53, 1957-59, 1961-

OWNERSHIP/MANAGEMENT
Operated By: Red Wings Management, LLC.
General Manager: Travis Sick. **Assistant GM:** Mike Ewing. **Director, Stadium Operations:** Don Rock. **Director, Merchandise:** Barbara Moore. **Clubhouse Manager:** John Versage.

FIELD STAFF
Manager: Angel Espada. **Hitting Coach:** Rich Arena. **Pitching Coach:** Brendan Sagara. **Trainer:** Michael Bibbo.

GAME INFORMATION
Radio Announcer: Matthew Coller. **No. of Games Broadcast:** Home-38 Away-20. **Flagship Station:** WBTA 1490-AM.
PA Announcer: Wayne Fuller. **Official Scorer:** Paul Bisig.
Stadium Name: Dwyer Stadium. **Location:** I-90 to exit 48, left on Route 98 South, left on Richmond Avenue, left on Bank Street. **Standard Game Times:** 7:05 pm, Sun 1:05/5:05. **Ticket Price Range:** $5.50-7.50.
Visiting Club Hotel: Days Inn of Batavia, 200 Oak St, Batavia, NY 14020. **Telephone:** (585) 344-6000.

BROOKLYN CYCLONES

Office Address: 1904 Surf Ave, Brooklyn, NY 11224.
Telephone: (718) 37-BKLYN. **Fax:** (718) 449-6368.
E-Mail Address: info@brooklyncyclones.com. **Website:** www.brooklyncyclones.com.
Affiliation (first year): New York Mets (2001). **Years in League:** 2001-

OWNERSHIP/MANAGEMENT
Chairman, CEO: Fred Wilpon.
President: Saul Katz. **COO:** Jeff Wilpon.
General Manager: Steve Cohen. **Assistant GM:** Kevin Mahoney.
Director, Communications: Billy Harner. **Director, New Business Development:** Gary J Perone. **Manager, Ticket Operations:** Greg Conway. **Graphics Manager:** Kevin Jimenez. **Operations Manager:** Vladimir Lipsman. **Community Relations Manager:** Josh Mevorach. **Manager, Marketing/Promotions:** Dan Pecoraro. **Head Groundskeeper:** Kevin Ponte. **Community Outreach/Promotions:** King Henry. **Account Executives:** Danny Diaz, Nicole Kneessy, Craig Coughlin, Madison Gallagher, Josh Hernandez, Ricky Viola. **Staff Accountant:** Tatiana Isdith. **Administrative Assistant, Community Relations:** Sharon Lundy-Ross.

FIELD STAFF
Manager: Rich Donnelly. **Coach:** Bobby Malek. **Pitching Coach:** Marc Valdes.

GAME INFORMATION

Radio Announcer: Unavailable. **No. of Games Broadcast:** Home-38, Away-38. **Flagship Station:** WKRB 90.3-FM. **PA Announcer:** Mark Frotto. **Official Scorer:** Tom Emberley.
Stadium Name: MCU Park. **Location:** Belt Parkway to Cropsey Ave South, continue on Cropsey until it becomes West 17th St, continue to Surf Ave, stadium on south side of Surf Ave; By subway, west/south to Stillwell Ave./Coney Island station. **Ticket Price Range:** $8-17.
Visiting Club Hotel: Holiday Inn Express, 279 Butler Street, Brooklyn, NY 11217. **Telephone:** (718) 855-9600.

CONNECTICUT TIGERS

Office Address: 14 Stott Avenue, Norwich, CT 06360.
Mailing Address: 14 Stott Avenue, Norwich, CT 06360.
Telephone: (860) 887-7962. **Fax:** (860) 886-5996.
E-Mail Address: info@cttigers.com. **Website:** www.cttigers.com.
Affiliation (first year): Detroit Tigers (1999). **Years in League:** 1966-

OWNERSHIP/MANAGEMENT

Operated By: Oneonta Athletic Corp.
President: Miles Prentice. **Vice President/General Manager:** CJ Knudsen. **VP/Assistant GM:** Eric Knighton. **Director, Community Relations/Promotions:** Dave Schermerhorn. **Director, Concessions/Merchandise:** Heather Bartlett. **Director, Facilities/Turf Management:** Bryan Barkley. **Box Office Manager:** Josh Postler. **Group Sales Manager:** Jack Kasten. **Group Sales Account Executive:** Kano Kinnaman.

FIELD STAFF

Manager: Andrew Graham. **Coach:** Mike Rabelo. **Pitching Coach:** Mark Johnson. **Trainer:** Jason Schwartzmann.

GAME INFORMATION

Radio: Jon Versteeg, Eric Knighton. **PA Announcer:** Ed Weyant. **Official Scorer:** Chris Cote. **Stadium Name:** Dodd Stadium. **Location:** Exit 82 off I-395. **Standard Game Times:** 7:05 pm, Sun 4:05. **Ticket Price Range:** $7-20.

HUDSON VALLEY RENEGADES

Office Address: Dutchess Stadium, 1500 Route 9D, Wappingers Falls, NY 12590.
Mailing Address: PO Box 661, Fishkill, NY 12524.
Telephone: (845) 838-0094. **Fax:** (845) 838-0014.
E-Mail Address: info@hvrenegades.com. **Website:** www.hvrenegades.com.
Affiliation (first year): Tampa Bay Rays (1996). **Years in League:** 1994-.

OWNERSHIP/MANAGEMENT

Operated by: Keystone Professional Baseball Club Inc.
Principal Owner: Marv Goldklang. **President:** Jeff Goldklang.
Senior Vice President/General Manager: Eben Yager.
VP/Assistant GM: Corey Whitted. **Assistant GM:** Kristen Huss. **Director, Special Events:** Rick Zolzer. **Director, Stadium Operations:** Tom Hubmaster. **Director, Baseball Communications:** Joe Ausanio. **Director, Business Operations:** Vicky DeFreese. **Director, Corporate Partnerships:** Andy Willmert. **Director, Group Sales:** Sean Kammerer. **Manager, Community Marketing/Communications:** Corinne Adams. **Manager, New Business Development:** Dave Neff. **Manager, Stadium Operations:** Kyle Mondschein. **Director, Food/Beverage:** Chris Yager. **Head Groundskeeper:** Time Merante. **Community Relations Specialist:** Bob Outer.

FIELD STAFF

Manager: Mike Johns. **Bench Coach:** Dan DeMent. **Pitching Coach:** Steve Watson. **Trainer:** Brian Newman.

GAME INFORMATION

Radio Announcer: Unavailable. **No. of Games Broadcast:** Home-38, Away-38.
Flagship Stations: WBNR 1260-AM/WLNA 1420-AM. **PA Announcer:** Rick Zolzer. **Official Scorers:** Unavailable.
Stadium Name: Dutchess Stadium. **Location:** I-84 to exit 11 (Route 9D North), north one mile to stadium.
Standard Game Times: 7:05 pm, Sun 5:05.
Visiting Club Hotel: Days Inn, 20 Schuyler Blvd and Route 9, Fishkill, NY 12524. **Telephone:** (845) 896-4995.

JAMESTOWN JAMMERS

Office Address: 485 Falconer St, Jamestown, NY 14701.
Mailing Address: PO Box 638, Jamestown, NY 14702.
Telephone: (716) 664-0915. **Fax:** (716) 664-4175.
E-Mail Address: email@jamestownjammers.com. **Website:** www.jamestownjammers.com.
Affiliation (first year): Pittsburgh Pirates (2013). **Years in League:** 1939-57, 1961-73, 1977-.

OWNERSHIP/MANAGEMENT
Operated By: Rich Baseball Operations.
President: Robert Rich Jr. **Chief Operating Officer:** Jonathon Dandes.
General Manager: Matthew Drayer. **Assistant GM:** John Pogorzelski. **Head Groundskeeper:** Josh Waid.

FIELD STAFF
Manager: Dave Turgeon. **Coach:** Kory DeHaan. **Pitching Coach:** Mike Steele.

GAME INFORMATION
Radio: Unavailable.
PA Announcer: Unavailable. **Official Scorers:** Jim Riggs, Scott Eddy.
Stadium Name: Russell E Diethrick Jr Park. **Location:** From I-90, south on Route 60, left on Buffalo Street, left on Falconer Street. **Standard Game Times:** 7:05 pm, Sun 6:05. **Ticket Price Range:** $5-7.
Visiting Club Hotel: Red Roof Inn, 1980 Main St, Falconer, NY 14733. **Telephone:** (716) 665-3670.

LOWELL SPINNERS

Office Address: 450 Aiken St, Lowell, MA 01854.
Telephone: (978) 459-2255. **Fax:** (978) 459-1674.
E-Mail Address: info@lowellspinners.com. **Website:** www.lowellspinners.com.
Affiliation (first year): Boston Red Sox (1996). **Years in League:** 1996-

OWNERSHIP/MANAGEMENT
Operated By: Diamond Action Inc.
Owner/CEO: Drew Weber.
President/General Manager: Tim Bawmann. **VP, Business Operations:** Brian Lindsay. **VP/Controller:** Patricia Harbour. **VP, Corporate Communications:** Jon Goode. **VP, Stadium Operations:** Dan Beaulieu. **Director, Facility Management:** Gareth Markey. **Director, Media Relations:** Jon Boswell. **Director, Merchandising:** Jeff Cohen. **VP, Group Ticketing:** Jon Healy. **Director, Ticket Operations:** Justin Williams. **Director, Game Day Entertainment:** Matt Steinberg. **Head Groundskeeper:** Jeff Paolino. **Director, Creative Services:** Jarrod FitzGerald. **Clubhouse Manager:** Del Christman. **Marketing Assistant:** Matt Berthiaume. **Assistant Comptroller:** Taylor Gillette. **Concession Assistant:** Ronnie Wallace.

FIELD STAFF
Manager: Bruce Crabbe. **Hitting Coach:** Noah Hall. **Pitching Coach:** Walter Miranda. **Athletic Trainer:** Satoshi Kajiyama.

GAME INFORMATION
Radio Announcer: John Leahy. **No. of Games Broadcast:** Home-38 Away-38. **Flagship Station:** WCAP 980-AM.
PA Announcers: Mike Riley, George Brown. **Official Scorer:** David Rourke.
Stadium Name: Edward A LeLacheur Park. **Location:** From Route 495 and 3, take exit 35C (Lowell Connector), follow connector to exit 5B (Thorndike Street) onto Dutton Street, left onto Father Morrissette Boulevard, right on Aiken Street. **Standard Game Times:** 7:05 pm. **Ticket Price Range:** $6-10.
Visiting Club Hotel: Radisson of Chelmsford, 10 Independence Dr, Chelmsford, MA 01879. **Telephone:** (978) 356-0800.

MAHONING VALLEY SCRAPPERS

Office Address: 111 Eastwood Mall Blvd, Niles, OH 44446.
Telephone: (330) 505-0000. **Fax:** (303) 505-9696.
E-Mail Address: info@mvscrappers.com. **Website:** www.mvscrappers.com.
Affiliation (first year): Cleveland Indians (1999). **Years in League:** 1999-

OWNERSHIP/MANAGEMENT
Operated By: HWS Baseball Group.
Managing General Partner: Michael Savit.
General Manager: Jordan Taylor. **Assistant GM, Marketing:** Heather Sahil. **Director, Sales:** Matt Thompson.

MINOR LEAGUES

Manager, Box Office/Merchandise: Stephanie Novak. **Director, Stadium Operations:** Brad Hooser. **Group Sales Manager:** Chris Sumner. **Head Groundskeeper:** Matt Rollins.

FIELD STAFF
Manager: Ted Kubiak. **Coach:** Shaun Larkin. **Pitching Coach:** Juan Alvarez.

GAME INFORMATION
Radio Announcer: Unavailable. **No. of Games Broadcast:** Home-38, Away-38. **Flagship Station:** 1570 WHTX. **PA Announcer:** Unavailable. **Official Scorer:** Craig Antush.
Stadium Name: Eastwood Field. **Location:** I-80 to 11 North to 82 West to 46 South; stadium located behind Eastwood Mall. **Ticket Price Range:** $5-11.
Visiting Club Hotel: Days Inn & Suites, 1615 Liberty St, Girard, OH 44429. **Telephone:** (330) 759-9820.

STATE COLLEGE SPIKES

Office Address: 112 Medlar Field, Lubrano Park, University Park, PA 16802.
Telephone: (814) 272-1711. **Fax:** (814) 272-1718.
Website: www.statecollegespikes.com.
Affiliation (first year): St. Louis Cardinals (2013). **Years in League:** 2006-.

OWNERSHIP/MANAGEMENT
Operated By: Spikes Baseball LP.
Chairman/Managing Partner: Chuck Greenberg.
Senior Vice President/General Manager: Jason Dambach.
VP, Sales: Scott Walker. **Director, Ticket Sales:** Kris McDonough. **Director, Promotions/Community Relations:** David Wells. **Director, Ballpark Operations:** Dan Petrazzolo. **Accounting Manager:** Karen Mahon. **Specialist, Accounting/Business Operations:** Steve Christ. **Ticket Account Executives:** Will West, Colby Miller. **Senior Sales Executive:** Steve Kassimer. **Sports Turf Manager:** Matt Neri.

FIELD STAFF
Manager: Oliver Marmol. **Hitting Coach:** Ramon Ortiz. **Pitching Coach:** Dernier Orozco. **Trainer:** Dan Martin.

GAME INFORMATION
Radio Announcers: Steve Jones, Joe Putnam. **No of Games Broadcast:** Home-38 Road-38. **Flagship Station:** WZWW 95.3-FM. **PA Announcer:** Jeff Brown. **Official Scorers:** Dave Baker, John Dixon, Justin Fraker.
Stadium Name: Medlar Field at Lubrano Park. **Location:** From west, US 322 to Mount Nittany Expressway, I-80 to exit 158 (old exit 23/Milesburg), follow Route 150 South to Route 26 South;From east, I-80 to exit 161 (old exit 24/Bellefonte) to Route 26 South or US 220/I-99 South. **Standard Game Times:** 7:05 pm, Sun 6:05. **Ticket Price Range:**$6-14.
Visiting Club Hotel: Ramada Conference Center State College, 1450 Atherton St, State College, PA 16801.Telephone: (814) 238-3001.

STATEN ISLAND YANKEES

Stadium Address: 75 Richmond Terrace, Staten Island, NY 10301.
Telephone: (718) 720-9265. **Fax:** (718) 273-5763.
Website: www.siyanks.com.
Affiliation (first year): New York Yankees (1999). **Years in League:** 1999-

OWNERSHIP/MANAGEMENT
Principal Owners: Nostalgic Partners.
President/General Manager: Jane Rogers.
Finance Manager: Tom Phillips. **Senior VP, Corporate Partnerships:** Kerry Atkinson. **VP, Ticket Sales:** Brian Levine. **Director, Ticket Sales/Operations:** Matt Gulino. **Assistant Director, Entertainment:** Mike Katz. **Managers, Sponsor Services:** Kerry Haley, Jill Wright. **Manager, Ticket Operations:** Matt Gulino. **Coordinator, Sales/Marketing:** Melissa Loughran. **Sales Executives:** John DeLuca, Evan Doyle, Tim Holder, Zach Johnston, Matthew Magnani, Steve McCann, Joe Mola, Kevin Ertel.

FIELD STAFF
Manager: Justin Pope. **Hitting Coach:** Ty Hawkins. **Pitching Coach:** Carlos Chantres. **Coach:** Danilo Valiente.

GAME INFORMATION
Radio Announcer: Unavailable. **No. of Games Broadcast:** Home-38, Away-38. **Flagship Station:** Unavailable. **PA Announcer:** Unavailable. **Official Scorer:** Unavailable.
Stadium Name: Richmond County Bank Ballpark at St George. **Location:** From I-95, take exit 13E (1-278 and Staten Island), cross Goethals Bridge, stay on I-278 East and take last exit before Verrazano Narrows Bridge, north on Father Cappodanno Boulevard, which turns into Bay Street, which goes to ferry terminal; ballpark next to Staten Island Ferry Terminal. **Standard Game Times:** 7 pm, Sun 4. **Visiting Club Hotel:** Unavailable.

TRI-CITY VALLEYCATS

Office Address: Joseph L Bruno Stadium, 80 Vandenburg Ave, Troy, NY 12180.
Mailing Address: PO Box 694, Troy, NY 12181.
Telephone: (518) 629-2287. **Fax:** (518) 629-2299.
E-Mail Address: info@tcvalleycats.com. **Website:** www.tcvalleycats.com.
Affiliation (first year): Houston Astros (2002). **Years in League:** 2002-

OWNERSHIP/MANAGEMENT

Operated By: Tri-City ValleyCats Inc.
Principal Owners: Martin Barr, John Burton, William Gladstone, Rick Murphy, Alfred Roberts, Stephen Siegel.
President: William Gladstone.
Vice President/General Manager: Rick Murphy. **Assistant GM:** Matt Callahan. **Fan Development/Community Relations Manager:** Michelle Skinner. **Stadium Operations Manager:** Keith Sweeney. **Media Relations Manager:** Chris Chenes. **Account Executives:** Ryan Burke, Chris Dawson, Michael Johnson, Phil Carr. **Food/Beverage Coordinator:** Dianna Blanchard. **Box Office Manager:** Jessica Kaszeta. **Accountant:** Ryun Girmindl.

FIELD STAFF

Manager: Ed Romero. **Hitting Coach:** Russ Steinhorn. **Pitching Coach:** Doug White. **Trainer:** Michael Rendon.

GAME INFORMATION

Radio Announcer: Unavailable. **No. of Games Broadcast:** Home-38. **Flagship Station:** MiLB.com.
PA Announcer: Anthony Pettograsso. **Official Scorer:** Unavailable.
Stadium Name: Joseph L Bruno Stadium. **Location:** From north, I-87 to exit 7 (Route 7), go east 1 1/2 miles to I-787 South, to Route 378 East, go over bridge to Route 4, right to Route 4South, one mile to Hudson Valley Community College campus on left; From south, I-87 to exit 23 (I-787), I-787 north six miles to exit for Route 378 east, over bridge to Route 4, right to Route 4 South, one mile to campus on left; Fromeast, Massachusetts Turnpike to exit B-1 (I-90), nine miles to Exit 8 (Defreestville), left off ramp to Route 4 North, five miles to campus on right; From west, I-90 to exit 24 (I-90 East), I-90 East for six miles to I-787 North (Troy), 2.2 miles to exit for Route 378 East, over bridge to Route 4, right to Route 4 south for one mile to campus on left. **Standard Game Times:** 7 pm, Sun 5. **Ticket Price Range:** $5-10.
Visiting Club Hotel: Travelodge, 831 New Loudon Road, Latham, NY 12110

VERMONT LAKE MONSTERS

Office Address: 1 King Street Ferry Dock, Burlington, VT 05401.
Telephone: (802) 655-4200. **Fax:** (802) 655-5660.
E-Mail Address: info@vermontlakemonsters.com. **Website:** www.vermontlakemonsters.com.
Affiliation (first year): Oakland Athletics (2011). **Years in League:** 1994-

OWNERSHIP/MANAGEMENT

Operated by: Vermont Expos Inc.
Principal Owner/President: Ray Pecor Jr. **Vice President:** Kyle Bostwick. **General Manager:** Nate Cloutier. **Assistant GM:** Joe Doud. **Accounts Manager/Merchandise Director:** Kate Echo. **Director, Business Operations:** Carney Daniels Jr. **Manager, Box Office:** Adam Matth. **Director, Fan Development/Promotions:** Lindsay Simmons. **Director, Media Relations:** Paul Stanfield. **Clubhouse Operations:** Phil Schelzo.

FIELD STAFF

Manager: Rick Magnante. **Hitting Coach:** Lloyd Turner. **Pitching Coach:** Craig Lefferts.

GAME INFORMATION

Radio Announcers: Chris Villani. **No. of Games Broadcast:** Home-38, Away-12. **Flagship Station:** 960 The Zone.
Stadium Name: Centennial Field. **Location:** I-89 to exit 14W, right on East Avenue for one mile, right at Colchester Avenue. **Standard Game Times:** 7:05 pm. **Ticket Price Range:** $5-8.
Visiting Club Hotel: Unavailable.

WILLIAMSPORT CROSSCUTTERS

Office Address: Bowman Field, 1700 W Fourth St, Williamsport, PA 17701.
Mailing Address: PO Box 3173, Williamsport, PA 17701.
Telephone: (570) 326-3389. **Fax:** (570) 326-3494.
E-Mail Address: mail@crosscutters.com. **Website:** www.crosscutters.com.
Affiliation (first year): Philadelphia Phillies (2007). **Years in League:** 1968-72, 1994-

OWNERSHIP/MANAGEMENT

Operated By: Geneva Cubs Baseball Inc.
Principal Owners: Paul Velte, John Schreyer.
President: Paul Velte. **Executive Vice President:** John Schreyer.
VP/General Manager: Doug Estes. **VP, Marketing/Public Relations:** Gabe Sinicropi. **Director, Concessions:** Bill Gehron. **Director, Ticket Operations/Community Relations:** Sarah Budd. **Director, Partner Services:** Jennifer Lorson.

FIELD STAFF

Manager: Nelson Prada. **Coach:** Lino Connell. **Pitching Coach:** Les Lancaster.

GAME INFORMATION

Radio Announcer: Todd Bartley. **No. of Games Broadcast:** Home-38, Away-38. **Flagship Station:** WLYC 1050-AM, 104.1-FM.
PA Announcer: Rob Thomas. **Official Scorer:** Ken Myers.
Stadium Name: Bowman Field. **Location:** From south, Route 15 to Maynard Street, right on Maynard, left on Fourth Street for one mile; From north, Route 15 to Fourth Street, left on Fourth. **Ticket Price Range:** $5-$8.
Visiting Club Hotel: Best Western, 1840 E Third St, Williamsport, PA 17701. **Telephone:** (570) 326-1981.

NORTHWEST LEAGUE

Mike Ellis

Office Address: 140 N Higgins Ave, No. 211, Missoula, MT, 59802.
Mailing Address: 140 N Higgins Ave, No. 211, Missoula, MT, 59802.
Telephone: (406) 541-9301. **Fax:** (406) 543-9463.
E-Mail Address: mellisnwl@aol.com. **Website:** www.northwestleague.com.
Years League Active: 1954-.
President/Treasurer: Mike Ellis.
Vice President: Dave Elmore (Eugene). **Corporate Secretary:** Jerry Walker (Salem-Keizer).
Directors: Dave Elmore (Eugene), Bobby Brett (Spokane), Tom Volpe (Everett), Jake Kerr (Vancouver), Mike McMurray (Hillsboro), Brent Miles (Tri-City), Jerry Walker (Salem-Keizer), Neil Leibman (Boise). **Administrative Assistant:** Judy Ellis.
Division Structure: South—Boise, Hillsboro, Eugene, Salem-Keizer. North—Everett, Spokane, Tri-City, Vancouver.
Regular Season: 76 games (split schedule).
2013 Opening Date: June 14. **Closing Date:** Sept 2. **Playoff Format:** First-half division winners meet second-half division winners in best-of-three series. Winners meet in best-of-three series for league championship. **All-Star Game:** Aug 6, in Everett.
Roster Limit: 30 active, 35 under control. **Player Eligibility Rule:** No more than three players on active list may have four or more years of prior service.
Brand of Baseball: Rawlings.
Umpires: Unavailable.

STADIUM INFORMATION

Club	Stadium	Opened	Dimensions			Capacity	2012 Att.
			LF	CF	RF		
Boise	Memorial Stadium	1989	335	400	335	3,426	91,167
Eugene	PK Park	2010	335	400	325	4,000	115,569
Everett	Everett Memorial Stadium	1984	324	380	330	3,682	95,929
* Hillsboro	Hillsboro Ballpark	2013	325	400	325	N/A	61,895
Salem-Keizer	Volcanoes Stadium	1997	325	400	325	4,100	101,785
Spokane	Avista Stadium	1958	335	398	335	7,162	183,458
Tri-City	Dust Devils Stadium	1995	335	400	335	3,700	86,095
Vancouver	Nat Bailey Stadium	1951	335	395	335	6,500	162,162

* Team relocates from Yakima, Wash.

BOISE HAWKS

Office Address: 5600 N Glenwood St Boise, ID 83714.
Telephone: (208) 322-5000. **Fax:** (208) 322-6846.
Website: www.boisehawks.com.
Affiliation (first year): Chicago Cubs (2001). **Years in League:** 1975-76, 1978, 1987-

OWNERSHIP/MANAGEMENT

Operated by: Boise Baseball LLC.
CEO: Neil Leibman.
President/General Manager: Todd Rahr.
Vice President/Business Operations: Dina Rahr. **VP, Sales:** Jinny Giery. **Sponsorship Sales Manager:** JD Bowers. **Ticket Sales Manager:** Brandon White. **Group Sales Assistant:** Dustin Gochenour. **Community Outreach/Event Manager:** Elizabeth Griffin. **Communications Manager:** Courtney Garner. **Creative Services/Brand Manager:** Kelly Kerkvliet. **Manager, Broadcast/Baseball Information:** Mike Safford. **Grounds Crew Manager:** Chuck Barto. **Stadium Operations Manager:** Raymond Stone. **Food Services Manager:** Geno George.

FIELD STAFF

Manager: Gary Van Tol. **Coach:** Bill Buckner. **Pitching Coach:** David Rosario. **Trainer:** Jonathan Fierro.

GAME INFORMATION

Radio Announcer: Mike Safford. **No. of Games Broadcast:** Home-38, Away-38.
Flagship Station: KTIK 1350-AM. **PA Announcer:** Unavailable. **Official Scorer:** Unavailable.
Stadium Name: Memorial Stadium. **Location:** I-84 to Cole Road, north to Western Idaho Fairgrounds at 5600 North Glenwood Street. **Standard Game Time:** 7:15 pm. **Ticket Price Range:** $6-14.
Visiting Club Hotel: Unavailable.

EUGENE EMERALDS

Office Address: 2760 Martin Luther King Jr Blvd, Eugene, OR 97401.
Mailing Address: PO Box 10911, Eugene, OR 97440.
Telephone: (541) 342-5367. **Fax:** (541) 342-6089.
E-Mail Address: info@emeraldsbaseball.com. **Website:** www.emeraldsbaseball.com.
Affiliation (first year): San Diego Padres (2001). **Years in League:** 1955-68, 1974-

OWNERSHIP/MANAGEMENT

Operated By: Elmore Sports Group Ltd.
Principal Owner: David Elmore.
General Manager: Allan Benavides.
Assistant GM: Sarah Heth. **Director, Corporate Sales:** Matt Dompe. **Director, Food/Beverage:** Kelly Hallquest. **Director, Mascot Operations:** Teigh Bowen. **Director, Finance:** Andy Hoedt. **Director, Tickets:** Fei Li. **Director, Corporate Events:** Tyler Tostenson. **Graphic Designer:** Danny Crowley.

FIELD STAFF

Manager: Jim Gabella. **Coach:** Ivan Cruz. **Pitching Coach:** Dave Rajsich.

GAME INFORMATION

Radio Announcer: Matt Dompe. **No. of Games Broadcast:** Home-38, Away-38. **Flagship Station:** 95.3—The Score.
PA Announcer: Ted Welker. **Official Scorer:** George McPherson.
Stadium Name: PK Park. **Standard Game Time:** 7:05 pm, Sun 1:05. **Ticket Price Range:** $6-12.
Visiting Club Hotel: Holiday Inn, 919 Kruse Way, Springfield, OR, 97477. **Telephone:** (541) 284-0707.

EVERETT AQUASOX

Mailing Address: 3802 Broadway, Everett, WA 98201.
Telephone: (425) 258-3673. **Fax:** (425) 258-3675.
E-Mail Address: info@aquasox.com. **Website:** www.aquasox.com.
Affiliation (first year): Seattle Mariners (1995). **Years in League:** 1984-

OWNERSHIP/MANAGEMENT

Operated by: 7th Inning Stretch, LLC
Directors: Tom Volpe, Pat Filippone.
Executive Vice President: Tom Backemeyer. **VP, Corporate Sponsorships:** Brian Sloan. **Director, Corporate Partnerships/Broadcasting:** Pat Dillon. **Director, Food/Beverage:** Nick Reuter. **Director, Community Relations:** Katie Crawford. **Director, Tickets:** Alex Dadisman. **Account Executives:** Alex Dadisman, Joe Haller, Erica Fensterbush, Duncan Jensen. **Head Groundskeeper:** Brian Burroughs.

FIELD STAFF

Manager: Rob Mummau. **Hitting Coach:** Rafael Santo Domingo. **Pitching Coach:** Rich Dorman. **Trainer:** Spyder Webb.

GAME INFORMATION

Radio Announcer: Pat Dillon. **No. of Games Broadcast:** Home-38, Away-38. **Flagship Station:** KRKO 1380-AM.
PA Announcer: Tom Lafferty. **Official Scorer:** Pat Castro.
Stadium Name: Everett Memorial Stadium. **Location:** I-5, exit 192. **Standard Game Times:** 7:05 pm, Sun 1:05/4:05.
Ticket Price Range: $7-17.
Visiting Club Hotel: Holiday Inn, Downtown Everett, 3105 Pine St, Everett, WA 98201. **Telephone:** (425) 339-2000.

HILLSBORO HOPS

Office Address: 6125 NE Cornell Road, Hillsboro, OR, 97124.
Mailing Address: 22115 NW Imbrie Dr, #223, Hillsboro, OR, 97124.
Telephone: (503) 640-0887.
E-Mail Address: info@hillsborohops.com. **Website:** www.hillsborohops.com.
Affiliation (first year): Arizona Diamondbacks (2001). **Years in League:** 1955-66, 1990-

OWNERSHIP/MANAGEMENT

Operated by: Short Season LLC.
Managing Partners: Mike McMurray, Mark Mays, Josh Weinman, Myron Levin.
President: Mike McMurray.
General Manager: KL Wombacher. **Assistant GM:** Aaron Arndt. **Chief Financial Officer:** Laura McMurray. **Director, Ballpark Operations:** Jared Jacobs. **Director, Merchandise:** Lauren Wombacher. **Director, Media Relations/Broadcasting:** John Hadden.

FIELD STAFF

Manager: Audo Vicente. **Hitting Coach:** JR House. **Pitching Coach:** Doug Drabek.

GAME INFORMATION

Stadium Name: Hillsboro Ballpark. **Location:** 4460 NW 229th, Hillsboro, OR, 97124. **Standard Game Times:** 7:05 pm, Sun 1:35. **Ticket Price Range:** $7-$16.
Visiting Club Hotel: Unavailable.

SALEM-KEIZER VOLCANOES

Street Address: 6700 Field of Dreams Way, Keizer, OR 97303.
Mailing Address: PO Box 20936, Keizer, OR 97307.
Telephone: (503) 390-2225. **Fax:** (503) 390-2227.
E-Mail Address: ticket_office@volcanoesbaseball.com. **Website:** www.volcanoesbaseball.com.
Affiliation (first year): San Francisco Giants (1997). **Years in League:** 1997-

OWNERSHIP/MANAGEMENT

Operated By: Sports Enterprises Inc.
Principal Owners: Jerry Walker, Bill Tucker.
General Manager: Jerry Walker. **Vice President, Operations:** Rick Nelson. **Senior Account Executive:** Jerry Howard. **Director, Ticket Office Operations:** Bea Howard. **Corportate Marketing Executive:** Michael Trevino. **Outside Sales Executive:** Marc Kaufman. **Director, Business Development:** Justin Lacche. **Director, Group Sales/Assistant Ticket Office Manager:** Jeff Turner.

FIELD STAFF

Manager: Gary Davenport. **Coach:** Ricky Ward. **Pitching Coach:** Jerry Cram. **Coach:** Hector Borg.

GAME INFORMATION

Radio Announcer: Rob Schreier. **No. of Games Broadcast:** Home-38, Away-38. **Flagship Station:** KBZY AM-1490.
PA Announcer: Michael Trevino. **Official Scorer:** Scott Sepich.
Stadium Name: Volcanoes Stadium. **Location:** I-5 to exit 260 (Chemawa Road), west one block to Stadium Way NE, north six blocks to stadium. **Standard Game Times:** 6:35 pm, Sun 5:05. **Ticket Price Range:** $7-11.
Visiting Club Hotel: Comfort Suites, 630 Hawthorne Ave SE, Salem, OR 97301. **Telephone:** (503) 585-9705.

SPOKANE INDIANS

Office Address: Avista Stadium, 602 N Havana, Spokane, WA 99202.
Mailing Address: PO Box 4758, Spokane, WA 99220.
Telephone: (509) 535-2922. **Fax:** (509) 534-5368.
E-Mail Address: mail@spokaneindiansbaseball.com. **Website:** www.spokaneindiansbaseball.com.
Affiliation (first year): Texas Rangers (2003). **Years in League:** 1972, 1983-

OWNERSHIP/MANAGEMENT

Operated By: Longball Inc.
Principal Owner: Bobby Brett. **Co-Owner/Senior Advisor:** Andrew Billig.
Vice President/General Manager: Chris Duff.
Senior VP: Otto Klein. **VP, Tickets:** Josh Roys. **Director, Business Operations:** Lesley DeHart. **Corporate Sponsorship Account Executive:** Jon Luke. **Promotions Coordinators:** Kyle Day, Alex Capeloto. **Group Sales Coordinators:** Nick Gaebe, Cody Rettinghouse. **Director, Concessions/Operations:** Justin Stottlemyre. **Director, Public Relations:** Bud Bareither. **CFO:** Greg Sloan. **Director, Accounting:** Dawnelle Shaw. **Head Groundskeeper:** Tony Lee. **Assistant Director, Stadium Operations:** Larry Blumer.

FIELD STAFF

Manager: Tim Hulett. **Hitting Coach:** Bobby Rose. **Pitching Coach:** Oscar Marin. **Coach:** Vinny Lopez. **Strength/Conditioning Coach:** Ed Yong. **Trainer:** Sean Fields.

GAME INFORMATION

Radio Announcer: Mike Boyle. **No. of Games Broadcast:** Home-38, Away-38. **Flagship Station:** 1510 KGA.
PA Announcer: Unavailable. **Official Scorer:** Peter Legner
Stadium Name: Avista Stadium at the Spokane Fair and Expo Center. **Location:** From west, I-90 to exit 283B (Thor/Freya), east on Third Avenue, left onto Havana; From east, I-90 to Broadway exit, right onto Broadway, left onto Havana. **Standard Game Time:** 6:30 pm, Sun 3:30. **Ticket Price Range:** $5-13.
Visiting Club Hotel: Mirabeau Park Hotel & Convention Center, N 1100 Sullivan Rd, Spokane, WA 99037. **Telephone:** (509) 924-9000.

TRI-CITY DUST DEVILS

Office Address: 6200 Burden Blvd, Pasco, WA 99301.
Telephone: (509) 544-8789. **Fax:** (509) 547-9570.
E-Mail Address: info@dustdevilsbaseball.com.
Website: www.dustdevilsbaseball.com.
Affiliation (first year): Colorado Rockies (2001). **Years in League:** 1955-1974, 1983-1986, 2001-

OWNERSHIP/MANAGEMENT

Operated by: Northwest Baseball Ventures.
Principal Owners: George Brett, Hoshino Dreams Corp, Brent Miles.
President: Brent Miles. **Vice President/General Manager:** Derrel Ebert. **VP, Business Operations:** Tim Gittel.
Assistant GM, Tickets: Dan O'Neill. **Director, Sponsorships:** Anne Brenner. **Group Sales Manager:** Andrew Klein.
Ticket Operations Manager: Austin Redman. **Group Services Manager:** Sam Spuhler. **Promotions Coordinator:** Heath Harshman. **Director, Concessions:** Pat Dorer. **Stadium Operations Coordinator:** Trevor Shively. **Head Groundskeeper:** Michael Angel.

FIELD STAFF

Manager: Drew Saylor. **Hitting Coach:** Warren Schaeffer. **Pitching Coach:** Frank Gonzales. **Trainer:** Casey Papas.

GAME INFORMATION

Radio Announcer: Chris King. **No. of Games Broadcast:** Home-38, Away-38. **Flagship Station:** Newstalk 870 AM KFLD.
PA Announcer: Patrick Harvey. **Official Scorers:** Tony Wise, Scott Tylinski. **Stadium Name:** Gesa Stadium. **Location:** I-182 to exit 9 (Road 68), north to Burden Blvd, right to stadium. **Standard Game Time:** 7:15 pm. **Ticket Price Range:** $6-9.
Visiting Club Hotel: Red Lion Hotel-Columbia Center, 1101 N Columbia Center Blvd, Kennewick, WA 99336. **Telephone:** (509) 783-0611

VANCOUVER CANADIANS

Office Address: Scotiabank Field at Nat Bailey Stadium, 4601 Ontario St, Vancouver, British Columbia V5V 3H4.
Telephone: (604) 872-5232. **Fax:** (604) 872-1714.
E-Mail Address: staff@canadiansbaseball.com. **Website:** www.canadiansbaseball.com.
Affiliation (first year): Toronto Blue Jays (2011). **Years in League:** 2000-

OWNERSHIP/MANAGEMENT

Operated by: Vancouver Canadians Professional Baseball LLP.
Principal Owners: Jake Kerr, Jeff Mooney. **President:** Andy Dunn.
General Manager: Jason Takefman. **Assistant GMs:** Rob Fai, JC Fraser, Allan Bailey. **VP, Sales/Marketing:** Graham Wall. **Manager, Sales/Promotions:** Grace Kim. **Coordinator, Sales/Community Relations:** Vanessa Williams. **Manager, Community Relations:** Jeff Holloway. **Financial Controller:** Eric Gounder. **Head Groundskeeper:** Tom Archibald.
Groundskeeper: Trevor Sheffield.

FIELD STAFF

Manager: Clayton McCullough. **Hitting Coach:** Dave Pano. **Pitching Coach:** Jim Czajkowski. **Trainer:** Regie Mungrue.

GAME INFORMATION

Radio Announcer: Rob Fai. **No. of Games Broadcast:** Home-38, Away-38. **Flagship Station:** The Team 1040-AM.
PA Announcer: Don Andrews. **Official Scorer:** Unavailable.
Stadium Name: Nat Bailey Stadium. **Location:** From downtown, take Cambie Street Bridge, left on East 25th Ave./King Edward Ave, right on Main Street, right on 33rd Ave, right on Ontario St to stadium; From south, take Highway 99 to Oak Street, right on 41st Ave, left on Main Street to 33rd Ave, right on Ontario St to stadium.
Standard Game Times: 7:05 pm, Sun 1:05. **Ticket Price Range:** $9-20.
Visiting Club Hotel: Accent Inns, 10551 Edwards Dr, Richmond, BC V6X 3L8. **Telephone:** (604) 273-3311.

APPALACHIAN LEAGUE
of professional baseball clubs

ROOKIE ADVANCED

Mailing Address: 759 182nd Avenue E, Redington Shores, FL 33708.
Telephone: 704-252-2656. **Fax:** None.
E-Mail Address: office@appyleague.net. **Website:** www.appyleague.com.
Years League Active: 1921-25, 1937-55, 1957-.
President/Treasurer: Lee Landers. **Corporate Secretary:** Jim Holland (Princeton).
Directors: Charlie Wilson (Bluefield), Nick Capra (Bristol), Scott Sharp (Burlington), Ronnie Richardson (Danville), Brad Steil(Elizabethton), Fred Nelson Quentin McCracken (Greeneville), Jon Vuch (Johnson City), Jon Miller (Kingsport), Mitch Lukevics (Princeton), Chris Gwynn (Pulaski).
Executive Committee: Wayne Carpenter (Pulaski), Ronnie Richardson (Atlanta), David Lane (Greeneville), Dan Moushon (Burlington), Jon Vuch (St. **Louis), Charlie Wilson (Toronto)**
Board of Trustee: Mitch Lukevics (Tampa Bay).
League Administrator: Bobbi Landers.
Division Structure: East—Bluefield, Burlington, Danville, Princeton, Pulaski. **West—Bristol, Elizabethton, Greeneville, Johnson City, Kingsport.**
Regular Season: 68 games. **2013 Opening Date:** June 20. **Closing Date:** Aug 30.
All-Star Game: None.

Lee Landers

Playoff Format: First round (best of three): East winner versus East second place; West winner versus West second place. Winners meet in best-of-three series for league championship.
Roster Limit: 30 active, 35 under control. **Player Eligibility Rule:** No more than three players on the active roster may have three or more years of prior minor league service.
Brand of Baseball: Rawlings.
Umpires: Unavailable

STADIUM INFORMATION

| Club | Stadium | Opened | Dimensions | | | Capacity | 2012 Att. |
			LF	CF	RF		
Bluefield	Bowen Field	1939	335	400	335	2,250	23,890
Bristol	DeVault Memorial Stadium	1969	325	400	310	2,000	23,387
Burlington	Burlington Athletic Stadium	1960	335	410	335	3,000	33,501
Danville	Dan Daniel Memorial Park	1993	330	400	330	2,588	27,628
Elizabethton	Joe O'Brien Field	1974	335	414	326	1,500	25,430
Greeneville	Pioneer Park	2004	331	400	331	2,400	42,303
Johnson City	Howard Johnson Field	1956	320	410	320	2,500	24,827
Kingsport	Hunter Wright Stadium	1995	330	410	330	2,500	26,408
Princeton	Hunnicutt Field	1988	330	396	330	1,950	26,110
Pulaski	Calfee Park	1935	335	405	310	2,500	25,301

BLUEFIELD BLUE JAYS

Office Address: Stadium Drive, Bluefield, WV 24701.
Mailing Address: PO Box 356, Bluefield, WV 24701.
Telephone: (304) 324-1326. **Fax:** (304) 324-1318.
E-Mail Address: babybirds1@comcast.net. **Website:** www.bluefieldjays.com.
Affiliation (first year): Toronto Blue Jays (2011). **Years in League:** 1946-55, 1957-

OWNERSHIP/MANAGEMENT
Director: Charlie Wilson (Toronto Blue Jays).
Vice President: Bill Looney. **Secretary:** MK Burton. **Counsel:** David Kersey.
President: George McGonagle. **General Manager:** Jeff Gray. **Director, Field Operations/Grounds:** Mike White.

FIELD STAFF
Manager: Dennis Holmberg. **Coach:** Ken Huckaby. **Pitching Coach:** Antonio Caceres.

GAME INFORMATION
Stadium Name: Bowen Field. **Location:** I-77 to Bluefield exit 1, Route 290 to Route 460 West, fourth light right onto Leatherwood Lane, left at first light, past Chevron station and turn right, stadium quarter-mile on left. **Ticket Price Range:** $4.
Visiting Club Hotel: Quality Inn Bluefield, 3350 Big Laurel Highway/460 West, Bluefield, WV 24701. **Telephone:** (304) 325-6170.

BRISTOL WHITE SOX

Ballpark Location: 1501 Euclid Ave, Bristol, VA 24201.
Mailing Address: PO Box 1434, Bristol, VA 24203.
Telephone: (276) 206-9946. **Fax:** (276) 669-7686.
E-Mail Address: brisox@btes.tv. **Website:** www.bristolsox.com.
Affiliation (first year): Chicago White Sox (1995). **Years in League:** 1921-25, 1940-55, 1969-

OWNERSHIP/MANAGEMENT
Owned by: Chicago White Sox.
Operated by: Bristol Baseball Inc.
Director: Buddy Bell (Chicago White Sox).
President/General Manager: Mahlon Luttrell. **Vice Presidents:** Lucas Hobbs, Perry Hustad, Jim Buckles.
Treasurers: Dorothy Cox, Delma Luttrell. **Secretary:** Tim Johnston.

FIELD STAFF
Manager: Bobby Magallanes. **Hitting Coach:** Greg Briley. **Pitching Coach:** Larry Owens. **Trainer:** James Kruk.
Conditioning Coach: Ibrahim Rivera.

GAME INFORMATION
Radio: Internet broadcast through milb.com.
PA Announcer: Unavailable. **Official Scorer:** Perry Hustad.
Stadium Name: DeVault Memorial Stadium. **Location:** I-81 to exit 3 onto Commonwealth Ave, right on Euclid Ave for half-mile. **Standard Game Time:** 7 pm. **Ticket Price Range:** $3-6.
Visiting Club Hotel: Holiday Inn, 3005 Linden Drive Bristol, VA 24202. **Telephone:** (276) 466-4100.

BURLINGTON ROYALS

Office Address: 1450 Graham St, Burlington, NC 27217.
Mailing Address: PO Box 1143, Burlington, NC 27216.
Telephone: (336) 222-0223. **Fax:** (336) 226-2498.
E-Mail Address: info@burlingtonroyals.com. **Website:** www.burlingtonroyals.com
Affiliation (first year): Kansas City Royals (2007). **Years in League:** 1986-

OWNERSHIP/MANAGEMENT
Operated by: Burlington Baseball Club Inc.
Director: Scott Sharp (Kansas City Royals).
President: Miles Wolff. **Vice President:** Dan Moushon.
General Manager: Ben Abzug. **Assistant GM:** Ryan Keur. **Director, Stadium Operations:** Mike Thompson.

FIELD STAFF
Manager: Tommy Shields. **Hitting Coach:** Abraham Nunez. **Pitching Coach:** Carlos Martinez.

GAME INFORMATION
Radio Announcer: Unavailable. **No. of Games Broadcast:** Home-34, Away-7. **Flagship:** www.burlingtonroyals.com.
PA Announcer: Tyler Williams. **Official Scorer:** Unavailable.
Stadium Name: Burlington Athletic Stadium. **Location:** I-40/85 to exit 145, north on Route 100 (Maple Avenue) for 1 1/2 miles, right on Mebane Street for 1 1/2 miles, right on Beaumont, left on Graham. **Standard Game Time:** 7 p.m.
Ticket Price Range: $4-8.

DANVILLE BRAVES

Office Address: Dan Daniel Memorial Park, 302 River Park Dr, Danville, VA 24540.
Mailing Address: PO Box 378, Danville, VA 24543.
Telephone: (434) 797-3792. **Fax:** (434) 797-3799.
E-Mail Address: info@dbraves.com. **Website:** www.dbraves.com.
Affiliation (first year): Atlanta Braves (1993). **Years in League:** 1993-

OWNERSHIP/MANAGEMENT
Operated by: Atlanta National League Baseball Club Inc. **Director:** Ronnie Richardson (Atlanta Braves). **General Manager:** David Cross. **Assistant GM:** Bob Kitzmiller. **Operations Manager:** Brandon Bennett.
Head Groundskeeper: Jon Hall.

FIELD STAFF
Manager: Jonathan Schuerholz. **Coach:** Rick Albert. **Pitching Coach:** Gabe Luckert. **Athletic Trainer:** Joe Luat.

GAME INFORMATION
   Radio Announcer: Nick Pierce. **No. of Games Broadcast:** Home-34 (internet only). **Flagship Station:** www.dbraves. com.
   PA Announcer: Jay Stephens. **Official Scorer:** Mark Bowman.
   Stadium Name: American Legion Field Post 325 Field at Dan Daniel Memorial Park. **Location:** US 29 Bypass to River Park Drive/Dan Daniel Memorial Park exit; follow signs to park. **Standard Game Times:** 7 pm, Sun 4. **Ticket Price Range:** $4-7. **Visiting Club Hotel:** Unavailable.

ELIZABETHTON TWINS

   Office Address: 300 West Mill Street, Elizabethton, TN 37643.
   Stadium Address: 208 N Holly Lane, Elizabethton, TN 37643. **Mailing Address:** 136 S Sycamore St, Elizabethton, TN 37643.
   Telephone: (423) 547-6441. **Fax:** (423) 547-6442.
   E-Mail Address: etwins@cityofelizabethton.org. **Website:** www.elizabethtontwins.com.
   Affiliation (first year): Minnesota Twins (1974). **Years in League:** 1937-42, 1945-51, 1974-

OWNERSHIP/MANAGEMENT
   Operator: City of Elizabethton.
   Director: Jim Rantz (Minnesota Twins).
   President: Harold Mains.
   General Manager: Mike Mains. **Clubhouse Operations/Head Groundskeeper:** David McQueen.

FIELD STAFF
   Manager: Ray Smith. **Coach:** Jeff Reed. **Pitching Coach:** Henry Bonilla. **Trainer:** Curtis Simondet.

GAME INFORMATION
   Radio Announcer: Unavailable. **No. of Games Broadcast:** Home-34, Away-6. **Flagship Station:** WBEJ 1240-AM.
   PA Announcer: Tom Banks. **Official Scorer:** Whitney Noble.
   Stadium Name: Joe O'Brien Field. **Location:** I-81 to Highway I-26, exit at Highway 321/67, left on Holly Lane. **Standard Game Time:** 7 pm. **Ticket Price Range:** $3-6.
   Visiting Club Hotel: Holiday Inn, 101 W Springbrook Dr, Johnson City, TN 37601. **Telephone:** (423) 282-4611.

GREENEVILLE ASTROS

   Office Address: 135 Shiloh Road, Greeneville, TN 37743.
   Mailing Address: PO Box 5192, Greeneville, TN 37743.
   Telephone: (423) 638-0411. **Fax:** (423) 638-9450.
   E-Mail Address: greeneville@astros.com. **Website:** www.greenevilleastros.com.
   Affiliation (first year): Houston Astros (2004). **Years in League:** 2004-

OWNERSHIP/MANAGEMENT
   Operated by: Houston Astros Baseball Club.
   Director: Quinton McCracken (Houston Astros).
   General Manager: David Lane. **Assistant GM:** Hunter Reed. **Head Groundskeeper:** Tyler Mittesteadt. **Clubhouse Operations:** Unavailable.

FIELD STAFF
   Manager: Josh Bonifay. **Hitting Coach:** Cesar Cedeno. **Pitching Coach:** Josh Miller. **Trainer:** Corey O'Brien.

GAME INFORMATION
   Internet Radio: Steve Wilhoit.
   PA Announcer: Bobby Rader. **Official Scorer:** Johnny Painter.
   Stadium Name: Pioneer Park. **Location:** On the campus of Tusculum College, 135 Shiloh Rd Greeneville, TN 37743.
Standard Game Time: 7 pm, Sat/Sun 6. **Ticket Price Range:** $5-7.
   Visiting Club Hotel: Jameson Inn, 3160 E Andrew Johnson Hwy, Greeneville, TN 37745. **Telephone:** (423) 638-7511.

JOHNSON CITY CARDINALS

Office Address: 111 Legion St, Johnson City, TN 37601.
Mailing Address: PO Box 179, Johnson City, TN 37605.
Telephone: (423) 461-4866. **Fax:** (423) 461-4864.
E-Mail Address: contact@jccardinals.com. **Website:** www.jccardinals.com.
Affiliation (first year): St. Louis Cardinals (1975). **Years in League:** 1911-13, 1921-24, 1937-55, 1957-61, 1964-

OWNERSHIP/MANAGEMENT
Owned by: St. Louis Cardinals.
Operated by: Johnson City Sports Foundation Inc.
President: Lee Sowers (JCSF).
Director: John Vuch (St. Louis Cardinals). **General Manager:** Chuck Arnold. **Assistant GM:** Sean Salemme.

FIELD STAFF
Manager: Joe Kruzel. **Coach:** Roberto Espinoza. **Pitching Coach:** Paul Davis.

GAME INFORMATION
Radio: None.
PA Announcer: Unavailable. **Official Scorer:** Gene Renfro.
Stadium Name: Howard Johnson Field at Cardinal Park. **Location:** I-26 to exit 23, left on East Main, through light onto Legion Street. **Standard Game Time:** 7 pm. **Ticket Price Range:** $4-$6.
Visiting Club Hotel: Holiday Inn, 101 W Springbrook Dr, Johnson City, TN 37601. **Telephone:** (423) 282-4611.

KINGSPORT METS

Office Address: 800 Granby Rd, Kingsport, TN 37660.
Mailing Address: PO Box 1128, Kingsport, TN 37662.
Telephone: (423) 378-3744. **Fax:** (423) 392-8538.
E-Mail Address: info@kmets.com. **Website:** www.kmets.com.
Affiliation (first year): New York Mets (1980). **Years in League:** 1921-25, 1938-52, 1957, 1960-63, 1969-82, 1984-

OWNERSHIP/MANAGEMENT
Operated By: S&H Baseball LLC.
Director: Adam Wogan (New York Mets).
President: Rick Spivey. **Vice President:** Steve Harville. **VP/General Manager:** Brian Paubeck. **Accountant:** Bob Dingus. **Director, Concessions:** Teresa Haywood. **Head Groundskeeper:** Josh Warner. **Clubhouse Manager:** Travis Baker. **Interns:** Mookie Jeter, JT Chadwell.

FIELD STAFF
Manager: Jon Debus. **Coach:** Yunir Garcia. **Pitching Coach:** Jonathan Hurst.

GAME INFORMATION
Radio: None.
PA Announcer: Don Spivey. **Official Scorer:** Eddie Durham.
Stadium Name: Hunter Wright Stadium. **Location:** I-81 to I-181 North, exit 1 (Stone Drive), left on West Stone Drive (US 11W), right on Granby Road. **Standard Game Time:** 6 pm, 7 (doubleheaders). **Ticket Price Range:** $2-5.
Visiting Club Hotel: The Jameson Inn, 3004 Bays Mountain Plaza, Kingsport, TN 37660. **Telephone:** (423) 282-4611.

PRINCETON RAYS

Office Address: 205 Old Bluefield Rd, Princeton, WV 24739.
Mailing Address: PO Box 5646, Princeton, WV 24740.
Telephone: (304) 487-2000. **Fax:** (304) 487-8762.
E-Mail Address: princetonrays@frontier.com . **Website:** www.princetonrays.net.
Affiliation (first year): Tampa Bay Rays (1997). **Years in League:** 1988-

OWNERSHIP/MANAGEMENT

Operated By: Princeton Baseball Association Inc.
Director: Mitch Lukevics (Tampa Bay Rays). **President:** Mori Williams.
General Manager: Jim Holland. **Director, Stadium Operations:** Mick Bayle. **Official Scorer:** Bob Redd. **Graphic Designer:** Warren Hypes. **Clubhouse Manager:** Anthony Dunagan. **Administrative Assistant:** Tommy Thomason. **Chaplain:** Craig Stout.

FIELD STAFF

Manager: Danny Sheaffer. **Coach:** Reinaldo Ruiz. **Pitching Coach:** Darwin Peguero. **Athletic Trainer:** Nick Flynn.

GAME INFORMATION

Radio Announcer: Bobby Iddings. **No. of Games Broadcast:** Home-34, Away-34. **Flagship Station:** WMTD 102.3-FM. **Official Scorer:** Bob Redd.
Stadium Name: Hunnicutt Field. **Location:** Exit 9 off I-77, US 460 West to downtown exit, left on Stafford Drive, stadium located behind Mercer County Technical Education Center. **Standard Game Times:** 7:05 pm, Sun 6:05 pm.
Ticket Price Range: $4-6.
Visiting Club Hotel: Days Inn, I-77 and Ambrose Lane, Princeton, WV 24740. **Telephone:** (304) 425-8100.

PULASKI MARINERS

Shipping Address: 700 South Washington Ave, Pulaski VA 24301.
Mailing Address: PO Box 676, Pulaski, VA 24301.
Telephone: (540) 980-1070. **Fax:** (540) 980-1850.
E-Mail Address: info@pulaskimariners.net.
Affiliation (first year): Seattle Mariners (2008). **Years in League:** 1946-50, 1952-55, 1957-58, 1969-77, 1982-92, 1997-2006, 2008-

OWNERSHIP/MANAGEMENT

Operated By: Pulaski Baseball Inc.
Director: Chris Gwynn (Seattle Mariners).
President: Tom Compton. **General Manager:** Ryan Kiel.

FIELD STAFF

Manager: Chris Prieto. **Hitting Coach:** Scott Steinmann. **Pitching Coach:** Nasusel Cabrera.

GAME INFORMATION

Radio: None.
PA Announcer: Unavailable. **Official Scorer:** Charles Altizer.
Stadium Name: Calfee Park. **Location:** Interstate 81 to Exit 89-B (Route 11), north to Pulaski, right on Pierce Avenue.
Standard Game Times: 7 pm.
Ticket Price Range: $4-6.
Visiting Club Hotel: Comfort Inn, 4424 Cleburne Blvd, Dublin, VA 24084. **Telephone:** (540) 674-1100.

PIONEER LEAGUE

Office Address: 2607 S Southeast Blvd, Building B, Suite 115, Spokane, WA 99223.
Mailing Address: PO Box 2564, Spokane, WA 99220.
Telephone: (509) 456-7615. **Fax:** (509) 456-0136.
E-Mail Address: fanmail@pioneerleague.com. **Website:** www.pioneerleague.com.
Years League Active: 1939-42, 1946-

President: Jim McCurdy.
Directors: Dave Baggott (Ogden), Matt Ellis (Missoula), DG Elmore (Helena), Kevin Greene (Idaho Falls), Michael Baker (Grand Junction), Jeff Katofsky (Orem), Vinny Purpura (Great Falls), Jim Iverson (Billings).
League Administrator: Teryl MacDonald. **Executive Assistant:** Mary Ann McCurdy.
Division Structure: North—Billings, Great Falls, Helena, Missoula. South—Grand Junction, Idaho Falls, Ogden, Orem.
Regular Season: 76 games (split schedule). **2013 Opening Date:** June 20. **Closing Date:** Sept 8.
Playoff Format: First-half division winners meet second-half division winners in best-of-three series. Winners meet in best-of-three series for league championship.
All-Star Game: None.
Roster Limit: 35 active, 30 dressed for each game. **Player Eligibility Rule:** No more than 17 players 21 and older, provided that no more than two are 23 or older (age limits waived). No player on active list may have three or more years of prior minor league service.
Brand of Baseball: Rawlings.
Umpires: Unavailable.

Jim McCurdy

STADIUM INFORMATION

Club	Stadium	Opened	Dimensions LF	CF	RF	Capacity	2012 Att.
Billings	Dehler Park	2008	329	410	350	3,071	112,602
Grand Junction	Sam Suplizio Field	1949	302	400	333	7,014	101,496
Great Falls	Centene Stadium at Legion Park	1956	335	414	335	3,800	66,106
Helena	Kindrick Field	1939	335	400	325	1,700	33,428
Idaho Falls	Melaleuca Field	1976	340	400	350	3,400	89,812
Missoula	Ogren Park at Allegiance Field	2004	309	398	287	3,500	89,812
Ogden	Lindquist Field	1997	335	396	334	5,000	123,625
Orem	Home of the Owlz	2005	305	408	312	4,500	87,392

BILLINGS MUSTANGS

Office Address: Dehler Park, 2611 9th Avenue North, Billings, MT 59101.
Mailing Address: PO Box 1553, Billings, MT 59103.
Telephone: (406) 252-1241. **Fax:** (406) 252-2968.
E-Mail Address: mustangs@billingsmustangs.com. **Website:** www.billingsmustangs.com .
Affiliation (first year): Cincinnati Reds (1974). **Years in League:** 1948-63, 1969-

OWNERSHIP/MANAGEMENT
Operated By: Billings Pioneer Baseball Club
President: Woody Hahn.
General Manager: Gary Roller. **Senior Director, Corporate Sales/Partnerships:** Chris Marshall. **Senior Director, Broadcasting/Media Relations:** Ryan Schuiling. **Senior Director, Food/Beverage Services:** Curt Prchal. **Senior Director, Field Maintenance/Facilities:** John Barta.

FIELD STAFF
Manager: Pat Kelly. **Hitting Coach:** Kevin Mahar. **Pitching Coach:** Tom Browning. **Strength/Conditioning Coach:** Rigo Febles. **Athletic Trainer:** Clete Sigwart.

GAME INFORMATION
Radio Broadcaster: Ryan Schuiling. **No. of Games Broadcast:** Home-38, Away-38. **Flagship Station:** KYSX 105.1 FM.
PA Announcer: Kyle Riley. **Official Scorer:** Matt Schoonover.
Stadium Name: Dehler Park. **Location:** I-90 to Exit 450, north on 27th Street North to 9th Avenue North.
Standard Game Times: 7:05 pm, Sun 2:05. **Ticket Price Range:** $3-9.
Visiting Club Hotel: Crowne Plaza, 27 N 27th St, Billings, MT, 59101. **Telephone:** (406) 252-7400.

GRAND JUNCTION ROCKIES

Office Address: 1315 North Ave, Grand Junction, CO 81501.
Telephone: (970) 255-7625. Fax: (970) 241-2374.
E-Mail Address: timray@gjrockies.com. Website: www.gjrockies.com.
Affiliation (first year): Colorado Rockies (2001). Years in League: 2001-

OWNERSHIP/MANAGEMENT

Principal Owners/Operated by: GJR LLC.
General Manager: Tim Ray. Assistant GM: Mike Ruvolo. Operations Manger: Stephanie Garcia-Hays.

FIELD STAFF

Manager: Anthony Sanders. Hitting Coach: Lee Stevens. Pitching Coach: Ryan Kibler. Trainer: Josh Guperman.

GAME INFORMATION

Radio Announcer: Unavailable. No. of Games Broadcast: Home-38, Away-38. Flagship Station: KNAM 92.3 FM..
Official Scorer: Dan Kenyon.
Stadium Name: Mike Lansing Field. Location: 1315 North Ave, Grand Junction, CO 81501.
Standard Game Times: 7:05 pm, Sun 2:05. Ticket Price Range: $7-10.
Visiting Club Hotel: Unavailable.

GREAT FALLS VOYAGERS

Office Address: 1015 25th St N, Great Falls, MT 59401.
Mailing Address: 1015 25th St N, Great Falls, MT 59401.
Telephone: (406) 452-5311. Fax: (406) 454-0811.
E-Mail Address: voyagers@gfvoyagers.com. Website: www.gfvoyagers.com.
Affiliation (first year): Chicago White Sox (2003). Years in League: 1948-1963, 1969-

OWNERSHIP/MANAGEMENT

Operated By: Great Falls Baseball Club, Inc.
President: Vinney Purpura.
General Manager: Kattie Meyer. Assistant GM: Scott Reasoner. Ticket Sales Manager: Kelly Wombacher.

FIELD STAFF

Manager: Pete Rose Jr. Coach: Charlie Poe. Pitching Coach: Brian Drahman.

GAME INFORMATION

Radio Announcer: Unavailable. No. of Games Broadcast: Home-38, Away-38. Flagship Station: Unavailable.
PA Announcer: Lance DeHaan. Official Scorer: Mike Lewis.
Stadium Name: Centene Stadium located at Legion Park. Location: From I-15 to exit 281 (10th Ave S), left on 26th, left on Eighth Ave North, right on 25th, ballpark on right, past railroad tracks. Ticket Price Range: $4-9.
Visiting Club Hotel: Quality Inn, 220 Central Ave N Great Falls, MT 59401. Telephone: (406) 761-3410.

HELENA BREWERS

Office Address: 1300 N Ewing, Helena, MT 59601.
Mailing Address: PO Box 6756, Helena, MT 59604.
Telephone: (406) 495-0500. Fax: (406) 495-0900.
E-Mail Address: info@helenabrewers.net. Website: www.helenabrewers.net.
Affiliation (first year): Milwaukee Brewers (2003). Years in League: 1978-2000, 2003-

OWNERSHIP/MANAGEMENT

Operated by: Helena Baseball Club LLC.
Principal Owner: DG Elmore.
General Manager: Paul Fetz. Director, Operations/Ticketing: Morgan Halpert. Director, Group Sales/Marketing: Nick Allen. Radio Announcer/Director, Broadcasting/Media Relations: Steve Wendt.

FIELD STAFF

Manager: Tony Diggs. Hitting Coach: Dwayne Hosey. Pitching Coach: Elvin Nina. Trainer: Unavailable.

GAME INFORMATION

Radio Announcer: Steve Wendt. No. of Games Broadcast: Home-38, Away-38. Flagship Station: KCAP 1340-AM.
PA Announcer: Randy Bowsher. Official Scorers: Kevin Higgens, Craig Struble, Jim Shope, Andrew Gideon.
Stadium Name: Kindrick Field. Location: Cedar Street exit off I-15, west to Last Chance Gulch, left at Memorial Park.
Standard Game Time: 7:05 pm, Sun 1:05. Ticket Price Range: $6-9.
Visiting Club Hotel: Red Lion Colonial. Telephone: 406-443-2100.

IDAHO FALLS CHUKARS

Office Address: 900 Jim Garchow Way, Idaho Falls, ID 83402.
Mailing Address: PO 2183, Idaho, ID 83403.
Telephone: (208) 522-8363. Fax: (208) 522-9858.
E-Mail Address: chukars@ifchukars.com. Website: www.ifchukars.com.
Affiliation (first year): Kansas City Royals (2004). Years in League: 1940-42, 1946-

OWNERSHIP/MANAGEMENT
Operated By: The Elmore Sports Group.
Principal Owner: David Elmore.
President/General Manager: Kevin Greene. Assistant GM, Merchandise: Andrew Daugherty.
Account Manager/Food Service Specialist: Paul Henderson. Clubhouse Manager: Josh Dibiase. Head Groundskeeper: Chris Sundvold.

FIELD STAFF
Manager: Omar Ramirez. Hitting Coach: Damon Hollins. Pitching Coach: Steve Merriman.

GAME INFORMATION
Radio Announcers: John Balginy, Aaron Cox. No. of Games Broadcast: Home-38 Road-38. Flagship Station: KUPI/ESPN 980-AM.
Official Scorer: John Balginy.
Stadium Name: Melaleuca Field. Location: I-15 to West Broadway exit, left onto Memorial Drive, right on Mound Avenue, 1/4 mile to stadium. Standard Game Times: 7:15 pm, Sun 4. Ticket Price Range: $6-9.
Visiting Club Hotel: Guesthouse Inn & Suites, 850 Lindsay Blvd, Idaho Falls, ID 83402. Telephone: (208) 522-6260.

MISSOULA OSPREY

Office Address: 140 N Higgins, Suite 201, Missoula, MT 59802.
Telephone: (406) 543-3300. Fax: (406) 543-9463.
E-Mail Address: info@missoulaosprey.com. Website: www.missoulaosprey.com.
Affiliation (first year): Arizona Diamondbacks (1999). Years in League: 1956-60, 1999-

OWNERSHIP/MANAGEMENT
Operated By: Mountain Baseball LLC.
President: Mike Ellis. Vice President: Judy Ellis.
Executive VP: Matt Ellis. VP, Finance/Merchandising: Shelly Ellis. GM/Operations: Jared Amoss. GM/Sales/Marketing: Jeff Griffin. Office Manager: Nola Hunter.

FIELD STAFF
Manager: Robby Hammock. Hitting Coach: Wilson Valera. Pitching Coach: Doug Bochtler. Strength/Conditioning: Sean Light. Trainer: Unavailable.

GAME INFORMATION
Radio Announcer: Ben Catley. No. of Games Broadcast: Home-38, Away-38. Flagship Station: KMPT 930-AM.
PA Announcer: Dan Stromme. Official Scorer: Dan Hunter, David Kinsey.
Stadium Name: Ogren Park at Allegiance Field. Location: 700 Cregg Lane. Directions: Take Orange Street to Cregg Lane, west on Cregg Lane, stadium west of McCormick Park. Standard Game Times: 7:05 pm, Sun 5:05. Ticket Price Range: $6-12.
Visiting Club Hotel: America's Best Value Inn, 420 W. Broadway, Missoula, Mt 59802. Telephone: (406) 728-4500

OGDEN RAPTORS

Office Address: 2330 Lincoln Ave, Ogden, UT 84401.
Telephone: (801) 393-2400. Fax: (801) 393-2473.
E-Mail Address: homerun@ogden-raptors.com. Website: www.ogden-raptors.com.
Affiliation (first year): Los Angeles Dodgers (2003). Years in League: 1939-42, 1946-55, 1966-74, 1994-

OWNERSHIP/MANAGEMENT
Operated By: Ogden Professional Baseball, Inc.
Principal Owners: Dave Baggott, John Lindquist.
President/General Manager: Dave Baggott.
Director Media Relations/Broadcaster: Brandon Hart. Director Stadium Operations/Merchandise: Geri Kopinski. Director, Food Service Personnel: Louise Hillard. Director, Security: Mark Ramsey. Director, Ticket Operations: Kylie Johnson. Director, Information Technology: Chris Greene. Public Relations: Pete Diamond. Groundskeeper: Kenny Kopinski. Assistant Groundskeeper: Bob Richardson.

FIELD STAFF

Manager: Damon Berryhill. **Hitting Coach:** Esteban Lopez. **Pitching Coach:** Scott Radinsky.

GAME INFORMATION

Radio Announcer: Brandon Hart. **No. of Games Broadcast:** Home-38, Away-38. **Flagship Station:** 97.5 FM.
PA Announcer: Pete Diamond. **Official Scorer:** Dennis Kunimura.
Stadium Name: Lindquist Field. **Location:** I-15 North to 21th Street exit, east to Lincoln Avenue, south three blocks to park. **Standard Game Times:** 7 pm, 4 pm (Sun). **Ticket Price Range:** $4-10.
Visiting Club Hotel: Unavailable.

OREM OWLZ

Office Address: 970 W University Parkway, Orem, UT 84058.
Telephone: (801) 377-2255. **Fax:** (801) 377-2345.
E-Mail Address: fan@oremowlz.com. **Website:** www.oremowlz.com.
Affiliation (first year): Los Angeles Angels (2001). **Years in League:** 2001-

OWNERSHIP/MANAGEMENT

Operated By: Bery Bery Gud To Me LLC.
Principal Owner: Jeff Katofsky.
General Manager: Unavailable. **Assistant General Manager:** Jillian Dingee. **IT Manager:** Julie Hatch. **Director, Ticket Office Manager/Group Sales:** Barry Winterton. **Director, Broadcasting/Media Relations:** Unavailable.

FIELD STAFF

Manager: Unavailable. **Hitting Coach:** Carson Vitale. **Pitching Coach:** Chris Gissell. **Trainer:** Matt Morrell.

GAME INFORMATION

Radio Announcer: Unavailable. **No. of Games Broadcast:** Home-38, Away-38. **Flagship Station:** Unavailable.
PA Announcer: Unavailable. **Official Scorer:** Unavailable.
Stadium Name: Home of the Owlz. **Location:** Exit 269 (University Parkway) off I-15 at Utah Valley University campus.
Ticket Price Range: $4-10.
Visiting Club Hotel: Courtyard Marriott 1600 N Freedom Blvd, Provo, UT 84604, (801)-373-2222

ARIZONA LEAGUE

Office Address: 620 W Franklin St, Boise, ID 83702.
Mailing Address: PO Box 1645, Boise, ID 83701.
Telephone: (208) 429-1511. **Fax:** (208) 429-1525. **E-Mail Address:** bobrichmond@qwestoffice.net
Years League Active: 1988-.
President/Treasurer: Bob Richmond.
Vice President: Tim Purpura (Rangers). **Corporate Secretary:** Ted Polakowski (Athletics).
Administrative Assistant: Rob Richmond.
Division Structure: East/Central/West divisions.
2013 Opening Date: June 20. **Closing Date:** Aug 29. **Regular Season:** 56 games. **Playoffs:** Aug 30, first half vs. **second half winners. Semifinals:** Aug 31. **Championship:** Sept 1. **Playoff Format:** Division champions from the first- and second-half of the season qualify. The two teams with the best overall records receive first-round bye and will meet first-round winners in the semifinals. Winners advance to a one-game championship. **All-Star Game:** None.
Roster Limit: 35 active. **Player Eligibility Rule:** No player may have three or more years of prior minor league service.
Brand of Baseball: Rawlings. **Standard Game Times:** 7 pm..

Clubs	Playing Site	Manager	Coach	Pitching Coach
Angels	Angels complex, Tempe	Denny Hocking	R. Barba/B. Betancourth	Matt Wise
Athletics	Papago Park Baseball Complex, Phoenix	Marcus Jensen	Juan Dilone	Carlos Chavez
Brewers	Maryvale Baseball Complex, Phoenix	Nestor Corredor	Unavailable	Steve Cline
Cubs	Fitch Park, Mesa	Bobby Mitchell	R Medina/J Gonzalez	Anderson Tavarez
D-backs	Salt River Fields at Talking Stick	Luis Urueta	Mark Grace	Jeff Bajenaru
Dodgers	Camelback Ranch, Glendale	P.J. Forbes	Leo Garcia	Kremlin Martinez
Giants	Giants complex, Scottsdale	Nestor Rojas	Billy Horton	L. McCall/Z. Zimmerman
Indians	Goodyear Ballpark	Anthony Medrano	J. Betances/D. Malave	S. Erickson/D. Swanson
Mariners	Peoria Sports Complex	Darrin Garner	Andy Bottin	Cibney Bello
Padres	Peoria Sports Complex	Michael Collins	Carlos Sosa	Nelson Cruz
Rangers	Surprise Recreation Campus	Corey Ragsdale	D. McDonald/B. Shouse	Jose Jaimes
Reds	Goodyear Ballpark	Eli Marrero	Luis Bolivar	D. Ebert/E. Dessens
Royals	Surprise Recreation Campus	Darryl Kennedy	Pedro Grifol	M. Davis/C. Reyes

GULF COAST LEAGUE

Operated By: Minor League Baseball.
Office Address: 9550 16th Street North, St Petersburg, FL 33716.
Telephone: 727-456-1734. **Fax:** 727-821-5819. **Website:** www.milb.com. **Email Address:** gcl@milb.com.
Vice President, Baseball/Business Operations: Tim Brunswick.
Assistant, Baseball Operations: Andy Shultz.
2013 Opening Date: June 21. **Closing Date:** Aug 29. **Regular Season:** 60 Games.
Divisional Alignment: East—Cardinals, Marlins, Mets, Nationals. Northeast—Astros, Braves, Tigers, Yankees 2. Northwest—Blue Jays, Phillies, Pirates, Yankees 1. South—Orioles, Rays, Red Sox, Twins.
Playoff Format: The division winner with the best record plays the division winner with the lowest record and the other two division winners meet in a one game semifinals. Should the Northeast and Northwest Divisions finish as the 1st and 4th division winners, the semifinal matchups would place 1st vs. 3rd and 2nd vs. 4th. The winners meet in a best-of-three series for the Gulf Coast League championship.
All-Star Game: None. **Roster Limit:** 35 active, only 30 of whom may be in uniform and eligible to play in any given game. At least 10 must be pitchers as of July 1. **Player Eligibility Rule:** No player may have three or more years of prior minor league service. **Brand of Baseball:** Rawlings. **Statistician:** Major League Baseball Advanced Media.

Clubs	Playing Site	Manager	Coach(es)	Pitching Coach
Astros	Astros Complex, Kissimmee	Edgar Alfonzo	Marty Malloy	Hector Mercado
Blue Jays	Mattick Training Center, Dunedin	John Schneider	P. Elliott/D. Solano	Dave Williams
Braves	ESPN Wide World of Sports, Orlando	Rocket Wheeler	Carlos Mendez	Willie Martinez
Cardinals	Cardinals Complex, Jupiter	Steve Turco	Jobel Jimenez	Darwin Marrero
Marlins	Roger Dean Stadium Complex, Jupiter	Julio Garcia	Bobby Bell	Jeremy Powell
Mets	Mets Complex, Port St Lucie	Jose Carreno	Ender Chavez	Unavailable
Nationals	Nationals Complex, Viera	Patrick Anderson	Amaury Garcia	Michael Tejera
Orioles	Ed Smith Stadium Complex, Sarasota	Orlando Gomez	Milt May	Wilson Alvarez
Phillies	Carpenter Complex, Clearwater	Roly DeArmas	R. Henderson/R. DeLima	Steve Schrenk
Pirates	Pirate City, Bradenton	Milver Reyes	M. Lum/W. Huyke	Miguel Bonilla
Rays	Charlotte Sports Park, Port Charlotte	Jim Morrison	W. Rincones/H. Torres	Marty DeMerritt
Red Sox	Jet Blue Park, Fort Myers	Darren Fenster	R. Gonzalez/D. Tomlin	T. Kotchman/D. Such
Tigers	Tigertown, Lakeland	Basilio Cabrera	Nelson Santovenia	Jorge Cordova
Twins	Lee County Sports Complex, Fort Myers	Ramon Borrego	R. Ingram/R. Hernandez	Ehren Wassermann
Yankees 1	Himes Complex, Tampa	Tom Nieto	E. Gonzalez/M. Hernandez	Jose Rosado
Yankees 2	Himes Complex, Tampa	Mario Garza	D. Henson/T. Chapman	Tim Norton

INDEPENDENT LEAGUES

AMERICAN ASSOCIATION

Office Address: 1415 Hwy 54 West, Suite 210, Durham, NC 27707.
Telephone: (919) 401-8150. **Fax:** (919) 401-8152. **Website:** www.americanassociationbaseball.com.
Year Founded: 2005.
Commissioner: Miles Wolff. **President:** Dan Moushon.
Director, Umpires: Kevin Winn.
Division Structure—North Division: Fargo-Moorhead RedHawks, St. Paul Saints, Sioux Falls Pheasants, Winnipeg Goldeyes.
Central Division: Gary SouthShore RailCats, Kansas City T-Bones, Lincoln Saltdogs, Sioux City Explorers, Wichita Wingnuts.
South Division: Amarillo Sox, El Paso Diablos, Grand Prairie AirHogs, Laredo Lemurs.
Regular Season: 100 games.
2013 Opening Date: May 16. **2012 Closing Date:** September 2.
Playoff Format: Three division winners and one wild card play in best-of-five series. Winners play for best-of-five American Association Championship.
Roster Limit: 22.
Eligibility Rule: Minimum of four first-year players; maximum of five veterans (at least six or more years of professional service).
Brand of Baseball: Rawlings.
Statistician: Pointstreak.com, 602-1595 16th Avenue, Richmond Hill, ON Canada L4B 3N9.

STADIUM INFORMATION

Club	Stadium	Opened	LF	CF	RF	Capacity	2012 Att.
Amarillo	Amarillo National Bank Sox Stadium	1949	355	429	355	7,500	133,380
El Paso	Cohen Stadium	1990	340	410	340	9,725	181,122
Fargo-Moorhead	Newman Outdoor Field	1996	314	408	318	4,513	187,438
Gary SouthShore	U.S. Steel Yard	2002	320	400	335	6,139	159,837
Grand Prairie	QuikTrip Park at Grand Prairie	2008	330	400	330	5,445	108,236
Kansas City	CommunityAmerica Ballpark	2003	300	396	328	6,537	260,620
Laredo	Uni-Trade Stadium	2012	335	405	335	6,000	187,845
Lincoln	Haymarket Park	2001	335	395	325	4,500	160,986
St. Paul	Midway Stadium	1982	320	400	320	6,069	240,616
Sioux City	Lewis and Clark Park	1993	330	400	330	3,630	55,627
Sioux Falls	Sioux Falls Stadium	1964	312	410	312	4,608	130,541
Wichita	Lawrence-Dumont Stadium	1934	344	401	312	6,055	152,727
Winnipeg	Shaw Park	1999	325	400	325	7,481	285,263

AMARILLO SOX

Office Address: 801 S Polk St, Amarillo, TX 79101.
Telephone: (806) 242-4653. **Fax:** (806) 322-1839.
E-Mail Address: mark.lee@amarillosox.com. **Website:** www.amarillosox.com.
VP/General Manager: Mark Lee.
Field Manager: Bobby Brown. **Pitching Coach:** Dennis Machado.

GAME INFORMATION
Stadium Name: Amarillo National Bank Sox Stadium. **Location:** Take Grand Street exit and proceed north on Grand Street; turn left onto SE 3rd Ave.
Standard Game Times: 7:05 pm, Sun 6:05.
Visiting Club Hotel: Holiday Inn, 1911 I-40 East, Amarillo, TX 79102. **Telephone:** 806-372-8741.

EL PASO DIABLOS

Office Address: 9700 Gateway North Blvd, El Paso, TX 79924.
Telephone: (915) 755-2000. **Fax:** (915) 757-0671.
E-Mail Address: info@diablos.com. **Website:** www.diablos.com.
Managing Partner/President: Matt LaBranche. **Business Manager:** Pat Hofman. **Director, Corporate Sponsorships:** Bernie Ricono. **Public Relations Director:** Lizette Espinosa. **Box Office Manager:** Steve Martinez. **Marketing & Events Manager:** Henry Quintana III. **Senior Account Executive:** Donna Blair. **Promotions Manager:** Victor Reta.
Manager: Tim Johnson. **Coaches:** Joe Torre, Brian Daley

GAME INFORMATION
Stadium Name: Cohen Stadium. **Location:** I-10 to U.S.54, Diana exit to Gateway North Boulevard.

Standard Game Times: 7:05 pm, Sun 6:05.
Visiting Club Hotel: Unavailable.

FARGO-MOORHEAD
REDHAWKS

Office Address: 1515 15th Ave N, Fargo, ND 58102.
Telephone: (701) 235-6161. **Fax:** (701) 297-9247.
E-Mail Address: redhawks@fmredhawks.com. **Website:** www.fmredhawks.com.
Operated by: Fargo Baseball LLC.
President: Bruce Thom. **Chief Executive Officer:** Brad Thom.
General Manager: Josh Buchholz. **Senior Accountant:** Rick Larson. **Director, Promotions:** Eric Jorgenson. **Director, Ticket Sales/Assistant Director, Marketing:** Michael Larson. **Director, Community Relations/Group Events:** Karl Hoium. **Director, Food/Beverage:** Sean Kiernan. **Account Executive:** Kole Zimmerman. **Head Groundskeeper:** Sam Petersen.
Manager/Director, Player Procurement: Doug Simunic. **Player Procurement Consultant:** Jeff Bittiger. **Pitching Coach:** Steve Montgomery. **Coaches:** Bucky Burgau, Kole Zimmerman. **Trainer:** Craig Brandenburger. **Home Clubhouse Manager:** Isaac Olson. **Visiting Clubhouse Manager:** Chris Krick

GAME INFORMATION

Radio Announcer: Scott Miller. **No. of Games Broadcast:** 100. **Flagship Station:** 740-AM The FAN.
Stadium Name: Newman Outdoor Field. **Location:** I-29 North to exit 67, east on 19th Ave North, right on Albrecht Boulevard. **Standard Game Times:** 7:02 pm, Sat 6, Sun 1.
Visiting Club Hotel: Howard Johnson Inn, 301 3rd Ave N, Fargo, ND 58102. **Telephone:** (701) 232-8850.

GARY SOUTHSHORE RAILCATS

Office Address: One Stadium Plaza, Gary, IN 46402.
Telephone: (219) 882-2255. **Fax:** (219) 882-2259.
E-Mail Address: info@railcatsbaseball.com. **Website:** www.railcatsbaseball.com.
Operated by: PLS Holdings.
Owner/CEO: Pat Salvi. **Owner:** Lindy Salvi.
President/General Manager: Kevin Spudic. **Assistant GM:** Becky Kremer. **Box Office Manager:** Adam Harris. **Director, Stadium Operations:** Nick Lampasona. **Director, Marketing/Promotions:** Natalie Kirby. **Manager, Merchandise:** Laura Blakeley. **Manager, Community Relations:** Radley Robinson. **Manager, Box Office:** Adam Harris. **Manager, Group Sales:** Aaron Pineda. **Account Executive:** Nikki Kimbrough. **Corporate Account Executive:** Percy Thornbor.
Manager, Media Relations/Broadcasting: Matt Friedman. **Graphic Designer:** Domonic Edwards. **Executive Assistant:** Arcella Moxley. **Stadium Maintenance:** Jim Kerr.
Manager: Greg Tagert.

GAME INFORMATION

No. of Games Broadcast: 100. **Flagship Station:** WLPR 89.1-FM.
Stadium Name: US Steel Yard. **Location:** I-80/94 to Broadway Exit (Exit 10), north on Broadway to Fifth Avenue, east one block to stadium. **Standard Game Times:** 7:10 pm, Sat 6:10, Sun 2:10.
Visiting Club Hotel: Radisson Hotel at Star Plaza, 800 East 81st Avenue, Merrillville, IN 46410. **Telephone:** (219) 769-6311.

GRAND PRAIRIE AIRHOGS

Office Address: 1600 Lone Star Parkway, Grand Prairie, TX 75050.
Telephone: (972) 504-9383. **Fax:** (972) 504-2288.
Websites: www.airhogsbaseball.com/www.quiktrippark.com.
Operated By: Southern Independent Baseball, LLC.
Owner: Gary Elliston. **President:** Scott Berry. **Vice President/General Manager:** John Bilbow. **VP, Communications:** David Hatchett. **Manager, Finance/Merchandise:** Trista Earlston. **Director, Ticket Operations:** Jeff Carman. **Director, Ballpark Oeprations:** TD Taylor. **Events Coordinator:** Matt Raffaele. **Director, Food/Beverage:** Chris Moriarty. **Receptionist:** Donna White.
Manager: Ricky VanAsselberg. **Coach:** Barrett Weaver.

GAME INFORMATION

No of Games Broadcast: 100. **Webcast:** www.airhogsbaseball.com.
Stadium Name: QuikTrip Park at Grand Prairie. **Location:** From I-30, take Beltline Road exit going north, take Lone Star Park entrance towards the stadium.

Standard Game Times: 7:05 pm, Sun 6:05.
Visiting Club Hotel: Hawthorn Suites by Wyndham, 2401 Brookhollow Plaza Drive, Arlington, TX 76006. **Telephone:** (817) 640-1188.

KANSAS CITY T-BONES

Office Address: 1800 Village West Parkway, Kansas City, KS 66111.
Telephone: (913) 328-5618. **Fax:** (913) 328-5674.
E-Mail Address: tickets@tbonesbaseball.com.
Website: www.tbonesbaseball.com.
Operated By: T-Bones Baseball Club, LLC; Ehlert Development.
Owner: John Ehlert. **President:** Adam Ehlert.
VP/General Manager: Chris Browne. **Senior Director, Corporate Sales:** Seth Alberg.
Assistant GM, Group Sales: Kurt Sieker. **Director, Media Relations/Press Box:** Matt Fulks. **Director, Promotions:** Emily Hoskins. **Director, Ticket Operations/Box Office Manager:** Jason Young. **Assistant Director, Group Sales:** Brad Holt. **Sales Executive:** Ryan Stos. **Bookkeeper:** Sherrie Stover. **Account Executive, Group Sales:** Jared Reid. **Head Groundskeeper:** Glen Averson. **Director, Broadcasting:** Brian Bruce.
Manager: Kenny Hook. **Coaches:** Frank White, Bill Sobbe, Andy Shipman. **Trainer:** Josh Adams.

GAME INFORMATION
Radio Announcer: Brian Bruce. **No. of Games Broadcast:** 100. **Flagship Station:** KUDL 1660-AM.
Stadium Name: CommunityAmerica Ballpark. **Location:** State Avenue West off I-435 and State Avenue. **Standard Game Times:** 7:05 pm (Mon-Sat), 5:05 pm (Sun).

LAREDO LEMURS

Office Address: 6320 Sinatra Drive, Laredo, TX 78045.
Telephone: (956) 753-6877. **Fax:** (956) 791-0672.
Website: www.laredolemurs.com.
Managing Partner: Mark Schuster.
President: Ruben Navas.
Director, Operations: Chuy Vela-Cuellar. **Corporate Sales:** Susan Gusman, Juan Salinas. **Office Manager/ Receptionist:** Victoria Cardenas. **Group Sales:** Monica Mendiola. **Promotions Coordinator:** Tanyn Walters. **Clubhouse Manager:** Gibby Vela-Cuellar.
Manager: Pete Incaviglia. **Coach:** Bill Bryk, Jr.

GAME INFORMATION
Announcer: Unavailable. **No. of Games Broadcast:** 100. **Webcast:** www.laredolemurs.com.
Stadium Name: Uni-Trade Stadium. **Location:** From North: I-35 to Exit 9 turn left onto Loop 20/Bob Bullock Blvd, south on Loop 20 for 3 miles, make right onto Sinatra Blvd, stadium on left; From South: I-35 to Exit 2 turn right onto Hwy 59 for 4 miles, turn left onto Loop 20 North for 2 miles, turn left onto Sinatra Drive, stadium on left.
Standard Game Times: 7:30 pm.
Visiting Club Hotel: La Posada Inn, 1000 Zaragoza Street, Laredo, TX 78040. **Telephone:** (956) 722-1701.

LINCOLN SALTDOGS

Office Address: 403 Line Drive Circle, Suite A, Lincoln, NE 68508.
Telephone: (402) 474-2255. **Fax:** (402) 474-2254.
E-Mail Address: info@saltdogs.com. **Website:** www.saltdogs.com.
Owner: Jim Abel. **President:** Charlie Meyer.
Vice President/General Manager: Tim Utrup. **Assistant GM/Director, Sales/ Marketing:** Bret Beer. **Director, Broadcasting/Communications:** Drew Bontadelli. **Director, Merchandising/ Promotions:** Anne Duchek. **Director, Season Tickets/Ticket Packages:** Toby Antonson. **Director, Stadium Operations:** Dave Aschwege. **Assistant Director, Stadium Operations:** Jeff Koncaba. **Office Manager:** Alicia Oakeson. **Athletic Turf Manager:** Josh Klute. **Assistant Turf Manager:** Jen Roeber.
Manager: Ken Oberkfell. **Coaches:** John Harris, Dan Reichert.

GAME INFORMATION
Radio Announcer: Drew Bontadelli. **No. of Games Broadcast:** 100. **Flagship Station:** KFOR 1240-AM. **Webcast Address:** www.kfor1240.com.
Stadium Name: Haymarket Park. **Location:** I-80 to Cornhusker Highway West, left on First Street, right on Sun Valley Boulevard, left on Line Drive.
Standard Game Times: 7:05 pm, Sun 5:05 pm.
Visiting Club Hotel: Country Inn & Suites, 5353 N 27th, Lincoln, NE 68521. **Telephone:** (402) 476-5353.

ST. PAUL SAINTS

Office Address: 1771 Energy Park Dr, St Paul, MN 55108.
Telephone: (651) 644-3517. **Fax:** (651) 644-1627.
E-Mail Address: funisgood@saintsbaseball.com.
Website: www.saintsbaseball.com.
Principal Owners: Marv Goldklang, Bill Murray, Mike Veeck. **Chairman:** Marv Goldklang. **President:** Mike Veeck.
Executive Vice President/General Manager: Derek Sharrer. **Executive VP:** Tom Whaley. **Assistant GMs:** Scott Bush, Chris Schwab. **VP, Customer Service/Community Partnerships:** Annie Huidekoper. **Director, Broadcast/Media Relations:** Sean Aronson. **Coordinator Director, Special Events:** Max Huber. **Director, Ticket Services:** Adam Lowler.
Director, New Media/Technology Services: Chelsey Wentz. **Director, Food/Beverage:** Curtis Nachtsheim. **Business Manager:** Leesa Anderson. **Office Manager:** Gina Kray. **Stadium Operations:** Bob Klepperich. **Groundskeeper:** Connie Rudolph.
Manager: George Tsamis. **Coaches:** Lamarr Rogers, Kerry Ligtenerg, TJ Wiesner.

GAME INFORMATION

Radio Announcer: Sean Aronson. **No. of Games Broadcast:** 100. **Flagship Station:** Club 1120 AM. **Webcast Address:** www.saintsbaseball.com.
Stadium Name: Midway Stadium. **Location:** From I-94, take Snelling Avenue North exit, west onto Energy Park Drive.
Standard Game Times: 7:05 pm, Sun 1:05.
Visiting Club Hotel: Crowne Plaza St Paul Riverfront, 11Kellogg Blvd, St Paul MN 55101. **Telephone:** (651)292-1900.

SIOUX CITY EXPLORERS

Office Address: 3400 Line Drive, Sioux City, IA 51106.
Telephone: (712) 277-9467. **Fax:** (712) 277-9406.
E-Mail Address: promotions@xsbaseball.com. **Website:** www.xsbaseball.com.
President: Matt Adamski.
General Manager: Shane M Tritz. **Assistant GM:** Ashley Schoenrock. **Sales Executive:** Tim Odle. **Office Manager:** Julie Stinger.
Field Manager: Stan Cliburn. **Director, Player Procurement:** Nick Belmonte.

GAME INFORMATION

Radio Announcer: Dave Nitz. **No. of Games Broadcast:** 100. **Flagship Station:** KSCJ 1360-AM. **Webcast Address:** www.xsbaseball.com.
Stadium Name: Lewis and Clark Park. **Location:** I-29 to Singing Hills Blvd, North, right on Line Drive.
Standard Game Times: 7:05 pm, Sun 6:05.
Visiting Club Hotel: Sioux City Hotel & Conference Center, 707 Fourth Street, Sioux City, IA 51101. **Telephone:** (712) 277-4101.

SIOUX FALLS PHEASANTS

Office Address: 1001 N West Ave, Sioux Falls, SD 57104.
Telephone: (605) 333-0179. **Fax:** (605) 333-0139.
E-Mail Address: info@sfpheasants.com. **Website:** www.sfpheasants.com.
Operated by: Sioux Falls Sports, LLC.
CEO/President/Managing Partner: Tom Garrity.
Vice President, Operations: Nate Welch. **Director, Stadium Operations:** Larry McKenney. **Office/Ticketing Manager:** Kim Hipple. **VP, Media/Public Relations:** Jim Olander. **VP, Sales:** Matt Ferguson.
Manager: Steve Shirley.

GAME INFORMATION

Radio Announcer: Scott Beatty. **No. of Games Broadcast:** 100. **Flagship Station:** KWSN 1230-AM. **Webcast Address:** www.kwsn.com.
Stadium Name: Sioux Falls Stadium. **Location:** I-29 to Russell Street, east one mile, south on West Avenue.
Standard Game Times: 7:05 pm, Sun 1:05.
Visiting Club Hotel: Comfort Inn & Suites 3708 Caroyln Ave., Sioux Falls, SD 57106. **Telephone:** (605) 361-2822.

WICHITA WINGNUTS

Office Address: 300 South Sycamore, Wichita, KS 67213.
Telephone: (316) 264-6887. Fax: (316) 264-2129.
Website: www.wichitawingnuts.com.
Owners: Steve Ruud, Dan Waller, Gary Austerman, Nick Easter, Nate Robertson.
President/General Manager: Josh Robertson. Assistant GM/Director, Corporate Sales: Ben Keiter. Assistant GM/Director, Ticket Sales: Jeremy Mock. Special Assistant to GM: Brian Holman. Director, Broadcast: Steve Schuster. Director, Finance: Kay Brown. Director, Stadium Operations: Jeff Kline. Director, Operations, Group Sales Manager: Brian Turner. Manager, Community Relations/Merchandise: Scott Johnson. Assistant Clubhouse Manager: Caleb Beeson.
Manager: Kevin Hooper. Coaches: Jose Amado, Brian Rose, Luke Robertson.

GAME INFORMATION
Radio Announcer: Steve Schuster. No. of Games Broadcast: 100. Games Broadcast: KWME 92.7-FM.
Webcast Address: www.wichitawingnuts.com.
Stadium Name: Lawrence-Dumont Stadium. Location: 135 North to Kellogg (54) West, Take Seneca Street exit North to Maple, Go East on Maple to Sycamore, Stadium is located on corner of Maple and Sycamore.
Standard Game Times: 7:05 pm, Sun 2:05 pm.
Visiting Club Hotel: North Rock Suites, 7856 E 36th St, N, Wichita, KS, 67226. Telephone: (316) 634-2303.

WINNIPEG GOLDEYES

Office Address: One Portage Ave E, Winnipeg, Manitoba R3B 3N3.
Telephone: (204) 982-2273. Fax: (204) 982-2274.
E-Mail Address: goldeyes@goldeyes.com. Website: www.goldeyes.com.
Operated by: Winnipeg Goldeyes Baseball Club, Inc.
Principal Owner/President: Sam Katz.
General Manager: Andrew Collier. Assistant GM: Regan Katz. Media Relations Manager: Scott Unger. Administrative Assistant: Bonnie Benson. Chief Financial Officer: Jason McRae-King. Controller: Judy Jones. Director, Sales/Marketing: Dan Chase. Sales/Marketing Coordinator: Angela Sanche. Account Representatives: Paul Edmonds, Dennis McLean, Blake Schultz, Scott Taylor. Promotions Coordinator: Sarah Wallace. Box Office Manager: Kevin Arnst. Retail Manager: Megan Tucker. Facility Manager/Head Groundskeeper: Don Ferguson.
Manager/Director, Player Procurement: Rick Forney. Coach: Tom Vaeth. Trainer: Shane Zdebiak.
Clubhouse Manager: Jamie Samson.

GAME INFORMATION
Radio Announcer: Paul Edmonds. No. of Games Broadcast: 100. Flagship Station: TSN Radio 1290ñAM.
Television Announcers: Scott Taylor.No. of Games Telecast: Home-20, Away-0. Station: Shaw TV Channel 9.
Stadium Name: Shaw Park. Location: North on Pembina Highway to Broadway, East on Broadway to Main Street, North on Main Street to Water Avenue, East on Water Avenue to Westbrook Street, North on Westbrook Street to Lombard Avenue, East on Lombard Avenue to Mill Street, South on Mill Street to ballpark.
Standard Game Times: 7 p.m., Sat 6, Sun 1:30.
Visiting Club Hotel: The Radisson Hotel Winnipeg Downtown, 288 Portage Ave, Winnipeg, Manitoba R3C 0B8. Telephone: (204) 956-0410.

ATLANTIC LEAGUE

Mailing Address: 401 N Delaware Ave Camden, NJ 08102.
Telephone: (856) 541-9400. **Fax:** (856) 541-9410.
E-Mail Address: info@atlanticleague.com. **Website:** www.atlanticleague.com.
Year Founded: 1998-
Chief Executive Officer/Founder: Frank Boulton. **President:** Peter Kirk. **Vice President:** Steven Kalafer.
Executive Director: Joe Klein.
Directors: Frank Boulton (Long Island, Bridgeport), Steve Kalafer (Somerset), Peter Kirk (Lancaster, York, Southern Maryland, Sugar Land), Frank Boulton/Peter Kirk (Camden).
Coordinator, League Operations/Latin: Ellie Rodriguez. **Director, Baseball Administration:** Patty MacLuckie.
Division Structure: Liberty Division—Bridgeport, Camden, Long Island, Southern Maryland; Freedom Division—Lancaster, Somerset, Sugar Land, York.
Regular Season: 140 games (split-schedule).
2013 Opening Date: April 18. **Closing Date:** Sept 15.
All-Star Game: July 10 at Southern Maryland.
Playoff Format: First-half division winners meet second-half winners in best of five series. Winners meet in best-of-five final for league championship.
Roster Limit: 25. Teams may keep 27 players from start of season until May 31.
Eligibility Rule: No restrictions.
Brand of Baseball: Rawlings.
Statistician: Statistician: Pointstreak.com, 602 - 1595 16th Avenue, Richmond Hill, ON, Canada L4B 3N9.

STADIUM INFORMATION

Club	Stadium	Opened	LF	CF	RF	Capacity	2012 Att.
Bridgeport	The Ballpark at Harbor Yard	1998	325	405	325	5,300	132,139
Camden	Campbell's Field	2001	325	405	325	6,425	231,987
Lancaster	Clipper Magazine Stadium	2005	372	400	300	6,000	307,431
Long Island	Citibank Park	2000	325	400	325	6,002	377,473
Somerset	Commerce Bank Ballpark	1999	317	402	315	6,100	350,295
So. Maryland	Regency Stadium	2008	305	400	320	6,000	229,094
Sugar Land	Constellation Field	2012	348	405	325	7,500	465,511
York	Sovereign Bank Stadium	2007	300	400	325	5,000	273,648

BRIDGEPORT BLUEFISH

Office Address: 500 Main St, Bridgeport, CT 06604. **Telephone:** (203) 345-4800.
Fax: (203) 345-4830. **Website:** www.bridgeportbluefish.com.
Operated by: Past Time Partners, LLC.
Principal Owner/CEO, Past Time Partners: Frank Boulton. **Senior VP, Past Time Partners:** Mike Pfaff. **Partners, Past Time Partners:** Tony Rosenthal, Fred Heyman, Jeffrey Serkes.
General Manager: Ken Shepard. **Assistant GM:** Jared Forma. **Finance Director:** Mary Jayne Wells. **Public Relations Director:** Paul Herrmann. **Ticket Manager:** Dan Cunningham. **Manager, Community Relations/Promotions:** Nicole Salcito. **Head Groundkeeper/Operations Coordinator:** Geremy Grate.
Manager: Willie Upshaw. **Coach:** Terry McGriff. **Pitching Coach:** Unavailable. **Trainer:** Ericka Ventura.

GAME INFORMATION

Radio Announcer: RJ Garcea. **No. of Games Broadcast:** 70 (webcast). **Flagship Station:** Unavailable. **PA Announcer:** Bill Jensen. **Official Scorer:** Chuck Sadowski.
Stadium Name: The Ballpark at Harbor Yard. **Location:** I-95 to exit 27, Route 8/25 to exit 1. **Standard Game Times:** 7:05 pm, Sat 6:05, Sun 1:05.
Visiting Club Hotel: Holiday Inn Bridgeport, 1070 Main St, Bridgeport, CT 06604. **Telephone:** (203) 334-1234.

CAMDEN RIVERSHARKS

Office Address: 401 N Delaware Ave, Camden, NJ 08102.
Telephone: (856) 963-2600. **FAX:** (856) 963-8534.
E-Mail Address: riversharks@riversharks.com. **Website:** www.riversharks.com.
Operated by: Camden Baseball, LLC
Principal Owners: Frank Boulton, Peter Kirk.
President: Jon Danos.
Controller: Emily Merrill. **President/General Manager:** Adam Lorber. **Assistant GM:** Lindsay Rosenberg. **Director, Group Events:** Bob Nehring. **Director, Group Sales:** Mark Schieber. **Director, Business Operations:** Amy Rotchford. **Director, Corporate Partnerships:** Drew Nelson. **Director, Marketing:** Kristin Segers. **Partnership Marketing Manager:** Mike Barone. **Creative Services Manager:** Meaghan Rhoades. **Group Sales Manager:** Kimberly Perno. **Group**

Sales Managers: Ross Anderson, David Koehler.

Box Office Manager: Dana Rommel. **Stadium Operations Manager:** Frank Slavinski. **Stadium Operations Assistant:** Jennifer Plankenhorn.

Manager: Ron Karkovice. **Bench Coach:** Brett Bonvechio. **Pitching Coach:** Chris Wedger.

GAME INFORMATION

Radio: www.riversharks.com / Z88.9 FM. **Riversharks Broadcaster:** Tim Saunders PA Announcer: Kevin Casey. **Official Scorer:** Dick Shute. **Stadium Name:** Campbell's Field.

Location: From Philadelphia, right on Sixth Street, right after Ben Franklin Bridge toll booth, right on Cooper Street until it ends at Delaware Ave; From Camden, I-676 to exit 5B, follow signs to field.

Standard Game Times: 7:05 pm, Sat 5:35, Sun 1:35. Gates open one hour prior to game time.

Visiting Club Hotel: Holiday Inn, Route 70 and Sayer Avenue, Cherry Hill, NJ 08002. **Telephone:** (856) 663-5300.

LANCASTER BARNSTORMERS

Office Address: 650 North Prince St, Lancaster, PA 17603.

Telephone: (717) 509-4487. **Fax:** (717) 509-4486.

E-Mail Address: info@lancasterbarnstormers.com. **Website:** www.lancasterbarnstormers.com.

Operated by: Lancaster Barnstormers Baseball Club, LLC.

Principal Owners: Opening Day Partners.

CEO: Jon Danos. **President:** Lisa Riggs. **Vice President, Business Development:** Vince Bulik. **Controller:** Emily Merrill. **General Manager:** Kristen Simon. **VP, Fan Experience:** Anthony DeMarco. **Director, Stadium Operations:** Don Pryer. **Finance Manager:** Brandi Garraffa. **Creative Services Manager:** Shaun Kreider. **Ticket Services Manager:** Maureen Wheeler. **Stadium Operations Manager:** Ed Snyder. **Stadium Operations Coordinator:** Tyler Swezey. **Marketing Manager:** Bryan Shaffer. **Director, Business Development:** Bob Ford. **Business Development Representatives:** Christopher Burton, Preston Moragne, Ben Smith. **Client Services Representative:** Liz Welch. **Administrative Assistant:** Holly Martin.

Manager: Butch Hobson. **Pitching Coach:** Marty Janzen. **Hitting Coach:** Lance Burkhart.

GAME INFORMATION

Radio Announcer: Dave Collins. **No. of Games Broadcast:** Home-70, Away-70. **Flagship Stations:** WLAN 1390 AM, WPDC 1600 AM. **PA Announcer:** John Witwer. **Official Scorer:** Joel Schreiner.

Stadium Name: Clipper Magazine Stadium. **Location:** From Route 30, take Fruitville Pike or Harrisburg Pike toward downtown Lancaster, stadium on North Prince between Clay Street and Frederick Street. **Standard Game Times:** 7 pm, Sun 1:30.

LONG ISLAND DUCKS

Mailing Address: 3 Court House Dr, Central Islip, NY 11722.

Telephone: (631) 940-3825. **Fax:** (631) 940-3800.

E-Mail Address: info@liducks.com. **Website:** www.liducks.com.

Operated by: Long Island Ducks Professional Baseball, LLC.

Founder/CEO: Frank Boulton. **Owner/Chairman:** Seth Waugh.

Owner/Senior VP, Baseball Operations: Bud Harrelson.

President/General Manager: Michael Pfaff. **Assistant GM/Senior VP, Sales:** Doug Cohen. **Director, Administration:** Gerry Anderson. **Director, Group Sales:** John Wolff. **Director, Season Sales:** Brad Kallman. **Manager, Box Office:** Ben Harper. **Manager, Merchandise/Client Services:** Jay Randall. **Manager, Media Relations/Broadcasting:** Michael Polak. **Manager, Corporate Sales:** Chris Burns. **Manager, Promotions:** Jordan Schiff. **Manager, Operations:** Scott Marshall. **Manager, Community Relations:** Taylor Turner.

Head Groundskeeper: Eric Ogden. **Coordinator, Administration:** Megan Gordon. **Account Executives:** Michael Kennedy, Brian Leavy. **Group Sales Assistant:** Anthony Rubino. **Ticket Assistants:** Sean Feminella, Anthony Vocaturo.

Manager: Kevin Baez. **Coaches:** Steve Foucault, Bud Harrelson. **Trainers:** Tony Amin, Adam Lewis, Dorothy Pitchford.

GAME INFORMATION

Radio Announcers: Michael Polak, Chris King, David Weiss. **No. of Games Broadcast:** 140 on www.liducks.com. **Flagship Station:** WRCN/103.9-FM. **PA Announcer:** Bob Ottone. **Official Scorers:** Michael Polak.

SOMERSET PATRIOTS

Office Address: One Patriots Park, Bridgewater, NJ 08807.
Telephone: (908) 252-0700. **Fax:** (908) 252-0776.
Website: www.somersetpatriots.com.
Operated by: Somerset Baseball Partners, LLC.
Principal Owners: Steve Kalafer, Jack Cust, Josh Kalafer, Jonathan Kalafer, Byron Brisby, Don Miller. **Chairman:** Steve Kalafer.
President/General Manager: Patrick McVerry. **Senior Vice President, Marketing:** Dave Marek. **VP/Assistant GM:** Rob Lukachyk. **VP, Public Relations:** Marc Russinoff. **VP, Ticketing:** Bryan Iwicki. **Head Groundskeeper:** Dan Purner. **Senior Director, Group Sales:** Matt Kopas. **Director, Community Relations:** Brian Cahill. **Director, Merchandise:** Rob Crossman. **Corporate Sales Manager:** Kevin Fleming. **Group Sales Manager:** Tom McCartney.
Account Executive: Deanna Liotard. **Ticket Sales Manager:** Joe Rafanelli. **Account Executive/Operations Manager:** Joshua Malakoff. **Executive Assistant to GM:** Michele DaCosta. **Controller:** Ron Schulz. **Accountant:** Stephanie Diez. **Receptionist:** Lorraine Ott. **GM, Centerplate:** Mike McDermott.
Manager: Brett Jodie. **Hitting:** Shane Spencer. **Pitching Coach:** Cory Domel. **Trainer:** Katie Reynolds. **Manager Emeritus:** Sparky Lyle.

GAME INFORMATION

Radio Announcer: Justin Antweil. **No. of Games Broadcast:** Home-70, Away-70. **Flagship Station:** WCTC 1450-AM. **PA Announcer:** Paul Spychala. **Official Scorer:** John Nolan.
Ballpark Name: TD Bank Ballpark. **Location:** Route 287 North to exit 13B/Route 287 South to exit 13 (Somerville Route 28 West); follow signs to ballpark. **Standard Game Times:** 7:05 pm, Sun 1:35/5:05.
Visiting Club Hotel: Hotel Somerset-Bridgewater.

SOUTHERN MARYLAND
BLUE CRABS

Office Address: 11765 St Linus Dr, Waldorf, MD 20602.
Telephone: 301-638-9788. **Fax:** 301-638-9788.
E-Mail address: info@somdbluecrabs.com. **Website:** www.somdbluecrabs.com.
Principal Owners: Opening Day Partners LLC, Brooks Robinson.
Chairman: Peter Kirk. **President:** Jon Danos. **Controller:** Emily Merrill.
General Manager: Patrick Day
Finance Manager: Theresa Coffey. **Sales Account Executives:** Joel Seiden, Sara Naar, Matthew Ammerman, Justin Miller.
Director, Corporate Sales: Candace Gick. **Creative Services:** Kevin Dove. **Marketing Manager:** Courtney Knichel. **Box Office:** Sean Maher. **Community Relations:** Amanda McComas. **Stadium Operations:** Steve Bowden. **GM, Centerplate Concessions/Merchandise:** Tim McGuire.
Manager: Patrick Osborn. **Hitting Coach:** Jeremy Owens (player/coach).

GAME INFORMATION

Radio: All Home and Away Games, www.somdbluecrabs.com. **Stadium:** Regency Furniture Stadium. **Standard Game Times:** 7:05 pm, Sat 6:35, Sun 2:05.

SUGAR LAND SKEETERS

Office Address: 1 Stadium Drive, Sugar Land Texas 77498.
Telephone: (281) 240-4487.
President: Matt O'Brien. **Assistant GM:** Lindsay Kirk. **Special Assistant to the President:** Deacon Jones.
Finance Manager: Purvi Shukla. **Human Resources:** Kimberly Ciszewski. **Senior Director, Sales:** Scott Podsim. **Senior Director, Community Development:** Kyle Dawson. **Director, Operations:** Michael Kirk. **Sponsorship Services Manager:** Jacqueline Holm. **Group Services Manager:** Chris Parsons. **Corporate Sales Manager:** Jeff Huebel. **Event Marketing Managers:** Ira Liebman, Tyler Stamm, Stefanie Nelson, Teneisha Hall, Taylor Galipp. **Director, Premium Services:** Paul Wallace. **Ticket Manager:** Jennifer Schwarz. **Customer Service Managers:** Jasmine Burns, Adam Mettler, Jonathan Berube.
Manager, Entertainment/Video: Gabriel Presas. **Director, Marketing/Communications:** MJ Burns. **Manager, Graphic Design/Web:** Todd Blair. **Manager, Community Relations/Outreach:** Taylor McFarland.
Head Groundskeeper: Brad Detmore. **Operations Manager:** Donnie Moore. **SEG Director:** Charlie Norton. **Special Events Manager:** Justin Roque. **Special Events Sales Manager:** Nikki Welsh. **Legends Hospitality General Manager:** Matt Coonrad.
Manager: Gary Gaetti. **Pitching Coach:** Jeff Scott. **Coach:** Victor Gutierrez.

GAME INFORMATION
Standard Game Times: 7:05 p.m., **Sat/Sun** 6:05.

YORK REVOLUTION

Office Address: 5 Brooks Robinson Way, York, PA 17401.
Telephone: (717) 801-4487. **Fax:** (717) 801-4499.
E-mail Address: ask@yorkrevolution.com.
Website: www.yorkrevolution.com.
Operated by: York Professional Baseball Club, LLC.
Principal Owners: Opening Day Partners.
President/General Manager: Eric Menzer. **Vice President/Business Development:** Neil Fortier. **Assistant GM/Business Operations:** John Gibson. **Finance Manager:** Lori Brunson. **Director, Ticketing:** Cindy Brown. **Box Office Manager:** Michael Foster. **Manager, Promotions/Communications:** Paul Braverman. **Director, Marketing:** Staci Wilkenson. **Director, Group Sales:** Mike Chatburn. **Corporate Partnerships Associates:** Yari Marte Natal, Amanda Seimer, Colin Cameron, Sam Nosoff, Sarah Blanchard. **Client Services Coordinator:** Reed Gunderson. **Stadium Operations Manager:** Ryan Long.

Head Groundskeeper: Zach Holm. **Creative Director:** Corey Shaud. **Legends Hospitality General Manager, Concessions/Merchandise/Catering:** Rob Wilson. **Legends Hospitality Catering Manager:** Adam Baumbach. **Legends Hospitality Chef:** Tiffany Eger.

Manager: Mark Mason. **Pitching Coach:** John Halama. **Infield Coach:** Enohel Polanco. **Baseball Operations Manager:** Andrew Ball.

GAME INFORMATION
Radio Announcer: Darrell Henry. **No. of Games Broadcast:** 140. **Flagship Station:** WOYK 1350 AM. **PA Announcer:** Chris DePatto, Merrill Spahn. **Official Scorer:** Brian Wisler.

Stadium Name: Sovereign Bank Stadium. **Location:** Take Route 30 West to North George Street. **Directions:** Turn left onto North George Street; follow that straight for four lights, Sovereign Bank Stadium is on left.

Standard Game Times: 6:30 p.m., **Sun** 5 p.m., **2 p.m.** (April/Sept). **Visiting Club Hotel:** The Yorktowne Hotel, 48 E Market Street, York, PA 17401. **Telephone:** (717) 848-1111.

CAN-AM LEAGUE

Office Address: 1415 Hwy 54 West, Suite 210, Durham, NC 27707.
Telephone: (919) 401-8150. **Fax:** (919) 401-8152. **Website:** www.canamleague.com.
Year Founded: 2004.
Commissioner: Miles Wolff. **President:** Dan Moushon.
Director, Umpires: Kevin Winn.
Regular Season: 100 games.
2013 Opening Date: May 16. **Closing Date:** Sept 2.
Playoff Format: Two teams with the best winning percentage meet in best-of-7 championship series.
Roster Limit: 22.
Eligibility Rule: Minimum of five and maximum of eight first-year players; minimum of five players must be an LS-4 or higher; a maximum of four may be veterans,
Brand of Baseball: Rawlings.
Statistician: Pointstreak.com.

STADIUM INFORMATION

| Club | Stadium | Opened | Dimensions | | | Capacity | 2012 Att. |
			LF	CF	RF		
Newark	Bears&Eagles Riverfront Stadium	1999	302	394	323	6,200	32,056
New Jersey	Yogi Berra Stadium	1998	308	398	308	3,784	87,206
Quebec	Stade Municipal	1938	315	385	315	4,800	152,663
Rockland	Provident Bank Park	2011	323	403	313	4,750	161,375
Trois-Rivieres	Stade Fernand-Bedard	1938	342	372	342	4,500	------

NEWARK BEARS

Office Address: 450 Broad St, Newark, NJ 07102.
Telephone: (973) 848-1000. **Fax:** (973) 621-0095.
E-Mail Address: info@newarkbears.com. **Website:** www.newarkbears.com.
Operated by: Danielle Dronet, Owner, CEO.
Owner/Partner: Douglas Spiel.
Manager: Garry Templeton.

GAME INFORMATION
No. of Games Broadcast: 100. **Webcast:** All-In Internet Broadcasting.
Stadium Name: Bears & Eagles Riverfront Stadium. **Location:** Garden State Parkway North/South to exit 145 (280 East), to exit 15; New Jersey Turnpike North/South to 280 West, to exit 15A.
Standard Game Times: 6:35 p.m., **Wed 11:**05, Sun 1:05.

NEW JERSEY JACKALS

Office Address: One Hall Dr, Little Falls, NJ 07424.
Telephone: (973) 746-7434. **Fax:** (973) 655-8006.
E-Mail Address: info@jackals.com. **Website:** www.jackals.com.
Operated by: Floyd Hall Enterprises, LLC.
Chairman: Floyd Hall.
President: Greg Lockard.
General Manager: Larry Hall. **Business Manager:** Jennifer Fertig. **Ticket Operations Manager:** Jeff Manahan. **Director, Group Sales:** Jordan Cascino. **Group Sales Representatives:** Michael Berhang, Shannon Koop. **Facilities Manager:** Aldo Licitra. **Concessions Manager:** Michelle Guarino.
Clubhouse Manager: Wally Brackett.
Manager: Joe Calfapietra. **Coaches:** Ed Ott, Ani Ramos

GAME INFORMATION
Webcast Announcer: No. **of Games Broadcast:** 100. **Webcast Address:** www.jackals.com.
Stadium Name: Yogi Berra Stadium. **Location:** On the campus of Montclair State University; Route 80 or Garden State Parkway to Route 46, take Valley Road exit to Montclair State University.
Standard Game Times: 7:05 pm, Sat 6:35, Sun 2:05.
Visiting Club Hotel: Ramada Inn, 130 Rte 10 West, East Hanover, NJ 07936. **Telephone:** (973) 386-5622.

QUEBEC CAPITALES

Office Address: 100 Rue du Cardinal Maurice-Roy, Quebec City, QC G1K8Z1.
Telephone: (418) 521-2255. **Fax:** (418) 521-2266.
E-Mail Address: info@capitalesdequebec.com. **Website:** www.capitalesdequebec.com.
Owner: Jean Tremblay.
President: Michel Laplante.
General Manager: Alex Harvey. **Assistant GM:** Julie Lefrancois. **Director, Media/Marketing:** Marc-Antoine Gariepy.
Sales Director: Pier-luc Nappert. **Assistant, Media/Marketing:** Maxime Aubry.
Manager: Patrick Scalabrini.

GAME INFORMATION

Webcast Address: www.capitalesdequebec.com.
Stadium Name: Stade Municipal de Quebec. **Location:** Highway 40 to Highway 173 (Centre-Ville) exit 2 to Parc Victoria.
Standard Game Times: 7:05 p.m., **Sun 1:**05.
Visiting Club Hotel: Le Cofortel, 6500 boul wilfrid-Hamel, Quebec, QC G2E 2j1

ROCKLAND BOULDERS

Office Address: 1 Provident Bank Park Drive, Pomona, NY 10970.†
Telephone: (845) 364-0009. **Fax:** (845) 364-0001.
E-Mail Address: info@rocklandboulders.com. **Website:** www.rocklandboulders.com.
President: Ken Lehner. **Executive Vice President:** Shawn Reilly. **Counsel:** Jonathan Fine. **Director of First Impressions:** Dana Fjermestad.† **Ticket Manager:** Bret Kaufman.
Corporate Partnership Manager: Seth Cantor.
Manager: Jamie Keefe. **Trainer:** Lori Rahim.

GAME INFORMATION

Radio Announcer: Seth Cantor.
Stadium Name: Provident Bank Park. **Location:** Take Exit 12 towards Route 45, make left at stop sign on Conklin Road, make left on Route 45, turn right on Pomona Road, take 1st right on Fireman's Memorial Drive.
Standard Game Times: 7:05 p.m., **Sun 2:**05/5:05.

TROIS-RIVIERES AIGLES

Office Address: 1760 Avenue Gilles-Villeneuve, Trois-Rivieres, QC G9A 5K8.
Telephone: (819) 379-0404. **Fax:** (819) 379-5087.
E-Mail Address: info@lesaiglestr.com. **Website:** www.lesaiglestr.com
President: Jean-Francois Picard. **General Manager:** Fred Lajoie. **Director, Stadium Facilities:** Real Lajoie. **Finance Director:** Steven Belanger. **Account Representatives:** Bobby Baril, Guylain Mailhot, Alexandre Ayotte.
Manager: Pete LaForest.

GAME INFORMATION

Stadium Name: Stade Fernand-Bedard. **Location:** Take exit Boul de forges/Centre-ville, keep right, turn right at light, turn right at stop sign.
Standard Game Times: 7:05 p.m., **Sun 2:**05.

FRONTIER LEAGUE

Office Address: 2041 Goose Lake Rd. **Suite 2A, Sauget, IL. 62206.**
Mailing Address: Same as above.
Telephone: (618) 215-4134. **Fax:** (618) 332-2115.
E-Mail Address: office@frontierleague.com. **Website:** www.frontierleague.com.
Year Founded: 1993.
Commissioner: Bill Lee.
Deputy Commissioner: Steve Tahsler.
President: Rich Sauget (Gateway). **Executive Committee:** Clint Brown (Florence), Steven Edelson (Lake Erie), Bryan Wickline (Rockford), Stu Williams (Washington).
Board of Directors: Tim Arseneau (Southern Illinois), Bill Bussing (Evansville), Steve Malliet (Normal/River City), Pat Salvi (Schaumburg), Josh Schaub (Joliet), Mike Stranczek (Windy City), Leslye Wuerfel (Traverse City).
Division Structure: East—Evansville, Florence, Frontier Greys, Lake Erie, Southern Illinois, Traverse City, Washington. West—Gateway, Joliet, Normal, River City, Rockford, Schaumburg, Windy City.
Regular Season: 96 games. **2013 Opening Date:** May 16. **Closing Date:** Sept 5.
All-Star Game: July 17 at Washington.
Playoff Format: Division winners and 2 wild card teams meet in best-of-five Divisional Series. Winners meet in best-of-five series for league championship.
Roster Limit: 24. **Eligibility Rule:** Minimum of eleven Rookie 1/Rookie 2 players. No player may be 27 prior to Jan. 1 of current season with the exception of one player that may not be 30 years of age prior to Jan. 1 of the current season.
Brand of Baseball: Wilson.
Statistician: Pointstreak, 602-1595 16th Avenue, Richmond Hill, ONT L4B 3N9

STADIUM INFORMATION

Club	Stadium	Opened	LF	CF	RF	Capacity	2012 Att.
Evansville	Bosse Field	1915	315	415	315	5,110	120,819
Florence	UC Health Stadium	2004	325	395	325	4,200	97,32
Gateway	GCS Ballpark	2002	318	395	325	5,500	150,745
Joliet	Silver Cross Field	2002	330	400	327	6,229	104,019
Lake Erie	All-Pro Freight	2009	325	400	325	5,000	127,124
Normal	The Corn Crib	2010	356	400	344	7,000	119,936
River City	T.R. Hughes Ballpark	1999	320	382	299	4,989	107,986
Rockford	RiverHawks Stadium	2006	315	393	312	3,279	97,453
Schaumburg	Schaumburg Stadium	1999	355	400	353	8,107	128,287
So. Illinois	Rent One Park	2007	325	400	330	4,500	129,936
Traverse City	Wuerfel Park	2006	320	400	320	4,600	175,284
Washington	CONSOL Energy Park	2002	325	400	325	3,200	81,836
Windy City	Standard Bank Stadium	1999	335	390	335	2,598	86,178

EVANSVILLE OTTERS

Mailing Address: 1701 N Main St, Evansville, IN 47711.
Telephone: (812) 435-8686.
Operated by: Evansville Baseball, LLC.
President: Bill Bussing.
Senior Vice President: Bix Branson. **General Manager:** Joel Padfield. **Director, Operations:** Jake Riffert. **Account Executive/Director, Media Relations/Broadcasting:** Mike Radomski. **Controller:** Casie Williams.
Sports Turf Manager: Lance Adler.
Manager, Baseball Operations: Andy McCauley.

GAME INFORMATION

Radio Announcer: Mike Radomski. **No. of Games Broadcast:** Home-51, Away-45. **Flagship Station:** WUEV 91.5-FM. **PA Announcer:** Zane Clodfelter. **Official Scorer:** Unknown.
Stadium Name: Bosse Field. **Location:** US 41 to Lloyd Expressway West (IN-62), Main St Exit, Right on Main St, ahead 1 mile to Bosse Field. **Standard Game Times:** 6:35 p.m., **Sun 5:**05; Doubleheaders 4:35.
Visiting Club Hotel: Econo Lodge Inn & Suites, 1930 North Cross Pointe Blvd, Evansville, IN 47715.

FLORENCE FREEDOM

Office Address: 7950 Freedom Way, Florence, KY 41042.
Telephone: (859) 594-4487. **Fax:** (859) 594-3194.
E-Mail Address: info@florencefreedom.com
Website: www.florencefreedom.com
Operated by: Canterbury Baseball, LLC.

President: Clint Brown. **GM:** Josh Anderson. **Assistant GM, Operations:** Kim Brown. **Director, Group Sales/ Promotions:** Kevin Schwab. **Baseball Operations/Manager:** Fran Riordan. **Pitching Coach:** Chris Homer.

GAME INFORMATION

Flagship Station: Unavailable. **Radio Broadcaster:** Unavailable. **PA Announcer:** Kevin Schwab. **Official Scorer:** Unavailable.

Stadium: University of Cincinnati Medical Center Stadium. **Location:** I-71/75 South to exit 180, left onto US 42, right on Freedom Way; I-71/75 North to exit 180. **Standard Game Times:** 6:35 p.m., **Sat/Sun 6:**05.

Visiting Club Hotel: Quality Inn.

FRONTIER GREYS

Mailing Address: 2041 Goose Lake Road, Suite 2A, Sauget, IL 62206.
Telephone: (618) 215-4134.
Operated by: Frontier League Baseball Travel Team, LLC.
President: Steve Tahsler.
Field manager: Brent Metheny. **Pitching coach:** Tom Waelchi. **Hitting Coach:** Doug Thennis. **Bench Coach:** Cliff Howe.

GATEWAY GRIZZLIES

Telephone: (618) 337-3000. **FAX:** (618) 332-3625
E-Mail Address: info@gatewaygrizzlies.com
Website: www.gatewaygrizzlies.com
Operated by: Gateway Baseball, LLC. **Managing Officer:** Richard Sauget.
General Manager: Steven Gomric. **Director, Stadium Operations:** Brent Pownall. **Director, Corporate Sales:** CJ Hendrickson. **Events Manager:** Jeff O'Neill. **Radio Broadcaster/Media Relations Director:** Adam Young. **Director, Marketing/Graphics:** Alex Wilson. **Director, Sales:** Craig Dohm. **Ticket Director:** Travis Holtkamp. **Assistant Director, Stadium Operations:** Jason Heinzmann. **Director, Merchandise:** Anna Grimm. **Sales Associate:** Brett Perkins. **Director, Promotions:** Hannah Harres.
Manager: Phil Warren. **Pitching Coach:** Randy Martz. **Hitting Coach:** Zach Borowiak. **Trainer:** Geof Manzo.

GAME INFORMATION

Radio Announcer: Adam Young. **No of Games Broadcast:** Home-48, Away-48. **Flagship Station:** 590-AM KFNS. **Affiliate Station:** 1400-AM KJFF. **PA Announcer:** Tom Calhoun.

Stadium Name: GCS Ballpark. **Location:** I-255 at exit 15 (Mousette Lane). **Standard Game Times:** 7:05 p.m., **Sun 6:**05/3:05.

Visiting Club Hotel: Ramada Inn, 6900 N Illinois St, Fairview Heights, IL 62208. **Telephone:** (618) 632-4747.

JOLIET SLAMMERS

Office Address: 1 Mayor Art Schultz Dr, Joliet, IL 60432
Telephone: (815)722-2287. **Fax:** (815) 726-4304.
E-Mail Address: info@jolietslammers.com . **Website:** www.jolietslammers.com .
Operated by: Joliet Community Baseball & Entertainment, LLC.
CEO: Josh Schaub
General Manager: Chris Franklin. **Assistant GM/Business:** Matt Gaddis. **Assistant GM/Promotions:** Kelli Drechsel. **Director, Ticket Sales/Service:** Kyle Wicks. **Director, Community Relations:** Ken Miller. **Stadium Operations:** Paul Rathje. **Head Groundskeeper:** Guy Massaro. **Box Office Manager:** Heather Mills
Manager: Mike Breyman. **Hitting Coach:** Dave Garcia. **Pitching Coach:** Eric Coleman. **Clubhouse Manager:** Greg Davison. **Trainer:** Andrew Gates: ATI Physical Therapy

GAME INFORMATION

Radio Announcer: Aaron Morse. **No. of Games Broadcast:** Home-51, Away-45. **Flagship Station:** WJOL (AM 1340). **PA. Announcer:** Mike Slodki. **Official Scorer:** Dave Laketa.

Stadium Name: Silver Cross Field. **Location:** Corner of Mayor Art Schultz Drive and Jefferson Street in downtown Joliet. **Standard Game Times:** 7:05 pm, Sat 6:05, Sun 2:05.

Visiting Club Hotel: Fairfield Inn, 3239 Norman Ave Joliet, IL 60431.

LAKE ERIE CRUSHERS

Mailing Address: 2009 Baseball Blvd, Avon, OH, 44011.
Telephone: (440) 934-3636. **Fax:** (440) 934-2458.

E-Mail Address: info@lakeeriecrushers.com. **Website:** www.lakeeriecrushers.com.
Operated by: Avon Pro Baseball LLC.
Managing Officer: Steven Edelson.
Vice President: Daniel Helm. **Assistant GM, Operations:** Paul Siegwarth. **Accountant:** Kathleen Hudson. **Box Office Manager:** Kelly Dolan. **Director, Group Sales:** Michael Link. **Director, Concessions/Catering:** Kevin Dailey. **Account Executives:** Matt Kendeigh, Whitney Goulish, Kate Walsh, Kim Deanovic. **Director, Broadcasting:** Andy Barch.
Manager: Jeff Isom.

GAME INFORMATION
Stadium Name: All Pro Freight Stadium. **Location:** Intersection of I-90 and Colorado Ave in Avon, OH. **Standard Game Times:** 7:05 pm, Sun 5:05.

NORMAL CORNBELTERS

Mailing Address:1000 West Raab Road, Normal, IL 61761.
Telephone: 309-454-2255 (BALL). **Fax:** 309- 454-2287 (BATS).
Ownership: Normal Baseball Group.
President: Steve Malliet. **General Manager:** Kyle Kreger.
Corporate Partnerships Director: Lori Johnson. **Vice President, Ticket Sales:** Joe Rejc. **Box Office Manager:** Justin Cartor. **Group Sales Manager:** Derek Johnston. **Stadium Operations Manager:** Ryan Eberle. **Business Manager:** Heather Manint.
Field Manager: Brooks Carey

GAME INFORMATION
Radio Announcer: Greg Halbleib. **Flagship Station:** 99.5 FM "The Ticket." **No. of Games Broadcast:** 0 (all games streaming online at http://www.995theticket.com). **Stadium Name:** The Corn Crib. **Location:** From I-55 North, go south on I-55 and take the 165 exit, turn left at light, turn right on Raab Road to ballpark on right; From I-55 South, go north on I-55 and take the 165 exit, merge onto Route 51 (Main Street), turn right on Raab Road to ballpark on right. **Standard Game Times:** 7 pm, Sun 6.

RIVER CITY RASCALS

Office Address: 900 TR Hughes Blvd, O'Fallon, MO 63366.
Telephone: (636) 240-2287. **Fax:** (636) 240-7313.
E-Mail Address: info@rivercityrascals.com. **Website:** www.rivercityrascals.com.
Operated by: PS and J Professional Baseball Club LLC.
Owners: Tim Hoeksema, Jan Hoeksema, Fred Stratton, Anne Stratton, Pam Malliet, Steve Malliet, Michael Veeck, Greg Wendt.
Executive Vice President/General Manager: Dan Dial. **Assistant GM/ Director, Corporate Sales:** Jody Sellers. **Senior Director, Ticket Operations:** Courtney Oakley. **Director, Stadium Operations:** Tom Bauer. **Director, Food/ Beverage:** Maureen Stranz. **Business Manager:** Sheri Livingston. **Senior Account Executives:** Ashley Phillips, Jeremy Cowen.
Team Manager: Steve Brook. **Assistant Coach:** Caleb Curry. **Assistant Coach:** Danny Sawyer.

GAME INFORMATION
No. of Games Broadcast: Home-51, Away-45. **PA Announcer:** Randy Moehlman.
Stadium Name: TR Hughes Ballpark. **Location:** I-70 to exit 219, north on TR Hughes Road, follow signs to ballpark. **Standard Game Times:** 7:05 pm, Sun 6:05.
Visiting Club Hotel: Days Inn 130 Salt Lick Road, Saint Peters, MO. **Telephone:** (636) 397-7101.

ROCKFORD AVIATORS

Office Address: 4503 Interstate Blvd Loves Park, IL 61111.
Telephone: (815) 885-2255. **Fax:** (815) 885-2204.
Website: www.rockfordaviators.com
Owned by: Rock River Valley Baseball. **CEO:** W Chris Hanners. **President:** Bryan Wickline.
General Manager: Brad Sholes. **Director, Media:** Jacob Wise. **Director, Group Sales:** Phil Racine. **Account Executive:** Evan Diece. **Head Groundskeeper:** Tyler Clay.
Field Manager: Rich Austin. **Hitting Coach:** Patrick O'Sullivan. **Pitching Coach:** Unavailable

GAME INFORMATION
Radio Announcer: Jacob Wise. **No. of Games Broadcast:** 96. **Flagship Station:** 100.5 NTAFM. **PA Announcer:** Brett Myhres. **Official Scorer:** Chris Etheridge.
Stadium Name: Aviators Stadium. **Location:** I-90 (Jane Addams Tollway) to Riverside Blvd exit (automatic toll booth), east to Interstate Dr, north on Interstate Drive to dead end. **Standard Game Times:** 7:05 pm, Sun 5:05.
Visiting Club Hotel: Best Western Clock Tower Resort, 7801 East State Street Rockford, Ill, 61108. **Telephone:** (800)

358-7666.

SCHAUMBURG BOOMERS

Office Address: 1999 Springinsguth Road, Schaumburg, IL 60193
E-Mail Address: info@boomersbaseball.com **Website:** www.boomersbaseball.com
Owned by: Pat and Lindy Salvi
President/General Manager: Andy Viano.
VP, Corporate Sales: Jeff Ney. **VP/Director, Marketing/Media:** Ed McCaskey.
Corporate Sales Manager: Jesse Zumbro. **Business Manager:** Todd Fulk. **Manager, Event Services/Merchandising:** Saralyn Locke. **Director, Facilities:** Mike Tlusty. **Creative Marketing Manager:** Dan Tomaszewski. **Community Relations Manager/Account Executive:** Sara Romano. **Promotions Manager/Account Executive:** Mike Kline. **Broadcaster:** Tim Calderwood. **Sponsor Services Specialist:** Kate Kleiva. **Stadium Event Specialist:** Kelly Nega. **Box Office Supervisor:** Mike Jacklich. **Stadium Operations Assistant:** Colt Schambach.
Manager: Jamie Bennett. **Hitting Coach:** C.J. Thieleke. **Pitching Coach:** T.J. Nall.

GAME INFORMATION
Broadcaster: Tim Calderwood. **No. of Games Broadcast:** Home-51, Away-45. **Flagship Station:** WRMN 1410 AM Elgin. **Official Scorer:** Drew Sauer.
Stadium: Schaumburg Boomers Stadium. **Location:** I-290 to Thorndale Ave Exit, head West on Elgin-O'Hare Expressway until Springinsguth Road Exit, second left at Springinsguth Road (shared parking lot with Schaumburg Metra Station). **Visiting Club Hotel:** Unavailable

SOUTHERN ILLINOIS MINERS

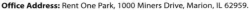

Office Address: Rent One Park, 1000 Miners Drive, Marion, IL 62959.
Telephone: (618) 998-8499. **Fax:** (618) 969-8550.
E-Mail Address: info@southernillinoisminers.com.
Website: www.southernillinoisminers.com.
Operated by: Southern Illinois Baseball Group. **Owner:** Jayne Simmons.
General Manager: Tim Arseneau. **Director, Ticket Operations:** Billy Leitner. **Corporate Partnerships/Promotions:** Terra Brenner. **Director, Sales:** Michael Bedokis. **Director, Video Production/Creative Services:** Heath Hooker. **Director, Finance:** Cathy Perry. **Director, Radio Broadcasting/Media Relations:** Michael Ventola. **Client Services Manager:** Grant Davis. **Account Executives:** Cory Lee, Eric Pionk. **Banquet Sales Manager:** Andrea Butler.
Manager: Mike Pinto. **Pitching Coach:** Brad Hall. **Hitting Coach:** Ralph Santana. **Coach/Advance Scout:** John Lakin.

GAME INFORMATION
No. of Games Broadcast: 96. **Flagship Station:** 97.7 WHET-FM.
Stadium Name: Rent One Park. **Location:** US 57 to Route 13 East, right at Halfway Road to Fairmont Drive. **Standard Game Times:** 7:05 pm, Sun 5:05.
Visiting Club Hotel: Days Inn 1802 Bittle Place, Marion, IL 62959.

TRAVERSE CITY BEACH BUMS

Office Address: 333 Stadium Dr, Traverse City, MI 49685.
Telephone: (231) 943-0100. **Fax:** (231) 943-0900.
E-Mail Address: info@tcbeachbums.com. **Website:** www.tcbeachbums.com.
Operated by: Traverse City Beach Bums, LLC.
Managing Partners: John Wuerfel, Leslye Wuerfel, Jason Wuerfel.
President/CEO: John Wuerfel. **Member/CFO:** Leslye Wuerfel. **Vice President/Director, Baseball Operations:** Jason Wuerfel.
Manager: Gregg Langbehn. **Hitting Coach:** Shannon Hunt. **Infield Coach:** Matt Pulley.

GAME INFORMATION
No. of Games Broadcast: Home-54, Away-42. **Flagship Stations:** WLDR 101.9-FM. **PA Announcer:** Chad Cooper.
Stadium Name: Wuerfel Park. **Location:** Three miles south of the Grand Traverse Mall just off US-31 and M-37 in Chums Village. **Stadium is visible from the highway. Standard Game Times:** 7:05 pm, Sun 5:05.
Visiting Club Hotel: Baymont Inn & Suites of Traverse City.

WASHINGTON WILD THINGS

Office Address: One Washington Federal Way, Washington, PA 15301.
Telephone: (724) 250-9555. **Fax:** (724) 250-2333.
E-Mail Address: info@washingtonwildthings.com.
Website: www.washingtonwildthings.com.
Owned by: Sports Facility, LLC. **Operated by:** Washington Frontier League Baseball, LLC. **President/Chief Executive Officer:** Stuart Williams. **General Manager:** Francine Williams
   Director, Marketing/Communications/Corporate Relations: Christine Blaine. **Assistant GM:** Steve Zavacky. **Corporate Partnership Manager:** Rick Minetti. **Corporate Partnership Account Executive:** Zack Kaminski. **Ticket Operations/Merchandise/Community Relations:** Kate Billings. **Ticket Manager:** Brian King. **Account Executives:** Jay Miller, Matt Banghart. **Promotions/Community Relations:** Kelly Williams. **Special Events/Operations:** Wayne Herrod. **Controller:** JJ Heider. **Administrative Assistant/Office Manager:** Malcolm Smith. **Creative Services:** Gloria Stone.
   Manager: Chris Bando. **Coach:** Bart Zeller.

GAME INFORMATION
   Radio Announcer: Randy Gore. **No. of Games Broadcast:** Home-53, Away-43.
   Flagship Station: WJPA 95.3-FM. **Official Scorer:** John Sacco. **Stadium Name:** CONSOL Energy Park. **Location:** I-70 to exit 15 (Chestnut Street), right on Chestnut Street to Washington Crown Center Mall, right at mall entrance, right on to Mall Drive to stadium. **Standard Game Times:** 7:05 Sunday 5:05 p.m.
   Visiting Club Hotel: Red Roof Inn

WINDY CITY THUNDERBOLTS

Office Address: 14011 South Kenton Avenue, Crestwood, IL 60445-2252.
Telephone: (708) 489-2255. **Fax:** (708) 489-2999.
E-Mail Address: info@wcthunderbolts.com. **Website:** www.wcthunderbolts.com.
Owned by: Crestwood Professional Baseball, LLC.
General Manager: Mike Lucas. **Director, Operations:** Mike VerSchave. **Director, Food/Beverage:** Steve Hasman.
Field Manager: Ron Biga. **Pitching Coach:** Brian Smith.

GAME INFORMATION
   Radio Announcer: Terry Bonadonna. **No. of Games Broadcast:** 96. **Flagship Station:** WXAV, 88.3 FM. **Official Scorer:** Steve Trotto.
   Stadium Name: Standard Bank Stadium. **Location:** I-294 to South Cicero Ave, exit (Route 50), south for 1 1/2 miles, left at Midlothian Turnpike, right on Kenton Ave; I-57 to 147th Street, west on 147th to Cicero, north on Cicero, right on Midlothian Turnpike, right on Kenton. **Standard Game Times:** 7:05 pm, Sat 6:05, Sun 5:05.
   Visiting Club Hotel: Georgioís Comfort Inn, 8800 W 159th St, Orland Park, IL 60462. **Telephone:** (708) 403-1100. **Fax:** (708) 403-1105.

ADDITIONAL LEAGUES

AMERICAN WEST BASEBALL LEAGUE

Mailing Address: 26632 Towne Centre Drive Suite 300 Foothill Ranch, CA 92610
Telephone: 888-932-2444. **E-Mail Address:** info@americanwestbl.com. **Website:** www.americanwestbl.com.
Year Founded: 2013.
Ownership Group: Embark Holdings, Inc.
Teams: Fullerton Flyers, North County Cannons, Desert Ghosts and Las Cruces.
Regular Season: 80 games. **Playoff Format:** Best of 3. **Roster Limit:** 22. **Eligibility Rules:** None. **Brand of Baseball:** Rawlings.

FREEDOM PRO BASEBALL LEAGUE

Mailing Address: PO B0X 5403 Scottsdale, AZ 85261.
Telephone: (480) 255-5696. **Fax:** (480) 947-4099.
E-Mail Address: info@FreedomProBaseballLeague.com. **Website:** www.FreedomProBaseballLeague.com.
Year Founded: 2012.
CEO/Founder: Joe Sperle.
Teams: Arizona Centennials, Phoenix CopperState Prospectors, Peoria Sonoran Explorers, Prescott Montezuma Federals.
Regular Season: 85 games.
2013 Opening Date: May 19. **Closing Date:** Sept 3. **Playoff Format:** Best-of-five series. **Roster Limit:** 22.

PACIFIC ASSOCIATION OF PROFESSIONAL BASEBALL CLUBS

Mailing address: 86 Granada Drive, Corte Madera, CA, 94904.
Telephone: (415) 485-1563. **Email:** info@pacificsbaseball.com. **Website:** www.pacificsbaseball.com.
Year Founded: 2013.
Ownership Group: Redwood Sports & Entertainment Group.
Teams: San Rafael Pacifics, Hawaii Stars, Maui Na Koa Ikaika, Vallejo Admirals.
Regular Season: 78 games. (Hawaii teams play interleague with Japanese Challenge League, California teams play interleague with Freedom League).
Roster Limit: 22. **Eligibility Rules:** None. **Brand of Baseball:** Rawlings. **Statistician:** Pointstreak.

UNITED LEAGUE

Mailing Address: 801 E Campbell Road Suite 638, Richardson, Texas 75081.
Telephone: (972) 792-8873. **Fax:** 972.792.8876. **E-Mail Address:** txproball@aol.com. **Website:** www.unitedleague-baseball.com.
Year Founded: 2006 (Operated as part of North American League in 2011-2012).
CEO/Founder: Reunion Sports Group. **Vice President:** Craig Brasfield.
Teams: Fort Worth Cats, San Angelo Colts, Rio Grande Valley Whitewings, Edinburg Roadrunners.
Regular Season: 96 games. **Playoff Format:** Top four teams. **Roster Limit:** 22 man roster. **Eligibility Rules:** Over 18 years old, no roster restrictions.
Brand of Baseball: Brett Baseballs. **Statistician:** Pointstreak.

INTERNATIONAL

AMERICAS

MEXICO

MEXICAN LEAGUE

Member, National Association
NOTE: The Mexican League is a member of the National Association of Professional Baseball Leagues and has a Triple-A classification. However, its member clubs operate largely independent of the 30 major league teams, and for that reason the league is listed in the international section.
Address: Av Insurgentes Sur #797 3er. piso. Col. Napoles. C.P. 03810, Benito Juarez, Mexico, D.F. **Telephone:** 52-55-5557-1007. **Fax:** 52-55-5395-2454. **E-Mail Address:** oficina@lmb.com.mx. **Website:** www.lmb.com.mx.
Years League Active: 1955-.
President: Plinio Escalante Bolio. **Operations Manager:** Nestor Alba Brito.
Division Structure: North—Aguascalientes, Laguna, Mexico City, Monclova, Monterrey, Puebla, Reynosa, Saltillo. South—Campeche, Ciudad del Carmen, Minatitlan, Oaxaca, Quintana Roo, Tabasco, Veracruz, Yucatan.
Regular Season: 110 games (split-schedule). **2013 Opening Date:** March 22. **Closing Date:** Aug 3.
All-Star Game: May 10-12, Oaxaca, Oaxaca.
Playoff Format: Eight teams qualify, including first- and second-half division winners plus wild-card teams with best overall records; Quarterfinals, semifinals and finals are all best-of-seven series.
Roster Limit: 28. **Roster Limit, Imports:** 6.

AGUASCALIENTE RAILROADS
Office Address: Blvd Juan Pablo II No 4506, Col Aeropuerto CP 31380. **Telephone:** (52) 614-459-0317. **Fax:** (52) 614-459-0336. **E-Mail Address:** icampos@doraslmb.com. **Website:** www.doradoslmb.com.
President: Mario Rodriguez. **General Manager:** Iram Campos Lara.
Manager: Arturo de Freitas.

CAMPECHE PIRATES
Office Address: Calle Filiberto Qui Farfan No. 2, Col. Camino Real, CP 24020, Campeche, Campeche. **Telephone:** (52) 981-827-4759. **Fax:** (52) 981-827-4767. **E-Mail Address:** piratas@prodigy.net.mx. **Website:** www.piratasdecampeche.com.mx.
President: Gabriel Escalante Castillo.
Manager: Dan Firova.

CIUDAD DEL CARMEN DOLPHINS
E-Mail Address: unionlag@prodigy.net.mx. **Website:** www.delfinesdelcarmen.com.
President: Carlos Mejía Berrio.
Manager: Felix Fermin.

LAGUNA COWBOYS
Office Address: Juan Gutenberg s/n, Col Centro, CP 27000, Torreon, Coahuila. **Telephone:** (52) 871-718-5515. **Fax:** (52) 871-717-4335. **E-Mail Address:** unionlag@prodigy.net.mx. **Website:** www.clubvaqueroslaguna.com.
President: Ricardo Martin Bringas. **General Manager:** Luis Dovalina.
Manager: Rafael Casteneda.

MEXICO CITY RED DEVILS
Office Address: Av Cuauhtemoc #451-101, Col Narvarte, CP 03020, Mexico DF. **Telephone:** (52) 555-639-8722. **Fax:** (52) 555-639-9722. **E-Mail Address:** diablos@

sportsya.com. **Website:** www.diablos.com.mx.
President: Roberto Mansur Galán. **General Manager:** Eduardo de la Cerda.
Manager: Daniel Fernandez.

MINATITLAN OILERS
Office Address: Av Avila Camacho esquina con H Colegio Militar, Estadio 18 de Marzo de 1938, Col De los Maestros, CP 96849, Minatitlan, Veracruz. **Telephone:** (52) 951-515-5522. **Fax:** (52) 951-515-4966. **E-Mail Address:** webmaster@petrolerosdeminatitlan.com.mx. **Website:** www.petrolerosdeminatitlan.com.mx.
President: Ranulfo Marquez Hernandez. **General Manager:** Edgar Santiago Chong Castillejos.
Manager: Alfonso Jimenez.

MONCLOVA STEELERS
Office Address: Cuauhtemoc #299, Col Ciudad Deportiva, CP 25750, Monclova, Coahuila. **Telephone:** (52) 866-636-2650. **Fax:** (52) 866-636-2688. **E-Mail Address:** acererosdelnorte@prodigy.net.mx. **Website:** www.aceros.com.mx.
President: Donaciano Garza Gutierrez. **General Manager:** Victor Favela Lopez.
Manager: Francisco Rodriguez.

MONTERREY SULTANS
Office Address: Av Manuel Barragan s/n, Estadio Monterrey, Apartado Postal 870, Monterrey, Nuevo Leon, CP 66460. **Telephone:** (52) 81-8351-0209. **Fax:** (52) 81-8351-8022. **E-Mail Address:** sultanes@sultanes.com.mx. **Website:** www.sultanes.com.mx.
President: José Maiz García. **General Manager:** Roberto Magdaleno Ramírez.
Manager: Felix Fermin.

OAXACA WARRIORS
Office Address: M Bravo 417 Col Centro 68000, Oaxaca, Oaxaca. **Telephone:** (52) 951-515-5522. **Fax:** (52) 951-515-4966. **E-Mail Address:** oaxacaguerreros@gmail.com. **Website:** www.guerrerosdeoaxaca.com.mx.
President: Luis Narchi Karam. **General Manager:** Guillermo Spindola Morales.
Manager: German Garcia.

PUEBLA PARROTS
Office Address: Calz Zaragoza S/N, Unidad Deportiva 5 de Mayo, Col Maravillas, CP 72220, Puebla, Puebla. **Telephone:** (52) 222-222-2116. **Fax:** (52) 222-222-2117. **E-Mail Address:** oficina@pericosdepuebla.com.mx. **Website:** www.pericosdepuebla.com.mx.
President: Rafael Moreno Valle Sanchez. **General Manager:** Edgar Ramirez Salazar.
Manager: Julio Franco Robles.

QUINTANA ROO TIGERS
Office Address: Av Mayapan Mz 4 Lt 1 Super Mz 21, CP 77500, Cancun, Quintana Roo. **Telephone:** (52) 998-887-3108. **Fax:** (52) 998-887-1313. **E-Mail Address:** tigres@tigrescapitalinos.com.mx. **Website:** www.tigresqr.com.
President: Cuauhtémoc Rodriguez. **General Manager:** Francisco Minjarez.
Manager: Matias Carrillo.

SALTILLO SARAPE MAKERS
Office Address: Blvd Nazario Ortiz Esquina con Blvd Jesus Sanchez, CP 25280, Saltillo, Coahuila. **Telephone:** (52) 844-416-9455. **Fax:** (52) 844-439-1330. **E-Mail Address:** aley@grupoley.com. **Website:** www.saraperos.com.mx.
President: Alvaro Ley Lopez. **General Manager:**

Eduardo Valenzuela Guajardo.
Manager: Derek Bryant.

TABASCO OLMECS

Office Address: Explanada de la Ciudad Deportiva, Parque de Beisbol Centenario del 27 de Febrero, Col Atasta de Serra, CP 86100, Villahermosa, Tabasco. **Telephone:** (52) 993-352-2787. **Fax:** (52) 993-352-2788. **E-Mail Address:** olmecastab@prodigy.net.mx. **Website:** www.olmecasdetabasco.com.mx.
President: Raul Gonzalez Rodriguez. **General Manager:** Luis Guzman Ramos.
Manager: Luis de los Santos.

REYNOSA BRONCOS

Office Address: Paris 511, Esq c/ Tiburcio Garza Zamora Altos, Locales 6 y 7, Col Beatty, Reynosa, Tamps. **Telephone:** (52) 922-3462. **Fax:** (52) 925-7118. **E-Mail Address:** broncosdereynosa@gmail.com. **Website:** www.broncosreynosa.com.
President: Eliud Villarreal Garza. **General Manager:** Leonardo Clayton Rodríguez.
Manager: Mario Mendoza.

VERACRUZ RED EAGLES

Office Address: Av Jacarandas S/N, Esquina España, Fraccionamiento Virginia, CP 94294, Boca del Rio, Veracruz. **Telephone:** (52) 229-935-5004. **Fax:** (229) 935-5008. **E-Mail Address:** rojosdelaguila@terra.com.mx. **Website:** www.aguiladeveracruz.com.
President: Jose Antonio Mansur Beltran. **General Manager:** Carlos Nahun Hernandez.
Manager: Pedro Mere.

YUCATAN LIONS

Office Address: Calle 50 #406-B, Entre 35 y 37, Col Jesus Carranza, CP 97109, Merida, Yucatán. **Telephone:** (52) 999-926-3022. **Fax:** (52) 999-926-3631. **E-Mail Addresses:** leones@prodigy.net.mx. **Website:** www.leonesdeyucatan.com.mx.
President: Ricalde Gustavo Durán. **General Manager:** Jose Rivero.
Manager: Lino Rivera.

MEXICAN ACADEMY

Rookie Classification
Mailing Address: Angel Pola No 16, Col Periodista, CP 11220, Mexico, DF Telephone: (52) 555-557-1007. **Fax:** (52) 555-395-2454. **E-Mail Address:** mbl@prodigy.net.mx. **Website:** www.academialmb.com.
Member Clubs: Celaya, Guanajuato, Queretaro, Salamanca.
Director General: Raul Martinez. **Administration:** Pela Villalobos.
Regular Season: 50 games. **Opening Date:** Oct 9. **Closing Date:** Dec 21.

DOMINICAN REPUBLIC
DOMINICAN SUMMER LEAGUE

Member, National Association
Rookie Classification
Mailing Address: Calle Segunda No 64, Reparto Antilla, Santo Domingo, Dominican Republic. **Telephone/Fax:** (809) 532-3619. **Website:** www.dominicansummerleague.com. **E-Mail Address:** ligadeverano@codetel.net.do.
Years League Active: 1985-.
President: Orlando Diaz.
Member Clubs/Division Structure: Boca Chica North—Marlins, Mets 2, Pirates 1, Rangers, Red Sox, Yankees 2. **Boca Chica South**—Cubs 2, Diamondbacks/Reds, Giants, Nationals, Mets 1, Phillies, Pirates 2, Yankees 1. **Boca Chica Northwest**—Astros, Athletics, Cardinals, Dodgers, Indians, Mariners, Rays, Royals. **Boca Chica Baseball City**—Cubs 1, Diamondbacks, Orioles, Padres, Reds, Rockies, Twins, White Sox. **San Pedro de Macoris**—Angels, Blue Jays, Braves, Brewers.
Regular Season: 72 games. **2013 Opening Date:** Unavailable. **Closing Date:** Unavailable.
Playoff Format: Six teams qualify for playoffs, including four division winners and two wild-card teams. Teams with two best records receive a bye to the semifinals; four other playoff teams play best-of-three series. Winners advance to best-of-three semifinals. Winners advance to best-of-five championship series.
Roster Limit: 35 active. **Player Eligibility Rule:** No player may have four or more years of prior minor league service. Draft-eligible players may not participate in the DSL or VSL, with the exception of two players from Puerto Rico. No age limits apply.

VENEZUELA
VENEZUELAN SUMMER LEAGUE

Member, National Association
Rookie Classification
Mailing Address: Torre Movilnet, Oficina 10, Piso 9, Valencia, Carabobo, Venezuela. **Telephone:** (58) 241-823-8101. **Fax:** (58) 241-824-3340. **Website:** www.vsl.com.ve.
Years League Active: 1997-.
Administrator: Saul Gonzalez. **Coordinator:** Ramon Feriera.
Participating Organizations: Mariners, Phillies, Rays, Tigers.
Regular Season: 70 games. **2013 Opening Date:** Unavailable. **Closing Date:** Unavailable.
Playoffs: Best-of-three series between top two teams in regular season.
Roster Limit: 35 active. **Player Eligibility Rule:** No player may have four or more years of prior minor league service. Draft-eligible players may not participate in the DSL or VSL, with the exception of two players from Puerto Rico. No age limits apply.

ASIA

CHINA
CHINA BASEBALL LEAGUE

Mailing Address: 5, Tiyuguan Road, Beijing 100763, China. **Telephone:** (86) 10-6716-9082. **Fax:** (86) 10-6716-2993. **E-Mail Address:** cga_cra@263.net.
Years League Active: 2002-.

Chairman: Hu Jian Guo. **Vice Chairmen:** Tom McCarthy, Shen Wei. **Executive Director:** Yang Jie. **General Manager, Marketing/Promotion:** Lin Xiao Wu.
Member Clubs: Beijing Tigers, Guangdong Leopards, Henan Elephants, Jiangsu Hopestars, Shanghai Golden Eagles, Sichuan Dragons, Tianjin Lions.
Regular Season: 28 games.
Playoff Format: Top two teams meet in one-game championship.

JAPAN

NIPPON PROFESSIONAL BASEBALL

Mailing Address: Imperial Tower, 14F, 1-1-1 Uchisaiwai-cho, Chiyoda-ku, Tokyo 100-0011. **Telephone:** 03-3502-0022. **Fax:** 03-3502-0140.
Website: www.npb.or.jp, www.npb.or.jp/eng
Commissioner: Ryozo Kato.
Executive Secretary: Kunio Shimoda. **Secretaries:** Atsushi Ihara, Shoji Numazawa. **Director, Baseball Operations:** Nobby Ito. **Director, Public Relations:** Katsuhisa Matsuzaki.
Director, Central League Operations: Kazunori Ogaki. **Director, Pacific League Operations:** Kazuo Nakano.
Nippon Series: Best-of-seven series between Central and Pacific League champions, begins Oct 26.
All-Star Series: July 19 at Sapporo Dome; July 20 at Jingu; July 22 at Iwaki.
Roster Limit: 70 per organization (one major league club, one minor league club). Major league club is permitted to register 28 players at a time, though just 25 may be available for each game.
Roster Limit, Imports: Four in majors (no more than three position players or pitchers); unlimited in minors.

CENTRAL LEAGUE

Regular Season: 144 games.
2013 Opening Date: March 29. **Closing Date:** Sept 27.
Playoff Format: Second-place team meets third-place team in best-of-three series. Winner meets first-place team in best-of-seven series to determine representative in Japan Series (first-place team has one-game advantage to begin series).

CHUNICHI DRAGONS

Mailing Address: Chunichi Bldg 6F, 4-1-1 Sakae, Naka-ku, Nagoya 460-0008. **Telephone:** 052-261-8811. **Fax:** 052-263-7696.
Chairman: Bungo Shirai. **President:** Katsuhiko Sakai. **General Manager:** Ryohei Sato. **Field Manager:** Morimichi Takagi.
2013 Foreign Players: Brad Bergesen, Daniel Cabrera, Matt Clark, Victor Diaz, Hector Luna.

HANSHIN TIGERS

Mailing Address: 2-33 Koshien-cho, Nishinomiya-shi, Hyogo-ken 663-8152. **Telephone:** 0798-46-1515. **Fax:** 0798-46-3555.
Chairman: Shinya Sakai. **President:** Nobuo Minami. **General Manager:** Eiichi Takano. **Field Manager:** Yutaka Wada.
2013 Foreign Players: Brooks Conrad, Randy Messenger, Matt Murton, Jason Standridge.

HIROSHIMA TOYO CARP

Mailing Address: 2-3-1 Minami Kaniya, Minami-ku, Hiroshima 732-8501. **Telephone:** 082-554-1000. **Fax:** 082-568-1190.
President: Hajime Matsuda. **General Manager:** Kiyoaki Suzuki. **Field Manager:** Kenjiro Nomura.
2013 Foreign Players: Brian Barden, Bryan Bullington, Brad Eldred, Fred Lewis, Kam Mickolio, Dennis Sarfate, Miguel Socolovich, Nick Stavinoha.

TOKYO YAKULT SWALLOWS

Mailing Address: Seizan Bldg, 4F, 2-12-28 Kita Aoyama, Minato-ku, Tokyo 107-0061. **Telephone:** 03-3405-8960. **Fax:** 03-3405-8961.
Chairman: Sumiya Hori. **President:** Tsuyoshi Klnugasa. **General Manager:** Junsei Atarashi. **Field Manager:** Junji Ogawa.

2013 Foreign Players: Wladimir Balentien, Tony Barnette, Lastings Milledge, Orlando Roman.

YOKOHAMA DeNA BAYSTARS

Mailing Address: Kannai Arai Bldg, 7F, 1-8 Onoe-cho, Naka-ku, Yokohama 231-0015. **Telephone:** 045-681-0811. **Fax:** 045-661-2500.
Chairman: Makoto Haruta. **President:** Jun Ikeda. **General Manager:** Shigeru Takada. **Field Manager:** Kiyoshi Nakahata.
2013 Foreign Players: Tony Blanco, Nyjer Morgan, Alex Ramirez, Wang Yi Cheng, Jorge Sosa, Enyelbert Soto.

YOMIURI GIANTS

Mailing Address: Otemachi Nomura Bldg, 7F, 2-1-1 Otemachi, Chiyoda-ku, Tokyo 100-8151. **Telephone:** 03-3246-7733. **Fax:** 03-3246-2726.
Chairman: Kojiro Shiraishi. **President:** Tsunekazu Momoi. **General Manager:** Atsushi Harasawa. **Field Manager:** Tatsunori Hara.
2013 Foreign Players: Manny Acosta, John Bowker, DJ Houlton, Lin Yi Hao, Jose Lopez, Scott Mathieson.

PACIFIC LEAGUE

Regular Season: 144 games.
2013 Opening Date: March 29. **Closing Date:** Oct 5.
Playoff Format: Second-place team meets third-place team in best-of-three series. Winner meets first-place team in best-of-seven series to determine league's representative in Japan Series (first-place team has one-game advantage to begin series).

CHIBA LOTTE MARINES

Mailing Address: 1 Mihama, Mihama-ku, Chiba-shi, Chiba-ken 261-8587. **Telephone:** 03-5682-6341.
Chairman: Takeo Shigemitsu. **President:** Iekuni Nakamura. **Field Manager:** Tsutomu Ito.
2013 Foreign Players: Dicky Gonzalez, Seth Greisinger, Wil Ledezma, Carlos Rosa, Josh Whitesell.

FUKUOKA SOFTBANK HAWKS

Mailing Address: Fukuoka Yahoo! Japan Dome, Hawks Town, Chuo-ku, Fukuoka 810-0065. **Telephone:** 092-847-1006. **Fax:** 092-844-4600.
Owner: Masayoshi Son. **Chairman:** Sadaharu Oh. **President:** Kazuhiko Kasai. **Field Manager:** Koji Akiyama.
2013 Foreign Players: Brian Falkenborg, Bryan LaHair, Vicente Padilla, Wily Mo Pena, Yang Yao-hsun.

HOKKAIDO NIPPON HAM FIGHTERS

Mailing Address: 1 Hitsujigaoka, Toyohira-ku, Sapporo 062-8655. **Telephone:** 011-857-3939. **Fax:** 011-857-3900.
Chairman: Hiroji Okoso. **President:** Junichi Fujii. **General Manager:** Masao Yamada. **Field Manager:** Hideki Kuriyama.
2013 Foreign Players: Micah Hoffpauir, Bobby Keppel, Dustin Molleken, Brian Wolfe.

ORIX BUFFALOES

Mailing Address: 3-Kita-2-30 Chiyozaki, Nishi-ku, Osaka 550-0023. **Telephone:** 06-6586-0221. **Fax:** 06-6586-0240.
Chairman: Yoshihiko Miyauchi. **President:** Hiroaki Nishina. **General Manager:** Yoshio Murayama. **Field Manager:** Hiroshi Moriwaki.
2013 Foreign Players: Aarom Baldiris, Brandon Dickson, Steve Hammond, Hsu Ming-Chie, Dae Ho Lee, Alex Maestri, Vinny Rottino.

SAITAMA SEIBU LIONS

Mailing Address: 2135 Kami-Yamaguchi, Tokorozawa-shi, Saitama-ken 359-1189. **Telephone:** 04-2924-1155. **Fax:** 04-2928-1919.
President: Hajime Igo. **Field Manager:** Hisanobu

Watanabe.

2013 Foreign Players: Esteban German, Jose Ortiz Dennis Sarfate, Brian Sikorski, Ryan Spilborghs, Randy Williams.

TOHOKU RAKUTEN GOLDEN EAGLES
Mailing Address: 2-11-6 Miyagino, Miyagino-ku, Sendai-shi, Miyagi-ken 983-0045. **Telephone:** 022-298-5300. **Fax:** 022-298-5360.
Chairman: Hiroshi Mikitani. **President:** Yozo Tachibana. **Field Manager:** Senichi Hoshino.
2013 Foreign Players: Brandon Duckworth, Jim Heuser, Andruw Jones, Casey McGehee, Darrell Rasner.

KOREA
KOREA BASEBALL ORGANIZATION

Mailing Address: 946-16 Dokokdong, Kangnam-gu, Seoul, Korea. **Telephone:** (02) 3460-4600. **Fax:** (02) 3460-4639.
Years League Active: 1982-.
Website: www.koreabaseball.com.
Commissioner: Shin Sang-woo. **Secretary General:** Ha Il-sung. **Deputy Secretary General:** Lee Sang-il.
Member Clubs: Doosan Bears, Hanwha Eagles, Kia Tigers, LG Twins, Lotte Giants, Samsung Lions, Seoul Heroes, SK Wyverns.
Regular Season: 133 games. **2013 Opening Date:** Unavailable.

Playoffs: Third- and fourth-place teams meet in best-of-three series; winner advances to meet second-place team in best-of-five series; winner meets first-place team in best-of-seven Korean Series for league championship.
Roster Limit: 26 active through Sept 1, when rosters expand to 31. **Imports:** Two active.

TAIWAN
CHINESE PROFESSIONAL BASEBALL LEAGUE

Mailing Address: 2F, No 32, Pateh Road, Sec 3, Taipei, Taiwan 10559. **Telephone:** 886-2-2577-6992. **Fax:** 886-2-2577-2606. **Website:** www.cpbl.com.tw.
Years League Active: 1990-.
Commissioner: Shou-Po Chao. **Secretary General:** Wen-pin Lee. **International Affairs:** Richard Wang. **E-Mail Address:** richard.wang@cpbl.com.tw.
Member Clubs: Brother Elephants, Uni Lions, Sinon Bulls, La New Bears.
Regular Season: 100 games. **2013 Opening Date:** March 28. **Playoffs:** Second- and third-place teams meet in best-of-five series; winner advances to meet first-place team in best-of-seven championship series.
Import Rule: Only three import players may be active, and only two may be on the field at the same time.

EUROPE

NETHERLANDS
DUTCH MAJOR LEAGUE

Mailing Address: Koninklijke Nederlandse Baseball en Softball Bond (Royal Dutch Baseball and Softball Association), Postbus 2650, 3430 GB Nieuwegein, Holland. **Telephone:** 31-30-751-3650. **Fax:** 31-30-751-3651. **Website:** www.knbsb.nl.
Member Clubs: ADO, Amsterdam Pirates, HCAW, Hoofddorp Pioniers, Kinheim, Neptunus, Sparta/Feyenoord, UVV.
President: Bob Bergkamp.

ITALY
SERIE A

Mailing Address: Federazione Italiana Baseball Softball, Viale Tiziano 74, 00196 Roma, Italy. **Telephone:** 39-06-32297201. **Fax:** 39-06-36858201. **Website:** www.fibs.it.
Member Clubs: Bologna, Godo, Grosseto, Nettuno, Parma, Paterno, Rimini, San Marino.
President: Riccardo Fraccari.

WINTER BASEBALL

CARIBBEAN BASEBALL CONFEDERATION

Mailing Address: Frank Feliz Miranda No 1 Naco, Santo Domingo, Dominican Republic. **Telephone:** (809) 381-2643. **Fax:** (809) 565-4654.
Commissioner: Juan Francisco Puello. **Secretary:** Benny Agosto.
Member Countries: Colombia, Dominican Republic, Mexico, Nicaragua, Puerto Rico, Venezuela (Colombia and Nicaragua do not play in the Caribbean Series).
2014 Caribbean Series: Venezuela, February.

DOMINICAN LEAGUE

Office Address: Estadio Quisqueya, 2da Planta, Ens La Fe, Santo Domingo, Dominican Republic. **Telephone:** (809) 567-6371. **Fax:** (809) 567-5720. **E-Mail Address:** ligadom@hotmail.com. **Website:** www.lidom.com.
Years League Active: 1951-.

President: Leonardo Matos Berrido. **Vice President:** Jose Rafael Alvarez Sanchez. **Administrator:** Marcos Rodríguez. **Public Relations Director:** Jorge Torres.
Member Clubs: Aguilas Cibaenas, Estrellas de Oriente, Gigantes del Cibao, Leones del Escogido, Tigres del Licey, Toros del Este.
Regular Season: 50 games. **2013 Opening Date:** Unavailable.
Playoff Format: Top four teams meet in 18-game round-robin. Top two teams advance to best-of-nine series for league championship. Winner advances to Caribbean Series.
Roster Limit: 30. **Imports:** 7.

MEXICAN PACIFIC LEAGUE

Mailing Address: Blvd Solidaridad No 335, Plaza las Palmas, Edificio A, Nivel 1, Local 4, Hermosillo, Sonora, Mexico CP 83246. **Telephone:** (52) 662-310-9714. **Fax:** (52) 662-310-9715. **E-Mail Address:** ligadelpacifico@liga-

delpacifico.com.mx. **Website:** www.ligadelpacifico.com.
mx.
Years League Active: 1958-.
President: Omar Canizales. **Administration:** Vanessa
Palacios. **Sports Manager:** Dennis Gonzalez Oviel.
Member Clubs: Culiacan Tomateros, Guasave
Algodoneros, Hermosillo Naranjeros, Los Mochis Caneros,
Mazatlan Venados, Mexicali Aguilas, Navojoa Mayos,
Obregon Yaquis.
Regular Season: 68 games. **2013 Opening Date:**
Unavailable.
Playoff Format: Six teams advance to best-of-seven
quarterfinals. Three winners and losing team with best
record advance to best-of-seven semifinals. Winners meet
in best-of-seven series for league championship. Winner
advances to Caribbean Series.
Roster Limit: 30. **Imports:** 5.

PUERTO RICAN LEAGUE

Office Address: Avenida Munoz Rivera 1056, Edificio
First Federal, Suite 501, Rio Piedras, PR 00925. **Mailing
Address:** PO Box 191852, San Juan, PR 00019. **Telephone:**
(787) 765-6285, 765-7285. **Fax:** (787) 767-3028. **Website:**
www.puertoricobaseballleague.com.
Years League Active: 1938-2007; 2008-
President: Joaquin Monserrate Matienzo. **Executive
Director:** Benny Agosto.
Member Clubs: Arecibo Lobos, Caguas Criollos,
Carolina Gigantes, Mayaguez Indios, Ponce Leones.
Regular Season: 42 games. **2013 Opening Date:**
Unavailable.
Playoff Format: Top four teams meet in best-of-seven
semifinal series. Winners meet in best-of-nine series for
league championship. Winner advances to Caribbean
Series.
Roster Limit: 30. **Imports:** 5.

VENEZUELAN LEAGUE

Mailing Address: Avenida Casanova, Centro Comercial
"El Recreo," Torre Sur, Piso 3, Oficinas 6 y 7, Sabana Grande,
Caracas, Venezuela. **Telephone:** (58) 212-761-6408. **Fax:**
(58) 212-761-7661. **Website:** www.lvbp.com.
Years League Active: 1946-.
President: Jose Grasso Vecchio. **Vice Presidents:**
Rafael Chaverogazdik, Gustavo Massiani. **General
Manager:** Domingo Alvarez.
Member Clubs: Anzoategui Caribes, Aragua Tigres,
Caracas Leones, La Guaira Tiburones, Lara Cardenales,
Magallanes Navegantes, Margarita Bravos, Zulia Aguilas.
Regular Season: 64 games. **2013 Opening Date:**
Unavailable.
Playoff Format: Top two teams in each division, plus
a wild-card team, meet in 16-game round-robin series.
Top two finishers meet in best-of-seven series for league
championship. Winner advances to Caribbean Series.
Roster Limit: 26. **Imports:** 7.

COLOMBIAN LEAGUE

Office/Mailing Address: Unavailable. **Telephone:**
Unavailable. **Website:** www.teamrenteria.com.
Member Clubs: Barranquilla, Cartagena, Monteria,

Sincelejo.
Regular season: 65 games. **2013 Opening Date:**
Unavailable.
Playoff Format: Top two teams meet in best-of-seven
finals for league championship.

NICARAGUAN LEAGUE

Office Address/Mailing Address: Canal 2 TV, Casa
#26, Managua, Nicaragua. **Telephone:** 505-2266-3645.
Website: www.lnbp.com.ni.
Commissioner: Noel Urcuyo Baez. **General Manager:**
Azalea Salmeron. **Marketing Director:** Jessica Market.
Member Clubs: Chinandega, Granada, Leon, Managua.
Regular Season: 40 games. **2013 Opening Date:**
Unavailable.
Playoff Format: Top two teams meet in best-of-seven
finals for league championship.

AUSTRALIA

AUSTRALIAN BASEBALL LEAGUE

Mailing Address: 1 Palm Meadows Drive, Carrara,
QLD, 4211, Australia. **Telephone:** 61-7-5510-6819. **Fax:**
61-7-5510-6855. **E-Mail Address:** admin@ableague.com.
au. **Website:** www.theabl.com.
CEO: Peter Wermuth. **Operations Manager:** Ben
Foster.
Teams: Adelaide, Brisbane, Canberra, Melbourne,
Perth, Sydney.
Playoff Format: First-place team plays second-place
team in major semifinal; third-place team plays fourth-
place team in minor semifinal, both best of three series.
Loser of major semifinal plays winner of minor semifinal
in best of three series. Winner of that series plays winner of major semifinal in best of three series for league
championship.

DOMESTIC LEAGUE

ARIZONA FALL LEAGUE

Mailing Address: 2415 E Camelback Road, Suite 850,
Phoenix, AZ 85016. **Telephone:** (602) 281-7250. **Fax:** (602)
281-7313. **E-Mail Address:** afl@mlb.com. **Website:** www.
mlb.com.
Years League Active: 1992-.
Operated by: Major League Baseball.
Executive Director: Steve Cobb. **Seasonal Assistant:**
Joan McGrath.
Teams: Mesa Solar Sox, Peoria Javelinas, Peoria
Saguaros, Phoenix Desert Dogs, Scottsdale Scorpions,
Surprise Rafters.
2013 Opening Date: Unavailable. **Play usually opens
in mid-October. Playoff Format:** Division champions
meet in one-game championship.
Roster Limit: 30. Players with less than one year of
major league service are eligible, with one foreign player
and one player below the Double-A level allowed per
team.

MINOR LEAGUE SCHEDULES

TRIPLE-A

INTERNATIONAL LEAGUE

BUFFALO

APRIL	
4-5	Rochester
6-7	at Rochester
8-10	Syracuse
11-14	Scranton/Wilkes-Barre
15-18	at Syracuse
19-22	at Lehigh Valley
23-26	Pawtucket
27-30	at Rochester

MAY	
2-5	Louisville
6-9	Norfolk
10-13	at Louisville
14-17	at Indianapolis
18-21	Charlotte
23-26	Indianapolis
27-30	at Durham
31	at Norfolk

JUNE	
1-3	at Norfolk
4-7	Lehigh Valley
8-11	at Scranton/Wilkes-Barre
13-16	at Pawtucket
17-20	Gwinnett
21-24	Durham
25-28	at Gwinnett
29-30	at Charlotte

JULY	
1-2	at Charlotte
3	Rochester
4-5	at Scranton/Wilkes-Barre
6-7	Syracuse
9-10	at Syracuse
11-12	at Lehigh Valley
13-14	Scranton/Wilkes-Barre
19-21	Toledo
22-25	Columbus
26-29	at Toledo
30-31	at Columbus

AUGUST	
1-2	at Columbus
3-6	Pawtucket
8-9	Scranton/Wilkes-Barre
10-11	at Scranton/Wilkes-Barre
12-13	Syracuse
14-16	Rochester
17-20	at Pawtucket
22-25	Lehigh Valley
26-27	at Lehigh Valley
28-29	Rochester
30-31	at Rochester

SEPTEMBER	
1-2	at Syracuse

CHARLOTTE KNIGHTS

APRIL	
4-7	at Gwinnett
8-10	at Norfolk
11-12	Gwinnett
13-16	Durham
17-18	at Durham
19-20	Gwinnett
21-22	at Gwinnett
23-26	Norfolk
27-30	Scranton/Wilkes-Barre

MAY	
2-5	at Toledo
6-9	at Columbus
10-13	Pawtucket
14-17	Louisville
18-21	at Buffalo
23-26	at Rochester
27-30	Toledo
31	Rochester

JUNE	
1-3	Rochester
4-7	at Pawtucket
8-11	at Lehigh Valley
13-16	Columbus
17-20	Syracuse
21-24	at Indianapolis
25-28	at Louisville
29-30	Buffalo

JULY	
1-2	Buffalo
3	Durham
4-5	at Gwinnett
6-7	Norfolk
8-9	Durham
10-11	at Durham
12-14	at Norfolk
18-19	Norfolk
20-21	at Norfolk
22-25	Indianapolis
26-29	Gwinnett
31	at Gwinnett

AUGUST	
1-2	at Gwinnett
3-4	at Norfolk
5-8	Lehigh Valley
9-11	at Durham
13-16	at Scranton/Wilkes-Barre
17-19	Durham
20-21	at Durham
22-25	at Syracuse
26-27	at Durham
28-30	Norfolk
31	Gwinnett

SEPTEMBER	
1-2	Gwinnett

COLUMBUS CLIPPERS

APRIL	
4-7	at Indianapolis
8-10	at Louisville
11-14	Indianapolis
15-17	Louisville
18-19	at Toledo
20-22	Toledo
23-26	at Scranton/Wilkes-Barre
27-30	at Pawtucket

MAY	
2-5	Rochester
6-9	Charlotte

10-13	at Rochester
14-17	at Syracuse
18-21	Scranton/Wilkes-Barre
23-26	Syracuse
27-30	at Louisville
31	Indianapolis

JUNE	
1-3	Indianapolis
4-5	Toledo
6-7	at Toledo
8-11	at Gwinnett
13-16	at Charlotte
17-20	Pawtucket
21-24	Lehigh Valley
25-28	at Norfolk
29-30	at Durham

JULY	
1-2	at Durham
3-4	at Toledo
5-7	Louisville
8-10	Indianapolis

DURHAM BULLS

APRIL	
4-7	at Norfolk
8-10	Gwinnett
11-12	Norfolk
13-16	at Charlotte
17-18	Charlotte
19-21	Norfolk
23-26	Toledo
27-30	at Syracuse

MAY	
2-5	at Pawtucket
6-9	Syracuse
10-13	Lehigh Valley
14-17	at Rochester
18-19	Norfolk
21-22	at Norfolk
23-26	at Scranton/Wilkes-Barre
27-30	Buffalo
31	Scranton/Wilkes-Barre

JUNE	
1-3	Scranton/Wilkes-Barre
4-7	at Indianapolis
8-11	at Louisville
13-16	Indianapolis
17-20	Louisville
21-24	at Buffalo
25-28	at Lehigh Valley
29-30	Columbus

GWINNETT BRAVES

APRIL	
4-7	Charlotte
8-10	at Durham
11-12	at Charlotte
13-14	at Norfolk
15-18	Norfolk
19-20	at Charlotte
21-22	Charlotte
23-26	at Louisville
27-30	at Indianapolis

MAY	
2-5	Scranton/Wilkes-Barre
6-9	Pawtucket
10-13	at Scranton/Wilkes-Barre
14-17	at Pawtucket
18-21	Louisville
23-26	Toledo

11-12	Toledo
13-14	at Indianapolis
18-21	at Lehigh Valley
22-25	at Buffalo
26-29	Durham
30-31	Buffalo

AUGUST	
1-2	Buffalo
3-5	at Toledo
6-7	Toledo
8-9	Louisville
10-11	at Louisville
13-16	at Indianapolis
17-20	Norfolk
22-25	Gwinnett
26-27	at Louisville
28-29	Louisville
30-31	at Toledo

SEPTEMBER	
1-2	Toledo

JULY	
1-2	Columbus
3	at Charlotte
4-5	Norfolk
6-7	at Gwinnett
8-9	at Charlotte
10-11	Charlotte
12-14	Gwinnett
18-21	Pawtucket
22-23	at Gwinnett
24-25	Gwinnett
26-29	at Columbus
30-31	at Toledo

AUGUST	
1-2	at Toledo
3-4	Gwinnett
5-8	Rochester
9-11	Charlotte
13-16	at Charlotte
17-19	at Charlotte
20-21	Charlotte
22-23	at Norfolk
24-25	Norfolk
26-27	Charlotte
28-30	at Gwinnett
31	at Norfolk

SEPTEMBER	
1-2	at Norfolk

27-30	at Syracuse
31	at Lehigh Valley

JUNE	
1-3	at Lehigh Valley
4-8	Rochester
9-11	Columbus
13-16	at Rochester
17-20	at Buffalo
21-23	Syracuse
25-28	Buffalo
29-30	at Norfolk

JULY	
1-3	at Norfolk
4-5	Charlotte
6-7	Durham
8-11	Norfolk
12-14	at Durham

18-21 . . . . . .Indianapolis
22-23 . . . . Durham
24-25 . . . . .at Toledo
26-29 . . . . . at Charlotte
31 . . . . Charlotte

AUGUST
1-2. . . . . Charlotte
3-4. . . . . . . .at Durham
5-8. . . . . at Norfolk

INDIANAPOLIS INDIANS

APRIL
4-7. . . . . Columbus
8-10 . . . . Toledo
11-14 . . . . . . at Columbus
15-17 . . . . .at Toledo
18-20 . . . . at Louisville
21-22 . . . . . Louisville
23-26 . . . . . Lehigh Valley
27-30 . . . . . . Gwinnett

MAY
2-5. . . . . at Lehigh Valley
6-9. . at Scranton/Wilkes-Barre
10-13 . . . . Toledo
14-17 . . . . Buffalo
18-21 . . . . . at Pawtucket
23-26 . . . . . at Buffalo
27-30 . . . . . Pawtucket
31 . . . . . . at Columbus

JUNE
1-3. . . . . . at Columbus
4-7. . . . . Durham
8-11 . . . . . . .Norfolk
13-16 . . . . . .at Durham
17-20 . . . . . at Norfolk
21-24 . . . . . . Charlotte
25-28 . . . . . . Rochester
29-30 . . . . . . Louisville

LEHIGH VALLEY IRONPIGS

APRIL
4-7. . . . . Syracuse
8-10 . . . . Pawtucket
12-14 . . . . at Syracuse
15-18 . . . . at Pawtucket
19-22 . . . . Buffalo
23-26 . . . at Indianapolis
27-30 . . . . at Louisville

MAY
2-5. . . . . . .Indianapolis
6-9. . . . . . . Louisville
10-13 . . . .at Durham
14-17 . . . . . at Norfolk
18-21 . . . . . . Rochester
23-26 . . . . . .Norfolk
27-30 . . . . at Rochester
31 . . . . Gwinnett

JUNE
1-3. . . . . Gwinnett
4-7. . . . . at Buffalo
8-11 . . . . Charlotte
13-16 . .Scranton/Wilkes-Barre
17-20 . . . . . . .at Toledo
21-24 . . . . at Columbus
25-28 . . . . . Durham
29-30 . . . . . . Toledo

LOUISVILLE BATS

APRIL
4-7. . . . . Toledo
8-10 . . . . Columbus
11-14 . . . . .at Toledo

9-12 . . . . . . Lehigh Valley
13-16 . . . . Durham
17-20 . . . . . .at Toledo
22-25 . . . . at Columbus
26-27 . . . . . . .Norfolk
28-30 . . . . Durham
31 . . . . .at Charlotte

SEPTEMBER
1-2. . . . . . . .at Charlotte

JULY
1 . . . . Louisville
2-3. . . . . . at Louisville
4 . . . . Louisville
5-7. . . . . .at Toledo
8-10 . . . . . at Columbus
11-12 . . . . . at Louisville
13-14 . . . . . . Columbus
18-21 . . . . at Gwinnett
22-25 . . . . . .at Charlotte
26-29 . . . . Syracuse
30-31 . .Scranton/Wilkes-Barre

AUGUST
1-2. . Scranton/Wilkes-Barre
3-5. . . . . Louisville
6-7. . . . . at Louisville
8-9. . . . . Toledo
10-11 . . . . . .at Toledo
13-16 . . . . . . Columbus
17-20 . . . . at Syracuse
22-25 . . . . at Rochester
26-27 . . . . Toledo
28-29 . . . . . .at Toledo
30-31 . . . . . . Louisville

SEPTEMBER
1-2. . . . . . . at Louisville

JULY
1-2 . . . . Toledo
3 . . . . Syracuse
4-5. . . . . at Syracuse
6-7. . at Scranton/Wilkes-Barre
8-10 . . . . . . .Pawtucket
11-12 . . . . Buffalo
13-14 . . . . at Syracuse
18-21 . . . . . . Columbus
22-25 . . . . at Rochester
26-29 . . . . at Pawtucket
30-31 . . . . . . Rochester

AUGUST
1-2. . . . . Rochester
3-4. . at Scranton/Wilkes-Barre
5-8. . . . . . . .at Charlotte
9-12 . . . . . .at Gwinnett
14-16 . . . . . . Syracuse
17-18 at Scranton/Wilkes-Barre
19-20 .at Scranton/Wilkes-Barre
22-25 . . . . . at Buffalo
26-27 . . . . Buffalo
28-29 . at Scranton/Wilkes-Barre
30-31 . .Scranton/Wilkes-Barre

SEPTEMBER
1-2. . . . . . . .Pawtucket

APRIL
15-17 . . . . . at Columbus
18-20 . . . . .Indianapolis
21-22 . . . .at Indianapolis
23-26 . . . . Gwinnett

27-30 . . . . . Lehigh Valley

MAY
2-5. . . . . at Buffalo
6-9. . . . . at Lehigh Valley
10-13 . . . . Buffalo
14-17 . . . . . .at Charlotte
18-21 . . . . . at Gwinnett
23-26 . . . . . .Pawtucket
27-30 . . . . . . Columbus
31 . . . . .at Toledo

JUNE
1-3. . . . . . . .at Toledo
4-7. . . . . .Norfolk
8-11 . . . . Durham
13-16 . . . . . at Norfolk
17-20 . . . . .at Durham
21-24 . . . . . . Rochester
25-28 . . . . . Charlotte
29-30 . . . at Indianapolis

JULY
1 . . . . . . at Indianapolis
2-3. . . . . . .Indianapolis

NORFOLK TIDES

APRIL
4-7. . . . . Durham
8-10 . . . . Charlotte
11-12 . . . . . .at Durham
13-14 . . . . . . Gwinnett
15-18 . . . . at Gwinnett
19-21 . . . . . .at Durham
23-26 . . . . at Charlotte
27-30 . . . . . . Toledo

MAY
2-5. . . . . Syracuse
6-9. . . . . . . at Buffalo
10-13 . . . . . at Syracuse
14-17 . . . Lehigh Valley
18-19 . . . . . .at Durham
21-22 . . . . . . Durham
23-26 . . . Lehigh Valley
27-30 . .Scranton/Wilkes-Barre
31 . . . . Buffalo

JUNE
1-3. . . . . Buffalo
4-7. . . . . . .at Louisville
8-11 . . . . . at Indianapolis
13-16 . . . . . Louisville
17-20 . . . . .Indianapolis
21-23 . at Scranton/Wilkes-Barre
25-28 . . . . Columbus

PAWTUCKET RED SOX

APRIL
4-7. . at Scranton/Wilkes-Barre
8-10 . . . . at Lehigh Valley
11-14 . . . . . . Rochester
15-18 . . . . Lehigh Valley
19-22 . . . . at Rochester
23-26 . . . . at Buffalo
27-30 . . . . . . Columbus

MAY
2-5. . . . . Durham
6-9. . . . . . .at Gwinnett
10-13 . . . . .at Charlotte
14-17 . . . . . . Gwinnett
18-21 . . . . .Indianapolis
23-26 . . . at Louisville
27-30 . . . . at Indianapolis
31 . . . . Syracuse

JUNE
1-3. . . . . Syracuse
4-7. . . . . . . Charlotte

---

4 . . . . at Indianapolis
5-7. . . . . . . at Columbus
8-10 . . . . . . .at Toledo
11-14 . . . . Toledo
18-21 . .at Scranton/Wilkes-Barre
22-25 . . . . . at Syracuse
26-29 . .Scranton/Wilkes-Barre
30-31 . . . . . . Syracuse

AUGUST
1-2. . . . . Syracuse
3-5. . . . at Indianapolis
6-7. . . . . . .Indianapolis
8-9. . . . . at Columbus
10-11 . . . . . Columbus
13-16 . . . . at Pawtucket
17-20 . . . . at Rochester
22-25 . . . . Toledo
26-27 . . . . . Columbus
28-29 . . . . at Columbus
30-31 . . . . at Indianapolis

SEPTEMBER
1-2. . . . . . . .Indianapolis

29-30 . . . . Gwinnett

JULY
1-3. . . . . Gwinnett
4-5. . . . . . .at Durham
6-7. . . . . . .at Charlotte
8-11 . . . . Gwinnett
12-14 . . . . . . Charlotte
18-19 . . . . at Charlotte
20-21 . . . . . Charlotte
22-25 . . . . . .Pawtucket
26-29 . . . . at Rochester
30-31 . . . . at Pawtucket

AUGUST
1-2. . . . . . at Pawtucket
3-4. . . . . . . Charlotte
5-8. . . . . Gwinnett
9-12 . . . . . . Rochester
13-16 . . . . . .at Toledo
17-20 . . . . at Columbus
22-23 . . . . . . Durham
24-25 . . . .at Durham
26-27 . . . . at Gwinnett
28-30 . . . . at Charlotte
31 . . . . Durham

SEPTEMBER
1-2. . . . . Durham

8-11 . . . . . . at Syracuse
13-16 . . . . Buffalo
17-20 . . . . at Columbus
21-24 . . . . . .at Toledo
25-28 . . . . Toledo
29-30 . .Scranton/Wilkes-Barre

JULY
1-3 . . Scranton/Wilkes-Barre
4-7. . . . . . at Rochester
8-10 . . . at Lehigh Valley
11-14 . . . . at Rochester
18-21 . . . . . .at Durham
22-25 . . . . . .at Norfolk
26-29 . . . Lehigh Valley
30-31 . . . . . . .Norfolk

AUGUST
1-2. . . . . .Norfolk
3-6. . . . . . . at Buffalo
8-11 . . . . . at Syracuse
13-16 . . . . . . Louisville

17-20 . . . . Buffalo
21-24. .at Scranton/Wilkes-Barre
25-27 Scranton/Wilkes-Barre

28-31 . . . . Syracuse
SEPTEMBER
1-2. . . . . at Lehigh Valley

ROCHESTER RED WINGS

APRIL	
4-5. . . . . at Buffalo	
6-7. . . . . Buffalo	
8-10 . .at Scranton/Wilkes-Barre	
11-14 . . . . . at Pawtucket	
15-18 . .Scranton/Wilkes-Barre	
19-22 . . . . Pawtucket	
23-26 . . . . . . at Syracuse	
27-30 . . . . Buffalo	

25-28 . . . . .at Indianapolis
29-30 . . . . . . at Syracuse
JULY
1-2. . . . . Syracuse
3 . . . . at Buffalo
4-7. . . . . .Pawtucket
8-10 . .at Scranton/Wilkes-Barre
11-14 . . . . . at Pawtucket
18-19 . . . . Syracuse
20-21 . . . . . at Syracuse
22-25 . . . . . Lehigh Valley
26-29 . . . . Norfolk
30-31 . . . at Lehigh Valley

MAY
2-5. . . . . . . at Columbus
6-9. . . . . .at Toledo
10-13 . . . . Columbus
14-17 . . . . Durham
18-21 . . . . at Lehigh Valley
23-26 . . . . Charlotte
27-30 . . . . . Lehigh Valley
31 . . . . at Charlotte

AUGUST
1-2. . . . . . at Lehigh Valley
3-4. . . . . .Syracuse
5-8. . . . . .at Durham
9-12. . . . . . . at Norfolk
14-16 . . . . . . at Buffalo
17-20 . . . . . . Louisville
22-25 . . . . .Indianapolis
26-27 . . . . . . .Syracuse
28-29 . . . . . at Buffalo
30-31 . . . . Buffalo

JUNE
1-3. . . . . at Charlotte
4-7. . . . . . . at Gwinnett
8-11 . . . . Toledo
13-16 . . . . . . Gwinnett
17-18 . .at Scranton/Wilkes-Barre
19-20 . .Scranton/Wilkes-Barre
21-24 . . . . at Louisville

SEPTEMBER
1-2. . Scranton/Wilkes-Barre

SCRANTON/WILKES-BARRE RAILRIDERS

APRIL	
4-7. . . . . .Pawtucket	
8-10 . . . . Rochester	
11-14 . . . . . . at Buffalo	
15-18 . . . . . at Rochester	
19-22 . . . . . . Syracuse	
23-26 . . . . . . Columbus	
27-30 . . . . . .at Charlotte	

MAY
2-5. . . . . at Gwinnett
6-9. . . . . . . .Indianapolis
10-13 . . . . . . Gwinnett
14-17 . . . . . . .at Toledo
18-21 . . . . at Columbus
23-26 . . . . . . Durham
27-30 . . . . at Norfolk
31 . . . . .at Durham

JUNE
1-3. . . . . .at Durham
4-5. . . . . Syracuse
6-7. . . . . . at Syracuse
8-11 . . . . Buffalo
13-16 . . . at Lehigh Valley
17-18 . . . . . . Rochester
19-20 . . . . at Rochester
21-23 . . . . . . .Norfolk
25-28 . . . . at Syracuse

29-30 . . . . . at Pawtucket
JULY
1-3. . . . . . . at Pawtucket
4-5. . . . . Buffalo
6-7. . . . . . . Lehigh Valley
8-10 . . . . Rochester
11-12 . . . . . . Syracuse
13-14 . . . . . at Buffalo
18-21 . . . . . . Louisville
22-25 . . . . Toledo
26-29 . . . . at Louisville
30-31 . . . .at Indianapolis

AUGUST
1-2. . . . . . .at Indianapolis
3-4. . . . . . . Lehigh Valley
6-7. . . . . . . at Syracuse
8-9. . . . . . . at Buffalo
10-11 . . . . Buffalo
13-16 . . . . . . Charlotte
17-18 . . . . . Lehigh Valley
19-20 . . . at Lehigh Valley
21-24 . . . . . .Pawtucket
25-27 . . . . at Pawtucket
28-29 . . . . . Lehigh Valley
30-31 . . . at Lehigh Valley

SEPTEMBER
1-2. . . . . . . at Rochester

SYRACUSE CHIEFS

APRIL	MAY
4-7. . . . . at Lehigh Valley	2-5. . . . . . . .at Norfolk
8-10 . . . . . . at Buffalo	6-9. . . . . . . .at Durham
12-14 . . . . . Lehigh Valley	10-13 . . . . . . .Norfolk
15-18 . . . . . . Buffalo	14-17 . . . . . . Columbus
19-22 . .at Scranton/Wilkes-Barre	18-21 . . . . . .at Toledo
23-26 . . . . . . Rochester	23-26 . . . . at Columbus
27-30 . . . . . . Durham	27-30 . . . . . . Gwinnett
	31 . . . . .at Pawtucket

JUNE

1-3. . . . . . . .at Pawtucket
4-5 at Scranton/Wilkes-Barre
6-7. . Scranton/Wilkes-Barre
8-11 . . . . .Pawtucket
13-16 . . . . Toledo
17-20 . . . . . .at Charlotte
21-23 . . . . . at Gwinnett
25-28 . .Scranton/Wilkes-Barre
29-30 . . . . . . Rochester

JULY
1-2. . . . . . . at Rochester
3 . . . . at Lehigh Valley
4-5. . . . . . Lehigh Valley
6-7. . . . . . . at Buffalo
9-10 . . . . Buffalo
11-12 . .at Scranton/Wilkes-Barre
13-14 . . . . . Lehigh Valley

TOLEDO MUD HENS

APRIL	
4-7. . . . . . . .at Louisville	
8-10 . . . .at Indianapolis	
11-14 . . . . . . Louisville	
15-17 . . . .Indianapolis	
18-19 . . . . . Columbus	
20-22 . . . . at Columbus	
23-26 . . . . .at Durham	
27-30 . . . . . . at Norfolk	

MAY
2-5. . . . . Charlotte
6-9. . . . . Rochester
10-13 . . . . at Indianapolis
14-17 . .Scranton/Wilkes-Barre
18-21 . . . . Syracuse
23-26 . . . . at Gwinnett
27-30 . . . .at Charlotte
31 . . . . Louisville

JUNE
1-3. . . . . Louisville
4-5. . . . . . at Columbus
6-7. . . . . . . Columbus
8-11 . . . . at Rochester
13-16 . . . at Syracuse
17-20 . . . . Lehigh Valley
21-24 . . . . . .Pawtucket
25-28 . . . . at Pawtucket

29-30 . . . . at Lehigh Valley
JULY
1-2. . . . . . at Lehigh Valley
3-4. . . . . Columbus
5-7. . . . . . . .Indianapolis
8-10 . . . . Louisville
11-12 . . . . at Columbus
13-14 . . . . .at Louisville
18-21 . . . . . . at Buffalo
22-25 . .at Scranton/Wilkes-Barre
26-29 . . . . Buffalo
30-31 . . . . Durham

AUGUST
1-2. . . . . Durham
3-5. . . . . Columbus
6-7. . . . . . at Columbus
8-9. . . . . .at Indianapolis
10-11 . . . . .Indianapolis
13-16 . . . . . . .Norfolk
17-20 . . . . Gwinnett
22-25 . . . .at Louisville
26-27 . . . . at Indianapolis
28-29 . . . . .Indianapolis
30-31 . . . . . . Columbus

SEPTEMBER
1-2. . . . . . . at Columbus

PACIFIC COAST LEAGUE

ALBUQUERQUE ISOTOPES

APRIL	
4-7. . . . . Iowa	
8-11 . . . . Omaha	
12-15 . . . . .at Iowa	
16-19 . . . . . . at Omaha	
20-23 . . . . Oklahoma City	
25-28 . . . . at Round Rock	
29-30 . . . . Memphis	

MAY
1-2. . . . . Memphis
3-6. . . . . . . New Orleans
7-10 . . . . . . at Tucson
11-14 . . . . . .at Las Vegas
16-19 . . . . Reno
20-23 . . . Colorado Springs
24-27 . . . . at Nashville
28-31 . . . . . at Memphis

JUNE
1-4. . . . . .Oklahoma City
6-9. . . . . .at New Orleans
10-13 . . . . at Round Rock
14-17 . . . . Memphis

18-21 . . . . at Omaha
22-25 . . . . . . .Round Rock
27-30 . . . . . .at Memphis
JULY
1-3. . . . at Oklahoma City
4-7. . . . . Iowa
8-10 . . . . .Nashville
11-14 . . . . . . .at Iowa
18-21 . . . . .Omaha
22-25 . . . . . at Nashville
26-29 . . . . . New Orleans
30-31 . . . at Sacramento

AUGUST
1-2. . . . . . . at Sacramento
3-6. . . . . .at Fresno
8-11 . . . . .Tacoma
12-15 . . . . Salt Lake
16-20 . . . at Oklahoma City
21-25 . . . . . . .Nashville
26-29 . . . . . .Round Rock
30-31 . . . . .at New Orleans

SEPTEMBER
1-2 . . . . . . .at New Orleans

COLORADO SPRINGS SKY SOX

APRIL	
4-7 . . . . Reno	
8-11 . . . . Tucson	
12-15 . . . . . .at Las Vegas	
16-19 . . . . .at Reno	
20-23 . . . . . . Las Vegas	
25-28 . . . . . . at Tucson	
29-30 . . . . . . at Salt Lake	

MAY	
1-2 . . . . . . at Salt Lake	
3-6 . . . . .at Fresno	
7-10 . . . . Iowa	
11-14 . . . . Omaha	
16-19 . . . . at Round Rock	
20-23 . . . . at Albuquerque	
24-27 . . . . Fresno	
28-31 . . . . .Tacoma	

JUNE	
1-4 . . . . at Salt Lake	
6-9 . . . . .at Reno	
10-13 . . . . .Salt Lake	
14-17 . . .at Las Vegas	
18-21 . . . . .Tacoma	

22-25 . . . . . at Sacramento	
27-30 . . . . Tucson	

JULY	
1-3 . . . . at Tacoma	
4-7 . . . . Reno	
8-10 . . . . . . .Sacramento	
11-14 . . . . .Salt Lake	
18-21 . . . . at Tucson	
22-25 . . . . at Sacramento	
26-29 . . . . Fresno	
30-31 . . . .at New Orleans	

AUGUST	
1-2 . . . . . .at New Orleans	
3-6 . . . . at Oklahoma City	
8-11 . . . . .Nashville	
12-15 . . . . Memphis	
16-20 . . . . at Tacoma	
21-25 . . . . . . .Sacramento	
26-29 . . . . . . Las Vegas	
30-31 . . . . .at Fresno	

SEPTEMBER	
1-2 . . . . .at Fresno	

FRESNO GRIZZLIES

APRIL	
4-7 . . . . .Tacoma	
8-11 . . . . Las Vegas	
12-15 . . . . at Tucson	
16-19 . . . . . . at Tacoma	
20-23 . . . . Tucson	
25-28 . . . . .at Reno	
29-30 . . . . . . Sacramento	

MAY	
1-2 . . . . .Sacramento	
3-6 . . . . Colorado Springs	
7-10 . . . . at Nashville	
11-14 . . . . . at Memphis	
16-19 . . . . New Orleans	
20-23 . . . .Oklahoma City	
24-27 . .at Colorado Springs	
28-31 . . . . . . at Tucson	

JUNE	
1-4 . . . . Las Vegas	
6-9 . . . . at Salt Lake	
10-13 . . . . Tucson	
14-17 . . . . . .Salt Lake	
18-21 . . . . .at Reno	

22-25 . . . . . . at Tacoma	
27-30 . . . . .Salt Lake	

JULY	
1-3 . . . . .at Las Vegas	
4-7 . . . . .Sacramento	
8-10 . . . . Reno	
11-14 . . . . at Sacramento	
18-21 . . . . .Tacoma	
22-25 . . . . .Salt Lake	
26-29 . .at Colorado Springs	
30-31 . . . . . . .Round Rock	

AUGUST	
1-2 . . . . .Round Rock	
3-6 . . . . Albuquerque	
8-11 . . . . .at Iowa	
12-15 . . . . . at Omaha	
16-20 . . . . Reno	
21-25 . . . . . .at Las Vegas	
26-29 . . . at Sacramento	
30-31 . . . Colorado Springs	

SEPTEMBER	
1-2 . . . . . Colorado Springs	

IOWA CUBS

APRIL	
4-7 . . . . . . at Albuquerque	
8-11 . . . . . .at Round Rock	
12-15 . . . . . Albuquerque	
16-19 . . . . .Nashville	
20-23 . . . . . at Memphis	
25-28 . . . . . . at Omaha	
29-30 . . . . . .Round Rock	

MAY	
1-2 . . . . .Round Rock	
3-6 . . . . . . .Oklahoma City	
7-10 . .at Colorado Springs	
11-14 . . . . .at Reno	
16-19 . . . . Tucson	
20-23 . . . . . Las Vegas	
24-27 . . . .Oklahoma City	
28-31 . . . . . . at Nashville	

JUNE	
1-4 . . . . New Orleans	
6-9 . . . . .Round Rock	
10-13 . . at Oklahoma City	
14-17 . . . . .Omaha	
18-21 . . . . .Nashville	
22-26 . . . . . at Memphis	
27-30 . . . . . . at Omaha	

JULY	
1-3 . . . . Memphis	
4-7 . . . . . at Albuquerque	
8-10 . . . .at New Orleans	
11-14 . . . . . Albuquerque	
18-21 . . . . at Round Rock	
22-25 . . . . . New Orleans	
26-29 . . at Oklahoma City	
30-31 . . . . . . at Salt Lake	

LAS VEGAS 51S

APRIL	
4-7 . . . . . . at Sacramento	
8-11 . . . . .at Fresno	
12-15 . . . Colorado Springs	
16-19 . . . . . .Sacramento	
20-23 . .at Colorado Springs	
25-28 . . . . .Tacoma	
29-30 . . . . .at Reno	

MAY	
1-2 . . . . .at Reno	
3-6 . . . . . . at Sacramento	
7-10 . . . . . . .Round Rock	
11-14 . . . . . Albuquerque	
16-19 . . . . . at Omaha	
20-23 . . . . . . .at Iowa	
24-27 . . . . . .Salt Lake	
28-31 . . . . Reno	

JUNE	
1-4 . . . . .at Fresno	
6-9 . . . . at Tacoma	
10-13 . . . . .Tacoma	
14-17 . . . Colorado Springs	
18-21 . . . . . . at Tucson	

22-25 . . . . .Salt Lake	
27-30 . . . . at Tacoma	

JULY	
1-3 . . . . Fresno	
4-7 . . . . at Tucson	
8-10 . . . . . . at Salt Lake	
11-13 . . . . at Tucson	
18-21 . . . . .at Reno	
22-25 . . . . Reno	
26-29 . . . . . . .Sacramento	
30-31 . . . . . at Nashville	

AUGUST	
1-2 . . . . at Nashville	
3-6 . . . . at Memphis	
8-11 . . . .Oklahoma City	
12-15 . . . New Orleans	
16-20 . . . . at Salt Lake	
21-25 . . . . Fresno	
26-29 . .at Colorado Springs	
30-31 . . . . Tucson	

SEPTEMBER	
1-2 . . . . Tucson	

MEMPHIS REDBIRDS

APRIL	
4-7 . . . . . . .Oklahoma City	
8-11 . . . . New Orleans	
12-15 . . . at Oklahoma City	
16-19 . . . .at New Orleans	
20-23 . . . . Iowa	
25-28 . . . . . . at Nashville	
29-30 . . . at Albuquerque	

MAY	
1-2 . . . . . at Albuquerque	
3-6 . . . . at Omaha	
7-10 . . . . . . .Sacramento	
11-14 . . . . Fresno	
16-19 . . . . . at Tacoma	
20-23 . . . . at Salt Lake	
24-27 . . . . . .Round Rock	
28-31 . . . . . Albuquerque	

JUNE	
1-4 . . . . at Omaha	
6-9 . . . . .Nashville	
10-13 . . . . . New Orleans	
14-17 . . . at Albuquerque	
18-21 . . . . . at Round Rock	

22-25 . . . . Iowa	
27-30 . . . . . Albuquerque	

JULY	
1-3 . . . . .at Iowa	
4-7 . . . . .Nashville	
8-10 . . . . .Omaha	
11-14 . . . . . at Nashville	
18-21 . . . . .Oklahoma City	
22-25 . . . . . . .Round Rock	
26-29 . . . . at Round Rock	
30-31 . . . . Tucson	

AUGUST	
1-2 . . . . Tucson	
3-6 . . . . Las Vegas	
8-11 . . . . .at Reno	
12-15 . .at Colorado Springs	
16-20 . . . . .Omaha	
21-25 . . . . .at Iowa	
26-29 . .at New Orleans	
30-31 . . . at Oklahoma City	

SEPTEMBER	
1-2 . . . . . at Oklahoma City	

NASHVILLE SOUNDS

APRIL	
4-7 . . . . New Orleans	
8-11 . . . . .Oklahoma City	
12-15 . . . . . . at Omaha	
16-19 . . . . at Iowa	
20-23 . . . . .Omaha	
25-28 . . . . . Memphis	
29-30 . . . at Oklahoma City	

MAY	
1-2 . . . . at Oklahoma City	
3-6 . . . . at Round Rock	
7-10 . . . . Fresno	
11-14 . . . . . .Sacramento	
16-19 . . . . . . at Salt Lake	

20-23 . . . . .at Tacoma	
24-27 . . . . . Albuquerque	
28-31 . . . . Iowa	

JUNE	
1-4 . . . . . . at Round Rock	
6-9 . . . . .at Memphis	
10-13 . . . . .Omaha	
14-17 . . . . New Orleans	
18-21 . . . . .at Iowa	
22-25 . . .at New Orleans	
27-30 . . . .Oklahoma City	

JULY	
1-3 . . . . .Round Rock	

AUGUST
1-2 . . . . at Salt Lake
3-6 . . . . at Tacoma
8-11 . . . . Fresno
12-15 . . . . . . .Sacramento
16-20 . . . . .at New Orleans
21-25 . . . . Memphis
26-29 . . . . .Omaha
30-31 . . . . . . at Nashville
SEPTEMBER
1-2 . . . . at Nashville

4-7 . . . . .at Memphis
8-10 . . . . at Albuquerque
11-14 . . . . . Memphis
18-21 . . .at New Orleans
22-25 . . . . . .Albuquerque
26-29 . . . . . . at Omaha
30-31 . . . . . Las Vegas

AUGUST
1-2 . . . . Las Vegas

NEW ORLEANS ZEPHYRS

APRIL
4-7 . . . . at Nashville
8-11 . . . . at Memphis
12-15 . . . . . .Round Rock
16-19 . . . . . Memphis
20-23 . . at Round Rock
25-28 . . at Oklahoma City
29-30 . . . . .Omaha

MAY
1-2 . . . . .Omaha
3-6 . . . . . at Albuquerque
7-10 . . . . .Salt Lake
11-14 . . . . .Tacoma
16-19 . . . . . . .at Fresno
20-23 . . at Sacramento
24-27 . . . . . . .Omaha
28-31 . . . . . .Round Rock

JUNE
1-4 . . . . .at Iowa
6-9 . . . . . Albuquerque
10-13 . . . . .at Memphis
14-17 . . . . at Nashville
18-21 . . . .Oklahoma City

22-25 . . . . .Nashville
27-30 . . . . . at Round Rock

JULY
1-3 . . . . at Omaha
4-7 . . . . . Oklahoma City
8-10 . . . . .Iowa
11-14 . . at Oklahoma City
18-21 . . . . .Nashville
22-25 . . . . .at Iowa
26-29 . . at Albuquerque
30-31 . . Colorado Springs

AUGUST
1-2 . . . . Colorado Springs
3-6 . . . . Reno
8-11 . . . . . at Tucson
12-15 . . . . . .at Las Vegas
16-20 . . . . Iowa
21-25 . . . . . at Omaha
26-29 . . . . . Memphis
30-31 . . . . . Albuquerque

SEPTEMBER
1-2 . . . . Albuquerque

OKLAHOMA CITY REDHAWKS

APRIL
4-7 . . . . . . .at Memphis
8-11 . . . . . . at Nashville
12-15 . . . . Memphis
16-19 . . . . .Round Rock
20-23 . . . . at Albuquerque
25-28 . . . . . New Orleans
29-30 . . . . . .Nashville

MAY
1-2 . . . . .Nashville
3-6 . . . . .at Iowa
7-10 . . . . .Tacoma
11-14 . . . . .Salt Lake
16-19 . . . . at Sacramento
20-23 . . . . . . .at Fresno
24-27 . . . . . at Iowa
28-31 . . . . .Omaha

JUNE
1-4 . . . . at Albuquerque
6-9 . . . . . . at Omaha
10-13 . . . . Iowa
14-17 . . . . .Round Rock
18-21 . . . .at New Orleans

OMAHA STORM CHASERS

APRIL
4-7 . . . . . . at Round Rock
8-11 . . . . . at Albuquerque
12-15 . . . . .Nashville
16-19 . . . . . Albuquerque
20-23 . . . . at Nashville
25-28 . . . . Iowa
29-30 . . . .at New Orleans

MAY
1-2 . . . . . .at New Orleans

3-6 . . . . Memphis
7-10 . . . . .at Reno
11-14 . .at Colorado Springs
16-19 . . . . . . Las Vegas
20-23 . . . . Tucson
24-27 . . . .at New Orleans
28-31 . . at Oklahoma City

JUNE
1-4 . . . . Memphis
6-9 . . . . . . Oklahoma City

10-13 . . . . . . at Nashville
14-17 . . . . .at Iowa
18-21 . . . . Albuquerque
22-25 . . at Oklahoma City
27-30 . . . . Iowa

JULY
1-3 . . . . New Orleans
4-7 . . . . . . at Round Rock
8-10 . . . . . .at Memphis
11-14 . . . . . .Round Rock
18-21 . . . . at Albuquerque
22-25 . . . .Oklahoma City
26-29 . . . . .Nashville

JULY
1-3 . . . . New Orleans
4-7 . . . . . . at Round Rock
8-10 . . . . . .at Memphis
11-14 . . . . . .Round Rock
18-21 . . . . at Albuquerque
22-25 . . . .Oklahoma City
26-29 . . . . .Nashville

RENO ACES

APRIL
4-7 . . .at Colorado Springs
8-11 . . . . . . at Salt Lake
12-15 . . . . .Sacramento
16-19 . . . Colorado Springs
20-23 . . . . at Sacramento
25-28 . . . . Fresno
29-30 . . . Las Vegas

MAY
1-2 . . . . . . Las Vegas
3-6 . . . . at Tacoma
7-10 . . . . .Omaha
11-14 . . . . Iowa
16-19 . . . at Albuquerque
20-23 . . . at Round Rock
24-27 . . . . .Tacoma
28-31 . . . . .at Las Vegas

JUNE
1-4 . . . . Tucson
6-9 . . . . Colorado Springs
10-13 . . . . . .Sacramento
14-17 . . . . at Tucson
18-21 . . . . Fresno

ROUND ROCK EXPRESS

APRIL
4-7 . . . . .Omaha
8-11 . . . . Iowa
12-15 . . . .at New Orleans
16-19 . . at Oklahoma City
20-23 . . . . . New Orleans
25-28 . . . . . Albuquerque
29-30 . . . . .at Iowa

MAY
1-2 . . . . .at Iowa
3-6 . . . . .Nashville
7-10 . . . .at Las Vegas
11-14 . . . . . . at Tucson
16-19 . . . Colorado Springs
20-23 . . . . Reno
24-27 . . . . .at Memphis
28-31 . . . .at New Orleans

JUNE
1-4 . . . . .Nashville
6-9 . . . . .at Iowa
10-13 . . . . . Albuquerque
14-17 . . at Oklahoma City
18-21 . . . . Memphis

SACRAMENTO RIVER CATS

APRIL
4-7 . . . . Las Vegas
8-11 . . . . .Tacoma
12-15 . . . . .at Reno
16-19 . . . .at Las Vegas
20-23 . . . . Reno
25-28 . . . . .Salt Lake

10-13 . . . . . . at Nashville
14-17 . . . . .at Iowa
18-21 . . . . . . Albuquerque
22-25 . . at Oklahoma City
27-30 . . . . Iowa

JULY
1-3 . . . . New Orleans
4-7 . . . . . . at Round Rock
8-10 . . . . . .at Memphis
11-14 . . . . . .Round Rock
18-21 . . . . at Albuquerque
22-25 . . . .Oklahoma City
26-29 . . . . .Nashville

22-25 . . . . Tucson
27-30 . . . . at Sacramento

JULY
1-3 . . . . .Salt Lake
4-7 . . .at Colorado Springs
8-10 . . . . .at Fresno
11-14 . . . . . . at Tacoma
18-21 . . . . . . Las Vegas
22-25 . . . . . .at Las Vegas
26-29 . . . . .Tacoma
30-31 . . . at Oklahoma City

AUGUST
1-2 . . . . . at Oklahoma City
3-6 . . . .at New Orleans
8-11 . . . . Memphis
12-15 . . . . .Nashville
16-20 . . . . . . .at Fresno
21-25 . . . . . . .Salt Lake
26-29 . . . . . at Tucson
30-31 . . . . . .at Salt Lake

SEPTEMBER
1-2 . . . . at Salt Lake

22-25 . . . . at Albuquerque
27-30 . . . . . New Orleans

JULY
1-3 . . . . at Nashville
4-7 . . . . .Omaha
8-10 . . . .Oklahoma City
11-14 . . . . . at Omaha
18-21 . . . . Iowa
22-25 . . . . . .at Memphis
26-29 . . . . . . Memphis
30-31 . . . . .at Fresno

AUGUST
1-2 . . . . .at Fresno
3-6 . . . . at Sacramento
8-11 . . . . .Salt Lake
12-15 . . . . .Tacoma
16-20 . . . . . at Nashville
21-25 . . . . . Oklahoma City
26-29 . . . at Albuquerque
30-31 . . . . . at Omaha

SEPTEMBER
1-2 . . . . .at Omaha

29-30 . . . . .at Fresno

MAY
1-2 . . . . .at Fresno
3-6 . . . . . Las Vegas
7-10 . . . . . . .at Memphis
11-14 . . . . . at Nashville
16-19 . . . .Oklahoma City

20-23	New Orleans
24-27	at Tucson
28-31	Salt Lake

JUNE

1-4	at Tacoma
6-9	at Tucson
10-13	at Reno
14-17	Tacoma
18-21	at Salt Lake
22-25	Colorado Springs
27-30	Reno

JULY

1-3	Tucson
4-7	at Fresno
8-10	at Colorado Springs
11-14	Fresno

18-21	at Salt Lake
22-25	Colorado Springs
26-29	at Las Vegas
30-31	Albuquerque

AUGUST

1-2	Albuquerque
3-6	Round Rock
8-11	at Omaha
12-15	at Iowa
16-20	Tucson
21-25	at Colorado Springs
26-29	Fresno
30-31	at Tacoma

SEPTEMBER

1-2	at Tacoma

16-19	Fresno
20-23	at Salt Lake
25-28	at Las Vegas
29-30	Tucson

MAY

1-2	Tucson
3-6	Reno
7-10	at Oklahoma City
11-14	at New Orleans
16-19	Memphis
20-23	Nashville
24-27	at Reno
28-31	at Colorado Springs

JUNE

1-4	Sacramento
6-9	Las Vegas
10-13	at Las Vegas
14-17	at Sacramento
18-21	at Colorado Springs
22-25	Fresno
27-30	Las Vegas

JULY

1-3	Colorado Springs
4-7	at Salt Lake
8-10	at Tucson
11-14	Reno
18-21	at Fresno
22-25	Tucson
26-29	at Reno
30-31	Omaha

AUGUST

1-2	Omaha
3-6	Iowa
8-11	at Albuquerque
12-15	at Round Rock
16-20	Colorado Springs
21-25	at Tucson
26-29	Salt Lake
30-31	Sacramento

SEPTEMBER

1-2	Sacramento

SALT LAKE BEES

APRIL

4-7	Tucson
8-11	Reno
12-15	at Tacoma
16-19	at Tucson
20-23	Tacoma
25-28	at Sacramento
29-30	Colorado Springs

MAY

1-2	Colorado Springs
3-6	Tucson
7-10	at New Orleans
11-14	at Oklahoma City
16-19	Nashville
20-23	Memphis
24-27	at Las Vegas
28-31	at Sacramento

JUNE

1-4	Colorado Springs
6-9	Fresno
10-13	at Colorado Springs
14-17	at Fresno
18-21	Sacramento

22-25	at Las Vegas
27-30	at Fresno

JULY

1-3	at Reno
4-7	Tacoma
8-10	Las Vegas
11-14	at Colorado Springs
18-21	Sacramento
22-25	Fresno
26-29	at Tucson
30-31	Iowa

AUGUST

1-2	Iowa
3-6	Omaha
8-11	at Round Rock
12-15	at Albuquerque
16-20	Las Vegas
21-25	at Reno
26-29	at Tacoma
30-31	Reno

SEPTEMBER

1-2	Reno

TACOMA RAINIERS

APRIL

4-7	at Fresno

8-11	at Sacramento
12-15	Salt Lake

TUCSON PADRES

APRIL

4-7	at Salt Lake
8-11	at Colorado Springs
12-15	Fresno
16-19	Salt Lake
20-23	at Fresno
25-28	Colorado Springs
29-30	at Tacoma

MAY

1-2	at Tacoma
3-6	at Salt Lake
7-10	Albuquerque
11-14	Round Rock
16-19	at Iowa
20-23	at Omaha
24-27	Sacramento
28-31	Fresno

JUNE

1-4	at Reno
6-9	Sacramento
10-13	at Fresno
14-17	Reno
18-21	Las Vegas

22-25	at Reno
27-30	at Colorado Springs

JULY

1-3	at Sacramento
4-7	Las Vegas
8-10	Tacoma
11-13	at Las Vegas
18-21	Colorado Springs
22-25	at Tacoma
26-29	Salt Lake
30-31	at Memphis

AUGUST

1-2	at Memphis
3-6	at Nashville
8-11	New Orleans
12-15	Oklahoma City
16-20	at Sacramento
21-25	Tacoma
26-29	Reno
30-31	at Las Vegas

SEPTEMBER

1-2	at Las Vegas

DOUBLE-A

EASTERN LEAGUE

AKRON AEROS

APRIL

4-7	Binghamton
8-10	Altoona
11-14	at Bowie
15-17	at Trenton
18-21	Bowie
22-24	Trenton
26-28	at Binghamton
29-30	at Altoona

MAY

1-2	at Altoona
3-5	Bowie
6-8	Erie
9-12	at Reading
13-15	at Binghamton
17-19	Erie
20-23	Bowie
24-27	at Erie
28-30	Harrisburg

31	at Reading

JUNE

1-2	at Reading
4-6	New Hampshire
7-9	Portland
11-13	at New Hampshire
14-16	at Portland
18-20	Trenton
21-23	New Britain
24-26	at Harrisburg
27-30	Altoona

JULY

1-3	at Bowie
4-8	at Richmond
11-14	Altoona
15-17	Erie
18-21	at Harrisburg
22-24	at Bowie

25-28	Richmond
30-31	at New Britain

AUGUST

1	at New Britain
2-4	at Altoona
6-8	New Britain
9-11	at Trenton
13-15	at Richmond

ALTOONA CURVE

APRIL

4-7	at Erie
8-10	at Akron
11-14	Harrisburg
15-17	Richmond
18-21	at Harrisburg
22-24	at Richmond
26-28	Erie
29-30	Akron

MAY

1-2	Akron
3-5	at Erie

16-18	Reading
19-21	at Erie
22-25	Binghamton
26-29	Erie
30-31	at Altoona

SEPTEMBER

1-2	at Altoona

6-8	at Harrisburg
9-12	Richmond
14-16	Trenton
17-19	at Richmond
20-23	at Reading
24-27	Richmond
28-30	at Binghamton
31	at Portland

JUNE

1-2	at Portland
4-6	Reading
7-9	Binghamton

11-13 . . . . . at New Britain
14-16 . . . . Trenton
18-20 . . . New Hampshire
21-23 . . . . at Bowie
24-26 . . . . . New Britain
27-30 . . . . at Akron

JULY
1-3 . . . . . .at Binghamton
4-8 . . . . Erie
11-14 . . . . . . at Akron
15-17 . . . . .Bowie
18-21 . . . . Erie
22-24 . . . . . . at Trenton
25-28 . . at New Hampshire

BINGHAMTON METS

APRIL
4-7 . . . . at Akron
8-10 . . . . at Erie
11-14 . . . New Hampshire
15-17 . . . . Portland
18-21 . . at New Hampshire
22-24 . . . . . at Portland
26-28 . . . . .Akron
29-30 . . . . Erie

MAY
1-2 . . . . Erie
3-5 . . . . at Harrisburg
6-8 . . . . at Trenton
9-12 . . . . . . .Harrisburg
13-15 . . . . .Akron
17-19 . . . . . at Portland
20-23 . . . at New Britain
24-27 . . . . . Portland
28-30 . . . . . . Altoona
31 . . . . at New Hampshire

JUNE
1-2 . . at New Hampshire
4-6 . . . . Trenton
7-9 . . . . . .at Altoona
11-13 . . . . . .at Trenton
14-16 . . . . .Bowie

BOWIE BAYSOX

APRIL
4-7 . . . . at Harrisburg
8-10 . . . . . at Richmond
11-14 . . . . .Akron
15-17 . . . . Erie
18-21 . . . . . . at Akron
22-24 . . . . . . at Erie
26-29 . . .Harrisburg
30 . . . . Richmond

MAY
1-2 . . . . Richmond
3-5 . . . . at Akron
6-8 . . . . . . at Richmond
9-12 . . . . Erie
14-16 . . . . . New Britain
17-19 . . . .at Trenton
20-23 . . . . at Akron
24-27 . . . . . Trenton
28-30 . . . . . Reading
31 . . . . . . at New Britain

JUNE
1-2 . . . . . at New Britain
4-6 . . . . . at Harrisburg
7-9 . . . . . New Britain
11-13 . . . . . .at Reading
14-16 . . . .at Binghamton

30-31 . . . . . . Binghamton

AUGUST
1 . . . . Binghamton
2-4 . . . . .Akron
6-8 . . . . . . at Binghamton
9-11 . . . . .Harrisburg
13-15 . . . . Portland
16-18 . . . . at Erie
19-21 . . . . Reading
22-25 . . . . at Richmond
26-29 . . . . at Harrisburg
30-31 . . . . .Akron

SEPTEMBER
1-2 . . . . .Akron

18-20 . . . . . at Richmond
21-23 . . . . Erie
24-26 . . . . . at Portland
27-30 . . . . . Trenton

JULY
1-3 . . . . Altoona
4-8 . . . . at New Hampshire
11-14 . . . . . Portland
15-17 . . . . . Richmond
18-21 . . . . at New Britain
22-24 . . . . . Reading
25-28 . . . . . . Trenton
30-31 . . . .at Altoona

AUGUST
1 . . . . at Altoona
2-4 . . . . at Harrisburg
6-8 . . . . Altoona
9-11 . . . . at Erie
13-15 . . . . .at Reading
16-18 . . . . New Britain
19-21 . . . . . . .Bowie
22-25 . . . . . at Akron
26-29 . . . . . at Bowie
30-31 . . . New Hampshire

SEPTEMBER
1-2 . . . . . New Hampshire

18-20 . . . . . . .Harrisburg
21-23 . . . . . Altoona
24-26 . . . at Richmond
27-30 . . . . . .Harrisburg

JULY
1-3 . . . . .Akron
4-8 . . . . . . at Harrisburg
11-14 . . . . . Richmond
15-17 . . . .at Altoona
18-21 . . . . at Richmond
22-24 . . . . . . .Akron
25-28 . . . . . at Erie
30-31 . . . New Hampshire

AUGUST
1 . . . . New Hampshire
2-4 . . . . Portland
6-8 . . . . at New Hampshire
9-11 . . . . . . at Portland
13-15 . . . . Erie
16-18 . . . . Richmond
19-21 . . . .at Binghamton
22-25 . . . . . New Britain
26-29 . . . . Binghamton
30-31 . . . . at Erie

SEPTEMBER
1-2 . . . . at Erie

ERIE SEAWOLVES

APRIL
4-7 . . . . Altoona
8-10 . . . . . . Binghamton
12-14 . . . . . .at Reading
15-17 . . . . . . at Bowie
18-21 . . . . Trenton
22-24 . . . . .Bowie
26-28 . . . .at Altoona
29-30 . . . .at Binghamton

MAY
1-2 . . . .at Binghamton
3-5 . . . . Altoona
6-8 . . . . . . at Akron
9-12 . . . . . . at Bowie
13-15 . . . . Reading
17-19 . . . . . . at Akron
20-23 . . . . . .Harrisburg
24-27 . . . . .Akron
28-30 . . . . . . at Trenton
31 . . . . . . at Richmond

JUNE
1-2 . . . . . at Richmond
4-6 . . . . Portland
7-9 . . . . . New Hampshire
11-13 . . . . . . at Portland
14-16 . . at New Hampshire

18-20 . . . . . . New Britain
21-23 . . . .at Binghamton
24-26 . . . . . at Trenton
27-30 . . . . . Richmond

JULY
1-3 . . . . .Harrisburg
4-8 . . . . at Altoona
11-14 . . . . . .Harrisburg
15-18 . . . . . . at Akron
19-21 . . . . . .at Altoona
22-24 . . . . . . Richmond
25-28 . . . . . . .Bowie
29-31 . . . .at Reading

AUGUST
1 . . . . .at Reading
2-4 . . . . at New Britain
6-8 . . . . Trenton
9-11 . . . . . . Binghamton
13-15 . . . . . . at Bowie
16-18 . . . . . . Altoona
19-21 . . . . .Akron
22-25 . . . . at Harrisburg
26-29 . . . . . at Akron
30-31 . . . . .Bowie

SEPTEMBER
1-2 . . . . .Bowie

HARRISBURG SENATORS

APRIL
4-7 . . . . .Bowie
8-10 . . . . . New Britain
11-14 . . . .at Altoona
15-16 . . . .at Reading
18-21 . . . . . Altoona
22-24 . . . . . Reading
26-28 . . . . . at Bowie
29-30 . . . at New Britain

MAY
1-2 . . . . . at New Britain
3-5 . . . . . . Binghamton
6-8 . . . . Altoona
9-12 . . . .at Binghamton
13-15 . . . . Richmond
17-19 . . . .at Reading
20-23 . . . . at Erie
24-27 . . . . . Reading
28-30 . . . . . at Akron
31 . . . . Trenton

JUNE
1-2 . . . . Trenton
4-6 . . . . .Bowie
7-10 . . . . . . .at Reading
11-13 . . . . Richmond
14-16 . . . at New Britain
18-20 . . . . . . at Bowie

21-23 . . . . New Hampshire
24-26 . . . . .Akron
27-30 . . . . . at Bowie

JULY
1-3 . . . . at Erie
4-8 . . . . .Bowie
11-14 . . . . . . at Erie
15-17 . . . New Britain
18-21 . . . . .Akron
22-24 . . at New Hampshire
25-28 . . . . . at Portland
30-31 . . . . . . at Trenton

AUGUST
1 . . . . at Trenton
2-4 . . . . Binghamton
6-8 . . . . Reading
9-11 . . . . . .at Altoona
13-15 . . . . . at Trenton
16-18 . . . . Portland
19-21 . . . . at Richmond
22-25 . . . . Erie
26-29 . . . . . . Altoona
30-31 . . . . at Richmond

SEPTEMBER
1-2 . . . . Richmond

NEW BRITAIN ROCK CATS

APRIL
4-7 . . . . at Richmond
8-10 . . . . . at Harrisburg
11-14 . . . . . . Portland
15-17 . . . New Hampshire
18-21 . . . . . . at Portland
23-25 . . at New Hampshire
26-28 . . . . Richmond
29-30 . . . . .Harrisburg

MAY
1-2 . . . . .Harrisburg
3-5 . . . . . . at Portland
6-8 . . . . at New Hampshire

9-12 . . . . Portland
14-16 . . . . at Bowie
17-19 . . . New Hampshire
20-23 . . . . Binghamton
24-27 . . at New Hampshire
28-30 . . . . . . Richmond
31 . . . . .Bowie

JUNE
1-2 . . . . .Bowie
4-6 . . . . at Richmond
7-9 . . . . at Bowie
11-13 . . . . Altoona
14-16 . . . . . . .Harrisburg
18-20 . . . . at Erie

21-23 . . . . at Akron
24-26 . . . . . . .at Altoona
27-30 . . . . Reading

JULY
1-3 . . . . . New Hampshire
4-8 . . . . at Portland
11-14 . . . . Trenton
15-17 . . . . . at Harrisburg
18-21 . . . . . Binghamton
22-24 . . . . Portland
25-28 . . . . . .at Reading
30-31 . . . . .Akron

NEW HAMPSHIRE FISHER CATS

APRIL
4-7 . . . . Reading
8-10 . . . . Trenton
11-14 . . . .at Binghamton
15-17 . . . . at New Britain
18-21 . . . . . Binghamton
23-25 . . . . . New Britain
26-28 . . . . .at Reading
29-30 . . . . . . at Trenton

MAY
1-2 . . . . at Trenton
3-5 . . . . Reading
6-8 . . . . New Britain
9-12 . . . . . . at Trenton
14-16 . . . . . Portland
17-19 . . . . at New Britain
20-23 . . . . . at Portland
24-27 . . . . . New Britain
28-30 . . . . at Portland
31 . . . . Binghamton

JUNE
1-2 . . . . . . Binghamton
4-6 . . . . at Akron
7-9 . . . . at Erie
11-13 . . . . . .Akron
14-16 . . . . . . Erie

18-20 . . . . . . .at Altoona
21-23 . . . at Harrisburg
24-26 . . . . . . Reading
27-30 . . . . . . Portland

JULY
1-3 . . . . . at New Britain
4-8 . . . . Binghamton
11-14 . . .at Reading
15-17 . . . . . Portland
18-21 . . . . at Trenton
22-24 . . . . .Harrisburg
25-28 . . . . . Altoona
30-31 . . . . at Bowie

AUGUST
1 . . . . at Bowie
2-4 . . . . . at Richmond
6-8 . . . . . . .Bowie
9-11 . . . . . Richmond
13-15 . . . . at New Britain
16-18 . . . . . Trenton
19-21 . . . . at Portland
22-25 . . . .at Reading
26-29 . . . . Portland
30-31 . . .at Binghamton

SEPTEMBER
1-2 . . . . . .at Binghamton

PORTLAND SEA DOGS

APRIL
4-7 . . . . Trenton
8-10 . . . . Reading
11-14 . . . . at New Britain
15-17 . . . .at Binghamton
18-21 . . . . . New Britain
22-24 . . . . . Binghamton
26-28 . . . . . at Trenton
29-30 . . . . . at Reading

MAY
1-2 . . . . . .at Reading
3-5 . . . . . New Britain
6-8 . . . . . . Reading
9-12 . . . . . at New Britain
14-16 . . at New Hampshire
17-19 . . . . Binghamton
20-23 . . . . New Hampshire
24-27 . . . .at Binghamton
28-30 . . . New Hampshire
31 . . . . Altoona

JUNE
1-2 . . . . Altoona
4-6 . . . . at Erie
7-9 . . . . at Akron
11-13 . . . . Erie
14-16 . . . . .Akron

18-20 . . . . . .at Reading
21-23 . . . . . .at Trenton
24-26 . . . . Binghamton
27-30 . . at New Hampshire

JULY
1-3 . . . . Trenton
4-8 . . . . New Britain
11-14 . . . .at Binghamton
15-17 . . at New Hampshire
18-21 . . . . Reading
22-24 . . . . at New Britain
25-28 . . . . .Harrisburg
30-31 . . . . at Richmond

AUGUST
1 . . . . at Richmond
2-4 . . . . at Bowie
6-8 . . . . .Richmond
9-11 . . . . .Bowie
13-15 . . . . . .at Altoona
16-18 . . . . at Harrisburg
19-21 . . . . New Hampshire
22-25 . . . . . . at Trenton
26-29 . . at New Hampshire
30-31 . . . . Trenton

SEPTEMBER
1-2 . . . . Trenton

READING FIGHTIN PHILS

APRIL
4-7 . . . at New Hampshire
8-10 . . . . . . at Portland
12-14 . . . . Erie
15-16 . . . . . .Harrisburg
18-21 . . . . at Richmond
22-24 . . . . at Harrisburg
26-28 . . . New Hampshire
29-30 . . . . . . Portland

MAY
1-2 . . . . Portland
3-5 . . . at New Hampshire
6-8 . . . . . . at Portland
9-12 . . . . .Akron
13-15 . . . . . . at Erie
17-19 . . . . . . .Harrisburg
20-23 . . . . Altoona
24-27 . . . . at Harrisburg
28-30 . . . . . at Bowie
31 . . . . .Akron

JUNE
1-2 . . . . .Akron
4-6 . . . . . .at Altoona
7-10 . . . . . .Harrisburg
11-13 . . . . .Bowie
14-16 . . . . at Richmond

18-20 . . . . Portland
21-23 . . . . . .Richmond
24-26 . . at New Hampshire
27-30 . . . . at New Britain

JULY
1-3 . . . . .Richmond
4-8 . . . . at Trenton
11-14 . . . New Hampshire
15-17 . . . . Trenton
18-21 . . . . . at Portland
22-24 . . . .at Binghamton
25-28 . . . . . New Britain
29-31 . . . . Erie

AUGUST
1 . . . . Erie
2-4 . . . . at Trenton
6-8 . . . . . . at Harrisburg
9-11 . . . . . New Britain
13-15 . . . . . Binghamton
16-18 . . . . . . at Akron
19-21 . . . . . .at Altoona
22-25 . . . New Hampshire
26-29 . . . . . . .Richmond
30-31 . . . at New Britain

SEPTEMBER
1-2 . . . . . . at New Britain

RICHMOND FLYING SQUIRRELS

APRIL
4-7 . . . . New Britain
8-10 . . . . .Bowie
11-14 . . . . . .at Trenton
15-17 . . . .at Altoona
18-21 . . . . . . Reading
22-24 . . . . . . Altoona
26-28 . . at New Britain
29-30 . . . . .at Bowie

MAY
1-2 . . . . . . at Bowie
3-5 . . . . . . Trenton
6-8 . . . . . . .Bowie
9-12 . . . . .at Altoona
13-15 . . . . at Harrisburg
17-19 . . . . . Altoona
20-23 . . . . . Trenton
24-27 . . . . at Altoona
28-30 . . . at New Britain
31 . . . . Erie

JUNE
1-2 . . . . Erie
4-6 . . . . . New Britain
7-9 . . . . at Trenton
11-13 . . . .at Harrisburg
14-16 . . . . . . Reading

18-20 . . . . . Binghamton
21-23 . . . . . .at Reading
24-26 . . . . . .Bowie
27-30 . . . . . at Erie

JULY
1-3 . . . . . .at Reading
4-8 . . . . .Akron
11-14 . . . . . at Bowie
15-17 . . . .at Binghamton
18-21 . . . . .Bowie
22-24 . . . . . at Erie
25-28 . . . . at Akron
30-31 . . . . Portland

AUGUST
1 . . . . Portland
2-4 . . . . . New Hampshire
6-8 . . . . . at Portland
9-11 . . at New Hampshire
13-15 . . . . . . .Akron
16-18 . . . . . at Bowie
19-21 . . . . . .Harrisburg
22-25 . . . . . . Altoona
26-29 . . . .at Reading
30-31 . . . . . .Harrisburg

SEPTEMBER
1-2 . . . . .Harrisburg

TRENTON THUNDER

APRIL
4-7 . . . . at Portland
8-10 . . at New Hampshire
11-14 . . . . . . Richmond
15-17 . . . . .Akron
18-21 . . . . . at Erie
22-24 . . . . . at Akron
26-28 . . . . . Portland
29-30 . . . New Hampshire

MAY
1-2 . . . . . New Hampshire
3-5 . . . . . . at Richmond
6-8 . . . . . . Binghamton
9-12 . . . . New Hampshire

14-16 . . . . . . .at Altoona
17-19 . . . . . . .Bowie
20-23 . . . at Richmond
24-27 . . . . . at Bowie
28-30 . . . . Erie
31 . . . . . . .at Harrisburg

JUNE
1-2 . . . . . at Harrisburg
4-6 . . . . . .at Binghamton
7-9 . . . . .Richmond
11-13 . . . . . Binghamton
14-16 . . . . . .at Altoona
18-20 . . . . . at Akron
21-23 . . . . . . Portland

24-26 . . . . Erie
27-30 . . . . . at Binghamton

JULY
1-3 . . . . at Portland
4-8 . . . . Reading
11-14 . . . . . at New Britain
15-17 . . . . at Reading
18-21 . . . New Hampshire
22-24 . . . . Altoona
25-28 . . . at Binghamton
30-31 . . . . .Harrisburg

AUGUST
1 . . . . .Harrisburg
2-4 . . . . Reading
6-8 . . . . at Erie
9-11 . . . . .Akron
13-15 . . . . . . .Harrisburg
16-18 . . at New Hampshire
19-21 . . . . at New Britain
22-25 . . . . Portland
26-29 . . . . . New Britain
30-31 . . . . . . at Portland

SEPTEMBER
1-2 . . . . at Portland

SOUTHERN LEAGUE

BIRMINGHAM BARONS

APRIL
4-8 . . . at Montgomery
10-14 . . . . . . .Mississippi
15-19 . . at Chattanooga
20-24 . . . . . . Huntsville
25-29 . . . at Montgomery

MAY
1-5 . . . . . Chattanooga
7-11 . . . . . at Tennessee
12-16 . . . . . Montgomery
17-20 . . . . . at Jackson
23-27 . . . . at Jacksonville
28-31 . . . . Tennessee

JUNE
1 . . . . Tennessee
2-6 . . . . at Huntsville
7-11 . . . . . Jacksonville
13-17 . . . . Jackson
19-23 . . . . . at Mississippi

24-28 . . . . Huntsville
29-30 . . . . .at Jackson

JULY
1-3 . . . . at Jackson
4-8 . . . . .Mississippi
10-14 . . . . . at Huntsville
18-22 . . . . . Chattanooga
23-27 . . . . Mobile
28-31 . . . . . at Tennessee

AUGUST
1 . . . . at Tennessee
2-6 . . . . Pensacola
8-12 . . . . at Mobile
13-17 . . . at Jacksonville
18-22 . . . . . . .Tennessee
23-27 . . . . at Pensacola
29-31 . . . . . Montgomery

SEPTEMBER
1-2 . . . . Montgomery

CHATTANOOGA LOOKOUTS

APRIL
4-8 . . . . Huntsville
10-14 . . . . . at Tennessee
15-19 . . . . . Birmingham
20-24 . . . at Jacksonville
25-29 . . . . Jackson

MAY
1-5 . . . . . .at Birmingham
7-11 . . . . Mobile
12-16 . . . . . at Pensacola
17-21 . . . . . . Tennessee
23-27 . . . . . Pensacola
28-31 . . . . . . at Mobile

JUNE
1 . . . . at Mobile
2-6 . . . . .Mississippi
7-11 . . . . .at Jackson
13-17 . . . . . at Huntsville
19-23 . . . . .Tennessee

HUNTSVILLE STARS

APRIL
4-8 . . . . . at Chattanooga
10-14 . . . . . Jacksonville
16-19 . . . . . Tennessee
20-24 . . at Birmingham
25-29 . . . . . . .Mississippi

MAY
1-5 . . . . at Mobile
7-11 . . . . . Jackson
12-16 . . . . at Mississippi
17-21 . . . . . Montgomery

24-28 . . . . . Montgomery
29-30 . . . . . at Huntsville

JULY
1-3 . . . . at Huntsville
4-8 . . . . Jacksonville
10-14 . . . . . at Mississippi
18-22 . . . .at Birmingham
23-27 . . . . Jackson
28-31 . . . . at Jacksonville

AUGUST
1 . . . . at Jacksonville
2-6 . . . . . . at Montgomery
7-11 . . . . Huntsville
13-17 . . . . . at Tennessee
18-22 . . . . . Jacksonville
23-27 . . . .at Jackson
29-31 . . . . . . .Tennessee

SEPTEMBER
1-2 . . . . Tennessee

23-27 . . . . . at Tennessee
28-31 . . . . . . .at Jackson

JUNE
1 . . . . at Jackson
2-6 . . . . . Birmingham
7-11 . . . . at Montgomery
13-17 . . . . Chattanooga
19-23 . . . . at Jacksonville
24-28 . . . .at Birmingham
29-30 . . . . . Chattanooga

JULY
1-3 . . . . Chattanooga
4-8 . . . . at Tennessee
10-14 . . . . . Birmingham
18-22 . . . . . at Pensacola
23-27 . . . . .Tennessee
28-31 . . . .at Jackson

AUGUST
1 . . . . .at Jackson

JACKSON GENERALS

APRIL
4-8 . . . . . at Jacksonville
10-14 . . . . . Montgomery
15-19 . . .at Mississippi
20-24 . . . . . . Pensacola
25-29 . . at Chattanooga

MAY
1-4 . . . . . . .Jacksonville
7-11 . . . . . . at Huntsville
12-16 . . . . Tennessee
17-20 . . . . . Birmingham
23-27 . . . at Montgomery
28-31 . . . . . . Huntsville

JUNE
1 . . . . Huntsville
2-6 . . . . . at Tennessee
7-11 . . . . Chattanooga
13-17 . . . .at Birmingham
19-23 . . . . Mobile

24-28 . . . . . at Tennessee
29-30 . . . . . Birmingham

JULY
1-3 . . . . Birmingham
4-8 . . . . . . at Pensacola
10-14 . . . . . . .Tennessee
18-22 . . . . . .Mississippi
23-27 . . . at Chattanooga
28-31 . . . . . Huntsville

AUGUST
1 . . . . Huntsville
2-6 . . . . at Mobile
7-11 . . . at Mississippi
13-17 . . . . . Montgomery
18-22 . . . . . at Mobile
23-27 . . . . Chattanooga
29-31 . . . . . at Huntsville

SEPTEMBER
1-2 . . . . . . at Huntsville

JACKSONVILLE SUNS

APRIL
4-8 . . . . Jackson
10-14 . . . . . at Huntsville
15-19 . . . . . at Pensacola
20-24 . . . Chattanooga
25-29 . . . . Mobile

MAY
1-4 . . . . . . .at Jackson
7-11 . . . . Pensacola
12-16 . . . . at Mobile
17-21 . . . . .at Mississippi
23-27 . . . . Birmingham
28-31 . . . . at Pensacola

JUNE
1 . . . . at Pensacola
2-6 . . . . Mobile
7-11 . . . .at Birmingham
13-17 . . . . . Montgomery
19-23 . . . . Huntsville

24-28 . . . . at Mobile
29-30 . . . Pensacola

JULY
1-3 . . . . Pensacola
4-8 . . . . . at Chattanooga
10-14 . . . . Mobile
18-22 . . . . at Tennessee
23-27 . . . at Montgomery
28-31 . . . . Chattanooga

AUGUST
1 . . . . Chattanooga
2-6 . . . . .Tennessee
7-11 . . . . . at Pensacola
13-17 . . . . . Birmingham
18-22 . . at Chattanooga
23-27 . . at Montgomery
29-31 . . . . . . .Mississippi

SEPTEMBER
1-2 . . . . .Mississippi

MISSISSIPPI BRAVES

APRIL
4-8 . . . . Mobile
10-14 . . .at Birmingham
15-19 . . . . . . Jackson
20-24 . . . . . . at Mobile
25-29 . . . . . . at Huntsville

MAY
1-5 . . . . Tennessee
7-11 . . . at Montgomery
12-16 . . . . . Huntsville
17-21 . . . . . Jacksonville
23-27 . . . . . at Mobile
28-31 . . . . Montgomery

JUNE
1 . . . . Montgomery
2-6 . . . . . at Chattanooga
7-11 . . . . Pensacola

13-17 . . . . . . at Tennessee
19-23 . . . . . Birmingham
24-28 . . . at Pensacola
29-30 . . . . Mobile

JULY
1-3 . . . . Mobile
4-8 . . . .at Birmingham
10-14 . . . . . Chattanooga
18-22 . . . . . .at Jackson
23-27 . . . . . Pensacola
28-31 . . . . . Montgomery

AUGUST
1 . . . . Montgomery
2-6 . . . . at Huntsville
7-11 . . . . . . Jackson
13-17 . . . . at Pensacola
18-22 . . . . at Montgomery

23-27 . . . . Huntsville
29-31 . . . . . at Jacksonville

MOBILE BAYBEARS

APRIL
4-8. . . . . . . .at Mississippi
10-14 . . . . Pensacola
15-19 . . . at Montgomery
20-24 . . . . . . .Mississippi
25-29 . . . at Jacksonville
MAY
1-5. . . . . Huntsville
7-11 . . . . at Chattanooga
12-16 . . . . . Jacksonville
17-21 . . . . . . at Pensacola
23-27 . . . . . .Mississippi
28-31 . . . . . Chattanooga
JUNE
1 . . . . Chattanooga
2-6. . . . . at Jacksonville
7-11 . . . . Tennessee
13-17 . . . . . . at Pensacola
19-23 . . . . . . .at Jackson

MONTGOMERY BISCUITS

APRIL
4-8. . . . . . Birmingham
10-14 . . . . . . .at Jackson
15-19 . . . . . . Mobile
20-24 . . . at Tennessee
25-29 . . . . . Birmingham
MAY
1-5. . . . . . . at Pensacola
7-11 . . . . . .Mississippi
12-16 . .at Birmingham
17-21 . . . . . at Huntsville
23-27 . . . . Jackson
28-31 . . . at Mississippi
JUNE
1 . . . . at Mississippi
2-6. . . . . Pensacola
7-11 . . . . . . Huntsville
13-17 . . . . at Jacksonville
19-23 . . . . Pensacola

PENSACOLA BLUE WAHOOS

APRIL
4-8. . . . . Tennessee
10-14 . . . . . . at Mobile
15-19 . . . . . . Jacksonville
20-24 . . . . . .at Jackson
25-29 . . . at Tennessee
MAY
1-5. . . . . Montgomery
7-11 . . . at Jacksonville
12-16 . . . . . Chattanooga
17-21 . . . . Mobile
23-27 . . . at Chattanooga
28-31 . . . . . Jacksonville
JUNE
1 . . . . Jacksonville
2-6. . . at Montgomery
7-11 . . . . . at Mississippi
13-17 . . . . Mobile
19-23 . . . at Montgomery

TENNESSEE SMOKIES

APRIL
4-8. . . . . . at Pensacola

SEPTEMBER
1-2. . . . . . at Jacksonville

24-28 . . . . .Jacksonville
29-30 . . . . . at Mississippi
JULY
1-3. . . . . . at Mississippi
4-8. . . . . . Montgomery
10-14 . . . . at Jacksonville
18-22 . . . . . Montgomery
23-27 . . . .at Birmingham
28-31 . . . . . at Pensacola
AUGUST
1 . . . . at Pensacola
2-6. . . . . Jackson
8-12 . . . . . . Birmingham
13-17 . . . . . at Huntsville
18-22 . . . . Jackson
23-27 . . . . at Tennessee
29-31 . . . . . . Pensacola
SEPTEMBER
1-2. . . . . Pensacola

24-28 . . . at Chattanooga
29-30 . . . . . . .Tennessee
JULY
1-3. . . . . . . Tennessee
4-8. . . . . . . at Mobile
10-14 . . . . . . Pensacola
18-22 . . . . . . at Mobile
23-27 . . . . . . Jacksonville
28-31 . . . . at Mississippi
AUGUST
1 . . . . at Mississippi
2-6. . . . . . Chattanooga
8-12 . . . . at Tennessee
13-17 . . . . . . .at Jackson
18-22 . . . . . .Mississippi
23-27 . . . . . Jacksonville
29-31 . . . .at Birmingham
SEPTEMBER
1-2. . . . . .at Birmingham

24-28 . . . . . .Mississippi
29-30 . . . . at Jacksonville
JULY
1-3. . . . . at Jacksonville
4-8. . . . . Jackson
10-14 . . at Montgomery
18-22 . . . . . . Huntsville
23-27 . . . at Mississippi
28-31 . . . . Mobile
AUGUST
1 . . . . Mobile
2-6. . . . .at Birmingham
7-11 . . . . . . Jacksonville
13-17 . . . . . .Mississippi
18-22 . . . . at Huntsville
23-27 . . . . . Birmingham
29-31 . . . . . . at Mobile
SEPTEMBER
1-2. . . . . . . at Mobile

10-14 . . . . . Chattanooga
15-19 . . . . . at Huntsville

20-24 . . . . . Montgomery
25-29 . . . . Pensacola
MAY
1-5. . . . . . .at Mississippi
7-11 . . . . . . Birmingham
12-16 . . . . . . .at Jackson
17-21 . . . at Chattanooga
23-27 . . . . Huntsville
28-31 . . . .at Birmingham
JUNE
1 . . . . . . .at Birmingham
2-6. . . . . Jackson
7-11 . . . . at Mobile
13-17 . . . . . . .Mississippi
19-23 . . . at Chattanooga
24-28 . . . . Jackson
29-30 . . at Montgomery

TEXAS LEAGUE
ARKANSAS TRAVELERS

APRIL
4-6. . . . . Frisco
7-9. . . . . Midland
11-13 . . . . . . at Frisco
14-16 . . . . . . at Midland
18-21 . . . . . Springfield
22-25 . . . . . . .at Tulsa
26-29 . . . . .at Springfield
30 . . . . Tulsa
MAY
1-3. . . . . Tulsa
4-7. .at Northwest Arkansas
8-9. . . . . .at Tulsa
11-12 . . . . .at Tulsa
13-16 . Northwest Arkansas
17-20 . . . . . . Springfield
22-24 . . . .at San Antonio
25-27 . . .at Corpus Christi
28-30 . . . . San Antonio
31 . . . . . Corpus Christi
JUNE
1-2. . . . . Corpus Christi
4-7. . . . . .at Springfield
8-11 .at Northwest Arkansas
12-15 . . . . Tulsa
16-19 . Northwest Arkansas

CORPUS CHRISTI HOOKS

APRIL
4-6. . . . . Springfield
7-9. . . . . Tulsa
11-13 . . . .at Springfield
14-16 . . . . .at Tulsa
18-21 . . . . .Frisco
22-25 . . . . . at Midland
26-29 . . . . . . at Frisco
30 . . . . Midland
MAY
1-3. . . . . Midland
4-7. . . . .at San Antonio
9-12. . . . . . . .Frisco
13-16 . . . . San Antonio
17-20 . . . . at Midland
22-24 . Northwest Arkansas
25-27 . . . . . . .Arkansas
28-30at Northwest Arkansas
31 . . . . at Arkansas
JUNE
1-2. . . . . . . at Arkansas
4-7. . . . . Midland
8-11 . . . . .at San Antonio

1-3. . . . . at Montgomery
4-8. . . . . Huntsville
10-14 . . . . . . .at Jackson
18-22 . . . . . . .Jacksonville
23-27 . . . . . at Huntsville
28-31 . . . . Birmingham
AUGUST
1 . . . . Birmingham
2-6. . . . at Jacksonville
8-12 . . . . . Montgomery
13-17 . . . . Chattanooga
18-22 . . . at Birmingham
23-27 . . . . Mobile
29-31 . . . at Chattanooga
SEPTEMBER
1-2. . . . . at Chattanooga

20-23 . . . . .at Springfield
26-28 . . . . .Frisco
29-30 . . . . . Midland
JULY
1 . . . . Midland
3-5. . . . . at Frisco
6-8. . . . . . at Midland
10-13 . . . . Tulsa
14-17 . . . .at Springfield
18-21 . . . . Tulsa
22-24at Northwest Arkansas
25-28 . . . . .at Tulsa
29-31 . Northwest Arkansas
AUGUST
1-4. . . . . Springfield
6-8. . . . . .at San Antonio
9-11 . . .at Corpus Christi
13-15 . . . . . San Antonio
16-18 . . . . Corpus Christi
20-23 . . . . .at Tulsa
24-26at Northwest Arkansas
27-30 . . . . . . Springfield
31 . . . Northwest Arkansas
SEPTEMBER
1-2. . . Northwest Arkansas

12-15 . . . . at Frisco
16-19 . . . . . San Antonio
20-23 . . . . . at Frisco
26-28 . . . . . Springfield
29-30 . . . . Tulsa
JULY
1 . . . . Tulsa
3-5. . . . .at Springfield
6-8. . . . . . . .at Tulsa
10-13 . . . . .Frisco
14-17 . . . . at Midland
18-21 . . . . .Frisco
22-24 . . . . . San Antonio
25-28 . . . . at Midland
29-31 . . .at San Antonio
AUGUST
1-4. . . . . Midland
6-8. . . Northwest Arkansas
9-11 . . . . .Arkansas
13-15at Northwest Arkansas
16-18 . . . . . at Arkansas
20-23 . . . . . . Midland
24-26 . . . .at San Antonio
27-30 . . . . at Frisco

31 . . . . San Antonio

FRISCO ROUGHRIDERS

APRIL	
4-6 . . . . at Arkansas	20-23 . . . . . Corpus Christi
7-9 . .at Northwest Arkansas	26-28 . . . . . at Arkansas
11-13 . . . . Arkansas	29-30at Northwest Arkansas
14-16 . Northwest Arkansas	**JULY**
18-21 . . . .at Corpus Christi	1 . . .at Northwest Arkansas
22-25 . . . . at San Antonio	3-5 . . . . Arkansas
26-29 . . . . . Corpus Christi	6-8 . .at Northwest Arkansas
30 . . . . San Antonio	10-13 . . . .at Corpus Christi
MAY	14-17 . . . . . San Antonio
1-3 . . . . . . San Antonio	18-21 . . . .at Corpus Christi
4-7 . . . . at Midland	22-24 . . . . Midland
9-12 . . . .at Corpus Christi	25-28 . . . at San Antonio
13-16 . . . . Midland	29-31 . . . . . . at Midland
17-20 . . . . . San Antonio	**AUGUST**
22-24 . . . .at Springfield	1-4 . . . . San Antonio
25-27 . . . . .at Tulsa	6-8 . . . . . . .at Springfield
28-30 . . . . Springfield	9-11 . . . . .at Tulsa
31 . . . . Tulsa	13-15 . . . . . Springfield
JUNE	16-18 . . . . Tulsa
1-2 . . . . Tulsa	20-23 . . . . at San Antonio
4-7 . . . . . at San Antonio	24-26 . . . . Midland
8-11 . . . . at Midland	27-30 . . . . Corpus Christi
12-15 . . . . . Corpus Christi	31 . . . . at Midland
16-19 . . . . Midland	**SEPTEMBER**
	1-2 . . . . at Midland

MIDLAND ROCKHOUNDS

APRIL	
4-6 . .at Northwest Arkansas	26-28at Northwest Arkansas
7-9 . . . . at Arkansas	29-30 . . . . . at Arkansas
11-13 . Northwest Arkansas	**JULY**
14-16 . . . . Arkansas	1 . . . . at Arkansas
18-21 . . . at San Antonio	3-5 . . . Northwest Arkansas
22-25 . . . . Corpus Christi	6-8 . . . . Arkansas
26-29 . . . . San Antonio	10-13 . . . . at San Antonio
30 . . . .at Corpus Christi	14-17 . . . . Corpus Christi
MAY	18-21 . . . at San Antonio
1-3 . . . . .at Corpus Christi	22-24 . . . . . . at Frisco
4-7 . . . . Frisco	25-28 . . . . Corpus Christi
9-12 . . . . at San Antonio	29-31 . . . . Frisco
13-16 . . . . . . at Frisco	**AUGUST**
17-20 . . . . Corpus Christi	1-4 . . . . .at Corpus Christi
22-24 . . . . . . .at Tulsa	6-8 . . . . .at Tulsa
25-27 . . . . .at Springfield	9-11 . . . . . .at Springfield
28-30 . . . . Tulsa	13-15 . . . . Tulsa
31 . . . . Springfield	16-18 . . . . . Springfield
JUNE	20-23 . . . .at Corpus Christi
1-2 . . . . Springfield	24-26 . . . . . . at Frisco
4-7 . . . . .at Corpus Christi	27-30 . . . . San Antonio
8-11 . . . . Frisco	31 . . . . Frisco
12-15 . . . . San Antonio	**SEPTEMBER**
16-19 . . . . . . at Frisco	1-2 . . . . Frisco
20-23 . . . . San Antonio	

NORTHWEST ARKANSAS NATURALS

APRIL	
4-6 . . . . Midland	9-12 . . . . .at Springfield
7-9 . . . . Frisco	13-16 . . . . . at Arkansas
11-13 . . . . . at Midland	17 . . . . .at Tulsa
14-16 . . . . . at Frisco	18-20 . . . . Tulsa
18-21 . . . . Tulsa	22-24 . . . .at Corpus Christi
22-25 . . . .at Springfield	25-27 . . . at San Antonio
26-29 . . . . .at Tulsa	28-30 . . . . Corpus Christi
30 . . . . Springfield	31 . . . . San Antonio
MAY	**JUNE**
1-3 . . . . Springfield	1-2 . . . . San Antonio
4-7 . . . . Arkansas	4-5 . . . . .at Tulsa
	6 . . . . Tulsa

SEPTEMBER	
1-2 . . . . San Antonio	

7 . . . . .at Tulsa
8-11 . . . . .Arkansas
12-15 . . . . . . Springfield
16-19 . . . . . at Arkansas
20-23 . . . . .at Tulsa
26-28 . . . . Midland
29-30 . . . . Frisco

JULY	
1 . . . . Frisco	
3-5 . . . . . . at Midland	
6-8 . . . . at Frisco	
10-13 . . . . . Springfield	
14-17 . . . . .at Tulsa	
18-21 . . . . . . Springfield	
22-24 . . . . . . .Arkansas	

SAN ANTONIO MISSIONS

APRIL	
4-6 . . . . Tulsa	20-23 . . . . . . at Midland
7-9 . . . . Springfield	26-28 . . . . Tulsa
11-13 . . . . . . .at Tulsa	29-30 . . . . . Springfield
14-16 . . . .at Springfield	**JULY**
18-21 . . . . Midland	1 . . . . Springfield
22-25 . . . . .Frisco	3-5 . . . . .at Tulsa
26-29 . . . . at Midland	6-8 . . . . . . .at Springfield
30 . . . . at Frisco	10-13 . . . . Midland
MAY	14-17 . . . . . . at Frisco
1-3 . . . . at Frisco	18-21 . . . . Midland
4-7 . . . . . Corpus Christi	22-24 . . .at Corpus Christi
9-12 . . . . Midland	25-28 . . . . Frisco
13-16 . . . .at Corpus Christi	29-31 . . . . . Corpus Christi
17-20 . . . . . . at Frisco	**AUGUST**
22-24 . . . . . . .Arkansas	1-4 . . . . at Frisco
25-27 . .Northwest Arkansas	6-8 . . . . .Arkansas
28-30 . . . . at Arkansas	9-11 . . Northwest Arkansas
31 . .at Northwest Arkansas	13-15 . . . . . at Arkansas
JUNE	16-18 . at Northwest Arkansas
1-2 . .at Northwest Arkansas	20-23 . . . . .Frisco
4-7 . . . . .Frisco	24-26 . . . . Corpus Christi
8-11 . . . . . . Corpus Christi	27-30 . . . . . at Midland
12-15 . . . . . at Midland	31 . . . . .at Corpus Christi
16-19 . . . .at Corpus Christi	**SEPTEMBER**
	1-2 . . . . .at Corpus Christi

SPRINGFIELD CARDINALS

APRIL	
4-6 . . . . . .at Corpus Christi	20-23 . . . . .Arkansas
7-9 . . . . . .at San Antonio	26-28 . . . .at Corpus Christi
11-13 . . . . . Corpus Christi	29-30 . . . .at San Antonio
14-16 . . . . . San Antonio	**JULY**
18-21 . . . . . at Arkansas	1 . . . . at San Antonio
22-25 . Northwest Arkansas	3-5 . . . . . . Corpus Christi
26-29 . . . . . . .Arkansas	6-8 . . . . San Antonio
30 . .at Northwest Arkansas	10-13 . at Northwest Arkansas
MAY	14-17 . . . . .Arkansas
1-3 . .at Northwest Arkansas	18-21at Northwest Arkansas
4-7 . . . . Tulsa	22-24 . . . . Tulsa
9-12 . . Northwest Arkansas	25-28 . Northwest Arkansas
13-16 . . . . .at Tulsa	29-31 . . . . .at Tulsa
17-20 . . . . . at Arkansas	**AUGUST**
22-24 . . . . .Frisco	1-4 . . . . at Arkansas
25-27 . . . . Midland	6-8 . . . . .Frisco
28-30 . . . . . . at Frisco	9-11 . . . . Midland
31 . . . . at Midland	13-15 . . . . at Frisco
JUNE	16-18 . . . . . at Midland
1-2 . . . . . . at Midland	20-23 . Northwest Arkansas
4-7 . . . . .Arkansas	24-26 . . . . .at Tulsa
8-11 . . . . .at Tulsa	27-30 . . . . at Arkansas
12-15 .at Northwest Arkansas	31 . . . . Tulsa
16-19 . . . . Tulsa	**SEPTEMBER**
	1-2 . . . . Tulsa

1-2 . . . . San Antonio

TULSA DRILLERS

APRIL
4-6. . . . . . at San Antonio
7-9. . . . . .at Corpus Christi
11-13 . . . . San Antonio
14-16 . . . . Corpus Christi
18-21 .at Northwest Arkansas
22-25 . . . . .Arkansas
26-29 . Northwest Arkansas
30 . . . . at Arkansas

MAY
1-3. . . . . at Arkansas
4-7. . . . . . .at Springfield
8-9. . . . . .Arkansas
11-12 . . . . .Arkansas
13-16 . . . . . . Springfield
17 . . . Northwest Arkansas
18-20 .at Northwest Arkansas
22-24 . . . . Midland
25-27 . . . . .Frisco
28-30 . . . . at Midland
31 . . . . at Frisco

JUNE
1-2. . . . . at Frisco
4-5. . . Northwest Arkansas
6 . . .at Northwest Arkansas
7 . . . Northwest Arkansas
8-11 . . . . Springfield

12-15 . . . . . . at Arkansas
16-19 . . . . .at Springfield
20-23 . Northwest Arkansas
26-28 . . . at San Antonio
29-30 . . . .at Corpus Christi

JULY
1 . . . .at Corpus Christi
3-5. . . . . . San Antonio
6-8. . . . . . Corpus Christi
10-13 . . . . . . at Arkansas
14-17 . Northwest Arkansas
18-21 . . . . at Arkansas
22-24 . . . . .at Springfield
25-28 . . . . . . .Arkansas
29-31 . . . . . Springfield

AUGUST
1-4. .at Northwest Arkansas
6-8. . . . . Midland
9-11 . . . . .Frisco
13-15 . . . . at Midland
16-18 . . . . . . at Frisco
20-23 . . . . . . .Arkansas
24-26 . . . . . Springfield
27-30. at Northwest Arkansas
31 . . . . . . .at Springfield

SEPTEMBER
1-2. . . . . . .at Springfield

CAROLINA LEAGUE

CAROLINA MUDCATS

APRIL
5-7. . . . . .Winston-Salem
8-10 . . . . . Wilmington
12-14 . . . at Winston-Salem
15-17 . . . . at Wilmington
18-21 . . . Myrtle Beach
22-25 . . . . .Potomac
26-28 . . . . . . at Frederick
29-30 . . . . . at Potomac

MAY
1-2. . . . . at Potomac
3-5. . . . . .Frederick
7-9. . . . . .at Salem
10-13 . . . . . .Lynchburg
14-16 . . . . .Salem
17-19 . . . . .at Lynchburg
21-23 . . . . at Myrtle Beach
24-26 . . . . Winston-Salem
27-30 . . . . . Wilmington
31 . . . . . at Winston-Salem

JUNE
1-2. . . . at Winston-Salem
3-6. . . . . . at Wilmington
7-9. . . . . . . Myrtle Beach
10-12 . . . . . . .Potomac
13-16 . . . . at Myrtle Beach

21-23 . . . . . . at Potomac
24-27 . . . . .Frederick
28-30 . . . . at Salem

JULY
1-3. . . . . .Lynchburg
4-7. . . . . .Salem
8-11 . . . . . at Lynchburg
12-15 . . . . . . at Frederick
17-20 . . . . Winston-Salem
21-23 . . . . Wilmington
24-27 . . . at Winston-Salem
28-30 . . . . at Wilmington

AUGUST
1-3. . . . . .Frederick
5-7. . . . . .Potomac
8-10 . . . . . . at Frederick
11-13 . . . . . at Potomac
14-16 . . . . . Myrtle Beach
17-20 . . . . at Salem
21-23 . . . . . . .Lynchburg
24-26 . . . . .Salem
28-30 . . . . at Lynchburg
31 . . . . . at Myrtle Beach

SEPTEMBER
1-2. . . . . at Myrtle Beach

FREDERICK KEYS

APRIL
5-7. . . . . .Salem
9-11 . . . . .Winston-Salem
12-14 . . . at Wilmington
15-17 . . . . . .Lynchburg
18-21 . . . . . . at Potomac
22-25 . . at Myrtle Beach
26-28 . . . . Carolina
29-30 . . . . . Myrtle Beach

MAY
1-2. . . . . . . Myrtle Beach

3-5. . . . . .at Carolina
6-8. . . . at Winston-Salem
10-13 . . . . Wilmington
14-16 . . . . .at Lynchburg
17-19 . . . . .at Salem
21-23 . . . . .Potomac
24-26 . . . . .Salem
27-30 . . . at Winston-Salem
31 . . . . . . .at Wilmington

JUNE
1-2. . . . . . at Wilmington

3-6. . . . . .Lynchburg
7-9. . . . . at Potomac
10-12 . . . . at Myrtle Beach
13-16 . . . . .Potomac
21-23 . . . . Myrtle Beach
24-27 . . . . . .at Carolina
28-30 . . . .Winston-Salem

JULY
1-3. . . . . Wilmington
4-6. . . . . . .at Lynchburg
8-11 . . . . at Wilmington
12-15 . . . . . . Carolina
17-20 . . . . .Salem
21-23 . . at Winston-Salem
24-27 . . . . .at Salem

LYNCHBURG HILLCATS

APRIL
5-7. . . . . at Potomac
9-11 . . . . . . Myrtle Beach
12-14 . . . . .Potomac
15-17 . . . . . at Frederick
18-21 . . . . .Salem
22-25 . . . at Winston-Salem
26-28 . . . . at Salem
29-30 . . . .Winston-Salem

MAY
1-2. . . . . .Winston-Salem
3-5. . . . . Wilmington
7-9. . . . at Myrtle Beach
10-13 . . . . . . .at Carolina
14-16 . . . . .Frederick
17-19 . . . . Carolina
21-23 . . . . at Wilmington
24-26 . . . . .Potomac
27-30 . . . Myrtle Beach
31 . . . . at Potomac

JUNE
1-2. . . . . at Potomac
3-6. . . . . at Frederick
7-9. . . . . .Salem
10-12 . . at Winston-Salem
13-16 . . . . at Salem

21-23 . . . .Winston-Salem
24-27 . . . . . . Wilmington
28-30 . . . . at Myrtle Beach

JULY
1-3. . . . . .at Carolina
4-6. . . . . .Frederick
8-11 . . . . Carolina
12-15 . . . . at Wilmington
17-20 . . . . . at Potomac
21-23 . . . . Myrtle Beach
24-27 . . . . .Potomac
29-31 . . . . . at Frederick

AUGUST
1-3. . . . . .Salem
5-7. . . . at Winston-Salem
8-10 . . . . . at Wilmington
11-13 . . . .Winston-Salem
14-16 . . . . . . Wilmington
17-20 . . . at Myrtle Beach
21-23 . . . . . . .at Carolina
24-27 . . . . .Frederick
28-30 . . . . Carolina
31 . . . . at Salem

SEPTEMBER
1-2. . . . . at Salem

MYRTLE BEACH PELICANS

APRIL
4-7. . . . . Wilmington
9-11 . . . . . .at Lynchburg
12-14 . . . . . at Salem
15-17 . . . .Winston-Salem
18-21 . . . . .at Carolina
22-25 . . . . .Frederick
26-28 . . . . .Potomac
29-30 . . . . . at Frederick

MAY
1-2. . . . . at Frederick
3-5. . . . . at Potomac
7-9. . . . . .Lynchburg
10-13 . . . . .Salem
14-16 . . . at Winston-Salem
17-19 . . . . at Wilmington
21-23 . . . . Carolina
25-26 . . . . . Wilmington
27-30 . . . at Lynchburg
31 . . . . at Salem

JUNE
1-2. . . . . at Salem
3-5. . . . . Potomac
7-9. . . . . . . .at Carolina
10-12 . . . . .Frederick
13-16 . . . . Carolina

21-23 . . . . . . at Frederick
24-27 . . . . . . at Potomac
28-30 . . . . . . .Lynchburg

JULY
1-3. . . . . .Salem
4-7. . . . at Winston-Salem
8-11 . . . . at Salem
12-15 . . . .Winston-Salem
17-20 . . . . . . Wilmington
21-23 . . . . .at Lynchburg
24-27 . . . . at Wilmington
29-31 . . . .Winston-Salem

AUGUST
1-3. . . . . at Potomac
4-6. . . . . .Frederick
8-10 . . . . .Potomac
11-13 . . . . . at Frederick
14-16 . . . . . .at Carolina
17-20 . . . . . .Lynchburg
21-23 . . . . .Salem
24-26 . . . at Winston-Salem
27-29 . . . . at Wilmington
31 . . . . Carolina

SEPTEMBER
1-2. . . . . Carolina

POTOMAC NATIONALS

APRIL	
5-7 . . . . .Lynchburg	21-23 . . . . Carolina
8-10 . . . . .Salem	24-27 . . . . . Myrtle Beach
12-14 . . . . . at Lynchburg	28-30 . . . . . at Wilmington
15-17 . . . . at Salem	JULY
18-21 . . . . .Frederick	1-3 . . . . . . .Winston-Salem
22-25 . . . . . .at Carolina	4-7 . . . . .Wilmington
26-28 . . . at Myrtle Beach	8-11 . . . at Winston-Salem
29-30 . . . . Carolina	12-15 . . . . at Salem
MAY	17-20 . . . . . . .Lynchburg
1-2 . . . . Carolina	21-23 . . . . .Salem
3-5 . . . . . . Myrtle Beach	24-27 . . . . at Lynchburg
7-9 . . . . . . at Wilmington	28-30 . . . . . . at Salem
10-13 . . . .Winston-Salem	AUGUST
14-16 . . . . . Wilmington	1-3 . . . . . Myrtle Beach
17-19 . . . at Winston-Salem	5-7 . . . . . .at Carolina
21-23 . . . . . at Frederick	8-10 . . . . at Myrtle Beach
24-26 . . . . at Lynchburg	11-13 . . . . Carolina
27-30 . . . . .Salem	14-16 . . . . . .Frederick
31 . . . . .Lynchburg	17-20 . . . . at Wilmington
JUNE	21-23 . . . .Winston-Salem
1-2 . . . . .Lynchburg	24-26 . . . . . Wilmington
3-6 . . . at Myrtle Beach	28-30 . . at Winston-Salem
7-9 . . . . .Frederick	31 . . . . at Frederick
10-12 . . . . .at Carolina	SEPTEMBER
13-16 . . . . . at Frederick	1-2 . . . . at Frederick

SALEM RED SOX

APRIL	
5-7 . . . . at Frederick	21-23 . . . . . at Wilmington
8-10 . . . . at Potomac	24-27 . . . at Winston-Salem
12-14 . . . . . Myrtle Beach	28-30 . . . . Carolina
15-17 . . . . .Potomac	JULY
18-21 . . . . . at Lynchburg	1-3 . . . . . at Myrtle Beach
22-25 . . . . . .Wilmington	4-7 . . . . . . .at Carolina
26-28 . . . . . .Lynchburg	8-11 . . . . Myrtle Beach
29-30 . . . . . at Wilmington	12-15 . . . . Potomac
MAY	17-20 . . . . . at Frederick
1-2 . . . . . . at Wilmington	21-23 . . . . . at Potomac
3-5 . . . . at Winston-Salem	24-27 . . . . . .Frederick
7-9 . . . . Carolina	28-30 . . . . . . .Potomac
10-13 . . at Myrtle Beach	AUGUST
14-16 . . . . .at Carolina	1-3 . . . . . .at Lynchburg
17-19 . . . . . .Frederick	5-7 . . . . . .Wilmington
21-23 . . . .Winston-Salem	8-10 . . . . .Winston-Salem
24-26 . . . . . at Frederick	11-13 . . . . at Wilmington
27-30 . . . . . at Potomac	14-16 . . at Winston-Salem
31 . . . . . . Myrtle Beach	17-20 . . . . Carolina
JUNE	21-23 . . . at Myrtle Beach
1-2 . . . . . . Myrtle Beach	24-26 . . . . .at Carolina
3-6 . . . .Winston-Salem	28-30 . . . . . .Frederick
7-9 . . . . . at Lynchburg	31 . . . . .Lynchburg
10-12 . . . . . . Wilmington	SEPTEMBER
13-16 . . . . . .Lynchburg	1-2 . . . . .Lynchburg

WILMINGTON BLUE ROCKS

APRIL	
4-7 . . . . at Myrtle Beach	21-23 . . . . .Salem
8-10 . . . . .at Carolina	24-27 . . . . . at Lynchburg
12-14 . . . . .Frederick	28-30 . . . . .Potomac
15-17 . . . . Carolina	JULY
18-21 . . . at Winston-Salem	1-3 . . . . at Frederick
22-25 . . . . at Salem	4-7 . . . . at Potomac
26-28 . . . . .Winston-Salem	8-11 . . . . .Frederick
29-30 . . . . .Salem	12-15 . . . . . . .Lynchburg
MAY	17-20 . . . at Myrtle Beach
1-2 . . . . .Salem	21-23 . . . . . .at Carolina
3-5 . . . . . at Lynchburg	24-27 . . . . Myrtle Beach
7-9 . . . . .Potomac	28-30 . . . . Carolina
10-13 . . . . . . at Frederick	AUGUST
14-16 . . . . . at Potomac	1-3 . . . . at Winston-Salem
17-19 . . . . Myrtle Beach	5-7 . . . . at Salem
21-23 . . . . . . .Lynchburg	8-10 . . . . .Lynchburg
25-26 . . . at Myrtle Beach	11-13 . . . . .Salem
27-30 . . . . . .at Carolina	14-16 . . . . at Lynchburg
31 . . . . .Frederick	17-20 . . . . Potomac
JUNE	21-23 . . . . . at Frederick
1-2 . . . . .Frederick	24-26 . . . . . at Potomac
3-6 . . . . Carolina	27-30 . . . . Myrtle Beach
7-9 . . . at Winston-Salem	31 . . . . . .Winston-Salem
10-12 . . . . . . at Salem	SEPTEMBER
13-16 . . . . .Winston-Salem	1-2 . . . . . .Winston-Salem

WINSTON-SALEM DASH

APRIL	
5-7 . . . . .at Carolina	21-23 . . . . . at Lynchburg
9-11 . . . . . at Frederick	24-27 . . . . .Salem
12-14 . . . . Carolina	28-30 . . . . . . at Frederick
15-17 . . . at Myrtle Beach	JULY
18-21 . . . . . . Wilmington	1-3 . . . . at Potomac
22-25 . . . . . . .Lynchburg	4-7 . . . . . . Myrtle Beach
26-28 . . . at Wilmington	8-11 . . . . .Potomac
29-30 . . . . . at Lynchburg	12-15 . . . at Myrtle Beach
MAY	17-20 . . . . . . .at Carolina
1-2 . . . . . at Lynchburg	21-23 . . . . . . .Frederick
3-5 . . . . .Salem	24-27 . . . . Carolina
6-8 . . . . .Frederick	29-31 . . . . at Myrtle Beach
10-13 . . . . . . at Potomac	AUGUST
14-16 . . . . Myrtle Beach	1-3 . . . . Wilmington
17-19 . . . . . . .Potomac	5-7 . . . . .Lynchburg
21-23 . . . . . . at Salem	8-10 . . . . at Salem
24-26 . . . . .at Carolina	11-13 . . . . at Lynchburg
27-30 . . . . . .Frederick	14-16 . . . . .Salem
31 . . . . Carolina	17-20 . . . . . at Frederick
JUNE	21-23 . . . . . at Potomac
1-2 . . . . Carolina	24-26 . . . . Myrtle Beach
3-6 . . . . at Salem	28-30 . . . . . . .Potomac
7-9 . . . . . . Wilmington	31 . . . . . at Wilmington
10-12 . . . . . . .Lynchburg	SEPTEMBER
13-16 . . . . at Wilmington	1-2 . . . . . . at Wilmington

HIGH CLASS A

CALIFORNIA LEAGUE

BAKERSFIELD BLAZE

APRIL	MAY
4-7 . . . . at Stockton	1-2 . . . . at San Jose
8-10 . . . . at Visalia	3-6 . . . . at Modesto
11-14 . . . . .Stockton	7-9 . . . . San Jose
15-17 . . . . . Inland Empire	10-13 . . . . .Modesto
18-21 . . . . . .at Lancaster	15-18 . . . . . at Stockton
23-25 . . . . at High Desert	19-21 . . . . .High Desert
26-28 . . . . Visalia	23-26 . . . . . . .Stockton
30 . . . . at San Jose	27-29 . . . . . at San Jose

30-31 . Rancho Cucamonga	7-9 . . . . .Modesto
JUNE	10-12 . . . . at Lake Elsinore
1-2 . . . Rancho Cucamonga	13-15at Rancho Cucamonga
3-5 . . . . at High Desert	17-19 . . . . Visalia
6-9 . . . . . Lake Elsinore	20-22 . . . . Lancaster
10-12 . . . . Visalia	23-25 . . . . . at Modesto
13-16 . . . . . at Modesto	26-28 . . . at Lake Elsinore
20-23 . . . . .High Desert	29-31 . . . . .Modesto
24-26 . . . . Lancaster	AUGUST
27-30 . . . . at Visalia	2-4 . . . . San Jose
JULY	6-8 . . . . at Stockton
1-3 . . . . .at Lancaster	9-11 . . . . . at San Jose
4-6 . . . . . . Lake Elsinore	12-14 . . . . Visalia
	16-18 . . . . . at Modesto

20-22 . . . . at Inland Empire
23-26 . . . . San Jose
27-29 . . . . Stockton
30-31 . . . . at Visalia

SEPTEMBER
1-2. . . . . at Visalia

HIGH DESERT MAVERICKS

APRIL
4-7. . . . . at Lancaster
8-10. . . . . at Inland Empire
11-14 . Rancho Cucamonga
15-17 . . . . Lancaster
18-21 .at Rancho Cucamonga
23-25 . . . . Bakersfield
26-28 . . . . Stockton
30 . . . . . . at Lake Elsinore

MAY
1-2. . . . . . at Lake Elsinore
3-6. . . . . Lancaster
8-9. . . . . at Visalia
10-13 . . . . at San Jose
15-18 . . . . . Inland Empire
19-21 . . . . . . at Bakersfield
22-25 . . . . San Jose
27-29 . . . . . . Lake Elsinore
30-31 . . . . at Modesto

JUNE
1-2. . . . . at Modesto
3-5. . . . . Bakersfield
6-9. . . . . at Inland Empire
10-12 . . . . at Lancaster
13-16 . . . . . Inland Empire
20-23 . . . . . . at Bakersfield
24-26 . . . . . . Lake Elsinore
27-30 . . . . Modesto

JULY
1-3. . . . . . at Lake Elsinore
4-6. . . Rancho Cucamonga
7-9. . . . . Lancaster
10-12. at Rancho Cucamonga
13-15 . . . . at Stockton
17-19 . . . . . . Lake Elsinore
20-21 . . . . Visalia
23-25 . . . . at Lake Elsinore
26-28 . . . . at Inland Empire
30-31 . . . . Stockton

AUGUST
1 . . . . Stockton
2-4. . . . . at Lancaster
6-8. . . . . . . Inland Empire
9-11 . . . . Lancaster
13-15. at Rancho Cucamonga
16-18 . . . . at Lancaster
20-22 . Rancho Cucamonga
23-26 . . . . at Inland Empire
27-29 .at Rancho Cucamonga
30-31 . . . . . . Lake Elsinore

SEPTEMBER
1-2. . . . . Lake Elsinore

INLAND EMPIRE 66ERS

APRIL
4-7. . . . . Modesto
8-10. . . . . High Desert
11-14 . . . . at Lake Elsinore
15-17 . . . . . . at Bakersfield
18-21 . . . . San Jose
23-25 . Rancho Cucamonga
26-28 . . . . at Lancaster
30 . . . . Lancaster

MAY
1-2. . . . . Lancaster
3-6. . . . . . at Lake Elsinore
7-9. .at Rancho Cucamonga
10-13 . . . . Visalia
15-18 . . . . . at High Desert
19-21 . . . . San Jose
23-26 . . . . at Lancaster
27-29 . . . . at Stockton
30-31 . . . . . . Lake Elsinore

JUNE
1-2. . . . . Lake Elsinore
3-5. .at Rancho Cucamonga
6-9. . . . . High Desert
10-12 . . . . Stockton
13-16 . . . . . at High Desert
20-23 . . . . . . Lake Elsinore
24-26 . Rancho Cucamonga
27-30 . . . . at Lake Elsinore

JULY
1-3. .at Rancho Cucamonga
4-6. . . . . Lancaster
7-9. . . Rancho Cucamonga
10-12 . . . . at Lancaster
13-15 . . . . at Visalia
17-19 . . . . Lancaster
20-22 . . . . Lake Elsinore
23-25. at Rancho Cucamonga
26-28 . . . . High Desert
30-31 . Rancho Cucamonga

AUGUST
1 . . . . Rancho Cucamonga
2-4. . . . . . at Lake Elsinore
6-8. . . . . . . at High Desert
9-11 . . . . Visalia
13-15 . . . . at Lancaster
16-18 . . . . at San Jose
20-22 . . . . Bakersfield
23-26 . . . . High Desert
27-29 . . . . at Modesto
30-31 . . . . at San Jose

SEPTEMBER
1-2. . . . . at San Jose

LAKE ELSINORE STORM

APRIL
4-7. .at Rancho Cucamonga
8-10. . . . . at Lancaster
11-14 . . . . . Inland Empire
15-17 . Rancho Cucamonga
18-21 . . . . at Visalia
23-25 . . . . Lancaster
26-28 .at Rancho Cucamonga
30 . . . . High Desert

MAY
1-2. . . . . High Desert
3-6. . . . . . . Inland Empire
7-9. . . . . at Lancaster
10-13 . Rancho Cucamonga
15-18 . . . . at Modesto
19-21 . . . . at Stockton
23-26 . . . . Modesto
27-29 . . . . . at High Desert
30-31 . . . . at Inland Empire

JUNE
1-2. . . . . at Inland Empire
3-5. . . . . Visalia
6-9. . . . . at Bakersfield
10-12 . Rancho Cucamonga
13-16 . . . . Lancaster
20-23 . . . . at Inland Empire
24-26 . . . . . at High Desert
27-30 . . . . . Inland Empire

JULY
1-3. . . . . High Desert
4-6. . . . . at Bakersfield
7-9. . . . . at San Jose
10-12 . . . . Bakersfield
13-15 . . . . San Jose
17-19 . . . . . at High Desert
20-22 . . . . at Inland Empire
23-25 . . . . High Desert
26-28 . . . . Bakersfield
30-31 . . . . at Lancaster

AUGUST
1 . . . . at Lancaster
2-4. . . . . . . Inland Empire
6-8. .at Rancho Cucamonga
9-11 . . Rancho Cucamonga
13-15 . . . . Stockton
16-18. at Rancho Cucamonga
20-22 . . . . Lancaster
23-26 . . . . Modesto
27-29 . . . . at Lancaster
30-31 . . . . . at High Desert

SEPTEMBER
1-2. . . . . . . at High Desert

LANCASTER JETHAWKS

APRIL
4-7. . . . . High Desert
8-10. . . . . . . Lake Elsinore
11-14 . . . . at Modesto
15-17 . . . . . at High Desert
18-21 . . . . Bakersfield
23-25 . . . . at Lake Elsinore
26-28 . . . . . Inland Empire
30 . . . . . . at Inland Empire

MAY
1-2. . . . . . at Inland Empire
3-6. . . . . . . at High Desert
7-9. . . . . Lake Elsinore
10-13 . . . . Stockton
15-18 . . . . at Visalia
19-21 . Rancho Cucamonga
23-26 . . . . . Inland Empire
27-29. at Rancho Cucamonga
30-31 . . . . Visalia

JUNE
1-2. . . . . Visalia
3-5. . . . . at Stockton
6-9. . . . . at San Jose
10-12 . . . . High Desert
13-16 . . . . at Lake Elsinore
20-23 . Rancho Cucamonga
24-26 . . . . . . at Bakersfield
27-30at Rancho Cucamonga

JULY
1-3. . . . . Bakersfield
4-6. . . . . . at Inland Empire
7-9. . . . . at High Desert
10-12 . . . . . Inland Empire
13-15 . . . . Modesto
17-19 . . . . at Inland Empire
20-22 . . . . . . at Bakersfield
23-25 . . . . San Jose
26-28 .at Rancho Cucamonga
30-31 . . . . . . Lake Elsinore

AUGUST
1 . . . . Lake Elsinore
2-4. . . . . High Desert
6-8. . . . . at Modesto
9-11 . . . . . . at High Desert
13-15 . . . . . Inland Empire
16-18 . . . . High Desert
20-22 . . . . at Lake Elsinore
23-26 . Rancho Cucamonga
27-29 . . . . . . Lake Elsinore
30-31 .at Rancho Cucamonga

SEPTEMBER
1-2. .at Rancho Cucamonga

MODESTO NUTS

APRIL
4-7. . . . . . at Inland Empire
8-10 .at Rancho Cucamonga
11-14 . . . . Lancaster
15-17 . . . . Visalia
18-21 . . . . at Stockton
23-25 . . . . at San Jose
26-28 . . . . San Jose
30 . . . . at Visalia

MAY
1-2. . . . . at Visalia
3-6. . . . . Bakersfield
7-9. . . . . Stockton
10-13 . . . . . . at Bakersfield
15-18 . . . . . . Lake Elsinore
19-21 . . . . Visalia
23-26 . . . . at Lake Elsinore
27-29 . . . . at Visalia
30-31 . . . . High Desert

JUNE
1-2. . . . . High Desert
3-5. . . . . San Jose
6-9. . . . . at Stockton
10-12 . . . . at San Jose
13-16 . . . . Bakersfield
20-23 . . . . Visalia
24-26 . . . . at San Jose
27-30 . . . . . . at High Desert

JULY
1-3. . . . . San Jose
4-6. . . . . at Stockton
7-9. . . . . at Bakersfield
10-12 . . . . Stockton
13-15 . . . . at Lancaster
17-19 . . . . at San Jose
20-22 . Rancho Cucamonga
23-25 . . . . Bakersfield
26-28 . . . . at Visalia
29-31 . . . . . . at Bakersfield

AUGUST
2-4. . . . . Stockton
6-8. . . . . Lancaster
9-11 . . . . at Stockton
13-15 . . . . San Jose
16-18 . . . . Bakersfield
20-22 . . . . at Visalia
23-26 . . . . at Lake Elsinore
27-29 . . . . . Inland Empire
30-31 . . . . Stockton

SEPTEMBER
1-2. . . . . Stockton

RANCHO CUCAMONGA QUAKES

APRIL
4-7 . . . . . . Lake Elsinore
8-10 . . . . Modesto
11-14 . . . . at High Desert
15-17 . . . at Lake Elsinore
18-21 . . . . . High Desert
23-25 . . . at Inland Empire
26-28 . . . . Lake Elsinore
30 . . . . at Stockton

MAY
1-2 . . . . at Stockton
3-6 . . . . at San Jose
7-9 . . . . . . Inland Empire
10-13 . . . at Lake Elsinore
15-18 . . . . San Jose
19-21 . . . . .at Lancaster
23-26 . . . . Visalia
27-29 . . . . . . Lancaster
30-31 . . . . .at Bakersfield

JUNE
1-2 . . . . . . .at Bakersfield
3-5 . . . . . . Inland Empire
6-9 . . . . .at Visalia
10-12 . . . at Lake Elsinore
13-16 . . . . . . .Stockton
20-23 . . . . . .at Lancaster

24-26 . . . .at Inland Empire
27-30 . . . . . . Lancaster

JULY
1-3 . . . . . . Inland Empire
4-6 . . . . . . at High Desert
7-9 . . . . .at Inland Empire
10-12 . . . . .High Desert
13-15 . . . . . Bakersfield
17-19 . . . . . at Stockton
20-22 . . . . . at Modesto
23-25 . . . . Inland Empire
26-28 . . . . . . Lancaster
30-31 . . . .at Inland Empire

AUGUST
1 . . . . .at Inland Empire
2-4 . . . . .at Visalia
6-8 . . . . . . Lake Elsinore
9-11 . . . . at Lake Elsinore
13-15 . . . . . .High Desert
16-18 . . . . . Lake Elsinore
20-22 . . . . at High Desert
23-26 . . . . . .at Lancaster
27-29 . . . . . .High Desert
30-31 . . . . Lancaster

SEPTEMBER
1-2 . . . . Lancaster

SAN JOSE GIANTS

APRIL
4-7 . . . . .at Visalia
8-10 . . . . at Stockton
11-14 . . . . Visalia
15-17 . . . . . .Stockton
18-21 . . . .at Inland Empire
23-25 . . . . . .Modesto
26-28 . . . . at Modesto
30 . . . . Bakersfield

MAY
1-2 . . . . Bakersfield
3-6 . . . Rancho Cucamonga
7-9 . . . . . .at Bakersfield
10-13 . . . . . .High Desert
15-18at Rancho Cucamonga
19-21 . . . .at Inland Empire
22-25 . . . . at High Desert
27-29 . . . . . Bakersfield
30-31 . . . . .Stockton

JUNE
1-2 . . . . .Stockton
3-5 . . . . . . at Modesto
6-9 . . . . Lancaster
10-12 . . . . . . Modesto
13-16 . . . . . .at Visalia
20-23 . . . . . at Stockton

24-26 . . . . Modesto
27-30 . . . . . . .Stockton

JULY
1-3 . . . . at Modesto
4-6 . . . . Visalia
7-9 . . . . . . Lake Elsinore
10-12 . . . . . . at Visalia
13-15 . . . at Lake Elsinore
17-19 . . . . . . .Modesto
20-22 . . . . . . .Stockton
23-25 . . . .at Lancaster
26-28 . . . . at Stockton
30-31 . . . . Visalia

AUGUST
1 . . . . Visalia
2-4 . . . . . .at Bakersfield
5-7 . . . . .at Visalia
9-11 . . . . Bakersfield
13-15 . . . . at Modesto
16-18 . . . . Inland Empire
20-22 . . . . . . .Stockton
23-26 . . . .at Bakersfield
27-29 . . . . Visalia
30-31 . . . . Inland Empire

SEPTEMBER
1-2 . . . . Inland Empire

STOCKTON PORTS

APRIL
4-7 . . . . Bakersfield
8-10 . . . . San Jose
11-14 . . . .at Bakersfield
15-17 . . . . at San Jose
18-21 . . . . . . Modesto
23-25 . . . . . .at Visalia
26-28 . . . . at High Desert
30 . . . Rancho Cucamonga

MAY
1-2 . . . Rancho Cucamonga
3-6 . . . . Visalia
7-9 . . . . at Modesto
10-13 . . . .at Lancaster

15-18 . . . . . . Bakersfield
19-21 . . . . . Lake Elsinore
23-26 . . . .at Bakersfield
27-29 . . . . Inland Empire
30-31 . . . . at San Jose

JUNE
1-2 . . . . at San Jose
3-5 . . . . Lancaster
6-9 . . . . .Modesto
10-12 . . . .at Inland Empire
13-16at Rancho Cucamonga
20-23 . . . . . . San Jose
24-26 . . . . Visalia
27-30 . . . . . . at San Jose

VISALIA RAWHIDE

APRIL
4-7 . . . . San Jose
8-10 . . . . Bakersfield
11-14 . . . . at San Jose
15-17 . . . . at Modesto
18-21 . . . Lake Elsinore
23-25 . . . . . .Stockton
26-28 . . .at Bakersfield
30 . . . . .Modesto

MAY
1-2 . . . . .Modesto
3-6 . . . . . at Stockton
8-9 . . . . . . .High Desert
10-13 . . . .at Inland Empire
15-18 . . . . Lancaster
19-21 . . . . at Modesto
23-26 .at Rancho Cucamonga
27-29 . . . . .Modesto
30-31 . . . . . .at Lancaster

JUNE
1-2 . . . . .at Lancaster
3-5 . . . at Lake Elsinore
6-9 . . . Rancho Cucamonga
10-12 . . . .at Bakersfield
13-16 . . . . . . San Jose
20-23 . . . . . . at Modesto

24-26 . . . . . . at Stockton
27-30 . . . . . Bakersfield

JULY
1-3 . . . . .Stockton
4-6 . . . . . . at San Jose
7-9 . . . . . . at Stockton
10-12 . . . . . . San Jose
13-15 . . . . Inland Empire
17-19 . . . .at Bakersfield
20-21 . . . at High Desert
23-25 . . . . . . .Stockton
26-28 . . . . Modesto
30-31 . . . . at San Jose

AUGUST
1 . . . . at San Jose
2-4 . . . Rancho Cucamonga
5-7 . . . . San Jose
9-11 . . . . .at Inland Empire
12-14 . . . .at Bakersfield
16-18 . . . . . .Stockton
20-22 . . . . . . .Modesto
23-26 . . . . at Stockton
27-29 . . . . at San Jose
30-31 . . . . . Bakersfield

SEPTEMBER
1-2 . . . . Bakersfield

FLORIDA STATE LEAGUE

BRADENTON MARAUDERS

APRIL
4 . . . . at Fort Myers
5 . . . . .Fort Myers
6 . . . . at Fort Myers
7 . . . . .Fort Myers
9-11 . . . . . . .at Charlotte
12-14 . . . . St. Lucie
15-17 . . . . . . at Jupiter
18-20 . . . . Palm Beach
21-23 . . . . Jupiter
25-27 . . . . . . at St. Lucie
28-30 . . . . Brevard County

MAY
1 . . . . Brevard County
2-4 . . . . . . at Palm Beach
5-8 . . . . . . at Dunedin
9-11 . . . . Charlotte
13-16 . . . .at Clearwater
17-19 . . . . St. Lucie
20-23 . . . . Tampa
24-26 . . . . . at St. Lucie
28 . . . . at Fort Myers
29 . . . . .Fort Myers
30 . . . . . .at Fort Myers
31 . . . . Jupiter

JUNE
1-2 . . . . Jupiter
3-6 . . . . Daytona

7 . . . . .Fort Myers
8 . . . . at Fort Myers
9 . . . . .Fort Myers
10-13 . . . . . .at Lakeland
17-19 . . . . at Jupiter
20-22 . . . . . . Charlotte
23-25 . . . . St. Lucie
26-28 . . . . .at Charlotte
29-30 . . . . Palm Beach

JULY
1 . . . . Palm Beach
2 . . . . .Fort Myers
3 . . . . at Fort Myers
5 . . . . .at Fort Myers
6-8 . . . . Charlotte
9-11 . . . . at Palm Beach
12-15 . . . . . . .at Tampa
17-20 . . . . . Clearwater
21-24 . . . . . . .Lakeland
25-28 . . . . Brevard County
29-31 . . . . Dunedin

AUGUST
1 . . . . .Dunedin
2-5 . . . . at Daytona
7-9 . . . . St. Lucie
10-12 . . . . . .at Charlotte
13-15 . . . . Palm Beach
16 . . . . .Fort Myers

17 . . . . at Fort Myers
18 . . . . . . .Fort Myers
20-22 . . . . Jupiter
23-25 . . . . . at Palm Beach
26-28 . . . . at Jupiter

BREVARD COUNTY MANATEES

APRIL
4 . . . . at Daytona
5 . . . . Daytona
6 . . . . at Daytona
7 . . . . Daytona
9-10 . . . . at Lakeland
11 . . . . .Lakeland
12-14 . . . . . . Clearwater
15-16 . . . . Lakeland
17 . . . . . . at Lakeland
18-20 . . . . . at Clearwater
21-23 . . . . .at Tampa
25-27 . . . . Dunedin
28-30 . . . . . . at Bradenton

MAY
1 . . . . at Bradenton
2-4 . . . . at Dunedin
5-8 . . . . Charlotte
9-11 . . . . Tampa
13-14 . . . . . at St. Lucie
15-16 . . . . . . St. Lucie
17-19 . . . . . . at Dunedin
20-23 . . . . . Palm Beach
24-26 . . . . . Clearwater
28-30 . . . .at Clearwater
31 . . . . Daytona

JUNE
1 . . . . at Daytona
2 . . . . at Daytona
3-6 . . . . . at Fort Myers
7 . . . . at Daytona
8 . . . . Daytona
9 . . . . at Daytona
10-13 . . . . Jupiter
17-19 . . . . . . .Lakeland

JULY
1 . . . . at Lakeland
3 . . . . Daytona
4 . . . . . . at Daytona
5 . . . . Daytona
6-8 . . . . Tampa
9-11 . . . . . . Clearwater
12-15 . . . at Palm Beach
17-18 . . . . St. Lucie
19-20 . . . . at St. Lucie
21-24 . . . . . .Fort Myers
25-28 . . . . . . .Bradenton
29-31 . . . . . at Jupiter

AUGUST
1 . . . . at Jupiter
2-5 . . . . . .at Charlotte
7-9 . . . . Tampa
10-12 . . . . . at Dunedin
13-15 . . . . . .at Tampa
16 . . . . . . at Daytona
17 . . . . Daytona
18 . . . . . . at Daytona
20-22 . . . . at Lakeland
23-25 . . . . . . Dunedin
26-28 . . . . . .Lakeland
29 . . . . Daytona
30 . . . . . at Daytona
31 . . . . . . at Daytona

SEPTEMBER
1 . . . . at Daytona

CHARLOTTE STONE CRABS

APRIL
4-5 . . . . . at Palm Beach
6-7 . . . . Palm Beach
9-11 . . . . . . .Bradenton
12-13 . . . . . .Fort Myers
14 . . . . . . at Fort Myers
15-17 . . . . at St. Lucie
18-20 . . . . . at Jupiter
21-23 . . . . . . St. Lucie
25 . . . . . . .Fort Myers
26-27 . . . . at Fort Myers
28-30 . . . . . . .Lakeland

MAY
1 . . . . .Lakeland
2-4 . . . . Jupiter
5-8 . . . .at Brevard County
9-11 . . . . . . at Bradenton
13-16 . . . . . at Daytona
17-19 . . . . .Fort Myers
20-23 . . . . . Clearwater
24-26 . . . . at Fort Myers
28-30 . . . at Palm Beach
31 . . . . St. Lucie

JUNE
1-2 . . . . St. Lucie
3-6 . . . . at Dunedin
7-9 . . . . Palm Beach
10-13 . . . . Tampa
17-19 . . . . at St. Lucie
20-22 . . . at Bradenton
23-25 . . . . Jupiter
26-28 . . . . . .Bradenton
29-30 . . . . at Jupiter

JULY
1 . . . . at Jupiter
3 . . . . Palm Beach
4-5 . . . . at Palm Beach
6-8 . . . . . at Bradenton
9-11 . . . . St. Lucie
12-15 . . . .at Clearwater
17-20 . . . . Daytona
21-24 . . . . Dunedin
25-28 . . . . . . .at Tampa
29-31 . . . . . at Lakeland

AUGUST
1 . . . . . . at Lakeland
2-5 . . . . . Brevard County
7 . . . . .Fort Myers
8-9 . . . . . . at Fort Myers
10-12 . . . . . . .Bradenton
13-15 . . . . at Jupiter
16 . . . . . at Palm Beach
17-18 . . . . . Palm Beach
20 . . . . . at Fort Myers
21-22 . . . . . .Fort Myers
23-25 . . . . Jupiter
26-28 . . . . at St. Lucie
29-30 . . . . Palm Beach
31 . . . . . . at Palm Beach

SEPTEMBER
1 . . . . . . at Palm Beach

29 . . . . .Fort Myers
30 . . . . . . at Fort Myers
31 . . . . . . .Fort Myers

SEPTEMBER
1 . . . . at Fort Myers

CLEARWATER THRESHERS

APRIL
4 . . . . at Dunedin
5 . . . . .Dunedin
6 . . . . at Dunedin
7 . . . . .Dunedin
9-11 . . . . . . at Daytona
12-14 . . .at Brevard County
15-17 . . . . Daytona
18-20 . . . . Brevard County
21-23 . . . . . . at Lakeland
24 . . . . .at Tampa
26-27 . . . . Tampa
28-30 . . . . . .Fort Myers

MAY
1 . . . . .Fort Myers
2 . . . . .at Tampa
3 . . . . Tampa
4 . . . . .at Tampa
5-8 . . . . . . at Palm Beach
9-11 . . . . . . .Lakeland
13-16 . . . . . . Bradenton
17-18 . . . . . . .at Tampa
19 . . . . Tampa
20-23 . . . . . at Charlotte
24-26 . . .at Brevard County
28-30 . . . . Brevard County
31 . . . . at Dunedin

JUNE
1 . . . . Dunedin
2 . . . . at Dunedin
3-6 . . . . at Jupiter
7 . . . . at Dunedin
8-9 . . . . Dunedin
10-13 . . . . . St. Lucie
17-19 . . . . . Daytona
20 . . . . .Lakeland

21-22 . . . . . . at Lakeland
23 . . . . Tampa
24 . . . . .at Tampa
25 . . . . Tampa
26-28 . . . . Brevard County
29-30 . . . . . at Daytona

JULY
1 . . . . at Daytona
3 . . . . Dunedin
4 . . . . at Dunedin
5 . . . . Dunedin
6-7 . . . . .Lakeland
8 . . . . at Lakeland
9-11 . . .at Brevard County
12-15 . . . . . . Charlotte
17-20 . . . . . at Bradenton
21-24 . . . . Jupiter
25-28 . . . . at Fort Myers
29-31 . . . . . Palm Beach

AUGUST
1 . . . . Palm Beach
2-5 . . . . . . at St. Lucie
7-9 . . . . Daytona
10-12 . . . . at Lakeland
13-15 . . . . at Daytona
16-17 . . . . . . Dunedin
18 . . . . . . at Dunedin
20 . . . . Tampa
21-22 . . . . . .at Tampa
23-25 . . . . . .Lakeland
26-27 . . . . . . Tampa
28 . . . . . . .at Tampa
29-30 . . . . at Dunedin
31 . . . . Dunedin

SEPTEMBER
1 . . . . at Dunedin

DAYTONA CUBS

APRIL
4 . . . . . . Brevard County
5 . . . . .at Brevard County
6 . . . . . . Brevard County
7 . . . . .at Brevard County
9-11 . . . . . . Clearwater
12-14 . . . . . .at Tampa
15-17 . . . .at Clearwater
18-20 . . . . . . Tampa
21-23 . . . . at Dunedin
25-27 . . . . . .Lakeland
28-30 . . . . . Palm Beach

MAY
1 . . . . Palm Beach
2-4 . . . . . . at Lakeland
5-8 . . . . . . at St. Lucie
9-11 . . . . Dunedin
13-16 . . . . . . Charlotte
17-19 . . . . at Lakeland
20-23 . . . . . . at Jupiter
24-26 . . . . . .Lakeland
28-30 . . . . . . Tampa
31 . . .at Brevard County

JUNE
1 . . . . . Brevard County
2 . . . .at Brevard County
3-6 . . . . . . at Bradenton
7 . . . . . . Brevard County
8 . . . .at Brevard County
9 . . . . . Brevard County
10-13 . . . . . .Fort Myers
17-19 . . . . at Clearwater
20-22 . . . . . . Dunedin

23-25 . . . . .Lakeland
26-28 . . . . . . .at Tampa
29-30 . . . . . Clearwater

JULY
1 . . . . Clearwater
3 . . . .at Brevard County
4 . . . . . Brevard County
5 . . . .at Brevard County
6-8 . . . . at Dunedin
9-11 . . . . . . at Lakeland
12-15 . . . . Jupiter
17-20 . . . . .at Charlotte
21-24 . . . . St. Lucie
25-28 . . . . at Palm Beach
29-31 . . . . at Fort Myers

AUGUST
1 . . . . at Fort Myers
2-5 . . . . .Bradenton
7-9 . . . . . . .at Clearwater
10-12 . . . . Tampa
13-15 . . . . . Clearwater
16 . . . . . Brevard County
17 . . . .at Brevard County
18 . . . .at Brevard County
20-22 . . . . . at Dunedin
23-25 . . . . . .at Tampa
26-28 . . . . . . Dunedin
29 . . . .at Brevard County
30 . . . . .at Brevard County
31 . . . .at Brevard County

SEPTEMBER
1 . . . . . . Brevard County

DUNEDIN BLUE JAYS

APRIL
4	Clearwater
5	at Clearwater
6	Clearwater
7	at Clearwater
9-11	Tampa
12-14	Lakeland
15-17	at Tampa
18-20	at Lakeland
21-23	Daytona
25-27	at Brevard County
28-30	at Jupiter

MAY
1	at Jupiter
2-4	Brevard County
5-8	Bradenton
9-11	at Daytona
13-16	at Fort Myers
17-19	Brevard County
20-23	St. Lucie
24	at Tampa
25	Tampa
26	at Tampa
28-30	at Lakeland
31	Clearwater

JUNE
1	at Clearwater
2	Clearwater
3-6	Charlotte
7	Clearwater
8-9	at Clearwater
10-13	at Palm Beach
17	Tampa
18	at Tampa
19	Tampa
20-22	at Daytona
23-25	at Brevard County
26-28	Lakeland
29-30	Tampa

JULY
1	Tampa
3	at Clearwater
4	Clearwater
5	at Clearwater
6-8	Daytona
9-11	at Tampa
12-15	at St. Lucie
17-20	Fort Myers
21-24	at Charlotte
25-28	Jupiter
29-31	at Bradenton

AUGUST
1	at Bradenton
2-5	Palm Beach
7-9	at Lakeland
10-12	Brevard County
13-15	Lakeland
16-17	at Clearwater
18	Clearwater
20-22	Daytona
23-25	at Brevard County
26-28	at Daytona
29-30	Clearwater
31	at Clearwater

SEPTEMBER
1	Clearwater

FORT MYERS MIRACLE

APRIL
4	Bradenton
5	at Bradenton
6	Bradenton
7	at Bradenton
9-11	Jupiter
12-13	at Charlotte
14	Charlotte
15-17	Palm Beach
18-20	at St. Lucie
21-23	at Palm Beach
25	at Charlotte
26-27	Charlotte
28-30	at Clearwater

MAY
1	at Clearwater
2-4	St. Lucie
5-8	Tampa
9-11	at Jupiter
13-16	Dunedin
17-19	at Charlotte
20-23	at Lakeland
24-26	Charlotte
28	Bradenton
29	at Bradenton
30	Bradenton
31	at Palm Beach

JUNE
1-2	at Palm Beach
3-6	Brevard County
7	at Bradenton
8	Bradenton
9	at Bradenton
10-13	at Daytona
17-19	Palm Beach
20-22	Jupiter
23-25	at Palm Beach
26-28	at Jupiter
29-30	St. Lucie

JULY
1	St. Lucie
2	at Bradenton
3	Bradenton
5	Bradenton
6-8	at St. Lucie
9-11	Jupiter
12-15	Lakeland
17-20	at Dunedin
21-24	at Brevard County
25-28	Clearwater
29-31	Daytona

AUGUST
1	Daytona
2-5	at Tampa
7	at Charlotte
8-9	Charlotte
10-12	at Jupiter
13-15	at St. Lucie
16	at Bradenton
17	Bradenton
18	at Bradenton
20	Charlotte
21-22	at Charlotte
23-25	St. Lucie
26-28	Palm Beach
29	at Bradenton
30	Bradenton
31	at Bradenton

SEPTEMBER
1	Bradenton

JUPITER HAMMERHEADS

APRIL
4-5	at St. Lucie
6-7	St. Lucie
9-11	at Fort Myers
12	Palm Beach
13	at Palm Beach
14	Palm Beach
15-17	Bradenton
18-20	Charlotte
21-23	at Bradenton
25-26	Palm Beach
27	at Palm Beach
28-30	Dunedin

MAY
1	Dunedin
2-4	at Charlotte
5-8	at Lakeland
9-11	Fort Myers
13-16	at Tampa
17	Palm Beach
18-19	at Palm Beach
20-23	Daytona
24	at Palm Beach
25	Palm Beach
26	at Palm Beach
28-30	at St. Lucie
31	at Bradenton

JUNE
1-2	at Bradenton
3-6	Clearwater
7-9	St. Lucie
10-13	at Brevard County
17-19	Bradenton

JULY
1	Charlotte
3	St. Lucie
4-5	at St. Lucie
6	at Palm Beach
7-8	Palm Beach
9-11	at Fort Myers
12-15	at Daytona
17-20	Tampa
21-24	at Clearwater
25-28	at Dunedin
29-31	Brevard County

AUGUST
1	Brevard County
2-5	Lakeland
7-8	at Palm Beach
9	Palm Beach
10-12	Fort Myers
13-15	Charlotte
16	at St. Lucie
17-18	St. Lucie
20-22	at Bradenton
23-25	at Charlotte
26-28	Bradenton
29-30	at St. Lucie
31	at St. Lucie

SEPTEMBER
1	at St. Lucie

LAKELAND FLYING TIGERS

APRIL
4	at Tampa
5	Tampa
6	at Tampa
7	Tampa
9-10	Brevard County
11	at Brevard County
12-14	at Dunedin
15-16	at Brevard County
17	Brevard County
18-20	Dunedin
21-23	Clearwater
25-27	at Daytona
28-30	at Charlotte

MAY
1	at Charlotte
2-4	Daytona
5-8	Jupiter
9-11	at Clearwater
13-16	at Palm Beach
17-19	Daytona
20-23	Fort Myers
24-26	at Daytona
28-30	Dunedin
31	Tampa

JUNE
1-2	at Tampa
3-6	at St. Lucie
7	at Tampa
8-9	Tampa
10-13	Bradenton
17-19	at Brevard County
20	at Clearwater

JULY
1	Brevard County
3	at Tampa
4-5	Tampa
6-7	at Clearwater
8	Clearwater
9-11	Daytona
12-15	at Fort Myers
17-20	Palm Beach
21-24	at Bradenton
25-28	St. Lucie
29-31	Charlotte

AUGUST
1	Charlotte
2-5	at Jupiter
7-9	Dunedin
10-12	Clearwater
13-15	at Dunedin
16	at Tampa
17	Tampa
18	at Tampa
20-22	Brevard County
23-25	at Clearwater
26-28	at Brevard County
29	at Tampa
30-31	Tampa

SEPTEMBER
1	at Tampa

PALM BEACH CARDINALS

APRIL
4-5	Charlotte
6-7	at Charlotte
9-11	St. Lucie

12 . . . . at Jupiter
13 . . . . Jupiter
14 . . . . at Jupiter
15-17 . . . . at Fort Myers
18-20 . . . . . at Bradenton
21-23 . . . . . .Fort Myers
25-26 . . . . . . at Jupiter
27 . . . . Jupiter
28-30 . . . . . . at Daytona

MAY

1 . . . . at Daytona
2-4 . . . . .Bradenton
5-8 . . . . Clearwater
9-11 . . . . . . at St. Lucie
13-16 . . . . .Lakeland
17 . . . . at Jupiter
18-19 . . . . Jupiter
20-23 . . .at Brevard County
24 . . . . Jupiter
25 . . . . at Jupiter
26 . . . . Jupiter
28-30 . . . . Charlotte
31 . . . . .Fort Myers

JUNE

1-2 . . . . .Fort Myers
3-6 . . . . .at Tampa
7-9 . . . . . at Charlotte
10-13 . . . . Dunedin
17-19 . . . at Fort Myers
20-22 . . . . St. Lucie
23-25 . . . . . . .Fort Myers

ST. LUCIE METS

APRIL

4-5 . . . . Jupiter
6-7 . . . . at Jupiter
9-11 . . . . at Palm Beach
12-14 . . . . . at Bradenton
15-17 . . . . . . Charlotte
18-20 . . . . . .Fort Myers
21-23 . . . at Charlotte
25-27 . . . . . .Bradenton
28-30 . . . . . . .at Tampa

MAY

1 . . . . .at Tampa
2-4 . . . . . . at Fort Myers
5-8 . . . . Daytona
9-11 . . . . . Palm Beach
13-14 . . . . Brevard County
15-16 . . .at Brevard County

17-19 . . . . . at Bradenton
20-23 . . . . . at Dunedin
24-26 . . . . . .Bradenton
28-30 . . . . Jupiter
31 . . . . .at Charlotte

JUNE

1-2 . . . . at Charlotte
3-6 . . . . .Lakeland
7-9 . . . . at Jupiter
10-13 . . . . .at Clearwater
17-19 . . . . Charlotte
20-22 . . . at Palm Beach
23-25 . . . . . . .Bradenton
26-28 . . . . . Palm Beach
29-30 . . . . at Fort Myers

JULY

1 . . . . at Fort Myers

26-28 . . . . . . at St. Lucie
29-30 . . . . . at Bradenton

JULY

1 . . . . at Bradenton
3 . . . . .at Charlotte
4-5 . . . . Charlotte
6 . . . . Jupiter
7-8 . . . . at Jupiter
9-11 . . . . .Bradenton
12-15 . . . Brevard County
17-20 . . . . . at Lakeland
21-24 . . . . Tampa
25-28 . . . Daytona
29-31 . . .at Clearwater

AUGUST

1 . . . . .at Clearwater
2-5 . . . . . . at Dunedin
7-8 . . . . Jupiter
9 . . . . at Jupiter
10-12 . . . . . at St. Lucie
13-15 . . . at Bradenton
16 . . . . Charlotte
17-18 . . . . .at Charlotte
20-22 . . . . . . St. Lucie
23-25 . . . . . .Bradenton
26-28 . . . . at Fort Myers
29-30 . . . . at Charlotte
31 . . . . Charlotte

SEPTEMBER

1 . . . . Charlotte

3 . . . . at Jupiter
4-5 . . . . Jupiter
6-8 . . . . .Fort Myers
9-11 . . . . . . .at Charlotte
12-15 . . . . Dunedin
17-18 . .at Brevard County
19-20 . . . Brevard County
21-24 . . . . at Daytona
25-28 . . . . at Lakeland
29-31 . . . . Tampa

AUGUST

1 . . . . Tampa
2-5 . . . . Clearwater

TAMPA YANKEES

APRIL

4 . . . . .Lakeland
5 . . . . . . at Lakeland
6 . . . . at Lakeland
7 . . . . . . at Lakeland
9-11 . . . . . at Dunedin
12-14 . . . . Daytona
15-17 . . . . Dunedin
18-20 . . . . at Daytona
21-23 . . . . Brevard County
24 . . . . Clearwater
26-27 . . . . at Clearwater
28-30 . . . . St. Lucie

MAY

1-2 . . . . Clearwater
3 . . . . .at Clearwater
4 . . . . .at Clearwater
5-8 . . . . . . at Fort Myers
9-11 . . . .at Brevard County
13-16 . . . . Jupiter
17-18 . . . . . . Clearwater
19 . . . . . . .at Clearwater
20-23 . . . . . at Bradenton
24 . . . . Dunedin
25 . . . . at Dunedin
26 . . . . Dunedin
28-30 . . . at Daytona
31 . . . . . . at Lakeland

JUNE

1-2 . . . . . . .Lakeland
3-6 . . . . Palm Beach
7 . . . . .Lakeland
8-9 . . . . . . at Lakeland
10-13 . . . . . . at Charlotte
17 . . . . . . at Dunedin
18 . . . . Dunedin

19 . . . . at Dunedin
20-22 . . . Brevard County
23 . . . . . .at Clearwater
24 . . . . Clearwater
25 . . . . . .at Clearwater
26-28 . . . . Daytona
29-30 . . . . at Dunedin

JULY

1 . . . . at Dunedin
3 . . . . .Lakeland
4-5 . . . . . . at Lakeland
6-8 . . .at Brevard County
9-11 . . . . . . .Dunedin
12-15 . . . . . .Bradenton
17-20 . . . . . at Jupiter
22-24 . . . . at Palm Beach
25-28 . . . . . Charlotte
29-31 . . . . at St. Lucie

AUGUST

1 . . . . at St. Lucie
2-5 . . . . .Fort Myers
7-9 . . .at Brevard County
10-12 . . . . . at Daytona
13-15 . . . Brevard County
16 . . . . .Lakeland
17 . . . . . at Lakeland
18 . . . . .Lakeland
20 . . . . . . .at Clearwater
21-22 . . . . . Clearwater
23-25 . . . . . . Daytona
26-27 . . .at Clearwater
28 . . . . . . Clearwater
29 . . . . .Lakeland
30-31 . . . . at Lakeland

SEPTEMBER

1 . . . . .Lakeland

7-9 . . . . . . at Bradenton
10-12 . . . . . . Palm Beach
13-15 . . . . .Fort Myers
16 . . . . Jupiter
17-18 . . . . . at Jupiter
20-22 . . . . at Palm Beach
23-25 . . . . at Fort Myers
26-28 . . . . . . Charlotte
29-30 . . . . . at Jupiter
31 . . . . Jupiter

SEPTEMBER

1 . . . . Jupiter

LOW CLASS A

MIDWEST LEAGUE

BELOIT SNAPPERS

APRIL

4-7 . . . . . at Cedar Rapids
8-10 . . . . . . .at Peoria
11-14 . . . . . . .Burlington
15-17 . . . . . Kane County
18-20 . . . . at Burlington
21-23 . . . . . . at Clinton
25-27 . . . . South Bend
28-30 . . . . West Michigan

MAY

1-3 . . . . . . at Great Lakes
4-6 . . . . . . .at Lansing
8-10 . . . . Peoria
11-13 . . . . . Cedar Rapids
14-16 . . . . . . at Clinton

17-20 . . . . at Quad Cities
22-24 . . . . . Cedar Rapids
25-27 . . . . at Kane County
28-30 . . . . Wisconsin
31 . . . . Quad Cities

JUNE

1-3 . . . . Quad Cities
5-7 . . . . at Wisconsin
8-10 . . . . . at Burlington
11-13 . . . . Wisconsin
14-16 . . . . Clinton
20-23 . . . . Peoria
25-28 . . . . at Kane County
29-30 . . . . .Burlington

JULY

1 . . . . .Burlington
2-3 . . . . Cedar Rapids
4-8 . . . . at Peoria
10-12 . . . . . . Lake County
13-15 . . . . . Fort Wayne
17-19 . . . . . . at Dayton
20-22 . . at Bowling Green
24-26 . . . . Kane City
27-29 . . . . . Quad Cities
30-31 . . . . at Clinton

AUGUST

1-2 . . . . at Clinton

BOWLING GREEN HOT RODS

APRIL

4-7 . . . . at South Bend
8-10 . . . . Lansing

3-6 . . . . at Wisconsin
7-9 . . . . Cedar Rapids
10-12 . . . . . at Burlington
14-16 . . . at Cedar Rapids
17-20 . . . . Wisconsin
21-23 . . at Kane County
24-27 . . . . .Clinton
28-30 . . . . .Burlington
31 . . . . . . at Quad Cities

SEPTEMBER

1-2 . . . . . . at Quad Cities

11-14 . . . . .West Michigan
16-18 . . . at Great Lakes
19-21 . . . . . . at Dayton

22-24 . . . . . . Fort Wayne
25-27 . . . . . . .Burlington
28-30 . . . . Peoria

MAY
1-3 . . . . . at Kane County
4-6 . . . . at Clinton
8-10 . . . . . West Michigan
11-13 . . . . Lake County
14-16 . . . . . .at Fort Wayne
17-20 . . . at West Michigan
22-24 . . . . . . Great Lakes
25-27 . . . . . Fort Wayne
28-30 . . . . .at Lake County
31 . . . . South Bend

JUNE
1-3 . . . . South Bend
5-7 . . . . Dayton
8-10 . . . . at Lake County
11-13 . . . . . at Dayton
14-16 . . . . . at Lansing
20-22 . . . . Lansing
23-25 . . . . . Lake County
26-28 . . . . at South Bend
29-30 . . . at West Michigan

BURLINGTON BEES

APRIL
4-7 . . . . Clinton
8-10 . . . . Quad Cities
11-14 . . . . at Beloit
15-17 . . . . .at Peoria
18-20 . . . . Beloit
21-23 . . . . . Cedar Rapids
25-27 . . at Bowling Green
28-30 . . . . at Dayton

MAY
1-3 . . . . Fort Wayne
4-6 . . . . Lake County
8-10 . . . . . . Kane County
11-13 . . . . . at Wisconsin
14-16 . . . at Cedar Rapids
17-20 . . . . . . Wisconsin
22-24 . . . . at Clinton
25-27 . . at Cedar Rapids
28-30 . . . . Peoria
31 . . . . at Clinton

JUNE
1-3 . . . . at Clinton
5-7 . . . . Kane County
8-10 . . . . Beloit
11-13 . . . . at Kane County
14-16 . . . . at Quad Cities
20-23 . . . . Clinton

CEDAR RAPIDS KERNELS

APRIL
4-7 . . . . Beloit
8-10 . . . . . . at Wisconsin
11-14 . . . . . . at Clinton
15-17 . . . . Wisconsin
18-20 . . . . .at Peoria
21-23 . . . . . at Burlington
25-27 . . . . . . Great Lakes
28-30 . . . . Lansing

MAY
1-3 . . . . at West Michigan
4-6 . . . . at South Bend
8-10 . . . . . at Quad Cities
11-13 . . . . at Beloit
14-16 . . . . . . .Burlington
17-20 . . . . . Kane County
22-24 . . . . . . at Beloit

JULY
1 . . . . . at West Michigan
2-3 . . . . .Dayton
4-5 . . . . at Dayton
6-8 . . . . Lansing
10-12 . . . . at Quad Cities
13-15 . . . . at Cedar Rapids
17-19 . . . . Wisconsin
20-22 . . . . Beloit
24-26 . . . . at Great Lakes
27-29 . . . . . .at Lansing
30-31 . . . . at Dayton

AUGUST
1-2 . . . . .Dayton
3-6 . . . . South Bend
7-9 . . . . Great Lakes
10-12 . . . .at Lake County
14-16 . . . . .at Fort Wayne
17-20 . . . . at South Bend
21-23 . . . . West Michigan
24-26 . . . . . . Fort Wayne
28-30 . . . . at South Bend
31 . . . . Lake County

SEPTEMBER
1-2 . . . . . Lake County

25-28 . . . . at Cedar Rapids
29-30 . . . . at Beloit

JULY
1 . . . . at Beloit
2-3 . . . . Peoria
4-5 . . . . at Clinton
6-8 . . . . Wisconsin
10-12 . . . . at Great Lakes
13-15 . . . . . .at Lansing
17-19 . . . . .West Michigan
20-22 . . . . . South Bend
24-26 . . . . . . Quad Cities
27-29 . . . . . at Wisconsin
30-31 . . . . . . Cedar Rapids

AUGUST
1-2 . . . . Cedar Rapids
3-6 . . . . .at Peoria
7-9 . . . . . at Kane County
10-12 . . . . Beloit
14-16 . . . . . . Kane County
17-20 . . . . at Quad Cities
21-23 . . . . Quad Cities
24-27 . . . . . . Quad Cities
28-30 . . . . at Beloit
31 . . . . Wisconsin

SEPTEMBER
1-2 . . . . Wisconsin

25-27 . . . . . . .Burlington
28-30 . . . . .Clinton
31 . . . . . at Kane County

JUNE
1-3 . . . . . at Kane County
5-7 . . . . Quad Cities
8-10 . . . . . . Kane County
11-13 . . . . at Quad Cities
14-16 . . . . Peoria
20-23 . . . . . at Wisconsin
25-28 . . . . . . .Burlington
29-30 . . . . Peoria

JULY
1 . . . . Peoria
2-3 . . . . at Beloit
4-5 . . . . Wisconsin
6-8 . . . . at Clinton

10-12 . . . . Dayton
13-15 . . . . . Bowling Green
17-19 . . . .at Lake County
20-22 . . . . .at Fort Wayne
24-26 . . . . Peoria
27-29 . . . . Clinton
30-31 . . . . . at Burlington

AUGUST
1-2 . . . . . . at Burlington
3-6 . . . . Quad Cities

CLINTON LUMBERKINGS

APRIL
4-7 . . . . . . at Burlington
8-10 . . . . at Kane County
11-14 . . . . . Cedar Rapids
15-17 . . . . at Quad Cities
18-20 . . . . Wisconsin
21-23 . . . . Beloit
25-27 . . .at Lake County
28-30 . . . . .at Fort Wayne

MAY
1-3 . . . . Dayton
4-6 . . . . . . Bowling Green
8-10 . . . . . at Wisconsin
11-13 . . . . . Kane County
14-16 . . . . Beloit
17-20 . . . . . . .at Peoria
22-24 . . . . . .Burlington
25-27 . . . . . Quad Cities
28-30 . . at Cedar Rapids
31 . . . . .Burlington

JUNE
1-3 . . . . .Burlington
5-7 . . . . .at Peoria
8-10 . . . . . at Wisconsin
11-13 . . . . Peoria
14-16 . . . . . . at Beloit
20-23 . . . . . at Burlington

DAYTON DRAGONS

APRIL
4-7 . . . . at West Michigan
8-10 . . . . at South Bend
11-14 . . . . . . Great Lakes
16-18 . . . .at Lake County
19-21 . . . . .Bowling Green
22-24 . . . . .at Lansing
25-27 . . . . Peoria
28-30 . . . . . . .Burlington

MAY
1-3 . . . . at Clinton
4-6 . . . . . at Kane County
8-10 . . . . Lansing
11-13 . . . . Fort Wayne
14-16 . . . . .West Michigan
17-20 . . . . . at South Bend
22-24 . . . . .West Michigan
25-27 . . . . at Great Lakes
28-30 . . . . . . South Bend
31 . . . . Lake County

JUNE
1-3 . . . . Lake County
5-7 . . . . at Bowling Green
8-10 . . . . . .at Fort Wayne
11-13 . . . . . Bowling Green
14-16 . . . . . at South Bend
20-22 . . . . . . Lake County
23-25 . . . . Lansing

7-9 . . . . at Beloit
10-12 . . . . at Kane County
14-16 . . . . .Beloit
17-20 . . . . .at Peoria
21-23 . . . . at Quad Cities
24-27 . . . . Peoria
28-30 . . . . at Kane County
31 . . . . at Clinton

SEPTEMBER
1-2 . . . . at Clinton

25-28 . . . . Wisconsin
29-30 . . . . at Quad Cities

JULY
1-3 . . . . at Quad Cities
4-5 . . . . .Burlington
6-8 . . . . Cedar Rapids
10-12 . . at West Michigan
13-15 . . . . at South Bend
17-19 . . . . Lansing
20-22 . . . . . . Great Lakes
24-26 . . . . . . at Wisconsin
27-29 . . at Cedar Rapids
30-31 . . . . .Beloit

AUGUST
1-2 . . . . .Beloit
3-6 . . . . Kane County
7-9 . . . . at Quad Cities
10-12 . . . . Peoria
14-16 . . . . . Quad Cities
17-20 . . . . at Kane County
21-23 . . . . Wisconsin
24-27 . . . . at Beloit
28-30 . . . . . . .at Peoria
31 . . . . Cedar Rapids

SEPTEMBER
1-2 . . . . Cedar Rapids

26-28 . . . at West Michigan
29-30 . . . . at South Bend

JULY
1 . . . . at South Bend
2-3 . . . at Bowling Green
4-5 . . . . . . Bowling Green
6-8 . . . . . at South Bend
10-12 . . . at Cedar Rapids
13-15 . . . at Quad Cities
17-19 . . . . .Beloit
20-22 . . . . at Wisconsin
24-26 . . . . . .at Lansing
27-29 . . . . . . Fort Wayne
30-31 . . . Bowling Green

AUGUST
1-2 . . . . . at Bowling Green
3-6 . . . . . at West Michigan
7-9 . . . . . . Lake County
10-12 . . . .at Fort Wayne
14-16 . . . . . Great Lakes
17-20 . . . .West Michigan
21-23 . . .at Lake County
24-26 . . . . . .at Lansing
28-30 . . . at Great Lakes
31 . . . . South Bend

SEPTEMBER
1-2 . . . . South Bend

FORT WAYNE TINCAPS

APRIL
4-7 . . . . . at Great Lakes
8-10 . . . at West Michigan
11-14 . . . . . Lake County
16-18 . . . . at South Bend
19-21 . . . . Lansing
22-24 . . . at Bowling Green
25-27 . . . . . Kane County
28-30 . . . . Clinton

MAY
1-3 . . . . . . at Burlington
4-6 . . . . at Peoria
8-10 . . . . . Great Lakes
11-13 . . . . . . at Dayton
14-16 . . . . Bowling Green
17-20 . . . . at Lake County
22-24 . . . . . . South Bend
25-27 . . at Bowling Green
28-30 . . . . Lansing
31 . . . . West Michigan

JUNE
1-3 . . . . . West Michigan
5-7 . . . . at Lansing
8-10 . . . . Dayton
11-13 . . . . . Lake County
14-16 . . at West Michigan
20-22 . . . . . South Bend
23-25 . . . . West Michigan

26-28 . . . . . . at Lansing
29-30 . . . . at Lake County

JULY
1 . . . . at Lake County
2-3 . . . . at South Bend
4-5 . . . . . . South Bend
6-8 . . . . . . Great Lakes
10-12 . . . . at Wisconsin
13-15 . . . . . . at Beloit
17-19 . . . . Quad Cities
20-22 . . . . Cedar Rapids
24-26 . . at West Michigan
27-29 . . . . at Dayton
30-31 . . . . . Lake County

AUGUST
1-2 . . . . . at Lake County
3-6 . . . . Lansing
7-9 . . . . . at South Bend
10-12 . . . . Dayton
14-16 . . . . Bowling Green
17-20 . . . at Great Lakes
21-23 . . . . . South Bend
24-26 . . at Bowling Green
28-30 . at West Michigan
31 . . . . Great Lakes

SEPTEMBER
1-2 . . . . Great Lakes

GREAT LAKES LOONS

APRIL
4-7 . . . . Fort Wayne
8-10 . . . . . Lake County
11-14 . . . . at Dayton
16-18 . . . . Bowling Green
19-21 . . . . . Lake County
22-24 . . . . at South Bend
25-27 . . at Cedar Rapids
28-30 . . . . at Quad Cities

MAY
1-3 . . . . Beloit
4-6 . . . . Wisconsin
8-10 . . . . .at Fort Wayne
11-13 . . . . . .at Lansing
14-16 . . . . . . South Bend
17-20 . . . . . .at Lansing
22-24 . . at Bowling Green
25-27 . . . . Dayton
28-30 . . at West Michigan
31 . . . . Lansing

JUNE
1-3 . . . . Lansing
5-7 . . . . at West Michigan
8-10 . . . . . . South Bend
11-13 . . . . West Michigan
14-16 . . . .at Lake County
20-22 . . . . West Michigan
23-25 . . . . . South Bend

26-28 . . . . .at Lake County
29-30 . . . . at Lansing

JULY
1 . . . . .at Lansing
2-3 . . . . . West Michigan
4-5 . . . . at West Michigan
6-8 . . . . . .at Fort Wayne
10-12 . . . . . . .Burlington
13-15 . . . . Peoria
17-19 . . . at Kane County
20-22 . . . . . . at Clinton
24-26 . . . . Bowling Green
27-29 . . . . . Lake County
30-31 . . . at West Michigan

AUGUST
1-2 . . . . . . West Michigan
3-6 . . . . . .at Lake County
7-9 . . . . at Bowling Green
10-12 . . . . Lansing
14-16 . . . . at Dayton
17-20 . . . . . . Fort Wayne
21-23 . . . . Lansing
24-26 . . . . at South Bend
28-30 . . . . Dayton
31 . . . . .at Fort Wayne

SEPTEMBER
1-2 . . . . . .at Fort Wayne

KANE COUNTY COUGARS

APRIL
4-7 . . . . Quad Cities
8-10 . . . . Clinton
11-14 . . . . . at Wisconsin
15-17 . . . . . . at Beloit
18-20 . . . . . Quad Cities
21-23 . . . . Peoria
25-27 . . . .at Fort Wayne
28-30 . . . .at Lake County

MAY
1-3 . . . . . .Bowling Green

4-6 . . . . Dayton
8-10 . . . . . at Burlington
11-13 . . . . . . at Clinton
14-16 . . . . Peoria
17-20 . . . at Cedar Rapids
22-24 . . . . . . at Peoria
25-27 . . . . Beloit
28-30 . . at Quad Cities
31 . . . . Cedar Rapids

JUNE
1-3 . . . . Cedar Rapids

LAKE COUNTY CAPTAINS

APRIL
4-7 . . . . Lansing
8-10 . . . . . at Great Lakes
11-14 . . . .at Fort Wayne
16-18 . . . . Dayton
19-21 . . . at Great Lakes
22-24 . . at West Michigan
25-27 . . . . Clinton
28-30 . . . . . Kane County

MAY
1-3 . . . . .at Peoria
4-6 . . . . . . at Burlington
8-10 . . . . . . South Bend
11-13 . . at Bowling Green
14-16 . . . . Lansing
17-20 . . . . . . Fort Wayne
21-23 . . . . . .at Lansing
25-27 . . . . West Michigan
28-30 . . . . Bowling Green
31 . . . . at Dayton

JUNE
1-3 . . . . at Dayton
5-7 . . . . at South Bend
8-10 . . . . Bowling Green
11-13 . . . .at Fort Wayne
14-16 . . . . . . Great Lakes
20-22 . . . . . . at Dayton
23-25 . . . .Bowling Green

26-28 . . . . . . Great Lakes
29-30 . . . . . . Fort Wayne

JULY
1 . . . . Fort Wayne
2-3 . . . . Lansing
4-5 . . . . . . .at Lansing
6-8 . . . . West Michigan
10-12 . . . . at Beloit
13-15 . . . . at Wisconsin
17-19 . . . . Cedar Rapids
20-22 . . . . Quad Cities
24-26 . . . . at South Bend
27-29 . . . at Great Lakes
30-31 . . . .at Fort Wayne

AUGUST
1-2 . . . . Fort Wayne
3-6 . . . . . . Great Lakes
7-9 . . . . at Dayton
10-12 . . . .Bowling Green
14-16 . . . . . . South Bend
17-20 . . . . . .at Lansing
21-23 . . . . .Dayton
24-26 . . at West Michigan
28-30 . . . . Lansing
31 . . . . at Bowling Green

SEPTEMBER
1-2 . . . . at Bowling Green

LANSING LUGNUTS

APRIL
4-7 . . . . . .at Lake County
8-10 . . . . Bowling Green
12-14 . . . . . . South Bend
16-18 . . . West Michigan
19-21 . . . .at Fort Wayne
22-24 . . . . Dayton
25-27 . . . . at Quad Cities
28-30 . . . at Cedar Rapids

MAY
1-3 . . . . Wisconsin
4-6 . . . . Beloit
8-10 . . . . . . at Dayton
11-13 . . . . . Great Lakes
14-16 . . .at Lake County
17-20 . . . . . Great Lakes
21-23 . . . . . Lake County
25-27 . . . at South Bend
28-30 . . .at Fort Wayne
31 . . . . . at Great Lakes

JUNE
1-3 . . . . . . at Great Lakes
5-7 . . . . Fort Wayne
8-10 . . . . West Michigan
11-13 . . . . . South Bend
14-16 . . . . Bowling Green
20-22 . . . at Bowling Green

23-25 . . . . at Dayton
26-28 . . . . . Fort Wayne
29-30 . . . . Great Lakes

JULY
1 . . . . Great Lakes
2-3 . . . .at Lake County
4-5 . . . . . Lake County
6-8 . . . . at Bowling Green
10-12 . . . . at Peoria
13-15 . . . . . . .Burlington
17-19 . . . . . . at Clinton
20-22 . . at Kane County
24-26 . . . . Dayton
27-29 . . . .Bowling Green
30-31 . . . . . South Bend

AUGUST
1-2 . . . . . at South Bend
3-6 . . . . . .at Fort Wayne
7-9 . . . . . West Michigan
10-12 . . . . at Great Lakes
14-16 . . at West Michigan
17-20 . . . . . Lake County
21-23 . . . . . Great Lakes
24-26 . . . . .Dayton
28-30 . . . .at Lake County
31 . . . . . . West Michigan

CHICAGO CUBS section (right column top)

5-7 . . . . . . at Burlington
8-10 . . . . at Cedar Rapids
11-13 . . . . . . .Burlington
14-16 . . . . Wisconsin
20-23 . . . at Quad Cities
25-28 . . . . Beloit
29-30 . . . . at Wisconsin

JULY
1-3 . . . . . . at Wisconsin
4-8 . . . . . . Quad Cities
10-12 . . . at South Bend
13-15 . . at West Michigan
17-19 . . . . . Great Lakes
20-22 . . . . Lansing
24-26 . . . . . at Beloit

26-28 . . . . . . at Lansing
29-30 . . . . . . Wisconsin

AUGUST
1-2 . . . . Wisconsin
3-6 . . . . at Clinton
7-9 . . . . .Burlington
10-12 . . . . . Cedar Rapids
14-16 . . . . at Burlington
17-20 . . . . .Clinton
21-23 . . . . Beloit
24-27 . . . at South Bend
28-30 . . . . at Cedar Rapids
31 . . . . Peoria

SEPTEMBER
1-2 . . . . Peoria

SEPTEMBER
1-2 . . . . . . West Michigan

PEORIA CHIEFS

APRIL	
4-7 . . . . Wisconsin	25-28 . . . . . at Quad Cities
8-10 . . . . Beloit	29-30 . . . at Cedar Rapids
11-14 . . . . at Quad Cities	**JULY**
15-17 . . . . . . Burlington	1 . . . . . . at Cedar Rapids
18-20 . . . . . Cedar Rapids	2-3 . . . . . at Burlington
21-23 . . . . at Kane County	4-8 . . . . Beloit
25-27 . . . . . . at Dayton	10-12 . . . . at Lansing
28-30 . . . at Bowling Green	13-15 . . . . at Great Lakes
MAY	17-19 . . . . . . South Bend
1-3 . . . . Lake County	20-22 . . . . . West Michigan
4-6 . . . . Fort Wayne	24-26 . . . at Cedar Rapids
8-10 . . . . at Beloit	27-29 . . . . Kane County
11-13 . . . . at Quad Cities	30-31 . . . . . at Quad Cities
14-16 . . . . at Kane County	**AUGUST**
17-20 . . . . Clinton	1-2 . . . . . at Quad Cities
22-24 . . . . Kane County	3-6 . . . . Burlington
25-27 . . . . . Wisconsin	7-9 . . . . Wisconsin
28-30 . . . . . at Burlington	10-12 . . . . . at Clinton
31 . . . . . . at Wisconsin	14-16 . . . . . at Wisconsin
JUNE	17-20 . . . . Cedar Rapids
1-3 . . . . . . at Wisconsin	21-23 . . . . . . Burlington
5-7 . . . . Clinton	24-27 . . . at Cedar Rapids
8-10 . . . . . . Quad Cities	28-30 . . . . Clinton
11-13 . . . . . at Clinton	31 . . . . . at Kane County
14-16 . . . at Cedar Rapids	**SEPTEMBER**
20-23 . . . . at Beloit	1-2 . . . . . at Kane County

QUAD CITIES RIVER BANDITS

APRIL	
4-7 . . . . . at Kane County	20-23 . . . . . Kane County
8-10 . . . . . . at Burlington	25-28 . . . . . at Peoria
11-14 . . . . Peoria	29-30 . . . . . . Clinton
15-17 . . . . Clinton	**JULY**
18-20 . . . at Kane County	1-3 . . . . Clinton
21-23 . . . . at Wisconsin	4-8 . . . . at Kane County
25-27 . . . . . . Lansing	10-12 . . Bowling Green
28-30 . . . . . Great Lakes	13-15 . . . . Dayton
MAY	17-19 . . . .at Fort Wayne
1-3 . . . . at South Bend	20-22 . . . .at Lake County
4-6 . . . . at West Michigan	24-26 . . . . at Burlington
8-10 . . . . . Cedar Rapids	27-29 . . . . . at Beloit
11-13 . . . . Peoria	30-31 . . . . Peoria
14-16 . . . . . at Wisconsin	**AUGUST**
17-20 . . . . Beloit	1-2 . . . . Peoria
22-24 . . . . . Wisconsin	3-6 . . . . at Cedar Rapids
25-27 . . . . . at Clinton	7-9 . . . . Clinton
28-30 . . . Kane County	10-12 . . . . . Wisconsin
31 . . . . at Beloit	14-16 . . . . . at Clinton
JUNE	17-20 . . . . . .Burlington
1-3 . . . . . . at Beloit	21-23 . . . . Cedar Rapids
5-7 . . . at Cedar Rapids	24-27 . . . at Burlington
8-10 . . . . . at Peoria	28-30 . . . at Wisconsin
11-13 . . . . . Cedar Rapids	31 . . . . Beloit
14-16 . . . . . . Burlington	**SEPTEMBER**
	1-2 . . . . Beloit

SOUTH BEND SILVER HAWKS

APRIL	MAY
4-7 . . . . . . Bowling Green	1-3 . . . . . . Quad Cities
8-10 . . . . Dayton	4-6 . . . . . Cedar Rapids
12-14 . . . . . at Lansing	8-10 . . . .at Lake County
16-18 . . . . . Fort Wayne	11-13 . . . West Michigan
19-21 . . at West Michigan	14-16 . . . at Great Lakes
22-24 . . . . . Great Lakes	17-20 . . . . . . Dayton
25-27 . . . . . . at Beloit	22-24 . . . .at Fort Wayne
28-30 . . . . . at Wisconsin	25-27 . . . . . Lansing
	28-30 . . . . . . at Dayton
	31 . . . . at Bowling Green

JUNE (continued under another column)

JUNE	
1-3 . . . . at Bowling Green	20-22 . . . . . at Burlington
5-7 . . . . . . Lake County	24-26 . . . . . Lake County
8-10 . . . . . at Great Lakes	27-29 . . . . West Michigan
11-13 . . . . at Lansing	30-31 . . . . at Lansing
14-16 . . . . Dayton	**AUGUST**
20-22 . . . .at Fort Wayne	1-2 . . . . Lansing
23-25 . . . . at Great Lakes	3-6 . . . . at Bowling Green
26-28 . . . . Bowling Green	7-9 . . . . Fort Wayne
29-30 . . . . Dayton	10-12 . . . at West Michigan
JULY	14-16 . . . .at Lake County
1 . . . . Dayton	17-20 . . . Bowling Green
2-3 . . . . . Fort Wayne	21-23 . . . .at Fort Wayne
4-5 . . . .at Fort Wayne	24-26 . . . . Great Lakes
6-8 . . . . . . at Dayton	28-30 . . . Bowling Green
10-12 . . . . Kane County	31 . . . . at Dayton
13-15 . . . . . . Clinton	**SEPTEMBER**
17-19 . . . . . at Peoria	1-2 . . . . . at Dayton

WEST MICHIGAN WHITECAPS

APRIL	
4-7 . . . . Dayton	26-28 . . . . Dayton
8-10 . . . . Fort Wayne	29-30 . . . . Bowling Green
11-14 . . . at Bowling Green	**JULY**
16-18 . . . . . . .at Lansing	1 . . . . .Bowling Green
19-21 . . . . . South Bend	2-3 . . . . at Great Lakes
22-24 . . . . . Lake County	4-5 . . . . . Great Lakes
25-27 . . . . . at Wisconsin	6-8 . . . . .at Lake County
28-30 . . . . at Beloit	10-12 . . . . . . Clinton
MAY	13-15 . . . . Kane County
1-3 . . . . . Cedar Rapids	17-19 . . . . at Burlington
4-6 . . . . . Quad Cities	20-22 . . . . . .at Peoria
8-10 . . . at Bowling Green	24-26 . . . . Fort Wayne
11-13 . . . at South Bend	27-29 . . . at South Bend
14-16 . . . . Dayton	30-31 . . . . . Great Lakes
17-20 . . . Bowling Green	**AUGUST**
22-24 . . . . . at Dayton	1-2 . . . . . at Great Lakes
25-27 . . .at Lake County	3-6 . . . . Dayton
28-30 . . . . Great Lakes	7-9 . . . . .at Lansing
31 . . . . . . .at Fort Wayne	10-12 . . . . . South Bend
JUNE	14-16 . . . . . . Lansing
1-3 . . . . .at Fort Wayne	17-20 . . . . . at Dayton
5-7 . . . . . Great Lakes	21-23 . . . at Bowling Green
8-10 . . . . . . Lansing	24-26 . . . . Lake County
11-13 . . . at Great Lakes	28-30 . . . . Fort Wayne
14-16 . . . . . Fort Wayne	31 . . . . .at Lansing
20-22 . . . at Great Lakes	**SEPTEMBER**
23-25 . . . . .at Fort Wayne	1-2 . . . . at Lansing

WISCONSIN TIMBER RATTLERS

APRIL	
4-7 . . . . .at Peoria	11-13 . . . . at Beloit
8-10 . . . . . Cedar Rapids	14-16 . . . at Kane County
11-14 . . . . Kane County	20-23 . . . . Cedar Rapids
15-17 . . . at Cedar Rapids	25-28 . . . . . at Clinton
18-20 . . . . . at Clinton	29-30 . . . . Kane County
21-23 . . . . . Quad Cities	**JULY**
25-27 . . . West Michigan	1-3 . . . . Kane County
28-30 . . . . . South Bend	4-5 . . . . at Cedar Rapids
MAY	6-8 . . . . . . at Burlington
1-3 . . . . .at Lansing	10-12 . . . . . Fort Wayne
4-6 . . . . at Great Lakes	13-15 . . . . Lake County
8-10 . . . . Clinton	17-19 . . . at Bowling Green
11-13 . . . . . .Burlington	20-22 . . . . . . at Dayton
14-16 . . . . Quad Cities	24-26 . . . . Clinton
17-20 . . . at Burlington	27-29 . . . . .Burlington
22-24 . . . at Quad Cities	30-31 . . . at Kane County
25-27 . . . . . . at Peoria	**AUGUST**
28-30 . . . . . at Beloit	1-2 . . . . at Kane County
31 . . . . Peoria	3-6 . . . . Beloit
JUNE	7-9 . . . . .at Peoria
1-3 . . . . Peoria	10-12 . . . at Quad Cities
5-7 . . . . Beloit	14-16 . . . . Peoria
8-10 . . . . Clinton	17-20 . . . . . . at Beloit
	21-23 . . . . . at Clinton

24-27 . . . . . . Kane County
28-30 . . . . . . Quad Cities
31 . . . . at Burlington

SEPTEMBER
1-2 . . . . at Burlington

SOUTH ATLANTIC LEAGUE

ASHEVILLE TOURISTS

APRIL	
4-7 . . . . . at West Virginia	
8-10 . . . . . at Lexington	
11-14 . . . . . West Virginia	
15-17 . . . . Hickory	
18-21 . . . . at Rome	
23-25 . . . . Lexington	
26-29 . . . . Lakewood	

MAY	
1-3 . . . . at Hickory	
4-7 . . . . at Augusta	
9-12 . . . . . . Kannapolis	
13-15 . . . . . . Greenville	
16-19 . . . . at Rome	
20-22 . . . . . at Lexington	
23-26 . . . . Rome	
27-29 . . . . . Hagerstown	
30-31 . . . . . at Greenville	

JUNE	
1-2 . . . . . . at Greenville	
4-6 . . . . Rome	
7-9 . . . . . at Charleston	
10-12 . . . . . at Savannah	
13-16 . . . . . . Lexington	

20-23 . . . . . at Delmarva
24-26 . . . . at Greensboro
27-30 . . . . Augusta

JULY
1-3 . . . . Greensboro
4-7 . . . . at Rome
9-11 . . . . . . Delmarva
12-15 . . . . . West Virginia
17-19 . . . . at Greenville
20-23 . . . . . . at Augusta
25-28 . . . . Rome
29-31 . . . . . . Savannah

AUGUST
1-4 . . . . at Hickory
5-7 . . . . . at Lexington
8-11 . . . . . . Greenville
13-15 . . . . . at Hickory
16-19 . . . at Hagerstown
20-22 . . . . Hickory
23-25 . . . . . Charleston
27-29 . . at West Virginia
30-31 . . . . Augusta

SEPTEMBER
1-2 . . . . Augusta

AUGUSTA GREENJACKETS

APRIL	
4-7 . . . . Lexington	
8-10 . . . . at Savannah	
11-14 . . . . . at Charleston	
15-17 . . . . . . Lexington	
18-21 . . . . . Kannapolis	
23-25 . . . at Hagerstown	
26-29 . . . . . at Lexington	

MAY	
1-3 . . . . Hagerstown	
4-7 . . . . Asheville	
9-12 . . . . at Greenville	
13-15 . . . . Rome	
16-19 . . . . . . Savannah	
20-22 . . . . . . at Rome	
23-26 . . . . . at Savannah	
27-29 . . . . Hickory	
30-31 . . . . . Charleston	

JUNE	
1-2 . . . . Charleston	
4-6 . . . . . at Greensboro	
7-9 . . . . . . Lexington	
10-12 . . . at Kannapolis	
13-16 . . . . at Charleston	

20-23 . . . . . . Kannapolis
24-26 . . . . . . Savannah
27-30 . . . . . at Asheville

JULY
1-3 . . . . . . at Kannapolis
4-7 . . . . Charleston
9-11 . . . . . at Savannah
12-15 . . . . at Charleston
17-19 . . . . . . Lakewood
20-23 . . . . . . Asheville
25-28 . . . . at Savannah
29-31 . . . . Rome

AUGUST
1-4 . . . . Charleston
5-7 . . . . at Rome
8-11 . . . . at Greensboro
13-15 . . . . . . Greenville
16-19 . . . . . . Savannah
20-22 . . . . at Lexington
23-25 . . . . . at Hickory
27-29 . . . . . Lexington
30-31 . . . . at Asheville

SEPTEMBER
1-2 . . . . at Asheville

CHARLESTON RIVERDOGS

APRIL	
4-7 . . . . at Greenville	
8-10 . . . . . at West Virginia	
11-14 . . . . Augusta	
15-17 . . . . Rome	
18-21 . . . . Hickory	
23-25 . . . . . West Virginia	
26-29 . . . . . Kannapolis	

MAY	
1-3 . . . . . . at Lakewood	
4-7 . . . . at Delmarva	
9-12 . . . . Hickory	

13-15 . . . . Savannah
16-19 . . . . . at Greenville
20-22 . . . . . at Savannah
23-26 . . . . Greenville
27-29 . . . . at Rome
30-31 . . . . . . at Augusta

JUNE
1-2 . . . . at Augusta
4-6 . . . . Greenville
7-9 . . . . Asheville
10-12 . . . . at Greenville
13-16 . . . . Augusta

20-23 . . . . at Rome
24-26 . . . . . at Greenville
27-30 . . . . Hickory

JULY
1-3 . . . . Rome
4-7 . . . . at Augusta
9-11 . . . . Greenville
12-15 . . . . Augusta
17-19 . . . . at Greensboro
20-23 . . . . . . at Hickory
25-28 . . . . . Greensboro
29-31 . . . . Hickory

AUGUST
1-4 . . . . at Augusta
5-7 . . . . . . .at Savannah
8-11 . . . . Rome
13-15 . . . . Lexington
16-19 . . . . at Rome
20-22 . . . . . West Virginia
23-25 . . . . . at Asheville
26-28 . . . . . at Greenville
30-31 . . . . Rome

SEPTEMBER
1-2 . . . . Rome

DELMARVA SHOREBIRDS

APRIL	
4-7 . . . . Hagerstown	
8-10 . . . . Kannapolis	
11-14 . . . . at Hagerstown	
15-17 . . . . .at Kannapolis	
18-21 . . . . . . Greensboro	
23-25 . . . .at Savannah	
26-29 . . . . at Greenville	

MAY	
1-3 . . . . Lexington	
4-7 . . . . Charleston	
9-12 . . . . at Hagerstown	
13-15 . . . . at Lakewood	
16-19 . . . . .Hickory	
20-22 . . . . . . Lakewood	
23-26 . . . at Greensboro	
27-29 . . . . at Lakewood	
30-31 . . . . . . Greensboro	

JUNE	
1-2 . . . . Greensboro	
4-6 . . . . . at West Virginia	
7-9 . . . . Lakewood	
10-12 . . . . West Virginia	
13-16 . . . . . at Hickory	

20-23 . . . . .Asheville
24-26 . . . . Lakewood
27-30 . . . . at Greensboro

JULY
1-3 . . . . at Lakewood
4-7 . . . . Hagerstown
9-11 . . . . . . at Asheville
12-15 . . . . . at Lexington
17-19 . . . . . Kannapolis
20-23 . . . . . . Savannah
25-28 . . . . at Lakewood
29-31 . . . at West Virginia

AUGUST
1-4 . . . . Greensboro
5-7 . . . . . . West Virginia
8-11 . . . . . .at Kannapolis
13-15 . . . . . Hagerstown
16-19 . . . . Lakewood
20-22 . . . at Greensboro
23-25 . . . . at Lakewood
27-29 . . . . . Kannapolis
30-31 . . . . . at Hickory

SEPTEMBER
1-2 . . . . at Hickory

GREENSBORO GRASSHOPPERS

APRIL	
4-7 . . . . at Hickory	
8-10 . . . . at Rome	
11-14 . . . . Lakewood	
15-17 . . . . . . Savannah	
18-21 . . . .at Delmarva	
23-25 . . . . .Hickory	
26-29 . . . . Rome	

MAY	
1-3 . . . . . at West Virginia	
4-7 . . . . . . .at Kannapolis	
9-12 . . . . . . .Lakewood	
13-15 . . . . . . Hagerstown	
16-19 . . . . . at Lakewood	
20-22 . . . at Hagerstown	
23-26 . . . . . . Delmarva	
27-29 . . . at West Virginia	
30-31 . . . .at Delmarva	

JUNE	
1-2 . . . . . .at Delmarva	
4-6 . . . . Augusta	
7-9 . . . . Kannapolis	
10-12 . . . . at Lakewood	
13-16 . . . . West Virginia	

20-23 . . . . . . at Hickory
24-26 . . . . .Asheville
27-30 . . . . Delmarva

JULY
1-3 . . . . at Asheville
4-7 . . . . Lakewood
9-11 . . . . . at Lexington
12-15 . . . . .at Kannapolis
17-19 . . . . . . Charleston
20-23 . . . . . . Hagerstown
25-28 . . . . at Charleston
29-31 . . . . . Greenville

AUGUST
1-4 . . . . . .at Delmarva
5-7 . . . . at Hickory
8-11 . . . . Augusta
13-15 . . . . at West Virginia
16-19 . . . . . . Kannapolis
20-22 . . . . Delmarva
23-25 . . . .at Hagerstown
27-29 . . . . .Hickory
30-31 . . . . . at Lakewood

SEPTEMBER
1-2 . . . . at Lakewood

GREENVILLE DRIVE

APRIL	
4-7 . . . . Charleston	
8-10 . . . . at Hickory	
11-14 . . . . . at Lexington	
15-17 . . . . . West Virginia	

18-21 . . . . . at Lexington
23-25 . . . . . . Lakewood
26-29 . . . . Delmarva

MAY
1-3 . . . . at Rome

MINOR LEAGUES

5-8 . . . . . at West Virginia	4-7 . . . . Savannah
9-12 . . . . Augusta	9-11 . . . . . at Charleston
13-15 . . . . . . at Asheville	12-15 . . . . . at Savannah
16-19 . . . . . Charleston	17-19 . . . . . . Asheville
20-22 . . . . . at Hickory	20-23 . . . . . Lexington
23-26 . . . . at Charleston	25-28 . . . . . at Lakewood
27-29 . . . . . Savannah	29-31 . . . . at Greensboro
30-31 . . . . . Asheville	**AUGUST**
JUNE	1-4 . . . . Savannah
1-2 . . . . Asheville	5-7 . . . . Kannapolis
4-6 . . . . . at Charleston	8-11 . . . . . at Asheville
7-9 . . . . Hickory	13-15 . . . . . at Augusta
10-12 . . . . . Charleston	16-19 . . . . . Lexington
13-16 . . . . at Asheville	20-22 . . . . Rome
20-23 . . . . . Hagerstown	23-25 . . . . at Lexington
24-26 . . . . . Charleston	26-28 . . . . . Charleston
27-30 . . . . at Kannapolis	30-31 . . . . at Savannah
JULY	**SEPTEMBER**
1-3 . . . . . at Lexington	1-2 . . . . . . at Savannah

HAGERSTOWN SUNS

APRIL	20-23 . . . . at Greenville
4-7 . . . . . . at Delmarva	24-26 . . . at West Virginia
8-10 . . . . . at Lakewood	27-30 . . . . . . Lexington
11-14 . . . . . Delmarva	**JULY**
15-17 . . . . . Lakewood	1-3 . . . . . West Virginia
18-21 . . . at West Virginia	4-7 . . . . . at Delmarva
23-25 . . . . . Augusta	9-11 . . . . Hickory
26-29 . . . . . at Hickory	12-15 . . . . Rome
MAY	17-19 . . . . at Hickory
1-3 . . . . . at Augusta	20-23 . . . . at Greensboro
4-7 . . . . at Rome	25-28 . . . . . Delmarva
9-12 . . . . . Delmarva	29-31 . . . . at Lakewood
13-15 . . . . at Greensboro	**AUGUST**
16-19 . . . . at Kannapolis	1-4 . . . . . . Kannapolis
20-22 . . . . . Greensboro	5-7 . . . . Lakewood
23-26 . . . . . Lexington	8-11 . . . . at Lexington
27-29 . . . . at Asheville	13-15 . . . . at Delmarva
30-31 . . . . at Lexington	16-19 . . . . . . Asheville
JUNE	20-22 . . . . at Lakewood
1-2 . . . . . at Lexington	23-25 . . . . . Greensboro
4-6 . . . . . Kannapolis	27-29 . . . . . Lakewood
7-9 . . . . at West Virginia	30-31 . . . . at Kannapolis
10-12 . . . . . . Hickory	**SEPTEMBER**
13-16 . . . . . Lakewood	1-2 . . . . . at Kannapolis

HICKORY CRAWDADS

APRIL	20-23 . . . . . Greensboro
4-7 . . . . Greensboro	24-26 . . . . . Lexington
8-10 . . . . Greenville	27-30 . . . . at Charleston
11-14 . . . . at Kannapolis	**JULY**
15-17 . . . . . at Asheville	1-3 . . . . . . at Savannah
18-21 . . . . . Charleston	4-7 . . . . . . Kannapolis
23-25 . . . . at Greensboro	9-11 . . . . at Hagerstown
26-29 . . . . at Hagerstown	12-15 . . . . . at Lakewood
MAY	17-19 . . . . . Hagerstown
1-3 . . . . Asheville	20-23 . . . . . Charleston
4-7 . . . . Savannah	25-28 . . . . at Kannapolis
9-12 . . . . . at Charleston	29-31 . . . . at Charleston
13-15 . . . . . West Virginia	**AUGUST**
16-19 . . . . at Delmarva	1-4 . . . . Asheville
20-22 . . . . . Greenville	5-7 . . . . Greensboro
23-26 . . . . . Kannapolis	8-11 . . . . at Savannah
27-29 . . . . at Augusta	13-15 . . . . . . Asheville
30-31 . . . . . at Rome	16-18 . . . at West Virginia
JUNE	20-22 . . . . at Asheville
1-2 . . . . . . at Rome	23-25 . . . . . . Augusta
4-6 . . . . Lakewood	27-29 . . . . at Greensboro
7-9 . . . . . at Greenville	30-31 . . . . . Delmarva
10-12 . . . . at Hagerstown	**SEPTEMBER**
13-16 . . . . . Delmarva	1-2 . . . . Delmarva

KANNAPOLIS INTIMIDATORS

APRIL	20-23 . . . . . at Augusta
4-7 . . . . . at Lakewood	24-26 . . . . . . at Rome
8-10 . . . . . at Delmarva	27-30 . . . . . . Greenville
11-14 . . . . Hickory	**JULY**
15-17 . . . . . . Delmarva	1-3 . . . . Augusta
18-21 . . . . . at Augusta	4-7 . . . . at Hickory
23-25 . . . . Rome	9-11 . . . . . West Virginia
26-29 . . . . at Charleston	12-16 . . . . . Greensboro
MAY	17-19 . . . . . at Delmarva
1-3 . . . . . . at Savannah	20-23 . . . at West Virginia
4-7 . . . . . . Greensboro	25-28 . . . . . . Hickory
9-12 . . . . . at Asheville	29-31 . . . . . Lexington
13-15 . . . . at Lexington	**AUGUST**
16-19 . . . . . Hagerstown	1-4 . . . . . at Hagerstown
20-22 . . . . West Virginia	5-7 . . . . . at Greenville
23-26 . . . . . at Hickory	8-11 . . . . . . Delmarva
27-29 . . . . at Lexington	13-15 . . . . . . Lakewood
30-31 . . . . . Savannah	16-19 . . . . at Greensboro
JUNE	20-22 . . . . . Savannah
1-2 . . . . . . Savannah	23-25 . . . . Rome
4-6 . . . . . at Hagerstown	27-29 . . . . . at Delmarva
7-9 . . . . . at Greensboro	30-31 . . . . . Hagerstown
10-12 . . . . . . Augusta	**SEPTEMBER**
13-16 . . . . Rome	1-2 . . . . . . Hagerstown

LAKEWOOD BLUECLAWS

APRIL	20-23 . . . . at West Virginia
4-7 . . . . . . Kannapolis	24-26 . . . . at Delmarva
8-10 . . . . . Hagerstown	27-30 . . . . West Virginia
11-14 . . . . at Greensboro	**JULY**
15-17 . . . . at Hagerstown	1-3 . . . . Delmarva
18-21 . . . . . Savannah	4-7 . . . . . at Greensboro
23-25 . . . . at Greenville	9-11 . . . . Rome
26-29 . . . . . at Asheville	12-15 . . . . Hickory
MAY	17-19 . . . . . at Augusta
1-3 . . . . . . Charleston	20-23 . . . . . at Rome
4-7 . . . . . . Lexington	25-28 . . . . . Greenville
9-12 . . . . at Greensboro	29-31 . . . . . Hagerstown
13-15 . . . . . Delmarva	**AUGUST**
16-19 . . . . . Greensboro	1-4 . . . . . at West Virginia
20-22 . . . . at Delmarva	5-7 . . . . . at Hagerstown
23-26 . . . at West Virginia	8-11 . . . . . West Virginia
27-29 . . . . . Delmarva	13-15 . . . . at Kannapolis
30-31 . . . . West Virginia	16-19 . . . . at Delmarva
JUNE	20-22 . . . . . Hagerstown
1-2 . . . . . . West Virginia	23-25 . . . . . Delmarva
4-6 . . . . . . at Hickory	27-29 . . . . at Hagerstown
7-9 . . . . . at Delmarva	30-31 . . . . . Greensboro
10-12 . . . . . Greensboro	**SEPTEMBER**
13-16 . . . at Hagerstown	1-2 . . . . Greensboro

LEXINGTON LEGENDS

APRIL	**JUNE**
4-7 . . . . . . at Augusta	1-2 . . . . . . Hagerstown
8-10 . . . . Asheville	4-6 . . . . . at Savannah
11-14 . . . . . Greenville	7-9 . . . . . . at Augusta
15-17 . . . . . at Augusta	10-12 . . . . Rome
18-21 . . . . . Greenville	13-16 . . . . at Asheville
23-25 . . . . at Asheville	20-23 . . . . . Savannah
26-29 . . . . . Augusta	24-26 . . . . at Hickory
MAY	27-30 . . . . at Hagerstown
1-3 . . . . . at Delmarva	**JULY**
4-7 . . . . . at Lakewood	1-3 . . . . Greenville
9-12 . . . . . West Virginia	4-7 . . . . at West Virginia
13-15 . . . . . Kannapolis	9-11 . . . . . Greensboro
16-19 . . . at West Virginia	12-15 . . . . . Delmarva
20-22 . . . . . . Asheville	17-19 . . . . . at Rome
23-26 . . . . at Hagerstown	20-23 . . . . at Greenville
27-29 . . . . . Kannapolis	25-28 . . . . West Virginia
30-31 . . . . . Hagerstown	29-31 . . . . at Kannapolis

AUGUST
1-4 . . . . at Rome
5-7 . . . . .Asheville
8-11 . . . . . .Hagerstown
13-15 . . . . .at Charleston
16-19 . . . . . at Greenville

20-22 . . . . Augusta
23-25 . . . . Greenville
27-29 . . . . . . at Augusta
30-31 . . . . . West Virginia

SEPTEMBER
1-2 . . . . West Virginia

ROME BRAVES

APRIL
4-5 . . . . .at Savannah
6-7 . . . . Savannah
8-10 . . . . Greensboro
11-12 . . . . Savannah
13-14 . . . . . .at Savannah
15-17 . . . . .at Charleston
18-21 . . . . .Asheville
23-25 . . . .at Kannapolis
26-29 . . . . at Greensboro

MAY
1-3 . . . . Greenville
4-7 . . . . .Hagerstown
9-12 . . . . . .at Savannah
13-15 . . . . . . at Augusta
16-19 . . . . . . .Asheville
20-22 . . . . Augusta
23-26 . . . . at Asheville
27-29 . . . . . . Charleston
30-31 . . . . .Hickory

JUNE
1-2 . . . . .Hickory
4-6 . . . . . . at Asheville
7-9 . . . . Savannah
10-12 . . . . . at Lexington

13-16 . . . . .at Kannapolis
20-23 . . . . . . Charleston
24-26 . . . . Kannapolis
27-30 . . . . .at Savannah

JULY
1-3 . . . . . . .at Charleston
4-7 . . . . .Asheville
9-11 . . . . at Lakewood
12-15 . . . . at Hagerstown
17-19 . . . . Lexington
20-23 . . . . Lakewood
25-28 . . . . . . at Asheville
29-31 . . . . . . at Augusta

AUGUST
1-4 . . . . Lexington
5-7 . . . . Augusta 8-11
at Charleston
13-15 . . . . . . Savannah
16-19 . . . . . . Charleston
20-22 . . . . at Greenville
23-25 . . . .at Kannapolis
27-29 . . . . . . Savannah
30-31 . . . .at Charleston

SEPTEMBER
1-2 . . . . . . .at Charleston

SAVANNAH SAND GNATS

APRIL
4-5 . . . . .Rome
6-7 . . . . at Rome
8-10 . . . . Augusta
11-12 . . . . . at Rome
13-14 . . . . .Rome
15-17 . . . . at Greensboro
18-21 . . . . . at Lakewood

23-25 . . . . Delmarva
26-29 . . . . . West Virginia

MAY
1-3 . . . . Kannapolis
4-7 . . . . at Hickory
9-12 . . . . .Rome
13-15 . . . .at Charleston

16-19 . . . . . . at Augusta
20-22 . . . . . . Charleston
23-26 . . . . Augusta
27-29 . . . . at Greenville
30-31 . . . . .at Kannapolis

JUNE
1-2 . . . . . .at Kannapolis
4-6 . . . . Lexington
7-9 . . . . at Rome
10-12 . . . . .Asheville
13-16 . . . . Greenville
20-23 . . . . at Lexington
24-26 . . . . at Augusta
27-30 . . . . .Rome

JULY
1-3 . . . . .Hickory
4-7 . . . . at Greenville
9-11 . . . . Augusta

WEST VIRGINIA POWER

APRIL
4-7 . . . . .Asheville
8-10 . . . . Charleston
11-14 . . . . . at Asheville
15-17 . . . . at Greenville
18-21 . . . . . .Hagerstown
23-25 . . . .at Charleston
26-29 . . . .at Savannah

MAY
1-3 . . . . Greensboro
5-8 . . . . Greenville
9-12 . . . . at Lexington
13-15 . . . . at Hickory
16-19 . . . . Lexington
20-22 . . . .at Kannapolis
23-26 . . . . . . Lakewood
27-29 . . . . . . Greensboro
30-31 . . . . . at Lakewood

JUNE
1-2 . . . . . . at Lakewood
4-6 . . . . Delmarva
7-9 . . . . .Hagerstown
10-12 . . . . . .at Delmarva
13-16 . . . . . at Greensboro

16-19 . . . . . . at Augusta
20-22 . . . . . . Charleston
23-26 . . . . Augusta
27-29 . . . . at Greenville
30-31 . . . .at Kannapolis

JUNE
1-2 . . . . . .at Kannapolis
4-6 . . . . Lexington
7-9 . . . . at Rome
10-12 . . . . . . .Asheville
13-16 . . . . Greenville
20-23 . . . . at Lexington
24-26 . . . . at Augusta
27-30 . . . . .Rome

JULY
1-3 . . . . .Hickory
4-7 . . . . at Greenville
9-11 . . . . Augusta

20-23 . . . . Lakewood
24-26 . . . . . .Hagerstown
27-30 . . . . . at Lakewood

JULY
1-3 . . . . . at Hagerstown
4-7 . . . . Lexington
9-11 . . . .at Kannapolis
12-15 . . . . . . at Asheville
17-19 . . . . Savannah
20-23 . . . . . Kannapolis
25-28 . . . . at Lexington
29-31 . . . . Delmarva

AUGUST
1-4 . . . . Lakewood
5-7 . . . . .at Delmarva
8-11 . . . . at Lakewood
13-15 . . . . . Greensboro
16-19 . . . . .Hickory
20-22 . . . .at Charleston
23-25 . . . .at Savannah
27-29 . . . . . .Asheville
30-31 . . . . at Lexington

SEPTEMBER
1-2 . . . . at Lexington

AUGUST
12-15 . . . . Greenville
17-19 . . . at West Virginia
20-23 . . . . . .at Delmarva
25-28 . . . . Augusta
29-31 . . . . . at Asheville

AUGUST
1-4 . . . . . . at Greenville
5-7 . . . . Charleston
8-11 . . . . .Hickory
13-15 . . . . . . at Rome
16-19 . . . . . at Augusta
20-22 . . . .at Kannapolis
23-25 . . . . West Virginia
27-29 . . . . . at Rome
30-31 . . . . Greenville

SEPTEMBER
1-2 . . . . Greenville

SHORT SEASON

NEW YORK-PENN LEAGUE

ABERDEEN IRONBIRDS

JUNE
17-19 . . . Hudson Valley
20-22 . . . . . . at Brooklyn
23-25 . . . . at Staten Island
26-27 . . . . . . .Brooklyn
28-30 . . . . . Staten Island

JULY
1-3 . . . . .at Hudson Valley
4-6 . . . . .Brooklyn
7-9 . . . . at Tri-City
10-12 . . . . State College
13-15 . . . . . Williamsport
17-19 . . . . . at Vermont
20-22 . . . . at Jamestown
23-25 . . . . Vermont
26-27 . . . .at Hudson Valley
28-29 . . . . at Staten Island

30-31 . . . .Mahoning Valley

AUGUST
1 . . . . .Mahoning Valley
2-4 . . . . Tri-City
6-8 . . . . at Auburn
9-11 . . . . at Batavia
14-15 . . . . . Staten Island
16-18 . . . . at Connecticut
19-20 . . . . Hudson Valley
21-22 . . . .at Hudson Valley
23-25 . . . . . . .Connecticut
26-28 . . . . .at Lowell
29-30 . . . . Hudson Valley
31 . . . . at Brooklyn

SEPTEMBER
1 . . . . at Brooklyn
2-4 . . . . Lowell

AUBURN DOUBLEDAYS

APRIL
17 . . . . Batavia
18 . . . . at Batavia
19 . . . . Batavia
20-22 . . . . . State College
23-25 . . at Mahoning Valley
26-27 . . . . . Williamsport
28-30 . . . . at Jamestown

JULY
1 . . . . at Batavia
2 . . . . Batavia
3 . . . . at Batavia
4-6 . . . . Jamestown
7-9 . . . . .at Williamsport
10-12 . . . . .Brooklyn
13-15 . . . . . Staten Island
17-19 . . . . . at Tri-City
20-22 . . . . . at Vermont
23-25 . . . . . Williamsport
26-27 . . . . at State College
28-29 . . . . . . Jamestown

30-31 . . . . .at Lowell

AUGUST
1 . . . . .at Lowell
2-4 . . . . .at Hudson Valley
6-8 . . . . Aberdeen
9-11 . . . . .Connecticut
14-15 . . . .at Williamsport
16-17 . . .Mahoning Valley
18-19 . . . . at Jamestown
20 . . . . Batavia
21-22 . . . . . at Batavia
23-25 . . . . at State College
26 . . . . Batavia
27 . . . . at Batavia
28 . . . . Batavia
29-30 . . at Mahoning Valley
31 . . . . State College

SEPTEMBER
1 . . . . State College
2-4 . . . . .Mahoning Valley

BATAVIA MUCKDOGS

JUNE
17 . . . . at Auburn
18 . . . . .Auburn
19 . . . . at Auburn
20-22 . . .Mahoning Valley
23-25 . . . .at Williamsport
26 . . . . . . at Jamestown
27 . . . . Jamestown
28-30 . . . . . State College

JULY
1 . . . . .Auburn
2 . . . . at Auburn
3 . . . . .Auburn
4-6 . . . . at State College
7 . . . . . . at Jamestown
8 . . . . . . at Jamestown
9 . . . . . . at Jamestown
10-12 . . . . Vermont
13-15 . . . . Tri-City
17-19 . . . . at Staten Island
20-22 . . . . . at Brooklyn
23-24 . . . . . . Jamestown
25 . . . . . . at Jamestown

26-27 . . at Mahoning Valley
28-29 . . . . . State College
30-31 . . . . .at Connecticut

AUGUST
1 . . . . at Connecticut
2-4 . . . . .at Lowell
6-8 . . . . . . Hudson Valley
9-11 . . . . Aberdeen
14 . . . . Jamestown
15 . . . . . . at Jamestown
16-17 . . . . . Williamsport
18-19 . . . . at State College
20 . . . . at Auburn
21-22 . . . . .Auburn
23-25 . . at Mahoning Valley
26 . . . . at Auburn
27 . . . . at Auburn
28 . . . . at Auburn
29-30 . . .at Williamsport
31 . . . . . .Mahoning Valley

SEPTEMBER
1 . . . . . .Mahoning Valley
2-4 . . . . Williamsport

BROOKLYN CYCLONES

JUNE
17 . . . . . at Staten Island
18 . . . . . . Staten Island
19 . . . . . at Staten Island
20-22 . . . . Aberdeen
23 . . . . . . Hudson Valley
24-25 . . .at Hudson Valley
26-27 . . . . . at Aberdeen
28 . . . . .at Hudson Valley
29 . . . . . . Hudson Valley
30 . . . . .at Hudson Valley

JULY
1 . . . . Staten Island
2 . . . . . . at Staten Island
3 . . . . Staten Island
4-6 . . . . at Aberdeen
7-9 . . . . Lowell
10-12 . . . . . . at Auburn
13-15 . . . .at Connecticut
17-19 . . .Mahoning Valley
20-22 . . . . Batavia
23-25 . . . . .at Lowell

26-27 . . . . at Staten Island
28-29 . . . . Hudson Valley
30-31 . . . .at Williamsport

AUGUST
1 . . . . . . .at Williamsport
2-4 . . . . . . at Jamestown
6-8 . . . . .Connecticut
9-11 . . . . . . State College
14 . . . . . . Hudson Valley
15 . . . . .at Hudson Valley
16-18 . . . . Vermont
19-20 . . . . . Staten Island
21 . . . . . at Staten Island
22 . . . . . . Staten Island
23-25 . . . . . at Vermont
26-28 . . . . Tri-City
29 . . . . . . Staten Island
30 . . . . at Staten Island
31 . . . . Aberdeen

SEPTEMBER
1 . . . . Aberdeen
2-4 . . . . at Tri-City

CONNECTICUT TIGERS

JUNE
17-18 . . . . Lowell
19 . . . . .at Lowell
20-22 . . . . . . at Vermont
23-25 . . . . Tri-City
26-27 . . . . Vermont
28-30 . . . . . . at Tri-City

JULY
1-3 . . . . .at Lowell
4-6 . . . . Vermont
7-9 . . . . . at Staten Island
10-12 . . . . Williamsport
13-15 . . . . Brooklyn
17-19 . . . at Jamestown
20-22 . . . . at State College
23-25 . . . . . Staten Island
26-27 . . . . Lowell
28-29 . . . . . . at Tri-City

30-31 . . . . Batavia

AUGUST
1 . . . . Batavia
2-4 . . .Mahoning Valley
6-8 . . . . at Brooklyn
9-11 . . . . at Auburn
14-15 . . . . Tri-City
16-18 . . . . . . Aberdeen
19-20 . . . . . . .at Lowell
21-22 . . . . Lowell
23-25 . . . . at Aberdeen
26-28 . . . . Hudson Valley
29 . . . . .at Lowell
30 . . . . Lowell
31 . . . . . . at Vermont

SEPTEMBER
1 . . . . at Vermont
2-4 . . . . . .at Hudson Valley

HUDSON VALLEY RENEGADES

JUNE
17-19 . . . . at Aberdeen
20 . . . . . at Staten Island
21 . . . . . . Staten Island
22 . . . . . at Staten Island
23 . . . . at Brooklyn
24-25 . . . . Brooklyn
26 . . . . . . Staten Island
27 . . . . at Staten Island
28 . . . . .Brooklyn
29 . . . . at Brooklyn
30 . . . . .Brooklyn

JULY
1-3 . . . . Aberdeen
4 . . . . . . at Staten Island
5 . . . . Staten Island
6 . . . . . . at Staten Island
7-9 . . . . . . at Vermont
10-12 . . . . . . Jamestown
13-15 . . . . State College
17-19 . . . .at Williamsport
20-22 . . . . . at Tri-City

23-25 . . . . Tri-City
26-27 . . . . . Aberdeen
28-29 . . . . . at Brooklyn
30-31 . . . . Vermont

AUGUST
1 . . . . Vermont
2-4 . . . . .Auburn
6-8 . . . . at Batavia
9-11 . . at Mahoning Valley
14 . . . . at Brooklyn
15 . . . . Brooklyn
16-18 . . . . . . .at Lowell
19-20 . . . . at Aberdeen
21-22 . . . . . Aberdeen
23-25 . . . . Lowell
26-28 . . . .at Connecticut
29-30 . . . . at Aberdeen
31 . . . . Staten Island

SEPTEMBER
1 . . . . Staten Island
2-4 . . . . .Connecticut

JAMESTOWN JAMMERS

JUNE
17-19 . . at Mahoning Valley
20-22 . . . . . . Williamsport
23-25 . . . . at State College
26 . . . . .Batavia
27 . . . . at Batavia
28-30 . . . . .Auburn

JULY
1-3 . . . . .Mahoning Valley
4-6 . . . . at Auburn
7 . . . . .Batavia
8 . . . . at Batavia
9 . . . . .Batavia
10-12 . . .at Hudson Valley
13-15 . . . . . .at Lowell
17-19 . . . . . . .Connecticut
20-22 . . . . . . Aberdeen
23-24 . . . . . at Batavia
25 . . . . Batavia
26-27 . . . .at Williamsport

28-29 . . . . at Auburn
30-31 . . . . Staten Island

AUGUST
1 . . . . Staten Island
2-4 . . . . .Brooklyn
6-8 . . . . . . at Vermont
9-11 . . . . . . at Tri-City
14 . . . . at Batavia
15 . . . . Batavia
16-17 . . . . . State College
18-19 . . . . .Auburn
20-22 . . at Mahoning Valley
23 . . . . . .at Williamsport
24-25 . . . . . Williamsport
26-28 . . .Mahoning Valley
29-30 . . . . at State College
31 . . . . .at Williamsport

SEPTEMBER
1 . . . . . . .at Williamsport
2-4 . . . . . . State College

LOWELL SPINNERS

JUNE
17-18 . . . . .at Connecticut
19 . . . . .Connecticut
20-22 . . . . Tri-City
23-25 . . . . . . at Vermont
26-27 . . . . . at Tri-City
28-30 . . . . Vermont

JULY
1-3 . . . . .Connecticut
4-6 . . . . at Tri-City
7-9 . . . . at Brooklyn
10-12 . . . . Staten Island
13-15 . . . . . Jamestown
17-19 . . . . at State College
20-22 . . .at Williamsport
23-25 . . . . .Brooklyn
26-27 . . . .at Connecticut
28-29 . . . . . at Vermont

30-31 . . . . .Auburn

AUGUST
1 . . . . .Auburn
2-4 . . . . Batavia
6-8 . . . .at Mahoning Valley
9-11 . . . . at Staten Island
14-15 . . . . Vermont
16-18 . . . . . Hudson Valley
19-20 . . . . . .Connecticut
21-22 . . . .at Connecticut
23-25 . . . .at Hudson Valley
26-28 . . . . . Aberdeen
29 . . . . .Connecticut
30 . . . . at Connecticut
31 . . . . Tri-City

SEPTEMBER
1 . . . . Tri-City
2-4 . . . . at Aberdeen

MAHONING VALLEY SCRAPPERS

JUNE
17-19 . . . . . . Jamestown
20-22 . . . . . . at Batavia

23-25 . . . . .Auburn
26-27 . . . . . State College
28-30 . . . . .at Williamsport

JULY	
1-3 . . . . . at Jamestown	2-4 . . . . . . at Connecticut
4-6 . . . . Williamsport	6-8 . . . . Lowell
7-9 . . . at State College	9-11 . . . . . Hudson Valley
10-12 . . . . Tri-City	14-15 . . . at State College
13-15 . . . . Vermont	16-17 . . . . at Auburn
17-19 . . . . . at Brooklyn	18-19 . . . .at Williamsport
20-22 . . at Staten Island	20-22 . . . . . . Jamestown
23-25 . . . . . State College	23-25 . . . . Batavia
26-27 . . . . Batavia	26-28 . . . . at Jamestown
28-29 . . . . . Williamsport	29-30 . . . . .Auburn
30-31 . . . . . at Aberdeen	31 . . . . at Batavia

AUGUST	SEPTEMBER
1 . . . . at Aberdeen	1 . . . . at Batavia
	2-4 . . . . at Auburn

STATE COLLEGE SPIKES

JUNE	
17 . . . . . . Williamsport	28-29 . . . . at Batavia
18 . . . . . .at Williamsport	30-31 . . . . Tri-City

	AUGUST
19 . . . . . . Williamsport	1 . . . . .Tri-City
20-22 . . . . . . at Auburn	2-4 . . . . Vermont
23-25 . . . . . . Jamestown	6-8 . . . . . at Staten Island
26-27 . . at Mahoning Valley	9-11 . . . . at Brooklyn
28-30 . . . . at Batavia	14-15 . . . .Mahoning Valley

JULY	
1 . . . . . . .at Williamsport	16-17 . . . . . at Jamestown
2 . . . . . . .at Williamsport	18-19 . . . . Batavia
3 . . . . . . .at Williamsport	20 . . . . . .at Williamsport
4-6 . . . . Batavia	21-22 . . . . . Williamsport
7-9 . . . . . .Mahoning Valley	23-25 . . . . .Auburn
10-12 . . . . . at Aberdeen	26-27 . . . .at Williamsport
13-15 . . .at Hudson Valley	28 . . . . Williamsport
17-19 . . . . Lowell	29-30 . . . . Jamestown
20-22 . . . . . .Connecticut	31 . . . . at Auburn
23-25 . . at Mahoning Valley	SEPTEMBER
26-27 . . . . .Auburn	1 . . . . at Auburn
	2-4 . . . . . . at Jamestown

STATEN ISLAND YANKEES

JUNE	
17 . . . . .Brooklyn	23-25 . . . . .at Connecticut
18 . . . . at Brooklyn	26-27 . . . . .Brooklyn
19 . . . . .Brooklyn	28-29 . . . . .Aberdeen
20 . . . . . . Hudson Valley	30-31 . . . . at Jamestown

	AUGUST
21 . . . . . .at Hudson Valley	1 . . . . at Jamestown
22 . . . . . . Hudson Valley	2-4 . . . . . .at Williamsport
23-25 . . . . .Aberdeen	6-8 . . . . . . State College
26 . . . . . .at Hudson Valley	9-11 . . . . Lowell
27 . . . . . . Hudson Valley	14-15 . . . . . at Aberdeen
28-30 . . . . . . at Aberdeen	16-18 . . . . Tri-City

JULY	
1 . . . . at Brooklyn	19-20 . . . . . at Brooklyn
2 . . . . .Brooklyn	21 . . . . .Brooklyn
3 . . . . at Brooklyn	22 . . . . at Brooklyn
4 . . . . . . Hudson Valley	23-25 . . . . . . at Tri-City
5 . . . . . .at Hudson Valley	26-28 . . . . Vermont
6 . . . . . . Hudson Valley	29 . . . . at Brooklyn
7-9 . . . . . . .Connecticut	30 . . . . .Brooklyn
10-12 . . . . . . .at Lowell	31 . . . . .at Hudson Valley
13-15 . . . . . . at Auburn	SEPTEMBER
17-19 . . . . Batavia	1 . . . . . .at Hudson Valley
20-22 . . . .Mahoning Valley	2-4 . . . . at Vermont

TRI-CITY VALLEYCATS

JUNE	
17-19 . . . . Vermont	7-9 . . . . Aberdeen
20-22 . . . . . . .at Lowell	10-12 . . at Mahoning Valley
23-25 . . . at Connecticut	13-15 . . . . . . at Batavia
26-27 . . . . Lowell	17-19 . . . . .Auburn
28-30 . . . . . . .Connecticut	20-22 . . . . Hudson Valley

JULY	
1-3 . . . . at Vermont	23-25 . . .at Hudson Valley
4-6 . . . . Lowell	26-27 . . . . . . at Vermont
	28-29 . . . . . .Connecticut
	30-31 . . . . at State College

AUGUST	
1 . . . . at State College	21-22 . . . . . . at Vermont
2-4 . . . . at Aberdeen	23-25 . . . . Staten Island
6-8 . . . . Wilmington	26-28 . . . . at Brooklyn
9-11 . . . . Jamestown	29-30 . . . . Vermont
14-15 . . . .at Connecticut	31 . . . . .at Lowell
16-18 . . at Staten Island	SEPTEMBER
19-20 . . . . Vermont	1 . . . . .at Lowell
	2-4 . . . . .Brooklyn

VERMONT LAKE MONSTERS

JUNE	
17-19 . . . . . . at Tri-City	30-31 . . .at Hudson Valley
20-22 . . . . . .Connecticut	AUGUST
23-25 . . . . Lowell	1 . . . . .at Hudson Valley
26-27 . . . . at Connecticut	2-4 . . . . . at State College
28-30 . . . . .at Lowell	6-8 . . . . Jamestown

JULY	
1-3 . . . . .Tri-City	9-11 . . . . Williamsport
4-6 . . . . . . at Connecticut	14-15 . . . . .at Lowell
7-9 . . . . . Hudson Valley	16-18 . . . . . . at Brooklyn
10-12 . . . . at Batavia	19-20 . . . . . . at Tri-City
13-15 . . at Mahoning Valley	21-22 . . . . .Tri-City
17-19 . . . . Aberdeen	23-25 . . . . .Brooklyn
20-22 . . . . .Auburn	26-28 . . at Staten Island
23-25 . . . . . at Aberdeen	29-30 . . . . . . at Tri-City
26-27 . . . . Tri-City	31 . . . . .Connecticut
28-29 . . . . Lowell	SEPTEMBER
	1 . . . . .Connecticut
	2-4 . . . . Staten Island

WILLIAMSPORT CROSSCUTTERS

JUNE	
17 . . . . . at State College	30-31 . . . . .Brooklyn
18 . . . . . at State College	AUGUST
19 . . . . . at State College	1 . . . . .Brooklyn
20-22 . . . at Jamestown	2-4 . . . . Staten Island
23-25 . . . . Batavia	6-8 . . . . at Tri-City
26-27 . . . . at Auburn	9-11 . . . . at Vermont
28-30 . . . .Mahoning Valley	14-15 . . . . .Auburn

JULY	
1 . . . . State College	16-17 . . . . . . at Batavia
2 . . . . . . at State College	18-19 . . . .Mahoning Valley
3 . . . . State College	20 . . . . State College
4-6 . . . at Mahoning Valley	21-22 . . . at State College
7-9 . . . . at Auburn	23 . . . . Jamestown
10-12 . . . . at Connecticut	24-25 . . . . . at Jamestown
13-15 . . . . . at Aberdeen	26-27 . . . . . State College
17-19 . . . . Hudson Valley	28 . . . . . . at State College
20-22 . . . . Lowell	29-30 . . . . Batavia
23-25 . . . . at Auburn	31 . . . . Jamestown
26-27 . . . . Jamestown	SEPTEMBER
28-29 . . at Mahoning Valley	1 . . . . Jamestown
	2-4 . . . . at Batavia

NORTHWEST LEAGUE

BOISE HAWKS

JUNE	
14-16 . . . . at Eugene	26-30 . . . . Spokane
17-19 . . . . . . Salem-Keiser	31 . . . . at Everett
20-24 . . . . . . at Spokane	AUGUST
25-27 . . . . .Hillsboro	1-4 . . . . at Everett
28-30 . . . . .Eugene	8-11 . . . . .Vancouver

JULY	
1-3 . . . . . at Salem-Keiser	13-15 . . . . .Eugene
4-8 . . . . Tri-City	16-20 . . . . . . at Tri-City
10-14 . . . . at Vancouver	21-23 . . . at Salem-Keiser
15-17 . . . . . at Hillsboro	24-26 . . . . . at Hillsboro
18-22 . . . . Everett	28-30 . . . . . Salem-Keiser
23-25 . . . . at Eugene	31 . . . . .Hillsboro

	SEPTEMBER
	1-2 . . . . .Hillsboro

EUGENE EMERALDS

JUNE
14-16 . . . . Boise
17-19 . . . . . . at Hillsboro
20-24 . . . . Tri-City
25-27 . . . . . Salem-Keizer
28-30 . . . . at Boise

JULY
1-3 . . . . .Hillsboro
4-8 . . . . at Spokane
10-14 . . . . Everett
15-17 . . . . at Salem-Keizer
18-22 . . . . . at Vancouver
23-25 . . . . Boise
26-30 . . . . .Vancouver
31 . . . . at Tri-City

AUGUST
1-4 . . . . at Tri-City
8-12 . . . . Spokane
13-15 . . . . at Boise
16-20 . . . . at Everett
21-23 . . . . .Hillsboro
24-26 . . . . . Salem-Keizer
28-30 . . . . . at Hillsboro
31 . . . . at Salem-Keizer

SEPTEMBER
1-2 . . . . at Salem-Keizer

EVERETT AQUASOX

JUNE
14-16 . . . . . . at Spokane
17-19 . . . . Tri-City
20-24 . . . . .Hillsboro
25-27 . . . . . . at Tri-City
28-30 . . . . Spokane

JULY
1-3 . . . . at Vancouver
4-8 . . . . . . Salem-Keizer
10-14 . . . . at Eugene
15-17 . . . . . .Vancouver
18-22 . . . . . . at Boise
23-25 . . . . Tri-City
26-30 . . . . . at Hillsboro
31 . . . . Boise

AUGUST
1-4 . . . . Boise
8-12 . . . . at Salem-Keizer
13-15 . . . . . at Vancouver
16-20 . . . . .Eugene
21-23 . . . . . . .Vancouver
24-26 . . . . . . at Tri-City
28-30 . . . . . at Spokane
31 . . . . Spokane

SEPTEMBER
1-2 . . . . Spokane

HILLSBORO HOPS

JUNE
14-16 . . . . at Salem-Keizer
17-19 . . . . .Eugene
20-24 . . . . . . at Everett
25-27 . . . . . . at Boise
28-30 . . . . . Salem-Keizer

JULY
1-3 . . . . at Eugene
4-8 . . . . . . .Vancouver
10-14 . . . . at Tri-City
15-17 . . . . Boise
18-22 . . . . Spokane
23-25 . . . . at Salem-Keizer
26-30 . . . . Everett
31 . . . . at Vancouver

AUGUST
1-4 . . . . . . at Vancouver
8-12 . . . . Tri-City
13-15 . . . . . Salem-Keizer
16-20 . . . . at Spokane
21-23 . . . . . . at Eugene
24-26 . . . . Boise
28-30 . . . . . . .Eugene
31 . . . . at Boise

SEPTEMBER
1-2 . . . . at Boise

SALEM-KEIZER VOLCANOES

JUNE
14-16 . . . . .Hillsboro
17-19 . . . . at Boise
20-24 . . . . . . .Vancouver
25-27 . . . . . . at Eugene

JULY
28-30 . . . . . . at Hillsboro
1-3 . . . . Boise
4-8 . . . . at Everett
10-14 . . . . Spokane

15-17 . . . . .Eugene
18-22 . . . . . at Tri-City
23-25 . . . . .Hillsboro
26-30 . . . . Tri-City
31 . . . . at Spokane

AUGUST
1-4 . . . . at Spokane
8-12 . . . . at Everett

SPOKANE INDIANS

JUNE
14-16 . . . . Everett
17-19 . . . . . at Vancouver
20-24 . . . . Boise
25-27 . . . . . . .Vancouver
28-30 . . . . . . at Everett

JULY
1-3 . . . . at Tri-City
4-8 . . . . .Eugene
10-14 . . . at Salem-Keizer
15-17 . . . . Tri-City
18-22 . . . . at Hillsboro
23-25 . . . . . .Vancouver
26-30 . . . . . . at Boise

TRI-CITY DUST DEVILS

JUNE
14-16 . . . . .Vancouver
17-19 . . . . . at Everett
20-24 . . . . . at Eugene
25-27 . . . . . . Everett
28-30 . . . . . at Vancouver

JULY
1-3 . . . . Spokane
4-8 . . . . at Boise
10-14 . . . . . .Hillsboro
15-17 . . . . at Spokane
18-22 . . . . Salem-Keizer
23-25 . . . . . at Everett

VANCOUVER CANADIANS

JUNE
14-16 . . . . at Tri-City
17-19 . . . . . . Spokane
20-24 . . . at Salem-Keizer
25-27 . . . . at Spokane
28-30 . . . . Tri-City

JULY
1-3 . . . . Everett
4-8 . . . . . . at Hillsboro
10-14 . . . . Boise
15-17 . . . . at Everett
18-22 . . . . .Eugene
23-25 . . . . . at Spokane

15-17 . . . . . . .Eugene
18-22 . . . . at Tri-City
23-25 . . . . . . .Hillsboro
26-30 . . . . Tri-City
31 . . . . at Spokane

AUGUST
1-4 . . . . at Spokane
8-12 . . . . at Everett

13-15 . . . . . . at Hillsboro
16-20 . . . . . at Vancouver
21-23 . . . . Boise
24-26 . . . . . . at Eugene
28-30 . . . . . at Boise
31 . . . . .Eugene

SEPTEMBER
1-2 . . . . .Eugene

31 . . . . Salem-Keizer

AUGUST
1-4 . . . . . Salem-Keizer
8-12 . . . . . . at Eugene
13-15 . . . . at Tri-City
16-20 . . . . . . .Hillsboro
21-23 . . . . Tri-City
24-26 . . . . at Vancouver
28-30 . . . . Everett
31 . . . . at Everett

SEPTEMBER
1-2 . . . . at Everett

26-30 . . . . at Salem-Keizer
31 . . . . .Eugene

AUGUST
1-4 . . . . .Eugene
8-12 . . . . . . at Hillsboro
13-15 . . . . . . Spokane
16-20 . . . . Boise
21-23 . . . . at Spokane
24-26 . . . . . . Everett
28-30 . . . . at Vancouver
31 . . . . . . .Vancouver

SEPTEMBER
1-2 . . . . . . .Vancouver

26-30 . . . . at Eugene
31 . . . . .Hillsboro

AUGUST
1-4 . . . . .Hillsboro
8-11 . . . . . . at Boise
13-15 . . . . . . Everett
16-20 . . . Salem-Keizer
21-23 . . . . at Everett
24-26 . . . . . Spokane
28-30 . . . . . Tri-City
31 . . . . . . at Tri-City

SEPTEMBER
1-2 . . . . . at Tri-City

ROOKIE

APPALACHIAN LEAGUE

BLUFIELD BLUE JAYS

JUNE
20-22 . . . . . . Greenville
23-25 . . . . . . at Pulaski
26-28 . . . . . .Burlington
29-30 . . . . . .at Danville

JULY
1 . . . . .at Danville

23-25 . . . . . . .at Danville
26-28 . . . . . Princeton
29-31 . . . . Danville

AUGUST
1-3 . . . . . .at Elizabethton
4 . . . . Princeton
6-8 . . . . .at Princeton

3 . . . . .at Princeton
4-6 . . . . . . Elizabethtown
7-9 . . . . Johnson City
10-12 . . . . at Burlington
13-15 . . . . at Pulaski
17-19 . . . . . . .Burlington
20-22 . . . . Bristol

9-11 . . . . . at Johnson City
12-14 . . . . .at Bristol
15-17 . . . . . Princeton
18-20 . . . . . . Pulaski
22-24 . . . . . . Kingsport
25-27 . . . . at Greenville
28-30 . . . . . at Kingsport

BRISTOL WHITE SOX

JUNE
20-22 . . . . .at Elizabethton

23-25 . . . . Kingsport
26-28 . . . . at Johnson City

29-30 . . . . at Pulaski

JULY
1 . . . . Pulaski
3 . . . . Pulaski
4-6 . . . . at Greeneville
7-9 . . . . Danville
10-12 . . . at Elizabethton
13-15 . . . . . Johnson City
17-19 . . . . . Elizabethton
20-22 . . . . . . at Bluefield
23-25 . . . . at Burlington
26-28 . . . . Kingsport

29-31 . . . . at Pulaski

AUGUST
1-3 . . . . Greenville
4 . . . . at Pulaski
6-8 . . . . Greenville
9-11 . . . . .at Danville
12-14 . . . . .Bluefield
15-17 . . . . at Kingsport
18-20 . . . . at Johnson City
22-24 . . . . . .at Princeton
25-27 . . . . .Burlington
28-30 . . . . Princeton

13-15 . . . . . Elizabethton
17-19 . . . . . . Princeton
20-22 . . . . at Johnson City
23-25 . . . . . Johnson City
26-28 . . . . Pulaski
29-31 . . . . . . .Burlington

AUGUST
1-3 . . . . at Bristol

JOHNSON CITY CARDINALS

JUNE
20-22 . . . . . . at Kingsport
23-25 . . . . Danville
26-28 . . . . Bristol
29-30 . . . . . .at Princeton

JULY
1 . . . . .at Princeton
3 . . . . . . .at Elizabethton
4-6 . . . . Kingsport
7-9 . . . . . . at Bluefield
10-12 . . . . Pulaski
13-15 . . . . at Bristol
17-19 . . . . . at Pulaski
20-22 . . . . . . Greenville

4 . . . . Kingsport
6-8 . . . . at Brtistol
9-11 . . . . Kingsport
12-14 . . . at Johnson City
15-17 . . . . . . at Pulaski
18-20 . . .at Elizabethton
22-24 . . . . . . .at Danville
25-27 . . . . .Bluefield
28-30 . . . . Danville

23-25 . . . . . at Greeneville
26-28 . . . . . Elizabethton
29-31 . . . . . . Princeton

AUGUST
1-3 . . . . at Kingsport
4 . . . . Elizabethton
6-8 . . . . . at Elizabethton
9-11 . . . . .Bluefield
12-14 . . . . . . Greenville
15-17 . . . .at Elizabethton
18-20 . . . . Bristol
22-24 . . . . at Burlington
25-27 . . . . . . .at Danville
28-30 . . . . . . .Burlington

BURLINGTON ROYALS

JUNE
20-22 . . . . Pulaski
23-25 . . . . . .at Princeton
26-28 . . . . . at Bluefield
29-30 . . . . Greenville

JULY
1 . . . . Greenville
3 . . . . .at Danville
4-6 . . . . Princeton
7-9 . . . .at Elizabethton
10-12 . . . . . .Bluefield
13-15 . . . . . . Kingsport
17-19 . . . . . at Bluefield
20-22 . . . . Pulaski

23-25 . . . . Bristol
26-27 . . . . . .at Danville
28 . . . . Danville
29-31 . . . . at Greenville

AUGUST
1-3 . . . . .at Princeton
4 . . . . .at Danville
6-8 . . . . Danville
9-11 . . . . . . Elizabethton
12-14 . . . . . at Pulaski
15-17 . . . . . . Danville
18-20 . . . . at Kingsport
22-24 . . . . Johnson City
25-27 . . . .at Bristol
28-30 . . . at Johnson City

DANVILLE BRAVES

JUNE
20-22 . . . . . . Princeton
23-25 . . . . at Johnson City
26-28 . . . . . . at Pulaski
29-30 . . . . . . .Bluefield

JULY
1 . . . . .Bluefield
3 . . . . .Burlington
4-6 . . . . at Pulaski
7-9 . . . . .at Bristol
10-12 . . . . . . Kingsport
13-15 . . . . . . Princeton
17-19 . . . . . at Kingsport
20-22 . . . .at Elizabethton

23-25 . . . . . . .Bluefield
26-27 . . . . . . .Burlington
28 . . . . . . at Burlington
29-31 . . . . . at Bluefield

AUGUST
1-3 . . . . Pulaski
4 . . . . .Burlington
6-8 . . . . . at Burlington
9-11 . . . . Bristol
12-14 . . . . . Elizabethton
15-17 . . . . at Burlington
18-20 . . . .at Princeton
22-24 . . . . . . Greenville
25-27 . . . . Johnson City
28-30 . . . . at Greenville

ELIZABETHTON TWINS

JUNE
20-22 . . . . . . Bristol
23-25 . . . . at Greenville
26-28 . . . . . . Princeton
29-30 . . . . at Kingsport

JULY
1 . . . . . . at Kingsport
3 . . . . . Johnson City
4-6 . . . . . . at Bluefield
7-9 . . . . . .Burlington
10-12 . . . . . . Bristol
13-15 . . . . at Greenville
17-19 . . . at Bristol
20-22 . . . . . Danville

23-25 . . . . at Kingsport
26-28 . . . at Johnson City
29-31 . . . . . Kingsport

AUGUST
1-3 . . . . .Bluefield
4 . . . . at Johnson City 6-8
Johnson City
9-11 . . . . . at Burlington
12-14 . . . . .at Danville
15-17 . . . Johnson City
18-20 . . . . . Greenville
22-24 . . . . at Pulaski
25-27 . . . .at Princeton
28-30 . . . . . Pulaski

GREENEVILLE ASTROS

JUNE
20-22 . . . . at Bluefield
23-25 . . . . . Elizabethton
26-28 . . . . . . Kingsport
29-30 . . . . at Burlington

JULY
1 . . . . . . at Burlington
3 . . . . . . at Kingsport
4-6 . . . . Bristol
7-9 . . . . . . at Kingsport
10-12 . . . . . .at Princeton

KINGSPORT METS

JUNE
20-22 . . . . . Johnson City
23-25 . . . . .at Bristol
26-28 . . . . . at Greenville
29-30 . . . . . Elizabethton

JULY
1 . . . . Elizabethton
3 . . . . Greenville
4-6 . . . . . at Johnson City
7-9 . . . . . . Greenville
10-12 . . . .at Danville
13-15 . . . . at Burlington
17-19 . . . . . Danville
20-22 . . . . .at Princeton

23-25 . . . . . Elizabethton
26-28 . . . . .at Bristol
29-31 . . . . . Elizabethton

AUGUST
1-3 . . . . . Johnson City
4 . . . . . at Greenville
6-8 . . . . . . Pulaski
9-11 . . . . at Greenville
12-14 . . . . . Princeton
15-17 . . . . . Bristol
18-20 . . . . .Burlington
22-24 . . . . at Bluefield
25-27 . . . . at Pulaski
28-30 . . . . .Bluefield

PRINCETON RAYS

JUNE
20-22 . . . . . . .at Danville
23-25 . . . . . . .Burlington
26-28 . . . .at Elizabethton
29-30 . . . . . Johnson City

JULY
1 . . . . Johnson City
3 . . . . .Bluefield
4-6 . . . . . . at Burlington
7-9 . . . . . . Pulaski
10-12 . . . . . Greenville
13-15 . . . . .at Danville
17-19 . . . at Greenville
20-22 . . . . . Kingsport
23-24 . . . . . Pulaski

25 . . . . at Pulaski
26-28 . . . . . at Bluefield
29-31 . . . at Johnson City

AUGUST
1-3 . . . . .Burlington
4 . . . . . at Bluefield
6-8 . . . . . . .Bluefield
9 . . . . Pulaski
10-11 . . . . . at Pulaski
12-14 . . . at Kingsport
15-17 . . . . at Bluefield
18-20 . . . . . . Danville
22-24 . . . . . . Bristol
25-27 . . . . Elizabethton
28-30 . . . . at Bristol

PULASKI MARINERS

JUNE
20-22 . . . . at Burlington
23-25 . . . . .Bluefield
26-28 . . . . . Danville
29-30 . . . . . at Bristol

JULY
1 . . . . . . at Bristol
3 . . . . . . at Bristol
4-6 . . . . . . Danville
7-9 . . . . .at Princeton

10-12 . . . at Johnson City
13-15 . . . . .Bluefield
17-19 . . . . Johnson City
20-22 . . . at Burlington
23-24 . . . .at Princeton
25 . . . . . . Princeton
26-28 . . . at Greeneville
29-31 . . . . . Bristol

AUGUST
1-3 . . . . . .at Danville

4 . . . . Bristol	15-17 . . . . Greenville	31 . . . . at Missoula	21-23 . . . . at Orem
6-8 . . . . at Kingsport	18-20 . . . . . . at Bluefield	**AUGUST**	24-27 . . . at Grand Junction
9 . . . . at Princeton	22-24 . . . . . Elizabethton	1-2 . . . . at Missoula	29-30 . . . . Missoula
10-11 . . . . Princeton	25-27 . . . . Kingsport	3-6 . . . . . . at Great Falls	31 . . . . Billings
12-14 . . . . . . .Burlington	28-30 . . . . .at Elizabethton	7-9 . . . . .Missoula	**SEPTEMBER**

PIONEER LEAGUE

BILLINGS MUSTANGS

JUNE		31 . . . . at Great Falls
20-21 . . . . . . .Great Falls		**AUGUST**
22-23 . . . . at Helena		1-2 . . . . . . at Great Falls
24-25 . . . . . . at Missoula		3-6 . . . . at Missoula
26-28 . . . . Helena		7-9 . . . . .Great Falls
29-30 . . . at Great Falls		10-12 . . . . Helena
JULY		13-16 . . . . at Idaho Falls
1 . . . . at Great Falls		17-19 . . . . at Ogden
2-3 . . . . at Missoula		21-23 . . . . . .Idaho Falls
4-7 . . . . Missoula		24-27 . . . . Ogden
9-12 . .at Grand Junction		29-30 . . . at Great Falls
13-15 . . . . at Orem		31 . . . . at Helena
17-19 . . . Grand Junction		**SEPTEMBER**
20-23 . . . . Orem		1-2 . . . . at Helena
24-26 . . . . . at Helena		3-4 . . . . Helena
27-29 . . . . . .Great Falls		5-8 . . . . .Missoula

GRAND JUNCTION ROCKIES

JUNE		29-31 . . . . . . at Ogden
20-21 . . . . Ogden		**AUGUST**
22-25 . . . . . . at Orem		1 . . . . at Ogden
26-27 . . . . . at Ogden		2-3 . . . . at Orem
28-30 . . . . Orem		4-7 . . . . Orem
JULY		8-11 . . . . . .Idaho Falls
1 . . . . Orem		13-16 . . . . . at Missoula
2-3 . . . . Ogden		17-19 . . . . at Helena
4-7 . . . . . at Idaho Falls		21-23 . . . . . . Missoula
9-12 . . . . Billings		24-27 . . . . Helena
13-15 . . . .Great Falls		28-31 . . . at Idaho Falls
17-19 . . . . at Billings		**SEPTEMBER**
20-23 . . at Great Falls		1-4 . . . . Ogden
25-28 . . .Idaho Falls		5-8 . . . . at Orem

GREAT FALLS VOYAGERS

JUNE		31 . . . . Billings
20-21 . . . . at Billings		**AUGUST**
22-23 . . . . . . Missoula		1-2 . . . . Billings
24-25 . . . . . . at Helena		3-6 . . . . Helena
26-28 . . . . . . Missoula		7-9 . . . . at Billings
29-30 . . . . . . Billings		10-12 . . . . . . Missoula
JULY		13-16 . . . . . at Ogden
1 . . . . Billings		17-19 . . . .Idaho Falls
2-3 . . . . . . at Helena		21-23 . . . . Ogden
4-7 . . . . Helena		24-27 . . . .Idaho Falls
9-12 . . . . . at Orem		29-30 . . . . . Billings
13-15 . .at Grand Junction		31 . . . . at Missoula
17-19 . . . . Orem		**SEPTEMBER**
20-23 . . . Grand Junction		1-4 . . . . . . at Missoula
24-26 . . . . at Missoula		5-8 . . . . at Helena
27-29 . . . . . at Billings		

HELENA BREWERS

JUNE		2-3 . . . . .Great Falls
20-21 . . . . . at Missoula		4-7 . . . . . . at Great Falls
22-23 . . . . Billings		9-12 . . . . . .Idaho Falls
24-25 . . . . . .Great Falls		13-15 . . . . . Ogden
26-28 . . . . . at Billings		17-19 . . at Idaho Falls
29-30 . . . . . at Missoula		20-23 . . . . at Ogden
JULY		24-26 . . . . . . Billings
1 . . . . at Missoula		27-29 . . . . . Missoula

IDAHO FALLS CHUKARS

JUNE		**AUGUST**
20-21 . . . . Orem		1 . . . . Orem
22-25 . . . . . at Ogden		2-3 . . . . at Ogden
26-27 . . . . . at Orem		4-7 . . . . Ogden
28-30 . . . . . . Ogden		8-11 . . . .at Grand Junction
JULY		13-16 . . . . . . Billings
1 . . . . Ogden		17-19 . . . . . .Great Falls
2-3 . . . . . . at Orem		21-23 . . . . . at Billings
4-7 . . . . Grand Junction		24-27 . . . at Great Falls
9-12 . . . . . . at Helena		28-31 . . . Grand Junction
13-15 . . . . at Missoula		**SEPTEMBER**
17-19 . . . . Helena		1-4 . . . . at Orem
20-23 . . . . Helena		5-6 . . . . . . at Ogden
25-28 . .at Grand Junction		7-8 . . . . Orem
29-31 . . . . . at Orem		

MISSOULA OSPREY

JUNE		31 . . . . Helena
20-21 . . . . Helena		**AUGUST**
22-23 . . . . at Great Falls		1-2 . . . . Helena
24-25 . . . . . . Billings		3-6 . . . . Billings
26-28 . . . at Great Falls		7-9 . . . . at Helena
29-30 . . . . . . Helena		10-12 . . . at Great Falls
JULY		13-16 . . . . Grand Junction
1 . . . . Helena		17-19 . . . . . . Orem
2-3 . . . . Billings		21-23 . . .at Grand Junction
4-7 . . . . . . at Billings		24-27 . . . . . at Orem
9-12 . . . . . . Ogden		29-30 . . . . . at Helena
13-15 . . . .Idaho Falls		31 . . . . .Great Falls
17-19 . . . . . at Ogden		**SEPTEMBER**
20-23 . . . . at Idaho Falls		1-4 . . . . .Great Falls
24-26 . . . . .Great Falls		5-8 . . . . at Billings
27-29 . . . . at Helena		

OGDEN RAPTORS

JUNE		**AUGUST**
20-21 . . .at Grand Junction		1 . . . . . . Grand Junction
22-25 . . . . . . .Idaho Falls		2-3 . . . . .Idaho Falls
26-27 . . . Grand Junction		4-7 . . . . . . at Idaho Falls
28-30 . . . at Idaho Falls		8-11 . . . . . . at Orem
JULY		13-16 . . . . . .Great Falls
1 . . . . at Idaho Falls		17-19 . . . . Orem
2-3 . . . at Grand Junction		21-23 . . . . at Great Falls
4-7 . . . . .Orem		24-27 . . . . . at Billings
9-12 . . . . . . at Missoula		28-31 . . . . Orem
13-15 . . . . . at Helena		**SEPTEMBER**
17-19 . . . . . . Missoula		1-4 . . . .at Grand Junction
20-23 . . . . . . Helena		5-6 . . . . . . .Idaho Falls
24-27 . . . . . at Orem		7-8 . . . . Grand Junction
29-31 . . . . Grand Junction		

OREM OWLZ

JUNE		4-7 . . . . at Ogden
20-21 . . . . . at Idaho Falls		9-12 . . . . . . .Great Falls
22-25 . . . Grand Junction		13-15 . . . . . at Great Falls
26-27 . . . .Idaho Falls		17-19 . . . at Great Falls
28-30 . . .at Grand Junction		20-23 . . . . . at Billings
JULY		24-27 . . . . Ogden
1 . . . . .at Grand Junction		29-31 . . . . . at Idaho Falls
2-3 . . . . .Idaho Falls		

AUGUST

1 . . . . at Idaho Falls
2-3 . . . . . . Grand Junction
4-7 . . . . at Grand Junction
8-11 . . . . Ogden
13-16 . . . . at Helena
17-19 . . . . . . at Missoula

21-23 . . . . Helena
24-27 . . . . Missoula
28-31 . . . . at Ogden

SEPTEMBER
1-4 . . . . Idaho Falls
5-6 . . . . . Grand Junction
7-8 . . . . at Idaho Falls

ARIZONA LEAGUE   * HOME GAMES ONLY

ANGELS

JUNE
23 . . . . Giants
24 . . . . Cubs
27 . . . . . . Diamondbacks
28 . . . . Athletics

JULY
3 . . . . Padres
5 . . . . Royals
7 . . . . Reds
9 . . . . Athletics
10 . . . . Rangers
12 . . . . Indians
14 . . . . . . Diamondbacks
18 . . . . Brewers
20 . . . . Cubs
23 . . . . Mariners

26 . . . . Cubs
28 . . . . Giants
31 . . . . Athletics

AUGUST
4 . . . . . . Diamondbacks
5 . . . . Dodgers
7 . . . . Padres
9 . . . . Cubs
13 . . . . Reds
15 . . . . Rangers
18 . . . . Indians
20 . . . . Athletics
23 . . . . Brewers
25 . . . . Giants
28 . . . . Royals
29 . . . . Athletics

ATHLETICS

JUNE
21 . . . . Giants
23 . . . . . Diamondbacks
25 . . . . Angels
29 . . . . Cubs

JULY
1 . . . . Mariners
4 . . . . . Diamondbacks
5 . . . . Padres
8 . . . . Rangers
10 . . . . Dodgers
14 . . . . Cubs
17 . . . . Giants
19 . . . . Royals
22 . . . . Indians

24 . . . . Reds
26 . . . . Giants
30 . . . . . Diamondbacks

AUGUST
1 . . . . Cubs
3 . . . . Angels
5 . . . . Mariners
8 . . . . Brewers
11 . . . . Royals
14 . . . . Angels
16 . . . . Dodgers
18 . . . . Brewers
19 . . . . Cubs
24 . . . . . Diamondbacks
26 . . . . Reds
28 . . . . Rangers

BREWERS

JUNE
21 . . . . Dodgers
23 . . . . Reds
25 . . . . Indians
27 . . . . Rangers

JULY
1 . . . . Royals
3 . . . . Giants
6 . . . . Dodgers
7 . . . . . Diamondbacks
11 . . . . Mariners
13 . . . . Athletics
15 . . . . Reds
19 . . . . Angels
22 . . . . Giants
24 . . . . Padres

26 . . . . Dodgers
28 . . . . Reds

AUGUST
1 . . . . Indians
3 . . . . Rangers
5 . . . . Royals
7 . . . . Cubs
10 . . . . Dodgers
13 . . . . . Diamondbacks
15 . . . . Mariners
17 . . . . Padres
21 . . . . Reds
22 . . . . Angels
25 . . . . Athletics
28 . . . . Indians

CUBS

JUNE
20 . . . . Angels
22 . . . . . Diamondbacks
26 . . . . Athletics
27 . . . . Giants

JULY
1 . . . . Dodgers
2 . . . . Brewers
4 . . . . Angels
5 . . . . Rangers

DIAMONDBACKS

JUNE
21 . . . . Cubs
24 . . . . Athletics
26 . . . . Giants
29 . . . . Angels

JULY
1 . . . . Indians
2 . . . . Mariners
8 . . . . Brewers
9 . . . . Cubs
11 . . . . Rangers
13 . . . . Royals
19 . . . . Reds
20 . . . . Athletics
22 . . . . Dodgers
25 . . . . Angels

28 . . . . Cubs
29 . . . . Athletics

AUGUST
2 . . . . Angels
3 . . . . Giants
8 . . . . Mariners
9 . . . . Athletics
11 . . . . Padres
12 . . . . Brewers
17 . . . . Royals
19 . . . . Angels
21 . . . . Cubs
22 . . . . Reds
27 . . . . Giants
29 . . . . Cubs

DODGERS

JUNE
20 . . . . Brewers
23 . . . . Indians
26 . . . . Reds
28 . . . . Royals
30 . . . . Angels

JULY
3 . . . . Rangers
5 . . . . Brewers
8 . . . . Mariners
11 . . . . Athletics
12 . . . . Giants
17 . . . . Indians
19 . . . . Padres
21 . . . . Cubs
23 . . . . Royals

27 . . . . Brewers
28 . . . . Indians
31 . . . . Reds

AUGUST
2 . . . . Royals
6 . . . . Cubs
7 . . . . Rangers
11 . . . . Brewers
12 . . . . Padres
15 . . . . Athletics
18 . . . . Giants
20 . . . . Indians
22 . . . . Mariners
26 . . . . . Diamondbacks
28 . . . . Reds

GIANTS

JUNE
20 . . . . Athletics
22 . . . . Angels
25 . . . . Cubs
28 . . . . . Diamondbacks

JULY
1 . . . . Padres
2 . . . . Reds
5 . . . . Mariners
8 . . . . Royals
10 . . . . Indians
13 . . . . Dodgers
15 . . . . Angels
18 . . . . Rangers
21 . . . . Brewers

24 . . . . . Diamondbacks
27 . . . . Athletics
29 . . . . Angels

AUGUST
1 . . . . . Diamondbacks
2 . . . . Cubs
5 . . . . Padres
8 . . . . Reds
11 . . . . Mariners
12 . . . . Royals
16 . . . . Indians
17 . . . . Dodgers
21 . . . . . . Athletics
23 . . . . Rangers
26 . . . . Cubs
28 . . . . . Diamondbacks

INDIANS

JUNE
20 . . . . Reds
22 . . . . Dodgers

26 . . . . Brewers
27 . . . . Padres
30 . . . . Cubs

AUGUST

4 . . . . Athletics
5 . . . . Indians
10 . . . . at Rangers
11 . . . . Rangers
12 . . . . Mariners
14 . . . . . Diamondbacks
16 . . . . Padres
20 . . . . Giants
22 . . . . Royals
24 . . . . Angels
27 . . . . Mariners

DIAMONDBACKS (MINOR)

10 . . . . Padres
12 . . . . Reds
15 . . . . Athletics
17 . . . . . Diamondbacks
22 . . . . Royals
23 . . . . Indians
25 . . . . Athletics
27 . . . . . Diamondbacks
30 . . . . Angels
31 . . . . Giants

MINOR LEAGUES

JULY		AUGUST	
3	Royals	3	Mariners
5	Reds	6	Diamondbacks
8	Padres	7	Royals
11	Giants	11	Reds
13	Angels	12	Rangers
15	Dodgers	15	Giants
19	Mariners	17	Angels
21	Athletics	21	Dodgers
24	Rangers	22	Padres
27	Reds	26	Brewers
29	Dodgers	27	Brewers
31	Brewers		

MARINERS

JUNE			
21	Padres	26	Padres
22	Royals	29	Royals
26	Rangers	31	Rangers
27	Reds	**AUGUST**	
30	Athletics	2	Indians
JULY		6	Athletics
3	Diamondbacks	7	Diamondbacks
6	Giants	10	Giants
7	Cubs	13	Dodgers
10	Brewers	16	Brewers
12	Rangers	18	Rangers
17	Padres	20	Royals
18	Dodgers	23	Indians
21	Reds	25	Dodgers
24	Angels	28	Padres

PADRES

JUNE			
20	Mariners	27	Mariners
22	Rangers	29	Rangers
25	Royals	**AUGUST**	
28	Brewers	1	Royals
30	Giants	3	Reds
JULY		6	Giants
2	Angels	8	Angels
6	Diamondbacks	10	Athletics
7	Dodgers	13	Indians
11	Cubs	15	Cubs
12	Brewers	18	Reds
15	Mariners	21	Rangers
18	Indians	22	at Indians
21	Rangers	23	Dodgers
22	at Rangers	26	Rangers
		27	Royals

RANGERS

JUNE			
21	Royals	26	Royals
23	Padres	28	Padres
25	Mariners	**AUGUST**	
28	Indians	1	Mariners
JULY		2	Brewers
1	Reds	5	Reds
2	Dodgers	8	Dodgers
6	Cubs	10	Cubs
7	Indians	13	Athletics
10	Angels	16	Diamondbacks
13	Mariners	17	Mariners
17	Royals	20	Padres
19	Giants	22	Giants
22	Padres	25	Indians
23	Brewers	27	Angels

REDS

JUNE			
21	Indians	22	Brewers
		25	Dodgers

28	Mariners	29	Brewers
30	Rangers	**AUGUST**	
JULY		1	Dodgers
3	Athletics	2	Padres
6	Indians	6	Rangers
8	Angels	7	Giants
11	Royals	10	Indians
13	Padres	12	Angels
17	Brewers	15	Royals
18	Diamondbacks	17	Cubs
19	at Diamondbacks	20	Brewers
22	Mariners	23	Diamondbacks
23	Giants	25	Cubs
26	Indians	27	Dodgers

ROYALS

JUNE			
20	Rangers	27	Rangers
23	Mariners	28	Mariners
26	Padres	31	Padres
27	Dodgers	**AUGUST**	
30	Brewers	3	Dodgers
JULY		6	Brewers
2	Indians	8	Indians
6	Athletics	10	Angels
7	Giants	13	Giants
10	Reds	16	Reds
12	Diamondbacks	18	Diamondbacks
15	Rangers	21	Mariners
18	Cubs	23	Athletics
21	Angels	25	Padres
24	Dodgers	26	Mariners

GULF COAST LEAGUE   * HOME GAMES ONLY

ASTROS

JUNE			
22	Braves	26	Tigers
25	Tigers	29	Yankees 2
26	Yankees 2	31	Pirates
28	Pirates	**AUGUST**	
JULY		2	Phillies
1	Phillies	5	Yankees 1
3	Yankees 1	8	Blue Jays
5	Blue Jays	10	Braves
8	Braves	12	Tigers
10	Tigers	15	Yankees 2
13	Yankees 2	17	Pirates
16	Pirates	20	Phillies
18	Phillies	22	Yankees 1
20	Yankees 1	23	Braves
22	Blue Jays	27	Tigers
25	Braves	28	Yankees 2

BLUE JAYS

JUNE			
22	Phillies	26	Pirates
24	Pirates	30	Yankees 1
27	Yankees 1	31	Braves
28	Braves	**AUGUST**	
JULY		2	Tigers
1	Tigers	6	Yankees 2
4	Yankees 2	7	Astros
6	Astros	10	Phillies
8	Phillies	13	Pirates
11	Pirates	14	Yankees 1
12	Yankees 1	17	Braves
16	Braves	20	Tigers
18	Tigers	21	Yankees 2
19	Yankees 2	24	Phillies
23	Astros	26	Pirates
24	Phillies	29	Yankees 1

BRAVES

JUNE	
21	Astros
24	Yankees 2
27	Tigers
29	Blue Jays

JULY	
2	Yankees 1
4	Phillies
6	Pirates
9	Astros
11	Yankees 2
12	Tigers
15	Blue Jays
17	Yankees 1
20	Phillies
22	Pirates
24	Astros
26	Yankees 2
30	Tigers

AUGUST	
1	Blue Jays
3	Yankees 1
6	Phillies
8	Pirates
9	Astros
13	Yankees 2
14	Tigers
16	Blue Jays
19	Yankees 1
21	Phillies
24	Astros
26	Yankees 2
28	Tigers

CARDINALS

JUNE	
22	Marlins
25	Mets
26	Nationals
28	Marlins

JULY	
1	Mets
4	Nationals
6	Marlins
8	Nationals
11	Mets
12	Marlins
16	Nationals
17	Mets
20	Marlins
23	Mets
24	Nationals
26	Marlins
29	Mets

AUGUST	
1	Nationals
3	Marlins
5	Nationals
8	Mets
9	Marlins
13	Nationals
14	Mets
17	Marlins
20	Mets
21	Nationals
23	Marlins
26	Mets
29	Nationals

MARLINS

JUNE	
21	Cardinals
24	Nationals
27	Mets
29	Cardinals

JULY	
2	Nationals
3	Mets
5	Cardinals
9	Mets
10	Nationals
13	Cardinals
15	Mets
18	Nationals
19	Cardinals
22	Nationals
25	Mets
27	Cardinals
30	Nationals
31	Mets

AUGUST	
2	Cardinals
6	Mets
7	Nationals
10	Cardinals
12	Mets
15	Nationals
16	Cardinals
19	Nationals
22	Mets
24	Cardinals
27	Nationals
28	Mets

METS

JUNE	
22	Nationals
24	Cardinals
26	Marlins
28	Nationals

JULY	
2	Cardinals
4	Marlins
6	Nationals
8	Marlins
10	Cardinals
12	Nationals
16	Marlins
18	Cardinals
20	Nationals
22	Cardinals
24	Marlins
26	Nationals
30	Cardinals

AUGUST	
1	Marlins
3	Nationals
5	Marlins
7	Cardinals
9	Nationals
13	Marlins
15	Cardinals
17	Nationals
19	Cardinals
21	Marlins
23	Nationals
27	Cardinals
29	Marlins

NATIONALS

JUNE	
21	Mets
25	Marlins
27	Cardinals
29	Mets

JULY	
1	Marlins
3	Cardinals
5	Mets
9	Cardinals
11	Marlins
13	Mets
15	Cardinals
17	Marlins
19	Mets
23	Marlins
25	Cardinals
27	Mets
29	Marlins
31	Cardinals

AUGUST	
2	Mets
6	Cardinals
8	Marlins
10	Mets
12	Cardinals
14	Marlins
16	Mets
20	Marlins
22	Cardinals
24	Mets
26	Marlins
28	Cardinals

ORIOLES

JUNE	
22	Rays
24	Red Sox
26	Twins
29	Rays

JULY	
2	Twins
4	Red Sox
5	Rays
8	Red Sox
10	Twins
13	Rays
16	Twins
18	Red Sox
19	Rays
22	Red Sox
24	Twins
27	Rays
30	Twins

AUGUST	
1	Red Sox
2	Rays
5	Red Sox
7	Twins
10	Rays
13	Twins
15	Red Sox
16	Rays
19	Red Sox
21	Twins
23	Rays
27	Red Sox
28	Twins

PHILLIES

JUNE	
21	Blue Jays
25	Yankees 1
26	Pirates
29	Tigers

JULY	
2	Astros
3	Braves
6	Yankees 2
9	Blue Jays
10	Yankees 1
12	Pirates
15	Tigers
17	Astros
19	Braves
22	Yankees 2
25	Blue Jays
27	Yankees 1
29	Pirates

AUGUST	
1	Tigers
3	Astros
5	Braves
8	Yankees 2
9	Blue Jays
12	Yankees 1
15	Pirates
17	Tigers
19	Astros
22	Braves
23	Blue Jays
27	Yankees 1
28	Pirates

PIRATES

JUNE	
22	Yankees 1
25	Blue Jays
27	Phillies
29	Astros

JULY	
1	Yankees 2
3	Tigers
5	Braves
8	Yankees 1
10	Blue Jays
13	Phillies
15	Astros
18	Yankees 2

MINOR LEAGUES

19 . . . . .Tigers	7 . . . . Braves	9 . . . . Yankees 2	21 . . . . Pirates
23 . . . . Braves	10 . . . . Yankees 1	13 . . . . .Astros	24 . . . . Yankees 2
25 . . . . Yankees 1	12 . . . . Blue Jays	15 . . . . Braves	26 . . . . .Astros
27 . . . . .Blue Jays	14 . . . . Phillies	16 . . . . Phillies	29 . . . . Braves
30 . . . . Phillies	16 . . . . Astros	19 . . . . .Blue Jays	

AUGUST
1 . . . . .Astros	20 . . . . Phillies
2 . . . . Yankees 2	22 . . . . .Tigers
6 . . . . .Tigers	23 . . . . Yankees 1
	27 . . . . .Blue Jays
	29 . . . . Phillies

TWINS

JUNE
21 . . . . Red Sox	25 . . . . Orioles
24 . . . . .Rays	26 . . . . Red Sox
27 . . . . Orioles	29 . . . . Orioles
28 . . . . Red Sox	

AUGUST
	1 . . . . .Rays

JULY
1 . . . . Orioles	3 . . . . Red Sox
4 . . . . .Rays	5 . . . . .Rays
6 . . . . Red Sox	8 . . . . Orioles
8 . . . . .Rays	9 . . . . Red Sox
11 . . . . Orioles	12 . . . . Orioles
12 . . . . Red Sox	15 . . . . .Rays
15 . . . . Orioles	17 . . . . Red Sox
18 . . . . .Rays	19 . . . . .Rays
20 . . . . Red Sox	22 . . . . Orioles
22 . . . . .Rays	24 . . . . Red Sox
	27 . . . . .Rays
	29 . . . . Orioles

RAYS

JUNE
21 . . . . Orioles	25 . . . . Red Sox
25 . . . . Twins	26 . . . . Orioles
26 . . . . .at Red Sox	29 . . . . Red Sox
27 . . . . Red Sox	31 . . . . Twins
28 . . . . Orioles	

AUGUST
	3 . . . . Orioles

JULY
1 . . . . Red Sox	6 . . . . Twins
3 . . . . Twins	8 . . . . Red Sox
6 . . . . Orioles	9 . . . . Orioles
9 . . . . Twins	12 . . . . Red Sox
11 . . . . Red Sox	14 . . . . Twins
12 . . . . Orioles	17 . . . . Orioles
15 . . . . Red Sox	20 . . . . Twins
17 . . . . Twins	22 . . . . Red Sox
20 . . . . Orioles	24 . . . . Orioles
23 . . . . Twins	26 . . . . Twins
	29 . . . . Red Sox

RED SOX

JUNE
22 . . . . Twins	27 . . . . Twins
25 . . . . Orioles	30 . . . . .Rays
26 . . . . .Rays	31 . . . . Orioles
29 . . . . Twins	

AUGUST
	2 . . . . Twins

JULY
2 . . . . .Rays	6 . . . . Orioles
3 . . . . Orioles	7 . . . . .Rays
5 . . . . Twins	10 . . . . Twins
9 . . . . Orioles	13 . . . . .Rays
10 . . . . .Rays	14 . . . . Orioles
13 . . . . Twins	16 . . . . Twins
16 . . . . .Rays	20 . . . . Orioles
17 . . . . Orioles	21 . . . . .Rays
19 . . . . Twins	23 . . . . Twins
23 . . . . Orioles	26 . . . . Orioles
24 . . . . .Rays	28 . . . . .Rays

TIGERS

JUNE
21 . . . . Yankees 2	16 . . . . Phillies
24 . . . . .Astros	17 . . . . .Blue Jays
26 . . . . Braves	20 . . . . Pirates
28 . . . . Phillies	23 . . . . Yankees 1
	24 . . . . Yankees 2

JULY
2 . . . . .Blue Jays	27 . . . . .Astros
4 . . . . Pirates	29 . . . . Braves
5 . . . . Yankees 1	31 . . . . Phillies
9 . . . . Yankees 2	

AUGUST
11 . . . . .Astros	3 . . . . .Blue Jays
13 . . . . Braves	5 . . . . Pirates
	7 . . . . Yankees 1

YANKEES 1

JUNE
21 . . . . Pirates	24 . . . . Pirates
24 . . . . Phillies	26 . . . . Phillies
26 . . . . .Blue Jays	29 . . . . .Blue Jays
29 . . . . Yankees 2	31 . . . . Yankees 2

JULY
1 . . . . Braves	2 . . . . Braves
4 . . . . .Astros	6 . . . . .Astros
6 . . . . .Tigers	8 . . . . .Tigers
9 . . . . Pirates	9 . . . . Pirates
11 . . . . Phillies	13 . . . . Phillies
13 . . . . .Blue Jays	15 . . . . .Blue Jays
16 . . . . Yankees 2	17 . . . . Yankees 2
18 . . . . Braves	20 . . . . Braves
19 . . . . .Astros	21 . . . . .Astros
22 . . . . .Tigers	24 . . . . Pirates
	26 . . . . Phillies
	28 . . . . .Blue Jays

AUGUST

YANKEES 2

JUNE
22 . . . . .Tigers	27 . . . . Braves
25 . . . . Braves	30 . . . . .Astros
27 . . . . .Astros	
28 . . . . Yankees 1	

AUGUST
	1 . . . . Yankees 1

JULY
2 . . . . Pirates	3 . . . . Pirates
3 . . . . .Blue Jays	5 . . . . .Blue Jays
5 . . . . Phillies	7 . . . . Phillies
8 . . . . .Tigers	10 . . . . .Tigers
10 . . . . Braves	12 . . . . Braves
12 . . . . .Astros	14 . . . . .Astros
15 . . . . Yankees 1	16 . . . . Yankees 1
17 . . . . Pirates	19 . . . . Pirates
20 . . . . .Blue Jays	22 . . . . .Blue Jays
23 . . . . Phillies	23 . . . . .Tigers
25 . . . . .Tigers	27 . . . . Braves
	29 . . . . .Astros

INDEPENDENT

AMERICAN ASSOCIATION   HOME GAMES ONLY

AMARILLO SOX

MAY	
20-22 . . . . Winnipeg	23-25 . . . . . Grand Prairie
	31 . . . . Grand Prairie

JUNE	JULY
1-2 . . . . . Grand Prairie	2-5 . . . . .Newark
3-5 . . . . Gary SouthShore	15-17 . . . . El Paso
14-16 . . . . Sioux Falls	18-21 . . . . . . Kansas City
17-19 . . . . El Paso	29-31 . . . . . Grand Prairie
24-27 . . . . El Paso	

AUGUST
1 . . . . Grand Prairie
2-4 . . . . Laredo

12-15 . . . . . Grand Prairie
16-18 . . . . Laredo
23-25 . . . . Lincoln

12-14 . . . . Lincoln
19-21 . . . . Rockland

27-30 . . . Gary SouthShore

EL PASO DIABLOS

MAY		JULY	
16-19	Amarillo	2-5	Laredo
20-22	Fargo-Moorhead	6-9	Grand Prairie
31	Gary SouthShore	18-21	Laredo
JUNE		29-31	Wichita
1-2	Gary SouthShore	**AUGUST**	
7-9	Grand Prairie	2-4	Grand Prairie
10-12	Amarillo	8-10	Amarillo
20-23	Sioux Falls	13-15	Laredo
		20-22	Lincoln
		23-25	Sioux City

FARGO-MOORHEAD REDHAWKS

MAY		JULY	
10	St. Paul	6-9	Sioux City
11-12	Winnipeg	15-17	Sioux Falls
24-26	Laredo	23-25	St. Paul
27-30	Sioux Falls	26-28	Sioux City
JUNE		**AUGUST**	
3-6	Lincoln	2-4	Winnipeg
7-9	Winnipeg	6-8	St. Paul
14-16	Gary SouthShore	12-15	Rockland
28-30	Kansas City	23-25	Kansas City
		27-30	Amarillo

GARY SOUTHSHORE RAILCATS

MAY		JULY	
16-19	Lincoln	11-14	Fargo-Moorhead
20-22	Wichita	22-25	Sioux City
27-29	Sioux City	**AUGUST**	
JUNE		2-4	St. Paul
7-9	Sioux Falls	5-7	Kansas City
10-12	Quebec	16-18	Sioux Falls
20-23	St. Paul	20-22	Wichita
24-27	Kansas City	31	El Paso
28-30	Winnipeg	**SEPTEMBER**	
		1-2	El Paso

GRAND PRAIRIE AIR HOGS

MAY			
17-19	Winnipeg	23-25	El Paso
28-30	Kansas City	26-28	Wichita
JUNE		**AUGUST**	
3-6	Laredo	5-7	Amarillo
10-12	Laredo	16-18	El Paso
20-23	Amarillo	20-22	Amarillo
28-30	Newark	26-29	El Paso
JULY		31	Lincoln
2-5	Wichita	**SEPTEMBER**	
11-14	St. Paul	1-2	Lincoln

KANSAS CITY T-BONES

MAY		JULY	
18-19	Wichita	2-5	Sioux Falls
20-22	Lincoln	12-13	Wichita
24-26	Gary SouthShore	15-17	Grand Prairie
JUNE		26-28	El Paso
3-6	Sioux City	29-31	Laredo
7-9	Quebec	**AUGUST**	
17-19	Grand Prairie	1	Laredo
21-23	Laredo	9-11	Fargo-Moorhead

LAREDO LEMURS

MAY		JULY	
16-19	Fargo-Moorhead	6-9	Newark
20-22	Grand Prairie	11-14	El Paso
31	Kansas City	15-17	St. Paul
JUNE		22-24	Kansas City
1-2	Kansas City	25-27	Amarillo
7-9	Amarillo	**AUGUST**	
13-16	El Paso	5-7	El Paso
17-19	Sioux Falls	8-11	Grand Prairie
28-30	Amarillo	20-22	Sioux City

LINCOLN SALTDOGS

MAY			
23-26	Winnipeg	10-13	Amarillo
27-29	El Paso	15-17	Gary SouthShore
JUNE		23-25	Trois-Rivieres
7-9	Sioux City	26-28	Sioux Falls
13-16	Kansas City	**AUGUST**	
17-19	Sioux City	6-8	Sioux Falls
28-30	El Paso	9-11	Gary SouthShore
JULY		16-18	Rockland
2-5	Fargo-Moorhead	27-30	Wichita

SIOUX CITY EXPLORERS

MAY		JULY	
16	Sioux Falls	2-5	Gary SouthShore
20-23	New Jersey	14-16	Wichita
24-26	Sioux Falls	18-21	Fargo-Moorhead
31	Lincoln	29-31	Gary SouthShore
JUNE		**AUGUST**	
1-2	Lincoln	2-4	Lincoln
10-12	Kansas City	12-15	Winnipeg
14-16	Grand Prairie	16-18	St. Paul
20-22	Wichita	27-28	Sioux Falls
25-27	Winnipeg	30	Sioux Falls

SIOUX FALLS PHEASANTS

MAY			
17-19	Sioux City	10-13	Sioux City
20-22	St. Paul	18-21	Gary SouthShore
31	Wichita	30-31	Troi-Rivieres
JUNE		**AUGUST**	
1-2	Wichita	1	Trois-Rivieres
3-6	Winnipeg	2-4	Kansas City
10-12	Lincoln	20-22	Fargo-Moorhead
25-27	Grand Prairie	23-25	Winnipeg
28-30	St. Paul	29	Sioux City
JULY		31	Amarillo
6-9	Lincoln	**SEPTEMBER**	
		1-2	Amarillo

ST. PAUL SAINTS

MAY			
16-19	New Jersey	18-21	Grand Prairie
24-26	El Paso	26-28	Gary SouthShore
JUNE		30-31	Fargo-Moorhead
7-9	Wichita	**AUGUST**	
10-12	Fargo-Moorhead	1	Fargo-Moorhead
17-19	Winnipeg	9-11	Sioux City
24-26	Lincoln	12-15	Sioux Falls
JULY		19-22	Winnipeg
6-9	Kansas City	23-25	Gary SouthShore
		31	Sioux City

SEPTEMBER
1-2 . . . . Sioux City

WICHITA WINGNUTS

MAY	
16-17 . . . . . . Kansas City	10-11 . . . . . Kansas City
23-25 . . . . . . New Jersey	18-21 . . . . Lincoln
27-29 . . . . Amarillo	22-24 . . . . Amarillo

JUNE	**AUGUST**
3-6 . . . . El Paso	13-15 . . . Gary SouthShore
14-16 . . . . St. Paul	16-18 . . .Fargo-Moorhead
17-18 . . Gary SouthShore	23-25 . . . . . Grand Prairie
24-26 . . . . Laredo	31 . . . . Kansas City
28-30 . . . . . . Sioux City	**SEPTEMBER**

JULY	
6-9 . . . . Amarillo	1-2 . . . . . Kansas City

WINNIPEG GOLDEYES

MAY	
27-29 . . . . Laredo	26-29 . . . . . Trois-Rivieres
31 . . . . .Fargo-Moorhead	30-31 . . . . Lincoln

JUNE	**AUGUST**
1-2 . . . .Fargo-Moorhead	1 . . . . Lincoln
10-12 . . . . Wichita	6-8 . . . . Sioux City
14-16 . . . . Quebec	9-11 . . . . Sioux Falls
20-23 . . . . Lincoln	16-18 . . . . . Kansas City
	27-30 . . . . St. Paul
JULY	31 . . . . .Fargo-Moorhead
2-5 . . . . St. Paul	**SEPTEMBER**
6-9 . . . . Gary SouthShore	1-2 . . . . .Fargo-Moorhead
23-25 . . . . . . Sioux Falls	

ATLANTIC LEAGUE

BRIDGEPORT BLUEFISH

APRIL	**JULY**
26-28 . . . . .York	2-4 . . . . .York
30 . . . Southern Maryland	12-14 . . . . . . Long Island
MAY	25-28 . . . . . . Long Island
1-2 . . Southern Maryland	30-31 . . . . Somerset
7-9 . . . . Camden	**AUGUST**
10-12 . . Southern Maryland	1 . . . . Somerset
23 . . . Southern Maryland	2-4 . . . . Sugar Land
24-27 . . . . Somerset	9-11 . . . . Camden
28-30 . . . . .York	12-14 . . Southern Maryland
JUNE	15-17 . . . . Lancaster
4-6 . . . . Long Island	26-29 . . . . Camden
7-9 . . . . Lancaster	**SEPTEMBER**
17-20 . . . . . . Sugar Land	3-5 . . . . Sugar Land
21-23 . . . . Lancaster	13-15 . . . . Camden

CAMDEN RIVERSHARKS

APRIL	28-30 . . . . . . Bridgeport
23-25 . . . . . . Bridgeport	**JULY**
26-28 . . . . Lancaster	15-17 . . . . Lancaster
MAY	22-24 . . . . . . Long Island
3-5 . . . Southern Maryland	25-28 . . . . Somerset
10-11 . . . . . . Sugar Land	**AUGUST**
13 . . . . Sugar Land	2-4 . . . . Lancaster
14-16 . . . . Lancaster	5-7 . . . . Sugar Land
20-23 . . . . . . Long Island	15-18 . . Southern Maryland
24-27 . . . . .York	19-21 . . . . . . Long Island
JUNE	30-31 . . . . . . Sugar Land
4-6 . . . . Somerset	**SEPTEMBER**
7-9 . . . . .York	1 . . . . Sugar Land
14-16 . . . . at Sugar Land	3-5 . . . . .York
17-20 . . . . . . Long Island	6-8 . . . . Somerset

LANCASTER BARNSTORMERS

APRIL	**JULY**
18-21 . . . . Camden	2-4 . . . . Sugar Land
23-25 . . . . . . Long Island	12-14 . . . . Camden
MAY	22-24 . . . . . . Sugar Land
6-9 . . . . Long Island	25-28 . . Southern Maryland
10-12 . . . . .York	**AUGUST**
21-23 . . . . Somerset	6-8 . . . . Long Island
24-27 . . . . . . Sugar Land	18-21 . . . . . . Bridgeport
31 . . . . Bridgeport	23-25 . . . . .York
JUNE	30-31 . . . . . . Bridgeport
1-3 . . . . Bridgeport	**SEPTEMBER**
4-6 . . Southern Maryland	1 . . . . Bridgeport
14-16 . . . . . . Long Island	3-5 . . . . Somerset
17-20 . . . . Somerset	6-8 . . . Southern Maryland
28-30 . . . . .York	

LONG ISLAND DUCKS

APRIL	**JULY**
26-28 . . . . . . Sugar Land	2-4 . . . . Somerset
30 . . . . Somerset	5-7 . . . . Bridgeport
MAY	15-17 . . Southern Maryland
1-2 . . . . Somerset	18-21 . . . . Camden
10-11 . . . . Somerset	29-31 . . Southern Maryland
14-16 . . . . .York	**AUGUST**
24-26 . . Southern Maryland	1 . . . . Southern Maryland
29-30 . . . . Camden	2-4 . . . . .York
JUNE	15-18 . . . . .York
7-9 . . Southern Maryland	22-25 . . . . Somerset
11-13 . . . . . . Bridgeport	26-29 . . . . Lancaster
21-23 . . . . . . Sugar Land	**SEPTEMBER**
24-27 . . . . . . Bridgeport	6-9 . . . . Sugar Land
	10-12 . . . . Lancaster

SOMERSET PATRIOTS

APRIL	**JULY**
18-21 . . Southern Maryland	1 . . . . Long Island
23-25 . . . . . . Sugar Land	5-7 . . . . Camden
MAY	18-21 . . . . Lancaster
3-5 . . . . Bridgeport	22-24 . . . . .York
14-16 . . Southern Maryland	**AUGUST**
17-19 . . . . Camden	2-4 . . Southern Maryland
28-30 . . . . Lancaster	6-8 . . . . Bridgeport
JUNE	12-14 . . . . Lancaster
7-9 . . . . Sugar Land	15-18 . . . . . . Sugar Land
11-13 . . . . .York	27-29 . . . . .York
14-16 . . . . . . Bridgeport	**SEPTEMBER**
24-27 . . . . Camden	10-12 . . . . . . Bridgeport
28-30 . . . . . . Long Island	13-15 . . . . . . Long Island

SOUTHERN MARYLAND BLUE CRABS

APRIL	**JULY**
24-25 . . . . .York	2-4 . . . . Camden
26-28 . . . . Somerset	5-7 . . . . Sugar Land
MAY	18-21 . . . . .York
6-9 . . . . Sugar Land	22-24 . . . . . . Bridgeport
17-19 . . . . . . Long Island	**AUGUST**
21-22 . . . . . . Bridgeport	6-8 . . . . .York
31 . . . . Camden	9-11 . . . . Somerset
JUNE	19-21 . . . . . . Sugar Land
1-3 . . . . Camden	22-25 . . . . . . Bridgeport
11-13 . . . . Lancaster	30-31 . . . . Somerset
14-16 . . . . .York	**SEPTEMBER**
21-23 . . . . Camden	1-2 . . . . Somerset
24-27 . . . . Lancaster	3-5 . . . . Long Island
	10-12 . . . . Camden
	13-15 . . . . Lancaster

SUGAR LAND SKEETERS

APRIL	
18-21 . . . . . . Long Island	
30 . . . . Lancaster	
MAY	
1 . . . . Lancaster	
3-5 . . . . Lancaster	
14-19 . . . . . . Bridgeport	
28-30 . . Southern Maryland	
31 . . . . Somerset	
JUNE	
1-3 . . . . Somerset	
10-12 . . . . Camden	
14-16 . . . . Camden	

24-27 . . . . York
28-30 . . Southern Maryland
JULY
12-17 . . . . Somerset
18-21 . . . . . . Bridgeport
29-31 . . . . Lancaster
AUGUST
1 . . . . Lancaster
9-14 . . . . Long Island
22-25 . . . . Camden
26-29 . . Southern Maryland
SEPTEMBER
10-15 . . . . York

YORK REVOLUTION

APRIL	
18-21 . . . . . . Bridgeport	
22-23 . . Southern Maryland	
30 . . . . Camden	
MAY	
1-2 . . . . Camden	
3-5 . . . . Long Island	
6-9 . . . . Somerset	
17-20 . . . . Lancaster	
21-23 . . . . . . Sugar Land	
31 . . . . Long Island	
JUNE	
1-3 . . . . Long Island	
4-6 . . . . Sugar Land	
18-20 . . Southern Maryland	
21-23 . . . . Somerset	

JULY
5-7 . . . . Lancaster
12-14 . . Southern Maryland
15-17 . . . . . . Bridgeport
25-28 . . . . . . Sugar Land
29-31 . . . . Camden
AUGUST
1 . . . . Camden
9-11 . . . . Lancaster
12-14 . . . . Camden
19-21 . . . . Somerset
30-31 . . . . . . Long Island
SEPTEMBER
1 . . . . Long Island
6-9 . . . . Bridgeport

CAN-AM LEAGUE

NEWARK BEARS

MAY	
17-19 . . . . Rockland	
28-30 . . . . Quebec	
31 . . . . Rockland	
JUNE	
3-6 . . . . Trois-Rivieres	
7-9 . . . . Rockland	
14-16 . . . . . . Trois-Rivieres	
17-19 . . . . . . New Jersey	
24-26 . . . Fargo-Moorhead	

JULY
11-13 . . . . Rockland
23-25 . . . . . . New Jersey
26 . . . . Rockland
29-31 . . . . Quebec
AUGUST
2-4 . . . . Wichita
9-11 . . . . Quebec
12-15 . . . . . . New Jersey
24-26 . . . . Laredo
27-30 . . . . . Trois-Rivieres

NEW JERSEY JACKALS

MAY	
28-30 . . . . Rockland	
31 . . . . Trois-Rivieres	
JUNE	
1-2 . . . . . . Trois-Rivieres	
11-13 . . . . Newark	
14 . . . . Newark	
20-23 . . . Fargo-Moorhead	
25-27 . . . . Rockland	
JULY	
6-9 . . . . Quebec	

11-14 . . . . . Trois-Rivieres
15-17 . . . . Newark
26-28 . . . . Quebec
31 . . . . Rockland
AUGUST
1 . . . . Rockland
5-8 . . . . Newark
9-11 . . . . Wichita
16-18 . . . . . Trois-Rivieres
20-22 . . . . Quebec
27-30 . . . . Loredo

QUEBEC CAPITALS

MAY	
16-19 . . . . . Trois-Rivieres	
21-23 . . . . Newark	
31 . . . . St. Paul	

JUNE
1-2 . . . . St. Paul
4-6 . . . . New Jersey
17-19 . . . . Rockland

20-23 . . . . Newark
JULY
2-3 . . . . . Trois-Rivieres
6 . . . . New Jersey
11-14 . . . . Winnipeg
18-21 . . . . . New Jersey
23-25 . . . . . . Rockland

ROCKLAND BOULDERS

MAY	
16 . . . . Newark	
22-23 . . . . . Trois-Rivieres	
24-27 . . . . Quebec	
JUNE	
1-2 . . . . Newark	
3-6 . . . . St. Paul	
15-16 . . . . . New Jersey	
20-23 . . . . . Trois-Rivieres	
28-30 . . . . Quebec	
JULY	
2-5 . . . . New Jersey	

14 . . . . Newark
15-17 . . . . Quebec
18-20 . . . . Winnipeg
27-28 . . . . Newark
30 . . . . . . New Jersey
AUGUST
5-8 . . . . Wichita
9-11 . . . . . Trois-Rivieres
23-26 . . . . . New Jersey
31 . . . . Newark
SEPTEMBER
1-2 . . . . Newark

TROIS-RIVIERES EAGLES

MAY	
24-26 . . . . Newark	
28-30 . . . . St. Paul	
JUNE	
4-5 . . . . Quebec	
7-9 . . . . New Jersey	
11-13 . . . . Rockland	
17-19 . . Fargo-Moorhead	
24-27 . . . . Quebec	
28-30 . . . . . New Jersey	
JULY	
6-9 . . . . Rockland	

15-17 . . . . Winnipeg
19-21 . . . . Newark
AUGUST
2-4 . . . . Rockland
14-15 . . . . Quebec
19-22 . . . . Newark
23-26 . . . . Quebec
31 . . . . . . New Jersey
SEPTEMBER
1-2 . . . . . . New Jersey

FRONTIER LEAGUE

EVANSVILLE OTTERS

MAY	
17-19 . . . . Normal	
24-26 . . . . . Windy City	
29-30 . . . . . . River City	
JUNE	
5-6 . . . . . Southern Illinois	
7-9 . . . . Florence	
19-20 . . . . Joliet	
21-23 . . . . Frontier	
JULY	
5-7 . . . . Washington	
22-24 . . . . . Traverse City	

28-29 . . . . Lake Erie
AUGUST
3-4 . . . . Florence
10-11 . . . . . Schaumburg
16-18 . . . . Gateway
21-22 . . . . Rockford
23-25 . . . . Frontier
30-31 . . . . . Schaumburg
SEPTEMBER
1 . . . . Schaumburg
3-5 . . . . River City

FLORENCE FREEDOM

MAY	
16-18 . . . . . . River City	
22-23 . . . . . Schaumburg	
31 . . . . Rockford	
JUNE	
1-2 . . . . Rockford	
5-6 . . . . Gateway	
11-13 . . . . . Traverse City	
14-16 . . . . Frontier	
25-27 . . . . . Washington	
JULY	
5-7 . . . . Frontier	

10-11 . . . . Evansville
12-14 . . . . . Washington
25-27 . . . . Joliet
31 . . . . Normal
AUGUST
1-2 . . . . Normal
7-9 . . . . Lake Erie
13-15 . . . . Evansville
21-22 . . . . . Windy City
23-25 . . Southern Illinois
30-31 . . . . . Washington
SEPTEMBER
3-5 . . . . Windy City

GATEWAY GRIZZLIES

MAY	
21-23	Joliet
24-26	Schaumburg
31	Traverse City

JUNE	
1-2	Traverse City
8	River City
11-13	Frontier
14-16	Normal
25-27	Evansville
28-30	Florence

JULY	
2-4	Washington

12-14	Evansville
19-21	Lake Erie
28-30	Frontier

AUGUST	
3-5	River City
7-9	Rockford
14-15	River City
23-25	Windy City
27-29	Southern Illinois
30-31	Rockford

SEPTEMBER	
1	Rockford

JOLIET SLAMMERS

MAY	
17-19	Traverse City
24-26	Florence
28-30	Washington

JUNE	
4-6	Windy City
11-13	River City
21-23	Gateway
28-30	Schaumburg

JULY	
2-4	Frontier

12-14	Rockford
19-21	Southern Illinois
22-24	Normal
31	Schaumburg

AUGUST	
1-2	Schaumburg
3-5	Windy City
10-12	Lake Erie
17-18	Southern Illinois
20-22	Frontier
27-29	Evansville

LAKE ERIE CRUSHERS

MAY	
17-19	Gateway
28-30	Florence
31	Joliet

JUNE	
1-2	Joliet
11-13	Evansville
18-20	Normal
25-27	Frontier

JULY	
2-4	Windy City
5-7	Rockford
12-14	Frontier

22-24	Southern Illinois
25-27	River City
31	Washington

AUGUST	
1-2	Washington
3-5	Traverse City
13-15	Washington
16-18	Frontier
23-25	Schaumburg
30-31	Frontier

SEPTEMBER	
1	Frontier
3-5	Traverse City

NORMAL CORNBELTERS

MAY	
21-23	Windy City
24-26	Frontier
31	River City

JUNE	
1-2	River City
7-9	Southern Illinois
11-13	Washington
21-23	Traverse City

JULY	
2-4	Florence
5-7	Gateway

9-11	Joliet
19-21	Evansville
25-27	Frontier

AUGUST	
7-9	Schaumburg
16-18	Rockford
20-22	Lake Erie
27-29	Florence
30-31	Windy City

SEPTEMBER	
1	Windy City
3-5	Rockford

RIVER CITY RASCALS

MAY	
21-23	Frontier
24-26	Lake Erie

MAY	
4-6	Schaumburg
7-9	Gateway
14-16	Schaumburg

18-20	Rockford
25-27	Southern Illinois
28-30	Windy City

JULY	
9-11	Gateway
19-21	Florence
22-24	Frontier

28-30	Joliet

AUGUST	
7-9	Evansville
10-11	Normal
20-22	Traverse City

ROCKFORD AVIATORS

MAY	
17-19	Frontier
21-23	Washington
28-30	Gateway

JUNE	
4-6	Normal
7-9	Windy City
14-16	Lake Erie
25-27	Joliet
28-30	Normal

23-25	Washington
30-31	Southern Illinois

SEPTEMBER	
1	Southern Illinois

JULY	
2-4	Evansville
9-11	Schaumburg
19-21	Frontier
25-27	Traverse City
28-30	Southern Illinois
31	Gateway

AUGUST	
1-2	Gateway
10-12	Florence
23-25	Joliet
27-29	River City

SCHAUMBURG BOOMERS

MAY	
16	Windy City
17-19	Washington
28-30	Normal
31	Evansville

JUNE	
1-2	Evansville
7-9	Joliet
18-20	Frontier
21-23	Lake Erie

JULY	
2-4	Southern Illinois

5-7	River City
12-14	Traverse City
23-24	Florence
25-27	Gateway
28-29	Windy City

AUGUST	
3-6	Rockford
13-15	Rockford
16-18	Traverse City
27-29	Frontier

SEPTEMBER	
3-5	Joliet

SOUTHERN ILLINOIS MINERS

MAY	
17-19	Windy City
21-23	Lake Erie
28-30	Traverse City
31	Frontier

JUNE	
1-2	Frontier
11-13	Rockford
18-20	Gateway
21-23	Florence
28-30	Evansville

JULY	
5-7	Joliet

12-14	Rockford
25-27	Washington
31	Evansville

AUGUST	
1-2	Evansville
3-5	Normal
10-12	Frontier
13-15	Normal
20-22	Schaumburg

SEPTEMBER	
3-5	Gateway

TRAVERSE CITY BEACH BUMS

MAY	
21-23	Evansville
24-26	Rockford

JUNE	
4-6	Lake Erie
7-9	Frontier
14-16	Joliet
25-27	Schaumburg
28-30	Lake Erie

JULY	
2-4	River City
9-11	Frontier
19-21	Windy City

28-30	Florence
31	Frontier

AUGUST	
1-2	Frontier
7-9	Southern Illinois
10-12	Gateway
13-15	Frontier
23-25	Normal
27-29	Washington
30-31	Joliet

SEPTEMBER	
1	Joliet

WASHINGTON WILD THINGS

MAY
24-26 . . . . Southern Illinois

JUNE
4-6 . . . . Frontier
7-9 . . . . Lake Erie
14-16 . . . . Evansville
18-20 . . . . . Traverse City
21-23 . . . . . . River City
28-30 . . . . Frontier

JULY
9-11 . . . . Lake Erie
19-21 . . . . . . Schaumburg

22-24 . . . . Rockford
28-30 . . . . Normal

AUGUST
3-4 . . . . Frontier
7-9 . . . . Joliet
10-12 . . . . . Windy City
16-18 . . . . Florence
20-22 . . . . Gateway
30-31 . . . . Florence

SEPTEMBER
1 . . . . Florence
3-5 . . . . Frontier

WINDY CITY THUNDERBOLTS

MAY
27-29 . . . . Frontier
31 . . . . Washington

JUNE
1-2 . . . . Washington
11-13 . . . . . Schaumburg
14-16 . . . . Southern Illinois
18-20 . . . . Florence
21-23 . . . . Rockford
25-27 . . . . Normal

JULY
5-7 . . . . . Traverse City

9-11 . . . . Southern Illinois
12-14 . . . . Normal
22-24 . . . . Gateway
25-27 . . . . Evansville
31 . . . . River City

AUGUST
1-2 . . . . River City
7-9 . . . . Frontier
13-15 . . . . Joliet
16-18 . . . . . . River City
27-29 . . . . . . Lake Erie

SPRING TRAINING SCHEDULES

ARIZONA CACTUS LEAGUE

ARIZONA DIAMONDBACKS

FEBRUARY
23 . . . . .Colorado
24 . . . . at Colorado
25 . . . . at Kansas City
26 . . . . . .at L.A. Angels
26 . . . . Oakland
27 . . . . Cincinnati
28 . . . . at Cincinnati

MARCH
1 . . . . . . at Chicago Cubs
2 . . . . Texas
3 . . . . . at San Francisco
4 . . . . Cincinnati
6 . . . . Kansas City
7 . . . . .at Milwaukee
8 . . . . . . .at L.A. Angels
9 . . . . Chicago White Sox
10 . . . . at Oakland
11 . . . . . . .Chicago Cubs

12 . . . . at Seattle
12 . . . . at Colorado
13 . . . . Milwaukee
15 . . . . Oakland
16 . . . . . . at San Diego
17 . . . . L.A. Dodgers
17 . . . . . . at San Diego
18 . . . . . .at L.A. Dodgers
19 . . . . San Diego
20 . .at Chicago White Sox
21 . . . . Cleveland
22 . . . . . . at Cleveland
23 . . . . . at Kansas City
24 . . . . Seattle
26 . . . . L.A. Angels
27 . . . . . .San Francisco
28 . . . . at Texas
29 . . . . Cincinnati
30 . . . . Cincinnati

CHICAGO CUBS

FEBRUARY
23 . . . . . .at L.A. Angels
24 . . . . . .San Francisco
25 . . . . .at L.A. Dodgers
26 . . . . .Colorado
27 . . . . . . L.A. Dodgers
28 . . . . Oakland

MARCH
1 . . . . .Arizona
2 . . . . . at San Francisco
3 . . . . . .at L.A. Angels
3 . . . . Milwaukee
4 . . . . Cleveland
5 . . . . at Colorado
6 . . . . at Texas
7 . . . . Chicago White Sox
8 . . . . at Cincinnati
9 . . . . Cleveland
10 . . . . San Diego
11 . . . . at Arizona

13 . . . . .Colorado
14 . . . . . . .at L.A. Dodgers
15 . .at Chicago White Sox
16 . . . . Kansas City
16 . . . . Texas
17 . . . . at Oakland
17 . . . . Texas
18 . . . . . at San Diego
19 . . . . Texas
21 . . . . . .at L.A. Dodgers
21 . . . . at Seattle
22 . . . . . .at Milwaukee
23 . . . . L.A. Angels
24 . . . . . . at Cleveland
25 . . . . . .San Francisco
26 . . . . Cincinnati
27 . . . . . at Kansas City
28 . . . . Seattle
29 . . . . at Houston
30 . . . . at Houston

CHICAGO WHITE SOX

FEBRUARY
23 . . . . . .at L.A. Dodgers
24 . . . . . . L.A. Dodgers
25 . . . . at San Francisco
26 . . . . at Texas
27 . . . . Texas
28 . . . . . .at Milwaukee

MARCH
1 . . . . at Cleveland
2 . . . . Cincinnati
3 . . . . at San Diego
4 . . . . . . .San Francisco
7 . . . . . . at Chicago Cubs

8 . . . . San Diego
9 . . . . at Arizona
10 . . . . at Seattle
10 . . . . Cincinnati
11 . . . . .Colorado
13 . . . . Cleveland
14 . . . . . .at L.A. Angels
15 . . . . . .Chicago Cubs
16 . . . . Oakland
17 . . . . . at Kansas City
19 . . . . . . at Cincinnati
20 . . . . .Arizona
21 . . . . Milwaukee
22 . . . . at Oakland

23 . . . . . .at L.A. Dodgers
24 . . . . Kansas City
25 . . . . L.A. Angels
26 . . . . at Texas

CINCINNATI REDS

FEBRUARY
22 . . . . . . at Cleveland
23 . . . . Cleveland
24 . . . . . . at Cleveland
25 . . . . Milwaukee
26 . . . . . at San Diego
27 . . . . at Arizona
28 . . . . .Arizona
28 . . . . . . at Colorado

MARCH
1 . . . . . . at Kansas City
2 . .at Chicago White Sox
3 . . . . Kansas City
4 . . . . at Arizona
5 . . . . . .at L.A. Angels
8 . . . . . . .Chicago Cubs
8 . . . . . .at L.A. Dodgers
9 . . . . Milwaukee
10 . . .at Chicago White Sox

12 . . . . L.A. Dodgers
13 . . . .San Francisco
14 . . . . at Seattle
15 . . . . .Colorado
16 . . . . . .at Milwaukee
16 . . . . at San Francisco
17 . . . . Cleveland
18 . . . . . . at Colorado
19 . . . Chicago White Sox
21 . . . . Oakland
22 . . . .at L.A. Dodgers
23 . . . . Texas
24 . . . . at Texas
25 . . . . Seattle
26 . . . . at Chicago Cubs
27 . . . . San Diego
28 . . . . Kansas City
29 . . . . at Arizona
30 . . . . . . at Cleveland
30 . . . . at Arizona

CLEVELAND INDIANS

FEBRUARY
22 . . . . Cincinnati
23 . . . . . . at Cincinnati
24 . . . . Cincinnati
24 . . . . . .at Milwaukee
25 . . . . at Oakland
26 . . . . . . Kansas City
27 . . . . Seattle
28 . . . . at Texas

MARCH
1 . . . . Chicago White Sox
2 . . . . San Diego
3 . . . . . .at L.A. Dodgers
4 . . . . at Chicago Cubs
5 . . . . at San Francisco
6 . . . . L.A. Dodgers
7 . . . . . . .San Francisco
8 . . . . . at Kansas City
9 . . . . . at Chicago Cubs

10 . . . . Texas
11 . . . . L.A. Angels
13 . .at Chicago White Sox
14 . . . . . . Kansas City
15 . . . . . .at Milwaukee
16 . . . . . .San Francisco
17 . . . . . at Cincinnati
18 . . . . Milwaukee
20 . . . . . .at L.A. Angels
21 . . . . at Arizona
22 . . . . .Arizona
23 . . . . at Seattle
24 . . . . . . .Chicago Cubs
25 . . . . . . at Colorado
26 . . . . Oakland
27 . .at Chicago White Sox
28 . . . . . . at San Diego
29 . . . . . at Kansas City
30 . . . . Cincinnati

COLORADO ROCKIES

FEBRUARY
23 . . . . at Arizona
24 . . . . .Arizona
25 . . . . Texas
26 . . . . at Chicago Cubs
27 . . . . . at San Diego
28 . . . . Cincinnati

MARCH
1 . . . . Milwaukee
2 . . . . at Oakland
3 . . . . Oakland
4 . . . . at Seattle
5 . . . . . . .Chicago Cubs

8 . . . . Kansas City
9 . . . . . . .at L.A. Angels
10 . . . . . . L.A. Dodgers
11 . .at Chicago White Sox
12 . . . . .Arizona
13 . . . . at Chicago Cubs
15 . . . . . . at Cincinnati
16 . . . . Seattle
17 . . . . at San Francisco
18 . . . . Cincinnati
19 . . . . at Kansas City
21 . . . . at San Francisco
22 . . . . at Texas

22 . . . . .San Francisco	26 . . . . . . .at L.A. Dodgers
23 . . . . San Diego	27 . . . . at Oakland
24 . . . . .at Milwaukee	28 . . . . Milwaukee
25 . . . . Cleveland	30 . . . . Seattle

KANSAS CITY ROYALS

FEBRUARY
22 . . . . at Texas	12 . . . . at Oakland
23 . . . . Texas	13 . . . . Seattle
24 . . . . at Texas	14 . . . . at Cleveland
25 . . . . .Arizona	15 . . . . San Diego
26 . . . . at Cleveland	15 . . . . . .at L.A. Dodgers
27 . . . . Milwaukee	16 . . . . . at Chicago Cubs
28 . . . . at San Diego	17 . . . Chicago White Sox

MARCH
1 . . . . Cincinnati	18 . . . . at Texas
2 . . . . .San Francisco	19 . . . . .Colorado
3 . . . . at Cincinnati	20 . . . . . . L.A. Dodgers
5 . . . . Oakland	22 . . . . . . .at L.A. Angels
6 . . . . at Arizona	23 . . . . .Arizona
7 . . . . Seattle	24 . . .at Chicago White Sox
8 . . . . Cleveland	25 . . . . L.A. Dodgers
8 . . . . at Colorado	26 . . . . at Seattle
9 . . . . . at San Francisco	27 . . . . . .at Milwaukee
10 . . . . L.A. Angels	27 . . . . .Chicago Cubs
	28 . . . . at Cincinnati
	29 . . . . Cleveland

LOS ANGELES ANGELS

FEBRUARY
23 . . . . . . .Chicago Cubs	11 . . . . at Cleveland
23 . . . . . .at San Francisco	13 . . . . at San Diego
24 . . . . Oakland	14 . . . . Chicago White Sox
25 . . . . at Seattle	15 . . . . Seattle
26 . . . . .Arizona	16 . . . . at Oakland
27 . . . . . . .San Francisco	17 . . . . San Diego
28 . . . . . .at L.A. Dodgers	19 . . . . . . .at Milwaukee

MARCH
1 . . . . L.A. Dodgers	20 . . . . Cleveland
2 . . . . .at Milwaukee	21 . . . . at Texas
3 . . . . .Chicago Cubs	22 . . . . Kansas City
4 . . . . at Oakland	23 . . . at Chicago Cubs
5 . . . . Cincinnati	23 . . . . Milwaukee
7 . . . . . . at San Diego	24 . . . . .San Francisco
8 . . . . .Arizona	25 . .at Chicago White Sox
9 . . . . .Colorado	26 . . . . at Arizona
10 . . . . . . at Kansas City	27 . . . . Texas
	28 . . . . L.A. Dodgers
	29 . . . . . .at L.A. Dodgers
	30 . . . . L.A. Dodgers

LOS ANGELES DODGERS

FEBRUARY
23 . . . . Chicago White Sox	12 . . . . at Cincinnati
24 . . .at Chicago White Sox	14 . . . . . . .Chicago Cubs
25 . . . . . . .Chicago Cubs	15 . . . . . . at San Diego
26 . . . . . . .San Francisco	15 . . . . Kansas City
27 . . . at Chicago Cubs	16 . . . . at Texas
28 . . . . L.A. Angels	17 . . . . Milwaukee
	17 . . . . at Arizona
	18 . . . . .Arizona

MARCH
1 . . . . .at L.A. Angels	19 . . . . Oakland
1 . . . . San Diego	20 . . . . . . at Kansas City
2 . . . . at Seattle	21 . . . . . . .Chicago Cubs
3 . . . . Cleveland	22 . . . . Cincinnati
5 . . . . . . at San Diego	23 . . . Chicago White Sox
6 . . . . at Cleveland	24 . . . . at Oakland
7 . . . . Texas	25 . . . . . . at Kansas City
8 . . . . . at San Francisco	26 . . . . .Colorado
8 . . . . Cincinnati	27 . . . . at Seattle
9 . . . . Seattle	28 . . . . . . .at L.A. Angels
10 . . . . . . .at Colorado	29 . . . . L.A. Angels
11 . . . . . . .at Milwaukee	30 . . . . . .at L.A. Angels

MILWAUKEE BREWERS

FEBRUARY
23 . . . . Oakland	7 . . . . .Arizona
24 . . . . Cleveland	8 . . . . Texas
25 . . . . . . at Cincinnati	9 . . . . at Cincinnati
25 . . . . San Diego	10 . . . . . . .San Francisco
26 . . . . Seattle	11 . . . . L.A. Dodgers
27 . . . . . . at Kansas City	12 . . . . at Texas
28 . . . . Chicago White Sox	13 . . . . at Arizona
	15 . . . . Cleveland

MARCH
1 . . . . at Colorado	16 . . . . Cincinnati
2 . . . . L.A. Angels	17 . . . .at L.A. Dodgers
3 . . . . . at Chicago Cubs	18 . . . . at Cleveland
6 . . . . at Seattle	19 . . . . L.A. Angels
	20 . . . . . at San Francisco
	21 . . .at Chicago White Sox

OAKLAND ATHLETICS

FEBRUARY
22 . . . . .Chicago Cubs	27 . . . . Kansas City
23 . . . . . . .at L.A. Angels	28 . . . . at Colorado
24 . . . . .Colorado	29 . . . Chicago White Sox
24 . . . . at San Diego	30 . . . Chicago White Sox
25 . . . . at Oakland	

FEBRUARY
23 . . . . . . .at Milwaukee	12 . . . . Kansas City
24 . . . . . .at L.A. Angels	14 . . . . Texas
25 . . . . Cleveland	15 . . . . at Arizona
26 . . . . at Arizona	16 . . . . L.A. Angels
27 . . . . San Diego	16 . .at Chicago White Sox
28 . . . . . at Chicago Cubs	17 . . . . .Chicago Cubs
	18 . . . . Seattle
	19 . . . . . .at L.A. Dodgers

MARCH
1 . . . . .San Francisco	21 . . . . at Cincinnati
2 . . . . .Colorado	22 . . . . Chicago White Sox
3 . . . . at Colorado	23 . . . at San Francisco
4 . . . . . . .at L.A. Angels	24 . . . . L.A. Dodgers
5 . . . . . at Kansas City	25 . . . . Milwaukee
7 . . . . Seattle	26 . . . . at Cleveland
8 . . . . at Seattle	27 . . . . .Colorado
9 . . . . at Texas	28 . . . . . at San Francisco
10 . . . . .Arizona	29 . . . . . at San Francisco
11 . . . . . . at San Diego	30 . . . . .San Francisco

SAN DIEGO PADRES

FEBRUARY
22 . . . . at Seattle	11 . . . . Oakland
23 . . . . at Seattle	12 . . . . at San Francisco
24 . . . . at Seattle	13 . . . . L.A. Angels
25 . . . . . .at Milwaukee	15 . . . . L.A. Dodgers
26 . . . . Cincinnati	15 . . . . . . at Kansas City
27 . . . . .Colorado	16 . . . . .Arizona
27 . . . . at Oakland	17 . . . . .Arizona
28 . . . . Kansas City	17 . . . . . .at L.A. Angels
	18 . . . . . . .Chicago Cubs
	19 . . . . at Arizona

MARCH
1 . . . . .at L.A. Dodgers	20 . . . . . . .San Francisco
2 . . . . at Cleveland	22 . . . . Seattle
3 . . . . Chicago White Sox	23 . . . . at Colorado
4 . . . . Arizona	24 . . . . Milwaukee
5 . . . . L.A. Dodgers	25 . . . . Texas
7 . . . . L.A. Angels	26 . . . . . at San Francisco
8 . .at Chicago White Sox	27 . . . . . . at Cincinnati
9 . . . . Texas	28 . . . . Cleveland
10 . . . . . at Chicago Cubs	29 . . . . at Texas
	30 . . . . at Texas

SAN FRANCISCO GIANTS

FEBRUARY
23 . . . . L.A. Angels	12 . . . . San Diego
24 . . . . at Chicago Cubs	13 . . . . at Cincinnati
25 . . . . . .Chicago Cubs	15 . . . . Texas
26 . . . .at L.A. Dodgers	16 . . . . Cincinnati
27 . . . . . .at L.A. Angels	16 . . . . at Cleveland
28 . . . . Seattle	17 . . . . .Colorado
	19 . . . . at Seattle
	20 . . . . Milwaukee

MARCH
1 . . . . at Oakland	20 . . . . . at San Diego
2 . . . . .Chicago Cubs	21 . . . . .Colorado
2 . . . . . . at Kansas City	22 . . . . at Colorado
3 . . . . .Arizona	23 . . . . Oakland
4 . .at Chicago White Sox	24 . . . . . . .at L.A. Angels
5 . . . . Cleveland	25 . . .at Chicago Cubs
7 . . . . at Oakland	26 . . . . San Diego
8 . . . . L.A. Dodgers	27 . . . . at Arizona
9 . . . . Kansas City	28 . . . . Oakland
10 . . . . . .at Milwaukee	29 . . . . Oakland
11 . . . . at Texas	30 . . . . at Oakland

SEATTLE MARINERS

FEBRUARY
22 . . . . San Diego	7 . . . . at Kansas City
23 . . . . . . at San Diego	7 . . . . at Oakland
24 . . . . San Diego	8 . . . . Oakland
25 . . . . L.A. Angels	9 . . . . . .at L.A. Dodgers
26 . . . . at Milwaukee	10 . . . . Chicago White Sox
27 . . . . at Cleveland	12 . . . . .Arizona
28 . . . . . at San Francisco	13 . . . . . . at Kansas City
	14 . . . . Cincinnati
	15 . . . . . . .at L.A. Angels

MARCH
1 . . . . Texas	16 . . . . at Colorado
2 . . . . L.A. Dodgers	17 . . . . Texas
3 . . . . at Texas	18 . . . . at Oakland
4 . . . . .Colorado	19 . . . . .San Francisco
6 . . . . Milwaukee	21 . . . . .Chicago Cubs
	22 . . . . at San Diego

23 .... Cleveland
24 .... at Arizona
25 .... at Cincinnati
26 .... Kansas City

27 .... L.A. Dodgers
28 .... at Chicago Cubs
30 .... at Colorado

20 .... at N.Y. Yankees
21 .... Philadelphia
22 .... at Toronto
23 .... Pittsburgh
24 .... at Philadelphia

25 .... at Baltimore
27 .... Miami
28 .... Minnesota
29 .... at Minnesota
30 .... Minnesota

TEXAS

FEBRUARY
22 .... Kansas City
23 .... at Kansas City
24 .... Kansas City
25 .... at Colorado
26 .... Chicago White Sox
27 .... at Chicago White Sox
28 .... Cleveland

MARCH
1 .... at Seattle
2 .... at Arizona
3 .... Seattle
4 .... San Diego
6 .... Chicago Cubs
7 .... at L.A. Dodgers
8 .... at Milwaukee
9 .... Oakland
9 .... at San Diego
10 .... at Cleveland
11 .... San Francisco
12 .... Milwaukee
14 .... at Oakland
15 .... at San Francisco
16 .... L.A. Dodgers
16 .... at Chicago Cubs
17 .... at Chicago Cubs
17 .... at Seattle
18 .... Kansas City
19 .... at Chicago Cubs
21 .... L.A. Angels
22 .... Colorado
23 .... at Cincinnati
24 .... Cincinnati
25 .... at San Diego
26 .... Chicago White Sox
27 .... at L.A. Angels
28 .... Arizona
29 .... San Diego
30 .... San Diego

FLORIDA GRAPEFRUIT LEAGUE

ATLANTA BRAVES

FEBRUARY
22 .... Detroit
23 .... N.Y. Yankees
24 .... at Pittsburgh
25 .... Miami
26 .... Washington
27 .... at Detroit
28 .... at Philadelphia

MARCH
1 .... Washington
2 .... at Houston
3 .... Detroit
4 .... at N.Y. Mets
5 .... at N.Y. Yankees
7 .... Detroit
8 .... at Houston
8 .... Toronto
9 .... at N.Y. Yankees
10 .... Miami
11 .... at Washington
12 .... St. Louis
13 .... at Miami
14 .... at St. Louis
15 .... N.Y. Mets
16 .... N.Y. Yankees
17 .... at N.Y. Mets
18 .... Philadelphia
20 .... Pittsburgh
21 .... Washington
22 .... at Philadelphia
23 .... at Toronto
23 .... Houston
24 .... at Washington
25 .... N.Y. Mets
26 .... at Detroit
27 .... at Washington
28 .... Houston

BALTIMORE ORIOLES

FEBRUARY
23 .... Minnesota
24 .... at Toronto
25 .... N.Y. Yankees
26 .... at Pittsburgh
27 .... at N.Y. Yankees
27 .... Boston
28 .... at Minnesota

MARCH
1 .... Pittsburgh
2 .... at Tampa Bay
3 .... Philadelphia
5 .... at Toronto
7 .... Toronto
8 .... at Pittsburgh
9 .... at Boston
10 .... Pittsburgh
11 .... at Pittsburgh
13 .... at Minnesota
14 .... Tampa Bay
15 .... Boston
16 .... at Toronto
17 .... at Philadelphia
17 .... Minnesota
19 .... at Boston
20 .... Toronto
21 .... Pittsburgh
22 .... at Tampa Bay
23 .... Philadelphia
24 .... at Pittsburgh
25 .... Boston
26 .... at Minnesota
27 .... N.Y. Yankees
28 .... Tampa Bay
30 .... N.Y. Mets

BOSTON RED SOX

FEBRUARY
23 .... Tampa Bay
24 .... at St. Louis
25 .... at Tampa Bay
25 .... at Toronto
26 .... St. Louis
27 .... at Baltimore
28 .... at Pittsburgh

MARCH
1 .... Pittsburgh
2 .... Minnesota
3 .... N.Y. Yankees
4 .... Tampa Bay
6 .... Pittsburgh
7 .... at Minnesota
8 .... Minnesota
9 .... at Tampa Bay
10 .... at Tampa Bay
11 .... at Miami
12 .... Toronto
14 .... at Minnesota
15 .... at Baltimore
15 .... Minnesota
16 .... at Tampa Bay
17 .... Tampa Bay
18 .... at Pittsburgh
19 .... Baltimore

DETROIT TIGERS

FEBRUARY
22 .... at Atlanta
23 .... Toronto
24 .... Philadelphia
25 .... at Philadelphia
26 .... at Houston
27 .... Atlanta
28 .... at Tampa Bay

MARCH
1 .... at N.Y. Mets
2 .... at N.Y. Yankees
2 .... Pittsburgh
3 .... at Atlanta
4 .... Houston
6 .... Toronto
7 .... at Atlanta
8 .... N.Y. Mets
9 .... at Toronto
10 .... Washington
11 .... N.Y. Mets
12 .... at Philadelphia
14 .... at N.Y. Mets
15 .... Toronto
16 .... at St. Louis
17 .... Washington
18 .... at Washington
19 .... Tampa Bay
21 .... Houston
22 .... at Washington
23 .... N.Y. Yankees
24 .... at N.Y. Mets
25 .... at Miami
26 .... Atlanta
27 .... Philadelphia
28 .... at Houston
29 .... Tampa Bay
30 .... at Tampa Bay

HOUSTON ASTROS

FEBRUARY
23 .... at Philadelphia
24 .... N.Y. Mets
25 .... at St. Louis
26 .... Detroit
26 .... at Tampa Bay
27 .... at Toronto
28 .... N.Y. Yankees

MARCH
1 .... St. Louis
2 .... Atlanta
3 .... at Pittsburgh
4 .... at Detroit
5 .... at Washington
7 .... Washington
8 .... Atlanta
9 .... at N.Y. Mets
10 .... Philadelphia
12 .... at Miami
13 .... Washington
14 .... at Washington
15 .... Pittsburgh
16 .... at Washington
17 .... Toronto
19 .... at Toronto
20 .... N.Y. Mets
21 .... at Detroit
22 .... St. Louis
23 .... at Atlanta
24 .... Miami
25 .... Washington
26 .... at N.Y. Yankees
27 .... at N.Y. Mets
28 .... Detroit
28 .... at Atlanta
29 .... Chicago Cubs
30 .... Chicago Cubs

MIAMI MARLINS

FEBRUARY
23 .... St. Louis
24 .... at Washington
25 .... at Atlanta
26 .... N.Y. Mets
27 .... at Washington
28 .... at St. Louis

MARCH
1 .... Minnesota
2 .... at N.Y. Mets
3 .... N.Y. Mets
6 .... at St. Louis
7 .... at N.Y. Mets
8 .... N.Y. Mets
9 .... at Washington
9 .... St. Louis
10 .... at Atlanta
11 .... Boston
12 .... Houston
13 .... Atlanta
15 .... at N.Y. Yankees
16 .... at N.Y. Mets
17 .... St. Louis
18 .... at Minnesota
19 .... at St. Louis
20 .... Washington
22 .... N.Y. Mets
23 .... St. Louis
24 .... at Houston
25 .... Detroit
26 .... Washington
27 .... at Boston
28 .... at St. Louis

MINNESOTA TWINS

FEBRUARY
23 .... at Baltimore
24 .... Tampa Bay
25 .... Pittsburgh
26 .... at Toronto
27 .... Philadelphia
28 .... Baltimore

MARCH
1 .... at Miami
2 .... Boston
3 .... at Tampa Bay
4 .... at St. Louis
5 .... Tampa Bay
7 .... Boston
7 .... at Philadelphia
8 .... at Boston
9 .... at Pittsburgh
10 .... Pittsburgh
11 .... at Tampa Bay
13 .... Baltimore
14 .... Boston
15 .... at Boston
16 .... Pittsburgh
17 .... at Baltimore
18 .... Miami
20 .... Tampa Bay
21 .... at N.Y. Mets
22 .... N.Y. Mets
23 .... St. Louis
24 .... Toronto
25 .... St. Louis
26 .... Baltimore
27 .... at Pittsburgh
28 .... at Boston
29 .... Boston
30 .... Boston

NEW YORK METS

FEBRUARY
23 . . . . .Washington
24 . . . . at Houston
25 . . . . .Washington
26 . . . . .at Miami
27 . . . . St. Louis
28 . . . . . . at Washington

MARCH
1 . . . . Detroit
2 . . . . Miami
3 . . . . at Miami
4 . . . . Atlanta
7 . . . . Miami
8 . . . . at Detroit
9 . . . . Houston
10 . . . . . . at St. Louis
11 . . . . at Detroit

13 . . . . . . at Washington
14 . . . . Detroit
15 . . . . at Atlanta
16 . . . . Miami
17 . . . . Atlanta
18 . . . . at St. Louis
20 . . . . at Houston
21 . . . . St. Louis
22 . . . . .at Miami
23 . . . . .Washington
24 . . . . . . at St. Louis
25 . . . . at Atlanta
26 . . . . St. Louis
27 . . . . Houston
28 . . . . . . at Washington
29 . . . . St. Louis
30 . . . . . . .at Baltimore

NEW YORK YANKEES

FEBRUARY
23 . . . . at Atlanta
24 . . . . Toronto
25 . . . . . .at Baltimore
26 . . . .at Philadelphia
27 . . . . Baltimore
28 . . . . at Houston
28 . . . . Toronto

MARCH
1 . . . . . . Philadelphia
2 . . . . Detroit
3 . . . . at Boston
5 . . . . Atlanta
7 . . . . . . at St. Louis
8 . . . . at Miami
9 . . . . Atlanta
10 . . . . . .at Toronto

11 . . . . St. Louis
12 . . . . . at Tampa Bay
13 . . . . . . Philadelphia
14 . . . . at Toronto
15 . . . . Miami
16 . . . . . . Philadelphia
16 . . . . at Atlanta
17 . . . . . at Pittsburgh
19 . . .at Philadelphia
20 . . . . Boston
21 . . . . Minnesota
22 . . . . . at Minnesota
23 . . . . at Detroit
24 . . . . . . Tampa Bay
26 . . . . Houston
27 . . . . .at Baltimore
28 . . . . Pittsburgh
29 . . . . at Washington

PHILADELPHIA PHILLIES

FEBRUARY
23 . . . . Houston
24 . . . . . . at Detroit
25 . . . . Detroit
26 . . . . .N.Y. Yankees
27 . . . . at Minnesota
28 . . . . Atlanta

MARCH
1 . . . . . at N.Y. Yankees
2 . . . . at Toronto
3 . . . . . .at Baltimore
3 . . . . Toronto
4 . . . . . at Pittsburgh
6 . . . . .Washington
7 . . . . Minnesota
8 . . . . at Tampa Bay
9 . . . . . . Tampa Bay
10 . . . . Houston

12 . . . . Detroit
13 . . . at N.Y. Yankees
14 . . . . . . .Pittsburgh
15 . . at Tampa Bay
16 . . . at N.Y. Yankees
17 . . . . Baltimore
18 . . . . . . at Atlanta
19 . . . . . .N.Y. Yankees
21 . . . . . . at Boston
22 . . . . Atlanta
23 . . . . . .at Baltimore
24 . . . . Boston
25 . . . . . . at Toronto
26 . . . . . Tampa Bay
27 . . . . . . at Detroit
28 . . . . Toronto
29 . . . . Toronto
30 . . . . Toronto

PITTSBURGH PIRATES

FEBRUARY
23 . . . . . at Tampa Bay
24 . . . . Atlanta
25 . . . . . at Minnesota
26 . . . . Baltimore
27 . . . . . . Tampa Bay
28 . . . . Boston

MARCH
1 . . . . . . .at Baltimore
1 . . . . at Boston
2 . . . . . . at Detroit
3 . . . . Houston
4 . . . . . . Philadelphia
6 . . . . at Boston
7 . . . . . . Tampa Bay
8 . . . . . . Baltimore
9 . . . . . . .Minnesota

10 . . . . . . .at Baltimore
10 . . . . . at Minnesota
11 . . . . . . Baltimore
13 . . . . . Tampa Bay
14 . . . .at Philadelphia
15 . . . . . at Houston
16 . . . . . at Minnesota
17 . . . . . . .N.Y. Yankees
18 . . . . Boston
20 . . . . . . at Atlanta
21 . . . . .at Baltimore
22 . . . . . . Tampa Bay
23 . . . . . . at Boston
24 . . . . Baltimore
25 . . at Tampa Bay
26 . . . . . at Toronto
27 . . . . . .Minnesota
28 . . . . at N.Y. Yankees

ST. LOUIS CARDINALS

FEBRUARY
23 . . . . at Miami
24 . . . . Boston
25 . . . . Houston
26 . . . . at Boston
27 . . . . at N.Y. Mets
28 . . . . Miami

MARCH
1 . . . . . . at Houston
2 . . . . . .Washington
3 . . . . at Washington
4 . . . . . .Minnesota
6 . . . . Miami
7 . . . . . .N.Y. Yankees
8 . . . . at Washington
9 . . . . at Miami
10 . . . . . . .N.Y. Mets

11 . . . . . at N.Y. Yankees
12 . . . . at Atlanta
14 . . . . Atlanta
15 . . . . . . .Washington
16 . . . . Detroit
17 . . . . .at Miami
18 . . . . . .N.Y. Mets
18 . . . . Miami
21 . . . . . at N.Y. Mets
22 . . . . . . at Houston
23 . . . . . . .at Miami
24 . . . . . .N.Y. Mets
25 . . . . . at Minnesota
26 . . . . . at N.Y. Mets
27 . . . . . .Washington
28 . . . . Miami
29 . . . . . at N.Y. Mets

TAMPA BAY RAYS

FEBRUARY
23 . . . . .Pittsburgh
23 . . . . at Boston
24 . . . . . at Minnesota
25 . . . . Boston
26 . . . . Houston
27 . . . . . at Pittsburgh
28 . . . . Detroit

MARCH
1 . . . . at Toronto
2 . . . . Baltimore
3 . . . . . . .Minnesota
4 . . . . at Boston
5 . . . . . at Minnesota
7 . . . . . at Pittsburgh
8 . . . . . . Philadelphia
9 . . . .at Philadelphia
10 . . . . Boston

11 . . . . .Minnesota
12 . . . . .N.Y. Yankees
14 . . . . . . .at Baltimore
15 . . . . . . Philadelphia
16 . . . . Boston
17 . . . . . . at Boston
19 . . . . at Detroit
20 . . . . . at Minnesota
21 . . . . Toronto
22 . . . . Baltimore
22 . . . . . at Pittsburgh
23 . . . . . . .Minnesota
24 . . . at N.Y. Yankees
25 . . . . . . .Pittsburgh
26 . . .at Philadelphia
27 . . . . Toronto
28 . . . . . .at Baltimore
29 . . . . . . at Detroit
30 . . . . Detroit

TORONTO BLUE JAYS

FEBRUARY
23 . . . . at Detroit
24 . . . . Baltimore
24 . . . at N.Y. Yankees
25 . . . . Boston
26 . . . . . .Minnesota
27 . . . . Houston
28 . . . at N.Y. Yankees

MARCH
1 . . . . . . Tampa Bay
2 . . . . . . Philadelphia
3 . . . .at Philadelphia
5 . . . . Baltimore
6 . . . . at Detroit
7 . . . . .at Baltimore
8 . . . . at Atlanta
9 . . . . Detroit
10 . . . . . .N.Y. Yankees

12 . . . . at Boston
13 . . . . . at Pittsburgh
14 . . . . . . .N.Y. Yankees
15 . . . . . . at Detroit
16 . . . . Baltimore
17 . . . . . . at Houston
19 . . . . Houston
20 . . . . . .at Baltimore
21 . . . . at Tampa Bay
22 . . . . Boston
23 . . . . Atlanta
24 . . . . . at Minnesota
25 . . . . . . Philadelphia
26 . . . . . . .Pittsburgh
27 . . .at Tampa Bay
28 . . . .at Philadelphia
29 . . . .at Philadelphia
30 . . . .at Philadelphia

WASHINGTON NATIONALS

FEBRUARY
23 . . . . at N.Y. Mets
24 . . . . Miami
25 . . . at N.Y. Mets
26 . . . . . . at Atlanta
27 . . . . Miami
28 . . . . . . .N.Y. Mets

MARCH
1 . . . . at Atlanta
2 . . . . . at St. Louis
3 . . . . . . St. Louis
5 . . . . Houston
6 . . . .at Philadelphia
7 . . . . . . at Houston
8 . . . . . . St. Louis
9 . . . . Miami
10 . . . . . at Detroit
11 . . . . Atlanta

13 . . . . .N.Y. Mets
13 . . . . . . at Houston
14 . . . . Houston
15 . . . . . at St. Louis
16 . . . . Houston
17 . . . . . . at Detroit
18 . . . . Detroit
20 . . . . . . .at Miami
21 . . . . . . at Atlanta
22 . . . . Detroit
23 . . . at N.Y. Mets
24 . . . . Atlanta
25 . . . . . at Houston
26 . . . . . . .at Miami
27 . . . . Atlanta
27 . . . . . at St. Louis
28 . . . . . . .N.Y. Mets
29 . . . . . . .N.Y. Mets

COLLEGES

COLLEGE ORGANIZATIONS

NATIONAL COLLEGIATE ATHLETIC ASSOCIATION

Mailing Address: P.O. Box 6222, Indianapolis, IN 46206. **Telephone:** (317) 917-6222. **Fax:** (317) 917-6826 (championships), 917-6710 (baseball). **E-Mail Addresses: Division I Championship:** dpoppe@ncaa.org (Dennis Poppe), dleech@ncaa.org (Damani Leech), jhamilton@ncaa.org (JD Hamilton), ctolliver@ncaa.org (Chad Tolliver), (kgiles@ncaa.org) Kim Giles; **Division II Championship:** kwillard@ncaa.org (Keith Willard), lhorvat@ncaa.org (Liz Horvat); **Division III:** jpwilliams@ncaa.org (J.P. Williams). **Websites:** www.ncaa.org, www.ncaa.com.

President: Dr. Mark Emmert. **Vice President, Division I Baseball/Football:** Dennis Poppe. **Director, Division I Baseball/Football:** Damani Leech. **Assistant Director, Division I Baseball/Football:** Chad Tolliver. **Division II Assistant Director, Championship and Alliances:** Keith Willard. **Division III Assistant Director, Championships:** J.P. Williams. **Media Contact, Division I Championship and College World Series:** J.D. Hamilton. **Statistics Contacts:** Jeff Williams (Division I and RPI); Gary Johnson (Division II); Sean Straziscar (Division III).

Chairman, Division I Baseball Committee: Dennis Farrell (Commissioner, Big West Conference). **Division I Baseball Committee:** Randy Buhr (Senior Associate Athletic Director, Washington State); Joel Erdmann (Athletics Director, South Alabama); Larry Gallo Jr (Senior Associate Athletic Director, North Carolina); Robert Goodman (Senior Associate Commissioner, Colonial Athletic Association); Rick Greenspan (Athletics Director, Rice); Dave Heeke (Athletics Director, Central Michigan); Eric Hyman (Athletics Director, Texas A&M); Mark LaBarbera (Director of Athletics, Valparaiso); Ed Scott (Associate Director of Athletics, Binghamton University). **Chairman, Division II Baseball Committee:** Jim Givens (Associate Athletic Director, University of Findlay, Ohio). **Chairman, Division III Baseball Committee:** Gregg Kaye (Commissioner, Commonwealth Coast Conference).

2014 National Convention: Jan. 15-18 at San Diego.

2013 CHAMPIONSHIP TOURNAMENTS

NCAA DIVISION I
67th College World Series . . . . .Omaha, June 15-25/26
Super Regionals (8) . . . . Campus sites, 7-10
Regionals (16). . . . . .Campus sites, May 31—June 3

NCAA DIVISION II
46th annual World Series . . . USA Baseball National Training Complex, Cary, N.C., May 25-June 1.
Regionals (8) . . . . Campus sites, May 16-19

NCAA DIVISION III
38th annual World Series . . . . . . .Times Warner Cable Field at Fox Cities Stadium—Appleton, Wis., May 24-28
Regionals (8) . . . . Campus sites, May 15-19

NATIONAL ASSOCIATION OF INTERCOLLEGIATE ATHLETICS

Mailing Address: 1200 Grand Blvd., Kansas City, MO 64106. **Telephone:** (816) 595-8000. **Fax:** (816) 595-8200. **E-Mail Address:** cwaller@naia.org. **Website:** www.naia. org.

President/CEO: Jim Carr. **Manager, Championship Sports:** Jason Ford. **Director, Sports Information:** Chad Waller. **President, Coaches Association:** Boyd Pitkin, (Briar Cliff, Iowa, College).

2013 NATIONAL CHAMPIONSHIP

Opening round: May 10-14, campus locations.
Avista-NAIA World Series: May 24-31, Lewiston, Idaho.

NATIONAL JUNIOR COLLEGE ATHLETIC ASSOCIATION

Mailing Address: 1631 Mesa Ave., Suite B, Colorado Springs, CO 80906. **Telephone:** (719) 590-9788. **Fax:** (719) 590-7324. **E-Mail Address:** mkrug@njcaa.org. **Website:** www.njcaa.org.

Executive Director: Mary Ellen Leicht. **Director, Division I Baseball Tournament:** Jamie Hamilton. **Director, Division II Baseball Tournament:** Billy Mayberry. **Director, Division III Baseball Tournament:** Tim Drain. **Director, Media Relations:** Mark Krug.

2013 CHAMPIONSHIP TOURNAMENTS

DIVISION I
World Series: Grand Junction, Colo., May 25-June 1
DIVISION II
World Series: Enid, Okla., May 25-June 1
DIVISION III
World Series: Tyler, Texas, May 25-30

CALIFORNIA COMMUNITY COLLEGE ATHLETIC ASSOCIATION

Mailing Address: 2017 O St., Sacramento, CA 95811-5211. **Telephone:** (916) 444-1600. **Fax:** (916) 444-2616. **E-Mail Addresses:** ccarter@cccaasports.org, jboggs@cccaasports.org. **Website:** www.cccaasports.org.

Executive Director: Carlyle Carter. **Director, Membership Services:** Debra Wheeler. **Director, Championships:** George Mategakis. **Assistant Director, Sports Information/Communications:** Jason Boggs.

2013 CHAMPIONSHIP TOURNAMENT

State Championship . . . . .Fresno, Calif., May 17-19

NORTHWEST ATHLETIC ASSOCIATION OF COMMUNITY COLLEGES

Mailing Address: Clark College TGB 121, 1933 Fort Vancouver Way, Vancouver, WA 98663-3598. **Telephone:** (360) 992-2833. **Fax:** (360) 696-6210. **E-Mail Address:** nwaacc@clark.edu. **Website:** www.nwaacc.org.

Executive Director: Marco Azurdia. **Executive Assistant:** Carol Hardin. **Director, Marketing:** Unavailable. **Sports Information Director:** Unavailable.

2013 CHAMPIONSHIP TOURNAMENT

NWAACC Championship,. . . . . Lower Columbia CC, Longview, Wash.,. . . . . .May 23-27

AMERICAN BASEBALL COACHES ASSOCIATION

Office Address: 108 S. University Ave, Suite 3, Mount Pleasant, MI 48858-2327. **Telephone:** (989) 775-3300. **Fax:** (989) 775-3600. **E-Mail Address:** abca@abca.org. **Website:** www.abca.org.

Executive Director: Dave Keilitz. **Assistant to Executive Director:** Betty Rulong. **Membership/Convention Coordinator:** Nick Phillips. **Marketing Director:** Juahn Clark. **Associate Membership/Convention Coordinator:** Jeff Franklyn.

Chairman: Mark Johnson. **President:** Tim Corbin (Vanderbilt).
2014 National Convention: Jan. 2-5 at Hilton Anatole in Dallas, TX.

NCAA DIVISION I CONFERENCES

AMERICA EAST CONFERENCE

Mailing Address: 215 First Street, Suite 140, Cambridge, MA 02142. **Telephone:** (617) 695-6369. **Fax:** (617) 695-6380. **E-Mail Address:** hager@americaeast.com. **Website:** www.americaeast.com.
Baseball Members (First Year): Albany (2002), Binghamton (2002), Hartford (1990), Maine (1990), Maryland-Baltimore County (2004), Stony Brook (2002).
Director, Strategic Media/Baseball Contact: Jared Hager.
2013 Tournament: Four teams, double-elimination. May 22-24 at highest-seeded team.

ATLANTIC COAST CONFERENCE

Mailing Address: 4512 Weybridge Lane, Greensboro, NC 27407. **Telephone:** (336) 851-6062. **Fax:** (336) 854-8797. **E-Mail Address:** sphillips@theacc.org. **Website:** www.theacc.com.
Baseball Members (First Year): Boston College (2006), Clemson (1954), Duke (1954), Florida State (1992), Georgia Tech (1980), Maryland (1954), Miami (2005), North Carolina (1954), North Carolina State (1954), Virginia (1955), Virginia Tech (2005), Wake Forest (1954).
Associate Director, Communications: Steve Phillips.
2013 Tournament: Eight teams, group play. May 22-26 at Durham Bulls Athletic Park, Durham, N.C.

ATLANTIC SUN CONFERENCE

Mailing Address: 3370 Vineville Ave., Suite 108-B, Macon, GA 31204. **Telephone:** (478) 474-3394. **Fax:** (478) 474-4272. **E-Mail Addresses:** pmccoy@atlanticsun.org. **Website:** www.atlanticsun.org.
Baseball Members (First Year): East Tennessee State (2006), Florida Gulf Coast (2008), Jacksonville (1999), Kennesaw State (2006), Lipscomb (2004), Mercer (1979), North Florida (2006), Northern Kentucky (2013) South Carolina-Upstate (2008), Stetson (1986).
Director, Sports Information: Patrick McCoy.
2013 Tournament: Eight teams, double-elimination. May 22-26 at Stetson.

ATLANTIC 10 CONFERENCE

Mailing Address: 11827 Canon Blvd., Suite 200, Newport News, VA 23606. **Telephone:** (757) 706-3059. **Fax:** (757) 706-3042. **E-Mail Address:** mkristofak@atlantic10.org. **Website:** www.atlantic10.com.
Baseball Members (First Year): Butler (2013), Charlotte (2006), Dayton (1996), Fordham (1996), George Washington (1977), LaSalle (1996), Massachusetts (1977), Rhode Island (1981), Richmond (2002), St. Bonaventure (1980), Saint Joseph's (1983), Saint Louis (2006), Temple (1983), Virginia Commonwealth (2013), Xavier (1996).
Commissioner: Bernadette V. McGlade. **Director of Communications:** Drew Dickerson. **Assistant Director of Communications/Baseball Contact:** Melissa Kristofak.
2013 Tournament: Seven teams, double elimination. May 22-25 at Robert and Mariam Hayes Stadium (Charlotte).

BIG EAST CONFERENCE

Mailing Address: 15 Park Row West, Providence, RI 02903. **Telephone:** (401) 453-0660. **Fax:** (401) 751-8540. **E-Mail Address:** csullivan@bigeast.org. **Website:** www.bigeast.org.
Baseball Members (First Year): Cincinnati (2006), Connecticut (1985), Georgetown (1985), Louisville (2006), Notre Dame (1996), Pittsburgh (1985), Rutgers (1996), St. John's (1985), Seton Hall (1985), South Florida (2006), Villanova (1985).
Director, Communications: Chuck Sullivan.
2013 Tournament: Eight teams, double-elimination. May 22-26 at Clearwater, Fla.

BIG SOUTH CONFERENCE

Mailing Address: 7233 Pineville-Matthews Rd., Suite 100, Charlotte, NC 28226. **Telephone:** (704) 341-7990. **Fax:** (704) 341-7991. **E-Mail Address:** nicb@bigsouth.org. **Website:** www.bigsouthsports.com.
Baseball Members (First Year): Campbell (2012), Charleston Southern (1983), Coastal Carolina (1983), Gardner-Webb (2009), High Point (1999), Liberty (1991), Longwood (2013), UNC Asheville (1985), Presbyterian (2009), Radford (1983), Virginia Military Institute (2004), Winthrop (1983).
Assistant Commissioner, Public Relations: Mark Simpson. **Assistant Director, Public Relations/Baseball Contact:** Nic Bowman.
2013 Tournament: Eight teams, double-elimination. May 21-25 at Liberty.

BIG TEN CONFERENCE

Mailing Address: 1500 W. Higgins Rd, Park Ridge, IL 60068. **Telephone:** (847) 696-1010. **Fax:** (847) 696-1110. **E-Mail Addresses:** svillatoro@bigten.org. **Website:** www.bigten.org.
Baseball Members (First Year): Illinois (1896), Indiana (1906), Iowa (1906), Michigan (1896), Michigan State (1950), Minnesota (1906), Nebraska (2012), Northwestern (1898), Ohio State (1913), Penn State (1992), Purdue (1906).
Bob Hammel Communications Intern: Stephen Villatoro
2013 Tournament: Six teams, double-elimination. May 22-25 at Target Field in Minneapolis, Minn.

BIG 12 CONFERENCE

Mailing Address: 400 E. John Carpenter Freeway, Irving, TX 75062. **Telephone:** (469) 524-1009. **E-Mail Address:** lrasmussen@big12sports.com. **Website:** www.big12sports.com.
Baseball Members (First Year): Baylor (1997), Kansas (1997), Kansas State (1997), Oklahoma (1997), Oklahoma State (1997), Texas Christian (2013), Texas (1997), Texas Tech (1997), West Virginia (2013).
Assistant Director, Communications: Laura Rasmussen.
2013 Tournament: Double-elimination division play. May 22-26 at Chickasaw Bricktown Ballpark, Oklahoma City.

BIG WEST CONFERENCE

Mailing Address: 2 Corporate Park, Suite 206, Irvine, CA 92606. **Telephone:** (949) 261-2525. **Fax:** (949) 261-2528. **E-Mail Address:** jstcyr@bigwest.org. **Website:** www.bigwest.org.

Baseball Members (First Year): Cal Poly (1997), UC Davis (2008), UC Irvine (2002), UC Riverside (2002), UC Santa Barbara (1970), Cal State Fullerton (1975), Cal State Northridge (2001), Hawaii (2013), Long Beach State (1970), Pacific (1972).

Director, Communications: Julie St. Cyr.

2013 Tournament: None.

COLONIAL ATHLETIC ASSOCIATION

Mailing Address: 8625 Patterson Ave., Richmond, VA 23229. **Telephone:** (804) 754-1616. **Fax:** (804) 754-1973. **E-Mail Address:** rwashburn@caasports.com. **Website:** www.caasports.com.

Baseball Members (First Year): Delaware (2002), George Mason (1986), Georgia State (2006), Hofstra (2002), James Madison (1986), UNC Wilmington (1986), Northeastern (2006), Old Dominion (1992), Towson (2002), William & Mary (1986).

Associate Commissioner/Communications: Rob Washburn.

2013 Tournament: Six teams, double-elimination. May 22-25 at Harrisonburg, Va. (James Madison).

CONFERENCE USA

Mailing Address: 5201 N. O'Connor Blvd., Suite 300, Irving, TX 75039. **Telephone:** (214) 774-1300. **Fax:** (214) 496-0055. **E-Mail Address:** rdanderson@c-usa.org. **Website:** www.conferenceusa.com.

Baseball Members (First Year): Alabama-Birmingham (1996), Central Florida (2006), East Carolina (2002), Houston (1997), Marshall (2006), Memphis (1996), Rice (2006), Southern Mississippi (1996), Tulane (1996).

Assistant Commissioner, Baseball Operations: Russell Anderson.

2013 Tournament: Eight-team, two-division pool play. May 22-26 at Rice.

GREAT WEST CONFERENCE

Mailing Address: P.O. Box 9344, Naperville, IL 60567. **Telephone:** (630) 428-4492. **Fax:** (630) 548-0705. **E-Mail Address:** cliff.c.martin@gmail.com. **Website:** www.greatwestconference.org.

Baseball Members (First Year): Chicago State (2010), Houston Baptist (2010), New Jersey Tech (2010), New York Tech (2010), North Dakota (2010), Northern Colorado (2010), Texas-Pan American (2010), Utah Valley (2010).

Media Relations Assistant Director: Cliff Martin.

2013 Tournament: Eight teams, double-elimination, May 21-25 at NJIT.

HORIZON LEAGUE

Mailing Address: 201 S. Capitol Ave, Suite 500, Indianapolis, IN 46225. **Telephone:** (317) 237-5604. **Fax:** (317) 237-5620. **E-Mail Address:** chammel@horizonleague.org. **Website:** www.horizonleague.org.

Baseball Members (First Year): Illinois-Chicago (1994), Valparaiso (2008), Wright State (1994), Wisconsin-Milwaukee (1994), Youngstown State (2002).

Assistant Director, Communications: Craig Hammel.

2013 Tournament: Five teams, double-elimination. May 22-25 at Youngstown State.

IVY LEAGUE

Mailing Address: 228 Alexander Rd., Second Floor, Princeton, NJ 08544. **Telephone:** (609) 258-6426. **Fax:** (609) 258-1690. **E-Mail Address:** trevor@ivyleaguesports.com. **Website:** www.ivyleaguesports.com.

Baseball Members (First Year): Rolfe—Brown (1948), Dartmouth (1930), Harvard (1948), Yale (1930). Gehrig—Columbia (1930), Cornell (1930), Pennsylvania (1930), Princeton (1930).

Interim Assistant Executive Director, Communications/Championships: Trevor Rutledge-Leverenz.

2013 Tournament: Best-of-three series between division champions. May 4-5 at team with best overall record.

METRO ATLANTIC ATHLETIC CONFERENCE

Mailing Address: 712 Amboy Ave., Edison, NJ 08837. **Telephone:** (732) 738-5455. **Fax:** (732) 738-8366. **E-Mail Address:** edward.clinton@maac.org. **Website:** www.maacsports.com.

Baseball Members (First Year): Canisius (1990), Fairfield (1982), Iona (1982), Manhattan (1982), Marist (1998), Niagara (1990), Rider (1998), Saint Peter's (1982), Siena (1990).

Assistant Commissioner, External Relations: Whitney Swab.

2013 Tournament: Four teams, double-elimination. May 23-26 at Waterfront Park, Trenton, N.J.

MID-AMERICAN CONFERENCE

Mailing Address: 24 Public Square, 15th Floor, Cleveland, OH 44113. **Telephone:** (216) 566-4622. **Fax:** (216) 858-9622. **E-Mail Address:** jguy@mac-sports.com. **Website:** www.mac-sports.com.

Baseball Members (First Year): Akron (1992), Ball State (1973), Bowling Green State (1952), Buffalo (2001), Central Michigan (1971), Eastern Michigan (1971), Kent State (1951), Miami (1947), Northern Illinois (1997), Ohio (1946), Toledo (1950), Western Michigan (1947).

Director, Communications: Jeremy Guy.

2013 Tournament: Eight teams (top three in each division and two teams with the next-best overall records, regardless of division), double-elimination. May 22-25 at All Pro Freight Stadium (Avon, Ohio).

MID-EASTERN ATHLETIC CONFERENCE

Mailing Address: 2730 Ellsmere Avenue, Norfolk, VA 23513. **Telephone:** (757) 951-2055. **Fax:** (757) 951-2077. **E-Mail Address:** rashids@themeac.com; porterp@themeac.com. **Website:** www.meacsports.com.

Baseball Members (First Year): Bethune-Cookman (1979), Coppin State (1985), Delaware State (1970), Florida A&M (1979), Maryland Eastern Shore (1970), Norfolk State (1998), North Carolina A&T (1970), North Carolina Central (1970-1977; 2012), Savannah State (2012).

Assistant Director, Media Relations/Baseball Contact: Sahar Abdur-Rashid.

2013 Tournament: Eight teams, double-elimination. May 15-19 at Norfolk State.

MISSOURI VALLEY CONFERENCE

Mailing Address: 1818 Chouteau Ave., St. Louis, MO 63103. **Telephone:** (314) 444-4300. **Fax:** (314) 444-4333. **E-Mail Address:** kbriscoe@mvc.org. **Website:** www.mvc-sports.com.

Baseball Members (First Year): Bradley (1955), Creighton (1976), Evansville (1994), Illinois State (1980),

Indiana State (1976), Missouri State (1990), Southern Illinois (1974), Wichita State (1945).

Assistant Commissioner for Communications: Kelli Briscoe.

2013 Tournament: Eight-team tournament with two four-team brackets mirroring the format of the College World Series, with the winners of each four-team bracket meeting in a single championship game. May 21-25 at Duffy Bass Field (Illinois State).

MOUNTAIN WEST CONFERENCE

Mailing Address: 15455 Gleneagle Dr., Suite 200, Colorado Springs, CO 80921. **Telephone:** (719) 488-4052. **Fax:** (719) 487-7241. **E-Mail Address:** jwillson@themwc.com. **Website:** www.themwc.com.

Baseball Members (First Year): Air Force (2000), Fresno State (2013), Nevada (2013), Nevada-Las Vegas (2000), New Mexico (2000), San Diego State (2000).

Associate Director, Communications: Judy Willson.

2013 Tournament: Six teams, double-elimination. May 22-26 at Fresno State.

NORTHEAST CONFERENCE

Mailing Address: 399 Campus Drive, Somerset, NJ 08873. **Telephone:** (732) 469-0440. **Fax:** (732) 469-0744. **E-Mail Address:** rventre@northeastconference.org. **Website:** www.northeastconference.org.

Baseball Members (First Year): Bryant (2010), Central Connecticut State (1999), Fairleigh Dickinson (1981), Long Island (1981), Monmouth (1985), Mount St. Mary's (1989), Quinnipiac (1999), Sacred Heart (2000), Wagner (1981).

Assistant Commissioner: Ralph Ventre.

2013 Tournament: Four teams, double-elimination. May 23-26 at Lakewood, N.J.

OHIO VALLEY CONFERENCE

Mailing Address: 215 Centerview Dr., Suite 115, Brentwood, TN 37027. **Telephone:** (615) 371-1698. **Fax:** (615) 371-1788. **E-Mail Address:** kschwartz@ovc.org. **Website:** www.ovcsports.com.

Baseball Members (First Year): Austin Peay State (1962), Belmont (2013), Eastern Illinois (1996), Eastern Kentucky (1948), Jacksonville State (2003), Morehead State (1948), Murray State (1948), Southeast Missouri State (1991), Southern Illinois-Edwardsville (2012), Tennessee-Martin (1992), Tennessee Tech (1949).

Assistant Commissioner: Kyle Schwartz.

2013 Tournament: Six teams, double-elimination. May 22-26 at Jackson, Tenn.

PACIFIC-12 CONFERENCE

Mailing Address: 1350 Treat Blvd., Suite 500. **Telephone:** (925) 932-4411. **Fax:** (925) 932-4601. **E-Mail Address:** akaufman@pac-12.org. **Website:** www.pac-12.com.

Baseball Members (First Year): Arizona (1979), Arizona State (1979), California (1916), UCLA (1928), Oregon (1916-1981, 2009) Oregon State (1916), Southern California (1923), Stanford (1918), Utah (2012), Washington (1916), Washington State (1919).

Public Relations Contact: Alex Kaufman.

2013 Tournament: None.

PATRIOT LEAGUE

Mailing Address: 3773 Corporate Pkwy., Suite 190, Center Valley, PA 18034. **Telephone:** (610) 289-1950. **Fax:** (610) 289-1951. **E-Mail Address:** mdougherty@patriot-league.com. **Website:** www.patriotleague.org.

Baseball Members (First Year): Army (1993), Bucknell (1991), Holy Cross (1991), Lafayette (1991), Lehigh (1991), Navy (1993).

Assistant Executive Director for Communications: Matt Dougherty.

2013 Tournament: Four teams, May 11-12 and May 18-19 at site of higher seeds.

SOUTHEASTERN CONFERENCE

Mailing Address: 2201 Richard Arrington Blvd. N., Birmingham, AL 35203. **Telephone:** (205) 458-3000. **Fax:** (205) 458-3030. **E-Mail Address:** cdunlap@sec.org. **Website:** www.secsports.com.

Baseball Members (First Year): East—Florida (1933), Georgia (1933), Kentucky (1933), Missouri (2013), South Carolina (1992), Tennessee (1933), Vanderbilt (1933). **West**—Alabama (1933), Arkansas (1992), Auburn (1933), Louisiana State (1933), Mississippi (1933), Mississippi State (1933), Texas A&M (2013).

Associate Director, Media Relations: Chuck Dunlap.

2013 Tournament: Ten teams, modified single/double-elimination. May 21-26 at Hoover, Ala.

SOUTHERN CONFERENCE

Mailing Address: 702 N. Pine St., Spartanburg, SC 29303. **Telephone:** (864) 591-5100. **Fax:** (864) 591-4282. **E-Mail Address:** pperry@socon.org. **Website:** www.soconsports.com.

Baseball Members (First Year): Appalachian State (1972), College of Charleston (1999), The Citadel (1937), Davidson (1992), Elon (2004), Furman (1937), Georgia Southern (1992), UNC Greensboro (1998), Samford (2009), Western Carolina (1977), Wofford (1998).

Media Relations: Phil Perry.

2013 Tournament: Eight teams, double-elimination, followed by a single-elimination championship game. May 22-26 at Fluor Field, Greenville, S.C.

SOUTHLAND CONFERENCE

Mailing Address: 2600 Network Blvd., Suite 150, Frisco, Texas 75034. **Telephone:** (972) 422-9500. **Fax:** (972) 422-9225. **E-Mail Address:** tlamb@southland.org. **Website:** www.southland.org.

Baseball Members (First Year): Central Arkansas (2007), Lamar (1999), McNeese State (1973), Nicholls State (1992), Northwestern State (1988), Oral Roberts (2013), Sam Houston State (1988), Southeastern Louisiana (1998), Stephen F. Austin (2006), Texas A&M-Corpus Christi (2007).

Baseball Contact/Assistant Commissioner: Todd Lamb.

2013 Tournament: Two four-team brackets, double-elimination. May 22-25 at Constellation Field, Sugar Land, Texas (neutral site).

SOUTHWESTERN ATHLETIC CONFERENCE

Mailing Address: 2101 6th Avenue North, Suite 700, Birmingham, AL 35203. **Telephone:** (205) 251-7573. **Fax:** (205) 297-9820. **E-Mail Address:** a.bell@swac.org. **Website:** www.swac.org.

Baseball Members (First Year): East Division—Alabama A&M (2000), Alabama State (1982), Alcorn State (1962), Jackson State (1958), Mississippi Valley State (1968). **West Division**—Arkansas-Pine Bluff (1999), Grambling State (1958), Prairie View A&M (1920), Southern (1934), Texas Southern (1954).

Director of Media Relations: Antoine Bell.

2013 Tournament: Eight teams, double-elimination.

May 15-19. Site TBD.

SUMMIT LEAGUE

Mailing Address: 340 W. Butterfield Rd., Suite 3-D, Elmhurst, IL 60126. **Telephone:** (630) 516-0661. **Fax:** (630) 516-0673. **E-Mail Address:** mette@thesummitleague.org. **Website:** www.thesummitleague.org.

Baseball Members (First Year): IPFW (2008), Nebraska-Omaha (2013), North Dakota State (2008), Oakland (2000), South Dakota State (2008), Western Illinois (1984).

Associate Director, Communications (baseball contact): Greg Mette.

2013 Tournament: Four teams, double-elimination. May 23-25 at Rochester, Mich. (Oakland).

SUN BELT CONFERENCE

Mailing Address: 601 Poydras St., Suite 2355, New Orleans, LA 70130. **Telephone:** (504) 299-9066. **Fax:** (504) 299-9068. **E-Mail Address:** nunez@sunbeltsports.org. **Website:** www.sunbeltsports.org.

Baseball Members (First Year): Arkansas State (1991), Arkansas-Little Rock (1991), Florida Atlantic (2007), Florida International (1999), Louisiana-Lafayette (1991), Louisiana-Monroe (2007), Middle Tennessee State (2001), South Alabama (1976), Troy (2006), Western Kentucky (1982).

Assistant Commissioner, Communications: Keith Nunez.

2013 Tournament: Eight teams, double-elimination. May 22-26 at Louisiana-Lafayette.

WEST COAST CONFERENCE

Mailing Address: 1111 Bayhill Dr., Suite 405, San Bruno, CA 94066. **Telephone:** (650) 873-8622. **Fax:** (650) 873-7846. **E-Mail Addresses:** jtourial@westcoast.org. **Website:** www.wccsports.com.

Baseball Members (First Year): Brigham Young (2012), Gonzaga (1996), Loyola Marymount (1968), Pepperdine (1968), Portland (1996), Saint Mary's (1968), San Diego (1979), San Francisco (1968), Santa Clara (1968).

Assistant Commissioner, Communications/New Media: Jeff Tourial. **Associate Director, Communications:** James Vega.

2013 Tournament: Four teams, May 23-25 at Banner Island Ballpark, Stockton, Calif.

WESTERN ATHLETIC CONFERENCE

Mailing Address: 9250 East Costilla Ave., Suite 300, Englewood, CO 80112. **Telephone:** (303) 799-9221. **Fax:** (303) 799-3888. **E-Mail Address:** jerickson@wac.org. **Website:** www.wacsports.com.

Baseball Members (First Year): Cal State Bakersfield (2013), Dallas Baptist (2013), Louisiana Tech (2002), New Mexico State (2006), Sacramento State (2006), San Jose State (1997), Seattle (2013), Texas-Arlington (2013), Texas-San Antonio (2013), Texas State (2013).

Interim Commissioner: Jeff Hurd. **Associate Commissioner:** Dave Chaffin. **Director of Media Relations:** Jason Erickson.

2013 Tournament: Eight teams, two-division pool play, May 22-26 at QuikTrip Park, Grand Prairie, Texas.

NCAA DIVISION I TEAMS
* Denotes recruiting coordinator

AIR FORCE FALCONS

Conference: Mountain West.
Mailing Address: 2169 Field House Drive, USAFA CO 80840. **Website:** www.goairforcefalcons.com.
Head Coach: Mike Kazlausky. **Telephone:** (719) 333-0835. **Baseball SID:** Nick Arseniak. **Telephone:** (719) 333-9251. **Fax:** (719) 333-3798.
Assistant Coaches: Toby Bicknell, *Tim Dixon. **Telephone:** (719) 333-7539.
Home Field: Falcon Field. **Seating Capacity:** 1,000. **Outfield Dimensions:** LF—340, CF—400, RF—327. **Press Box Telephone:** (719) 333-3472.

AKRON ZIPS

Conference: Mid-American (East).
Mailing Address: University of Akron, Rhodes Arena, Akron, OH 44325. **Website:** www.GoZips.com.
Head Coach: *Rick Rembielak. **Telephone:** (330) 972-7290. **Baseball SID:** Nick VanDemark. **Telephone:** (330) 972-7171. **Fax:** (330) 374-8844.
Assistant Coaches: Matt Ford, Fred Worth. **Telephone:** (330) 972-7290.
Home Field: Lee R. Jackson Baseball Field. **Seating Capacity:** 1,500. **Press Box Telephone:** (419) 769-3544.

ALABAMA CRIMSON TIDE

Conference: Southeastern (West).
Mailing Address: 323 Bryant Drive, Tuscaloosa, AL 35401. **Website:** www.rolltide.com.
Head Coach: Mitch Gaspard. **Telephone:** (205) 348-4029. **Baseball SID:** Rich Davi. **Telephone:** (205) 348-3550. **Fax:** (205) 348-8841.
Assistant Coaches: *Dax Norris, Andy Phillips. **Telephone:** (205) 348-1074.
Home Field: Sewell-Thomas Stadium. **Seating Capacity:** 6,571. **Outfield Dimensions:** LF—325, CF—400, RF—325. **Press Box Telephone:** (205) 348-4927.

ALABAMA A&M BULLDOGS

Conference: Southwestern Athletic.
Mailing Address: PO Box 342 Normal, AL 35762. **Website:** www.aamusports.com.
Head Coach: Michael Tompkins. **Telephone:** (256) 372-4004. **Baseball SID:** Brandon Willis. **Telephone:** (256) 372-4005. **Fax:** (256) 372-5919.
Assistant Coaches: *Mitch Hill, Preston Potter. **Telephone:** (256) 372-8744.
Home Field: Bulldog Field. **Seating Capacity:** 500. **Outfield Dimensions:** LF—325, CF—402, RF—315.

ALABAMA STATE HORNETS

Conference: Southwestern Athletic.
Mailing Address: 915 South Jackson Street, Acadome E-134, Montgomery, AL 36104. **Website:** www.bamastatesports.com.
Head Coach: Mervyl Melendez. **Telephone:** (334) 229-5600. **Baseball SID:** Duane Lewis. **Telephone:** (334) 229-5230. **Fax:** (334) 262-2971.
Assistant Coaches: Drew Clark, *Jose Vazquez. **Telephone:** (334) 229-5607.
Home Field: Wheeler-Watkins Baseball Complex. **Seating Capacity:** 500. **Outfield Dimensions:** LF—330, CF—400, RF—330. **Press Box Telephone:** (334) 229-8899.

ALABAMA-BIRMINGHAM BLAZERS

Conference: Conference USA.
Mailing Address: 1212 University Blvd, U236, Birmingham, AL 35294. **Website:** www.uabsports.com.
Head Coach: Brian Shoop. **Telephone:** (205) 934-5181. **Baseball SID:** Ben Warnick. **Telephone:** (205) 934-0725. **Fax:** (205) 934-7505.
Assistant Coaches: Josh Hopper, *Perry Roth. **Telephone:** (205) 934-5182.
Home Field: Young Memorial Field. **Seating Capacity:** 1,000. **Outfield Dimensions:** LF—330, CF—400, RF—330. **Press Box Telephone:** (205) 934-0200.

ALBANY GREAT DANES

Conference: America East.
Mailing Address: 1400 Washington Ave., P.E. Bldg 123, Albany, NY 12222. **Website:** www.ualbanysports.com.
Head Coach: Jon Mueller. **Telephone:** (518) 442-3014. **Baseball SID:** Elizabeth Barlow. **Telephone:** (518) 442-3359. **Fax:** (518) 442-3139.
Assistant Coaches: Jeff Kaier, *Drew Pearce. **Telephone:** (518) 442-3337.
Home Field: Varsity Field. **Seating Capacity:** 1,500. **Outfield Dimensions:** LF—346, CF—400, RF—325.

ALCORN STATE BRAVES

Conference: Southwestern Athletic.
Mailing Address: 1000 ASU Dr., #510, Alcorn State, MS 39096. **Website:** www.alcornsports.com.
Head Coach: Barret Rey. **Telephone:** (601) 877-4090. **Baseball SID:** Je'Kel Smith. **Telephone:** 601-877-6501. **Fax:** (601) 877-3821.
Assistant Coaches: *David Gomez. **Telephone:** (601) 877-4090.
Home Field: Willie "Rat" McGowan, Sr. Stadium/Bill Foster Field. **Seating Capacity:** 500. **Press Box Telephone:**(601) 443-1087.

APPALACHIAN STATE MOUNTAINEERS

Conference: Southern.
Mailing Address: Smith Baseball Stadium, ASU Box 32159, Boone, NC 28608. **Website:** www.goasu.com.
Head Coach: Billy Jones. **Telephone:** (828) 262-6097. **Baseball SID:** Mike Flynn. **Telephone:** (828) 262-2845. **Fax:** (828) 262-6106.
Assistant Coaches: Matt Payne, *Michael Rogers. **Telephone:** (828) 262-7165.
Home Field: Beaver Field at Jim and Bettie Smith Stadium. **Seating Capacity:** 1,000. **Outfield Dimensions:** LF—330, CF—400, RF—330. **Press Box Telephone:** (828) 262-2016.

ARIZONA WILDCATS

Conference: Pacific-12.
Mailing Address: 1 National Championship Drive, Tucson, AZ 85721-0096. **Website:** www.arizonaathletics.com.
Head Coach: Andy Lopez. **Telephone:** (520) 621-8808. **Baseball SID:** Blair Willis. **Telephone:** (520) 621-0914. **Fax:** (520) 621-2681.
Assistant Coaches: *Shaun Cole, Matt Siegel. **Telephone:** (520) 621-4714.
Home Field: Hi Corbett Field. **Seating Capacity:** 9,500. **Outfield Dimensions:** LF—366, CF—392, RF—349. **Press Box Telephone:** (520) 621-4440.

ARIZONA STATE SUN DEVILS

Conference: Pacific-12.
Mailing Address: 500 East Veteran's Way, Tempe, AZ 85287. **Website:** www.thesundevils.com.
Head Coach: Tim Esmay. **Telephone:** (480) 965-3677. **Baseball SID:** Thomas Lenneberg. **Telephone:** (480) 965-6594. **Fax:** (480) 965-5408.
Assistant Coaches: Mike Benjamin, *Ken Knutson. **Telephone:** (480) 965-3677.
Home Field: Winkles Field Packard Stadium at Brock Ballpark. **Seating Capacity:** 4,000. **Outfield Dimensions:** LF—335, CF—395, RF—335. **Press Box Telephone:** (480) 727-7253.

ARKANSAS RAZORBACKS

Conference: Southeastern (West).
Mailing Address: 1255 S. Razorback, Fayetteville, AR 72701. **Website:** www.arkansasrazorbacks.com.
Head Coach: Dave Van Horn. **Telephone:** (479) 575-3655. **Baseball SID:** Chad Crunk. **Telephone:** (479) 575-2753. **Fax:** (479) 575-7481.
Assistant Coaches: *Todd Butler, Dave Jorn. **Telephone:** (479) 575-3552.
Home Field: Baum Stadium. **Seating Capacity:** 10,737. **Outfield Dimensions:** LF—320, CF—400, RF—320. **Press Box Telephone:** (479) 575-4141.

ARKANSAS STATE RED WOLVES

Conference: Sun Belt.
Mailing Address: P.O. Box 1000, State University, AR 72467. **Website:** www.astateredwolves.com.
Head Coach: Tommy Raffo. **Telephone:** (870) 972-2700. **Baseball SID:** Chris Graddy. **Telephone:** (870) 972-2707. **Fax:** (870) 972-3367.
Assistant Coaches: Tighe Dickinson, *Anthony Everman. **Telephone:** (870) 972-2700.
Home Field: Tomlinson Stadium/Kell Field. **Seating Capacity:** 1,200. **Outfield Dimensions:** LF—335, CF—400, RF—335. **Press Box Telephone:** (870) 972-2541.

ARKANSAS-LITTLE ROCK TROJANS

Conference: Sun Belt.
Mailing Address: 2801 S. University Avenue, Little Rock, AR 72204. **Website:** www.ualrtrojans.com.
Head Coach: Scott Norwood. **Telephone:** (501) 663-8095. **Baseball SID:** Patrick Newton. **Telephone:** (501) 683-7003. **Fax:** (501) 683-7002.
Assistant Coaches: Chris Marx, *Brandon Rowan. **Telephone:** (501) 280-0759.
Home Field: Gary Hogan Field. **Outfield Dimensions:** LF—315, CF—390, RF—305. **Press Box Telephone:** (501) 351-1060.

ARKANSAS-PINE BLUFF GOLDEN LIONS

Conference: Southwestern Athletic.
Mailing Address: 1200 N. University Drive, Mail Slot 4891, Pine Bluff, AR 71601. **Website:** www.uapblionsroar.com.
Head Coach: Carlos James. **Telephone:** (870) 575-8995. **Baseball SID:** Edrin Nicholson. **Telephone:** (870) 575-7949. **Fax:** (870) 575-4655.
Assistant Coaches: *Marc MacMillan. **Telephone:** (870) 575-8995.
Home Field: Torii Hunter Baseball Complex. **Seating Capacity:** 2000. **Outfield Dimensions:** LF—325, CF—400, RF—325.

ARMY BLACK KNIGHTS

Conference: Patriot.
Mailing Address: 639 Howard Road, West Point, NY 10996. **Website:** www.goarmysports.com.
Head Coach: Joe Sottolano. **Telephone:** (845) 938-3712. **Baseball SID:** Christian Anderson. **Telephone:** (845) 938-6929. **Fax:** (845) 446-2556.
Assistant Coaches: Anthony DeCicco, *Matt Reid. **Telephone:** (845) 938-3712.
Home Field: Doubleday Field. **Seating Capacity:** 880. **Outfield Dimensions:** LF—327, CF—400, RF—327. **Press Box Telephone:** (845) 938-8168.

AUBURN TIGERS

Conference: Southeastern (West).
Mailing Address: P.O. Box 351, Auburn, AL 36849. **Website:** www.auburntigers.com.
Head Coach: John Pawlowski. **Telephone:** (334) 844-9758. **Baseball SID:** Dan Froehlich. **Telephone:** (334) 844-9803. **Fax:** (334) 844-9807.
Assistant Coaches: *Scott Foxhall, Ty Megahee. **Telephone:** (334) 844-9646.
Home Field: Plainsman Park. **Seating Capacity:** 4,096. **Outfield Dimensions:** LF—315, CF—385, RF—331. **Press Box Telephone:** (334) 844-4138.

AUSTIN PEAY STATE GOVERNORS

Conference: Ohio Valley.
Mailing Address: Austin Peay Baseball Office, Box 4515, Clarksville, TN 37044. **Website:** www.letsgopeay.com.
Head Coach: Gary McClure. **Telephone:** (931) 221-6266. **Baseball SID:** Cody Bush. **Telephone:** (931) 221-7561. **Fax:** (931) 221-7830.
Assistant Coaches: Derrick Dunbar, *Joel Mangrum. **Telephone:** (931) 221-7902.
Home Field: Raymond C Hand Park. **Seating Capacity:** 777. **Outfield Dimensions:** LF—319, CF—392, RF—327. **Press Box Telephone:** (931) 221-7406.

BALL STATE CARDINALS

Conference: Mid-American (West).
Mailing Address: H.P. 260, Muncie, IN 47306-0929. **Website:** www.ballstatesports.com.
Head Coach: Rich Maloney. **Telephone:** (765) 285-1425. **Baseball SID:** Joel Godett. **Telephone:** (765) 285-8242. **Fax:** (765) 285-8929.
Assistant Coaches: *Scott French, Todd Linklater. **Telephone:** (765) 285-1425.
Home Field: Ball Diamond. **Seating Capacity:** 1,700. **Outfield Dimensions:** LF—330, CF—400, RF—330. **Press Box Telephone:** (765) 285-8932.

BAYLOR BEARS

Conference: Big 12.
Mailing Address: 1612 S University Parks Dr, Waco TX 76706. **Website:** www.baylorbears.com.
Head Coach: Steve Smith. **Telephone:** (254) 710-3097. **Baseball SID:** Adam Revelette. **Telephone:** (254) 710-2743. **Fax:** (254) 710-1369.
Assistant Coaches: Steve Johnigan, *Trevor Mote. **Telephone:** (254) 710-3044.
Home Field: Baylor Ballpark. **Seating Capacity:** 5,000. **Outfield Dimensions:** LF—330, CF—400, RF—330. **Press Box Telephone:** (254) 754-5546.

BELMONT BRUINS

Conference: Ohio Valley.
Mailing Address: 1900 Belmont Blvd, Nashville, TN 37212. **Website:** www.belmontbruins.com.
Head Coach: Dave Jarvis. **Telephone:** (615) 460-6166. **Baseball SID:** Kristen Litchfield. **Telephone:** (615) 460-8023. **Fax:** (615) 460-5584.
Assistant Coaches: Matt Barnett, *Aaron Smith. **Telephone:** (615) 460-5586.
Home Field: ES Rose Park. **Seating Capacity:** 800. **Outfield Dimensions:** LF—330, CF—400, RF—330.

BETHUNE-COOKMAN WILDCATS

Conference: Mid-Eastern Athletic.
Mailing Address: 640 Mary McLeod Bethune Blvd., Daytona Beach, FL 32114. **Website:** www.bccathletics.com.
Head Coach: Jason Beverlin. **Telephone:** (386) 481-2224. **Baseball SID:** Michael Stambaugh. **Telephone:** (386) 481-2278. **Fax:** (386) 481-2238.
Assistant Coaches: *Barrett Shaft, Kenny Smith. **Telephone:** (386) 481-2242.
Home Field: Jackie Robinson Ballpark. **Seating Capacity:** 4,800. **Outfield Dimensions:** LF—317, CF—400, RF—325.

BINGHAMTON BEARCATS

Conference: America East.
Mailing Address: Binghamton University, Events Center Office #110, Binghamton, NY, 13902. **Website:** www.bubearcats.com.
Head Coach: Tim Sinicki. **Telephone:** (607) 777-2525. **Baseball SID:** John Hartrick. **Telephone:** (607) 777-6800. **Fax:** (607) 777-4597.
Assistant Coaches: *Ryan Hurba. **Telephone:** (607) 777-5808, (607) 777-4552.
Home Field: Varsity Field. **Seating Capacity:** 1,200. **Outfield Dimensions:** LF—325, CF—390, RF—325. **Press Box Telephone:** (607) 777-3600.

BOSTON COLLEGE EAGLES

Conference: Atlantic Coast (Atlantic).
Mailing Address: 140 Commonwealth Ave., Chestnut Hill, MA 02467. **Website:** www.bceagles.com.
Head Coach: Michael Gambino. **Telephone:** (617) 552-2674. **Baseball SID:** Zanna Ollove. **Telephone:** (617) 552-2004. **Fax:** (617) 552-4903.
Assistant Coaches: *Scott Friedholm, Greg Sullivan. **Telephone:** (617) 552-3092.
Home Field: Pellagrini Diamond at Commander Shea Field. **Seating Capacity:** 1000. **Outfield Dimensions:** LF—330, CF—400, RF—320. **Press Box Telephone:** (978) 828-9221.

BOWLING GREEN STATE FALCONS

Conference: Missouri Valley.
Mailing Address: Bowling Green State University, Sebo Athletic Center—Baseball, Bowling Green, OH 43403. **Website:** www.bgsufalcons.com.
Head Coach: Danny Schmitz. **Telephone:** (419) 372-7065. **Baseball SID:** Scott Swegan. **Telephone:** (419) 372-7105. **Fax:** (419) 372-6969.
Assistant Coaches: *Rick Blanc, Spencer Schmitz. **Telephone:** (419) 372-7641.
Home Field: Steller Field. **Seating Capacity:** 1,100. **Outfield Dimensions:** LF—340, CF—400, RF—340. **Press Box Telephone:** (419) 372-1234.

BRADLEY BRAVES

Conference: Missouri Valley.
Mailing Address: 1501 W Bradley Ave., Peoria, IL 61625. **Website:** www.bradleybraves.com.
Head Coach: Elvis Dominguez. **Telephone:** (309) 677-2684. **Baseball SID:** Bobby Parker. **Telephone:** (309) 677-2624. **Fax:** (309) 677-2626.
Assistant Coaches: *John Corbin, Sean Lyons. **Telephone:** (309) 677-4583.
Home Field: O'Brien Stadium. **Seating Capacity:** 7500. **Outfield Dimensions:** LF—310, CF—400, RF—310. **Press Box Telephone:** (309) 680-4045.

BRIGHAM YOUNG COUGARS

Conference: West Coast.
Mailing Address: 30 S.F.H., BYU, Provo, UT 84602. **Website:** www.byucougars.com.
Head Coach: Mike Littlewood. **Telephone:** (801) 422-5049. **Baseball SID:** Ralph Zobell. **Telephone:** (801) 422-9769. **Fax:** (801) 422-0633.
Assistant Coaches: *Brent Haring, Trent Pratt. **Telephone:** (801) 422-5064.
Home Field: Larry H. Miller Field. **Seating Capacity:** 2,204. **Outfield Dimensions:** LF—345, CF—400, RF—345. **Press Box Telephone:** (801) 422-4041.

BROWN BEARS

Conference: Ivy League (Rolfe).
Mailing Address: Brown University Baseball, 235 Hope St., Box 1932, Providence, RI 02912. **Website:** www.brown-bears.com.
Head Coach: Marek Drabinski. **Telephone:** (401) 863-3090. **Baseball SID:** Caitlin Grant. **Telephone:** (401) 863-6069. **Fax:** (401) 863-1436.
Assistant Coaches: *Grant Achilles, Mike McCormack. **Telephone:** (401) 863-3090.
Home Field: Murray Stadium. **Seating Capacity:** 1,500. **Outfield Dimensions:** LF—340, CF—405, RF—325. **Press Box Telephone:** (401) 863-9427.

BRYANT BULLDOGS

Conference: Northeast.
Mailing Address: 1150 Douglas Pike, Smithfield RI 02917. **Website:** www.bryantbulldogs.com.
Head Coach: Steve Owens. **Telephone:** (401) 232-6397. **Baseball SID:** Tristan Hobbes. **Telephone:** (401) 232-6558 Ext. **2. Fax:** (401) 232-5158.
Assistant Coaches: *Ryan Fecteau, Michael Gedman. **Telephone:** (401) 232-6967.
Home Field: Conaty Park. **Seating Capacity:** 500. **Outfield Dimensions:** LF—330, CF—400, RF—330.

BUCKNELL BISON

Conference: Patriot.
Mailing Address: Langone Athletics and Recreation Center, Bucknell University, 1 Dent Drive, Lewisburg, PA 17837. **Website:** www.bucknellbison.com.
Head Coach: Scott Heather. **Telephone:** 570-577-1059. **Baseball SID:** Todd Merriett. **Telephone:** (570) 577-3488. **Fax:** (570) 577-1660.
Assistant Coaches: *Jason Neitz. **Telephone:** 570-577-1059.
Home Field: Depew Field. **Seating Capacity:** 500. **Outfield Dimensions:** LF—330, CF—400, RF—330. **Press Box Telephone:** (570) 428-5393.

BUFFALO BULLS

Conference: Mid-American (East).
Mailing Address: University at Buffalo, Division of Athletics, 175 Alumni Arena, Buffalo, NY 14260. **Website:** www.buffalobulls.com.
Head Coach: Ron Torgalski. **Telephone:** (716) 645-6834. **Baseball SID:** Joe Kepler. **Telephone:** (716) 645-5523.
Assistant Coaches: *Brad Cochrane, Steve Ziroli. **Telephone:** (716) 645-3437.
Home Field: Amherst Audubon Field. **Seating Capacity:** 500. **Outfield Dimensions:** LF—330, CF—400, RF—330. **Press Box Telephone:** (716) 867-1908.

BUTLER BULLDOGS

Conference: Atlantic 10.
Mailing Address: 510 W 49th St., Indianapolis, IN 46208. **Website:** www.butlersports.com.
Head Coach: Steve Farley. **Telephone:** (317) 940-9721. **Baseball SID:** Josh Rattray. **Telephone:** (317) 940-9994. **Fax:** (317) 940-9808.
Assistant Coaches: *Brian Hiscox, Miles Miller. **Telephone:** (317) 940-6536.
Home Field: Bulldog Park. **Seating Capacity:** 1,000. **Outfield Dimensions:** LF—330, CF—400, RF—330. **Press Box Telephone:** (317) 940-9817.

CALIFORNIA GOLDEN BEARS

Conference: Pacific-12.
Mailing Address: Haas Pavilion, Berkeley, CA 94720. **Website:** www.calbears.com.
Head Coach: David Esquer. **Telephone:** (510) 643-6006. **Baseball SID:** Scott Ball. **Telephone:** (510) 643-1741. **Fax:** (510) 643-7778.
Assistant Coaches: Tony Arnerich, *Mike Neu. **Telephone:** (510) 643-6006.
Home Field: Evans Diamond. **Seating Capacity:** 2,500. **Outfield Dimensions:** LF—320, CF—395, RF—320. **Press Box Telephone:** (510) 642-3098.

UC DAVIS AGGIES

Conference: Big West.
Mailing Address: One Shields Ave. Davis, CA 95616. **Website:** www.ucdavisaggies.com.
Head Coach: Matt Vaughn. **Telephone:** (530) 752-7513. **Baseball SID:** Amanda Piechowski. **Telephone:** (530) 752-2663. **Fax:** (530) 752-6681.
Assistant Coaches: Brett Lindgren, *Tony Schifano. **Telephone:** (530) 752-7513.
Home Field: Dobbins Stadium. **Seating Capacity:** 3,500. **Outfield Dimensions:** LF—310, CF—400, RF—310. **Press Box Telephone:** (530) 752-3673.

UC IRVINE ANTEATERS

Conference: Big West.
Mailing Address: UC Irvine Athletics, 903 W. Peltason Drive, Irvine, CA 92697. **Website:** www.ucirvinesports.com.
Head Coach: Mike Gillespie. **Telephone:** (949) 824-0132. **Baseball SID:** Fumi Kimura. **Telephone:** (949) 824-9474. **Fax:** (949) 824-5260.
Assistant Coaches: Bob Macaluso, *Pat Shine. **Telephone:** (949) 824-9521.
Home Field: Anteater Ballpark. **Seating Capacity:** 1200. **Outfield Dimensions:** LF—330, CF—400, RF—330. **Press Box Telephone:** (949) 824-9905.

UCLA BRUINS

Conference: Pacific-12.
Mailing Address: 325 Westwood Plaza, Los Angeles, CA 90095. **Website:** www.uclabruins.com.
Head Coach: John Savage. **Telephone:** (310) 794-2470. **Baseball SID:** Mike Leary. **Telephone:** (310) 206-7873. **Fax:** (310) 206-6831.
Assistant Coaches: *T.J. Bruce, Rex Peters. **Telephone:** (310) 794-8210.
Home Field: Jackie Robinson Stadium. **Seating Capacity:** 1,820. **Outfield Dimensions:** LF—330, CF—395, RF—330. **Press Box Telephone:** (310) 794-8213.

CAL POLY MUSTANGS

Conference: Big West.
Mailing Address: 1 Grand Ave., San Luis Obispo, CA 93407-0388. **Website:** www.gopoly.com.
Head Coach: Larry Lee. **Telephone:** (805) 756-6367. **Baseball SID:** Eric Burdick. **Telephone:** (805) 756-6550. **Fax:** (805) 756-2650.
Assistant Coaches: Thomas Eager, *Teddy Warrecker. **Telephone:** (805) 756-1201.
Home Field: Baggett Stadium. **Seating Capacity:** 1,734. **Outfield Dimensions:** LF—335, CF—405, RF—335. **Press Box Telephone:** (805) 756-7456.

UC RIVERSIDE HIGHLANDERS

Conference: Big West.
Mailing Address: 900 University Ave., Riverside, CA 92521. **Website:** www.gohighlanders.com.
Head Coach: Doug Smith. **Telephone:** (951) 827-5441. **Baseball SID:** John Maxwell. **Telephone:** (951) 827-5438. **Fax:** (951) 827-3569.
Assistant Coaches: *Bobby Applegate, Bryson LeBlanc. **Telephone:** (951) 827-5441.
Home Field: Riverside Sports Complex. **Seating Capacity:** 2,500. **Outfield Dimensions:** LF—330, CF—400, RF—330.

UC SANTA BARBARA GAUCHOS

Conference: Big West.
Mailing Address: UCSB Intercollegiate Athletics Department, ICA Building, Santa Barbara, CA 93106-5200. **Website:** www.ucsbgauchos.com.
Head Coach: Andrew Checketts. **Telephone:** (805) 893-3690. **Baseball SID:** Andrew Wagner. **Telephone:** (805) 893-8603. **Fax:** (805) 893-5477.
Assistant Coaches: *Eddie Cornejo, Jason Hawkins. **Telephone:** (805) 893-2021.
Home Field: Caesar Uyesaka Stadium. **Seating Capacity:** 1,000. **Outfield Dimensions:** LF—335, CF—400, RF—335. **Press Box Telephone:** (805) 893-4671.

CAL STATE BAKERSFIELD ROADRUNNERS

Conference: Western Athletic.
Mailing Address: 9001 Stockdale Highway, Bakersfield, CA 93311. **Website:** www.csub.edu.
Head Coach: Bill Kernen. **Telephone:** (661) 654-2678. **Baseball SID:** Matt Turk. **Telephone:** (661) 654-3071. **Fax:** (661) 654-6978.
Assistant Coaches: *Head Coach, Jody Robinson. **Telephone:** (661) 654-2678.
Home Field: Hard Field. **Seating Capacity:** 2,000. **Outfield Dimensions:** LF—325, CF—390, RF—325. **Press Box Telephone:** (515) 240-0483.

CAL STATE FULLERTON TITANS

Conference: Big West.
Mailing Address: 800 N. State College Blvd., Fullerton, CA, 92831. **Website:** www.fullertontitans.com.
Head Coach: Rick Vanderhook. **Telephone:** (657) 278-3780. **Baseball SID:** Andria Wenzel. **Telephone:** (657) 278-3970. **Fax:** (657) 278-3141.
Assistant Coaches: Jason Dietrich, *Mike Kirby. **Telephone:** (657) 278-2492.
Home Field: Goodwin Field. **Seating Capacity:** 3,500. **Outfield Dimensions:** LF—330, CF—400, RF—330. **Press Box Telephone:** (657) 278-5327.

CAL STATE NORTHRIDGE MATADORS

Conference: Big West.
Mailing Address: 18111 Nordhoff St., Northridge, CA 91330. **Website:** gomatadors.com.
Head Coach: Matt Curtis. **Telephone:** (818) 677-7055. **Baseball SID:** Kevin Strauss. **Telephone:** (818) 677-3860. **Fax:** (818) 677-4762.
Assistant Coaches: *Sergio Brown, Sam Peraza. **Telephone:** (818) 677-3218.
Home Field: Matador Field. **Seating Capacity:** 1000. **Outfield Dimensions:** LF—325, CF—395, RF—325. **Press Box Telephone:** (909) 730-2076.

CAMPBELL FIGHTING CAMELS

Conference: Atlantic Sun.
Mailing Address: P.O. Box 10 Buies Creek, NC 27506. **Website:** www.gocamels.com.
Head Coach: Greg Goff. **Telephone:** (910) 893-1354. **Baseball SID:** Jason Williams. **Telephone:** (910) 814-4367. **Fax:** (910) 814-5530.
Assistant Coaches: *Justin Haire, Rick McCarty. **Telephone:** (910) 814-4335.
Home Field: Jim Perry Stadium. **Seating Capacity:** 1,000.
Fax: (716) 888-8444.

CANISIUS GOLDEN GRIFFINS

Conference: Metro Atlantic.
Mailing Address: 2001 Main St., Buffalo, NY 14208. **Website:** www.gogriffs.com.
Head Coach: Mike McRae. **Telephone:** (716) 888-8485. **Baseball SID:** Matt Lozar. **Telephone:** (716) 888-8266. **Fax:** (716) 888-8444.
Assistant Coaches: *Matt Mazurek. **Telephone:** (716) 888-8479.
Home Field: Demske Sports Complex. **Seating Capacity:** 1,000. **Outfield Dimensions:** LF—325, CF—405, RF—325. **Press Box Telephone:** (440) 477-3777.

CENTRAL ARKANSAS BEARS

Conference: Southland.
Mailing Address: 2401 College Ave., Conway, AR 72034. **Website:** www.ucasports.com.
Head Coach: Allen Gum. **Telephone:** (501) 450-3147. **Baseball SID:** Steve East. **Telephone:** (501) 450-5743. **Fax:** (501) 450-5740.
Assistant Coaches: *Dallas Black, Kirk Kelley. **Telephone:** (501) 339-0101.
Home Field: Bear Stadium. **Seating Capacity:** 2,000. **Press Box Telephone:** (501) 450-5972.

CENTRAL CONNECTICUT STATE BLUE DEVILS

Conference: Northeast.

Mailing Address: 16151 Stanley St., New Britain, CT 06050. **Website:** www.ccsubluedevils.com.
Head Coach: Charlie Hickey. **Telephone:** (860) 832-3074. **Baseball SID:** Tom Pincince. **Telephone:** (860) 832-3089. **Fax:** (860) 832-3754.
Assistant Coaches: *Patrick Hall. **Telephone:** (860) 832-3075.
Home Field: Balf Savin Baseball Field.

CENTRAL FLORIDA KNIGHTS

Conference: Conference USA.
Mailing Address: 4000 Central Florida Blvd., Orlando, FL 32816. **Website:** www.ucfathletics.com.
Head Coach: Terry Rooney. **Telephone:** (407) 823-0141. **Baseball SID:** Eric DeSalvo. **Telephone:** (407) 823-6489. **Fax:** (407) 823-5266.
Assistant Coaches: Ryan Klosterman, *Kevin Schnall. **Telephone:** (407) 823-4320.
Home Field: Jay Bergman Field. **Seating Capacity:** 3,900. **Outfield Dimensions:** LF—330, CF—390, RF—320. **Press Box Telephone:** (407) 823-4487.

CENTRAL MICHIGAN CHIPPEWAS

Conference: Mid-American (West).
Mailing Address: 100 Rose Center, Mount Pleasant, MI 48859. **Website:** www.cmuchippewas.com.
Head Coach: Steve Jaksa. **Telephone:** (989) 774-4392. **Baseball SID:** Kyle Kelley. **Telephone:** (989) 774-1128. **Fax:** (989) 774-5391.
Assistant Coaches: Brett Haring, *Jeff Opalewski. **Telephone:** (989) 774-2123.
Home Field: Theunissen Stadium. **Seating Capacity:** 2,500. **Outfield Dimensions:** LF—330, CF—400, RF—330. **Press Box Telephone:** (989) 774-3579.

CHARLESTON SOUTHERN BUCCANEERS

Conference: Big South.
Mailing Address: 9200 University Blvd., North Charleston, SC 29406. **Website:** www.csusports.com.
Head Coach: Stuart Lake. **Telephone:** (843) 863-7591. **Baseball SID:** Zeke Beam. **Telephone:** (843) 863-7687. **Fax:** (843) 863-7676.
Assistant Coaches: *Sid Fallaw, Adam Ward. **Telephone:** (843) 863-7832.
Home Field: CSU Ballpark. **Seating Capacity:** 1,500. **Outfield Dimensions:** LF—330, CF—400, RF—330. **Press Box Telephone:** (843) 863-7591.

CHARLOTTE 49ERS

Conference: Atlantic 10.
Mailing Address: 9201 University City Blvd., Charlotte, NC 28223. **Website:** www.charlotte49ers.com.
Head Coach: Loren Hibbs. **Telephone:** (704) 687-0727. **Baseball SID:** Ryan Rose. **Telephone:** (704) 687-1023. **Fax:** (704) 687-4918.
Assistant Coaches: *Brandon Hall, Kris Rochelle. **Telephone:** (704) 687-0728.
Home Field: Robert and Mariam Hayes Stadium. **Seating Capacity:** 1,100 (seats); 3,200 (standing room). **Outfield Dimensions:** LF—335, CF—390, RF—335. **Press Box Telephone:** (704) 687-5959.

CHICAGO STATE COUGARS

Conference: Great West.
Mailing Address: 9501 S. Michigan, Chicago, IL. **Website:** www.gocsucougars.com.
Head Coach: Steve Joslyn. **Telephone:** (773) 995-3637.

Baseball SID: Derrick Sloboda. **Telephone:** (773) 995-2217. **Fax:** (773) 995-3656.
Assistant Coaches: *Ray Napientek, Dan Pirillo. **Telephone:** (773) 995-2817.
Home Field: Cougar Field. **Seating Capacity:** 1000. **Outfield Dimensions:** LF—330, CF—390, RF—330.

CINCINNATI BEARCATS

Conference: Big East.
Mailing Address: 2751 O'Varsity Way, Suite 764 Cincinnati, OH 45221. **Website:** www.gobearcats.com.
Head Coach: Brian Cleary. **Telephone:** (513) 556-1577. **Baseball SID:** Jeff Geiser. **Telephone:** (513) 556-0618. **Fax:** (513) 556-0619.
Assistant Coaches: *J.D. Heilmann, Greg Mamula. **Telephone:** (513) 556-1577.
Home Field: Marge Schott Stadium. **Seating Capacity:** 3,085. **Outfield Dimensions:** LF—325, CF—400, RF—325. **Press Box Telephone:** (513) 556-9645.

CITADEL BULLDOGS

Conference: Big South.
Mailing Address: 171 Moultrie Street, Charleston, SC 29409. **Website:** www.citadelsports.com.
Head Coach: Fred Jordan. **Telephone:** (843) 953-5901. **Baseball SID:** Mike Hoffman. **Telephone:** (843) 953-5353. **Fax:** (843) 953-6727.
Assistant Coaches: *David Beckley, Britt Reames. **Telephone:** (843) 953-7265.
Home Field: Joseph P. Riley Jr. Park. **Seating Capacity:** 6,000. **Outfield Dimensions:** LF—305, CF—398, RF—337. **Press Box Telephone:** (843) 302-6193.

CLEMSON TIGERS

Conference: Atlantic Coast (Atlantic).
Mailing Address: Jervey Athletic Center, 100 Perimeter Road, Clemson, SC 29633. **Website:** www.clemsontigers.com.
Head Coach: Jack Leggett. **Telephone:** (864) 656-1947. **Baseball SID:** Brian Hennessy. **Telephone:** (864) 656-1921. **Fax:** (864) 656-0299.
Assistant Coaches: *Bradley LeCroy, Dan Pepicelli. **Telephone:** (864) 656-1948.
Home Field: Doug Kingsmore Stadium. **Seating Capacity:** 6,346. **Outfield Dimensions:** LF—320, CF—400, RF—330. **Press Box Telephone:** (864) 656-7731.

COASTAL CAROLINA CHANTICLEERS

Conference: Big South.
Mailing Address: P.O. Box 261954, Conway, SC 29528. **Website:** www.goccusports.com.
Head Coach: Gary Gilmore. **Telephone:** (843) 349-2524. **Baseball SID:** Mike Cawood. **Telephone:** (843) 349-2822. **Fax:** (843) 349-2819.
Assistant Coaches: *Joe Hastings, Drew Thomas. **Telephone:** (843) 349-2849.
Home Field: TicketReturn.com Field at Pelicans Ballpark (for 2013). **Seating Capacity:** 5,200. **Outfield Dimensions:** LF—308, CF—400, RF—328. **Press Box Telephone:** (843) 234-3474.

COLLEGE OF CHARLESTON COUGARS

Conference: Southern.
Mailing Address: 66 George Street, Charleston, SC 29424. **Website:** www.cofcsports.com.
Head Coach: Monte Lee. **Telephone:** (843) 953-5916. **Baseball SID:** Will Bryan. **Telephone:** (843) 953-3683. **Fax:**

(843) 953-6534.
Assistant Coaches: *Matt Heath, Chris Morris. **Telephone:** (843) 953-7013.
Home Field: Patriots Point. **Seating Capacity:** 2,000. **Outfield Dimensions:** LF—300, CF—400, RF—330. **Press Box Telephone:** (843) 819-7429.

COLUMBIA LIONS

Conference: Ivy League (Gehrig).
Mailing Address: 3030 Broadway, Mail Code 1930, New York, NY 10027. **Website:** www.gocolumbialions.com.
Head Coach: Brett Boretti. **Telephone:** (212) 854-8448. **Baseball SID:** Lauren Boots. **Telephone:** (212) 851-5643. **Fax:** (212) 854-8168.
Assistant Coaches: *Pete Maki, Dan Tischler. **Telephone:** (212) 854-7772.
Home Field: Satow Stadium. **Seating Capacity:** 600. **Press Box Telephone:** (917) 678-3621.

CONNECTICUT HUSKIES

Conference: Big East.
Mailing Address: 2095 Hillside Road, Storrs, CT 06269. **Website:** www.uconnhuskies.com.
Head Coach: Jim Penders. **Telephone:** (860) 486-4089. **Baseball SID:** Brendan Flynn. **Telephone:** (860) 486-1496. **Fax:** (860) 486-5085.
Assistant Coaches: *Jeff Hourigan, Josh MacDonald. **Telephone:** (860) 486-5771.
Home Field: J.O. Christian Field. **Seating Capacity:** 2,000. **Outfield Dimensions:** LF—337, CF—400, RF—325. **Press Box Telephone:** (203) 415-5381.

COPPIN STATE EAGLES

Conference: Mid-Eastern Athletic.
Mailing Address: 2500 W. North Avenue Baltimore, MD 21216. **Website:** www.coppinstatesports.com.
Head Coach: Sherman Reed, Sr. **Telephone:** (410) 951-3723. **Baseball SID:** Roger McAfee. **Telephone:** (410) 951-3729. **Fax:** (410) 951-3717.
Assistant Coaches: *Gregory Beckman. **Telephone:** (410) 951-6941.
Home Field: Joe Cannon Stadium. **Seating Capacity:** 1,500. **Outfield Dimensions:** LF—310', CF—410', RF—310'. **Press Box Telephone:** (410) 608-6396.

CORNELL BIG RED

Conference: Ivy League (Rolfe).
Mailing Address: Cornell Baseball, Teagle Hall, Campus Rd, Ithaca, NY 14853. **Website:** www.cornellbigred.com.
Head Coach: Bill Walkenbach. **Telephone:** (607) 255-3812. **Baseball SID:** Brandon Thomas. **Telephone:** (607) 255-5627. **Fax:** (607) 255-9791.
Assistant Coaches: Tom Ford, *Scott Marsh. **Telephone:** (607) 255-6604.
Home Field: Hoy Field. **Seating Capacity:** 1,000. **Outfield Dimensions:** LF—315, CF—405, RF—325.

CREIGHTON BLUEJAYS

Conference: Missouri Valley.
Mailing Address: 2500 California Plaza, Omaha, NE 68178. **Website:** www.gocreighton.com.
Head Coach: Ed Servais. **Telephone:** (402) 280-2483. **Baseball SID:** Glen Sisk. **Telephone:** (402) 280-2433. **Fax:** (402) 280-2495.
Assistant Coaches: *Spencer Allen, Thomas Lipari. **Telephone:** (402) 280-5545.

Home Field: TD Ameritrade Park Omaha. **Seating Capacity:** 24,000. **Outfield Dimensions:** LF—335, CF—408, RF—335. **Press Box Telephone:** (402) 546-0702.

DALLAS BAPTIST PATRIOTS

Conference: Western Athletic.
Mailing Address: 3000 Mountain Creek Pkwy., Dallas, TX 75211. **Website:** www.dbu.edu.
Head Coach: Dan Heefner. **Telephone:** (214) 333-5327. **Baseball SID:** Nate Frieling. **Telephone:** (214) 333-5590. **Fax:** (214) 333-5306.
Assistant Coaches: *Dan Fitzgerald, Wes Johnson. **Telephone:** (214) 333-6957.
Home Field: Horner Ballpark. **Seating Capacity:** 2,000. **Outfield Dimensions:** LF—330, CF—390, RF—330. **Press Box Telephone:** (214) 333-5542.

DARTMOUTH BIG GREEN

Conference: Ivy League (Rolfe).
Mailing Address: 6083 Alumni Gym, Hanover, NH 03755. **Website:** www.dartmouthsports.com.
Head Coach: Bob Whalen. **Telephone:** (603) 646-2477. **Baseball SID:** Rick Bender. **Telephone:** (603) 646-1030. **Fax:** (603) 646-3348.
Assistant Coaches: *Jonathan Anderson, Evan Wells. **Telephone:** (603) 646-9775.
Home Field: Biondi Park at Red Rolfe Field. **Seating Capacity:** 2,000. **Outfield Dimensions:** LF—325, CF—403, RF—340. **Press Box Telephone:** (603) 646-6937.

DAVIDSON WILDCATS

Conference: Southern.
Mailing Address: Box 7158 Davidson College, Davidson, NC 28035. **Website:** www.davidsonwildcats.com.
Head Coach: Dick Cooke. **Telephone:** (704) 894-2368. **Baseball SID:** Mark Brumbaugh. **Telephone:** (704) 894-2931. **Fax:** (704) 894-2636.
Assistant Coaches: Wayne Miller, *Rucker Taylor. **Telephone:** (704) 894-2772.
Home Field: Wilson Field. **Seating Capacity:** 700. **Outfield Dimensions:** LF—320, CF—385, RF—325. **Press Box Telephone:** (704) 894-2740.

DAYTON FLYERS

Conference: Atlantic 10.
Mailing Address: Baseball Office 300 College Park, Dayton, OH 45469. **Website:** www.daytonflyers.com.
Head Coach: Tony Vittorio. **Telephone:** (937) 229-4456. **Baseball SID:** Ross Bagienski. **Telephone:** (937) 229-4431. **Fax:** (937) 229-4461.
Assistant Coaches: Jim Roberson, *Matt Talarico. **Telephone:** (937) 229-4788.
Home Field: Time Warner Cable Stadium. **Seating Capacity:** 500.

DELAWARE FIGHTIN' BLUE HENS

Conference: Colonial Athletic.
Mailing Address: 116 Delaware Field House, Newark, DE 19716. **Website:** www.bluehens.com.
Head Coach: Jim Sherman. **Telephone:** (302) 831-8596. **Baseball SID:** Adam Nichols. **Telephone:** (302) 831-2186. **Fax:** (302) 831-8653.
Assistant Coaches: Dan Hammer, *Brian Walker. **Telephone:** (302) 831-2723.
Home Field: Bob Hannah Stadium. **Seating Capacity:** 1,300. **Outfield Dimensions:** LF—330, CF—400, RF—330.

DELAWARE STATE HORNETS

Conference: Mid-Eastern Athletic.
Mailing Address: 1200 N. Dupont Hwy., Dover, DE 19901. **Website:** www.dsuhornets.com.
Head Coach: J.P. Blandin. **Telephone:** (302) 857-7809.
Baseball SID: Dennis Jones. **Telephone:** (302) 857-6068.
Fax: (302) 857-6069.
Assistant Coaches: *Russ Steinhorn. **Telephone:** (302) 857-7809.
Home Field: Soldier Field. **Seating Capacity:** 250.
Outfield Dimensions: LF—320, CF—400, RF—310.

DUKE BLUE DEVILS

Conference: Atlantic Coast (Coastal).
Mailing Address: 118 Cameron Indoor Stadium, Durham, NC 27708. **Website:** www.goduke.com.
Head Coach: Chris Pollard. **Telephone:** (919) 668-0255.
Baseball SID: Ashley Wolf. **Telephone:** (919) 668-4393.
Fax: (919) 684-2489.
Assistant Coaches: *Josh Jordan, Andrew See. **Telephone:** (919) 668-5735.
Home Field: Durham Bulls Athletic Park. **Seating Capacity:** 10,000. **Outfield Dimensions:** LF—305, CF—400, RF—327.

EAST CAROLINA PIRATES

Conference: Conference USA.
Mailing Address: 102 Clark-LeClair Stadium Greenville NC 27858. **Website:** www.ecupirates.com.
Head Coach: Billy Godwin. **Telephone:** (252) 737-1985.
Baseball SID: Malcolm Gray. **Telephone:** (252) 737-4523.
Fax: (252) 737-4528.
Assistant Coaches: Dan Roszel, *Ben Sanderson. **Telephone:** (252) 737-1467.
Home Field: Clark-LeClair Stadium. **Seating Capacity:** 5,000. **Outfield Dimensions:** LF—320, CF—400, RF—320.
Press Box Telephone: (252) 328-0068.

EAST TENNESSEE STATE BUCCANEERS

Conference: Atlantic Sun.
Mailing Address: P.O. Box 70707, Johnson City, TN 37614. **Website:** www.etsubucs.com.
Head Coach: Tony Skole. **Telephone:** (423) 439-4496.
Baseball SID: Kevin Brown. **Telephone:** (423) 439-5263.
Fax: (423) 439-6138.
Assistant Coaches: *Xan Barksdale, Kyle Bunn. **Telephone:** (423) 439-4485.
Home Field: Thomas Stadium. **Outfield Dimensions:** LF—330, CF—400, RF—330.

EASTERN ILLINOIS PANTHERS

Conference: Ohio Valley.
Mailing Address: 600 Lincoln Avenue, Charleston, IL 61920. **Website:** www.eiupanthers.com.
Head Coach: Jim Schmitz. **Telephone:** (217) 581-8510.
Baseball SID: Greg Lautzenheiser. **Telephone:** (217) 581-7020. **Fax:** (217)-581-6434.
Assistant Coaches: Jason Anderson, Ben Wolgamot. **Telephone:** (217) 581-8510.
Home Field: Coaches Stadium. **Seating Capacity:** 500.
Outfield Dimensions: LF—340, CF—380, RF—340. **Press Box Telephone:** (419) 605-8512.

EASTERN KENTUCKY COLONELS

Conference: Ohio Valley.
Mailing Address: 521 Lancaster, 115 Alumni Coliseum,
Richmond, KY 40475. **Website:** www.ekusports.com.
Head Coach: Jason Stein. **Telephone:** (859) 622-2128.
Baseball SID: Kevin Britton. **Telephone:** (859) 622-2006.
Fax: (859) 622-5108.
Assistant Coaches: Steven Brown, *John Peterson. **Telephone:** (859) 622-4996.
Home Field: Turkey Hughes Field. **Seating Capacity:** 300. **Outfield Dimensions:** LF—340, CF—410, RF—330.
Press Box Telephone: (859) 358-8359.

EASTERN MICHIGAN EAGLES

Conference: Mid-American (West).
Mailing Address: 799 Hewitt Rd., Ypsilanti, MI 48197.
Website: www.emueagles.com.
Head Coach: Jay Alexander. **Telephone:** (734) 487-0315. **Baseball SID:** Chris Puzzuoli. **Telephone:** (734) 487-0137. **Fax:** (734) 485-3840.
Assistant Coaches: Aaron Hepner, *Andrew Maki. **Telephone:** (734) 487-0315.
Home Field: Oestrike Stadium. **Seating Capacity:** 1,200. **Outfield Dimensions:** LF—330, CF—390, RF—330.
Press Box Telephone: (731) 481-9328.

ELON PHOENIX

Conference: Southern.
Mailing Address: 2500 Campus Box, 100 Campus Drive, Elon, NC 27244. **Website:** www.elonphoenix.com.
Head Coach: Mike Kennedy. **Telephone:** (336) 278-6741. **Baseball SID:** Chris Rash. **Telephone:** (336) 278-6712. **Fax:** (336) 278-6768.
Assistant Coaches: Robbie Huffstetler, *Greg Starbuck. **Telephone:** (336) 278-6794.
Home Field: Latham Park. **Seating Capacity:** 2,000.
Outfield Dimensions: LF—326, CF—385, RF—327. **Press Box Telephone:** (336) 278-6788.

EVANSVILLE PURPLE ACES

Conference: Missouri Valley.
Mailing Address: 1800 Lincoln Ave., Evansville, IN 47722. **Website:** www.gopurpleaces.com.
Head Coach: Wes Carroll. **Telephone:** (812) 488-2059.
Baseball SID: Dustin Hall. **Telephone:** (812) 488-1152.
Fax: (812) 488-2199.
Assistant Coaches: *Ben Bachmann, Andy Pascoe. **Telephone:** (812) 488-2764.
Home Field: Braun Stadium. **Seating Capacity:** 1,200.
Outfield Dimensions: LF—330, CF—400, RF—330. **Press Box Telephone:** (812) 479-2587.

FAIRFIELD STAGS

Conference: Metro Atlantic.
Mailing Address: 1073 North Benson Road, Fairfield, CT 06824. **Website:** www.fairfieldstags.com.
Head Coach: Bill Currier. **Telephone:** (203) 254-4000, ext 2605. **Baseball SID:** Kelly McCarthy. **Telephone:** (203) 254-4000. **Fax:** (203) 254-4117.
Assistant Coaches: Trevor Brown. **Telephone:** (203) 254-4000, ext 3178.
Home Field: Alumni Baseball Diamond. **Outfield Dimensions:** LF—330, CF—400, RF—330.

FAIRLEIGH DICKINSON KNIGHTS

Conference: Northeast.
Mailing Address: 1000 River Road, H-AT1-01, Teaneck, NJ 07666. **Website:** www.fduknights.com.
Head Coach: Gary Puccio. **Telephone:** (201) 692-2245.
Baseball SID: Chris Strauch. **Telephone:** (201) 692-2499.

Fax: (201) 692-9361.
Assistant Coaches: *Justin McKay. Telephone: (201) 692-2245.
Home Field: Naimoli Family Baseball Complex. Seating Capacity: N/A. Outfield Dimensions: LF—321, CF—368, RF—320.

FLORIDA GATORS

Conference: Southeastern.
Mailing Address: P.O. Box 14485 Gainesville, FL 32604. Website: www.gatorzone.com.
Head Coach: Kevin O'Sullivan. Telephone: (352) 375-4683. Baseball SID: John Hines. Telephone: (352) 375-4683. Fax: (352) 375-4809.
Assistant Coaches: *Craig Bell, Brad Weitzel. Telephone: (352) 375-4683.
Home Field: Alfred A. McKethan Stadium. Seating Capacity: 5,500. Outfield Dimensions: LF—326, CF—365, RF—400. Press Box Telephone: (352) 375-4683.

FLORIDA A&M RATTLERS

Conference: Mid-Eastern Athletic.
Mailing Address: 1835 Wahnish Way, Tallahassee, FL 32307. Website: www.famuathletics.com.
Head Coach: Willie Brown. Telephone: (850) 599-3202. Baseball SID: Ronnie Johnson. Telephone: (850) 599-3736. Fax: (850) 599-3206.
Assistant Coaches: Kevin Clethen. Telephone: (850) 412-7391.
Home Field: Moore-Kittles Field. Seating Capacity: 500.

FLORIDA ATLANTIC OWLS

Conference: Sun Belt.
Mailing Address: 777 Glades Road, Boca Raton, FL 33431. Website: www.fausports.com.
Head Coach: John McCormack. Telephone: (561) 297-1055. Baseball SID: Dale Long. Telephone: 561-756-0653. Fax: (561) 291-3956.
Assistant Coaches: Dickie Hart, *Jason Jackson. Telephone: (561) 297-1055.
Home Field: FAU Baseball Stadium. Seating Capacity: 2,000. Outfield Dimensions: LF—330, CF—400, RF—330. Press Box Telephone: (561) 756-0653.

FLORIDA GULF COAST EAGLES

Conference: Atlantic Sun.
Mailing Address: 10501 FGCU Boulevard South, Fort Myers, Fla. 33965. Website: www.fgcuathletics.com.
Head Coach: David Tollett. Telephone: (239) 590-7051. Baseball SID: Matt Farhadi. Telephone: (239) 590-7097. Fax: (239) 590-7014.
Assistant Coaches: Forrest Martin, *Rusty McKee. Telephone: (239) 590-7059.
Home Field: Swanson Stadium. Seating Capacity: 1,500. Outfield Dimensions: LF—330, CF—400, RF—330. Press Box Telephone: (239) 357-2390.

FLORIDA INTERNATIONAL PANTHERS

Conference: Sun Belt.
Mailing Address: 11200 S.W. 8th St., Miami, Fl. 33199. Website: www.fiusports.com.
Head Coach: Turtle Thomas. Telephone: (305) 348-3166. Baseball SID: Matt Ratner. Telephone: (305) 348-1496. Fax: (305) 348-2963.
Assistant Coaches: *Frank Damas, Drew French. Telephone: (305) 348-2145.

Home Field: FIU Baseball Stadium. Seating Capacity: 2,000. Outfield Dimensions: LF—325, CF—400, RF—325. Press Box Telephone: (561) 441-8057.

FLORIDA STATE SEMINOLES

Conference: Atlantic Coast (Atlantic).
Mailing Address: 403 Stadium Drive West, Room D0107, Tallahassee, FL 32306. Website: www.seminoles.com.
Head Coach: Mike Martin. Telephone: (850) 644-1073. Baseball SID: Jason Leturmy. Telephone: (850) 644-3920. Fax: (850) 644-3820.
Assistant Coaches: Mike Bell, *Mike Martin Jr. Telephone: (850) 644-1072.
Home Field: Mike Martin Field at Dick Howser Stadium. Seating Capacity: 6,700. Outfield Dimensions: LF—340, CF—400, RF—320. Press Box Telephone: (850) 644-1073.

FORDHAM RAMS

Conference: Atlantic 10.
Mailing Address: 441 East Fordham Road, Bronx, NY 10458. Website: www.fordhamsports.com.
Head Coach: Kevin Leighton. Telephone: (718) 817-4292. Baseball SID: Scott Kwiatkowski. Telephone: (718) 817-4219. Fax: (718) 817-4244.
Assistant Coaches: *Jimmy Jackson. Telephone: (718) 817-4292.
Home Field: Houlihan Park. Seating Capacity: 1,000. Outfield Dimensions: LF—338, CF—400, RF—338. Press Box Telephone: (718) 817-3373.

FRESNO STATE BULLDOGS

Conference: Mountain West.
Mailing Address: 1620 E. Bulldog Ln., Fresno, CA 93720. Website: www.gobulldogs.com.
Head Coach: Mike Batesole. Telephone: (559) 278-2178. Baseball SID: Stephen Trembley. Telephone: (559) 278-6178. Fax: (559) 278-4689.
Assistant Coaches: *Ryan Overland, Steve Rousey. Telephone: (559) 278-2178.
Home Field: Beiden Field. Seating Capacity: 5,757. Outfield Dimensions: LF—330, CF—400, RF—330. Press Box Telephone: (559) 278-7678.

FURMAN PALADINS

Conference: Southern.
Mailing Address: 3300 Poinsett Highway, Greenville, S.C. 29613. Website: www.furmanpaladins.com.
Head Coach: Ron Smith. Telephone: (864) 294-2146. Baseball SID: Hunter Reid. Telephone: (864) 294-2061. Fax: (864) 294-3061.
Assistant Coaches: Mike Ranson, *Jeff Whitfield. Telephone: (864) 294-2243.
Home Field: Latham Stadium. Seating Capacity: 2,000. Outfield Dimensions: LF—330, CF—393, RF—330. Press Box Telephone: (864) 294-3066.

GARDNER-WEBB RUNNIN' BULLDOGS

Conference: Atlantic Sun.
Mailing Address: P.O. Box 877, Boiling Springs, NC 28017. Website: www.gwusports.com.
Head Coach: Rusty Stroupe. Telephone: (704) 406-4421. Baseball SID: Marc Rabb. Telephone: (704) 406-4355. Fax: (704) 406-4739.
Assistant Coaches: *Kent Cox, Ray Greene. Telephone: (704) 406-3557.
Home Field: John Henry Moss Stadium. Seating

Capacity: 550.

GEORGE MASON PATRIOTS

Conference: Colonial Athletic.
Mailing Address: 4400 University Dr. MS 3A5, Fairfax, VA 22030. **Website:** www.gomason.com.
Head Coach: Bill Brown. **Telephone:** (703) 993-3282. **Baseball SID:** Rachel Buck. **Telephone:** (703) 993-3264. **Fax:** (703) 993-3259.
Assistant Coaches: *Steve Hay, Lucas Jones. **Telephone:** (703) 993-3281.
Home Field: Spuhler Field. **Seating Capacity:** 900. **Outfield Dimensions:** LF—320, CF—400, RF—320.

GEORGE WASHINGTON COLONIALS

Conference: Atlantic 10.
Mailing Address: 619 22nd Street NW Washington D.C. 20052. **Website:** www.gwsports.com.
Head Coach: Gregg Ritchie. **Telephone:** (202) 994-7399. **Baseball SID:** Dan DiVeglio. **Telephone:** (202) 994-0339. **Fax:** (202) 994-2713.
Assistant Coaches: *Dave Lorber, Tom Sheridan. **Telephone:** (202) 994-0327.
Home Field: Barcroft Park. **Seating Capacity:** 450. **Outfield Dimensions:** LF—330, CF—380, RF—330.

GEORGETOWN HOYAS

Conference: Big East.
Mailing Address: 37th & O Streets, NW, Washington, D.C. 20057. **Website:** www.guhoyas.com.
Head Coach: Pete Wilk. **Telephone:** (202) 687-2462. **Baseball SID:** Michael. **Telephone:** (202) 687-2475. **Fax:** (202) 687-2491.
Assistant Coaches: *Curtis Brown, Phil Disher. **Telephone:** (202) 687-6406.
Home Field: Shirley Povich Field. **Seating Capacity:** 1,500. **Outfield Dimensions:** LF—330, CF—375, RF—330. **Press Box Telephone:** (917) 576-7445.

GEORGIA BULLDOGS

Conference: Southeastern (East).
Mailing Address: P.O. Box 1472, Athens, Ga. 30603-1472. **Website:** www.georgiadogs.com.
Head Coach: David Perno. **Telephone:** (706) 542-7971. **Baseball SID:** Christopher Lakos. **Telephone:** (706) 542-1621. **Fax:** (706) 542-9339.
Assistant Coaches: Jason Eller, *Allen Osborne. **Telephone:** (706) 542-7971.
Home Field: Foley Field. **Seating Capacity:** 3,291. **Outfield Dimensions:** LF—350, CF—404, RF—314. **Press Box Telephone:** (706) 542-6161.

GEORGIA SOUTHERN EAGLES

Conference: Southern.
Mailing Address: 590 Herty Drive, Room 1125, Statesboro, Ga. 30460. **Website:** www.georgiasoutherneagles.com.
Head Coach: Rodney Hennon. **Telephone:** (912) 478-7360. **Baseball SID:** Barrett Gilham. **Telephone:** (912) 478-5448. **Fax:** (912) 478-1063.
Assistant Coaches: *B.J. Green, Chris Moore. **Telephone:** (912) 478-5188.
Home Field: J.I. Clements Stadium. **Seating Capacity:** 3,000. **Outfield Dimensions:** LF—330, CF—385, RF—330. **Press Box Telephone:** (912) 478-5764.

GEORGIA STATE PANTHERS

Conference: Colonial Athletic.
Mailing Address: P.O. Box 3875, Atlanta, GA 30302-3975. **Website:** www.georgiastatesports.com.
Head Coach: Greg Frady. **Telephone:** (404) 413-4143. **Baseball SID:** Allison George. **Telephone:** (404) 413-4032. **Fax:** (404) 413-4035.
Assistant Coaches: *Willie Stewart, Edwin Thompson. **Telephone:** (404) 413-4077.
Home Field: GSU Baseball Complex. **Seating Capacity:** 1,000. **Outfield Dimensions:** LF—334, CF—385, RF—338. **Press Box Telephone:** (518) 817-3564.

GEORGIA TECH YELLOW JACKETS

Conference: Atlantic Coast (Coastal).
Mailing Address: 150 Bobby Dodd Way NW, Atlanta, Ga. 30324. **Website:** www.ramblinwreck.com.
Head Coach: Danny Hall. **Telephone:** (404) 894-5471. **Baseball SID:** Mike DeGeorge. **Telephone:** (404) 894-5445. **Fax:** (404) 894-1248.
Assistant Coaches: Jason Howell, *Bryan Prince. **Telephone:** .
Home Field: Russ Chandler Stadium. **Seating Capacity:** 4,157. **Outfield Dimensions:** LF—328, CF—400, RF—334. **Press Box Telephone:** (404) 894-3167.

GONZAGA BULLDOGS

Conference: West Coast.
Mailing Address: 502 E. Boone Ave Spokane, WA 99258. **Website:** www.gozags.com.
Head Coach: Mark Machtolf. **Telephone:** (509) 313-4209. **Baseball SID:** Justin Trujillo. **Telephone:** (509) 313-4227. **Fax:** (509) 313-5730.
Assistant Coaches: Steve Bennett, *Danny Evans. **Telephone:** (509) 313-3597.
Home Field: Patterson Baseball Complex at Washington Trust Field. **Seating Capacity:** 1,500. **Outfield Dimensions:** LF—328, CF—398, RF—328. **Press Box Telephone:** (509) 279-1005.

GRAMBLING STATE TIGERS

Conference: Southwestern Athletic.
Mailing Address: 403 Main Street, P.O. Box 4252, Grambling, La 71245. **Website:** www.gsutigers.com.
Head Coach: James Cooper. **Telephone:** (318) 274-6566. **Baseball SID:** Santoria Black. **Telephone:** 318-274-6562.
Assistant Coaches: Davin Pierre. **Telephone:** (318) 274-2416.
Home Field: Jones Field at Ellis Park. **Seating Capacity:** 3,000. **Outfield Dimensions:** LF—315, CF—400, RF—350.

HARTFORD HAWKS

Conference: America East.
Mailing Address: 200 Bloomfield Ave., West Hartford, CT. **Website:** www.hartfordhawks.com.
Head Coach: Justin Blood. **Telephone:** (860) 768-5760. **Baseball SID:** Dan Ruede. **Telephone:** (860) 768-4501.
Assistant Coaches: *Steve Malinowski, Mike Nemeth. **Telephone:** (860) 768-4972.
Home Field: Fiondella Field. **Seating Capacity:** 1,500. **Outfield Dimensions:** LF—325, CF—400, RF—325.

HARVARD CRIMSON

Conference: Ivy League (Rolfe).
Mailing Address: Murr Center, 65 North Harvard St.,

Boston, MA -2163. **Website:** www.gocrimson.com.
Head Coach: Bill Decker. **Telephone:** (617) 495-2629.
Baseball SID: Kurt Svoboda. **Telephone:** (617) 495-2206.
Fax: (617) 495-2130.
Assistant Coaches: John Birtwell, *Jeff Calcaterra.
Telephone: (617) 496-1435.
Home Field: O'Donnell Field. **Seating Capacity:** 1,000.
Outfield Dimensions: LF—335, CF—410, RF—335.

HAWAII RAINBOWS

Conference: Big West.
Mailing Address: 1337 Lower Campus Rd,. Honolulu,
HI 96822. **Website:** www.hawaiiathletics.com.
Head Coach: Mike Trapasso. **Telephone:** (808) 956-
6247. **Baseball SID:** John Barry. **Telephone:** (808) 956-
7506. **Fax:** (808) 956-4470.
Assistant Coaches: *Chad Konishi, Rusty McNamara.
Telephone: (808) 956-6247.
Home Field: Les Murakami Stadium. **Seating Capacity:**
4312. **Outfield Dimensions:** LF—325, CF—385, RF—325.

HIGH POINT PANTHERS

Conference: Big South.
Mailing Address: 884 Montlieu Avenue, High Point,
NC 27262. **Website:** www.highpointpanthers.com.
Head Coach: Craig Cozart. **Telephone:** (336) 841-9190.
Baseball SID: Joe Arancio. **Telephone:** (336) 841-4638.
Fax: (336) 841-9182.
Assistant Coaches: Bryan Peters, *Rich Wallace.
Telephone: (336) 841-4614.
Home Field: Williard Stadium. **Seating Capacity:** 550.
Outfield Dimensions: LF—350, CF—400, RF—330. **Press
Box Telephone:** (336) 841-9192.

HOFSTRA PRIDE

Conference: Colonial Athletic.
Mailing Address: 240 Hofstra University, Hempstead,
NY 11549. **Website:** www.gohofstra.com.
Head Coach: John Russo. **Telephone:** (516) 463-3759.
Baseball SID: Len Skoros. **Telephone:** (516) 463-4602.
Fax: (516) 463-5033.
Assistant Coaches: *Kelly Haynes, Christopher Johns.
Telephone: (516) 463-5065.
Home Field: University Field. **Seating Capacity:** 600.
Outfield Dimensions: LF—322, CF—382, RF—337. **Press
Box Telephone:** (516) 463-1896.

HOLY CROSS CRUSADERS

Conference: Patriot.
Mailing Address: 1 College Street, Worcester, MA
01610. **Website:** www.goholycross.com.
Head Coach: Greg DiCenzo. **Telephone:** (508) 793-
2753. **Baseball SID:** Jim Sarkisian. **Telephone:** (508) 793-
2583. **Fax:** (508) 793-2309.
Assistant Coaches: *Jeff Kane, Ron Rakowski.
Telephone: (508) 793-2753.
Home Field: Fitton Field. **Seating Capacity:** 3,000.
Outfield Dimensions: LF—332, CF—385, RF—313.

HOUSTON COUGARS

Conference: Conference USA.
Mailing Address: 3100 Cullen Blvd., Houston, Texas
77204. **Website:** www.uhcougars.com.
Head Coach: Todd Whitting. **Telephone:** (713) 743-
9416. **Baseball SID:** Allison McClain. **Telephone:** (713)
743-9406. **Fax:** (713) 743-9411.
Assistant Coaches: Frank Anderson, *Trip Couch.

Telephone: (713) 743-9415.
Home Field: Cougar Field. **Seating Capacity:** 3,500.
Outfield Dimensions: LF—330, CF—390, RF—330. **Press
Box Telephone:** (713) 743-0840.

HOUSTON BAPTIST HUSKIES

Conference: Great West.
Mailing Address: 7502 Fondren, Houston, TX 77074.
Website: www.hbuhuskies.com.
Head Coach: Jared Moon. **Telephone:** (281) 649-3332.
Baseball SID: Russ Reneau. **Telephone:** (281) 649-3098.
Fax: (281) 649-3496.
Assistant Coaches: *Xavier Hernandez, Russell
Stockton. **Telephone:** (281) 649-3264.
Home Field: Husky Field. **Seating Capacity:** 500.
Outfield Dimensions: LF—340, CF—400, RF—340. **Press
Box Telephone:** (281) 923-0813.

ILLINOIS FIGHTING ILLINI

Conference: Big Ten.
Mailing Address: 1700 S. Fourth St., Champaign, IL
61820. **Website:** www.fightingillini.com.
Head Coach: Dan Hartleb. **Telephone:** (217) 244-8144.
Baseball SID: Ben Taylor. **Telephone:** (217) 244-5045. **Fax:**
(217) 333-5540.
Assistant Coaches: Drew Dickinson, *Eric Snider.
Telephone: (217) 244-5539.
Home Field: Illinois Field. **Seating Capacity:** 1,500.
Press Box Telephone: (217) 333-1227.

ILLINOIS STATE REDBIRDS

Conference: Missouri Valley.
Mailing Address: 211 Horton Field House, Campus
Box 7130, Normal, IL, 61790-7130. **Website:** www.gore-
dbirds.com.
Head Coach: Mark Kingston. **Telephone:** (309) 438-
5709. **Baseball SID:** Ronan O'Shea. **Telephone:** (309)
438-5746. **Fax:** (309) 438-5634.
Assistant Coaches: *Bo Durkac, Billy Mohl. **Telephone:**
(309) 438-5151.
Home Field: Duffy Bass Field. **Seating Capacity:** 2,000.
Outfield Dimensions: LF—330, CF—400, RF—330.

ILLINOIS-CHICAGO FLAMES

Conference: Horizon.
Mailing Address: 839 West Roosevelt Road, Chicago, IL
60608. **Website:** www.uicflames.com.
Head Coach: Mike Dee. **Telephone:** (312) 996-8645.
Baseball SID: Mike Laninga. **Telephone:** (312) 996-5881.
Fax: (312) 996-8349.
Assistant Coaches: *John Flood, Sean McDermott.
Telephone: (312) 355-1757.
Home Field: Les Miller Field. **Seating Capacity:** 1,500.
Outfield Dimensions: LF—330, CF—401, RF—330. **Press
Box Telephone:** (312) 355-1190.

INDIANA HOOSIERS

Conference: Big Ten.
Mailing Address: 1001 E. 17th St., Bloomington, IN
47408. **Website:** www.iuhoosiers.com.
Head Coach: Tracy Smith. **Telephone:** (812) 855-1680.
Baseball SID: Kyle Kuhlman. **Telephone:** (812) 855-4770.
Fax: (812) 855-9401.
Assistant Coaches: Ben Greenspan, *Ty Neal.
Telephone: (812) 855-9790.
Home Field: Bart Kaufman Field. **Seating Capacity:**
2,500. **Outfield Dimensions:** LF—330, CF—400, RF—340.

Press Box Telephone: (419) 308-8292.

INDIANA STATE SYCAMORES

Conference: Missouri Valley.
Mailing Address: 401 N 4th St., ISU Arena, Terre Haute, IN 47809. **Website:** www.gosycamores.com.
Head Coach: Rick Heller. **Telephone:** (812) 237-4051. **Baseball SID:** Danny Pfrank. **Telephone:** (812) 237-4159. **Fax:** (812) 237-4157.
Assistant Coaches: *Tyler Herbst, Brian Smiley. **Telephone:** (812) 237-4630.
Home Field: Bob Warn Field. **Seating Capacity:** 2000. **Outfield Dimensions:** LF—335, CF—395, RF—335. **Press Box Telephone:** (812) 237-4187.

IONA GAELS

Conference: Metro Atlantic.
Mailing Address: 715 North Ave., New Rochelle, NY 10801. **Website:** www.icgaels.com.
Head Coach: Pat Carey. **Telephone:** (914) 633-2319. **Baseball SID:** Brian Beyrer. **Telephone:** (914) 633-2334. **Fax:** (914) 633-2072.
Assistant Coaches: Rob DiToma, Scott McGrath. **Telephone:** (914) 633-2319.
Home Field: Salesian Field. **Seating Capacity:** 450. **Press Box Telephone:** (914) 497-3136.

IOWA HAWKEYES

Conference: Big Ten.
Mailing Address: 1 Elliott Drive, Iowa City, IA. **Website:** www.hawkeyesports.com.
Head Coach: Jack Dahm. **Telephone:** (319) 335-9743. **Baseball SID:** James Allan. **Telephone:** (319) 335-9411. **Fax:** (319) 335-9417.
Assistant Coaches: Jim Brownlee, *Zach Dillon. **Telephone:** (319) 335-9743.
Home Field: Duane Banks Field. **Seating Capacity:** 3,000. **Outfield Dimensions:** LF—329, CF—395, RF—329. **Press Box Telephone:** (319) 335-9520.

IPFW MASTODONS

Conference: Summit.
Mailing Address: 2101 E. Coliseum Blvd., Fort Wayne, IN 46805. **Website:** www.gomastodons.com.
Head Coach: Bobby Pierce. **Telephone:** (260) 481-5480. **Baseball SID:** Kit Stetzel. **Telephone:** (260) 481-6646. **Fax:** (260) 481-6002.
Assistant Coaches: *Grant Birely, Alex Rinearson. **Telephone:** (260) 481-5455.
Home Field: Mastodon Park. **Seating Capacity:** 1,000. **Outfield Dimensions:** LF—330, CF—405, RF—330. **Press Box Telephone:** (260) 402-6599.

JACKSON STATE TIGERS

Conference: Southwestern Athletic.
Mailing Address: JSU Box 18060, Jackson, MS 39217-0660. **Website:** www.jsutigers.com.
Head Coach: Omar Johnson. **Telephone:** (601) 979-3930. **Baseball SID:** Wesley Peterson. **Telephone:** (601) 979-5899.
Assistant Coaches: Chris Stamps. **Telephone:** (601) 979-3928.
Home Field: Robert "Bob" Braddy Sr Field. **Seating Capacity:** 600. **Outfield Dimensions:** LF—325, CF—401, RF—325.

JACKSONVILLE DOLPHINS

Conference: Atlantic Sun.
Mailing Address: 2800 University Blvd. N., Jacksonville, FL 32211. **Website:** www.judolphins.com.
Head Coach: Terry Alexander. **Telephone:** (904) 256-7412. **Baseball SID:** Tom Leonard. **Telephone:** (904) 256-7616. **Fax:** (904) 256-7424.
Assistant Coaches: Tim Montez, *Talmadge Nunarri. **Telephone:** (904) 256-7367.
Home Field: John Sessions Stadium. **Seating Capacity:** 3,000. **Outfield Dimensions:** LF—340, CF—405, RF—340. **Press Box Telephone:** (904) 256-7588.

JACKSONVILLE STATE GAMECOCKS

Conference: Ohio Valley.
Mailing Address: 700 Pelham Road North, Jacksonville, AL 36265. **Website:** www.jsugamecocksports.com.
Head Coach: Jim Case. **Telephone:** (256) 782-5367. **Baseball SID:** Greg Seitz. **Telephone:** (256) 782-5279. **Fax:** (256) 782-5958.
Assistant Coaches: Mike Murphree, *Brandon Romans. **Telephone:** (256) 782-8141.
Home Field: Rudy Abbott Field. **Seating Capacity:** 3,500. **Press Box Telephone:** (256) 782-5533.

JAMES MADISON DUKES

Conference: Colonial Athletic.
Mailing Address: 395 South High Street, Memorial Hall, Harrisonburg, VA 22801. **Website:** www.jmusports.com.
Head Coach: Spanky McFarland. **Telephone:** (540) 568-5510. **Baseball SID:** Kevin Warner. **Telephone:** (540) 568-4263. **Fax:** (540) 568-3703.
Assistant Coaches: Brandon Cohen, *Ted White. **Telephone:** (540) 568-3630.
Home Field: Eagle Field at Veterans Memorial Park. **Seating Capacity:** 1,200. **Outfield Dimensions:** LF—340, CF—400, RF—320. **Press Box Telephone:** (540) 568-6545.

KANSAS JAYHAWKS

Conference: Big 12.
Mailing Address: 1651 Naismith Drive, Lawrence, KS 66045. **Website:** www.kuathletics.com.
Head Coach: Ritch Price. **Telephone:** (785) 864-4196. **Baseball SID:** Mike Cummings. **Telephone:** (785) 864-3575. **Fax:** (785) 864-7944.
Assistant Coaches: *Ryan Graves, Ritchie Price. **Telephone:** (785) 864-7135.
Home Field: Hoglund Ballpark. **Seating Capacity:** 2,500. **Outfield Dimensions:** LF—330, CF—400, RF—330. **Press Box Telephone:** (785) 331-6307.

KANSAS STATE WILDCATS

Conference: Big 12.
Mailing Address: 1800 College Ave., Manhattan, KS 66502. **Website:** www.kstatesports.com.
Head Coach: Brad Hill. **Telephone:** (785) 532-6735. **Baseball SID:** Ryan Lackey. **Telephone:** (785) 532-7708. **Fax:** (785) 532-6093.
Assistant Coaches: *Mike Clement, Josh Reynolds. **Telephone:** (785) 532-6735.
Home Field: Tointon Family Stadium. **Seating Capacity:** 2,331. **Outfield Dimensions:** LF—340, CF—400, RF—325. **Press Box Telephone:** (785) 532-5801.

KENNESAW STATE OWLS

Conference: Atlantic Sun.
Mailing Address: 1000 Chastain Rd., Mailbox 0201, Kennesaw, GA 30144. **Website:** www.ksuowls.com.
Head Coach: Mike Sansing. **Telephone:** (770) 423-6264. **Baseball SID:** Brian Harper. **Telephone:** (770) 794-7789. **Fax:** (770) 423-6665.
Assistant Coaches: Kevin Erminio, *Derek Simmons. **Telephone:** (678) 797-2099.
Home Field: Stillwell Stadium. **Seating Capacity:** 1,200. **Outfield Dimensions:** LF—330, CF—400, RF—330.

KENT STATE GOLDEN FLASHES

Conference: Mid-American (East).
Mailing Address: 234 MAC Center, Kent, OH 44242. **Website:** www.kentstatesports.com.
Head Coach: Scott Stricklin. **Telephone:** (330) 672-8432. **Baseball SID:** Mollie Radzinski. **Telephone:** (330) 672-8419. **Fax:** (330) 672-2112.
Assistant Coaches: Mike Birkbeck, *Scott Daeley. **Telephone:** (330) 672-8433.
Home Field: Schoonover Stadium. **Seating Capacity:** 1,200. **Outfield Dimensions:** LF—320, CF—415, RF—320. **Press Box Telephone:** (330) 672-2110.

KENTUCKY WILDCATS

Conference: Southeastern (East).
Mailing Address: Commonwealth Stadium, Lexington, KY 40506. **Website:** www.ukathletics.com.
Head Coach: Gary Henderson. **Telephone:** (859) 257-2880. **Baseball SID:** Brent Ingram. **Telephone:** (859) 257-8504. **Fax:** (859) 323-4310.
Assistant Coaches: *Brad Bohannon, Brian Green. **Telephone:** (859) 257-3013.
Home Field: Cliff Hagan Stadium. **Seating Capacity:** 3,000. **Outfield Dimensions:** LF—340, CF—390, RF—310. **Press Box Telephone:** (859) 257-9011.

LA SALLE EXPLORERS

Conference: Atlantic 10.
Mailing Address: 1900 West Olney Avenue, Philadelphia, PA 19141. **Website:** www.goexplorers.com.
Head Coach: Mike Lake. **Telephone:** (215) 951-1995. **Baseball SID:** Paul Hembekides. **Telephone:** (215) 991-2886. **Fax:** (215) 951-1694.
Assistant Coaches: *John Duffy, Bryan Torresani. **Telephone:** (215) 951-1995.
Home Field: Hank DeVincent Field. **Seating Capacity:** 1,000.

LAFAYETTE LEOPARDS

Conference: Patriot.
Mailing Address: Kirby Sports Center, Pierce & Hamilton Streets, Easton, PA 18042. **Website:** www.goleopards.com.
Head Coach: Joe Kinney. **Telephone:** (610) 330-5476. **Baseball SID:** Mark Mohrman. **Telephone:** (610) 330-5003. **Fax:** (610) 330-5519.
Assistant Coaches: *Ian Law. **Telephone:** (610) 330-5945.
Home Field: Hilton Rahn '51 Field at Kamine Stadium. **Seating Capacity:** 500. **Outfield Dimensions:** LF—332, CF—403, RF—335.

LAMAR CARDINALS

Conference: Southland.

Mailing Address: P.O. Box 10066, Beaumont, TX 77710. **Website:** lamarcardinals.com.
Head Coach: Jim Gilligan. **Telephone:** (409) 880-8315. **Baseball SID:** Clay Trainum. **Telephone:** (409) 880-7845. **Fax:** (409) 880-2338.
Assistant Coaches: Scott Hatten, *Jim Ricklefson. **Telephone:** (409) 880-8974.
Home Field: Vincent-Beck Stadium. **Seating Capacity:** 3,500. **Press Box Telephone:** (409) 880-8327.

LEHIGH MOUNTAIN HAWKS

Conference: Patriot.
Mailing Address: 641 Taylor St., Bethlehem, PA 18015. **Website:** www.lehighsports.com.
Head Coach: Sean Leary. **Telephone:** (610) 758-4315. **Baseball SID:** Chris Martrich. **Telephone:** (610) 758-5101. **Fax:** (610) 758-4407.
Assistant Coaches: *John Fugett. **Telephone:** (610) 758-6629.
Home Field: Lehigh Field. **Seating Capacity:** 500. **Outfield Dimensions:** LF—320, CF—400, RF—320.

LIBERTY FLAMES

Conference: Big South.
Mailing Address: 1971 University Blvd., Lynchburg, VA 24502. **Website:** www.libertyflames.com.
Head Coach: Jim Toman. **Telephone:** (434) 582-2305. **Baseball SID:** Ryan Bomberger. **Telephone:** (434) 582-2605. **Fax:** (434) 582-2205.
Assistant Coaches: *Jason Murray, Garrett Quinn. **Telephone:** (434) 582-2119.
Home Field: Worthington Stadium. **Seating Capacity:** 1,000. **Press Box Telephone:** (434) 582-2914.

LIPSCOMB BISONS

Conference: Atlantic Sun.
Mailing Address: One University Park Drive, Nashville, TN 37204. **Website:** www.lipscombsports.com.
Head Coach: Jeff Forehand. **Telephone:** (615) 966-5716. **Baseball SID:** Jamie Gilliam. **Telephone:** (615) 966-5166. **Fax:** (615) 966-1806.
Assistant Coaches: Paul Phillips, *Tyler Shrout. **Telephone:** (615) 966-5879.
Home Field: Dugan Field. **Seating Capacity:** 1,500. **Outfield Dimensions:** LF—330, CF—405, RF—330. **Press Box Telephone:** (615) 479-6133.

LONG BEACH STATE DIRTBAGS

Conference: Big West.
Mailing Address: 1250 Bellflower Blvd., Long Beach, CA 90840. **Website:** www.longbeachstate.com.
Head Coach: Troy Buckley. **Telephone:** (562) 985-4661. **Baseball SID:** Roger Kirk. **Telephone:** (562) 985-7565. **Fax:** (562) 985-1549.
Assistant Coaches: Shawn Gilbert, *Jesse Zepeda. **Telephone:** (562) 985-7548.
Home Field: Blair Field. **Seating Capacity:** 3,000. **Outfield Dimensions:** LF—348, CF—400, RF—348. **Press Box Telephone:** (562) 505-0975.

LONG ISLAND-BROOKLYN BLACKBIRDS

Conference: Northeast.
Mailing Address: 1 University Plaza, Brooklyn, NY 11201. **Website:** www.liuathletics.com.
Head Coach: Donald Maines. **Telephone:** (718) 488-1538. **Baseball SID:** Daniel Lobacz. **Telephone:** (718) 488-1420. **Fax:** (718) 488-1669.

Assistant Coaches: Jesse Marsh, *Craig Noto. **Telephone:** (718) 488-1000.
    Home Field: LIU Field. **Seating Capacity:** 600. **Outfield Dimensions:** LF—315, CF—410, RF—310.

LONGWOOD LANCERS

Conference: Big South.
Mailing Address: 201 High Street Farmville, VA 23901. **Website:** www.longwoodlancers.com.
Head Coach: Buddy Bolding. **Telephone:** (434) 395-2352. **Baseball SID:** Greg Prouty. **Telephone:** (434) 395-2097. **Fax:** (434) 395-2568.
Assistant Coaches: Jon Benick, *Brian McCullough. **Telephone:** (434) 395-2351.
    Home Field: Charles Buddy Bolding Stadium. **Seating Capacity:** 500. **Outfield Dimensions:** LF—335, CF—400, RF—335. **Press Box Telephone:** (434) 395-2710.

LOUISIANA STATE FIGHTING TIGERS

Conference: Southeastern (West).
Mailing Address: Athletic Administration Bldg., Baton Rouge, LA 70803. **Website:** www.lsusports.net.
Head Coach: Paul Mainieri. **Telephone:** (225) 578-4148. **Baseball SID:** Bill Franques. **Telephone:** (225) 578-2527. **Fax:** (225) 578-1861.
Assistant Coaches: Alan Dunn, *Javi Sanchez. **Telephone:** (225) 578-2524.
    Home Field: Alex Box Stadium. **Seating Capacity:** 10,326. **Outfield Dimensions:** LF—330, CF—405, RF—330. **Press Box Telephone:** (225) 578-4149.

LOUISIANA TECH BULLDOGS

Conference: Western Athletic.
Mailing Address: Louisiana Tech University, P.O. Box 3166, Ruston, LA 71272. **Website:** www.latechsports.com.
Head Coach: Wade Simoneaux. **Telephone:** (318) 257-5318. **Baseball SID:** Anna Claire Thomas. **Telephone:** (318) 257-5314. **Fax:** (318) 257-3757.
Assistant Coaches: Fran Andermann, *Brian Rountree. **Telephone:** (318) 257-5312.
    Home Field: J.C. Love Field at Pat Patterson Park. **Seating Capacity:** 3,000. **Outfield Dimensions:** LF—315, CF—385, RF—325. **Press Box Telephone:** (318) 257-3144.

LOUISIANA-LAFAYETTE RAGIN' CAJUNS

Conference: Sun Belt.
Mailing Address: 201 Reinhardt Dr., Lafayette, LA 70506. **Website:** www.ragincajuns.com.
Head Coach: Tony Robichaux. **Telephone:** (337) 482-6189. **Baseball SID:** Matt Hebert. **Telephone:** (337) 482-6331. **Fax:** (337) 482-6529.
Assistant Coaches: Anthony Babineaux, *Matt Deggs. **Telephone:** (337) 482-6093.
    Home Field: ML 'Tigue' Moore Field. **Seating Capacity:** 3,600. **Press Box Telephone:** (337) 851-2255.

LOUISIANA-MONROE WARHAWKS

Conference: Sun Belt.
Mailing Address: 308 Warhawk Way, Monroe, LA 71209. **Website:** www.ulmwarhawks.com.
Head Coach: Jeff Schexnaider. **Telephone:** (318) 342-5396. **Baseball SID:** Tony Jones. **Telephone:** (318) 342-5461.
Assistant Coaches: *Cory Barton, Justin Hill. **Telephone:** (318) 342-3589.
    Home Field: Warhawk Field. **Seating Capacity:** 2,000. **Outfield Dimensions:** LF—330, CF—405, RF—330. **Press**

Box Telephone: (318) 342-5476.

LOUISVILLE CARDINALS

Conference: Big East.
Mailing Address: 215 Central Ave., Louisville, KY 40292. **Website:** www.uoflsports.com.
Head Coach: Dan McDonnell. **Telephone:** (502) 852-0103. **Baseball SID:** Garett Wall. **Telephone:** (502) 852-3088. **Fax:** (502) 852-7401.
Assistant Coaches: *Chris Lemonis, Roger Williams. **Telephone:** (502) 852-3929.
    Home Field: Jim Patterson Stadium. **Seating Capacity:** 4,000. **Outfield Dimensions:** LF—330, CF—402, RF—330. **Press Box Telephone:** (502) 852-3700.

LOYOLA MARYMOUNT LIONS

Conference: West Coast.
Mailing Address: 1 LMU Drive, Los Angeles, CA 90045. **Website:** www.lmulions.com.
Head Coach: Jason Gill. **Telephone:** (310) 338-2949. **Baseball SID:** Tyler Geivett. **Telephone:** (310) 338-7638. **Fax:** (310) 338-2703.
Assistant Coaches: Dan Ricabal, *Bryant Ward. **Telephone:** (310) 338-4511.
    Home Field: Page Stadium. **Seating Capacity:** 600. **Outfield Dimensions:** LF—326, CF—413, RF—330. **Press Box Telephone:** (310) 338-3046.

MAINE BLACK BEARS

Conference: America East.
Mailing Address: 5747 Memorial Gym, Orono, ME 04469. **Website:** www.goblackbears.com.
Head Coach: Steve Trimper. **Telephone:** (207) 581-1090. **Baseball SID:** Laura Reed. **Telephone:** (207) 581-3646. **Fax:** (207) 581-3297.
Assistant Coaches: Billy Cather, *Jason Spaulding. **Telephone:** (207) 581-1097.
    Home Field: Mahaney Diamond. **Seating Capacity:** 4,400. **Outfield Dimensions:** LF—330, CF—400, RF—330. **Press Box Telephone:** (207) 581-1049.

MANHATTAN JASPERS

Conference: Metro Atlantic.
Mailing Address: 4513 Manhattan College Parkway, Riverdale NY 10471. **Website:** www.gojaspers.com.
Head Coach: Jim Duffy. **Telephone:** (718) 862-7821. **Baseball SID:** Steve Dombroski. **Telephone:** (718) 862-7228. **Fax:** (718) 862-8020.
Assistant Coaches: Elvys Quezada, *Rene Ruiz. **Telephone:** (718) 862-7218.
    Home Field: Van Cortlandt Park. **Seating Capacity:** 1000. **Outfield Dimensions:** LF—330, CF—400, RF—330.

MARIST RED FOXES

Conference: Metro Atlantic.
Mailing Address: 3399 North Road, Poughkeepsie, NY 12601. **Website:** www.goredfoxes.com.
Head Coach: Chris Tracz. **Telephone:** (845) 575-3000 Ext 2570. **Baseball SID:** Mike Ferraro. **Telephone:** (845) 575-3321.
Assistant Coaches: Justin Haywood, *Thomas Seay. **Telephone:** (845) 575-3000 Ext 7583.
    Home Field: McCann Field. **Seating Capacity:** 1,000. **Press Box Telephone:** (914) 456-3447.

MARSHALL THUNDERING HERD

Conference: Conference USA.

Mailing Address: P.O. Box 1360, Huntington, WV 25715. **Website:** www.herdzone.com.
Head Coach: Jeff Waggoner. **Telephone:** (304) 696-5277. **Baseball SID:** Daniel Manget. **Telephone:** (304) 696-5276. **Fax:** (304) 696-2325.
Assistant Coaches: *Tim Donnelly, Joe Renner. **Telephone:** (304) 696-3885.
Home Field: Appalachian Power Park. **Seating Capacity:** 4,500. **Outfield Dimensions:** LF—330, CF—400, RF—320.

MARYLAND TERRAPINS

Conference: Atlantic Coast (Atlantic).
Mailing Address: Comcast Center, 1 Terrapin Trail, College Park, MD 20742. **Website:** www.umterps.com.
Head Coach: John Szefc. **Telephone:** (301) 314-7003. **Baseball SID:** Matt Bertram. **Telephone:** (301) 314-8093. **Fax:** (301) 314-9094.
Assistant Coaches: Jim Belanger, *Rob Vaughn. **Telephone:** (301) 314-1286.
Home Field: Shipley Field at Bob "Turtle" Smith Stadium. **Seating Capacity:** 2,500. **Outfield Dimensions:** LF—320, CF—380, RF—325. **Press Box Telephone:** (301) 314-0379.

MARYLAND-BALTIMORE COUNTY RETRIEVERS

Conference: America East.
Mailing Address: Department of Athletics, RAC Arena, 1000 Hilltop Circle, Baltimore, MD 21250. **Website:** www.umbcretrievers.com.
Head Coach: Bob Mumma. **Telephone:** (410) 455-2239. **Baseball SID:** Daniel LaHatte. **Telephone:** (410) 455-1530. **Fax:** (410) 455-3994.
Assistant Coaches: *Liam Bowen, Larry Williams. **Telephone:** (410) 455-5845.
Home Field: Baseball Factory Field. **Seating Capacity:** 1,000. **Outfield Dimensions:** LF—330, CF—365, RF—340. **Press Box Telephone:** (443) 928-3343.

MARYLAND-EASTERN SHORE HAWKS

Conference: Mid-Eastern.
Mailing Address: 1 College Backbone Road William P. Hytche Athletic Center, Princess Anne, MD 21853. **Website:** www.umeshawks.com.
Head Coach: Pedro Swann. **Telephone:** (410) 651-8158. **Baseball SID:** Dave Vatz. **Telephone:** (410) 621-1108. **Fax:** (410) 651-7514.
Assistant Coaches: *John O'Neil. **Telephone:** (410) 651-8908.
Home Field: Hawks Stadium. **Seating Capacity:** 1,000. **Outfield Dimensions:** LF—340, CF—400, RF—340.

MASSACHUSETTS MINUTEMEN

Conference: Atlantic 10.
Mailing Address: 131 Commonwealth Ave., Amherst, MA 01003. **Website:** umassathletics.com.
Head Coach: Mike Stone. **Telephone:** (413) 545-3120. **Baseball SID:** Jillian Jakuba. **Telephone:** (413) 577-0053. **Fax:** (413) 545-1404.
Assistant Coaches: *Mike Sweeney. **Telephone:** (413) 545-3766.
Home Field: Earl Lorden Field. **Seating Capacity:** 1,500. **Press Box Telephone:** (413) 420-3116.

McNEESE STATE COWBOYS

Conference: Southland.
Mailing Address: Box 92735, McNeese State, Lake Charles, LA 70609. **Website:** mcneesesports.com.
Head Coach: Terry Burrows. **Telephone:** (337) 475-5484. **Baseball SID:** Matthew Bonnette. **Telephone:** (337) 475-5207. **Fax:** (337) 475-5202.
Assistant Coaches: *Bubbs Merrill, Matt Collins. **Telephone:** (337) 475-5903, (337) 475-5904.
Home Field: Cowboy Diamond. **Seating Capacity:** 2,000. **Press Box Telephone:** (337) 475-8007.

MEMPHIS TIGERS

Conference: Conference USA.
Mailing Address: 207 Athletic Office Bldg., Memphis TN 38152. **Website:** www.gotigersgo.com.
Head Coach: Daron Schoenrock. **Telephone:** (901) 678-4137. **Baseball SID:** Mark Taylor. **Telephone:** (901) 678-5108. **Fax:** (901) 678-4134.
Assistant Coaches: Fred Corral, *Clay Greene. **Telephone:** (901) 678-4139.
Home Field: FedEx Park. **Seating Capacity:** 2,000. **Outfield Dimensions:** LF—318, CF—379, RF—317. **Press Box Telephone:** (901) 678-1301.

MERCER BEARS

Conference: Atlantic Sun.
Mailing Address: 1400 Coleman Ave., Macon, GA 31207. **Website:** www.mercerbears.com.
Head Coach: Craig Gibson. **Telephone:** (478) 301-2396. **Baseball SID:** Jason Farhadi. **Telephone:** (478) 301-5218. **Fax:** (478) 301-5350.
Assistant Coaches: *Brent Shade. **Telephone:** (478) 301-2738.
Home Field: Claude Smith Field. **Seating Capacity:** 500. **Outfield Dimensions:** LF—330, CF—400, RF—320. **Press Box Telephone:** (478) 301-2339.

MIAMI HURRICANES

Conference: Atlantic Coast (Coastal).
Mailing Address: 6201 San Amaro Dr., Coral Gables, FL 33146. **Website:** www.hurricanesports.com.
Head Coach: Jim Morris. **Telephone:** (617) 284-4171. **Baseball SID:** Camron Ghorbi. **Telephone:** (305) 284-3230. **Fax:** (305) 284-2807.
Assistant Coaches: J.D. Arteaga, *Gino DiMare. **Telephone:** (305) 284-4171.
Home Field: Alex Rodriguez Park at Mark Light Field. **Seating Capacity:** 4,999. **Outfield Dimensions:** LF—330, CF—400, RF—330. **Press Box Telephone:** (305) 284-8192.

MIAMI (OHIO) REDHAWKS

Conference: Mid-American (East).
Mailing Address: 120 Withrow Court, Oxford, OH 45056. **Website:** www.muredhawks.com.
Head Coach: Dan Simonds. **Telephone:** (513) 529-6631. **Baseball SID:** Jim Stephan. **Telephone:** (513) 529-4330. **Fax:** (513) 529-6729.
Assistant Coaches: *Jeremy Ison, Tom Kinkelaar. **Telephone:** (513) 529-7293.
Home Field: McKie Field at Hayden Park. **Seating Capacity:** 1,000. **Press Box Telephone:** (513) 529-4331.

MICHIGAN WOLVERINES

Conference: Big Ten.
Mailing Address: 1000 S State St., Ann Arbor, MI 48109. **Website:** www.mgoblue.com.
Head Coach: Erik Bakich. **Telephone:** (734) 647-4614. **Baseball SID:** Kent Reichert. **Telephone:** (734) 647-1726. **Fax:** (734) 647-1188.

Assistant Coaches: Sean Kenny, *Nick Schnabel. Telephone: (734) 647-4585.
Home Field: Wilpon Complex/Fisher Stadium. Seating Capacity: 3,500. Outfield Dimensions: LF—312, CF—395, RF—320. Press Box Telephone: (734) 548-0878.

MICHIGAN STATE SPARTANS

Conference: Big Ten.
Mailing Address: 304 Jenison Field House, East Lansing, MI 48824. Website: www.msuspartans.com.
Head Coach: Jake Boss, Jr. Telephone: (517) 355-4486.
Baseball SID: Ben Phlegar. Telephone: (517) 355-2271. Fax: (517) 353-9636.
Assistant Coaches: *Graham Sikes, Mark Van Ameyde. Telephone: (517) 355-3419.
Home Field: McLane Stadium at Kobs Field. Seating Capacity: 3,000. Outfield Dimensions: LF—340, CF—403, RF—305. Press Box Telephone: (517) 353-3009.

MIDDLE TENNESSEE STATE BLUE RAIDERS

Conference: Sun Belt.
Mailing Address: MTSU P.O. Box 90, Murfreesboro, TN 37132. Website: www.goblueraiders.com.
Head Coach: Jim McGuire. Telephone: (615) 898-2961.
Baseball SID: Leslie Wilhite. Telephone: (615) 904-8115. Fax: (615) 898-5626.
Assistant Coaches: *Scott Hall, Skylar Meade. Telephone: (615) 904-8796.
Home Field: Reese Smith Jr. Field. Seating Capacity: 2,300. Outfield Dimensions: LF—330, CF—390, RF—330. Press Box Telephone: (615) 898-2117.

MINNESOTA GOLDEN GOPHERS

Conference: Big Ten.
Mailing Address: University of Minnesota 516 15th Avenue S.E., Minneapolis, MN 55455. Website: www.gophersports.com.
Head Coach: John Anderson. Telephone: (612) 625-4057. Baseball SID: Michelle Traen. Telephone: (612) 624-0522.
Assistant Coaches: *Rob Fornasiere, Todd Oakes. Telephone: (612) 625-3568.
Home Field: Siebert Field. Seating Capacity: 1,400.

MISSISSIPPI REBELS

Conference: Southeastern (West).
Mailing Address: Ole Miss Baseball Office, University Place, University, MS 38677. Website: www.olemisssports.com.
Head Coach: Mike Bianco. Telephone: (662) 915-6643.
Baseball SID: Bill Bunting. Telephone: (662) 915-1083. Fax: (662) 915-7006.
Assistant Coaches: Cliff Godwin, *Carl Lafferty. Telephone: (662) 915-6643.
Home Field: Oxford-University Stadium. Seating Capacity: 10,323. Outfield Dimensions: LF—330, CF—390, RF—330. Press Box Telephone: (662) 236-1931.

MISSISSIPPI STATE BULLDOGS

Conference: Southeastern (West).
Mailing Address: Box 5327, Mississippi State, MS 39762. Website: www.mstateathletics.com.
Head Coach: John Cohen. Telephone: (662) 325-3597.
Baseball SID: Joe Dier. Telephone: (662) 325-8040. Fax: (662) 325-3600.
Assistant Coaches: *Nick Mingione, Butch Thompson. Telephone: (662) 325-3597.

Home Field: Dudy Noble Field. Seating Capacity: 15,000. Outfield Dimensions: LF—330, CF—390, RF—326. Press Box Telephone: (662) 325-3776.

MISSISSIPPI VALLEY STATE DELTA DEVILS

Conference: Southwestern Athletic.
Mailing Address: 14000 Hwy. 82 West, Itta Bena, MS 38941. Website: www.mvsu.edu.
Head Coach: Doug Shanks. Telephone: (662) 254-3834. Baseball SID: Kenneth Mister. Telephone: (662) 254-3011. Fax: (662) 254-3639.
Assistant Coaches: Aaron Stevens, *Luke Walker. Telephone: 662-254-3342.
Home Field: Shanks Field. Seating Capacity: 300. Outfield Dimensions: LF—334, CF—410, RF—347.

MISSOURI TIGERS

Conference: Southeastern (East).
Mailing Address: 100 MATC, Columbia, MO 65211. Website: www.mutigers.com.
Head Coach: Tim Jamieson. Telephone: (573) 882-1917. Baseball SID: Shawn Davis. Telephone: (573) 882-0711.
Assistant Coaches: Matt Hobbs, *Kerrick Jackson. Telephone: (573) 882-0731.
Home Field: Simmons Field. Seating Capacity: 3,000. Outfield Dimensions: LF—330, CF—400, RF—340. Press Box Telephone: (573) 884-8912.

MISSOURI STATE BEARS

Conference: Missouri Valley.
Mailing Address: 901 S. National, Springfield, MO 65897. Website: www.missouristatebears.com.
Head Coach: Keith Guttin. Telephone: (417) 836-4497.
Baseball SID: Eric Doennig. Telephone: (417) 836-4586. Fax: (417) 836-4868.
Assistant Coaches: Paul Evans, *Brent Thomas. Telephone: (417) 836-4496.
Home Field: Hammons Field. Seating Capacity: 8,000. Outfield Dimensions: LF—315, CF—400, RF—330. Press Box Telephone: (417) 832-3029.

MONMOUTH HAWKS

Conference: Northeast.
Mailing Address: 400 Cedar Ave., West Long Branch, NJ 07764. Website: .
Head Coach: Dean Ehehalt. Telephone: (732) 263-5186. Baseball SID: Greg Ott. Telephone: (732) 263-5834. Fax: (732) 571-3535.
Assistant Coaches: George Brown, *Rick Oliveri. Telephone: (732) 263-5347.
Home Field: MU Baseball Field. Seating Capacity: 500. Outfield Dimensions: LF—325, CF—395, RF—320. Press Box Telephone: (732) 263-5401.

MOREHEAD STATE EAGLES

Conference: Ohio Valley.
Mailing Address: 156 AAC Morehead, KY 40351. Website: www.msueagles.com.
Head Coach: Mike McGuire. Telephone: (606) 783-2882. Baseball SID: Brent Fritzmeier. Telephone: (606) 783-5481. Fax: (606) 783-5035.
Assistant Coaches: Adam Brown, *Jeff Stanek. Telephone: (606) 783-2881.
Home Field: Allen Field. Seating Capacity: 750. Outfield Dimensions: LF—315, CF—365, RF—320.

MOUNT ST. MARY'S MOUNTAINEERS

Conference: Northeast.
Mailing Address: 16300 Old Emmitsburg Rd., Emmitsburg, MD 21727. **Website:** www.mountathletics.com.
Head Coach: Scott Thomson. **Telephone:** (301) 447-3806. **Baseball SID:** Mark Vandergrift. **Telephone:** (301) 447-5384. **Fax:** (301) 447-5300.
Assistant Coach: David Brooks, Greg White. **Telephone:** (301) 447-3806.
Home Field: ET Straw Family Stadium.

MURRAY STATE TOUROUGHBREDS

Conference: Ohio Valley.
Mailing Address: 217 Stewart Stadium, Murray, KY. **Website:** goracers.com.
Head Coach: Rob McDonald. **Telephone:** (270) 809-4892. **Baseball SID:** John Brush. **Telephone:** (270) 809-7044. **Fax:** (270) 809-6814.
Assistant Coaches: *Chris Cole, Dan Skirka. **Telephone:** (270) 809-3475.
Home Field: Johnny Reagan Field. **Seating Capacity:** 800. **Press Box Telephone:** (270) 809-5650.

NAVY MIDSHIPMEN

Conference: Patriot.
Mailing Address: 566 Brownson Rd., Annapolis, MD 21402. **Website:** www.navysports.com.
Head Coach: Paul Kostacopoulos. **Telephone:** (410) 293-5571. **Baseball SID:** Jeff Barnes. **Telephone:** (410) 293-8771. **Fax:** (410) 293-8954.
Assistant Coaches: Ryan Mau, *Matt Reynolds. **Telephone:** (410) 293-5428.
Home Field: Max Bishop Stadium. **Seating Capacity:** 1,500. **Outfield Dimensions:** LF—322, CF—397, RF—304. **Press Box Telephone:** (410) 293-5430.

NEBRASKA CORNHUSKERS

Conference: Big 12.
Mailing Address: One Memorial Stadium, Lincoln NE 68588. **Website:** www.huskers.com.
Head Coach: Darin Erstad. **Telephone:** (402) 472-2269. **Baseball SID:** Jeremy Foote. **Telephone:** (402) 472-7778. **Fax:** (402) 472-2005.
Assistant Coaches: Will Bolt, *Ted Silva. **Telephone:** (402) 472-2269.
Home Field: Hawks Field at Haymarket Park. **Seating Capacity:** 8,486. **Outfield Dimensions:** LF—335, CF—395, RF—325. **Press Box Telephone:** (402) 472-6861.

NEBRASKA-OMAHA MAVERICKS

Conference: Summit.
Mailing Address: 6001 Dodge Street, Omaha, NE, 68182. **Website:** www.omavs.com.
Head Coach: Bob Herold. **Telephone:** (402) 554-3388. **Baseball SID:** Bonnie Ryan. **Telephone:** (402) 554-3267. **Fax:** (402) 554-2555.
Assistant Coaches: *Chris Gadsden, Evan Porter. **Telephone:** (402) 554-3388.
Home Field: Ballpark at Boys Town.

NEVADA WOLF PACK

Conference: Mountain West.
Mailing Address: 1664 North Virginia St., Reno, NV 89557. **Website:** www.nevadawolfpack.com.
Head Coach: Gary Powers. **Telephone:** (775) 682-6978.

Baseball SID: Jack Kuestermeyer. **Telephone:** (775) 682-6984. **Fax:** (775) 784-4387.
Assistant Coaches: Pat Flury, *Buddy Gouldsmith. **Telephone:** (775) 682-6979.
Home Field: Peccole Park. **Seating Capacity:** 3,000. **Outfield Dimensions:** LF—340, CF—401, RF—340. **Press Box Telephone:** (775) 784-1585.

NEVADA-LAS VEGAS REBELS

Conference: Mountain West.
Mailing Address: 4505 S. Maryland Parkway, Las Vegas, NV 89154. **Website:** www.unlvrebels.com.
Head Coach: Tim Chambers. **Telephone:** (702) 895-3499. **Baseball SID:** Sage Sammons. **Telephone:** (702) 895-3764. **Fax:** (702) 895-0989.
Assistant Coaches: *Kevin Higgins, Stan Stolte. **Telephone:** (702) 895-3835.
Home Field: Earl E Wilson Stadium. **Seating Capacity:** 3,000. **Outfield Dimensions:** LF—335, CF—400, RF—335. **Press Box Telephone:** (702) 739-1595.

NEW JERSEY TECH HIGHLANDERS

Conference: Great West.
Mailing Address: NJIT University Heights, Newark, NJ 07102. **Website:** www.njithighlanders.com.
Head Coach: Brian Guiliana. **Telephone:** (973) 596-5827. **Baseball SID:** Tim Camp. **Telephone:** (973) 596-8461. **Fax:** (973) 596-8295.
Assistant Coaches: *Robbie McClellan, Grant Neary. **Telephone:** (973) 596-8396.
Home Field: Riverfront Stadium. **Seating Capacity:** 6,500.

NEW MEXICO LOBOS

Conference: Mountain West.
Mailing Address: Colleen J. Maloof Administration Building, 1 University of New Mexico, MSC04 2680, Albuquerque, NM 87131. **Website:** www.golobos.com.
Head Coach: Ray Birmingham. **Telephone:** (505) 925-5725. **Baseball SID:** Terry Kelly. **Telephone:** (505) 925-5520. **Fax:** (505) 925-5609.
Assistant Coaches: *Ken Jacome, Dan Spencer. **Telephone:** (505) 925-5725.
Home Field: Lobo Field. **Seating Capacity:** 1,000. **Outfield Dimensions:** LF—350, CF—420, RF—350.

NEW MEXICO STATE AGGIES

Conference: Western Athletic.
Mailing Address: P.O. Box 30001, Dept 3145, Las Cruces NM 88003. **Website:** www.nmstatesports.com.
Head Coach: Rocky Ward. **Telephone:** (575) 646-5813. **Baseball SID:** Eddie Morelos. **Telephone:** (575) 646-1885. **Fax:** (575) 646-2425.
Assistant Coaches: *Mike Evans, Nate Shaver. **Telephone:** (575) 646-7693.
Home Field: Presley Askew Field. **Seating Capacity:** 1,000. **Outfield Dimensions:** LF—335, CF—400, RF—335. **Press Box Telephone:** (575) 646-5100.

NEW ORLEANS PRIVATEERS

Conference: Independent.
Mailing Address: Lakefront Arena, Baseball Office, 2000 Lakeshore Dr, New Orleans, LA 70148. **Website:** www.unoprivateers.com.
Head Coach: Bruce Peddie. **Telephone:** (504) 280-7253. **Baseball SID:** Jason Plotkin. **Telephone:** (504) 280-6284.

Assistant Coaches: Justin Garcia, *James Jurries.
Home Field: Maestri Field. **Seating Capacity:** 600.
Outfield Dimensions: LF—330, CF—405, RF—330.

NEW YORK INSTUTE OF TECHNOLOGY BEARS

Conference: Great West.
Mailing Address: Sports Complex, Northern Blvd., P.O. Box 8000, Old Westbury, NY 11568. **Website:** www.nyit.edu/athletics.
Head Coach: Bob Malvagna. **Telephone:** (516) 686-7513. **Baseball SID:** Sabrina Polidoro. **Telephone:** (516) 686-7504. **Fax:** (516) 686-1219.
Assistant Coaches: *Chris Rojas. **Telephone:** (516) 686-7513.
Home Field: President's Field. **Seating Capacity:** 500. **Outfield Dimensions:** LF—315, CF—395, RF—315. **Press Box Telephone:** (516) 686-7886.

NIAGARA PURPLE EAGLES

Conference: Metro Atlantic.
Mailing Address: P.O. Box 2009, UL Gallagher Ctr., Niagara University, NY 14109. **Website:** www.purpleeagles.com.
Head Coach: Rob McCoy. **Telephone:** (716) 286-7361. **Baseball SID:** Bob Vail. **Telephone:** (716) 286-8586. **Fax:** (716) 286-8609.
Assistant Coaches: *Matt Spatafora, Jeff Ziemecki. **Telephone:** (716) 286-8624.
Home Field: Sal Maglie Stadium. **Seating Capacity:** 4,000. **Outfield Dimensions:** LF—325, CF—408, RF—325.

NICHOLLS STATE COLONELS

Conference: Southland.
Mailing Address: www.geauxcolonels.com. **Website:** www.geauxcolonels.com.
Head Coach: Seth Thibodeaux. **Telephone:** (985) 449-7149. **Baseball SID:** Clyde Verdin. **Telephone:** (985) 448-4813. **Fax:** (985) 448-4814.
Assistant Coaches: Rudy Darrow, *Chris Prothro. **Telephone:** (985) 448-4808.
Home Field: Ray E. Didier Field. **Seating Capacity:** 2,200. **Outfield Dimensions:** LF—330, CF—405, RF—330. **Press Box Telephone:** (985) 448-4794.

NORFOLK STATE SPARTANS

Conference: Mid-Eastern Athletic.
Mailing Address: 700 Park Ave., Norfolk, VA 23504. **Website:** www.nsuspartans.com.
Head Coach: Claudell Clark. **Telephone:** (757) 676-3082. **Baseball SID:** Matt Michalec. **Telephone:** (757) 823-2628. **Fax:** (757) 823-8218.
Assistant Coaches: Joey Seal. **Telephone:** (757) 812-2409.
Home Field: Marty L. Miller Field. **Seating Capacity:** 1,500. **Outfield Dimensions:** LF—330, CF—404, RF—318. **Press Box Telephone:** (757) 823-8196.

NORTH CAROLINA TAR HEELS

Conference: Atlantic Coast (Coastal).
Mailing Address: P.O. Box 2126, Chapel Hill, NC 27515. **Website:** www.goheels.com.
Head Coach: Mike Fox. **Telephone:** (919) 962-2351. **Baseball SID:** Dave Schmidt. **Telephone:** (919) 962-0084. **Fax:** (919) 962-0612.
Assistant Coaches: Scott Forbes, *Scott Jackson. **Telephone:** (919) 962-5451.
Home Field: Bryson Field at Boshamer Stadium.

Seating Capacity: 4,500. **Outfield Dimensions:** LF—325, CF—400, RF—330. **Press Box Telephone:** (919) 962-3509.

NORTH CAROLINA A&T AGGIES

Conference: Mid-Eastern Athletic.
Mailing Address: 1601 E. Market Street, Greensboro, NC 27411. **Website:** www.ncataggies.com.
Head Coach: Joel Sanchez. **Telephone:** (336) 285-4272. **Baseball SID:** Kristin Pratt. **Telephone:** (336) 334-7141. **Fax:** (336) 334-7181.
Assistant Coaches: Jeremy Jones, *Wes Timmons. **Telephone:** (336) 285-4272.
Home Field: War Memorial Stadium. **Seating Capacity:** 2,000. **Press Box Telephone:** (336) 328-6710.

NORTH CAROLINA CENTRAL EAGLES

Conference: Mid-Eastern Athletic.
Mailing Address: 1801 Fayetteville Street, Durham, NC 27707. **Website:** www.nccueaglepride.com.
Head Coach: Jim Koerner. **Telephone:** (919) 530-6723. **Baseball SID:** Chris Hooks. **Telephone:** (919) 530-6017. **Fax:** (919) 530-5426.
Assistant Coaches: Tyler Hanson, *Jerry Shank. **Telephone:** (919) 530-5439.
Home Field: Durham Athletic Park. **Seating Capacity:** 2,000. **Outfield Dimensions:** LF—330, CF—395, RF—290.

NORTH CAROLINA STATE WOLFPACK

Conference: Atlantic Coast (Atlantic).
Mailing Address: 1081 Varsity Drive, Raleigh, NC 27695. **Website:** gopack.com.
Head Coach: Elliott Avent. **Telephone:** (919) 515-3613. **Baseball SID:** Cavan Fosnes. **Telephone:** (919) 515-1180. **Fax:** (919) 515-3624.
Assistant Coaches: *Chris Hart, Tom Holliday. **Telephone:** (919) 515-3613.
Home Field: Doak Field at Dail Park. **Seating Capacity:** 3,000. **Press Box Telephone:** (919) 819-3035.

UNC ASHEVILLE BULLDOGS

Conference: Big South.
Mailing Address: Justice Center, CPO #2600, One University Heights, Asheville, NC 28804. **Website:** www.uncabulldogs.com.
Head Coach: Tom Smith. **Telephone:** (828) 251-6920. **Baseball SID:** Mike Gore. **Telephone:** (828) 575-6649. **Fax:** (828) 251-6923.
Assistant Coaches: *Jeremey Plexico, Brent Walsh. **Telephone:** (828) 251-6903.
Home Field: Greenwood Field. **Seating Capacity:** 1,000. **Outfield Dimensions:** LF—330, CF—400, RF—330.

UNC GREENSBORO SPARTANS

Conference: Southern.
Mailing Address: 1408 Walker Ave., 337 HHP Building, P.O. Box 26168, Greensboro, NC 27403. **Website:** www.uncgspartans.com.
Head Coach: Link Jarrett. **Telephone:** (336) 334-3247. **Baseball SID:** Chip Welch. **Telephone:** (336) 334-5615. **Fax:** (336) 334-3182.
Assistant Coaches: *Matt Boykin, Jerry Edwards. **Telephone:** (336) 334-3247.
Home Field: UNCG Baseball Stadium. **Seating Capacity:** 3,500. **Outfield Dimensions:** LF—340, CF—405, RF—340. **Press Box Telephone:** (336) 334-5625.

UNC WILMINGTON SEAHAWKS

Conference: Colonial Athletic.
Mailing Address: 601 South College Road, Wilmington, NC 28403. **Website:** www.uncwsports.com.
Head Coach: Mark Scalf. **Telephone:** (910) 962-3570. **Baseball SID:** Tom Riordan. **Telephone:** (910) 962-4099. **Fax:** (910) 962-3001.
Assistant Coaches: *Randy Hood, Robert Woodard. **Telephone:** (910) 962-7471.
Home Field: Brooks Field. **Seating Capacity:** 3,500. **Outfield Dimensions:** LF—340, CF—380, RF—340. **Press Box Telephone:** (910) 395-5141.

NORTH DAKOTA

Conference: Great West.
Mailing Address: Hyslop Sports Center Room 120, 2751 2nd Ave. N., Stop 9013, Grand Forks, ND 58202. **Website:** www.fightingsioux.com.
Head Coach: Jeff Dodson. **Telephone:** (701) 777-4038. **Baseball SID:** Mitch Wigness. **Telephone:** (701) 777-4210. **Fax:** (701) 777-2285.
Assistant Coaches: Brian DeVillers, *JC Field. **Telephone:** (701) 777-2937.
Home Field: Kraft Field. **Seating Capacity:** 2,000. **Outfield Dimensions:** LF—330, CF—410, RF—330. **Press Box Telephone:** (701) 746-2762.

NORTH DAKOTA STATE BISON

Conference: Summit.
Mailing Address: NDSU Dept 1200, P.O. Box 6050, Fargo, ND 58108-6050. **Website:** www.gobison.com.
Head Coach: Tod Brown. **Telephone:** (701) 231-8853. **Baseball SID:** Ryan Perreault. **Telephone:** (701) 231-8331. **Fax:** (701) 231-8022.
Assistant Coaches: Jake Angier, *David Pearson. **Telephone:** (701) 231-7817.
Home Field: Newman Outdoor Field. **Seating Capacity:** 4,419. **Outfield Dimensions:** LF—318, CF—408, RF—314. **Press Box Telephone:** (701) 235-5204.

NORTH FLORIDA OSPREYS

Conference: Atlantic Sun.
Mailing Address: 1 UNF Drive, Jacksonville, FL 32224. **Website:** www.unfospreys.com.
Head Coach: Smoke Laval. **Telephone:** (904) 620-1556. **Baseball SID:** Chris Whitehead. **Telephone:** (904) 620-4029. **Fax:** (904) 620-2836.
Assistant Coaches: *Judd Loveland, Tim Parenton. **Telephone:** (904) 620-2556.
Home Field: Harmon Stadium. **Seating Capacity:** 1,000. **Outfield Dimensions:** LF—330, CF—400, RF—330. **Press Box Telephone:** (904) 620-2556.

NORTHEASTERN HUSKIES

Conference: Colonial Athletic.
Mailing Address: 360 Huntington Ave., Boston, MA 02115. **Website:** www.gonu.com.
Head Coach: Neil McPhee. **Telephone:** (617) 373-3657. **Baseball SID:** Michael Black. **Telephone:** (617) 373-4252. **Fax:** (617) 373-3152.
Assistant Coaches: Kevin Cobb, *Mike Glavine. **Telephone:** (617) 373-5256.
Home Field: Friedman Diamond. **Seating Capacity:** 3,000. **Outfield Dimensions:** LF—330, CF—435, RF—342.

NORTHERN COLORADO BEARS

Conference: Great West.
Mailing Address: Butler Hancock Sports Complex, Greeley, CO 80639. **Website:** www.uncbears.com.
Head Coach: Carl Iwasaki. **Telephone:** (970) 351-1714. **Baseball SID:** Heather Kennedy. **Telephone:** (970) 351-1065. **Fax:** (970) 351-2018.
Assistant Coaches: Patrick Perry, *RD Spiehs. **Telephone:** (970) 351-1714.
Home Field: Jackson Field. **Seating Capacity:** 1,500. **Outfield Dimensions:** LF—348, CF—410, RF—340. **Press Box Telephone:** (970) 978-0675.

NORTHERN ILLINOIS HUSKIES

Conference: Mid-American (West).
Mailing Address: 1525 W. Lincoln Hwy., DeKalb, IL 60115. **Website:** www.niuhuskies.com.
Head Coach: Ed Mathey. **Telephone:** (815) 753-2225. **Baseball SID:** Matt Sheerer. **Telephone:** (815) 753-1708. **Fax:** (815) 753-7700.
Assistant Coaches: Tom Carcione, *Todd Coryell. **Telephone:** (815) 753-0147.
Home Field: Ralph McKinzie Field. **Seating Capacity:** 1,500. **Outfield Dimensions:** LF—312, CF—395, RF—322. **Press Box Telephone:** (360) 931-1132.

NORTHERN KENTUCKY NORSE

Conference: Atlantic Sun.
Mailing Address: 133 The Bank of Kentucky Center, 500 Nunn Drive, Highland Heights, KY 41099. **Website:** nkunorse.com.
Head Coach: Todd Asalon. **Telephone:** (859) 572-6474. **Baseball SID:** Kelli Marksbury. **Telephone:** (859) 572-7850. **Fax:** (859) 572-6089.
Assistant Coaches: Dizzy Peyton, Kent Shartzer. **Telephone:** (859) 572-5940.
Home Field: Bill Aker Baseball Complex at Friendship Field. **Seating Capacity:** 500. **Outfield Dimensions:** LF—330, CF—395, RF—330.

NORTHWESTERN WILDCATS

Conference: Southland.
Mailing Address: 1501 Central St., Evanston, IL 60208. **Website:** www.nusports.com.
Head Coach: Paul Stevens. **Telephone:** (847) 491-4652. **Baseball SID:** Dan Yopchick. **Telephone:** (847) 467-3418. **Fax:** (847) 491-8818.
Assistant Coaches: *Jon Mikrut, Tim Stoddard. **Telephone:** (847) 491-4651.
Home Field: Rocky Miller Park. **Seating Capacity:** 1,000. **Press Box Telephone:** (847) 491-4200.

NORTHWESTERN STATE DEMONS

Conference: Southland.
Mailing Address: 468 Caspari Street, Natchitoches, LA 71497. **Website:** www.nsudemons.com.
Head Coach: Lane Burroughs. **Telephone:** (318) 357-4139. **Baseball SID:** Matt Fowler. **Telephone:** (318) 357-6467. **Fax:** (318) 357-4515.
Assistant Coaches: Chris Curry, *Andy Morgan. **Telephone:** (318) 357-4176.
Home Field: Brown-Stroud Field. **Seating Capacity:** 1,500. **Outfield Dimensions:** LF—320, CF—400, RF—330. **Press Box Telephone:** (318) 357-4606.

NOTRE DAME FIGHTING IRISH

Conference: Big East.
Mailing Address: 202 Joyce Center, Notre Dame, IN 46556. **Website:** und.com.
Head Coach: Mik Aoki. **Telephone:** (574) 631-8466. **Baseball SID:** Michael Bertsch. **Telephone:** (574) 631-8642. **Fax:** (574) 631-7941.
Assistant Coaches: *Joe Hastings, Jesse Woods. **Telephone:** (574) 631-3375.
Home Field: Frank Eck Stadium. **Seating Capacity:** 2,500. **Press Box Telephone:** (574) 631-9018.

OAKLAND GOLDEN GRIZZLIES

Conference: Summit.
Mailing Address: 201 Athletics Center, Rochester, MI 48309. **Website:** www.ougrizzlies.com.
Head Coach: John Musachio. **Telephone:** (248) 370-4059. **Baseball SID:** Scott Dunford. **Telephone:** (248) 370-3123. **Fax:** (248) 370-4056.
Assistant Coaches: Ryan Hilton, *Ty Rogers. **Telephone:** (248) 370-4228.
Home Field: OU Baseball Field. **Seating Capacity:** 500. **Press Box Telephone:** (248) 688-7646.

OHIO BOBCATS

Conference: Mid-American (East).
Mailing Address: N117 Convocation Center, Athens, OH 45701. **Website:** www.ohiobobcats.com.
Head Coach: Rob Smith. **Telephone:** (740) 593-1180. **Baseball SID:** Tom Symonds. **Telephone:** (740) 593-1298.
Assistant Coaches: Chris Berry, *Craig Moore. **Telephone:** (740) 593-1207.
Home Field: Bob Wren Stadium. **Seating Capacity:** 5,000. **Press Box Telephone:** (740) 593-0526.

OHIO STATE BUCKEYES

Conference: Big Ten.
Mailing Address: 250 Bill Davis Stadium, 650 Borror Dr., Columbus, OH 43210. **Website:** www.ohiostatebuckeyes.com.
Head Coach: Greg Beals. **Telephone:** (614) 292-1075. **Baseball SID:** Brett Rybak. **Telephone:** (614) 292-1112. **Fax:** (614) 292-8547.
Assistant Coaches: *Chris Holick, Mike Stafford. **Telephone:** (614) 292-1075.
Home Field: Nick Swisher Field at Bill Davis Stadium. **Seating Capacity:** 4,450. **Outfield Dimensions:** LF—330, CF—400, RF—330. **Press Box Telephone:** (614) 292-0021.

OKLAHOMA SOONERS

Conference: Big 12.
Mailing Address: 401 W. Imhoff, Norman, OK 73019. **Website:** www.soonersports.com.
Head Coach: Sunny Golloway. **Telephone:** (405) 325-8354. **Baseball SID:** Mike Ashcraft. **Telephone:** (405) 325-6449. **Fax:** (405) 325-7623.
Assistant Coaches: Jack Giese, *Aric Thomas. **Telephone:** (405) 325-8354.
Home Field: L. Dale Mitchell Park. **Seating Capacity:** 3,180. **Outfield Dimensions:** LF—335, CF—411, RF—335. **Press Box Telephone:** (405) 325-8363.

OKLAHOMA STATE COWBOYS

Conference: Big 12.
Mailing Address: 220 Athletics Center, Stillwater, OK 74078. **Website:** www.okstate.com.

Head Coach: Josh Holliday. **Telephone:** (405) 744-7141. **Baseball SID:** Wade McWhorter. **Telephone:** (405) 744-7853. **Fax:** (405) 744-7754.
Assistant Coaches: *Marty Lees, Rob Walton. **Telephone:** (405) 744-5968.
Home Field: Allie P. Reynolds Stadium. **Seating Capacity:** 4,000. **Outfield Dimensions:** LF—330, CF—398, RF—330. **Press Box Telephone:** (405) 744-5757.

OLD DOMINION MONARCHS

Conference: Colonial Athletic.
Mailing Address: Bud Metheny Baseball Complex, Norfolk, VA 23529-0201. **Website:** www.odusports.com.
Head Coach: Chris Finwood. **Telephone:** (757) 683-4230. **Baseball SID:** Carol Hudson, Jr. **Telephone:** (757) 683-3395. **Fax:** (757) 683-3119.
Assistant Coaches: Tim LaVigne, *Karl Nonemaker. **Telephone:** (757) 683-4230.
Home Field: Bud Metheny Complex. **Seating Capacity:** 2,000. **Outfield Dimensions:** LF—325, CF—395, RF—325. **Press Box Telephone:** (757) 683-5036.

ORAL ROBERTS GOLDEN EAGLES

Conference: Southland.
Mailing Address: 7777 S. Lewis Ave., Tulsa, OK 74147. **Website:** www.orugoldeneagles.com.
Head Coach: Ryan Folmar. **Telephone:** (918) 495-7639. **Baseball SID:** Eric Scott. **Telephone:** (918) 495-6646. **Fax:** (918) 495-7142.
Assistant Coaches: *Ryan Neill, Sean Snedeker. **Telephone:** (918) 495-7205.
Home Field: J.L. Johnson Stadium. **Seating Capacity:** 2,418. **Outfield Dimensions:** LF—330, CF—400, RF—330. **Press Box Telephone:** (918) 495-7165.

OREGON DUCKS

Conference: Pacific-12.
Mailing Address: Len Casanova Center, 2727 Leo Harris Parkway, Eugene, OR 97401. **Website:** www.goducks.com.
Head Coach: George Horton. **Telephone:** (541) 346-5235. **Baseball SID:** Todd Miles. **Telephone:** (541) 346-0962. **Fax:** (541) 346-5449.
Assistant Coaches: Jay Uhlman, *Mark Wasikowski. **Telephone:** (541) 346-5768. **Home Field:** PK Park. **Seating Capacity:** 4,000. **Outfield Dimensions:** LF—335, CF—400, RF—325. **Press Box Telephone:** (541) 346-6309.

OREGON STATE BEAVERS

Conference: Pacific-12.
Mailing Address: 103 Gill Coliseum, Corvallis, OR 97331. **Website:** www.osubeavers.com.
Head Coach: Pat Casey. **Telephone:** (541) 737-2825. **Baseball SID:** Hank Hager. **Telephone:** (541) 737-7472. **Fax:** (541) 737-3072.
Assistant Coaches: Pat Bailey, Nate Yeskie. **Telephone:** (541) 737-7484.
Home Field: Coleman Field. **Seating Capacity:** 3,248. **Outfield Dimensions:** LF—330, CF—400, RF—330. **Press Box Telephone:** (541) 737-7475.

PACIFIC TIGERS

Conference: Big West.
Mailing Address: 3601 Pacific Ave., Stockton, CA 95211. **Website:** www.pacifictigers.com.
Head Coach: Ed Sprague. **Telephone:** (209) 946-2709. **Baseball SID:** Kevin Wilkinson. **Telephone:** (209) 946-

2289. **Fax:** (209) 946-2757.
Assistant Coaches: *Don Barbara, Mike McCormick.
Telephone: (209) 946-2386.
Home Field: Klein Family Field. **Seating Capacity:** 2,500. **Outfield Dimensions:** LF—335, CF—405, RF—325. **Press Box Telephone:** (209) 946-2722.

PENN STATE NITTANY LIONS

Conference: Big Ten.
Mailing Address: Medlar Field at Lubrano Park, Suite 230, University Park, PA 16802. **Website:** www.gopsusports.com.
Head Coach: Robbie Wine. **Telephone:** (814) 863-0239. **Baseball SID:** Annie Plunkett. **Telephone:** (814) 865-1757. **Fax:** (814) 863-3165.
Assistant Coaches: Jason Bell, *Eric Folmar. **Telephone:** (814) 865-8605.
Home Field: Medlar Field at Lubrano Park. **Seating Capacity:** 5,406. **Outfield Dimensions:** LF—325, CF—399, RF—320. **Press Box Telephone:** (814) 865-2552.

PENNSYLVANIA QUAKERS

Conference: Ivy League (Gehrig).
Mailing Address: 235 S. 33rd St., Philadelphia, PA 19104. **Website:** www.pennathletics.com.
Head Coach: John Cole. **Telephone:** (215) 898-6282. **Baseball SID:** Alex Keil. **Telephone:** (215) 898-6128. **Fax:** (215) 898-1747.
Assistant Coaches: Mike Santello, *John Yurkow. **Telephone:** (215) 746-2325.
Home Field: Meiklejohn Stadium. **Seating Capacity:** 1,000. **Outfield Dimensions:** LF—330, CF—380, RF—330.

PEPPERDINE WAVES

Conference: West Coast.
Mailing Address: 24255 Pacific Coast Hwy., Malibu, CA 90263. **Website:** www.pepperdinesports.com.
Head Coach: Steve Rodriguez. **Telephone:** (310) 506-4371. **Baseball SID:** Ryan McCrary. **Telephone:** (310) 506-4333. **Fax:** (310) 506-7459.
Assistant Coaches: Rick Hirtensteiner, *Jon Strauss. **Telephone:** (310) 506-4404.
Home Field: Eddy D. Field Stadium. **Seating Capacity:** 1,800. **Outfield Dimensions:** LF—330, CF—390, RF—330. **Press Box Telephone:** (310) 506-4598.

PITTSBURGH PANTHERS

Conference: Big East.
Mailing Address: 212 Fitzgerald Fieldhouse, Pittsburgh, PA 15261. **Website:** www.pittsburghpanthers.com.
Head Coach: Joe Jordano. **Telephone:** (412) 648-8208. **Baseball SID:** Matt Haas. **Telephone:** (412) 648-8240. **Fax:** (412) 648-8248.
Assistant Coaches: *Danny Lopaze, Jerry Oakes. **Telephone:** (412) 648-3825.
Home Field: Charles L. Cost Field at the Petersen Sports Complex. **Seating Capacity:** 900. **Outfield Dimensions:** LF—330, CF—405, RF—330.

PORTLAND PILOTS

Conference: West Coast.
Mailing Address: 5000 N. Willamette Blvd., Portland, OR 97203. **Website:** www.portlandpilots.com.
Head Coach: Chris Sperry. **Telephone:** (503) 943-7707. **Baseball SID:** Adam Linnman. **Telephone:** (503) 943-7731. **Fax:** (503) 943-8082.

Assistant Coaches: Tucker Brack, *Larry Casian. **Telephone:** (503) 943-7732.
Home Field: Joe Etzel Field. **Seating Capacity:** 1,000. **Outfield Dimensions:** LF—350, CF—390, RF—340. **Press Box Telephone:** (503) 943-7253.

PRAIRIE VIEW A&M Panthers
Conference: Southwestern Athletic.
Mailing Address: P.O. Box 519 MS 1500, Prairie View, TX 77446. **Website:** sports.pvamu.edu.
Head Coach: Waskyla Cullivan. **Telephone:** (936) 261-9121. **Baseball SID:** Ryan McGinty. **Telephone:** (936) 261-9140. **Fax:** (936) 261-9159.
Assistant Coach: *Byron Carter. **Telephone:** (936) 261-9115.
Home Field: Panther Baseball Field. **Seating Capacity:** 1,000. **Outfield Dimensions:** LF—330, CF—400, RF—330.

PRESBYTERIAN BLUE HOSE

Conference: Big South.
Mailing Address: 105 Ashland Ave., Clinton, SC 29325. **Website:** www.gobluehose.com.
Head Coach: Elton Pollock. **Telephone:** (864) 833-8236. **Baseball SID:** Ryan Real. **Telephone:** (864) 833-7095. **Fax:** (864) 833-8323.
Assistant Coaches: Mark Crocco, *Josh Davis. **Telephone:** (864) 833-7134.
Home Field: PC Baseball Complex. **Seating Capacity:** 500. **Outfield Dimensions:** LF—375, CF—400, RF—375. **Press Box Telephone:** (864) 833-8527.

PRINCETON TIGERS

Conference: Ivy League (Gehrig).
Mailing Address: P.O. Box 71, Princeton University, Princeton, NJ 08544. **Website:** www.goprincetontigers.com.
Head Coach: Scott Bradley. **Telephone:** (609) 258-5059. **Baseball SID:** Diana Chamorro. **Telephone:** (609) 258-2630. **Fax:** (609) 258-4477.
Assistant Coaches: *Lloyd Brewer, Hank Coogan. **Telephone:** (609) 258-5684.
Home Field: Clarke Field. **Seating Capacity:** 1,000. **Outfield Dimensions:** LF—335, CF—400, RF—320. **Press Box Telephone:** (609) 462-0248.

PURDUE BOILERMAKERS

Conference: Big Ten.
Mailing Address: 900 N. John Wooden Drive, West Lafayette IN 47909. **Website:** www.purduesports.com.
Head Coach: Doug Schreiber. **Telephone:** (765) 494-3998. **Baseball SID:** Ben Turner. **Telephone:** (765) 494-3198. **Fax:** (765) 494-5447.
Assistant Coaches: *Jeff Duncan, Tristan McIntyre. **Telephone:** (765) 496-3442.
Home Field: Alexander Field. **Seating Capacity:** 2,000. **Outfield Dimensions:** LF—340, CF—408, RF—330. **Press Box Telephone:** (217) 549-7965.

QUINNIPIAC BOBCATS

Conference: Northeast.
Mailing Address: 275 Mount Carmel Ave., Hamden, CT 06518. **Website:** www.quinnipiacbobcats.com.
Head Coach: Dan Gooley. **Telephone:** (203) 582-8966. **Baseball SID:** Ken Sweeten. **Telephone:** (203) 582-8625. **Fax:** (203) 582-5385.
Assistant Coaches: *John Delaney. **Telephone:** (203) 582-6546.
Home Field: Quinnipiac Field. **Seating Capacity:** 1,000. **Press Box Telephone:** (203) 859-8529.

RADFORD HIGHLANDERS

Conference: Big South.
Mailing Address: Radford University, Dedmon Center, P.O. Box 6913, Radford, VA 24142. **Website:** www.ruhighlanders.com.
Head Coach: Joe Raccuia. **Telephone:** (540) 831-5881. **Baseball SID:** Tom Galbraith. **Telephone:** (540) 831-5726. **Fax:** (540) 831-6095.
Assistant Coaches: *Brian Anderson, Ryan Connolly. **Telephone:** (540) 831-6581.
Home Field: Radford Baseball Field. **Seating Capacity:** 1200. **Outfield Dimensions:** LF—335, CF—400, RF—335. **Press Box Telephone:** (540) 831-6062.

RHODE ISLAND RAMS

Conference: Atlantic 10.
Mailing Address: 3 Keaney Rd., Suite One, Kingston, RI 02881. **Website:** www.gorhody.com.
Head Coach: Jim Foster. **Telephone:** (401) 874-4550. **Baseball SID:** Jodi Pontbriand. **Telephone:** (401) 874-5356. **Fax:** (401) 874-5354.
Assistant Coaches: *Raphael Cerrato, Matt Untiet. **Telephone:** (401) 874-4888.
Home Field: Bill Beck Field. **Seating Capacity:** 1,000. **Outfield Dimensions:** LF—330, CF—400, RF—330. **Press Box Telephone:** (401) 481-6648.

RICE OWLS

Conference: Conference USA.
Mailing Address: 6100 Main, Houston, TX 77251. **Website:** www.riceowls.com.
Head Coach: Wayne Graham. **Telephone:** (713) 348-8864. **Baseball SID:** John Sullivan. **Telephone:** (713) 348-5636. **Fax:** (713) 348-6019.
Assistant Coaches: *Patrick Hallmark, Clay Van. **Telephone:** (713) 348-8859.
Home Field: Reckling Park. **Seating Capacity:** 6,193. **Outfield Dimensions:** LF—330, CF—400, RF—330. **Press Box Telephone:** (713) 348-4931.

RICHMOND SPIDERS

Conference: Atlantic 10.
Mailing Address: Robins Center, University of Richmond, Richmond, VA 23173. **Website:** www.richmondspiders.com.
Head Coach: Mark McQueen. **Telephone:** (804) 289-8391. **Baseball SID:** Scott Burns. **Telephone:** (804) 287-6313. **Fax:** (804) 289-8820.
Assistant Coaches: Charlie Goens, *Tag Montague. **Telephone:** (804) 289-8391.
Home Field: Pitt Field. **Seating Capacity:** 600. **Outfield Dimensions:** LF—328, CF—390, RF—328. **Press Box Telephone:** (804) 289-8714.

RIDER BRONCS

Conference: Metro Atlantic.
Mailing Address: 2083 Lawrenceville Rd., Lawrenceville, NJ 08648. **Website:** www.gobroncs.com.
Head Coach: Barry Davis. **Telephone:** (609) 896-5055. **Baseball SID:** Bud Focht. **Telephone:** (609) 896-5138. **Fax:** (609) 896-0341.
Assistant Coaches: Jaime Steward. **Telephone:** (609) 895-5703.
Home Field: Sonny Pittaro Field. **Seating Capacity:** 1,000.

RUTGERS SCARLET KNIGHTS

Conference: Big East.
Mailing Address: 83 Rockafeller Rd., Piscataway, NJ 08854. **Website:** www.scarletknights.com.
Head Coach: Fred Hill. **Telephone:** (732) 445-7834. **Baseball SID:** Trey Miller. **Telephone:** (732) 445-7886. **Fax:** (732) 445-3063.
Assistant Coaches: Casey Gaynor, *Joe Litterio. **Telephone:** (732) 445-7834.
Home Field: Bainton Field. **Seating Capacity:** 1,500. **Outfield Dimensions:** LF—330, CF—410, RF—320. **Press Box Telephone:** (732) 921-1067.

SACRAMENTO STATE HORNETS

Conference: Western Athletic.
Mailing Address: 6000 J. Street, Sacramento, CA 95819-6099. **Website:** www.hornetsports.com.
Head Coach: Reggie Christiansen. **Telephone:** (916) 278-4036. **Baseball SID:** Joe Waltasti. **Telephone:** (916) 278-6896. **Fax:** (916) 278-5429.
Assistant Coaches: *Steve Holm, Jake Mckinley. **Telephone:** (916) 278-4036.
Home Field: John Smith Field. **Seating Capacity:** 2,500. **Outfield Dimensions:** LF—333, CF—400, RF—333. **Press Box Telephone:** (916) 889-6643.

SACRED HEART PIONEERS

Conference: Northeast.
Mailing Address: 5151 Park Ave., Fairfield, CT 06825. **Website:** www.sacredheartpioneers.com.
Head Coach: Nick Giaquinto. **Telephone:** (203) 365-7632. **Baseball SID:** Jim Sheehan. **Telephone:** (203) 365-4813. **Fax:** (203) 371-7889.
Assistant Coaches: *Tyler Kavanaugh, Wayne Mazzoni. **Telephone:** (203) 365-4469.
Home Field: Ballpark at Harbor Yard. **Seating Capacity:** 5,500.

ST. BONAVENTURE BONNIES

Conference: Atlantic 10.
Mailing Address: P.O. Box G., Reilly Center, St. Bonaventure, NY 14778. **Website:** www.gobonnies.com.
Head Coach: Larry Sudbrook. **Telephone:** (716) 375-2641. **Baseball SID:** Jason MacBain. **Telephone:** (716) 375-4019. **Fax:** (716) 375-2383.
Assistant Coaches: *Larry Sudbrook, Jamie Wallschlaeger. **Telephone:** (716) 375-2699.
Home Field: Fred Handler Park. **Outfield Dimensions:** LF—330, CF—402, RF—330.

ST. JOHN'S RED STORM

Conference: Big East.
Mailing Address: 8000 Utopia Parkway, Queens, NY 11439. **Website:** www.redstormsports.com.
Head Coach: Ed Blankmeyer. **Telephone:** (718) 990-6148. **Baseball SID:** Tim Brown. **Telephone:** (718) 990-1521. **Fax:** (718) 969-8468.
Assistant Coaches: *Mike Hampton, Corey Muscara. **Telephone:** (718) 990-7523.
Home Field: Jack Kaiser Stadium. **Seating Capacity:** 3,500. **Outfield Dimensions:** LF—325, CF—400, RF—325. **Press Box Telephone:** (718) 990-2724.

ST. JOSEPH'S HAWKS

Conference: Atlantic 10.
Mailing Address: 5600 City Avenue, Philadelphia, PA

19131. **Website:** www.sjuhawks.com.
Head Coach: Fritz Hamburg. **Telephone:** (610) 660-1718. **Baseball SID:** Joe Greenwich. **Telephone:** (610) 660-1738. **Fax:** (610) 660-1724.
Assistant Coaches: Matt Allison, *Kyle Werman. **Telephone:** (610) 660-1704.
Home Field: Smithson Field. **Seating Capacity:** 400. **Outfield Dimensions:** LF—327, CF—400, RF—331.

SAINT LOUIS BILLIKENS

Conference: Atlantic 10.
Mailing Address: 3330 Laclede Ave., St. Louis, MO 63103. **Website:** www.slubillikens.com.
Head Coach: Darin Hendrickson. **Telephone:** (314) 977-3172. **Baseball SID:** Jake Gossage. **Telephone:** (314) 977-2524. **Fax:** (314) 977-3178.
Assistant Coaches: Will Bradley, *Kevin Moulder. **Telephone:** (314) 977-3260.
Home Field: Billiken Sports Center. **Seating Capacity:** 500. **Outfield Dimensions:** LF—330, CF—403, RF—330. **Press Box Telephone:** (314) 956-1265.

ST. MARY'S GAELS

Conference: West Coast.
Mailing Address: 1928 Saint Mary's Road, Moraga, CA 94575. **Website:** www.smcgaels.com.
Head Coach: Jedd Soto. **Telephone:** (925) 878-9857. **Baseball SID:** Mark Oshidari. **Telephone:** (925) 631-8722. **Fax:** (925) 376-0829.
Assistant Coaches: *Lloyd Acosta, Gabe Zappin. **Telephone:** (925) 457-6357.
Home Field: Louis Guisto Field. **Seating Capacity:** 500. **Outfield Dimensions:** LF—330, CF—395, RF—330. **Press Box Telephone:** (925) 376-3906.

ST. PETER'S PEACOCKS

Conference: Metro Atlantic.
Mailing Address: 2641 Kennedy Blvd., Jersey City, NJ 07306. **Website:** www.spc.edu.
Head Coach: Sean Cashman. **Telephone:** (201) 761-7319. **Baseball SID:** Lily Rodriguez. **Telephone:** (201) 761-7322. **Fax:** (201) 761-7301.
Assistant Coaches: Ryan Cohen, *Jon Ubbenga. **Telephone:** (201) 761-7318.
Home Field: Jaroshack Field. **Outfield Dimensions:** LF—318, CF—405, RF—310.

SAM HOUSTON STATE BEARKATS

Conference: Southland.
Mailing Address: 620 Bowers Blvd., Huntsville, TX 77340. **Website:** www.gobearkats.com.
Head Coach: David Pierce. **Telephone:** (936) 294-1731. **Baseball SID:** Paul Ridings. **Telephone:** (936) 294-1764. **Fax:** (936) 294-3538.
Assistant Coaches: *Sean Allen, Philip Miller. **Telephone:** (936) 295-4435.
Home Field: Don Sanders Stadium. **Seating Capacity:** 3,000. **Outfield Dimensions:** LF—330, CF—400, RF—330. **Press Box Telephone:** (936) 294-4132.

SAMFORD BULLDOGS

Conference: Southern.
Mailing Address: 800 Lakeshore Dr., Birmingham AL 35229. **Website:** www.samfordsports.com.
Head Coach: Casey Dunn. **Telephone:** (205) 726-2134. **Baseball SID:** Joey Mullins. **Telephone:** (205) 726-2799. **Fax:** (205) 726-2132.

Assistant Coaches: *Tony David, Mick Fieldbinder. **Telephone:** (205) 726-2134.
Home Field: Joe Lee Griffin Field. **Seating Capacity:** 1,000. **Press Box Telephone:** (205) 726-4167.

SAN DIEGO TOREROS

Conference: West Coast.
Mailing Address: 5998 Alcala Park, San Diego, CA 92110. **Website:** www.usdtoreros.cstv.com.
Head Coach: Rich Hill. **Telephone:** (619) 260-5953. **Baseball SID:** Chris Loucks. **Telephone:** (619) 260-7930. **Fax:** (619) 260-2213.
Assistant Coaches: *Jay Johnson, Tyler Kincaid. **Telephone:** (619) 260-5989.
Home Field: Fowler Park. **Outfield Dimensions:** LF—312, CF—391, RF—329.

SAN DIEGO STATE AZTECS

Conference: Mountain West.
Mailing Address: 5302 55th St., Room 3014, San Diego, CA 92182. **Website:** www.goaztecs.com.
Head Coach: Tony Gwynn. **Telephone:** (619) 594-6889. **Baseball SID:** Dave Kuhn. **Telephone:** (619) 594-5242. **Fax:** (619) 582-6541.
Assistant Coaches: Mark Martinez, *Eric Valenzuela. **Telephone:** (619) 593-3357.
Home Field: Tony Gwynn Stadium. **Seating Capacity:** 2,500. **Outfield Dimensions:** LF—340, CF—410, RF—340. **Press Box Telephone:** (619) 594-4103.

SAN FRANCISCO DONS

Conference: West Coast.
Mailing Address: USF Athletics, 2130 Fulton Street, San Francisco, CA 94117. **Website:** www.usfdons.com.
Head Coach: Nino Giarratano. **Telephone:** (415) 422-2934. **Baseball SID:** Sam Cohn. **Telephone:** (415) 422-9045. **Fax:** (415) 422-2510.
Assistant Coaches: Greg Moore, *Troy Nakamura. **Telephone:** (415) 422-2934.
Home Field: Benedetti Diamond. **Seating Capacity:** 1,500. **Press Box Telephone:** (415) 422-2919.

SAN JOSE STATE SPARTANS

Conference: Western Athletic.
Mailing Address: 1393 S. 7th Street, San Jose, CA 95112. **Website:** www.sjuspartans.com.
Head Coach: Dave Nakama. **Telephone:** (408) 924-1255. **Baseball SID:** Dominic Urrutia. **Telephone:** (408) 924-1211. **Fax:** (408) 924-1291.
Assistant Coaches: Nicholas Enriquez, *Brad Sanfilippo. **Telephone:** (408) 924-1262.
Home Field: San Jose Municipal Stadium. **Seating Capacity:** 4,200. **Outfield Dimensions:** LF—341, CF—390, RF—340. **Press Box Telephone:** (408) 924-7276.

SANTA CLARA BRONCOS

Conference: West Coast.
Mailing Address: 500 El Camino Real, Santa Clara, CA 95050. **Website:** www.santaclarabroncos.com.
Head Coach: Dan O'Brien. **Telephone:** (408) 554-4882. **Baseball SID:** Joey Karp. **Telephone:** (408) 554-4670. **Fax:** (408) 554-6969.
Assistant Coaches: Keith Beauregard, *Gabe Ribas. **Telephone:** (408) 554-4151.
Home Field: Schott Stadium. **Seating Capacity:** 1,500. **Outfield Dimensions:** LF—340, CF—400, RF—335. **Press Box Telephone:** (408) 554-5587.

SAVANNAH STATE TIGERS

Conference: Mid-Eastern Athletic.
Mailing Address: 3219 College Street, Savannah, GA 31404. **Website:** www.ssuathletics.com.
Head Coach: Carlton Hardy. **Telephone:** (912) 358-3082. **Baseball SID:** Opio Mashariki. **Telephone:** (912) 358-3430. **Fax:** (912) 358-3583.
Assistant Coaches: Anthony Macon. **Telephone:** (912) 358-3082.
Home Field: Tiger Field. **Seating Capacity:** 800. **Outfield Dimensions:** LF—330, CF—400, RF—330.

SEATTLE REDHAWKS

Conference: Western Athletic.
Mailing Address: 901 12th Ave., P.O. Box 222000, Seattle, WA 98122. **Website:** www.goseattleu.com.
Head Coach: Donny Harrel. **Telephone:** (206) 398-4399. **Baseball SID:** Jason Behenna. **Telephone:** (206) 296-5915. **Fax:** (206) 296-2154.
Assistant Coaches: *Casey Powell, Dave Wainhouse. **Telephone:** (206) 398-4396.
Home Field: Bannerwood Park. **Seating Capacity:** 2,000. **Outfield Dimensions:** LF—330, CF—410, RF—330.

SETON HALL PIRATES

Conference: Big East.
Mailing Address: 400 South Orange Ave. South Orange, NJ 07079. **Website:** www.shupirates.com.
Head Coach: Rob Sheppard. **Telephone:** (973) 761-9557. **Baseball SID:** Matt Sweeney. **Telephone:** (973) 761-9556. **Fax:** (973) 761-9061.
Assistant Coaches: *Phil Cundari, Mark Pappas. **Telephone:** (973) 275-6437.
Home Field: Owen T. Carroll Field. **Seating Capacity:** 800. **Outfield Dimensions:** LF—315, CF—400, RF—330. **Press Box Telephone:** (973) 943-8434.

SIENA SAINTS

Conference: Metro Atlantic.
Mailing Address: 515 Loudon Rd., Loudonville, NY 12211. **Website:** www.sienasaints.com.
Head Coach: Tony Rossi. **Telephone:** (518) 786-5044. **Baseball SID:** Jason Rich. **Telephone:** (518) 783-2411. **Fax:** (518) 783-2992.
Assistant Coaches: *Mike Kellar. **Telephone:** (518) 782-6875.
Home Field: Siena Field. **Seating Capacity:** 1,000. **Outfield Dimensions:** LF—300, CF—400, RF—325. **Press Box Telephone:** (518) 542-7240.

SOUTH ALABAMA JAGUARS

Conference: Sun Belt.
Mailing Address: 5950 Old Shell Rd., 1209 MC, Mobile, AL 36688. **Website:** www.usajaguars.com.
Head Coach: Mark Calvi. **Telephone:** (251) 414-8243. **Baseball SID:** Charlie Nichols. **Telephone:** (251) 414-8017. **Fax:** (251) 460-7297.
Assistant Coaches: Bob Keller, *Jerry Zulli. **Telephone:** (251) 414-8209.
Home Field: Stanky Field. **Seating Capacity:** 3,775. **Outfield Dimensions:** LF—330, CF—400, RF—330. **Press Box Telephone:** (251) 461-1842.

SOUTH CAROLINA GAMECOCKS

Conference: Southeastern (East).
Mailing Address: Carolina Stadium, 431 Williams Street, Columbia, SC 29208. **Website:** www.gamecocksonline.com.
Head Coach: Chad Holbrook. **Telephone:** (803) 777-0116. **Baseball SID:** Andrew Kitick. **Telephone:** (803) 777-5257. **Fax:** (803) 777-2967.
Assistant Coaches: *Sammy Esposito, Jerry Meyers. **Telephone:** (803) 777-7913.
Home Field: Carolina Stadium. **Seating Capacity:** 8,242. **Outfield Dimensions:** LF—325, CF—400, RF—325. **Press Box Telephone:** (803) 777-6648.

SOUTH CAROLINA-UPSTATE SPARTANS

Conference: Atlantic Sun.
Mailing Address: 800 University Way, Spartanburg, SC 29303. **Website:** www.upstatespartans.com.
Head Coach: Matt Fincher. **Telephone:** (864) 503-5135. **Baseball SID:** David Beall. **Telephone:** (864) 503-5166. **Fax:** (864) 503-5127.
Assistant Coaches: *Grant Rembert, Wes Wrenn. **Telephone:** (864) 503-5164.
Home Field: Harley Park. **Seating Capacity:** 500. **Outfield Dimensions:** LF—335, CF—402, RF—335. **Press Box Telephone:** (864) 503-5815.

SOUTH DAKOTA STATE JACKRABBITS

Conference: Summit.
Mailing Address: 2820 HPER Center, Brookings, SD 57006. **Website:** www.gojacks.com.
Head Coach: David Schrage. **Telephone:** (605) 688-5027. **Baseball SID:** Jason Hove. **Telephone:** (605) 688-4623. **Fax:** (605) 688-5999.
Assistant Coaches: *Brian Grunzke, Ben Norton. **Telephone:** (605) 688-5778.
Home Field: Erv Heuther Field. **Seating Capacity:** 1,500. **Outfield Dimensions:** LF—330, CF—400, RF—330. **Press Box Telephone:** (605) 695-1827.

SOUTH FLORIDA BULLS

Conference: Big East.
Mailing Address: University of South Florida, ATH 100, 4202 East Fowler, Tampa FL 33620. **Website:** www.gousfbulls.com.
Head Coach: Lelo Prado. **Telephone:** (813) 974-2504. **Baseball SID:** Casey Goldstein. **Telephone:** (813) 974-0415. **Fax:** (813) 974-4029.
Assistant Coaches: Lance Carter, *Chris Heintz. **Telephone:** (813) 974-2507.
Home Field: USF Baseball Stadium. **Seating Capacity:** 3,211. **Press Box Telephone:** (813) 410-1194.

SOUTHEAST MISSOURI STATE REDHAWKS

Conference: Ohio Valley.
Mailing Address: One University Plaza, MS0200, Cape Girardeau, MO 63701. **Website:** www.gosoutheast.com.
Head Coach: Steve Bieser. **Telephone:** (573) 986-6002. **Baseball SID:** Nick Seeman. **Telephone:** (573) 651-2294. **Fax:** (573) 651-2810.
Assistant Coaches: Dillon Lawson, *Lance Rhodes. **Telephone:** (573) 986-6002.
Home Field: Capaha Field. **Seating Capacity:** 2,000. **Outfield Dimensions:** LF—330, CF—400, RF—330. **Press Box Telephone:** (573) 651-9130.

SOUTHEASTERN LOUISIANA LIONS

Conference: Southland.
Mailing Address: 800 Galloway Dr., Hammond, LA 70402. **Website:** www.lionsports.net.

Head Coach: Jay Artigues. **Telephone:** (985) 549-3566. **Baseball SID:** Damon Sunde. **Telephone:** (985) 549-3774. **Fax:** (985) 549-3773.
Assistant Coaches: Daniel Latham, *Matt Riser. **Telephone:** (985) 549-5130.
Home Field: Pat Kenelly Diamond at Alumni Field. **Seating Capacity:** 2,500. **Outfield Dimensions:** LF—330, CF—400, RF—330. **Press Box Telephone:** (985) 549-2431.

SOUTHERN JAGUARS

Conference: Southwestern Athletic.
Mailing Address: P.O. Box 10850, Baton Rouge, LA 70813. **Website:** www.gojagsports.com.
Head Coach: Roger Cador. **Telephone:** (225) 771-2513. **Baseball SID:** Chris Jones. **Telephone:** (225) 771-3495.
Assistant Coaches: *Fernando Puebla. **Telephone:** (225) 771-3712.
Home Field: Lee-Hines Stadium. **Seating Capacity:** 1,500. **Outfield Dimensions:** LF—360, CF—395, RF—325.

SOUTHERN CALIFORNIA TROJANS

Conference: Pacific-12.
Mailing Address: 1021 Childs Way, Los Angeles, CA 90089. **Website:** www.usctrojans.com.
Head Coach: Frank Cruz. **Telephone:** (213) 740-5762. **Baseball SID:** Rachel Caton. **Telephone:** (213) 740-3809. **Fax:** (213) 740-7584.
Assistant Coaches: Gabe Alvarez, *Dan Hubbs. **Telephone:** (213) 740-8448.
Home Field: Dedeaux Field. **Seating Capacity:** 2,500. **Outfield Dimensions:** LF—375, CF—395, RF—365. **Press Box Telephone:** (213) 748-3449.

SOUTHERN ILLINOIS SALUKIS

Conference: Missouri Valley.
Mailing Address: 425 Saluki Dr., Carbondale, IL 62901. **Website:** www.siusalukis.com.
Head Coach: Ken Henderson. **Telephone:** (618) 453-3794. **Baseball SID:** Scott Gierman. **Telephone:** (618) 453-5470. **Fax:** (618) 453-5470.
Assistant Coaches: *P.J. Finigan, Ryan Strain. **Telephone:** (618) 453-7646.
Home Field: Abe Martin Field. **Seating Capacity:** 2,000. **Outfield Dimensions:** LF—340, CF—390, RF—340. **Press Box Telephone:** (618) 751-3400.

SOUTHERN ILLINOIS-EDWARDSVILLE COUGARS

Conference: Ohio Valley.
Mailing Address: 1 University Drive, Edwardsville, IL 62026. **Website:** www.siuecougars.com.
Head Coach: Tony Stoecklin. **Telephone:** (618) 650-2331. **Baseball SID:** Joe Pott. **Telephone:** (618) 650-2860. **Fax:** (618) 650-3369.
Assistant Coaches: *Danny Jackson. **Telephone:** (618) 650-2032.
Home Field: Simmons Baseball Complex. **Seating Capacity:** 1,000. **Press Box Telephone:** (314) 707-1712.

SOUTHERN MISSISSIPPI GOLDEN EAGLES

Conference: Conference USA.
Mailing Address: 118 College Dr., #5017, Hattiesburg, MS 39406. **Website:** www.southernmiss.com.
Head Coach: Scott Berry. **Telephone:** (601) 266-6542. **Baseball SID:** Jack Duggan. **Telephone:** (601) 266-4503. **Fax:** (601) 266-4507.
Assistant Coaches: *Chad Caillet, Michael Federico. **Telephone:** (601) 266-6542.

Home Field: Pete Taylor Park at Hill Denson Field. **Seating Capacity:** 5,500. **Outfield Dimensions:** LF—340, CF—400, RF—340. **Press Box Telephone:** (601) 266-5684.

STANFORD CARDINAL

Conference: Pacific-12.
Mailing Address: 641 E. Campus Dr., Stanford, CA 94305. **Website:** www.gostanford.com.
Head Coach: Mark Marquess. **Telephone:** (650) 723-4528. **Baseball SID:** Alan George. **Telephone:** (650) 725-2959. **Fax:** (650) 725-2957.
Assistant Coaches: Rusty Filter, *Dean Stotz. **Telephone:** (650) 723-9528.
Home Field: Sunken Diamond. **Seating Capacity:** 4,000. **Outfield Dimensions:** LF—335, CF—400, RF—335. **Press Box Telephone:** (650) 723-4629.

STEPHEN F. AUSTIN STATE LUMBERJACKS

Conference: Southland.
Mailing Address: P.O. Box 13010, SFA Station, Nacogdoches, TX 75962. **Website:** www.sfajacks.com.
Head Coach: Johnny Cardenas. **Telephone:** (936) 468-5982. **Baseball SID:** Ben Rikard. **Telephone:** (936) 468-5801. **Fax:** (936) 468-4593.
Assistant Coaches: *Chris Connally, Chad Massengale. **Telephone:** (936) 468-7796.
Home Field: Jaycees Field. **Seating Capacity:** 1,000. **Outfield Dimensions:** LF—320, CF—400, RF—320. **Press Box Telephone:** (936) 559-8344.

STETSON HATTERS

Conference: Atlantic Sun.
Mailing Address: 421 N. Woodland Blvd., Unit 8359, DeLand, FL, 32723. **Website:** www.gohatters.com.
Head Coach: Pete Dunn. **Telephone:** (386) 822-8106. **Baseball SID:** Ricky Hazel. **Telephone:** (386) 822-8130. **Fax:** (386) 822-7486.
Assistant Coaches: *Mark Leavitt, Chris Roberts. **Telephone:** (386) 822-8733.
Home Field: Melching Field at Conrad Park. **Seating Capacity:** 2,500. **Outfield Dimensions:** LF—335, CF—403, RF—335. **Press Box Telephone:** (386) 736-7360.

STONY BROOK SEAWOLVES

Conference: America East.
Mailing Address: Indoor Sports Complex, Stony Brook NY 11794-3500. **Website:** goseawolves.org.
Head Coach: Matt Senk. **Telephone:** (631) 632-9226. **Baseball SID:** Thomas Chen. **Telephone:** (631) 632-7289. **Fax:** (631) 632-8841.
Assistant Coaches: Mike Marron, *Joe Pennucci. **Telephone:** (631) 632-4755.
Home Field: Joe Nathan Field. **Seating Capacity:** 1,000. **Outfield Dimensions:** LF—330, CF—390, RF—330. **Press Box Telephone:** (860) 690-3482.

TEMPLE OWLS

Conference: Atlantic Sun.
Mailing Address: 1700 North Broad Street, Philadelphia, PA 19122. **Website:** www.owlsports.com.
Head Coach: Ryan Wheeler. **Telephone:** (215) 204-8639. **Baseball SID:** Steve Helm. **Telephone:** (215) 204-7446. **Fax:** (215) 933-5257.
Assistant Coaches: *Brian Pugh, Kevin Small. **Telephone:** (215) 204-8640.
Home Field: Skip Wilson Field. **Seating Capacity:** 1,000. **Press Box Telephone:** (609) 969-0975.

TENNESSEE VOLUNTEERS

Conference: Southeastern (East).
Mailing Address: 1511 Pat Summitt Drive, Knoxville, TN 37996. **Website:** www.utsports.com.
Head Coach: Dave Serrano. **Telephone:** (865) 974-2057. **Baseball SID:** Cameron Harris. **Telephone:** (865) 974-8876. **Fax:** (865) 974-8875.
Assistant Coaches: Greg Bergeron, *Bill Mosiello. **Telephone:** (865) 974-2057.
Home Field: Lindsey Nelson Stadium. **Seating Capacity:** 3,800. **Outfield Dimensions:** LF—320, CF—390, RF—320. **Press Box Telephone:** (865) 974-3376.

TENNESSEE TECH GOLDEN EAGLES

Conference: Ohio Valley.
Mailing Address: Box 5057 1100 McGee Blvd, Cookeville, TN 38505-0001. **Website:** www.ttusports.com.
Head Coach: Matt Bragga. **Telephone:** (931) 372-6546. **Baseball SID:** Mike Lehman. **Telephone:** (931) 372-3883.
Assistant Coaches: Cody Church, *Brandon Turner. **Telephone:** (931) 372-6546.
Home Field: Bush Stadium at Averitt Express Baseball Complex. **Seating Capacity:** 1,100.

TENNESSEE-MARTIN SKYHAWKS

Conference: Ohio Valley.
Mailing Address: 1022 Elam Center, 15 Mt. Pelia Road, Martin, TN 38238. **Website:** www.utmsports.com.
Head Coach: *Bubba Cates. **Telephone:** (731) 881-7337. **Baseball SID:** Joe Lofaro. **Telephone:** (731) 881-7632. **Fax:** (731) 881-7624.
Assistant Coaches: Brad Goss. **Telephone:** (731) 881-3691.
Home Field: Skyhawk Field. **Seating Capacity:** 300. **Outfield Dimensions:** LF—330, CF—385, RF—330. **Press Box Telephone:** (270) 703-2601.

TEXAS LONGHORNS

Conference: Big 12.
Mailing Address: 2100 San Jacinto Boulevard, Bellmont Hall 327, Austin, TX 78712. **Website:** www.texassports.com.
Head Coach: Augie Garrido. **Telephone:** (512) 471-5732. **Baseball SID:** Thomas Dick. **Telephone:** (512) 471-6039. **Fax:** (512) 471-6040.
Assistant Coaches: Skip Johnson, *Tommy Nicholson. **Telephone:** (512) 471-5732.
Home Field: UFCU Disch-Falk Field. **Seating Capacity:** 6,649.

TEXAS A&M AGGIES

Conference: Southeastern (West).
Mailing Address: 161 Wellborn Road, College Station, TX 77843. **Website:** www.aggieathletics.com.
Head Coach: Rob Childress. **Telephone:** (979) 845-4810. **Baseball SID:** Thomas Dick. **Telephone:** (979) 862-5486. **Fax:** (979) 845-6825.
Assistant Coaches: Andy Sawyers, *Justin Seely. **Telephone:** (979) 845-4810.
Home Field: Blue Bell Park. **Seating Capacity:** 6,100. **Outfield Dimensions:** LF—330-375, CF—400, RF—375-330. **Press Box Telephone:** (979) 458-3604.

TEXAS A&M-CORPUS CHRISTI ISLANDERS

Conference: Southland.
Mailing Address: 6300 Ocean Drive, Unit 5719, Corpus Christi, TX 78412. **Website:** www.goislanders.com.
Head Coach: Scott Malone. **Telephone:** (361) 825-3413. **Baseball SID:** Josh Brown. **Telephone:** (361) 825-3411. **Fax:** (361) 825-3218.
Assistant Coaches: *Chris Ramirez, Marty Smith. **Telephone:** (361) 825-3252.
Home Field: Chapman Field. **Seating Capacity:** 1,200. **Outfield Dimensions:** LF—330, CF—404, RF—330. **Press Box Telephone:** (337) 302-4722.

TEXAS CHRISTIAN HORNED FROGS

Conference: Big 12.
Mailing Address: 2900 Stadium Dr., Fort Worth, TX 71629. **Website:** www.gofrogs.com.
Head Coach: Jim Schlossnagle. **Telephone:** (817) 257-5354. **Baseball SID:** Brandie Davidson. **Telephone:** (817) 257-7479. **Fax:** (817) 257-7964.
Assistant Coaches: Kirk Saarloos, *Tony Vitello. **Telephone:** (817) 257-5656.
Home Field: Lupton Stadium. **Seating Capacity:** 4,500. **Outfield Dimensions:** LF—330, CF—390, RF—325. **Press Box Telephone:** (817) 257-7966.

TEXAS SOUTHERN TIGERS

Conference: Southwestern Athletic.
Mailing Address: 3100 Cleburne Street, Houston, TX 77004. **Website:** www.tsu.edu.
Head Coach: Michael Robertson. **Telephone:** (713) 313-4315. **Baseball SID:** Rodney Bush. **Telephone:** (713) 313-7603. **Fax:** (713) 313-1045.
Assistant Coaches: *Marqus Johnson, Ehren Moreno. **Telephone:** (713) 313-4315.
Home Field: Macgregor Park. **Seating Capacity:** 500. **Outfield Dimensions:** LF—315, CF—390, RF—315.

TEXAS STATE BOBCATS

Conference: Western Athletic.
Mailing Address: 601 University Dr., San Marcos, TX 78666. **Website:** www.txstatebobcats.com.
Head Coach: Ty Harrington. **Telephone:** (512) 245-7566. **Baseball SID:** Steve Appelhans. **Telephone:** (512) 245-4387. **Fax:** (512) 245-8387.
Assistant Coaches: *Jeremy Fikac, Mike Silva. **Telephone:** (512) 245-4345.
Home Field: Bobcat Baseball Stadium. **Seating Capacity:** 2,500. **Outfield Dimensions:** LF—330, CF—404, RF—330. **Press Box Telephone:** (512) 245-5739.

TEXAS TECH RED RAIDERS

Conference: Big 12.
Mailing Address: 2901 Drive of Champions, Lubbock, TX 79409. **Website:** www.texastech.com.
Head Coach: Tim Tadlock. **Telephone:** (806) 742-2770. **Baseball SID:** Scott Lacefield. **Telephone:** (806) 742-2770. **Fax:** (806) 742-1970.
Assistant Coaches: Ray Hayward, *J-Bob Thomas. **Telephone:** (806) 742-2770.
Home Field: Dan Law Field at Rip Griffin Park. **Seating Capacity:** 4,368. **Outfield Dimensions:** LF—330, CF—404, RF—330. **Press Box Telephone:** (817) 691-3786.

TEXAS-ARLINGTON MAVERICKS

Conference: Western Athletic
Mailing Address: 1309 West Mitchell Street, Arlington, TX 76019. **Website:** utamavs.com.
Head Coach: Darin Thomas. **Telephone:** (817) 272-2542. **Baseball SID:** Art Garcia. **Telephone:** (817) 272-

2239. **Fax:** (817) 272-5037.
Assistant Coaches: K.J. Hendricks, *Jay Sirianni. **Telephone:** (817) 272-0111, (817) 272-7625.
Home Field: Clay Gould Ballpark. **Seating Capacity:** 1,600. **Press Box Telephone:** (817) 462-4225.

TEXAS-PAN AMERICAN BRONCS

Conference: Great West.
Mailing Address: 1201 W. University Dr., Edinburg, TX 78539. **Website:** www.utpabroncs.com.
Head Coach: Manny Mantrana. **Telephone:** (956) 665-2235. **Baseball SID:** Jonah Goldberg. **Telephone:** (956) 665-2240. **Fax:** (956) 665-2261.
Assistant Coaches: Robert Clayton, *Norberto Lopez. **Telephone:** (956) 665-2891.
Home Field: Edinburg Baseball Stadium. **Seating Capacity:** 5,500. **Outfield Dimensions:** LF—325, CF—405, RF—325.

TEXAS-SAN ANTONIO ROADRUNNERS

Conference: Western Athletic.
Mailing Address: One UTSA Circle, San Antonio, TX 78249. **Website:** www.goutsa.com.
Head Coach: Jason Marshall. **Telephone:** (210) 458-4811. **Baseball SID:** Tony Baldwin. **Telephone:** (210) 458-6460. **Fax:** (210) 458-4569.
Assistant Coaches: *Jim Blair, Brett Lawler. **Telephone:** (210) 458-4195.
Home Field: Roadrunner Field. **Seating Capacity:** 800. **Outfield Dimensions:** LF—335, CF—405, RF—340. **Press Box Telephone:** (210) 458-4612.

TOLEDO ROCKETS

Conference: Mid-American (West).
Mailing Address: 2801 West Bancroft St., MS-408, Toledo, OH 43606. **Website:** www.utrockets.com.
Head Coach: Cory Mee. **Telephone:** (419) 530-6263. **Baseball SID:** Brian Debenedictis. **Telephone:** (419) 530-4919. **Fax:** (419) 530-4428.
Assistant Coaches: *Josh Bradford, Nick McIntyre. **Telephone:** (419) 530-3097.
Home Field: Scott Park. **Seating Capacity:** 1,000. **Outfield Dimensions:** LF—330, CF—400, RF—330. **Press Box Telephone:** (419) 530-3089.

TOWSON TIGERS

Conference: Colonial Athletic.
Mailing Address: 8000 York Road, Towson, MD 21252. **Website:** www.towsontigers.com.
Head Coach: Mike Gottlieb. **Telephone:** (410) 704-3775. **Baseball SID:** Dan O'Connell. **Telephone:** (410) 704-3102. **Fax:** (410) 704-3861.
Assistant Coaches: Lance Mauck, Scott Roane. **Telephone:** (410) 704-4587.
Home Field: John B. Schuerholz Park. **Seating Capacity:** 500. **Press Box Telephone:** (410) 704-5810.

TROY TROJANS

Conference: Sun Belt.
Mailing Address: 5000 Veterans Stadium Drive, Troy, AL, 36082. **Website:** www.troytrojans.com.
Head Coach: Bobby Pierce. **Telephone:** (334) 670-3489. **Baseball SID:** Adam Prendergast. **Telephone:** (334) 670-3832. **Fax:** (334) 670-5665.
Assistant Coaches: Brad Phillips, *Mark Smartt. **Telephone:** (334) 670-5705.
Home Field: Riddle-Pace Field. **Seating Capacity:**

2,200. **Outfield Dimensions:** LF—340, CF—400, RF—310. **Press Box Telephone:** (334) 670-5701.

TULANE GREEN WAVE

Conference: Conference USA.
Mailing Address: James W. Wilson Center, New Orleans, LA 70118. **Website:** www.tulanegreenwave.com.
Head Coach: Rick Jones. **Telephone:** (504) 862-8239. **Baseball SID:** Curtis Akey. **Telephone:** (504) 862-7271. **Fax:** (504) 862-8554.
Assistant Coaches: *Jake Gautreau, Chad Sutter. **Telephone:** (504) 862-7203.
Home Field: Greer Field at Turchin Stadium. **Seating Capacity:** 5,000. **Outfield Dimensions:** LF—330, CF—400, RF—330. **Press Box Telephone:** (504) 862-8244.

UTAH UTES

Conference: Pacific-12.
Mailing Address: 1825 E. South Campus Dr., Salt Lake City, UT 84112-0900. **Website:** www.utahutes.com.
Head Coach: Bill Kinneberg. **Telephone:** (801) 581-3526. **Baseball SID:** Brooke Frederickson. **Telephone:** (801) 581-8302.
Assistant Coaches: *Mike Crawford, Bryan Kinneberg. **Telephone:** (801) 581-3024.
Home Field: Spring Mobile Ballpark. **Seating Capacity:** 15,000. **Outfield Dimensions:** LF—345, CF—420, RF—315.

UTAH VALLEY WOLVERINES

Conference: Great West.
Mailing Address: 800 W. University Pkwy., Orem, UT, 84058. **Website:** www.wolverinegreen.com.
Head Coach: Eric Madsen. **Telephone:** (801) 863-6509. **Baseball SID:** Clint Burgi. **Telephone:** (801) 863-8644. **Fax:** (801) 863-8813.
Assistant Coaches: *Dave Carter, Cooper Fouts. **Telephone:** (801) 863-8647.
Home Field: Brent Brown Ballpark. **Seating Capacity:** 5,000. **Outfield Dimensions:** LF—312, CF—408, RF—315. **Press Box Telephone:** (801) 362-1548.

VALPARAISO CRUSADERS

Conference: Horizon.
Mailing Address: 1700 Chapel Drive, Valparaiso, IN 46383-4543. **Website:** www.valpoathletics.com.
Head Coach: Tracy Woodson. **Telephone:** (219) 464-5239. **Baseball SID:** Brad Collignon. **Telephone:** (219) 464-6953. **Fax:** (219) 464-5762.
Assistant Coaches: Adam Piotrowicz, *Brian Schmack. **Telephone:** (219) 465-7961.
Home Field: Emory G. Bauer Field. **Seating Capacity:** 500. **Outfield Dimensions:** LF—330, CF—400, RF—330. **Press Box Telephone:** (219) 464-6006.

VANDERBILT COMMODORES

Conference: Southeastern (East).
Mailing Address: 2601 Jess Neely Drive, Nashville, TN 37212. **Website:** www.vucommodores.com.
Head Coach: Tim Corbin. **Telephone:** (615) 322-7725. **Baseball SID:** Kyle Parkinson. **Telephone:** (615) 343-0020. **Fax:** (615) 343-7064.
Assistant Coaches: Scott Brown, *Travis Jewett. **Telephone:** (615) 322-3074.
Home Field: Hawkins Field. **Seating Capacity:** 3,626. **Outfield Dimensions:** LF—310, CF—400, RF—335. **Press Box Telephone:** (615) 320-0436.

VILLANOVA WILDCATS

Conference: Big East.
Mailing Address: 800 E. Lancaster Avenue, Jake Nevin Field House, Villanova, PA 19085. **Website:** www.villanova.com.
Head Coach: Joe Godri. **Telephone:** (610) 519-4529. **Baseball SID:** David Berman. **Telephone:** (610) 519-4122. **Fax:** (610) 519-7323.
Assistant Coaches: *Derek Shunk, Nick Weisheipl. **Telephone:** (610) 519-5520.
Home Field: Villanova Ballpark at Plymouth. **Seating Capacity:** 750. **Outfield Dimensions:** LF—330, CF—405, RF—330. **Press Box Telephone:** (860) 490-6398.

VIRGINIA CAVALIERS

Conference: Atlantic Coast (Coastal).
Mailing Address: P.O. Box 400853, Charlottesville, VA 22904-4853. **Website:** www.virginiasports.com.
Head Coach: Brian O'Connor. **Telephone:** (434) 982-4932. **Baseball SID:** Andy Fledderjohann. **Telephone:** (434) 982-5131. **Fax:** (434) 982-5500.
Assistant Coaches: Karl Kuhn, *Kevin McMullan. **Telephone:** (434) 982-5776.
Home Field: Davenport Field. **Seating Capacity:** 4,980. **Outfield Dimensions:** LF—332, CF—404, RF—332. **Press Box Telephone:** (434) 244-4071.

VIRGINIA COMMONWEALTH RAMS

Conference: Atlantic 10.
Mailing Address: 1300 W. Broad Street, P.O. Box 842003, Richmond, VA 23284. **Website:** www.vcuathletics.com.
Head Coach: Shawn Stiffler. **Telephone:** (804) 828-4822. **Baseball SID:** Andrew Phillips. **Telephone:** (804) 828-9567. **Fax:** (804) 828-4938.
Assistant Coaches: Kurt Elbin, *Jeff Palumbo. **Telephone:** (804) 828-4821.
Home Field: The Diamond. **Seating Capacity:** 9,560. **Outfield Dimensions:** LF—330, CF—402, RF—330. **Press Box Telephone:** (804) 840-4439.

VIRGINIA MILITARY INSTITUTE KEYDETS

Conference: Big South.
Mailing Address: Cameron Hall, Lexington, VA 24450. **Website:** www.vmikeydets.com.
Head Coach: Marlin Ikenberry. **Telephone:** (540) 464-7609. **Baseball SID:** Brad Salois. **Telephone:** (540) 464-7015. **Fax:** (540) 464-7583.
Assistant Coaches: Travis Beazley, *Jonathan Hadra. **Telephone:** (540) 464-7605.
Home Field: Gray-Minor Stadium. **Seating Capacity:** 1,400. **Outfield Dimensions:** LF—325, CF—390, RF—335. **Press Box Telephone:** (540) 460-6920.

VIRGINIA TECH HOKIES

Conference: Atlantic Coast (Coastal).
Mailing Address: 460 Jamerson Athletic Center, Blacksburg, VA 24061-0502. **Website:** www.hokiesports.com.
Head Coach: Pete Hughes. **Telephone:** (540) 231-3671. **Baseball SID:** Marc Mullen. **Telephone:** (540) 231-1894. **Fax:** (540) 231-6984.
Assistant Coaches: Mike Kunigonis, *Pat Mason. **Telephone:** (540) 231-3098.

Home Field: English Field. **Seating Capacity:** 4,000. **Outfield Dimensions:** LF—330, CF—400, RF—330. **Press Box Telephone:** (540) 231-8974.

WAGNER SEAHAWKS

Conference: Northeast.
Mailing Address: Spiro Sports Center, One Campus Road, Staten Island, NY 10301. **Website:** www.wagner-athletics.com.
Head Coach: Jim Carone. **Telephone:** (718) 390-3154. **Baseball SID:** Kevin Ross. **Telephone:** (718) 390-3215. **Fax:** (718) 420-4015.
Assistant Coaches: *Chris Collazo, Joe Mercurio. **Telephone:** (718) 420-4121.
Home Field: Richmond County Bank Ballpark. **Seating Capacity:** 7,171. **Outfield Dimensions:** LF—320, CF—390, RF—318. **Press Box Telephone:** (716) 969-6126.

WAKE FOREST DEMON DEACONS

Conference: Atlantic Coast (Atlantic).
Mailing Address: 1834 Wake Forest Drive, Winston-Salem, NC 27103. **Website:** wakeforestsports.com.
Head Coach: Tom Walter. **Telephone:** (336) 758-5570. **Baseball SID:** Steven Wright. **Telephone:** (336) 758-4120. **Fax:** (336) 758-5140.
Assistant Coaches: Bill Cilento, *Dennis Healy. **Telephone:** (336) 758-5645.
Home Field: Wake Forest Baseball Park. **Seating Capacity:** 6,000. **Outfield Dimensions:** LF—310, CF—400, RF—300. **Press Box Telephone:** (336) 759-7373.

WASHINGTON HUSKIES

Conference: Pacific-12.
Mailing Address: Graves Annex Box 354080, Seattle, WA 98195-4080. **Website:** www.gohuskies.com.
Head Coach: Lindsay Meggs. **Telephone:** (206) 616-4335. **Baseball SID:** Jeff Bechtold. **Telephone:** (206) 685-7910. **Fax:** (206) 543-5000.
Assistant Coaches: *Jason Kelly, Jordon Twohig. **Telephone:** (206) 685-7016.
Home Field: Husky Ballpark. **Seating Capacity:** 2,000. **Outfield Dimensions:** LF—327, CF—395, RF—317. **Press Box Telephone:** (206) 685-1994.

WASHINGTON STATE COUGARS

Conference: Pacific-12.
Mailing Address: 195 Bohler Athletic Complex, Pullman, WA 99164-1602. **Website:** www.wsucougars.com.
Head Coach: Donnie Marbut. **Telephone:** (509) 335-0332. **Baseball SID:** Craig Lawson. **Telephone:** (509) 335-0265. **Fax:** (509) 335-0267.
Assistant Coaches: Gregg Swenson, *Pat Waer. **Telephone:** (509) 335-0216.
Home Field: Bailey-Brayton Field. **Seating Capacity:** 3,500. **Outfield Dimensions:** LF—330, CF—400, RF—330. **Press Box Telephone:** (509) 432-9063.

WEST VIRGINIA MOUNTAINEERS

Conference: Big 12.
Mailing Address: P.O. Box 0877, Morgantown, WV 26507-0877. **Website:** www.wvusports.com.
Head Coach: Randy Mazey. **Telephone:** (304) 293-9881. **Baseball SID:** Grant Dovey. **Telephone:** (304) 293-2821. **Fax:** (304) 293-4105.
Assistant Coaches: *Derek Matlock, Steven Trout. **Telephone:** (304) 293-0067.

Home Field: Hawley Field. **Seating Capacity:** 1,500. **Outfield Dimensions:** LF—325, CF—390, RF—325. **Press Box Telephone:** (304) 293-5988.

WESTERN CAROLINA CATAMOUNTS

Conference: Southern.
Mailing Address: 92 Catamount Rd., Ramsey Center, Cullowhee, NC 28723. **Website:** www.catamountsports. com.
Head Coach: Bobby Moranda. **Telephone:** (828) 227-2021. **Baseball SID:** Daniel Hooker. **Telephone:** (828) 227-2339. **Fax:** (828) 227-7688.
Assistant Coaches: *Alan Beck, Bruce Johnson. **Telephone:** (828) 227-2022.
Home Field: Childress Field at Hennon Stadium. **Seating Capacity:** 1,500. **Outfield Dimensions:** LF—325, CF—390, RF—325. **Press Box Telephone:** (828) 227-7020.

WESTERN ILLINOIS FIGHTING LEATHERNECKS

Conference: Summit.
Mailing Address: 209 Western Hall, 1 University Circle, Macomb, IL 61455. **Website:** www.wiuathletics.com.
Head Coach: Ryan Brownlee. **Telephone:** (309) 298-1521. **Baseball SID:** Sean Ingrassia. **Telephone:** (309) 298-1133. **Fax:** (309) 298-1960.
Assistant Coaches: *Shane Davis, Dusty Napoleon. **Telephone:** (309) 298-1521.
Home Field: Alfred D. Boyer Stadium. **Seating Capacity:** 500. **Outfield Dimensions:** LF—330, CF—400, RF—330. **Press Box Telephone:** (309) 298-3492.

WESTERN KENTUCKY HILLTOPPERS

Conference: Sun Belt.
Mailing Address: 1605 Avenue of Champions, Bowling Green, KY 42104. **Website:** www.wkusports.com.
Head Coach: Matt Myers. **Telephone:** (270) 745-2277. **Baseball SID:** Kyle Allen. **Telephone:** (270) 745-3756. **Fax:** (270) 745-2573.
Assistant Coaches: *Blake Allen, Brendan Dougherty. **Telephone:** (270) 745-2274.
Home Field: Nick Denes Field. **Seating Capacity:** 1,500. **Outfield Dimensions:** LF—330, CF—400, RF—330. **Press Box Telephone:** (270) 745-6941.

WESTERN MICHIGAN BRONCOS

Conference: Mid-American (West).
Mailing Address: 1903 W. Michigan Avenue, Kalamazoo, MI 49008. **Website:** www.wmubroncos.com.
Head Coach: Billy Gernon. **Telephone:** (269) 276-3207. **Baseball SID:** Kristin Keirns. **Telephone:** (269) 387-4123. **Fax:** (269) 387-7063.
Assistant Coaches: *Blaine McFerrin, Matt Rademacher. **Telephone:** (269) 276-3208.
Home Field: Hyames Field at Robert J. Bobb Stadium. **Seating Capacity:** 1,500. **Outfield Dimensions:** LF—310, CF—395, RF—335.

WICHITA STATE SHOCKERS

Conference: Missouri Valley.
Mailing Address: 1845 Fairmount, Box 18, Wichita, KS 67260-0018. **Website:** www.goshockers.com.
Head Coach: Gene Stephenson. **Telephone:** (316) 978-3636. **Baseball SID:** Tami Cutler. **Telephone:** (316) 978-5559. **Fax:** (316) 978-3336.
Assistant Coaches: *Brent Kemnitz, Jim Thomas. **Telephone:** (316) 978-3636.
Home Field: Eck Stadium. **Seating Capacity:** 7,851.

Outfield Dimensions: LF—330, CF—390, RF—330. **Press Box Telephone:** (316) 978-3390.

WILLIAM & MARY TRIBE

Conference: Colonial Athletic.
Mailing Address: P.O. Box 399, Williamsburg, VA 23187. **Website:** www.tribeathletics.com.
Head Coach: Jamie Pinzino. **Telephone:** (757) 221-3492. **Baseball SID:** Travis Lawson. **Telephone:** (757) 221-3344. **Fax:** (757) 221-2989.
Assistant Coaches: Brian Casey, *Brian Murphy. **Telephone:** (757) 221-3475.
Home Field: Plumeri Park. **Seating Capacity:** 1,000. **Press Box Telephone:** (757) 221-3998.

WINTHROP EAGLES

Conference: Big South.
Mailing Address: 1162 Eden Terrace, Rock Hill, SC 29733. **Website:** www.winthropeagles.com.
Head Coach: Tom Riginos. **Telephone:** (803) 323-2129. **Baseball SID:** Jack Frost. **Telephone:** (803) 323-2129. **Fax:** (803) 323-2303.
Assistant Coaches: *Clint Chrysler, Ben Hall. **Telephone:** (803) 323-2129.
Home Field: Winthrop Ball Park. **Seating Capacity:** 1,500. **Outfield Dimensions:** LF—325, CF—390, RF—325. **Press Box Telephone:** (803) 323-2155.

WISCONSIN-MILWAUKEE PANTHERS

Conference: Horizon.
Mailing Address: UWM Athletics, The Pavilion—Room 150, 3409 N. Downer Ave., Milwaukee, WI 53211. **Website:** www.uwmpanthers.com.
Head Coach: Scott Doffek. **Telephone:** (414) 229-5670. **Baseball SID:** Chris Zills. **Telephone:** (414) 229-4593. **Fax:** (414) 229-4593.
Assistant Coaches: *Cory Bigler. **Telephone:** (414) 229-2433.
Home Field: Henry Aaron Field. **Outfield Dimensions:** LF—320, CF—390, RF—320. **Press Box Telephone:** (414) 750-2090.

WOFFORD TERRIERS

Conference: Southern.
Mailing Address: 429 N. Church St., Spartanburg, SC 29303. **Website:** athletics.wofford.edu.
Head Coach: Todd Interdonato. **Telephone:** (864) 597-4497. **Baseball SID:** Brent Williamson. **Telephone:** (864) 597-4093. **Fax:** (864) 597-4112.
Assistant Coaches: *Jason Burke, J.J. Edwards. **Telephone:** (864) 597-4499.
Home Field: Russell C. King Field. **Seating Capacity:** 2,500. **Outfield Dimensions:** LF—325, CF—395, RF—325. **Press Box Telephone:** (864) 597-4487.

WRIGHT STATE RAIDERS

Conference: Horizon.
Mailing Address: 3640 Colonel Glenn Highway, Dayton, OH 45435. **Website:** www.wsuraiders.com.
Head Coach: Rob Cooper. **Telephone:** (937) 775-3667. **Baseball SID:** Matt Zircher. **Telephone:** (937) 775-2831. **Fax:** (937) 775-2368.
Assistant Coaches: *Greg Lovelady, Ross Oeder. **Telephone:** (937) 775-4188.
Home Field: Nischwitz Stadium. **Seating Capacity:** 750. **Outfield Dimensions:** LF—330, CF—400, RF—330. **Press Box Telephone:** (937) 304-6586.

XAVIER MUSKETEERS

Conference: Atlantic 10.
Mailing Address: 3800 Victory Parkway, Cincinnati, OH 45207-7530. **Website:** www.goxavier.com.
Head Coach: Scott Googins. **Telephone:** (513) 745-2891. **Baseball SID:** Bryan McEldowney. **Telephone:** (513) 745-3388. **Fax:** (513) 745-2825.
Assistant Coaches: Dan Hayden, *Nick Otte. **Telephone:** (513) 745-2890.
Home Field: Hayden Field. **Seating Capacity:** 500. **Outfield Dimensions:** LF—310, CF—380, RF—310. **Press Box Telephone:** (937) 478-5027.

YALE BULLDOGS

Conference: Ivy League (Rolfe).
Mailing Address: 20 Tower Parkway, New Haven, CT 06511. **Website:** yalebulldogs.com.
Head Coach: John Stuper. **Telephone:** (203) 432-1466. **Baseball SID:** Jon Erickson. **Telephone:** (203) 432-4747.
Assistant Coaches: *Tucker Frawley, Kevin Huber. **Telephone:** (203) 432-1467.
Home Field: Yale Field. **Seating Capacity:** 6,000.

YOUNGSTOWN STATE PENGUINS

Conference: Horizon.
Mailing Address: 1 University Plaza, Youngstown, OH 44555. **Website:** www.ysusports.com.
Head Coach: Steve Gillispie. **Telephone:** (330) 941-3485. **Baseball SID:** John Vogel. **Telephone:** (330) 941-1480. **Fax:** (330) 941-3191.
Assistant Coaches: *Jason Neal, Kevin Smallcomb. **Telephone:** (304) 633-8150.
Home Field: Eastwood Field. **Seating Capacity:** 6,000. **Outfield Dimensions:** LF—335, CF—405, RF—335. **Press Box Telephone:** (330) 505-0000, ext 229.

AMATEUR & YOUTH

INTERNATIONAL ORGANIZATIONS

INTERNATIONAL BASEBALL FEDERATION

Headquarters: Maison du Sport International—54, Avenue de Rhodanie, 1007 Lausanne, Switzerland. **Telephone:** (+41-21) 318-82-40. **Fax:** (41-21) 318-82-41.
Website: www.ibaf.org. **E-Mail:** office@ibaf.org.
Year Founded: 1938.
President: Riccardo Fraccari.
1st Vice President: Kazuhiro Tawa. **2nd Vice President:** Alonso Perez Gonzalez. **3rd Vice President:** Antonio Castro. **Secretary General:** Israel Roldan. **Treasurer:** Rene Laforce. **Members at Large:** Luis Melero, Tom Peng, Paul Seiler. **Continental VP, Africa:** Ishola Williams. **Continental VP, Americas:** Jorge Otsuka. **Continental VP, Asia:** Kang Seung Kyoo. **Continental VP, Europe:** Petr Ditrich (Acting). **Continental VP, Oceania:** Rob Finlay. **Executive Director:** Michael Schmidt.
Assistant to the President: Oscar Lopez. **Media Relations Coordinator:** Riccardo Schiroli. **Assistant, Media Relations/Webmaster:** Philipp Wuerfel. **Manager, Marketing/Tournaments:** Masaru Yokoo. **Account, Tournaments:** Anna Di Luca. **Account, Anti-Doping:** Victor Isola. **Account, Office Operations:** Francesca Fabretto. **Coordinator, Administration Department:** Jacques Adrien Clermont. **Assistant, Administration/Accounting:** Sandrine Pennone.

CONTINENTAL ASSOCIATIONS

CONFEDERATION PAN AMERICANA DE BEISBOL (COPABE)

Mailing Address: Calle 3, Francisco Filos, Vista Hermosa, Edificio 74, Planta Baja Local No. 1, Panama City, Panama. **Telephone:** (507) 229-8684. **Fax:** Unavailable. **Website:** www.copabe.net. **E-Mail:** copabe@sinfo.net.
President: Eduardo De Bello (Panama). **Secretary General:** Hector Pereyra (Dominican Republic).

AFRICAN BASEBALL/SOFTBALL ASSOCIATION

Mailing Address: Paiko Road, Changaga, Minna, Niger State, PMB 150, Nigeria. **Telephone:** (234-66) 224-555. **Fax:** (234-66) 224-555. **E-Mail Address:** absasecretariat@yahoo.com.
President: Ishola Williams (Nigeria). **Executive Director:** Friday Ichide (Nigeria). **Secretary General:** Mabothobile Shebe (Lesotho).

BASEBALL FEDERATION OF ASIA

Mailing Address: No. 946-16 Dogok-Dong, Kangnam-Gu, Seoul, 135-270 Korea. **Telephone:** (82-2) 572-8413.

Fax: (82-2) 572-8416.
President: Seung-Kyoo Kang (Korea). **Vice Presidents:** Suzuki Yoshinobu (Japan), Chen Tai Cheng (Taipei), Shen Wei (China). **Secretary General:** Sang-Hyun Lee (Korea). **Members At Large:** Allan Mak Nin Fung (Hong Kong), Hector Navasero (Phillippines), Khawar Shah (Pakistan).

EUROPEAN BASEBALL CONFEDERATION

Mailing Address: Otto-FleckSchneise 12, D—60528 Frankfurt, Germany. **Telephone:** +49-69-6700-284. **Fax:** +49-69-67724-212. **E-Mail Address:** office@baseballeurope.com. **Website:** baseballeurope.com.
Acting President: Petr Ditrich (Czech Republic). **1st Vice President:** Unavailable. **2nd Vice President:** Alexander Ratner (Russia). **3rd Vice President:** Mick Manning (Ireland). **Secretary General:** Unavailable. **Treasurer:** Rene Laforce (Belgium). **Vocals:** Mats Fransson (Sweden), Attila Borbely (Hungary), Monique Schmitt (Switzerland), Juan Garcia (Spain), Rainer Husty (Austria).

BASEBALL CONFEDERATION OF OCEANIA

Mailing Address: 48 Partridge Way, Mooroolbark, Victoria 3138, Australia. **Telephone:** 613 9727 1779. **Fax:** 613 9727 5959. **E-Mail Address:** bcosecgeneral@baseballoceania.com. **Website:** www.baseballoceania.com.
President: Ron Finlay (Australia). **1st Vice President:** Bob Steffy (Guam). **2nd Vice President:** Laurent Cassier (New Caledonia). **Secretary General:** Chet Gray (Australia). **Executive Committee:** David Ballinger (New Zealand), Ronald Seeto (Fiji), Rose Igitol (Commonwealth of Northern Mariana Islands).

ORGANIZATIONS

INTERNATIONAL GOODWILL SERIES, INC.

Mailing Address: 982 Slate Drive, Santa Rosa, CA 95405. **Telephone:** (707) 538-0777. **E-Mail Address:** bobw.24@goodwillseries.org. **Website:** www.goodwillseries.org.
President, Goodwill Series, Inc.: Bob Williams.

INTERNATIONAL SPORTS GROUP

Mailing Address: 3135 South Vermont Ave., Milwaukee, WI 53207. **Telephone:** (541) 882-4293. **E-Mail Address:** isgbaseball@yahoo.com. **Website:** www.isg-baseball.com.
President: Jim Jones. **Vice President:** Tom O'Connell.
President, Goodwill Series, Inc.: Bob Williams.
President: Jim Jones. **Vice President:** Tom O'Connell.
Secretary/Treasurer: Randy Town.

NATIONAL ORGANIZATIONS

USA BASEBALL

Mailing Address, Corporate Headquarters: 403 Blackwell St., Durham, NC 27701. **Telephone:** (919) 474-8721. **Fax:** (919) 474-8822. **E-Mail Address:** info@usabaseball.com. **Website:** www.usabaseball.com.
President: Mike Gaski. **Treasurer:** Jason Dobis, John McHale, Jr. (Major League Baseball), Steven Cloud (American Legion), Steve Tellefsen (Babe Ruth), Damani Leech (NCAA); Jenny Dalton-Hill (Recent Athlete), John Gall (Recent Athlete), George Grande (At Large).
Executive Director/Chief Executive Officer: Paul Seiler. **Director, National Team Development Programs & Women's National Team:** Ashley Bratcher. **General Manager, National Teams:** Eric Campbell. **Chief Financial Officer:** Ray Darwin. **Director, Travel Services:** Jocelyn Fern. **Director, Digital & Social Media:** Kevin Jones. **Chief Operating Officer:** David Perkins. **Director, Development:** Rick Riccobono. **Director, Community Relations:** Lindsay Robertson. **Director, 18U National

Team/Alumni: Brant Ust.

National Members: Amateur Athletic Union (AAU), American Amateur Baseball Congress (AABC), American Baseball Coaches Association (ABCA), American Legion Baseball, Babe Ruth Baseball, Dixie Baseball, Little LeagueBaseball, National Amateur Baseball Federation (NABF), National Association of Intercollegiate Athletics (NAIA), National Baseball Congress (NBC), National Collegiate Athletic Association (NCAA), National Federation of State High School Athletic Associations, National High School Baseball Coaches Association (BCA), National Junior College Athletic Association (NJCAA), Police Athletic League (PAL), PONY Baseball, T-Ball USA, United States Specialty Sports Association (USSSA), YMCAs of the USA.

Events: www.usabaseball.com/events/schedule.jsp.

BASEBALL CANADA

Mailing Address: 2212 Gladwin Cres., Suite A7, Ottawa, Ontario K1B 5N1. **Telephone:** (613) 748-5606. **Fax:** (613) 748-5767. **E-Mail Address:** info@baseball.ca. **Website:** www.baseball.ca.

Director General: Jim Baba. **Head Coach/Director,**

National Teams: Greg Hamilton. **Manager, Baseball Operations:** Andre Lachance. **Program Coordinator:** Kelsey McIntosh. **Manager, Media/Public Relations:** Andre Cormier. **Administrative Coordinator:** Denise Thomas. **Administrative Assistant:** Penny Baba.

NATIONAL BASEBALL CONGRESS

Mailing Address: 300 S. Sycamore, Wichita, KS 67213. **Telephone:** (316) 264-6887. **Fax:** (316) 264-2129. **Website:** www.nbcbaseball.com.

Year Founded: 1931.

General Manager: Josh Robertson. **Tournament Director:** Casey Walkup.

ATHLETES IN ACTION

Mailing Address: 651 Taylor Dr., Xenia, OH 45385. **Telephone:** (937) 352-1000. **Fax:** (937) 352-1245. **E-Mail Address:** baseball@athletesinaction.org. **Website:** www. aiabaseball.org.

Director, AIA Baseball: Jason Lester. **U.S. Teams Director:** Chris Beck. **International Teams Director:** John McLaughlin. **General Manager, Great Lakes:** John Henschen. **Athletic Trainer:** Natalie McLaughlin.

SUMMER COLLEGE LEAGUES

NATIONAL ALLIANCE OF COLLEGE SUMMER BASEBALL

Telephone: (508) 404-7403. **E-Mail Address:** pgalop@comcast.net. **Website:** www.nacsb.org.

Executive Directors: Bobby Bennett (Sunbelt Baseball League), Immediate Past, Jeff Carter (Southern Collegiate Baseball League). **Assistant Executive Director:** David Biery (Valley Baseball League). **Treasurer:** Larry Tremitiere (Southern Collegiate Baseball League). **Director, Public Relations/Secretary:** Stefano Foggi (Florida Collegiate Summer League). **Compliance Officer:** Kim Lance (Great Lakes Summer Collegiate League).

Member Leagues: Atlantic Collegiate Baseball League, Cal Ripken Collegiate Baseball League, Cape Cod Baseball League, Florida Collegiate Summer League, Great Lakes Summer Collegiate League, New England Collegiate Baseball League, New York Collegiate Baseball League, Southern Collegiate Baseball League, Sunbelt Baseball League, Valley Baseball League.

ALASKA BASEBALL LEAGUE

Mailing Address: 435 West 10th Avenue, Suite B, Anchorage, AK 99501. **Telephone:** (907) 283-6186. **Fax:** (907) 746-5068. **E-Mail Address:** mikebaxter@acsalaska. net.

Year Founded: 1974 (reunited, 1998).

President: Shawn Maltby (Anchorage Bucs). **VP, Secretary:** James Clark (Peninsula Oilers). **VP, Rules/Membership:** Chris Beck (Chugiak-Eagle River Chinooks). **3rd VP:** Pete Christopher (Mat-Su Miners). **VP, Marketing:** Jon Dyson (Anchorage Glacier Pilots). **VP, Umpiring/Scheduling:** Don Dennis (Goldpanners). **League Spokesperson:** Mike Baxter. **League Stats:** Dick Lobdell.

Regular Season: 40 league games and approximately 5 non-league games. **2013 Opening Date:** June 9. **Closing Date:** Aug 1.

Playoff Format: Regular-season league champion qualifies for National Baseball Congress World Series if desired. Also, a round robin end-of-season tournament

with a best 2-of-3 final determines playoff champion.

Roster Limit: 26 plus exemption for Alaska residents. **Player Eligibility:** Open except drafted college seniors.

ANCHORAGE BUCS

Mailing Address: P.O. Box 240061, Anchorage, AK 99524-0061. **Telephone:** (907) 561-2827. **Fax:** (907) 561-2920. **E-Mail Address:** gm@anchoragebucs.com. **Website:** anchoragebucs.com. **General Manager:** Shawn Maltby. **Head Coach:** Tony Cappuccilli (Irvine Valley, Calif, CC).

ANCHORAGE GLACIER PILOTS

Mailing Address: 435 West 10th Avenue, Suite A, Anchorage, AK 99501. **Telephone:** (907) 274-3627. **Fax:** (907) 274-3628. **E-Mail Address:** gpilots@alaska. net. **Website:** glacierpilots.com. **General Manager:** Jon Dyson. **Head Coach:** Conor Bird (CC of Marin, Calif.).

CHUGIAK-EAGLE RIVER CHINOOKS

Mailing Address: 651 Taylor Dr., Xenia, OH 45385. **Telephone:** (937) 352-1237. **Fax:** (937) 352-1245. **E-Mail Address:** chris.beck@athletesinaction.org. **Website:** www.aiabaseball.org. **General Manager:** Chris Beck. **Head Coach:** Jon Groth (Tyler, Texas, CC).

FAIRBANKS ALASKA GOLDPANNERS

Mailing Address: P.O. Box 71154, Fairbanks, AK 99707. **Telephone:** (907) 451-0095, (619) 561-4581. **Fax:** (907) 456-6429, (619) 561-4581. **E-Mail Address:** todd@goldpanners.com. **Website:** goldpanners.com. **General Manager:** Todd Dennis. **Head Coach:** Bryan Harris (Santa Ana, Calif, JC).

MAT-SU MINERS

Mailing Address: P.O. Box 2690, Palmer, AK 99645-2690. **Telephone:** (907) 746-4914; (907) 745-6401. **Fax:**

(907) 746-5068. **E-Mail Address:** generalmanager@
matsuminers.org. **Website:** matsuminers.org. **General
Manager:** Pete Christopher. **Assistant GM:** Bob Plumley.
Head Coach: Unavailable.

PENINSULA OILERS

Mailing Address: 601 S. Main St., Kenai, AK 99611.
Telephone: (907) 283-7133. **Fax:** (907) 283-3390. **E-Mail
Address:** gm@oilersbaseball.com. **Website:** oilersbase-
ball.com. **General Manager:** James Clark. **Head Coach:**
Kyle Richardson (Yuba, Calif, CC).

ATLANTIC COLLEGIATE
BASEBALL LEAUGE

Mailing Address: 1760 Joanne Drive, Quakertown, PA
18951. **Telephone:** (215) 536-5777. **Fax:** (215) 536-5777.
E-Mail: tbonekemper@verizon.net. **Website:** www.acbl-
online.com.
Year Founded: 1967.
Commissioner: Ralph Addonizio. **President:** Tom
Bonekemper. **Vice President:** Doug Cinella. **Secretary:**
Nick Rizzacasa. **Treasurer:** Bob Hoffman.
Regular Season: 40 games. **2013 Opening Date:** June
1. **Closing Date:** Aug 8. **All-Star Game:** July 22, 7 pm,
Memorial Park, Quakertown, Pa.
Roster Limit: 25.

ALLENTOWN RAILERS

Mailing Address: Suite 202, 1801 Union Blvd.,
Allentown, PA 18109. **E-Mail Address:** ddando@lehighval-
leybaseballacademy.com. **Field Manager:** Dylan Dando.

JERSEY PILOTS

Mailing Address: 401 Timber Dr., Berkeley Heights,
NJ 07922. **Telephone:** (908) 464-8042. **E-Mail Address:**
bensmookler@aol.com. **President/General Manager:**
Ben Smookler. **Field Manager:** Aaron Kalb.

LEHIGH VALLEY CATZ

Mailing Address: 103 Logan Dr., Easton, PA 18045.
Telephone: (610) 533-9349. **Website:** www.lvcatz.com.
General Manager: Pat O'Connell. **Field Manager:** Dennis
Morgan.

NORTH JERSEY EAGLES

Mailing Address: 107 Pleasant Avenue, Upper Saddle
River, NJ 07458. **General Manager:** Brian Casey. **Field
Manager:** Jorge Hernandez.

QUAKERTOWN BLAZERS

Telephone: (215) 679-5072. **E-Mail Address:**
gbonekemper@yahoo.com. **Website:** www.quaker-
townblazers.com. **General Manager:** Jerry Mayza. **Field
Manager:** Mark Angelo.

STATEN ISLAND TIDE

Website: www.statenislandtide.com. **General
Manager:** Gary Sutphen. **Field Manager:** Tommy Weber.

TRENTON GENERALS

E-Mail Address: gally22@aol.com. **General Manager:**
Dave Gallagher. **Field Manager:** Jim Maher.

CALIFORNIA COLLEGIATE LEAGUE

Mailing Address: 806 W Pedregosa St., Santa Barbara,
CA 93101. **Telephone:** (805) 680-1047. **Fax:** (805) 684-
8596. **Email Address:** burns@calsummerball.com.
Website: www.calsummerball.com.
Year Founded: 1993.
Commissioner: Pat Burns.
Division Structure: North Division—Bakersfield
Sound, Conejo Oaks, San Luis Obispo Blues, Santa Barbara
Foresters. **South**—Academy Barons, Los Angeles Brewers,
Southern California Catch, Team Vegas Baseball Club.
Regular Season: 36 games (24 divisional games, 12
inter-divisional games).
2013 Opening Date: June 1. **Closing Date:** July 31.
Playoff Format: Divisional champions meet in a best two-
out-of-three championship series.
Roster Limit: 33.

ACADEMY BARONS

Address: 901 E. Artesia Blvd., Compton, CA 90221.
Telephone: (310) 635-2967.
Website: www.academybarons.org. **Email Address:**
tavelli08@gmail.com.
Director: Don Buford. **Field Manager:** Tip Lefebvre.

BAKERSFIELD SOUND

Address: P.O. Box 20760, Bakersfield, CA 93390.
Telephone: (661) 343-2616.
Website: www.calsummerball.com. **Email Address:**
bakersfieldsound.baseball@yahoo.com.
General Manager: Dave Packer. **Field Manager:** Rob
Paramo.

CONEJO OAKS

Address: 1710 N. Moorpark Rd., #106, Thousand Oaks,
CA91360. **Telephone:** (805) 797-7889. **Fax:** (805) 529-
9862. **Email Address:** oaksbaseball@roadrunner.com.
Website: www.oaksbaseball.org.
General Managers: Randy Riley, Verne Merrill. **Field
Manager:** David Soilz.

LOS ANGELES BREWERS

Address: 2312 Park Ave., #413, Tustin CA 92626.
Telephone: (949) 278-2458.
Email Address: jwicks@labrewersbaseball.com.
Website: www.labrewersbaseball.com. **General
Manager/Field Manager:** Jameson Wicks.

SAN LUIS OBISPO BLUES

Address: 241-B Prado Rd., San Luis Obispo, CA 93401.
Telephone: (805) 215-6660. **Fax:** (805) 528-1146. **Email
Address:** chal@bluesbaseball.com. **Website:** www.blues-
baseball.com. **General Manager:** Adam Stowe. **Field
Manager:** Chal Fanning.

SANTA BARBARA FORESTERS

Address: 4299 Carpinteria Ave., Suite 201, Carpinteria,
CA 93013. **Telephone:** (805) 684-0657. **Email Address:**
foresters19@dock.net. **Website:** www.sbforesters.org.
General Manager/Field Manager: Bill Pintard.

SOUTHERN CALIFORNIA CATCH

Address: 14830 Grayville Drive, La Mirada, CA 90638.
Telephone: (562) 686-8262. **Email Address:** borr@fca.org.
Website: www.socalfcabaseball.org. **General Manager:**
Ben Orr.

TEAM VEGAS BASEBALL CLUB

Address: 9265 Euphoria Rose Ave., Las Vegas NV 89166. **Telephone:** (702) 575-9394. **Email Address:** rangerbuck2002@yahoo.com. **Website:** www.teamvegasbaseball.com. **General Manager/Field Manager:** Buck Thomas.

CAL RIPKEN COLLEGIATE LEAGUE

Address: 5804 Inman Park Circle #370, Rockville, MD 20852. **Telephone:** (301) 793-1311. **E-Mail:** athompson@calripkenleague.org. **Website:** www.calripkenleague.org. **Year Founded:** 2005. **Commissioner:** Alex Thompson. **Deputy Commissioner:** Jerry Wargo.

Regular Season: 44 games. **2013 Opening Date:** June 6. **Closing Date:** July 28. **All-Star Game:** July 17 at Povich Field in Bethesda, MD. **Playoff Format:** Six-team, first round single-elimination, then double-elimination tournament, July 30-Aug 4. **Roster Limit:** 30 (college-eligible players 22 and under).

ALEXANDRIA ACES

Address: 600 14th Street NW, Suite 400, Washington, DC 20005. **Telephone:** (202) 255-1683. **E-Mail:** ddinan@ralaw.com. **Website:** www.alexandriaaces.org. **President/General Manager:** Donald Dinan. **Head Coach:** David DeSilva. **Ballpark:** Frank Mann Field at Four Mile Run Park.

BALTIMORE REDBIRDS

Address: 2208 Pine Hill Farms Lane, Cockeysville, MD 21030. **Telephone:** (410) 802-2220. **Fax:** (410) 785-6138. **E-Mail:** johntcarey@hotmail.com. **Website:** www.baltimoreredbirds.org. **President:** John Carey. **Head Coach:** Michael Carter. **Ballpark:** Carlo Crispino Stadium at Calvert Hall High School.

BETHESDA BIG TRAIN

Address: 5420 Butler Road, Bethesda, MD 20816. **Telephone:** (301) 983-1006. **Fax:** (301) 229-8362. **E-Mail:** faninfo@bigtrain.org. **Website:** www.bigtrain.org. **General Manager:** Adam Dantus. **Head Coach:** Sal Colangelo. **Ballpark:** Shirley Povich Field.

D.C. GRAYS

Address: 900 19th Street NW, 8th floor, Washington, DC 20006. **Telephone:** (202) 327-8116. **Fax:** (202) 327-8101. **Website:** www.dcgrays.com. **E-Mail Address:** barbera@acg-consultants.com. **President/Chairman:** Michael Barbera. **General Manager:** Antonio Scott. **Head Coach:** Arlan Freeman. **Ballpark:** Hoy Field at Gallaudet University.

GAITHERSBURG GIANTS

Address: 10 Brookes Avenue, Gaithersburg, MD 20877. **Telephone:** (240) 888-6810. **Fax:** (301) 355-5006. **E-Mail:** alriley13@gmail.com. **Website:** www.gaithersburggiants.org. **General Manager:** Alfie Riley. **Head Coach:** Jeff Rabberman. **Ballpark:** Kelley Park.

FCA HERNDON BRAVES

Address: 1305 Kelly Court, Herndon, VA 20170-2605. **Telephone:** (702) 909-2750. **Fax:** (703) 783-1319. **E-Mail:** fcaherndonbraves@yahoo.com. **Website:** www.herndonbraves.com. **President/General Manager:** Todd Burger. **Head Coach:** Justin Janis. **Ballpark:** Alan McCullock Field at Herndon High School.

PRESSTMAN CARDINALS

Address: 10441 Hickory Ridge Road L, Columbia, MD 21044. **Telephone:** (410) 782-5708. **Fax:** (410) 730-4620. **E-Mail:** presstmancards@hotmail.com. **Website:** www.presstmancardinals.org. **President/Head Coach:** Reginald Smith. **General Manager:** Ray Hale. **Ballpark:** Joe Cannon Stadium.

ROCKVILLE EXPRESS

Address: P.O. Box 10188, Rockville, MD 20849. **Telephone:** (301) 367-9435. **E-Mail:** info@rockvilleexpress.org. **Website:** www.rockvilleexpress.org. **President/GM:** Jim Kazunas. **Vice President:** Brad Botwin. **Head Coach:** Rick Price. **Ballpark:** Knights Field at Montgomery College-Rockville.

SILVER SPRING-TAKOMA T-BOLTS

Address: 906 Glaizewood Court, Takoma Park, MD 20912. **Telephone:** (301) 270-0794. **E-Mail:** tboltsbaseball@gmail.com. **Website:** www.tbolts.org. **General Manager:** David Stinson. **Head Coach:** Doug Remer. **Ballpark:** Blair Stadium at Montgomery Blair High School.

SOUTHERN MARYLAND NATIONALS

Address: 2243 Garrity Rd., Saint Leonard, MD 20685. **Telephone:** (301) 751-6299. **E-Mail:** winegard@erols.com. **Website:** www.somdnationals.com. **President:** Chuck Winegardner. **General Manager:** Don Herbert. **Head Coach:** Doug Creek. **Ballpark:** Regency Furniture Stadium.

VIENNA RIVER DOGS

Address: 12703 Hitchcock Ct., Reston, VA 20191. **Telephone:** (703) 615-4396. **Fax:** (703) 904-1723. **E-Mail Address:** tickets@brucehallsports.com. **Website:** www.viennariverdogs.org. **President/General Manager/Head Coach:** Bruce Hall. **Ballpark:** James Madison High School.

YOUSE'S ORIOLES

Address: 3 Oyster Court, Baltimore, MD 21219. **Telephone:** (410) 477-3764. **E-Mail:** tnt017@comcast.net. **Website:** www.youseorioles.com. **General Manager/Head Coach:** Tim Norris. **Ballpark:** Bachman Park.

CAPE COD LEAGUE

Mailing Address: P.O. Box 266, Harwich Port, MA 02646. **Telephone:** (508) 404-8597. **E-Mail:** info@capecodbaseball.org. **Website:** www.capecodbaseball.org.

Year Founded: 1885.

Commissioner: Paul Galop. **President:** Judy Walden Scarafile. **Treasurer/Webmaster:** Steven Wilson. **Secretary:** Kim Wolfe. **Senior VP:** Jim Higgins. **VP/Deputy Commissioner:** Bill Bussiere. **VP:** Peter Ford. **Senior Deputy Commissioner/Director, Officiating:** Sol Yas. **Deputy Commissioner-West:** Jim McNally. **Deputy Commissioner-East:** Peter Hall. **Deputy Commissioner Emeritus:** Dick Sullivan.

Director, Public Relations/Broadcasting: John Garner Jr. **Director, Communications:** Jim McGonigle. **Director, Publications:** Lou Barnicle. **Director, Memorabilia:** Dan Dunn. **Editor, Publications:** Rich Plante. **Assistant to the Officers:** Bill Watson. **Assistants, Marketing:** Melissa Ellis, Sue Pina. **Director, Social Media:** Ashley Crosby. **Coordinator, Special Events/Projects:** Joe Sherman. **Website Editor:** Victoria Martin.

Division Structure: **East**—Brewster, Chatham,

Harwich, Orleans, Yarmouth-Dennis. **Western—**Bourne, Cotuit, Falmouth, Hyannis, Wareham. **Regular Season:** 44 games. **2013 Opening Date:** June 14. **Closing Date:** Aug 15. **All-Star Game:** July 28. **Playoff Format:** Top four teams in each division qualify. Three rounds of best-of-three series. **Roster Limit:** 25 (college-eligible players only).

BOURNE BRAVES

Mailing Address: P.O. Box 895, Monument Beach, MA 02553. **Telephone:** (508) 345-1013. **E-Mail Address:** bournebravesgm@hotmail.com. **Website:** www.bournebraves. org. **President:** Nicole Norkevicius. **General Manager:** Chuck Sturtevant. **Head Coach:** Harvey Shapiro.

BREWSTER WHITECAPS

Mailing Address: P.O. Box 2349, Brewster, MA 02631. **Telephone:** (508) 896-8500, ext 147. **Fax:** (508) 896-9845. **E-Mail Address:** cagradone@comcast.net. **Website:** www.brewsterwhitecaps.com. **President:** Claire Gradone. **General Manager:** Ned Monthie. **Head Coach:** John Altobelli.

CHATHAM ANGLERS

Mailing Address: P.O. Box 428, Chatham, MA 02633. **Telephone:** (508) 241-8382. **Fax:** (508) 430-8323. **Website:** www.chathamas.com. **President:** Doug Grattan. **General Manager:** Bob Sherman. **Head Coach:** John Schiffner.

COTUIT KETTLEERS

Mailing Address: P.O. Box 411, Cotuit, MA 02635. **Telephone:** (508) 428-3358. **Fax:** (508) 420-5584. **E-Mail Address:** info@kettleers.org. **Website:** www.kettleers.org. **President:** Paul Logan. **General Manager:** Bruce Murphy. **Head Coach:** Mike Roberts.

FALMOUTH COMMODORES

Mailing Address: P.O. Box 808 Falmouth, MA 02541. **Telephone:** (508) 472-7922. **Fax:** (508) 862-6011. **Website:** www.falcommodores.org. **President:** Steve Kostas. **General Manager:** Eric Zmuda. **Head Coach:** Jeff Trundy.

HARWICH MARINERS

Mailing Address: P.O. Box 201, Harwich Port, MA 02646. **Telephone:** (508) 432-2000. **Fax:** (508) 432-5357. **E-Mail Address:** mehendy@comcast.net. **Website:** www.harwichmariners.org. **President:** Mary Henderson. **General Manager:** Ben Layton. **Head Coach:** Steve Englert.

HYANNIS HARBOR HAWKS

Mailing Address: P.O. Box 852, Hyannis, MA 02601. **Telephone:** (508) 364-3164. **Fax:** (508) 534-1270. **E-Mail Address:** bbussiere@harborhawks.org. **Website:** www. harborhawks.org. **President:** Brad Pfeifer. **General Manager:** Tino DiGiovanni. **Head Coach:** Chad Gassman.

ORLEANS FIREBIRDS

Mailing Address: P.O. Box 504, Orleans, MA 02653. **Telephone:** (508) 255-0793. **Fax:** (508) 255-2237. **Website:** www.orleansfirebirds.com. **President:** Steven Garran. **General Manager:** Sue Horton. **Head Coach:** Kelly Nicholson.

WAREHAM GATEMEN

Mailing Address: P.O. Box 287, Wareham, MA 02571. **Telephone:** (508) 748-0287. **Fax:** (508) 880-2602. **E-Mail Address:** sheri.gay4gatemen@comcast.net. **Website:** www.gatemen.org. **President/General Manager:** Thomas Gay. **Head Coach:** Cooper Farris.

YARMOUTH-DENNIS RED SOX

Mailing Address: P.O. Box 814, South Yarmouth, MA 02664. **Telephone:** (508) 394-9387. **Fax:** (508) 398-2239. **E-Mail Address:** jimmartin321@yahoo.com. **Website:** www.ydredsox.org. **President:** Steve Faucher. **General Manager:** Jim Martin. **Head Coach:** Scott Pickler.

COASTAL PLAIN LEAGUE

Mailing Address: 125 Quantum Street, Holly Springs, NC27540. **Telephone:** (919) 852-1960. **Fax:** (919) 516-0852. **Email Address:** justins@coastalplain.com. **Website:** www.coastalplain.com.

Year Founded: 1997.

Chairman/CEO: Jerry Petitt. **President:** Pete Bock. **Commissioner:** Justin Sellers. **Director, On-Field Operations:** Jeff Bock.

Division Structure: East—Edenton, Fayetteville, Morehead City, Peninsula, Petersburg, Wilmington, Wilson. **West—**Asheboro, Columbia, Florence, Forest City, Gastonia, Martinsville, Thomaville.

Regular Season: 56 games (split schedule). **2013 Opening Date:** May 28. **Closing Date:** August 17. **All-Star Game:** July 8. **Playoff Format:** Three rounds, best of three in each round (August 7-17).

Roster Limit: 30 (college-eligible players only).

ASHEBORO COPPERHEADS

Mailing Address: P.O. Box 4006, Asheboro, NC 27204. **Telephone:** (336) 460-7018. **Fax:** (336) 629-2651. **E-Mail Address:** info@teamcopperhead.com. **Website:** www. teamcopperhead.com. **Owners:** Ronnie Pugh, Steve Pugh, Doug Pugh, Mike Pugh. **General Manager:** David Camp. **Head Coach:** Donnie Wilson (Cal State-Dominguez Hills).

COLUMBIA BLOWFISH

Mailing Address: P.O. **Box 1328, Columbia, SC 29202. Telephone:** (803) 254-3474. **Fax:** (803) 254-4482. **E-Mail Address:** info@blowfishbaseball.com. **Website:** www.blowfishbaseball.com. **Owner:** HWS Baseball V (Michael Savit, Bill Shanahan). **General Manager:** Skip Anderson. **Head Coach:** Unavailable.

EDENTON STEAMERS

Mailing Address: P.O. Box 86, Edenton, NC 27932. **Telephone:** (252) 482-4080. **Fax:** (252) 482-1717. **E-Mail Address:** edentonsteamers@hotmail.com. **Website:** www.edentonsteamers.com. **Owner:** Edenton Steamers Inc. **President:** Wallace Evans. **General Manager:** Chip Pruden. **Head Coach:** Dan Pirillo (Chicago State).

FAYETTEVILLE SWAMPDOGS

Mailing Address: P.O. Box 64691, Fayetteville, NC 28306.**Telephone:** (910) 426-5900. **Fax:** (910) 426-3544. **E-Mail Address:** info@fayettevilleswampdogs. com. **Website:** www.goswampdogs.com. **Owners:** Lew Handelsman, Darrell Handelsman. **General Manager:** Jeremy Aagard. **Head Coach:** Darrell Handelsman.

FLORENCE REDWOLVES

Mailing Address: P.O. Box 809, Florence, SC 29503. **Telephone:** (843) 629-0700. **Fax:** (843) 629-0703. **E-Mail Address:** jamie@florenceredwolves.com. **Website:** www.florenceredwolves.com. **Owners:** Kevin Barth, Donna Barth. **General Manager:** Jamie Young. **Head Coach:** Jared Barkdoll (Francis Marion).

FOREST CITY OWLS

Mailing Address: P.O. Box 1062, Forest City, NC 28043. **Telephone:** (828) 245-0000. **Fax:** (828) 245-6666. **E-Mail Address:** forestcitybaseball@yahoo.com. **Website:** www.forestcitybaseball.com. **Owner/President:** Ken Silver. **Managing Partner:** Jesse Cole. **General Manager:** Jeremy Boler. **Head Coach:** David Tufo (Menlo College).

GASTONIA GRIZZLIES

Mailing Address: P.O. Box 177, Gastonia, NC 28053. **Telephone:** (704) 866-8622. **Fax:** (704) 864-6122. **E-Mail Address:** jesse@gastoniagrizzlies.com. **Website:** www.gastoniagrizzlies.com. **President:** Ken Silver. **Managing Partner/General Manager:** Jesse Cole. **Head Coach:** Jason Wood (Southeastern CC).

MARTINSVILLE MUSTANGS

Mailing Address: P.O. Box 1112, Martinsville, VA 24114. **Telephone:** (276) 403-5250. **Fax:** (276) 403-5387. **E-Mail Address:** jesse@teamcoleandassociates.com. **Website:** www.martinsvillemustangs.com. **Owner:** City of Martinsville. **General Manager:** Unavailable. **Head Coach:** Matt Duffy.

MOREHEAD CITY MARLINS

Mailing Address: 1921 Oglesby Road, Morehead City, NC 28557. **Telephone:** (252) 269-9767. **Fax:** (252) 727-9402. **E-Mail Address:** mitch@mhcmarlins.com. **Website:** www.mhcmarlins.com. **President:** Buddy Bengel. **General Manager:** Mitch Kluver. **Head Coach:** Jamie Sheetz (Missouri State).

PENINSULA PILOTS

Mailing Address: P.O. Box 7376, Hampton, VA 23666. **Telephone:** (757) 245-2222. **Fax:** (757) 245-8030. **E-Mail Address:** jeffscott@peninsulapilots.com. **Website:** www.peninsulapilots.com. **Owner:** Henry Morgan. **General Manager:** Jeffrey Scott. **Head Coach/Vice President:** Hank Morgan.

PETERSBURG GENERALS

Mailing Address: 1981 Midway Ave., Petersburg, VA 23803. **Telephone:** (804) 722-0141. **Fax:** (804) 733-7370. **E-Mail Address:** petggenerals@earthlink.net. **Website:** www.generals.petersburgsports.com. **Owner:** City of Petersburg. **General Manager:** Ryan Massenburg. **Head Coach:** Bob Smith.

THOMASVILLE HI-TOMS

Mailing Address: P.O. Box 3035, Thomasville, NC 27361. **Telephone:** (336) 472-8667. **Fax:** (336) 472-7198. **E-Mail Address:** info@hitoms.com. **Website:** www.hitoms.com. **Owner:** Richard Holland. **President:** Greg Suire. **Director, Business Relations:** Nick Gaski. **Head Coach:** Zach Brown (Furman).

WILMINGTON SHARKS

Mailing Address: P.O. Box 15233, Wilmington, NC 28412. **Telephone:** (910) 343-5621. **Fax:** (910) 343-8932. **E-Mail Address:** info@wilmingtonsharks.com. **Website:** www.wilmingtonsharks.com. **Owners:** Lew Handelsman, Darrell Handelsman. **General Manager:** TBD. **Head Coach:** Ryan McCleney (UNC Pembroke).

WILSON TOBS

Mailing Address: P.O. Box 633, Wilson, NC 27894. **Telephone:** (252) 291-8627. **Fax:** (252) 291-1224. **E-Mail Address:** wilsontobs@gmail.com. **Website:** www.wilsontobs.com. **Owner:** Richard Holland. **President:** Greg Suire. **General Manager:** Thomas Webb. **Head Coach:** Austin Love.

FLORIDA COLLEGIATE SUMMER LEAGUE

Mailing Address: 55 West Crystal Lake Street, Suite 50, Orlando, FL 32806. **Telephone:** (321) 206-9174. **Fax:** (407) 574-7926. **E-Mail Address:** info@floridaleague.com. **Website:** www.floridaleague.com.

Year Founded: 2004.

CEO: Sara Whiting. **President/COO:** Rob Sitz. **Vice President:** Stefano Foggi. **League Operations:** Phil Chinnery. **Marketing Director:** Jay Hatch. **Regular Season:** 45 games. **2013 Opening Date:** June 5. **Closing Date:** Aug 4. **All-Star Game:** July 11. **Playoff Format:** Five teams, No. 4 and No. 5 seed play-in game. Second round features two best-of-three series, with winners meeting in winner-take-all championship game. **Roster Limit:** 27 (college-eligible players only).

DELAND SUNS

Operated through league office. **E-Mail Address:** delandsuns@floridaleague.com. **Head Coach:** Rick Hall.

LEESBURG LIGHTNING

Mailing Address: 318 South 2nd St., Leesburg, FL 34748. **Telephone:** (352) 728-9885. **E-Mail Address:** leesburglightning@floridaleague.com. **President:** Bruce Ericson. **Head Coach:** Dave Therneau.

ORLANDO FREEDOM

Operated through league office. **E-Mail Address:** orlandofreedom@floridaleague.com. **Head Coach:** Scott Makarewicz.

ORLANDO MONARCHS

Operated through league office. **E-Mail Address:** orlandomonarchs@floridaleague.com. **President:** Rickie Weeks Sr. **Head Coach:** Unavailable.

SANFORD RIVER RATS

Operated through league office. **E-Mail Address:** sanfordriverrats@floridaleague.com. **Head Coach:** Ken Kelly.

WINTER PARK DIAMOND DAWGS

Operated through league office. **E-Mail Address:** winterparkdiamonddawgs@floridaleague.com. **Head Coach:** Kevin Davidson.

FUTURES COLLEGIATE LEAGUE OF NEW ENGLAND

Mailing Address: 46 Chestnut Hill Rd., Chelmsford, MA 01824. **Telephone:** (617) 593-2112. **E-Mail Address:** futuresleague@yahoo.com. **Website:** www.thefutures-league.com.

Year Founded: 2010.
Commissioner: Chris Hall.
Member Clubs (team contact): Brockton Rox, Martha's Vineyard Sharks, Nashua Silver Knights, North Shore Navigators, Old Orchard Beach Raging Tide, Pittsfield Suns, Seacoast Mavericks, Torrington Titans, Wachusett Dirt Dogs. **Regular Season:** 54 games. **2013 Opening Date:** June 6. **Closing Date:** Aug 8. **Playoff Format:** Top six teams make playoffs. Top two teams get byes. No. 3 seed plays No. 6 seed and No. 4 seed plays No. 5 seed in one-game playoffs. Winners play top two seeds in best-of-three semifinal series. Winners meet in best-of-three championship series. Roster Limit: 30. Half must be from New England or play collegiately at a New England college.

GREAT LAKES SUMMER COLLEGIATE LEAGUE

Mailing Address: 133 W. Winter St., Delaware, OH 43015. **Telephone:** (740) 368-3527. **Fax:** (740) 368-3999. **E-Mail Address:** kalance@owu.edu. **Website:** www.great-lakesleague.org. **Year Founded:** 1986.
President/Commissioner: Kim Lance.
Regular Season: 40 games. **2013 Opening Date:** June 6. **Closing Date:** July 28. **All-Star Game:** July 10 at Western Hills High School, Cincinnati, OH. **Playoff Format:** Top six teams meet in playoffs.
Roster Limit: 30 (college-eligible players only).

CINCINNATI STEAM

Mailing Address: 2745 Anderson Ferry Rd., Cincinnati, OH 45238. **Telephone:** (513) 922-4272. **Website:** www.cincinnatisteam.com. **GeneralManager:** Max McLeary. **Head Coach:** Billy O'Connor.

DAYTON DOCS

Mailing Address: Dayton Docs Baseball Club, P.O. Box 773, Greenville, OH 45331. **Telephone:** (937) 423-3053. **Website:** www.docsbaseball.com. **President/General Manager:** Joe Marker. **Head Coach:** Burt Davis.

GRAND LAKE MARINERS

Mailing Address: 1460 James Drive, Celina, OH 45822. **Telephone:** (419) 586-3187. **Website:** www.grandlake-mariners.com. **General Manager:** Betty Feliciano. **Head Coach:** Mike Goldschmidt.

HAMILTON JOES

Mailing Address: 6218 Greens Way, Hamilton, OH 45011. **Telephone:** (513) 267-0601. **E-mail address:** darrelgrissom@fuse.net. **Website:** www.hamiltonjoes.com. **General Manager:** Josh Manley. **Head Coach:** Darrel Grissom.

LAKE ERIE MONARCHS

Mailing Address: 2220 West Sigler Road, Carleton, MI 48117. **Telephone:** (734) 626-1166. **Website:** www.lakeeriemonarchs.com. **General Manager:** Jim DeSana. **Head Coach:** Brian Lewis

LEXINGTON HUSTLERS

Mailing Address: 2061 Lexington Road, Nicholasville, KY 40356. **Telephone:** (859) 335-0928. **Fax:** (859) 881-0598. **Website:** lexingtonhustlers.wordpress.com. **Email Address:** lexigntonhustlers@gmail.com. **General Manager:** Jeff Adkins. **Head Coach:** Kyle Medley

LICKING COUNTY SETTLERS

Mailing Address: 958 Camden Dr., Newark, OH 43055. **Telephone:** (678) 367-8686. **Website:** www.settlersbaseball.com. **General Manager:** Sean West. **Head Coach:** Andy Levell.

LIMA LOCOS

Mailing Address: 3588 South Conant Rd., Spencerville, OH 45887. **Telephone:** (419) 647-5242. **Website:** www.limalocos.com. **General Manager:** Steve Meyer. **Head Coach:** Dan Furuto.

SOUTHERN OHIO COPPERHEADS

Mailing Address: P.O. Box 442, Athens, OH 45701. **Telephone:** (740) 541-9284. **Website:** www.copperheadsbaseball.com. **General Manager:** David Palmer. **Head Coach:** Chris Moore.

XENIA SCOUTS

Mailing Address: 651 Taylor Dr., Xenia, OH 45385. **Telephone:** (937) 352-1000. **E-Mail Address:** john.henschen@athletesinaction.org **Website:** www.aiabaseball.org. **General Manager:** John Henschen. **Head Coach:** JD Arndt.

JAYHAWK LEAGUE

Mailing Address: 865 Fabrique, Wichita, KS 67218. **Telephone:** (316) 942-6333. **Fax:** (316) 942-2009. **Website:** www.jayhawkbaseballleague.org. **Year Founded:** 1976.
Commissioner: Jim Foltz. **President:** JD Schneider. **Vice President:** Frank Leo. **Public Relations/Statistician:** Gary Karr. **Secretary:** Cheryl Kastner.
Regular Season: 32 games. **2013 Opening Date:** June 3. **Closing Date:** July 25. **Playoff Format:** Top two teams qualify for National Baseball Congress World Series. **Roster Limit:** 30 to begin season; 28 at midseason.

DERBY TWINS

Mailing Address: 1245 N. Pine Grove, Wichita, KS 67212. **Telephone:** (316) 992-3623. **E-mail Address:** jwells@riadatrading.com, jwells53@att.net. **Website:** www.derbytwins.com. **General Manager:** Jeff Wells. **Head Coach:** Billy Hall.

DODGE CITY A'S

Mailing Address: 1715 Central Ave., Dodge City, KS 67801. **Telephone:** 620-225-0238. **Website:** www.dodgecityas.com. **General Manager/Head Coach:** Phil Stevenson.

EL DORADO BRONCOS

Mailing Address: Box 168, El Dorado, KS 67042. **Telephone:** (316) 323-5098. **Website:** www.360eldorado.com. **General Manager:** Doug Bell. **Head Coach:** Pat Hon.

HAYS LARKS

Mailing Address: 2715 Walnut, Hays, KS 67601.

Telephone: (785) 259-1430. **Fax:** (630) 848-2236. **Website:** www.hdnews.net/larks. **General Manager/Head Coach:** Frank Leo.

LIBERAL BEE JAYS

Mailing Address: P.O. Box 793, Liberal, KS 67901. **Telephone:** (620) 629-1162. **Fax:** (620) 624-1906. **Head Coach:** Mike Silva. **Website:** beejays.net.

WELLINGTON HEAT

Mailing Address: Unavailable. **Telephone:** (928) 854-4092. **Website:** www.wellingtonheat.com. **Email Address:** wellingtonheat@yahoo.com. **General Manager/Owner/Head Coach:** Rick Twyman.

MIDWEST COLLEGIATE LEAGUE

Mailing Address: P.O. Box 172, Flossmoor, IL 60422. **E-Mail Address:** commissioner@midwestcollegiateleague.com. **Website:** www.midwestcollegiateleague.com. **Year Founded:** 2010. **President/Commissioner:** Don Popravak. **Regular Season:** 46 games. **2013 Opening Date:** May 31. **Closing Date:** Aug 4. **All-Star Game:** July 10. **Playoff Format:** Top four teams meet in best-of-three series. Winners meet in best-of-three championship series. **Roster Limit:** 28.

CHICAGO ZEPHYRS

Mailing Address: 3 S. 517 Winfield Road, Suite B, Warrenville, IL 60555. **Telephone:** (630) 327-9295. **E-Mail Address:** emmo2512@me.com. **Website:** www.zephyrsbaseball.com. **General Manager/Head Coach:** Marco Fajardo.

CHICAGO SOUTHLAND VIKINGS

Mailing Address: P.O. Box 172, Flossmoor, IL 60422. **Telephone:** (312) 420-1268. **E-Mail Address:** don@southlandvidings.com. **Website:** www.southlandvikings.com. **General Manager:** Don Popravak. **Head Coach:** Chris Cunningham.

DUPAGE COUNTY HOUNDS

Mailing Address: 17-8 Squirrel Trail, Cary, IL 60013. **Telephone:** (815) 704-3839. **E-Mail Address:** tickets@dupagehounds.com. **Website:** www.DuPageHounds.com. **General Managers:** Joe Stevani, Josh VanSwol. **Head Coach:** Sean Osborne.

LEXINGTON SNIPES

Mailing Address: 216 Prairie Ridge Drive, Lexington, IL 61753. **Telephone:** (309) 287-1668. **E-Mail Address:** billyd_73@yahoo.com. **Website:** www.lexingtonsnipes.com. **General Manager/Head Coach:** Billy Dubois.

NORTHWEST INDIANA OILMEN

Mailing Address: 1500 119th Street, Whiting, IN 46394. **Telephone:** (219) 659-1000. **E-Mail Address:** info@nwioilmen.com. **Website:** www.nwioilmen.com. **General Manager:** Jim Taipalus. **Head Coach:** Justin Huisman.

ROCKFORD FORESTERS

Mailing Address: P.O. Box 611, Rockford, IL 61104. **Telephone:** (815) 312-2115. **E-Mail Address:** tickets@rockfordforesters.com. **Website:** www.rockfordforesters.com. **General Manager:** Joe Stefani. **Head Coach:** Kevin Tyrrell.

M.I.N.K. LEAGUE (MISSOURI, IOWA, NEBRASKA, KANSAS)

Mailing Address: P.O. Box 601, Nevada, MO 64772. **Telephone:** (417) 667-6159. **Fax:** (417) 667-4210. **E-mail Address:** jpost@morrisonpost.com. **Website:** www.minkleaguebaseball.com.
Year Founded: 1995.
Commissioner: Bob Steinkamp. **President:** Jeff Post. **Vice President:** Arden Rakosky. **Secretary:** Edwina Rains. **Regular Season:** 42 games. **2013 Opening Date:** May 31. **Closing Date:** July 27. **Playoff Format:** Top team in North and South divisions play best-of-three series for league championship. Top team in each division qualifies for National Baseball Congress World Series. **Roster Limit:** 30.

CHILLICOTHE MUDCATS

Mailing Address: 426 E. Jackson, Chillicothe, MO 64601. **Telephone:** (660) 247-1504. **Fax:** (660) 646-6933. **E-Mail Address:** doughty@greenhills.net. **Website:** www.chillicothemudcats.com. **General Manager:** Doug Doughty. **Head Coach:** Eric Peterson.

CLARINDA A'S

Mailing Address: 225 East Lincoln, Clarinda, IA 51632. **Telephone:** (712) 542-4272. **E-Mail Address:** m.everly@mchsi.com. **Website:** www.clarindaiowa-as-baseball.org. **General Manager:** Merle Eberly. **Head Coach:** Ryan Eberly.

JOPLIN OUTLAWS

Mailing Address: 5860 North Pearl, Joplin, MO 64801. **Telephone:** (417) 825-4218. **E-Mail Address:** merains@mchsi.com. **Website:** www.joplinoutlaws.com. **President/General Manager:** Mark Rains. **Head Coach:** Rob Vessell.

NEVADA GRIFFONS

Mailing Address: P.O. Box 601, Nevada, MO 64772. **Telephone:** (417) 667-6159. **E-Mail Address:** jpost@morrisonpost.com. **Website:** www.nevadagriffons.org. **President:** Bob Hawks. **General Manager:** Jeff Post. **Head Coach:** Ryan Mansfield.

OMAHA DIAMOND SPIRIT

Mailing Address: 4618 N. 135th Ave., Omaha, NE 68164. **Telephone:** (402) 679-0206. **E-Mail Address:** arden@omahadiamondspirit.com. **Website:** www.omahadiamondspirit.com. **General Manager:** Arden Rakosky. **Head Coach:** Adam Steyer.

OZARK GENERALS

Mailing Address: 1336 W. Farm Road 182, Springfield, MO 65810. **Telephone:** (417) 832-8830. **Fax:** (417) 877-4625. **E-Mail Address:** rda160@yahoo.com. **Website:** www.generalsbaseballclub.com. **General Manager/Head Coach:** Rusty Aton.

ST. JOSEPH MUSTANGS

Mailing Address: 2600 SW Parkway, St. Joseph, MO 64503. **Telephone:** (816) 279-7856. **Fax:** (816) 749-4082. **E-Mail Address:** rmuntean717@gmail.com. **Website:** www.stjoemustangs.com. **President:** Dan Gerson. **General Manager:** Rick Muntean. **Manager/Director, Player Personnel:** Matt Johnson.

SEDALIA BOMBERS

Mailing Address: 2205 S. Grand, Sedalia, MO 65301. **Telephone:** (660) 287-4722. **E-Mail Address:** jkindle@knobnoster.k12.mo.us. **Website:** www.sedaliabombers.com. **President/General Manager/Head Coach:** Jud Kindle. **Vice President:** Ross Dey.

MOUNTAIN COLLEGIATE LEAGUE

E-mail Address: info@mcbl.net. **Website:** www.mcbl.net. **Year Founded:** 2005. **Directors:** Kurt Colicchio, Ron Kailey, Aaron McCreight, Ryan Kolo, Paul Birge. **Commissioner:** Karl Holden. **Director of Umpires:** Gary Weibert.

Regular Season: 48 games. **2013 Opening Date:** June 1. **Closing Date:** August 4 (last game of LCS). **Playoff Format:** Second-place and third-place teams meet in one-game playoff; winner advances to best-of-three league championship series against first-place team. **All-Star Game:** Unavailable. **Roster limit:** 31 total, 25 active (college-eligible players only).

CASPER CUTTHROATS

Telephone: (307) 277-9159. **Email Address:** aaron@caspercutthroats.com. **Website:** www.caspercutthrpoats.com. **Owner/General Manager:** Aaron McCreight. **Head Coach:** Steve Stutzman.

CHEYENNE GRIZZLIES

Telephone: (307) 631-7337. **E-mail Address:** rkaide@aol.com. **Website:** www.cheyennegrizzlies.com. **Owner/General Manager:** Ron Kailey. **Head Coach:** Jared Franklin.

COLORADO BOBCATS

Telephone: 575-779-0928. **E-Mail Address:** pcbirge@gmail.com. **Website:** coloradobobcats.com. **Owner/General Manager:** Paul Birge. **Head Coach:** Kellen Mitts.

COLORADO SPRINGS BLUE SOX

Telephone: (719) 200-5692. **E-Mail Address:** steven@coloradobaseballacademy.com. **Website:** www.csbluesox.com. **General Manager:** Steven Locket. **Head Coach:** Lou Trujillo.

FORT COLLINS FOXES

Telephone: (970) 225-9564. **E-Mail Address:** info@fortcollinsfoxes.com. **Website:** www.fortcollinsfoxes.com. **Owner/General Manager:** Kurt Colicchio. **Head Coach:** Brad Averitte.

NORTHERN COLORADO TOROS

Telephone: 970-775-3676. **E-Mail Address:** onefifteenbaseballclub@yahoo.com. **Website:** onefifteenbaseball.com. **Owner/General Manager:** Ryan Kolo. **Head Coach:** Steve Gerrard.

NEW ENGLAND COLLEGIATE LEAGUE

Mailing Address: 28 Kateley Lane, North Adams, MA 01247. **Telephone:** (413) 652-1031. **Fax:** (413) 473-0012. **E-Mail Address:** smcgrath@necbl.com. **Website:** www.necbl.com.

Year founded: 1993.

President: John DeRosa. **Commissioner:** Sean McGrath. **Deputy Commissioners:** Brian Hamm, Gregg Hunt. **Secretary:** Max Pinto. **Treasurer:** Brigid Schaffer.

Regular Season: 44 games. **2013 Opening Date:** June 6. **Closing Date:** Aug 13. **All-Star Game:** July 21 at 5:30 in Laconia, NH.

Roster Limit: 30 (college-eligible players only).

DANBURY WESTERNERS

Mailing Address: 9 Pleasant View, New Milford, CT 06776. **Telephone:** (203) 502-9167. **E-Mail Address:** jspitser@msn.com. **Website:** www.danburywesterners.com. **President:** Paul Schaffer. **General Manager:** Jon Pitser. **Field Manager:** Jamie Shevchik.

HOLYOKE BLUE SOX

Mailing Address: 100 Congress St., Springfield, MA 01104. **Telephone:** (413) 652-9014. **E-Mail Address:** Barry@Holyokesox.com **Website:** www.holyokesox.com. **CEO/COO:** Barry Wadsworth. **General Manager:** Kirk Fredriksson. **Field Manager:** Darryle Morhardt.

KEENE SWAMP BATS

Mailing Address: P.O. Box 160, Keene, NH 13431. **Telephone:** (603) 357-5464. **Fax:** (603) 357-5090. **E-Mail Address:** kwatterson@ne.rr.com. **Website:** www.swamp-bats.com. **President:** Kevin Watterson. **VP/General Manager:** Walt Kilburn.

LACONIA MUSKRATS

Mailing Address: 134 Stevens Rd., Lebanon, NH 03766. **Telephone:** (864) 380-2873. **E-Mail Address:** noah@laconiamuskrats.com. **Website:** www.laconiamuskrats.com. **President:** Jonathan Crane. **General Manager:** Noah Crane. **Field Manager:** Matt Alison.

MYSTIC SCHOONERS

Mailing Address: P.O. Box 432, Mystic, CT 06355. **Telephone:** (860) 608-3287. **E-Mail Address:** dlong@mysticbaseball.org. **Website:** www.mysticbaseball.org. **President:** Tom Marra. **General Manager:** Dennis Long. **Field Manager:** Phil Orbe.

NEW BEDFORD BAY SOX

Mailing Address: 17 Sawmill Road, Jericho, VT 05465. **Telephone:** (774) 930-1481. **E-Mail Address:** mfriar@nbbaysox.com. **Website:** www.nbbaysox.com. **President:** Pat O'Connor. **General Manager:** Mike Friar. **Field Manager:** Rick Miller.

NEWPORT GULLS

Mailing Address: P.O. Box 777, Newport, RI 02840. **Telephone:** (401) 845-6832. **E-Mail Address:** gm@newportgulls.com. **Website:** www.newportgulls.com. **President/General Manager:** Chuck Paiva. **Field Manager:** Mike Coombs.

NORTH ADAMS STEEPLECATS

Mailing Address: P.O. Box 540, North Adams, MA 01247. **Telephone:** (413) 884-4100. **E-Mail Address:** dan.bosley@verizon.net. **Website:** www.steeplecats.com. **President:** Dan Bosley. **Field Manager:** Bryan Adamski.

OCEAN STATE WAVES

Mailing Address: 1174 Kingstown Rd., Wakefield, RI 02879. **Telephone:** (401) 360-2977. **E-Mail Address:** mattfin09@yahoo.com. **Website:** www.oceanstatewaves.com. **President:** Jeff Sweenor. **General Manager:** Matt

Finlayson. **Field Manager:** Phil Davidson.

PLYMOUTH PILGRIMS

Mailing Address: 134 Court Street, Plymouth, MA 02360. **Telephone:** (401) 862-3711. **Fax:** (508) 830-1621. **E-Mail Address:** chris@pilgrimsbaseball.com.
Website: www.pilgrimsbaseball.com. **President:** Dave Dittmann. **General Manager:** Chris Patsos. **Field Manager:** Greg Zackrison.

SANFORD MAINERS

Mailing Address: P.O. Box 26, 4 Washington St., Sanford, ME 04073. **Telephone:** (207) 324-0010. **Fax:** (207) 324-2227. **E-Mail Address:** jwebb@nicholswebb.com. **Website:** www.sanfordmainers.com. **CEO:** Steve Cabana. **General Manager:** John Webb. **Field Manager:** Aaron Izaryk.

SARATOGA BRIGAIDE

Mailing Address: 254 Wolf Road, Latham, NY 12110. **Telephone:** (518) 598-9131. **E-Mail Address:** saratoga.brigade@yahoo.com. **Website:** www.SaratogaBrigade.com. **President:** Dan Scaring. **General Manager:** Keith Rogers. **Field Manager:** Garrett Baron.

VERMONT MOUNTAINEERS

Mailing Address: P.O. Box 57, East Montpelier, VT 05651. **Telephone:** (802) 223-5224. **E-Mail Address:** gmvtm@comcast.net. **Website:** www.thevermontmountaineers.com. **President:** Katheran Thayer. **General Manager:** Brian Gallagher. **Field Manager:** Joe Brown.

NEW YORK COLLEGIATE BASEBALL LEAGUE

Mailing Address: 4 Creekside Ln., Rochester, NY 14624-1059. **Telephone:** (585) 314-1122. **E-Mail Address:** slehman@nycbl.com. **Website:** www.nycbl.com.
Year founded: 1978.
President/Commissioner/Executive Director: Stan Lehman. **Vice President:** Cal Kern. **Treasurer:** Dan Russo. **Secretary:** Paul Welker. **Director of Baseball Operations:** Jake Dennstedt. **Franchise Development:** Cal Kern.
Franchises: Geneva Red Wings, Geneva Twins, Hornell Dodgers, Niagara Power, Olean Oilers, Oneonta Outlaws, Rochester Ridgemen, Sherrill Silversmiths, Syracuse Junior Chiefs, Syracuse Salt Cats, Wellsville Nitros.
Regular season starts: June 3. **Regular season ends:** July 22. **All-Star Game/Scout Day:** July 9 at McDonough Field, Geneva, New York. **Playoff Format:** Round 1: one playoff game between the fourth and fifth-place teams. **Round 2:** two three-game playoffs between first-place team and the winner of Round 1 and second-place vs third place. The winners of the two Round 2 series play in a three-game playoff for the NYCBL championship. **Roster Limit:** 30 (college-eligible players only)

GENEVA RED WINGS

Mailing Address: P.O. Box 17624, Rochester, NY 14617. **Telephone:** 585-342-5750. **Fax:** 585-342-5155. **E-Mail Address:** gwings@rochester.rr.com. **Website:** genevaredwings.com. **President/Manager:** David Herbst. **Executive GM:** John Oughterson.

GENEVA TWINS

Mailing Address: P.O. BOX 17624, Rochester, NY 14617. **Telephone:** 585-342-5750. **Fax:** 585-342-5155. **E-Mail**

Address: gwings@rochester.rr.com. **Website:** genevaredwings.com. **President/Manager:** David Herbst. **Executive GM:** John Oughterson.

HORNELL DODGERS

Mailing Address: P.O. Box 235, Hornell, NY 14843. **Telephone:** (607) 661-4173. **Fax:** (607) 661-4173. **E-Mail Address:** gm@hornelldodgers.com. **Website:** www.hornelldodgers.com. **General Manager:** Paul Welker. **Field Manager:** Jake Tenhouse (Quincy University).

NIAGARA POWER

Mailing Address: 2905 Staley Road, Grand Island, NY 14072. **Telephone:** (716) 773-1748. **Fax:** (716) 773-1748. **E-Mail Address:** ckern@fca.org **Website:** www.niagarapower.org. **General Manager:** Cal Kern. **Field Manager:** Josh Rebandt.

OLEAN OILERS

Mailing Address: 126 N. 10th, Olean, NY 14760. **Telephone:** 716-378-0641. **E-Mail Addresses:** baseball@oleanoilers.com, Bellr41@yahoo.com. **General Manager:** Bobby Bell. **Field Manager:** Unavailable.

ONEONTA OUTLAWS

Mailing Address: P.O. Box 608, Oneonta, NY 13820. **Telephone:** (607) 432-6326. **Fax:** (607) 432-1965. **E-Mail Address:** stevepindar@oneontaoutlaws.com. **Website:** www.oneontaoutlaws.com. **General Manager:** Steve Pindar. **Field Manager:** Joe Hughes.

ROCHESTER RIDGEMEN

Mailing Address: 651 Taylor Dr., Xenia, OH 45385. **Telephone:** (937) 352-1225. **E-Mail Addresses:** baseball@athletesinaction.org, chris.rainwater@athletesinaction.org. **Website:** www.aiabaseball.org. **General Manager:** Chris Rainwater. **Field Manager:** Taylor Hargrove.

SHERRILL SILVERSMITHS

Mailing Address: P.O. Box 111, Sherrill, NY 13440. **Telephone:** (315) 264-4334. **E-Mail Address:** sherrillsilversmiths@hotmail.com. **Website:** www.leaguelineup.com/silversmiths. **General Manager:** Matthew Rafte. **Field Manager:** Unavailable.

SYRACUSE JR CHIEFS

Mailing Address: 227 Walters Dr., Liverpool, NY 13088. **Telephone:** (315) 263-3777. **E-Mail Address:** perfect.practice@yahoo.com. **General Manager:** Mike DiPaulo. **Field Manager:** Unavailable.

SYRACUSE SALT CATS

Mailing Address: 208 Lakeland Ave., Syracuse, NY 13209. **Telephone:** (315) 727-9220. **Fax:** (315) 488-1750. **E-Mail Address:** mmarti6044@yahoo.com. **Website:** www.leaguelineup.com/saltcats. **General Manager:** Manny Martinez. **Field Manager:** Mike Martinez.

WELLSVILLE NITROS

Mailing Address: 2848 O'Donnell Rd., Wellsville, NY 14895. **Telephone:** 585-596-9523. **Fax:** 585-593-5260. **E-Mail Address:** ackley8122@roadrunner.com. **Website:** www.nitros baseball.com. **General Manager:** Steven J. Ackley. **Assistant Manager:** Shelley Butler.

NORTHWOODS LEAGUE

Office Address: 2900 4th St. SW, Rochester, MN 55902. **Telephone:** (507) 536-4579. **Fax:** (507) 536-4597. **E-Mail Address:** info@northwoodsleague.com. **Website:** www.northwoodsleague.com.

Year Founded: 1994.

President: Dick Radatz Jr. **Vice President, Business Development:** Matt Bomberg. **VP, Operations:** Glen Showalter.

Division Structure: North—Alexandria, Duluth, Mankato, Rochester, St. Cloud, Thunder Bay, Waterloo, Willmar. **South**—Battle Creek, Eau Claire, Green Bay, La Crosse, Lakeshore, Madison, Rochester, Wisconsin, Wisconsin Rapids.

Regular Season: 70 games (split schedule). **2013 Opening Date:** May 29. **Closing Date:** Aug 11. **All-Star Game:** July 23 at Eau Claire. **Playoff Format:** First-half and second-half division winners meet in best-of-three series. Winners meet in best-of-three series for league championship. **Roster Limit:** 30 (college-eligible players only).

ALEXANDRIA BEETLES

Mailing Address: 2900 4th St. SW, Rochester, MN 55902. **Telephone:** (507) 536-4579. **Fax:** (507) 536-4597. **E-Mail Address:** info@northwoodsleague.com. **Website:** www.alexandriabeetles.com. **Field Manager:** Drew Saberhagen.

BATTLE CREEK BOMBERS

Mailing Address: 189 Bridge Street, Battle Creek, MI 49017. **Telephone:** (269) 962-0735. **Fax:** (269) 962-0741. **Email Address:** info@battlecreekbombers.com. **Website:** www.battlecreekbombers.com. **General Manager:** Brian Colopy. **Assistant General Manager:** Anthony Iovieno. **Field Manager:** Brandon Higelin.

DULUTH HUSKIES

Mailing Address: 207 W. Superior St., Suite 206, Holiday Center Mall, Duluth, MN 55802. **Telephone:** (218) 786-9909. **Fax:** (218) 786-9001. **E-Mail Address:** huskies@duluthhuskies.com. **Website:** www.duluthhuskies.com. **Owners:** Andy Karon, Michael Rosenzweig. **General Manager:** Craig Smith. **Field Manager:** Daniel Hersey.

EAU CLAIRE EXPRESS

Mailing Address: 108 E. Grand Ave., Eau Claire, WI 54701. **Telephone:** (715) 839-7788. **Fax:** (715) 839-7676. **E-Mail Address:** info@eauclaireexpress.com. **Website:** www.eauclaireexpress.com. **Owner:** Bill Rowlett. **General Manager:** Andy Neborak. **Director, Operations/Field Manager:** Dale Varsho.

GREEN BAY BULLFROGS

Mailing Address: 1306 Main Street, Green Bay, WI 54302. **Telephone:** (920) 497-7225. **Fax:** (920) 437-3551. **Email Address:** info@greenbaybullfrogs.com. **Website:** www.greenbaybullfrogs.com. **President:** Jeffrey L Royle. **Director, Sales/Marketing:** Shannon Krein. **Field Manager:** Karl Johnston.

LA CROSSE LOGGERS

Mailing Address: 1225 Caledonia St., La Crosse, WI 54603. **Telephone:** (608) 796-9553. **Fax:** (608) 796-9032. **E-Mail Address:** info@lacrosseloggers.com. **Website:** www.lacrosseloggers.com. **Owner:** Dan Kapanke. **General Manager:** Chris Goodell. **Assistant GM:** Ben

Kapanke. **Field Manager:** Jason Nell.

LAKESHORE CHINOOKS

Mailing Address: P.O. Box 227, 995 Badger Circle, Grafton, WI 53024. **Telephone:** (262) 618-4659. **Fax:** (262) 618-4362. **E-Mail Address:** info@lakeshorechinooks.com. **Website:** www.lakeshorechinooks.com. **Owner:** Jim Kacmarcik. **General Manager:** Dean Rennicke. **Assistant GM:** Chad Bauer. **Field Manager:** Eddy Morgan.

MADISON MALLARDS

Mailing Address: 2920 N. Sherman Ave., Madison, WI 53704. **Telephone:** (608) 246-4277. **Fax:** (608) 246-4163. **E-Mail Address:** conor@mallardsbaseball.com. **Website:** www.mallardsbaseball.com. **Owner:** Steve Schmitt. **President:** Vern Stenman. **General Manager:** Conor Caloia. **Field Manager:** Donnie Scott.

MANKATO MOONDOGS

Mailing Address: 1221 Caledonia Street, Mankato, MN 56001. **Telephone:** (507) 625-7047. **Fax:** (507) 625-7059. **E-Mail Address:** office@mankatomoondogs.com. **Website:** www.mankatomoondogs.com. **Owner:** Mark Ogren. **Vice President:** Kyle Mrozek. **General Manager:** Greg Weis. **Director:** Scott Ogren. **Field Manager:** Mike Orchard.

ROCHESTER HONKERS

Mailing Address: P.O. Box 482, Rochester, MN 55903. **Telephone:** (507) 289-1170. **Fax:** (507) 289-1866. **E-Mail Address:** honkers@rochesterhonkers.com. **Website:** www.rochesterhonkers.com. **Owner/General Manager:** Dan Litzinger. **Field Manager:** Brian Aguilar (Oral Roberts).

ST. CLOUD ROX

Mailing Address: 5001 Veterans Drive, Saint Cloud, MN 56303. **Telephone:** (320) 240-9798. **Fax:** (320) 255-5228. **E-Mail Address:** info@stcloudrox.com. **Website:** www.stcloudrox.com. **President:** Scott Schreiner. **GM:** Wes Sharp. **Field Manager:** Augie Rodriguez.

THUNDER BAY BORDER CATS

Mailing Address: P.O. Box 29105, Thunder Bay, ON P7B 6P9. **Telephone:** (807) 766-2287. **Fax:** (807) 345-8299. **E-Mail Address:** baseball@tbaytel.net. **Website:** www.bordercatsbaseball.com. **President/General Manager:** Brad Jorgenson. **Field Manager:** Andy Judkins.

WATERLOO BUCKS

Mailing Address: P.O. Box 4124, Waterloo, IA 50704. **Telephone:** (319) 232-0500. **Fax:** (319) 232-0700. **E-Mail Address:** waterloobucks@waterloobucks.com. **Website:** www.waterloobucks.com. **General Manager:** Dan Corbin. **Field Manager:** Travis Kiewiet.

WILLMAR STINGERS

Mailing Address: P.O. Box 201, Willmar, MN, 56201. **Telephone:** (320) 222-2010. **E-Mail Address:** ryan@willmarstingers.com. **Website:** www.willmarstingers.com. **Owners:** Marc Jerzak, Ryan Voz. **General Manager:** Nick McCallum. **Field Manager:** Matt Hollod.

WISCONSIN WOODCHUCKS

Mailing Address: P.O. Box 6157, Wausau, WI 54402. **Telephone:** (715) 845-5055. **Fax:** (715) 845-5015. **E-Mail

Address: info@woodchucks.com. Website: www.wood-chucks.com. Owner: Mark Macdonald. General Manager: Ryan Treu. Field Manager: Erik Supplee.

WISCONSIN RAPIDS RAFTERS

Mailing Address: 521 Lincoln St., Wisconsin Rapids, WI 54494. Telephone: (715) 424-5400. E-Mail Address: info@raftersbaseball.com. Website: www.raftersbaseball.com. Owner/President: Vern Stenman. General Manager: Liz Kern. Field Manager: Jake Martin (Coffeyville CC, Kansas).

PACIFIC INTERNATIONAL LEAGUE

Mailing Address: 4400 26th Ave. W, Seattle, WA 98199. Telephone: (206) 623-8844. Fax: (206) 623-8361. E-Mail Address: spotter@potterprinting.com. Website: www.pacificinternationalleague.com.

Year Founded: 1992.

President: Mike MacColloch. Vice President: Steve Peterson. Commissioner: Brian Gooch. Secretary: Steve Potter. Treasurer: Mark Dow. Member Clubs: Northwest Honkers, Everett Merchants, Kamloops Sundevils, Kelowna Jays, Langley Blaze, Seattle Studs, Trail (BC) franchise, Burnaby Collegiate. Regular Season: 20 league games. 2013 Opening Date: June 1. Closing Date: July 31. Playoff Format: The top team is invited to NBC World Series. Roster Limit: 30; 25 eligible for games (players must be at least 18.

PERFECT GAME COLLEGIATE BASEBALL LEAGUE

Mailing Address: 8 Michaels Lane, Old Brookville, NY 11545. Telephone: (516) 521-0206. Fax: (516) 801-0818. E-Mail Address: valkun@aol.com. Website: www.pgcbl.com.

Year Founded: 2010.

President: Jeffrey Kunion. Executive Committee: Tom Hickey (Cooperstown Hawkeyes), Bob Ohmann (Newark Pilots), Paul Samulski (Albany Dutchmen). Member Teams: East Division—Albany Dutchmen, Amsterdam Mohawks, Cooperstown Hawkeyes, Glens Falls Golden Eagles, Mohawk Valley DiamondDawgs. West Division—Adirondack Trail Blazers, Elmira Pioneers, Newark Pilots, Utica Brewers, Watertown Wizards.

Regular Season: 48. 2013 Opening Date: June 5. Closing Date: July 31. All-Star Game: July 24 at Colburn Park, Newark, N.Y. Playoff Format: Top three teams in each division qualify for the three-round postseason. Second and third-place finishers have a one-game playoff, then the next two series are best-of-three. Roster Limit: 30 (maximum of two graduated high school players per team).

PROSPECT LEAGUE

Mailing Address: 10011 Woodland Birth Drive, Arlington, TN 38002. Telephone: (901) 218-3386. Fax: (480) 247-5068. E-Mail Address: commissioner@prospectleague.com. Website: www.prospectleague.com.

Year Founded: 1963 as Central Illinois Collegiate League; 2009 as Prospect League.

Commissioner: Dave Chase.

Regular Season: 60 games. 2013 Opening Date: May 28. Closing Date: Aug 4. All-Star Game: July 17 at Pullman Park, Butler, Pa. Championship Series: Aug 9-12. Roster Limit: 28.

BUTLER BLUESOX

Mailing Address: 6 West Diamond Street, Butler, PA 16001. Telephone: (724) 282-2222 or (724) 256-9994. Fax: (724) 282-6565. E-Mail Address: frontoffice@butlerbluesox.net. Website: www.butlerbluesox.com. League Director: Wink Robinson. General Manager: Matt Cunningham. Field Manager: Anthony Rebyanski.

CHILLICOTHE PAINTS

Mailing Address: 59 North Paint Street, Chillicothe, OH 45601. Telephone: (740) 773-8326. Fax: (740) 773-8338. E-Mail Address: paints@bright.net. Website: www.chillicothepaints.com. League Director/General Manager: Bryan Wickline. Field Manager: Unavailable.

DANVILLE DANS

Mailing Address: 138 East Raymond, Danville, IL 61832. Telephone: (217) 918-3401. Fax: (217) 446-9995. E-Mail Address: danvilledans@comcast.net. Website: www.danvilledans.com. League Director: Jeannie Cooke. Co-General Managers: Jeanie Cooke, Rick Kurth. Field Manager: Jamie Sailors.

HANNIBAL CAVEMEN

Mailing Address: 403 Warren Barrett Drive, Hannibal, MO 63401. Telephone: (573) 221-1010. Fax: (573) 221-5269. E-Mail Address: hannibalbaseball@sbcglobal.com. Website: www.hannibalcavemen.com. President: Robert Hemond. League Director/General Manager: John Civitate. Field Manager: Jay Hemond.

LORAIN COUNTY IRONMEN

Mailing Address: 2840 Meister Road, Lorain, OH 44052. Telephone: (440) 752-0372. Email Address: info@lcironmen.com. Website: loraincountyironmen.com. League Director: Kevin Rhomberg. General Manager: Unavailable. Field Manager: Unavailable.

QUINCY GEMS

Mailing Address: 300 Civic Center Plaza, Suite 237, Quincy, IL 62301. Telephone: (217) 223-1000. Fax: (217) 223-1330. E-Mail Address: rebbing@quincygems.com. Website: www.quincygems.com. League Director: Rob Ebbing. General Manager: Terry Martin. Field Manager: Chris Martin.

RICHMOND RIVERRATS

Mailing Address: 201 NW 13th Street, Richmond, IN 47374. Telephone: (765) 935-7287. Fax: (765) 935-7529. E-Mail Address: dbeaman@richmondriverrats.com. Website: www.richmondriverrats.com. League Director: Duke Ward. General Manager: Deanna Beaman. Field Manager: Tyler Lairson.

SLIPPERY ROCK SLIDERS

Mailing Address: P.O. Box 496, Slippery Rock, PA 16057. Telephone: (724) 458-8831. Fax: (724) 458-8831. E-Mail Address: mbencic@zoominternet.net. Website: www.theslipperyrocksliders.com. League Director/General Manager: Mike Bencic. Field Manager: Brad Neffendorf.

SPRINGFIELD SLIDERS

Mailing Address: 1415 North Grand Avenue East, Suite B, Springfield, IL 62702. Telephone: (217) 679-

3511. **Fax:** (217) 679-3512. **E-Mail Address:** slidersfun@springfieldsliders.com. **Website:** www.springfieldsliders.com. **League Director:** Shane Martin. **General Manager:** Dennis Martin. **Field Manager:** Pete Romero.

TERRE HAUTE REX

Mailing Address: 30 North 5th Street, Terre Haute, IN 47807. **Telephone:** (812) 514-8557. **Fax:** (812) 514-8551. **E-mail Address:** threxbaseball@indianastatefoundation.org. **Website:** www.threxbaseball.com. **League Director:** Roland Shelton. **General Manager:** Casey DeGroote. **Field Manager:** Ronnie Prettyman.

WEST VIRGINIA MINERS

Mailing Address: 476 Ragland Road, Suite 1, Beckley, WV 25801. **Telephone:** (304) 252-7233. **Fax:** (304) 253-1998. **E-mail Address:** wvminers@wvminersbaseball.com. **Website:** www.wvminersbaseball.com. **President:** Doug Epling. **League Director/General Manager/Field Manager:** Tim Epling.

SOUTHERN COLLEGIATE BASEBALL LEAGUE

Mailing Address: 9723 Northcross Center Court, Huntersville, NC 28078. **Telephone:** (704) 635-7126. **Fax:** (704) 234-8448. **E-Mail Address:** SCBLCommissioner@aol.com. **Website:** www.scbl.org.

Year Founded: 1999.

Commissioner: Bill Capps. **President:** Jeff Carter. **Executive Vice President:** Brian Swords. **VP, Marketing/Development:** Dave Collins. **Secretary:** James Bradley. **Treasurer:** Brenda Templin. **League Historian:** Larry Tremitiere. **Umpire in Chief:** Tom Haight.

Regular Season: 40 games. **2013 Opening Date:** June 3. **Closing Date:** July 23. **Playoff Format:** Seven-team single-elimination tournament with best-of-three championship series between final two teams.

Roster Limit: 30 (College-eligible players only).

BALLANTYNE SMOKIES

Mailing Address: 31014 Executive Point, Fort Mill, SC 29708. **Telephone:** (704) 996-1367. **Email Address:** jspencer@ballantynesmokies.com. **General Manager:** John Spencer. **Head Coach:** JD Vidal.

CAROLINA CHAOS

Mailing Address: 142 Orchard Drive, Liberty, SC 29657. **Telephone:** (864) 843-3232, (864) 901-4331. **E-Mail Address:** brian_swords@carolinachaos.com. **Website:** www.carolinachaos.com. **General Manager:** Brian Swords. **Head Coach:** Guy Howard.

LAKE NORMAN COPPERHEADS

Mailing Address: P.O. Box 9723, Northcross Center Court, Huntersville, NC 28078. **Telephone:** (704) 892-1041, (704) 564-9211. **E-Mail Address:** jcarter@copperheadsports.org. **Website:** www.copperheadsports.org. **General Manager:** Jeff Carter. **Head Coach:** Derek Shoe.

MORGANTON AGGIES

Mailing Address: P.O. Box 3448, Morganton, NC 28680. **Telephone:** (828) 438-5351. **Fax:** (828) 438-5350. **E-Mail Address:** gleonhardt@ci.morganton.nc.us. **General Manager:** Gary Leonhardt. **Head Coach:** Travis Howard.

PINEVILLE PIONEERS

Mailing Address: 10229 Rodney Street, Pineville, NC 28134. **Telephone:** (704) 889-2287. **E-Mail Address:** brian.hoop96@gmail.com. **General Manager:** Garry Hill. **Assistant GM:** Brian Hoop. **Head Coach:** Terry Brewer.

STATESVILLE OWLS

Mailing Address: P.O. Box 17637, Asheville, NC 28816. **Telephone:** (828) 320-5100. **Email Address:** brian.suarez@statesvilleowls.com. **General Manager:** Brian Suarez. **Head Coach:** Ryan Smith.

CAROLINA VIPERS

Mailing Address: 10800 Sikes Place, Suite 225, Charlotte, NC 28277. **Telephone:** (704) 246-8620. **E-Mail Address:** mpolito@tprsolutions.com. **General Manager:** Keith Bray. **Head Coach:** Aaron Bray.

SUNBELT BASEBALL LEAGUE

Mailing Address: 3022 Liberty Way, Atlanta, GA 30318. **Telephone:** (770) 490-7912. **E-mail Address:** info@sunbeltleague.com. **Website:** www.sunbeltleague.com. **Year Founded:** 2006.

Commissioner: Bobby Bennett. **Email:** bobbybennett27@me.com. **Executive Director:** Marty Kelly. **Director, Player Development:** Todd Pratt. **Director, Operations:** Karl Garcia.

Regular Season: 28 games. **2013 Opening Date:** June 1. **Closing Date:** July 30. **All-Star Game:** July 13 at Lawrenceville, Ga. **Playoff Format:** division championship series and league championship series, best of 3. **Roster Limit:** 30 (college-eligible players 22 and under).

ATLANTA CRACKERS

Telephone: (770) 380-1461. **E-Mail:** kmeistickle@gmail.com. **General Manager:** Steve Autry. **Head Coach:** Kevin Meistickle

BERKLEY LAKE TIDES

Telephone: (678) 409-3977. **E-Mail:** kgarcia10@hotmail.com. **General Manager:** Karl Garcia. **Head Coach:** Scott Ward.

BROOKHAVEN BUCKS

Telephone: (404) 840-0039. **E-Mail:** jdbravo@bellsouth.net. **General Manager:** John Davis. **Head Coach:** Nick Hogan.

DOUGLASVILLE BULLS

Telephone: (770) 990-6686. **E-Mail:** tpratt2829@bellsouth.net. **General Manager:** Todd Pratt. **Head Coach:** Austin Janowski.

6-4-3 DP COUGARS

Telephone (678) 883-4629. **E-Mail:** coachroy10@hotmail.com. **General Manager:** Jay Andrews. **Head Coach:** Roy Anderson.

SOUTH ATLANTA BEARCATS

Telephone: (404) 291-0094. **Email:** dilowe@comcast.net. **General Manager:** Scott Fletcher. **Head Coach:** Dion Lowe

PEACHTREE CITY CHUKARS

Telephone: (404) 245-3580. **Email:** homeplate318@bellsouth.net. **General Manager:** Lloyd Thompson. **Head Coach:** Rodney Dickenson.

WINDWARD BRAVES

Telephone: (404) 403-0812. **E-Mail:** rube@windwardbaseball.com. **General Manager:** Eric Ruben. **Head Coach:** Davis May.

TEXAS COLLEGIATE LEAGUE

Mailing Address: 735 Plaza Blvd., Suite 200, Coppell, TX 75019. **Telephone:** (979) 985-5198. **Fax:** (979) 779-2398. **E-Mail Address:** info@tclbaseball.com. **Website:** www.texascollegiateleague.com.

Year Founded: 2004.
President: Uri Geva.
Regular Season: 60 games (split schedule). **2013 Opening Date:** May 30. **Closing Date:** Aug 13. **Playoff Format:** The first- and second-half champions will be joined in the TCL playoffs by two wild card teams. Winners of the one-game divisional round meet in the best-of-three championship series.
Roster Limit: 30 (College-eligible players only).

ACADIANA CANE CUTTERS

Telephone: (337) 451-6582. **Fax:** (337) 451-6581. **E-Mail Address:** info@canecuttersbaseball.com. **Website:** www.canecuttersbaseball.com. **Owners:** Richard Chalmers, Sandi Chalmers. **General Manager:** Jacob Andrews. **Head Coach:** Lonny Landry.

ALEXANDRIA ACES

Mailing Address: 1 Babe Ruth Dr., Alexandria, LA 71301. **Telephone:** (318) 473-2273. **Website:** www.myacesbaseball.com. **President/Chief Executive Officer:** Eric Moran.

BRAZOS VALLEY BOMBERS

Mailing Address: 405 Mitchell St., Bryan, TX 77801. **Telephone:** (979) 799-7529. **Fax:** (979) 779-2398. **E-Mail Address:** info@bvbombers.com. **Website:** www.bvbombers.com. **Owners:** Uri Geva, Chris Clark. **General Manager:** Chris Clark. **Head Coach:** Curt Dixon.

EAST TEXAS PUMP JACKS

Mailing Address: P.O. Box 2369, Kilgore, TX 75663. **Telephone:** (903) 218-4638. **Fax:** (866) 511-5449. **E-mail Address:** info@pumpjacksbaseball.com. **Website:** www.pumpjacksbaseball.com. **Owners:** Alan Poff, Brett Cox, Mike Lieberman. **General Manager:** Mike Lieberman. **Head Coach:** Mark Kertenian.

TEXAS MARSHALS

Mailing Address: 7920 Beltline Rd., Suite 1005 Dallas, TX 75254. **Telephone:** (214) 578-4388. **E-Mail Address:** info@texasmarshals.com. **Website:** www.texasmarshals.com. **Owner:** Marc Landry. **General Manager:** Kendrick Moore. **Head Coach:** Dax Powell.

WOODLANDS STRYKERS

Mailing Address: 25009 OakHurst Dr., Spring, TX 77386. **Telephone:** (713) 724-9825. **Fax:** (281) 465-0748. **Owner/General Manager:** Ramiro Lozano. **Head Coach:** Freddy Rodriguez.

VICTORIA GENERALS

Mailing Address: 1307 E. Airline Road, Suite H, Victoria, TX 77901. **Telephone:** (361) 485-9522. **Fax:** (361) 485-0936. **E-Mail Address:** info@baseballinvictoria.com, tkyoung@victoriagenerals.com. **Website:** www.victoriagenerals.com. **President:** Tracy Young. **VP/General Manager:** Blake Koch. **Head Coach:** Stephen Flora.

VALLEY BASEBALL LEAGUE

Mailing Address: Valley Baseball League, 3006 Preston Lake Boulevard, Harrisonburg, VA 22801. **Telephone:** (540) 810-9194. **Fax:** (540) 434-5083. **E-Mail Addresses:** don@lemish.com & baseball@shentel.net **Website:** www.valleyleaguebaseball.com.

Year Founded: 1961.
President: Donald L. Lemish. **Assistant to the President:** Don Harper. **Executive Vice President:** Bruce Alger. **Media Relations Director:** Brian Hansen. **Secretary:** Megan Smith. **Treasurer:** Gene Davis.
Regular Season: 44 games. **2013 Opening Date:** May 31. **Closing Date:** July 30. **All-Star Game:** North vs South, July 7 at Harrisonburg. **Playoff Format:** Eight teams; best-of-three quarterfinals and semifinals; best-of-five finals.
Roster Limit: 28 (college eligible players only)

COVINGTON LUMBERJACKS

Mailing Address: P.O. Box 30, Covington, VA 24426. **Telephone:** (540) 969-9923, (540) 962-1155. **Fax:** (540) 962-7153. **E-Mail Address:** covingtonlumberjacks@valleyleaguebaseball.com. **Website:** www.lumberjacksbaseball.com. **President:** Dizzy Garten. **Head Coach:** Dan Scott.

ALDIE SENATORS

Mailing Address: 42020 Village Center Plaza, Suite 120-50, Stoneridge, VA 20105. **Telephone:** (703) 542-2110, (703) 989-5009. **Fax:** (703)327-7435. **E-Mail Address:** haymarketsenators@valleyleaguebaseball.com. **Website:** www.haymarketbaseball.com. **President:** Scott Newell. **General Manager:** BernieSchaffler. **Head Coach:** Justin Aspegren.

CHARLES TOWN CANNONS

Mailing Address: 2862 Northwestern Pike, Capon Bridge, WV 26711.. **Telephone:** (540) 743-3338, (540) 843-4472. **Fax:** (304) 856-1619. **E-Mail Address:** bigdaddy432@verizon.net. **Website:** www.charlestowncannons.com. **President:** Brett Fuller. **Recruiting Coordinator:** Brett Fuller. **General Manager:** Steve Sabins.

FRONT ROYAL CARDINALS

Mailing Address: 382 Morgans Ridge Road, Front Royal, VA 22630. **Telephone:** (703) 244-6662, (540) 905-0152. **E-Mail Address:** DonnaSettle@centurylink.net-frontroyalcardinals@valleyleaguebaseball.com. **Website:** www.valleyleaguebaseball.com. **President:** Donna Settle. **Head Coach:** Jake Weghorst.

HARRISONBURG TURKS

Mailing Address: 1489 S. Main St., Harrisonburg, VA 22801. **Telephone:** (540) 434-5919. **Fax:** (540) 434-5919. **E-Mail Address:** turksbaseball@hotmail.com. **Website:** www.harrisonburgturks.com. **Operations Manager:** Teresa Wease. **General Manager/Head Coach:** Bob Wease.

NEW MARKET REBELS

Mailing Address: P.O. Box 902, New Market, VA 22844. **Telephone:** (304) 856-1623. **Fax:** (540) 740-9486. **E-Mail Address:** nmrebels@shentel.net. **Website:** www.rebels-baseball.biz. **President/General Manager:** Bruce Alger. **Head Coach:** C.J. Rhodes.

ROCKBRIDGE RAPIDS

Mailing Address: P.O. Box 600, Lexington, VA 24450. **Telephone:** (540) 460-7502, (540) 462-7521. **E-Mail Address:** rockbridgerapids@valleyleaguebaseball.com. **Website:** www.rockbridgerapids.com. **President:** Bill Luton. **General Manager:** Ken Newman. **Head Coach:** Greg Keaton.

STAUNTON BRAVES

Mailing Address: 14 Shannon Place, Staunton, VA 24401.Telephone: (540) 886-0987, (540) 885-1645. **Fax:** (540) 886-0905. **E-Mail Address:** sbraves@hotmail.com. **Website:** www.stauntonbravesbaseball.com. **General Manager:** Steve Cox. **Head Coach:** George Laase.

STRASBURG EXPRESS

Mailing Address: P.O. Box 417, Strasburg, VA 22657. **Telephone:** (540) 325-5677, (540) 459-4041. **Fax:** (540) 459-3398. **E-Mail Address:** neallaw@shentel.net. **Website:** www.strasburgexpress.com. **General manager:** Jay Neal. **Head coach:** Butch Barnes.

WAYNESBORO GENERALS

Mailing Address: 435 Essex Ave., Suite 105, Waynesboro VA 22980. **Telephone:** (540) 932-2300. **Fax:** (540) 932-2322. **E-Mail Address:** waynesborogenerals@valleyleaguebaseball.com. **Website:** www.waynesboro-generals.com. **Chairman:** David T. Gauldin II. **Head Coach:** Mike Bocock.

WINCHESTER ROYALS

Mailing Address: P.O. Box 2485, Winchester, VA 22604. **Telephone:** (540) 539-8888, (540) 664-3978. **Fax:** (540) 662-1434. **E-Mail Addresses:** winchesterroyals@valleyleaguebaseball.com, jimphill@shentel.net.Website: www.winchesterroyals.com. **President:** Todd Thompson. **Operations Director:** Jimmie Shipp. **Coach:** Kyle Phelps

WOODSTOCK RIVER BANDITS

Mailing Address: P.O. Box 227, Woodstock, VA 22664. **Telephone:** (540) 481-0525. **Fax:** (540) 459-8227. **E-Mail Address:** woodstockriverbandits@valleyleaguebaseball.com. **Website:** www.woodstockriverbandits.org. **General Manager:** R.W. Bowman Jr. **Head Coach:** Phil Betterly.

WEST COAST LEAGUE

Mailing Address: P.O. Box 8395, Portland, OR 97207. **Telephone:** (503) 764-9510. **E-Mail Address:** wilson@westcoastleague.com. **Website:** www.westcoastleague.com.

Year Founded: 2005.
President: Ken Wilson. **Vice President:** Eddie Poplawski. **Secretary:** Jerry Walker. **Treasurer:** Tony Bonacci. **Supervisor of Umpires:** Tom Hiler.
Division Structure: North—Bellingham, Kelowna, Walla Walla, Wenatchee, Victoria. **South**—Bend, Corvallis, Cowlitz, Kitsap, Klamath Falls, Medford.
Regular Season: 54 games. **2013 Opening Date:** June

5. **Closing Date:** August 11. **All-Star Game:** July 23 at Victoria. **Playoff Format:** First- and second-place teams in each division meet in best-of-three semifinal series; winners advance to best-of-three championship series.
Roster Limit: 25 (college-eligible players only).

BELLINGHAM BELLS

Mailing Address: 1221 Potter Street, Bellingham, WA 98229. **Telephone:** (360) 746-0406. **E-Mail Address:** info@bellinghambells.com. **Website:** www.bellinghambells.com. **Owner:** Eddie Poplawski. **General Manager:** Nick Caples. **Head Coach:** Gary Hatch.

BEND ELKS

Mailing Address: P.O. Box 9009, Bend, OR 97708. **Telephone:** (541) 312-9259. **E-Mail Address:** richardsj@bendcable.com. **Website:** www.bendelks.com. **Owner/ General Manager:** Jim Richards. **Head Coach:** Joe Dominiak.

CORVALLIS KNIGHTS

Mailing Address: P.O. Box 1356, Corvallis, OR 97339. **Telephone:** (541) 752-5656. **E-Mail Address:** dan.segel@corvallisknights.com. **Website:** www.corvallisknights.com. **President:** Dan Segel. **General Manager:** Bre Kerkvliet. **Head Coach:** Brooke Knight.

COWLITZ BLACK BEARS

Mailing Address: P.O. Box 1255, Longview, WA 98632. **Telephone:** (360) 703-3195. **E-Mail Address:** gwilsonagm@gmail.com. **Website:** www.cowlitzblackbears.com. **Owner/ General Manager:** Tony Bonacci. **Head Coach:** Tim Matz (Santa Ana, Calif., JC).

KELOWNA FALCONS

Mailing Address: 201-1014 Glenmore Dr., Kelowna, BC, V1Y 4P2. **Telephone:** (250) 763-4100. **E-Mail Address:** mark@kelownafalcons.com. **Website:** www.kelownafalcons.com. **Owner:** Dan Nonis. **General Manager:** Mark Nonis. **Head Coach:** Geoff White.

KITSAP BLUEJACKETS

Mailing Address: P.O. Box 68, Silverdale, WA 98383. **Telephone:** (360) 692-5566.
E-Mail Address: rsmith@kitsapbluejackets.com. **Website:** www.kitsapbluejackets.com. **Managing Partner/General Manager:** Rick Smith. **Head Coach:** Ryan Parker (Olympic, Wash., JC).

KLAMATH FALLS GEMS

Mailing Address: 2001 Crest Street, Klamath Falls, Oregon 97603. **Telephone:** (541) 883-4367. **E-Mail Address:** grant@klamathfallsgems.com. **Website:** www.klamathfallsgems.com. **Owners:** Jerry and Lisa Walker. **General Manager:**
Grant Wilson. **Head Coach:** Mitch Karraker (Oregon).

MEDFORD ROGUES

Mailing Address: P.O. Box 699, Medford, Oregon 97501. **Telephone:** (541) 973-2883. **E-Mail Address:** chuck@medfordrogues.com. **Website:** www.medfordrogues.com. **Owner:** CSH International. **General Manager:** Chuck Heeman. **Head Coach:** Josh Hogan (Lane, Ore., CC).

VICTORIA HARBOURCATS

Mailing Address: 1014 Caledonia Avenue, Victoria, BC, V8T 1G1. **Telephone:** (250) 216-0006. **E-Mail Address:** holly@harbourcats.com. **Website:** www.harbourcats.com. **Owner:** John McLean. **General Manager:** Holly Jones. **Head Coach:** Dennis Rogers (Riverside, Calif., **CC).**

WALLA WALLA SWEETS

Mailing Address: 109 E. Main Street, Walla Walla, WA 99362. **Telephone:** (509) 522-2255. **E-Mail Address:** Zachary.Fraser@pacificbaseballventures.com. **Website:** www.wallawallabaseball.com. **Owner:** Pacific Baseball Ventures, LLC. **General Manager:** Zachary Fraser. **Head Coach:** JC Biagi (Walla Walla, Wash., CC).

WENATCHEE APPLESOX

Mailing Address: P.O. Box 5100, Wenatchee, WA 98807. **Telephone:** (509) 665-6900. **E-Mail Address:** sales@applesox.com. **Website:** www.applesox.com. **Owner/General Manager:** Jim Corcoran. **Head Coach:** Ed Knaggs.

WCL PORTLAND

Mailing Address: 2811 N.E. Holman, Portland, Oregon 97211. **Telephone:** (503) 280-8691. **E-Mail Address:** rvance@cu-portland.edu. **Website:**www.wccbl.com/portland.
Year Founded: 2009.
Commissioner: Rob Vance.
Regular Season: 30 games. **2013 Opening Date:** June 8. **Closing Date:** August 3. **All-Star Game:** None. **Playoff Format:** First-place team faces fourth-place team and second-place team faces third-place team in first round. **Winners advance to championship game.**
Roster Limit: 24 (college-eligible players only).
Teams: Bucks, Dukes, Lobos, Ports, Stars, Toros.

HIGH SCHOOL BASEBALL

NATIONAL FEDERATION OF STATE HIGH SCHOOL ASSOCIATIONS

Mailing Address: P.O. Box 690, Indianapolis, IN 46206. **Telephone:** (317) 972-6900. **Fax:** (317) 822-5700. **E-Mail Address:** baseball@nfhs.org. **Website:** www.nfhs.org.
Executive Director: Bob Gardner. **Chief Operating Officer:** James Tenopir. **Assistant Director/Baseball Rules Editor:** Elliot Hopkins. **Director, Publications/Communications:** Bruce Howard.

NATIONAL HIGH SCHOOL BASEBALL COACHES ASSOCIATION

Mailing Address: P.O. Box 12843, Tempe, AZ 85284. **Telephone:** (602) 615-0571. **Fax:** (480) 838-7133. **E-Mail Address:** rdavini@cox.net. **Website:** www.baseballcoaches.org. **Executive Director:** Ron Davini. **President:** Art Griffith (Winslow, Ariz., HS). **First Vice President:** John Lowery Sr (Jefferson HS, Shepherdstown, W.Va.). **Second Vice President:** Tim Saunders (Dublin Coffman HS, Dublin, Ohio).
2013 National Convention: Dec. 5-8, at Tucson, Ariz.

NATIONAL TOURNAMENTS

IN-SEASON

HORIZON NATIONAL INVITATIONAL

Mailing Address: Horizon High School, 5653 Sandra Terrace, Scottsdale, AZ 85254. **Telephone:** (602) 867-9003. **E-mail:** huskycoach1@yahoo.com. **Website:** www.horizonbaseball.com
Tournament Director: Eric Kibler.
2013 Tournament: March 25-29.

INTERNATIONAL PAPER CLASSIC

Mailing Address: 4775 Johnson Rd., Georgetown, SC 29440. **Telephone:** (843) 527-9606, (843) 546-3807. **Fax:** (843) 546-8521. **Website:** www.ipclassic.com.
Tournament Director: Alicia Johnson.
2013 Tournament: March 7-10 (eight teams).

LIONS INVITATIONAL

Mailing Address: 3502 Lark St., San Diego CA 92103. **Telephone:** (619) 602-8650. **Fax:** (619) 239-3539. **Website:** www.anaheimlionstourney.com
Tournament Director: Rod Wallace.
2013 Tournament: March 30, April 1-3.

NATIONAL CLASSIC BASEBALL TOURNAMENT

Mailing Address: P.O. Box 338, Placentia, CA 92870. **Telephone:** (714) 993-2838. **Fax:** (714) 993-5350. **E-Mail Address:** placentiamustang@aol.com. **Website:** www.national-classic.com
Tournament Director: Marcus Jones.
2013 Tournament: April 1-4 (16 teams).

USA BASEBALL NATIONAL HIGH SCHOOL INVITATIONAL

Mailing Address: 403 Blackwell St., Durham, NC 27701. **Telephone:** (919) 474-8721. **Fax:** (919) 474-8822. **Email:** rickriccobono@usabaseball.com. **Website:** www.usabaseball.com.
Tournament Director: Rick Riccobono.
2013 Tournament: March 27-30 at USA Baseball National Training Complex, Cary, NC (16 teams).

USA CLASSIC NATIONAL HIGH SCHOOL INVITATIONAL

Mailing Address: P.O. Box 247, Millington, TN 38043. **Telephone:** (901) 873-5880. **Fax:** (901) 873-5885. **Email:** jwaits@cityofmillington.org. **Website:** www.millingtontn.gov.
Tournament Organizers: Jeff Waits, Johnny Ray.
2013 Tournament: Unavailable.

POSTSEASON

SUNBELT BASEBALL CLASSIC SERIES

Mailing Address: 505 North Blvd., Edmond, OK 73034. **Telephone:** (405) 348-3839. **Fax:** (405) 340-7538. **Email:** lyngor@aol.com. **Website:** www.sunbeltclassicbaseball.com.
Chairman: John Schwartz.
2013 Senior Series: Unavailable.
2013 Junior Series: Unavailable.
2013 Sophomore Series: Unavailable.

ALL-STAR GAMES/AWARDS

PERFECT GAME ALL-AMERICAN CLASSIC

Mailing Address: 1932 Wynnton Road, Columbus, Georgia 31999. **Telephone:** (706) 763-2827. **Fax:** (706) 320-2288. **Event Organizer:** Blue Ridge Sports & Entertainment. **Vice President, Events:** Lou Lacy. **2013 Game:** Unavailable.

UNDER ARMOUR ALL-AMERICA GAME, POWERED BY BASEBALL FACTORY

Mailing Address: 9212 Berger Rd., Suite 200, Columbia, MD 21046. **Telephone:** 410-715-5080. **E-Mail Address:** jason@baseballfactory.com. **Website:** baseballfactory.com. **Event Organizers:** Baseball Factory, Team One Baseball. **2013 Game:** Aug 24.

GATORADE CIRCLE OF CHAMPIONS
(National HS Player of the Year Award)

Mailing Address: The Gatorade Company, 321 N. Clark St., Suite 24-3, Chicago, IL, 60610. **Telephone:** 312-821-1000. **Website:** www.gatorade.com.

SHOWCASE EVENTS

ALL-AMERICAN BASEBALL TALENT SHOWCASES

Mailing Address: 333 Preston Ave., Unit 1, Voorhees, NJ 08043. **Telephone:** (856) 354-0201. **Fax:** (856) 354-0818. **E-Mail Address:** hitdoctor@thehitdoctor.com. **Website:** thehitdoctor.com. **National Director:** Joe Barth.

ARIZONA FALL CLASSIC

Mailing Address: 6102 W. Maui Lane, Glendale, AZ 85306. **Telephone:** (602) 978-2929. **Fax:** (602) 439-4494. **E-Mail Address:** azbaseballted@msn.com.
Website: www.azfallclassic.com.
Directors: Ted Heid, Tracy Heid.

2013 Events

Four Corner Classic . . . . .Peoria, AZ, May 30-June 2
Arizona Summer Classic . . . . Peoria, AZ, July 11-14
Arizona Summer Classic (16U) . . . . .July 18-21
Arizona Fall Invitational . . . . Oct. 4-6
Arizona Fall Classic (16U). . . . . Oct. 4-6
AZ Senior Fall Classic (HS seniors) . . . . Peoria, AZ, Oct. 10-13
AZ Junior Fall Classic (HS juniors) . . . . Peoria, AZ, Oct. 17-20
AZ Sophomore Fall Classic
(HS soph. and under) . . . . Peoria, AZ, Oct. 24-27

BASEBALL FACTORY

Office Address: 9212 Berger Rd., Suite 200, Columbia, MD 21046. **Telephone:** (800) 641-4487, (410) 715-5080. **Fax:** (410) 715-1975. **E-Mail Address:** info@baseballfactory.com. **Website:** www.baseballfactory.com. **Chief Executive Officer/Founder:** Steve Sclafani. **President:** Rob Naddelman. **Executive VP/Chairman, Under Armour All-America Game Selection Committee:** Steve Bernhardt. **Senior VP, Marketing/Brand:** Jason Budden. **Senior VP, Baseball Operations:** Jim Gemler. **VP, Creative:** Matt Kirby. **VP, Player Development:** Dan Forester. **VP, Youth Baseball:** Jeff Brazier. **VP, Finance:** Gene Mattingly. **Senior Director, Baseball Operations:** Andy Ferguson. **Senior Director, College Recruiting:** Dan Mooney. **Senior Multimedia Producer:** Brian Johnson. **Executive Player Development Coordinator:** Steve Nagler. **Senior Player Development Coordinators:** Dave Packer, John Perko. **Regional Player Development Coordinators:** Patrick Wuebben, Chris Brown, Adam Darvick, Will Bach, Rob Onolfi, Ryan Schweikert, Scott Ritter, Jesse Tome, Drew Baldwin, Ed Bach, Jeff Gossett. **Director, Client Services:** Cecile Banas. **Director, On-Field Operations:** Joe Lake. **Director, PVP Program/National Tryouts:** Bryan Dunkel. **Director, Event/Online**

Marketing: Dave Lax.
Under Armour All-America Pre-Season Tournament: January 18-20 in Tucson, AZ (Kino Sports Complex).
Under Armour All-America Game: August 24, in Chicago, IL (Wrigley Field).
2013 Under Armour Baseball Factory National Tryouts/Premium Video Program: Various locations across the country. Year round. Open to high school players, ages 14–18 and a separate division for pre-high school players, ages 12–14. For full schedule, visit www.baseballfactory.com/tryouts.

BLUE-GREY CLASSIC

Mailing address: 68 Norfolk Road, Mills MA 02054. **Telephone:** (508) 376-1250. **E-Mail address:** impactprospects@comcast.net. **Website:** www.impactprospects.com.
2013 events: Various dates, locations June-Sept 2013.

BOBBY VALENTINE ALL-AMERICAN CAMPS

Address: 72 Camp Avenue, Stamford, CT 06907. **Telephone:** (203) 517-1277. **Fax:** (203) 517-1377.
Website: www.allamericanfoundation.com

COLLEGE SELECT BASEBALL

Mailing Address: P.O. Box 783, Manchester, CT 06040. **Telephone:** (800) 645-9854. **E-Mail Address:** TRhit@msn.com. **Website:** www.collegeselect.org.
Consulting Director: Tom Rizzi.

EAST COAST PROFESSIONAL SHOWCASE

Website: www.eastcoastproshowcase.com.
Tournament Directors: John Castleberry.
Tournament Coordinator: Shannon Follett.
2013 Showcase: July 31-Aug 3, Syracuse, N.Y.

IMPACT BASEBALL

Mailing Address: P.O. Box 47, Sedalia, NC 27342. **E-Mail Address:** andypartin@aol.com. **Website:** impactbaseball.com.
Operator: Andy Partin.
2013 Events: Various dates, May-Aug 2013.

NEW BALANCE BASEBALL GAMES

Mailing Address: 23954 Madison Street, Torrance,

CA 90505. **Telephone:** 310-791-1142 x 4426. **Website:** newbalancegames.com

Event Organizer: Kirsten Leetch.

2013 Area Code Games: Aug 5-10 at Blair Field in Long Beach, Calif.

PACIFIC NORTHWEST CHAMPIONSHIPS

Mailing Address: 2035 Celeen Ave. SW, Salem, Ore. **Telephone:** (541) 896-0841. **E-Mail Address:** mckay@baseballnorthwest.com. **Website:** www.baseballnorthwest.com. **Tournament Organizer:** Jeff McKay.

PERFECT GAME USA

Mailing Address: 1203 Rockford Road SW, Cedar Rapids, IA 52404. **Telephone:** (319) 298-2923 Fax: (319) 298-2924. **E-Mail Address:** jerry@perfectgame.org. **Website:** www.perfectgameusa.com.

President/Director: Jerry Ford. **Vice Presidents:** Andy Ford, Jason Gerst, Tyson Kimm. **Director, Crosscheckers:** Allan Simpson. **International Scouting Coordinator:** Kentaro Yasutake. **National Director:** Jim Arp. **National Tournament Director:** Taylor McCollough. **Scouting Director:** David Rawnsley. **National BCS Director:** Ben Ford. **Iowa League Director:** Steve James. **Northeast Director:** Dan Kennedy. **Western Tournament Director:** Matt Bliven. **Scouting Coordinators:** Greg Sabers, Jason Piddington, Kenny Gardner, Justin Hlubek.

2013 Showcase/Tournament Events: Sites across the United States, Jan 9-Nov 7.

PROFESSIONAL BASEBALL INSTRUCTION—BATTERY INVITATIONAL

(for top high school pitchers and catchers)

Mailing Address: 107 Pleasant Avenue, Upper Saddle River N.J. 07458. **Telephone:** (800) 282-4638. **Fax:** (201) 760-8720. **E-Mail Address:** info@baseballclinics.com. **Website:** www.baseballclinics.com/batteryinvitational.html.

President: Doug Cinnella.

Senior Staff Administrator: Greg Cinnella. **General Manager/PR/Marketing:** Jim Monaghan.

SELECTFEST BASEBALL

Mailing Address: 60 Franklin Pl., Morris Plains, NJ 07950. **Telephone:** (862) 222-6404. **E-Mail Address:** selectfest@optonline.net. **Website:** www.selectfestbaseball.org. **Camp Directors:** Bruce Shatel.

2013 Showcase: Unavailable.

TEAM ONE BASEBALL (A DIVISION OF BASEBALL FACTORY)

Office Address: 1000 Bristol Street North, Box 17285, Newport Beach, CA 92660. **Telephone:** (800) 621-5452, (805) 451-8203. **Fax:** (949) 209-1829. **E-Mail Address:** jroswell@teamonebaseball.com. **Website:** www.teamonebaseball.com.

Senior Director: Justin Roswell. **Executive VP:** Steve Bernhardt. **Senior VP, Baseball Operations:** Jim Gemler. **VP, Player Development:** Dan Forester.

2013 Under Armour Showcases: Team One Florida: June 12-13 in Jupiter, FL (Roger Dean Sports Complex); **Team One West:** July 8–9 in Costa Mesa, CA (Vanguard University); **Team One South:** July 12–13 in Peachtree City, GA (The Chuck at Homeplate); **Team One North:** July 26–27 in Plymouth, PA (Ballpark at Plymouth Meeting); **Team One Futures East:** September 21 in Jupiter, FL (Roger Dean Stadium); **Team One Futures West:** October 25 in Azusa, CA (Azusa Pacific University)

2013 Under Armour Tournaments: Under Armour Memorial Day Classic: May 24-27 in Jupiter, FL (Roger Dean Sports Complex); **Under Armour Southeast Championships:** June 7–11 in Jupiter, FL (Roger Dean Sports Complex); **Under Armour Firecracker Classic:** July 1–5 in Jupiter, FL (Roger Dean Sports Complex); **Under Armour Southwest Championships:** July 31-Aug 4 in Azusa, CA (Azusa Pacific University/Citrus College); **Under Armour Fall Classic:** Sept 20–22 in Jupiter, FL (Roger Dean Sports Complex); **Under Armour Invitational:** Oct 13–14 in St. Petersburg, FL (Walter Fuller Complex); **Under Armour SoCal Classic:** Oct 25–27 in Azusa, CA (Azusa Pacific University/Citrus College).

TOP 96 COLLEGE COACHES CLINICS

Mailing Address: 6 Foley Dr. Southboro, MA 01772. **Telephone:** 508-481-5935.

E-Mail Address: doug.henson@top96.com. **Website:** www.top96.com.

Directors: Doug Henson, Dave Callum.

2013 Clinics: Various clinics throughout the United States; see website for schedule.

YOUTH BASEBALL

ALL AMERICAN AMATEUR BASEBALL ASSOCIATION

Mailing Address: 331 Parkway Dr., Zanesville, OH 43701. **Telephone:** (740) 453-8531. **E-Mail Address:** clw@aol.com. **Website:** www.aaaba.us.
Year Founded: 1944.
President: Lou Tiberi. **Executive Director/Secretary:** Bob Wolfe.
2013 Events: Dates unavailable.

AMATEUR ATHLETIC UNION OF THE UNITED STATES, INC.

Mailing Address: P.O. Box 22409, Lake Buena Vista, FL 32830. **Telephone:** (407) 828-3459. **Fax:** (407) 934-7242. **E-Mail Address:** debra@aausports.org. **Website:** www.aaubaseball.org.
Year Founded: 1982. **Sports Manager, Baseball:** Debra Horn.

AMERICAN AMATEUR BASEBALL CONGRESS

National Headquarters: 100 West Broadway, Farmington, NM 87401. **Telephone:** (505) 327-3120. **Fax:** (505) 327-3132. **E-Mail Address:** aabc@aabc.us. **Website:** www.aabc.us.
Year Founded: 1935.
President: Richard Neely.

AMERICAN AMATEUR YOUTH BASEBALL ALLIANCE

Mailing Address: 1703 Koala Drive, Wentzville, MO 63385. **Telephone:** (636) 332-7799. **E-Mail Address:** clwjr28@aol.com. **Website:** www.aayba.com.
President, Baseball Operations: Carroll Wood. **President, Business Operations:** Greg Moore.

AMERICAN LEGION BASEBALL

National Headquarters: American Legion Baseball, 700 N Pennsylvania St., Indianapolis, IN 46204. **Telephone:** (317) 630-1213. **Fax:** (317) 630-1369. **E-Mail Address:** baseball@legion.org **Website:** www.baseball.legion.org/baseball.
Year Founded: 1925.
Program Coordinator: Jim Quinlan.
2013 World Series (19 and under): Dates unavailable. At Veteran's Field, Shelby, N.C.
2013 Regional Tournaments (Aug 8-12): **Northeast**—Middletown, Conn; **Mid-Atlantic**—Brooklawn, NJ; **Southeast**—Asheboro NC; **Mid-South**—North Little Rock, Ark; **Great Lakes**—Terre Haute, Ind; **Central Plains**—Fargo, ND; **Northwest**—Eugene, Ore; **Western**—Surprise, Ariz.

BABE RUTH BASEBALL

International Headquarters: 1770 Brunswick Pike, P.O. Box 5000, Trenton, NJ 08638. **Telephone:** (609) 695-1434. **Fax:** (609) 695-2505. **E-Mail Address:** info@baberuthleague.org. **Website:** www.baberuthleague.org.
Year Founded: 1951.
President/Chief Executive Officer: Steven Tellefsen.

CONTINENTAL AMATEUR BASEBALL ASSOCIATION

Mailing Address: 1173 French Court, Maineville, Ohio 45039. **Telephone:** (513) 677-1580. **Fax:** 513-677-2586. **E-Mail Address:** lred-wine@cababaseball.com. **Website:** www.cababaseball.com.
Year Founded: 1984.
Executive Director: Larry Redwine. **Commissioner:** John Mocny. **Executive Vice President:** Fran Pell.

DIXIE YOUTH BASEBALL

Mailing Address: P.O. Box 877, Marshall, TX 75671. **Telephone:** (903) 927-2255. **Fax:** (903) 927-1846. **E-Mail Address:** dyb@dixie.org. **Website:** www.dixie.org.
Year Founded: 1955.
Commissioner: Wes Skelton.

DIXIE BOYS BASEBALL

Mailing Address: P.O. Box 8263, Dothan, Alabama 36304. **Telephone:** (334) 793-3331. **E-Mail Address:** jjones29@sw.rr.com. **Website:** http://baseball.dixie.org.
Commissioner/Chief Executive Officer: Sandy Jones.

DIZZY DEAN BASEBALL

Mailing Address: P.O. Box 856, Hernando, MS 38632. **Telephone:** (662) 429-4365, (423) 596-1353. **E-Mail Address:** DPhil10513@aol.com, jimmywahl@bellsouth.net, Bdunn39270@comcast.net, hsuggsdizzydean@aol.com. **Website:** www.dizzydeanbbinc.org.
Year Founded: 1962.
Commissioner: Danny Phillips. **President:** Jimmy Wahl. **VP:** Bobby Dunn. **Secretary:** Billy Powell. **Treasurer:** Houston Suggs.

HAP DUMONT YOUTH BASEBALL (A DIVISION OF THE NATIONAL BASEBALL CONGRESS)

E-Mail Address: bruce@prattrecreation.com,gbclev@hapdumontbaseball.com. **Website:** www.hapdumont-baseball.com.
Year Founded: 1974.
President: Bruce Pinkall

LITTLE LEAGUE BASEBALL

International Headquarters: P.O. Box 3485, Williamsport, PA 17701. **Telephone:** (570) 326-1921. **Fax:** (570) 326-1074. **Website:** www.littleleague.org.
Year Founded: 1939.
Chairman: Dr. Davie Jane Gilmour.
President/Chief Executive Officer: Stephen D. Keener. **Chief Financial Officer:** David Houseknecht. **Vice President, Operations:** Patrick Wilson. **Treasurer:** Melissa Singer. **Senior Communications Executive:** Lance Van Auken.

NATIONAL AMATEUR BASEBALL FEDERATION

Mailing Address: P.O. Box 705, Bowie, MD 20718. **Telephone:** (410) 721-4727. **Fax:** (410) 721-4940. **E-Mail Address:** nabf1914@aol.com.
Website: www.nabf.com.
Year Founded: 1914.
Executive Director: Charles Blackburn.

AMATEUR/YOUTH

NATIONAL ASSOCIATION OF POLICE ATHLETIC LEAGUES
Mailing Address: 658 W. Indiantown Road #201, Jupiter, FL 33458. **Telephone:** (561) 745-5535. **Fax:** (561) 745-3147. **E-Mail Address:** copnkid@nationalpal.org. **Website:** www.nationalpal.org.
Year Founded: 1914.
President: Christopher Hill.

PONY BASEBALL
International Headquarters: P.O. Box 225, Washington, PA 15301. **Telephone:** (724) 225-1060. **Fax:** (724) 225-9852. **E-Mail Address:** info@pony.org.
Website: www.pony.org.
Year Founded: 1951.
President: Abraham Key.

REVIVING BASEBALL IN INNER CITIES
Mailing Address: 245 Park Ave., New York, NY 10167. **Telephone:** (212) 931-7800. **Fax:** (212) 949-5695. **Year Founded:** 1989. **Director, Reviving Baseball in Inner Cities:** David James (David.James@mlb.com). **Vice President, Community Affairs:** Thomas C Brasuell. **Email:** rbi@mlb.com. **Website:** www.mlb.com/rbi.

SUPER SERIES BASEBALL OF AMERICA
National Headquarters: 3449 East Kael St., Mesa, AZ 85213-1773. **Telephone:** (480) 664-2998. **Fax:** (480) 664-2997. **E-Mail Address:** info@superseriesbaseball.com. **Website:** www.superseriesbaseball.com.
President: Mark Mathew.

TRIPLE CROWN SPORTS
Mailing Address: 3930 Automation Way, Fort Collins, CO 80525. **Telephone:** (970) 223-6644. **Fax:** (970) 223-3636. **Websites:** www.triplecrownsports.com. **E-Mail:** thad@triplecrownsports.com.
Director, Baseball Operations: Thad Anderson.

U.S. AMATEUR BASEBALL FEDERATION
Mailing Address: P.O. Box 531216, San Diego, CA 92153. **Telephone:** (619) 934-2551. **Fax:** (619) 271-6659. **E-Mail Address:** usabf@cox.net. **Website:** www.usabf.com.
Year Founded: 1997.
Senior Chief Executive Officer/President: Tim Halbig.

UNITED STATES SPECIALTY SPORTS ASSOCIATION
Executive Vice President, Baseball: Don DeDonatis III, 33600 Mound Rd., Sterling Heights, MI 48310. **Telephone:** (810) 397-6410. **E-Mail Address:** michusssa@aol.com.
Executive Vice President, Baseball Operations: Rick Fortuna, 6324 N. Chatham Ave., #136, Kansas City, MO 64151. **Telephone:** (816) 587-4545. **E-Mail Address:** rick@kcsports.org. **Website:** www.usssabaseball.org. **Year Founded:** 1965/Baseball 1996.

WORLD WOOD BAT ASSOCIATION (A DIVISION OF PERFECT GAME USA)
Mailing Address: 1203 Rockford Road SW, Cedar Rapids, IA 52404. **Telephone:** (319) 298-2923. **Fax:** (319) 298-2924. **E-Mail Address:** taylor@perfectgame.org. **Website:** www.worldwoodbat.com.
Year Founded: 1997.
President: Jerry Ford. **National Director:** Taylor McCollough. **Scouting Director:** David Rawnsley.

BASEBALL USA
Mailing Address: 2626 West Sam Houston Pkwy. N., Houston, TX 77043. **Telephone:** (713) 690-5055. **E-Mail Address:** info@baseballusa.com. **Website:** www.baseballusa.com.
Tournament Director: Steve Olson

CALIFORNIA COMPETITIVE YOUTH BASEBALL
Mailing Address: P.O. Box 338, Placentia, CA 92870. **Telephone:** (714) 993-2838. **E-Mail Address:** ccybnet@aol.com. **Website:** www.ccyb.net.
Tournament Director: Todd Rogers.

COCOA EXPO SPORTS CENTER
Mailing Address: 500 Friday Road, Cocoa, FL 32926. **Telephone:** (321) 639-3976. **Fax:** (407) 390-9435. **E-Mail Address:** athleticdirector@cocoaexpo.com. **Website:** www.cocoaexpo.com.
Athletic Director: Matt Yurish.
Activities: Spring training program, spring & fall leagues, instructional camps, team training camps, youth tournaments.

COOPERSTOWN BASEBALL WORLD
Mailing Address: P.O. Box 646, Allenwood, NJ 08723. **Telephone:** (888) CBW-8750. **Fax:** (888) CBW-8720. **E-Mail:** cbw@cooperstownbaseballworld.com. **Website:** www.cooperstownbaseballworld.com.
Complex Address: Cooperstown Baseball World, SUNY-Oneonta, Ravine Parkway, Oneonta, NY 13820.
President/Chairman: Eddie Einhorn. **Vice President:** Debra Sirianni.
2013 Tournaments (15 Teams Per Week): Open to 11U, 12U, 13U, 14U, 15U, 16U

COOPERSTOWN DREAMS PARK
Mailing Address: 330 S. Main St., Salisbury, NC 28144. **Telephone:** (704) 630-0050. **Fax:** (704) 630-0737. **E-Mail Address:** info@cooperstowndreamspark.com. **Website:** www.cooperstowndreamspark.com.
Complex Address: 4550 State Highway 28, Cooperstown, NY 13807.
Chief Executive Officer: Lou Presutti. **Program Director:** Geoff Davis.
2013 Tournaments: Weekly June 2–Aug 31.

COOPERSTOWN ALL STAR VILLAGE
Mailing Address: P.O. Box 670, Cooperstown, NY 13326. **Telephone:** (800) 327-6790. **Fax:** (607) 432-1076. **E-Mail Address:** info@cooperstownallstarvillage.com. **Website:** www.cooperstownallstarvillage.com.
Team Registrations: Jim Rudloff. **Hotel Room Reservations:** Shelly Yager. **Presidents:** Martin and Brenda Patton.

DISNEY'S WIDE WORLD OF SPORTS
Mailing Address: P.O. Box 470847, Celebration, Fl 34747. **Telephone:** (407) 938-3802. **Fax:** (407) 938-3442. **E-mail address:** wdw.sports.baseball@disneysports.com.

Website: www.disneybaseball.com.
Manager, Sports Events: Scott St. George. Senior Sports Manager: Emily Moak. Tournament Director: Al Schlazer.

KC SPORTS TOURNAMENTS

Mailing Address: KC Sports, 6324 N. Chatham Ave., No. 136, Kansas City, MO 64151.
Telephone: (816) 587-4545. Fax: (816) 587-4549.
E-Mail Address: info@kcsports.org.
Website: www.kcsports.org.
Activities: USSSA Youth tournaments (ages 6-18).

U.S. AMATEUR BASEBALL FEDERATION

Mailing Address: P.O. Box 531216, San Diego, CA 92153. Telephone: (619) 934-2551. Fax: (619) 271-6659. E-Mail Address: usabf@cox.net. Website: www.usabf.com.
Year Founded: 1997. Senior Chief Executive Officer/ President: Tim Halbig.

INSTRUCTIONAL SCHOOLS/ PRIVATE CAMPS

ACADEMY OF PRO PLAYERS

Mailing Address: 140 5th Avenue, Hawthorne, NJ 07506. Telephone: (973) 304-1470. Fax: (973) 636-6375. E-Mail Address: proplayer@nji.com. Website: www.academypro.com. Camp Director: Dan Gilligan.

ALL-STAR BASEBALL ACADEMY

Mailing Addresses: 650 South Parkway Blvd., Broomall, PA 19008; 52 Penn Oaks Dr., West Chester, PA 19382, 3 Esterbrook Lane, Cherry Hill, NJ 08003, 417 Boot Rd., Downington, PA 19335, 1537 Campus Drive, Warminster, PA 18974. Telephone: (610) 355-2411, (856) 433-8312, (610) 518-7400, (215) 672-1826, (610) 399-8050. Fax: (610) 355-2414. E-Mail Address: basba@allstarbaseballacademy.com. Website: www.allstarbaseballacademy.com. Directors: Mike Manning, Jim Freeman.

AMERICAN BASEBALL FOUNDATION

Mailing Address: 2660 10th Ave. South, Suite 620, Birmingham, AL 35205. Telephone: (205) 558-4235. Fax: (205) 918-0800. E-Mail Address: abf@asmi.org. Website: www.americanbaseball.org. Executive Director: David Osinski.

THE BASEBALL ACADEMY

Mailing Address: IMG Academies, 5500 34th St. W., Bradenton, FL 34210. Telephone: (941) 739-7480. Fax: (941) 739-7484. E-Mail Address: acad_baseball@imgworld.com. Website: www.imgacademies.com.

AMERICA'S BASEBALL CAMPS

Mailing Address: 3020 ISSQ Pine Lake Road #12, Sammamish, WA 98075. Telephone: (800) 222-8152. Fax: (888) 751-8989. E-Mail Address: info@baseballcamps.com. Website: www.baseballcamps.com.

CHAMPIONS BASEBALL ACADEMY

Mailing Address: 5994 Linneman Street Cincinnatti, OH 45228. Telephone: (513) 831-8873. Fax: (513) 247-0040. E-Mail Address: championsbaseball@ymail.com. Website: www.championsbaseball.net.

DOYLE BASEBALL ACADEMY

Mailing Address: P.O. Box 9156, Winter Haven, FL 33883. Telephone: (863) 439-1000. Fax: (863) 294-8607. E-Mail Address: info@doylebaseball.com.
Website: www.doylebaseball.com. President: Denny Doyle. CEO/CFO: Blake Doyle.

ELEV8 SPORTS INSTITUTE

Mailing Address: 490 Dotterel Road, Delray Beach, FL 33444. Telephone: (561) 265-0280. Fax: (561) 278-6679. E-Mail Address: staff@dentbaseball.com. Website: http://elev8si.com.com

FROZEN ROPES TRAINING CENTERS

Mailing Address: 24 Old Black Meadow Rd., Chester, NY 10918. Telephone: (845) 469-7331. Fax: (845) 469-6742. E-Mail Address: info@frozenropes.com. Website: www.frozenropes.com.

MARK CRESSE BASEBALL SCHOOL

Mailing Address: 58 Fulmar Lane, Aliso Viego, CA 92656. Telephone: (714) 892-6145. Fax: (949) 600-9807. E-Mail Address: info@markcresse.com. Website: www.markcresse.com.
Owner/Founder: Mark Cresse.

US SPORTS CAMPS

Mailing Address: 750 Lindaro Street, Suite 220, San Rafael, CA 94901. Telephone: (415) 479-6060. Fax: (415) 479-6061. E-Mail Address: baseball@ussportscamps.com. Website: www.ussportscamps.com.

MOUNTAIN WEST BASEBALL ACADEMY

Mailing Address: 389 West 10000 South, South Jordan, UT 84095. Telephone: (801) 561-1700. Fax: (801) 561-1762. E-Mail Address: kent@utahbaseballacademy.com. Website: www.mountainwestbaseball.com. Director: Bob Keyes

NORTH CAROLINA BASEBALL ACADEMY

Mailing Address: 1137 Pleasant Ridge Road, Greensboro, NC 27409. Telephone: (336) 931-1118. E-Mail Address: info@ncbaseball.com. Website: www.ncbaseball.com.
Owner/Director: Scott Bankhead.

PENNSYLVANIA DIAMOND BUCKS

Mailing Address: 2320 Whitetail Court, Hellertown, PA 18055. Telephone: (610) 838-1219, (610) 442-6998. E-Mail Address: janciganick@yahoo.com. Camp Director: Jan Ciganick. Head of Instruction: Chuck Ciganick.

PROFESSIONAL BASEBALL INSTRUCTION

Mailing Address: 107 Pleasant Ave., Upper Saddle River, NJ 07458. Telephone: (800) 282-4638 (NY/NJ), (877) 448-2220 (rest of U.S.). Fax: (201) 760-8820. E-Mail Address: info@baseballclinics.com. Website: www.baseballclinics.com. President: Doug Cinnella.

RIPKEN BASEBALL CAMPS

Mailing Address: 1427 Clarkview Rd., Suite 100, Baltimore, MD 21209. Telephone: (410) 823-0808. Fax: (410) 823-0850. E-Mail Address: information@ripkenbaseball.com. Website: www.ripkenbaseball.com.

SHO-ME BASEBALL CAMP

Mailing Address: P.O. Box 2270, Branson West, MO 65737. **Telephone:** (417) 338-5838. **Fax:** (417) 338-2610. **E-Mail Address:** info@shomebaseball.com. **Website:** www.shomebaseball.com.

COLLEGE CAMPS

Almost all of the elite college baseball programs have summer/holiday instructional camps. Please consult the college section for listings.

SENIOR BASEBALL

MEN'S SENIOR BASEBALL LEAGUE

(25 and Over, 35 and Over, 45 and Over, 55 and Over)
Mailing Address: One Huntington Quadrangle, Suite 3N07, Melville, NY 11747. **Telephone:** (631) 753-6725. **Fax:** (631) 753-4031.
President: Steve Sigler. **Vice President:** Gary D'Ambrisi.
E-Mail Address: info@msblnational.com.
Website: www.msblnational.com.

MEN'S ADULT BASEBALL LEAGUE

(18 and Over)
Mailing Address: One Huntington Quadrangle, Suite 3N07, Melville, NY 11747. **Telephone:** (631) 753-6725. **Fax:** (631) 753-4031.
E-Mail Address: info@msblnational.com. **Website:** www.msblnational.com.
President: Steve Sigler. **Vice President:** Gary D'Ambrisi.

NATIONAL ADULT BASEBALL ASSOCIATION

Mailing Address: 5944 S. Kipling St., Suite 200, Littleton, CO 80127. **Telephone:** (800) 621-6479. **Fax:** (303) 639-6605. **E-Mail:** nabanational@aol.com. **Website:** www.dugout.org.
President: Shane Fugita.

NATIONAL ADULT BASEBALL ASSOCIATION

Mailing Address: 3609 S. Wadsworth Blvd., Suite 135, Lakewood, CO 80235. **Telephone:** (800) 621-6479.
Fax: (303) 639-6605. **E-Mail:** nabanational@aol.com. **Website:** www.dugout.org.
President: Shane Fugita.

NATIONAL AMATEUR BASEBALL FEDERATION

Mailing Address: P.O. Box 705, Bowie, MD 20718. **Telephone:** (410) 721-4727. **Fax:** (410) 721-4940. **E-Mail Address:** nabf1914@aol.com. **Website:** www.nabf.com.
Year Founded: 1914.
Executive Director: Charles Blackburn.

ROY HOBBS BASEBALL

Open (18-over), Veterans (38-over), Masters (48-over), Legends (55-over); Classics (60-over), Seniors (65-over), Timeless (70-over), Women's open.
Mailing Address: 2048 Akron Peninsula Rd., Akron, OH 44313. **Telephone:** (330) 923-3400. **Fax:** (330) 923-1967. **E-Mail Address:** rhbb@royhobbs.com.
Website: www.royhobbs.com.
President: Tom Giffen. **Vice President:** Ellen Giffen.

DIRECTORIES
- **AGENT**
- **SERVICE**

AGENT DIRECTORY

ACES INC
188 Montague St.
Brooklyn, NY 11201
Phone: (718)-237-2900
Fax: (718)-522-3906
www.acesinc1.com
aces@acesinc1.com
Seth Levinson, Esq.
Sam Levinson
Keith Miller
Peter Pedalino, Esq.
Josh Yates
Mike Zimmerman
Brandon O'Hearn
Jamie Appel

METIS SPORTS MANAGEMENT, LLC
132 North Old Woodward Ave.
Birmingham, MI 48009
Phone: (248)-594-1070
Fax: (248)-281-5150
www.metissports.com
storm@metissports.com
hector@metissports.com
Storm T. Kirschenbaum, Esq.
Hector Faneytt

PRO AGENTS, INC
90 Woodbridge Center Dr, Ste 901
Woodbridge, NJ 07095
Phone: (800)-795-3454
Fax: (732)-726-6688
www.proagentsinc.com
dpepe@proagentsinc.com
David P. Pepe
Billy Martin, Jr.

PRO STAR MANAGEMENT, INC
1600 Scripps Center
312 Walnut St.
Cincinnati, OH 45202
Phone: (513)-762-7676
Fax: (513)-721-4628
www.prostarmanagement.com
prostar@fuse.net
Joe Bick, President
Brett Bick, Executive VP
Ryan Bick, VP

SOSNICK COBBE SPORTS
712 Bancroft Rd, #510
Walnut Creek, CA 94598
Phone: (925)-890-5283
Fax: (925)-476-0130
www.sosnickcobbesports.com
Mattsoz@aol.com, PaulCobbe@me.com
Matt Sosnick
Paul Cobbe
Adam Karon
Matt Hofer
Tripper Johnson
Jonathan Pridie

THE L. WARNER COMPANIES, INC
9690 Deereco Rd., Ste 650
Timonium, MD 21093
Phone: (410)-252-0808
Fax: (443)-281-5554
www.lwarner.com/baseball
baseball@lwarner.com
Rick Oliver, President
Jay Witasick, Vice President
Joe Gaza, Director of Baseball Operations
Lee Warner, Chairman and CEO

THE LEGACY AGENCY
200 Madison Ave., Ste 2225
New York, NY 10016
Phone: (212)-334-6880
Fax: (212)-334-6895
www.legacy-agency.com
Peter E. Greenberg, Esq.
Edward L. Greenberg
Chris Leible

THE LEGACY AGENCY
500 Newport Center Dr., Ste 800
Newport Beach, CA 92660
Phone: (949)-720-8700
Fax: (949)-720-1331
www.legacy-agency.com
Greg Genske
Brian Peters
Brodi Scoffield
R.J. Hernandez
Kenny Felder
Joe Mizzo
Joe Brennan
Hiram Bocachica
Mike Maulini

VERRILL DANA SPORTS LAW GROUP
One Portland Square
Portland, ME 04101
Phone: (207)-774-4000
Fax: (207)-774-7499
www.verrilldana.com
dabramson@verrilldana.com
David S. Abramson, Esq

SERVICE DIRECTORY

ACCESSORIES

M^POWERED BASEBALL
P.O. Box 2391
Danville, CA 94526
Phone: (925) 915-9393
Fax: (516) 333-1811
www.mpoweredbaseball.com
info@mpoweredbaseball.com

SOUTHERN ATHLETIC FIELDS, INC
1309 Mainsail Dr.
Columbia, TN 38401
Phone: (800) 837-8062
Fax: (931) 380-0145
www.safdirt.com
saf@safdirt.com

WILSON SPORTING GOODS
8750 West Bryn Mawr Ave., 13th Floor
Chicago, IL 60631
Phone: (800) 333-8326
Fax: (773) 714-4565
www.wilson.com
askwilson@wilson.com

APPAREL

DEMARINI
6435 N.W. Croeni Rd.
Hillsboro, OR 97124
Phone: (800) 937-BATS (2287)
Fax: (503) 531-5506
www.demarini.com

MINOR LEAGUES, MAJOR DREAMS
P.O. Box 6098
Anaheim, CA 92816
Phone: (800) 345-2421
Fax: (714) 939-0655
www.minorleagues.com
mlmd@minorleagues.com

BAGS

DEMARINI
6435 N.W. Croeni Rd.
Hillsboro, OR 97124
Phone: (800) 937-BATS (2287)
Fax: (503) 531-5506
www.demarini.com

DIAMOND SPORTS
1880 E. St. Andrew Place
Santa Ana, CA 92705
Phone: (714) 415-7600
Fax: (714) 415-7601
www.diamond-sports.com
info@diamond-sports.com

GERRY COSBY AND COMPANY
11 Pennsylvania Plaza
New York, NY 10001
Phone: (877) 563-6464
Fax: (212) 967-0876
www.cosbysports.com
gcsmsg@cosbysport.com

LOUISVILLE SLUGGER
800 W. Main St.
Louisville, KY 40202
Phone: (800) 282-2287
Fax: (502) 585-1179
www.slugger.com
customer.service@slugger.com

SCHUTT SPORTS
710 S. Industrial Dr.
Litchfield, IL 62056
Phone: (800) 426-9784
Fax: (217) 324-2732
www.schuttsports.com
sales@schutt-sports.com

WILSON SPORTING GOODS
8750 West Bryn Mawr Ave., 13th Floor
Chicago, IL 60631
Phone: (800) 333-8326
Fax: (773) 714-4565
www.wilson.com
askwilson@wilson.com

BASEBALLS

DIAMOND SPORTS
1880 E. St. Andrew Place
Santa Ana, CA 92705
Phone: (714) 415-7600
Fax: (714) 415-7601
www.diamond-sports.com
info@diamond-sports.com

M^POWERED BASEBALL
P.O. Box 2391
Danville, CA 94526
Phone: (925) 915-9393
Fax: (516) 333-1811
www.mpoweredbaseball.com
info@mpoweredbaseball.com

WILSON SPORTING GOODS
8750 West Bryn Mawr Ave., 13th Floor
Chicago, IL 60631
Phone: (800) 333-8326
Fax: (773) 714-4565
www.wilson.com
askwilson@wilson.com

BASES

BEAM CLAY
See our ad on the inside back cover!
One Kelsey Park
Great Meadows, NJ 07838
Phone: (800) 247-BEAM (2326)
Fax: 908-637-8421
www.beamclay.com
sales@partac.com

SCHUTT SPORTS
710 S. Industrial Dr.
Litchfield, IL 62056
Phone: (800) 426-9784
Fax: (217) 324-2732
www.schuttsports.com
sales@schutt-sports.com

BATS

B45 - THE ORIGINAL YELLOW BIRCH BAT COMPANY
281 Edward-Assh
Ste-Catherine-de-la-Cartier,
QC, Canada G3N 1A3
Phone: (888) 669-0145
www.b45online.com
info@b45online.com
*Pro/MLB Contact: Rick Kramer
301-346-1046 rkramer@b45online.com

BWP BATS, LLC
80 Womeldorf Ln.
Brookville, PA 15825
Phone: (814) 849-0089
Fax: (814) 849-8584
www.bwpbats.com
sales@bwpbats.com

CARRERA SPORTS
4857 Palm Beach Blvd., Ste. 4
Fort Myers, FL 33905
Phone: (716) 785-0023
www.carrerasportsint.com
sales@carrerasportsint.com

DEMARINI
6435 N.W. Croeni Rd.
Hillsboro, OR 97124
Phone: (800) 937-BATS (2287)
Fax: (503) 531-5506
www.demarini.com

DIAMOND SPORTS
1880 E. St. Andrew Place
Santa Ana, CA 92705
Phone: (714) 415-7600
Fax: (714) 415-7601
www.diamond-sports.com
info@diamond-sports.com

HOOSIER BAT CO
P.O. Box 432
4511 Evans Ave.
Valparaiso, IN 46384
Phone: (800) 228-3787/(219) 531-1006
Fax: (219) 465-0877
www.hoosierbat.com
baseball@netnico.com

LOUISVILLE SLUGGER
800 W. Main St.
Louisville, KY 40202
Phone: (800) 282-2287
Fax: (502) 585-1179
www.slugger.com
customer.service@slugger.com

M^POWERED BASEBALL
P.O. Box 2391
Danville, CA 94526
Phone: (925) 915-9393
Fax: (516) 333-1811
www.mpoweredbaseball.com
info@mpoweredbaseball.com

OLD HICKORY BAT COMPANY
P.O. Box 588
White House, TN 37188
Phone: (615) 285-0588
Fax: (615) 285-0512
www.oldhickorybats.com
mail@oldhickorybats.com

PHOENIX BATS
7801 Corporate Blvd. Ste. E
Plain City, OH 43064
Phone: (614) 873-7776
Fax: (614) 932-2313
www.phoenixbats.com
customercare@phoenixbats.com

RAWLINGS
510 Maryville University Dr. Ste. 110
St. Louis, MO 63141
Phone: (314) 819-2800
Fax: (314) 819-2990
www.rawlings.com
contact@rawlings.com

SAM BAT
110 Industrial Ave.
Carleton Place, ON K7C 3T2
Phone: (888) SAM-BATS
Fax: (613) 257-8577
www.sambat.com
bats@sambat.com

TRINITY BAT COMPANY
2493 E. Orangethorpe Ave.
Fullerton, CA 92831
Phone: (714) 449-1275
Fax: (714) 449-1285
www.trinitybats.com
bats@trinitybat.com

ZINGER BAT COMPANY
3155 N. Nevada St. Ste. 4
Chandler AZ 85225
Phone: (602) 751-5895
Fax: (416) 663-3797
www.zingerbats.com
jason@zingerbats.com

BATTING CAGES

BEAM CLAY
See our ad on the inside back cover!
One Kelsey Park
Great Meadows, NJ 07838
Phone: (800) 247-BEAM (2326)
Fax: 908-637-8421
www.beamclay.com
sales@partac.com

C&H BASEBALL, INC
10615 Technology Terrace, #100
Bradenton, FL 34211
Phone: (800) 248-5192
Fax: (941) 727-0588
www.chbaseball.com
info@chbaseball

DIAMOND SPORTS
1880 E. St. Andrew Place
Santa Ana, CA 92705
Phone: (714) 415-7600
Fax: (714) 415-7601
www.diamond-sports.com
info@diamond-sports.com

GOLF RANGE NETTING, INC
40351 U.S. Hwy. 19N #303
Tarpon Springs, FL 34689
Phone: (727) 938-4448
Fax: (727) 938-4135
www.golfrangnetting.com
info@golfrangenetting.com

JUGS SPORTS
11885 S.W. Herman Rd.
Tualatin, OR 97062
Phone: (800) 547-6843
Fax: (503) 691-8907
www.jugssports.com
stevec@jugssports.com

MASTER PITCHING MACHINE, INC
4200 N.E. Birmingham Rd.
Kansas City, MO 64117
Phone: (816) 452-0228/(800) 878-8228
Fax: (816) 452-7581
www.masterpitch.com
joeg@masterpitch.com

NATIONAL SPORTS PRODUCTS
3441 S. 11th Ave.
Eldridge, IA 52807
Phone: (800) 478-6497
Fax: (800) 443-8907
www.nationalsportsproducts.com
sales@nationalsportsproducts.com

PROMATS ATHLETICS
P.O. Box 2489
Salisbury, NC 28145
Phone: (800) 617-7125
Fax: (704) 603-4138
www.promatsathletics.com
mcross@promatsathletics.com

WEST COAST NETTING
5075 Flightline Dr.
Kingman, AZ 86401
Phone: (928) 692-1144
Fax: (928) 692-1501
www.westcoastnetting.com
info@westcoastnetting.com

BATTING GLOVES

DEMARINI
6435 N.W. Croeni Rd.
Hillsboro, OR 97124
Phone: (800) 937-BATS (2287)
Fax: (503) 531-5506
www.demarini.com

BUNTING, PLEATED FANS AND FLAGS

INDEPENDENCE BUNTING & FLAG CORP
44 W. Jefryn Blvd., Ste. T
Deer Park, NY 11729
Phone: (800) 995-9129
Fax: (888) 824-1060
www.independence-bunting.com
independencebunting@gmail.com

CAMPS/SCHOOLS

PROFESSIONAL BASEBALL INSTRUCTION
107 Pleasant Ave.
Upper Saddle River, NJ 07458
Phone: (800) 282-4638
Fax: (201) 760-8820
www.baseballclinics.com
info@baseballclinics.com

CAPS/HEADWEAR

MINOR LEAGUES, MAJOR DREAMS
P.O. Box 6098
Anaheim, CA 92816
Phone: (800) 345-2421
Fax: (714) 939-0655
www.minorleagues.com
mlmd@minorleagues.com

CONCESSION OPERATIONS

CONCESSION SOLUTIONS, INC
16022-26th Ave. N.E.
Shoreline, WA 98155
Phone: (206) 440-9203
Fax: (206) 440-9213
www.concessionsolutions.com
theresa@concessionsolutions.com

IOWA ROTO PLASTICS, INC
1712 Moellers Dr.
P.O. Box 320
Decorah, IA 52101
Phone: (800) 553-050
Fax: (563) 382-3016
www.irpinc.com
irp@irpinc.com

CONFETTI/STREAMERS

PYROTECNICO
P.O. Box 149
New Castle, PA 16103
Phone: (800) 854-4705
Fax: (724) 652-1288
www.pyrotecnico.com
mbriggs@pyrotecnico.com

EMBROIDED EMBLEMS

THE EMBLEM SOURCE
4575 Westgrove, #500
Addison, TX 75001
Phone: (972) 248-1909
Fax: (972) 248-1615
www.theemblemsource.com
larry@theemblemsource.com

ENTERTAINMENT

BIRDZERK!
P.O. Box 36061
Louisville, KY 40233
Phone: (800) 219-0899/(502) 458-4020
Fax: (502) 458-0867
www.birdzerk.com
dom@birdzerk.com

BREAKIN' BBOY McCOY
P.O. Box 36061
Louisville, KY 40233
Phone: (800) 219-0899/(502) 458-4020
Fax: (502) 458-0867
www.bboymccoy.com
dom@theskillegroup.com

INFLATAMANIACS
8004 Sycamore Creek
Louisville, KY 40222
Phone: (502) 417-8659
www.inflatamaniacs.com
steven@inflatamaniacs.com

MYRON NOODLEMAN
P.O. Box 36061
Louisville, KY 40233
Phone: (800) 219-0899/(502) 458-4020
Fax: (502) 458-0867
www.myronnoodleman.com
dom@theskillegroup.com

RAYMOND ENTERTAINMENT
62 N. Chapel St., Ste. 004
Newark, DE 19711
Phone: (302) 731-2000
Fax: (302) 731-8772
www.raymondentertainment.com

RB3-RUSSIAN BAR TRIO
P.O. Box 36061
Louisville, KY 40233
Phone: (800) 219-0899/(502) 458-4020
Fax: (502) 458-0867
www.rb3usa.com
dom@theskillegroup.com

SCOLLON PRODUCTIONS/ SCOLLON LIVE EVENTS
P.O. Box 486
White Rock, SC 29177
Phone: (803) 345-3922
Fax: (803) 345-9313
www.scollon.com
rick@scollon.com

SWEETRIGHT ENTERTAINMENT
8328 Plano Ct.
Raleigh, NC 27616
Phone: (919) 744-8131
Fax: (919) 896-8981
www.sweetrightbrothers.com
npriddy@sweetrightent.com

ZOOPERSTARS!
P.O. Box 36061
Louisville, KY 40233
Phone: (800) 219-0899/(502) 458-4020
Fax: (502) 458-0867
www.zooperstars.com
dom@zooperstars.com

FIELD COVERS/TARPS

BEAM CLAY
See our ad on the inside back cover!
One Kelsey Park
Great Meadows, NJ 07838
Phone: (800) 247-BEAM (2326)
Fax: 908-637-8421
www.beamclay.com
sales@partac.com

C&H BASEBALL, INC
10615 Technology Terrace, #100
Bradenton, FL 34211
Phone: (800) 248-5192
Fax: (941) 727-0588
www.chbaseball.com
info@chbaseball

COVERMASTER, INC
100 Westmore Dr. 11-D
Rexdale, ON M9V5C3
Phone: (800) 387-5808
Fax: (416) 742-6837
www.covermaster.com
info@covermaster.com

NATIONAL SPORTS PRODUCTS
3441 S. 11th Ave.
Eldridge, IA 52807
Phone: (800) 478-6497
Fax: (800) 443-8907
www.nationalsportsproducts.com
sales@nationalsportsproducts.com

REEF INDUSTRIES, INC
9209 Almeda Genoa Rd.
Houston, TX 77075
Phone: (713) 507-4251
Fax: (713) 507-4251
www.reefindustries.com
myoung@reefindustries.com

SOUTHERN ATHLETIC FIELDS, INC
1309 Mainsail Dr.
Columbia, TN 38401
Phone: (800) 837-8062
Fax: (931) 380-0145
www.safdirt.com
saf@safdirt.com

FIELD CONSTRUCTION/ RENOVATION

ALPINE SERVICES, INC
5313 Brookeville Rd.
Gaithersburg, MD 20882
Phone: (800) 292-8420
Fax: (301) 963-7901
www.alpineservices.com
asi@alpineservices.com

FIELD EQUIPMENT

DIAMOND SPORTS
1880 E. St. Andrew Place
Santa Ana, CA 92705
Phone: (714) 415-7600
Fax: (714) 415-7601
www.diamond-sports.com
info@diamond-sports.com

FIELD WALL PADDING

BEAM CLAY
See our ad on the inside back cover!
One Kelsey Park
Great Meadows, NJ 07838
Phone: (800) 247-BEAM (2326)
Fax: 908-637-8421
www.beamclay.com
sales@partac.com

C&H BASEBALL, INC
10615 Technology Terrace, #100
Bradenton, FL 34211
Phone: (800) 248-5192
Fax: (941) 727-0588
www.chbaseball.com
info@chbaseball

COVERMASTER, INC
100 Westmore Dr. 11-D
Rexdale, ON M9V5C3
Phone: (800) 387-5808
Fax: (416) 742-6837
www.covermaster.com
info@covermaster.com

NATIONAL SPORTS PRODUCTS
3441 S. 11th Ave.
Eldridge, IA 52807
Phone: (800) 478-6497
Fax: (800) 443-8907
www.nationalsportsproducts.com
sales@nationalsportsproducts.com

PROMATS ATHLETICS
P.O. Box 2489
Salisbury, NC 28145
Phone: (800) 617-7125
Fax: (704) 603-4138
www.promatsathletics.com
mcross@promatsathletics.com

WEST COAST NETTING
5075 Flightline Dr.
Kingman, AZ 86401
Phone: (928) 692-1144
Fax: (928) 692-1501
www.westcoastnetting.com
info@westcoastnetting.com

FIREWORKS

PYROTECNICO
P.O. Box 149
New Castle, PA 16103
Phone: (800) 854-4705
Fax: (724) 652-1288
www.pyrotecnico.com
mbriggs@pyrotecnico.com

FOAM HANDS AND NOVELTY GIFTS

RICO INDUSTRIES, INC
7000 N. Austin
Niles, IL 60714
Phone: (800) 423-5856
Fax: (312) 427-0313
www.ricoinc.com
jimz@ricoinc.com

FOOD SERVICE

IOWA ROTO PLASTICS, INC
1712 Moellers Dr.
P.O. Box 320
Decorah, IA 52101
Phone: (800) 553-0050
Fax: (563) 382-3016
www.irpinc.com
irp@irpinc.com

FUNDRAISING

LITTLE CAESARS PIZZA KIT FUNDRAISING PROGRAM
2211 Woodward Ave.
Detroit, MI 48201
Phone: (888) 4-LC-KITS
Fax: (313) 471-6101
www.pizzakit.com
service@pizzakit.com

GIVEAWAY ITEMS

RICO INDUSTRIES, INC
7000 N. Austin
Niles, IL 60714
Phone: (800) 423-5856`
Fax: (312) 427-0313
www.ricoinc.com
jimz@ricoinc.com

GLOVES

AMPAC ENTERPRISES/ ALL-STAR
1 Main St.
P.O. Box 1356
Shirley, MA 01464
Phone: (978) 425-6266
Fax: (978) 425-4068
www.all-starsports.com
customerservice@all-starsports.com

FRANK'S SPORT SHOP
430 E. Tremont Ave.
Bronx, NY 10457
Phone: (718) 299-5223/
(212) 945-0020
Fax: (718) 583-1653
www.frankssportshop.com

See our ad on the insert!

LOUISVILLE SLUGGER
800 W. Main St.
Louisville, KY 40202
Phone: (800) 282-2287
Fax: (502) 585-1179
www.slugger.com
customer.service@slugger.com

M^POWERED BASEBALL
P.O. Box 2391
Danville, CA 94526
Phone: (925) 915-9393
Fax: (516) 333-1811
www.mpoweredbaseball.com
info@mpoweredbaseball.com

OLD HICKORY BAT COMPANY
P.O. Box 588
White House, TN 37188
Phone: (615) 285-0588
Fax: (615) 285-0512
www.oldhickorybats.com
mail@oldhickorybats.com

RAWLINGS
510 Maryville University Dr. Ste. 110
St. Louis, MO 63141
Phone: (314) 819-2800
Fax: (314) 819-2990
www.rawlings.com
contact@rawlings.com

WILSON SPORTING GOODS
8750 West Bryn Mawr Ave., 13th Floor
Chicago, IL 60631
Phone: (800) 333-8326
Fax: (773) 714-4565
www.wilson.com
askwilson@wilson.com

INSURANCE

K&K INSURANCE
1712 Magnavox Way
Fort Wayne, IN 46804
Phone: (800) 637-4757
Fax: (260) 459-5120
www.kandkinsurance.com
kk-sports@kandkinsurance.com

See our ad on the inside front cover!

LIGHTING

GOLF RANGE NETTING, INC
40351 U.S. Hwy. 19N #303
Tarpon Springs, FL 34689
Phone: (727) 938-4448
Fax: (727) 938-4135
www.golfrangnetting.com
info@golfrangenetting.com

MASCOTS

OLYMPUS GROUP
9000 West Heather Ave.
Milwaukee, WI 53224
Phone: (414) 355-2010
Fax: (414) 355-1931
www.olympusgrp.com
sales@olympusgrp.com

SCOLLON PRODUCTIONS / SCOLLON LIVE EVENTS
P.O. Box 486
White Rock, SC 29177
Phone: (803) 345-3922
Fax: (803) 345-9313
www.scollon.com
rick@scollon.com

MASCOT DOCTOR

RAYMOND ENTERTAINMENT
62 N. Chapel St., Ste. 004
Newark, DE 19711
Phone: (302) 731-2000
Fax: (302) 731-8772
www.raymondentertainment.com

MOUND CLAY

SOUTHERN ATHLETIC FIELDS, INC
1309 Mainsail Dr.
Columbia, TN 38401
Phone: (800) 837-8062
Fax: (931) 380-0145
www.safdirt.com
saf@safdirt.com

MUSIC / SOUND EFFECTS

CLICK EFFECTS
2408 Felts Ave.
Nashville, TN 37211
Phone: (615) 460-7330
Fax: (615) 460-7331
www.clickeffects.com
sales@clickeffects.com

SOUND DIRECTOR, INC
2918 S.W. Royal Way
Gresham OR 97080
Phone: (503) 665-6869/(888) 276 0078
Fax: (503) 914-1812
www.sounddirector.com
info@sounddirector.com

NETTING/POSTS

BEAM CLAY
One Kelsey Park
Great Meadows, NJ 07838
Phone: (800) 247-BEAM (2326)
Fax: 908-637-8421
www.beamclay.com
sales@partac.com

See our ad on the inside back cover!

C&H BASEBALL, INC
10615 Technology Terrace, #100
Bradenton, FL 34211
Phone: (800) 248-5192
Fax: (941) 727-0588
www.chbaseball.com
info@chbaseball

GOLF RANGE NETTING, INC
40351 U.S. Hwy. 19N #303
Tarpon Springs, FL 34689
Phone: (727) 938-4448
Fax: (727) 938-4135
www.golfrangnetting.com
info@golfrangenetting.com

JUGS SPORTS
11885 S.W. Herman Rd.
Tualatin, OR 97062
Phone: (800) 547-6843
Fax: (503) 691-1110
www.jugssports.com
stevec@jugssports.com

L.A. STEELCRAFT PRODUCTS, INC
1975 Lincoln Ave.
Pasadena, CA 91103
Phone: (800) 371-2438
Fax: (626) 798-1482
www.lasteelcraft.com
info@lasteelcraft.com

NATIONAL SPORTS PRODUCTS
3441 S. 11th Ave.
Eldridge, IA 52807
Phone: (800) 478-6497
Fax: (800) 443-8907
www.nationalsportsproducts.com
sales@nationalsportsproducts.com

PROMATS ATHLETICS
P.O. Box 2489
Salisbury, NC 28145
Phone: (800) 617-7125
Fax: (704) 603-4138
www.promatsathletics.com
mcross@promatsathletics.com

WEST COAST NETTING
5075 Flightline Dr.
Kingman, AZ 86401
Phone: (928) 692-1144
Fax: (928) 692-1501
www.westcoastnetting.com
info@westcoastnetting.com

NOVELTY GIFTS

RICO INDUSTRIES, INC
7000 N. Austin
Niles, IL 60714
Phone: (800) 423-5856
Fax: (312) 427-0313
www.ricoinc.com
jimz@ricoinc.com

PENNANTS

RICO INDUSTRIES, INC
7000 N. Austin
Niles, IL 60714
Phone: (800) 423-5856`
Fax: (312) 427-0313
www.ricoinc.com
jimz@ricoinc.com

PITCHING MACHINES

ATHLETIC TRAINING EQUIPMENT COMPANY - ATEC
655 Spice Island Dr.
Sparks, NV 89431
Phone: (800) 998-ATEC (2832)
Fax: (800) 959-ATEC (2832)
www.atecsports.com
askATEC@wilson.com

C&H BASEBALL, INC
10615 Technology Terrace, #100
Bradenton, FL 34211
Phone: (800) 248-5192
Fax: (941) 727-0588
www.chbaseball.com
info@chbaseball

JUGS SPORTS
11885 S.W. Herman Rd.
Tualatin, OR 97062
Phone: (800) 547-6843
Fax: (503) 691-8907
www.jugssports.com
stevec@jugssports.com

MASTER PITCHING MACHINE, INC
4200 N.E. Birmingham Rd.
Kansas City, MO 64117
Phone: (816) 452-0228/(800) 878-8228
Fax: (816) 452-7581
www.masterpitch.com
joeg@masterpitch.com

PROBATTER SPORTS
49 Research Dr.,, Ste. A
Milford, CT 06460
Phone: (203) 874-2772
Fax: (818) 972-9651
www.probatter.com
abattersby@probatter.com

SPORTS TUTOR
3300 Winona Ave.
Burbank, CA 91504
Phone: (818) 972-2772
Fax: (818) 972-9651
www.sportsmachines.com
orders@sportstutor.com

PLAYING FIELD PRODUCTS

BEAM CLAY
One Kelsey Park
Great Meadows, NJ 07838
Phone: (800) 247-BEAM (2326)
Fax: 908-637-8421
www.beamclay.com
sales@partac.com

See our ad on the inside back cover!

C&H BASEBALL, INC
10615 Technology Terrace, #100
Bradenton, FL 34211
Phone: (800) 248-5192
Fax: (941) 727-0588
www.chbaseball.com
info@chbaseball

EWING IRRIGATION PRODUCTS, INC
3441 E. Harbour Dr.
Phoenix, AZ 85074
Phone: (800) 343-9464
Fax: (602) 437-0446
www.ewing1.com
csinacori@ewing1.com

SOUTHERN ATHLETIC FIELDS, INC
1309 Mainsail Dr.
Columbia, TN 38401
Phone: (800) 837-8062
Fax: (931) 380-0145
www.safdirt.com
saf@safdirt.com

STALKER RADAR (APPLIED CONCEPTS)
2609 Technology Dr.
Plano, TX 75074
Phone: (888) stalker
www.stalkerradar.com
sales@stalkerradar.com

See our ad on page 7!

PITCHING AIDS

THROWTHECURVE.COM
107 Pleasant Ave.
Upper Saddle River, NJ 07458
Phone: (800) 282-4638
Fax: (201) 760-8820
www.throwthecurve.com

POINT OF SALE ITEMS

GERRY COSBY AND COMPANY
11 Pennsylvania Plaza
New York, NY 10001
Phone: (877) 563-6464
Fax: (212) 967-0876
www.cosbysports.com
gcsmsg@cosbysport.com

IOWA ROTO PLASTICS, INC
1712 Moellers Dr.
P.O. Box 320
Decorah, IA 52101
Phone: (800) 553-050
Fax: (563) 382-3016
www.irpinc.com
irp@irpinc.com

MICROS SYSTEMS, INC
7031 Columbia Gateway Dr.
Columbia, MD 21046
Phone: (866) 287-4736
www.micros.com
info@micros.com

PRINTING

OLYMPUS GROUP
9000 West Heather Ave.
Milwaukee, WI 53224
Phone: (414) 355-2010
Fax: (414) 355-1931
www.olympusgrp.com
sales@olympusgrp.com

PROFESSIONAL SERVICES

GERRY COSBY AND COMPANY
11 Pennsylvania Plaza
New York, NY 10001
Phone: (877) 563-6464
Fax: (212) 967-0876
www.cosbysports.com
gcsmsg@cosbysport.com

PROMOTIONAL ITEMS

C&H BASEBALL, INC
10615 Technology Terrace, #100
Bradenton, FL 34211
Phone: (800) 248-5192
Fax: (941) 727-0588
www.chbaseball.com
info@chbaseball

RICO INDUSTRIES, INC
7000 N. Austin

Niles, IL 60714
Phone: (800) 423-5856`
Fax: (312) 427-0313
www.ricoinc.com
jimz@ricoinc.com

PROMOTIONS

SCA PROMOTIONS
3030 LBJ Frwy., #300
Dallas, TX 75234
Phone: (888) 860-3700
Fax: (214) 860-3437
www.scapromotions.com
sports@scapromo.com

PROTECTIVE EQUIPMENT

AMPAC ENTERPRISES/ ALL-STAR
1 Main St.
P.O. Box 1356
Shirley, MA 01464
Phone: (978) 425-6266
Fax: (978) 425-4068
www.all-starsports.com
customerservice@all-starsports.com

BEAM CLAY
One Kelsey Park
Great Meadows, NJ 07838
Phone: (800) 247-BEAM (2326)
Fax: 908-637-8421
www.beamclay.com
sales@partac.com

See our ad on the inside back cover!

C&H BASEBALL, INC
10615 Technology Terrace, #100
Bradenton, FL 34211
Phone: (800) 248-5192
Fax: (941) 727-0588
www.chbaseball.com
info@chbaseball

DIAMOND SPORTS
1880 E. St. Andrew Place
Santa Ana, CA 92705
Phone: (714) 415-7600
Fax: (714) 415-7601
www.diamond-sports.com
info@diamond-sports.com

SCHUTT SPORTS
710 S. Industrial Dr.
Litchfield, IL 62056
Phone: (800) 426-9784
Fax: (217) 324-2732
www.schuttsports.com
sales@schutt-sports.com

WEST COAST NETTING
5075 Flightline Dr.
Kingman, AZ 86401
Phone: (928) 692-1144
Fax: (928) 692-1501
www.westcoastnetting.com
info@westcoastnetting.com

WILSON SPORTING GOODS
8750 West Bryn Mawr Ave., 13th Floor
Chicago, IL 60631
Phone: (800) 333-8326
Fax: (773) 714-4565
www.wilson.com
askwilson@wilson.com

RADAR EQUIPMENT

JUGS SPORTS
11885 S.W. Herman Rd.
Tualatin, OR 97062
Phone: (800) 547-6843
Fax: (503) 691-8907
www.jugssports.com
stevec@jugssports.com

SPORTS SENSORS INC
11351 Embassy Dr.

Cincinnati, OH 45240
Phone: (888) 542-9246
Fax: (513) 825-8532
www.sportssensors.com
adilz@cinci.rr.com

See our ad on page 7!

STALKER RADAR (APPLIED CONCEPTS)
2609 Technology Dr.
Plano, TX 75074
Phone: (888) stalker
www.stalkerradar.com
sales@stalkerradar.com

SEATING

STURDISTEEL CO
P.O. Box 2655
Waco, TX 76702
Phone: (800) 433-3116
Fax: (254) 666-4472
www.sturdisteel.com
rgroppe@sturdisteel.net

SHOES

See our ad on the insert!

FRANK'S SPORT SHOP
430 E. Tremont Ave.
Bronx, NY 10457
Phone: (718) 299-5223/(212) 945-0020
Fax: (718) 583-1653
www.frankssportshop.com

SHOWCASES/PLAYER DEVELOPMENT

PROFESSIONAL BASEBALL INSTRUCTION: BATTERY INVITATIONAL
(pitchers/catchers-early November)
107 Pleasant Ave.
Upper Saddle River, NJ 07458
Phone: (800) 282-4638
Fax: (201) 760-8820
greg@baseballclinics.com

SOFTWARE

STADIUM ONE
13479 Polo Trace Dr.
Delray Beach, FL 33446
Phone: (561) 498-8356
Fax: (561) 498-8358
www.stadium1.com
bquinn@stadium1.com

SPECIAL EFFECTS & LASERS

PYROTECNICO
P.O. Box 149
New Castle, PA 16103
Phone: (800) 854-4705
Fax: (724) 652-1288
www.pyrotecnico.com
mbriggs@pyrotecnico.com

SPORTING GOODS

JUGHEAD SPORTS
107 Pleasant Ave.
Upper Saddle River, NJ 07458
Phone: (800) 282-4638
Fax: (201) 760-8820
www.jugheadsports.com

TEXT MESSAGE MARKETING

84444.COM & 84444.CA
996 Old Eagle School Rd., Ste. 1105
Wayne, PA 19087

www.8444.com
www.8444.ca
sales@84444.com

TICKETS

INDIANA TICKET CO
P.O. Box 823
Muncie, IN 47308
Phone: (800) 428-8640
Fax: (888) 428-8640
www.indianaticket.com
info@indianaticket.com

TOURNAMENTS

COOPERSTOWN ALL STAR VILLAGE
P.O. Box 670
Cooperstown, NY 13328
Phone: (607) 432-7483
Fax: (607) 432-1076
www.cooperstownallstarvillage.com
info@cooperstownallstarvillage.com

TRAINING EQUIPMENT

ATHLETIC TRAINING EQUIPMENT COMPANY - ATEC
655 Spice Island Dr.
Sparks, NV 89431
Phone: (800) 998-ATEC (2832)
Fax: (800) 959-ATEC (2832)
www.atecsports.com
askATEC@wilson.com

JUGS SPORTS
11885 S.W. Herman Rd.
Tualatin, OR 97062
Phone: (800) 547-6843
Fax: (503) 691-8907
www.jugssports.com
stevec@jugssports.com

LOUISVILLE SLUGGER
800 W. Main St.
Louisville, KY 40202
Phone: (800) 282-2287
Fax: (502) 585-1179
www.slugger.com
customer.service@slugger.com

PICKLE BALL, INC
810 N.W. 45th St., Ste. 2
Seattle, WA 98107
Phone: (206) 632-0119
Fax: (206) 632-0126
www.pickleball.com
janet@pickleball.com

SCHUTT SPORTS
710 S. Industrial Dr.
Litchfield, IL 62056
Phone: (800) 426-9784
Fax: (217) 324-2732
www.schuttsports.com
sales@schutt-sports.com

SPORTS SENSORS INC
11351 Embassy Dr.
Cincinnati, OH 45240
Phone: (888) 542-9246
Fax: (513) 825-8532
www.sportssensors.com
adilz@cinci.rr.com

TRAVEL

BROACH BASEBALL TOURS
3235 South Blvd.
Charlotte, NC 28209
Phone: (800) 849-6345
Fax: (704) 365-3800
www.baseballtoursusa.com
info@broachsportstours.com

UNIFORMS

AIS ATHLETIC UNIFORMS
2460 E. 57th St.
Huntington Park, CA 90058
Phone: (323) 582-3005
Fax: (323) 582-2831
www.aisathleticuniforms.com
info@aisathleticuniforms.com

RAWLINGS
510 Maryville University Dr. Ste. 110
St. Louis, MO 63141
Phone: (314) 819-2800
Fax: (314) 819-2990
www.rawlings.com
contact@rawlings.com

WILSON SPORTING GOODS
8750 West Bryn Mawr Ave., 13th Floor
Chicago, IL 60631
Phone: (800) 333-8326
Fax: (773) 714-4565
www.wilson.com
askwilson@wilson.com

WINDSCREENS

See our ad on the inside back cover!

BEAM CLAY
One Kelsey Park
Great Meadows, NJ 07838
Phone: (800) 247-BEAM (2326)
Fax: 908-637-8421
www.beamclay.com
sales@partac.com

C&H BASEBALL, INC
10615 Technology Terrace, #100
Bradenton, FL 34211
Phone: (800) 248-5192
Fax: (941) 727-0588
www.chbaseball.com
info@chbaseball

GOLF RANGE NETTING, INC
40351 U.S. Hwy. 19N #303
Tarpon Springs, FL 34689
Phone: (727) 938-4448
Fax: (727) 938-4135
www.golfrangnetting.com
info@golfrangenetting.com

NATIONAL SPORTS PRODUCTS
3441 S. 11th Ave.
Eldridge, IA 52807
Phone: (800) 478-6497
Fax: (800) 443-8907
www.nationalsportsproducts.com
sales@nationalsportsproducts.com

PROMATS ATHLETICS
P.O. Box 2489
Salisbury, NC 28145
Phone: (800) 617-7125
Fax: (704) 603-4138
www.promatsathletics.com
mcross@promatsathletics.com

SOUTHERN ATHLETIC FIELDS, INC
1309 Mainsail Dr.
Columbia, TN 38401
Phone: (800) 837-8062
Fax: (931) 380-0145
www.safdirt.com
saf@safdirt.com

WEST COAST NETTING
5075 Flightline Dr.
Kingman, AZ 86401
Phone: (928) 692-1144
Fax: (928) 692-1501
www.westcoastnetting.com
info@westcoastnetting.com

INDEX

MAJOR LEAGUE TEAMS

MINOR LEAGUE TEAMS

INDEPENDENT TEAMS

OTHER ORGANIZATIONS

INDEX